Management Control in Nonprofit Organizations

Management Control in Nonprofit Organizations

Seventh Edition

Robert N. Anthony, D.B.A.

*Professor Emeritus
Graduate School of Business
Administration
Harvard University*

David W. Young, D.B.A.

*Professor of Accounting and Control
Health Care Management and Public and
Nonprofit Management Programs
School of Management
Boston University*

Boston   Burr Ridge, IL   Dubuque, IA   Madison, WI   New York   San Francisco   St. Louis
Bangkok   Bogotá   Caracas   Kuala Lumpur   Lisbon   London   Madrid   Mexico City
Milan   Montreal   New Delhi   Santiago   Seoul   Singapore   Sydney   Taipei   Toronto

McGraw-Hill Higher Education

A Division of The **McGraw-Hill** Companies

MANAGEMENT CONTROL IN NONPROFIT ORGANIZATIONS
Published by McGraw-Hill/Irwin, a business unit of The McGraw-Hill Companies, Inc., 1221 Avenue of the Americas, New York, NY, 10020. Copyright © 2003, 1999, 1994, 1988, 1984, 1980, 1975 by The McGraw-Hill Companies, Inc. All rights reserved. No part of this publication may be reproduced or distributed in any form or by any means, or stored in a database or retrieval system, without the prior written consent of The McGraw-Hill Companies, Inc., including, but not limited to, in any network or other electronic storage or transmission, or broadcast for distance learning.

Some ancillaries, including electronic and print components, may not be available to customers outside the United States.

This book is printed on acid-free paper.

1 2 3 4 5 6 7 8 9 0 DOC/DOC 0 9 8 7 6 5 4 3 2

ISBN 0-07-250825-6

Publisher: *Brent Gordon*
Sponsoring editor: *Steve DeLancey*
Developmental editor: *Kelly Odom*
Marketing manager: *Ryan Blankenship*
Project Manager: *Jim Labeots*
Production supervisor: *Gina Hangos*
Coordinator freelance design: *Mary L. Christianson*
Supplement producer: *Joyce J. Cappetto*
Typeface: *10.5/12 Times Roman*
Compositor: *GAC Indianapolis*
Printer: *R. R. Donnelley & Sons Company*

Library of Congress Cataloging-in-Publication Data
Anthony, Robert Newton, 1916-
     Management control in nonprofit organizations / Robert N. Anthony, David W. Young.—7th ed.
         p. cm.
     Includes index.
     ISBN 0-07-250825-6 (alk. paper)
     1. Nonprofit organizations—Accounting 2. Managerial accounting. I. Young, David W. II. Title.
     HF5686.N56 A57 2003

                                                                          2002020031

www.mhhe.com

Preface

Courses for which this text has been designed have existed for over 25 years in many universities. As the field of management control in nonprofit organizations has developed, so have our own ideas about the material in this book. In addition, in the four years that have passed since the Sixth Edition, a great deal of literature has been published relating to both the management of nonprofit organizations in general, and *management control* in those organizations in particular. Finally, changes have taken place in the environments of most nonprofit organizations, forcing many of them to rethink the way they conduct their operations.

As a result of these developments, several substantive changes have been made in the content of the book. A chapter, Analyzing Financial Statements (Chapter 4), has been added, and two chapters from the Sixth Edition (Chapters 8 and 9) have been combined into one (Chapter 9). In addition, based on requests from faculty users of the book, we have included one or more practice cases at the end of nine of the more technical chapters. These cases allow students to practice using a chapter's techniques and concepts before beginning to analyze the more substantive cases.

Organizationally, the book remains structured into three parts—introduction, management control principles, and management control systems. Some chapters have been rewritten, and some appendices have been updated. In addition, in several of the chapters, we have introduced some new concepts being developed in both the management field in general, and management accounting and control in particular. We look at how these emerging concepts relate to the management control effort in nonprofit organizations.

In addition to the practice cases, we have introduced 9 new cases into this edition, and have revised 16 cases from the Sixth Edition. Overall, this edition has 63 cases. This large number of cases permits instructors to use the book in courses for either beginning or advanced students. It also permits instructors to explore a particular subject in some depth, beginning on a relatively elementary level, and moving to a more advanced one.

USE OF THE BOOK

We wish to emphasize that this is *not* primarily a book on accounting. Rather, it is intended for a course on management control problems in nonprofit organizations in general. Such a course is often offered by an accounting department, but the book has also been used in courses offered by economics and finance departments, and by management departments in schools of education, medicine, public health, social work, theology, and public administration. Out goal is to put accounting-like issues into their broader organizational context.

Although written to apply to all types on nonprofit organizations, including governmental entities, the book can easily be adapted for a course that focuses on a single type, such as education or health care, by the selection of cases appropriate to that type. The book also may be used in short programs designed for managers of nonprofit organizations. The selection of chapters and cases for such programs depends on the nature of the short program. In one type of program the principal topics of the whole book may be discussed; in another type, the focus might be on a specific area of management control, such as programming, budgeting, or the evaluation of performance. Finally, the book may also be used by individual managers in nonprofit organizations as background reading or for reference purposes.

CASE REPRODUCTION

The 63 cases included in this book are listed in the index in alphabetical order. The first page of each case indicates its authors' names and affiliations, the copyright holder(s), and the source from which copies of the case may be obtained. For Harvard Business School cases, the first page also indicates the case number.

Individuals wishing to obtain additional copies of cases should contact the source shown on the first page on the case. Harvard Business School cases are available from Harvard Business School Publishing, Customer Service, Boston, MA 02163. The Crimson Press Curriculum Center cases are available from The Crimson Press Curriculum Center, Suite 323, 1770 Massachusetts Avenue, Cambridge, MA 02140. Permission to reproduce other cases should be sought from the copyright holder.

Comments on the text or cases, or new ideas for teaching the cases, are welcomed, and should be sent to Professor Young at the Boston University School of Management, 595 Commonwealth Avenue, Boston, MA 02215.

ACKNOWLEDGMENTS

We are grateful to many individuals for assistance in the preparation of both the text and the cases that we authored. These include Charles A. Anderson; Richard J. Anthony; Michael Blaszyk; Charles Bowsher; Eleanor Chelimsky, Professor Charles J. Christenson, Harvard Business School; William E. Cotter and Douglas Reinhardt, Colby College; Richard Depp, MD, Thomas Jefferson Medical School, Philadelphia; Gregory Dorf, Nancy Fisk, William Wubbenhorst, and Dean Rakoff, (former MBA students at Boston University School of Management); Professor Patricia Douglas, University of Montana; James Farnhum, Henry Harbury, and Richard Showalter, Dartmouth-Hitchcock Medical Center; Professor Antoni Garcìa-Prat, Instituto de Estudios Superiores de la Empresa, Barcelona, Spain; Neil E. Harlan; Emily Hayden; Professor Martin Ives, Pace University; Miriam Jost; Professor Nancy Kane, Harvard School of Public Health; John Lordan, Johns Hopkins University; Sheila M. McCarthy, The Crimson Group; Richard A. Morse;

Dean Patricia A. O'Brien, Simmons Graduate School of Business; Professor Leslie Pearlman Breitner, John F. Kennedy School of Government; Margaret B. Reber; Alexander Stankowicz; Pamela Sytkowski; Stan Trecker, Art Institute of Boston; and Eoin Trevelyan, Harvard School of Public Health.

We are also appreciative of the support we received from Boston University and Harvard University, and from the following sources for the preparation of certain cases:

Wyeth-Ayerst Laboratories for a grant to the Medical Education Foundation of the Association of Professors of Gynecology and Obstetrics (Croswell University Hospital and Brookstone Ob-Gyn Associates).

The Boston Foundation (Boulder Public Schools, Jefferson High School, Moray Junior High School, and Timilty Middle School).

Department of Health Policy and Management, Harvard School of Public Health (Fletcher Allen Health Care).

The Edwin Gould Foundation for Children (Bureau of Child Welfare).

Line Publications (Carlsbad Home Care).

Marion Merrill Dow and the Curriculum Development Project of the Public Management Program of the Boston University School of Management (Boston University Medical Center Hospital).

Massachusetts Health Data Consortium (Union Medical Center).

The Alliance for Academic Internal Medicine (Abbington Medical Education Programs).

The BEST Program at Boston University (Barrington High School).

Finally, we greatly appreciate the editorial assistance of Audrey Barrett, and Heather Sabo, and the staff assistance provided by Betty Waterman, Anita Warren, and Megan Weiss.

We, of course, accept full responsibility for the final product.

Robert N. Anthony

David W. Young

Brief Contents

Table of Contents

CHAPTER 6
Measurement and Use of Differential Costs   272

CHAPTER 7
Pricing Decisions   313

PART THREE
MANAGEMENT CONTROL SYSTEMS 371

CHAPTER 8
The Management Control Environment 372

CHAPTER 9
Strategic Planning and Program Analysis 422

## Part 1

Introduction

Management control in nonprofit organizations—as an academic subject—is relatively new. Historically, many nonprofit organizations survived on the strength of their mission and their ability to attract increasing amounts of public and private support for their activities. Over the past 20 to 25 years, there has been a gradual change in the prevailing attitude toward nonprofit management on the part of both professionals (physicians, educators, artists, and so on) and managers (who generally are professionals themselves). It was not until recently, however, that these individuals recognized their need for stronger management skills. One of these skills is management control.

In this introductory section we discuss the scope of the material covered in this book and the nature of the organizations to which we intend to apply it. Chapter 1 outlines the territory of the field of management control, indicating both what it includes and, equally important, what it does not include. Chapter 2 discusses the nature and size of nonprofit organizations, as well as the types of services they offer.

Chapter 1

The Management Control Function

Any organization, even the tiniest, has a management control function. In large organizations management control tends to be formal; in smaller ones it is often quite informal. Management control has existed as long as organizations have been in existence, but it has not been the subject of much systematic study and analysis until quite recently. One of the early works on the subject was Chester Barnard's *The Functions of the Executive.*[1] Originally published in 1938, this landmark book dealt with management control as well as other management functions. Since then, managers and academics have contributed to the evolution and definition of principles for designing management control systems and carrying out the management control function.

As with most principles of management, the tenets of management control are incomplete, inconclusive, tentative, vague, contradictory, and inadequately supported by experimental or other evidence. Some initial *truths* have been proven wrong. Other principles, however, have shown sufficient validity in terms of managerial and organizational performance that managers increasingly are taking them into account.

Most studies of management control have been conducted in for-profit businesses, where most management control techniques originally were developed. Consequently, descriptions of management control tend to assume that the primary objective of the enterprise is earning a profit. This book, by contrast, looks at management control in nonprofit organizations. Our thesis is that the basic concepts of management control are the same in both for-profit and nonprofit organizations, but, because of the special characteristics

[1]Chester I. Barnard, *The Functions of the Executive,* 30th anniversary ed. (Cambridge, MA: Harvard University Press, 1968).

of nonprofit organizations, the way managers apply these concepts will differ in some important respects.

Planning and Control Activities

Managers engage in a wide variety of activities. They lead, teach, organize, influence, plan, and control. In this book, we focus on the latter two activities. In the planning activity, managers decide what should be done and how it should be done. In the control activity, managers attempt to assure that the desired results are obtained.

There are three different types of planning and control activities: (1) strategy formulation, (2) task control, and (3) management control. Since our focus is on management control, we will describe the other two types of activities briefly. Our purpose in doing so is to clarify the boundaries of management control.[2]

Strategy Formulation

An organization exists for the purpose of accomplishing something; that is, it has one or more goals. Senior management generally determines both the organization's goals and the general nature of the activities it will undertake to achieve them—the organization's strategies. *Strategy formulation* is the process of deciding on the goals of the organization and on the strategies that are to be followed in attaining them.

Many nonprofits have difficulty determining a strategy that rules out certain activities or programs. But a strategy involves trade-offs, which many nonprofits are reluctant to make.[3]

Example

The United Way of Southeastern New England (UWSENE) needed to choose between being donor-focused, agency-focused, or community-focused. Trying to be all three was risky since a community focus might make some donors unhappy, an agency focus might make some communities unhappy, and so forth. In the end, the UWSENE decided to be donor-focused, reasoning that if the donors were satisfied the agencies would have their needs met, and this would benefit the communities.[4]

Nevertheless, at any given time, an organization has a set of goals and strategies. Strategies can be changed when senior management perceives (*a*) a threat to the organization, (*b*) new opportunities for the organization, or (*c*) a better way to achieve the goals. Since threats and opportunities do not arise in

---

[2]For a more thorough description of these activities, see Robert N. Anthony, *The Management Control Function* (Boston: Harvard Business School Press, 1988).
[3]Michael Porter, "What is Strategy?" *Harvard Business Review,* November–December 1996, pp. 61–78
[4]R. S. Kaplan and E. L. Kaplan, "United Way of Southeastern New England," Boston, Harvard Business School Case 9-197-036,1997.

orderly, predictable ways, strategic decisions are not made according to a prescribed timetable. The *strategy formulation* process therefore is essentially irregular and in many respects unsystematic.[5]

Task Control

At the other extreme are control processes used in carrying out the day-to-day operations of the organization, in particular the performance of specific tasks. Task control is the process of assuring that these operations are carried out effectively and efficiently.

Task control activities vary with the nature of the organization's operations. In a hospital, for example, maintaining an adequate inventory in the pharmacy is task control. So is assuring adequate patient care procedures on the wards. Many task control activities do not involve managers. If they are automated, they do not even involve human beings, except to assure that the task control system is functioning properly and to deal with matters not included in the automated process. For example, in many organizations with sizable inventories, when the quantity of an item on hand decreases to a preset limit, a computer places a replacement order directly with the appropriate vendor.

Management Control

Management control sits between strategy formulation and task control. Management control accepts the goals and strategies determined in the strategy formulation process as given. It focuses on the implementation of the strategies and the attainment of the goals. As such, management control attempts to assure that the organization designs effective programs and implements them efficiently. An effective program is one that moves the organization toward its goals. An efficient program is one that accomplishes its purposes at the lowest possible cost.

Unlike strategy formulation, management control is a regular, systematic process with steps repeated in a predictable way. And, unlike task control, which may not even involve human beings, management control is fundamentally behavioral. It requires managers to interact with other people in the organization, particularly other managers. In many organizations, especially nonprofits, it also depends on managers interacting with the organization's professional staff.

In part, the management control function assists managers to decide on the optimum allocation of resources. In this respect, it is governed by the principles of *economics*. Management control also looks at the influence of accounting and reporting systems on the behavior of people in organizations. In

---

[5]For additional details on the strategic planning process, see Kenneth R. Andrews, *The Concept of Corporate Strategy* (Homewood, IL: Dow Jones-Irwin, 1980), and Michael Porter, *Competitive Strategy* (New York: Free Press, 1980). The Suggested Additional Readings at the end of this chapter contain several books focued on the application of strategic planning to nonprofits.

this respect, it is governed by the principles of *social psychology*. Managers who experience initial difficulty in understanding the subject of management control should take comfort in the recognition that the principles found in these two disciplines are quite different, and that their relative importance to the management control function varies greatly in different situations. Throughout this book, we hope to help managers cultivate the ability to ask the critical questions that will enable them to incorporate the optimal mix of economic and behavioral factors in their management control efforts.

Many nonprofits have a difficult time making the link between strategy formulation and management control. Some define their mission and vision quite clearly, but then move to a list of programs and initiatives rather than some indication of outcomes or goals that can be measured by the management control system.[6] Others are able to make the linkage more directly.

Example

Between 1992 and 1997, CARE, a large international relief and development nonprofit, undertook a transformation effort. The effort comprised both strategic planning and management control. Once the strategic planning process had been completed, CARE turned to the management control activities needed to achieve the strategic goals. These activities included reengineering, restructuring of responsibility centers, improved information flows, and implementation of "best practices" models.[7]

The Management Control Environment

The way the management control function is carried out in an organization is influenced by that organization's external and internal environments. The external environment is important because management control must be concerned with matters such as the actions of customers or clients, the constraints imposed by funding providers and legislative bodies, and the customs and norms of the society in which the organization exists. The internal environment is important because management control affects and is affected by the organization's structure, its members' behavior, its information systems, and its cultural norms. We discuss some of these aspects briefly here.

Organizational Structure

Organizations can be structured in a variety of ways, generally determined by the tasks that managers and employees need to perform. Some organizations have a *functional* structure, in which employees and managers are grouped according to common tasks such as production, marketing, or finance. Other

---

[6]Robert S. Kaplan, "Strategic Performance Measurement and Management in Nonprofit Organizations," *Nonprofit Management and Leadership,* Spring 2001.
[7]Marc Lindenberg, "Are We at the Cutting Edge or the Blunt Edge? Improving NGO Organizational Performance with Private and Public Sector Strategic Management Frameworks," *Nonprofit Management and Leadership,* Spring 2001.

organizations have a *program* structure, in which employees and managers who perform different functions (or tasks) are grouped according to common programs or services. Still others have a *matrix* structure in which programs and functional responsibilities have equal or reasonably equal weight.[8]

Some nonprofits have adopted an organizational structure much like that of many corporations, in which each division's performance potential is enhanced by being a part of the larger entity. For example, before the United Way of America (UWA) scandal broke, William Aramony had conceived of the UWA as a unified social service organization in which each division worked toward achieving common system goals, such as improving children's lives, eliminating cancer, and so forth. Aramony's goal was to have the various member entities work in a coordinated fashion. This is a quite different model from one in which several nonprofits band together in an association-like structure to improve their bargaining position with suppliers or third-party payers.[9]

However the organizational structure is defined, the management control function takes it as given, and overlays it with a network of *responsibility centers*. A responsibility center is a group of people working toward some organizational objective. It is headed by a manager who is responsible for the actions of its members. The network of responsibility centers is called the *management control structure*. We will discuss the management control structure later in the chapter.

Organizational Relationships and Members' Behavior

Line and Staff

Organization units can be classified as either line or staff units. Line units are directly responsible for carrying out the work of the organization. Staff units provide advice and assistance to the line units. Line managers are the focal points in management control. Their judgment is incorporated into the approved plans, they must work with others to accomplish their objectives, and their performance is measured via their responsibility center's performance.

Staff people collect, summarize, and present information that is useful in the management control function, and they make calculations that translate management judgments into the format of the management control system. Such a staff may be large in numbers; indeed, the control department is often the largest staff department in an organization. However, the significant program and control decisions are made by line managers, not by staff people.

---

[8]For a thorough discussion of these matters and other organizational issues in a health care context, see Martin P. Charns and Laura J. Smith-Tewksbury, *Collaborative Management in Health Care: Implementing the Integrative Organization* (San Francisco: Jossey-Bass, 1993).
[9]Dennis R. Young, "Organizational Identify and the Structure of Nonprofit Umbrella Organizations," *Nonprofit Management and Leadership,* Spring 2001.

Controller

The person responsible for the design and operation of the management control system is the controller.[10] In practice, the controller may have other titles, such as chief financial officer or chief accountant.

The idea that the controller has a broader responsibility than merely keeping the books is a fairly recent one in for-profit organizations, and it is not yet well accepted in many nonprofit organizations. Not too long ago, controllers were invariably called *chief accountants* and expected to confine their activities to collecting and reporting historical data. With the development of formal management control systems, and the increased emphasis on information needed for planning and decision making, the controller's function has broadened.

The controller is still a staff person, however, and thus does not make management control decisions. The job of the staff is to provide information that will facilitate good decision making by line managers. Sometimes an operating manager with a problem of inadequate resources is told, "Go see the controller." In making such a statement, senior management effectively has shifted line responsibility, and the controller has been put into a line capacity. The controller then becomes a de facto manager, with a corresponding diminution in the responsibility of the organization's other line managers. This usually leads to less than optimal management of the whole organization.[11]

Information

An important part of the management control environment is information. Information is a resource, and, as with any resource, its use involves both costs and benefits. Senior management must attempt to assure that the value of the information exceeds the cost of collecting and disseminating it.

Information may be either quantitative or qualitative; a report that "Ms. X is doing a good job" is qualitative information. A report that "Ms. X delivered 25 hours of client service" is quantitative information. Quantitative information may be either monetary or nonmonetary. A report that "Ms. X earned $200" is monetary information; a report that "Ms. X worked 15 hours" is nonmonetary information. Much of the information used in management control is monetary information. The system that collects, summarizes, analyzes, and reports such information is the *accounting system*.

Nature of Accounting Information

An accounting system provides historical information; that is, what has happened, and what the organization's revenues and costs actually were. This

---

[10]The preferred term is *controller.* However, in some organizations, the word is spelled *comptroller.* In any event, the term is always pronounced as if it were spelled controller. Pronouncing it "*compt*roller" is archaic.

[11]Senior management may decide to assign responsibility for certain detailed decisions, such as approval of travel vouchers, to the controller. This is different from assigning line responsibility to the controller.

system collects information for three purposes: management control, reporting to outside parties, and special analyses.

Management Control   Information for management control purposes usually is classified in two ways: by responsibility centers and by programs. As we discuss later, the management control system must have an ability to integrate these two sets of information.

Reporting to Outside Parties   Some accounting information is contained in general-purpose financial reports. Principles governing the preparation of these reports are described in Chapter 3. Other information is prepared for outside agencies according to reporting requirements that they specify. State and local government agencies that accept funds from the federal government, for example, must prepare reports on their use of these funds. The content of these reports is specified by the agency that grants the funds. Ideally, the information contained in these special-purpose reports simply summarizes information in the management control system. This is because the information needs of outside agencies presumably do not exceed or vary greatly from those of management. The ideal is not always the case, however. The appropriation structure specified by the Congress for federal agencies, for example, rarely results in reporting configurations that are useful for the information and control needs of managers in those organizations.

Special Analyses   Special analyses include information used in connection with litigation or other one-time studies. In many organizations, for example, the accounting system collects information that is useful in strategic planning. Strategic decisions are made only occasionally, however, and each decision requires tailor-made information. This information cannot ordinarily be collected in any routine, recurring fashion. Rather, it must be assembled when the need arises and in the form required for the specific issue.

Although the management control system includes information found in the accounting system, it also provides two types of information not found in the accounting system: (1) estimates of what will happen in the future and (2) estimates of what should happen. The former are called forecasts, and the latter are called *standards* or *budgets*.

Cost Information

The accounting system collects information on the resources used in an organization. This is information on inputs. Inputs can be expressed as physical quantities, such as hours of labor, quarts of oil, reams of paper, or kilowatt-hours of electricity. If these physical quantities are converted to monetary units, they are called *costs*. Money provides a common denominator that permits the quantities of individual resources to be combined.

Cost is a measure of the amount of resources used for a purpose. In accounting terms, this purpose is called a *cost object*. The education of a student, the care of a patient, the completion of a research project, and the development of a museum exhibit are all examples of cost objects. Ordinarily, responsibility centers work on cost objects.

Inputs are resources *used* by a responsibility center in working on a cost object. Thus, the patients in a hospital or the students in a school are not the inputs of a responsibility center. Rather, a responsibility center's inputs are the resources it uses in accomplishing its objectives of treating patients or educating students.

Input information consists of three basic types of cost construction: full, differential, and responsibility. Each is used for a different purpose, and considerable misunderstanding can arise if the cost construction for one purpose is used inappropriately for another. Full costs and responsibility costs ordinarily are collected in the accounts. For reasons discussed below, differential costs are not collected in the accounts.

Full Cost   The total amount of resources used for a cost object is the cost object's full cost. Since cost objects often are programs, full costs often are called program costs. The full cost of a cost object is the sum of its direct costs plus a fair share of the organization's indirect costs.

Direct costs are costs that can be traced to a single cost object. For example, the salaries and fringe benefits of persons who work exclusively on a single program (cost object) are direct costs of that program. *Indirect costs* are costs incurred jointly for two or more cost objects, and a fair share of these indirect costs must be allocated to each cost object to obtain its full cost. These matters are discussed in greater detail in Chapter 5.

Differential Costs   Costs that are different under one set of conditions from what they would be under another are differential costs. These costs are useful in many problems involving a choice among alternative courses of action. The analysis of such problems involves estimates of how costs would be different if different proposed alternatives were adopted. Since the costs that are relevant to a given problem depend on the nature of that problem, there is no general way of labeling a given item of cost as differential or nondifferential, and therefore no way of recording differential costs as such in the formal accounts. The analyst uses information from the program structure or the responsibility structure as raw material for estimating the differential costs of a particular proposed alternative.

In many alternative choice problems, an important classification of costs is whether they are variable or fixed. *Variable costs* are those that change proportionally with changes in volume. Since teaching two fifth-grade students requires twice the number of workbooks needed to teach one, the cost of books used in education is a variable cost. By contrast, the amount of depreciation expense for the school building does not change with the number of students, so depreciation is a fixed cost. Other costs, such as teachers' salaries share features of both, changing as volume increases or decreases but not in direct proportion. Differential costs are the subject of Chapter 6.

Responsibility Costs   Costs incurred by or on behalf of a responsibility center are responsibility costs. They provide managers information on the cost of the responsibility center as an organizational unit, rather than on the program or programs with which the responsibility center is involved. When measured in monetary terms, the total resources consumed by a responsibility center for a specific period of time are the full costs of that responsibility center. However, total recorded costs are at best an approximation of total inputs. Some inputs are not included as costs, either because the effort required to translate them into monetary terms is not worthwhile (e.g., minor supplies and services or small amounts of borrowed labor) or because measurement is not possible (e.g., certain types of executive or staff assistance, or training).

Responsibility costs are classified as either controllable or noncontrollable. An item of cost is *controllable* if it is significantly influenced by the actions of the manager of the responsibility center in which it was incurred. Note that *controllable* always refers to a specific responsibility center, since all items of cost are ultimately controllable by someone in the organization. Note also that the definition refers to a significant amount of influence, rather than complete influence. Few managers have complete influence over any item of cost.

Output Information

Although inputs almost always can be measured in terms of cost, outputs are much more difficult to measure. In many responsibility centers, outputs cannot be measured at all. In a for-profit organization, revenue is often an important measure of output. But such a measure is rarely a complete expression of output, since it does not encompass everything that the organization does. For example, it might exclude such activities as pollution control and environmental cleanup, which may be important outputs from a societal perspective.

Many nonprofit organizations do not have a good quantitative measure of output. A school can easily measure the number of students graduated, but it is much more difficult (usually impossible) to measure how much education each of them acquired. Although outputs may not be measurable, it is a fact that every organization unit has outputs; that is, it does something.

The degree to which outputs can be measured quantitatively varies greatly with circumstances. If the quantity of output is relatively homogeneous (e.g., membership certificates in an association), it often can be measured precisely. If the goods or services are heterogeneous (e.g., different types of health care services), however, problems arise in summarizing the separate outputs into a meaningful measure of total output. Converting dissimilar physical goods to monetary equivalents is one way of solving this problem. Such a monetary measure is called *revenue*. If fees are structured properly, the total quantity of output of a client-serving organization is reliably measured by the fees charged to clients; that is, by revenues. This is true even though the services rendered consist of dissimilar activities (e.g., the use of beds, nursing care, operating rooms, and various laboratory, X-ray, and other technical procedures in a hospital).

At best, revenue measures the *quantity* of output. Measurement of the *quality* of output is much more difficult, and often cannot be made at all. In many situations, quality is determined strictly on a judgmental basis. In some, there is a go-no-go measurement—either the output is of satisfactory quality or it is not. Moreover, it is always difficult, and often unfeasible, to measure, or even estimate, the outputs of such staff units as the legal or research departments of a company, or the outputs of schools, government agencies, or churches.

In addition to goods and services thought of as outputs, responsibility centers produce intangible effects—sometimes intentionally and sometimes unintentionally. They may prepare employees for advancement, for example, or instill attitudes of loyalty and pride of accomplishment (or, alternatively, attitudes of disloyalty and indolence). They may also affect the image of the organization as perceived by the outside world. Some of these outputs, such as better trained employees, are created in order to benefit operations in future periods; that is, they will become inputs at some future time. Such outputs are therefore *investments,* since an investment is a commitment of current resources in the expectation of deriving future benefits. Because of inherent obstacles to measurement, however, investments in intangibles are rarely recorded in the formal accounting system. We discuss output measures more fully in Chapter 12.

Efficiency and Effectiveness

Efficiency and effectiveness are the two criteria for judging the performance of a responsibility center. These criteria are almost always used in a relative, rather than absolute, sense. We do not ordinarily say that Organization Unit A is 80 percent efficient, for example. Rather, we say that Unit A is more (or less) efficient than Unit B, or that it is more (or less) efficient now than it was in the past, or that it was more (or less) efficient than planned or budgeted.

Efficiency

Efficiency is the ratio of a responsibility center's outputs to its inputs; that is, its output per unit of input. Unit A is more efficient than Unit B if it (1) uses fewer resources than Unit B but has the same output, or (2) uses the same resources as Unit B but has more output. Note that the first measure of efficiency does not require us to quantify output; it only requires a reasonable judgment that the outputs of the two units are approximately equal. If management is satisfied that Units A and B are both doing a satisfactory job, and if their jobs are of comparable magnitude, then the unit with fewer inputs (i.e., lower costs) is more efficient. For example, if two elementary schools are judged to be furnishing adequate education, the one with lower per student costs is more efficient.

The second type of efficiency measure, which contrasts different levels of output given approximately equal levels of input, requires some quantitative indication of output. It is therefore more difficult to use in many situations. If two elementary schools have the same costs, for example, one can be said to be more efficient than the other only if it provides more education, but this is inherently difficult to measure.

In many responsibility centers, measures of efficiency can be developed that relate actual costs to some standard. The standard expresses the costs that should be incurred for a given level of output. Managers often find such measures useful as indicators of efficiency.

Effectiveness

The relationship between a responsibility center's output and its objectives is an indication of its effectiveness. The more its outputs contribute to its objectives, the more effective a responsibility center is. Since both outputs and success in meeting objectives may be difficult to quantify, measures of effectiveness are often difficult to obtain. Effectiveness, therefore, is usually expressed in qualitative, judgmental terms, such as "College A is doing a first-rate job" or "College B has slipped somewhat in recent years."

An organization unit should attempt to be both efficient and effective; it is not a matter of being one or the other. A manager who meets a responsibility center's objectives with the least resources may be efficient; but if the center's output is inadequate in its contribution to the unit's objectives, the manager is ineffective. If, for example, the employees in a welfare office are invariably busy, processing claims and applications with little wasted motion, the office is efficient. If the personnel have the attitude that their function is to ensure that every form is made out perfectly, however—rather than to help clients obtain welfare services—the office is ineffective.

The Role of Profit

One important goal in a for-profit organization is to earn a satisfactory profit, and the amount of profit is therefore an important measure of effectiveness. Since profit is the difference between revenue, which is a measure of output, and expense, which is a measure of input, profit is also a measure of efficiency. Thus, in a for-profit organization, profit measures both effectiveness and efficiency. Since, by definition, earning a profit is not a goal of a nonprofit organization, the difference between revenue and expense says nothing about either effectiveness or efficiency.

The Management Control Structure

As discussed previously, the management control structure is an organization's network of responsibility centers. Large organizations usually have complicated hierarchies of responsibility centers: units, sections, departments, branches, and divisions. With the exception of those at the bottom of the organization, each responsibility center consists of aggregations of smaller responsibility centers, and the entire organization is itself a responsibility center. One function of senior management is to plan and control the work of all these responsibility centers.

Example

A university consists of a number of responsibility centers, such as its Schools of Law and Medicine and its College of Arts and Sciences. Each school or college is in turn composed of separate responsibility centers, such as the language department or the physics department. These departments may in turn be divided into separate responsibility centers; the language department may, for example, be composed of sections for each language. The management control function is to plan, coordinate, and control the work of all these responsibility centers.

As discussed above, a responsibility center exists to accomplish one or more purposes; these are its objectives. These objectives should help the organization achieve its overall goals, which were decided in the *strategy formulation* process. A responsibility center also has inputs of labor, material, and services. The language department in the above example has inputs of faculty, staff, educational materials, and maintenance services. The department uses these inputs to produce its outputs. If the responsibility center is effective, its outputs will be closely related to its objectives. One output of the language department is the knowledge and skill in language acquired by the students; another might be instructional recordings or tapes for use outside the university. These outputs are related to the language department's objectives and presumably help satisfy one or more of the university's goals.

Exhibit 1–1 shows the essence of what a responsibility center does, using a steam-generating plant as an analogy. The plant exists for a purpose, namely, to generate electrical energy. To accomplish this objective, it employs furnaces, turbines, smokestacks, and other physical resources which, in operating, use fuel. These are its inputs. The energy the plant generates is its output.

Types of Responsibility Centers

There are four principal types of responsibility centers: (1) revenue, (2) expense, (3) profit, and (4) investment. The principal factor in the selection of one type over another is control. That is, senior management's objective in choosing a given type of responsibility center is to hold the center's manager accountable for only those inputs and outputs over which he or she can exercise a reasonable amount of control (not necessarily total control, however).

Revenue Centers

A revenue center is a responsibility center in which the manager is charged primarily with attaining some predetermined amount of revenue. Of course, a revenue center incurs expenses, and these are agreed upon between the manager and his or her superiors. However, the manager's *performance* is measured in terms of the amount of revenue earned by the responsibility center. Many marketing departments are revenue centers. A university's development office frequently is a revenue center.

EXHIBIT 1–1
Nature of a
Responsibility Center

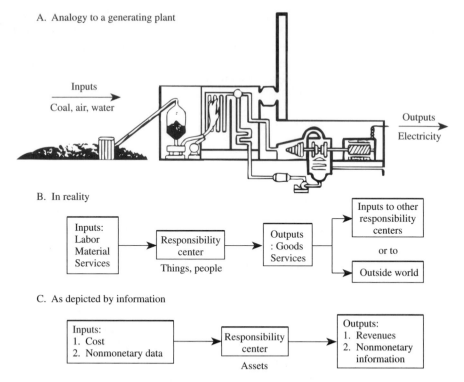

A. Analogy to a generating plant

B. In reality

C. As depicted by information

Expense Centers

In an expense center, the manager is held responsible for the expenses incurred during a specified time period.[12] This means that the management control system is concerned with the center's inputs.

There are two types of expense centers: discretionary expense centers and standard expense centers. A *discretionary expense center* ordinarily is used when there is no easy way to measure the center's outputs, such as in an accounting department. If this is the case, the manager is held responsible for a fixed amount of expenses for the month (or other reporting period) and is expected not to exceed this amount unless there are compelling reasons to do so.

A *standard expense center* is used when the units of output can be rather easily identified and measured, such as in a radiology department in a hospital. With a standard expense center, the manager is not responsible for a fixed amount of expenses, but for a predetermined expense for each unit of output. A standard expense center ordinarily is used when the manager cannot control the amount of output that his or her department is required to produce. Instead, the

---

[12]The term *expense* is not synonymous with cost. Cost is a measure of resources consumed for any specified purpose, whereas expense always refers to resources that are consumed in operations of a specified time period. Outlays to manufacture a product are costs in the period in which the product is manufactured, but they become expenses only in the period in which the product is sold and the related revenue is earned. This distinction is discussed more fully in Chapter 3.

amount of output is determined by requests from other responsibility centers. When this happens, the manager's budget for each reporting period is determined by multiplying the actual output produced by the standard expense per unit. His or her performance is measured against this figure.

Example

During a particular month, a department of radiology received requests from the department of pediatrics for 500 chest X-rays and 200 skull X-rays. The agreed-upon expenses were $25 per chest X-ray and $50 per skull X-ray. The expense budget against which the radiology manager's performance is measured is $12,500 (500 × $25) for chest X-rays and $10,000 (200 × $50) for skull X-rays, for a total of $22,500.[13]

In a business enterprise most individual production departments are standard expense centers, and most staff units are discretionary expense centers. In many nonprofit organizations, both types of departments are discretionary expense centers. For these, the accounting system records expenses incurred, but not revenue earned or output produced.

Profit Centers

In a profit center, the manager is responsible for both revenue (a monetary measure of output) and expense (a monetary measure of input, or resources consumed). Profit is the difference between revenue and expense. Thus, a profit center manager's performance is measured in terms of both the revenue his or her center earns and the expenses it incurs.

Many nonprofit organizations have responsibility centers that charge fees for their services and incur expenses in delivering those services. This is the case with many hospital departments; with the housing, dining, and other auxiliary services of a university; and with utilities, refuse collection, and similar enterprises of a municipality. In these instances, the responsibility center can be thought of as a profit center, even though use of the term *profit center* in a nonprofit organization may seem contradictory.

Investment Centers

In an investment center, a manager is responsible for both profit and the assets used in generating the profit. This responsibility frequently is measured in terms of a return on assets (ROA), which is a ratio of profit earned to assets employed. The former usually is expressed as a percentage of the latter. Thus, an investment center adds more to a manager's scope of responsibility than does a profit center, just as a profit center involves more than an expense center. Although investment centers are rarely used in nonprofit organizations, they are nevertheless quite appropriate for those situations in which a manager is responsible for a clearly identified set of assets. This can happen in nonprofit organizations as well as in for-profit ones.

[13]The computations are somewhat more complicated than this. We will return to this issue in Part 3.

Mission Centers and Service Centers

Regardless of type, responsibility centers can be classified as either mission centers or service centers. The output of a *mission center* contributes directly to the objectives of the organization. The output of a *service center* contributes to the work of other responsibility centers, which may be either mission centers or service centers; its output is thus one of the inputs of these responsibility centers. A service center is often called a *support center.*

Example

In a museum, the curatorial and education departments ordinarily are designated as mission centers—they contribute directly to the objectives of the museum. Finance and personnel departments usually are designated as service centers—they contribute to the work of other responsibility centers but do not contribute *directly* to the objectives of the museum.

Many mission centers are also profit centers, although some are designated as revenue or expense centers. A service center may be a discretionary expense center, a standard expense center, or a profit center. If the latter, it *sells* its services to other units, and its output is measured by the revenue generated from its sales. Its objective usually is not to make a profit (i.e., an excess of revenue over expenses) but rather to break even. The extension of the profit center concept to service centers is relatively new in nonprofit organizations. When properly designed, however, service centers functioning as profit centers can provide a powerful instrument for management control.

Responsibility Centers and Programs

Many organizations distinguish between responsibility centers and programs. These organizations have both program structures and responsibility center structures in their management control systems. The responsibility center structure contains information classified by responsibility center. This information is used for: (1) planning the activities of individual responsibility centers, (2) coordinating the work of several responsibility centers in the organization, and (3) measuring the performance of the responsibility center managers.

Information about the programs that the organization undertakes or plans to undertake is contained in the program structure. Managers use the program structure for three principal purposes:

1. To make decisions about the programs to be undertaken and the amount and kind of resources that should be devoted to each.

2. To provide a basis for setting fees charged to clients or for reimbursement of costs incurred.

3. To permit comparisons with similar programs in other organizations. For example, managers in a hospital with an open-heart surgery program might wish to compare its costs with those of similar programs in other hospitals.

EXHIBIT 1–2   **Relationship between Responsibility Centers and Programs**

Responsibility Centers	Programs			
	Sports Medicine	*Alcohol Detoxification*	*Drug Rehabilitation*	*Open-Heart Surgery*
Mission centers:				
Routine care	3,800 days	1,200 days	300 days	8,000 days
Surgery	1,000 operations	—	—	500 operations
Laboratory	2,000 tests	500 tests	300 tests	2,000 tests
Radiology	8,000 procedures	—	—	1,500 procedures
Outpatient care	12,500 visits	10,000 visits	8,500 visits	—
Service centers:				
Housekeeping	Costs allocated to mission centers			
Dietary	for purposes of measuring the full			
Laundry	cost of mission centers and the			
Administration	programs using the resources of			
Social service	these mission centers.			

When there is both a responsibility center structure and a program structure, the management control system must identify their interactions. In some instances, a responsibility center may work solely on one program, and it may be the only responsibility center working on that program. If so, the program structure corresponds to the responsibility center structure. This is the case in most municipal governments. One organization unit is responsible for providing police protection, another for education, another for solid waste disposal, and so on.

One-to-one correspondence between programs and responsibility centers does not always exist, however. For example, a regional office of the U.S. Department of Health and Human Services (HHS), which is a responsibility center, works on several HHS programs. When this happens, the management control system must identify the relationships between the organization's responsibility centers and its programs.

Exhibit 1–2 uses a hospital to depict the relationship between responsibility centers and programs. In this organization, responsibility centers are divided between mission centers and service centers. A given mission center, such as the outpatient department, can work for several programs. Here, it provides 12,500 visits for the sports medicine program, 10,000 visits for the alcohol detoxification program, and 8,500 visits for the drug rehabilitation program. At the same time, a given program, such as the drug rehabilitation program, can receive services from several mission and service centers. Here, it receives 300 days of care from the routine care mission center, 300 tests from the laboratory, and 8,500 visits from the outpatient department. It also receives housekeeping, dietary, laundry, administrative, and social services from the hospital's service centers. If these departments were established as profit centers, they might sell their services to both mission centers and programs; otherwise, their costs would be allocated to mission centers and programs.

The Management Control Process

The management control process takes place in the context of an organization's goals and the broad strategies senior management has chosen for achieving them. As discussed previously, decisions on goals and strategies are made in the strategy formulation process, which is largely unsystematic and informal.

Much of the management control process also is informal. It occurs by memoranda, meetings, conversations, and even such signals as facial expressions—control devices not amenable to systematic description. Most organizations also have a formal system, however, with information on planned and actual outputs and inputs. Prior to a given operating period, decisions and estimates (budgets) are made that specify desired levels of these outputs and inputs. During the operating period, records of actual levels are collected and reports are then prepared that compare actual and planned levels. If necessary, corrective action is taken on the basis of these reports.

The formal management control process has four principal phases:

1. Strategic planning (sometimes called *programming*).

2. Budget preparation.

3. Operating and measurement.

4. Reporting and evaluation.

These phases occur in a regular cycle, and together they constitute a closed loop, as indicated in Exhibit 1–3.

Strategic Planning

In the strategic planning phase, senior management determines the major programs the organization will undertake during the coming period and the approximate expenses that each will incur. These decisions are made within the context of the goals and strategies that emerged from the strategy formulation activity. If a new program represents a change in strategy, the decision to initiate it effectively is part of the strategy formulation activity, rather than the management control process. Strategy formulation and management control merge in the strategic planning (or programming) phase.

Many organizations prepare a strategic plan that contains planned revenues and expenses for several years in the future—usually five years, but possibly as few as three, or (in the case of public utilities) as many as 20. Other organizations do not have a formal *mechanism* for describing their overall future programs. They rely instead on reports or understandings as to specific,

EXHIBIT 1–3
Phases of
Management Control

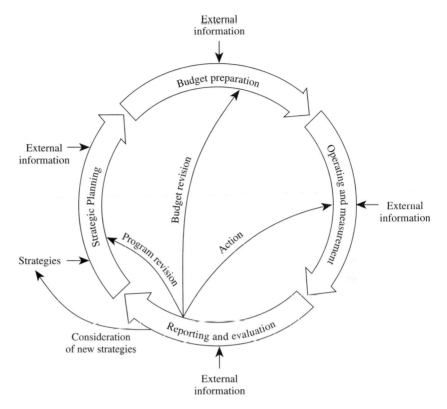

important facets of their programs, especially the amounts to be invested in capital assets and the means of financing these assets.

Programs in industrial companies are usually products or product lines, plus activities (such as research) that cannot be related to specific products. The plans state the amount and character of resources (inputs) that are to be devoted to each program and the planned uses of these resources. In a nonprofit organization, programs define the types of services the organization has decided to provide.

To the extent feasible, program decisions are based on economic analyses, which compare estimated revenues or other benefits from a proposed program with the program's estimated costs. In many for-profit companies, as well as in most nonprofit organizations, reliable estimates of a program's benefits cannot be made. Decisions on these programs tend to rest on senior management's ability to exercise sound judgment in the face of sometimes persuasive program advocates, political considerations, and the frequently parochial interests of external constituencies.

Budget Preparation

A budget is a plan, expressed in quantitative, usually monetary, terms. It covers a specified period, usually a year. In the budget preparation phase of the management control process, each program's objectives are translated into terms that correspond to the spheres of responsibility of the managers charged with implementing them. Thus, during the budget preparation phase, plans made in program terms are converted into responsibility terms.

Example	In a university, an art program will have several interrelated goals: train a certain number of students, provide some cross-cultural experiences, raise a designated amount of support from alumni, and so forth. During the budget preparation process, the university determines the faculty and staff resources that are to be committed to the program, the budgeted operating expenses (e.g., travel) for the program, and, perhaps, some program objectives (e.g., admit a certain number of international students to the program). The manager of the program assumes responsibility for accomplishing these objectives within some specified amount of resources (the budget), department chairs assume responsibility for providing the requisite faculty to teach in the program, and the program manager may obtain commitments from his or her subordinates to achieve certain objectives (e.g., send three newsletters to 90 percent of alumni; develop a fund raising campaign).

The process of arriving at the budget is essentially one of negotiation between responsibility center managers and their superiors. The end product of these negotiations is a statement of the outputs expected during the budget year and the resources (inputs) to be used to achieve these outputs. As such, the agreed-upon budget is a *bilateral commitment.* Responsibility center managers commit to producing the planned output with the agreed amount of resources, and their superiors commit to agreeing that such performance is satisfactory. Both commitments are subject to the qualification "unless circumstances change significantly."

Operating and Measurement

During the period of actual operations, managers supervise what is going on and the accounting staff keep records of actual inputs and outputs. In many organizations, the records of inputs (i.e., resources consumed) are maintained so as to reflect the costs incurred by both programs and responsibility centers. Program cost records are used as a basis for future programming; responsibility cost records are used to measure the performance of responsibility center managers.

Reporting and Evaluation

Accounting information, along with a variety of other information, is summarized, analyzed, and reported to those responsible for knowing what is happening in the organization as well as those charged with attaining agreed-upon levels of performance. The reports enable managers to compare planned outputs and inputs with actual results. The information in these reports is used for three purposes.

Operations

First, the reports help senior managers coordinate and control current operations of the organization. Using this information, together with information obtained from conversations or other informal sources, managers can identify situations that may warrant intervention. They can investigate these situations and initiate corrective action where necessary and feasible.

Performance Evaluation

Second, the reports are used as a basis for evaluating operating performance. Such evaluations lead to actions related to responsibility center managers: praise for a job well done; constructive criticism if warranted; or promotion, reassignment, or, in extreme cases, termination. Such information is also used to guide managers of responsibility centers in the development of improved methods of operating.

Program Evaluation

Third, the reports are used as a basis for program evaluation. For any of a number of reasons, the plan for a program may be suboptimal. If so, individual budgets or entire programs may need to be revised.

The reporting-and-evaluation phase thus closes the loop of the management control process. Evaluation of actual performance can lead back to the first phase, a revision of the program, or to the second phase, a revision of the budget, or to the third phase, a modification in operations. It can also lead senior management to reconsider the organization's strategies for achieving its goals, or even to revise the organization's goals.

Characteristics of a Good Management Control System

Management control systems differ considerably from one organization to the next. In some organizations they work well; in others they are in need of considerable redesign if they are to play a significant role in helping the organization to achieve its goals and strategies. In assessing the quality of a management control system, analysts tend to focus on several criteria. The absence of one or more of these criteria is an indication that the system is in need of redesign.

A Total System

Properly designed, a management control system is a *total* system; that is, it embraces all aspects of an organization's operations. It needs to be a total system because an important management function is to assure that all parts of the operation are in balance with one another. To monitor and maintain this balance, senior management must have information about all parts of the organization's operations.

Goal Congruence

A basic principle of social psychology is that persons act according to their perceived best interests. Because of this, one characteristic of a good management control system is that it encourages managers to act in accordance with *both* their own best interests *and* the best interests of the organization as a whole. In the language of social psychology, the system should encourage *goal congruence*. It should be structured so that the goals of individual managers are consistent with the goals of the organization as a whole.

Perfect congruence between individual goals and organizational goals rarely exists. At a minimum, however, the system should not include evaluation and reward criteria that make the individual's best interests inconsistent with the best interests of the organization. For example, a lack of goal congruence exists if the management control system emphasizes reduced costs and, in doing so, encourages managers to sacrifice quality, provide inadequate service, or engage in activities that reduce costs in one department but cause more than an offsetting increase in another.

Financial Framework

With rare exceptions a management control system should be built around a financial structure; that is, estimates and measures are stated in monetary amounts. This does not mean that accounting information is the sole, or even the most important, part of the control system; it means only that the accounting system provides a unifying core to which managers can relate other types of information. Although the financial structure is usually the central focus, nonmonetary measures, such as minutes per operation, number of persons served, percentage of applicants admitted, and recidivism and drop-out rates are also important parts of the system.

Rhythm

The management control process tends to be rhythmic; it follows a definite pattern and timetable, month after month, year after year. In budget preparation, certain steps are taken in a prescribed sequence and at certain dates each year: dissemination of guidelines, preparation of original estimates, transmission of these estimates up through the several echelons of the organization, review of these estimates, final approval by senior management, and dissemination back through the organization.

Integration

A management control system should be a coordinated, integrated system. Although it is a single system, it is perhaps more useful to think of it as two interlocking subsystems—one focused on programs and the other on responsibility centers. Furthermore, much of the data used in the management control system are also used in preparing a variety of other reports and analyses used by both line managers and professional staff.

Boundaries of this Book

Management control is an important function, but it is by no means the whole of management. Managers also must make judgments about people: their integrity, their ability, their potential, their fitness for a given job, or their compatibility with colleagues. Senior management is responsible for building an effective organization and for motivating the people who comprise that organization to work toward its goals.

Similarly, while the management control function helps an organization to reach its goals, it does not have anything to do directly with the existence of the organization or the formulation of its goals. This book therefore is not concerned with whether there should be an organization, or whether it should have its existing goals—be they good or bad. The management control function occurs both in UNICEF and the Mafia. Our focus thus precludes criticism of the goals themselves, on moral, public policy, or other grounds. We do not, for example, debate the question of the extent to which the government should be responsible for health care. We accept the fact that the Congress has assigned certain health care responsibilities to the Department of Health and Human Services, and start our analysis with this as a given.

Exclusion of Systems Approach

The focus on management control in an existing organization means that some exciting topics are not given the attention that their importance might otherwise warrant. Of these, perhaps the most important is the systems approach. Health care, for example, should be viewed as a system, comprising all the individuals, organizations, and policies that are intended to provide an optimal level of health care. When viewed in this way, it is apparent that the healthcare system in the United States is deficient. Our morbidity rates, infant mortality rates, and other indicators of health status rank nowhere near the top of the list of industrialized countries, despite the fact that we spend more on health care per capita than do most other nations. Healthcare facilities are poorly distributed. Many ill people who could be treated inexpensively in a clinic are sent unnecessarily to expensive hospitals. Many people cannot afford adequate health care.

All these facts are indications that the healthcare *system* needs a drastic overhaul. It should be possible to provide better health care at substantially lower cost by emphasizing new organizational arrangements, such as more ambulatory care facilities; a new mix of personnel, such as more nurse practitioners and physician extenders; and more emphasis on preventive medicine. In short, a focus on health care as a system is fascinating, and an analysis of this system can lead to major improvements in its functioning. Similarly, governmental organizations, higher educational facilities, and volunteer organizations are all best understood when viewed in a systemic perspective.

This book takes a narrower focus, however, concerning itself with the activities of individual organizations. Within the healthcare system, our focus will be limited to a hospital, clinic, or nursing home, for example. Within the educational system, we will focus on individual schools, colleges, or universities. The book accepts the role of an organization and its goals essentially as given, and concentrates on how improvements in the management control function might help the organization to perform more effectively and efficiently.

Such a focus tends to be less than satisfying to many people because it rules out discussion of certain current, sometimes glamorous, high-payoff topics. These topics should, of course, be discussed, but in another context. Thus, in the chapters that follow, we put a relatively low emphasis on the systems in which nonprofit organizations exist, focusing instead on the individual organizations that comprise those systems. It is tempting to focus on global systems' problems and to neglect the problems of individual organizations, but we try to resist that temptation.

Suggested Additional Readings

Anthony, Robert N., and V. G. Govindarajan. *Management Control Systems,* 10th ed. Chicago: Irwin/McGraw-Hill, 2000.

Berman, Evan M., and William B. Werther, Jr. *Third Sector Management: The Art of Managing Nonprofit Organizations.* Washington, DC: Georgetown University Press, 2001.

Brinckerhoff, Peter C. *Social Entrepreneurship: The Art of Misson-Based Venture Development.* New York: John Wiley & Sons, 2000.

Bryson, John M. *Strategic Planning for Public and Nonprofit Organizations.* San Francisco: Jossey-Bass Publishers, 1995.

Dees, J. Gregory, Jed Emerson, and Peter Economy. *Enterprising Nonprofits: A Toolkit for Social Entrepreneurs.* New York: John Wiley & Sons, 2001.

Drucker, Peter Ferdinand, Frances Hesselbein, and Max De Pree. *Excellence in Nonprofit Leadership.* San Francisco: Jossey-Bass, 1998.

Firstenberg, Paul B. *The 21st Century Nonprofit: Remaking the Organization in the Post-Government Era.* New York: Foundation Center, 1996.

Herman, Robert D. *The Jossey-Bass Handbook of Nonprofit Leadership and Management.* San Francisco: Jossey-Bass, 1994.

Kluger, Miriam P. *Innovative Leadership in the Nonprofit Organization: Strategies for Change.* Washington, DC: Child Welfare League of America, 1994.

Letts, Chrstine W., William P. Ryan, and Allen S. Grossman. *High Performance Nonprofit Organizations: Managing Upstream for Greater Impact.* New York: John Wiley & Sons, 1998.

Light, Paul Charles. *Making Nonprofits Work: A Report on the Tides of Nonprofit Management Reform.* Washington, DC: Brookings Institute, 2000.

Migliore, R. Henry. *Strategic Planning for Not-for-Profit Organizations.* New York: Haworth Press, 1995.

Oster, Sharon M. *Strategic Management for Nonprofit Organizations: Theory and Cases.* New York: Oxford University Press, 1995.

Pappas, Alceste T. *Re-engineering Your Nonprofit Organization: A Guide to Strategic Transformation.* New York: John Wiley & Sons, 1996.

Case 1–1

Hamilton Hospital*

> This has been one of the ugliest things I've ever done—all the personal abuse, just for following the damn rules the university sent down. It is the closest I've come to quitting my job . . .

In September 1996, Dr. Richard Wells, Chief of Surgery at Hamilton Hospital in Chicago, Illinois, announced that all full-time doctors in the Department of Surgery were required to join the Surgical Group Practice or leave the hospital premises. In his eight years as chief, Dr. Wells had initiated numerous changes in the department, but never one as controversial as the Group Practice.

Dr. Wells had established the Group Practice or "trust" in 1994 to serve two purposes. First, it was intended to regulate each surgeon's professional income to comply with the Kent Medical School Salary Regulation, and secondly, it would augment the department's income with funds not otherwise attainable. Additionally, Dr. Wells was convinced that as an academic department of Kent Medical School, the Department of Surgery needed guidelines to ensure a standard of excellence:

> I think this has to be done in any academic institution. Doctors here are supposed to provide ongoing patient care, carry on research, and teach. Now if you're at all good as a surgeon, your private practice will skyrocket, and your research and teaching will lose out. It's fun and lucrative to practice medicine, but in a teaching hospital you have other responsibilities, too.

*This case was prepared by Patricia O'Brien under the direction of Professor David W. Young. It subsequently was modified by Professor Young. Copyright © by David W. Young.

Background

The Department of Surgery was a clinical department of the 95-year-old Hamilton Hospital in Chicago. A private, 450-bed hospital, Hamilton had been a teaching affiliate of Kent Medical School since 1925. In its more than 70 years as a teaching hospital, Hamilton had demonstrated a firm commitment to teaching and research as well as patient care. Insisting that the three were interdependent units which together enhanced the quality of medical care, Hamilton's medical staff had distinguished itself among hospital teaching staffs. In 1990, Hamilton was the most popular hospital among Kent medical students and attracted graduates of the top medical schools for its 175 intern and resident positions.

As part of the teaching hospital, Hamilton's clinical departments were subject to the guidelines of Kent Medical School. Prior to 1990, Kent's guidelines, which primarily stressed Kent's commitment to scholastic achievement, had had little effect on the school's clinical departments. Dr. Wells explained:

> For years, we'd had what you'd call a "Gentleman's Agreement" with the medical school. They gave the department a modest budget and paid doctors something for their teaching and research. Other than that, doctors could work for the hospital and carry on a private practice making about as much money as they wanted. There was some innocuous stipulation in our agreement allowing doctors to make as much money as "didn't interfere with their scholarly activities."

By 1990, Kent Medical School was feeling the financial constraints besetting most academic institutions. Unable to continue supporting their clinical departments, they altered the agreement, asking that patient fees support hospital clinical departments. The school issued a Salary Statement Regulation, from which the following is excerpted.

> Total Compensation paid to full-time members of the Faculty of Medicine as of December 1, 1991, may not exceed the level set for each individual in the *Appointments and Compensation Requirements for the Faculty of Medicine at Kent University*. The member's total income is equal to the sum of his/her Academic Salary plus Additional Compensation plus Other Personal Professional Income and may not at any level exceed twice the member's Academic Salary.
>
> Each Clinical Department head shall be responsible for maintaining the records and reporting the income of all full-time members of the Department. . . . Fees earned that are in excess of an individual's compensation level must be reported and disposed of as directed by the institution responsible for setting the level of compensation in consultation with the Dean of the Medical School.
>
> Inasmuch as the System was adopted by the faculty and approved by the Kent Corporation, it is understood that no Faculty member may continue in the full-time system unless he/she is in full conformity with the system and the procedures designed to implement it.

According to Dr. Wells, this was a difficult confirmation for the chiefs to give:

The new guidelines caused quite a commotion, as you can imagine. Doctors were critical of the policy because they now had to report their salaries—something they'd never had to do before.

When I asked people in my department for income disclosures, some of them tried everything to get around the rules. They were giving me their salaries after taxes and expenses—and it was *unreal* what they were calling "expenses." They were, of course, making just what they had been before. And it was becoming clear to me that I couldn't enforce the regulation.

Meanwhile, the Department of Surgery's income, now derived from the hospital and grants, was not meeting the department's needs. Some surgeons joined Dr. Wells in his concern about their financial problems. Dr. Eleanor Robinson, Associate Director of the Department of Surgery, explained:

We were finding the department had needs, mostly of an academic nature, that we didn't have the money to support. Occasionally, we'd want to send residents to meetings or postgraduate educational programs but couldn't afford to. Or someone would need financial assistance for a small research project that wasn't covered by long-term NIH grants and the money just wasn't there.

The Group Practice

Responding to these administrative and financial problems, in 1993, Dr. Wells decided to establish a group practice. He intended to structure the practice as a department fund that could pool surgeons' professional fees and pay them salaries, according to Kent's regulation. Any surplus of fees would be retained by the department for its use.

The Group Practice was organized as an educational and charitable trust fund with nonprofit, tax-exempt status. Although the hospital and medical school became the trust's beneficiaries, the trust maintained total responsibility for its policies and budget. Dr. Wells commented:

I watched the Department of Anesthesia at Memorial Hospital form a group through their hospital about eight years ago. Everything goes into the hospital, and they give the group a yearly budget. The chief there is now having difficulty getting a rundown from the hospital on the department's contribution margin when he knows the department is making money. If he wants another anesthetist, he has to justify it to the hospital. I don't want to crawl to the hospital for what I need if I've got the space. Because of their problems, I chose not to do that.

Dr. Robinson, who aided in administering the trust, added:

We generally agreed that patient income for the department's use should be administered outside of the hospital budget. Surgeons sometimes view themselves as more hardworking than the rest of the hospital and we didn't want our money used to subsidize other departments. We hadn't had problems with the hospital but it was a preventive measure.

The Surgical Trust offered members a salary in accordance with the medical school guidelines plus benefits and a conditional overage expense account. As an incentive, salaries were graded down from the guideline ceiling with increases based on yearly evaluation meetings between Dr. Wells and the doctor concerned. Dr. Wells explained:

> A doctor's salary is a function of his or her overall contribution to the department plus academic rank. What the medical school gave us is a maximum for each position. At the evaluation conferences, I decide, with the doctor, where he or she falls on that scale. In reality, we're all pretty close to our maximums but it's an incentive to get the work done.
>
> It's important to realize though, that salaries don't reflect the patient fees generated by the doctor. If a surgeon has a steady practice and generates an average income in patient fees but is an invaluable teacher or researcher, he or she might be promoted academically and hence be paid more than another surgeon whose best skills are in seeing patients.

Dr. Wells acknowledged that this could also be a disadvantage:

> There's a practical problem with tying salaries to academic rank. It isn't always possible for people to do all three things equally well. If they don't do the academics, their salaries suffer. For example, we have some super neurosurgeons—absolutely super—but they don't have time to write academic papers. Their salaries are stuck at their academic rank, whatever happens.
>
> But the fact is, this is an academic hospital and if doctors are interested in making money, they shouldn't be here. They can move up the street and make as much money as they want.

The trust's benefits were health, life, and malpractice insurance, long-term disability insurance, and a tax-deferred annuity program. The plan was designed to provide members with benefits that had previously been purchased with members' after-tax dollars. Thus, it sought both to maximize members' income potentials within the Kent ceiling and to offer tax advantages.

If doctors generated more income than their salaries reflected, they received an overage account for professional expenses. That is, 50 percent of a doctor's surplus income would be credited to the doctor to cover expenses such as subscriptions, books, and conference travel. According to the by-laws of the trust, however, overage money could not be converted into salary. The remaining surplus income was to be used for department expenses.

The department would collect supplemental income from "chief-service patients." Prior to the trust, those patients who did not have private physicians were the responsibility of the chief resident and received free professional services. Because chief-service patients were admitted to the hospital without private physicians, the surgical services they received did not qualify for Blue Shield reimbursement.

When the department established the trust, they employed the senior chief resident as the Group's "junior-staff surgeon" and admitted all junior-staff patients as patients of the professional group practice. The trust could then bill junior-staff patients through its provider status. As a result, the trust collected fees that were not available when each doctor maintained an independent practice.

The trust was to be governed by a board of trustees. The five-member board would be responsible for trust policies and approving loans and budgets. Board members were to be Dr. Wells, who held a permanent position, two trustees appointed by him, and two trustees elected by the department. In addition, Dr. Wells would hold periodic meetings for all trust members.

Membership

By the winter of 1995, there were four members of the Surgical Group Practice: the junior-staff surgeon, Dr. Wells, and two other young surgeons. Critical of the trust's organization and planning methods, four or five doctors opposed joining. Dr. Melvin Jefferson, a general surgeon at Hamilton for 10 years, was the most vocal about his position:

> I was not going to join the trust until I knew exactly what was being proposed. A number of the important issues were left extremely vague. The reasons for establishing the trust were even vague, in my mind at least, and our meetings did little to clarify the specifics. Some of the important issues, especially reconciling salaries, faculty rank, and academic and financial contributions to the department, were unresolved. I don't think these things had been thoroughly thought out, yet we were being asked to join. So a few other doctors and I refused to join until we knew more about the details.

In the spring of 1996, Dr. Wells asked all surgeons to join the trust. A few doctors who had verbally committed themselves to the trust but had postponed joining became members. But because attitudes in the department continued to differ, Dr. Wells decided membership had to be mandatory for all full-time academic surgeons. He explained:

> Membership had to be a prerequisite for remaining in the department because I knew what was going to happen. I had a few nice guys, resigned to the idea of the trust, carrying the department. And there were these other fellows, you know, friends of everyone; they'd been here a long time and didn't want to join the group. Some of them were taking home $300,000 a year. Others, their friends, were toeing the line.
>
> I knew that some people wouldn't go along with it, and maybe for good reasons. You have to be realistic about the specialty you're talking about; if cardiologists can make $300,000 a year, how can you keep them down on the farm? In another one of our subdepartments, everyone is leaving. They're moving down the street to private offices. They're good specialists and it's too bad we're losing them, but if they're interested in making money, that's where they should be.

At the announcement of mandatory participation, every surgeon was forced to make a decision. Dr. Ben Lewis, head of the urology subdepartment, explained his decision to join the trust:

We were TOLD by Dr. Wells that the department was not in compliance with the medical school's financial guidelines. He TOLD us that we had to change our system to comply and that if we didn't want to, we'd have to leave.

I said fine. I trusted Dr. Wells totally, I admired him greatly, and I liked my work. I was willing to change even though I knew the financial and emotional costs. I knew the financial cost because I subtracted their guideline figure from my salary and . . . that was my loss. The emotional cost, loss of independence, is harder to evaluate and still troubles me.

It makes you wonder why people stay here. Why do they? I guess it's because they like Wells—I think that's the main reason everyone stays. He's created a good faculty and a relatively favorable environment.

Other surgeons, however, were still opposed to the Group Practice. Dr. Jefferson, the most reluctant to join, explained that his reticence stemmed from his impression of the trust's operational structure:

In thinking about the Group Practice earlier, I'd had exalted goals in mind. I thought we could use the trust to make a more unified and cohesive Department of Surgery. We could spread the operative experience to the younger surgeons and improve the department academically by removing some of the economic motivations. Somehow the trust got sidetracked into an instrument whose *sole* purpose was to collect chief-service fees for the department, which resulted in a lot of divisiveness in the department.

For example, look at the method of remuneration as initially spelled out: a salary based on faculty rank and an admittedly extremely modest fringe benefit package. That left the question of overages and benefits essentially unresolved. We were being asked to sign a document involving a significant financial decision that could theoretically and legally involve making considerably less money than before, without having the specifics spelled out. We were just told that "no one would be hurt."

I also thought it was absurd to erect a gigantic administrative superstructure on what is essentially a small department. If the purpose was simply to conform to the medical school guideline and earn a little extra money for the department, we didn't need this whole organization with a billing office and everything else. I think we should have started small and built up—the fact is, we just don't have any big earners who can support a trust of this size.

From Dr. Wells' perspective, the trust had by then become

. . . a tremendous can of worms. I had doctors philosophizing about everything, you should have heard them. All upset because of their "loss of control." It wasn't loss of control at all, it was loss of money. The absurd part of it was that a lot of those people weren't losing money. Believe me, surgeons can be a difficult bunch to work with.

Unfortunately, there's no uniformity in the way clinical departments interpreted the guidelines so doctors could point to other departments and claim that they weren't complying the way we were. They were right, particularly in this school, because the dean is afraid to interfere too much in the autonomy of the hospitals.

Billing System

At the outset of the trust, Dr. Wells intended to have all members' billing managed by a central billing office. In the spring of 1993, he hired a business manager to administer billings, collections, and reports for members. He planned that each doctor would submit a daily "activity sheet" to the business office, detailing services rendered, patient names, and fees.

However, because of considerable opposition to the centralized billing plan, Dr. Wells postponed implementing it. Instead, upon joining the trust, each doctor had the choice of centralized billing through the business office or their previous system wherein secretaries billed for doctors' private practices. Given the choice, half the surgeons chose central billing and half chose to remain with the old system. Ann Miller, the business manager explained:

> Doctors really hold a spectrum of opinions on billing; some don't care at all about their bills while others want to see and discuss every one. I think some doctors don't like the business aspect of medicine—they prefer not having to handle it. The others don't like not having control of it. They feel removed from their practice if they don't see the bills go out.

The doctors who remained with private billing were to submit duplicate bills and their monthly collections to the business office. But most doctors never forwarded their duplicate bills, leaving the office with incomplete billing information. Ms. Miller was forced to establish a bill-receipt record system, posting bills and receipts simultaneously and setting them equal to each other.

> It was a crazy system and we knew it, but what could we do? Surgeons set their own fees, and we had no idea what they were. At the end of the month they would send us money with a record of patients' names and amounts paid. So we'd record that amount as billed and paid.
>
> But it was no way to run a business office. For example, one day a doctor brought in $15,000 in checks, just like that. We hadn't expected it at all. We never had any idea of our accounts receivable or collection rates.

However, Ms. Miller added that centralized billing had developed its own complications:

> Our main problem was that the information we received from doctors varied immensely from doctor to doctor. We didn't provide them with a formal activity sheet, so the doctors used their own systems of recording. As you can imagine, we were receiving dissimilar information from all of them.
>
> From what they gave us, my three assistants would compile standard data sheets which was unbelievably time-consuming. On top of that, we were billing for 5 doctors, collecting and recording for 11 doctors, and attempting individual monthly reports for 11. It was taking us three weeks to do just the monthly reports.

It was also becoming obvious to Dr. Wells that the trust billing had to be uniform and managed by a central computer system:

> Finally, I'd had it. The only efficient way to collect money for so many people was through one system. It had to be cheaper and more accurate plus it would keep everyone honest. I figured that if collections changed at all, they should increase because one office was handling all the data.

Many surgeons disagreed with Dr. Wells on this issue. Among them was Dr. Lewis:

> I felt all along that it was crucial that we do our billing independently. Very simply, no one is more interested in his collections than the person who worked for it: I can do it better because I *care.*
>
> Secondly, there are complications in people's billings, which can only be settled by the doctor. A patient is on welfare and can't pay. After one bill, I'd know enough to drop it. A professional courtesy charge—I'm never sure what the billing office charged or if they understand my intention.
>
> Sometimes people come in and say, "Doctor, I've been in here three times and I haven't received a bill yet, why?" I have to say, "I don't know," which makes me feel foolish. When my secretary did billing, I'd just step out, ask her and get the answer. Now with the business office all the way over in Talbot, geographically remote from the department, it is very difficult to know what the current situation is.

In January of 1997, the trust hired a computer company to manage all billings. The company was to receive billing and payment information from the business office and would process it by batches into claims and collections. They would apply claims and collections to physicians' balances and maintain a continual record of the trust's financial status. The computer company agreed to produce monthly printouts, by provider, so that doctors would have accurate records of their accounts.

Despite this contract, the computer company never produced the information. Ms. Miller explained:

> We had a terrible time with that company. The first problem was they never produced any reports according to doctor. We kept asking and they kept agreeing, but they never gave us anything useful.
>
> By the time we realized that we weren't going to get that out of them, we had a more serious problem: they had dropped $15,000 in payments from the records. They just hadn't applied it to any accounts, so although we had the money, we didn't know which accounts, i.e., doctors, it belonged to. That meant that the rates we had manually calculated were also meaningless. Well, we got rid of the company then, but I'm afraid it was too late.

Some doctors, affected by these errors, were already furious. With minimal billing information and startling fluctuations in collection rates, doctors blamed the centralized billing procedure. In an attempt to trace the problems, Dr. Robinson studied the collection data. After analyzing patient mix, payor class, and service mix, she reached no conclusion:

I felt that centralized billing should, if anything, improve collections, but that wasn't our experience. Of course, with our other computer problems the issue became more complicated because our information was incomplete.

Nevertheless, I think we have to separate questions of administrative efficiency from problems with the system itself. This is difficult to do, but we can't treat them as all one big problem with the billing system. Of course, we also have to consider that when surgeons turn their bills over to a collection office, they feel like they're losing control. That's the motive for doing the billing ourselves.

Dr. Wells considered the billing problem to be one of administrative oversights:

Obviously, there were problems with that computer company but I don't see why this would be inherent to centralized billing systems. I've discussed the problem with other groups and our experience is atypical. It happened though, and we can't explain it.

There's also the issue of overhead; doctors are seeing it now like never before. They can see costs that the hospital and department formerly picked up, like secretaries, coming directly out of the trust, and they're not pleased.

Other surgeons, including Dr. Lewis who had become an elected member of the board of trustees, maintained their opposition to the system. He commented:

I've been against centralized billing from the start, and I think time has borne me out. For one year I've worked with no idea of what my collections have been. As a result, I don't know my overage, or if I even have one. If I submit receipts, I don't know if they'll be covered.

I got some information for a few months last year and according to that, my collections had fallen by 33 percent. Yet, Dr. Wells calls this a more efficient system . . .

This method must be costing us more. My secretary still prepares the background information on bills and sends that to the billing office to finish. She might as well do the whole thing. It's unnecessary and inefficient to involve that whole office.

Dr. Jefferson thought that, for himself, the system was less efficient than his previous one:

Last year I tried to get some information about my collections and was appalled at how little they'd collected and how little they knew. They couldn't even give me records on patient payments. I did find out though that overhead was about 19 percent of my salary. We all agreed that this was excessive.

Dr. Lewis added that, in his opinion, the controversy over billing methods and other administrative matters was indicative of the trust's overall administrative policies:

What happened with billing is typical of the way the trust is run. I like and respect Dr. Wells, but our finances are in shambles because he isn't interested in and doesn't have financial skills. For example, look at what happened with the computer company he and Ms. Miller engaged.

What it comes down to is that the trust is really Dr. Wells's. It reflects his personality, plus he controls the majority of votes. Of the five board members, three are Dr. Wells and his two appointments, giving him 3/5 of any vote—it would be impossible to beat him. Not that there has been a showdown but the fact is, he's playing with a loaded deck. It's OK as long as you like and trust him, but it makes for an uncertain future.

Evaluation

By the winter of 1998, all 14 full-time surgeons at Hamilton had joined the trust. Five doctors had left the department in the previous two years for reasons both related and unrelated to the trust. Some joined the staffs at other hospitals, others left to establish independent private practices. Dr. Wells gradually filled their positions with surgeons who joined the trust upon joining the department.

Although reactions in the department still differed on some aspects of the trust, there were also points of general agreement among members. One such area concerned the trust's effect on the department's economic condition. Dr. Robinson commented on it:

> One of the most important results of the trust has been the increased revenue generated for the department. It remains to be seen whether any of this is from the changes in the billing system, but collecting chief-service patient fees has certainly helped us financially.
>
> Before the trust, the department was stretching to take care of the usual expenses. In the past few years we've not only covered our usual costs but we've been able to pay for postgraduate education and extend interest-free loans to residents. We even lent travel money to a resident so that his family could go to England with him when he was studying there.
>
> The problems in the trust were really administrative and business problems. People here are devoted to academic pursuits so they're not concerned about who is generating the most income—that's not the point of medicine. I think these problems are getting smoothed out and the trust will run much better in the future. I also think it will improve as more people join the department.

Dr. Jefferson agreed with Dr. Robinson that the trust had helped the department, but he remained critical of the trust's operations:

> It's still difficult to get a handle on precisely what's going on. The process of forming the trust was not salutary on communication problems within the department, and these problems remain.
>
> In a way, the trust has had no real effect on me. I do exactly what I did before and am not significantly better or worse off because of it. The available funds have allowed the department to survive, which was important, but when the trust was formed, Dr. Wells was never as frank as he should have been about the economic problems of the department. He said "we'd make a little extra money" but we

never knew that there was a significant economic problem. If we had, we might have all discussed it and come up with an agreeable solution. The emphasis was always on the Medical School guidelines.

I think Dr. Wells is a much better chief of surgery than a businessman. There are many business issues and it was preposterous to go about them in an unbusinesslike way. I think Wells had the attitude that it isn't nice to talk about money. So, because he can't talk about it, we have a major communication problem. We still need frankness about this because we're getting new people into the trust and they have to know the details.

Dr. Lewis gave his opinion of the trust's shortcomings:

It's a nice feature of the department to have supplemental funds. I've set up a library in my office for medical students and residents in urology. I've also used money for honoraria and visual aids, and residents have been reimbursed for expenses from urological meetings.

I'd eventually like to see more money spent on teaching and conference equipment. We have considered a closed-circuit TV in the operating room.

As for the other side, I would say that reduced personal income and loss of independence are disadvantages of the trust. And there have been mistakes. The whole concept of centralized billing was a big mistake. I've voted against it every time it's come up, but it exists. Of course, the mistake was exacerbated by Wells's choice of computer companies.

I believe the real problem in organizing the trust was asking people to change. People were asked to go from a liberal, laissez-faire system to a structured one, and resisted. That's not unusual and could have been predicted.

Commenting on the trust four years after he'd organized it, Dr. Wells noted that some questions remained unanswered:

It's a difficult situation because there still is no uniformity in the medical school. I did what I thought had to be done to keep a Department of Surgery functioning academically, but some departments haven't done anything. And realistically, I know academic rank doesn't always reflect someone's contribution. But what could I do?

Then there's always been the budget problem. We never really know where we stand with any of our four budgets. We have budgets for the hospital, the medical school, the grants, and the trust; research funds for this department alone are $1 million. That's big business, and we're not trained for that.

Questions

1. Classify the activities of Dr. Wells into the categories of strategy formulation, management control, and task control. How, if at all, does this assist you in understanding the problems faced by the trust?

2. How would you characterize the management control structure of the trust? Was it well designed? If not, how would you change it?

3. What is your assessment of the management control process of the trust? How, if at all, would you change it?

Case 1–2

Boulder Public Schools*

Edward Caton, a teacher in a midsize elementary school in Boulder, Oklahoma, hoped someday to rise through the administrative ranks to serve as a principal of his own school, but he felt that in order to do so, he should understand more about the position to which he aspired. This was especially important to him in terms of the control he might have over the budget, which he knew was central to real power in many organizations.

In an effort to learn more about the operations of the Boulder Public Schools, he set up some informational interviews with the principal/headmaster of an elementary school, a middle school, and a high school. Before making those rounds, however, he visited the headquarters of the Boulder School Committee to obtain background information for his interviews.

Background

Mr. Caton learned that the department of implementation (DI) made school enrollment projections each December for the coming fiscal year (which ran from July to June). These projections were important since annual staffing needs for each school were determined by a rather complex formula that used the DI's projections as the starting point. Moreover, since personnel formed the bulk of the budget, these projections effectively determined a school's budget. Each school had a few weeks to challenge the DI projections, and, if a convincing argument could be made, the projections would be modified. Final enrollment projections were established by mid-January of each year.

Mr. Caton learned that Boulder had seen declining enrollments. The decline was caused by a slowing of the birthrate, and the flight of middle class families from the city. The result was not only a drop in enrollments, but also a change in the composition of the school system population. Specifically, the proportion of white students had dropped from 64 percent some 15 years ago to only 27 percent. Black students, by contrast, had increased during those same years from 30 to 48 percent, and Hispanics from 4 to 17 percent. Moreover, the proportion of students termed very poor had increased, by one estimate, to two-thirds of the total; 60 percent of the families of Boulder public school students were classified as being at the poverty level of income as defined in federal guidelines.

*This case was prepared by Dena Rakoff under the supervision of Professor David W. Young. Copyright © by David W. Young.

Retrenchment had been necessary in the face of these shrinking enrollments, and pink slips to staff and closing of school buildings had become almost commonplace during this era. Last year, the BPS operated 77 elementary schools grades K–5, and 1 grades K–8; 22 middle schools grades 6–8, and 1 grades 7–8; and 17 high schools. Nearly 4,000 teachers worked in these schools.

The Current Budget

Recently, the city had witnessed the beginnings of a rise in enrollments, and the DI was forecasting an increase to 58,625 students in the current fiscal year. The budget had been set at $293 million, divided between two funds: Fund Number 017 (General School Purposes [GSP]/City Funds), which comprised $285 million of the total, and Fund Number 027 (Facilities Management/Alterations and Repairs [A&R]), which accounted for the remaining $8 million.

The Special Education and Bilingual Education chapters of the Oklahoma State Laws mandated certain levels of spending for their constituents; the portion of the Boulder School Committee budget assigned to those laws was 28 percent. Despite some state financial support for these mandates, much of the funding had to be provided by the School Committee, thereby limiting the funds available for regular education programs.

The State constitution prescribed a formula which determined the amount that the City of Boulder was required to provide to Boulder Public Schools; the school system received this automatically, without being required to make a justification. For the current fiscal year, this "constitutional base" figure was $224.5 million. For additional revenue, the school system had to convince the city of its needs. For the current year, this "supplemental appropriation" from the city was $57.9 million. In addition, the school system expected revenues from miscellaneous sources, mostly federal government entitlement programs, of $10.6 million. These amounts equaled the $293 million budgeted expenditures.

Control of the Budget Formulation Process

Much of the control of the budget process appeared to Mr. Caton to derive from the Central Office, which emphasized centralized decision making. The office advocated a tripartite objective—quality education, equal access, and accountability—and it wanted to reduce so-called *operational inefficiencies.* Two years ago, the office had launched a new budget system with new procedures and committees. This new budgeting system was explained in a document of about 100 pages entitled *Budget Perspective for the Boulder Public Schools,* and was supplemented with two budget manuals, each about 30–50 pages long. The current year's budget document itself was some 75 pages long.

In January, in accordance with the new budgeting system, the principals and headmasters of each school had been given budget packets to assist them in preparing their budgets for the fiscal year beginning in July. These packets included forms such as a school profile, requesting formulation of goals and program directions; a program summary on which to detail plans for using allotted staff; and a programmatic reductions form, which allowed the principals and headmasters to make an argument for restoring previously withdrawn funds by documenting the impact of the cut. The principals and headmasters had about 20 days to complete these documents and to submit them to district superintendents; about a month after that, the district superintendents had been required to submit the packets to the Central Office. Reviews and hearings had taken place on several community and committee levels, as well as on the Central level, prior to arriving at a final budget.

Mr. Caton had read that the longer term objective for the budget formulation process was to rely on a zero-based budgeting model, where all spending would begin with an empty line and build on a program-by-program basis, in accordance with the rationale for each program. However, that plan had not been in place for the current budget, which had been simply a maintenance budget, keeping stable spending levels from the previous year, combined with a few initiatives and a few cuts. The result was an increase of about 8 percent over the prior year's $270 million budget.

Mr. Caton noticed that of the $293 million, $190 million consisted of personnel expenditures, including $121 million for teachers and substitutes. He assumed that this money, and much but not all of the administrative support costs, were quite difficult to reduce, given enrollment levels and union contracts for salary levels and student-teacher ratios. Moreover, budget maneuverability appeared to him to be quite restricted by a variety of "givens" within the system: curriculum requirements, accompanied by citywide tests; promotion and graduation requirements; and even length-of-class-period dictates. All of these requirements were handed down by the school committee. He even had heard of rumors of an initiative being developed by the State Department of Education to require schools to report on matters such as truant days, suspension days, dropouts, and high school seniors' postgraduation plans. He wondered what this would imply for the availability of state funds for individual schools within the system.

Mr. Caton also had observed what he thought to be a troublesome dichotomy within the system. On the one hand, he had seen a recent memorandum from Finance and Administration, describing some options that gave principals and headmasters greater budget flexibility (Exhibit 1). But on the other hand, Mr. Caton noted that the superintendent was in some ways decreasing the autonomy of schools. He continually heard, for instance, about the slowing of progress toward *School-Based Management,* a program that had made great strides in placing the locus for much decision making in the hands of each school and local community.

EXHIBIT 1
Memorandum to Principals and Headmasters from Finance and Administration

Subject: Budget Flexibility

One major outgrowth of surveys and interviews done in connection with the Finance and Administration Task Force is that desire for budget flexibility continues to be one of the highest priorities of principals and headmasters.

The School-Based Management Project had already given considerable impetus to this concept, and piloted it in certain schools. The Office of School Site Management has emphasized it as a priority for this school year.

The current fiscal year promises to be a very tight budget period throughout. While the schools and programs appear to be adequately staffed, lack of appropriate initial funding and unanticipated large-scale costs in transportation and other areas will put a yearlong squeeze on the total school budget. However, since we will more than likely be in tight budget situations for years to come, we should not use that as a reason for totally avoiding the issue of budget flexibility. Therefore we will undertake initial moves on a systemwide basis this year.

The budget flexibility options open to all principals and headmasters will include:

a. *Ability to move positions* within the individual school budget throughout the school year as long as there is compliance with state and federal mandates. This can be done by submission of a budget transfer (FA-01) and accompanying explanation to the Budget Office through the respective community superintendent.

b. *Use of lag funds* within the 312 account at all levels, and within the lunch monitor account at the elementary school level. This can be done beginning immediately by written request to the Budget Office through the community superintendent.

c. *Return to schools* of one-third of what is saved in substitute monies once we have factored out the use of district substitutes or building substitutes. This will be done early enough in the spring to enable principals and headmasters to use any funds saved in late spring.

d. *Flexible use of 620 funds* to buy equipment, to pay part-time stipends to teachers for special programs for contracted services, for consultants, for tutors, or for hiring temporary help during peak periods. Use of 620 funds in this manner will be by submission of the appropriate FA-01 and explanation to the Budget Office through the community superintendent. (It should be noted that 620 funds cannot be used for creating extra permanent positions, whether full- or part-time.)

e. *Pooling of resources between schools.* Savings that accrue to an individual school may prove small but pooling resources among several facilities might offer opportunities that might not otherwise prove possible. For example, two or three small schools might find it possible to purchase jointly audio/visual equipment that neither could buy individually. In fact, smaller schools are most likely to obtain maximum benefits from these proposals only if they do cooperate and dovetail their efforts with each other.

> This initial movement toward providing flexibility while small at first, will enable school principals and headmasters to purchase some important materials and to try some innovative approaches. It will also allow us as a system to test out ways to provide budget flexibility in a more comprehensive manner in the future.

Perspective of the Principals and Headmasters

Armed with some sense of the school system at large, and toting a set of documents gathered from the Central Office, Mr. Caton next ventured out into the field to interview some school principals. He decided to first visit a senior high school, followed by an elementary school and a middle school.

The Senior High School

The senior high school Mr. Caton visited was a relatively new one, with an enrollment of some 900 students. He began by attempting to learn more about the matter of budgetary discretion:

Caton: What I'd like to know is where you feel that you have any budgetary discretion. Is the entire procedure out of your hands?

Headmaster: Well, no, not entirely. Look, for instance, at my 620 account. That's the budgetary line that covers Instructional Materials. It's fairly broad, including mainly supplies—books, paper, that sort of thing. The total amount assigned to me in September—or actually in late spring—is determined by my projected student enrollment. A fixed part is removed from my allocation before I ever get the opportunity to assign it; that part covers equipment rental and that sort of thing. Let's say I get about an $85,000 allotment; $8,000–$9,000 of that might be assigned before I see the funds.

Then I have the rest to spend as I see fit. No, let me modify that. I have control over the items purchased with the rest and over the timing of that spending—but within certain guidelines. I must order books that appear on the list of School Committee–approved publications. I must use the vendors identified by them as approved. If there is something I want under $2,000, I can arrange my own vendor. However, I still have to go through the central purchasing format. And, to order books not on the list, I have to get approval from the Department of Curriculum and Instruction, which is quite time consuming.

In terms of when I spend my funds, there is some pressure to use up the money quickly. You never know when the Central

Office might issue a spending freeze, and those monies you were saving for a particular midyear purchase vanish. What's more, sometimes, your money is needed elsewhere—and it's wiped out of your account. So, spend quickly is my motto.

I very much wish I could use the money in a more measured way. Rolling over funds from year to year is a good example of a power that would enable me to save for items greatly needed, or to not spend when the need wasn't strong. But, we cannot keep any surplus till the following year, so I spend now!

If I could choose my vendors, I'm sure I could make more informed choices than the Central people can. I'm sure I could get better prices. But, as I said before, as soon as I make a purchase of over $2,000, I must use the approved sellers, or if no appropriate ones are listed, put the proposed purchase out to bid, which makes for a very lengthy procedure.

Caton: Tell me, I think I heard about money held for payment of substitutes, which reverts to you during the year if you do not call upon your full allotment of subs. Is that useful to you?

Headmaster: Sometimes, a portion of the unspent balance does come to the school for us to use as we see fit. We've gotten as much as $7,000 in a year that way. I leave the spending decision to the faculty senate. But, again, we bump up against the issue of inability to choose vendors by ourselves. And, you should consider the pressure felt by the faculty in knowing that their absences determine just how much of these funds all of us will have to use. Sometimes there are legitimate reasons to be out— personal sickness, ill children, etc. And, the teachers' union rises in agitation when they worry about too much pressure being put on people not to take advantage of their legitimate benefits. To tell you the truth, I'd rather spend my time solving real problems than focus too much on this "boon."

Caton: Is there any opportunity to handle your own money more directly when you are awarded grant money?

Headmaster: Yes and no. I recently got an outside grant, funded by the Bank of Boulder and administered by the Central Office. In that case, I had to comply with the usual spending procedures. However, I also had a Carnegie grant of $30,000, and since that was not administered by Central, I could dispense the money as I saw fit.

Caton: I understand that your budget's size is determined by the projected student enrollment. What happens if you take in more students than either you or the Department of Implementation foresaw?

Headmaster: An addendum to the budget is possible. I do feel very strongly, though, that needs and program offerings, rather than numbers, should drive the budget. I'd like to be able to fund a program to train teachers to focus on problem-solving skills here, for instance.

Caton: Is there any way that you, here in your school, can control the numbers reported to Central?

Headmaster: Yes. I try to clean up my DNRs quickly. That stands for "Did Not Report"—in other words, students who were supposed to come to our school but either moved or are attending another school. I don't want them on my rolls any longer than necessary. I send out an attendance officer early to investigate those who do not report, and to drop them early.

Caton: But, doesn't that penalize you when it comes to determining your enrollment?

Headmaster: I run into union trouble if I don't drop them: they make the classes look unrealistically large. My truancy rate looks too large, also. I like clean books.

Caton: What control do you have over changes in budget procedure? How would you go about getting some of these revisions made?

Headmaster: I have a policy of always keeping parent groups informed. It's most important to know how to utilize your constituencies.

The Elementary School

Next, Mr. Caton visited an elementary school, built some 15 years ago, with an enrollment of about 700.

Principal: So, you want to know where I have any discretionary spending power. The 620 account, that's key. Maybe 12% of that is preassigned; the rest is mine to do with as I see fit.

Look, here's a copy of the latest expenditure report for this school from Central (Exhibit 2). As you can see, here's my 620 line. It shows me budgeted for about $59,000. Supposedly, according to this, $20,000 has already been spent by me—not by Central on its predetermined purchases. But I know that I've spent more than $20,000. It's very important for you to keep records in-house. That's the only way you can answer them downtown when they say you've overspent, or when they try to assign your funds elsewhere, or when you don't know how much you have left because the expenditure reports don't arrive in a very timely manner.

Caton: Don't you get funds from unfilled vacancies to use within your school?

Principal: They don't come here.

Caton: What about unspent substitute money?

Principal: I think that gets reassigned. I don't spend it. But, maybe the reason is that my per diem line gets charged for the long-term substitutes I seem to need each year.

   I don't suffer, though. I manage to make things happen. I came into this school when it was a shambles. I've managed to create a very good faculty. Some of the people who contributed very little left.

Caton: How did you bring that about?

EXHIBIT 2   School Expenditure Report

EXP OBJ	ACCOUNT DESCRIPTION	CURRENT BUDGET	RE-SERVED	ENCUM-BERED	EXPEN-DED	ADJUST-MENTS	PCT YTD	AVLBLE BUDGET
	GSP/CITY FUNDS							
131	REG. EDUCATION TCHR	690,289			58,151		8	632,137
133	PER DIEM SUBS	32,340						32,340
141	KDG TEACHER	121,752			9,214		7	112,537
161	BILINGUAL KDG TCHR	22,180			2,272		10	19,907
171	SPED RESOURCE TCHR	94,146			6,225		6	87,920
181	SPED SUB/SEP. TCHR	245,174			19,721		8	225,452
191	BILINGUAL TEACHER	202,642			17,893		8	184,748
312	SCH/DIST. ADMINIS.	123,714			30,629		24	93,804
341	PROGRAM SUPPORT	32,777			3,300		10	29,476
381	ATHLETIC INSTRUC.	24,976			2,272		9	22,703
391	P.T. PROF/STIPEND	588						588
521	CUSTODIAN	157,341			35,919		22	121,421
576	LUNCH MONITOR	24,486			858		3	23,627
577	BUS MONITOR	4,236						4,236
578	INSTRUCTIONAL AIDE	8,482						8,482
586	SPED RESOURCE AIDE	9,282						9,282
587	SPED SUB/SEP. AIDE	64,972			2,037		3	62,934
588	BILINGUAL ED. AIDE	30,809			564		1	30,244
620	INSTRUC. SUPPLIES	58,850	1,432	21,909	20,507		74	14,999
730	RPRS/MAINT. B&G							
810	INSTR. EQUIPMENT	1,750	985	753			99	11
820	NON-INSTR. EQUIP.							
	-DISTRICT C/E	1,950,786	2,417	22,663	209,570		12	1,716,134

Principal: I simply let my expectations be known; if people wanted to work with me, they stayed; if they didn't, most of them left. Of course there are exceptions.

It took me a few years to get the support of the community. But look, now I can get parents in to help with the video workshop or with field trips any time I need them. I'm about to launch a program for parents to train them in carrying on at home the teaching that we begin here during the day.

Caton: Do you have any other sources of funds?

Principal: Grants. Grant application-writing, that's something my teachers spend a lot of time on. One of my teachers is presenting a workshop on that during the upcoming Teacher Professional Workshop Day. They really produce.

Grants give us some discretionary money. We sometimes get them for schoolwide use, and sometimes individual teachers get them for use with specific classes.

We really must look to external sources. Sales of candy or the like are another place where we turn up money we can use for whatever ends we choose. Parents and children help, last year we raised almost $7,500 through sales. That allows us to buy new blackboards, bulletin boards, to take field trips, and to do some repair of the facilities, which happen to be in fairly poor shape. Fortunately, neither this money, nor our 188 money from the State carry any vendor requirements.

As a matter of fact, look at the 730 account, repairs and maintenance of buildings and grounds. You can see I have an empty line there. The School Committee isn't paying for nonemergencies.

As I say, though, I'm able to get what I need. And, if a teacher needs something, and makes a good case to me for that need, I can provide it. There's always a way.

But, I do have somewhere in my head a list of changes I feel are necessary. One item on that list is the method of determining the budget in the first place. What we need is a program-based budget. We should be able to designate the needs we must meet from the level of the school, and then be given the means and the responsibility to meet them. We shouldn't have to work on what Central says to work on. They claim they understand our programs, but then they do something like what they did this morning—send me a seventh "Behavior Lab" student when six is the limit.

As you know enrollment predictions are very important in determining the budget. Central sends me their estimate every year, and I'm allowed to counter it with my own predictions. In fact, my predictions for the past few years have been right on target. I've worked hard to prove to Central that my predictions are the accurate ones.

Once the budget is set, I can move teachers and use aides to cover if I need to. And, I've been able to distribute enrichment subjects among the student body in a fair way by creating a seven-day roster week; with that, each student gets music or art not once a week in the traditional way, but once every seven-day rotation. Thereby I keep my classes down to a manageable size.

The Middle School

Finally, Mr. Caton went to a middle school of about 600 pupils, constructed about 25 years ago. Some people had told him that middle schools were particularly difficult to manage because of their unstable demographics. He also had learned that high schools received more resources than middle schools; this was due, in part, to the fact that high schools operated with departmentalized systems and differentiated staffing. But he also had been informed that, in the past few years, the middle schools had received funding for some additional positions, such as Directors of Instruction, Instructional Support teachers, and Targeted Reading teachers. He was anxious therefore to learn more about the perspective of a principal of a middle school.

Principal: You have to understand, Boulder has a system of priorities in its school department. Most important is the high school. They get more personnel, more budget, and more discretionary funding; that's probably because the media features them, and media attention must be respected.

Next come the elementary schools, and finally the middle schools. Historically, our size and importance have been determined by the surges and retractions in the elementary school populations. As you probably know, the junior high schools, which middle schools supplanted, ran from grades 7 through 9. Because of this dependency on elementary school enrollment, we, at times, have been as inclusive as grades 4 through 8; sometimes we're 6 through 8. That variation has made it difficult to focus on an age group, and the abrupt changes have been disruptive to teachers as well.

Middle school years, especially 7th and 8th grades, are important years; those are when the decision to drop out is made. We're beginning to get some funds and programs now to combat middle-school-specific problems like overage students, dropouts, and teenage pregnancy.

Caton: Speaking of money, have you been able to take advantage of the "lag funds," that is, the unspent money from unfilled vacancies in your school that I understand reverts to you for your own use?

Principal: That's tricky. I have a vacancy right now for an assistant principal. I do get some of the salary money now, about three months' worth to cover August through this month of October, if I take a new person. But if I take a recall, I lose whatever funds are necessary to pay that person retroactively for the difference between his or her previous salary and this one. So, it's likely not to be as much money as you might expect.

But if I do get some money, I can file a Form FA-01, asking for the money to be transferred to my 620 account, and from there I have some discretion as to what it will buy.

You might think that leaving a position vacant could buy you the money you need for programs or whatever. Not really. The union has come in when positions remain unfilled if there are any unassigned teachers within that certificate area. They worry about their members not being utilized—and paid. And, what's more, if you leave a position unfilled for too long, Central might deem your need for the position reduced, and eliminate the funding for it in the coming budget year.

Numbers, in particular enrollments, are all-important. Special Education and Bilingual Education, both of which are programs mandated by the state, but only partially reimbursed by state or federal funds, put a drain on our resources. When it comes to regular education programs, we have trouble making a case for them.

The Department of Implementation each winter projects our enrollment for next year. My projected and actual enrollment figures are never the same. If you think the figures generated for your school are too small when the March budget figures are announced, you can petition to have the projections altered by making a good statistical argument. If your argument is considered valid, your teacher allotment will be raised, but your 620 account will not—it will be calculated on the basis of the original enrollment projections. Teacher allotments are contractual according to class size; instructional materials are not. The result is that if I get enough students to push a special education class over its limit, for example, I'm given an extra teacher, but I do not necessarily get enough extra 620 money to provide the students with books.

Caton: Do you find the 620 account something you can use to increase expenditures where you feel they're needed?

Principal: Yes, to some extent. But some of those expenditures are fixed: paper, Xerox supplies, art supplies, membership in various organizations; all those things are taken from your 620 account before the line is open to you. Prediction of costs is a bit difficult here also. Some years, for instance, maintenance of the Xerox is done by Central; some years, you have to absorb the costs yourself. It's important to stay in touch with Central each year to learn the current procedures.

After this final interview Mr. Caton looked forward to the evening, when he would sit back in his favorite armchair, notes in hand. From that vantage point, he would attempt to make a coherent whole from the various parts.

Questions

1. Define the key features of the management control system in the Boulder Public Schools.

2. As the manager (principal or headmaster) of a Boulder public school, what changes would you like to see made in the management control system? (Your proposals should, of course, be limited to those that you think might be acceptable to headquarters.)

3. As the Superintendent of Schools, what would be your reaction to these proposals?

Chapter 2

Characteristics of Nonprofit Organizations

A nonprofit organization is an organization whose goal is something other than earning a profit for its owners. Usually its goal is to provide services. This definition corresponds approximately to that found in most state statutes.[1]

The definition also emphasizes a basic distinction between for-profit and nonprofit organizations—a distinction that is the cause of many management control problems in nonprofit organizations. In a for-profit company, decisions made by management are intended to increase (or at least maintain) profits. Success is measured, to a significant degree, by the amount of profit the organization earns. By contrast, in a nonprofit organization, decisions made by management ordinarily are intended to produce the best possible service with the available resources. Success in a nonprofit organization is measured primarily by how much service the organization provides and by how well these services are rendered. More basically, the success of a nonprofit organization is measured by how much it contributes to the public well-being.

Since service is a more vague, less measurable concept than profit, it is more difficult to measure performance in a nonprofit organization. It is also more difficult to make clear-cut choices among alternative courses of action

---

[1]Some people prefer the term *not-for-profit* on the grounds that a business enterprise with a net loss is literally a nonprofit organization. *Black's Law Dictionary, Kohler's Dictionary for Accountants, Webster's Third New International Dictionary, Funk and Wagnalls Dictionary,* and *American Heritage Dictionary* do not list "not-for-profit," however. Practice varies widely among states and is not uniform for the statutes of a given state. In federal statutes, the usual term is *nonprofit*. In income tax regulations, *not-for-profit* refers to a corporation that is operated as a hobby of the owners.

in such an organization; relationships between service costs and benefits, and even the amount of benefits, usually are hard to measure. Despite these complications, management must do what it can to assure that resources are used efficiently and effectively. Thus, the central problem is to find out what management control policies and practices are useful for nonprofit organizations.

The distinction between for-profit and nonprofit organizations is not black and white. A for-profit company must render services that its customers find adequate if it is to earn a profit. A nonprofit organization must receive funds from operating revenues or other sources that are at least equal to its expenses if it is to continue to render services. Thus, the distinction is not based on the *need* for funds, per se, but on the predominant attitude toward the *uses* of funds.

Nor does the distinction relate solely to the types of services provided. Some hospitals, medical clinics, schools, even religious organizations operate as for-profit organizations, even though the services they provide often are thought of as being provided by nonprofit organizations. Moreover, in addition to proprietary (i.e., for-profit) hospitals, an increasing number of nonprofit hospitals are being managed by for-profit companies.

Nature of the Nonprofit Sector

Any categorization of nonprofit organizations is certain to have gray areas.[2] Nevertheless, the categories shown in Exhibit 2–1 will serve as a useful frame of reference for this book. As this exhibit indicates, an important distinction exists between public (governmental) and private nonprofit organizations. Within the public category, the division among federal, state, and local government entities provides a useful organizing scheme; any of these entities can have agencies, commissions, or authorities.

Within the private category, an important distinction is between charitable organizations, for which donor contributions are tax deductible, and commercial and membership organizations, for which donor contributions ordinarily are not tax deductible. The former category includes health, educational, social service, religious, cultural, and scientific organizations; in the latter are social clubs, fraternal organizations, labor unions, and similar entities.

To encourage educational, charitable, and other social welfare activities, the Internal Revenue Service (IRS) has made it relatively easy to obtain tax-exempt status. It also revokes the tax-exempt status of only about 100 nonprofits a year.[3]

[2]Some work has been done to develop a common language to define, describe, and classify nonprofit organizations by major function and type. See Virginia A. Hogdkinson and Christopher Toppe, "A New Research and Planning Tool for Managers: The National Taxonomy of Exempt Entities," *Nonprofit Management & Leadership* 1, no. 4 (Summer 1991).
[3]For additional information, see John R. Emshwiller, "More Small Firms Complain About Tax-Exempt Rivals," *Wall Street Journal,* August 8, 1995.

EXHIBIT 2–1 **Categories of Nonprofit Organizations**

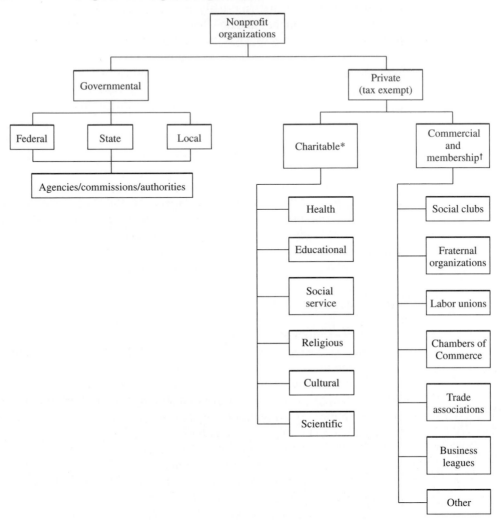

*Donor contributions are tax deductible.
†Donor contributions are not tax deductible.

Diversity of Demands on Managers

As Exhibit 2–1 suggests, the nonprofit sector comprises many different types of entities, with diverse activities, clientele, technological resources, and funding sources. Because of these and many other differences, any discussion of management control in nonprofit organizations must be viewed as a highly contingent one. That is, a management control system that works for one nonprofit organization quite likely will not work for another. Nevertheless, there are certain management control principles that are applicable to almost all nonprofit organizations, and certain issues that all nonprofit managers invariably confront as they attempt to improve the effectiveness and efficiency of their organizations. These are the focus of this book.

Size and Composition of the Nonprofit Sector

As of 1999, the Internal Revenue Service recognized some 275,000 nonprofit organizations with total equity (net assets) in excess of $600 million. Support came in the form of income from investments, grants and fees, and public support. These organizations all fall into Section 501(c) of the Internal Revenue Code in that they are exempt from paying taxes on the income generated by their tax-exempt activities. Exhibit 2–2 shows the seven 501(c) categories, the approximate number of organizations in each, and the approximate amount of equity on their collective balance sheets.

As indicated in Exhibit 2–2, Section 501(c)(3) of the code accounts for more organizations than all other sections combined; these are commonly called 501(c)(3) organizations. If these organizations meet certain criteria, evidenced by a letter that they receive from the IRS, contributions to them for the exempt purpose are tax deductible by the contributor. The contribution must be just that, however—a contribution and not a payment for services—and it must be for the tax-exempt purpose. For example, a contribution to a

EXHIBIT 2–2   Section 501(c) Organizations

Source: Cecelia Hilgert, "Charities and Other Tax-Exempt Organizations, 1994," Washington, D.C., Internal Revenue Service, Special Studies Special Projects Section, March, 1999.

Category		Approximate Number	Total Equity
501(c)(3)	Religious, educational, charitable, scientific, or literary organizations; testing for public safety organizations; organizations preventing cruelty to children or animals, or fostering national or international amateur sports competition.	175,000	$530 million
501(c)(4)	Civic leagues, social welfare organizations, and local associations of employees.	22,000	$13 million
501(c)(5)	Labor, agriculture, horticultural organizations.	20,000	$16 million
501(c)(6)	Business leagues, chambers of commerce, and real estate boards	25,000	$13 million
501(c)(7)	Social and recreational clubs	15,000	$8 million
501(c)(8)	Fraternal beneficiary societies and associations	8,000	$6 million
501(c)(9)	Voluntary employee beneficiary associations (including federal employees' voluntary beneficiary associations).	10,000	$40 million

EXHIBIT 2–3 Number of Employees in Nonprofit Organizations

Source: U.S. Department of Commerce, Census Bureau, *Statistical Abstract of the United States* (Washington, DC: Government Printing Office, 2000).

	Number of Employees (Millions)			Percentage Change	
	1980	1990	1999	1980-90	1990-99
Government:					
Federal..	2.9	3.1	2.7	6.9	-12.9
State..	3.6	4.3	4.7	19.4	9.3
Local..	9.8	10.9	12.8	11.2	17.4
Health services:					
Physicians' offices and clinics..............	0.8	1.3	1.9	62.5	46.2
Nursing and personal care facilities.......	1.0	1.4	1.8	40.0	28.6
Hospitals	2.8	3.5	4.0	25.0	14.3
Home health care services	n.a.	2.5	3.4	n.a.	36.0
Education	1.1	1.7	2.3	54.5	35.3
Social services....................................	1.1	1.7	2.8	54.5	64.7
Membership organizations	1.5	1.9	2.4	26.7	26.3
Total nonprofit...................................	24.6	32.3	38.8	31.3	20.1
Total nonagricultural workforce	90.4	109.4	128.6	21.0	17.6
Nonprofit as percent of total.................	27.2%	29.5%	30.2%	8.5	2.2

college to provide scholarships is tax deductible, but a tuition payment for a specified student is not.

In general, these organizations are tax-exempt. However, they must pay income taxes on their "unrelated business income," which is the profit from units whose purpose is earning income rather than providing tax-exempt services. Such units include manufacturing facilities and certain types of marketing and service entities.

Employment in the Nonprofit Sector

Exhibit 2–3 gives some idea of the magnitude of employment in the nonprofit sector. The figures are not exact because the census categories do not quite conform to the definition of nonprofit that is used here. They are, however, satisfactory as a basis for some general impressions.

As can be seen, nonprofit organizations employ about a quarter of the nation's nonagricultural workforce. Local governments are by far the largest employers, with hospitals the largest nongovernmental employers (although the numbers for this category are somewhat overstated since they include for-profit organizations). However, because many nonprofits make extensive use of volunteer labor, this exhibit, which looks only at paid employees, understates the amount of effort expended on behalf of these organizations' clientele.

Characteristics of Nonprofit Organizations

In the remainder of this chapter we discuss characteristics of nonprofit organizations that affect the management control process. These characteristics are arranged under the following headings:

1. The absence of a *profit* measure.

2. Different *tax and legal* considerations.

3. A tendency to be *service* organizations.

4. Greater *constraints* on goals and strategies.

5. Less dependence on clients for *financial support.*

6. The dominance of *professionals.*

7. Differences in *governance.*

8. Importance of *political influences.*

9. A *tradition* of inadequate management controls.

The absence of a profit measure is the most important characteristic. Since it affects all nonprofit organizations, we will discuss it at length. The other characteristics affect many, but not all, nonprofit organizations. They do so to varying degrees and are not unique to nonprofit organizations; they therefore are tendencies rather than pervasive characteristics.

The Profit Measure

All organizations use resources to produce goods and services; that is, they use inputs to produce outputs. As we discussed in Chapter 1, an organization's effectiveness is measured by the extent to which its outputs accomplish its goals, and its efficiency is measured by the relationship between inputs and outputs. In a for-profit organization, profit provides an overall measure of both effectiveness and efficiency. The absence of a single, satisfactory, overall measure of performance comparable to the profit measure is the most serious problem nonprofit managers face in developing effective management control systems for their organizations. To appreciate the significance of this statement, we need to consider the usefulness and the limitations of the profit measure in for-profit organizations.

Usefulness of the Profit Measure

The profit measure has the following advantages: (1) it provides a single criterion that can be used in evaluating proposed courses of action; (2) it permits a quantitative analysis of those proposals in which benefits can be directly compared with costs; (3) it provides a single, broad measure of performance;

(4) it facilitates decentralization; and (5) it permits comparisons of perform-ance among entities that are performing dissimilar functions. We discuss each of these points below, and contrast them with the situation in a nonprofit organization.

Single Criterion

In a for-profit business, profit provides a way of focusing the considerations involved in choosing among alternative courses of action. The analyst and the decision maker can address such questions as: Is the proposal likely to pro-duce a satisfactory level of profits? Is Alternative A likely to add more to prof-its than Alternative B?

The decision maker's analysis is rarely as simple and straightforward as the profit criterion might imply. Even in a for-profit organization, most proposals cannot be analyzed solely in terms of their effect on profits—almost all pro-posals involve considerations that cannot be measured in monetary terms. Nevertheless, these qualifications do not invalidate the general point: profit provides a focus for decision making.

In a nonprofit organization, there often is no clear-cut objective criterion that can be used in analyzing proposed alternative courses of action. Members of the management team of a nonprofit organization often will not agree on the relative importance of various objectives. Thus, in a municipality, all members of the management team may agree that the addition of a new pumper will add to the effectiveness of the fire department. Nevertheless, some may disagree on the importance of an expenditure to increase the effec-tiveness of the fire department as compared to a comparable expenditure on parks, streets, or welfare.

Quantitative Analysis

The easiest type of proposal to analyze is one in which estimated costs can be compared directly with estimated benefits. Such an analysis is possible when the objective is profitability: profit is the difference between expense and rev-enue, and revenue is equated to benefits.

For most important decisions in a nonprofit organization, managers have no accurate way of estimating the relationship between costs and benefits; that is, they have difficulty judging what effect the expenditure of X dollars will have on achieving the goals of the organization. Would the addition of another professor increase the value of the education that a college provides by an amount that exceeds the cost of that individual? How much should be spent on a program to retrain unemployed persons? Issues of this type are difficult to analyze in quantitative terms because there is no good way of estimating the benefits of a given increment in spending.

Performance Measurement

Profit provides a measure that incorporates a great many separate aspects of performance. The best manager is not the one who generates the most sales volume, considered by itself; nor the one who uses labor, material, or capital most efficiently; nor who has the best control of overhead. Rather, the best manager is the one who, on balance, does best on the combination of all these separate activities. Profit incorporates these separate elements. The key consideration is not the details of the operating statement, but the *bottom line.* This measure provides managers with a current, frequent, easily understood signal as to how well they are doing, and it provides others with an objective basis for judging a given manager's performance.

The principal goal of a nonprofit organization is to render service. Since the amount and quality of service rendered cannot be quantified easily, however, performance with respect to goals is difficult and sometimes impossible to measure. The success of an educational institution depends more on the ability and diligence of its faculty than on such measurable characteristics as the number of courses offered or the ratio of faculty to students, for example.

Decentralization

For-profit organizations have a well-understood goal. The performance of many individual managers can be measured in terms of their contribution toward that goal. Because of this, senior management can safely decentralize, thereby delegating many decisions to lower levels in the organization.

If an organization has multiple goals and no good way of measuring performance in attaining them, it cannot delegate as many important decisions to lower level managers. For this reason, many problems in government organizations must be resolved in Washington or in state capitals rather than in local offices. The paperwork and related procedures involved in sending problems to senior management, and in transmitting the resulting decisions back to the field can be quite elaborate, giving rise to part of the criticism that is levied against bureaucracy. Such criticism is often unwarranted because, in the absence of something corresponding to the profit measure, there is no feasible way for governmental organizations to decentralize.

Comparison of Unlike Units

The profit measure permits a comparison of the performance of heterogeneous operations that is not possible with any other measure. The performance of a department store can be compared with the performance of a paper mill in terms of a single criterion: Which was more profitable? This usually is measured in terms of return on equity or return on assets.

Profitability therefore provides a way of combining heterogeneous elements of performance within a company, and a way of making valid comparisons among organizations. Organizations that have a goal of profitability can be compared, at least roughly, even though the size, technology, products, and markets of these companies are quite different from one another.

Nonprofit organizations can be compared with one another only if they have similar functions. One fire department can be compared with other fire departments, and one general hospital with other general hospitals. There is no way of comparing the effectiveness of a fire department with the effectiveness of a hospital, however.

Tax and Legal Considerations

Most nonprofit organizations benefit from certain provisions of tax legislation. In this section, we summarize the general nature of these benefits. We also discuss briefly some of the legal implications of nonprofit status, particularly with regard to the generation and distribution of a financial surplus and the development of for-profit subsidiaries. The reader should use this information as a broadbrush approach only; it is not a substitute for a legal or tax opinion.

Tax Considerations

Nonprofit organizations ordinarily are exempt from income, property, and sales taxes. In some instances, individuals who lend money to these organizations are exempt from paying taxes on the interest income they earn from their loans. Contributions and gifts to nonprofit organizations also may be tax deductible. We will discuss each item separately.

Income Taxes

Most nonprofit organizations are exempt from paying federal, state, and municipal taxes on income related to their nonprofit activity.[4] They do, however, pay taxes on income generated from activities that fall outside their nonprofit charters. Such activities are known as unrelated business activities.

A nonprofit organization can lose its tax-exempt status if it engages in activities that are considered "inappropriate." These include substantial lobbying or participation in political campaigns. A nonprofit organization also can lose its tax-exempt status if a "substantial part" of its income results from activities that are unrelated to its charter.

The line between unrelated activities and tax-exempt activities frequently is not clear. For example, most YMCAs do not pay taxes on the income from their gymnasiums and swimming pools, even though these facilities compete directly with for-profit physical fitness centers that offer similar services. If, on the other hand, a YMCA shifts its service and program mix too radically, its tax-exempt status may be called into question.

There are essentially two ways a nonprofit organization can conduct for-profit activities and maintain its tax-exempt status: it can pursue a venture that is either (1) related to its tax-exempt purpose or (2) unrelated, but insubstantial. If the organization's for-profit activity falls into the first category, it will preserve its tax-exempt status and pay no federal income taxes. If the activity

---

[4]They report their revenues, expenses, and compensation paid to key executives to the Internal Revenue Service on Form 990.

falls into the second category, the organization will pay "unrelated business" income taxes on the portion of its activity that is unrelated, but will maintain its general tax-exempt status. Many nonprofit organizations that engage in for-profit activities organize in such a way that these activities are carried out in separate, wholly owned subsidiaries. The key advantage of a separate corporate entity is that, for income tax purposes, it minimizes the risk to the parent organization's tax-exempt status. It does not necessarily eliminate the risk that the organization's nonprofit status will be challenged by its state or municipality for property or sales taxes, however.

There is a fine line between related an unrelated income. For example, the profit on books sold in a college bookstore is tax-exempt, but the profit on emblems and clothing is taxable. In addition, a nonprofit's venture into unrelated business activities can have implications that extend beyond the tax consequences. Some observers, for example, have expressed concern about potential conflicts of interest.

Example	In an effort to earn money from the test-preparation field, The College Board launched a website to compete with such firms as Kaplan, Inc., and Princeton Review. The dot-com company was set up as a for-profit subsidiary, with 70 percent ownership by the Board. Competitors argued that the website was a conflict of interest since it was 70 percent owned by the nonprofit entity that prepared the tests. The Board argued that it needed the capital and stock options to compete for top talent.

The college board is not alone in setting up for-profit subsidiaries, some of which engender conflict-of-interest concerns, and some of which cause concern about the future of the nonprofit mission. The American Association of Retired Persons (through its for-profit subsidiary, AARP Services) sells insurance, credit cards, and other services to its members. The American Medical Association (through Medem) links doctors with patients for a profit. Columbia University (through Fathom) provides online educational and information resources, and the National Geographic Society (through National Geographic Ventures) has wholly owned for-profit television and film production, mapping, and retail store subsidiaries.[5]

State and Municipal Taxes

Government, charitable, religious, scientific, and educational organizations are exempt from local property taxes. In many states and municipalities, they are also exempt from sales taxes on the goods and services they sell. In addition, some are exempt from social security contributions and enjoy reduced postal rates. In comparing the costs of a nonprofit organization with those of a for-profit one in the same industry, the nonprofit's costs are inherently lower for these reasons.

---

[5]Diane Brady, "When Nonprofits Go After Profits," *Business Week,* June 26, 2000.

Taxation requirements vary considerably among states. Most states permit municipalities to levy property taxes on nonprofit organizations that do not meet certain criteria. For example, a hospital may be subject to a property tax if it doesn't provide enough charity care or does not meet "community care standards" in other ways. In addition, although nonprofit organizations may be exempt from state or local sales taxes on certain items, sometimes these exemptions can be complicated. For example, in some states, revenues from food sales to college students at an on-campus convenience shop are exempt from sales tax, but revenues from food sales to faculty are not.

Some nonprofits make voluntary contributions to their municipalities as payment for services that the municipality furnishes. For example, a college may pay what it and the municipality agree is its fair share of the cost of fire and police protection, or a fair share of water and sewage if these costs are not charged directly to users. As might be imagined, these discussions can sometimes become controversial.

Example	According to an article in the *Boston Globe,* Harvard University purchased a 30-acre site in Watertown, Massachusetts, a small suburb just outside of Cambridge, for which it paid a private developer $162 million. However, more than $100 million in state and federal money had gone into cleaning up the site and getting it ready for development and inclusion on Watertown's tax roles. Had it been purchased by a for-profit entity, it would have constituted one-third of the town's commercial and real estate tax base. As a nonprofit organization, Harvard was not obligated to pay any real estate taxes. Although Harvard was discussing with Watertown how much it would pay "in lieu of taxes," Watertown's town manager was quoted as saying that the university's proposal was "confusing and unworkable. They are asking for rights no other taxpayer in the country would be granted."[6]

Tax-Exempt Bonds

Individuals who purchase bonds issued by states and municipalities do not pay federal or state taxes on the bond interest income they receive. Some states issue bonds whose proceeds are used by nonprofit hospitals and educational institutions, and the income on these bonds usually is tax exempt also. Because holders of these bonds do not pay taxes on the interest income they receive, they are willing to accept a lower interest rate than they would on a bond of similar grade whose interest was taxable.

Contributions

Individuals and corporations that make contributions to charitable organizations can itemize and deduct these contributions in calculating their taxable

[6]Joan Vennochi, "Rich Old Harvard is Jeopardizing Watertown's Security," *Boston Globe,* July 13, 2001.

income. The organizations that qualify for these deductions are spelled out in detail in Sections 170 and 501(c)(3) of the Internal Revenue Code. As Exhibit 2–1 indicates, they include entities established for religious, charitable, health, scientific, literary, or educational purposes. Nonprofit veterans' groups, cemeteries, and day care centers also are included. States, municipalities, and fraternal organizations are included in this group if the contributions they receive are designated for the above purposes.

Legal Considerations

Three legal issues are of great concern to nonprofit managers: (1) ownership of the entity, (2) generation and distribution of a profit or surplus, and (3) legal obligations under a nonprofit charter.

Ownership of the Entity

A for-profit organization is owned by its shareholders, who expect to receive dividends and stock price appreciation as a return on the equity capital they furnish. By contrast, nonprofits cannot obtain equity capital from outside investors. Instead, the equity capital they obtain from outside sources must be from donations. Moreover, a nonprofit organization cannot distribute assets or income to, or otherwise operate for the benefit of, any individual (trustees usually serve without monetary compensation). There is nothing comparable to stock options, for example, which constitute an important employee incentive in many for-profit organizations. However, under the current tax code, neither high salaries nor large cash reserves are *necessarily* a violation of these requirements. Considerable judgment is required, of course, in determining what is too high or too large.

When a nonprofit organization is dissolved, the entity's value is transferred to another nonprofit organization or to the state or municipality where the organization operates, never to private individuals. In the case of a conversion from nonprofit to for-profit status, the determination of the amount of value is a central concern of the state agency charged with regulating nonprofit organizations. This is because the entity's market value may be greater than the difference between its recorded assets and liabilities, and, when this is the case, the determination of the appropriate amount becomes a matter of judgment.[7]

Sales of nonprofit organizations to for-profit enterprises appear to be on the rise in the health care field. During 1996, more than 100 hospitals once controlled by state and local governments, schools, churches, synagogues, and community boards had affiliated with, or had been purchased by, a for-profit corporation.[8]

[7]For a discussion of this point, see David W. Young, "Ownership Conversions in Health Care Organizations: Who Should Benefit?" *Journal of Health Politics, Policy, and Law* 10, no. 4 (Winter 1986.) See also James C. Robinson, "Capital Finance and Ownership Conversions in Health Care," *Health Affairs,* January–February. 2000.
[8]Monica Langley and Anita Sharpe, "As Big Hospital Chains Take Over Nonprofits, a Backlash Growing," *Wall Street Journal,* October 18, 1996.

In most instances, the purchase requires the creation of a charitable foundation to continue the nonprofit mission. However, this doesn't always happen.

The $150 million Rose Foundation, formed by Columbia/HCA's purchase of Denver's Jewish-affiliated Rose Health Care System, targeted preservation of Jewish identity as a priority funding area. The Jackson Foundation, created as part of Columbia/HCA's $80 million purchase of Goodlark Regional Medical Center, was considering financing a sports-training complex, an arts center, and a foreign language program.[9]

Mergers

In part because of declining philanthropy, and in part because of corporate leaders serving on their boards, some nonprofit organizations also have begun to merge.

Second Harvest and Foodchain, two nonprofits concerned with fighting hunger, were, in the view of many, a perfect merger. Second Harvest distributed mainly canned goods, while Foodchain specialized in handling hot foods. Second Harvest was facing declines in contributions of canned goods, with many of its donors preferring to shift to prepared meals. Their clients were asking for more hot meals rather than ingredients that had to be mixed and prepared. Foodchain was facing a growing demand for its services but did not have enough staff or funding to meet the demand. Although the two organizations had contrasting cultures and financial stability, they were being strongly encouraged to merge by their donors and board members. The merger was announced in April 2000. For similar reasons, Family Services of America and the National Association of Homes and Services for Children merged in October 1998 under the name "Alliance for Children and Families."[10]

Surplus Generation and Distribution

Legally, a nonprofit organization is allowed to earn an excess of revenues over expenses, sometimes called a *surplus* or an *increase in net assets.* This is one means of accumulating the equity capital that may be needed for *(a)* expansion, *(b)* the replacement of fixed assets, or *(c)* a buffer in the case of hard times. A nonprofit organization is prohibited from paying out any of its surplus as cash dividends.

As indicated previously, some nonprofit organizations create for-profit subsidiaries, which are permitted to pay dividends. For example, a nonprofit research laboratory may have a subsidiary that holds patents developed by its employees. It gives these employees ownership shares in the subsidiary,

---

[9]Harris Meyer, "Selling or Selling Out," *Trustee,* September 1996.
[10]Jonathan Eig, "The Urge to Merge Hits Charities," *Wall Street Journal,* April 18, 2000.

and thereby rewards them with a share of license fees for patented products they develop.

The Internal Revenue Service allows nonprofit organizations to establish profit-sharing plans for employees under certain conditions. In making this determination, the IRS decided that profit-sharing plans could have a favorable effect on employees' performance, and thus could further a nonprofit organization's charitable purposes. The IRS prohibits a nonprofit organization from distributing a portion of its surplus to its managers after the fact, however. That is, there must be a profit-sharing plan in place prior to any sort of distribution.

The need for a preexisting plan arises because, under federal tax codes, no earnings of a tax-exempt organization may "inure," or benefit, a private individual. In this regard, the *Taxpayer Bill of Rights,* which became effective in September 1996, greatly expands public access to the annual federal tax filings of all tax-exempt organizations, and gives the IRS greater authority to punish tax-exempt organizations that engage in prohibited "private inurement" activities. Previously, the only available penalty under federal statutes for private inurement violations was stripping the organization of its tax exemption. Because of the severity of the penalty, IRS officials had been reluctant to use it.

Under the 1996 law, the IRS also is able to assess penalty excise taxes against organization executives who arrange "excess benefit transactions" and people who receive them.[11] Beneficiaries of such transactions are subject to a 25 percent tax on the amount of compensation determined to be in excess of fair market value. Managers of an organization who arrange such transactions are subject to a 10 percent tax on the same amount. And insiders would face a 200 percent tax on the amount if the organization failed to take corrective action to avoid problems in the future.[12] All excess benefit transactions and any penalties paid by the individuals involved are reported on IRS Form 990.

Legal Obligations under a Nonprofit Charter

In exchange for their tax-exempt status, nonprofit organizations are required to provide benefits to their communities. A subject of some considerable debate among nonprofits concerns the nature and extent of these benefits. During the early 1990s, some states and municipalities, facing fiscal difficulties, began to look to the possibility of revoking the tax-exempt status of certain nonprofits. The argument they used was that these nonprofits were not providing sufficient benefits to their communities.

---

[11]An excess benefit transaction is one in which an "insider" receives compensation or another form of economic benefit that exceeds the fair market value of the service for which the payment was intended. Such transactions also include those in which the amount of the compensation or economic benefit paid to the insider was based on the revenues of the tax-exempt organization.

[12]David Burda, "New Tax Law Opens Books of Non-Profits," *Modern Healthcare,* August 1996.

Example

Some cities require hospitals to meet "community care standards" before being exempted from property taxes. Hospitals wishing to retain their tax-exempt status are required to contribute to their communities in a variety of ways, such as by accepting medicaid patients or running a 24-hour emergency room.

Service Organizations

Most nonprofit organizations are service organizations and thus do not have the same management control advantages as companies that manufacture and sell tangible goods. There are several important differences between the two types of organizations:

- Services cannot be stored. Goods can be stored in inventory, awaiting a customer's order. If facilities and personnel available to provide a service today are not used today, the potential revenue is lost forever.

- Service organizations tend to be labor intensive. Although such organizations require relatively little capital per unit of output, controlling this output requires managing the people who deliver the services, which generally is more difficult than managing an operation whose work flow is paced or dominated by machines.

- It is not always easy to measure the quantity of services. Keeping track of a quantity of tangible goods, both during the production process or when goods are sold, is usually easy. By contrast, a medical group practice can measure the number of patients a physician treats in a day, for example, and even classify patient visits by type of presenting problem. However, this is by no means equivalent to measuring the amount of service the physician provides to each of these patients.

- The quality of a service cannot be inspected in advance. The quality of tangible goods can be inspected in most cases before the goods are released to customers, and any defects are usually physically evident. At best, the quality of a service can be inspected during the time it is rendered to the client. Judgments as to the quality of most services are subjective, however, since for the most part, objective measurement instruments and unambiguous quality standards do not exist.

Constraints on Goals and Strategies

Within wide limits, a for-profit organization can select the industry or industries in which it will do business. It can choose any of a number of different ways of competing in its industry, and it can change these strategies fairly easily should its management choose to do so. Most nonprofit managers have much less freedom of choice, and tend to change strategies slowly, if at all. A university adds or closes a professional school less frequently than a large corporation adds or divests an operating division. A municipality is expected to provide certain services for its residents, such as education, public safety, or welfare. It usually can make decisions about the amounts of these services it will provide, but it cannot as easily decide to discontinue them.

Furthermore, many nonprofit organizations must provide services as directed by an outside agency, rather than as decided by their own management or governing boards. Private social service organizations must conform to state or municipal guidelines. Many hospitals must obtain a certificate of need to undertake a large-scale capital project. Organizations receiving support from the government must conform to the terms of the contract or grant. Moreover, the charters of many nonprofit organizations specify in fairly explicit terms the types of services that they can provide.

Finally, federal and state legislatures may limit total spending for an organization or certain programs. They also may dictate spending limits for certain cost objects, such as travel. Similarly, donors to nonprofit organizations may restrict management's options on the uses to which their contributions may be put.

Diversification through New Ventures

Despite the various constraints they face, many nonprofit organizations have grown and diversified considerably during the past decade. Many have done so through the formation of for-profit subsidiaries. The process a nonprofit follows in its decision to undertake a new venture is invariably complex, involving legal, strategic, and managerial concerns. We introduce some of these issues here and discuss them further in Chapter 9.

In many instances, new ventures have helped nonprofit organizations subsidize activities that otherwise would not have been financially feasible. Indeed, during the 1980s and 1990s, faced with substantial reductions in federal assistance, many nonprofits saw diversification strategies as crucial to their survival.

For some nonprofits, the production of new types of goods and services has put them in direct competition with for-profit organizations, particularly small ones. Many small businesses argue that, since nonprofit organizations pay no taxes, there is unfair competition.[13]

Example

The nonprofit MacNeal Hospital, near Chicago, entered into a joint venture with Damon Corp., a diversified biotechnology company in Massachusetts, to conduct blood and urine tests, as well as cell and tissue studies. Damon splits its profits from commercial medical testing with MacNeal, and MacNeal saved an estimated $750,000 in purchasing costs because of the greater scale of operations at its testing lab.[14]

[13]For a discussion of this point, see Emshwiller, "More Small Firms Complain About Tax-Exempt Rivals."
[14]Udayan Gupta, "Hospitals Enlist Profit-Minded Partners for Ventures to Gnerate New Business," *Wall Street Journal*, January 23, 1987.

Example

The nonprofit Metro Washington Park Zoo in Oregon sells cans of "Zoo Doo," elephant manure that is used as fertilizer. Washington's National Zoo hosts champagne breakfasts in its reptile house. And the Minnesota Zoo charges crosscountry skiers $4 to traverse its grounds.[15]

Increasingly, nonprofit organizations are aligning their efforts with for-profit firms. In many instances, a nonprofit will license its name to a corporation and take a share of the royalties from sales for doing so.[16]

Example

In 1996 the New York Parks Commission announced a $2 million alliance with Coca Cola Co., whose products became the official soft drink of the state's park system. The Commission also persuaded Saturn dealerships to donate $250,000 of playground equipment for three parks in return for small signs at each facility advertising their donation.[17]

The issue of competition between nonprofit and for-profit organizations is complicated by the presence of for-profit companies in activities traditionally conducted by nonprofit organizations. This is particularly true in health care, where considerable debate has raged over the merits of such a shift and its impact on the cost and quality of care.

Competition of nonprofits with small businesses is further muddied because analysts attempting to address its financial consequences have not distinguished clearly among three types of growth by nonprofits: (1) expanded sales of goods and services that do not compete with small businesses (e.g., hospital care), (2) expanded sales of goods and services that already were competing with small businesses (e.g., Girl Scout cookies), and (3) sales of goods and services that are relatively new to the nonprofit arena (e.g., tanning salons at a YMCA). Until a distinction of this sort is made, interested parties will not be able to address the issue fully.

Entrepreneurial Behavior

Regardless of the category, these sorts of activities are suggestive of a new, somewhat oxymoronic, focus of nonprofit organizations: entrepreneurial behavior.

Example

Ashoka: Innovators for the Public, a nonprofit international venture-capital foundation, based in Arlington, Virginia, has provided financial and professional backing for more than 1,000 social entrepreneurs in 34 countries. These individuals use business techniques and expertise to help people help themselves. In the view of William Drayton, Ashoka's founder and chairman, there is no difference between those who use their skills in business and those who use them in the pursuit of social goals. In addition,

---

[15]Michael Allen, "Let's Hope Pythons Don't Enjoy a Sip of Veuve Clicquot," *Wall Street Journal,* February 12, 1990.
[16]Jeff Smyth, "Nonprofits Get Market-Savvy," *Advertising Age,* May 29, 1995.
[17]Terzah Ewing, "Meet the New Entrepreneurs: State Parks," *Wall Street Journal,* February 11, 1997.

many U.S. business schools now have courses on social entrepreneurship, and graduates are engaging in such diverse activities as assisting with the small nonprofit start-ups, improving the efficiency of city government, and developing innovative new product lines in shelters for the homeless.[18]

Source of Financial Support

A for-profit company obtains financial resources from the sales of goods and services. If the flow of this revenue is inadequate, the company does not survive. A company cannot survive for very long if it makes a product that the market does not want. Moreover, it cannot sell products unless their quality is acceptable, and their selling prices are in line with what the market is willing to pay. Thus, the market dictates the limits within which the management of a for-profit company can operate.

Some nonprofit organizations also obtain all, or substantially all, of their financial resources from sales revenue. This is the case with most hospitals (which depend on patient care revenue), private schools and colleges (which depend on tuition), and research organizations (which depend on contracts for specific projects). These client-supported nonprofit organizations are subject to much the same forces as are their for-profit counterparts, such as proprietary hospitals, private schools, and for-profit research organizations.

Other nonprofit organizations receive significant financial support from sources other than revenue for services rendered. In these public-supported organizations, there is no direct connection between the amount of services received by clients and the amounts of resources provided to the organization. Individuals receive essentially the same services from a government unit whether they pay high taxes or no taxes. Unrestricted grants by a foundation are not made because of services provided by the grantee. Appropriations made by a state legislature to a university or hospital are not related directly to the services received by the taxpayers from these organizations.

Gifts: A Two-Edged Sword

Many nonprofits solicit and accept gifts. However, accepting gifts is not always as financially beneficial as it may seem at first.

Example

In one instance a YMCA received a donation of a corner lot at a busy intersection. When they tried to sell it, they found that the property had been used as a service station and the YMCA was liable for the cleanup. The donor took a $500,000 charitable deduction and the Y had to spend about $1 million to clean up the property. They then had difficulty selling it because of the bad press, and they were unlikely to build on it themselves due to the potential liability should a child become sick.[19]

[18]Emily Mitchell, "Getting Better at Doing Good," *Time,* February 21, 2000.
[19]IRS Regs re Contribution Acknowledgement," *Institute for Management Accoutants, Not-for-Profit E-Mail Exchange,* Nonprofit@Lists-IMANet.org, November 19, 1999.

Contrast between Client-Supported and Public-Supported Organizations

In almost all instances, client-supported organizations want more customers. More customers imply more revenues, and more revenues imply greater success. In public-supported organizations there is no such relationship between the number of clients and the success of the organization. Indeed, additional clients may place a strain on resources. This is especially true when a nonprofit's available resources are fixed by appropriations (as in the case of government agencies) or by income from endowment or annual giving (as in the case of many educational, religious, and charitable organizations). Thus, in a public-supported organization, a new client may be only a burden— to be accepted with misgivings. In most for-profit, or client-supported nonprofit organizations, by contrast, a new client is an opportunity to be pursued vigorously.

This negative attitude toward clients gives rise to complaints about the poor service and surly attitude of bureaucrats. Clients of client-supported organizations tend to hear "please" and "thank you" more often than clients of public-supported organizations.

In some public-supported organizations, the contrast with the motivations associated with market forces is even stronger. A welfare organization should be motivated to decrease its clientele, rather than increase it; that is, it should seek ways of rehabilitating clients, and removing them from the welfare rolls. The Small Business Administration (SBA) should work to change high-risk businesses into low-risk businesses that will no longer need the special services of the SBA. The idea that an organization should deliberately set out to reduce its clientele is foreign to the thinking of for-profit managers.

Competition provides a powerful incentive to use resources wisely. Profits will decline if a firm in a competitive industry permits its costs to get out of control, its product line to become obsolete, or its quality to decrease. A public-supported organization has no such automatic danger signal.

As a substitute for the market mechanism for allocating resources, managers of public-supported organizations compete with one another for available resources. The sanitation, the parks, and the road maintenance departments all try to get as large a slice as possible of a city's budget pie. In responding to their requests, senior management tries to judge what services clients should have, or what is best in terms of the public interest, rather than what the market wants. In the public interest, Amtrak provides railroad service to areas where it is not economically warranted. Similarly, the U.S. Postal Service maintains rural post offices even though they are not profitable.

Just as the success of a client-supported organization depends upon its ability to satisfy clients, the success of a public-supported organization depends on its ability to satisfy those who provide resources. Thus, a state university may maintain close contact with the state legislature, and a private university may place somewhat more emphasis on athletics than the faculty thinks is warranted so as to satisfy contributors to the alumni fund. Similarly, a sanitation department may place considerable emphasis on removing the mayor's garbage in a timely way. Furthermore, acceptance of support from the public frequently carries with it a responsibility for accounting to the public. In many instances, this accounting must be done to a greater degree than exists in a client-supported organization.

Professionals

In many nonprofit organizations, success in achieving goals depends upon the behavior of professionals (e.g., physicians, scientists, combat commanders, teachers, pilots, artists, ministers). Professionals often have motivations that are inconsistent with good resource utilization. This creates a dilemma that has important implications for senior managers in nonprofit organizations.

Professionals are motivated by two sets of standards: those of their organizations and those of their colleagues. The former are related to organizational objectives; the latter may be inconsistent with organizational objectives. In fact, the rewards for achieving organizational objectives may be much less potent than those for achieving professional objectives. The reluctance of university faculty to serve on school or department committees is a direct reflection of this reward structure.

Many professionals, by nature, prefer to work independently. Examples are academicians, researchers, and physicians. Because the essence of management is getting things done through people, professionals with such a temperament are not naturally suited to the role of manager. This is one reason why managers in professional organizations are less likely to have come up through the ranks than are those in for-profit organizations.

Although leadership in a nonprofit organization may require more management skills than professional skills, custom often requires that the manager be a professional. Traditionally, the head of a research organization has been a scientist; the president of a university, a professor; the head of a hospital, a physician. This tradition seems to be diminishing, however.

In a professional organization, the professional quality of the people is of primary importance and other considerations are secondary. Promotion is often geared to the criteria established by the profession rather than those of the organization per se. To the extent that these criteria reflect an individual's worth to the profession but not to the organization, they may run counter to the efficiency and effectiveness of the organization as a whole. Moreover, professionals tend to need a longer time to prove their worth to the profession than managers need to prove their worth to the organization.

Traditionally, a professional's education has not included a management component. Most educators believe that training in the skills of the profession is far more important than training in the skills needed to manage organizations employing members of the profession. Consequently, professionals often underestimate the importance of the management function. While education and external pressures for better organizational performance are working to change this perception, the culture of many organizations has reinforced the tendency to look down on managers.

Financial incentives tend to be less effective with professional people. This is both because professionals usually consider their current compensation to be adequate and because their primary satisfaction ordinarily comes from their work. Professionals also tend to give inadequate weight to the financial implication of their decisions. Many physicians, for example, feel that no limit should be placed on the amount spent to save a human life. Unfortunately, in a world of limited resources, such an attitude is unrealistic.

Governance

Although the statement that shareholders control a corporation is an oversimplification, shareholders do have the ultimate authority. They may exercise this authority only in times of crisis, but it nevertheless is there. The movement of stock prices is an immediate and influential indication of what shareholders think of management. In for-profit organizations, policy and management responsibilities are vested in the board of directors, which derives its power from the shareholders. In turn, the board delegates power to the chief executive officer (CEO), who serves at the board's pleasure, acts as the board's agent in the management of the organization, and is replaced if there are serious differences of interest or opinion.

Governing Boards in Nonprofit Organizations

In many nonprofit organizations the corresponding line of responsibility is often not clear. There are no shareholders, members of the governing body are seldom paid for their services, and they may be chosen for political or financial reasons rather than for their ability to exercise sound judgment about the organization's management. The governing body frequently is insufficiently informed about major issues facing the organization, and its decisions therefore are not always optimal. Thus, governing boards tend to be less influential in nonprofit organizations than in for-profit ones.[20]

At an absolute minimum, the governing board of a nonprofit organization has the responsibility to act when the organization is in trouble. Since there is no profit measure to provide an obvious warning, the personal appraisal by board members of the health of the organization is much more important in a nonprofit organization than in a for-profit one. In order to have a sound basis for such an appraisal, board members need to spend a considerable amount of

---

[20]For a thorough discussion of the differences between for-profit and nonprofit boards, see F. Warren McFarlan, "Working on Nonprofit Boards: Don't Assume the Shoe Fits," *Harvard Business Review,* November–December 1999.

time learning what is going on in the organization, and they need to have enough expertise to understand the significance of what they learn.

The juxtaposition of the previous two paragraphs points to one of the most serious governance problems faced by many nonprofit organizations. For reasons indicated in the first paragraph, many governing boards do an inadequate job of fulfilling the responsibilities outlined in the second. Frequently, there is not even a general recognition of the board's responsibility. In universities, for example, a widely quoted maxim is that "The function of a Board is to hire a president and then back him, period."[21] In hospitals, boards frequently are dominated by physicians who are qualified to oversee the quality of care but who have neither the expertise nor the willingness to assess the effectiveness and efficiency of hospital management. In government organizations at all levels, auditors verify compliance with statutory rules on spending, but few oversight agencies pay attention to how well management performs its functions. Although legislative committees look for headline-making sins, many committees do not have the staff or the inclination to arrive at an informed judgment on management performance.

Example

Press accounts of Empire Blue Cross in New York regularly referred to the lack of proper oversight on the part of outside directors. According to some accounts, board scrutiny did not adhere to the basic standards of the corporate world.[22]

The *New York Times* reported that while insurance rates skyrocketed, the Maryland Blue Cross-Blue Shield plan bought a $300,000 skybox at a baseball park. The New York State plan spent $15,000 on a silver punch bowl for board members.[23]

Government Organizations

In government organizations, external influences tend to come from a number of sources, leading to a diffusion of power. In state and federal governments, for example, there is a division of authority among executive, legislative, and judicial branches. Consequently, there are often conflicting judgments about objectives and the means of attaining them. In a for-profit company the board of directors and the chief executive officer usually have similar objectives.

---

[21]Perhaps because the academic environment encourages writing, more has been written about college and university trustees than about other types of governing boards. Publications of the Association of Governing Boards of Colleges and Universities, One Dupont Circle, Washington, D.C., contain much material about the governance of colleges and universities. The classic book is still Beardsley Ruml and Donald M. Morrison, *Memo to a College Trustee* (New York: McGraw-Hill, 1959).

[22]William G. Bowen, "When a Business Leader Joins a Nonprofit Board," *Harvard Business Review,* September–October 1994.

[23]Regina E. Herzlinger, "Effective Oversight: A Guide for Nonprofit Directors," *Harvard Business Review,* July–August 1994.

There may also be a vertical division of authority among levels of government (federal, state, and local), each responsible for facets of the same problem. For example, the federal government finances major and many minor highways, whereas local governments construct and maintain other highways.

Agencies, or units within agencies, may have their own special-interest clienteles (e.g., Maritime Administration and shipping interests) with political power that is stronger than that of the chief executive of the agency. Similarly, senior-management authority may be divided, particularly in states where expenditure authority is vested in committees of independently elected officials. The same problem occurs in localities governed by commissions whose members each administer a particular segment of the organization (e.g., streets or health). By contrast, elected officials, such as the attorney general, the treasurer, the secretary of state, or the director of education, each may manage their organizations fairly independently.

A manager's latitude also may be determined by political boundaries that are structural in nature. For example, the mayor of Los Angeles has much narrower responsibility than does the mayor of New York because county government in California is responsible for many services that in New York fall under the city organization.

Often, too, government bureaucracy is insulated from senior management by virtue of job security and rules. Career civil servants may know that they will outlast the term of office of the elected or appointed chief executive. If a particular project cannot be sold to the current boss, the project's sponsors may bide their time and hope to sell it to the next one. Conversely, if they dislike a new policy, they may drag their heels long enough to allow new management to take over and possibly rescind the policy.

This fragmentation of authority complicates management control. A particularly significant consequence is that the public administrator comes to depend upon political power to influence those who cannot be controlled directly. Consequently, managers must focus on their political credit as well as their financial credit; they must measure the political costs and benefits of alternatives, as well as their financial costs and benefits. On the other hand, as the U.S. Constitution states, there are strong advantages to divided authority, with each branch serving as a check on the activities of the others.

Political Influences

Many nonprofit organizations are political—they are responsible to the electorate or to a legislative body that presumably represents the electorate. Some of the consequences of this status are discussed below.

Necessity for Reelection

In government organizations, decisions result from multiple, often conflicting, pressures. In part, these political pressures are inevitable, and up to a point desirable. In effect, since elected officials are accountable to voters, these pressures presumably represent the forces of the marketplace. Elected officials cannot function if they are not reelected. In order to be reelected, they must advocate the perceived needs of their constituents. In order to gain support for programs important to their constituents, however, elected officials must often support certain of their colleagues' programs, even though they personally do not favor them. This logrolling phenomenon is also present in for-profit organizations, but to a lesser extent.

Public Visibility

In some instances, the need for improved management arises not because a nonprofit organization is large and complex but because it is highly visible.

Example

KERA/Channel 13 is one of two television stations that broadcast programs prepared by North Texas Public Broadcasting (NTBP). In the words of Gerry Ferral, president and CEO of NTPB, "KERA has about 150 employees and a budget of slightly under $20 million, which is not very big in terms of major companies. And if our products were widgets or thingamajigs, no one would ever notice us. But because PBS is very public, we must deal with many of the same workplace issues and public relations needs that very, very large companies deal with."[24]

More generally, in a democratic society, the press and the public feel they have a right to know everything there is to know about a government organization. In the federal government and some state governments, this feeling is reinforced by "freedom of information" statutes, but the channels for distributing this information are not always unbiased. Although some media stories describing mismanagement are fully justified, others tend to be exaggerated or to give inadequate recognition to the inevitability of mistakes in any organization. To reduce the potential for unfavorable media stories, government managers may take steps to reduce the amount of sensitive information that flows through the formal management control system. Unfortunately, this also lessens the usefulness of the system.

Multiple External Pressures

The electoral process, with institutionalized public review through the media and opposing political parties, results in a wider variety of pressures on managers of public organizations than on managers of private ones, whether nonprofit or for-profit. In general, elected public officials generate more controversy about their decisions than do business managers. In the absence of profit as a clear-cut measure of performance, these pressures may be erratic, illogical, or even influenced by momentary fads. Frequently, these pressures

[24]Judy Corwin, "Managing a Nonprofit—The Case of Public Broadcasting" *Baylor Business Review,* Spring 2000.

tend to induce an emphasis on short-term goals and on program decisions devoid of careful analysis. Shareholders demand satisfactory earnings, whereas the public and governing bodies of nonprofit organizations do not always channel their pressures toward good resource utilization.

Legislative Restrictions

Government organizations must operate within statutes enacted by the legislative branch, which are much more restrictive than the charter and bylaws of corporations, and which often prescribe detailed practices. In many instances it is relatively difficult to change these statutes.

Management Turnover

In some public organizations senior management tends to turn over rapidly because of administration changes, political shifts, military orders, and managers who only dabble in government jobs. Each change requires learning lead time and frequently a change in priorities. This rapid turnover can result in short-run plans and programs that quickly produce visible results, rather than substantive long-range programs.

Civil Service

There is widespread belief that Civil Service regulations operate to inhibit good management control. It is by no means clear, though, that Civil Service regulations are different in any important respect from personnel regulations in some large companies. One important difference in many state and municipal governments is that Civil Service laws effectively inhibit the use of both the carrot and the stick. As a result, a Civil Service Syndrome may develop: "You need not produce success; you need merely to avoid making major mistakes." This attitude is a major barrier to employees and managers who wish to improve organizational effectiveness.

Nevertheless, Civil Service regulations in many government organizations may be no more dysfunctional than union regulations and norms in for-profit organizations. Examples are the restrictive and inefficient union rules regarding work assignments, such as the number of engineers and other personnel aboard trains, or the division between electricians and plumbers on a joint repair job. An important difference is that union rules generally affect individuals near the bottom of the organization, whereas Civil Service rules affect individuals throughout the organization, including most managers.

Tradition

In the 19th century, accounting was primarily fiduciary in nature; that is, its purpose was to keep track of funds entrusted to an organization to ensure that they were spent honestly. In the 20th century, accounting in business organizations has assumed much broader functions. It furnishes useful information to interested outside parties as well as to management. Nonprofit organizations have been slow to adopt 20th-century accounting and management control concepts and practices, particularly the accrual concept.[25]

Barriers to Progress

Since nonprofit organizations lack the semiautomatic control provided by the profit mechanism, they need good management control systems even more than businesses. Why, then, have many such organizations, particularly government organizations, lagged behind? For government, there seem to be three principal explanations.

First, for many years, there was a prevalent attitude that the differences between government and business were so great that government could not use management control techniques developed by business. This attitude continues to be implicit in some texts on government accounting.

Second, at the federal level, the Congress, particularly the House Committee on Appropriations, is reluctant to shift to a new budget format. Because of the importance of the budget, this reluctance affects the whole management control system. A similar problem exists in many states. In part the reluctance is based on simple inertia, but it also reflects a suspicion—generally unwarranted—that the change is an attempt by the executive branch to conceal something from the legislative branch.

Third, many career officials recognize that a good management control system is double-edged: it provides new information for management, but it also provides new information for outside agencies such as the Office of Management and Budget (OMB), the Congress, special interest groups, and the media. Sometimes, these officials are not anxious for outside agencies to have access to new and better information.

It is important to note that the first reason is based on the premise that good management control systems cannot be developed in the public sector. The second reason is based on the premise that the proposed formats provide poorer information. The third reason is based on the premise that a revised management control system will provide better information. All three reasons cannot be correct.

Summary

The characteristics of nonprofit organizations described in this chapter can be grouped into two classes—technical and behavioral. Both are important to the material in this book.

Technical characteristics relate to the difficulty of measuring outputs and assessing the relationship between inputs and outputs. This difficulty is unique to a nonprofit organization. Great improvements in output measurement are possible, however, and managers need to spend considerable efforts to make such

[25]For a brief history of the accounting function and its development in the last century, see William Steinberg, "Cooked Books," *The Atlantic Monthly,* January 1992.

improvements. Nevertheless, it must be recognized at the outset that the resulting system will never provide as good a basis for planning or measuring performance as does the profit measure in for-profit organizations.

Behavioral characteristics encompass all the other topics in the book. The significance of these characteristics is twofold. First, most behavioral factors that impede good management control can be overcome by improved understanding and education. Second, unless these problems are overcome, any improvement in the technical area is likely to have little real impact on the management control function.

Differences among Nonprofit Organizations

The description of nonprofit organizations in this chapter is intended to apply to nonprofit organizations in general. Clearly, the characteristics we discussed do not fit all such organizations equally well. In this appendix, we attempt to relate the broad description of nonprofit organizations contained in the text to each of the principal nonprofit sectors. Of course, these too are broadbrush generalizations to which many exceptions can he found in individual organizations.

Health Care Organizations

Nonprofit hospitals, nursing homes, health maintenance organizations, clinics, and similar health care organizations closely resemble their for-profit counterparts. Indeed, were it not for the difference in objectives—service rather than profit—their management control problems would be identical to those of their for-profit counterparts. There are few differences between a voluntary hospital and a proprietary hospital.

The health care environment is changing dramatically, and competition among health care organizations of all kinds has become much more intense in the past few years than ever before. Nevertheless, most health care organizations still have fewer competitive pressures than the typical for-profit business. Much of their revenue is still received from third parties (e.g., Blue Cross, commercial insurance companies, and the government) rather than directly from clients. Additionally, they are dominated by professionals, and they have no clear-cut line of responsibility to a defined group of owners. Spurred on by public concern about the rising cost of health care and by the necessity of justifying their fees on the basis of a plausible measurement of cost, many hospitals have made dramatic improvements in their cost accounting systems in recent years.[26]

Educational Organizations

Private colleges and universities whose tuition approximates the cost of education also resemble for-profit educational entities. To the extent that colleges and universities are supported by contributions and endowment earnings, however, the relationship between tuition revenues and the cost of services is less direct. Like hospitals, they are dominated by professionals, and their governing boards tend to be relatively uninfluential. They are also subject to increasing competitive pressures—in their case because of the decline in student population. In recent years, under the leadership of the National Association of College and University Business Officers (NACUBO), many have made substantial improvements in their management control systems.

State colleges and universities are supported primarily by appropriations from state legislatures. Although these appropriations may be based on a formula that takes into account the number of students or the number of credit hours, they are not the same as fees charged to clients because the individual student (or parent) ordinarily does not make the decision that the education received is worth the amount charged. In other respects, state institutions are similar to private colleges and universities. In recent years, the legislative oversight bodies of some states have paid much attention to the financial management of their colleges and universities, and this has led to great improvements in their management control systems.

Membership Organizations

Membership organizations are those whose purpose is to render services to their members. They include religious organizations, labor unions, trade associations, professional associations, fraternal organizations, social and country clubs, cemetery societies, and political organizations. To the extent that they are supported by membership dues, fluctuations in the amount of such dues is an indication of the perceived value of services rendered by the organization. This is true even though there is rarely a direct connection between an individual's dues and the services he or she receives.

Many membership organizations are dominated by professionals and have weak governing boards. Certain membership organizations, such as religious organizations and some labor organizations, face strong competitive pressures. Others, such as professional associations, have no effective competition.

---

[26]For a discussion of these improvements, see David W. Young and Leslie K. Pearlman, "Managing the Stages of Hospital Cost Accounting," *Healthcare Financial Management,* April 1993.

Historically, religious organizations have had notoriously weak management control systems. In recent years, however, several denominations have developed good systems and encouraged their use at local levels. Religious organizations have a particularly difficult problem in deciding on the programs to be undertaken and in measuring the value of services rendered. ("Souls saved per pew hour preached" is not a feasible measurement!)

Human Service and Arts Organizations

Human service organizations include family and child service agencies, the Red Cross, scouting and similar youth organizations, and various other charitable organizations. Arts organizations include museums, public broadcasting stations, symphony orchestras, theaters, and ballet companies.

Although they have quite different missions, human service and arts organizations share a characteristic that unites them from a management control perspective. With some notable exceptions, these organizations rely heavily on public support, either from the government or from contributions by individuals, companies, and foundations. Their revenues therefore do not directly measure the value of services provided to clients. Those who provide support tend to exercise an increasing amount of influence over the financial affairs of these organizations.

Considerable improvements have been made over the past several years in the management control systems of these organizations. These improvements are primarily a result of the influence of such organizations as the United Way of America and professional associations of museums and broadcasting stations. Significant opportunities for further improvement remain, however.

The Federal Government

Except for certain businesslike activities, such as the U.S. Postal Service, the federal government does not receive fees from clients. Its goals are multiple and fuzzy, and the value of its services is especially difficult to measure.

The federal government is subject to more external power and political influence than other nonprofit organizations. These forces make management control especially difficult. Furthermore, many federal agencies are unique (there is only one State Department), so there is no basis for comparing their performance with that of other units. Some improvements have occurred in recent years, but much remains to be done.

State and Local Governments

Collectively, state and local governments are by far the largest category of nonprofit organizations. Like the federal government, they are subject to a variety of external powers and political influences, and therefore have difficult management control problems.

Generally, their revenue is not directly related to services provided to clients. Although the person whose house is on fire is a client in one sense, the main function of the fire department is to protect the whole community. Proposals for specific programs are often political in nature, and frequently are not subject to economic analysis. The objectives of these organizations are difficult to define in ways that permit measurements of attainment. (What is adequate fire or police protection?)

Because management control in state and local government is inherently difficult, good systems are especially necessary. With a few notable exceptions, such systems currently do not now exist in most government units. Tradition has greatly hampered development of adequate systems. Many government units keep their accounts solely on a cash receipts and disbursements basis, a practice that has been obsolete since the 19th century. Only recently has pressure for change—public dissatisfaction with rising taxes and revelations of poor management—begun to emerge. There also are pressures from the federal government to implement revenue-sharing programs. Moreover, the Governmental Accounting Standards Board (GASB) is in the process of making substantial improvements in its accounting systems. These pressures seem likely to lead to improvements in the relatively near future.

Suggested Additional Readings

Austin, James E. *The Collaborative Challenge.* San Francisco: Jossey-Bass, 2000.

Ben-Ner, Avner, and Benedetto Gui. *The Nonprofit Sector in the Mixed Economy.* Ann Arbor: University of Michigan Press, 1993.

Bryce, Herrington J. *Financial and Strategic Management for Nonprofit Organizations.* San Francisco: Jossey-Bass, 2000.

Connors, Tracy Daniel (ed.). *The Nonprofit Handbook: Management.* New York: John Wiley & Sons, 2001.

Dees, J. Gregory. "Enterprising Nonprofits." *Harvard Business Review,* January–February 1998.

Drucker, Peter F. *Managing the Non-Profit Organization: Practices and Principles.* New York: HarperCollins, 1990.

Duca, Diane J. *Nonprofit Boards: Roles, Responsibilities, and Performance.* New York: John Wiley & Sons, 1996.

Eldridge, Grant. *National Directory of Nonprofit Organizations 2001.* New York: Gale Group, 2000.

Grobman, Gary. *The Nonprofit Organization's Guide to E-Commerce.* New York: White Hat Communications, 2000.

Hopkins, Bruce R., and D. Benson Tesdahl. *Intermediate Sanctions: Curbing Nonprofit Abuse.* New York: John Wiley & Sons, 1997.

Kearns, Kevin. *Managing for Accountability: Preserving the Public Trust in Public and Nonprofit Organizations.* San Francisco: Jossey-Bass, 1996.

Malavo, Marie C. *Museum Governance: Mission, Ethics, Policy.* Washington, DC: Smithsonian Institutional Press, 1994.

Oleck, Howard Leoner. *Nonprofit Corporations, Organizations and Associations,* 6th ed. Englewood Cliffs, NJ: Prentice Hall, 1994.

Ott, J. Steven (ed.). *The Nature of the Nonprofit Sector.* Boulder, CO: Westview Press, 2001.

Ott, J. Steven (ed.). *Understanding Nonprofit Organizations: Governance, Leadership, and Management.* Boulder, CO: Westview Press, 2001.

Roche, George Charles. *The Fall of the Ivory Tower: Government Funding, Corruption, and the Bankruptcy of American Higher Education.* Washington, DC: Regnery Publishing, 1994.

Steckel, Richard, Jennifer Lehman, and Alan Shrader. *In Search of America's Best Nonprofits.* San Francisco: Jossey-Bass, 1997.

Young, Dennis. *Economics for Non-profit Managers.* New York: Foundation Center, 1995.

Zeff, Robin. *The Nonprofit Guide to the Internet.* New York: John Wiley & Sons, 1996.

http://www.mapnp.org/library A free management library for nonprofits and for-profits.

http://www.nonprofit.gov A network of links to federal government information and services.

http://www.nccs.urban.org Contains statistics on the nonprofit sector.

http://www.guidestar.org A national database of nonprofit organizations. Contains copies of Form 990 for several thousand nonprofits.

Case 2-1

Granville Symphony Orchestra[*]

If it weren't for the special fund drive in conjunction with our 100th Anniversary, this would have been our fifth year in a row with a deficit. Even with the fund drive, the total deficit for the last five years has totaled well over $4 million, which

[*]This case was prepared by Professor Robert N. Anthony and revised by Professor David W. Young. Copyright © by Osceola Institute.

we've had to withdraw from capital funds. If we continue at the pre-anniversary rate, our capital funds will soon be exhausted.

The speaker was William Johnson, Chair of the Board of Trustees of the Granville Symphony Orchestra (GSO). He continued:

We've got to stop the hemorrhaging. Our plan is to put in place a series of measures that will both help us out on the revenue side and keep our expenses in check. Although we've outlined that plan in our most recent annual report, and I'm sure the board and staff are committed to it, I'm not completely convinced that it's attainable.

Background

GSO owned two properties. One was Concert Hall in Granville. The orchestra performed there, except in the summer and when it performed in other cities. When Concert Hall was not needed for performances, rehearsals, or recording sessions, it often was rented to other organizations.

The other property was Greenwood, a large complex in the Beaumont Hills, about 130 miles from Granville. The orchestra performed there for nine weeks in the summer. Several hundred students participated in training programs at Greenwood each summer. (The principal buildings at Greenwood were not winterized and could be used only in the summer.) In the summer of 1997, attendance at Greenwood totaled 308,000.

In 1996–97, in addition to Greenwood, the orchestra gave 107 concerts, of which 13 were in foreign countries and 14 in other American cities. The Granville Players Orchestra, formed from symphony orchestra players, gave 63 concerts in Concert Hall and 7 free concerts at an outdoor concert shell in Granville, known as the Terrace. Nearly all orchestra and Players performances were sold out.

Management estimated that Concert Hall was used 165 evenings a year, of which 130 were for GSO concerts and rehearsals, and 35 were for rentals to outside groups. In the afternoons there were 22 symphony orchestra concerts and approximately 25 rentals to outside groups. The orchestra used the hall on 125 to 150 afternoons annually for rehearsals, recording, or television sessions.

Proposed Plan

The "GSO/100" fund drive raised about $20 million of capital funds (primarily endowment) over a five-year period. Management recognized, however, that the special stimulus of the 100th Anniversary could not be counted on to provide the funds needed to balance the budget in the future.

Alternative ways of financing operations were discussed, and the trustees eventually agreed on the plan given in Exhibit 1. In the GSO annual report for 1997 (i.e., for the fiscal year ended August 31, 1997), this plan was described as follows:

EXHIBIT 1

GRANVILLE SYMPHONY ORCHESTRA, INC.
ANALYSIS OF REVENUE CONTRIBUTION TO FIXED COSTS
FOR THE YEAR ENDED AUGUST 31
(IN $000)

	Actual						Projections						
	1993	1994	1995	1996	1997	1998	1999	2000	2001	2002	2003	2004	2005
Fixed costs:													
Artistic	3,902	4,243	4,514	5,176	5,608								
Facilities	920	1,005	1,160	1,318	1,348								
Administration	1,377	1,472	1,768	1,940	2,204								
Total fixed costs	6,199	6,720	7,442	8,434	9,160	10,140	10,850	11,800	12,425	13,300	14,225	15,225	16,300
Results from operations:													
Operations:													
Concerts	2,666	2,986	3,161	3,827	4,006								
Radio	125	145	160	185	185								
Recording	320	384	510	543	827								
Television	139	225	289	223	246								
Occupancies	101	91	186	252	244								
Education	(100)	(60)	(87)	(34)	(77)								
Other Income	0	12	32	35	278								
Marginal contribution	3,251	3,783	4,251	5,031	5,709	6,160	6,675	7,325	7,775	8,375	9,025	9,750	10,500
Percent fixed costs	52.4%	56.3%	57.1%	59.7%	62.3%	60.7%	61.5%	62.1%	62.6%	63.0%	63.4%	64.0%	64.4%
Operating (deficit)	(2,948)	(2,937)	(3,191)	(3,403)	(3,451)	(3,980)	(4,175)	(4,475)	(4,650)	(4,925)	(5,200)	(5,475)	(5,800)
Percent fixed costs	47.6%	43.7%	42.9%	40.3%	37.7%	39.3%	38.5%	37.9%	37.4%	37.0%	36.6%	36.0%	35.6%
Endowment Income:	981	1,221	1,358	1,691	1,893								
Percent fixed costs	15.8%	18.2%	18.2%	20.0%	20.7%								

EXHIBIT 1 (continued)

GRANVILLE SYMPHONY ORCHESTRA, INC.
ANALYSIS OF REVENUE CONTRIBUTION TO FIXED COSTS
FOR THE YEAR ENDED AUGUST 31
(IN $000)

	Actual						Projections						
	1993	1994	1995	1996	1997	1998	1999	2000	2001	2002	2003	2004	2005
Annual fund-raising:													
Total annual gifts	1,133	1,121	1,211	1,334	1,786								
Special-purpose gifts transferred to operations	(162)	(302)	(268)	(299)	(355)								
General-purpose gifts	971	819	943	1,035	1,431								
Net project revenues	176	209	229	264	723								
	1,147	1,028	1,172	1,299	2,154								
Fund-raising expenses	(549)	(441)	(414)	(553)	(442)								
Total	598	587	758	746	1,712								
Percent fixed costs	9.6%	8.7%	10.2%	8.8%	18.7%								
Total endowment income and annual fund-raising	1,579	1,808	2,116	2,437	3,605	3,865	4,175	4,475	4,650	4,925	5,200	5,475	5,800
Percent fixed costs	25.5%	26.5%	28.4%	28.9%	39.4%	38.1%	38.5%	37.9%	37.4%	37.0%	36.6%	36.0%	35.6%
Surplus (deficit)	(1,369)	(1,129)	(1,075)	(966)	154	(115)	0	0	0	0	0	0	0
Percent fixed costs	22.1%	16.8%	14.4%	11.5%	−1.7%	1.1%							
Capital analysis:													
Additions to endowment	442	1,750	1,433	1,308	3,709	3,500	3,500	3,500	3,500	3,500	3,500	3,500	3,500
Funding of deficit	(1,369)	(1,129)	(1,075)	(966)		(115)							
Net change in endowment fund	(927)	621	358	342	3,709	3,385							
Contributions for plant additions	433	980	493	1,641	367	1,021	500	500	500	500	500	500	500
Pooled investments:													
Cost	10,343	12,018	13,850	15,822	19,465	23,000	26,500	30,000	33,500	37,000	40,500	44,000	47,500
Market	11,645	14,015	15,817	16,356	20,536								

As the orchestra embarks on the first decade of its second century, Trustees, Overseers, and Friends must make plans based upon the experience of the past and their best estimate of the economic climate in the years ahead. The single most important assumption in making such a projection is the rate at which "fixed costs" of maintaining the present organization and properties will increase due to inflation. Included in the Analysis of Revenue Contribution to Fixed Costs are projections based upon several assumptions:

1. That "fixed costs" will increase at a compound annual rate of approximately 7 percent through fiscal 2004–05.
2. That management will be able to increase the percentage of "fixed costs" financed by concert activities by 1/2 of 1 percent per year.
3. That the Investment Committee and the Resources Committee working together will be able to increase the percentage of "fixed costs" covered by endowment income by 1/2 of 1 percent per year.
4. That the Resources Committee will be able to raise on average about $6,000,000 per year, of which $2,000,000 per year will be available to balance the budget.
5. That the Buildings and Grounds Committee will be able to limit capital expenditures for depreciation, for necessary improvements, and for new facilities to $500,000 per year.

Perhaps the most significant conclusions to draw from the projections [Exhibit 1] are:

1. That, in the absence of some new source of revenue, ticket prices will have to continue to increase so that the marginal contribution from concert activities can increase from $5,709,000 in 1996–97 to $10,500,000, or 64.5 percent of "fixed costs," in 2004–05.
2. That Endowment Income available for unrestricted use must increase from $1,893,000 in 1996–97 to $4,000,000, or 24.5 percent of "fixed costs," in 2004–05.
3. That the book value of Pooled Investments must be increased from $19,465,000 at August 31, 1997, to $47,500,000 in 2005 if the yield on endowment funds averages slightly over 8 percent over the period.

During the past five years the orchestra raised a total of $20,000,000 for GSO/100 and $7,000,000 from Annual Fund Drives for a grand total of $27,000,000.

The goal of $6,000,000 per year, or $30,000,000 over the next five years, is challenging, but the task is not much greater than the task already accomplished during the period of the GSO/100 campaign, and the organization is in place to do the job.

The financial projections in the Analysis of Revenue Contribution to Fixed Costs and the above assumptions and conclusions will have to be reexamined annually in the light of economic conditions and the financial results of each year's operations, but the nature of the task facing management and volunteer fundraisers will probably not be materially changed by modest differences from the assumptions.

Contributions to Fixed Costs

The concept of "contributions to fixed costs" referred to in the above description was explained in the Annual Report as follows:

Each year the Trustees are faced with certain relatively fixed costs which are scheduled in the Analysis of Revenue Contribution to Fixed Costs report. These are primarily for the annual compensation of orchestra members, the general administration of the orchestra, and the basic costs of maintaining Concert Hall and Greenwood. Management earns a percentage of these "fixed costs" by presenting concert programs, through radio, television, and recordings, and through other projects which involve both direct expenses and related income from ticket sales, fees, and royalties.

Each program or activity, of which there are over 40, is expected to make a "marginal contribution" to "fixed costs." The "marginal contribution" is the difference between direct income and direct costs of the particular program or activity. The orchestra continued to make progress toward its goal of increasing the percentage of "fixed costs" contributed from operation activities.

The "marginal contribution" from all operations in 1996–97 covered 62.3 percent of "fixed costs" as compared to 59.7 percent last year and 43.0 percent in 1986–87.

In fiscal 1996–97, the "fixed costs" amounted to $9,160,000, compared to $8,434,000 in 1995–96, an increase of 8.6 percent. Operations earned $5,709,000, compared to $5,031,000 last year, a 13.1 percent increase. This left an "operating deficit" to be funded from other sources, e.g., endowment income and unrestricted contributions, of $3,451,000 in 1996–97, compared to $3,403,000 last year.

Other Information

The 1997 Annual Report contained the following explanation of endowment income:

Investment Income reached an all-time high of $2,134,000 as compared to $1,838,000 in the prior year. Of this amount, $219,000 was used for restricted purposes, e.g., supporting the winter season programs ($35,000), providing fellowships for the Beaumont Music Center and other BMC activities ($101,000), supporting the Terrace concerts ($47,000), underwriting the Prelude Series ($29,000), and other miscellaneous activities. An additional $22,000 went to nonoperational uses, leaving $1,893,000 for unrestricted use in support of operations. This compares to $1,690,000 in 1995–96, a 12 percent increase.

The Annual Report also explained how the budget for 1997 was balanced, as follows:

The percentage of "fixed costs" that had to be provided by unrestricted gifts was reduced from 20.3 percent in 1995–96 to 17.0 percent in 1996–97, amounting to $1,558,000.

The sources of the $1,558,000 required to balance revenues and expenses in 1996-97 were:

EXHIBIT 2

GRANVILLE SYMPHONY ORCHESTRA, INC.
BALANCE SHEETS
AUGUST 31, 1997 AND 1996

Assets

	1997	1996
Unrestricted Fund		
Cash (including savings accounts of $49,835 in 1997 and $463,320 in 1996)	$ 119,888	$ 501,962
Short-term cash investments	2,600,000	1,666,222
Participation in pooled investments, at market	1,979,960	1,681,781
Accounts receivable—less allowance for doubtful accounts of $10,000 in 1997 and $32,000 in 1996	994,969	1,228,087
Prepaid salaries and wages	343,962	345,195
Total current assets	6,038,779	5,423,247
Deferred charges	163,893	40,111
Properties and equipment at cost, less accumulated depreciation of $2,209,622 in 1997 and $1,956,005 in 1996	4,766,216	4,693,885
Prepayments and other assets	251,077	506,858
Total assets	$11,219,965	$10,664,101
Endowment Fund		
Cash management fund—annuities	120,409	179,390
Real estate and other property held for sale	712,223	862,233
Pooled investments at market	20,536,010	16,356,225
Less participation in pooled investments by other funds	(1,979,960)	(1,681,791)
Total assets	$19,388,682	$15,716,057

Liabilities and Fund Balances

	1997	1996
Unrestricted Fund		
Accounts payable	$ 564,677	$ 591,559
Accrued expenses and other liabilities	619,008	189,972
Advanced ticket sales and other receipts	2,781,005	2,516,114
Advance receipts—special events	137,983	803,015
Total current liabilities	$ 4,102,673	$ 4,100,660
Accrued pension liability	221,116	187,775
Total liabilities	$ 4,323,789	$ 4,288,435
Net assets	6,896,176	6,375,666
Total liabilities and net assets	$11,219,965	$10,664,101
Endowment Fund		
Annuity payable	$ 67,778	$ 103,662
Net assets	19,320,904	15,612,395
Total liabilities and net assets	$19,388,682	$15,716,057

1. Annual Fund (net): $989,000, up $250,000 or 34 percent over the previous year.
2. Projects (net): $723,000, up $459,000 or 174 percent over the previous year.

   Since funds available from these two sources totaled $1,712,000, it was possible to transfer the excess gifts of $154,000 for other needs.

Exhibit 2 gives the balance sheet, taken from the Annual Report.

Questions

1. What is the strategy of the GSO? Please be as specific as you can in identifying both the GSO's environmental constraints, and how it differs both from other symphony orchestras and professional sports teams (which have many similar constraints and objectives). Why do these differences exist?

2. Reconstruct Exhibit 1 into a more traditional operating statement. What does this tell you about how well the GSO is achieving the strategy you identified in Question 1? What additional financial information would you like to have in making this assessment?

3. How has the GSO managed its financial affairs over the past five years? What criteria did you use in making this assessment?

4. Do the plans for 1998–2005 seem attainable? If so, why? If not, what changes would you propose?

Case 2-2
New England Trust*

Sandra Connor, Vice President of New England Trust's Nonprofit Lending and Charities Department, found herself sifting through scores of résumés to hire an assistant manager. Facing a glut of mostly MBA applicants for the position, Ms. Connor devised a system to test the applicants' understanding of the nonprofit sector, and their ability to analyze financial statements for lending and investment decisions. She gave each of the selected candidates for the position 90 minutes to complete the following exercise.

Exhibit 1 contains summarized financial information for 10 local and regional organizations, representing a diverse range of the nonprofit sector. The exhibit includes both balance sheet and operating statement information as well as a set of common ratios. You may find that other ratios are useful, and, if so, you should calculate them.

*This case was prepared by Gregory Dorf under the supervision of Professor David W. Young, using information available from public sources. Copyright © by David W. Young.

EXHIBIT 1

NEW ENGLAND TRUST
SELECTED FINANCIAL INFORMATION AND RATIOS
($ IN THOUSANDS)

	1	2	3	4	5	6	7	8	9	10
Balance Sheet										
Assets										
Cash and Equivalents	21,003	1,323	4,232	962	185	138,213		5,737	1,388	6,114
Accounts Receivable (less b.d.)	1,790	13,696	50,715	2,721	954	17,292	1,466		2,193	8,318
Investments	31,777	151,896	61,034	6,158,191	2,431	38,677	159,212	1,154	61,223	
Inventories			3,900			6,300	6,811	92		816
Other current assets	3,211	19,705	119,764	70,922	104	18,307	1,258	30	2,047	412
Total Current Assets	57,781	186,620	239,645	6,232,796	3,674	218,789	168,747	7,013	66,851	15,660
Plant & Equipment (less dep.)	2,541	559,416	274,213	20,210	1,267	175,084	78,779	949	17,321	12,039
All Other Assets	1,068		170,315			40,833	7,694	757	7,930	35,702
Total Assets	61,390	746,036	684,173	6,253,006	4,941	434,706	255,220	8,719	92,102	63,401
Liabilities and Fund Balance										
Current liabilities	43,801	44,817	132,187	193,679	981	182,472	8,707	2,986	8,127	16,118
Long-Term Liabilities		288,815	347,091		344	180,760	42,241		10,068	35,451
Total Fund Balance	17,589	412,404	204,895	6,059,327	3,616	71,474	204,272	5,733	73,907	11,832
Total Liability and Fund	61,390	746,036	684,173	6,253,006	4,941	434,706	255,220	8,719	92,102	63,401
Operating Statement										
Operating Revenues	230,491	176,378	527,444	303,394	5,141	828,667	49,761	467	25,235	44,342
Expenses	224,514	157,180	522,604	333,772	8,273	813,085	61,653	12,740	31,546	44,194
Operating Income	5,977	19,198	4,840	(30,378)	(3,132)	15,582	(11,892)	(12,273)	(6,311)	148
Non-Operating gain (loss)		3,057	12,694	884,570	2,695		13,476	13,340	6,839	652
Net Income	5,977	22,255	17,534	854,192	(437)	15,582	1,584	1,067	528	800
Profitability Ratios										
Operating Profit Margin	.03	.11	.01	(.10)	(.61)	.02	(.24)	(26.28)	(.25)	.00
Net Profit Margin	.03	.13	.03	2.82	(.09)	.02	.03	2.28	.02	.02
ROA	.10	.03	.03	.14	(.09)	.04	.01	.12	.01	.01
ROE	.34	.05	.09	.14	(.12)	.22	.01	.19	.01	.07
Activity Ratios										
Average Collection	2.83	28.34	35.10	3.27	67.73	7.62	10.75	0.00	31.72	68.47
Asset Turnover	3.75	.24	.77	.05	1.04	1.91	.19	.05	.27	.70
Liquidity Ratios										
Current Ratio	1.32	4.16	1.81	32.18	3.75	1.20	19.38	2.35	8.23	.97
Quick Ratio	1.32	4.16	1.78	32.18	3.75	1.16	18.60	2.32	8.23	.92
Leverage Ratios										
Debt Ratio	.71	.45	.70	.03	.27	.84	.20	.34	.20	.81
Debt-Equity	.00	.70	1.69	.00	.10	2.53	.21	.00	.14	3.00

To report financial statements in a consistent manner, the following procedures were applied:

- Accounts receivable are shown net of bad debt allowances.

- Plant and equipment is shown net of depreciation.

- Operating income includes fees for service, investment income, and specific public funding for operations. All other sources of funding, such as public and private contributions and sales of assets, are classified as nonoperating gains.

The organizations included on Exhibit 1 are the following:

Boston Symphony Orchestra

Brigham and Women's Hospital

Quincy City Hospital

The Ford Foundation

Family Service of Greater Boston

Tufts Associated Health Maintenance Organization

Harvard Community Health Plan, Inc., and Affiliates

Museum of Fine Arts, Boston

MassPort Authority

Oxfam America, Inc.

A brief description of each organization follows.

Boston Symphony Orchestra (BSO)

The BSO provides live musical performances to over one million admissions annually, and is heard by countless others through numerous radio broadcasts each year. BSO owns its performance facilities, which include Boston's Symphony Hall (much of which has been depreciated), and Tanglewood in Lenox, Massachusetts, where outdoor summer events and other activities are hosted. Although ticket sales account for a large portion of total revenues, operating costs are subsidized by endowment and other investment earnings, foundation support, and annual public contributions.

Brigham and Women's Hospital (B&W)

Brigham and Women's is a 750-bed urban teaching hospital affiliated with Harvard University's School of Medicine. Like most hospitals in the United

States, the B&W attempts to at least break even from the fees it receives from operating activities. One of the challenges hospitals face is collecting unpaid bills, many of which get written off as bad debt. Furthermore, a certain portion of hospital services are delivered as "charitable care." The B&W owns all of its buildings and is currently rebuilding its labor and delivery ward, the largest of its kind in the Greater Boston Area.

Quincy City Hospital

Quincy City is a 302-bed municipal hospital serving a local community with a rapidly growing immigrant population. Although the hospital can break even from patient fees, a large portion of fees go unpaid as charitable services and bad debt. Quincy City owns its buildings and most of its fixed equipment. The hospital's assets have been funded largely by long-term Series A Bonds issued by the City of Quincy, as well as by mortgage loans for both existing buildings and relatively large-scale construction in progress.

The Ford Foundation

Like any large charitable foundation, The Ford Foundation is in the business of granting proceeds from its large pool of investments to a wide range of solicitants. Ford's operating income comes strictly from the interest and dividends from its investments. Capital appreciation of its investments is classified as an additional source of nonoperating income. Each year Ford grants millions of dollars to support all kinds of organizations around the world. Typical grants include community development, medical research, education, the arts, and many other charitable causes.

Family Service of Greater Boston

One of Boston's largest community service providers, this association emphasizes the improvement of conditions affecting family life. Many of these services are reimbursed by federal and state government contracts. Last year, government contracts represented 35 percent of total funding support. Nearly the same amount of revenues are generated from client fees, which may take considerable time to collect. With large operating expenses, Family Service is very reliant on both outside support and returns generated by its investments. This past year it allocated significantly more to current operations than actual returns from investments. Outside support comes from a variety of sources, most notably, the United Way of Massachusetts.

Tufts Associated Health Maintenance Organization (TAHMO)

TAHMO is a Massachusetts nonprofit corporation that arranges for the delivery of comprehensive health care services, on a prepaid basis, to subscribing individuals and groups. To cover costs, TAHMO must at least break even from its operating activities. Since TAHMO does not directly provide health care service, most of its asset base is financial, and a large portion of its liabilities are unearned revenues.

Harvard Community Health Plan, Inc., and Affiliates (HCHP)

HCHP, a Massachusetts nonprofit corporation, and its New England affiliates provide comprehensive medical services to their members mainly through their own health care professionals but also through contracts with established multi-specialty medical groups. Typical of health maintenance organizations, HCHP relies entirely on operating revenues both to cover its costs and to reinvest as it continues to grow as a service provider. Unlike typical health insurers and other HMOs, however, HCHP owns and rents its own buildings, equipment, supplies, and inventories as necessary. Since HCHP memberships are either prepaid or paid for in regular installments by an employer, its accounts receivable are typically small. On the other hand, since many services are provided outside of HCHP facilities, such as hospital emergencies and surgical procedures, accounts payable add considerably to the company's current liabilities.

Museum of Fine Arts (MFA)

The MFA of Boston provides exhibits and other activities for both members and paying customers. Its large Huntington Avenue facilities continue to expand allowing the museum to widen its mix of services. Retail merchandise is also stocked by the museum and sold to the public. Like most museums, these sources of revenue are not sufficient to support operating activities. The MFA is fortunate to have investments and an endowment from which interest and dividends are transferred to the current fund. Both annual donations and capital gains from investments constitute additional sources of income. In accordance with general practices of art museums, the cost of works of art are not capitalized. Rather they are charged directly to the funds available for such purposes.

Massport Authority

MassPort owns and operates large-scale air, land, and sea transportation facilities throughout the state of Massachusetts. MassPort maintains and collects revenues from Logan and Hanscom Field airports, the Port of Boston, Tobin Memorial Bridge, World Trade Center, Boston Fish Pier, Constitution Plaza, Revere Sugar, and the Boston Shipyard. All of these facilities give MassPort a rather large asset base relative to operating revenues and expenses. Annual surpluses from operations are an important part of financing expansionary projects such as the Central Artery Tunnel.

Oxfam America, Inc.

Oxfam is a publicly supported, nonprofit Massachusetts corporation, whose primary purpose is to promote long-term, self-sustaining development among low-income people throughout the world. It also engages in development education activities to increase knowledge and awareness of the basic needs of the world's poor. Oxfam receives nearly all of its financial support from public contributions, which are classified as nonoperating sources of funding. Operating revenues consist primarily of its return on investments, with program reimbursements accounting for only 1 percent of total sources of funding. Other than accounts payable and deferred revenues, Oxfam has virtually no liabilities due to its reliance on fund-raising activities.

Questions

1. Using the above information in conjunction with the financial information in Exhibit 1, identify each organization on Exhibit 1. What criteria did you use in making your assessment?

2. Assuming more than one applicant accurately identifies all of the organizations, what other criteria related to the analysis of these organizations might Ms. Connor use to select someone for the job?

Part 2

Management Control Principles

Before discussing management control systems and their implementation, we first outline some of the principles on which these systems are based. In Chapter 3, we describe general-purpose financial statements—the vehicles by which nonprofit organizations report their financial activities and results to outside parties. In Chapter 4, we discuss financial management issues in nonprofit organizations. In Chapter 5 we look at full-cost accounting in terms of the decisions managers must make to establish a full-cost system. Chapter 6 takes up the topic of differential costs, discussing different types of costs and how they are calculated. Finally, in Chapter 7, we examine one of the more important aspects of management control in nonprofit organizations: pricing decisions. We discuss some considerations for managers who make these decisions.

A common theme in Chapters 5, 6, and 7 is cost (and expense) measurement. Cost information plays a central role in many management decisions in nonprofit organizations. These decisions include:

- Determining the financial viability of programs, which requires full-cost information.

- Choosing among alternative courses of action, which relies on differential costs.

- Pricing, which uses a combination of full costs and differential costs.

Cost information is also important in decisions about the management control system. In setting up the management control system, senior management structures costs in terms of the managers who are responsible for incurring them. Costs structured in this way are called responsibility costs. Responsibility costs are discussed in Part 3.

Full costs and responsibility costs are incorporated into an organization's accounts so that they can be collected on a regular basis. By contrast, a differential cost analysis is specific to the issue under consideration; therefore, differential costs, as such, are not included in the accounts.

Chapter 3

Published Financial Statements

There are two types of accounting information. Management accounting deals with information that is useful to an organization's managers. Financial accounting deals with financial information published for use by parties outside the organization. This chapter focuses on financial accounting. Most of the other chapters in this book focus on management accounting.

Characteristics of Financial Accounting

Financial accounting follows established rules.[1] There are three rule-making agencies in the United States. The Financial Accounting Standards Board (FASB) develops rules for businesses and nonprofit organizations. The Governmental Accounting Standards Board (GASB) develops rules for state and municipal organizations. The Federal Accounting Standards Advisory Board (FASAB) develops rules for federal agencies.

The principal reason for having these rules is to provide comparability for the information published by individual entities. Unless the numbers had the same meaning in all financial statements, it would not be possible to compare numbers of one organization with those of another or to add individual numbers to provide averages and ratios. Even with the best rules, the reports of

---

[1]For additional information on these standards, see the FASB Continuing Professional Education course: "Accounting and Reporting by Not-for-Profit Organizations." See also Thomas A. Ratcliffe and John Stephen Grice, "New Accounting and Auditing Guidance for Not-for-Profit Organizations." *The National Public Accountant,* February–March 2000. For a criticism of the standards see Robert N. Anthony, "The Nonprofit Accounting Mess," *Accounting Horizons,* June 1995, and Robert N. Anthony, "Coping with Nonprofit Accounting Rules," *CPA Journal,* August 1996.

two or more organizations cannot be exactly comparable since so much of what happens in them is too complicated to permit direct comparisons.

Organizations publish at least two reports annually. One is a statement of the organization's status as of the last day of the year. The other is a statement of flows of financial amounts within the year. In business entities, these are called the *balance sheet* and the *income statement,* respectively. In nonprofit and governmental organizations, they have different titles, as will be described below. These differences and many others exist because the rules for business and nonprofit organizations were developed by different people. This does not mean that the numbers are inherently different; many differences are only in the labels for the items.

The balance sheet has two sides. The left side lists assets, which are the resources owned or controlled by the organization. The right side lists the sources of the funds used to acquire these resources. The right side has two sections: liabilities (the amounts obtained from nonowner sources) and equity (the amounts obtained from contributors of capital and from the organization's operations).

The totals of the two sides must balance; that is, assets must equal liabilities plus equity. There is no exception to this equality. If assets do not equal liabilities plus equity, there is something wrong with the organization's recordkeeping. At the same time, the equality does not mean that performance was good or bad; it simply is a fundamental characteristic of accounting.

The income statement reports changes in equity during the accounting period. The bottom line, net income, is the difference between revenues and expenses. Revenues are amounts earned from the sale of goods and services, contributions for operating purposes, and certain gains relating to assets. Expenses are resources consumed during the period and certain losses.

There are only two fundamental differences between for-profit and nonprofit organizations. First, for-profit businesses have transactions with shareholders, whereas nonprofit organizations do not. Second, nonprofit organizations receive contributed capital, which businesses do not.

Despite the inherent similarities between for profit and nonprofit accounting, many nonprofit organizations divide income statement items into operating and nonoperating sections. Unfortunately, there is no general agreement as to the meaning of *operating.* It is not defined by any rule-making body and therefore depends on each organization's preference.

Important Concepts

Accounting rules are developed and promulgated by standards-setting bodies. *Accounting concepts,* by contrast, provide general guidance for determining the rules. Several of the more important concepts are discussed below.

Historical

The amounts reported on the balance sheet are the amounts as of the end of the period. This date has, of course, passed by the time financial statements are made public. The income statement reports the activities during the period; they are not estimates of future activities or future status or performance. Some estimates of future performance are necessary, but these are kept to a minimum.

Example

Accounts receivable is an asset that states the amounts customers *probably* will pay. The amount actually owed is reduced by an estimate of the amounts that will not be collected, called an allowance for bad debts. If the accountants did not make this reduction, the accounts receivable amount would overstate the actual asset.

Monetary

All the numbers on the financial statements are monetary. Without this common denominator, they could not be added or subtracted from one another. This point is obvious but its significance sometimes is not recognized.

Example

The real assets of an organization include its skilled employees, the ability of its management, its reputation with the public, and the value of products being developed. These amounts are taken into account by analysts in judging the value of an organization, but they are not stated in the financial statements.

Realization

Revenue is recognized when goods are delivered to customers, when services are performed, or when contributions are made that are related to the period. The receipt of a grant to conduct a project in the future is not revenue of the period when it was received. Instead, it is a liability at the time of receipt. Its revenue will be realized in the period or periods when the associated work is done.

Matching

Expenses are recognized in the period in which the related work is performed. In effect, they are matched to the revenue that was earned during the period. This does not mean that the expenses need to be equal to the revenue, but rather that any expenses incurred in conjunction with the revenue must be included on the same income statement.

Example

Claims expense in a managed care organization must be matched against the premium revenue received during the period. In almost all managed care organizations, there are some claims that have been incurred but that have not yet been received by the organization at the time it prepares its financial statements. The matching concept requires that the accountants estimate the amount of claims incurred but not received and place this amount on the same income statement that contains the premium revenues.

Standards for Nonprofit Organizations[2]

Until 1980 there were separate standards for four different private nonprofit industries: colleges and universities, health care organizations, voluntary health and welfare organizations, and all other nonprofits. There were many inconsistencies among these standards. In 1980 the FASB accepted jurisdiction for all nonprofit organizations except governments.

The important FASB standards are No. 93 ("Accounting for Depreciation"), No. 116, ("Accounting for Contributions Received and Contributions Made"), No. 117, ("Financial Statements of Not-for-Profit Organizations"), and No. 124 ("Accounting for Certain Investments Held by Not-for-Profit Organizations").

These standards required radical changes in the accounting numbers developed using the earlier rules. Based on the public's reactions to these new forms of reporting, the FASB probably will make changes in them. Their current requirements are discussed below.

Classification

Financial Accounting Standard 116 (or *FAS 116*) requires that transactions in nonprofit organizations be reported in one of three classes: unrestricted, temporarily restricted, or permanently restricted. Unrestricted items are resource inflows that can be used for any purpose; that is, they are not legally restricted. Expenses of the period are also unrestricted. Temporarily restricted items are revenues that initially are restricted to a specified future project or future period. They are similar to prepaid liabilities (e.g., magazine subscriptions) in a business. Permanently restricted items are revenues that will never be reclassified as unrestricted. They include additions to endowment, works of art and other museum objects, and other long-lived assets. (In a business, only additions to the unrestricted class would be called revenue; additions to the other classes would be either liabilities or contributed capital.)

Operating versus Nonoperating Transactions

Most nonprofit accounting systems that were superseded by the FASB's nonprofit standards distinguished between contributions that were operating transactions and those that were nonoperating. Contributions for current operations, such as donations to a college's annual fund, were considered to be

---

[2]Our discussion is brief. Readers who are not familiar with accounting principles may want to read Anthony and Pearlman, *Essentials of Accounting,* 7th ed. (Prentice Hall, 2002). This is a programmed text focusing on accounting in business organizations. Readers who are familiar with the basics of accounting, but who want a refresher, including some of the specific aspects of accounting that are applicable to nonprofit organizations, and some practice cases for analysis, should see David W. Young, *Primer on Financial Accounting for Nonprofit Organizations* (Cambridge, MA: The Crimson Press Curriculum Center, 1997). The address for the Curriculum Center is contained in the Preface.

operating transactions and were included in the organization's revenues. Contributions with a longer-term focus, such as gifts to endowment or for new buildings, were considered to be nonoperating and were recorded in the equity section of the balance sheet, much like contributed capital in a business organization. The operating statement summarized the operating transactions only. Nonoperating transactions were summarized in one or more *statements of changes in fund balances.*

The new FASB nonprofit rules require that all contributions be reported as revenues. Moreover, rather than distinguishing between operating and nonoperating contributions, the new rules distinguish between unrestricted and legally restricted contributions. The latter are those contributions specifically restricted by the donors, using one of two types of restrictions: temporary and permanent.

A temporarily restricted contribution, as its name implies, is a contribution for use in a specified future period or for a specific purpose. Once the period has passed or the expenses associated with the purpose have been incurred, the contribution is reclassified as unrestricted. A foundation or government grant is an example of an item in this category. If, on the other hand, a donor specifically states that the principal of his or her contribution is to be preserved indefinitely, it is recorded as permanently restricted. Examples of items in this category are endowment contributions and contributions of museum objects.

The FASB rules require that nonprofits prepare a *statement of unrestricted activities,* but this is not the same as an operating statement. It includes both contributions for operating purposes, such as gifts from an annual fund drive, and also contributions that, although not intended for operating purposes, were not legally restricted by the donor. This approach is a marked deviation from past practice. In the past, if a donor made a large bequest—so large that it obviously was not intended to be spent in the current year—the nonprofit's board generally added it to endowment funds as *board-designated endowment* (sometimes called *quasi-endowment*), reasoning that the donor meant it for endowment even though he or she did not specifically say so. Similarly, contributions to a campaign to build a new building obviously are not intended for operating purposes, even though the donors do not say so. Nevertheless, under the new FASB rules, any contribution that is not specifically restricted by the donor is classified as unrestricted revenue.

If a nonprofit organization does not have endowments, contributed buildings, or other contributed capital items, the problem of distinguishing between operating and nonoperating transactions does not arise. In this case, the organization's financial statements closely resemble those of a for-profit business.

Unrestricted Revenues and Expenses

Revenues from Services

Revenues in nonprofit organizations should be recognized in accordance with the realization concept, just as in business entities. Patient charges in a community health center, for example, are revenues of the period in which the patient received the center's services, even though this is not necessarily the same period in which the patient (or a third-party payer) was billed or when payment actually was received. The amount of revenue recognized is the amount that is highly likely to be received. If some patients are unlikely to pay their bills, the organization should include an estimate of bad debts. Similarly, if third-party payers disallow certain items on a bill, revenue is the amount billed less these *contractual allowances*.[3]

Membership Dues   Some nonprofit organizations, such as industry or professional associations, have members who pay dues. These dues are revenues of the membership period, whether they are collected prior to (as is often the case), during, or after the period. If fees are not collected until after the period, the asset *dues receivable* must be adjusted downward at the end of the period to allow for the amount that may not be received. If the collection of dues is fairly uncertain (as in an organization with high membership turnover), these dues are recorded as revenues only when cash is received.

Lifetime membership dues present a special problem. Conceptually, a part of the total should be recorded as revenue in each year of the member's expected life. As a practical matter, this calculation is complicated and requires considerable recordkeeping. Many organizations, therefore, take the simple solution of recording life memberships as revenues in the year received.

Pledges   In accordance with the basic revenue concept, pledges of support of the current year's operating activities are revenues in the current year, even if the cash is not received in that year. Unpaid pledges are adjusted downward to allow for estimated uncollectible amounts, just as is done with other accounts receivable. Some people argue that the basic revenue concept should not apply to pledges because, unlike accounts receivable, they are not legally enforceable claims. Others maintain that it is so difficult to estimate the amount of uncollectible pledges that a revenue amount incorporating such an estimate is unreliable. Neither group would count unpaid pledges as revenues.[4]

Endowment Earnings   FAS 124 requires that the earnings on endowment, including increases in the fair value of the principal, be reported in the unrestricted class. This can result in a huge amount of unrestricted income, compared with the previous practice. Many entities therefore continue to use the total return method (described below) and adjust the *statement of activities* accordingly.

---

[3]Nonprofit organizations sometimes use the term *income* instead of revenue, as in patient care income, interest income, and so on. This usage is incorrect and potentially confusing. *Income* is the difference between revenues and expenses—not the revenues themselves.
[4]Note that this paragraph relates only to pledges for the current year. Pledges for future years are described in the FASB's Statement of Financial Standards (FAS) No. 116.

In the total return method, an organization computes the gain on its investments by summing its interest revenue, dividend receipts, and the gain on the fair market value of its securities. This contrasts with using only interest revenue and dividend receipts as the gain on investments, which some nonprofit organizations continue to do.

The method used to evaluate the return on a nonprofit's portfolio must be contrasted with the method used to determine how much of that return to spend in a given year. Although they may use the total return method to measure the investment performance of their endowments, most organizations use only a fraction of that return as operating revenue (i.e., for spending purposes). To do so, they determine the amount of operating revenue to be transferred from the endowment by using a *spending rate*. The spending rate is usually about 5 or 6 percent of the average market value of the endowment, generally using a moving average over a period of three to five years. The remainder of the total return stays in the principal of the endowment.

There are two reasons for using a spending rate. First, if all endowment earnings were used for operating purposes, the purchasing power of the endowment fund would decrease because of inflation. A spending rate of 5 percent assumes that if there were no inflation, invested funds would earn 5 percent. Earnings in excess of 5 percent are implicitly expected to approximate the rate of inflation and are added to the principal of the endowment fund to maintain its purchasing power. Second, the spending rate provides the organization's senior management with a reasonably predictable flow of operating revenues for annual budgeting purposes.

Use of the total return method and the application of a spending rate are not permitted by FASB rules. As a result, organizations have developed different ways to explain the differences.

Contributed Services Volunteers donate their services to many nonprofit organizations. Although these services are valuable, they are recognized as revenues only if they (*a*) create or enhance nonfinancial assets, such as helping to construct a building, or (*b*) require specialized skills, which the volunteers possess and which the organization would need to purchase in the absence of volunteers. When one of these conditions is met, the services are measured at the going wage rate. If it counts services as revenues, however, the organization also must report an equal amount as an expense so there is no net effect on the bottom line.

Expenses

Nonprofit organizations report most expenses according to Generally Accepted Accounting Principles (GAAP) for businesses; that is, they record expenses when resources are consumed or otherwise used up. Some organizations do not follow this principle. For example, they report *purchases* of inventory as expenses. With minor supplies, the approach can be justified on grounds of materiality. Otherwise, the practice is inconsistent with GAAP.

Similarly, some small nonprofits use a cash-basis accounting system; that is, they report cash disbursement and receipts rather than expenses and revenues. This also is not in accordance with GAAP, but in organizations that have small fixed assets and mostly cash transactions, the difference may not be great.

When fixed assets are sizable, there is a problem with the cash-based method. By definition, fixed assets provide service for several years after the organization has purchased them, and GAAP requires that depreciation be used to recognize the associated expenses in the year they provide service. If depreciation is not used, net income is understated in the year the asset is purchased and overstated in succeeding years. Nevertheless, some nonprofits do not depreciate their long-lived assets, arguing that the practice of expensing an asset in the year of purchase is conservative. This is not consistent with GAAP.

Donated Long-Lived Assets   Donated long-lived assets are a special case. When an asset is donated, FAS 93 requires that it be recorded at its fair market value at the time it was received (even though its cost to the organization was zero) and depreciated over its useful life. Some organizations object to this requirement. They argue that because a fixed asset was donated, the organization did not—and never will—require the use of revenues to finance it. Therefore, the inclusion of a depreciation component as an expense item on the operating statement would result in understating the amount of income earned through operating activities. FAS 93 is based on the premise that fixed assets are used for operating purposes; therefore, omitting depreciation would understate the organization's real operating expense.

FAS 116 added a further complication to the accounting effort. For contributed long-lived assets or for assets acquired with contributed funds, an organization may take either of two approaches. (1) It may report the cost of the asset as unrestricted revenue in the year it is placed in service and depreciate this cost over the asset's useful life. (2) It may report the asset as restricted initially and then report depreciation as an operating expense in each year of the asset's economic life, while reporting an equal amount as revenue each of those years. With the former approach, there will be a large positive impact on the organization's bottom line in the year of the asset's acquisition, and small negative effects in each year of the asset's economic life. With the latter, there is no net effect on the bottom line from either the acquisition or depreciation of the asset.

FASB Statement No. 136   FAS 136, issued in June, 1999, concerns transfers of assets to a nonprofit organization when the nonprofit accepts the assets from a donor and agrees to use them on behalf of a specified unaffiliated beneficiary (or subsequently transfer the assets to that beneficiary). In those instances, the assets' fair value must be shown as a liability to the beneficiary.

Example

A foundation receives a contribution of $1 million from an estate. The terms of the bequest stipulate that the foundation is to transfer the contribution, as well as any investment income realized from it, to the ABC hospital. The foundation has no economic interest in the hospital. In this instance, the foundation's balance sheet would show an increase in its assets (cash) of $1 million and an increase in its liabilities of $1 million, indicating its obligation to transfer $1 million to the hospital. Any investment income earned prior to the transfer would increase both cash and the liability.[5]

Equity

Although nonprofit organizations report assets and liabilities in essentially the same way as their for-profit counterparts, they report equity quite differently. Specifically, because nonprofit organizations have no investors, their balance sheets have no paid-in capital amount. Some nonprofits receive contributions, however, and many generate earnings from their operations, both of which increase equity. Since they are legally prohibited from paying dividends, equity only decreases through operating losses.[6]

Some nonprofit organizations do not use the term *equity* on their balance sheets. Instead, they label this amount *net assets.* Whatever the label, the amount is conceptually the same as equity in a for-profit corporation. Nevertheless, there are some tricky concepts and terminology.

Contributed Capital

There are two general types of contributed capital: contributions for endowment and contributions for plant. As described above, only the earnings on the endowment or some fraction thereof are used for operating purposes; the principal is not used. Similarly, when a donor contributes money to acquire a building or other item of plant, this contribution must be used for the specified purpose; it is not available to finance operating activities.

Financial Statement Presentation

The above description has focused on the distinction between operating and nonoperating items; this distinction is important for management purposes. FAS 116 and 117 require organizations to publish a *statement of activities* that shows separately the inflows and outflows during the accounting period for each of the three classes—unrestricted, temporarily restricted, and permanently restricted. Inflows to all three classes are called revenues. All expenses are reported in the unrestricted class. In a business, revenues relate only to operating activities; however, as noted above, under FAS 117, the unrestricted class includes both operating items and certain restricted contributions. Exhibit 3–1 is a sample *statement of activities* that abides by the new rules.

---

[5]Randall W. Luecke and David T. Meeting, "FASB Statement No. 136 Clarifies Transfer of Assets," *Healthcare Financial Management,* March 2000.
[6]In some rare instances, equity also can decrease through a reduction in the market value of the endowment fund's invested assets.

EXHIBIT 3–1

ANDERSON COLLEGE STATEMENT OF ACTIVITIES FOR THE YEAR ENDED JUNE 30, 2002, WITH COMPARATIVE FIGURES FOR 2001 (IN THOUSANDS)				
	Unrestricted	Temporarily Restricted	Permanently Restricted	Total 2002	Total 2001
Operating Activities:					
Operating Revenues					
Tuition and fees	$20,064			$ 20,064	$ 18,291
Student aid........................	(4,340)			(4,340)	(3,873)
Net tuition and fees.................	15,724			15,724	14,418
Contributions	983			983	989
Endowment used for operations	2,498			2,498	2,242
Other investment income..............	462			462	310
Auxiliary enterprises	6,793			6,793	6,455
Equity released from restrictions	1,292			1,292	1,000
Other revenue	457			457	450
Total operating revenues..............	28,209			28,209	25,864
Expenses					
Instruction and research	10,477			10,477	9,740
Academic support....................	2,622			2,622	2,386
Student services	4,667			4,667	4,341
Institutional support	3,510			3,510	3,282
Auxiliary enterprises	6,237			6,237	5,856
Total operating expenses..............	27,513			27,513	25,605
Operating surplus	696			696	259
Nonoperating activities:					
Contributions.......................	564	$ 4,087	$ 2,371	7,022	12,400
Investment income...................	766	2,042	146	2,954	2,484
Net realized and unrealized gains	3,473	6,650	1,068	11,191	9,399
Endowment used for operations			(2,498)	(2,498)	(2,242)
Other revenue		11	1	12	31
Capital campaign expenses..............	(333)			(333)	(349)
Investment expenses..................	(294)			(294)	(269)
Other expenses......................	(334)			(334)	(138)
Net change in annuity and life income funds		(867)	25	(842)	(391)
Equity released from restriction (Note 15)....	10,472	(11,764)		(1,292)	(1,000)
Equity reclassified to permanently restricted .	(876)	(99)	974	(1)	
Change in equity from nonoperating activities. . .	13,438	60	2,087	15,585	19,925
Cumulative effect of change in accounting for land, buildings and equipment (Note 13)	(2,655)			(2,655)	
Total change in equity	11,479	60	2,087	13,626	20,184
Equity, beginning of year.................	65,796	14,962	35,715	116,473	96,289
Equity, end of year.....................	$77,275	$15,022	$37,802	$130,099	$116,473

FAS 117 also requires a balance sheet that shows the assets, liabilities, and equity for the organization as a whole—that is, without showing each class separately. The equity section of the balance sheet reports each category's net assets, however, as is shown in Exhibit 3–2.

EXHIBIT 3–2

ANDERSON COLLEGE
BALANCE SHEET
AS OF JUNE 30, 2002 AND 2001
(IN THOUSANDS)

	2002	2001
Assets		
Cash and cash equivalents........................	$ 2,038	$ 1,664
Accrued income receivable	39	104
Accounts receivable.............................	574	429
Funds held by trustee...........................	664	561
Inventories......................................	257	453
Prepaid expenses and deferred charges	354	345
Notes receivable	3,140	3,211
Pledges receivable and bequests in probate..........	6,775	7,403
Investments, endowment	78,140	67,783
Investments, annuity and life income funds..........	6,269	4,811
Investments, funds held in trust by others	5,048	4,687
Investments, other..............................	4,126	3,550
Total investments............................	93,583	80,831
Land, buildings and equipment (less allowance for depreciation of $10,194 in 2002 and $11,678 in 2001)	37,102	34,861
Total assets	$144,526	$129,862
Liabilities		
Accounts payable and accrued liabilities.............	$3,094	$2,204
Student deposits	664	898
Government advances for student loans	2,072	1,976
Annuity obligations	2,423	1,880
Bonds payable..................................	5,925	6,303
Obligation under capital lease	77	128
Postretirement benefit obligation..................	172	
Total liabilities...............................	14,427	13,389
Equity		
Unrestricted....................................	77,275	65,796
Temporarily restricted	15,022	14,962
Permanently restricted..........................	37,802	35,715
Total equity	130,099	116,473
Total liabilities and equity.......................	$144,526	$129,862

The FASB also requires nonprofit organizations to provide a *statement of cash flows* (SCF) similar to that published by business organizations. Since the SCF has this similarity and since it does not make a distinction among the three categories of funds, we do not show an example here.

As Exhibits 3–1 and 3–2 show, the equity (i.e., the net asset amount) of a nonprofit organization is divided into three classes: permanently restricted, temporarily restricted, and unrestricted. Each is discussed below.

Permanently Restricted Net Assets

This class contains any amounts whose use the donor has restricted permanently and any fixed assets that do not depreciate. It includes all legally restricted endowments as well as land and most art and museum objects.

Unless the donor specifies that the gift of art or a museum object can be sold and the proceeds used for operating purposes, the contribution is reported as a separate fund. The amount reported on the balance sheet is the fair value of the asset at the time of the contribution. The asset is not depreciated unless it has a limited life, which is unusual. The donor may permit the organization to sell the object and reinvest the proceeds in similar assets, but this is not the same as allowing the proceeds to be used for operating purposes.

Temporarily Restricted Net Assets

As indicated previously, this class is used when donors place temporary restrictions on the way an organization may use their contributions. This class includes term *endowments* (endowments that are used up within a time period specified by the donor, which may span several years), *annuities* (contributions that provide a return to the contributor for a period of several years and then revert to the nonprofit organization), advance payments for work to be performed in future years, and any donated fixed assets (unless the organization selects the alternative of including them in the unrestricted fund).

Unrestricted Net Assets

This class includes all equity that is not restricted by the donor. It therefore includes equity items related to the regular operations of the organization. It also includes contributions that, although intended for purposes other than ongoing operations, were not legally restricted by the donor. As indicated above, unless donors make their intentions clear, their contributions must be included in the unrestricted category.

FAS 116 permits organizations to report an operating statement *within* the *statement of activities,* but not as a separate statement. Many organizations do prepare an unrestricted statement, but it does contain an operating section. These organizations regard operating performance as more important than unrestricted performance because several revenue items designated unrestricted are not related to operating activities of the current period.

Standards for State and Local Governments

State and local governments collectively are the largest category of nonprofit organizations. They are subject to a variety of external forces and political influences and, therefore, have difficult management control problems. Traditionally, they have used an accounting system called fund accounting, a system that was designed to regulate spending. In this system, each type of activity is a separate fund with its own statement of financial status and statement of financial flows. Each fund was established with appropriated amounts from some other source. When the total additions were spent, no more could be spent.

Generally, in state and local governments, revenues are not directly related to services provided to clients. Although the person whose house is on fire is a client in one sense, the fire department's main function is to protect the whole community. Specific programs proposed to state and local government agencies are often political in nature and frequently not subject to economic analysis. The objectives of these organizations are difficult to define in ways that permit measurement of attainment. What constitutes adequate fire or police protection, for example, is inherently difficult to determine.

Because management control in state and local governments is so difficult, good accounting systems are especially necessary. With a few notable exceptions, such systems do not now exist in most government units. Tradition has greatly hampered development of adequate systems. Many government units keep their accounts solely on a cash-receipts-and-disbursements basis, for example, a practice that has been obsolete since the 19th century. Only recently has pressure for change—public dissatisfaction with rising taxes and revelations of poor management—begun to emerge. There are also pressures from the federal government to implement revenue-sharing programs. Moreover, the Governmental Accounting Standards Board (GASB) has made substantial improvements in governmental accounting systems, and these will be implemented over the next few years.

The GASB has been in existence only since 1979. Its role was to take a fresh look at the system that should be used for government accounting. During its first year, it issued a concepts statement, which is drastically different from fund accounting. The statement had two principal concepts: accountability and interperiod equity. *Accountability* meant that the organization should account for all its resources. *Interperiod equity* meant that the taxpayers in the current year should pay for all the resources used in that year; that is, current taxpayers should not put the burden for this year's services on taxpayers in future years. (This general concept actually permitted averaging over several periods.)

In 1999 the GASB issued Statement No. 34, which described the required accounting system. This statement called for two sets of financial statements: (1) government-wide statements that are similar to the financial statements used by businesses, and (2) a set that is essentially the same as the fund-accounting statements.

These statements are supposed to be implemented by 2003. For the fund-accounting statements, meeting this date is easy because this is the system currently in use. The government-wide statements will be somewhat slower in coming, however.

Government-wide Statements

The two principal government-wide financial statements are called the *statement of net assets* and the *statement of activities*. Each is discussed below.

Statement of Net Assets

This is a status statement similar to a business balance sheet, with some modification to take into account the special conditions of some government assets. It contains information for all the units in the reporting government, such as a municipality. Like a business balance sheet, it has assets in one section and liabilities plus net assets in another. *Net assets* means the same as equity in a business. Like a business balance sheet, the statement conforms to the equation Assets = Liabilities + Net Assets.

There is one column for the primary government and another column for component units, such as schools, parks and recreation, and cemeteries. There is a third column for businesslike activities—activities financed by revenues from services rendered, such as water, sewer, and electrical services.

The rules for reporting most assets are the same as in business. Capital assets (i.e., long-lived assets) are reported at cost less accumulated depreciation. If the asset was donated, it is shown at its fair value at the time of acquisition.

Capital assets that are stationary, that have an extremely long life, and that meet certain other conditions are called infrastructure assets and are not depreciated. They include roads, bridges, tunnels, dams, and sewer systems. Works of art and historical treasures also are reported at cost or fair value when donated and are not depreciated.

Statement of Activities

The *statement of activities* reports revenues and expenses for the year. In general, the rules for recognition and measurement are the same as those for business income statements. There are special rules for items unique to government, however, such as taxes and contributions.

Revenues and expenses are reported separately for principal government functions (e.g., public safety, public works, health and sanitation). They are also reported separately for each type of business activity (e.g., water and sewer).

Revenues are defined approximately the same as in business—that is, they are the inflows of resources from operating activities during the period. There are specific definitions for revenues from taxation and for contributions.

Expenses are reported at the cost of resources consumed during the period, as in business. Extraordinary items—items that are unusual and/or that occur infrequently—are reported at the bottom of the *statement of activities,* as in business.

Fund Financial Statements

Governmental accounting systems consist of a number of separate funds, each of which is a self-balancing set of accounts. The general fund, which accounts for governmental operating transactions, and enterprise funds, which account for businesslike activities such as public utilities, are the principal funds. Many governmental organizations also have some special-purpose funds.

General Fund

The items in the general fund are essentially the same items as those in the government's operating budget and form the basis for controlling the organization's operating activities.[7] In preparing this budget, the organization generally estimates revenues from nontax sources and then computes taxes as the difference between them and total operating expenses.[8]

Revenues

Revenues are the amounts received from taxes, grants and contracts, fines, parking meters, and other sources. In cases where estimates are difficult or impossible to make, revenues are measured in terms of cash received during the period. This is true for a state's income tax revenue, where there is considerable difficulty estimating in advance the revenues that the taxes will generate, as well as for fines and other miscellaneous sources of revenue.

In general, however, revenues are measured by the accrual concept.[9] For example, property tax revenue is the amount of the tax applicable to the current period (not the period in which the bills were sent out, which frequently is an earlier period), less an allowance for uncollectable amounts. Similarly, the amount for grants and contracts is the revenue earned from the grant or contract work done during the period, not the amount of cash received during the period for new grants and contracts.[10]

---

[7]Since 1997, the GASB has been considering a drastic change in the governmental model. Because no decision had been made as of the date this chapter was written, discussion of it in this section would be highly speculative.

[8]This section of the general fund is labeled *expenses* in some entities and *expenditures* in others. Usually, it is a mixture of both types of outflows.

[9]Because some revenues are reported on a cash basis, the GASB describes its requirement as a *modified revenue concept.* Actually, most business organizations with similar uncertainties also would report these items on a cash basis.

[10]See GASB Statement No. 24, *"Accounting and Financial Reporting for Certain Grants and Other Financial Assistance,"* for the rules pertaining to grants and contracts, and also for rules concerning food stamps and payments of certain fringe benefits and salaries.

Expenditures

Resource outflows reported in the general fund differ from those reported in business accounting in two respects: (1) they are expenditures rather than expenses,[11] and (2) they do not include noncurrent transactions. In the case of supplies, operations for the current period are charged with the cost of goods *received* during the period, rather than with the goods that were *used.*

Pension costs and other postemployment benefits are special cases. Historically, they were treated as expenditures in the period when the payments were made, which was a much later period than when the expenses were incurred. This practice seriously understated the cost of operating government organizations, sometimes by millions or even billions of dollars. In 1996 for example, the District of Columbia had an unfunded pension benefit of $4.7 billion. These benefits now are recorded in the period in which employees work and thereby become entitled to them. This change, implemented in 1998, makes government practice consistent with the private sector's treatment of these benefits.[12]

The current practice reflects the fact that governments tend to acquire major long-lived assets by borrowing an amount that is approximately equal to the asset's acquisition cost. Often, the terms of a bond issue or other form of borrowing require annual payments be made to retire the debt over the useful life of the assets acquired. The annual payments, called *debt service,* include both the interest on the amount of the loan outstanding and a portion of the principal. Under GAAP, interest on the loan is properly an expense of the period, but the principal payment is not.

If, however, the loan is for the full cost of the asset, and if the term of the loan and the economic life of the asset are about equal, each year's principal payment will approximate the annual amount of depreciation that otherwise would have been charged as an expense. Under these circumstances, treating principal as an expense will have roughly the same effect on the government's surplus as using depreciation. The validity of such treatment depends, of course, on how closely the principal payments come to the amount that would have been charged as depreciation.

In summary, general fund transactions are limited to revenues and expenditures that are strictly related to governmental activities. In addition, these transactions are limited to current items as contrasted with capital ones. All other activities are accounted for in some other fund.

Enterprise Funds

Some governments operate electric, gas, water, sewer, or other utilities, or have other units that generate substantial amounts of revenue, such as a subway, toll

---

[11]For a description of the difference between expenditures and expenses, see the *Primer on Financial Accounting for Nonprofit Organizations,* cited in footnote 2.

[12]See GASB Statement No. 27, *"Accounting for Pensions by State and Local Governmental Employees."* GASB Statements Nos. 25 and 26 have other requirements for pensions and postemployment benefits.

bridge, lottery, or hospital. Accounting for these enterprise funds is basically the same as accounting for business entities. The bottom line on the operating statement for such a fund is equivalent to a business organization's net income.

An enterprise fund is one type of what are called proprietary funds. Another type is the *internal service fund,* which is used for governmental units that sell goods and services to other units; a maintenance garage is an example. In business accounting, the sale of these services is handled by direct charges to the organizational units that receive them, rather than by creating a separate fund.[13]

Other Funds

Separate funds are used for each type of resource inflow wherein spending is limited to a specified purpose. For example, a government does not account for the acquisition of capital assets in the general fund. Instead, it uses a *capital projects fund* for this purpose. Authorized capital expenditures are described in a capital budget. As noted above, *debt service funds* are used to record borrowing and the associated principal and interest payments. *Special revenue funds* record the revenues and related expenditures for work on projects that are not included in the general fund, such as the cost of building a road that is to be paid by the developer of the property. *Fiduciary funds* account for assets that the governmental unit holds as a trustee or agent for another party. Federal tax withholding amounts are an example.

Account Groups

In addition to funds, there are two account groups, one for fixed assets and the other for long-term debt. Because the transactions for these items are recorded in one of the funds discussed above, the account groups serve only as memorandum, or single-entry, groups. They do not appear on the balance sheet of the government organization.

Federal Government Accounting

Several commissions have recommended that the federal government shift its accounting system from a focus on obligations to a focus on expenses. Legislation to this effect was enacted in 1984, but nothing actually happened for several years thereafter.

Federal Accounting Standards Advisory Board

In 1990, the Federal Accounting Standards Advisory Board (FASAB) issued its first pronouncement. The FASAB consisted of executives from the three agencies that set rules for federal accounting: Department of the Treasury,

---

[13]This charge is called a *transfer price.* It is discussed in detail in Chapter 7.

General Accounting Office, and Office of Management and Budget. The FASAB standards are tentatively expected to be implemented by 2003. They are applicable both to the overall financial statements of the federal government and to individual agencies. They therefore apply to financial accounting, as described earlier, and also to management accounting.

The FASAB requires three principal financial statements: a *balance sheet,* a *statement of operations and changes in net position,* and *statement of net cost.*

The balance sheet reports assets, liabilities, and net position (i.e., equity). It does not, by any means, report all the assets owned by the government. The items omitted are described in a separate section of the financial report. Examples include more than 700 million acres of land used for forests, national parks, grazing, and wildlife refuges; heritage assets, such as buildings of historical significance and battlefields; Social Security and retirement funds, for which the government is in effect a trustee; military and space hardware; and mineral resources located on the continental shelf. Although the balance sheet reports a negative net position, taking the omitted assets into account would surely make it a strong positive.

The *statement of operations and net position* is a form of income statement; it includes revenues and expenses for the government as a whole. The *statement of net cost* consists of costs for each major program.

In businesses, private nonprofit organizations, and governmental organizations, the most important single number on the financial statements is the difference between revenues and expenses for a period. This is the bottom line, called *net income (loss)* in a business and *surplus (deficit)* or *change in net assets* in nonprofit organizations.

This is not the case for the federal government as a whole. Instead, it can and usually does operate at a deficit. Within limits, there is no cause for concern, because of the government's unique power to print money.[14] The focus of financial accounting in the federal government as a whole, therefore, is not on the measurement of net income or its equivalent.

Management Accounting

The rules for the overall financial statements also apply to financial statements prepared by each government agency. The FASAB has published additional rules for these statements; for example, there is a section on cost accounting. Standards for businesses and nonprofit organizations do not go into this level of detail.

This generalization applies to the federal government as a whole. Individual agencies, however, may have quite different circumstances. Some, such as the Internal Revenue Service, generate tax revenues that are far greater than their expenses. Others, such as the postal service and the Tennessee Valley Authority, are essentially businesses whose expenses are financed by their

[14]The term *within limits* is key here. There have been many instances throughout history of the irresponsible printing of money leading to high rates of inflation.

revenues (and, in some cases, by a government subsidy). Most agencies have little or no revenue; their activities are financed by congressional appropriations.[15] Nevertheless, all agencies need an accounting system that measures and controls their expenses and, where relevant, measures and controls their revenues. In addition, the system must control capital expenditures in all agencies.

Because of these multiple needs, the federal government has two accounting systems. One, the *budgetary system,* provides the information used to prepare the budget and to control spending. The other, the *federal accounting system,* is, in most respects, similar to the accounting systems used by many private nonprofit organizations.

Budgetary System

The budget is the primary financial planning and control tool of the government. Government managers and members of Congress are interested mainly in financial reports that show how much an agency actually spent compared with what it was authorized to spend.

The rules for these reports are given in OMB Circular A-34. They differ in two respects from expenses as this term is used in the government-wide system: (1) the time and (2) the responsible party.

For example, a contract for widgets written by the contracting office at Meriden Supply Center in 2001 is an obligation of the center. If the widgets are used at the Clavis base in 2002, they are an expense in 2002 of the Clavis base. If a contract to paint a building is signed in 2001, it is an obligation in 2001. If the building is painted in 2002, it is an expense in 2002. An employee's pay is an obligation of the unit showing the employee on its payroll even if the employee actually works in another unit.

As will be discussed in later chapters, expenses are a better measure than obligations of resources used. Expenses permit comparisons with a prior period and they often can measure efficiency, that is, the cost per unit of work. Because of this, the budgetary accounting system—which reflects the "power of the purse"—is much more important than the federal accounting system.[16] It starts with appropriations, which are the authority that Congress grants to spending agencies. There are several types of appropriations, each requiring somewhat different accounting procedures.

Annual Appropriations

The operating activity of most agencies, including their authority to make certain types of grants and contracts, is financed by annual appropriations. An

---

[15]Some of these agencies have units within them that generate revenues from sales to the outside world or other government agencies, but, in general, these are small. The Passport Office in the State Department, for example, generates revenue from the sale of passports.
[16]Federal Accounting Standards Advisory Board, *Statement of Recommended Accounting Standards No. 7,* April 1996, Paragraph 75.

annual appropriation, sometimes called *budget authority,* is the authority to obligate funds during the fiscal year. An agency obligates funds by such activities as writing contracts and grants or hiring employees. Since agencies lose any annual appropriations that are not fully obligated by September 30, they tend to write many contracts and grants shortly before this date.[17] In business accounting, there is no counterpart to the obligation activity.

No-Year Appropriations

Appropriations for the acquisition of major items, such as buildings, ships, airplanes, and equipment, are continuing, or "no-year", appropriations. They grant authority to spend a specified amount of money on the particular project rather than in a particular year. If a project turns out to be more costly than originally anticipated, either an additional appropriation is made or the project stops. Stories about cost overruns do not mean that more than the appropriated amount was spent on the project; they usually mean that the amount originally appropriated was too low and that additional appropriations subsequently were made.[18]

Entitlement Programs

Amounts spent for entitlement programs are governed by formulas set by Congress. These include Social Security, Medicare, Medicaid, and most subsidies. Agencies have the authority to spend whatever the formula permits, and the amounts set forth in the approved budget are estimates rather than ceilings that cannot be exceeded.

Cost Accounting

Government grants and contracts prescribe the type of costs that the government will reimburse for a given program. The recipients of these grants and contracts must keep records of costs incurred according to principles established by the granting agency, the Cost Accounting Standards Board (CASB), or the Office of Management and Budget in the Executive Office of the President. The CASB, located in the Office of Federal Procurement Policy, publishes Federal Acquisition Regulations, which prescribe detailed rules for all cost-type defense contracts and for many contracts made by other agencies.

Implementation

The new federal accounting rules require substantial educational programs, both for accountants who must provide the information and, more importantly, for users of the information. The federal system was required by law to be operational in 1997. The system did produce a financial report for 1997 and

---

[17]Although rarely the case, an individual who overobligates an appropriation is subject to a fine or other penalty under the Antideficiency Act (31 U.S.C. 665).

[18]As with annual appropriations, if more than the appropriated amount is spent, the person responsible can suffer the penalties of the Antideficiency Act, but this rarely happens.

has done so for every year thereafter, but none of these reports have met the minimum requirements established by the American Institute of Certified Public Accountants.

The changes require new software programs, and the market for these programs is huge. Some developers for federal programs have invested more than $100 million each in developing the software.

Providing the necessary resources for the FASAB program is especially difficult, but this program must compete with the budgetary program already in existence, which has the power of the purse. As this is written, the current estimate is that the Federal system will be operational by 2003. It is highly unlikely that a satisfactory set of financial statements will be published by that date, however.

Suggested Additonal Readings

Anthony, Robert N., and Leslie Pearlman. *Essentials of Accounting,* 7th edition. Englewood Cliffs, NJ: Prentice Hall, 2002.

Bailey, Larry. *Miller Governmental GAAP Guide, 2002.* San Diego: Harcourt Brace Professional Publishing, 2001.

Chan, James L., Rowan H. Jones, and Klaus G. Lüder (eds.). *Research in Governmental and Non-Profit Accounting.* Greenwich, CT: JAI Press, 1985– . An annual publication.

Engstrom, John, and Paul A. Copley. *Essentials of Accounting for Governmental and Not-for-Profit Organizations.* New York: McGraw-Hill, 2000.

Foster, Mary F., Howard Becker, and Richard Terrano. *GAAP for Not-for-Profit Organizations.* San Diego: Harcourt Brace Professional Publishing, 1998. (Also available on CDROM.)

Freeman, Robert J., and Craig D. Shoulders. *Governmental and Nonprofit Accounting: Theory and Practice.* Upper Saddle River, NJ: Prentice Hall, 1996.

Gross, Malvern J., Richard F. Larkin, and John H. McCarthy. *Financial and Accounting Guide for Non-for-Profit Organizations.* New York: John Wiley & Sons, 2000.

Henke, Emerson O. *Introduction to Nonprofit Organization Accounting,* 4th ed. Cincinnati: South-Western Publishing Co., 1996.

Larkin, Richard F., and Marie Ditommaso. *Wiley Not-for-Profit GAAP 2001: Interpretation and Application of Generally Accepted Accounting Standards for Not-for-Profit Organizations 2001.* New York: John Wiley & Sons, 2001.

McKinney, Jerome B. *Effective Financial Management in Public and Nonprofit Agencies: A Practical and Integrative Approach.* Westport, CT: Quorum Books, 1995.

Ostrom, John S. *Accounting for Contributions: Understanding the Requirements of FASB Statement No. 116.* Washington, D.C.: National Association of College and University Business Officers, 1996.

Razek, Joseph R. *Introduction to Governmental and Not-for-Profit Accounting.* Englewood Cliffs, NJ: Prentice Hall, 2000.

Wilson, Earl R., Leon E. Hay and Sojan C. Kattelus. *Accounting for Governmental and Nonprofit Entities.* Chicago: Irwin, 1999.

Young, David W. *Primer on Financial Accounting in Nonprofit Organizations.* Cambridge, MA: The Crimson Press Curriculum Center, 1997.

http://www.mapnp.org/library

Education

Everett, Ronald E., Donald Johnson, and Raymond L. Lows. *Managerial and Financial Accounting for School Administrators.* Reston, VA: Association of School Business Officials International, 1996.

Jenny, Jans H. *Cost Accounting in Higher Education: Simplified Macro- and Micro-Costing Techniques.* Washington, D.C.: NACUBO, 1996.

Jones, Leigh, and Mary Joan McCarthy. *The Impact of FASB Standards 116 & 117 on Development Operations: An Overview with Questions and Answers.* Washington, D.C.: National Association of College and University Business Officers, 1995.

National Association of College and University Business Officers (NACUBO). *Financial Accounting and Reporting Manual for Higher Education.* Washington, D.C.

Federal Government

Joint Financial Management Improvement Program. *Report on Financial Management Improvements.* Washington, DC: JFMIP: 1987– . Microform; also available in paper. Annual.

U.S. Congress. Senate. Committee on Governmental Affairs. *Federal Financial Management Improvement Act of 1996.* Washington, DC: Government Printing Office, 1996.

U.S. Department of Transportation. *U.S. Government Standard General Ledger.* Washington, DC: Government Printing Office.

U.S. Federal Accounting Standards Advisory Board. *Statements of Recommended Accounting Standards.* Washington, DC: Executive Office of the President, Office of Management and Budget.

U.S. General Accounting Office. *GAO Policy and Procedures Manual, Title 2, Accounting.* Washington DC: Government Printing Office, 1988– . Updated regularly.

State and Local Government

Governmental Accounting Standards Board. *Codification of the Governmental Accounting and Financial Reporting Standards Board.* Stamford, CT: GASB. Updated regularly.

Health Care

Berman, Howard J. *The Financial Management of Hospitals.* Ann Arbor, MI: Health Administration Press, Steven F. Kukla, and Lewis E. Weeks. 1998.

Cleverley, William O. *Essentials of Health Care Finance,* 4th ed. Gaithersburg, MD: Aspen Publishers, Inc., 1997.

Other Sectors

Club Managers Association of America. *Uniform System of Accounts for Clubs.* Dubuque, IA: Kendall/Hunt Pub. Co., 1990.

Henry, Jack A. *Basic Accounting for Churches: A Turnkey Manual.* Nashville: Broadman & Holman, 1994.

McMillan, Edward J. *Model Accounting and Financial Policies and Procedures Handbook for Not-for-Profit Organizations.* Washington, DC: American Society of Association Executives, 1994.

Smith, G. Stevenson. *Managerial Accounting for Librarians and Other Not-for-Profit Managers.* Chicago: American Library Association, 1991.

Practice Case

Oceanside Nursing Home*

Oceanside Nursing Home began operating on January 1, 1997. It is now December 31, 1998, the end of the second fiscal year. With a good reputation, a competent staff, and fairly good patient revenue, Oceanside did well financially during both years. Bob Holmes and George Nichols, who manage the

*This case was prepared by Elizabeth O'Brien under the supervision of Professor David W. Young. Copyright © by David W. Young.

home, were completely dedicated to providing the best care possible to their clients, but they were not the least bit interested in keeping accurate financial records.

Seeing a low cash balance in the check book, Holmes and Nichols asked their local bank for a loan. The bank requested Oceanside's financial statements. The statements were presented in the format shown in Exhibit 1.

EXHIBIT 1

| OCEANSIDE NURSING HOME |
| FINANCIAL STATEMENTS DECEMBER 31, 1998 |

Operating Statement		Balance Sheet	
Patient revenue	$110,000	Assets:	
Expenses:.		Cash	$ 1,500
Salaries.	$ 40,000	Receivables	13,000
Maintenance	25,000	Supplies.	4,000
Other expenses	35,000	Property & equipment . .	48,000
Total.	100,000	Other assets	12,000
		Total assets	$78,500
Surplus	$ 10,000		
		Liabilities:	
		Accounts payable	9,000
		Net assets:	
		Contributions.	45,000
		Retained earnings	24,500
			$78,500

Upon viewing the statements provided, the bank officers found them to be much too general. They insisted on additional information before a loan could even be considered—information dealing with depreciation, accruals, inventory counts, etc.

Holmes and Nichols were amazed. They had not anticipated any problems regarding their loan request. After feverishly reviewing their records and supporting statements (with some expert assistance), the following information was discovered:

(a)The inventory of supplies should have been $3,000 instead of the $4,000 shown on December 31, 1998.

(b) Prepaid insurance at December 31, 1998, amounted to $2,000. All of the insurance premium had been debited to Other Expense.

(c)The property and equipment was purchased in January 1997 at a cost of $48,000. It had an estimated useful life of 20 years. Salvage value was estimated to be $8,000.

(d) Unpaid salaries at December 31, 1998, amounted to $4,000.

(e) Unearned patient revenue at December 31, 1998, amounted to $4,000. This had been credited to Patient Revenue.

(f) Bad debts were estimated to be $800 for the year. No entry had been made to the financial statements to reflect this.

Questions

1. Prepare corrected financial statements, taking the above information into account.

2. What do the corrected statements tell you about operations of Oceanside?

Case 3–1

National Association of Accountants*

Each December the incoming members of the board of directors of the National Association of Accountants (NAA) met in joint session with the outgoing board as a means of smoothing the transition from one administration to another. At the meeting in December 2000, questions were raised about whether the board had adhered to the general policies of the association. The ensuing discussion became quite heated.

NAA was a nonprofit professional association with 3,000 members. The association published two professional journals, arranged an annual meeting and several regional meetings, appointed committees that developed positions on various topics of interest to the membership, and represented the members before standards-setting bodies.

The operating activities of the association were managed by George Tremble, its executive secretary. Mr. Tremble reported to the board of directors. The board consisted of four officers and seven other members. Six members of the 2001 board (i.e., the board that assumed responsibility on January 2001) were also on the 2000 board; the other five members were newly elected. The president served a one-year term.

The financial policy of the association was that each year should "stand on its own feet"; that is, expenses of the year should approximately equal the revenues of the year. If there was a deficit in 2000, this amount would normally be made up by a dues increase in 2001.

At the meeting in December 2000, Mr. Tremble presented an estimated income statement for 2000 (Exhibit 1). Although some of the December transactions were necessarily estimated, Mr. Tremble assured the board that the actual totals for the year would closely approximate the numbers shown.

*This case was prepared by Professor Robert N. Anthony of a disguised organization. Copyright © by Robert N. Anthony.

EXHIBIT 1

ESTIMATED INCOME STATEMENT YEAR ENDING DECEMBER 31, 2000	
Revenues:	
Membership dues....................................	$287,500
Journal subscriptions................................	31,000
Publication sales...................................	11,900
Foundation grant...................................	54,000
1994 annual meeting, profit..........................	3,400
Total revenues..................................	387,800
Expenses:	
Printing and mailing publications.....................	92,400
Committee meeting expense..........................	49,200
Annual meeting advance.............................	10,800
Desktop publishing system...........................	27,000
Administrative salaries and expenses...................	171,500
Miscellaneous.....................................	25,000
Total expenses..................................	375,900
Surplus..	$ 11,900

Wilma Fosdick, one of the newly elected board members, raised a question about the foundation grant of $54,000. She questioned whether this item should be counted as revenue. If it were excluded, there was a deficit; and this showed that the 2000 board had, in effect, eaten into reserves and thus made it more difficult to provide the level of service that the members had a right to expect in 2001. This led to detailed questions about items on the income statement, which brought forth the following information from Mr. Tremble.

1. In 2000 NAA received a $54,000 cash grant from the Beckwith Foundation for the purpose of financing a symposium to be held in June 2001. During 2000 approximately $2,700 was spent in preliminary planning for this symposium and was included in Committee Meeting Expenses. When asked why the $54,000 had been recorded as revenue in 2000 rather than in 2001, Mr. Tremble said that the grant was obtained entirely by the initiative and persuasiveness of the 2000 president, so 2000 should be given credit for it. Further, although the grant was intended to finance the symposium, there was no legal requirement that the symposium be held; if for any reason it was not held, the money would be used for the general operations of the association.

2. In early December 2000 the association took delivery of, and paid for, a new desktop publishing system costing $27,000. This system would greatly simplify the work of preparing membership lists, correspondence, and manuscripts submitted for publication. Except for this new system,

the personal computers, desks, and other equipment in the association office were quite old.

3. Ordinarily, members paid their dues during the first few months of the year. Because of the need to raise cash to finance the purchase of the desktop publishing system, the association announced in September 2000 that members who paid their 2001 dues before December 15, 2000, would receive a free copy of the book of papers presented an the special symposium to be held in June 2001. The approximate per-copy cost of publishing this book was $16, and it was expected to be sold for $18. Consequently, $32,400 of 2001 dues were received by December 15, 2000; they were included in 2000 revenue.

4. In July 2000 the association sent a membership directory to members. Its long-standing practice was to publish such a directory every two years. The cost of preparing and printing this directory was $23,200. Of the 4,000 copies printed, 3,000 were mailed to members in 2000. The remaining 1,000 were held to meet the needs of new members who would join before the next directory came out; they would receive a free copy of the directory when they joined.

5. Members received the association's journals at no extra cost, as a part of the membership privileges. Some libraries and other nonmembers also subscribed to the journals. The $31,000 reported as subscription revenue was the cash received in 2000. Of this amount, about $8,100 was for journals that would be delivered in 2001. Offsetting this was $5,400 of subscription revenue received in 1999 for journals delivered in 2000; this $5,400 had been reported as 1999 revenue.

6. The association had advanced $10,800 to the committee responsible for planning the 2000 annual meeting held in late November. This amount was used for preliminary expenses, and was included as 2000 Committee Meeting Expense. Registration fees at the annual meeting were set so as to cover all convention costs; it was expected that the $10,800, plus any profit, would be returned to the association after the committee had finished paying the convention bills. The 1999 convention had resulted in a $3,400 profit, but the results of the 2000 convention were not known, although the revenues and expenses were about as anticipated.

Questions

1. Did the association have a surplus (revenues greater than expenses) or a deficit (expenses greater than revenues) in 2000?

2. Should the amount of surplus or deficit in 2000 affect the decision to change the annual dues for 2001?

Case 3–2

The Athenaeum School*

In November 1996, Rachel Cognatta, a member of the board of directors of The Athenaeum School was reviewing the organization's 1996 financial statements and auditors' report. The next meeting of the board was to be devoted entirely to a discussion of the financial statements. In complying with her fiduciary responsibilities as a member of the board, Ms. Cognatta wished to make sure that everything was in order and that the organization's finances were being managed appropriately.

Background

The Athenaeum School was located in a former public school building in Waterville, Oregon. It bordered a park with a playground and playing field. The Athenaeum offered educational programs for prekindergarten through sixth grade children. Afterschool care was also offered for all children, prekindergarten through sixth grade, beginning immediately after each regular school day.

   The school's underlying theme was "respect the environment, respect others, respect yourself." It strove for cultural diversity among its students. Indeed, diversity was seen as an essential aspect of education, and the school welcomed children of any race, color, national or ethnic origin. Like other schools of its type, The Athenaeum charged tuition according to grade, ranging from $5,500 for kindergarten and prekindergarten to $7,025 for grades 4 through 6. Financial aid was awarded on the basis of need. However, unlike its peer schools, The Athenaeum selected qualified applicants for admission through a lottery.

   The school offered a full and integrated curriculum that included mathematics, language, arts and music, natural, social, and physical sciences, and physical education. In keeping with its philosophy concerning diversity, the school mixed ages in classrooms, small groups, and lunch rooms, and it encouraged team teaching, partnered classes, senior citizen aides, and parental involvement.

Recent Developments

When he assumed the directorship of The Athenaeum School in April 1994, Vic Daniels inherited an organization in some considerable financial difficulty. Although he attempted to institute some controls on spending

*This case was prepared by Professor David W. Young. Copyright © by David W. Young.

immediately after being hired, there was little he could do about the financial condition for the fiscal year ending in August 1994. That year showed a deficiency of revenue over expenses of some $34,000. He commented on the situation he faced:

> The $34,000 is a bit misleading since it included expenses for a paid sabbatical leave for my predecessor, but even without it, we had an operating deficit of some $25,000. Nevertheless, the deficit was the full $34,000, and, because of it, our fund balance fell from a negative $55,000 at the beginning of 1994 to a negative $89,000 as of the end of the year.
>
> We also had some fairly serious accounting problems. Prior to 1994, we were using a cash accounting system, and each year we depended on tuition payments for the next year to keep the checkbook in a positive state. No one really knew how deeply we had been digging into each year's surplus to keep the checkbook in balance.
>
> When we converted to an accrual basis of accounting for the 1994 fiscal year, we found that we had almost $300,000 in liabilities. We owed over $100,000 to parents for tuition deposits, $90,000 to the bank on a line of credit, $92,000 in payroll, including the $9,000 to my predecessor, and a few other smaller items. I remember going home one day and saying to my wife, "My God, what have I gotten myself into?"
>
> Even without good financial information, the staff and I worked hard in 1995 to turn the situation around, and we ended fiscal 1995 with a $13,000 surplus. We were all real proud of that. We also had a really good year financially in 1996. We finished with a surplus of over $100,000.

Financial Data

The auditors' opinion letter for the 1995 audit, dated September 15, 1995, stated that the financial statements (shown in Exhibit 1):

> . . . present fairly, in all material respects, the financial position of The Athenaeum School, Inc., as of June 30, 1995 and 1994, and the results of its operations and its cash flows for the years then ended, in accordance with generally accepted accounting principles.

Extracts from the auditors' notes to the financial statements also are contained in Exhibit 1.

The auditor's opinion letter for the 1996 audit contained a similar statement. The financial statements, along with extracts from the notes, are contained in Exhibit 2.

Of some confusion to Ms. Cognatta was the fact that the 1995 financial statements seemed to differ between the two audits. She commented:

> I recall the discussion we had last year about the audit. Vic was proud of the surplus and we were proud of him for having turned the school's finances around. We also were quite distressed, however, at the presence of a negative fund balance. Christopher [the board's treasurer] told us that a negative fund balance meant that, technically, the school was bankrupt.

Now I look at the 1995 financials on the 1996 audit, and there's no negative fund balance. I know we had a good year financially in 1996. Everyone's been talking about the fact that the higher enrollments created a real windfall surplus, and that's fine, I guess. But that's for 1996. The figures for 1995 should be the same, shouldn't they? Why is it that the 1995 audit showed a negative fund balance of $75,856 and the 1995 figures in the 1996 audit show a $143,472 *positive* fund balance, or *net assets,* as they now seem to call it.

The Board Meeting

Ms. Cognatta had been told that both the auditors and the school's director would be at the upcoming board meeting. In preparation for the meeting, she decided that she would prepare some questions for both. She knew she could ask the auditors about anything to do with the accounting process that had been followed in preparing the statements. Her questions for the director would need to be related to the information the statements revealed about the financial condition of the school.

One of the major issues on Ms. Cognatta's mind was an accreditation report prepared in February 1996 by a visiting committee of the state's Independent School Association (ISA). In its report, the committee had commended the school for its mission and impact on its community, but had expressed some concerns about the board's ability to oversee the school's financial management. Indeed, the committee stated "We see some serious financial 'squeezes' ahead for the Athenaeum . . ." and had recommended that the board strengthen its financial management capabilities.

The visiting committee also had expressed concern about the school's physical plant as an area in need of special attention:

The . . . concern is the long-term rental costs to Athenaeum. . . . The problem is that a greater portion of the operating budget will be dedicated to the physical plant expenses and Athenaeum will not have improved space or a permanent home.

Our sense is that the goal should be for the school to be able to control its plant, not only in its costs, but in its occupancy. A long-term lease or direct ownership are the only ways we can envision for this control to be gained. We feel that this is a potentially disastrous financial problem for the school. *We strongly recommend that the Board and Director continue its study of this issue and formulate a plan of action to resolve the matter of owning or leasing a permanent site for the school* (emphasis in original).

Questions

1. Explain why the negative $75,856 *fund balance* on the 1995 balance sheet in the 1995 audit became a positive $143,472 *net assets* on the 1995 balance sheet in the 1996 audit. Please be specific. Exactly what items changed to account for the difference? Which of the two gives a more accurate portrayal of the school's financial condition?

2. What questions should Ms. Cognatta ask the accountants about the school's financial statements?

3. What should Ms. Cognatta ask the director about the school's financial situation?

4. What is your assessment of the financial condition of The Athenaeum School?

EXHIBIT 1

THE ATHENAEUM SCHOOL
1995 AUDITED FINANCIAL STATEMENTS
BALANCE SHEETS
AS OF JUNE 30, 1995 AND 1994

	1995	1994
Assets		
Current assets:		
Cash	$ 91,607	$ 85,166
Accounts receivable	39,694	61,586
Prepaid expenses and other	5,654	4,059
Total current assets	136,955	150,811
Equipment and improvements	43,604	47,498
Other assets:		
Deposit	500	500
Restricted cash	147,982	103,219
Pledges receivable	71,346	98,421
Total other assets	219,828	202,140
Total assets	$400,387	$400,449
Liabilities and Fund Balance		
Current liabilities:		
Note payable, bank		$ 80,000
Current portion of capital lease obligation	$ 7,119	3,375
Accounts payable and accrued expenses	15,001	444
Current portion of tuition deposits	10,800	11,400
Accrued payroll and payroll taxes	114,060	92,393
Prepaid revenue	8,235	
Total current liabilities	$155,215	$187,612
Capital lease obligation, net of current portion		7,119
Other liabilities:		
Tuition deposits	101,700	93,050
Unexpended restricted funds	219,328	201,640
Total other liabilities	321,028	294,690
Fund balance	(75,856)	(88,972)
Total liabilities and fund balance	$400,387	$400,449

See notes to financial statements.

EXHIBIT 1
(Continued)

THE ATHENAEUM SCHOOL 1995 AUDITED FINANCIAL STATEMENTS STATEMENTS OF REVENUES AND EXPENSES YEARS ENDED JUNE 30, 1995 AND 1994		
	1995	*1994*
Revenue and support:		
Tuition	$1,451,945	$1,241,573
Program revenue and other fees.	195,712	167,957
Annual fund	87,639	94,867
Capital campaign.	10,077	29,662
Interest.	3,798	1,126
Financial aid	(146,900)	(116,042)
	$1,602,271	$1,419,143
Expenses:		
Staff		
Salaries and payroll taxes	$1,023,731	$ 902,343
Payroll taxes	89,507	79,046
Staff development.	15,310	22,694
Staff welfare	14,265	15,875
Consultants and substitute teachers	27,324	43,963
Students		
Class supplies	49,244	44,946
Field trips and assemblies	3,652	684
Program expense	3,893	5,489
Depreciation.	17,677	18,189
Fund-raising		
Capital campaign	10,077	29,662
Annual fund and other	7,753	1,828
Occupancy		
Rent	163,317	155,117
Utilities	24,578	25,850
Maintenance and grounds	30,723	28,330
Office and general management expense		
Office supplies and expense	28,912	26,899
Printing, publications, and advertising	9,262	4,712
Insurance	15,991	19,658
Legal and accounting	5,250	4,650
Memberships	4,750	3,954
Contingency.	637	3,064
Bad debt expense.	36,990	9,838
Board expenses.	4,217	2,844
Interest expense	2,095	3,604
	$1,589,155	$1,453,239
Excess (deficiency) of revenue over expenses	$ 13,116	$ (34,096)
Fund balance, beginning	(88,972)	(54,876)
Fund balance, ending	$ (75,856)	$ (88,972)
See notes to financial statements.		

EXHIBIT 1
(Continued)

THE ATHENAEUM SCHOOL
1995 AUDITED FINANCIAL STATEMENTS
STATEMENTS OF CASH FLOWS
YEARS ENDED JUNE 30, 1995 AND 1994

	1995	1994
Cash flows from operating activities		
Excess (deficiency) of revenue over expenses	$ 13,116	$(34,096)
Adjustments to reconcile excess (deficiency) of revenue over expenses to net cash provided (used) by operations		
Depreciation	17,677	18,189
Allowance for doubtful accounts	5,000	5,000
Changes in operating assets and liabilities:		
Decrease (increase) in assets:		
Accounts receivable	16,893	(14,688)
Prepaid expenses and other	(1,595)	8,732
Loan receivable, employee		13,853
Restricted cash	(44,763)	(73,034)
Pledges receivable	27,075	1,579
Increase (decrease) in liabilities:		
Accounts payable and accrued expenses	14,557	(55,165)
Tuition deposits	8,050	11,450
Accrued payroll and payroll taxes	21,667	1,549
Prepaid revenue	8,235	(13,823)
Unexpended restricted funds	17,688	69,978
Net cash provided (used) by operating activities.	$103,600	$(60,476)
Cash flows from investing activities		
Purchases of equipment and improvements	(13,784)	(13,204)
Cash flows from financing activities		
Proceeds of note payable, bank.		80,000
Repayments of note payable, bank	(80,000)	
Principal payments under capital lease obligations . .	(3,375)	(2,932)
Net cash provided (used) by financing activities	$ (83,375)	$ 77,068
Net increase (decrease) in cash.	$6,441	$3,388
Cash, beginning of year	85,166	81,778
Cash, ending	$ 91,607	$ 85,166

See notes to financial statements.

Notes To Financial Statements
Years Ended June 30, 1995 and 1994

1. Summary of operations and significant accounting policies:

Operations: The Athenaeum School, Inc. (the "School") is a private elementary educational institution founded in 1982, providing educational services for prekindergarten through sixth grade.

Nature of organization: The School is exempt from federal income taxes under Internal Revenue Code Section 501 (c) (3), and qualifies for the 50% charitable contribution deduction for individual donors.

Cash: cash deposits in excess of the Federal Deposit Insurance Corporation's coverage limits were held at a Portland, Oregon, bank during the year. Excess deposits amounted to $159,114 at June 30, 1995.

Equipment and improvements: Equipment and improvements are stated at cost if acquired by purchase and at fair market value if acquired by gift.

Equipment is depreciated using straight line and accelerated methods over the estimated useful lives of the assets. Improvements are amortized using the straight-line method over the lease term, including options.

Accrued payroll: The School's policy is to give teachers the option of receiving their salary over a nine- or twelve-month period. Accrued payroll represents teachers' salaries that are earned but unpaid at year end.

Prepaid revenue: Prepaid revenue represents student tuition received in advance. Tuition is recognized as revenue when the services have been provided.

Contribution revenue: Unrestricted contributions are generally recorded as revenue upon receipt of cash or other property subject to compliance with specified terms. Restricted contributions are recorded as revenue when the School has incurred expenditures in compliance with the specific restrictions. Such amounts received but not yet earned are reported as unexpended restricted funds. The School's policy is to treat interest earned on restricted funds as restricted interest income. Unexpended restricted funds are presented as a noncurrent liability consistent with the School's plans to allow the funds to grow through additional contributions and earnings.

Reclassifications: Certain amounts reported on the 1994 financial statements have been reclassified to conform to the 1995 classification.

2. Accounts receivable:

Accounts receivable consist of the following:

	1995	1994
Tuitions receivable	$69,694	$86,586
Less allowance for doubtful accounts	30,000	25,000
	$39,694	$61,586

3. Equipment and improvements:

Equipment and improvements consist of the following:

	1995	1994
Furniture and fixtures	$ 63,360	$ 61,356
Office and classroom equipment	86,826	80,876
Leasehold improvements	32,973	27,143
Motor vehicles	19,500	19,500
	202,659	188,875
Less accumulated depreciation	159,055	141,377
	$ 43,604	$ 47,498

4. Pledges receivable:

Pledges receivable consist of pledges received but not yet collected for the School's 1995 capital campaign, as follows:

	1995	1994
Pledges receivable	$81,346	$108,421
Less allowance for uncollectible pledges	10,000	10,000
	$71,346	$ 98,421

5. Unexpended restricted funds:

Unexpended restricted funds consist of the following:

	1995	1994
Capital Campaign Fund.	$175,199	$168,407
Headmaster Fund.	6,163	0
Larry Daniels Memorial Fund.	6,274	6,109
Tom Peters Memorial Fund.	7,221	4,688
Staff Development Fund	16,099	15,381
K. Dvorak Diversity Fund.	7,970	6,653
Tide Grant	402	402
	$219,328	$201,640

Unexpended restricted funds include pledges receivable for the School's 1995 Capital Campaign and other Capital Campaign and restricted gifts collected but not yet expended. Cash received and held for restricted purposes amounted to $147,982 and $103,219 at June 30, 1995 and 1994, respectively.

6. Line of credit:

Annually, the School arranged for short term borrowing from Portland Trust Company. In July, 1993, the School borrowed $80,000 which was repaid in August, 1993, with interest at 7.5% per annum. In May, 1994, $80,000 was borrowed with interest at 8.25% per annum, and was repaid in August, 1994. In July, 1995, the School borrowed $50,000 which was repaid in August, 1995, with interest at 9.25% per annum.

7. Tuition deposits:

The School collects a tuition deposit of $600 per student which is refundable in the student's final year of enrollment. These deposits are expected to be refunded as follows:

Year Ending June 30	Amount
1996	$ 10,800
1997	14,100
1998	15,900
1999	11,100
2000	15,900
2001	16,800
2002	17,100
2003	10,800
	112,500
Less current portion	(10,800)
	$101,700

8. Loan payable, officer:

The School has an unsecured, interest free loan from its Founder (a trustee), made June 4, 1987, and originally due September 1, 1988. The loan was extended each year without penalty. During 1994, the trustee applied the unpaid loan balance toward partial satisfaction of her pledge to the Capital Campaign.

EXHIBIT 2

THE ATHENAEUM SCHOOL
1996 AUDITED FINANCIAL STATEMENTS
BALANCE SHEETS
AS OF JUNE 30, 1996 AND 1995

	1996	1995
Assets		
Current assets:		
Cash.	$428,800	$239,589
Accounts receivable, net of allowance for doubtful accounts of $17,000 and $30,000 at 1996 and 1995, respectively	16,924	39,694
Prepaid expenses and other	11,392	5,654
Deposit.		500
Pledges receivable, net of allowance for uncollectible pledges of $5,000 and $10,000 at 1996 and 1995, respectively	52,146	71,346
Total current assets	$509,262	$356,783
Equipment and improvements.	42,801	43,604
Total assets.	$552,063	$400,387
Liabilities and Fund Balance		
Current liabilities:		
Accounts payable and accrued expenses	$ 35,848	$ 15,001
Current portion of capital lease obligation		7,119
Current portion of tuition deposits	14,100	10,800
Accrued payroll and payroll taxes	137,022	114,060
Prepaid revenue	1,230	8,235
Total current liabilities	$188,200	$155,215
Tuition deposits	97,700	101,700
Net assets:		
Unrestricted	217,191	115,844
Temporarily restricted.	48,972	27,628
	$266,163	$143,472
Total liabilities and net assets	$552,063	$400,387

See notes to financial statements.

EXHIBIT 2
(Continued)

THE ATHENAEUM SCHOOL
1996 AUDITED FINANCIAL STATEMENTS
STATEMENTS OF REVENUES AND EXPENSES
YEARS ENDED JUNE 30, 1996 AND 1995

	1996			
	Unrestricted	Temporarily Restricted	Total	1995
Revenue and support:				
Tuition	$1,629,131		$1,629,131	$1,451,945
Program revenue and other fees . . .	194,442		194,442	195,712
Annual fund	77,824	$20,494	98,318	97,568
Capital campaign	36,898		36,898	14,472
Interest	11,945	850	12,795	7,162
Financial aid	(186,500)		(186,500)	(146,900)
	$1,763,740	$21,344	$1,785,084	$1,619,959
Expenses:				
Staff				
Salaries and payroll taxes	$1,102,698		$1,102,698	$1,023,731
Payroll taxes	95,149		95,149	89,507
Staff development	15,052		15,052	15,310
Staff welfare	13,075		13,075	14,265
Consultants and substitute teachers	25,621		25,621	27,324
Students				
Class supplies	45,466		45,466	49,244
Field trips and assemblies	3,729		3,729	3,652
Program expense	6,754		6,754	3,893
Depreciation	18,413		18,413	17,677
Fund-raising				
Capital campaign				10,077
Annual fund and other	7,973		7,973	7,753
Occupancy				
Rent	172,265		172,265	163,317
Utilities	23,786		23,786	24,578
Maintenance and grounds	25,201		25,201	30,723
Office and general management expense				
Office supplies and expense	30,745		30,745	28,912
Printing, publications, and advertising	13,411		13,411	9,262
Insurance	20,948		20,948	15,991
Legal and accounting	6,610		6,610	5,250
Memberships	4,181		4,181	4,750
Contingency	706		706	637
Bad debt expense	28,527		28,527	36,990
Board expenses	1,404		1,404	4,217
Interest expense	679		679	2,095
	$1,662,393		$1,662,393	$1,589,155
Excess (deficiency) of revenue over expenses	$ 101,347	$21,344	$ 122,691	$ 30,804
Fund balance, beginning	115,844	27,628	143,472	112,668
Fund balance, ending	$ 217,191	$48,972	$ 266,163	$ 143,472

See notes to financial statements.

EXHIBIT 2
(Continued)

THE ATHENAEUM SCHOOL 1996 AUDITED FINANCIAL STATEMENTS STATEMENTS OF CASH FLOWS YEARS ENDED JUNE 30, 1996 AND 1995		
	1996	*1995*
Cash flows from operating activities		
Excess (deficiency) of revenue over expenses.	$122,691	$ 30,804
Adjustments to reconcile excess (deficiency) of revenue over expenses to net cash provided (used) by operations		
Depreciation	18,413	17,677
Changes in operating assets and liabilities:		
Decrease (increase) in assets:		
Accounts receivable	22,770	21,893
Prepaid expenses and other	(5,738)	(1,595)
Deposits.	500	
Pledges receivable	19,200	27,075
Increase (decrease) in liabilities:		
Accounts payable and accrued expenses	20,847	14,557
Tuition deposits	(700)	8,050
Accrued payroll and payroll taxes.	22,962	21,667
Prepaid revenue	(7,005)	8,235
Net cash provided (used) by operating activities.	$213,940	$148,363
Cash flows from investing activities		
Purchases of equipment and improvements	(17,610)	(13,784)
Cash flows from financing activities		
Repayments of note payable, bank		(80,000)
Principal payments under capital lease obligations . . .	(7,119)	(3,375)
Net cash provided (used) by financing activities	$ (7,119)	$ (83,375)
Net increase (decrease) in cash.	$189,211	$ 51,204
Cash, beginning of year	239,589	188,385
Cash, ending	$428,800	$239,589
Cash paid for interest	$ 679	$ 2,095

**Notes To Financial Statements
Years Ended June 30, 1996 and 1995
(Excludes items that are the same as 1995/1994)**

1. Summary of operations and significant accounting policies:

Use of estimates: The preparation of financial statements in conformity with generally accepted accounting principles requires management to make estimates that affect certain reported amounts. Accordingly, actual results could differ from these estimates.

Financial statement presentation: The School adopted the provisions of *Statement of Financial Accounting Standards (SFAS) No. 117,* "Financial Statements of Not-for-Profit Organizations." Under *SFAS No. 117,* the School is required to report information regarding its financial position and activities according to three classes of net assets: unrestricted, temporarily restricted and permanently restricted. In addition, the School is required to present a statement of cash flows. The School has discontinued its use of fund accounting and has reformatted its financial statements to present the classes of net assets, as appropriate in the circumstances.

Contributions: The School also adopted the provisions of *SFAS No. 116,* "Accounting for Contributions Received and Contributions Made." In accordance with *SFAS No. 116,* contributions received and receipts of unconditional promises to give are recorded as unrestricted, temporarily restricted or permanently restricted support depending on the existence and/or nature of any donor restrictions. Restricted net assets are reclassified to unrestricted net assets upon satisfaction of the time or purpose restrictions. As permitted by *SFAS No. 116,* the School retroactively applied the provisions of *SFAS No. 116* by restating net assets as of June 30, 1994. The adjustment of $201,640 made to net assets as of June 30, 1994, represents unexpended restricted funds previously recorded as a liability. The effect of adopting *SFAS No. 116* on the School's change in net assets for 1996 and 1995 was an increase of $63,121 and $17,688 respectively, from what would have been reported under prior accounting principles.

Cash: cash deposits in excess of the Federal Deposit Insurance Corporation's coverage limits were held at a Portland, Oregon bank during the year. Excess deposits amounted to $354,702 and $159,114 at June 30, 1996 and 1995, respectively.

Reclassifications: Certain amounts reported in the 1995 financial statements have been reclassified to conform with the 1996 presentation.

2. Equipment and improvements:

Equipment and improvements consist of the following:

	1996	1995
Furniture and fixtures	$ 70,390	$ 63,360
Office and classroom equipment	94,456	86,826
Leasehold improvements	35,923	32,973
Motor vehicles	19,500	19,500
	220,269	202,659
Less accumulated depreciation	177,468	159,055
	$ 42,801	$ 43,604

3. Line of credit:

Annually, the School arranged for short term borrowing from Portland Trust Company. In May, 1994, $80,000 was borrowed with interest at 8.25% per annum, and was repaid in August, 1994. In July, 1995 the School borrowed $50,000 which was repaid in August, 1995, with interest at 9.25% per annum.

4. Tuition deposits:

The School collects a tuition deposit of $600 per student which is refundable in the student's final year of enrollment. These deposits are expected to be refunded as follows:

Year Ending June 30	Amount
1997	$ 14,100
1998	15,900
1999	11,100
2000	15,900
2001	16,800
2002	17,100
2003	10,800
2004	10,100
	111,800
Less current portion	(14,100)
	$ 97,700

5. Temporarily restricted net assets:

Temporarily restricted net assets are for the following purposes:

	1996	1995
Music program	$ 5,670	
Science and technology programs	5,169	
Activities of the school	5,000	
Purpose to be decided	33,133	27,628
	$48,972	$27,628

Case 3–3

Boise Park Health Care Foundation*

I'd like to know if Boise Park is financially sound. We don't want our members to be left high and dry if it goes under.

Mr. Lawrence Kern, Executive Director of the Idaho Consumer Health Advocacy Program, put down the phone following a call from a representative of Local 285 of the Service Employees' International Union, the union representing Idaho state employees. A new health plan, Boise Park Health Care Foundation, an independent practice association (IPA)-type health maintenance organization, had recently been offered to 48,000 state employees as a health insurance option. The union representative wanted to know whether to recommend the plan to union members, and he had asked Mr. Kern to assist him. Mr. Kern thought that his first step should be to examine Boise Park's financial statements for its two most recent fiscal years (Exhibit 1).

*This case was prepared by Margaret B. Reber, Research Assistant, under the supervision of Professor David W. Young. It subsequently was modified by Professor Young. Copyright © by David W. Young.

EXHIBIT 1

BOISE PARK HEALTH CARE FOUNDATION, INC. FINANCIAL STATEMENTS BALANCE SHEETS AS OF SEPTEMBER 30, 1996 AND 1997		
	1997	1996
Assets		
Cash	$147,861	$ 147
Investments, at cost which approximates market	202,433	
Accounts receivable	75,344	34,699
Demand notes receivable (Note 2)	151,848	
Reinsurance recoverable (Note 6)	16,950	
Prepaid program expenses (Note 2)	46,123	
Total current assets	640,559	34,846
Fixed assets, net of depreciation	28,952	14,830
Total Assets	$669,511	$ 49,676
Liabilities and Reserves and Unassigned Surplus		
Liabilities and reserves:		
Reserve for hospital claims (Note 2)	$ 71,729	
Reserve for medical claims (Note 2)	61,325	
Risk fund (Note 3)	27,761	
Premium reserves	4,892	
Accounts payable and accrued expenses	37,845	$ 68,942
Advanced premium deposits	759	
Installments payable	5,773	
Total liabilities & reserves	$210,084	$ 68,942
Unassigned Surplus	459,427	(19,266)
Total liabilities, reserves and surplus	$669,511	$ 49,676
The accompanying notes are an integral part of the financial statements.		

EXHIBIT 1
(Continued)

BOISE PARK HEALTH CARE FOUNDATION, INC.
FINANCIAL STATEMENTS
STATEMENTS OF REVENUES AND EXPENSES
AND UNASSIGNED SURPLUS
FOR THE YEARS ENDED SEPTEMBER 30, 1996 AND 1997

	1997	1996
Revenues		
Premiums (Note 2)	$195,674	
Membership fees (Note 2)	637,296	$ 43,325
Interest	16,596	1,937
Consulting	2,960	5,920
Miscellaneous	983	2,741
Total revenues	$853,509	$ 53,923
Expenses:		
Hospital claims paid	$8,692	
Medical claims paid	8,165	
Increase in hospital and medical claim reserves	133,054	
Increase in risk fund (Note 3)	27,761	
Reinsurance recoveries (Note 6)	(16,950)	
Reinsurance	17,446	
Premium reserves	4,892	
Program management (Note 2)	170,190	$165,259
Audit and actuarial	12,902	18,380
Data Processing	4,803	
Marketing	3,861	
Total expenses	$374,816	$183,639
Program gain (loss)	478,693	(129,716)
Unassigned surplus, beginning of period	(19,266)	110,450
Unassigned surplus, end of period	$459,427	($ 19,266)

The accompanying notes are an integral part of the financial statements.

EXHIBIT 1
(Continued)

BOISE PARK HEALTH CARE FOUNDATION, INC. FINANCIAL STATEMENTS STATEMENTS OF CASH FLOWS FOR THE YEARS ENDED SEPTEMBER 30, 1996 AND 1997		
	1997	*1996*
Cash from (used by) operations		
Program gain (loss)	$478,693	($129,716)
Plus (minus)		
Depreciation	4,302	2,331
Changes in accounts receivables	(40,645)	(6,999)
Change in demand notes receivable.	(151,848)	
Change in reinsurance recoverable.	(16,950)	
Change in prepaid program expenses	(46,123)	
Change in accounts payable and accrued expenses .	(31,097)	23,518
Change in reserve for hospital claims	71,729	
Change in reserve for medical claims	61,325	
Change in premium reserves	4,892	
Change in risk fund	27,761	
Change in installments payable	5,773	
Change in advance premium deposits	759	1,107
Cash provided (used) by operations.	$368,571	($109,759)
Cash from (to) investing		
Sale of long-term asset		$ 24,880
Purchase of fixed assets	($ 18,424)	(2,555)
Cash provided (used) by investing.	($ 18,424)	$ 22,325
Increase (decrease) in cash and short-term securities . .	350,147	(87,434)
Plus beginning balance	147	87,581
Equals ending balance.	350,294	147
Breakdown		
Cash	147,861	147
Short-term securities	202,433	—
	$350,294	$ 147

Background

IPAs are health maintenance organizations (HMOs) with membership open to physicians whose practice habits are sufficiently cost-effective to meet its standards. Member physicians are not salaried by the IPA. Instead, they "join" it by paying a one-time membership fee and agreeing to abide by its policies and procedures.

A successful IPA must set realistic yet competitive premiums. If its premiums are too high, it will not attract subscribers; if they are too low, it will incur operating deficits and possible resignation of the member physicians. IPA premiums typically are approximately $2,500 a year for a single individual, and $5,000 a year for a family, regardless of size.

Most IPA members are primary care physicians (PCPs), who act as "gate-keepers" to care. Subscribers (patients) are required to see a PCP initially for all illnesses, and are not covered for care provided by physicians outside the IPA's physician "network." The PCP is responsible for determining whether to (*a*) treat the patient without referrals or a hospitalization, (*b*) refer the patient to a specialist, or (*c*) place the patient in a hospital. Overall, the PCP is responsible for assuring that medical treatment and hospital costs do not exceed IPA premium revenue.

An IPA negotiates fee arrangements with specialists and charge arrangements with hospitals. Usually, this entails obtaining favorable per-unit rates. In the case of specialists, the rate usually is a fee for a visit. For hospital care, the IPA must negotiate rates for a wide variety of services, such as per-diem rates for inpatient care, per-test or per-procedures rates for laboratory and radiological services, per-minute rates for operating room use, and per-visit rates for emergency room use, occupational therapy treatments, and so forth. Increasingly, IPAs are negotiating "bundled" or "global" rates for a single hospitalization. The bundled rate puts the hospital and the specialists at risk for any costs that exceed the rate.

If an IPA's cost of hospital and medical services exceeds its premium revenue, the member physicians usually absorb a proportionate share of the deficit, typically the first 15 to 20 percent, with the remainder covered by reinsurance. The IPA provides a "reserve" for these deficits by discounting the PCPs' (and sometimes the specialists') usual fees. If the IPA's expenses are at or below its premium revenue, its member physicians receive full reimbursement up to the agreed upon limits, and frequently also receive a bonus. Member physicians who have consistently high rates of specialist referrals and/or hospitalizations are either assessed a surcharge or asked to resign their membership in the IPA.

Financial Information

Boise Park's financial statements were audited by a national firm of public accountants, and its opinion letter contained the following comments:

> To the Board of Directors
> Boise Park Health Care Foundation, Inc.:
>   We have examined the balance sheets of Boise Park Health Care Foundation, Inc., as of September 31, 1996 and 1997, and the related statements of revenues and expenses and unassigned surplus (deficit) and statements of cash flows for the years then ended. Our examinations were made in accordance with generally accepted auditing standards and, accordingly, included such tests of the accounting records and such other auditing procedures as we considered necessary in the circumstances.

The Foundation has established reserves for hospital and medical claims expense as described in Note 2. While management believes that sufficient reserves have been recorded, the Foundation began issuing group health service contracts in April 1996 and has no historical claims experience. The sufficiency of the reserve is dependent upon the future assertion and resolution of claims which cannot presently be determined.

In our opinion, subject to the effects of such adjustments, if any, on the 1996 financial statements as might have been required had the outcome of the uncertainty referred to in the preceding paragraph been known, the financial statements referred to above present fairly the financial position of Boise Park Health Care Foundation, Inc., as of September 30, 1996 and 1997, and the results of its operation and the changes in its financial position for the years then ended in conformity with generally accepted accounting principles applied on a consistent basis.

Questions

1. What is the meaning of the account called "Reserve for hospital claims"? How does it relate to the account called "Increase in hospital & medical claim reserves"? Give a hypothetical accounting transaction that would take place in order for a credit entry to be made to this account. A debit to the account.

2. What concerns, if any, do you have about the account called "Membership fees"? Give the transaction that Boise Park uses to record an initial deposit of $667, and the deferral of the remaining $333. How else might this transaction be recorded?

3. Given the information currently available, is Boise Park a good deal for the members (i.e., the physicians who provide care to patients)? Is it a good deal for subscribers (i.e., the patients)?

BOISE PARK HEALTH CARE FOUNDATION, INC.
Notes to Financial Statements

---

1. Organization

Boise Park Health Care Foundation, Inc., was created as an incorporated, nonprofit, professionally sponsored management system for the delivery of health care services.

Membership in the Foundation is voluntary and is comprised of qualified doctors with registered certificates and qualified dentists with an office in the state of Idaho. The Foundation has received a license to operate a Health Maintenance Organization ("Boise Park Health Care") as defined under Idaho General Laws, Chapter 176G.

Membership is granted upon receipt of a one-time $1,000 membership fee, agreement to serve in equitable rotation on the Peer Review Committees of the Foundation, and acceptance of the decisions of the Committees as binding upon their own practice and conduct.

2. Summary of Significant Accounting Policies

Membership fees are recorded as revenue upon payment of the fees or upon receipt of an initial deposit of $667 with the remaining $333 being deferred in the form of notes unconditionally payable to the Foundation upon demand. Such demand notes do not bear interest.

Subscribers are billed on a monthly basis in advance of the coverage, which begins on the first day of each month. Premiums are reported as earned during the period of coverage.

The Foundation follows the practice of capitalizing all expenditures for furniture and equipment in excess of $100. Depreciation is provided over the estimated useful lives of the assets on a straight-line basis.

Investments are recorded at cost, which approximates market.

Program expenses relating to printing of policy contracts and certain promotional material have been capitalized and expensed based upon actual usage. Program management expenses consist principally of salaries.

The Foundation has no loss experience as of September 30, 1996, upon which to base a reasonable estimate of hospital and medical claim reserves. Until the Foundation has built up sufficient experience upon which to base such estimates, the hospital and medical claims reserves will be based upon the actuarial assumptions used in establishing premium rates.

3. Physicians Risk Fund

Payments to participating physicians for certain medical claims are subject to retention by the Foundation at a rate of 30 percent. Final payment of such retainage is contingent upon the program attaining certain service utilization levels. Failure to attain such levels will allow the Foundation to use the retained funds to eliminate or reduce any program deficits.

4. Tax Status

Under provisions of the Internal Revenue Code Section 501 (c) (6), the Foundation is exempt from federal income taxes.

5. Lease Commitments

The Foundation is obligated under two separate leases for office space until September 1, 1998, and August 1, 2000. Minimal annual rentals under these leases amount to $3,500 and $11,000, respectively.

6. Reinsurance

The Foundation reinsures all group service contracts against losses over a stipulated amount arising from any one occurrence. A contingent liability exists with respect to reinsurance which would become a liability of the Foundation in the event that the reinsurer is unable to meet its obligations under the reinsurance agreement.

Case 3–4
Merced College*

> Last year the administration tells us they're happy with our spending policy. Now they tell us it's inadequate and they have to cut the Latin American Studies Program, which is a key element of our strategy. What's right here? How do we set a policy that we all can live with without having to reexamine this issue every few years?

The speaker was Samuel Scribner, Chair of the Budget Committee of the Board of Trustees of Merced College. He was commenting on the policy the college used to determine the amount of endowment earnings that should be used as revenue in the college's operating budget. For the past several years Merced had been attempting to determine a policy that would be appropriate in light of the dual demands of preserving the purchasing power of the endowment fund, while simultaneously providing the college's central administration with some predictability of revenues for the operating budget.

*This case was prepared by Professor David W. Young. Copyright © by David W. Young.

Background

Merced College was a 150-year-old, 4-year undergraduate institution with an enrollment of approximately 2,000 full-time residential students. It offered a liberal arts education with a full complement of athletic programs and a variety of special programs, including Latin American studies, communications, and meteorology.

Over the years, its alumni, many of whom had assumed positions of leadership in business, had donated generously to the college, with the result that Merced's endowment fund had grown considerably. Data for the past 17 years are contained in Exhibit 1.

The Spending Policy

Prior to 1988, the board's spending policy had been to provide the administration with all dividends and interest earned on the endowment. All other earnings were reinvested in the endowment fund. In 1988, in response to complaints from the college's administration that dividends and interest fluctuated widely, depending on the kinds of investments being made with the endowment fund's portfolio, the board shifted to a policy of providing the administration with 5 percent of the beginning balance of the fund, lagged one year. The lag was needed to allow budget preparation activities to proceed with complete certainty of the amount to be transferred from the endowment fund.

In 1993, noting the dividends and interest were much greater than the amount being transferred to operations under the 5 percent policy, the administration convinced the board to return to a dividends and interest policy. The result, beginning in 1994, was a sharp increase in the transfers from the endowment fund to operations.

The current crisis had arisen because the administration, noting that dividends and interest transfers were below what the transfers would have been under the 5 percent approach, once again was requesting a shift in the policy. It now was recommending a return to the 5 percent approach. Mr. Scribner commented:

> Our policy for decades has been that the college will have a balanced budget each year. Since revenue transferred from our endowment fund is an important element in balancing the budget, the central administration counts on it every year. For some time now the controller has complained that she has no predictability of the endowment fund revenue, and hence cannot prepare a meaningful budget. Of course, predictability is not the only issue since we moved away from predictability in 1994 when we shifted back to dividends and interest. However, it seems as though her goal is to maximize the transfers, which of course is difficult since so much depends on the mix of investments in the endowment fund's investment portfolio.

EXHIBIT 1

MERCED COLLEGE
ENDOWMENT FUND PERFORMANCE AND TRANSFERS ($000)

Year Ending June 30	Beginning Fund Value	Contributions to Principal	Stock Appreciation	Dividends & Interest	Ending Fund Value	Realized Gains	Unrealized Gains	Total Gains	Available Cash	Transferred to Operations	Basis of Transfer
	1	2	3	4	5 = 1 + 2 + 3 + 4 − 10	6	7	8 = 6 + 7 / 8 = 3	9 = 4 + 6	10	
1980	6,435	750	112	115	7,297	35	77	112	150	115	D&I*
1981	7,297	1,400	(426)	334	8,271	883	(1,309)	(426)	1,217	334	D&I
1982	8,271	955	1,287	223	10,513	889	398	1,287	1,112	223	D&I
1983	10,513	1,235	1,239	350	12,988	432	807	1,239	782	350	D&I
1984	12,988	2,350	(277)	890	15,061	1,233	(1,510)	(277)	2,123	890	D&I
1985	15,061	55	2,390	580	17,506	2,009	381	2,390	2,589	580	D&I
1986	17,506	600	1,888	379	19,995	1,589	299	1,888	1,968	379	D&I
1987	19,995	40	244	440	20,279	125	119	244	565	440	D&I
1988	20,279	3,300	1,500	680	24,760	347	1,153	1,500	1,027	1,000	5% of BB‡ in t-1
1989	24,760	125	3,472	955	28,297	481	2,991	3,472	1,436	1,014	5% of BB in t-1
1990	28,297	88	(622)	1,345	27,870	2,378	(3,000)	(622)	3,723	1,238	5% of BB in t-1
1991	27,870	375	3,629	1,567	32,026	1,223	2,406	3,629	2,790	1,415	5% of BB in t-1
1992	32,026	580	718	1,655	33,586	1,545	(827)	718	3,200	1,394	5% of BB in t-1
1993	33,586	1,100	2,864	1,955	37,904	2,668	196	2,864	4,623	1,601	5% of BB in t-1
1994	37,904	5,000	460	2,056	43,364	1,975	(1,515)	460	4,031	2,056	D&I
1995	43,364	35	8,184	1,945	51,583	4,658	3,526	8,184	6,603	1,945	D&I
1996	51,583	110	6,481	1,955	58,173	3,219	3,262	6,481	5,174	1,955	D&I
1997	58,173										
Totals		18,098	33,145	17,424		25,689	7,456	33,145	43,113	16,928	

*Dividends and interest
‡ Beginning fund balance

Other Perspectives

Several other members of the board, as well as the college president and the independent auditor, had some views on the matter. For example, according to George Lawrence, the chair of the board's investment committee, the main issue was the college's investment objectives:

> I have believed all along that our goal is to maximize the value of the portfolio, consistent, of course, with prudence. We should not be investing in biotech stocks, for example, as some universities have done, but we definitely should be investing in growth stocks when we believe that the market is growing, and in bonds and income stocks when we believe that growth is slowing. The problem is that when we had a dividends and interest policy, our committee was regularly pressured by the central administration to shift the mix of the portfolio to income stocks and bonds even when we felt that this was not the best investment policy. A big issue for us is how we keep our investment policy "pure," that is, independent of the central administration's need for cash to help balance the budget.

Mario Nadalini, a philosophy professor, and one of two faculty representatives on the board's budget committee, was concerned principally about matters of equity:

> If we don't include increases in market value in our assessment of the performance of the endowment portfolio, we are violating the principle of intergenerational equity: we are stealing from the present generation of students to provide benefits for future generations. At the same time, if we use all of the earnings of the endowment fund for this year's budget, we are effectively depleting the value of the fund, since inflation will be eroding its purchasing power. Thus, we must leave something in the fund each year to compensate for the effects of inflation. The greater the size of the endowment fund, the larger this amount needs to be.

Benjamin Culley, the college president, had a slightly different perspective.

> We need predictability. How can we mount and run programs if we don't know from one year to the next how much will be transferred to operations from the endowment fund? Also, even if we have predictability, we also need consistency. It's not enough to know with great certainty that we'll have less this year than last. What do I tell my program directors and department chairs under these circumstances? A decline in transfers from the endowment fund can be devastating to our programs.

Jonathan Larson, a board member and investment advisor to many wealthy people in the area, had a slightly different perspective:

> Total return. That's the key. It's the only way to measure the performance of the endowment fund. Dividends and interest miss the whole point of capital appreciation. To measure the performance of the investment committee, we need to look at all aspects of the portfolio, which means computing appreciation—both realized and unrealized—as well as dividends and interest. Otherwise, we're missing the whole point of sound investment policy.

George Augustus, a professor of economics and the other faculty representative on the budget committee, shed some additional light on the issue:

> Investment policy should be totally separate from revenue transfers. Investment decisions should not be influenced in any way by a need to generate a certain amount of funds for operational purposes. At the same time, we must preserve the purchasing power of the endowment fund, and we must do so deliberately, not by coincidence. If you believe that inflation is about 3 to 4 percent a year, and earnings on the endowment fund are 8 to 10 percent, that leaves about 5 percent to be used for operational purposes. Of course, we are constantly getting new donations, so we need to incorporate them into the formula. I know that some universities use a moving average to even out the volatility that otherwise would exist. Maybe that's what we should do.

Finally, William Glenn, the accounting firm partner who was in charge of the audit of the college's financial statements, had yet a different perspective:

> SFAS 117 and 124 have totally changed the picture. SFAS 124 says that all unrealized gains are to be included on the balance sheet, and treated as revenue in the endowment fund. SFAS 117 says that all revenue from the permanently restricted fund, which is the endowment fund, is to be transferred to the unrestricted fund, and treated as unrestricted. You put those two together, and, in a year of high capital appreciation, whether realized or not, you're talking about massive transfers from the endowment fund to the unrestricted fund. The central administration will be thrilled, but the board won't. How is it going to preserve the purchasing power of the endowment fund in the face of inflation if it has to transfer all revenue to the unrestricted fund, *including* unrealized gains? How is the college going to achieve any sort of consistent flow of funds for the operating budget under these circumstances?

The March board meeting was about two weeks away, and Mr. Scribner knew that his committee needed to make a recommendation so that a vote could be taken and the central administration could move ahead with preparation of its operational budget for the upcoming academic year. He knew that there would be some acrimony at the meeting, but he felt that the acrimony could be lessened if his committee could clarify what he saw as several separate but interrelated issues that were on the table.

Questions

1. What are the issues that face the committee? Be specific in separating the issues, and then showing how they relate to each other.

2. What policy would you recommend the board adopt to deal with each of the issues you identified in your answer to Question 1? In doing this, you should compare your recommendation with the board's policy over the past 19 years to show how the transfers from the endowment fund would have been affected.

Case 3–5

City of Douglas*

Claire Dexter was appointed by the mayor of Douglas to a three-year term on the city's finance committee. The finance committee acted as an adviser to city officials and as a "watchdog" on behalf of the city's citizens. Under certain circumstances it could propose city budgets, and it had to approve large proposed capital expenditures. Its views were given considerable weight by city officials.

Ms. Dexter was senior vice president of the region's largest bank. She had extensive experience in analyzing corporate financial statements. As preparation for her committee work, she asked the city controller for financial statements. The controller promptly furnished a 102-page book, titled "Comprehensive Annual Financial Report, City of Douglas, Fiscal Year Ended June 30, 1987." The financial statements had been examined by a national public accounting firm, and in its opinion letter the firm stated that they "present fairly the financial position and results of operations . . . in conformity with generally accepted accounting principles."

Ms. Dexter searched through the book looking for an operating statement or income statement, which was in her opinion the most important financial statement for any organization. She did not find one. The closest to it appeared to be an exhibit with the title "Combined Statement of Revenues, Expenditures, and Changes in Fund Balances: All Governmental Fund Types." She decided to recast this statement, as closely as possible, to the form and content of a business operating statement.

She particularly wanted to determine whether Douglas operated at a surplus or a deficit. Specifically, she believed that the financial goal of a municipality should be that the revenues applicable to a given year are approximately equal to the expenses of that year. She also wanted numbers for the various city programs so that spending on these programs could be compared with amounts for previous years and with amounts spent by other municipalities.

Exhibit 1 is adapted from the statement referred to above. Ms. Dexter had her secretary modify the actual statement in two ways. First, the numbers on the report were carried out to the last dollar, which she modified by rounding them to thousands of dollars. Second, there was a column on the statement headed "Totals (Memorandum only)," which contained the totals of the amounts in each row. It seemed to her that these totals were "adding apples and oranges," and she eliminated them.

Funds

Next, she read the notes accompanying the financial statements to determine whether the fund types listed in the report did in fact relate to operations. A

*This case was prepared by Professor Robert N. Anthony. Copyright © by Robert N. Anthony.

EXHIBIT 1

CITY OF DOUGLAS
COMBINED STATEMENT OF REVENUES, EXPENDITURES, AND CHANGES IN FUND BALANCES
ALL GOVERNMENTAL FUND TYPES
YEAR ENDED JUNE 30, 1987
($000)

	General	Special Revenue	Debt Service	Capital Project	Special Assess- ments
Revenues:					
Taxes and assessments........................	$32,015	$ —	$ —	$ —	$ 82
Penalties	377	—	—	—	31
Licenses and permits	164	—	—	—	—
Intergovernmental...........................	11,637	2,712	23	1,071	—
Charges for services.........................	332	582	—	—	—
Investment earnings	960	128	—	166	154
Contributions	—	30	—	—	—
Miscellaneous	551	4	—	—	1
Total revenues.........................	46,036	3,456	23	1,237	268
Expenditures:					
General government	1,435	415	—	—	—
Public safety	5,400	112	—	—	—
Public works	4,579	667	—	—	—
Health and welfare..........................	1,461	634	—	—	—
Libraries...................................	435	49	—	—	—
Parks and recreation	726	188	—	—	—
Education	23,028	1,958	—	—	—
Citywide:					
Employee benefits and pensions..............	3,793	—	—	—	—
General insurance	542	—	—	—	—
Capital outlay		—	—	1,937	8
Debt service:					
Principal retirement	—	—	1,872	—	—
Interest and fiscal charges	—	—	1,034	—	108
Miscellaneous	619	—	—	—	—
Total expenditures	42,018	4,023	2,906	1,937	116
Excess of revenues over (under) expenditures	4,018	(567)	(2,883)	(700)	152
Other financing sources (uses):					
Operating transfers in	160	952	2,693	142	—
Operating transfers out	(3,434)	(134)	—	(379)	—
Total...................................	(3,274)	818	2,693	(237)	—
Net excess (under)*..........................	744	251	(190)	(937)	152
Fund balance, July 1, 1987	2,955	1,984	1,259	2,115	(60)
Fund balance, June 30, 1988..................	$ 3,699	$2,235	$1,069	$1,178	$ 92

*The label for this line was "Excess of revenues and other sources over (under) expenditures and other uses."

summary of the description of these funds and Ms. Dexter's conclusions about them follows:

General Fund

"The General Fund is the general operating fund of the City. It is used to account for all financial resources except those required to be accounted for in another fund. The General Fund accounts for the normal recurring activities of the city." Ms. Dexter concluded that the amounts in this column clearly related to operations.

Special Revenue Funds

"Special Revenue Funds are used to account for the proceeds of specific revenue sources (other than special assessments or major capital projects) that are legally restricted to expenditures for specified purposes." An exhibit in the financial report showed that the amount reported in Exhibit 1 was the total of 13 separate funds, the largest of which were revenue sharing (amounts received from the federal government), special education grants (grants from the state), and school lunch program (grants from both state and federal sources). Ms. Dexter concluded that the amounts in the special revenue column were substantially related to operating activities.

Debt Service Fund

"The Debt Service Fund is used to account for the accumulation of resources for, and the payment of, general long-term debt principal, interest, and related costs." Ms. Dexter learned from the report used to construct Exhibit 1 that $2,693,000 was transferred to the Debt Service Fund from the General Fund. She concluded that this amount was probably related to operations and that to include the Debt Service Fund column would be double counting; she therefore eliminated it.

Capital Project Fund

"The Capital Project Fund is used to account for financial resources to be used for the acquisition or construction of major capital facilities." Ms. Dexter concluded that the expenditures recorded for this fund were similar to those for the account "construction in progress" in a business balance sheet, and that they related to fixed asset acquisitions, which are not operating activities.

Special Assessments Fund

"The Special Assessment Fund has been established to account for the financing and construction of various sewer extension projects deemed to benefit the properties against which special assessments are levied." Ms. Dexter concluded that this fund also related to the acquisition of fixed assets rather than to operating activities.

Ms. Dexter therefore combined the amounts in the general fund and special revenue fund columns of Exhibit 1 to obtain a first approximation to an operating statement.

Revenues

General Property Taxes

The report stated: "In accordance with GAAP, general property taxes are recorded as revenues in the period in which they become measurable and available. Taxes for the year that are not received within 60 days of year-end are assumed not to be 'available.'" These unpaid taxes, reduced by an allowance for bad debts, were recorded as assets on the balance sheet, with an offsetting credit to a liability, deferred revenue.

Ms. Dexter concluded that the tax revenue for the year 1987 should be the amount assessed for 1987 (reduced by an allowance for bad debts). A table in the report gave information about tax assessments for the past 10 years. From it she learned that the assessment for 1987 was $32,015,000, and that the bad debt experience over the period averaged 0.49 percent of the amount assessed. She therefore took $31,858,000 (99.51 percent of $32,015,000) as the amount of 1987 tax revenue, a decrease of $157,000 from the amount reported.

Other Revenues

The report stated that certain special revenue items were grants from government agencies that were recognized as revenues in the same period as that in which the expenditure was incurred, because this was required by the terms of the grant. Ms. Dexter viewed this treatment as appropriate.

Expenditures

The Douglas statement had the heading "expenditures," whereas the term *expenses* was used for similar items in business operating statements. In general, expenditures were recognized in the period in which the liability was incurred. Ms. Dexter concluded that regardless of the label, expenditures were the same as expenses, with the exceptions noted below.

Inventories

Inventories were recognized when the inventory items were received by the city. A business would recognize an expense in the period in which the items were consumed, which often would be a later period. However, the Douglas accounting system did not track the consumption of inventory items, so there was no way of making an adjustment for this.

Accumulated Unpaid Vacation and Sick Pay

In accordance with GAAP, Douglas recorded these amounts as a "long-term obligation," a memorandum account that did not affect the operating statement. In a business, the amounts earned by employees because of work done in the year would be recorded as an expense of the year. The amount of the obligation as of June 30, 1987, was $3,272,000. However, this was only $100,000 more than the amount reported a year earlier. Ms. Dexter decided that an adjustment for this amount was not worth the effort.

Pensions

Under business GAAP, the pension expense recognized for a given year an amount equal to the present value of that part of the benefits that employees would receive after they retired that was earned because of the work they did in that year. If the pension benefits were increased, the employee would be entitled to an additional amount for the earnings of prior years, and a fraction of this "past service liability" also would be included as pension expense of the current year. Douglas used a quite different approach to its calculation of pension expenditures. It contributed to its pension fund an amount "reasonably necessary to meet expenditures and benefits payable."

In 1987, the city paid $2,668,000 to its pension fund under this provision and recognized this amount as an expenditure. The pension fund at year-end had assets of $36,216,000, and the estimated present value of the pension benefits to which employees would become entitled by virtue of their earnings through 1987 was $46,739,000. Ms. Dexter therefore concluded that the amount that had been contributed to the fund in this and prior years was about $10,500,000 too low. However, this deficiency related to several prior years, and she did not have data that would permit a calculation of the amount attributable to 1987. Pending further study, she decided to add $1,000,000 to the 1987 pension expenditure.

Program Expenditures

Exhibit 1 contained an item under "Citywide" for employee benefits and pensions, amounting to $3,793,000. Ms. Dexter decided that this amount, plus the $1,000,000 of inadequate pension expense, properly were part of the compensation earned by employees and therefore should be recorded as expenses in the programs to which their salaries were charged. (Programs were the items listed on Exhibit 1, from "general government" through "education.") She hoped to obtain information on the salary expense for each program, but lacking this information, she decided to allocate the $4,793,000 in proportion to the amount reported as expenditures for each program.

Depreciation

GAAP does not permit depreciation accounting in government activities. The city did have a record of the cost of depreciable assets, which totaled

$85,737,000 as of June 30, 1985. However, a note to the financial statement listed some $48,000,000 of new projects that currently were in various stages of completion, which indicated to Ms. Dexter that the $85,737,000 cost of all assets in use was too low; these assets had been acquired over the past 50 years or more.

As another clue, a note to the statement indicated that $2,693,000 had been transferred from the General Fund to the Debt Service Fund, and that the Debt Service Fund had retired $1,872,000 principal amount of bonds during the year. If all the fixed assets had been acquired with borrowed funds, and if the repayment schedule corresponded to the life of the asset, the $1,872,000 would correspond to a depreciation charge. Since some assets were acquired with government grants and others with operating funds, and since the bond issues typically were for a shorter period than the life of the assets acquired with the proceeds of the bonds, this amount clearly was too low. Nevertheless, Ms. Dexter decided to use $1,872,000 as an indication of depreciation expense. Because of the uncertainty involved in this amount, she decided to show it as a separate item, rather than spreading it among the several programs.

Operating Transfers

The items labeled *transfers* apparently were something different from revenues and expenditures because they were shown separately. Of the transfers "in" and "out" of the General and Special Revenue Funds, $2,693,000 was the transfer to the Debt Service Fund already mentioned. Most of the other transfers were between the General and Special Revenue funds, which largely offset one another. Other transfers were to or from Capital Project and Special Assessment Funds, and Ms. Dexter believed that they were related to fixed assets rather than to operating expenditures. In constructing her statement, she therefore disregarded transfers other than the debt service item described above.

Proprietary Fund Type

In a separate section of the Douglas annual financial report, Ms. Dexter discovered a "Combined Statement of Revenues, Expenses, and Changes in Retained Earnings/Fund Balances—Proprietary Fund types," with a column headed "Enterprise Fund." A note stated: "The Enterprise Fund is used to account for the operations of the Douglas Water Department. These operations are financed and operated in a manner similar to that of a private business enterprise where the intent is that all costs, including depreciation, related to the provision of goods and services to the general public on a continuing basis be financed or recovered primarily through user charges."

As the title implied, this statement was a conventional business-type operating statement, recognizing revenues when earned and expenses as the amounts of resources applicable to the year, including depreciation. The bottom line reported a net loss of $420,000. Ms. Dexter concluded that the water

EXHIBIT 2

CITY OF DOUGLAS
OPERATING STATEMENT
YEAR ENDED JUNE 30, 1987
(WITH ADJUSTMENTS MADE BY CLAIRE DEXTER)
($000)

	General	+ Special Revenue	= Subtotal	+ Other	= Total
Revenues:					
Property taxes	$32,015	$ —	$32,015	$ (157)	$31,858
Penalties	377	—	377	—	377
Licenses and permits	164	—	164	—	164
Intergovernmental	11,637	2,712	14,349	—	14,349
Charges for services	332	582	914	—	914
Investment earnings	960	128	1,088	—	1,088
Contributions	—	30	30	—	30
Miscellaneous	551	4	555	—	555
Total revenues	$46,036	$3,456	$49,492	$ (157)	$49,335
Expenses:					
General government	1,435	415	1,850	239	2,089
Public safety	5,400	112	5,512	624	6,136
Public works	4,579	667	5,246	623	5,869
Health and welfare	1,461	634	2,095	239	2,334
Libraries	435	49	484	48	532
Parks and recreation	726	188	914	96	1,010
Education	23,028	1,958	24,986	2,924	27,910
Benefits and pensions	3,793	—	3,793	(3,793)*	—
General insurance	542	—	542	—	542
Depreciation	—	—	—	1,872	1,872
Interest	—	—	—	1,034	1,034
Miscellaneous	619	—	619	—	619
Total expenses	$42,018	$4,023	$46,041	$ 3,906	$49,947
Operating income, government	$ 4,018	$ (567)	$ 3,451	$(4,063)	(612)
Loss, Water Department				(420)	(420)
Net loss					$ (1,032)

*3,793 + 1,000 = 4,793 assigned to programs.

department was a part of the City of Douglas, so she incorporated this loss in her operating statement.

Revised Operating Statement

Exhibit 2 summarizes the changes she made to Exhibit 1 to arrive at an operating statement. (If this type of statement were adopted, the reconciliation to

Exhibit 1 would not be shown.) Her operating statement showed a net loss of $1,032,000, compared with the "Excess of revenues over expenditures" of $3,451,000, or the "Excess of revenues and other sources over expenditures and other uses" of $995,000, both numbers being the sum of the amounts in the General and Special Revenue Fund columns in Exhibit 1.

Discussions with Controller

Ms. Dexter explained to the controller what she had done and asked for his comment. He took issue principally with two items, pension expense and depreciation (although Ms. Dexter got the impression that he did not agree with any of the adjustments and refrained from saying so out of politeness).

With respect to pension expense, the controller said that taxpayers should not be asked to finance pension payments that might be made many years in the future. Proper provision should be made for the payments to retirees that were made in the current year, and that was enough.

He also said that the retirement of the current year's debt service principal is the amount for which this year's taxpayers should be responsible. Depreciation in excess of this amount would be misleading, especially for assets that have been paid for from other funds such as grants from the federal government. No present or future taxpayer would have to pay for these amounts.

The controller also pointed out that if Douglas did not prepare its reports in accordance with municipal GAAP, it would not receive a Certificate of Compliance from the Municipal Finance Officers Association. He said credit rating agencies gave favorable treatment to cities with this certificate.

Questions

1. Do you agree with Ms. Dexter's decision to eliminate the Debt Service Fund, the Capital Project Fund, and the Special Assessments Fund? Her decision to combine the General and Special Revenue Funds?

2. Should the amount reported as pensions in Exhibit 1 be increased? If so, how should the increase be calculated?

3. Should depreciation be recognized, or is the "principal retirement" of Debt Service an adequate substitute? If you favor depreciation, how would you respond to the controller's remark about assets acquired with grants?

4. In your opinion, did the city of Douglas operate with a surplus or a loss in 1987?

5. In general, which type of operating statement do you prefer? Should the city of Douglas prepare an operating statement like that in Exhibit 2?

Chapter 4

Analyzing Financial Statements

Much has been written on techniques for financial statement analysis. The purpose of this chapter is to provide a framework for the use of these techniques in nonprofit organizations. In particular, the chapter looks at the relationship between the accounting issues discussed in Chapter 3 and the broader topic of financial management. The chapter also discusses ratio analysis, including the issue of the quality of the data used for ratio calculations. It then builds upon ratio analysis to consider some additional aspects to analyzing a set of financial statements. Finally, the chapter looks at two issues of particular importance to nonprofit organizations: leverage and the role of a surplus. The Appendix contains a primer on ratio analysis.

The Analytical Process

The purpose of financial statement analysis is not to determine how well or poorly an organization has followed generally accepted accounting principles. Nevertheless, prior to undertaking an analysis of a set of financial statements, it is important to identify any accounting issues that would affect the analysis.

Distinction between Accounting and Financial Management Issues

The distinction between accounting and financial management issues, although frequently ignored, is extremely important. There is little use in calculating a current ratio in the normal fashion, for example, if there is evidence to suggest that the organization has misclassified either its current assets or current liabilities. Similarly, calculating a profit margin is of little value if the organization has some significant estimated expenses where the estimates may be either unduly high or unduly low. In either case, the profit margin will be quite misleading. Similar problems can exist for other ratios as well.

Identifying Accounting Issues

An important step in the process of financial statement analysis, then, is to identify those accounts on the balance sheet and the operating statement that might have misleading numbers. Frequently, these will be accounts whose totals are derived via estimates. Some accounts that are candidates for having misleading numbers are the following:

- Bad debts, contractual allowances, and the allowance for doubtful accounts. These accounts rely on estimates that will affect both the profit margin and the net accounts receivable figure.

- Inventory, where obsolescence, spoilage, or other forms of shrinkage may mean that the *saleable* inventory is much less than the reported figure.

- Depreciation and accumulated depreciation, where choices about economic lives and residual values of fixed assets affect both accounts.

- Any asset where amortization is involved and where the amortization schedule can make the book value for the asset diverge considerably from its market value.

- Any other asset or liability account involving estimates, where the estimates affect both the surplus on the operating statement and the size of the asset or liability account on the balance sheet.

Example	An estimated expense on an operating statement that affects a liability account on the balance sheet is the expense associated with an insurance claim *incurred* during an accounting period but not yet received by the insurer. This is a typical account for a managed care organization or other health insurer, such as Blue Cross and was the subject of Case 3–3. Since the insurer has earned premium revenue during the accounting period, it must match the associated expenses to that revenue, one of which is the claims that have been incurred but not yet received. In this respect, the estimate of expenses for claims incurred but not received is quite similar to the estimate of bad debt expenses. The difference is that the account corresponding to the bad debt expense estimate—the allowance for doubtful accounts—is a contra account to the accounts receivable asset, whereas in the insurance industry the corresponding account is a liability, usually called something like Claims Incurred but Not Received (or IBNR).

Notes to the Financial Statements

An important source of information concerning accounting estimates and their effects on the associated accounts is the notes to the financial statements. The notes are the means by which an organization's independent auditors describe some of the underlying detail in the financial statements, disclose important accounting policies, and identify any special or unusual accounting practices that the organization has followed in preparing its financial statements. The notes should be read with care since they provide an analyst with a reasonably good idea of the kinds of accounting problems and issues the organization faces, and how they affect the financial statements.

Example

In a community mental health center, the notes might contain a description of the organization's different types of payers, and the expectations for payment from each group. If an analyst were assessing the accounts receivable collection period for the center, he or she might see that there are some extended payment plans for certain clients. The analyst also might find that the percent of the total that each third-party payer comprises had changed over time, and therefore would expect to see the accounts receivable collection periods shifting in conjunction with the shift in payers.

Frequently, the notes give a fair amount of information about the organization's debt structure, which can facilitate an analysis of long-term solvency. They also explain the reasons for "extraordinary items," that is, activities that occur outside an organization's normal course of operations and that affect its financial statements. For example, an expense associated with a major fire in an organization would affect its surplus (or deficit) from operations. But this would not be included as part of ordinary operations. Rather, it would be identified separately, listed below the surplus from operations, and discussed in the notes.

Making Adjustments

Once significant accounting issues have been identified, an analyst can take one of three actions: (1) adjust the accounts to provide more appropriate totals, (2) ignore the accounting issues, or (3) keep them in mind in drawing conclusions. The first is risky since it rarely is possible to obtain enough information to make appropriate adjustments. Even if it were possible to obtain the information, the analyst would then need to be consistent in comparing the resulting totals to prior years or to other organizations.

The second option would be appropriate if the accounting issues were relatively minor or if they affected accounts that were relatively unimportant in conducting the rest of the analysis. If this is not the case, then the third option probably is the most reasonable. That is, when ratios are calculated, the analyst would need to keep in mind that a more accurate accounting effort would result in slightly (or significantly) different ratio results.

Financial Analysis

Having identified the significant accounting issues, and having made any necessary adjustments to the financial statements, an analyst can then undertake an assessment of the organization's financial management. As indicated above, the distinction between accounting and financial management is an important one: the accounting issues relate to the *accuracy* of the figures on the financial statements, whereas financial management focuses on the *meaning* of those figures. Properly analyzed, with appropriate allowances made for any inaccuracies, the operating statement, balance sheet, and statement of cash flows can convey a great deal of information about an organization's operations and financial management.

In general, conducting an analysis of an organization's financial management requires undertaking ratio analysis, assessing the statement of cash flows (SCF), and relying on whatever other information is available. Each activity is discussed below.

Ratio Analysis

One technique used to assess an organization's financial management is ratio analysis, which focuses on mathematical comparisons between or among the accounts on a set of financial statements. Ratios allow us to look at the relationships among various parts of a single statement, such as the balance sheet, or to look at the relationships between elements on two different statements, generally the operating statement and the balance sheet. The current ratio—which examines the relationship between current assets and current liabilities—is an example of the former; the return-on-assets ratio—where the surplus (or increase in net assets) from the operating statement) is compared with assets (from the balance sheet—is an example of the latter.

The principal purpose of ratio analysis is to allow us to look closely at four categories of financial management: profitability, liquidity, asset management, and long-term solvency. Indeed, although dozens of ratios can be used for purposes of analyzing a set of financial statements, most fall into one of these four categories. Some of the more important questions that ratios can help to answer are discussed below, by category.

Profitability

An organization's profitability (i.e., its surplus or change in net assets on its operating statement) can be thought about along two dimensions:

- How large was the surplus relative to revenue? Is this amount about right or too small?

- What were the returns on assets and equity? Are these about right, given the risks that the organization faces in doing business, or are they too low?

Liquidity

The issue of liquidity is essentially one of cash availability and use. Among the questions we might ask are the following:

- How well is the organization using its cash? Does it have enough cash on hand to meet its current obligations? Does it have too much cash sitting idle?

- How well is the organization managing its accounts receivable? Are collection periods too long? Are they lengthening?

- How well is the organization managing its inventory? Does it have too much, thereby tying up cash in an otherwise unproductive asset, or does it have too little inventory?

Asset Management

Assessing an organization's assets requires examining both the current and noncurrent sections of the left side of the balance sheet. The current sections were looked at under the heading of liquidity. With regard to noncurrent assets, several questions emerge:

- What is the nature of fixed assets? Are they appropriate to the organization's strategy?

- How well are assets being utilized? For example, how much revenue is being generated for every dollar of assets?

- How old are the fixed assets? Are they in need of replacement? If so, does the organization have funds available to replace them or plans in place to obtain the funds?

Long-Term Solvency

To determine if the organization has made good financing decisions, and thereby has provided for its solvency over the long-term, we must look at the right side of the balance sheet as well as the operating statement. Here, we are attempting to answer the following sorts of questions:

- How well have current liabilities been managed? Will the organization be able to meet these obligations when they become due?

- How much long-term debt is there relative to the amount of equity? Is this about right? Is there too much debt given the inherent riskiness of the organization's operations? Could the organization take on more debt without jeopardizing its ability to repay both the new and existing debt?

Standards for Comparison

Although ratios can assist us in analyzing a set of financial statements, they do not provide all the answers. One important question that emerges in the use of ratios is the standard to which each ratio should be compared. For example, as indicated in the Appendix, the current ratio should give us some indication of an organization's liquidity, and therefore can assist us in assessing the way the organization is managing its current assets. A figure of 2.0 was suggested as about right.

Suppose we calculate the current ratio and find that it is 1.5; that is, current assets are 1.5 times greater than current liabilities. Is this too low? Are there circumstances that would make 1.5 acceptable? Is it possible that under some circumstances 1.5 might be too high? Answering these questions requires that we have some standard for comparison. In general, three possible standards exist: industry, historical, and managerial.

Industry Standards Industry standards are popular and can form an easy basis for assessing the quality of an organization's financial ratios. However, industry standards also can be misleading. Typically we have several concerns when using industry standards. The first is whether the organization we are analyzing is truly a member of the "industry" for which the standards have been developed. For example, considerable work has been expended developing industry norms for hospitals, and yet within this so called industry there may be a number of subindustries that are more relevant for analysis. There are teaching hospitals and community hospitals, rural hospitals and urban hospitals, investor-owned hospitals and nonprofit hospitals, hospitals in the Southwest and hospitals in the Northeast.

For a variety of reasons, such as regulatory requirements, regional payment patterns by insurance companies, and so on, a hospital in a particular region of the country may, by necessity, have a ratio that diverges from the so-called norm. Certainly, we would expect the financial ratios for a nonprofit teaching hospital in an urban setting in the Northeast to be somewhat, if not considerably, different from those of an investor-owned, rural community hospital in the Southwest.

Second, industry norms generally have been derived from published data, and it is important to ascertain that the ratios for both the organization under analysis and the industry have been calculated in the same, or approximately the same, way. With some ratios, there is only one method of calculation, and there are no problems. With others, there may be several different ways the ratio can be calculated, each of which is legitimate, but each of which will produce slightly different results. Moreover, despite the presence of generally accepted accounting principles, there is a lack of a uniform chart of accounts or uniform reporting for almost all industries. This means there is a good possibility that some ratio comparisons will not be valid even if we think the same elements are being included.

Finally, we must be certain that the ratios are for roughly the same time period. This is particularly important if there have been changes in the organization's environment or its strategy. For example, assume that the industry norm for an accounts receivable collection ratio for a nonprofit organization contracting with a state government had been calculated during a period when the state's resources were plentiful and payments were being made in a timely way. It would be quite misleading to compare that ratio with one calculated when the state's fiscal resources were less plentiful and its payments less timely. As many organizations have learned quite painfully, changes of this sort frequently do not happen gradually but, quite dramatically instead, such that a comparison of ratios to an industry norm that was developed only one year previously could be quite misleading.

These latter concerns suggest that, apart from the regional variations and calculation differences, an industry norm is not necessarily the right level for a ratio. Some studies that have attempted to develop industry norms, for example, have looked at organizations that ultimately went bankrupt; this hardly provides a standard to aspire to. Moreover, as interest rates rise and fall, many companies will shift the mix of their permanent capital, sometimes having high debt and sometimes shifting away from debt into a greater proportion of equity. Thus, what was a norm 5 or 10 years ago may no longer be appropriate. In short, managers should view industry norms with considerable skepticism.

Historical Standards Historical standards avoid many of the problems associated with industry norms. Since they consist of ratios calculated over time for the same organization, there is no question that the industry is the same (unless the organization has had a major strategic shift and moved into a new industry). It is also quite easy to avoid the problem of calculating the ratios in different ways.

The weakness of historical ratios, of course, is that they have no external validation. For example, an organization's accounts receivable collection period may have remained at 60 days for a number of years, but management may be unaware of a technique that other similar organizations in the same industry are using to accelerate collections to, say, 30 days. Without some sort of external validation, management may continue to think that a 60-day collection period is appropriate.

Managerial Standards Industry ratios are not the only way an organization's management learns of practices in its industry. For example, consider the above situation in which a 60-day collection period was thought to be reasonable when other organizations in the industry had achieved a 30-day period. It should not be necessary to bring information of this sort to management's attention via an industry norm for an accounts receivable collection period. Managers generally engage in a variety of activities that make them aware of how other organizations in their industry are being managed. It would be a rare case, indeed, for the manager of an organization with a 60-day collection period not to be aware of the fact that many other organizations in the same industry were achieving 30 days, even if no published industry data were available.

Because of the availability of external information such as the above, and because different organizations have different strategic objectives, an organization's senior management may establish certain standards that deviate from historical patterns, but that are consistent with its chosen strategic directions and its own sense of how the organization's balance sheet needs to be managed. It is even possible, of course, that where industry norms are available, management will decide that it wishes to deviate from these norms for one reason or another. It may wish, for example, to tolerate longer collection periods for its accounts receivable than other organizations in its industry because it knows that many of its clients have financial difficulties. Rather than insist on timely payment (which effectively would result in a loss of the client), it chooses instead to accept a longer collection period. Without knowing this kind of information, it is extremely difficult for an external analyst to be critical of a particular organization's financial management practices.

The Need for Judgment

In summary, the use of ratio analysis to make comparisons among several similar organizations must be done with great care. Not all organizations, even those in the same industry, prepare their financial statements in the same way or incorporate the same information into accounts with similar names. Thus, when ratios are used to compare two or more organizations, even if the ratios included in the comparison utilize very specific accounts on the financial statement, the results should be viewed with some skepticism. In general, then, while comparisons among organizations *can* be made, or the ratios of a given organization *can* be related to some industry norm, the most valid comparisons usually are those that are made over time for a single organization.

Even when ratios are calculated historically for the same organization, however, changes in the organization's environment, strategy, or managerial tactics may invalidate the comparisons. In short, it seems quite clear that an external analyst must exercise considerable caution in interpreting an organization's ratios. About all the analyst can do is raise questions about the quality of the organization's profitability, liquidity, asset management, or long-term solvency decisions, but it is quite difficult to be critical or judgmental without some understanding of the organization's environment, strategy, and overall management.

Using the SCF

Apart from ratios, the statement of cash flows can be a very powerful tool for understanding the kinds of financing decisions that management has made during an accounting period, as well as assessing management's ability to make effective and efficient use of the organization's assets. In particular, the SCF can be used to determine the extent to which an organization is financing itself appropriately (i.e., using short-term debt to finance its seasonal and other short-term needs, and long-term debt and equity to finance its fixed assets).

Compiling Other Information

Many nonprofit organizations publish annual reports or promotional literature that provide descriptive information about their operations. This can be quite helpful to the analyst in determining the nature of the organization's activities, its environment, its strategy, and other matters relevant to the quality of its financial statements. Of course, if the analyst has an opportunity to interview the organization's management, he or she may be able to determine other factors that bear upon the financial management decisions being taken and the rationale that underlies them. All of these factors are important ingredients in a thorough analysis of an organization's financial statements. Taken together, they give the analyst some indication of the organization's financial management goals and constraints, and therefore some basis to use for identifying and analyzing the quality of management's performance in achieving these goals.

Beyond the use of ratios and a reliance on supplemental information, such as the SCF and the notes to the financial statements, an analyst also must have an understanding of some of the fundamental financing issues that are faced by almost all organizations. Two of these issues in particular stand out as significant: leverage and the role of surplus. They relate to two questions that must be addressed in any good analysis of an organization's financial management: (1) How much debt (or leverage) is appropriate for this organization? and (2) How large a surplus (or change in net assets) must the organization have?

Leverage

Leverage is a subject of great concern to managers of many organizations. Recall that in the Appendix, it is defined as Assets ÷ Equity. Therefore, according to the basic accounting equation (Assets = Liabilities + Equity), if an organization had no debt whatsoever, its assets and equity would be equal. Its leverage ratio, therefore, would be 1. As an organization begins to rely on debt to finance its assets, the ratio increases. Exhibit 4–1 illustrates this phenomenon with a simple example, beginning with a balance sheet in which assets and equity are equal, and moving to a situation in which total debt and equity are equal. As can be seen, the ratio increases to a level of 2.0 under these circumstances.

As Exhibit 4–1 shows, leverage allows an organization to finance more assets than would be possible if it relied only on its own equity. Note that equity has remained unchanged in this example while assets have doubled. In a very real sense, the organization is using its equity as a "lever" to obtain funds from outsiders and, thus, to expand its asset base. This, in turn, allows it to deliver more services (or to produce more goods) than otherwise would be possible, and therefore to earn more revenue.

Drawbacks to Leverage

Leverage does not come without some drawbacks. Funds borrowed must be repaid, and generally there is an interest charge. Organizations that rely heavily on borrowed funds spend considerable time and effort predicting and managing their cash flows so as to assure themselves of sufficient cash on hand to meet their debt service obligations.

Financial Risk versus Business Risk

One way to think about leverage is in terms of the *financial risk* it creates as compared with the organization's overall *business risk*. Financial risk and

Exhibit 4–1
Examples of Leverage

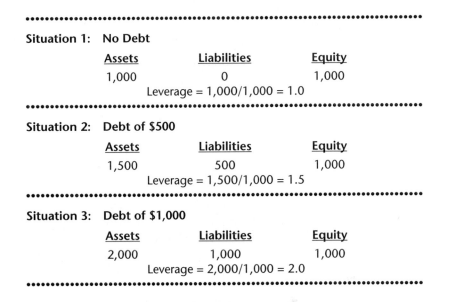

Situation 1: No Debt

Assets	Liabilities	Equity
1,000	0	1,000

Leverage = 1,000/1,000 = 1.0

Situation 2: Debt of $500

Assets	Liabilities	Equity
1,500	500	1,000

Leverage = 1,500/1,000 = 1.5

Situation 3: Debt of $1,000

Assets	Liabilities	Equity
2,000	1,000	1,000

Leverage = 2,000/1,000 = 2.0

leverage are synonymous. That is, other things being equal, the higher an organization's leverage, the higher its debt service obligation, and the greater the risk that it will be unable to meet this obligation.

Business risk, by contrast, refers to the certainty of an organization's annual cash flows. Specifically, organizations that have a relatively high business risk have a high degree of *uncertainty* about their cash flows. An example of an organization with high business risk is a social service agency that relies on one or two large government grants for much of its revenue. An example of an organization with low business risk is a child care center located in a neighborhood with many dual-career families. The social service agency quite likely would face a great deal of uncertainty from one year to the next about its annual cash flows, whereas the child care center would be almost completely certain of its.

Example

Tuckman and Chang identified four indicators of business risk: (1) small amounts of equity balances, (2) few revenue sources, (3) low administrative costs (leaving little room for cutbacks if revenue should fall), and (4) low operating margins.[1] Testing these indicators has proven to be difficult, but in one study, Greenlee and Trussel found that the model was most useful for senior managers and boards during a strategic planning process, for potential creditors in determining a nonprofit's creditworthiness, and for funders in deciding on the amount and timing of contributions.[2]

[1]H. Tuckman and C. Chang, "A Methodology for Measuring the Financial Vulnerability of Charitable Nonprofit Organizations," *Nonprofit and Voluntary Sector Quarterly,* 1991.
[2]Janet S. Greenlee and John M. Trussel, "Predicting the Financial Vulnerability of Charitable Organizations," *Nonprofit Management and Leadership,* Winter 2000.

EXHIBIT 4–2
Business Risk versus
Financial Risk

	Low Business Risk	High Business Risk
High Financial Risk	*Possible*	*Danger Zone*
Low Financial Risk	*Very Safe*	*Necessary*

The combined effect of financial and business risk is illustrated in Exhibit 4–2. As it suggests, other things being equal, an organization with low business risk can have a fairly high financial risk. Assuming the organization does not take on more debt service obligations than its cash flow can support, the relative certainty of its annual cash flows gives it some reasonable assurance that it will be able to meet these obligations from one year to the next. By contrast, an organization with a high business risk generally would find it unwise to have high financial risk (i.e., a great deal of leverage). Since debt service obligations remain constant each year, the organization could quite easily find itself in a situation where, because of events beyond its control, cash flows were not sufficient to meet these obligations. The result could be detrimental to the organization's continued existence as a financially viable entity.

The Role of Surplus

Economists frequently cite profit as the fundamental characteristic of capitalism. According to them it motivates, measures success, and rewards. Indeed, economists see an adequate profit as a legitimate cost of operating an organization. It is excess profits (i.e., those greater than a normal return) that provide an impetus for new organizations to enter a market. In the purely competitive model, excess profits entice new organizations to enter a market and increase the supply of goods and services. This goes on until prices fall to a level at which all organizations can earn a normal profit. At that point, the market is in equilibrium.

Accountants and managers see profit somewhat differently For them, it is simply the numerical difference between revenues and expenses. In addition, besides providing a return to the owners of an organization, one of profit's principal purposes is to finance asset acquisitions. In fact, a basic financial-management maxim is that an organization should finance its fixed assets with some combination of long-term debt and equity. For nonprofits, direct contributions by donors as well as operating surpluses are the sources of equity.

This financing role of profits is an important one. Museums, libraries, universities, hospitals, port authorities, and the like, that must add to plant capacity, purchase new and more sophisticated equipment, or upgrade their facilities, have large fixed-asset bases that require significant amounts of financing. But even small nonprofit organizations, which must add office equipment, microcomputers, and other assets as they develop and grow, have financing needs. Moreover, any organization that wishes to remain in a steady state must provide for the replacement of assets, since inflation, however slight, effectively serves to erode an organization's asset base.

Organizations could avoid the need for profits (or surpluses) by relying exclusively on long-term debt. In general, however, this is not an adequate approach. Many organizations, have increased their debt to the maximum prudent levels (i.e., where annual cash flows are about equal to debt service obligations). For these organizations, equity is the only additional source of funds.

Surplus and Growth

Independent of its need for fixed assets, an organization experiencing growth in its revenues also requires increasing amounts of cash. For example, because of the time lag in collecting accounts receivable, an organization that is both growing and extending credit to its clients has an increasing amount of cash tied up in accounts receivable. Moreover, for organizations that require a sizable inventory, the time that passes between acquiring inventory and either selling or using it also requires cash.

They key idea is that an organization must finance the cash outflows that take place between the acquisition of inventory or the prevision of service and the subsequent collection of accounts receivable. If managers of growing organizations use debt to finance these increases in inventory and receivables, the organization's indebtedness will continue to expand until such time as growth slows or stops.

While a variety of financing or strategic options other than debt exists for a rapidly growing organization, the five that have the greatest impact are (1) slowing growth, (2) shortening the collection period for accounts receivable, (3) shortening the inventory holding period, (4) extending the period for paying accounts payable, or (5) generating equity via either surplus or additional contributions. For managers to rely on debt—either long-term or short-term—instead of one or more of these other options ordinarily will not suffice. The debt will not be repayable until management invokes one of the five options.

How Much Surplus Is Needed?

Because these two uses of surplus—asset replacement and growth—are so different, managers need to take different approaches to assess how much surplus is sufficient for each. The first is related to the financing of fixed assets; the second concerns provision of adequate cash to cover the cash needs associated with growth.

Financing Fixed Assets

Most organizations, including many nonprofits, establish selling prices to provide for the desired amount of surplus so that retained earnings can help to

EXHIBIT 4–3

A System of Ratios

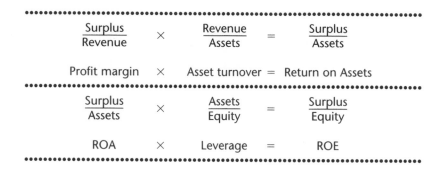

$$\frac{\text{Surplus}}{\text{Revenue}} \times \frac{\text{Revenue}}{\text{Assets}} = \frac{\text{Surplus}}{\text{Assets}}$$

Profit margin $\times$ Asset turnover = Return on Assets

$$\frac{\text{Surplus}}{\text{Assets}} \times \frac{\text{Assets}}{\text{Equity}} = \frac{\text{Surplus}}{\text{Equity}}$$

ROA $\times$ Leverage = ROE

meet capital needs. The organization's price thus becomes one element of the "surplus formula," a formula that includes both volume and cost. Further, the required surplus level generally is related to the organization's desired return on equity.

As indicated in the Appendix, ROE is closely related to another ratio of concern to managers: return on assets, or ROA. Indeed, as indicated in the discussion of ROA in the Appendix, if an organization does not obtain a sufficiently high return on assets, it will be unable to sustain itself over the long term. That is, as assets wear out or become technologically obsolete, management must replace them and, because of inflation, doing so requires more funds than depreciation provides.

One way to analyze this problem is to combine several of the ratios discussed in the Appendix. The set of ratios contained in Exhibit 4–3 demonstrates some important relationships and also highlights some key managerial concerns. In particular, two important questions emerge from a careful analysis of the distinction between ROA and ROE: (1) Which is the preferable measure? and (2) How much is enough? The first question is not trivial. By using leverage, an organization can transform a low ROA into a high ROE. A high ROE, however, is no guarantee that assets can be replaced as they wear out. Indeed, if an organization is highly leveraged, and if managers wish to replace assets without a decline in ROE, they must maintain their organization's leverage at the initial level, but they often cannot either obtain more debt or refinance existing debt. As a result, it may not be possible to provide for asset replacement.

The second question can be answered by recognizing that an ROA equivalent to the rate of inflation is necessary to replace assets as they wear out. Therefore, the desired ROA figure needs to be at least as high as the rate of inflation, and higher if the organization is expanding its asset base.

Once a desired ROA figure has been selected, it can be attained by using a variety of combinations of margin and asset turnover. In general, the easiest approach to take is to determine a reasonable asset turnover level—based on, say, past performance—and to use it, in conjunction with the desired ROA figure, to calculate the necessary profit margin percentage. This, in turn, can be used to set *desired* prices at an appropriate level above expenses. While

EXHIBIT 4–4

Cash Needs Associated with Growth

Assumptions:

1. Growth in revenue and expenses of approximately 2% a month.
2. Accounts receivable collection lag of two months.
3. Accounts payable paid immediately.
4. Inventory, prepaid expenses, and other current assets grow at same rate as revenue.
5. Current liabilities (other than payables) grow at same rate as inventory, prepaid expenses, and other current assets.

	Month					
	1	**2**	**3**	**4**	**5**	**6**
Operating statement:						
Revenue	100	102	104	106	108	110
Expenses	100	102	104	106	108	110
Surplus	0	0	0	0	0	0
Cash flow:						
Cash collections*	96	98	100	102	104	106
Cash payments†	100	102	104	106	108	110
Change in cash	(4)	(4)	(4)	(4)	(4)	(4)
Cumulative change	(4)	(8)	(12)	(16)	(20)	(24)

Notes:
*From revenue earned two months ago that went into accounts receivable.
†Same as expenses due to Assumptions 3, 4, and 5 above.

market forces and third-party payers clearly will affect the prices an organization actually can charge, such an approach nevertheless provides a starting point. Moreover, it allows a manager to determine which services are priced below their desired level, and therefore to better manage the needed cross-subsidization from other services.

Provision of Cash Needs

The need for cash arises from a combination of three factors: profit margin, changes in current assets (especially accounts receivable and inventory), and changes in current liabilities (especially accounts payable). Exhibit 4–4 illustrates why organizations need additional cash. The exhibit looks at a situation where there is no surplus. It shows the resulting effect of growth on cash that arises *only* out of the time lag in collecting accounts receivable. Although additional cash requirements will result from the difference between the growth rate of remaining current assets and that of current liabilities, the most significant factor in many growing nonprofit organizations generally is accounts receivable.

As this exhibit indicates, under the assumed set of circumstances, there is a constant need for cash. As a result, if managers use debt to finance their cash needs, they will not be able to repay the debt unless the growth rate slows or they take other measures (such as accelerating the collection of accounts receivable or delaying the payment of expenses) to lessen their need for cash. Therefore, under these circumstances, managers generally consider debt to be an undesirable alternative. As with the purchase and replacement of fixed assets, a surplus is needed. In the simplified example in Exhibit 4–4, a surplus figure equivalent to the "Change in cash" line would be satisfactory.

The Analytical Process

Most people will develop their own process for analyzing a set of financial statements. Some will begin by immediately calculating some ratios. Others will begin with a careful reading of the notes to the financial statements. Regardless of the sequence of steps taken, three general categories of activities are necessary: (1) assessment of the organization's strategy, (2) analysis of the significant accounting issues, and (3) analysis of the significant financial management issues. Each is discussed below.

Strategic Assessment

Understanding an organization's overall strategy is helpful if the analyst is to put its financial statements into a context. Doing so includes assessing the organization's environment and determining, for example, (1) the relevant competitive and regulatory forces, (2) the nature of the organization's clients or customers, and (3) possible changes in client needs in the future. In conducting this analysis, the analyst typically is attempting to answer two sets of questions:

- What are this organization's critical success factors? That is, what must the organization do well in order to succeed? How, if at all, will these factors show up on the financial statements?

- What are the important and tricky accounting issues for this organization? Does it need to estimate an expense for claims incurred but not received, for example? Does it have volatile accounts receivable, such that the bad debt expense estimate is tricky?

Accounting Issues

In assessing the accounting issues the organization faces, many analysts focus on the notes to the financial statements. What accounting issues do the notes mention? How important do they seem? One fairly easy technique to use in assessing the importance of an accounting issue is to identify the relatively large numbers on the financial statements, and then ask whether a change in accounting policies would affect any of these numbers in a significant way. For example, if accounts receivable comprise 50 percent of assets, the analyst no doubt would want to know about the process for estimating bad debts.

Clearly there are gray areas, such that it is not possible to say with total certainty how one goes about determining significance. In general, however, the steps to follow are as follows:

- Read the notes to the financial statements. What accounting issues do they suggest are present?

- Look for the large numbers on the financial statements. Are any of them influenced by estimates? What do the notes say about the estimates?

- Are any of the assets influenced by a distinction between book value and market value? What do the notes say about this distinction? What does intuition say? If, for example, the organization purchased a building in Beverly Hills, California, in 1960, the chances are good that the market value exceeds the book value.

- To what extent is the surplus figure valid? That is, was the figure based on estimates? For example, was there an estimate of bad debts, and, if so, is any information available on its accuracy? If there is a depreciation expense, does it appear to be a reasonably accurate representation of the using up of the associated assets?

- What is the nature of the organization's liabilities? Are they truly obligations that must be repaid or are they the result of higher-than-appropriate estimates (e.g., with the IBNR discussed above)? Have some liabilities, such as pensions, been underestimated, such that there may be unanticipated drains on cash in the future?

Financial Management Issues

In assessing the significant financial management issues, many analysts conduct their investigation along the lines of the ratios discussed in the Appendix, using the SCF and other information to support the analysis. A set of questions for each of the four ratio areas was given above. Some further considerations are given below.

Profitability

The analysis here relies primarily on the set of ratios shown in Exhibit A–1 (in the Appendix), and focuses on the following questions:

- How does this organization generate a surplus? Selling many units of items with a relatively low margin, or selling a few units of items with relatively high margin?

- How do the ratios compare to the conclusions from the strategic analysis?

- Is the organization earning a sufficiently high return on assets to counteract the forces of inflation? If not, what steps has it taken to correct for the deficiencies? What else might be done?

Liquidity

The analysis here relies on both the statement of cash flows and some of the liquidity ratios. Some questions are as follows:

- Is this organization generating cash from operations? If not, why not?

- What other sources of cash does the organization have? Are these likely to continue into the future? How are these other sources of cash being managed over time?

- What is the business risk of this organization? Are its cash flows fairly predictable and certain from year to year (low business risk) or is there considerable uncertainty (high business risk)?

Asset Management

The analysis here uses the investing portion of the statement of cash flows, two asset management ratios, and the accounts receivable and inventory turnover ratios, and attempts to answer the following questions:

- Does the asset turnover ratio seem about right for this organization? For example, is this an industry with low profit margins where high asset turnover is key to success, and, if so, how is this organization doing?

- How is the organization managing its current assets, particularly accounts receivable? Has this turnover rate been improving or worsening over the time period for which financial statements are available? Why?

Long-Term Solvency

The analysis here uses the financing portion of the statement of cash flows and some of the long-term solvency ratios. It focuses on the following questions:

- How has this organization structured its debt? Has it done a good job of matching the term of its debt to the life of its assets?

- How much leverage does this organization have? Does it have too much financial risk compared to its business risk (i.e., is it in the "danger zone" on Exhibit 4–2)?

- What kind of debt-service coverage does the organization have? Is there a reasonable margin for safety given its business risk?

- What does an environmental assessment indicate about the future for this organization? Are any of the circumstances surrounding its business risk likely to change? If so, how will they affect it? What does this suggest for its debt?

Summary   This chapter has provided an overview of some important aspects of financial statement analysis. Essentially, this analysis consists of assessing the quality of an organization's financial statements—and thus its overall financial performance—through the use of ratio analysis, the statement of cash flows, and other related information. The SCF, although not always used as fully as it might be by analysts, provides some valuable insight into the way an organization has financed its activities over the course of the most recent accounting period.

Financing considerations inevitably result in the need to pay some attention to the issue of leverage, and the chapter addressed both the advantages and some of the risks of leverage. Indeed, one of the most important aspects of the managerial process is the management of debt, or leverage. Further, however, managers must be aware of the need to earn a sufficiently large surplus to provide for both asset replacement and the cash needs associated with growth, since to incur debt for these activities is to flirt with serious financial difficulties.

Appendix

A Primer on Ratio Analysis

To understand ratio analysis and its use, one must recall that the asset side of the balance sheet contains those items that an organization owns or has claim to, whereas the liability and equity side shows how the assets were financed. Since the balance sheet is the result of all of the organization's historical financial activities viewed at a given point in time, it provides what might be thought of as the long-run view of an organization's asset acquisition and financing decisions.

This long-run view can be supplemented by an analysis of the statement of cash flows, which shows management's specific financing choices and activities over the course of a given accounting period (usually a year). Recall that the SCF gives specific information concerning the sources of funds during a year and the uses to which those funds were put. Thus, by using the SCF, a reader of financial statements can determine the extent to which an organization acquired more fixed assets or current assets during a year, and how those assets were financed (e.g., from operations, short-term debt, long-term debt, annual contributions). Consequently, the SCF and the balance sheet together provide a reader of financial statements with some indication of the financing decisions made by an organization's management, both over time and during the course of the most recent accounting period.

By contrast, the operating statement lets one look at the quality of the organization's *profitability* during a given accounting period. As discussed below, ratios involving both the operating statement and the balance sheet can help us to assess relationships among surplus, assets, and liabilities.

Role of Ratios

Image yourself with, say, $1,000 to invest in one of two for-profit companies: Company A or Company B. You are given the following information about each company:

	Company A	Company B
Profit last year	$100,000	$1,000,000
Current assets as of the end of last year	$50,000	$500,000

In which company would you invest your $1,000? Is there any additional information from the financial statements you would like to have before making your decision?

Before answering the question, let's ask another question. Suppose you now were given the following information about the two companies:

	Company A	Company B
Shareholders' equity as of the end of the last year	$500,000	$100,000,000
Current liabilities as of the end of last year	$25,000	$10,000,000

Would this make any difference in your investment decision? Why or why not?

In effect, the additional information has told us about two factors that might be of considerable importance to an investor: the relationship between profit and equity, and the relationship between current assets and current liabilities. Each is important for different reasons. If, for example, you are interested in investing in a company that will earn the highest return possible on your $1,000, you presumably would prefer to have it invested in Company A, where profit is 20 percent of equity ($100,000 ÷ $500,000), rather than Company B, where profit is only 1 percent of equity ($1 million ÷ $100 million). Of course, these are the figures for last year only, and the future may be quite different from the past. Nevertheless, the notion of a *return on investment* would lead you in a quite different direction than simply looking at profit in isolation.

Similarly, if you are interested in investing in a company that can meet its current obligations when they come due, you presumably would be somewhat more concerned about Company B than Company A. That is, Company B has $10 million of liabilities that are current (will be due and payable sometime in the next year), and only $500,000 of current assets at the moment to provide the cash needed to meet those obligations. Company A, by contrast, while having only $50,000 in current assets, has only $25,000 in current liabilities. Thus, it seems to have a comfortable margin of safety.

Clearly there are many other factors you would consider in making an investment decision. The purpose of this example is only to illustrate that the absolute dollar amounts, by themselves, tell you relatively little about an organization's financial strength. Moreover, if we are to make comparisons of any sort—between two or more organizations, or between different years of operations for the same organization—we must use something other than flat dollar amounts. Ratios allow us to do this. For a variety of reasons, many of which are discussed in the text, even ratios have limitations, and we must move beyond them if we are to fully understand and analyze an organization's financial statements. Nevertheless, by permitting us to move beyond the absolute magnitude of the numbers on the financial statements to *a set of relationships between and among the numbers,* ratios can assist us greatly in the analytical effort.

Ratios can be classified into four categories for purposes of discussion: profitability, liquidity, asset management, and long-term solvency. Each is discussed below. Exhibit A–1 summarizes the ratios and the items used in their computations.

Profitability Ratios

Profitability ratios attempt to measure the ability of an organization to generate sufficient funds from its operations to both sustain itself and, in the case of a for-profit entity, provide an acceptable return to its owners. The former aspect is important to both for-profit and nonprofit organizations. That is, over the long term, all organizations must generate enough funds from operations to allow them to (1) replace fixed assets as they wear out, (2) purchase new fixed assets as revenues grow, (3) service debt, and (4) provide for the cash needs associated with growth. Profitability ratios provide some partial evidence of how well an organization is satisfying these requirements.

The first profitability measure is *profit margin.*

$$\text{Profit margin} = \frac{\text{Surplus}^3}{\text{Revenue}}$$

This ratio effectively measures how much of each dollar in revenue received by the organization ultimately becomes surplus. Profit margins tend to vary widely from one industry to the next. An organization in an industry with commodity-like product, such as a museum, will tend to have a relatively low profit margin; it earns a surplus by having a high volume of sales relative to its assets.[4] By contrast, an organization in an industry which is highly capital-intensive, such as a port authority, will tend to have a larger profit

---

[3]The term *surplus* is used here. Other terms include *change in net assets* and *excess of revenue over expenses.*
[4]Of course, many nonprofits that have commodity-like services are unable to earn a surplus on operations. They rely on contributions to compensate for a deficit on operations.

margins; its sales volume tends to be much lower relative to assets than, say, a museum.

A second profitability ratio is *return on assets*.

$$\text{Return on assets} = \frac{\text{Surplus}}{\text{Total assets}}$$

Since depreciation recognizes the expense associated with the using up of an asset, it is based on the historical cost of the asset, and in no way compensates for the effects of inflation. Although there are a variety of other factors to consider with respect to the replacement of assets, the return-on-assets ratio provides at least a rudimentary indication of whether an organization—nonprofit or for profit—is earning a sufficiently large excess of revenues over expenses to maintain itself in a steady state. Accordingly, one would hope to see a return-on-assets ratio that is at least as high as the rate of inflation in an organization's service area.

The final profitability measure is *return on equity*.

$$\text{Return on equity} = \frac{\text{Surplus}}{\text{Total equity}}$$

This ratio, generally abbreviated as ROE (or sometimes ROI, for return on investment), is perhaps the most commonly used indicator of profitability. In the for-profit world, it allows investors or potential investors to compare the earnings on their investment in one organization with a variety of alternative uses (e.g., savings certificates, treasury notes) of the investment funds. It is of less value in the nonprofit world.

Liquidity Ratios

As the name implies, liquidity ratios measure the extent to which an organization has an ability to convert its noncash assets into cash (i.e., to "liquidate" its assets). Liquidity ratios generally are computed with some portion of an organization's current assets, occasionally comparing them with its current liabilities. Recall that current assets are those assets that will be, or have a reasonable expectation to be, converted into cash within a year; current liabilities are those obligations that must be paid within a year. Consequently, the most commonly used liquidity ratio is the *current ratio*.

$$\text{Current ratio} = \frac{\text{Current assets}}{\text{Current liabilities}}$$

Although many considerations govern the appropriate size of this ratio for any given company, and there tend to be wide variations across industries, a figure of 2.0 often is used as an appropriate level. That is, current assets should be roughly twice as large as current liabilities.

A variety of other liquidity ratios can be computed to measure some portion of the current ratio. The most frequently used is the *quick ratio* (sometimes called the *acid-test ratio*).

$$\text{Quick ratio} = \frac{\text{Cash} + \text{Marketable securities} + \text{Net accounts receivable}}{\text{Current liabilities}}$$

The purpose of the quick ratio is to eliminate those current assets that, for one reason or another, may *not* be readily or fully convertible into cash. In particular, the quick ratio excludes inventory and prepaid expenses. If a quick ratio is below 1.0, it suggests that the organization may encounter some difficulties in meeting its current liabilities when they come due.

Although included in both the current and quick ratios, accounts receivable frequently can be a somewhat questionable asset. Both ratios attempt to compensate for this uncertainty by using a *net* accounts receivable figure (i.e., gross accounts receivable less the allowance for doubtful accounts). Nevertheless, more detail on accounts receivable frequently is helpful. A third liquidity ratio, *average days receivable,* allows us to make an assessment of how quickly, on average, an organization is collecting its accounts receivable.

$$\text{Average days receivable} = \frac{\text{Net accounts receivable}}{(\text{Revenue} \div 365)}$$

The denominator of this ratio gives us the average revenue earned per day (ideally, using credit sales only). When this figure is divided into net accounts receivable, we have an estimate of the average number of days of revenue that are included in the net accounts receivable figure. This gives us a rough estimate of the average number days needed to collect an account receivable. This figure can be compared with the organization's payment policies to determine how well clients (or third parties on behalf of clients), on average, are abiding by the organization's payment expectations.

A final liquidity ratio is one that is comparable to the average days receivable ratio: *average days inventory.*

$$\text{Average days inventory} = \frac{\text{Inventory}}{(\text{Cost of goods sold} \div 365)}$$

As with revenue in the average-days-receivable ratio, cost of goods sold, when divided by 365 gives the average cost of goods sold per day. When this is divided into inventory, the result is the average number of days that inventory remains on hand before being sold.

Most nonprofit organizations do not sell their inventory. Rather, they use up an inventory of supplies (e.g., office supplies) in order to conduct their business. In these cases, there will be no cost-of-goods-sold figure. When this happens, total expenses (or, better yet, total expenses less salaries and depreciation) can be used in place of cost of goods sold. Although some precision is lost, such a ratio, when used in a comparative way over several years, may help to reveal potential weaknesses in inventory management.

Asset Management Ratios

The average-days-receivable and average-days-inventory ratios lie at the intersection of liquidity and asset management, since they have aspects of each included in them. Asset management ratios help us to assess how effectively an organization is using its assets (which include accounts receivable and inventory). In addition to average days receivable and average days inventory, a commonly used asset management ratio is *asset turnover.*

$$\text{Asset turnover} = \frac{\text{Revenue}}{\text{Total assets}}$$

This ratio allows us to determine how many dollars of revenue the organization has earned for each dollar it has invested in assets. Organizations that have an asset base consisting largely of accounts receivable and inventory would be expected to have a relatively high asset turnover; that is, each item in the asset base is used up and replaced many times a year, and revenue is earned each time an inventory item is sold and a new accounts receivable is created. By contrast, organizations with a high proportion of fixed assets, such as plant and equipment, generally would have a low asset turnover, since it takes several years for a fixed asset to be used up (via depreciation) and replaced.

If an organization is fairly capital intensive, such as a hospital, a university, or a port authority, a modified ratio may shed more light on the quality of its asset management; this is the *fixed-asset turnover ratio.*

$$\text{Fixed-asset turnover} = \frac{\text{Revenue}}{\text{Net fixed assets}}$$

In a rough sense, this ratio permits us to assess the relative productivity of new plant and equipment, compared to plant and equipment assets that are highly depreciated. One would expect that, as assets depreciated (and, hence, *net* fixed assets fell), the ability of those assets to earn revenue also would fall. The magnitude of this fall can be assessed by use of this ratio. A comparison might be made to the organization's past performance (when the assets were newer), for example, or to other organizations with relatively new assets.

Long-Term Solvency Ratios

Long-term solvency ratios provide an indication of the way an organization has financed its assets over the long term (i.e., for the period extending beyond one year). Generally, two issues are of concern here. The first is the balance between debt and equity financing. The former consists of loans, mortgages, bonds, and similar debt instruments; the latter of contributions and retained earnings. The second is the ability of the organization to meet its debt obligations.

In looking at the balance between debt and equity, the most commonly used ratio is the *debt/equity ratio.*

$$\text{Debt/Equity} = \frac{\text{Total liabilities}}{\text{Equity}}$$

The higher this ratio, the greater the organization's "leverage," that is, the greater the extent to which it has utilized external funds (debt) to supplement its internal funds (equity).

Several other measures of leverage exist also. One of the most common is obtained by dividing total assets by equity.

$$\text{Leverage} = \frac{\text{Total assets}}{\text{Equity}}$$

Effectively, this ratio is the same as the debt/equity ratio plus one.[5]

Because of the need to make both short- and long-term assessments, analysts frequently distinguish between short- and long-term debt (i.e., between current and long-term liabilities). This gives rise to a modified—and more frequently used—version of the debt/equity ratio: the *long-term debt/equity ratio.*

$$\text{Long-term debt/equity} = \frac{\text{Noncurrent liabilities}}{\text{Equity}}$$

Looked at over time, this ratio can reveal the extent to which an organization is relying increasingly on long-term debt to finance asset acquisition.

As indicated above, debt—either long- or short-term—gives rise to a debt service obligation (i.e., the payment of both principal and interest). An organization's ability to meet its debt service obligation in a timely way can be measured by a ratio called *debt service coverage.*

$$\text{Debt service coverage} = \frac{\text{Surplus} + \text{Depreciation} + \text{Interest payments}}{\text{Principal payments} + \text{Interest payments}}$$

The numerator of this ratio is a rough estimate of the cash available to meet debt service obligations; the denominator is the debt service obligation itself. Depreciation is included in the numerator because it is a noncash expense (i.e., for the same reason we add it back to surplus when preparing the SCF). Interest payments are included because we want to determine the funds available to meet principal *and* interest payments, and surplus measures the funds left *after* interest payments have been made; therefore, we must add interest

---

[5]This is true by virtue of the fundamental accounting identity: Assets = Liabilities + Equity. If A = L + E, then A/E = L/E + E/E, or A/E = L/E + 1, that is, assets/equity is debt/equity plus one.

payments back. Thus, the ratio provides some indication of the extent to which the debt service obligation is "covered" by available cash, subject, of course, to the caveat that not all of surplus is available in the form of cash.

Since principal payment amounts frequently are not known to individuals outside an organization (although they usually can be found on the SCF), a surrogate ratio, called *times-interest-earned,* occasionally is used by outside analysts in lieu of debt service coverage.

$$\text{Times-interest-earned} = \frac{\text{Surplus} + \text{Interest payments}}{\text{Interest payments}}$$

Since it does not include the principal payments on the debt, this ratio can be a misleading measure of an organization's ability to meet its debt service obligations. To illustrate this phenomenon, consider the following situation:

Surplus (S)	$20
Depreciation (D)	5
Interest (I)	2
Principal payment (P)	8

Under these circumstances, the organization's debt service coverage ratio is 2.7:

$$\frac{S + D + I}{P + I} = \frac{27}{10} = 2.7$$

Its times-interest-earned ratio, by contrast, is 11.0:

$$\frac{S + I}{I} = \frac{22}{2} = 11.0$$

Thus, while the organization has earned enough cash to cover its interest payment 11 times, it can only cover its *debt service* obligation about 3 times. Since *all* debt service payments must be made (not just interest), this discrepancy can be of some concern.

From a cash management perspective, we are most interested in debt service coverage. Yet unless we have information on principal payments (which frequently we do not), we cannot calculate the debt-service-coverage ratio. However, as the above example suggests, to calculate only the times-interest-earned ratio could give a misleading sense of comfort about the organization's ability to meet its debt service obligations.

Even when the debt-service ratio is used, we must bear in mind that most organizations have many more cash obligations than debt service. It therefore is extremely important that the debt-service-coverage ratio (or the times-interest-earned ratio) be analyzed in the context of other related ratios, most notably those relating to liquidity.

As indicated previously, there are many other ratios that could be calculated. For completeness, several of these are discussed below. Interested readers can find more information on ratio calculations and ratio analysis in books dedicated specifically to that topic.[6]

$$\text{Gross margin percentage} = \frac{\text{Gross margin}}{\text{Sales revenues}}$$

This is a variation on profit margin, looking only at sales revenue and only at gross margin (i.e. sales revenue minus cost of goods sold). It is a measure of profitability before the inclusion of operating expenses, sales and administrative expenses, interest, and taxes.

$$\frac{\text{Earnings per}}{\text{share}} = \frac{\text{Surplus–Dividends to preferred shareholders}}{\text{Average shares of common stock outstanding for the year}}$$

$$\text{Price-earnings ratio} = \frac{\text{Average market price of common stock}}{\text{Earnings per share}}$$

Earnings-per-share computations are required on the operating statements of all publicly traded for-profit companies. The price-earnings ratio is used frequently by the investment community to judge whether a stock price is appropriate considering a company's earnings. Neither of these is appropriate for a nonprofit organization.

$$\text{Return on permanent capital} = \frac{\text{Surplus + interest + taxes}}{\text{Equity + noncurrent liabilities}}$$

This ratio is a variation on return on equity. It, like return on equity, sometimes is called ROI. Recall that permanent capital is defined as equity plus long-term debt (or noncurrent liabilities). Therefore, this ratio measures the earnings on all sources of long-term financing (debt and equity). It also does so before taxes and interest are deducted. Interest is added back since we are interested in the return on debt capital as well as equity capital. Therefore, we must include the earnings before the interest payment (i.e., the cost of the debt capital). For for-profit organizations, adding back taxes allows us to look at how well the company performed despite its particular tax situation.

The numerator of this ratio frequently is called earnings before interest and taxes, or *EBIT,* and EBIT is used quite frequently in finance and by the investment community.

$$\text{EBIT margin} = \frac{\text{EBIT}}{\text{Sales revenues}}$$

This is another variation on profit margin, using EBIT instead of surplus. Again, however, its use for nonprofit organizations is limited.

---

[6]One of the most popular books is Erich A. Helfert, *Techniques of Financial Analysis: A Guide to Value Creation* (Burr Ridge, IL: McGraw-Hill Higher Education, 1999).

EXHIBIT A–1
Summary of Ratio Computations

Profitability Ratios

$$\text{Profit margin} = \frac{\text{Surplus}}{\text{Operating revenues}}$$

$$\text{Return on assets} = \frac{\text{Surplus}}{\text{Total assets}}$$

$$\text{Return on equity} = \frac{\text{Surplus}}{\text{Equity}}$$

Liquidity Ratios

$$\text{Current ratio} = \frac{\text{Current assets}}{\text{Current liabilities}}$$

$$\text{Quick ratio} = \frac{\text{Cash} + \text{Marketable securities} + \text{Net accounts receivable}}{\text{Current liabilities}}$$

$$\text{Average days receivable} = \frac{\text{Net accounts receivable}}{\text{Revenue} \div 365}$$

$$\text{Average days inventory} = \frac{\text{Inventory}}{\text{Cost of goods sold} \div 365}$$

Asset Management Ratios

$$\text{Asset turnover} = \frac{\text{Revenue}}{\text{Total assets}}$$

$$\text{Fixed-asset turnover} = \frac{\text{Revenue}}{\text{Net fixed assets}}$$

Long-Term Solvency Ratios

$$\text{Debt/Equity} = \frac{\text{Total liabilities}}{\text{Equity}}$$

$$\text{Leverage} = \frac{\text{Total assets}}{\text{Equity}}$$

$$\text{Long-term debt/equity} = \frac{\text{Noncurrent liabilities}}{\text{Equity}}$$

$$\text{Debt-service coverage} = \frac{\text{Surplus} + \text{Depreciation} + \text{Interest payments}}{\text{Principal payments} + \text{Interest payments}}$$

$$\text{Times-interest-earned} = \frac{\text{Surplus} + \text{Interest payments}}{\text{Interest payments}}$$

A Disclaimer

There is no general agreement that the four categories of ratios discussed in this chapter are the most appropriate ones. In addition, some writers and analysts would classify some of the ratios into categories differently than is done here. Still others would calculate the ratios themselves somewhat differently. They would use different numerators or denominators, for example, or they would use averages rather than ending amounts for balance sheet items.

You should be aware of these different approaches to ratio analysis. But, more importantly, you should not lose sight of the fundamental thrust of ratio analysis. Its purpose is not to arrive at the right ratio or the right classification of a ratio. Rather, the purpose is to help us analyze a set of financial statements so that we can understand how an organization is being managed financially. In this regard, the goal is to see what sort of story a *set* of ratios tells about the company. In general, greater precision in calculating certain ratios or a reclassification of some of the ratios into different categories will not change that story much, if at all. We thus must beware of the trap that many analysts fall into of worrying about the precision of specific ratio calculations and classifications rather than the overall story itself.

Suggested Additional Readings

Finkler, Steven A. *Financial Management for Public Health, and Not-for-Profit Organizations.* Englewood Cliffs, NJ: Prentice Hall, 2000.

Granof, Michael H. *Government and Not-for-Profit Accounting: Concepts and Practices.* New York: John Wiley & Sons, 2000.

Randall, Adrian, and Paul Palmer. *Financial Management in the Voluntary Sector: An Introduction.* New York: Routledge, 2001.

http://www.mapnp.org/library. Contains a basic guide to nonprofit financial management.

Practice Case

Energy Associates (A)*

Energy Associates (EA) was a nonprofit agency that purchased energy-saving devices in bulk, repackaged them, and sold them to low-income consumers. Its products consisted of shower nozzles that restrict the flow of water, thermostats with timers, and storm windows.

Exhibit 1 contains the agency's balance sheets as of December 31, 1997 and 1998, and its operating statement for 1998.

*This case was prepared by Professor David W. Young. Copyright © by David W. Young.

EXHIBIT 1

ENERGY ASSOCIATES (A)
Comparative Balance Sheets
As of December 31 of Each Year

	1997	1998
Assets		
Cash	$ 19,000	$ 30,000
Accounts receivable	24,000	15,000
Inventory	31,000	59,000
Total current	$ 74,000	$104,000
Plant and equipment	$ 48,000	$ 72,000
Accumulated depreciation	(12,000)	(24,000)
Land	20,000	20,000
Total	$130,000	$172,000
Liabilities and Equity		
Accounts payable	$ 16,000	$ 20,000
Notes payable (short-term)	7,000	0
Total current	$ 23,000	$ 20,000
Bonds payable	$ 0	$ 20,000
Net assets (equity)	107,000	132,000
Total	$130,000	$172,000

Operating Statement
For the Year Ended December 31, 1998

Revenues		$200,000
Less: Cost of goods sold		130,000
Gross margin		$ 70,000
Other expenses:		
Administrative and general salaries	$ 17,000	
Depreciation	12,000	
Other (all cash)	14,100	43,100
Surplus from operations		$ 26,900
Interest expense		1,900
Change in net assets		$ 25,000

Questions

1. Prepare a statement of cash flows (SCF) for the year ending December 31, 1998. Use both the direct and indirect methods.

2. Calculate all relevant ratios for EA.[†]

3. What do the SCF and the ratios tell you about EA that you couldn't learn from the other financial statements or that you didn't already know?

4. What additional information would you like to have about EA to better analyze their financial statements?

Case 4–1

Coolidge Corner Theatre Foundation[*]

I'm confused. I just got this memo in the mail [Exhibit 1], and the spreadsheet wasn't attached. I tried to contact the treasurer but I can't reach her. Will you please see what you can do with the information in the memo's text to prepare the spreadsheet for me. I'll need it in a couple of hours since I need to leave for the meeting then.

Lynda McGahan, a member of the board of The Coolidge Corner Theatre Foundation, was speaking to Max Bessenov, her recently hired executive assistant—an MBA with knowledge of nonprofit organizations. She continued:

The memo suggests that we need a pretty sizable surplus, yet the Coolidge is a nonprofit organization. Whether you call it a surplus or a profit, the result is the same, an excess of revenue over expenses. Yet, it seems to me that as a nonprofit organization, the Coolidge should not be earning a surplus. I'm not sure I buy any of the arguments given in the memo, so I'd like your views on those too.

With that, Mr. Bessenov set out to see what he could do.

Background

The Coolidge Corner Theatre was a greater-Boston icon. Located in Brookline, a suburb just outside of Boston, the Coolidge was the last surviving art deco movie house in the area, and was considered a landmark. The Coolidge Corner Theatre Foundation had been incorporated as a nonprofit organization in 1988 to operate the theatre. It's mission was to promote public interest in

---

[†]Try to set up a spreadsheet to calculate the ratios. Set it up to be as "formula driven" as possible (i.e., in such a way that you need to enter as few items as possible from the financial statements). Then use the spreadsheet for other cases when you need to calculate ratios. If you set up the spreadsheet correctly, you should be able to calculate ratios for the next organization you analyze by copying the EA file and entering the numbers from the new set of financial statements. All relevant ratios then should be calculated automatically by the spreadsheet formulas.

[*]This case was prepared by Professor David W. Young. Copyright © by David W. Young.

film and to operate the theatre as a multifunctional community cultural center to promote the performing arts.

Over the several decades prior to the late 1990s, the Theatre had lapsed into a state of disrepair and the foundation has incurred several operating deficits. In early 1999, the board had hired a new director, Joe Zina, whose job was to breathe new life into the Theatre and return the foundation to a viable entity. According to a local newspaper, the *Brookline Tab,* Zina was "the man who can lead the venerable cinema into the 21st century."

Mr. Zina began with some basic improvements: painting walls, replacing carpets, and renovating the concession stands. He also began to raise funds for some of the larger projects that were needed in the restoration effort: bathroom renovations, electric and lighting upgrades, ceiling repairing and repainting, handrail replacement, aisle lighting installation, new heating and air conditioning, life/safety system upgrades, and a host of others.

Within two years, Mr. Zina had raised close to $200,000 in grants and contributions to support the renovations. He also had turned the Theatre's deficit operations into profitable ones.

The question that he knew the board now needed to address was how to sustain the theatre once the contributions abated. He had raised the issue at a meeting of the board's executive committee, and the board's treasurer has volunteered to take on the task. The result was the memo contained in Exhibit 1.

Questions

1. Prepare a spreadsheet that addresses the issues discussed in Exhibit 1. Is the figure of $25,740 for a cash surplus correct? If not, what should it be?

2. What are your reactions to the other three requirements discussed in the memo? Is the treasurer's reasoning correct? If not, how would you modify her recommendations?

3. How much cash should the Coolidge maintain in its cash reserve account?

4. What important issues, if any, has the treasurer failed to address?

EXHIBIT 1
Coolidge Corner
Theatre Foundation:
Memorandum

To: Members of the Coolidge Board
From: The Treasurer
Subject: Proposed Policy for Operating Surpluses

At yesterday's Executive Committee meeting, I agreed to draft a proposal on how we might best deal with our cash reserves and operating surpluses. What follows is a first cut at a policy. This should be treated as a draft for discussion purposes, and it is subject to change. Following the discussion at the next board meeting, I will prepare something more formal for a vote at the December 2001 or January 2002 meeting. Of importance, I am only

EXHIBIT 1
(Continued)

addressing here the funds associated with operations. Restricted donations or other contributions that are for capital projects are a separate (although somewhat related) matter.

With regard to operations, cash reserves and the operating surplus are rather tightly linked. That is, without a surplus it is very difficult for an organization like the Coolidge to generate operating cash reserves. Most of our revenue is in the form of cash as are most of our expenses. Thus, to generate cash, we must have an excess of revenue over expenses.

The accounting and financial management literature on nonprofit organizations is in considerable agreement that organizations like ours need adequate financial surpluses for four reasons:*

1. Assist the organization to obtain the funds necessary to replace assets that wear out or become obsolete.

2. Finance the cash needs associated with a growth in revenues in conjunction with its charitable or nonprofit purposes.

3. Provide the organization with the funds necessary to expand and diversify its fixed assets as it expands its charitable activities.

4. Protect the organization from fluctuations in revenues from year to year, and from general economic and other uncertainties surrounding its ongoing operations.

In short, the question is not *whether* we should have an operating surplus, but rather what amount is *reasonable*. This question can be addressed from the perspective of each of the above four requirements.

Requirement #1. Fixed Asset Replacement

The surplus requirements associated with replacing fixed assets (principally plant and equipment) arise because, at some point, these assets wear out or become technologically obsolete. Because of inflation, their replacement cost usually is more than their initial cost.

Some have argued that sufficient funds would be available for fixed asset replacement if their depreciation were "funded," i.e., if an equivalent amount of cash were sequestered each year in a special fund dedicated to fixed asset replacement. However, funded depreciation would be sufficient only if there were no inflation. In an inflationary economy, the inflation base is the asset's purchase price, whereas the earnings on the funded depreciation come from a base that is only a fraction of the asset's purchase price.

At present, we do not fund depreciation. For this reason, our operating (or income) statement each year, which is prepared on an accrual basis and includes depreciation, will, other things being equal, show a smaller surplus than our budget report shows. Happily, depreciation is not a cash expense, so, from a cash perspective, our cash balance will increase each year by an amount that is virtually the same as the surplus on our budget

*Regina E. Herzlinger and Denise Nitterhouse, *Financial Accounting and Managerial Control for Nonprofit Organizations* (Cincinnati: South-Western Publishing Co., 1994), p. 152. See also Mary T. Ziebell and Don T. DeCoster, *Management Control Systems in Nonprofit Organizations* (San Diego: Harcourt Brace Jovanovich, 1991), and David W. Young. "Nonprofits Need Surplus Too," *Harvard Business Review,* January–February 1982.

EXHIBIT 1
(Continued)

report. Regardless of these accounting machinations, if we are to be conservative about asset replacement, we must put some cash into an "asset replacement fund" each year.

How Much Cash? To determine our required cash surplus in light of Requirement #1, we must look at it in comparison to our fixed assets and the earnings we can achieve on the resulting fund. if we do not use our cash surplus to create an asset replacement fund, our only other options are capital campaigns, donations, or debt. Capital campaigns are infrequent, donations of the magnitude necessary to replace fixed assets are rare, and debt probably is imprudent.

As of 31 October 2000, our leasehold improvements and equipment assets had an acquisition cost totaling about $200,000. Let's assume that their replacement cost is inflating at about 5 percent a year Let's also assume that we can earn 5 percent on the funds we invest in our asset replacement fund.

The result of these assumptions, combined with a $200,000 beginning value of assets (for simplicity, I assumed they all were purchased in year 1), is contained in the attached exhibit. As it indicates, those assets would require $210,000 to replace at the end of year 1. With continued inflation at the 5 percent rate, they would cost $325,779 to replace at the end of year 10. By funding the annual depreciation of $20,000 ($200,000 ÷ 10 years) on these assets, and with annual earnings on the fund of 5 percent, we would need an *accrued* surplus of $5,740 to have the funds on hand to replace the assets at the end of year 10. In other words, our cash surplus (which is what our budget report shows) would need to be $25,740. Thus, the projected budget surplus for FY2002 of $25,586 is just about right on a steady state basis (assuming no more than $200,000 in fixed assets).

These percentages are a bit high in light of the current rate of inflation and the rates of interest we can earn on our funds. However, on an ongoing basis, we can adjust the percentages each year to reflect our best guess of what they will be like in the upcoming year, and we can couple those adjustments with our actual cash surpluses in prior years to determine the amount of surplus we need to earn in any given budget year. (In this spreadsheet, the funded surplus is the "plug figure" to make the numbers work.)

Requirement #2. Cash Needs Associated with Growth

When an organization is both growing and selling its goods and services on credit—a common situation for many nonprofit organizations—this requirement translates into a need to have sufficient cash on hand to meet financial obligations. That is, nonprofit organizations that are expanding their operations and that have cash tied up in accounts receivable and inventory must earn surpluses to finance the cash needs associated with their growth. This is not a problem that we have at the Coolidge, since almost all of what we do is on a cash or near-cash basis. Thus, no surplus is needed for this purpose.

Requirement #3. Expand and Diversify Fixed Assets

In general, we are using grants and the capital campaign for these purposes. Once we have the theatre where we want it to be as far as fixed

EXHIBIT 1
(Continued)

assets are concerned, we will need to rely on our surpluses for asset replacement. This is not to suggest that we should cease seeking grants or large donations for purposes of replacing some assets, but only that our surplus gives us greater certainty that we will have the funds when we need them.

Requirement #4. Provide for Economic Uncertainties

In general, the surplus needed for meeting Requirement #4 involves an analysis of an organization's financial history, including the stability of its prices and its mixture of operating surpluses and deficits over time. The presence of wide swings in prices for an organization's goods or services, for example, or the occasional occurrence of an operating deficit, usually indicates that a surplus is necessary whenever feasible. These surpluses, in turn, can help to fund any future deficits.

We are in the fortunate position of having had three years of surpluses in a row. This looks to be a sustainable position, but one never knows. Thus, it seems to me that we need to think about this requirement in terms of how many days of cash we should have on hand at all times.

Some large nonprofits that I know of attempt to have about three months of cash on hand. I'm not sure we need that much since our risk of revenue shortfalls is pretty low (lots of small-ticket sales to a population that is pretty consistent in its movie-going behavior). Nevertheless, it seems to me that we need to have enough cash on hand to allow us to weather any unanticipated revenue shortfalls. if such shortfalls occurred, we would need to curtail expenses quickly, but we would not be able to do so overnight.

My guess is that one month of cash would be sufficient, but to be on the safe side, I would suggest that we have two months on hand. Since our budgeted expenses for FY2002 are about $1.2 million, or about $100,000 a month, we therefore should have $200,000 of cash on hand. Most of this cash can be kept in reasonably liquid, low-risk funds, where we can get as much interest as possible consistent with our liquidity requirements.

Summary

Once the board has reached agreement on a set of general principles we can get more specific about the amounts involved. However, overall, here is the approach I would suggest, along with some approximate amounts:

1. We should use our surpluses each year to build our cash reserve to a level of $200,000. We already have most of this in place, so we only need to grow the reserve by the difference. This should be invested conservatively in a liquid fund with no more than $100,000 in a single checking account.

2. Once the cash reserve has reached $200,000, we should use our surpluses to build an asset replacement reserve. We do not need to do this immediately, since we have the capital campaign underway and most of what we do in terms of fixed assets will be covered by it and other contributions. While this reserve also should be invested conservatively, we do not have the liquidity needs with it that we have with our cash reserves. Thus, it can be invested in less liquid (and presumably higher interest earning) instruments.

3. The asset replacement reserve should grow indefinitely, although each year we likely will use a portion of it to fund asset replacements (or even asset expansion if no external funds are available). In effect, this fund will become the major source of financing for our capital budget, and perhaps the *only* source at some point in the future. Each year, we will prepare a capital budget based on a combination of the amount available in this fund and our anticipated needs.

4. Once the cash reserve has reached $200,000, we should budget for a cash surplus of at least $26,000 a year for the next 10 years (i.e., the amount needed to cover the effects of inflation on our fixed assets). Additionally, once our new fixed assets are in place, we will need to set a slightly higher surplus target to cover the higher level of assets needing replacement. Finally, as our fixed assets grow over time, we will need to earn greater and greater cash surpluses. As the spreadsheet indicates, beginning with a base of $200,000 in fixed assets, we would need to increase our cash surplus from $25,767 in years 1–10 to $41,933 in years 11–20 simply to provide for the effects of inflation.

I look forward to discussing these issues with you at the next board meeting.

Case 4–2

Gotham Meals on Wheels*

"We're a success!" exclaimed Ethan McCall, executive director of Gotham Meals on Wheels, upon seeing that his March surplus had reached $2,000. "And if our projections for the next six months are accurate, we'll have earned enough to rent facilities in Newburytown and double our service area. My only concern is whether we'll have the cash on hand to do so."

With that, Mr. McCall set about predicting how his cash would change in accordance with his projected growth in volume of activity. Although March had been a good month, cash had been falling since December, and he was concerned about making sure he had enough on hand to purchase supplies and meet payroll for the remainder of the year.

Background

Gotham Meals on Wheels was a nonprofit agency that specialized in preparing and delivering nutritious yet appetizing meals to home-bound people. Its clientele included many elderly individuals plus victims of AIDS who, because of the debilitating nature of their disease, were unable to leave their homes, and did not have enough strength to prepare their own meals. Convinced that there was a large market for a specialized meal service, and

*This case was prepared by Professor David W. Young. Copyright © by David W. Young.

supported by a $25,000 grant from a local foundation, the agency had begun operations in early October.

In order to assure that it wouldn't run short during any given month, the agency prepared its meals one month in advance and froze them. By basing production on the following month's anticipated sales, the agency had found that it could assure its clients of uninterrupted service. All the costs associated with these meals were paid in the month in which production took place.

Another advantage of freezing the meals was that they could be delivered in bulk to each client. The meals were easily stored in the freezing compartments of clients' refrigerators. From the agency's perspective, freezing the meals and delivering several of them at a time had allowed it to keep its transportation costs at a minimum. Clients seemed to have no complaints about the food being frozen, and many, in fact, had written Mr. McCall to tell him how much they enjoyed the meals.

Sales Results

November sales had been 325 meals, and December sales had been 450 meals. Mr. McCall had expected that 500 meals would be sold in January, and that sales would increase by 250 meals per month after that through the end of the year. Thus, by May, sales would be 1,500 meals, and by September they would reach 2,500 meals. His exuberance expressed in the first paragraph was because sales for January through March had been on target, and 1,250 meals had been produced and frozen for delivery in April.

Because of the relatively low volume of sales, the first two months had been somewhat difficult, and the agency had run small deficits in both October and November. But in December it had earned a surplus that was enough to erase the October and November deficits. The balance sheet as of December 31 is shown in Exhibit 1.

EXHIBIT 1

GOTHAM MEALS ON WHEELS			
Balance Sheet			
As of December 31			
Assets		**Liabilities and Equity**	
Cash..............	$12,975	Contributed capital	$25,000
Accounts receivable ...	8,525	Retained surpluses	0
Inventory	3,500		
Total assets.........	$25,000	Total liabilities and equity...	$25,000

Financial Data

The ingredients and labor needed to produce each meal cost the agency $7.00. In addition, the agency incurred some monthly administrative costs, such as rent, that were not directly associated with the meals. These costs had grown from only $300 in October, when Mr. McCall had used his own home to produce and freeze the November meals, to $1,400 in November and December, and $1,600 in January. In February and March, they had reached $2,000, and were expected to remain at that level for the rest of the year. These monthly costs were incurred whether the agency sold any meals at all, whereas the $7.00 per meal was incurred only when meals actually were sold. The meals were sold at a price of $11.00 each.

Because many of the agency's clients were on limited incomes, Mr. McCall did not insist upon immediate payment. Instead, he billed the clients monthly. Because of some office inefficiencies the bills usually were not sent out until a month after the meals had been delivered, and most clients took a full month to pay their bills. So, for example, bills for January meals actually were sent in February, and payment was not received until March. All clients were extremely conscientious about paying on time, however, and none exceeded the 30-day time limit for payment.

Questions

1. What problems, if any, does Gotham Meals on Wheels have? Please be as specific as you can, clearly identifying the *cause(s)* of any problems you identify. To do so, you should do the following:[*]

   a. Reconcile Equity, Accounts Receivable, and Inventory for each month, beginning in November, and, for each account, using the basic formula:

   $$BB$$
   $$+ \text{Additions}$$
   $$- \text{Reductions}$$
   $$= EB$$

   b. Prepare actual balance sheets and operating statements for November through March, and pro forma balance sheets and operating statements for April through September. Remember that, because of the matching principle, cost of goods sold is recognized as an expense only when the meals actually are sold, not when they are produced.

   c. Prepare actual statements of cash flows (SCFs) for January through March, and pro forma SCFs for April through September.

2. What advice would you give Mr. McCall?

[*]In doing so, try to set up a spreadsheet containing the balance sheet, the operating statement, and the statement of cash flows in such a way that they are all interconnected. That is, try to make the spreadsheet as "formula driven" as possible.

Case 4–3

Brookstone Ob-Gyn Associates[*]

In mid-July 2001, Dr. Mark Amsted, chair of the department of obstetrics and gynecology at Brookstone Medical School, chief of Ob-Gyn at Brookstone Medical Center, and president of Brookstone Ob-Gyn Associates (BOGA), was concerned about his upcoming meeting with the Harris National Bank. He planned to present a request for an increase in BOGA's line of credit. As had happened in the past, the bank's approval of his request was critical to BOGA's continued operations. Although the dean of the medical school had approved his request to approach the bank, Dr. Amsted was uncertain about the bank's reaction.

In conjunction with Dr. Amsted's January request for a $300,000 line of credit, the bank had asked him to prepare some projections for the 2001 operating year. He had done this, indicating that he expected 2001 revenue to be 30 percent greater than 2000 revenue. After switching to an accrual system of accounting, Dr. Amsted had been pleased to learn that 2000 had been a profitable year for the group. His projections indicated that 2001 also would be profitable.

Problems

Despite the growth in revenues and the group's profitability, BOGA's cash flow was once again becoming an issue. Indeed, as he began to prepare for the meeting with the bank, Dr. Amsted realized that he faced two problems related to BOGA's cash flows. He commented:

> In January, I established a $300,000 line of credit with the Harris Bank. We expected to have some cash flow difficulties, and I thought this would help us cope with them until our cash caught up with our profitability. Now I'm not sure $300,000 is enough!
>
> There's a related problem, too. Until 2000, we kept our financial records on what the accountants called a modified cash basis. That was pretty simple. Revenues were recorded when we received a cash payment from a patient or third-party payer. Expenses were recorded when the cash was paid out. The only exception was plant and equipment purchases, where the accountants said we needed to use depreciation instead of cash as the expense.
>
> When I applied to the Harris Bank for the line of credit, Ms. Tanshel [the bank's loan officer] told me that a modified cash basis was not an acceptable way to present our financial statements. The bank required us to submit our statements on an accrual basis. According to our accountants, the most significant change needed to satisfy the bank's requirement was to record revenue when a patient received services, rather than when we actually received the related cash payment.

---

*This case was prepared by Professor David W. Young. Copyright © by David W. Young.

EXHIBIT 1

	BROOKSTONE OB/GYN ASSOCIATES						
	Operating Statements (Accrual Basis)						
	($000)						

	2001 Projected	2001 Actual					
		January	February	March	April	May	June
Revenue:							
Professional services..............	$8,252.3	$678.2	$693.1	$704.9	$719.0	$732.7	$748.8
Less: allowances and bad debts ..	1,650.5	135.6	138.6	141.0	143.8	146.5	149.8
Net revenue	$6,601.8	$542.6	$554.5	$563.9	$575.2	$586.1	$599.0
Expenses:							
Physician payments..............	$1,573.6	$110.2	$113.3	$118.0	$122.7	$125.9	$130.6
Administrative salaries	820.8	57.5	61.6	61.6	65.7	65.7	73.9
Benefits..........................	396.8	27.8	28.8	29.8	31.1	31.7	33.5
Medical supplies	123.8	10.2	10.4	10.6	10.8	11.0	11.2
Rent and utilities.................	523.2	43.6	43.6	43.6	43.6	43.6	43.6
Billing/collection fees	660.2	54.3	55.5	56.4	57.5	58.6	59.9
Equipment depreciation	29.7	2.0	2.0	2.0	2.4	2.4	2.4
Office expense...................	60.0	5.0	5.0	5.0	5.0	5.0	5.0
Liability insurance................	1,237.8	101.7	104.0	105.7	107.9	109.9	112.3
Contracted services	127.2	10.6	10.6	10.6	10.6	10.6	10.6
Other...........................	54.0	4.5	4.5	4.5	4.5	4.5	4.5
Contribution to Dean	726.2	59.7	61.0	62.0	63.3	64.5	65.9
Total expenses..................	$6,333.3	$486.9	$500.2	$509.8	$525.1	$533.4	$553.5
Surplus (Deficit)...................	$ 268.5	$ 55.6	$ 54.3	$ 54.2	$ 50.2	$ 52.8	$ 45.6

2001 Expectations

Exhibit 1 contains a projected operating statement for calendar year 2001 (prepared by Mr. Weber [BOGA's business manager] and Dr. Amsted in January 2001), and actual operating statements for each of the first six months of 2001. The projected operating statement confirmed Dr. Amsted's expectation that 2001 revenue would grow by 30 percent over the 2000 level. Exhibit 2 contains actual balance sheets as of the end of each month for the first six months of 2001.

As the exhibits show, Dr. Amsted expected that 2001 would add $268,500 to retained surpluses. These retained surpluses, plus the medical center's start-up contribution of $1 million, would give BOGA equity (or a fund balance) of some $3 million as of the end of 2001.

2001 Results

The first six months of 2001 had gone much better than expectations. In fact, Dr. Amsted had expected that the annual surplus in 2001 would be about 4 percent of net revenue, and the monthly surpluses had been averaging

EXHIBIT 2

	BROOKSTONE OB/GYN ASSOCIATES Balance Sheets (Accrual Basis) ($000)					
	2001 Actual					
	As of Jan. 31	As of Feb. 28	As of Mar. 31	As of Apr. 30	As of May 31	As of June 30
Assets						
Cash	$ 44.3	$ 0.0	$ 0.0	$ 0.0	$ 0.0	$ 0.0
Accounts receivable (net)	1,932.2	2,025.0	2,105.3	2,171.5	2,223.0	2,279.5
Medical supply inventory	135.0	145.0	155.0	165.0	167.0	170.0
Prepaid insurance	275.0	300.0	320.0	320.0	330.0	340.0
Total current assets	$2,386.5	$2,470.0	$2,580.3	$2,656.5	$2,720.0	$2,789.5
Equipment (net)	1,248.0	1,246.0	1,294.0	1,291.6	1,289.2	1,306.8
Total assets	$3,634.5	$3,716.0	$3,874.3	$3,948.1	$4,009.2	$4,096.3
Liabilities and Equity						
Bank loan (line of credit)	$ 0.0	$ 15.5	$ 139.2	$ 153.9	$ 155.2	$ 218.8
Accounts payable	76.5	78.0	79.6	81.2	82.7	84.4
Payable to Dean	141.2	151.4	160.3	167.5	173.2	179.4
Total current liabilities	$ 217.7	$ 244.9	$ 379.1	$ 402.7	$ 411.1	$ 482.5
Note payable	630.0	630.0	600.0	600.0	600.0	570.0
Fund balance						
Start-up contribution	1,000.0	1,000.0	1,000.0	1,000.0	1,000.0	1,000.0
Retained surpluses	1,786.7	1,841.1	1,895.2	1,945.4	1,998.2	2,043.8
Total liabilities + Fund balance	$3,634.5	$3,716.0	$3,874.3	$3,948.1	$4,009.2	$4,096.3

between 8 and 10 percent. Although the surpluses had fallen off slightly in April, May, and June, Dr. Amsted expected them to grow, along with revenue increases, during the second half of the year.

Surpluses were not the problem, however. In January, shortly after Dr. Amsted had arranged for the line of credit, BOGA's cash balance declined from $110,000 as of the end of 2000 to just over $44,000. In February, BOGA used up all of its cash, and drew down $15,500 of its line of credit. The trend had continued, and by the end of June the line of credit had reached some $219,000. These figures are shown in Exhibit 2. Dr. Amsted commented on them:

> If we had continued with the modified cash basis of accounting this wouldn't have happened. How can it be that we earn a surplus in each month of the year and run out of cash? It just doesn't compute. When we used the cash basis, my life was much simpler. If we had a surplus, we had cash in the bank. No surplus, no cash.

It was BOGA's problem with cash that had led Dr. Amsted to arrange for the meeting with Ms. Tanshel. Ms. Tanshel had readily agreed to meet, but she also had insisted that Dr. Amsted think about BOGA's future plans. In particular, she wanted to know if BOGA would need more than $300,000 in its line of credit and, if so, how much more it would need. She also asked Dr. Amsted to think about a repayment plan, since the bank usually required its customers to fully repay a line of credit at least once a year.

Review of the Financial Statements

To respond to Ms. Tanshel's request, Dr. Amsted met with Mr. Weber to review the current situation and project figures for the remainder of 2001. Despite the problems with cash, Dr. Amsted was optimistic. One reason was salaries. The number of physicians and administrative staff in the group had grown slightly during the first six months of 2001, and some physician compensation arrangements had changed slightly. These changes had caused some increases in salary expenses. Salaries had more or less stabilized as of June 30, however, and Dr. Amsted expected they would remain constant for the rest of the year despite the expected increases in revenue.

In reviewing the financial statements, Mr. Weber and Dr. Amsted saw nothing surprising. In March and June, they had made the quarterly payments of $30,000 on the long-term note payable. They also had made some planned equipment purchases of $50,000 in March and $20,000 in June; both of these were cash purchases. The payments on the note and the equipment purchases were reflected on the balance sheet. Dr. Amsted's plans called for a cash purchase of another $30,000 of equipment in September. Mr. Weber expected that all equipment items would have a 10-year economic life with no salvage value.

Dr. Amsted also knew that the group's medical supply inventory and prepaid insurance payments needed to grow with the increase in the number of patients and physicians. For example, with the greater volume of patients being seen, the group needed to have a larger supply of inventory on hand. Similarly, as new physicians joined the group, BOGA needed to make some advance premium payments to the insurance companies for malpractice coverage.

Dr. Amsted realized that the growth in BOGA's accounts receivable was a result of both the accrual system and patients' paying patterns. The average collection period for a bill was five months, which meant that as volume grew (as it had been doing), accounts receivable would need to grow also. In fact, he was pleased that the entire $1,831,200 in net accounts receivable owed as of December 31, 2000, had been collected by the end of May. (*Net* accounts receivable is the portion of billings that BOGA actually expected to collect from patients and third parties.)

A Lack of Cash

Despite all of this, the decline in cash was perplexing. One problem was that, although the average time necessary to collect an account receivable was approximately five months, almost all of BOGA's expenses had to be paid immediately. Dr. Amsted had asked some of his medical supply vendors to wait a bit longer for their payments, but most were insistent on 30-day terms. Since billings were growing, however, so were the expenses related to billings.

Because of this, accounts payable had been growing by about 2 percent a month for the first six months of 2001. Similarly, since BOGA's payment to the dean was based on cash collections, the account called *Payable to Dean* also was growing. Nevertheless, according to Mr. Weber, because this growth in the two payables accounts was so slow, there still was a strain on cash.

Dr. Amsted did not know how much larger the line of credit needed to be to cover BOGA's cash shortfalls in the next six months. Ms. Tanshel had indicated a reluctance to increase the ceiling above the current $300,000 level, but Dr. Amsted felt he could convince her to raise it if he presented her with a solid financial analysis. This meant he would need to give careful consideration to projecting the next six months of activity. As a first step in this effort, he asked Mr. Weber to address the behavior of each item on the financial statements. Mr. Weber reached the conclusions shown in Exhibit 3.

EXHIBIT 3   Projected Revenue, Expense, Asset, and Liability Behavior for July–December 2001

Revenue:
Professional services	Will grow at 2 percent a month for the rest of the year.
Allowances and bad debts	Will be 20 percent of revenue from professional services.

Expenses:
Physician payments	$141,600 per month for the rest of the year.
Administrative wages	$73,900 per month for the rest of the year.
Benefits	$0.20 per MD salary dollar; $0.10 per administrative salary dollar.
Medical supplies	1.5 percent of professional services revenue.
Rent and utilities	$43,600 per month for the rest of the year.
Billing and collection fees	8 percent of gross billings (i.e., the professional services line)
Equipment depreciation	$2,600 per month for July–September; $2,900 per month for October–December.
Office expenses	$5,000 per month for the rest of the year.
Liability insurance	15 percent of gross billings.*
Contracted services	$10,600 per month for the rest of the year.
Other	$4,500 per month for the rest of the year (includes interest on the long-term note and the line of credit).
Contribution to Dean	11 percent of net revenue.

Assets:
Accounts receivable	The five-month collection lag will continue for the rest of the year.
Medical supply inventory	Will grow by $3,000 per month for the rest of the year.
Prepaid insurance	Will remain constant at $340,000 for the rest of the year.
Equipment	Will increase with additional purchases in a given month, and decrease by the amount of the monthly depreciation expense.

Liabilities:
Accounts payable	Will grow by 2 percent a month for the rest of the year.
Payable to Dean	Will increase by 11 percent of net revenues and decrease by 11 percent of cash collections.
Note payable	Payment of $30,000 is scheduled for September.

*This item actually is related to the number of physicians, but 15 percent of gross billings provides a satisfactory approximation.

EXHIBIT 4

BROOKSTONE OB/GYN ASSOCIATES
Worksheets
($000s)

Operating Statements

		2001 Forecast					Total for
	July	August	September	October	November	December	2001
Revenue:							
Professional services							
Less: allowances and bad debts							
Net revenue							
Expenses:							
Physician payments							
Administrative wages							
Benefits							
Medical supplies							
Rent and utilities							
Billing/collection fees							
Equipment depreciation							
Office expense							
Liability insurance							
Contracted services							
Other							
Contribution to Dean							
Total expenses							
Surplus (Deficit)							

Balance Sheets

	2001 Forecast					
	As of July 31	As of Aug. 31	As of Sept. 30	As of Oct. 31	As of Nov. 30	As of Dec. 31
Assets:						
Cash						
Accounts receivable						
Medical supply inventory						
Prepaid insurance						
Total current assets						
Equipment (net)						
Total assets						
Liabilities and Equity Liabilities:						
Bank loan (line of credit)						
Accounts payable						
Payable to Dean						
Total current liabilities						
Note payable						
Equity:						
Start-up contribution						
Retained surpluses						
Total liabilities + fund balance						

As they began to prepare for the meeting, Dr. Amsted and Mr. Weber realized that their request would need to incorporate more than just the cash needs associated with the timing differences of revenue and expenses. It also would need to include the changes they had forecasted in all of the current accounts on the balance sheet, as well as BOGA's cash needs for paying off the note and purchasing the equipment. Unless they included all this information, their analysis would not reflect BOGA's true cash needs.

Questions

1. Using the data in Exhibit 3 and the worksheets in Exhibit 4, project the changes in the line of credit during July–December 2001. Note that the line of credit effectively is negative cash. It will increase in any given month by the same amount that cash otherwise would decrease for that month.

2. What is causing the decline in cash? How big does the line of credit need to be to accommodate the cash shortfalls? When will BOGA be able to repay the line of credit to the bank? Would a return to a modified cash system eliminate the problem?

3. What should Dr. Amsted do?

Case 4–4

Menotomy Home Health Services*

In November 1997, Ms. Carolyn Ringer, treasurer of the Menotomy Home Health Services (MHHS), was preparing a loan request to go to the Norten Municipal Bank. Less than eight months earlier, MHHS had expanded their staff by 30 percent. At that time, the home health service had been in a secure financial position and Ms. Ringer, anticipating no financial problems, had spoken to the agency's board of directors in favor of the increase in services. However, in July, Ms. Ringer realized that although MHHS had begun training and paying their new staff in June, the agency would not receive the additional revenue generated by the new staff until later in the year. With the staff totaling about 30 employees (full- and part-time), Ms. Ringer realized that MHHS could not always have on hand the cash they would require.

Faced with these unexpected expenses, Ms. Ringer had gone to the Norten Municipal Bank to apply for a short-term line of credit to cover the additional costs. Mr. Jansen, the bank officer, had granted MHHS a line of credit which

*This case was prepared by Patricia O'Brien under the supervision of Professor David W. Young. It subsequently was modified and updated by David W. Young. Copyright © by David W. Young.

EXHIBIT 1

MENOTOMY HOME HEALTH SERVICES Balance Sheet As of September 30, 1995–1997			
	1995	*1996*	*1997*
Assets			
Cash	$143,460	$ 32,805	$ 22,860
Accounts receivable	52,650	58,140	68,100
Inventory.	26,622	30,780	39,960
Prepaid expenses	32,118	34,303	41,585
Total current assets.	$254,850	$156,028	$172,505
Property and equipment (net)	315,345	411,735	468,946
Other assets.	13,590	15,975	16,650
Total assets	$583,785	$583,738	$658,101
Liabilities and Fund Balances			
Line of credit	$ 0	$ 0	$ 65,400
Accounts payable.	2,745	3,542	2,925
Salaries and benefits payable	31,050	32,400	35,100
Due to third-party payer	12,060	13,153	14,086
Note payable, current	21,240	26,235	29,070
Mortgage, current	11,250	11,250	11,250
Total current liabilities.	$ 78,345	$ 86,580	$157,831
Mortgage payable	168,750	157,500	146,250
Other long-term debt	270,000	270,000	270,000
Total liabilities.	$517,095	$514,080	$574,081
Fund balances	66,690	69,658	84,020
Total liabilities and fund balances.	$583,785	$583,738	$658,101

had reached almost $66,000 by September 1997. Although he had allowed the agency to continue using its line of credit into its next fiscal year,[1] he had raised some important considerations.

He explained that the bank was willing to continue a line of credit for the agency but he was concerned that Ms. Ringer had not adequately anticipated the agency's cash needs. He asked Ms. Ringer to present the bank at the outset with a detailed monthly statement of MHHS's projected cash needs for fiscal year 1998. Consequently, Ms. Ringer began to review the agency's financial statements (contained in Exhibits 1 and 2) and collect data that would help her plan for MHHS's future cash requirements.

[1]MHHS's fiscal year ran from October 1 to September 30. Fiscal year 1997 ran from October 1, 1996, to September 30, 1997.

EXHIBIT 2

MENOTOMY HOME HEALTH SERVICES Income Statements Fiscal Years 1995–1997			
	1995	*1996*	*1997*
Gross patient revenue	$649,462	$722,493	$838,524
Less: Contractual allowances and			
uncollectible accounts.	114,892	130,278	140,034
Net patient revenue	$534,570	$592,215	$698,490
Operating expenses:			
Salary and benefits	$372,600	$388,800	$421,200
Overhead and administration	63,129	89,807	136,310
Cost of medical supplies	24,477	27,967	34,471
Contract services	8,123	8,640	10,230
Equipment rental	17,250	18,750	19,650
Depreciation.	22,500	28,500	33,000
Interest.	–0–	15,947	14,935
Other expenses	3,058	10,836	14,332
Total operating expenses	$511,137	$589,247	$684,128
Excess of revenue over expenses	$ 23,433	$ 2,968	$ 14,362
Fund balance, September 30	$ 66,690	$ 69,658	$ 84,020

Background

Menotomy Home Health Services was a private, nonprofit home health agency founded in 1975 by four retired nurses. Each founder had between 10 and 35 years of experience working with elderly and disabled patients in Norten's hospitals. Realizing that a majority of their patients would not have needed hospitalization if Norten or the near vicinity had had a home health service, the nurses started their own agency. At first, MHHS was small and operated out of one person's home. The agency then employed the four founders, a part-time social worker, and six home health aides, three of whom were volunteers.

By 1984, the organization had outgrown its "office space" as well as its organizational structure and objectives. Although two visiting nurse associations had sprung up in Norten in the early 1980s, there was still a greater demand for MHHS's services than the agency could provide. Demand had risen at an average rate of 10 percent per year, and forecasts at that time indicated a steady increase at the 10 percent level.

During the mid-80s, MHHS underwent a gradual expansion. They purchased a small building in downtown Norten for management offices, employee training programs, and headquarters. They also bought some of the vehicles and equipment they had previously rented. In the subsequent 10 years, the staff grew from 10 to 20 people.

In the mid-1990s, in conjunction with increased pressures on hospitals to discharge their patients earlier, MHHS was again faced with an increasing demand for home health services. A poll taken at Norten's three hospitals in March 1997 indicated that there would be a 20 percent increase for them in home health care patients. MHHS management estimated that net patient revenue would reach $810,000 in FY 1998, an increase of 16 percent over the 1997 level. Further growth of between $75,000 and $100,000 a year was expected during the 1999–2000 period.

Consequently, MHHS was forced to decide whether to hold staff and services steady and hope that other health service organizations would fill in the gaps or to launch an expansion program aimed at providing more services to a greater number of patients in the Norten area. After examining MHHS's financial position and talking to Norten's health care providers about the agency's services, the board voted overwhelmingly to expand.

Data

Demand for MHHS's services, like that for many other home health agencies, was seasonal. Over two-thirds of the agency's annual home visits were made during the late fall and winter months. Exhibit 3 contains the forecasted monthly revenue for FY 1998 based on the number of visits during FY 1997. In making these projections, Ms. Ringer took into account the contractual adjustments and bad debts from MHHS's third-party payers and indigent patients.

Although demand for the agency's services tended to be seasonal, MHHS's employee salaries and benefits were expected to be relatively steady throughout the year. The agency had a firm policy of regular employment for both full- and part-time employees which, according to management, enabled MHHS to maintain a highly skilled and committed staff. MHHS's management also believed that its employment policy contributed significantly to the agency's reputation for quality home health care. Employees were paid on the first of each month for earnings from the previous month. Starting in October, employee salary and benefit earnings were expected to be $41,250 a month except for June when many employees would be on vacation and some part-time wages would be eliminated; payments in July would thus decrease to about $30,000.

Disbursements related to overhead and administration were scheduled at $15,000 a month throughout FY 1998. Included in that $15,000 a month was Ms. Ringer's estimate of the monthly interest on the Norten Municipal Bank loan. The initial depreciation expense was forecasted to be $33,000. Medical and office supply purchases were projected at $3,420 per month. The agency's policy was to charge these items and pay for each month's purchases in the following month. Contract service expenses were forecast at $900 a month. Other miscellaneous expenses were projected to total about $1,500 per month.

EXHIBIT 3
Estimated Monthly
Revenue and
Month-End Accounts
Receivable for
FY 1997–98

	Gross Patient Revenue	Net Revenue*	Accounts Receivable End-of-Month
October............	$ 67,500	$ 55,800	$117,450
November	96,000	78,750	148,050
December	135,600	111,150	212,850
January	139,950	114,750	257,400
February	156,450	128,250	278,100
March	88,350	72,450	235,800
April	73,500	60,300	143,100
May	61,350	50,400	117,450
June	53,400	43,800	76,500
July	32,850	27,000	59,550
August............	34,500	28,350	60,000
September.........	47,550	39,000	89,700
	$987,000	$810,000	

*After adjustments for contractual allowances and bad debts.

The new van, ordered for the meals-on-wheels program, was due for delivery in December. The van cost $18,000 and would be paid for in four equal monthly installments, beginning on delivery. The vehicle had an economic life of four years, at the end of which its salvage value would be zero. Depreciation would begin in the month of delivery.

In FY 1998, MHHS would owe Dr. Wilson, one of the board members, $29,070 for a short-term, interest-free loan she had made to the agency. This amount was payable in equal installments in December and March. The agency was also the lessee on long-term leases of furniture, equipment, and automobiles, with terms ranging from three to five years, beginning at various dates. The payments owed on these operating leases totaled $22,500, payable in equal installments in December and June.

In October 1995, MHHS had borrowed $180,000 from a life insurance company under a 16-year mortgage loan secured by the property and equipment. The current portion of the loan was repayable in equal installments in March and September of each year. Interest of 9 percent per annum on the unpaid balance was payable at the same time. In preparing her financial forecasts, Ms. Ringer planned to show separately the two principal payments, totaling $11,250, and the two interest payments, totaling $13,922, due in FY 1998.

The only other expenditure Ms. Ringer anticipated was $14,086 due to medicare for payments received exceeding reimbursable costs for the period ending September 30, 1997. The sum payable was noninterest-bearing and due in equal installments in June and September. She did not expect to incur a liability of this sort during FY 1998. Inventory, prepaid expenses, other assets, and other long-term debt were expected to remain essentially unchanged during FY 1998.

EXHIBIT 4

MENOTOMY HOME HEALTH SERVICES
Cash Flow Worksheet

	Oct.	Nov.	Dec.	Jan.	Feb.	Mar.	Apr.	May	June	July	Aug.	Sept.
CASH IN												
CASH OUT:												
Salaries and benefits												
Overhead and administration												
Payment of A/P												
Contract services												
Miscellaneous expense												
Vehicle expenditure												
Payment of note/P												
Equipment leases												
Payment of mortgage/P												
Mortgage interest												
Payment of third-party/P												
TOTAL OUT												
Net inflow (+) or outflow (−)												
Financing:												
(1) cash drawn down (+) or increase (−)												
(2) Line of credit change												
Beginning balance, line of credit												
Ending balance, line of credit												

Although Mr. Jansen had not hesitated to grant MHHS a line of credit, he had stressed the importance of the bank's credit regulations. The bank required that for a line of credit of $200,000 or less, the agency maintain a compensating cash balance of $20,000 at all times. Second, the entire line of credit, including the $65,400 currently owed by MHHS, was to be completely liquidated for at least one month during the year.

Using the worksheet in Exhibit 4, Ms. Ringer began to prepare a monthly cash flow forecast for FY 1998 that, she hoped, would show how much money the agency would need on a monthly basis.

Questions

1. Prepare the cash flow worksheet contained in Exhibit 4. What does this tell you about the operations of MHHS?

2. Prepare pro forma financial statements for FY 1998. What do these tell you about the operations of MHHS? How can you reconcile the information in the cash flow worksheet with that in the financial statements?

3. How do the cash flow problems being experienced by Menotomy Home Health Services compare with those of Gotham Meals on Wheels or Brookstone OB/GYN Associates? Please be as specific as you can: What is causing the problems in each organization? Is the solution the same for each?

4. What recommendations would you make to Ms. Ringer?

Case 4–5

CareGroup, Inc.*

On December 30, 1998, Ernst and Young, LLP issued the *Report of Independent Auditors* for CareGroup, Inc., and its subsidiaries, known collectively as CareGroup. CareGroup's operating statement showed a loss on operations of over $34 million and a decline in the entity's net assets of more than $104 million.

These losses contrasted sharply with comparable figures for the prior two years. In 1997, there was a gain on operations of almost $28 million and an increase in net assets of over $50 million. In 1996, the operating gain was over $45 million and the net asset increase was over $101 million. In effect, the worsening financial performance between 1996 and 1997 had become even more severe between 1997 and 1998.

*This case was prepared by Sheila M. McCarthy, MBA, and Professor David W. Young using information from public records. Copyright © by David W. Young.

Background

In the early 1990s, the passage of a Massachusetts law known as *Chapter 495,* had eliminated a great deal of state regulation, resulting in intense competition within the healthcare industry. Similar to many other parts of the country, the Northeast had seen a significant shift from indemnity insurance to managed care. The result was the existence of several dominant managed care organizations, including Harvard Pilgrim Health Care, Blue Cross and Blue Shield of Massachusetts, and Tufts Associated Health Plan. In addition, changes in the Medicare payment system had put increasing pressure on providers, especially hospitals. The state's Medicaid program, as in many other states, remained a below-cost payer for most hospitals.

These changes, as well as other environmental pressures to reduce healthcare costs and increase the level of accountability, had led to a series of mergers and strategic alliances in the greater Boston area. Two major hospital-based systems—Partners Healthcare and CareGroup, Inc.—dominated the market, although there also were several other key players, including Lahey Clinic, Caritas Christi Health System, and a number of independent providers that continued to compete in the market.

The two large systems as well as the smaller ones were constantly forming alliances with local community-based hospitals and physician practices. Thus, while the hospital-based systems appeared quite different on the surface, they all were focused on gaining market share by expanding their community based networks.

CareGroup

CareGroup, formed in 1996, was considered to be a leading hospital system in the Boston area. It was affiliated through research, teaching, and clinical care with Harvard Medical School.

In August, 1997, the CareGroup system comprised approximately 1,800 physicians (including about 450 primary care physicians in 38 communities). It served about 600,000 patients, and had 11.1 percent of hospital admissions in its market area.

CareGroup's operating statements for 1996, 1997, and 1998 are in Exhibit 1. Statements of changes in net assets and statements of cash flows for the same three years are contained in Exhibits 2 and 3 respectively. Exhibit 4 contains balance sheets for the three years, each with an effective date of September 30. Exhibit 5 contains selected portions of the Notes to the Consolidated Financial Statements.

In addition to describing significant accounting policies, the notes to the financial statements contained the following:

> CareGroup is an organized health care delivery system of teaching and community hospitals, physician groups and other care givers. It is committed to personalized, patient-centered care, excellence in medical education and research, and the creation

of a regional network that adds value to the health care system. CareGroup serves the health needs of patients and communities extending from north and south of Boston to the western suburbs beyond the Route 495 belt, and is comprised of:

- Six [Massachusetts] hospitals—Beth Israel Deaconess Medical Center, Inc. [formed through the merger of Beth Israel Hospital and New England Deaconess Hospital], Deaconess-Glover Hospital Corporation [in Needham], Deaconess-Nashoba Hospital [in Ayer], Deaconess-Waltham Hospital [in Waltham], Mount Auburn Hospital [in Cambridge], and New England Baptist Hospital [in Boston].

- A committed medical staff offering community-based primary care and a wide range of specialty services, and

- A broad spectrum of comprehensive health services ranging from wellness programs to hospice care.

A New CEO

A major focus for early 1998 had been the search for a new chief executive officer, after its original CEO, Mitchell Rabkin, M.D. (who had led Beth Israel for over 20 years prior to the merger), announced he would be retiring. A new CEO was named in May 1998.

Physician Contributions

The notes to the auditors' report also indicated that many of the academic physicians had made an investment in the formation of CareGroup:

> On May 1, 1998 and July 1, 1998, portions of the operations of 11 academic physician group practices foundations affiliated with the former Beth Israel Hospital Association joined with Deaconess Professional Practice Group, Inc., and was renamed Harvard Medical Faculty Physicians at Beth Israel Deaconess Medical Center, Inc. This transaction was accounted for as contributions from the affiliated academic physician group practice foundations which aggregated $8,529,000. As such, this amount is reported as contribution revenue in the accompanying 1998 consolidated statement of operations.

Questions

1. Starting with the $45,789 excess in revenues over expenses for 1996 in Exhibit 1, make sure you see how the four statements are linked. That is, the $45,789 is also included on Exhibit 2, and is combined to give totals for the unrestricted fund. The increase in net assets for 1996 for all funds is then contained on Exhibit 3 and is reconciled to the change in cash, which is used to compute the cash balance that appears on the balance sheet on Exhibit 4. Make sure you understand all of these linkages.

2. Note that, although there was $27,878 excess of revenue over expenses in 1997, the cash balance declined by $5,287. Why is this?

3. Explain the causes of the decline in excess of revenues over expenses between 1996 and 1998.

4. Perform a ratio analysis, using the unrestricted fund only. To do so, assume that the entire net asset figure for temporarily and permanently restricted funds each year is contained in the asset account labeled "Held for specific purposes and endowments."

5. What are the three most significant accounting issues that CareGroup faced in assembling its 1996, 1997, and 1998 financial statements? How have the auditors addressed these issues?

6. What, in your opinion, are the three most significant financial management issues that CareGroup faces as it enters its 1999 fiscal year?

EXHIBIT 1

CAREGROUP, INC. Operating Statements for the Years Ended 30 September (In Thousands)			
	1996	**1997**	**1998**
Unrestricted revenue, gains, and other support:			
Net patient services revenue	$ 932,191	$ 958,002	$ 963,626
Research revenue	79,969	85,020	88,169
Contributions, investment income, and gains	58,432	73,300	69,447
Other revenues	59,351	71,593	80,156
	$1,129,943	$1,187,915	$1,201,398
Expenses:			
Salaries and benefits	$ 549,917	$ 569,378	$ 638,170
Supplies and other expenses	335,277	374,320	373,878
Uncompensated care	65,730	78,920	85,606
Depreciation	86,872	94,388	97,858
Interest	37,793	39,455	40,222
Merger and restructuring expense . . .	8,565	3,576	0
	$1,084,154	$1,160,037	$1,235,734
Excess of revenue over expenses	$ 45,789	$ 27,878	$ (34,336)
Change in unrealized gains on investments	8,130	20,260	(50,134)
Net assets released from restructions used for purchase of property and equipment	54,719	2,742	403
Extraordinary loss on advance refunding of long-term debt	(3,811)	0	(20,054)
Cumulative effect of change in accounting principle	(3,061)	0	0
Increase (decrease) in unrestricted net assets	$ 101,766	$ 50,880	$ (104,121)

EXHIBIT 2

CARE GROUP, INC.
Statements of Changes in Net Assets
(In Thousands)

	Unrestricted	Temporarily Restricted	Permanently Restricted	Total
Net assets at 1 October 1995	$538,674	$173,972	$27,803	$740,449
Excess (deficiency) of 1996 revenue over expenses	45,789			45,789
Contributions		18,092	736	18,828
Restricted investment income and realized gains		17,172	25	17,197
Change in net unrealized gains on investments	8,130	651		8,781
Net assets released from restrictions used for operations. .		(14,260)		(14,260)
Net assets released from restrictions used for purchase of property and equipment.	54,719	(54,719)		0
Extraordinary loss on advance refunding of long-term debt	(3,811)			(3,811)
Cumulative effect of change in accounting principle.	(3,061)			(3,061)
Total changes	$101,766	($33,064)	$761	$ 69,463
Net assets at 30 September 1996	$640,440	$140,908	$28,564	$809,912
Excess (deficiency) of 1997 revenue over expenses	27,878			27,878
Contributions		13,857	559	14,416
Restricted investment income and realized gains		22,028		22,028
Change in net unrealized gains on investments	20,260	10,780		31,040
Net assets released from restrictions used for operations. .		(12,170)	(265)	(12,435)
Net assets released from restrictions used for purchase of property and equipment.	2,742	(2,742)		0
Total changes	$ 50,880	$ 31,753	$ 294	$ 82,927
Net assets at 30 September 1997.	$691,320	$172,661	$28,858	$892,839
Excess (deficiency) of 1998 revenue over expenses	(34,336)			(34,336)
Contributions		8,282	12,751	21,033
Restricted investment income and realized gains		20,372		20,372
Change in net unrealized gains on investments	(50,134)	(24,437)		(74,571)
Net assets released from restrictions used for operations. .		(17,745)		(17,745)
Net assets released from restrictions used for purchase of property and equipment.	403	(403)		0
Extraordinary loss on advance refunding of long-term debt	(20,054)			(20,054)
Total changes	($104,121)	($13,931)	$12,751	($105,301)
Net assets at 30 September 1998	$587,199	$158,730	$41,609	$787,538

EXHIBIT 3

CAREGROUP, INC.			
Statements of Cash Flows for the Years Ended 30 September			
(In Thousands)			

	1996	1997	1998
Operating Activities			
Increase in net assets	$ 69,463	$82,927	($105,301)
Adjustments to reconcile increase in net assets to change in cash:			
Depreciation and amortization	89,245	95,592	97,858
Change in net unrealized gains on investment	(8,781)	(31,040)	74,571
Net realized gains on investments	(51,744)	(63,449)	(57,201)
Restructed contributions and investment income	(22,953)	(20,013)	(25,756)
Extraordinary loss on advance refunding of long-term debt	3,811		20,054
Cumulative effect of change in accounting principle	3,061		
Contributions from affiliated academic physician group practice foundations			(8,529)
Increase (decrease) in cash resulting from changes in:			
Patient accounts receivable	(17,159)	(51,565)	43,084
Other current assets	1,174	5,272	(16,616)
Accounts payable and accrued expenses	(3,092)	10,730	9,201
Estimate settlements with third-party payers	(11,280)	13,977	(6,817)
Other liabilities	4,484	1,962	(2,422)
Net cash provided by operating activities	$ 56,229	$44,393	$ 22,126
Investing Activities			
Purchase of property and equipment	($136,894)	($82,675)	($125,306)
Decrease in investments and assets whose use is limited or restricted	83,890	18,671	(88,672)
Increase (decrease) in other assets	(2,540)	12,068	(603)
Acquisition of physician group practices	(4,069)	(8,491)	
Net cash used in investing activities	($ 59,613)	($60,427)	($214,581)
Financing Activities			
Payments on long-term debt	($ 14,401)	($16,800)	($ 15,979)
Proceeds from issuance of long-term debt	34,726	7,818	399,380
Advance refunding of long-term debt	(25,170)		(219,570)
Debt issuance costs	(2,072)		(6,131)
Cash advanced under note receivable	(92)	(284)	
Restricted contributions and investment income	22,953	20,013	25,756
Net cash provided by financing activities	$ 15,944	$10,747	$183,456
Net increase (decrease) in cash and cash equivalents	$ 12,560	($ 5,287)	($ 8,999)
Cash and cash equivalents at beginning of year	23,846	36,406	31,119
Cash and cash equivalents at end of year	$ 36,406	$31,119	$ 22,120

EXHIBIT 4

CARE GROUP, INC.
Balance Sheets as of 30 September
(In Thousands)

	1996	1997	1998
Assets			
Current Assets:			
Cash and cash equivalents	$ 36,406	$ 31,119	$ 22,120
Investments	105,857	114,907	83,647
Current portion of assets limited as to use	302,680	339,206	339,635
Gross patient accounts receivable	$187,590	$257,282	$241,281
Allowance for doubtful accounts	(32,722)	(47,755)	(62,900)
Net patient accounts receivable	154,868	209,527	178,381
Other current assets	43,500	35,369	52,782
Total current assets	$ 643,311	$ 730,128	$ 676,565
Assets limited or restricted as to use:			
Held by trustees under debt and other agreements	$ 41,744	$ 41,666	$ 146,203
Held for specific purposes and endowments	167,694	198,214	195,810
	$ 209,438	$ 239,880	$ 342,013
Noncurrent assets:			
Property and equipment	$ 804,405	$ 789,326	$ 819,342
Contributions receivable	19,337	14,693	9,890
Debt issuance costs	10,990	10,267	12,869
Other assets	23,243	19,995	25,911
	$ 857,975	$ 834,281	$ 868,012
Total assets	$1,710,724	$1,804,289	$1,886,590
Liabilities and Net Assets			
Current liabilities:			
Current portion of long-term debt	$ 18,914	$ 20,397	$ 22,171
Accounts payable and accrued expenses	141,454	152,069	165,474
Current portion of estimated settlements with third-party payers	27,298	36,854	41,668
Unexpended research grants	4,461		
Total current liabilities	$ 192,127	$ 209,320	$ 229,313
Long-term debt	626,856	612,877	796,784
Estimated settlements with third-party payers	25,322	29,743	18,112
Professional liability	14,452	14,149	13,893
Postretirement medical benefits	23,901	23,660	23,166
Other liabilities	18,134	21,701	17,784
Total liabilities	$ 900,812	$ 911,450	$1,099,052
Net assets:			
Unrestricted	$ 640,440	$ 691,320	$ 587,199
Temporarily restricted	140,908	172,661	158,730
Permanently restricted	28,554	28,858	41,609
Total net assets	809,912	892,839	787,538
Total liabilities and net assets	$1,710,724	$1,804,289	$1,886,590

EXHIBIT 5

CAREGROUP, INC.
Selected Notes to Consolidated Financial Statements
for CareGroup, Inc. and Subsidiaries
September 30, 1999 and 1998*

1. Organization and Mission

The accompanying consolidated financial statements include the accounts of CareGroup, Inc. (CareGroup) and its subsidiaries (collectively, the Corporation). Intercompany balances and transactions are eliminated in consolidation. . . .

On May 1, 1998 and July 1, 1998, portions of 11 academic physician group practice foundations affiliated with the former Beth Israel Hospital Association joined with Deaconess Professional Practice Group, Inc., and the corporation was renamed Harvard Medical Faculty Physicians at Beth Israel Deaconess Medical Center, Inc. The transaction was accounted for as contributions from the affiliated academic physician group practice foundations, which aggregated $8,529,000. As such, this amount is reported as contribution revenue m the accompanying 1998 consolidated statement of operations.

2. Summary of Significant Accounting Policies

Cash and Cash Equivalents

Cash and cash equivalents include investments in highly liquid debt instruments with a maturity of three months or less when purchased, excluding amounts whose use is limited by internal designation or other arrangements under trust agreements or by donors.

Assets Limited or Restricted as to Use

Assets limited or restricted as to use primarily include assets restricted by donors, assets set aside by the Board, and assets held by trustees under long-term debt and other agreements. Internally designated assets may, at the Board's discretion, subsequently be used for other purposes. Internally designated assets are classified as current assets because such amounts are available to meet the Corporation's cash requirements.

Investments and Investment Income

Investments in equity securities with readily determinable fair values and all investments in debt securities are measured at fair value in the consolidated balance sheets. Investment income or loss (including realized gains and losses on investments, interest and dividends) is included in the excess of revenue over expenses unless the income is restricted by donor or law. Unrealized gains and losses on investments are excluded from the excess of revenue over expenses. Certain investments are included in investment pools managed by the Corporation. Pooled investment income and gains and losses are allocated to participating funds based upon their respective shares of the pool.

Property and Equipment

Property and equipment are stated at cost less accumulated depreciation. Depreciation is computed using the straight-line method over the estimated useful lives of depreciable assets. Equipment under capitalized leases is amortized using the straight-line method over the shorter period of the lease term or the estimated useful life of the equipment. Such amortization is included with depreciation expense.

Gifts of long-lived assets such as land, buildings or equipment are reported as unrestricted support and are excluded from the excess of revenue over expenses unless explicit donor stipulations specify how the donated assets must be used. Gifts of long-lived assets with explicit restrictions that specify how the assets are to be used and gifts of cash or other assets that must be used to acquire long-lived assets are reported as restricted support.

Absent explicit donor stipulations about how long these long-lived assets must be maintained, expiration of donor restrictions are reported when the donated or acquired long-lived assets are placed in service.

Other Assets

The Corporation purchased certain physician group practices and recorded the excess of the purchase price over the fair value of the net assets acquired as goodwill. The goodwill is being amortized on a straight-line basis over five years and is included with supplies and other expenses. The Corporation also holds an investment in a joint venture, which owns a physician group practice. The Corporation accounts for this investment under the equity method of accounting.

Self-Insurance

The Corporation is self-insured for certain health insurance and workers' compensation benefit programs. Estimated losses and claims are accrued as incurred.

*For pedagogical purposes, certain portions of the notes have been omitted.

EXHIBIT 5
(Continued)

2. Summary of Significant Accounting Policies (Continued)

Temporarily and Permanently Restricted Net Assets

Temporarily restricted net assets are those whose use by the Corporation has been limited by donors to a specific time period or purpose. Permanently restricted net assets have been restricted by donors to be maintained by the Corporation in perpetuity.

The Corporation has interpreted state law as requiring realized and unrealized gains of permanently restricted net assets to be retained in a temporarily restricted net asset classification until appropriated by the Board and expended. State law allows the Board to appropriate so much of the net appreciation of permanently restricted net assets as is prudent considering the Corporation's long- and short-term needs, present and anticipated financial requirements, expected total return on its investments, price level trends, and general economic conditions.

Deficiency of Revenue Over Expenses

The consolidated statements of operations include the deficiency of revenue over expenses. Changes in unrestricted net assets which are excluded from the deficiency of revenue over expenses include unrealized gains or losses on investments, contributions of long-lived assets (including assets acquired using contributions which by donor restriction were to be used for the purposes of acquiring such assets) and extraordinary items.

Revenue Recognition

The Corporation has entered into payment agreements with Medicare, Blue Cross, Medicaid and various commercial insurance carriers, health maintenance organizations, and preferred provider organizations. The basis for payment under these agreements varies and includes prospectively determined rates per discharge, discounts from established charges, capitated rates, cost (subject to limits), fee screens, and prospectively determined daily rates.

Net patient service revenue is reported at the estimated net realizable amounts from patients, third-party payors and others for services rendered. Under the terms of various agreements, regulations, and statutes, certain elements of third-party reimbursement are subject to negotiation, audit and/or final determination by the third-party payors. Variances between preliminary estimates of net patient service revenue and final third-party settlements are included in the consolidated statements of operations in the year in which the settlement or change in estimate occurs. Changes in prior year estimated settlements increased net patient service revenue by approximately $16,025,000 in 1999 and $15,393,000 in 1998.

Donations

Unconditional promises to give cash and other assets to the Corporation are reported at fair value at the date the promise is received. Conditional promises to give and indications of intentions to give are reported at fair value at the date the gift is received or the conditional promise becomes unconditional. The gifts are reported as either temporarily or permanently restricted support if they are received with donor stipulations that limit the use of the donated assets. When a donor restriction expires, that is, when a stipulated time restriction ends or purpose restriction is accomplished, temporarily restricted net assets are reclassified as unrestricted net assets and recorded as net assets released from restrictions (which are included with other revenue or as direct additions to net assets if for capital).

Costs of Borrowing

Debt issuance costs and original issue discounts are amortized over the period the related obligation is outstanding generally using the interest method. Amortization of such amounts during the period of construction of capital assets is capitalized as a component of the cost of acquiring such assets. Interest costs, net of interest income, incurred on borrowed funds during the period of construction of capital assets are capitalized as a component of the cost of acquiring such assets. Capitalized interest was $1,214,000 in 1999 and $335,000 in 1998.

Research Grants and Contracts

Revenue related to research grants and contracts is recognized as the related costs are incurred. Indirect costs relating to certain government grants and contracts are reimbursed at fixed rates negotiated with the government agencies. Amounts received in advance of incurring the related expenditures are recorded as unexpended research grants and are included with accounts payable and accrued expenses.

Professional Liability

The Corporation insures its professional liability risks on a claims-made basis in cooperation with several other Harvard-affiliated health care organizations through a captive insurance company, of which CareGroup holds a 10% ownership interest. The Corporation maintains a program of self-insurance to cover professional liability claims incurred but not reported to the captive insurance company at year end. The estimated amount of accrued unasserted claims has been determined by consulting actuaries on a discounted basis using an interest rate of 7.5%.

Income Tax Status

CareGroup and substantially all of its subsidiaries have previously been determined by the Internal Revenue Service to be organizations described in Internal Revenue Code (the Code) Section 501 (c)(3) and, therefore, are exempt from federal income taxes on related income pursuant to Section *501 (a)* of the Code. One of CareGroup's subsidiaries has for-profit subsidiaries. The income tax provisions for these entities are reported as an operating expense because the amount is not material.

EXHIBIT 5
(Continued)

2. Summary of Significant Accounting Policies (Continued)

Use of Estimates

The preparation of financial statements in conformity with generally accepted accounting principles requires management to make estimates and assumptions that affect the reported amounts of assets and liabilities and disclosure of contingent assets and liabilities at the date of the financial statements. Estimates also affect the reported amounts of revenue and expenses during the reporting period. Actual results could differ from those estimates.

Fair Value of Financial Instruments

The carrying amounts of the Corporation's financial instruments as reported in the accompanying consolidated balance sheets other than long-term debt (see Note 7) approximate their fair value.

Reclassifications

Certain amounts in the 1998 consolidated financial statements have been reclassified to conform to the 1999 presentation.

3. Community Service and Uncompensated Care . . .

Unreimbursed Charity Care

The Corporation provides care without charge or at amounts less than its established rates to patients who meet certain criteria under its charity care policy. Because the Corporation does not pursue collection of amounts determined to qualify as charity care, they are not reported as revenue except to the extent reimbursed by the statewide Uncompensated Care Pool (the Pool).

Community Benefit Programs

The Corporation also provides resources to foster a partnership with the community to deliver quality care and services. This active community benefit program provides financial and educational support to community activities and programs dealing with a variety of health issues. . . .

6. Property and Equipment

Property and equipment consisted of the following (in thousands of dollars):

	September 30	
	1999	*1998*
Land	$ 45,620	$ 44,260
Buildings and improvements	758,144	682,220
Equipment	924,135	896,478
Construction in progress	20,025	41,285
	1,747,924	1,664,243
Less accumulated depreciation	(939,095)	(844,901)
	$ 808,829	$ 819,342

In 1999, the Corporation recorded a write-off of fixed assets aggregating $18,486,000. The write-off was primarily attributable to the abandonment of certain information system projects that were in progress and consisted of hardware, software and other related costs. The write-off was reported as restructuring expense in the consolidated statement of operations.

7. Long-Term Debt

	September 30	
	1999	*1998*
Fixed-rate debt:		
Massachusetts Health and Educational Facilities Authority (MHEFA) Revenue Bonds:		
CareGroup Issue, Series A	$287,590	$293,175
Beth Israel Hospital Issue Series G	154,765	158,605
Beth Israel Issue, Series E	69,220	72,905
Mount Auburn Hospital Issue Series B	49,495	49,495
Massachusetts Wellness and Fitness, L.L.C		
Taxable Revenue Bonds, Series 1998	31,400	31,400
Other	9,716	11,829
	602,186	617,409
Less unamortized original issue discounts	(6,838)	(7,309)
Total fixed-rate debt	595,348	610,100

**EXHIBIT 5
(Continued)**

7. Long-Term Debt (Continued)

	September 30	
	1999	*1998*
Variable-rate debt:		
MHEFA Revenue Bonds:		
CareGroup Issue, Series B.	$ 75,000	$ 75,000
Beth Israel Issue, Series G.	64,700	64,700
Beth Israel Issue, Series F	32,100	32,100
Beth Israel Issue, Series H.	22,800	23,800
New England Deaconess Hospital Issue, Series F . . .	9,700	9,700
Other	1,510	3,555
Total variable-rate debt	205,810	208,955
	801,158	818,955
Less current portion.	(23,695)	(22,171)
	$777,463	$796,784

. . .

The Corporation's Revenue Bonds bear interest, mature and are redeemable prior to maturity as follows:

Issue	Interest Rate	Maturity	Redemption Terms
CareGroup:			
Series A	4.0% to 5.5%	2025	Beginning in 2008 at 102% and at decreasing amounts to 100% in 2010 and thereafter
Series B	Variable, currently 3.1%	2028	Currently at 100%
Beth Israel Hospital:			
Series E	6.5%to7.0%	2014	Beginning in 1999 at 102% and at decreasing amounts to 100% in 2001 and thereafter
Series F	Variable, currently 3.2%	2013	Currently at 100%
Series G	4.2% to 6.0%	2025	Beginning in 2002 at 102% and at decreasing amounts to 100% in 2004 and thereafter
Series H	Variable, currently 3.5%	2015	Currently at 100%
New England Deaconess Hospital:			
Series F	Variable, currently 3.2%	2013	Currently at 100%
Mount Auburn Hospital:			
Series B	5.3% to 6.3%	2024	Beginning in 2004 at 102% and at decreasing amounts to 100% in 2006 thereafter
Massachusetts Wellness and Fitness, L.L.C.			
Series 1998	6.8%	2019	Beginning in 2008 at 102% and at decreasing amounts to 100% in 2010 and thereafter

Scheduled principal repayments and sinking fund requirements on long-term debt for the next five years are as follows (in thousands of dollars):

Year Ending September 30	
2000	$23,695
2001	22,000
2002	23,000
2003	21,000
2004	22,000

Based upon borrowing rates available to the Corporation for bonds with similar terms and average maturities, the market value of long-term debt, including the portion classified as a current liability, is approximately $790,000,000 at September 30, 1999.

Interest paid on all outstanding debt amounted to $40,688,000 in 1999 and $38,644,000 in 1998.

The Corporation has guaranteed certain debt obligations of other organizations totaling approximately $20,000,000 in outstanding principal. As of September 30, 1999, there have not been any requirements to honor calls under these guarantees.

EXHIBIT 5
(Continued)

8. Assets Held by Trustees

Assets held by trustees include amounts held in trust for professional liability risks and under the requirements of various debt agreements. The terms of MHEFA Revenue Bonds require the establishment of certain reserve funds, which are held by trustees. These funds, principally comprised of cash, cash equivalents and government securities, are carried at fair market value and are as follows (in thousands of dollars):

	September 30	
	1999	1998
Professional liability......................	$11,565	$ 11,121
Debt agreements:		
Construction funds......................	51,445	128,830
Debt service reserve funds................	9,973	10,147
Debt service funds	9,604	4,519
	82,587	154,617
Less Current portion......................	(8,291)	(7,981)
	$74,296	$146,636

9. Employee Benefit Plans

Pension Benefits

The Corporation sponsors several noncontributory defined benefit pension plans and defined contribution plans covering substantially all of its employees.

Defined Benefit Plans

During 1998, Beth Israel Deaconess Medical Center's two noncontributory defined benefit pension plans were merged into a single plan, and the plan was renamed the CareCroup, Inc., Pension Plan (the Plan). The Plan covers employees of Beth Israel Deaconess Medical Center, CareGroup and certain other of its subsidiaries. Provisions for future benefits were adjusted to be consistent for all participants under the new Plan. These adjustments reduced the projected benefit obligation by approximately $16 million as of September 30, 1998. Under the Plan, participants retirement accounts are credited annually with service credits of between 3% and 9% of participants' compensation (based on age and years of service) and interest credits equal to the one year Treasury bill rate but not less than 5%. The funding policy of the Plan is to make contributions at least equal to the minimum amount required under the law. Pension plan assets are invested in a variety of equity and fixed-income securities.

During 1999, the Plan recognized a settlement gain of $2,787,000 as a result of the transition of certain participants employed by Harvard Medical Faculty Physicians at Beth Israel Deaconess Medical Center (HMFP) to a new plan sponsored by HMFP. During 1998, the Plan recognized curtailment and settlement gains totaling $2,689,000 as a result of this transition.

Defined benefit pension plans are also sponsored by New England Baptist Hospital and Deaconess Waltham Hospital.

Net pension cost for the defined benefit pension plans included the following components (in thousands of dollars):

	Year Ending September 30	
	1999	1998
Service cost for benefits earned during the year ..	$ 8,567	$ 9,421
Interest cost on projected benefit obligation	15,669	15,056
Expected return on plan assets................	(21,211)	(20,061)
Net amortization..........................	(4,292)	(5,187)
Effect of curtailment		(1,813)
Effect of settlement	(2,787)	(876)
Net pension cost (income)..................	$(4,054)	$ (3,460)

EXHIBIT 5
(Continued)

9. Employee Benefit Plans (Continued)

The following tables set forth the plans funded status and amounts recognized in the consolidated balance sheets (in thousands of dollars):

	Year Ending September 30	
	1999	1998
Change In benefit obligation:		
Benefit obligation at beginning of year	$222,283	$205,795
Service cost	8,567	9,421
Interest cost	15,669	15,054
Benefits paid..........................	(15,321)	(11.683)
Plan changes...........................		(17,250)
Effect of settlement	(11,104)	(3,935)
Effect of curtailment....................		(1,636)
Actuarial loss (gain)......................	(8,051)	26,517
Benefit obligation at end of year	$212,043	$222,283

	September 30	
	1999	1998
Change In plan assets:		
Fair value of plan assets at beginning of year .	$279,283	$251,231
Actual return on plan assets	24,310	43,670
Effect of settlement	(11,104)	(3,935)
Benefits paid..........................	(15,321)	(11,683)
Fair value of plan assets at end of year	$277,168	$279,283
Funded status of the Plan	$65,125	$ 57,000
Unrecognized net transition asset...........	(33,154)	(30,472)
Unrecognized prior service cost (benefit)	(15,033)	(16,167)
Unrecognized actuarial gain...............	(22,309)	(19,786)
Accrued pension expense..................	$ (5,371)	$ (9,425)

The following table sets forth the assumptions used by the actuaries in determining the above:

	September 30	
	1999	1998
Weighted-average discount rate	7.25% - 7.75%	7.25% - 7.75%
Rate of increase in future compensation...............	4.0 – 4.5	4.0 – 4.5
Expected long term rate of return on plan assets	8.25	8.25

Defined Contribution Plans

The Corporation has defined contribution plans, which provide the Corporation with the ability to make annual contributions based on specified percentages of annual compensation and employee contributions. The Corporation contributed $19,024,000 and $11,966,000 to the plans in 1999 and 1998, respectively.

Post-retirement Medical Benefits

The Corporation has defined post retirement medical benefit plans covering certain of its current and former employees. The plans generally provide medical benefits to retired employees of certain of the institutions who meet age and years of service requirements. The plans are not funded.

Net periodic post-retirement medical benefit cost is comprised of the components listed below (in thousands of dollars):

	Year Ended September 30	
	1999	1998
Service cost for benefits attributed to service during the year	$ 1	$ 9
Interest cost on accumulated post-retirement benefit obligation	1,024	1,086
Net amortization and deferral	(451)	(601)
Net periodic post-retirement medical benefit cost	$ 574	$ 494

The following tables set forth the components of the components of the accumulated post-retirement benefit obligation shown in the Corporation's financial statements (in thousands of dollars):

EXHIBIT 5
(Continued)

9. Employee Benefit Plans (Continued)

	September 30	
	1999	*1998*
Change in Post-retirement Benefit Obligation		
Benefit obligation at beginning of year	$18,195	$17,257
Service cost	1	9
Interest cost	1,024	1,086
Benefits paid.	(1,063)	(1,095)
Actuarial loss (gain).	(1,393)	938
Benefit obligation at end of year	16,764	18,195
Unrecognized net transition asset.	3,463	3,848
Unrecognized actuarial gain.	2,460	1,243
Accrued post-retirement cost	$22,687	$23,286

In determining the accumulated post-retirement medical benefit obligation, the Corporation used discount rates of 7.25% to 8% in 1999 and 7.25% in 1998. The Plan assumed a range of 5% to 10% annual rates of increase in the per capita cost of covered health care benefits for the plans during 1999. The rates are assumed to decrease gradually down to between 5% and 6% on a graded scale, becoming fixed between 2000 and 2012. Increasing the assumed health care cost trend rates by one percentage point in each year would increase the accumulated post-retirement medical benefit obligation as of September 30, 1999, by $1,100,000 and the net periodic post-retirement medical benefit cost for the year then ended by $80,000.

10. Temporarily Restricted Net Assets

Temporarily restricted net assets consisted of the following (in thousands of dollars):

	September 30	
	1999	*1998*
Donor restricted for research	$ 78,789	$ 77,463
Donor restricted for operations	18,385	16,163
Donor restricted for capital	3,894	4,662
Accumulated net realized and unrealized gains on permanently restricted donations	71,775	60,442
	$172,843	$158,730

11. Concentration of Credit Risk

The Corporation grants credit without collateral to its patients, many of whom are local residents and are insured under third-party payor agreements. Management estimates that accounts receivable, net of contractual allowances, were comprised as follows:

	September 30	
	1999	*1998*
Medicare.	14%	18%
Medicaid.	10	9
Blue Cross	13	13
Commercial insurance and managed care	34	20
Patient.	21	25
Other.	8	5
	100%	100%

13. Contingencies

Laws and regulations governing the Medicare, Medicaid, and federal research programs are complex, and compliance with such laws ad regulations can be subject to future government review and interpretation as well as significant regulatory action, including fines, penalties, and exclusion from the Medicare and Medicaid programs. In 1998, the Beth Israel Deaconess Medical Center, Inc., Mount Auburn Hospital, and HMFP, along with a number of other health care providers, received Civil Investigation Demands (CID) from the United States Department of Justice issued under the Civil False Claims Act in connection with an investigation of the billing practices to the Medicare program for the services of teaching physicians. The CIDs consist of requests for certain documents and interrogatories related to such billing practices. The Corporation has responded to these requests. Because the investigation is still in a preliminary stage, the ultimate outcome cannot be presently determined. Accordingly, no provision for any liability that may result from this investigation has been made in the accompanying consolidated financial statements.

EXHIBIT 5
(Continued)

14. Year 2000 (Unaudited)

The Corporation has modified or replaced certain portions of its software, hardware, and patient care equipment so that its systems and equipment will function properly with respect to dates in the Year 2000 and thereafter. Affected systems include clinical and biomedical instrumentation and equipment used within the Corporation for purposes of direct or indirect patient care such as imaging, laboratory, pharmacy, and respiratory devices; cardiology measurement and support devices; emergency care devices (including monitors, defibrillators, dialysis equipment, and ventilators); operating room equipment (including lasers, transfusion equipment, anesthesia equipment, and pumps); automated implants and/or devices used to program them; and general patient care devices (including telemetry and endoscopy equipment and IV pumps). The Corporation utilized both internal and external resources to reprogram, or replace, and test the software and patient care equipment for Year 2000 readiness.

The Corporation has substantially completed the Year 2000 remediation efforts. The incremental cost of the Year 2000 project was $23,007,000 in 1999, including $8,244,000 that was capitalized as part of property and equipment and $14,763,000 that was charged to expense. Year 2000 costs were not significant in 1998. Costs to be incurred subsequent to September 30, 1990, are not expected to be significant.

15. Harvard Pilgrim Health Care Receivership

On January 4, 2000, under an order by the Massachusetts Supreme Judicial Court, Harvard Pilgrim Health Care (HPHC) was placed in receivership under the control of the Commissioner of Insurance of the Commonwealth of Massachusetts. Under the receivership order, all providers of health care services to HPHC members have been ordered to continue to provide services. The Commissioner, as receiver, has been ordered to file a plan of proposed further action within 30 days. At September 30, 1999, CareGroup institutions had accounts receivable of $26.5 million outstanding from HPHC against which advance payments of $10.5 million have been received. In addition, estimated receivables under risk sharing settlements of $3.4 million are outstanding on September 30, 1999.

Case 4–6

Northridge*

The meeting of the Northridge board of directors on January 8, 1997, unexpectedly evolved into a heated discussion of what one member called a philosophical issue, namely, the role of surplus in a nonprofit organization.

Background

Northridge was a continuing care retirement community (CCRC) located in a small college town. Its impetus came from members of a local church, who persuaded the national headquarters of that denomination to take on the project. The denomination headquarters had built other CCRCs. It supervised design and construction, arranged the initial financing, and selected and trained management personnel. Construction started in 1989, and the first residents moved in on July 1, 1991.

Construction and start-up costs were financed by two bond issues totaling $42,990,000. One issue, in the amount of $15,000,000, was redeemed on

*This case was prepared by Professor Robert N. Anthony. Copyright © by Robert N. Anthony.

October 1, 1994. The other issue had an interest rate of 8 percent, due October 1, 2019, with annual mandatory redemption of $440,000 in FY 1997 (the year ended March 31, 1997), increasing by approximately 10 percent each year thereafter. The bonds were secured by a letter of credit, at an annual fee of 1 percent.

The 60-acre property consisted of a residential complex of 248 apartments with a health center. The apartments were studio, one bedroom, two bedrooms, and two bedrooms and den. In late 1996, there were 369 residents. The complex included a dining room, cafeteria, auditorium seating 150 people, library, indoor pool, beauty/barber shop, branch bank, gift shop, and facilities for crafts, woodworking, painting, and other activities. These apartments and facilities were in a connected group of buildings.

The health care center was in a building connected to the residential complex. There were 76 nursing beds, but one section, consisting of 20 beds, was not open in 1996. It was expected that this section would be opened in 1998 or soon thereafter. The health care center included an employee day care center, exercise and physical therapy rooms, and a clinic with medical, dental, ophthalmology, podiatry, and laboratory facilities.

Northridge residents paid an entrance fee and a monthly fee. In FY 1997 the entrance fee for single occupancy ranged from $78,800 to $267,300, median of $225,100; for double occupancy, the entrance fee was 5 percent higher. Monthly fees for single occupancy ranged from $1,581 to $2,802, median of $2,451; for double occupancy, the fee was 40 percent higher. An occupant of the health care center paid the same monthly fee as he or she paid when in an apartment. The monthly fee covered one meal per day, housekeeping, utilities (including cable TV, but not telephone), and complete health care. Part of a resident's health care costs was reimbursed by Medicare or Medicaid.

When it opened, Northridge was the only CCRC in its marketing area, which it defined as an area with a radius of about 60 miles. Since then, three other CCRCs had opened in the area. Although Northridge had a lengthy waiting list of persons who had paid a refundable fee of $1,000, experience had shown that several names on the list had to be contacted to locate someone who wanted the type of apartment available and who was willing to move in the near future. For some prospective residents, the problem was the difficulty of selling their home in order to provide funds for the entrance fee. There were 18 new entrants to apartments (each with one or two persons) in FY 1995 and 25 in FY 1996.

Northridge was a nonprofit organization exempt from federal taxes under Section 501(c) of the Internal Revenue Code, but subject to local property taxes on the residential facilities. It was governed by an unpaid board of directors; 11 members were local residents, 2 were residents of Northridge, and 1 was a member of the national board of the denomination.

Grover Porter was the executive director of Northridge. He joined Northridge in January 1996. His previous job had been as executive director of a smaller CCRC.

Financial Statements

At its quarterly meeting on January 8, the board discussed the financial statements in Exhibits 1, 2, and 3.[†]

On the statement of revenues and expenses, the item "Health Center Fees: Resident" was the amount of the resident's monthly fee that was allocated to the health center.

"Entry Fees Earned" was the amortization of the entrance fees applicable to the year. This amount was obtained by amortizing each resident's entrance fee over his or her expected life on a straight-line basis.

"Shared Services Fee" was the amount paid to the denomination headquarters for providing assistance.

On the balance sheet, the assets under "Trustee Held Funds" were assets held by a trustee as required by the bond indenture.

The January 8 Meeting

After disposing of a few routine matters, the meeting was devoted to the budget for FY 1998 (year ending March 31, 1998). The budget had been discussed and approved at an earlier meeting of the finance committee. Mr. Porter, presented the administration's recommended budget. It called for an increase in the monthly fee of 2.5 percent, with no change in the entrance fee. Several members raised questions about the need for this increase. A summary of the executive directors comments, made throughout the meeting, follows.

- **Fee History.** Monthly fees were increased by 4.3 percent in FY 1993, 5.0 percent in 1994, 4.0 percent in 1995, 4.3 percent in 1996, and 3.0 percent in 1997. The proposed increase of 2.5 percent for 1998 is the lowest ever. The same percentage increases were made in the entrance fee; no increase in the entrance fee is proposed for 1998.

- **Refinancing.** We probably can refinance our debt at a net $2.5 million saving in interest (and letter-of-credit fee) through 2019. However, prospective underwriters will be concerned about our heavy reliance on entrance fees. They will want to see a surplus of $500,000 to $800,000 annually. If the numbers don't show this, our chances of refinancing will be unrealistic.

- **Staffing.** The proposed cost-of-living increase for staff is 3.25 percent, the same as for 1997. The full-time-equivalent (FTE) staff in the 1998 budget included an increase of six FTEs in the health care facility; otherwise, the numbers are approximately the same as the projected actual for 1997.

[†]The actual numbers on these exhibits were shown to the dollar. They have been rounded to thousands of dollars.

- **Relation to Inflation.** The fee increase is lower than the inflation rate for expenses assumed in the budget. Budgeting a lower increase for fees would challenge the financial viability of the organization.

- **Relation to long-range plan.** The long-range plan assumes an annual increase in fees of 3.5 percent. Unless there are compelling reasons to do otherwise, we should stick with the approved plan.

- **Relation to Cash Flow.** Maintaining a positive cash flow is of utmost importance. In order to generate a positive cash flow, a reasonable bottom-line surplus should be budgeted, and we must obtain an adequate amount of new entrance fees.

- **Deficit.** Until FY 1996, Northridge operated at an annual deficit; the sum of these deficits was negative equity of $3.3 million as of the end of 1996. Operating surpluses reduced this deficit thereafter, but $1.5 million will remain at the beginning of FY 1998. Lenders do not like to see a balance sheet with negative equity.

- **Desirable Surplus.** The budgeted surplus is less than 4 percent of operating revenues; this is reasonable for a nonprofit organization.

- **Capital Expenditures.** As our fixed assets age, we must provide increasing amounts for renewals and replacements. Budgeting a surplus in effect provides a nest egg that will help finance these expenditures.

- **Actuarial Study.** A careful actuarial study was made recently. It extrapolated the revenues of each resident for his or her expected life and the related expenditures for the total period from now until the years in which the oldest current resident is expected to live. The numbers were based on the same estimates of cost of living, fee increases, and other factors included in the FY 1998 budget. It shows that the present value of the revenues exceeds the present value of the expenses and expenditures by only $1 million. This is a small margin of safety as a percentage of revenues; total revenues for this period will exceed $100 million.

- **Competition.** Three CCRCs have opened in our marketing area, and we can expect more. Their fees are a little lower than ours. Although we now have 98 percent occupancy, we might experience an unexpected reduction at any time. In anticipation of this possibility, the budget is based on occupancy of 96 percent. The surplus will help us deal with a situation of operating at less than capacity if it arises.

- **Health Care.** As our residents age, we must anticipate that the demand for health care will increase. We must soon face the need to open additional beds, with a drastic increase in health care costs. The surplus will help cushion the impact of these costs.

EXHIBIT 1

NORTHRIDGE
Operating Statements

	Budget FY 1997	Projected FY 1997	Budget FY 1998	% Change Between Budgets 98/97
Operating Revenues				
Operating Revenues:				
Residential Fees	$ 7,220	$ 7,291	$ 7,239	0.26%
Charity Care.	(40)	(38)	(50)	25%
Health Center Fees:				
Resident	1,309	1,344	1,585	21.08%
Medicare & Other Insurance.	377	322	324	-14.06%
Nonresident	29	57	32	10.34%
Entry Fees Earned	3,398	3,398	3,466	2.00%
Investment Income	691	766	776	12.30%
Restricted Assets Released to Operations	0	45	50	N/A
Other Program Services.	180	177	183	1.67%
Other Operating Revenue	10	10	9	-10.00%
Total Operating Revenues	$13,174	$13,372	$13,614	3.34%
Operating Expenses				
Health Services.	2,061	2,057	2,295	11.35%
Food Services.	1,546	1,455	1,538	-0.52%
General and Administrative	1,012	941	1,033	2.08%
Employee Benefits	592	524	582	1.69%
Utilities.	592	601	633	6.93%
Housekeeping	633	581	632	-0.16%
Maintenance	754	733	813	7.82%
Shared Services Fee	469	469	486	3.62%
Real Estate Taxes	772	752	789	2.20%
Depreciation and Amortization.	1,856	1,798	1,837	-1.02%
Interest.	2,400	2,418	2,344	-2.33%
Contingency Expense.	88	0	125	42.05%
Total Operating Expenses	12,775	12,329	13,107	2.60%
Excess (Deficiency) Of Operating Revenues over Operating Expenses	399	1,043	507	27.07%

EXHIBIT 2

	NORTHRIDGE Balance Sheets		
	Actual March 96	Projected March 97	Budgeted March 98
Assets			
Current Assets:			
Cash and Equivalents...............	$ 823	$ 830	$ 830
Short-Term Investments.............	4,526	6,500	7,235
Accounts Receivable	675	753	767
Accrued Income	79	65	65
Deposits & Prepaid Expenses	183	266	277
Supplies Inventory..................	72	81	84
Trustee Held DSI Account...........	902	1,090	1,056
Trustee Held DSP Account	410	440	475
Total Current Assets	$ 7,670	$10,025	$10,789
Trustee Held Funds:			
Debt Reserve Fund.................	4,607	4,520	4,520
Working Capital Reserve	1,549	1,601	1,601
Liquid Asset Reserve...............	496	860	860
Investment Valuation Account	0	18	0
Accrued Income	107	72	74
Total Trustee Held Funds.............	$ 6,759	$ 7,071	$ 7,055
Property Plant and Equipment:			
Land	1,155	1,155	1,155
Buildings and Improvements	47,982	48,034	48,646
Equipment	2,916	3,052	3,244
Total PP&E.......................	$52,053	$52,241	$53,045
Less Accumulated Depreciation.........	(7,757)	(9,441)	(11,163)
Net PP&E........................	$44,296	$42,800	$41,882
Other Assets:			
Organizational & Licenses Net	659	577	496
Deferred Financing Costs Net.........	667	634	601
Total Other Assets..................	$ 1,326	$ 1,211	$ 1,097
Total Assets.....................	$60,051	$61,107	$60,823
Liabilities and Fund Balance			
Current Liabilities:			
Accounts Payable..................	$ 232	$ 255	$ 268
Accrued Expenses	157	245	257
Current Portion of Long-Term Debt	410	440	475
Advance Billing for Residence Care.....	734	745	770
Interest Payable...................	1,090	1,074	1,056
Total Current Liabilities	$2,623	$2,759	$2,826
Long-Term Debt....................	26,740	26,305	25,835
Deferred Entry Fees	32,821	33,148	32,744
Advance Deposits...................	420	405	420
Total Liabilities	$62,604	$62,617	$61,825
Fund Balance:			
Prior Year........................	($ 3,270)	($ 2,553)	($ 1,509)
Current Period....................	717	1,043	507
Total Fund Balance	($2,553)	($ 1,510)	($ 1,002)
Total Liabilities and Fund Balance......	$60,051	$61,107	$60,823

EXHIBIT 3

	NORTHRIDGE Statement of Cash Flows		
	Actual March 96	Projected March 97	Budgeted March 98
Operating Activities			
Excess (Deficit) of Revenues over Expenses	$ 717	$ 1,043	$ 507
Earned Entrance Fees	(3,166)	(3,398)	(3,466)
Entrance Fees Received	2,928	3,725	3,062
Depreciation & Amortization	1,803	1,798	1,837
NonCash Interest Items	5	5	5
Incr(Decr) Accounts Payable	(71)	23	13
Decr(Incr) Accounts Receivable	(23)	(78)	(14)
Decr(Incr) Accrued Income	(85)	48	(2)
Incr(Decr)Accrued Expenses	(427)	88	12
Decr(Incr) Prepaid Exp/Inven	(11)	(92)	(14)
Incr(Decr) Interest Payable	(15)	(16)	(18)
Incr(Decr) Advance Billing	27	10	26
Net Cash Provided (Used) by Operating Activities	$ 1,682	$ 3,156	$ 1,948
Investing Activities			
Acquisition Property & Plant	(346)	(55)	(612)
Equipment Additions	(112)	(132)	(192)
Net Cash (Used) by Investing Activities	($ 458)	($ 187)	($ 804)
Financing Activities			
Change in Long-Term Debt	(375)	(410)	(440)
Change in Priority Deposits	(24)	(15)	15
Change in Other LT Liabilities	(22)	0	0
Net Cash Provided (Used) by Financing Activities	(421)	(425)	(425)
Increase (Decrease) in Cash and Cash Investments	803	2,545	719
Cash and Cash Investments at Beginning of Year	12,510	13,313	15,858
At End of Year	$13,313	$15,858	$16,577

- **Regulatory Uncertainties.** We cannot know what the state and federal regulatory agencies will do to us. For example, the state may require that we maintain a specified amount of liquid assets.

- **Policy.** Our parent organization, with many years of experience, strongly recommends that we plan on a surplus of between $500,000 and $800,000 annually.

Questions

1. Is Exhibit 1 the best set of numbers to use as a basis for arriving at the fee? If not, what improvements would you suggest?

2. Appraise the validity and relevance of each of the points made by the executive director.

3. What is the desirable ultimate amount of surplus?

4. As a director, what change in the FY 1997 fees would you recommend for FY 1998?

Chapter 5

Full-Cost Accounting

"What did it cost?" is one of the most slippery questions for managers in both for-profit and nonprofit organizations. Although the cost of *acquiring* resources, such as supplies and labor, usually can be obtained readily from invoices and other documents, measuring the *use* of those resources for various purposes is another matter. Calculating a total cost per unit produced—be it a newsletter or 50 minutes of psychotherapy—is relatively easy as long as the organization produces a single product.[1] Complications arise when an organization produces different types of products, because each type uses *different* amounts of resources, and each therefore has *different* costs.

This chapter discusses some of these complications. We begin with an overview of the uses to which full-cost information can be put. Next, we look at several decisions that managers make in developing full-cost accounting systems. We conclude the chapter with a discussion of several factors that complicate a full-cost analysis.

Uses of Full-Cost Information

Information on the full cost of carrying out a particular endeavor has three basic uses: pricing, profitability assessments, and comparative analyses.

Pricing

One of the functions of full-cost information is to assist management in setting prices. Clearly, full-cost information is not the only information that management uses for this purpose, but it is an important ingredient in the decision-making process. Many nonprofit organizations are *price takers;* that is, they must accept whatever price a third party or client can pay. In these instances,

---

[1]As defined by the Institute of Management Accountants, the term *product* refers to both goods and services. Goods are tangible products; services are intangible products. Some people define *products* to include only tangible items, but this is incorrect.

prices are not based on full costs, but on the market. For other organizations, full-cost information is much more important to the pricing decision. These include organizations whose reimbursement from clients or third parties is calculated on a cost basis. We discuss pricing issues in greater detail in Chapter 7.

Profitability Assessments

Even nonprofit organizations that are price takers must calculate full costs if management is to know whether a particular program or service is making or losing money. In Chapter 6, we will examine what management might do if a program or service is losing money on a full-cost basis, but for the moment, it is sufficient to say that if a product is not covering its full costs, it is, by definition, a *loss leader.* Full-cost accounting highlights where cross subsidization is taking place, which allows management to assess its consistency with the organization's strategy.

Comparative Analyses

Many organizations can benefit from comparing their costs with those of similar organizations that deliver the same sorts of products. Full-cost information can assist in this effort.

In undertaking such analyses, managers need to be aware of potential problems. For example, they need to know whether the organizations with which they are comparing themselves measure their costs in the same way they do. As the discussion in this chapter will indicate, there can be a variety of complexities in undertaking comparative analyses.

Example

Northern College, a small private liberal arts college, is interested in comparing its cost per student with the cost per student in some other similar colleges. In making the comparisons, the college must consider issues such as average class size, the existence of specialized programs in athletics, art, music or other subjects, special services (such as career counseling), whether it wishes to include room and board costs in the comparison, the method used to calculate the cost of its library (e.g., whether it amortizes its collections, and if so, over what time period), whether it wishes to include the library cost in the comparison, and a wide variety of similar issues.

As this example suggests, even the definition of what is to be included in a full-cost calculation requires a managerial decision. Indeed, because there is such a wide range of choices embedded in an organization's full-cost accounting system, managers frequently find it difficult to compare their costs with those of other organizations.

Cost Accounting System Decisions

Conceptually, the goal of full-cost accounting in nonprofit organizations is quite basic: to measure the amount of resources consumed in the delivery of each service. Putting this concept into practice is difficult, however, because of several decisions that must be made in designing a cost accounting system. These include: defining the final cost object, specifying intermediate cost objects, determining cost centers, assigning costs, selecting allocation bases, deciding on an allocation method, attaching costs to intermediate cost objects, and summing intermediate cost objects.

These decisions frequently are made by an organization's accounting staff rather than its managers, which is not optimal. Senior management must take an active role in cost accounting decisions if it is to have a cost accounting system that meets its needs.

Final Cost Object

A central question in designing a cost accounting system concerns the unit for which we wish to know the cost. In a hospital, for example, the unit might be a day of care, an admission, or any of a variety of other outputs.[2] The choices in an educational context might include the cost of a classroom hour, a student-year, a course, or a department. In cost accounting terminology this unit is called the *final cost object* or sometimes a *final product cost.*[3]

In many instances, the choice of a final cost object is constrained by limitations of available data. In a community health center (CHC), for example, some managers believe that an episode of illness is the most appropriate final cost object.[4] Most CHCs do not have data systems that permit easy retrieval of complete episode information, however. As a result, the final cost object usually is a visit or an encounter, for which data can be obtained more easily.

Intermediate Cost Objects

A second question concerns the activities that take place to produce the final cost object. A day of care in a hospital encompasses a wide range of activities, for example, including differences in levels of nursing care provided, types of laboratory tests and radiological procedures conducted, and amenities furnished. In a school system, the cost of educating a student in a given grade will depend on activities such as provision of special instruction, involvement in athletics, and use of counseling services. Each of these activities is an intermediate cost object, and its costs should be included in the final cost object.

In effect, differences in intermediate cost objects represent what might be called product differences. That is, for a given final cost object—such as the

---

[2]A day of care is a day spent in a hospital as an inpatient. An admission usually spans several days, and includes all activities associated with the hospitalization, workup, treatment, and discharge of a patient.

[3]Cost accounting terminology is not completely uniform. The Appendix contains definitions of some key terms used in the chapter. For additional discussion of terminology and methodological considerations, see Charles Horngren, George Foster, and Srikant Datar, *Cost Accounting: A Managerical Emphasis* (Englewood Cliffs, NJ: Prentice Hall, 1999).

[4]An episode of illness includes all activities that take place from the time a person gets sick (with an acute, i.e., non-chronic, illness) until he or she is cured. It can include both in-hospital (inpatient) and out-of-hospital (outpatient) activities (and costs).

education of a student for one academic year or the discharge of a healthy patient—the final product can be quite different from one individual to the next, depending on the aggregation of intermediate products. For example, to treat a patient with a particular diagnosis or diagnosis-related group (DRG)[5] some physicians might order a surgical procedure, while others might not; some might order one combination of tests and procedures, while others might order a different combination. These different combinations of intermediate products affect the cost of the final cost object, even though the end product—the discharge of a patient—is the same.

Cost Centers

Before being attached to intermediate products, costs are first collected in cost centers.[6] Cost centers might be thought of as "buckets" into which an organization's costs are classified and accumulated for purposes of full-cost analysis. Frequently, an organization's departments are its cost centers. For example, in a hospital, the department of radiology might be one cost center, the social work department another, the housekeeping department a third, and so on. But this is not always the case. The department of radiology, for instance, might be divided into several separate cost centers: CT scanning, angiography, and so on. Or a language laboratory in a high school, while not a department, might be a cost center.

There are two broad types of cost centers: mission centers and service centers. *Mission centers* are directly related to the purposes of the organization. *Service centers* provide support to both mission centers and other service centers. In a hospital, the housekeeping, plant maintenance, and dietary departments are service centers, while the pediatrics, obstetrics, and medical/surgical departments are mission centers. A good rule of thumb for client-serving organizations is that mission centers charge clients for their services while service centers do not. For this reason, mission centers frequently are called *revenue-producing centers.*[7] In some instances, service centers may charge both mission centers and other service centers for their support activities, but they do not charge clients directly.[8]

The distinction between intermediate products and mission centers is occasionally quite subtle since both may be viewed as purposes for which costs are collected.

Example	The annual cost of caring for a child in the Western Home for Children (the final cost object) depends upon the services (intermediate products) the child receives. There are four basic types of services: foster home care,

[5]A DRG is a group of related diagnoses. There are several hundred DRGs.
[6]Strictly speaking, as we discuss in the Appendix, a cost center is also a type of cost object.
[7]This rule of thumb works for all client-serving organizations, even those that do not charge clients directly. Where there are no charges, the accounting system nevertheless can calculate a cost that *could be used* as a basis for the charge.
[8]This internal charge is called a *transfer price.* It is discussed in greater detail in Chapter 8.

psychological testing, social work counseling, and psychotherapy. Each of these services also is a mission center, where a variety of costs are accumulated. The psychological testing center, for example, includes the costs of part-time psychologists, testing materials, and the fee the agency pays to an outside organization to have the tests processed and scored. The costs in the psychological testing mission center are accumulated for the year, and are divided by the number of children tested to give a cost per child tested. Each child who was tested has this cost added to his or her other costs to arrive at the total cost of caring for him or her for the year.

Cost Assignment

An appropriate analysis of costs should allow us to identify both the costs directly associated with (or that can be physically traced to) a particular cost center, as well as those that are associated with more than one. A full-cost accounting system should distinguish between these direct and indirect costs. That is, direct costs are unambiguously associated with a specific cost center. Indirect costs apply to more than one.

To carry out the full-cost accounting effort, the accounting staff must *assign* all costs to cost centers. Direct costs, by definition, can be assigned quite easily. Indirect costs, because they are not clearly associated with a particular mission or service center, pose problems, however. Ordinarily, the accounting staff uses formulas to assign them as fairly as possible to the appropriate cost centers.[9] Sometimes, however, by developing improved measurement techniques and appropriate records, the staff can convert an indirect cost into a direct one.[10]

Example

A social worker in the foster home care department of Western Home for Children is supervised by a person who also supervises the psychologists in the testing department. Unless the time the supervisor spends in each department is traced, his or her salary is an indirect cost of the two departments—it applies to activities in both. To distribute the cost between the two, the accountants might develop a formula, using, say, relative hours of service or number of personnel in each cost center as the distribution mechanism. Alternatively, the supervisor might be asked to maintain careful records of the time spent in each cost center, which the accountants

---

[9]This assignment process sometimes is called *allocation*. It contrasts with another type of allocation, discussed later in this chapter, of service center costs to mission centers.
[10]Government contracts normally permit the recovery of service center costs via an *indirect overhead rate*. When this happens, an organization receiving government funding for a particular project first calculates the direct costs of the project—usually personnel, supplies, transportation, equipment, and the like—and then adds its allowable (as determined by prior audits) indirect overhead rate to determine the full amount of funding to be received. In such a contract, the cost elements to be included in direct costs must be spelled out clearly.

then could use to distribute the salary. In this latter case, the cost (time) would be direct, since it is now traceable to each cost center.

Bases of Allocation

A full-cost analysis would be incomplete if it stopped with the assignment of costs to cost centers. We would then know the cost in each service and mission center, but not the full cost of each mission center. Therefore, once all costs have been assigned, the accounting staff must *allocate* service center costs to mission centers.[11]

Allocation is the process of distributing service center costs to mission centers, to determine the full cost of each mission center. To accomplish this, the staff must select a *basis of allocation* for each service center. In general, the best basis for allocating the costs of a given service center is the one that most accurately measures its use by the cost centers that receive its services. Here, the main issue is *causality*. That is, to the extent possible the basis of allocation should reflect the receiving cost center's usage of a service center.

Example

The basis for allocating the costs of the laundry service center in a hospital usually is pounds processed. In the dietary service center, the usual basis is number of meals served. In each instance, the hospital is seeking a basis of allocation that measures the *usage* of the laundry and dietary service centers by the cost centers receiving the allocations.

In selecting a service center's allocation basis, managers should carefully assess the need for precision, since, in general, greater precision increases the expense of operating the cost accounting system.

Example

Housekeeping costs in a hospital frequently are allocated on the basis of the number of square feet occupied by the cost centers that use housekeeping services. Alternatively, and more accurately, housekeeping costs could be allocated on the basis of hours of service rendered to each cost center by the housekeeping department. Although hours of service is a more accurate measure of the cause of the cost, it requires the housekeeping department and the accounting staff to maintain records of hours; this recordkeeping expense is not necessary in the simpler system.

The Allocation Method

Several methods are available for allocating service center costs. The easiest is known as *single-step* allocation. With this method, each service center's

---

[11]This is one area where terminology can be particularly confusing. The terms *assign, apportion,* and *allocate* sometimes are used interchangeably. Moreover, many managers consider all mission center costs to be direct and all service center costs to be indirect. Additionally, service center costs frequently are called *overhead costs,* although the definition of *overhead* varies considerably among organizations. In general, the context will make clear how the terms are being used.

costs are allocated to the various mission centers that use its services, but not to any other service centers. For example, in a hospital, housekeeping would be allocated to pediatrics, surgery, and so forth based on, say, their share of the institution's square feet. However, this method fails to recognize that some service centers provide services to other service centers; for instance, housekeeping cleans the medical records department, another service center.

The Stepdown Method

The *stepdown* method corrects for this deficiency. With this method, sometimes called a "two stage" method, the costs of the service centers are "trickled down" to other service centers and the mission centers using the chosen allocation bases. This method is illustrated in Exhibit 5–1. Typically, it begins with the service center that serves the greatest number of other service centers in the organization, and spreads its costs over the remaining cost centers. It continues in this fashion with all other service centers.

Clearly, Exhibit 5–1 is quite simple—it has only three service centers and two mission centers. The allocation process used would be the same, however, in a system with many cost centers. It begins with the first service cost center, depreciation of buildings and fixtures in this case, and distributes its assigned costs across all remaining cost centers. The column labeled "Depreciation, Buildings and Fixtures" shows this distribution. The amount to be distributed from the next service center (Housekeeping) now includes not only its

EXHIBIT 5–1 The Stepdown Method*

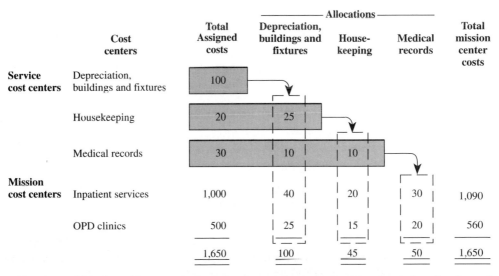

*The three solid horizontal bars contain the assigned costs of each service center plus, in housekeeping and medical records, those amounts allocated from the previous cost center(s). The three dotted vertical bars contain the individual amounts allocated to each cost center from the three service centers. Note that, as the arrows indicate, the total amount in each horizontal bar has been redistributed within a vertical bar. This redistribution is done in accordance with the chosen allocation basis; for example, by square feet for housekeeping.

assigned costs ($20) but also the amount allocated to it from the previous step ($25 of depreciation). The column "Housekeeping" allocates this total ($45) to the remaining cost centers. The third step, "Medical Records," includes its assigned costs ($30), plus the amount of depreciation ($10) and housekeeping ($10) allocated to it, for a total of $50. The "Medical Records" column shows how this total was allocated to the two mission centers.

Exhibit 5–1 does not show the bases of allocation for the service centers. For example, the basis of allocation for depreciation might be square feet. The housekeeping department's share of depreciation then would be calculated based on its share of the hospital's total square footage.

Two important aspects of the stepdown method are (1) no reverse allocation takes place; that is, once a service center's costs have been allocated, that service center receives no additional allocations from other service centers; and (2) service center costs are allocated both to other service centers and to mission centers, but mission center costs are not allocated to other mission centers.

Because no reverse allocation takes place, the sequence of the steps in the stepdown is an important cost accounting decision. Although the effect of different stepdown sequences often is not great, in some circumstances the choice may have a significant influence on the costs allocated to the various mission centers.

The Reciprocal Method

The need to select a stepdown sequence can be obviated by using the *reciprocal method.* With this method, service center costs are not stepped down. Rather, the accountants develop a set of simultaneous equations that measure and allocate each service center's costs based on the use of its services by *all* other cost centers, not just those below it in a stepdown sequence. This technique thus avoids the problem with the stepdown method that no reverse allocation can take place. The reciprocal method is discussed in most cost accounting texts.

Attaching Mission Center Costs to Intermediate Cost Objects

The next step in the cost accounting process is to determine the cost of each intermediate cost object. Since a mission center frequently works on several intermediate products, its costs must be attached to each.[12] These intermediate cost objects are then summed to give the cost of the final cost object. Sometimes this is relatively easy, and sometimes it can be complicated.

Example

The research department of a university (a mission center) may work on several different research projects (final cost objects), and each project must be costed-out individually.

---

[12]The term *attached* is not widespread. A more frequently used term is *assigned.* We use *attached* here so not to confuse this step with the step (discussed earlier) that *assigns* costs to cost centers.

Example

The counseling department of a social service agency (a mission center) comes into contact with many clients (final cost objects), and wishes to know the cost associated with each.

The special education department of a junior high school (a mission center) provides services to many students (final cost objects) and wishes to know the cost for each student.

The internal medicine department of a rural group practice (a mission center) sees many patients each day and wants to know the cost of each patient's visit (the final cost object).

Process Costing and Job Order Costing

In the above situations and other similar ones where mission center costs must be attached to either intermediate or final cost objects, organizations are faced with two principal choices, each of which has several variations: the process method and the job order method. In manufacturing, the process method is used when all units of output are essentially identical, such as the production of chairs, phone directories, and fertilizer—activities that often are performed on a production line or in a chemical process. The job order method is used when the units of output are quite different, such as in an automobile repair garage or a specialty machine shop.

With the process costing method, all mission center costs for a given accounting period are calculated, totaled, and then divided by the total number of units produced to give an average cost per unit.[13] With the job order method, the labor, material, and other direct costs associated with each job are collected separately on a job cost record, and indirect costs are distributed to each job using one or more overhead rates.

In general, the choice between the two methods depends upon the significance of an average cost figure.

Example

Most hospitals use a job order system. They sum the costs from several mission centers for each patient, based on the patient's actual use of those mission centers. Medications, special dietary services, operating room usage, ancillary procedures, special nursing care, and intensive care unit usage are accumulated on a patient's medical (job cost) record to obtain the cost of treating that individual. Each patient's final cost will differ depending on the intermediate products used, and the cost of each.

---

[13]The accounting process actually is considerably more complicated than this, since (*a*) units frequently move through several production stages, each of which is a cost center, (*b*) at any given time there are partially completed units in each cost center, and (*c*) spoilage (both normal and abnormal) must be taken into account. For details, see Horngren, Foster, and Datar, *Cost Accounting.*

<table>
<tr><td>

Example

</td><td>

Third-party payers that reimburse a hospital on the basis of an all-inclusive per diem amount assume (perhaps implicitly) that the hospital is using a process method. The reimbursement system treats the entire hospital as a mission center, calculates all costs for the hospital, and determines the average cost per day by dividing the number of patient days delivered into total costs. The assumption underlying in this approach is that all patients served receive roughly similar services, and therefore an average cost per day is a meaningful figure.

A school with a special education (SPED) program lies between a pure process system and a job order system. It recognizes that a student in the SPED program will use resources that are different from those used by a student in a regular education program, but it assumes that all students using the SPED program will use roughly the same services (i.e., that this average is a meaningful figure). The system does not attempt to find the cost of individual products (i.e., students).

</td></tr>
</table>

In choosing between process and job order methods, managers must weigh the higher cost of the job order method against its benefits, such as improved competitive pricing information and cost control potential. Differences among clients and services are important in making the choice. For example, most client- or patient-serving nonprofit organizations would benefit from a method that approximates job order, while most membership-type organizations or associations would find a process method acceptable.

An Illustration

To illustrate how the full-cost accounting process works, assume that we want to know the full cost of educating a senior in high school. This is our final cost object. To get this figure, we need to sum several intermediate costs objects, namely the per-student cost of each course (or extracurricular activity) the student took or engaged in. Since different seniors will take different courses and engage in different extracurricular activities, each will have a different cost; that is, the total of the final cost object will differ from one student to the next depending on the mix and unit costs of the intermediate products.

Assume that each course and extracurricular activity is part of a mission center, and there are five mission centers: the English, Science, History, Math, and Athletic Departments. Also, assume that there are four service centers: building depreciation, building maintenance, janitorial services, and school administration.

To begin, we *assign* all of the school's costs to cost centers, either mission centers or service centers. As Exhibit 5–2 indicates, the school has $1,290,000 of costs, all of which have been assigned to the cost centers shown in the leftmost column.

We next *allocate* service center costs both to other service centers and to mission centers. In this instance, we are using the stepdown method, which was

EXHIBIT 5–2 Determining the Full Cost per Mission Center

Cost Centers	Assigned Costs	Allocated Costs	Costs to be Allocated	Allocations				Full Cost
				Depreciation (Sq Ft)	Maintenance (Hours)	Janitorial (Hours)	Administration (Salary $)	
	1	$2 = 4 + 5 + 6 + 7$	$3 = 1 + 2$	4	5	6	7	$8 = 1 + 2$
Service Centers								
Building depreciation......	150,000	0	150,000					
Building maintenance......	115,000	9,000	124,000	9,000				
Janitorial services	50,000	14,500	64,500	7,500	7,000			
School administration......	100,000	48,600	148,600	21,000	18,600	9,000		
Mission Centers								
English Department.........	175,000	74,755		18,000	17,360	9,675	29,720	249,755
Science Department.........	200,000	84,293		15,000	20,280	14,835	34,178	284,293
History Department.........	125,000	59,359		16,500	13,640	8,415	20,804	184,359
Math Department	150,000	73,037		19,500	18,600	9,675	25,262	223,037
Athletic Department.........	225,000	123,556		43,500	28,520	12,900	38,636	348,556
Total cost	1,290,000			150,000	124,000	64,500	148,600	1,290,000

EXHIBIT 5–3
Calculating
Intermediate Product
Costs

Mission Center	Mission Center Cost 1	Number of Courses 2	Cost per Course 3 = 1 ÷ 2
Mission Center			
English Department	249,755	15	16,650
Science Department	284,293	15	18,953
History Department	184,359	12	15,363
Math Department.	223,037	15	14,869
Athletic Department	348,556	10	34,856
Total cost.	1,290,000		

shown schematically in Exhibit 5–1, and has been expanded in Exhibit 5–2 to meet the high school's needs. For example, "Janitorial services" has $50,000 of assigned costs and $14,500 of allocated costs, for a total of $64,500. Of the $14,500 in allocated costs, $7,500 came from "Building depreciation" (allocated on the basis of square feet) and $7,000 from "Building maintenance" (allocated on the basis of hours of service).

The $64,500 total of "Janitorial services" costs is then allocated to the remaining service center ("School administration"), and the five mission centers; these allocations are based on hours of service, and are shown in column 6. The same process is followed for the school Administration service center (as had been followed for the service centers above "Janitorial services"), but using salary dollars as the basis of allocation; that is, the more salary dollars in a given cost center, the higher its allocation of "School administration." The result is shown in column 7.

The end result of this process is that all service center costs have been allocated to mission centers. The same $1,290,000 we began with is contained in the rightmost column, but it now consists only of costs in mission centers.

Once all costs are contained in mission centers, we then must attach them to intermediate products—in this case, courses. If we assume that each course consumes roughly the same amount of the mission center's costs (we will relax this assumption later), then we simply divide the mission center's full costs by the number of courses offered, to get a cost per course.

This step is shown in Exhibit 5–3. Here, the full cost figure for each mission center (from Exhibit 5–2) is divided by the number of courses (or sports in the case of the Athletic Department) to give a cost per course or sport; that is, the intermediate cost object. This differs for each department depending on its full cost and the number of courses it offered.

Once we know the cost of each course, we divide it by the number of students taking the course to get the cost per student per course. For any given student, we then add the relevant per-student intermediate costs objects to get the full cost—his or her education for the year (or other period, such as a semester).

EXHIBIT 5–4

Calculating the Final
Product Cost

Student #1 Course	Cost per Course	Course Enrollment	Cost per Student
English 101	16,650	15	1,110
Science 102	18,953	12	1,579
History 103	15,363	20	768
Football Team	34,856	30	1,162
Basketball Team	34,856	15	2,324
Final Product Cost			6,943

Student #2 Course	Cost per Course	Course Enrollment	Cost per Student
English 401	16,650	30	555
Science 402	18,953	25	758
Science 403	18,953	20	948
Math 420	14,869	30	496
Math 480	14,869	20	743
Final Product Cost			3,500

This last step is shown in Exhibit 5–4 which calculates the full cost for each of two students. As it indicates, lower enrollments lead to higher per student costs even though the intermediate cost objects may be the same (such as with the two English courses). As Exhibit 5–4 also indicates, the mix of intermediate products influences the full cost for any given student. For example, Student #1, an athlete, took only three academic courses (two of which had low enrollments), and played two sports, which have relatively high per-student costs (due largely to their high intermediate product costs, but also, in the case of basketball, to a low number of students playing the sport). He thus had a relatively high full cost. By contrast, Student #2, a scholar, took mainly math and science courses with average enrollments, and hence had a relatively low full cost.

Relaxing the Homogeneity Assumption

In Exhibit 5–3, we assumed that each course (intermediate product) consumed roughly the same amount of a mission center's resources; that is, that the intermediate products in each mission center were homogeneous. However not all cost centers are like this.

Assume, for example, that the science department offers some courses that make extensive use of laboratories, while others do not. Those courses require more square footage (the classroom plus the lab), more maintenance (since many experiments cause damage to the facilities), and more janitorial services (since cleaning a lab takes more time than cleaning a classroom). Assume also

EXHIBIT 5–5
Calculating the Final
Product Cost
Assuming No
Product
Heterogeneity

Student #2 Course	Intermediate Product Cost	Course Enrollment	Cost per Student
English 401	16,650	30	555
Science 402.	18,953	25	758
Science 403.	18,953	20	948
Math 420	14,869	30	496
Math 480	14,869	20	743
Final Product Cost			3,500

Student #3 Course	Intermediate Product Cost	Course Enrollment	Cost per Student
English 401	16,650	30	555
Science 402.	18,953	25	758
Science 550.	18,953	20	948
Math 420	14,869	30	496
Math 480	14,869	20	743
Final Product Cost			3,500

that each course using a lab needs a lab assistant, and hence has higher personnel costs.

Exhibit 5–5 illustrates the nature of the dilemma. Science 403 is a nonlaboratory course, whereas Science 550 is a laboratory-based course. As the cost accounting system is now structured, both courses have an intermediate product cost of $18,953, yet Science 550 requires more direct costs from the Science Department (the lab assistant) and more overhead (from building depreciation, building maintenance, and janitorial services). In effect, while students #2 and #3 would appear to have the same full cost, we know that the cost of student #3 actually is higher due to the lab course.

The above situation occurs anytime a mission center has a heterogeneous mix of intermediate products, that is, a mix where some products consume more resources (direct and/or indirect) than others. To resolve the dilemma, we need to refine the process for computing the cost of the intermediate cost objects. To do so, we must focus on the means by which mission center costs are attached to intermediate products.

Ordinarily, a mission center's *direct* costs can be attached to an intermediate product relatively easily—by recording the amount of labor and raw materials that went into the product. In the above example it should not be difficult to record the personnel expenses associated with each course, including both the lab assistants and anyone else, as well as to distinguish, if we wished, between different salaries for different faculty. We also should be able to identify any other expenses associated directly with the lab, such as supplies and other materials.

The overhead costs for intermediate products present a more difficult problem. These costs include both service center costs that have been allocated to the mission center, and costs within the mission center that, while direct for the mission center, are not direct for the center's products.[14]

Activity-Based Costing

One approach taken to attach these overhead costs to intermediate products is activity-based costing, or ABC. ABC is needed when a single activity (such as machine hours in a factory, test hours in a laboratory, or courses in a school) is inadequate to assign the mission center's overhead to products.[15] In general, this situation occurs when there is either *product diversity* or *volume diversity.* Product diversity exists when different products use overhead-related services in different proportions, and when the costs of those services are significantly different. Volume diversity exists if the products are manufactured in batches of different sizes, and overhead activities are affected by the size of the batch being produced.[16] In the example of the high school, there is considerable product diversity, such that lab courses in the Science Department consume more depreciation, maintenance, and cleaning services than nonlab courses.

Increasingly, nonprofit and other service organizations have begun to use the principles of ABC to attach overhead costs to their intermediate products.[17] For example, a laboratory or radiology department in a hospital has considerable diversity among its tests and procedures (its intermediate products), making it much like a manufacturing organization. A school in a university has diversity among its programs—different programs may use considerably more or less overhead than the average. A health insurer may have volume diversity when, for example, it must process batches of claims that, for one reason or another, are larger or smaller than the usual batch size.

---

[14]All of these costs are sometimes call *indirect costs* of the intermediate products. In the latter situation, they may be directly associated with the mission center, although not with any given intermediate product worked on in the mission center. An example would be the department's secretary.

[15]For a discussion of the characteristics of a system where a single rate is inappropriate see Robin Cooper, "You Need a New Cost System When . . . ," *Harvard Buisness Review,* January–February 1989, pp. 77–82.

[16]For a detailed discussion of these factors, see Robin Cooper, "The Rise of Activity-Based Costing—Part Three: How Many Cost Drivers Do You Need, and How Do You Select Them?" *Journal of Cost Management,* Winter 1989, pp. 34–46.

[17]For a description of how such an approach was used at Union Pacific, a service organization that is similar to many nonprofit organizations, see Robin Cooper and Robert S. Kaplan, "Activity-Based Systems: Measuring the Costs of Resource Usage," *Accounting Horizons,* September 1992. For a discussion of the applicability of ABC to service organizations in general, see Don Lambert and John Whitworth, "How ABC Can Help Service Organizations," *CMA Magazine* 70, no. 4, May 1996. For a health care focus, see Timothy D. West and David A. West, "Applying ABC to Healthcare," *Management Accounting,* February 1997.

When ABC is used, the analysis usually begins with the activities that cause the costs for one batch of services (or products) to be different from those for another. Each activity is then given its own *cost driver.* If, for example, one type of test in a laboratory requires considerably more setup time than another, the appropriate cost driver would be something associated with setups. If a high degree of supervision is needed for one type of program or service but not for another, the appropriate cost driver would be something like supervisory hours. In this way each cost driver measures a program's or service's use of the overhead resources that are needed for its delivery.

By having an ABC system to attach mission center overhead costs to the center's products, senior management not only can be assured that the accounting system is measuring costs more accurately than before, but it can begin to concentrate on controlling costs by controlling the cost drivers; that is, by *managing activities rather than costs.*[18] It is this shift in thinking—from measurement to control—that is one of the most powerful benefits of an activity-based cost system.

Example

Activity-based cost management (ABCM) in the Internal Revenue Service used activity-based costing (ABC) to guide managers in decision making. In one office the activity pools were (1) managing accounts, (2) informing, educating, and assisting, (3) ensuring compliance, and (4) resourcing. The activity drivers included volume and cycle time.[19]

Of course, ABC also is helpful for other cost accounting–related activities, such as pricing and profitability analysis. Indeed, the use of ABC can help senior management in many nonprofit organizations to identify more clearly the nature and extent of cross subsidization taking place among the organization's programs and services. Thus, ABC can help link cost measurement and control to an organization's overall strategy. Several cases illustrate aspects of ABC, but especially Case 5–4, "Neighborhood Servings."

Interactive Effects

As the above discussion indicates, the decisions involved in developing a full-cost accounting system may be quite difficult. Regardless of the difficulty, it is important to note that changes in the system that increase the cost of one cost object will always decrease the cost of one or more other cost objects. This is because the total costs of operating the organization are unaffected; the cost accounting system merely divides this total among the cost objects. Nevertheless, changes in cost accounting definitions and techniques can have a significant effect on the costs reported for a given cost center or cost object. In

---

[18]For additional discussion of this idea, see H. Thomas Johnson, "Activity-Based Information: A Blueprint for World-Class Management Accounting," *Management Accounting,* June 1988, pp. 23–30.

[19]John B. MacArthur, "Cost Management at the IRS," *Management Accounting,* November 1996.

many organizations, managers' ability to analyze these effects is facilitated by computer software packages. The packages allow a manager or analyst to vary cost accounting decisions, and to examine the impact of such changes on individual cost centers and cost objects.

Complicating Factors

In practice, the general framework described above has many variations and complications. While most of them are appropriately dealt with in a cost accounting course, there are a few worth noting.

Defining Direct Costs

There are significant differences in the ways different organizations draw the line between direct and indirect costs. For example, in calculating the cost of university research projects, one university may count pension and other fringe benefits of researchers as direct costs, while another may count these items as indirect costs; one may charge secretarial assistance directly to projects, but another may charge all secretarial help to a common pool (a service center). Similarly, if heat, light and other utilities are metered for each cost center, they are direct costs; if not, they are indirect costs.

These differences in accounting treatment may have no material effect on the *total cost* of a research project because approximately the same amount may wind up as a cost, whether charged directly or indirectly. They do, however, affect the *relationship* between direct and indirect costs. Because of this, comparisons of this relationship among organizations are of little use.

Example

Assume the research costs in four universities showed the following percentages of indirect costs to direct salary and wages:

University	Overhead Percentage
A.	86
B.	80
C	57
D	54

While it is possible that Universities A and B had much more overhead than C and D, it also is possible that the differences are simply due to variations in the method of distinguishing between direct and indirect costs.

Appropriateness of Indirect Costs

Frequently, the issue is not one of distinguishing between direct and indirect costs, but of the appropriateness of the indirect costs themselves. For example, in the case of universities, critics say indirect costs have been rising unchecked for years. These costs now total over 50 percent of direct costs for most major research universities, and have been reported to be as high as 74 percent in some cases. University officials contend that such costs are needed to run the university. At issue are several questions: (1) what costs should be allowable, (2) which projects should pay for them, and (3) what kinds of efficiency standards should be used (such as how many librarians are needed to run the library).

Because of these questions, many resource providers have published rules governing the way costs are to be measured for reimbursement purposes. The most broadly applicable set is that of the Cost Accounting Standards Board in the Office of Federal Procurement Policy, but there are many other rules for specific types of reimbursement. The Department of Health and Human Services prescribes rules for health care organizations. The Office of Revenue Sharing of the Treasury Department prescribes principles for state and local governmental units. The Office of Management and Budget (OMB) sets forth principles for educational institutions. These principles are not completely consistent with one another, and an organization must be thoroughly familiar with the specific rules that are applicable to its situation.

Example

Much university research is supported by the federal government through contracts or grants. If the support comes in the form of a contract, the university is reimbursed in accordance with principles set forth in OMB Circular A-21, *Cost Principles for Educational Institutions.* These principles provide for direct costs plus an equitable share of indirect costs, including a use allowance for depreciation of buildings and equipment, operations and maintenance of plant, general administration and general expenses, departmental administration, student administration and services, and library.

Despite the presence of the OMB document, university overhead costs have presented an ongoing problem, and claims of overcharging for indirect costs are frequent. In some instances, the debate has reached the faculty ranks, with faculty expressing concern that high indirect rates impede a university's ability to obtain research funding.

Example

In a flurry of letters and emotional meetings, [Stanford University faculty] deluged the administration with bitter complaints that a bloated bureaucracy and campuswide building fever was burdening them with costs that would strangle their research. The tinder for the explosion was the news that Stanford's overhead—already among the highest in the nation at 74 percent—would rise to 84 percent.[20]

Similar claims have surfaced in other nonprofit organizations as well. In health care, for example, concerns have been voiced about the indirect costs that teaching hospitals charge Medicare for medical education. Teaching hospital administrators claim that these costs are appropriate ones for Medicare

[20]Marcia Barinaga, "Stanford Erupts over Indirect Costs," *Science* 248 (April 20, 1990), p. 292.

to pay in that, over the long term, they benefit Medicare patients. This, of course, is not a debate that will be resolved by improved cost accounting alone.

Standard Costs

Increasingly, nonprofit organizations are adopting cost accounting approaches that have proven to be successful in manufacturing settings. One such approach is the use of standard costs. In a standard cost system, each unit of product in a mission center is charged a predetermined (or standard) cost for direct labor, direct materials, and overhead. When this procedure is followed, the mission center's total standard cost for a given month (or other accounting period) is obtained by multiplying the standard unit cost by the number of units that flowed through the mission center for the month.

When a standard cost system is in place, management can use a technique called *variance analysis,* to identify whether deviations from the standard cost figure in a particular mission center are the result of volume changes (more or fewer units than anticipated), mix changes (a different combination of services than anticipated), efficiency changes (more or less time or materials needed per unit of service), or price changes (higher or lower wage rates and material prices).

As a consequence of using standard costs and variances, managers can gain much greater understanding of cost behavior in their organizations, as well as improved ability to control costs. Variance analysis is discussed in greater detail in Chapter 13.

Capital Costs

As discussed in Chapters 3 and 4, because of inflation, the full cost of using fixed assets is greater than the assets' depreciation expense. In effect, the need for a surplus is based on the idea that capital is tied up in these assets, even though a charge for the use of capital is not identified as a cost item in many accounting systems. Similarly, all organizations need working capital to operate, which also has a cost. Indeed, there are many situations that entail a cost of using capital.

Example

If a university borrowed $1 million at 10 percent to finance the construction of a building, the $100,000 annual interest expense would be considered part of the cost of using the building. Suppose, however, that the university used $1 million of its own funds to finance the building's construction. Some would argue that there is a capital cost associated with this transaction because, if the university had not used the funds to finance the building, it would have continued to invest them, earning perhaps $100,000 a year. Therefore, the "opportunity cost" of those lost earnings is appropriately part of the annual cost of using the building.

These cost elements are important in situations in which it is agreed that a client will reimburse the organization for the full cost of the service rendered as, for example, in a research contract. Unless the reimbursement includes an allowance for items such as the above, the organization's revenues will be insufficient to allow it to maintain its capital. Alternatively, there will be an incentive to finance all new fixed assets with debt, which may increase the organization's leverage above prudent levels.

Opportunity Costs

As indicated above, one way to measure the cost of capital employed is with *opportunity costs*. Opportunity costs also may be appropriate as a supplement to monetary outlays for some programs, especially in the public sector.

Example

As water becomes an increasingly scarce resource, the expense of some programs, such as waterfowl refuges, may come to be measured as the opportunity cost of water consumption rather than solely in terms of monetary outlays. Similar instances can be cited for public lands and public controls of private land.

Imputed Costs

In certain situations, imputed costs, which are a form of opportunity costs, need to be incorporated into the cost accounting system. Both cost measurement and control are facilitated if imputed costs are converted to actual monetary outlays.

Example

In the United States the cost of polluting water is usually an imputed cost; that is, companies generally have not been charged for the social cost of the rivers that they pollute. In the Ruhr Valley in Germany, by contrast, polluters pay a charge based on the effect of the effluent on the river's biochemical oxygen demand. The revenue derived from this charge is used to provide for water treatment. The effect is to convert an imputed cost into a monetary cost. In one study, conducted 30 years ago, the amount involved was about $60 million per year.[21] That amount would be considerably higher in today's prices.

The Dutch government developed a system of national accounting to reflect the damage done to the air, water, soil, and animal and plant life, and to account for the cost of maintaining or restoring them. Sweden, France, and Norway also have begun similar efforts at what is now called *green accounting.* In the United States, the Congress directed the Department of Commerce to work on a new system of calculating environmental costs and benefits.[22]

---

[21]From Barbara Ward and René Dubos, *Only One Earth,* an official report commissioned by the secretary general of the United Nations Conference on Human Environment (New York: W. W. Norton, 1972), chap. 7.
[22]Marlise Simons, "Europeans Begin to Calculate the Price of Pollution," *New York Times,* December 9, 1990.

Statistical System Costs

Some organizations base prices on cost, but they obtain cost data from a statistical system. Since a statistical system is not tied directly to the accounts, such cost data are likely to be of dubious validity. Furthermore, since prices are not related to the actual costs incurred in responsibility centers, managers of these centers are unlikely to accept them as reliable. Once designed and implemented, a cost system tied directly to the accounts requires about the same work to maintain as a statistical cost system.

Implications

Full costs are necessary if costs are to be used as a basis for pricing an organization's services, as in the TVA, the U.S. Postal Service, hospitals, and universities. They are also useful if judgments need to be made about the extent to which a program should "pay for itself," which is conceptually almost the same problem. Full-cost information may also facilitate the comparison of the cost of performing certain services in nonprofit organizations with the costs of comparable services in for-profit organizations.

The innate difficulties of making comparisons such as the above are considerable, however. Because of them, and in light of some of the complications discussed above, some people believe that the techniques of full-cost accounting do not actually provide a reasonable approximation of full cost. This is particularly important when, as will be discussed more fully in Chapter 7, full costs are a significant factor in setting prices.

Summary

Accountants engage in three distinct activities in a cost accounting effort. First, they define cost centers. Second, they assign all costs to a cost center—either a mission center or a service center. With direct costs, this is easy; with indirect costs it is more complicated. Third, they *allocate* service center costs to mission centers.

To carry out the allocation process, the accountants must take two steps. First, they must choose a *basis of allocation* (such as square feet) for each service center; this basis attempts to measure the use of the center's services by the other cost centers. Second, they must select a *method* of allocation (such as the step-down method) to distribute service center costs among other cost centers and ultimately to mission centers. Sometimes this process can become quite complex.

In many instances, service center costs are called *overhead costs,* although terminology is not consistent across all organizations. In some instances, for example, *overhead* is used to describe any cost element that is not directly associated with a final cost object. In this regard, the easiest approach usually is to determine the methodology being used rather than to attempt to discern the meaning of the terminology.

Once costs have been allocated to mission centers, they must be attached to cost objects. Doing so entails a choice between a process and job order method. In all of these activities there are a variety of complicating factors, such as capital costs, opportunity costs, and imputed costs. These factors are reflective of a cost accounting effort that entails many managerial choices.

Cost Accounting Terminology

As discussed in the text, cost accounting terminology can be confusing and occasionally contradictory. This appendix discusses several particularly tricky terms and concepts. It is not meant to be the final word, and readers usually must determine the precise meaning of a particular term from the context in which it is used.

A *cost object* is anything whose cost is collected. The Cost Accounting Standards Board (CASB) uses the term *cost objective* to mean the same thing. A *cost center,* therefore, is a cost object; *revenue (or mission) centers* and *service centers* are types of cost centers and, hence, also are cost objects. In many situations, a product is a *final cost object,* and cost centers are *intermediate cost objects.* Sometimes, there are several layers of cost objects, as when a final product consists of several intermediate products, each of which is produced in one or more cost centers.

A *cost item* is something that has been purchased: a pound of supplies, an hour of labor, a month of rent. It is expressed in units of currency (e.g., dollars) rather than some other measure. *Assign* is a verb referring to any recording of a cost item in a cost object. There are two ways a cost item can be assigned: (1) it can be assigned directly or (2) it can be allocated.

A cost item is *assigned directly* if it is traced to a single cost object. Such an item is a *direct cost* component of that cost object. If a cost item relates to two or more cost objects, it can still be assigned directly if appropriate measurement devices are used. For example, if a social worker carries out activities in two programs (cost objects) but keeps careful time records, his or her salary can be assigned directly to the two programs based on the percent of time spent in each. If a cost item cannot be assigned directly to a single cost object, it must be *allocated.* Therefore, a cost item is allocated if it is assigned to two or more cost objects. When this happens, the cost item is an *indirect cost* of each cost object. Thus, all indirect costs are allocated costs and vice versa; but not all assigned costs are allocated costs—some assigned costs are direct.

These definitions are slightly different from those used by the CASB. The CASB says that costs are *assigned to accounting periods.* They then are allocated to cost objects within the accounting period. They may be either directly or indirectly allocated.

We believe our usage conforms to the ordinary usage of *allocated.* Few people would say (as the CASB does) that direct labor or direct material is *allocated* to a product. Moreover, almost everyone refers to the *basis of allocation,* which refers to indirect costs only. If the CASB were to be consistent, it would need to use the term *basis of **indirect** allocation,* which it does not.

Suggested Additional Readings

Bodnar, George H. *Accounting Information Systems,* 6th ed. Englewood Cliffs, NJ: Prentice Hall, 1995.

Cooper, Robin, and Robert S. Kaplan. *The Design of Cost Management Systems: Text, Cases, and Readings.* Englewood Cliffs, NJ: Prentice Hall, 1991.

Horngren, Charles, George Foster, and Srikant Datar. *Cost Accounting: A Managerial Emphasis.* Englewood Cliffs, NJ: Prentice Hall, 1999.

Neumann, Bruce and Keith E. Boles. *Management Accounting for Health Care Organizations,* 5th ed. Chicago: Precept Press, 1998.

Practice Case 1

Mossy Bog Transportation Agency*

The Mossy Bog Transportation Agency (MBTA) had two service departments (maintenance and administration) and two mission departments (rapid transit and slow transit). Rapid Transit used high-speed trains and was highly equipment-intensive, while Slow Transit, using rickshaws, was highly labor intensive. Management had decided to allocate maintenance costs on the basis of depreciation dollars in each department, and administration costs on the basis of labor hours worked by the employees in each department.

The following data (dollar amounts in thousands) appeared in the agency's records for the current period:

	Service Centers		Production Centers		
	Mainten-ance	Admini-stration	Rapid Transit	Slow Transit	Total Costs
Direct plus distributed costs	$1,160	$2,400	$8,000	$4,000	$15,560
Depreciation dollars*	$ 200	$2,000	$3,000	$ 800	$ 6,000
Labor hours	20,000	10,000	10,000	40,000	

*Note: Depreciation dollars included in direct cost figures. Example: $1,160,000 in maintenance department includes $200,000 of depreciation.

*This case was prepared by Professor David W. Young. Copyright © by David W. Young

Questions

1. Allocate the service center costs to production centers using the stepdown method, and determine the relevant total costs. Begin with the maintenance department.

2. To what use would you put this information? Please be specific: What are the next steps you would take as a manager based on this information?

Practice Case 2

Museum of Frozen History[*]

The Museum of Frozen History was a nonprofit organization dedicated to educating the public about the history of ice cream. Instead of an admission price, the museum actually sold ice cream, using the proceeds to fund its expenses. It produced 15 different flavors that it offered to patrons in 1-pint cartons. The museum bought special ingredients from around the world, and then blended them with cream from its own cows, and packaged them for sale in a small shop situated at the end of the tour.

The museum's major cost was raw materials (the special flavors and the cream). However, there was a substantial amount of manufacturing overhead in the process of turning cream into ice cream, blending the flavors, and packaging the resulting product into the cartons. Most of these activities were highly automated, and the museum used very little direct labor. In fact, one of its displays showed how the manufacture of ice cream had been transformed from a highly labor-intensive activity into one that was almost completely automated.

Some of the flavors were very popular and sold in large volumes; however, a few of the more esoteric blends had very low volumes. The museum priced its ice cream at full production cost, plus a markup of 30 percent.

The museum's 2001 budget included manufacturing overhead of $3 million. This was allocated on the basis of each product's direct-labor cost. The budgeted direct-labor cost for 2001 was $600,000. Based on the sales budget and raw materials budget, the controller estimated that purchases and use of raw materials would total $6 million.

Exhibit 1 shows the expected direct manufacturing cost for a one-pint carton of two of the museum's ice creams. Upon reviewing this, the controller believed that the traditional product-costing system was providing misleading cost information. He developed an analysis of the 2001 budgeted manufacturing overhead costs, shown in Exhibit 2. Data for the 2001 production of Colombian Cocoa and Miami Mango are shown in Exhibit 3.

*This case was prepared by Professor David W. Young. Copyright © by David W. Young

EXHIBIT 1

MUSEUM OF FROZEN HISTORY		
Direct Manufacturing Costs for a 1-Pint Carton of Ice Cream		
	Colombian Cocoa	**Miami Mango**
Direct material	$4.20	$3.20
Direct labor	.30	.30

EXHIBIT 2

MUSEUM OF FROZEN HISTORY			
Analysis of 2001 Budgeted Manufacturing Overhead Costs			
Activity	**Cost Driver**	**Budgeted Activity**	**Budgeted Cost**
Purchasing	Purchase orders	1,158	$ 579,000
Material handling	Setups	1,800	720,000
Quality control	Batches	720	144,000
Cream freezing	Machine hours	96,100	961,000
Flavor blending	Blending hours	33,600	336,000
Packaging	Packaging hours	26,000	260,000
Total manufacturing overhead costs			$3,000,000

EXHIBIT 3
2001 Production Data

	Colombian Cocoa	**Miami Mango**
Budgeted production and sales	100,000 pints	2,000 pints
Batch size	10,000 pints	500 pints
Setups	3 per batch	3 per batch
Purchase order size	25,000 pints	500 pints
Cream freezing time	1 hour per 100 pints	1 hour per 100 pints
Flavor blending time	1/2 hour per 100 pints	1/2 hour per 100 pints
Packaging time	1/10 hour per 100 pints	1/10 hour per 100 pints

Questions

1. Compute the museum's predetermined overhead rate under the current system, and use it to determine the full product cost and selling price of 1 pint of Colombian Cocoa ice cream and 1 pint of Miami Mango.

2. Compute the full production cost for 1 pint of Colombian Cocoa ice cream and 1 pint of Miami Mango using an ABC approach.

3. What are the pros and cons of adopting the ABC system? Should the museum adopt it?

Case 5–1

Croswell University Hospital*

Ann Julian, M.D., chief of the department of obstetrics and gynecology at Croswell University Hospital (CUH), was reviewing the hospital's most recent cost report. Disappointed with its contents, she was meeting with Jonathan Haskell, the director of fiscal affairs, whose department had generated the report. She was not pleased.

> This report doesn't describe where our costs are generated. We're applying one standard to all patients, regardless of their level of care. What incentive is there to identify and account for the costs of each type of procedure? Unless I have better cost information, all our attempts to control costs will focus on decreasing the number of days spent in the hospital. This limits our options. In fact, it's not even an appropriate response to the hospital's reimbursement constraints.

Background

With the advent of DRGs and reimbursement limits by managed care organizations, CUH had felt the pinch of third parties' attempts to control hospital costs. The third parties effectively had placed hospitals at risk for their own costs. Croswell, like many other tertiary care institutions, had extended the cost control responsibility to its middle managers. It required each department head to become involved in the hospital's budgeting process, and to become accountable for the share of costs associated with his or her department's activities.

After considerable discussion with the board, the vice president for Medical Affairs had agreed that each clinical department chief should assume responsibility for the share of costs associated with the care of patients in his or her specialty. By enlisting the participation of chiefs in the cost control efforts, Croswell's senior management hoped to improve the hospital's overall financial performance.

The Present System

The hospital's present cost accounting system was based on an average standard costing unit applied to each department. For inpatient costs, the system used a cost-per-bed-per-day, known as a *bed/day*. For operating rooms (both inpatient and emergency), the standard unit was a cost-per-operation or procedure.

*This case was prepared by Emily Hayden, R.N., MBA, under the supervision of Professor David W. Young. It was prepared with assistance from Richard Depp, M.D., and with financial support from the Association of Professors of Gynecology and Obstetrics. Development of the case was made possible by a grant from Wyeth-Ayerst Laboratories to the APGO Medical Education Foundation. Copyright © by David W. Young.

To calculate the unit cost, the fiscal affairs department began with the direct costs of each department, as shown in Exhibit 1. It then allocated indirect costs, such as maintenance and depreciation, according to a predetermined method. It had developed this method in order to report costs to third parties such as medicare. The method used allocation bases such as size of plant, number of employees, salary dollars, and the total number of bed/days. For a given cost, the basis of allocation was designed to distribute indirect costs as fairly as possible across departments.

EXHIBIT 1
Cost Center Report
for 2001

Cost Center: Inpatient Surgery-Gynecology		
Number of available bed/days	16,425	
Number of occupied bed/days	14,602	
Occupancy rate	88.9%	
Direct costs:		
Wages:		
Nursing service	$3,182,330	
Clinical support staff	902,790	
Administrative staff	132,605	$ 4,217,725
Supplies:		
Pharmaceutical	$2,518,643	
Medical supplies	670,050	3,188,693
Diagnostic/Therapeutic:		
Diagnostic imaging	$ 687,361	
Laboratory tests	923,986	
Radiotherapy	279,486	1,890,833
Total direct costs		$ 9,297,251
Indirect costs:		
Patient services:		
Dietary	$ 626,430	
Laundry	169,575	
Housekeeping	154,260	
Medical records	127,720	
Social service	120,897	$ 1,198,882
Capital equipment:		
Depreciation on major purchases	$ 174,000	
Minor purchases	34,000	208,000
General services:		
Operation of plant	$ 236,450	
Plant depreciation	382,680	
Employee benefits	469,950	
Administration	$1,205,450	
Liability insurance	541,000	$ 2,835,530
Total indirect costs		$ 4,242,412
Total direct and indirect costs		$13,539,663
Average cost per day at full capacity		$824.33
Average cost per day at occupied capacity .		$927.25

Once all direct costs had been assigned to departments, and indirect costs had been allocated, the fiscal staff would calculate the average cost per unit by dividing the department's total costs by the number of activity units for that department. Exhibit 2 shows the average cost per unit for several surgical specialty departments.

After reviewing the costs and activities of the department of Ob/Gyn, Dr. Julian felt that obstetrical procedures were fairly well defined in terms of their costs. By contrast, gynecological procedures were a problem. She commented:

> Gynecological procedures are less amenable to assignment into cost categories. This is mainly because of the age range and diversity of the patients, but it's also due to the distinctions among the surgical subspecialties in gynecology. Because of this, the present cost accounting system is of little use for gynecology cases. This is extremely frustrating, especially since the hospital is expecting me to utilize the average cost per day approach to manage costs in the department. The average figure simply does not account for the real use of clinical resources by gynecology patients.

Mr. Haskell disagreed.

> Dr. Julian just doesn't understand. This system is ideal for comparative purposes. It allows me to quickly compare the costs of services among different departments within the hospital. It also helps me to compare the cost of a particular department at Croswell with a similar department at another hospital. Additionally, I can use the information to estimate the cost of treating an entire illness at Croswell. For example, I can easily determine the approximate cost of treating a patient having a total abdominal hysterectomy [TAH].*

According to Mr. Haskell's figures, the cost of a nononcology TAH would be about $3,709 ($927.25 × 4), since an average procedure of this type required four days in the hospital. To this would be added the cost of a major operation with general anesthesia, or $1,197. This procedure might also be performed with epidural or spinal anesthesia at the discretion of the anesthesia staff, in which case the total cost of the procedure would be slightly less.

The inpatient operating room costs of specific operative procedures were based on a three-year study. These figures were updated regularly by the fiscal affairs department. Dr. Julian was not presently held accountable for these costs, nor for the costs of anesthesia management. She was held responsible only for the costs associated with the pre- and postoperative care of the patients in her department. These costs were the ones causing her difficulty. According to her:

> Some patients, especially those undergoing treatment for cancer, use more resources than others. This is mainly because the testing and therapeutic treatment of patients varies widely. Some require more or fewer diagnostic and therapeutic

---

*This is a procedure in which the uterus, fallopian tubes, and ovaries are removed. If the procedure is done for reasons other than cancer, then it is classified as a *nononcology procedure.*

EXHIBIT 2   Cost Summary for Surgical Specialties

Specialty	Costing Unit	Total Cost	Average Cost at Occupied Capacity	Average Cost at Full Capacity
General	Bed/day	$11,871,305	$ 797.36	$721.32
Orthopedic	Bed/day	12,274,636	938.24	794.56
Neurosurgery.	Bed/day	15,837,594	1,105.80	808.80
Gynecology	Bed/day	13,539,663	927.25	824.33
Obstetrics	Bed/day	9,483,625	819.12	733.80
Pediatrics.	Bed/day	11,847,364	882.28	802.68
Inpatient operating rooms		$13,789,475		
Major/general anesthesia.	Procedure		$ 1,197	
Major/epidural or spinal.	Procedure		1,163	
Major/local or regional.	Procedure		760	
Minor/general anesthesia.	Procedure		589	
Minor/epidural or spinal	Procedure		485	
Minor/local or regional	Procedure		274	
Emergency operating rooms		$ 4,842,631		
Minor/general anesthesia.	Procedure		$ 486	
Minor/local or regional	Procedure		388	
Minor/no anesthesia	Procedure		178	
Total costs		$93,486,293		

interventions, depending upon their admitting diagnoses. For example, radiation therapy is utilized almost exclusively by oncology patients.

Somehow, a good cost accounting system must recognize these differences. I also don't want my department to appear overly costly simply because some patients don't conform to the norm. The current cost accounting system just does not account for the differences among patients, and it doesn't give me the data I need to manage costs.

The Use of Clinical Distinctions

After some discussion, Dr. Julian convinced Mr. Haskell that the average unit cost calculation could be revised to account for the differences among patients having different gynecology procedures. In an effort to address these clinical differences, Mr. Haskell suggested that the gynecology patients be divided into three categories according to clinical subspecialty:

1. General gynecology/urogynecology (Nononco Gyn).

2. Reproductive/in vitro fertilization (RE-IVF).

3. Oncology.

With the help of Dr. Julian, Mr. Haskell calculated time and material estimates for each type of patient stay. For example, he estimated that, in general, more medication was used on oncology patients than on general gynecology patients. Also, oncology patients were likely to need more of a variety of other resources, such as lab tests, drugs, and X-rays.

Mr. Haskell conferred with his staff regarding the best method to apportion indirect costs among the three subspecialties. After much discussion, they decided to apportion most of these costs according to the number of patient days in each subspecialty. They made a few adjustments, however, to reflect unusual circumstances.

Although this new system maintained bed/days as the standard costing unit, Mr. Haskell pointed out that it was more accurate than the one currently in use because there were now three average costs per bed/day: one for general gynecology/urogynecology, another for RE-IVF, and a third for oncology. Exhibit 3 contains this information.

Dr. Julian and Mr. Haskell performed some calculations and compared the differences between the two systems. They computed the cost of an abdominal hysterectomy (nononcology) using each system. Dr. Julian estimated that an uncomplicated TAH generally required a four-day stay under general gynecology. They also compared the costs of patients undergoing two other fairly frequent procedures. One was a tuboplasty, a procedure in which the fallopian tube is opened or its lumen (passage) is reestablished. The other procedure was a total abdominal hysterectomy (TAH) with lymph node dissection. In this operation, the lymph nodes in the pelvic region are also excised. The tuboplasty would be categorized in the RE-IVF category, while, in this instance, the TAH with lymph node dissection would be classified in the oncology category.

Although their findings were based on only three of the departments many procedures, Dr. Julian and Mr. Haskell concluded that this specialty-based system could greatly increase Dr. Julian's ability to identify and control costs.

Intensities of Care

After Dr. Julian had compared a few more specialty-based costs of care, she continued to harbor some concerns about the system. Although it was an improvement over the average bed/day calculation, it still had problems. She was particularly disturbed about the intensities of medical and nursing attention given to patients within each subspecialty category. Dr. Julian explained to Mr. Haskell that, for example, a TAH patient with cancer required more nursing and medical care on the second postoperative day than did a laparoscopy patient, even if both patients were classified in the oncology category.

The new system did not address these differences. The system made it appear as if all oncology patients received the same amount of care on a given day in the hospital. From a clinical perspective, this clearly was not the

EXHIBIT 3   Department of Gynecology Cost Breakdown by Surgical Specialty

Costs	General Gynecology	Reproductive/ IVF	Oncology	Total
Direct:				
Wages:				
Nursing	$1,040,160	$ 903,080	$1,239,090	$ 3,182,330
Clinical support	302,900	247,210	352,680	902,790
Administration.	41,825	37,475	53,305	132,605
Supplies:				
Pharmaceutical	650,422	595,277	1,272,944	2,518,643
Medical supplies	119,470	238,940	311,640	670,050
Diagnostic/therapeutic:				
Diagnostic imaging	229,564	153,838	303,959	687,361
Laboratory tests.	295,384	241,745	386,857	923,986
Radiotherapy	0	0	279,486	279,486
Total direct	$2,679,725	$2,417,565	$4,199,961	$ 9,297,251
Indirect:				
Patient services:				
Dietary.	$ 180,480	$ 136,490	$ 309,460	$ 626,430
Laundry.	57,495	45,535	66,545	169,575
Housekeeping	49,090	43,030	62,140	154,260
Medical records.	30,930	31,850	64,940	127,720
Social services	32,567	28,465	59,865	120,897
Capital equipment:				
Major equipment depreciation	36,692	82,540	54,768	174,000
Minor	7,564	13,875	12,561	34,000
General services:				
Operation of plant.	79,160	59,155	98,135	236,450
Plant depreciation	102,230	113,370	167,080	382,680
Employee benefits	141,550	153,280	175,120	469,950
Administration.	235,510	480,530	489,410	1,205,450
Liability insurance	195,771	187,243	157,986	541,000
Total indirect	$1,149,039	$1,375,363	$1,718,010	$ 4,242,412
Total direct and indirect	$3,828,764	$3,792,928	$5,917,971	$13,539,663
Number of bed/days	4,002	5,023	5,577	
Cost per bed/day	$ 956.71	$ 755.11	$ 1,061.14	

case. Because of this, Dr. Julian felt that the subspecialty breakdown was still not a sufficiently accurate measure of the costs of care rendered to different patients. Working on her own, she developed a third cost accounting method based on levels of care delivered by the nursing and medical teams. In developing this new method, she divided the department's costs into three categories that were quite different from those used by Mr. Haskell:

1. Daily patient maintenance.

2. Medical treatment.

3. Nursing care.

Dr. Julian decided that medical treatment could be measured with an index of non-nursing clinical intensity. She worked with two other physicians in the department to determine the amount of laboratory, diagnostic radiology, therapeutic radiology, and pharmacy resources that would be used by a typical patient with a TAH (nononcology), a TAH (oncology), and a tuboplasty. She

EXHIBIT 4 Levels of Nursing Care

Level 1. Basic Assistance (mainly for ambulatory patients)	**1–3 units**
Feeds self without supervision or with family member.	
Toilets independently.	
Vital signs routine—daily temperature, pulse, and respiration.	
Bedside humidifier or blow bottle.	
Routine postoperation suction standby.	
Bathes self, bed straightened with minimal or no supervision.	
Exercises with assistance, once in eight hours.	
Treatments once or twice in eight hours.	
Level 2. Periodic Assistance	**4–7 units**
Feeds self with staff supervision; or tubal feeding by patient.	
Toilets with supervision or specimen collection, or uses bedpan. Hemovac output.	
Vital signs monitored; every two to four hours.	
Mist or humidified air when sleeping, or cough and deep breathe every two hours.	
Nasopharyngeal or oral suction prn.	
Bathed and dressed by personnel or partial bath given; daily change of linen.	
Up in chair with assistance twice in eight hours or walking with assistance.	
Treatments three or four times in eight hours.	
Level 3. Continual Nursing Care	**8–10 units**
Total feeding by personnel or continuous IV or blood transfusions or instructing the patient.	
Tube feeding by personnel every three hours or less.	
Up to toilet with standby supervision or output measurement every hour. Initial hemovac setup.	
Vital signs and observation every hour or vital signs monitored plus neuro check. Blood pressure, pulse, respiration, and neuro check every 30 minutes.	
Continuous oxygen, trach mist or cough and deep breathe every hour. IPPB with supervision every four hours.	
Tracheostomy suction every two hours or less.	
Bathed and dressed by personnel, special skin care, occupied bed.	
Bed rest with assistance in turning every two hours or less, or walking with assistance of two persons twice in eight hours.	
Treatments more than every two hours.	

Source: Adapted from M. Poland et al., "PETO—A System for Assisting and Meeting Patient Care Needs," *American Journal of Nursing* 70 (July 1970), p. 1479.

then translated these resources into units that could be counted and totaled easily. Dr. Julian knew that this type of information was not completely accurate. For example, a TAH (nononcology) patient in relatively good health would need fewer tests and drugs than a somewhat older patient, or a patient with complications. This could result in higher or lower medical intensity, even though the number of medical treatment units in the system would be the same for all patients with the same procedure. Despite these problems, she felt that she now had a way to measure medical resource use fairly accurately.

Levels of nursing care proved to be a similarly complicated issue. Dr. Julian consulted with nurses on the gynecology floors and, with them, developed a system to measure patient care needs. They defined three basic levels of nursing care, which are described in Exhibit 4. A patient could change levels during his or her stay. Within each level, a patient could be assigned a range of units, depending upon the intensity of nursing services being provided.

In this third method, Dr. Julian expected to use not only bed/days as a costing unit, but also, the average number of medical treatment and nursing units per procedure. She enlisted the assistance of Mr. Haskell in devising a means to apportion costs to each of the categories in her new system. The resulting cost summary is shown in Exhibit 5.

Comparison of Costs

To compare her new system with the others, Dr. Julian again calculated costs for the same three procedures. According to her calculations, each required the following:

Procedure	Bed/Days	Total Medical Treatment Units	Total Nursing Units
TAH-Nononcology	4	12	10
Tuboplasty	3	10	5
TAH-Oncology	7	20	38

Dr. Julian was satisfied with the results of this cost accounting system. She believed that it accurately distinguished among the surgical procedures in the gynecologic subspecialties, and that the differences in costs reflected the actual differences in resources used by patients. She commented:

> With this new information, I can identify cost problems easily since all costs are now categorized according to the nature as well as the intensity of the services. I plan to develop this system even further so that standard unit requirements for each type of procedure become well-known by the attendings and residents in my department. Then I'll be able to analyze gynecology costs according to the

EXHIBIT 5   Department of Gynecology Level of Care System

Costs	Daily Patient Maintenance	Medical Treatment	Nursing Care	Total
Direct:				
Wages:				
Nursing			$3,182,330	$ 3,182,330
Clinical support	$ 17,345	$ 429,756	455,689	902,790
Administration	132,605			132,605
Supplies:				
Pharmaceutical.		$2,518,643		2,518,643
Medical supplies.	229,310	328,140	112,600	670,050
Diagnostic/therapeutic:				
Diagnostic imaging		687,361		687,361
Laboratory tests		923,986		923,986
Radiotherapy		279,486		279,486
Total direct	$ 379,260	$5,167,372	$3,750,619	$ 9,297,251
Indirect:				
Patient services:				
Dietary.	$ 626,430			626,430
Laundry	169,575			169,575
Housekeeping.	154,260			154,260
Medical records	85,145	28,575	14,000	127,720
Social services.	72,100	30,050	18,747	120,897
Capital equipment:				
Major equipment depreciation	35,276	138,724		174,000
Minor.	6,748	17,928	9,324	34,000
General services:				
Operation of plant	236,450			236,450
Plant depreciation	382,680			382,680
Employee benefits		194,490	275,460	469,950
Administration	1,205,450			1,205,450
Liability insurance.		502,000	39,000	541,000
Total indirect.	$2,974,114	$ 911,767	$ 356,531	$ 4,242,412
Total direct and indirect costs	$3,353,374	$6,079,139	$4,107,150	$13,539,663
Total days care.	14,602			
Cost per bed/day	$ 230			
Total medical treatment units		36,180		
Cost per medical treatment unit		$ 168		
Total nursing units.			49,754	
Cost per nursing unit.			$ 83	

particular patient mix being treated, and in terms of the services being provided by different physicians in the department.

Mr. Haskell agreed with Dr. Julian that this third system might work well in gynecology and in other departments having surgical subspecialties. However, he doubted that it could be transferred to all departments within the hospital. He felt that some departments would not be able to develop standard medical and nursing requirements since their patient diagnoses and procedures were less well-defined than in surgery. Furthermore, he was concerned about the complexity of the system, especially for department chiefs. Chiefs, in his view, might not have the inclination to use the system effectively or might not feel it worth the time to collect all of the necessary information.

Dr. Julian disagreed. She contacted the vice president of medical affairs and offered to present her system at the next meeting of chiefs of service. She was convinced that the other chiefs would see the value of the system.

Questions

1. What is the cost in Dr. Julian's department of a TAH (nononcology) under each of the cost accounting systems? A tuboplasty? A TAH (oncology)? What accounts for the changes from one system to the next?

2. Which of the three systems is the best? Why?

3. From a managerial perspective, of what use is the information in the second and third systems? That is, how, if at all, would this additional information improve Dr. Julian's ability to control costs? How might it help chiefs in nonsurgical specialties?

4. How should Dr. Julian present her system at the next meeting of chiefs of service?

Case 5–2

Jefferson High School*

"I'm sorry, but I'm having a very difficult time using the information on this cost report," said Adam King, principal of Jefferson High School. "I mean, salary totals and the average unit cost may be useful to you and the people in the central office, but I need to know more detail. We have so many different types of activities at Jefferson that I need to know the unit cost for each if I'm going to do anything about cost control."

*This case was prepared by Professor David W. Young. Copyright © by David W. Young.

Mr. King was discussing the Los Diablos school system's cost accounting system with Michael Abbott, director of the fiscal affairs department. Mr. King had requested the meeting because he felt he needed more information than that contained on his school's cost report, shown in Exhibit 1. Interested in improving cost control methods at Jefferson High, Mr. King argued that the average per-student cost calculation was not an accurate measure of Jefferson's costs because the type and content of a student's educational activities varied greatly depending on the student's grade, interests, and special needs. According to Mr. King, the school system's cost accounting system needed to be revised in order to identify the specific unit costs of various student-based activities. During the discussion, Mr. Abbott became interested in Mr. King's approach, and agreed to help him design a cost accounting system that made these distinctions.

Background

In 2001, in conjunction with the Los Diablos school system's move toward decentralizing its educational activities, a school-based cost accounting system had been developed. As one of the system's largest schools, Jefferson was among the first to implement such a system, which required the assistance of principals in monitoring their school's expenditures. By involving principals in the budgeting and expenditure review process, Nell Chamberlain, Los Diablos' school superintendent, hoped to gain more control over school-based costs and to improve the system's overall financial performance.

The school-based cost accounting system (SBCAS) was based on a standard costing unit which each school could use to measure its overall costs. SBCAS used a student as the basic cost calculation unit. To calculate an average cost per student for any given school, SBCAS first collected the direct costs on the school-based cost report (SBCR), as shown in Exhibit 1. The fiscal affairs department then allocated the central office costs, such as depreciation, health and life insurance, and administration to each school according to a predetermined method. These allocation methods for indirect costs had been determined by Mr. Abbott, and included classroom space, number of student days, number of employees, and salary dollars. The basis of allocation for any given cost was designed to provide the fairest means possible for distributing it to the various schools in the system.

Once all costs had been allocated to schools, the fiscal staff would calculate the average cost per student by dividing each school's total costs by the appropriate number of students. These calculations also are shown on Exhibit 1.

According to Mr. Abbott, the main advantage of this system was that it allowed him to quickly compare the cost of educating a child in different schools. He also thought the system could be used to calculate the cost of educating the students in a particular grade. For example, to determine the cost

EXHIBIT 1
School-Based Cost
Report, 2000–2001

Statistics:		
Number of registered students	750	
Number of days in academic year	170	
Number of potential student days	127,500	
Actual number of student days	115,350	
Attendance rate	90.5%	
Direct costs—Instruction		
Regular teacher salaries	$1,175,000	
Special education teacher salaries	480,000	
Aide salaries	58,500	
Substitute teacher salaries	37,700	
Instructional supplies and library	85,200	
Other services*	327,500	
Total		$2,163,900
Direct costs—Administration		
Administrative salaries	$ 125,000	
Administrative supplies	15,500	
Operations and maintenance	270,000	
Other	7,500	
Total		418,000
Total direct costs		$2,581,900
Indirect costs—Allocated from central office		
School committee	$ 3,500	
Administration	43,300	
Health/life insurance	135,200	
Operation and maintenance	7,400	
Rent and depreciation	3,500	
Contract services	2,200	
Travel	850	
Total		195,950
Total direct and indirect costs		$2,777,850
Average cost per registered student		$ 3,704

*Includes athletics, transportation, and counseling.

of educating students in the 12th grade, Mr. Abbott could multiply the number of students in that grade at Jefferson High by Jefferson's average cost per student, perform similar calculations for all other high schools in the system, and add the results together.

For Ms. Chamberlain, the SBCAS was to be the basis for greater fiscal accountability, and she had notified the principals in each school that she expected them to work with the SBCAS data in attempting to control costs. This was the main source of concern for Mr. King, since he thought that the average cost per student was not an accurate measure for most of the students at Jefferson High. According to him, the actual cost of a student varied because students at different grade levels required different types and levels of education. Mr. King argued that the average cost per student misrepresented the resource needs of most students, and, because of this, the SBCAS did not provide him with the data he needed for accurate budgeting and planning.

Grade-Based System

In an effort to address this problem, Mr. Abbott suggested that the SBCAS for Jefferson be based on grade distinctions. He therefore divided the school's students into three categories based on their grade levels—10th, 11th, and 12th—and, with Mr. King's help, calculated personnel and supply estimates for each grade level. For example, he estimated that although there were fewer students in the 12th grade than the 10th or 11th, many students in the 12th grade regularly used the school's career counselor, whereas most students in the 10th and 11th grades did not. From these estimates, Mr. Abbott assigned Jefferson's direct costs to each grade level.

Next, Mr. Abbott set about devising a method for allocating the indirect costs. After much discussion with Mr. King and his staff, he decided to allocate all these costs according to the number of students in each grade. His calculations are contained in Exhibit 2.

Although the new system maintained a student as the standard costing unit, Mr. Abbott argued that it was a more accurate approach than the system currently in use. Instead of an average cost per student, he now had three average cost figures: one for each grade level.

In evaluating the new cost accounting system, Mr. King and Mr. Abbott explored the differences in cost calculations resulting from the two systems. Some quick computations by the two pointed out the differences in the cost per student under different accounting procedures. From these findings, Mr. Abbott concluded that his "grade-based" system could greatly increase a principal's ability to budget and control costs.

As Mr. King reflected on the new system, a few problems continued to bother him. Although he agreed that the grade-based costs were more accurate than the school-based per-student calculations, he felt there were further distinctions in resource use that the system did not sufficiently address. He was particularly disturbed about the varying intensities of special education, athletics, and counseling received within each grade. Mr. King explained to Mr. Abbott that, according to the new accounting system, it appeared as though all students in the 12th grade received the same amount of educational resources, but from his perspective this clearly was not the case. He pointed out by way of example that a student in varsity athletics received far more athletic resources than one taking only regular physical education classes. Similarly, a

EXHIBIT 2   Grade-Based Cost Report, 2000–2001

	Grade 10	*Grade 11*	*Grade 12*	*Total*
Direct costs—Instruction				
Regular teacher salaries.	$ 470,000	$411,250	$293,750	$1,175,000
Special education teacher salaries	240,000	144,000	96,000	480,000
Aide salaries	35,100	14,625	8,775	58,500
Substitute teacher salaries.	15,080	13,195	9,425	37,700
Instructional supplies and library.	34,080	29,820	21,300	85,200
Other services.	65,500	81,875	180,125	327,500
Total	$ 859,760	$694,765	$609,375	$2,163,900
Direct costs—Administration				
Administrative salaries.	$ 50,000	$ 43,750	$ 31,250	$ 125,000
Administrative supplies	6,200	5,425	3,875	15,500
Operations and maintenance	67,500	108,000	94,500	270,000
Other	3,000	2,625	1,875	7,500
Total	$ 126,700	$159,800	$131,500	$ 418,000
Indirect costs—Allocated from central office				
School committee.	$ 1,400	$ 1,223	$ 877	$ 3,500
Administration	17,320	15,126	10,854	43,300
Health/life insurance	54,080	47,230	33,890	135,200
Operation and maintenance.	2,960	2,585	1,855	7,400
Rent and depreciation.	1,400	1,223	877	3,500
Contract services.	880	769	551	2,200
Travel	340	297	213	850
Total	$ 78,380	$ 68,453	$ 49,117	$ 195,950
Total direct and indirect costs.	$1,064,840	$923,018	$789,992	$2,777,850
Number of registered students.	300	262	188	
Average cost per registered student . . . . $	3,550	$ 3,523	$ 4,202	

student whose behavior resulted in a need to see the school counselor regularly used more counseling resources than one who was well-behaved. These sorts of distinctions could be made, he argued, for special education as well. As such, the grade-based breakdown was not a sufficiently accurate measure.

Service-Based System

Unable to convince Mr. Abbott of the importance of this additional refinement, Mr. King himself began experimenting with a third cost accounting method—based on levels of educational services received—that he thought might be more accurate. As the first step in his calculations, he divided the school's costs according to the type of service provided: regular education, special education, athletics, and counseling. He decided that a student's use of the regular education component could be measured most easily and accurately in terms of the number of days of school attendance during the academic year.

Examining Jefferson's student records, he decided that it was more complicated to measure special education. He consulted with some of the special education teachers and, with them, developed a system based on levels of special education needs. They decided to define special education intensity on three levels: one unit represented occasional assistance only; two units were for a student who received special education services for one or two days a week; three units represented three or more days a week.

Athletics and counseling were measured in a similar fashion. Students who participated in after-school athletic programs but did not play either junior varsity or varsity sports received one unit; two units were given for junior varsity; three units for varsity. Students who used counseling services on an infrequent basis received one unit; those who used them more regularly received two units; those who used them continually received three units.

Having developed these classifications, Mr. King solicited Mr. Abbott's assistance in allocating indirect costs; their cost summary is contained in Exhibit 3. In this analysis, Mr. King expected to use more than student days as the costing unit. For each student, he would need to calculate the number of days of school attendance, and estimate the number of units required for special education, athletics, and counseling.

To compare this system with the others, Mr. King chose three students at random in order to determine their costs. According to his calculations, each required the following:

Student	Grade	Regular Education	Special Education	Athletics	Counseling
Larry B	10	170 days	2 units	0 units	0 units
Michael R	11	150	0	3	2
Anna B	12	165	3	1	3

Mr. King was satisfied with the results of this cost accounting system. He thought that it accurately distinguished among the various types of services available, and that the differences in costs reflected actual differences in services received. He felt that because he could now isolate costs by both the nature and intensity of the service provided, he would be able to locate and manage cost problems in the school more easily, thereby complying more effectively with Ms. Chamberlain's expectations.

Mr. Abbott, however, remained skeptical. Although he thought Mr. King might be able to make effective use of the system at Jefferson, he doubted that it could be transferred to other schools since, in his view, other schools would not be able to develop resource utilization units for the various services. Furthermore, he was afraid that the system was too complicated to be

EXHIBIT 3   Service-Based Cost Report, 2000–2001

	Regular Education	Special Education	Athletics	Counseling	Total
Direct costs—Instruction					
Regular teacher salaries	$1,112,300		$ 62,700		$1,175,000
Special education teacher salaries.		$480,000			480,000
Aide salaries	15,300	43,200			58,500
Substitute teacher salaries	25,700	12,000			37,700
Instructional supplies and library	60,200	25,000			85,200
Other services	18,200	50,300	204,000	$55,000	327,500
Total	$1,231,700	$610,500	$266,700	$55,000	$2,163,900
Direct costs—Administration					
Administrative salaries	$ 71,750	$ 35,266	$ 15,406	$ 3,178	$ 125,000
Administrative supplies.	8,823	4,373	1,910	394	15,500
Operations and maintenance	153,685	76,175	33,277	6,863	270,000
Other.	4,269	2,116	924	191	7,500
Total	$ 237,927	$117,930	$ 51,517	$10,626	$ 418,000
Indirect costs—Allocated from central office					
School committee	$ 1,992	$ 987	$ 431	$ 89	$ 3,500
Administration	24,648	12,216	5,337	1,101	43,300
Health/life insurance.	76,956	38,144	16,663	3,436	135,200
Operation and maintenance.	4,212	2,088	912	188	7,400
Rent and depreciation	1,992	987	431	89	3,500
Contract services	1,252	621	271	56	2,200
Travel	484	240	105	22	850
Total	$ 111,536	$ 55,283	$ 24,150	$ 4,981	$195,950
Total direct and indirect costs	$1,581,163	$783,713	$342,367	$70,607	$2,777,850
Total number of units.	127,500	1,200	1,500	300	
Cost per unit	$ 12.40	$ 653.09	$ 280.13	$ 235.36	

implemented in all schools. Finally, he seriously questioned the ability of principals to use the system effectively.

Questions

1. What is the cost for each of the three students Mr. King chose at random? What explains the differences?

2. Which of the three systems is the best? Why?

3. What other systems, if any, would you propose?

4. Should Mr. King's system be implemented in all schools?

Case 5–3

Harbor City Children's Center*

> Our deficit is increasing, and we obviously have to reverse this trend if we're going to become solvent. But, for that, we have to know where our costs are, in particular the cost of each of the services we offer.

In March 1998, Liz Conaway, executive director of Harbor City Children's Center, expressed concern to Ted Roberts, her new accountant, about the center's cost accounting system. The extensive funding Harbor City had received during its early years was decreasing, and Ms. Conaway wanted to prepare the center to be self-sufficient, yet she lacked critical cost information.

Background

Harbor City Children's Center was established in 1983 by a consortium of community groups. Situated in Torrance, a residential neighborhood near Los Angeles, California, the center was intended to provide counseling and related services to residents of Torrance and neighboring communities. Fifteen years after its inception, the center maintained strong ties with the community groups responsible for its development and subsequent acceptance in Torrance.

Funding for Harbor City was initially provided by the federal government as part of the Department of Health and Human Services' attempt to provide social services to inner-city poverty areas in the United States. When these operating funds were depleted in 1996, the city of Torrance supplemented Harbor City's income with a small three-year grant. Because Ms. Conaway realized that government support could not continue indefinitely, she intended to make the center self-sufficient as soon as possible. Harbor City's income statement is contained in Exhibit 1.

The center was composed of eight client-service departments: Homemaker Service, Family Planning, Counseling, Parents' Advocacy, Mental Health, Alcohol Rehabilitation, Community Outreach, and Referral and Placement. In addition, the center had a Training and Education Department, which saw no clients, and a Client Records Department. The center had 22 paid employees and a volunteer staff of 6–10 students acquiring clinical and managerial experience.

Community Outreach, which had been designed by Harbor City's consumers, was a multidisciplinary department providing a link between the health and social services at the center and the schools and city services of the community. The department was staffed by a part-time speech pathologist, a part-time learning specialist, and a full-time nutritionist.

*This case was prepared by Professor David W. Young. Copyright © by David W. Young.

EXHIBIT 1

HARBOR CITY CHILDREN'S CENTER INCOME STATEMENT For the Year Ended December 31, 1997	
Revenue from patient fees	$1,381,800
Other revenues	20,000
Total revenue	$1,401,800
Expenses:	
Program services	$ 940,000
Recordkeeping	40,000
Training and education	100,000
General and administrative	368,000
Total expenses	$1,448,000
Surplus (deficit)	$ (46,200)

The Referral and Placement Service was for clients whom the center felt, at the time it received a referral, it could not serve; the staff attempted to locate another agency that could serve the client. Parents' Advocacy did not serve clients directly but rather worked on behalf of clients who were having difficulty with housing, schools, and so forth.

The Existing Information System

Harbor City's previous accountant had established a system to determine the cost per client visit (or related activity such as advocacy). According to this method, shown in Exhibit 2, the cost was a yearly average for all client visits. The accountant would first determine the direct cost of each department. He would then add overhead costs, such as administration, rent, and utilities, to the total cost of all the departments to determine the center's total costs. Finally, he would divide that total by the number of visits. Increased by an anticipated inflation figure for the following year, this number became the projected cost per client visit for the subsequent year.

In reviewing this method with Mr. Roberts, Ms. Conaway explained the problems she perceived. She said that although she realized this was not a precise method of determining costs for clients, the center's cost per visit had to be held at a reasonable level to keep the services accessible to as many community residents as possible. Additionally, she anticipated complications in determining the cost per visit for each of Harbor City's departments:

> You have to consider that our overhead costs, like administration and rent, have to be included in the cost per visit. That's easy to do when we have a single cost, but I'm not certain how to go about it when determining costs on a departmental basis. Furthermore, it's important to point out that some of our departments provide services to others. Parents' Advocacy, for example. There are three social workers in that department, all earning the same salary. But one works exclusively for

EXHIBIT 2 Costs and Client Visits for 1997, by Department*

Department	Number Client Visits	Expenses Salaries†	Expenses Other‡	Expenses Total
Homemaker Service	5,000	$ 80,000	$ 32,000	$ 112,000
Family Planning	10,000	20,000	60,000	80,000
Counseling.	2,100	120,000	64,000	184,000
Parents' Advocacy	4,000	108,000	24,000	132,000
Mental Health	1,400	60,000	32,000	92,000
Alcohol Rehabilitation.	1,500	128,000	32,000	160,000
Community Outreach	2,500	20,000	40,000	60,000
Referral and Placement.	6,400	80,000	40,000	120,000
Subtotal	32,900	616,000	324,000	940,000
Administration		152,000	8,000	160,000
Rent.			144,000	144,000
Utilities.			40,000	40,000
Training and Education.		64,000	36,000	100,000
Cleaning			24,000	24,000
Recordkeeping		28,000	12,000	40,000
Total		$860,000	$588,000	$1,448,000
Number of patient visits.				32,900
Average cost per visit				$ 44.00

*Client visits rounded to nearest 100; expenses rounded to nearest $1,000.
†Includes fringe benefits.
‡Materials, supplies, contracted services, depreciation, and other nonpersonnel expenses.

Counseling, another divides her time evenly between Family Planning and Homemaker Service. Only the third spends his entire time in the Advocacy Department seeing clients who don't need other social services, although he occasionally refers clients to other social workers. In the Alcohol Rehabilitation Department, the situation is more complicated. We have two MSWs, each earning $48,000 a year, and one bachelor degree social worker earning $32,000. The two MSWs yearly see about 1,500 clients who need counseling, but they also spend about 50 percent of their time in other departments. The BA social worker cuts pretty evenly across all departments except Referral and Placement, of course.

Mr. Roberts added further dimensions to the problems:

I've spent most of my time so far trying to get a handle on allocating these overhead costs to the departments. It's not an easy job, you know. Administration, for example, seems to help everyone about equally, yet I suppose we might say more administrative time is spent in the departments where we pay more salaries. Rent, on the other hand, is pretty easy: that can be done on a square-foot basis. We could classify utilities according to usage if we had meters to measure electricity, phone usage, and so forth, but because we don't we have to do that on a square-foot basis as well. This applies to cleaning too, I guess. It seems to me that

EXHIBIT 3
Floor Space and
T&E Usage, by
Department

Department	Floor Space*	T&E Usage†
Homemaker Service.	1,000	1,000
Family Planning.	1,300	200
Counseling	1,800	2,400
Parents' Advocacy	300	100
Mental Health	1,000	—
Alcohol Rehabilitation	500	—
Community Outreach	1,100	100
Referral and Placement	1,000	200
Administration.	500	—
Recordkeeping	300	—
Training and Education (T&E)	1,200	—
Total	10,000	4,000

*In square feet, rounded to nearest 100.
†In hours per year, rounded to nearest 100.

recordkeeping can be allocated on the basis of the number of records, and each department generates one record per client visit.

Training and Education (T&E) is the most confusing. Some departments don't use it at all, while others use it regularly. I guess the fairest would be to charge for T&E on an hourly basis. Since there are two people in the department, each working about 2,000 hours a year, the charge per hour would be about $16.00. But this is a bit unfair since the T&E Department also uses supplies, space, and administrative time. So we should include those other costs in its hourly rate. Thus, the process is confusing and I haven't really decided how to sort it out. However, I have prepared totals for floor space and T&E usage [Exhibit 3].

The Future

As Ms. Conaway looked toward the remainder of 1998, she decided to calculate a precise cost figure for each department. The center was growing, and she estimated that total client volume would increase by about 10 percent during 1998, spread evenly over each department. She anticipated that costs would also increase by about 10 percent. She asked Mr. Roberts to prepare a stepdown analysis for 1997 so that they would know the costs for each department. She planned to use this information to assist her in projecting costs for 1998.

Questions

1. What is the cost per visit for each department?

2. How might this information be used by Ms. Conaway?

Case 5–4

Neighborhood Servings*

A few years ago, I didn't think we'd make it. Some other agencies and several small restaurants were competing with us, and were undercutting our prices. So a year ago we decided to begin making specialty meals for AIDS and cancer patients, and for other people with special dietary needs. I thought that strategy was working. Certainly sales were up. But now a consultant tells me that our cost accounting system is giving us misleading results, and we may actually be losing money on our specialty meals. On top of that, some of our regular customers are complaining about our prices.

The speaker was George Larson, CEO of Neighborhood Servings (NS), a nonprofit organization that produced and delivered meals to homes throughout the greater Kansas City area. He continued:

I realize that we now need to dig into our costs. We established our prices based on these costs. If the costs for speciality meals are higher than we thought, then our prices are too low, and our whole new strategy is in jeopardy. In addition, if our costs for regular meals are too high, then we're setting our prices too high and we'll lose out to the competition even more. Also, we use our cost data for budgeting each year, so if the data are bad, then our budget will be unrealistic.

Background

NS had been in business for over 10 years. It began as a "meals on wheels" agency, providing dinners to elderly people and individuals who were permanently or temporarily homebound. Almost all of its clients were single and lived alone. Over the years, its menu had expanded, although, based on extensive market research into customer preferences, NS continued to provide its clients with only one meal a day. All meals were sold in "collections" of seven—a different meal for each day of the week, and deliveries (of seven meals each) were made once per week to each client (clients often froze a few of the meals for use in the latter half of the week).

During the past few years, NS had encountered some competition for its services. One or two other nonprofits that had been successful in other parts of either Kansas or Missouri had expanded their operations into the Kansas City area. In addition, some of the local fast-food restaurants, realizing that they could use their kitchen staffs to provide basic fare for delivery to nearby homes, had begun providing meals in certain neighborhoods that were close to their restaurants.

*This case was prepared by Professor David W. Young. Copyright © by David W. Young.

In response, and after considerable debate, NS decided to offer specialty meals. There were two main differences between NS's specialty meals and its regular meals: (1) specialty meals used a variety of nonstandard ingredients, frequently including organically grown fruits and vegetables, and often being meatless, and (2) because of a greater need for freshness, specialty meals were delivered daily (one per customer).

The new strategy seemed to be working. During the past year, approximately 80,000 of NS's 200,000 meals were specialty meals. The remainder were regular meals.

The Cost Accounting System

NS's cost accounting system calculated the cost of a meal by summing its direct and indirect costs. Direct costs included ingredients, packaging materials, and kitchen labor. When a new meal was introduced, NS's accounting staff spent considerable time determining exactly what ingredients it contained, and measuring the time it took both the prep staff and the line staff to actually prepare the ingredients and cook the meal. Prep staff were those kitchen workers who washed and cut the ingredients, prepared sauces, and took care of other tasks needed prior to actually cooking the meals. Line staff cooked and assembled the ingredients for each meal.

Indirect costs were classified into two categories: administration and general (A&G), and occupancy. A&G included the costs of the administrative staff, as well as the purchasing staff, drivers, and dietitians. Occupancy included rent, utilities, and cleaning. Gus Janeway, NS's accountant, explained the process he followed to arrive at a per meal cost:

> For years, we had only one overhead rate, but we realized that we got much greater accuracy by having two rates. Our studies have shown that A&G is always about 220 percent of kitchen labor, and occupancy is always about 20 percent of direct costs. In fact, once we know our budgeted kitchen labor and other direct costs for the year, we use this information to set the budgets for A&G and occupancy. Sometimes the actual budgeted amounts are slightly more or less than these standards, but we always come pretty close.
>
> Our overhead rates were quite handy when we shifted to the special-meal strategy. Both ingredient and kitchen labor costs were higher with the special meals than with our regular meals, and our overhead rates were quite helpful in showing us the higher *total* cost of the special meals. That, of course, helped us with preparing our budget for the year.

Mr. Janeway's computations are shown in Exhibit 1. As this exhibit indicates, the cost of ingredients for special meals was about three times greater than for regular meals, and there were higher kitchen labor costs. The result was higher overhead allocations, and a total cost per meal of $11.70 as compared to only $6.90 for a regular meal.

EXHIBIT 1 Cost Accounting Data

Total Costs			
Ingredients	$ 426,200		
Packaging materials	57,000		
Kitchen labor (prep and line)	348,000		
Overhead			
Admin and General	764,500		
Occupancy	170,000		
Total	$1,765,700		

Per meal costs	Regular	Special	
Ingredients	$ 1.21	$ 3.53	
Packaging materials	0.28	0.28	
Kitchen labor (prep and line)	1.50	2.09	
Total direct costs	$ 2.99	$ 5.90	
Admin and General	3.30	4.59	219.7% of kitchen labor
Occupancy	0.61	1.21	20.5% of direct costs
Total	$ 6.90	$ 11.70	
Price	$ 8.28	$ 14.04	120% of total cost
Number of meals	120,950	79,600	200,550
Total revenue	$1,001,184	$1,117,861	$2,119,046
Total cost	834,320	931,551	1,765,871
	$ 166,864	$ 186,310	$ 353,174

Pricing Policy

As Exhibit 1 indicates, NS's pricing policy was to add 20 percent to the total cost of a meal. Since demand fluctuated slightly during the year, and since no costs were completely predictable, Mr. Larson believed that the 20 percent margin was about right. He commented:

> It gives us enough to cover seasonal and other fluctuations. It also to helps to provide the funds needed to upgrade or replace our kitchen equipment, which includes some large items, but also small items, such as pots, pans, and cooking utensils. The prices of these items seem to go up at about 5 percent a year. And, of course, for items where there are constant improvements in quality and functionality, the inflation rate is even greater.

Pricing Problems

The problem that Mr. Larson alluded to in his opening comments had arisen because a growing number of regular customers were complaining about NS's prices. Some said that they had tried the meals of competing organizations and found them comparable, with prices about $1.00 to $1.50 below those of NS.

It was because of these complaints that Mr. Larson had called in a consult-ant, who subsequently had told him that the cost accounting system was giv-ing misleading information. The result was Mr. Larson's concern not only about having his regular meals priced too high, but having his special meals priced too low.

The Consultant's Report

According to Ramona Canard, Mr. Larson's consultant, the problem with NS's accounting system was that overhead was divided into only two "pools," as she called them:

> Two overhead pools could work if all overhead activities were about the same regardless of the kind of meal produced. That seems to be true for occupancy, but A&G is another matter. Purchasing, for example, is quite different for special meals. This is because purchasing people need to work very closely with local farmers to make sure that the food is organically grown, which takes much more of their time than when they're purchasing for regular meals, which only requires a few phone calls.
>
> Similarly, the dietitians have to spend a lot more time and effort designing the meals around the organic foods that are available during each season. That takes a whole lot longer than when they can just specify a meal's ingredients without concern for product availability—these days you can buy anything at almost any time of the year as long as you don't care where it comes from.
>
> Finally, delivering special meals is a lot different than delivering regular meals. Each customer for a special meal receives only one meal per delivery, whereas a customer for the regular meals gets seven meals at a time. So the per-meal delivery cost is a lot higher.
>
> What all this means is that we need different overhead pools for the different costs. My goal was to not only create the pools, but to identify a "driver" for each—that is, an activity that would cause the pool to increase or decrease.

Ms. Canard's overhead pools are contained in Exhibit 2. As this exhibit in-dicates, she moved $447,500 from the original A&G line, and distributed it among three new lines: purchasing, dietitians, and delivery. Purchasing con-tained not only the salaries of the purchasing agents, but transportation asso-ciated with trips to farms, and other purchasing-related expenses. She did the same for the dietitians, including both their salaries and associated expenses. Finally the pool for delivery included not only drivers' salaries, but deprecia-tion on the delivery vehicles, and expenses for fuel, repairs, maintenance, and garaging. Ms. Canard commented on this effort:

> Creating the pools was relatively easy, although pretty time-consuming. The hard part was the "cost drivers," as I call them. I talked with purchasing people, dietitians, and van drivers to try to get a sense of what would cause their costs to rise. At the end I reached what I think are some pretty solid conclusions. Purchasing costs are related to purchase orders, and because there are many small local organic farmers, the number of purchase orders for special meals is

EXHIBIT 2 New Cost Pools

	Before	After	% of Total Cost Before	% of Total Cost After
Ingredients....................................	$ 426,200	$ 426,200	24.1%	24.1%
Packaging materials...........................	57,000	57,000	3.2%	3.2%
Kitchen labor (prep and line)...................	348,000	348,000	19.7%	19.7%
Overhead				
Admin and General........................	764,500	317,000	43.3%	18.0%
Occupancy..............................	170,000	170,000	9.6%	9.6%
Purchasing..............................		132,500		7.5%
Dietitians...............................		121,000		6.9%
Delivery................................		194,000		11.0%
Total......................................	$1,765,700	$1,765,700	100.0%	100.0%

considerably greater than for regular meals. I verified this by going through two years' worth of purchase orders, and comparing them prior to and after the switch to special meals.

Dietitian costs are related to the number of special ingredients, and, again, special meals have more special ingredients than regular meals. That was easy to figure out. The hard part here was verifying that, as the number of special meals increased, the company's dietitian-related costs rose, not linearly, of course, but in a way that seemed pretty directly related.

Delivery was the easiest; it's pretty clearly related to the number of trips that the drivers must make to customers. Now, it's true that a driver can take many meals with him when he goes out in the van, so a "trip" wasn't a driver leaving the plant and returning. Rather, it was a "stop" at a customer's house. With regular meals, one stop was needed to deliver seven meals, but with special meals, one stop resulted in only one meal being delivered. This obviously causes delivery costs to be higher for special meals than for regular meals.

Ms. Canard's cost driver data are contained below:

	Regular	Special	Total
Number of meals..................	120,950	79,600	200,550
Number of purchase orders..........	150	500	650
Special ingredients per meal.........	2	8	
Number of "trips".................	17,279	79,600	96,879

She continued:

It's pretty clear when you use my new overhead pools and cost drivers that the per-meal costs are quite different than George and Gus think they are. I plan to present my conclusions to them this afternoon. I expect that this information will help George to rethink not only NS's prices, but perhaps the agency's whole strategy.

Mr. Larson, in thinking about the upcoming meeting, had some reactions to Ms. Canard's work:

I think Ramona is on to something here, and I guess when we run the numbers, her approach will make a difference, but is it a big enough difference to be meaningful? Assuming it is, what do we do with this new information? Should we compute these costs once a year as part of preparing the budget, and should we use the information to assist us with pricing? If so, we don't need a new cost accounting system—we just need an annual analysis of the sort that Ramona did. Or should we compute these figures on a monthly basis to assist us with controlling our costs? If so, it looks as though we'll need to completely update our cost accounting system so that we can produce monthly reports. Of course, the question then is whether it's worth the time and effort. What would it cost to prepare monthly reports using this new information, and what kinds of decisions would I make on the basis of these reports that I couldn't make without them?

Questions

1. Compute the cost of a regular and special meal using the new overhead pools and cost drivers. What explains the differences between these costs and the ones in Exhibit 1?

2. What is your assessment of the overhead pools and cost drivers that Ms. Canard has chosen? How, if at all, might they be improved?

3. Assuming the overhead pools and cost drivers give a better indication of actual costs, what should Mr. Larson do with this information? In answering this question, you should address the questions he raises at the end of the case.

Chapter 6

Measurement and Use of Differential Costs

One of the most significant principles of cost accounting is the notion that "different costs are used for different purposes." The full-cost accounting principles discussed in Chapter 5 are valuable for activities such as pricing, profitability analysis, and reimbursement. They are inappropriate, however, for a variety of decisions—called *alternative choice decisions*—made regularly in both for-profit and nonprofit organizations. Examples of alternative choice decisions include:

1. Keep or drop a service or program.

2. Expand or reduce the amount of a service provided.

3. Perform work in-house or outsource it.

4. Accept or reject a special request.

5. Sell or scrap obsolete supplies and equipment.

Alternative choice decisions frequently have strategic, organizational, and political dimensions; they also have a financial dimension. As we discuss in this chapter, the appropriate information to use for analyzing the financial dimension is differential costs, rather than full costs.

We begin the chapter with an assessment of the kinds of cost analyses that must be undertaken in an alternative choice decision. We then move to a discussion of cost behavior, addressing the distinction between costs used for a full-cost analysis and those used for a differential cost analysis. Next, we take up the topic of breakeven analysis, a special application of differential cost analysis. Following this, we review four important assumptions that underlie cost behavior in a breakeven analysis. We then discuss some of the techniques that analysts use to estimate the relationship between volume of activity and costs.

We are then ready to examine the factors that can complicate a differential cost analysis. We conclude the chapter by examining some of the issues that can surface in an outsourcing (sometimes called *make-or-buy*) decision—a type of alternative choice decision that most organizations make quite frequently. We include a discussion of a special form of contracting out: privatization. This section highlights some recent developments in the nonprofit field that call for managers to be especially attuned to the need for sophisticated and thoughtful analyses of differential costs.

The Nature of Cost Analyses for Alternative Choice Decisions

A key financial question in an alternative choice analysis is: "How will costs (and revenues) change under the proposed set of circumstances?" That is, what costs and revenues will be *different?* In the keep/drop, expand/reduce, and in-house/outsource decisions, for example, certain costs and revenues will be eliminated. Other costs may be incurred, however, and additional revenues may be realized. In the special-request or obsolete-asset situations, certain revenues will be received, but costs will change only minimally or not at all.

The use of full-cost information as a basis for deciding which costs will change can be misleading. Indeed, using full-cost information can lead to decisions that will be more, rather than less, costly to the organization.

Example

The full cost of educating a child in a certain public school system is $5,700 a year. This figure includes teachers' salaries, curriculum supplies and materials, a fair share of individual school overhead expenses (e.g., a principal's or headmaster's salary), and a fair share of the school system's overhead expenses (e.g., the school system superintendent's salary). The decision to reduce enrollment by 10 students clearly would not save $57,000 (= $5,700 × 10), since it is unlikely that teachers' salaries, individual school overhead expenses, and the school system's overhead expenses would be changed at all with a reduction of 10 students.

Even the decision to close an entire school would not save $5,700 per student, since it is unlikely that the school system's overhead expenses would be reduced. Moreover, if closing a given school resulted in shifting tax revenues that had been assigned to the school system to some other use, and these revenues amounted to $5,700 per student, the school system would be worse off as a result of the closing. That is, its revenues would have declined by more than its costs. It is for reasons such as this that an understanding of cost behavior is essential to a differential cost analysis.

Cost Behavior

Fundamental to the analysis of any alternative choice decision is the question of how costs behave with changes in volume. Chapter 5 described the distinction between direct and indirect costs; this chapter uses a different view, dividing costs among fixed, variable, and some intermediate possibilities. This latter view gives us a better perspective on how an organization's costs actually will behave under various scenarios, and therefore can assist us to identify the differential or nondifferential nature of those costs.

Fixed Costs

Fixed costs are those costs that do not vary with changes in the number of units of service delivered, at least in the short run. They can be graphed as shown in segment A of Exhibit 6–1.

An example of a fixed cost in most organizations is rent. Regardless of the volume of activity, the amount of rent that an organization pays in a given year will remain the same. Clearly, no cost is completely fixed. As such, there is a *relevant range* of volume implicit in any statement that a cost is fixed. We will discuss this idea in greater detail later in the chapter.

Step-Function Costs

Step-function costs are similar to fixed costs, except that each step has a much narrower relevant range. As such, they increase in relatively small "lumps" as

EXHIBIT 6–1

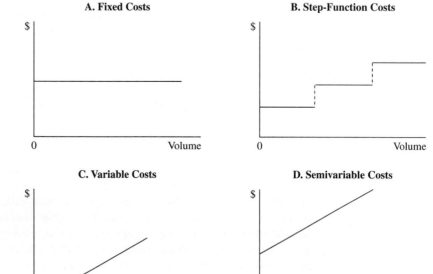

A. Fixed Costs   B. Step-Function Costs

C. Variable Costs   D. Semivariable Costs

volume increases. Graphically, step-function costs behave as shown in segment B of Exhibit 6–1.

An example of a step-function cost is supervision. In a hospital or social service agency, for instance, as the number of nurses, social workers, and the like, increases, supervisory personnel must be added, but not on a one-to-one basis. Since it is difficult for most organizations to add part-time supervisory help, the cost function for supervisors usually will behave in a steplike fashion. Similarly, in a school system or university, new faculty members are added in steplike increments when the total number of students either in the school or in a given course reaches a certain level.

Variable Costs

Variable costs behave in a roughly linear fashion with changes in volume. That is, as volume increases, total variable costs will increase in the same proportion. The result is a straight line, whose slope is determined by the amount of variable costs associated with each unit of activity, as shown in segment C of Exhibit 6–1.

An example of variable costs is supplies, such as textbooks for students in a public school system. Some organizations have relatively high variable costs per unit, resulting in a line that slopes upward quite steeply. Other organizations have variable costs that are relatively low for each unit of output, with a variable cost line that slopes upward more slowly.

Semivariable Costs

Semivariable costs have a fixed component that is unrelated to the level of volume, plus a variable component. Consequently, they intersect the cost axis of a graph at some point above zero, and then slope upward in a linear fashion, as is shown in segment D of Exhibit 6–1.

For many organizations, utilities are semivariable costs, since the organization typically pays a basic monthly service charge, followed by increments in cost according to use of the utility. Electricity, for example, typically has both a base (or demand) component, which is fixed, and a use component, which is variable.

Total Costs

Total costs are the sum of the fixed, step-function, variable, and semivariable components. Because cost analyses combining all four types of costs are quite complex and difficult to work with, most analysts generally classify all costs as either fixed or variable. For semivariable costs, this can be accomplished by incorporating the fixed element into total fixed costs and adding the variable element to the variable costs. For step-function costs, the width of the relevant range typically dictates whether the cost is added to fixed costs or incorporated into the variable cost amount.

Example

The Abbington Youth Center has annual rent and other fixed costs of $50,000, and variable supply and material costs of $100 per student. Its annual meal costs have a fixed element (a part-time dietitian) of $7,000, and a variable component (food and beverages) of $500 per student.

In constructing a graphical representation of Abbington's costs, we can incorporate the fixed and variable components of the semivariable cost function for meals into the separate fixed and variable components, as follows:

Cost Element	Fixed Amount	Variable Amount (per student)
Rent, etc.	$50,000	$ 0
Supplies and materials	0	100
Meals	7,000	500
Total	$57,000	$600

Abbington also has student-teacher ratios of 3:1 for its infants and toddlers program and 15:1 for its adolescent after-school program. Faculty salaries are $15,000 per year. The step-function relationships for these two programs are shown in Exhibit 6–2.

The narrow steps in the infant and toddlers program suggest that the relationship is close enough to a linear one that the costs can be treated as variable, whereas the wider steps in the adolescent after-school program would appear to call for these costs being treated as fixed, even though they have a shorter relevant range than, say, rent.

EXHIBIT 6–2 **Step-Function Costs of Abbington Youth Center**

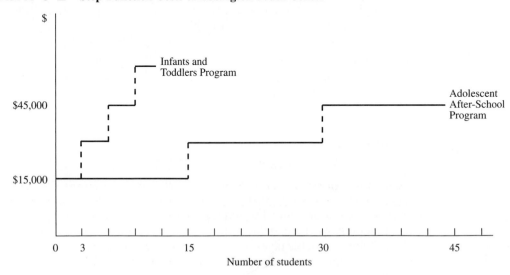

Once teacher salaries are simplified in this manner, they can be added to either the variable cost per student totals or the fixed cost totals, as follows:

Program	Fixed Amount	Variable Amount per Year
Infant and toddlers.................	0	$5,000 per student
Adolescent after-school (30-45 students).................	$45,000	0

With these simplifications, total costs then are as follows:

Cost Element	Fixed Amount	Variable Amount per Student
Rent, etc.	$ 50,000	$ 0
Supplies and materials................	0	100
Meals	7,000	500
Teachers		
Infant and toddlers	0	5,000
Adolescent after-school (30-45 students)	45,000	
	$102,000	$5,600

Note that the fixed costs are only valid within a range of 30 to 45 students in the adolescent after-school program. Above 45 students, they jump to a higher step; below 30 students, they fall to a lower step. Also, the variable cost of $5,600 for each additional student is not quite accurate, since $5,000 is actually a portion of a step-function change. Nevertheless, because the steps in the infants and toddlers program are so small, the amount is a reasonable representation of the pattern of cost changes that are associated with volume. Of course, we must also be concerned with the mix of students since the cost impact of, say, three more students will depend on whether they are infants and toddlers or adolescents. We discuss this point later in the chapter.

Breakeven Analysis

The purpose of breakeven analysis is to determine the volume of activity at which total revenue equals total costs. This usually is done for a program or other activity within an organization. A breakeven analysis begins with the fundamental equation:

$$\text{Total revenue} = \text{Total costs}$$

EXHIBIT 6–3
Breakeven Analysis

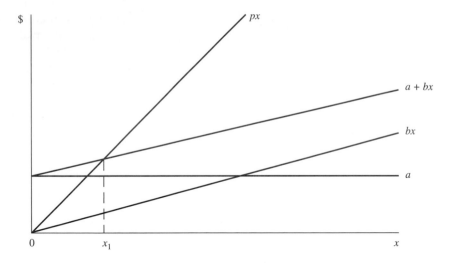

Since, as indicated above, total costs can be expressed as the sum of fixed and variable costs, the equation can be expanded as follows:

$$\text{Total revenue} = \text{Fixed costs} + \text{Variable costs}$$

Total revenue for most activities is quite easy to calculate. If we assume that an organization's charge or price per unit is represented by p and its volume by x, then total revenue is unit price times volume, or

$$\text{Total revenue} = px$$

Algebraically, fixed costs generally are represented by a and variable costs per unit by b. Thus, total variable costs can be represented by the term bx where, as before, x represents volume. The resulting breakeven formula can be shown as follows:

$$px = a + bx$$

Graphically, we can represent the formula as follows: First, revenue is an upwardly sloping straight line, whose slope is determined by price. Variable costs are similar, but with a less steep slope. Fixed costs are represented by a horizontal line. Total costs are shown by adding the variable cost line to the fixed cost line. Exhibit 6–3 is the result. Point x_1 where $px = a + bx$ is the breakeven volume; that is, it is the point at which total revenue (px) equals total costs ($a + bx$). Thus, if we know unit price, fixed costs, and variable costs per unit, we can solve the formula algebraically for x, which would be our breakeven volume.

Example

The Valley Wine Association has fixed costs of $10,000, variable costs per member of $18, and charges a $38 annual membership fee. What is its breakeven volume (number of members)?

Analysis

$$px = a + bx$$
$$\$38x = \$10,000 + \$18x$$
$$\$20x = \$10,000$$
$$x = 500$$

Breakeven thus would be 500 members. To confirm:

Revenue	$38(500)	=	$19,000
Less: costs:			
Variable	$18(500)	=	9,000
Fixed			10,000
Total			$19,000
Surplus (deficit).			$ 0

Unit Contribution

An alternative way to think of a breakeven analysis is in terms of the contribution that each unit sold makes to the recovery of fixed costs. Returning to the basic breakeven formula, we can see that unit contribution is the difference between price and unit variable cost, or $p - b$. Thus, by rearranging some of the terms, we can see that breakeven is simply fixed costs divided by unit contribution, as follows:

$$px = a + bx$$
$$px - bx = a$$
$$x(p - b) = a$$
$$x = \frac{a}{(p - b)}$$

In effect, price less unit variable cost tells us how much each additional unit of service contributes to the coverage of our fixed costs. Since breakeven volume is the level where all our fixed costs are being covered, we simply need to divide fixed costs by the unit contribution margin to determine the amount.

Example

The Federated Milk Producers Association has fixed costs of $900,000 and variable costs of $200 per member. Its annual membership dues are $500. Therefore its breakeven volume is

$$\$900,000 \div (\$500 - \$200) = 3,000 \text{ members}$$

Fundamental Assumptions of Breakeven Analysis

There are four important assumptions about cost behavior in a breakeven analysis: relevant range, linearity, homogeneity of volume, and underlying conditions.

Relevant Range

As mentioned in the discussion of fixed costs, an implicit assumption made for analytical purposes is that cost behavior does not change within a specified range of volume, called the *relevant range.* With fixed costs, the graphs in Exhibits 6–1 and 6–3 give the impression that costs are fixed from a level of zero volume to whatever number is shown at the far right of the graph.

Clearly, this impression is not realistic, since at near-zero volume, some so-called *fixed costs* probably could be eliminated. Basic clerical staff, cleaning staff, and so forth, while generally considered fixed, most likely could be reduced if a very low level of services were being delivered. By contrast, once volume exceeds a certain level, an organization will find it necessary to incur additional fixed costs. For example, once its activities grow beyond a certain level of volume, an organization will need additional space. At that point, rent—the prototypical fixed cost—will increase. Consequently, in a differential cost analysis, one must stipulate the assumptions about the range within which fixed costs are considered to be fixed.

As discussed earlier, identifying the relevant range is especially important for step-function costs. If the range is narrow enough, the step-function costs can be treated as variable; indeed the narrower the width of the steps, the more the line looks like a variable cost line. On the other hand, if the steps are relatively wide, step-function costs must be considered as fixed costs and added to the other fixed costs for analytical purposes.

The distinction between fixed and variable costs is also greatly influenced by the length of the time period that is used in the analysis. If the time period is short, such as a week, almost all costs are fixed. If the time period is a year, fewer costs are fixed. This point is sometimes overlooked in an analysis because of the design of an organization's cost accounting system. For example, in some systems, direct labor costs are classified as variable, but if volume falls within a given week, it is unlikely that employees will be laid off. Moreover, even if there are layoffs, they probably will not be proportionate to the change in volume.

Linearity

In most differential cost analyses, the assumption is made that the relationship between volume and cost is a linear one. That is, each cost, even if fixed, can be depicted by a straight line. Clearly this is not true for step-function costs, and, of course, there can be situations in which the relationship between volume and cost is curvilinear; that is, the cost line is curved.

Calculating costs when the cost line is curvilinear is complicated, and unless the curvilinear force is strong, an assumption usually is made that a linear relationship is close enough for analytical purposes. On the other hand, a linear assumption may not be adequate with step-function costs. Moreover, if a step-function cost is assumed to be fixed, the analyst must then check the resulting breakeven figure to determine if it is within the relevant range. If not, it will be necessary to move up or down the step function and recalculate the breakeven volume until a figure is reached that satisfies the relevant range of the step-function relationship.

Example

Recall that the Valley Wine Association charges its members $38 per year, has fixed costs of $10,000 and variable costs per member of $18. Assume that it also has supervisory costs that behave as follows:

Members	Costs
0–500	$ 5,000
501–1,000	10,000
1,001–1,500	15,000
1,501–2,000	20,000

To calculate a breakeven membership volume, we must determine the appropriate level of supervisory (i.e., step-function) costs to use. This means that we must assume some level of membership. If we begin with the first level, we add the $5,000 in supervisory costs to our fixed costs of $10,000 and undertake the breakeven analysis, which looks as follows:

$$px = a + bx$$
$$\$38x = \$10,000 + \$5,000 + \$18x$$
$$\$20x = \$15,000$$
$$x = 750$$

The problem is that, although the breakeven volume is 750 members, the relevant range for the step-function costs was only 0 to 500 members. Thus, the solution is invalid, and we must move to the next step on the step function, which gives us the following equation:

$$\$38x = \$10,000 + \$10,000 + \$18x$$
$$\$20x = \$20,000$$
$$x = 1,000$$

This solution is within the relevant range for step 2 and therefore is valid.

The conclusion we can draw from this example is that the incorporation of step-function costs in the breakeven formula requires a trial-and-error process to reach the breakeven volume; that is, each time a breakeven volume is determined, it must be checked against the step used in the calculation to be certain it is within the relevant range. If it is not, another step must be used for the calculation until a breakeven volume is found that is within the range of the step used in the calculation.

Homogeneity of Volume

In conducting breakeven analyses, an assumption is made that the units of volume being considered are all essentially identical. In the above analysis, for example, we assumed that all members were treated equally and, thus, that the $18-per-member variable costs and the step-function supervisory costs would be affected in an identical manner any time a new member was added to the organization.

Clearly this is not always the case. In many instances the differences average out so that the assumption of volume homogeneity is adequate. In others, however, separate analyses may be necessary for different types of service units.

Example	In the analysis of the Abbington Youth Center described earlier in this chapter, the presence of different step-function relationships for the Infant and Toddler Program and the Adolescent After-School Program means that there is an absence of volume homogeneity. Thus, although the fixed, variable, and semivariable cost relationships may be analyzed with this assumption, the step-function relationship may not. That is, under the step-function relationships described above, the addition of one child to the Infant and Toddler Program is assumed to add $5,000 to costs, while the addition of an adolescent to the Adolescent After-School Program will not add anything to costs unless the relevant range is exceeded. Therefore, each program should be considered separately. This creates another complication, namely the need to determine how much, if any, of the $57,000 in fixed costs is applicable to each program.

When there is an absence of volume homogeneity, the breakeven analysis becomes considerably more complex. Techniques for dealing with this complexity are discussed in many cost accounting textbooks.[1]

Underlying Conditions

A *ceteris paribus* (other things being equal) set of assumptions underlies a breakeven analysis. If any underlying conditions should change, the analysis becomes obsolete and must be recalculated using the new set of conditions. For example, if the above variable cost per unit of $18 is derived from certain supply prices for stationery, photocopying, and so forth, and if those prices increase, a new breakeven analysis must be undertaken using the new prices.

Estimating the Cost-Volume Relationship

To construct a cost-volume graph, an analyst estimates the costs that will be incurred at various levels of volume. These estimates often are made as part of the operations budgeting process, described in Chapter 10. Frequently, the analyst relies on historical data, modified as appropriate for the changing circumstances the organization expects to face in the future. Any of five methods can be used to construct a cost line.

---

[1]See, for example, Charles Horngren, George Foster, and Srikant Datar, *Cost Accounting: A Managerial Emphasis,* 9th ed. (Englewood Cliffs, NJ: Prentice Hall, 1999).

High-Low Method

Under the high-low method, total costs are determined for each of two volume levels. This establishes two points on the total cost line. Next, the costs at the lower volume are subtracted from the costs at the higher volume, and the difference in units between the two levels is determined. The difference in costs is then divided by the difference in units to obtain the variable cost per unit, that is, the slope of the variable cost line, or b in the breakeven formula. Finally, for either of the two volumes, the variable cost per unit is multiplied by the volume, and the result is subtracted from the total cost figure initially determined. The difference between the two is the fixed component.

Example

Two years ago, the Federated Producers Association had total costs of $1,500,000 with a membership of 3,000. Last year, its costs were $1,700,000 with a membership of 4,000. To determine its cost line, it can take the following steps:

1. Difference in total costs:

$$\$1,700,000 - \$1,500,000 = \$200,000$$

2. Difference in volume:

$$4,000 - 3,000 = 1,000$$

3. Variable cost per unit:

$$\$200,000 \div 1,000 = \$200$$

4. Total variable costs with 3,000 members:

$$\$200 \times 3,000 = \$600,000$$

5. Total fixed costs with 3,000 members:

$$\$1,500,000 - \$600,000 = \$900,000$$

Therefore fixed costs are $900,000 and variable costs per unit are $200. The formula for its cost line is:

$$\text{Total costs} = \$900,000 + \$200x$$

Scatter Diagram Method

Instead of using the high-low method with just two points, it is possible to plot several historical cost points on a graph, with total costs on the vertical axis and volume on the horizontal axis. The number of data points varies depending on the information available. Outliers—or unusual circumstances (e.g., the presence of a strike during a particular year that required using outside contractors to perform work normally done by employees)—usually are omitted. Using visual inspection, the analyst then fits a line to the points. Two points then can be chosen from this line to use for the high-low method.

Least Squares or Linear Regression Method

This is a modification of the scatter diagram method in which the line is fitted by a statistical technique rather than by visual inspection. This method is more mathematically correct than visual inspection and, if outliers are omitted, is probably more accurate. However, because much of the process of estimating the cost-volume relationship is necessarily judgmental, many analysts prefer the visual inspection approach over a mathematical one.[2]

Incremental Method

This method is used when there is only one data point; that is, one total cost figure and its associated volume. When this is the case, the analyst must estimate how an assumed increment in volume would affect total costs. Once this has been done, two data points are available, and the high-low method can be used.

Element Analysis

This method is used when there are no historical data points available. The analyst therefore must estimate each cost category separately (e.g., salaries and wages) and dissect it into its various cost elements: fixed, step-function, variable, semivariable. Once this is done, simplifying assumptions can be made concerning step-function and semivariable costs, and the totals for each cost element can be summed to produce a total cost equation.

This type of analysis is necessary when a new program or new service is being considered. It frequently is accompanied by a "sensitivity analysis," in which the various assumptions are tested with best- and worst-case scenarios.

Complicating Factors

In addition to the difficulties associated with estimating costs and dividing them into their various elements, an analyst may encounter several other complications in a differential cost analysis. Some of these are associated with the need on occasion to use full-cost reports as the source of cost information;

---

[2]A more detailed discussion of the least squares and linear regression methods can be found in Robert N. Anthony, David F. Hawkins, and Kenneth A. Merchant, *Accounting: Text and Cases,* 10th ed. (Burr Ridge, IL: Richard D. Irwin, 1998).

others are associated with the contrast between an organization's fixed and variable costs, on the one hand, and its differential-costs, on the other.

Use of Information from Full-Cost Reports

Two potential problems arise when information for differential-cost analyses is obtained from full-cost reports: cost distinctions and the behavior of allocated costs. Each of these potential problems calls for the analyst to exercise caution in obtaining and working with full-cost data.

Cost Distinctions

The analysis of differential costs would be simplified if, as occasionally is assumed, all indirect costs were fixed and all direct costs were variable. This is not always the case. Exhibit 6–4 contains an illustration of four different cost types and their fixed/variable, direct/indirect distinctions. Note that each of the four cells in the matrix contains a possible cost, leading to the conclusion that all direct and indirect costs in a full-cost accounting system must be analyzed individually to determine how they can be expected to behave as volume changes.

Behavior of Allocated Costs

Three problems exist in differential cost analysis when allocated costs are associated with a particular effort for which the differential analysis is to be made: misleading allocation bases, shared savings, and complexities of the stepdown methodology.

Misleading Allocation Bases   The bases of allocation used in the full-cost accounting system do not necessarily reflect actual resource use by mission or service cost centers. Thus, if the costs of a particular mission center are reduced, the service center costs *allocated* to that mission center automatically will be reduced. However, the service center costs themselves will not necessarily be reduced proportionately, and they may not be reduced at all.

EXHIBIT 6–4   Cost Examples: Fixed/Variable versus Direct/Indirect in the Foster Home Program of a Social Service Agency

	Fixed	*Variable*
Direct	Supervisor's salary in the foster home care program	Payments to foster parents for room and board
Indirect	Portion of executive director's salary (which is a cost of administration) that is allocated to the foster home program	Electric bills, which are mainly variable costs, and are part of administration, a service center whose costs are allocated to the foster home program

Example

A reduction of staff in a given mission center will lead to a reduction in total salaries in that center. If general and administration (G&A) costs are allocated to cost centers on the basis of salary dollars, there also will be a reduction in the amount of G&A costs allocated to the center. It is unlikely, however, that there will be a proportionate reduction in the staff or other costs associated with the G&A service cost center.

Shared Savings While some service center costs actually may be reduced as a result of reduced activity in a given mission center, the reduction may not accrue entirely to that mission center. Indeed, when the allocation basis does not change, the savings will be shared with other cost centers.

Example

A reduction in volume in a given mission center may reduce that mission center's need for housekeeping services, and result in some housekeeping cost savings. If housekeeping costs are allocated on a square footage basis, however, and the space used by the mission center does not change, the housekeeping allocation will not change by the full amount of housekeeping's savings. Instead, the savings will be shared with other mission centers that receive housekeeping allocations. Thus, although costs allocated to the mission center will fall as a result of the lower amount of housekeeping costs overall, the reduction *indicated* on the full-cost report will be much less than the *real* reduction that took place.

Complexities of the Stepdown Methodology When the stepdown methodology is used, it blurs the impact of cost changes. Specifically, since each service center is allocated to all remaining cost centers as one moves down the steps in the stepdown, the service centers farthest down in the report will have allocations from the cost centers above them included in their totals. And, since the total to be allocated from each service center includes both its direct costs and the costs that have been allocated to it from previous "steps" in the stepdown, the allocation from a service center far down in the stepdown will include cost from several other cost centers.

Example

If social service is far down on the list in a stepdown, the total social service cost allocated to a particular mission center likely will carry a significant allocated component with it (e.g., administration, housekeeping, laundry and linen, and so on). In a health care organization, for example, while it may be possible to reduce the use of social workers in a mission center by reducing the number of patients treated, the full impact of that reduction on the costs in the social service cost center will be overstated if one uses the fully allocated social services totals (including both direct and previously allocated costs). That is, the allocated component from social services contains costs from a variety of other cost centers that may not be affected at all by the reduction in patient volume.

Recognizing these problems and incorporating them into analytic efforts is extremely challenging. Determining which costs are indeed differential, and by how much, is difficult, particularly when a full-cost report is the principal source of information.

Differential Costs versus Variable and Fixed Costs

Another erroneous assumption that frequently is made in the analysis of differential costs is that there is no change in *unit* variable costs. In some situations, for example, volume will not change at all, but alternative cost scenarios will be possible for the same volume of activity. Similarly, a reduction in volume may increase the unit cost of supplies because of a loss of volume discounts, or, an increase in volume may result in a volume discount. Both of these scenarios will change unit variable costs.

Some analysts assume that fixed costs are not differential. That is, when they analyze the various alternatives under consideration, they assume that the only cost changes they need to consider are those associated with variable costs, semivariable costs, and step-function costs. Actually, many alternative choice problems faced by an organization involve movements outside the relevant range for fixed costs, and, hence, changes in fixed costs as well. The following example illustrates the nature of this problem as well as one of the problems associated with incorporating allocated costs into a differential cost analysis.

Example

Clearwater Transport Service operates two minivans that it uses to transport senior citizens on errands and shopping trips. It charges $1 per mile for each service mile driven. Van 1 drives 60,000 service miles a year; Van 2 drives 30,000 service miles a year. The variable cost per mile for each van is 30 cents. The organization's revenues and costs are as follows:

Item	Van 1	Van 2	Total
Revenue	$1.00×60,000 =$60,000	$1.00×30,000 =$30,000	$90,000
Costs:			
Variable costs.........	.30×60,000 =$18,000	.30×30,000 =$ 9,000	27,000
Drivers..............	15,000	15,000	30,000
Overhead costs (rent and administration)....	20,000	10,000	30,000
Total costs	53,000	34,000	87,000
Surplus (Deficit).........	$ 7,000	$ (4,000)	$ 3,000

Question

Would the profitability of Clearwater Transport Service be improved if Van 2, which is losing money, were discontinued?

Analysis

The question is not whether Van 2 is losing money on a full-cost basis, but rather the nature of its differential costs and revenues. More specifically, if Van 2 were discontinued, which revenues and costs would be eliminated and which would remain.

It appears that if we eliminate Van 2, we discontinue all of its revenue, all of its variable costs, and the fixed cost of the driver. From all indications, however, the rent and administrative costs will remain; that is, they are nondifferential. The result is a shift from an overall *surplus* of $3,000 to a *deficit* of $3,000, as the analysis below indicates.

Item		*Van 1*
Revenue ($1.00 × 60,000).		$60,000
Costs:		
Variable costs (.30 × 60,000)	$18,000	
Driver.	15,000	
Overhead costs (rent and administration)	30,000	
Total costs.		63,000
Surplus (Deficit)		$ (3,000)

This example illustrates several important points. First, full-cost information can produce misleading results if used for differential cost decisions—in this instance a keep/drop decision. In the case of the Clearwater Transport Service, the full-cost data would seem to indicate that we could increase the surplus by dropping Van 2, but this clearly was not so.

Second, differential costs can include both fixed and variable costs. In the above example, the driver generally would be considered a fixed cost, but the elimination of Van 2 eliminates this fixed cost. The key point here is that as long as we operate the van, we have the fixed cost of the driver's salary; it does not fluctuate in accordance with the number of miles driven within the relevant range. But when we eliminate the van, we also eliminate this cost in its entirety; it is thus differential in terms of the decision we are analyzing. In effect, we have dropped below the relevant range for this cost.

A third point is that differential cost analysis invariably requires assumptions. Since we do not have perfect knowledge of the future, we must make some guesses about how costs will behave. In this example, there are three important assumptions: (1) the number of miles driven by Van 1 will not increase with the elimination of Van 2; (2) we will not be able to reduce or eliminate any overhead costs with the elimination of Van 2; and (3) the unit costs and revenues will be the same in the future as in the past.

Changes in these assumptions clearly would have an impact on the new surplus (deficit) figure, and might in fact actually make it financially feasible to eliminate van 2. It is therefore important in undertaking any form of differential cost analysis both to clarify the assumptions one is making and to explore how changes in these assumptions would affect the conclusions of the analysis. This latter activity is another example of *sensitivity analysis.*

Contribution to Overhead Costs

In discussing breakeven analysis earlier in this chapter, we introduced the notion of unit contribution, defining it as the amount that each unit sold contributes to the recovery of fixed costs. The concept of contribution also can be used in differential cost analyses.

As the Clearwater Transport example indicated, a key question in many differential cost analyses is the behavior of overhead costs. In this illustration, we assumed that overhead costs (rent and administration) for the transport service would not be reduced if the second van were eliminated. As indicated above, and as will be discussed in greater detail later, an assumption of this sort is not necessarily valid. Nevertheless, in most instances an analysis of differential costs is most easily performed when the direct fixed and variable costs of the particular activity itself are analyzed separately from the overhead costs of the organization. Such an analysis can be structured in terms of the contribution of the particular service or program to the organization's overhead costs.

More specifically, a program (a van in this instance) provides some revenues and incurs some direct costs. The difference between the revenue provided and the direct costs (both fixed and variable) is the contribution of that program to the organization's overhead costs.

Returning to the example above, the cost data for the transport service could be structured in the following way:

Item	Van 1	Van 2	Total
Revenue	$60,000	$30,000	$90,000
Less: Variable costs	18,000	9,000	27,000
Margin (for fixed and overhead costs).	$42,000	$21,000	$63,000
Less: Fixed costs (drivers).	15,000	15,000	30,000
Contribution (to overhead costs).	$27,000	$ 6,000	$33,000
Less: Overhead costs	20,000	10,000	30,000
Surplus (Deficit)	$ 7,000	$ (4,000)	$ 3,000

As this example indicates, both Van 1 and Van 2 are contributing to the coverage of overhead costs. Consequently, elimination of either van will reduce the total contribution to overhead, thereby either reducing the organization's surplus or increasing its deficit. In fact, it is the $6,000 contribution from Van 2 that led to the change from a $3,000 surplus to a $3,000 deficit when we considered the impact of eliminating it.

The Outsourcing Decision

Up to this point, we have discussed the use of differential costs in situations where an alternative choice decision involved a change in volume. This is the characteristic of most keep/drop and special-request decisions. Many other types of alternative choice decisions do not involve a change in volume. Perhaps the most common of these is what is called the *outsourcing* (or *make-or-buy* or *contract-out*) decision. We discuss the general nature of this decision below, and provide some illustrations of a special form of outsourcing decision making—called *privatization*—that has become increasingly popular in government organizations.

Nature of the Outsourcing Decision

An organization provides some services by using its own resources, and it obtains other services by buying them from other organizations. Almost all of the things it does internally conceivably could be done for it by an outside organization. At the extreme, the total operation could be contracted out, as the federal government does in the operation of certain nuclear generating plants that it owns. Conversely, a large organization could rely on its own resources for most of its needs, even building a power plant to generate electricity, rather than buying electricity from a public utility. At any given time, there is a balance between what an organization makes and what it buys. Management frequently must reexamine whether this balance is the most appropriate one.

A wide variety of considerations generally enters into the outsourcing decision, one of which is the applicable costs and revenues. That is, management wishes to identify the alternative that has the lower costs and/or higher revenues. The relevant revenues and costs are the differential ones associated with each alternative.

Example	A trade association cleans its headquarters with employees who are hired for this purpose. Someone has proposed that an outside cleaning crew be engaged. The differential cost of contracting with an outside organization is relatively easy to determine; it is the amount specified in the proposed contract. Finding the differential cost of continuing to use the association's own employees is more complicated, however. The salaries and benefits of the cleaning crew and the supplies they use obviously are differential costs; they would disappear if the cleaning were contracted out. The other differential costs associated with this activity are more difficult to estimate. Would there be a reduction of costs in the payroll accounting department? The personnel department? In other overhead costs? In estimating the amount of differential overhead costs, management must be aware of the cautions made in earlier sections of this chapter about possible misinterpretations of the effects of overhead allocations.

General Principles

There are few general principles for deciding what items of cost are differential in a contract-out problem. Although each problem is unique, and must be analyzed separately to decide what costs would be different under the particular circumstances, one generalization can be made: the longer the time period involved, the more costs are differential. If the alternative being considered is to contract out a single printing job rather than use in-house facilities, for instance, the only reduction in costs might be the savings in paper and ink; the printing presses remain, payment to employees probably would not be reduced, and no overhead costs would be affected. If, however, the proposal is to discontinue the in-house print shop permanently, all the costs associated with operating that shop, both direct and overhead, would be saved.

Role of Depreciation

A common error in calculating differential costs for outsourcing problems is to include depreciation on existing plant and equipment as a cost that would be saved if the organization bought the service from an outside contractor. Depreciation is not a differential cost, however. Once assets have been acquired, the costs incurred to purchase them are *sunk costs*. Depreciation is simply an accounting mechanism to charge the expense of using up an asset to each year of its useful life. The expenditure itself took place at the time the asset was acquired. Unfortunately, the past cannot be undone, and money spent cannot be recovered. Therefore, eliminating the use of an asset does not result in a saving of its depreciation. Of course, if an asset is sold, the amount realized can be a differential gain associated with the outsourcing decision, but this amount rarely corresponds to the asset's book value.

If the outsourcing time frame is a sufficiently long one, such that the acquisition of additional assets would be required under the *make* option but not under the *buy* option, then depreciation might be used as a surrogate for the cost associated with replacing existing assets as they wear out. If this is done, the analyst must be certain that the existing depreciation figure is adjusted for changes in prices, technology, and other factors that would cause replacement assets to cost more or less than existing ones. Again, the replacement amount rarely corresponds to the existing depreciation expense. Moreover, if asset acquisition is a significant aspect of the decision—if, that is, assets must be acquired for the *make* option to be pursued—then depreciation alone will not suffice. Rather, a technique known as net present value is required. This technique is discussed in Chapter 8.

The Move toward Privatization

In government—federal, state, and local—the strategy of contracting out has become extremely popular during the past 20 to 25 years. Called *privatization,* this activity has touched on a wide variety of services that only a few years ago were seen as the exclusive domain of a federal, state, or local government agency. In almost all instances, the principal driving force behind the decision to contract out has been cost savings.

The privatization movement has been characterized by two quite different activities: (1) the divestment of assets or programs, such as national land, railroads, and the post office, and (2) actual outsourcing for services, such as prison operations, health care delivery, garbage collection, and dog catching. The former has a one-time effect only, whereas the latter has the potential for ongoing savings over many years. In this latter area, it seems clear that privatization is on the rise, as the data in Exhibit 6–5 indicate:

EXHIBIT 6–5
Privatized Jobs.
Share of Public
Services Handled by
Contract Workers

	1987	1995
Waste collection	30%	50%
Building maintenance	32	42
Bill collection	10	20
Data processing	16	31
Health/medical	15	27
Street cleaning	9	18
Street repair	19	37

Source: Mercer Group, Inc.

Example

In Indianapolis, outsourcing reduced public employment by 40 percent over three years in fields outside of police and fire services. Sunnyvale, California, relied on a temporary employment company for 25 percent of its workforce. Massachusetts, New Jersey, and Georgia developed ambitious plans for outsourcing. Pennsylvania had its own pool of temporary employees that supplied hundreds of secretaries to state agencies.[3]

Butte, Montana, saved $600,000 a year by contracting with a private firm to run its municipal hospital. Newark, New Jersey, used a private firm to collect about one-third of its refuse, at a [reported] annual savings of over $200,000, and hired private contractors to provide services such as tree trimming, garbage collection, building demolition, snow plowing, and street sweeping. The Southern California coastal community of Rancho Palos Verdes paid a private law firm to act as town prosecutor. Farmington, New Mexico, contracted with an independent firm to run its airport control tower at a cost of $99,000 per year, compared with the $287,000 the Federal Aviation Administration had been paying out. A private paramedic/ambulance service saved Newton, Massachusetts, some $500,000 a year. New York, Philadelphia, Washington, D.C., and 70 other cities used private *meter persons* to enforce parking regulations. And, Scottsdale, Arizona,—the first U.S. city to use a private company for fire protection—boasted of better-than-average fire response times, at less than half the cost to cities of comparable size.[4]

Privatization Concerns

One of the main questions that emerges when a government agency decides to privatize is which services to contract out. A related concern is the difficulty of making comparisons between the contractor's charge and the cost of maintaining services inhouse. A third is the private contractor's possible lack of commitment to, and involvement with, the organization and its goals.[5]

[3]G. Pascal Zachary, "Two-Edged Sword: Some Public Workers Lose Well-Paying Jobs as Agencies Outsource," *Wall Street Journal,* August 6, 1996.
[4]Neil A. Martin, "When Public Services Go Private," *World,* May–June 1986, pp. 26–28.
[5]For a discussion of these points, see Mary Kelaher, "Commercializing the Public Sector," *Australian Accountant* 61, no. 2 (March 1991).

With regard to costs, the usual goal is to save money, although the savings can come in a variety of forms. For example, in a study of privatizing corrections, Demone and Gibelman found that no matter whether the focus was on prevention, deterrence, incarceration, or postincarceration rehabilitation, the goals were similar: to save money, reduce capital expenditures, provide more effective and efficient services, and bypass the rigidity, slowness, and lack of responsiveness of public bureaucracies.[6]

The cost computations can be tricky, however. One complication is with the distinction between wage *rate* and total wage cost. For example, in New York, some computer programmers earned $400 a day as contractors, about a third more than civil servants were paid,[7] yet the city was moving toward privatizing computer programming, presumably because the contract programmers were sufficiently more productive to justify the higher daily rate.

In an effort to assure that costs are considered appropriately, the federal Office of Management and Budget *Circular A-76* directs departments and agencies to study privatization possibilities, and gives detailed rules for estimating the differential costs appropriate for such a study. In general, *Circular A-76* focuses on the differential costs associated with personnel, although it emphasizes the need to consider all significant costs, including overhead items.[8]

Example	Increasingly, municipalities are privatizing the management of their zoos. Typically, the city retains ownership of the zoo infrastructure, and makes reduced contributions to the operating budget. According to the American Zoo and Aquarium Association, of the nation's 110 zoos, one-third are privatized in this way.[9] Since a zoo is a freestanding programmatic entity and the city makes reduced contributions from its own budget to the zoo's budget, the cost computations are relatively easy.

Problems with a shared commitment are particularly apparent when a government agency contracts with the private sector. In particular, some concerns have been raised about quality and other delivery-related issues associated with converting what is essentially a public-sector responsibility into a private enterprise. In addition, although both for-profit and nonprofit contractors have been employed to carry out privatization, many nonprofit professionals are especially concerned when the contract is with a for-profit organization.

[6]Harold Demone, Jr., and Margaret Gibelman, "'Privatizing' the Treatment of Criminal Offenders," *Journal of Offender Counseling, Services & Rehabilitation* 15, no. 1, 1990.
[7]Zachary, "Two-Edged Sword".
[8]For a summary of *Circular A-76* and its intent, see "Enhancing Government Productivity through Competition: Targeting for Annual Savings of One Billion Dollars by 1988," Office of Management and Budget, March 1984. For an example of an analysis carried out under *Circular A-76,* see David R. Solenberger, "The Cost of a Federal Employee: An Input to Economic Analysis," *GAO Review,* Spring 1985. See also Jerome S. Gabig, Jr., "Privatization: A Coming Wave for Federal Information Technology Requirements," *National Contract Management Journal* 27, no. 1, 1996.
[9]Beth Wade, "The Economic Poop on Municipal Zoos," *American City & County* 109, no. 2, February 1994.

Indeed, this concern extends outside of government into nonprofit organizations that contract out for services with for-profit vendors.

Despite these concerns, there are instances where privatization has produced superior quality services.

<table>
<tr>
<td>Example</td>
<td>Fifteen countries have experimented successfully with private, nonprofit air traffic control system corporations. Germany privatized its system in 1993, and since then, air traffic delays have dropped 25 percent without any impact on safety.[10]</td>
</tr>
</table>

Moreover, there also are instances where the use of for-profit companies to carry out the effort has received some considerable support. For example, companies seeking to locate plants often have been frustrated by bureaucratic barriers, infighting, and jurisdictional disputes among layers of government. More and more, these companies are opting to deal peer-to-peer with a private group, one that they believe is more sensitive to their business concerns.[11]

While privatization issues frequently evoke more passion than substance, the phenomenon nevertheless is an important aspect of nonprofit management—particularly for city, state, and federal agencies. From the perspective of this chapter, the critical question is that of cost analysis. Later chapters will introduce issues related to designing and using appropriate and effective management control systems to manage private contractors.

Summary

Differential costs provide the proper analytical focus for keep/drop, expand/reduce, outsource, special request, or obsolete asset decisions. However, they do not make either the decisions themselves or the analytical efforts that underlie them easy. Indeed, a variety of strategic and other nonquantifiable factors usually enter into these decisions which go beyond financial analysis and which create highly complex situations. An adequate differential analysis must incorporate all of these factors.

Suggested Additional Readings

Anthony, Robert N., David F. Hawkins, and Kenneth A. Merchant. *Accounting: Text and Cases.* Burr Ridge, IL, Irwin-McGraw Hill, 1998.

Donahue, John D. *The Privatization Decision, Public Ends, Private Means.* New York: Basic Books, 1991.

Gibelman, Margaret, and Harold W. Demone, Jr., eds. *The Privatization of Social Services: Policy and Practice Issues.* Springer Series on Social Work, Vol. 1, New Brunswick, NJ: Rutgers University Press, 1997.

---

[10]Randall Lane, "FAA, Inc.," *Forbes* 158, no. 5, August 26, 1996.
[11]Jim Schriner, "Is the Fox Guarding the Hen House?" *Industry Week* 245, no. 11, June 3, 1996.

Henke, Emerson O. *Introduction to Nonprofit Organization Accounting.* Cincinnati, OH: South-Western Publishing, 1992.

McKinney, Jerome B. *Effective Financial Management in Public and Nonprofit Agencies: A Practical and Integrative Approach,* 2nd ed. Westport, CN: Greenwood Publishing Group, Incorporated, 1995.

Riska, Stacey. *Outsourcing: Using Outside Resources to Get More Done.* New York: American Society of Association Executives, 2001.

U.S. General Accounting Office. *Privatization: Lessons Learned by State and Local Governments,* GGD 97–48, 1997.

U.S. Department of Education. *Tough Choices: A Guide to Administrative Cost Management in Colleges and Universities.* Washington, D.C.: Government Printing Office, 1991.

Practice Case

Energy Associates (B)[*]

Energy Associates (EA), a nonprofit agency, purchased energy-saving devices in bulk, repackaged them, and sold them to low-income consumers. Its products in the past consisted of shower nozzles that restricted the flow of water and thermostats with timers. It was considering the addition of storm windows. In addition to a price of $100 and a variable cost of $95, the new product line was expected to add $2,000 to the organization's overhead costs (such as warehouse personnel, shipping and receiving personnel, and the billing staff).

Preliminary budgeted figures, by product line, are shown below:

	Shower Nozzles	Thermo-stats	Storm Windows	Total
Number of items	800	200	500	1,500
Price per item.	$ 10	$ 80	$ 100	
Total revenue	$ 8,000	$16,000	$ 50,000	$ 74,000
Purchase cost per item	8	70	95	
Total purchase costs	6,400	14,000	47,500	67,900
Allocated overhead (includes all labor)	27,040	6,760	16,900	50,700
Total costs	$ 33,440	$20,760	$ 64,400	$118,600
Profit (loss).	$(25,440)	$ (4,760)	$(14,400)	$ (44,600)

*This case was prepared by Professor David W. Young. Copyright © by David W. Young.

Questions

1. What is breakeven for storm windows? What concerns, if any, do you have about this figure?

2. Given that its preliminary budget shows a sizable loss, EA must consider ways to eliminate this loss. What budgetary options should management consider?

3. EA thinks it can increase the sales of its products by advertising in local newspapers, and has decided to spend $1,000 on advertising. To get the most out of its advertising dollar, it has decided to concentrate on one product only. Given financial concerns only, please discuss how it should decide which product to emphasize?

4. One of EA's managers has suggested that, since the storm windows line is budged to lose money, the organization should not sell them. What advice would you give EA about this decision?

Case 6–1

Carlsbad Home Care*

In December, Mr. Joseph Blanchard became the controller of Carlsbad Home Care (CHC). After 10 years in the accounting department of a consumer products firm, Mr. Blanchard decided to move into the nonprofit field where he felt his expertise would be needed. CHC, a small agency in Southern New Mexico, offered him that opportunity.

Before Mr. Blanchard accepted the position of controller, Ms. Louise Tucker, the director of the agency, briefed him on the agency's financial position. Like many home care agencies, CHC had become affiliated with a large health maintenance organization (HMO). The HMO paid a fixed fee of $110 to CHC for each home visit.

Ms. Tucker was concerned because CHC's per-visit costs exceeded that amount, and she had hired Mr. Blanchard with the hope that he could resolve this problem. CHC's average cost per visit calculation is contained in Exhibit 1.

Background

CHC had been established in 1980 to provide home health visits to elderly and disabled residents of Carlsbad and neighboring towns. Several years ago, in response to community need, it had expanded its services to include physical

*This case was prepared by Patricia O'Brien under the supervision of Professor David W. Young. It subsequently was revised by Professor Young. Copyright © by David W. Young.

FXHIBIT 1
Expense Record

	Detail	Total
1. Salaries		$567,994
Director, assistant director, controller	$165,140	
Nurses (2)	105,920	
Psychologist (1)	56,000	
Social workers (2).............................	77,000	
Physical therapists (2).........................	90,334	
Support staff (3).............................	73,600	
2. Transportation costs		56,000
Automobile operation and insurance	16,000	
Automobile allowance for staff..................	40,000	
3. Purchased services.............................		4,700
4. Medical and nursing supplies		14,800
5. Space occupancy costs		34,660
6. Office costs (telephone, postage, stationery)		25,312
7. Other general costs (depreciation, insurance, legal).....		35,720
Total cost		$739,186
Number of visits		6,384
Average cost per visit.............................		$ 115.79

therapy and social service visits. Because another organization in town, The Canyon Home Service, provided home health aide care, CHC did not offer aide services.

CHC had a staff of 13. Two registered nurses, two physical therapists, and two social workers were responsible for the home health visits. The administration consisted of a director, an assistant director, a supervising psychologist the newly appointed controller, and a support staff of three. The skilled nursing care visits were handled by the two registered nurses. The two physical therapists worked exclusively on patient visits. The social workers, under the guidance of the psychologist, provided all the social service visits.

The two registered nurses who handled all nursing visits could provide as many as seven visits a day each. However, because the case visits varied significantly in time, effort, and location, the nurses averaged only 5.5 visits per day. The physical therapists averaged 3.3 visits per day, although Ms. Tucker thought their capacity could be increased by at least 33 percent if they had the demand. CHC's social service visits were the most complicated. The social workers averaged 4.5 visits a day, but Ms. Tucker thought these could be increased to about 5.5 a day. The psychologist who supervised the social workers, made no visits. All CHC staff worked an average of 240 days a year.

Data

In his first few weeks, Mr. Blanchard reviewed CHC's financial statements, employee service sheets, and other working papers to become familiar with the agency's financial status and planning needs. He realized the agency had been operating without any cost goals. After a cursory review of past records, he decided that his first priority was to ensure that revenue met costs.

Examining CHC's expense record, shown in Exhibit 1, Mr. Blanchard determined that the agency had two types of costs: those that changed according to the number of visits provided and those that were unchanged, regardless of volume. He reasoned that at their breakeven point, CHC's revenue of $110 per visit would equal the total cost of the expenses generated by each visit plus the fixed expenses.

Mr. Blanchard reviewed each item on the expense record to determine which type of cost it was. He thought the medically related salaries and the medical and nursing supplies were items that varied directly with the number of visits. When he discussed his analysis with Ms. Tucker, she suggested that staff automobile allowance also varied with the number of visits because it referred to mileage incurred by the medical staff in making home visits.

"Terrific," thought Mr. Blanchard. "Now I can calculate a variable cost per visit and in no time I'll know the breakeven point. I can show them their costs and revenues, and where we'll have to operate to keep this agency in business."

Questions

1. Identify the fixed and variable costs.

2. What is the breakeven point?

3. What assumptions were necessary in answering questions 1 and 2?

Case 6–2

Abbington Youth Center*

Mark Thomas, a recently graduated MBA, had been hired three months ago as assistant director of the Abbington Youth Center. Prior to earning his MBA, he had worked in several manufacturing firms, but he had never worked in a nonprofit organization. He knew little about Abbington's programs or the educational and social theories in use by the professional staff, but had decided to take the job since he had been impressed with the center's attempts to provide high-quality programs for the children in his community.

Despite his lack of experience in organizations like Abbington, Mr. Thomas had brought some much-needed management skills to the center's

---

*This case was prepared by Professor David W. Young. It is based in part on the case "Bill French" by R. C. Hill and N. E. Harlan, Harvard Business School. Copyright © by David W. Young.

operations. In his short tenure with the center he not only had introduced some new management techniques, but had regularly made attempts to educate the professional staff about the use of those techniques.

This afternoon's staff meeting was no exception. In attendance would be the center's director, Helen Fineberg, and the coordinators of the center's three programs: Fiona Mosteller (Infants and Toddlers Program), Joanne Olivo (Preschool Program), and Don Harris (After-School Program). As the names suggested, each program was aimed toward a different age-group: the first accepted children up to the age of three; the second from three to five years of age; and the third from five to seven years.

Mr. Thomas planned to instruct the program directors in the concept of breakeven analysis. To do so, he had gathered some data on the revenues and costs of the three programs (see Exhibit 1). Using this information, he determined that each student contributed $4,348 to fixed costs after covering his or her variable costs. Given total fixed costs of $498,700 ($328,000 in the programs and $170,700 for the center overall), he had calculated that approximately 115 students were needed to break even.

He had prepared the breakeven chart, shown in Exhibit 2, which he planned to distribute to everyone at the meeting prior to giving a short lecture on the concept of breakeven analysis. His intent was to make clear to everyone that enrollment was exactly breakeven, which did not allow any margin of safety, and to encourage the program directors to expand the size of their programs by a few students each so as to provide a more comfortable margin and, if all went well, a surplus for the center.

EXHIBIT 1   Program Cost Analysis, Normal Year[1]

	Infants and Toddlers	Preschool	After-School	Aggregate
Students at full capacity.				150
Actual number of students.	50	40	25	115
Fee per student	$ 4,520	$ 5,320	$ 5,970	$ 5,113
Total revenue.	226,000	212,800	149,250	588,050
Variable cost per student	480	1,040	896	765
Total variable cost	24,000	41,600	22,400	88,000
Contribution to program fixed costs	$202,000	$171,200	$126,850	$500,050
Less: Program fixed costs.	130,000	118,000	80,000	328,000
Contribution to allocated fixed costs	$ 72,000	$ 53,200	$ 46,850	$172,050
Less: Allocated fixed costs[2].	42,675	51,210	76,815	170,700
Surplus (deficit)	$ 29,325	$ 1,990	$(29,965)	$ 1,350

[1]All figures rounded to the nearest dollar.
[2]Allocated on the basis of square feet.

EXHIBIT 2
Breakeven Chart—All Programs

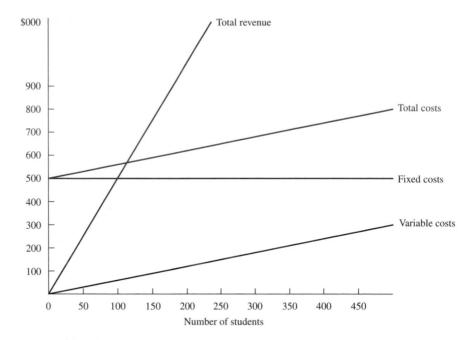

The Meeting

At the meeting, several issues arose that Mr. Thomas had not anticipated, and a rather hostile atmosphere developed. Ms. Mosteller pointed out that 50 students was the maximum her program could accommodate, given current classroom space, and wondered exactly how Mr. Thomas expected her to increase the program's size. Ms. Olivo said she would be happy to expand her program by another 10 students, but to do so, she would need to hire another teacher, at a cost of $22,000. She wondered how Mr. Thomas might include this fact in his analysis, and, under the circumstances, whether the teacher should be considered a fixed or a variable cost. Mr. Harris told Mr. Thomas that he had been planning all along to add another 15 students to his program, and wondered why Mr. Thomas had not checked with him about this prior to preparing the figures and the chart. He too would need to hire another teacher, however, at a cost of $25,000, and also wondered whether this was a fixed or variable cost.

Ms. Fineberg seemed quite perplexed by the discussion, and began her comments by asking Mr. Thomas why he was using averages when the center had three separate programs. She also indicated that $1,350 was far too low a surplus, since she was hoping to have some extra money available during the year for painting and some minor renovations, which would cost about $10,000. She asked Mr. Thomas how he might incorporate this need into his analysis. She also expressed some concern about Mr. Thomas's per-student fees, stating that in conversations with people in other centers she had learned that Abbington's fees were about 10 percent below what others were charging. She thought an across-the-board increase to make up the difference was called for.

Finally, all three program directors queried Mr. Thomas about his variable-cost-per-student figure. They asked him how he had derived these figures and whether they included some recent price increases of about 5 percent in educational supplies. Mr. Thomas stated that they included both supplies and food, divided about 75 percent/25 percent between the two, but he confessed that he had not included any price increase in his calculations.

Next Steps

The meeting ended on a less-than-happy note. Mr. Thomas had not had an opportunity to give his lecture, the program managers felt frustrated that their concerns and plans had not been included in his analysis, and Ms. Fineberg was quite upset because it appeared as though the center would not have the funds necessary to pay for the much-needed painting and renovations.

Mr. Thomas returned to his office and wondered whether his decision to work at the center had been a wise one. Perhaps, he thought, life would be simpler in a manufacturing firm.

Questions

1. What assumptions are implicit in Mr. Thomas's determination of a break-even point?

2. Using the data in Exhibit 1, calculate a breakeven point for *each* of the three programs. Why is the sum of these three volumes not equal to the aggregate breakeven volume?

3. On the basis of the suggestions and comments made at the meeting, and making assumptions where necessary, prepare revisions to Exhibit 1. What is the new breakeven volume for the center? What is it for each of the three programs?

4. Based on the information in Exhibit 1, Ms. Fineberg is considering eliminating the After-School Program. What advice would you give her?

Case 6–3

Museo de la Casa*

If a department can't cover all of its costs, we should get rid of it. It's that simple! The speaker was Ricardo Delgado, controller of Museo de la Casa, a

*This case was prepared by Professor David W. Young. Copyright © by David W. Young.

EXHIBIT 1

MUSEO DE LA CASA Income Statement for 2000 (In U.S. Dollar Equivalents, Rounded to the Nearest Thousand

Revenues	$3,000,000
Operating expenses	2,820,000
Operating income	$ 180,000
Interest expense	21,000
Surplus (deficit)	$ 159,000

museum devoted to the display of advances in home appliances. He was discussing the poor financial performance of the museum's video department at a monthly meeting of department managers.

Background

Museo de la Casa received donations of a wide variety of appliances which it then organized into displays showing the history of each appliance's development. It had three departments: audio (which contained record players, stereo tuners, CD players, and radios), video (including televisions, hand-held cameras, and VCRs), and portable communication devices (such as cell phones and electronic pagers). Patrons who came to the museum paid to enter each department, and each department accounted for about one-third of the museum's total revenue. An income statement for the most recent year is contained in Exhibit 1.

Recently, under Sr. Delgado's leadership, Museo de la Casa had begun to prepare departmental income statements. The video department's income statement for the first quarter of 2001 is contained in Exhibit 2. Of the three departments, only the video department lost money during the quarter. The other two had surpluses.

Reactions

Ernesto Gallardo, the video department's manager was not pleased with Sr. Delgado's conclusions:

> This so called income statement may show a loss, but it misses a lot of important factors. First, it's just for three months, and a slow three months at that, coming just after the holidays. Second, the video department helps out the other departments a lot. People come to my department to look at the history of TVs, and they sometimes wander into the audio department or the communication department, where they purchase additional entry tickets. How do you measure that on our department's income statement.

EXHIBIT 2

MUSEO DE LA CASA Video Department Income Statement First Quarter 2001 (In U.S. Dollar Equivalents, Rounded to the Nearest Thousand)		
Revenues		$229,000
Expenses:		
Warehouse personnel (1)	27,000	
Delivery personnel (2)	29,000	
Department manager's office (3)	70,000	
Rent and utilities (4)	50,000	
Insurance (5)	15,000	
Administrative costs (6)	60,000	
Total operating expenses		251,000
Surplus (deficit)		$ (22,000)

Notes:

(1) This amount is one-third of the total warehouse personnel payroll. Warehouse personnel were not assigned to any particular department, and they worked for all three departments on most days. The video department's items were not as extensive as those of other departments, but they were much more cumbersome to carry. As a result, the personnel spent about one-third of their time handling the video department's items.

(2) This amount was assigned to each department on the basis of its share of total revenues. The museum had two delivery trucks and each truck required a driver and an assistant. When a delivery truck came in with items for the museum, it usually contained items for all three departments.

(3) This line included the salaries of the department manager and his office staff, all of whom worked exclusively for the video department.

(4) The museum's rent and utilities were allocated to each department on the basis of its share of total square footage. The museum had a 50-year noncancelable lease for its facilities.

(5) Insurance was based on the museum's inventory. It varied slightly depending on how fragile the items were, but generally was about 6.5 percent of revenue.

(6) These were the costs of the museum central administration, such as the salary of the managing director, the salaries of her office staff, the museum's accounting and legal departments, consulting fees, and other administrative items in the central office. Each department was allocated a share of these costs based on its percentage of revenue.

Juana Fuentes, the museum's managing director, responded to Mr. Gallardo, and raised some additional concerns:

Let's forget the loss-leader argument, Ernesto. Video revenues are helped by the audio and communications departments, too. Also, since we don't have any other data to go on, let's assume the first quarter is representative of the year, even though it may not be. I'm still not convinced that the museum would be better off by getting rid of the video department.

I think your job, Ernesto, as manager of the department, is to look closely at the operating expenses on Ricardo's income statement and to analyze them. Assume that this quarter is representative of the year, and forget the revenue in other departments. Try to get back to me by the end of this week with your assessment of the financial impact of getting rid of your department.

Questions

1 Assume that the video department's revenue in the first quarter of 2001 was one-third of the museum's total revenues, and that each of the other two department's had margins of 8 percent (i.e., their surpluses were 8 percent of their revenues). What was Museo de la Casa's surplus or deficit for the quarter?

2. Analyze what the museum's surplus or deficit would have been *without* the video department? Be specific in explaining the differences, addressing each of the notes contained in Exhibit 2.

3. How should Mr. Gallardo present the information about the video department to Ms. Fuentes? How do you think Mr. Delgado would react to this presentation?

4. What should be done about the video department?

Case 6–4

Lakeside Hospital*

> A hospital just can't afford to operate a department at 50 percent capacity. If we average 20 dialysis patients, it costs us $425 per treatment, and we're only paid $250. If a department can't cover its costs, including a fair share of overhead, it isn't self-sufficient and I don't think we should carry it.

Peter Lawrence, M.D., Director of Specialty Services at Lakeside Hospital, was addressing James Newell, M.D., Chief Nephrologist of Lakeside's Renal Division, concerning a change in Medicare's payment policies for hemodialysis treatments. Recently, Medicare had begun paying independent dialysis clinics for standard dialysis treatments, and the change in policy had caused patient volume in Lakeside's dialysis unit to decrease to about 50 percent of capacity, producing a corresponding increase in per-treatment costs. By February of the current fiscal year,[1] Dr. Lawrence and Lakeside's Medical Director were considering closing the hospital's dialysis unit.

Dr. Newell, who had been Chief Nephrologist since he'd helped establish the unit, was opposed to closing it. Although he was impressed by the quality of care that independent centers offered, he was convinced that Lakeside's unit was necessary for providing back-up and emergency services for the outpatient centers, as well as for treatment for some of the hospital's seriously ill inpatients. Furthermore, although the unit could not achieve the low costs of the

---

*This case was prepared by Patricia O'Brien under the supervision of Professor David W. Young. It subsequently was revised by Professor Young. Copyright © by David W. Young.
[1]Lakeside's fiscal year (FY) ran from October 1 to September 30.

independent centers, he disagreed with Dr. Lawrence's cost figure of $425 per treatment. He resolved to prepare his own cost analysis for their next meeting.

Background

Approximately twenty years ago, at Dr. Newell's initiative, Lakeside had opened the dialysis unit, largely in response to the growing number of patients with chronic kidney disease. The hospital's renal division had long provided acute renal failure care and kidney transplants, but the most common treatment for end-stage renal disease was hemodialysis. During dialysis, a portion of a patient's blood circulates through an artificial kidney machine and is cleansed of waste products. Used three times a week for four to five hours, the kidney machine allows people with chronic kidney disease to lead almost normal lives.

Lakeside's dialysis unit had 14 artificial kidney machines. Because of space limitations, they used only 10 at any one time, reserving the other 4 for breakdowns and emergencies. Open six days a week with two shifts of patients daily, the unit could provide 120 treatments a week, which meant they could accommodate 40 regular patients.

From 1973, the year that Medicare began reimbursing for dialysis, all dialysis patients at Lakeside had been covered by Medicare. Until recently, the unit had been operating at almost 100 percent capacity, even extending its hours to accept emergency cases and to avoid turning away patients.

Patients typically spent their first three months of dialysis in a hospital facility. If there were no complications when this "start-up" period had passed, they were then required to transfer to an independent center.

Most independent dialysis centers were centrally owned and operated, and were organized into satellite groups spread throughout urban and suburban areas. The facilities were modern and attractively designed and, because they were separate from hospitals' institutional environments, they offered psychological advantages to patients. Centrally managed with low overhead, they could achieve economies unobtainable by similar hospital units. Supplies and equipment were purchased in bulk, for example, and administrators watched staff scheduling and other costs closely. As a result, their per-treatment costs were significantly lower than those in a hospital facility. For example, a treatment in a center operating at 100 percent capacity with 40 patients could cost as little as $160.

Lakeside Data

Lakeside's direct and allocated costs for the Renal Dialysis Unit in the previous fiscal year are detailed in Exhibit 1. Dr. Newell also obtained the unit's cost center report for the same fiscal year (Exhibit 2), which provided a breakdown of the unit's direct costs.

EXHIBIT 1

LAKESIDE HOSPITAL
Cost Allocation Report
Prior Fiscal Year

Cost Center	Direct Expenses	Apportioned Expenses	Total for Apportionment	Depreciation (Sq. Footage)	Admin. and General (Payroll $)	Employee Health and Welfare (Payroll $)	Operation of Plant (Sq. Footage)	Laundry and Linen (Lbs. Processed)	Housekeeping (No. of Meals)	Dietary (Payroll $)	Maintenance of Personnel (Hrs. of Service)	Nursing Service (Hrs. of Service)	Physician Salaries (Dir. Supp. $)	Medical Supplies (Phrm. Rev. $)	Pharmacy (No. of Records)	Medical Records (Hrs. of Service)	Social Services (Hrs. of Service)	Intern Resident Services	Total Expense
1. General Services																			
2. Depreciation	3,185,102		3,185,102																
3. Admin. and general	7,416,669	85,998	7,502,667	85,998															
4. Employee health and welfare	4,774,196	956	4,775,152	956	72,626														
5. Operation of plant	2,379,838	295,941	2,675,779	177,092	23,934	46,223													
6. Laundry and linen	530,249	106,312	636,561	35,036	344,372	15,233	32,109												
7. Housekeeping	1,364,177	642,554	2,006,731	38,221	349,174	219,179	35,053	5,729											
8. Dietary	98,735	989,973	1,088,708	153,203	17,106	222,236	140,211	17,187	107,962										
9. Maint. of personnel	204,327	838,166	1,042,493	306,725		10,887	280,957	6,366	216,125										
10. Professional Care—General																			
11. Nursing service	604,183	84,327	688,510	27,392				1,591	19,305	2,289									
12. Physician salaries	1,237,980	485,096	1,723,076		251,790	160,254	25,152			8,598	39,302								
13. Medical supplies	352,954	1,041,454	1,394,408	181,869	306,859	195,304	166,701	14,641	128,230		47,850								
14. Pharmacy (general)	932,181	285,848	1,218,029	36,310	105,037	66,852	33,180	891	25,566		16,367			1,645					
15. Medical records	276,355	345,465	621,820	53,510	114,791	73,060	48,967		37,727		17,410								
16. Social services	221,804	286,975	508,779	23,888	125,144	79,650	21,941		16,857		19,495								
17. Intern-resident services	438,547	630,658	1,069,205	89,820	143,676	91,444	82,146	1,082	63,292	136,089	23,039			70					
18.																			
19. Professional Care—Special																			
20. Operating rooms	3,179,736	1,877,383		178,366	424,651	270,274	163,490	177,601	100,337		66,615		143,015	78,645	114,008			160,381	5,057,119
21. Electrocardiology	349,552	101,372		18,155	27,760	17,668	16,590	159	12,843		4,378		1,723	418	609			1,069	450,924
22. Anesthesiology	1,232,988	807,737		37,583	327,866	208,674	28,898	1,082	26,489		54,210		12,062	2,468	108,405				2,040,725
23. Radiology	2,909,080	1,622,683		188,876	579,206	368,642	173,123	14,577	134,451	15,242	90,384		5,169	7,251	45,067			695	4,531,763
24. Laboratory	4,173,298	1,878,882		245,890	656,483	417,826	225,301	7,639	173,181		102,373			3,904	46,285				6,052,180
25. Blood bank	889,190	414,876		65,932	131,297	83,565	60,473	1,719	46,556		20,433			516	4,385				1,304,066
26. Physical therapy	775,470	183,484		22,296	61,822	39,347	20,336	6,175	15,653		9,591		5,169	42			3,053		958,954
27. Pharmacy (special)	508,852	673,570													673,570				1,182,422
28. Renal dialysis	1,050,048	277,267		4,778	69,550	44,266	4,281	1,782	3,411	9,471	10,842		65,477	279	1,827		50,878	10,425	1,327,315
29. Oxygen therapy	1,065,514	30,086		5,733	7,728	4,918	5,352	318	4,013		1,251			42	731				1,095,600
30.																			
31. Professional Care—Ambulatory																			
32. Emergency	446,164	921,647		16,881	118,542	75,447	15,252	12,094	11,839		18,452		177,477	28,864	20,706	52,233	7,123	366,737	1,367,811
33. Other (OPD)	1,592,046	1,854,084		168,492	316,613	201,511	155,195	2,419	118,397		49,414		286,031	10,319	13,520	171,000	132,791	228,382	3,446,130
34.																			
35. Routine Services—Inpatients																			
36. Adults and children	9,620,154	8,902,811		438,589	1,546,300	984,159	401,367	327,861	321,077	883,269	241,233	688,510	937,353	1,191,424	138,977	310,910	285,425	206,357	18,522,965
37. Intensive care	776,834	1,456,321		102,879	492,925	313,727	94,187	35,011	72,242		76,415			68,186	48,721	27,360	29,509	95,159	2,233,155
38. Nonpatient		3,015,094		480,632	887,415	564,806	445,517	637	351,178		133,439		89,600	335	1,218	60,317			3,015,094
39.																			
Total	52,586,223			3,185,102	7,502,667	4,775,152	2,675,779	636,561	2,006,731	1,088,708	1,042,493	688,510	1,723,076	1,394,408	1,218,029	621,820	508,779	1,069,205	52,586,223

EXHIBIT 2

		LAKESIDE HOSPITAL					
		Cost Center Report—Dialysis Unit					
		Prior Fiscal Year					
Expense Item	*Oct–Nov*	*Dec–Jan*	*Feb–Mar*	*Apr–May*	*June–July*	*Aug–Sept*	*Total*
Medical supplies:	$83,904	$81,800	$81,810	$81,612	$82,400	$82,280	$ 493,806
Purchased lab services.	4,232	4,052	4,000	3,988	4,084	4,120	24,476
Salaries and wages:							
Nursing	35,000	35,000	35,000	35,000	35,000	35,000	
Technicians	30,680	30,680	30,680	30,680	30,680	30,680	
Administration.	7,120	7,120	7,120	7,120	7,120	7,120	
Total	$72,800	$72,800	$72,800	$72,800	$72,800	$72,800	436,800
Employee expense							
(fringe benefits).	6,170	6,170	6,170	6,170	6,170	6,170	37,020
Water usage	3,528	3,480	3,456	3,440	3,496	3,496	20,896
Administrative supplies	1,800	1,800	1,800	1,800	1,800	1,800	10,800
Major equipment							
depreciation	4,375	4,375	4,375	4,375	4,375	4,375	26,250
Total costs.							$1,050,048
Number of treatments	980	956	944	940	956	960	5,736

Dr. Newell intended to use the prior year's costs to calculate the per-treatment cost at various volume levels for the current year. He also wanted to find the point at which the unit's revenue would meet its costs. He commented:

I plan to use only those costs that can be traced directly to dialysis treatments, and not any overhead costs. If the unit's revenue meets its direct costs, it is self-sufficient. Peter's treatment cost of $425 is misleading since it includes substantial overhead, and this year's overhead will differ from last year's because of the unit's decrease in volume. Also, even though this year's overhead can't be calculated until the end of the fiscal year, I think I can come up with an estimate. First, though, I plan to calculate the "real" cost of a treatment and, from there, define a "fair share" of overhead.

In reviewing the cost center report, Dr. Newell realized that the nature of the costs varied.

There are three types of costs I need to consider in this analysis: those that vary in proportion to volume, those that vary with significant changes in volume, and those that remain the same regardless of the unit's volume. The first and the last are pretty clear. Medical supplies, purchased laboratory services, and water usage all change according to the number of treatments provided. The other nonpersonnel expenses will stay essentially the same regardless of the number of treatments.

Salary and wages, and employee expense costs are more complicated. Although they didn't change during the last year, the unit's number of treatments also remained fairly steady. However, the significant reduction in volume this year might cause a corresponding reduction in salary and employee expenses. Last year, we employed seven hemodialysis technicians, seven nurses, and one administrator (our nephrologists are all on the hospitals' physicians' payroll). However, since I had anticipated that volume would fall, I didn't replace the nurse and two technicians who left in January of this year. So, as of February, our monthly salaries and employee expenses have decreased by about $7,500.

Finally, just as a precaution, in case Peter asks, I had my secretary call a hospital equipment supply manufacturer to discuss the resale value of our 14 machines. They told her that machines used for four years or more could not be sold, even for scrap. We purchased all 14 machines five years ago for $210,000.

Questions

1. What is the breakeven volume for the dialysis unit? What assumptions are necessary for calculating it?

2. What is a fair share of overhead at the current level of activity in the unit?

3. What will happen to total costs and revenues at Lakeside if the dialysis unit is closed? What other options are available and what are their financial consequences?

4. What should Dr. Newell do?

5. What should Dr. Lawrence do?

Case 6–5

Town of Belmont*

It was 10 A.M., January 4th. Mr. James Castanino, the newly promoted head of the Highway Department, sat at his desk looking out across the sloping park toward the town's busy main shopping district. Opposite him was a member of his staff who had recently begun a project to determine the appropriate mix of town-owned and subcontract snow removal equipment.

The study came at an opportune time. The town's aging six Walther Snow Fighters were rapidly reaching the point of replacement, and it was Mr. Castanino's intention to replace them at a rate of one per year. Belmont, like most town governments, was finding it ever more difficult to increase its revenues rapidly enough to maintain previous levels of service. All of the town's departments were undertaking sustained cost cutting measures. The Highway Department had been a leader in such cost savings, doing volume purchasing and repairing all its vehicles. However, further cost cutting was necessary.

*This case was prepared by Professor Roy D. Shapiro, Harvard Business School. Copyright © by the President and Fellows of Harvard College. Harvard Business School case 9-182-046.

With snow removal being the largest component of the department's budget, a reexamination of its snow removal subcontracting policies might yield significant savings.

In simplified terms, the decision Mr. Castanino faced contained two options. The first option was to replace the six Walther Snow Fighters on a one-to-one basis. The second was to not replace the Walthers and subcontract six more vehicles. Before making his decision he felt a number of important variables needed to be considered.

Belmont (triple A bond rating) was a suburb of Boston. Its population was predominantly middle class, with a high proportion of professional people. The town had a well-deserved reputation for providing its citizens with high-quality services, and the maintenance of this reputation was important. Indeed, during the two large blizzards of 1978 the Highway Department had managed to keep all roads passable and was one of the first in the state to have restored road conditions to normal.

The department heads reported to a part-time Board of Selectmen. This provided them with considerable autonomy in their day-to-day decision making. Capital expenditures greater than $5,000 required approval by the selectmen, the warrant committee, and the town meeting. As a result, Mr. Castanino was aware that any capital expenditure would face searching scrutiny before approval. The town also desired to maintain good relations with its employees. Thus, any cost-saving measure which improved working conditions would be highly attractive.

The town had 90 miles of roads, of which 40 were considered main thoroughfares. When salting or sanding was required, the main thoroughfares were covered each hour by four trucks equipped with spreaders.

The use of spreaders varied according to conditions. If only a trace of snow was expected, road conditions were watched closely. If road conditions seemed likely to worsen, one truck would be dispatched to cover the steeper gradients. If more than a trace but less than an inch was expected, four trucks with spreaders would be dispatched to cover the main thoroughfares. They would generally have to make two sweeps (at 10 miles an hour). If greater than an inch but less than three inches fell, seven trucks with spreaders would be dispatched to cover all roads. They would generally spend an hour per inch with an hour for mopping-up operations. If greater than three inches were expected, snowplowing procedures were initiated. Exhibit 1 contains relevant snowfall data, averaged for 30 years.

The department's resources consisted of its own vehicles and subcontractors. Belmont had 15 vehicles which could be used for snowplowing. They consisted of the six Walther Snow Fighters and nine other vehicles that were used for other purposes in addition to snowplowing. On the average, 13 were available during a storm. Also on call were 15 subcontracted vehicles. Typically, 90 percent of those called in any storm would turn out. To ensure good relations with the subcontractors, Castanino's policy was to divide them into two groups—one group of seven and one of eight. If the expected snowfall

EXHIBIT 1
Snowfall Data,
30-Year Average

November

11 percent of November days had snow, sleet, or hail; of these days, measured snowfall was as follows:

Snowfall (inches)	Proportion of Days Having that Amount
Trace	72%
Under 1	18
Over 1	10

December

34 percent of December days had snow, sleet, or hail; of these days, measured snowfall was as follows:

Snowfall (inches)	Proportion of Days Having that Amount
Trace	54%
Under 1	27
1–3	9
3–5	5
5–10	1
10–15	1
Over 15	0.5

January

41 percent of January days had snow, sleet, or hail; of these days, measured snowfall was as follows:

Snowfall (inches)	Proportion of Days Having that Amount
Trace	47%
Under 1	29
1–3	11
3–5	7
5–10	4
10–15	1
Over 15	0.2

February

39 percent of February days had snow, sleet, or hail; of these days, measured snowfall was as follows:

Snowfall (inches)	Proportion of Days Having that Amount
Trace	47%
Under 1	30
1–3	11
3–5	5
5–10	4
10–15	1
Over 15	1

EXHIBIT 1
(Concluded)

March

28 percent of March days had snow, sleet, or hail; of these days, measured snowfall was as follows:

Snowfall (inches)	*Proportion of Days Having that Amount*
Trace	50%
Under 1	27
1–3	12
3–5	6
5–10	4
10–15	1
Over 15	0.4

Source: Local Climatological Data Monthly Survey (for Boston Logan International Airport) compiled by the National Oceanic and Atmospheric Administration Environmental Data Service.

EXHIBIT 2
Cost of Operating a Town Vehicle, Salting and Sanding

Labor	2 persons per vehicle*
Salt	$27 per ton at 3 tons per hour[†]
or	
Sand	$3 per ton at 3 tons per hour[†]
Fuel	$6/hour
Repairs and maintenance	$10/hour

Snow Removal with New Vehicles

Labor	1 person per vehicle*
Fuel	$6/hour
Repairs and maintenance	$10/hour
Cost of new 18 GVW vehicle	$30,000

*Labor costs were $6 per hour, time-and-a-half for overtime.
[†]Normally half of the material spread was salt and half was sand.

was greater than three inches but less than five inches, he would call in only one group. The two groups would be chosen on an alternating basis. If greater than five inches was expected, all 15 subcontractor vehicles would be called. Subcontractors only performed plowing services, not the salting and sanding of roads. Like town employees, subcontractors would work until the snow was cleared, but they did not receive overtime pay. While the size and rental cost of subcontracted vehicles varied, an appropriate average was $34 per hour. Cost data for a town vehicle is contained in Exhibit 2.

Normal procedures called for the employees and/or subcontractors to work until the storm was cleared up. For all storms, this took roughly an hour for each inch of snow. "Mop-up" for a three-inch storm required an additional three-hour shift of all vehicles. For an 8-inch snowfall, an additional four hours was required for mop-up, and for a snowfall greater than 16 inches, an additional eight hours was required. For any storm which dumped more than 12 inches, the usual policy required working 16-hour shifts. This meant that only two-thirds of the vehicles would be on the road at any time. For snowfall in excess of two feet, all crews would be sent home for eight hours rest before clean-up operations were resumed. It was not a surprising demonstration of the innate perversity of weather conditions that, historically, 70 percent of all town employees' time spent on snow removal had been at overtime rates.

It also had come to Mr. Castanino's attention that if the Walthers were retired but not replaced, it would be possible to redeploy their drivers as replacements for other drivers, reducing the expected time any individual driver would spend on the road in a 12-inch storm by 6.5 hours without increasing labor costs. The total labor cost per town vehicle would, however, remain the same.

Having discussed operating procedures, Mr. Castanino and his assistant began to discuss ways of determining the costs of these two options.

Questions

1. What are the relevant annual costs to consider for each option?

2. What factors other than annual costs are important in making the decision?

3. What action would you recommend?

Chapter 7

Pricing Decisions

Management control in a for-profit company does not usually encompass decisions about prices for the company's products. By contrast, for reasons we discuss in this chapter, pricing decisions are an important aspect of management control in nonprofit organizations. Nevertheless, many nonprofit managers have given insufficient thought to pricing policies. In fact, many tend to regard all marketing activity as something to be ignored. Such an attitude can result in their giving insufficient attention to client needs and decision-making behavior. It also can result in the organization pricing its services in a way that is unfair to some of its clients, or developing pricing policies that inhibit the achievement of its strategic goals.

In the first section of this chapter we explain why pricing decisions are important to management control in nonprofit organizations. We then describe the basis of normal pricing, which is a product's full cost plus a profit margin. Finally, we describe two variations from normal pricing: services provided at subsidized prices and services provided at no charge.

Relevance of Pricing to Management Control

In for-profit companies, pricing is usually the responsibility of the marketing department. Apart from the provision of relevant cost information from company accounts, the topic rarely is mentioned in a description of management control practices. In most nonprofit organizations, however, prices are an important consideration in management control. There are three reasons for this:

- Prices influence the behavior of clients.

- Prices provide a measure of output.

- Prices influence the behavior of managers.

Client Behavior

The amount that a client (or third party on behalf of a client) pays for a service indicates that the service is worth at least that much to the client. Indeed, the better a pricing scheme fits with client decision-making options, the more powerful its impact on client behavior.

Example	Residents of a city or town can be charged for use of water in one of at least three different ways: (1) everyone can be charged the same amount (or, at the extreme, nothing); (2) everyone can be charged a monthly or quarterly flat rate, based on the number of bathrooms and kitchens in their residences; or (3) everyone can be charged individually for the water they actually consume, as measured by a meter. In the first case, residents are not motivated to conserve water, and consumers who use little water subsidize those who use more. In the second case, the charge is somewhat more equitable because water usage tends to vary with the number of outlets. However, such a system does not motivate consumers to conserve water (although it may influence their decisions to add or delete bathrooms). If meters are installed, consumers are more likely to give thought to conserving water. This occurred in New York City some time ago when, after meters were installed, water consumption fell by nearly 50 percent.

Strength of Motivation

Prices that affect clients directly tend to have the greatest influence on consumption. Normally, as the price for a unit of service increases, clients consume fewer units. The influence may not be as strong if charges are paid by third parties, however. Some observers claim, for example, that third-party insurance for health care services, by insulating patients from the full cost of those services, has contributed to escalating health care costs.

In other situations, price is a mere bookkeeping charge with no direct effect on client behavior. Some universities, for example, allocate computer resources by providing students and faculty with monetary allowances that entitle them to a certain amount of computer time. These allowances may be set so high or may be so easily supplemented, however, that they do not motivate at all, and do little more than track computer usage. The motivating force of such systems would be much stronger if clients were allowed to trade *dollars* of computer time for other resources, or receive a refund for time not used.

Price can sometimes provide an automatic means of rationing a service. For example, if motorists who renew their automobile registrations in person are charged more than those who complete their renewal by mail, fewer are likely to use the window services of the registry.

Measure of Output

Measurements of output in nonmonetary terms, such as the number of visitors to a community health center or the number of hours faculty spend in contact with students, are likely to be cruder than monetary measurements. If, on the other hand, each service furnished by an organization is priced at its full cost plus a margin to cover the cost of capital, the total revenue for a period approximates the total amount of service provided. Even if reported revenue does not measure the real value of an organization's services to individual clients or society, the revenue-based approximation may provide useful information to managers. For example, if revenue one year is lower than that of the previous year (after adjustments for inflation), managers have a good indication that the organization's real output has decreased.

If the quantity of service provided varies among an organization's clients, a single price will not accurately measure the variations. At one time, for example, hospital patients were charged a flat rate per day, even though the services they received varied greatly based on their illnesses. Today, most hospital charges vary directly with the quantity of services provided. If the unit price of a service reflects the relative magnitude of that service, then total revenue, which is the aggregate of these prices, is in effect a weighted measure of output. That is, total revenue incorporates differences in the types of services rendered.[1]

Behavior of Managers

If services are sold, the responsibility center that sells them frequently is designated as a profit center.[2] In general, profit center managers are motivated to think of ways to: (*a*) render additional services so as to increase revenue, (*b*) reduce costs, or (*c*) change prices. Under these circumstances, the manager of a profit center in a nonprofit organization behaves much like a manager in a for-profit company.

Example

In an organization with a computer center, if computer services are furnished without charge, assignment of computer time is the responsibility of the manager of the center, and time assignments are made according to his or her perception of users' needs (or, sometimes, friendship with users). In any case, the manager has little financial incentive to provide quality computer services in a cost-effective manner.

[1]While most health care managers and policymakers consider this evolution an improvement, we caution against pursuing such precision in all pricing and control situations. For reasons we will describe later, linking prices directly to the types of services provided may not be optimal in all circumstances.
[2]Recall that a profit center is an organizational unit in which both outputs and inputs are measured in monetary terms. The manager of a profit center is responsible for operating the unit in such a way that it achieves the budgeted difference between revenues and expenses.

If the computer center is set up as a profit center, however, and dissatisfied users are free to go elsewhere, the manager is motivated to offer quality services at competitive prices—or risk underutilized facilities, unmet revenue goals, and poor performance. In addition, when internal clients must pay for their use of computer resources (which reduces the profit in their profit centers), they tend to think much more carefully about their use of those resources.

In this and other pricing situations, if customers do not buy a product in the quantity that managers think is reasonable, there is an indication that something is wrong. Perhaps not enough people believe the product is worthwhile at the stated price. Perhaps they can obtain a similar or better product at a lower price elsewhere. Whatever the reason, management will want to reexamine the product and its price. Can its costs be reduced? Is there a need for better marketing? Can the product be made more attractive? If not, should it be discontinued?

Prospective Prices

As a general rule, management control is facilitated when the price is set prior to the performance of a service. When this happens, prices provide an incentive for managers to keep costs within prescribed amounts. No such incentive exists for managers who know that costs will be recouped no matter how high they are.

This principle can be applied, of course, only when it is feasible to estimate the cost of a service. With many research-and-development projects, for example, there is no reliable basis for estimating how much money should be spent to achieve the desired result. Even so, it is usually possible to establish overhead rates based on budgeted overhead costs and to require adherence to these rates.

Opponents of prospective pricing assert that it leads to an overemphasis on cost control, with a consequent lowering of the quality of service. Advocates counter that a well-designed management control system should help managers and service providers overcome any tendency to emphasize reduced cost at the expense of quality.

Normal Pricing

In general, the price of a product provided by a nonprofit organization should be its full cost plus a surplus, or margin. This is the same approach that is used in normal pricing in for-profit companies, except that in a for-profit company delivering similar services, the margin ordinarily is higher so as to provide a return to shareholders.

Full Cost

As we discussed in Chapter 5, the full cost of a product is the sum of its direct costs and its allocated share of the service center costs incurred jointly for it and any other products. In arriving at prices, the relevant costs are estimates of *future* costs, not historical costs.

Recall from Chapter 5 that direct costs are those that can be traced directly to a single cost object. In nonprofit organizations, a frequent cost object is a service or a program. Service center costs, although incurred in part for that cost object, are not traced directly to it. They are allocated to cost objects by means of overhead rates. These rates are set so that at the expected volume, 100 percent of service center costs are allocated to the cost objects whose prices are being calculated. Pricing principles assume, therefore, that a specified volume of output will be attained.

Depreciation

In nonprofit organizations, there is a difference of opinion as to whether depreciation on buildings and equipment that were financed with contributions should be included as an element of cost. Some people argue that such buildings and equipment were acquired at zero cost and that, because the purpose of depreciation is to recover an organization's cost, there is nothing to depreciate. Others maintain that depreciation is necessary to help provide for replacement of these assets. Also, some people argue that the services a nonprofit organization provides are just as valuable as the services provided by a for-profit company, and that clients should pay a comparable amount for them. Thus, by including depreciation as an element of cost, a nonprofit's pricing practice is similar to the pricing practices of for-profit companies. Indeed, many clients of nonprofit organizations, including government agencies, are willing to include depreciation on contributed assets (or its equivalent as a *use charge*) as an element of cost. (The government does not permit inclusion of depreciation on equipment it has already paid for in the prices it is charged, however; to do so would be double counting.)

As discussed in Chapter 3, many organizations do not depreciate fixed assets. Instead, they approximate depreciation by using the principal payments on borrowed funds. They supplement this approach with a policy of expensing all fixed assets except major equipment purchases. They argue that this adds up to approximately the same amount as depreciation in an average year.

Revenue Offsets

Some services are partially financed by revenue from endowment or other contributed sources. Opinions differ as to whether these *revenue offsets* should be deducted from costs to arrive at the price a client should pay.

If revenue is directly related to a service—as is the case with endowment that is specifically designated for financial aid to students—a good case can be made for taking this revenue into account in arriving at the price. Even if this is done, however, it may be desirable to report this amount as a component of the service's revenue on the operating statement, rather than as an expense. Then the operating statement will show the total resources earned by and for the service.

If the contributed revenue is for general operating purposes rather than for a specific service, many organizations do not treat some fraction of it as an offset to full cost in calculating the price for a specific service. Rather, they prefer to reduce the required margin included in the price of all services by the amount of this revenue.

Need for a Satisfactory Margin

As discussed in earlier chapters, a nonprofit organization's basic goal is to provide services. To survive, however, it must generate revenues that at least equal its expenses. Otherwise, it will go bankrupt. Moreover, as discussed in Chapter 4, a nonprofit needs an excess of revenue over expenses to finance fixed asset growth and replacement, plus needed working capital (such as for inventories and receivables).

Many nonprofit organizations can finance some of their fixed asset and working capital needs by borrowing, just as for-profit companies do. However, there is a limit to the amount that any organization can borrow. Consequently, nonprofits need equity capital for basically the same reason that for-profit companies do: because lenders are unwilling to provide amounts that equal an organization's total capital needs. Indeed, many nonprofits believe that financing fixed assets entirely with borrowed funds is too risky. Therefore, they need to generate equity from either contributions or operations. In the absence of a constant and predictable source of contributions from donors or other sources, the organization will need to generate additional equity in the form of a surplus from its own operations. Thus, although nonprofit organizations do not have stockholders who expect returns, they nevertheless must generate equity from operations as a source of financing.

Estimating the Margin

Conceptually, the best way for managers to estimate the margin component of a price is to calculate the cost of using the equity capital that the organization needs, and to include this cost in the total cost of a service. Most managers do not make such calculations, however. Instead, they rely on rules of thumb. For example, there is a widespread belief among managers of hospital and research organizations that their organizations' margin should be 3 or 4 percent of revenue. It is not clear that this belief is grounded in a thorough analysis of the underlying needs, however.

Some organizations base their prices on a conservative estimate of volume, and plan for no surplus. When actual volume exceeds the estimate, the incremental amount (i.e., revenues minus variable expenses) provides the necessary margin. For example, a college may base its tuition on an enrollment that is 5 percent lower than what it actually expects. If its actual enrollment reaches the expected level, the difference is its surplus for the year. Similarly, an organization may make a conservative estimate of its revenue from annual giving, with the expectation that the anticipated excess will be its surplus.

This approach works when the estimate of volume is truly conservative. Difficulties arise when volume falls below the anticipated level. When this happens, an organization's revenues do not cover its expenses. In such circumstances continued existence is precarious and often rests on the hope that, in times of crisis, special appeals to donors will bail the organization out.

Example

It is said that for many years the Metropolitan Museum of Art presented its annual deficit to its board of trustees, and the trustees then wrote personal checks that totaled the needed amount. Today, few nonprofit organizations (including the Metropolitan Museum) are able to do this.

Danger of Normal Pricing

If a nonprofit organization provides a worthwhile service, clients are usually willing to pay the normal price. In this case, the organization usually will earn its desired margin. This is so even if the organization has competitors with lower-priced services, because clients often do not select a service provider on the basis of price alone.

The danger of this situation is that the normal price may conceal cost inefficiencies. For-profit companies must face the test of the marketplace; an inadequate profit is a danger signal that may not exist in a nonprofit organization. Because of the absence of such a danger signal, the nonprofit governing board has the responsibility of ensuring operating efficiency in other ways. It does this by careful analysis of proposed budgets (as explained in later chapters), by comparing the costs with the costs of comparable organizations if this is feasible, and by other devices that lead management to "get the message" that efficiency is important.

The Pricing Unit

In general, the smaller and more specific the unit of service that is priced, the better. It improves senior management's decisions about the allocation of resources, and it measures output for control purposes more accurately. A price that includes several discrete services with different costs is not a good measure of output because it masks the actual mix of services rendered. The practice of isolating progressively smaller units of service for pricing purposes is called *unbundling*.

There is considerable disagreement about this practice. Those who reject it argue that price should reflect an average mix of services, and that detailed information needed for management control can be obtained in other ways.

Managers who decide to unbundle services should be mindful of two qualifications: First, beyond a certain point, the paperwork and other costs associated with pricing tiny units of service obviously exceed the benefits. Some hospitals charge for individual aspirin tablets, a practice that is difficult to defend. The precise location of this point is, of course, uncertain.

The second qualification for managers considering unbundled prices is that the consequences of such pricing should be consistent with the organization's overall policy and goals. This qualification extends beyond the size of the unit to matters that are much more strategic in nature.

Example

Undergraduate English instruction costs less than undergraduate physics instruction, and these differences could be reflected by charging different prices for these courses. However, a separate price for each course might cause students to select courses in a way that university management considers to be educationally unsound. By contrast, in most universities there are significant differences in the overall costs of graduate and undergraduate programs. Thus, there may be good reasons for charging different tuition rates for graduate and undergraduate students. University administrators who unbundle in this way do not feel that these differences motivate individual students to make unwise choices.

The Port Authority of New York and New Jersey charges the same amount for a tunnel crossing of the Hudson River as for a crossing using the George Washington Bridge, despite a lower full cost per vehicle for bridge traffic. The pricing decision is based on transportation policy, rather than on the cost of the separate services.

Hospital Pricing as an Example of Unbundling

Exhibit 7–1 shows several approaches that could be used in pricing the services provided by a hospital. Moving from Column A to Column D, one can see pricing practices that involve (1) an increase in recordkeeping, (2) a corresponding increase in the amount of output information for use in management control, and (3) a basis for charging to clients that more accurately reflects the services they received.

At one extreme, the hospital could charge an all-inclusive rate, say $1,500 per day. This practice is advocated by some people on the grounds that patients then know in advance what their bills will be (assuming their lengths of stay can be estimated), and because recordkeeping, at least for billing purposes, is simplified. They point out that detailed information required for administration can be collected in the management control system, even though such information would not be reflected in the prices charged. The weakness of the latter argument is that if detailed information is going to be collected for management anyway, an all-inclusive price will not result in significant savings in recordkeeping (unless shortcuts and estimates are substituted for sound

EXHIBIT 7–1   **Pricing Alternatives in a Hospital**

(A) All-Inclusive Rate	(B) Daily Charge plus Special Services	(C) Type of Service	(D) Detailed

$1,500/day	Patient care....... $700/day
	Operating room $300/hour
	Pharmacy......... $7/dosage
	Radiology........ $ 35/film
	Special nurses...... $ 75/day
	Etc.
		Medical/surgical:
		  1st day $750
		  Other days 575
		Maternity:.............
		  1st day $450
		  Other days 400
		(Plus special services as in *B*)
			Admittance............ $500
			Work-up, per hour 50
			Medical/surgical bed,
			  per day 500
			Maternity bed, per day 250
			Bassinet, per day......... 125
			Nursery care, per hour 30
			Meals, per day 40
			Discharge 50
			(Plus special services as in B)

data collection methods). The only savings would be in the billing process, which is a small part of a hospital's total accounting function.

A common variation on the all-inclusive price is shown in Column B. Here the hospital charges separately for the cost of each easily identifiable special service, and makes a blanket daily charge for everything else. Radiology prices, for example, are frequently calculated according to a rather detailed point system that takes into account the size of the radiology plate and the complexity of the procedure; each point is worth a few cents. There is some incongruity, however, in calculating prices for certain services in terms of points worth a few cents each, while lumping other service costs into an over-all rate of, say, $700 per day.

Column C unbundles the daily charge. Different charges are made for each department, and more is charged for the first day than for subsequent days. This pricing policy accounts for the admitting and work-up costs associated only with the first day of a patient's stay.

Column D is the job-cost approach that managers in many for-profit companies use. Managers of automobile repair shops, for example, cost each repair job separately. Each repair is charged for the services of mechanics according to the number of hours they work on the job, as well as for each part and significant item of supply required for the job's completion. The sum of these separate charges is the basis for the price the customer pays. Customers of a repair garage would not tolerate any other approach. They would not, for example, tolerate paying a flat daily rate for repairs, regardless of the service provided.

Variations from Normal Prices

There are many situations in nonprofit organizations where circumstances call for variations from the normal approach to setting prices. In some instances, these situations arise because of the presence of third-party payers. In others, they arise because the organization wishes to distinguish between services provided as part of its main mission and those that are more peripheral.

Prices Influenced by Outside Forces

Some prices are set by outside agencies. Examples are the diagnosis related group (DRG) prices that are used by Medicare to reimburse hospitals, and the price ceilings sometimes specified by government agencies as a condition for providing services funded by government grants. In these instances, managers still need to make cost calculations even though their selling price is given. If, for example, a hospital's full cost of treating a patient with a particular diagnosis is greater than the associated DRG price, the hospital will need to determine whether it wishes to avoid accepting patients with that diagnosis. Of course, this decision is subject to the hospital's legal and ethical obligations.

DRG prices also affect the way physicians behave. Consciously or unconsciously, they may treat the patient in a way that generates the most income, rather than in the most clinically appropriate way.

Example
A General Accounting Office study of 264 oncologists found that 64 percent of them administered chemotherapy in hospitals rather than in their private offices, although the treatment in many cases could have been conducted equally well in a private office. Payments for office treatment were low, however, compared to payments (and costs) in a hospital.[3]

Price may also be indirectly influenced by outside forces. For example, no college could charge much more than its competitors; to do so would indicate that it was inefficient. Nor would a college charge less than its competitors because it could make good use of any additional amount to strengthen its curriculum. Furthermore, most colleges are convinced that small differences in tuition do not influence a student's decision as to which college to attend.

Example
In 1990 the Department of Justice considered investigating the possible incidence of illegal price fixing by a group of colleges whose tuition charges were within 5 percent of one another. Its decision not to pursue this matter was probably influenced by the recognition that such a situation is likely among competing organizations.

Similarly, if a ceiling price required by a government grant is lower than the full cost of the service to be provided, the organization has to decide whether to accept the grant. It may decide to do so if the price exceeds the variable costs of providing the service; that is, if the grant makes a contribution to overhead.

Cost Reimbursement

Revenue for many services consists of reimbursement for costs actually incurred, rather than a preset selling price. Although the intent of the buyer usu-

[3]U.S. General Accounting Office, "Medicare Reimbursement Policies Can Influence the Setting and Cost of Chemotherapy" (GAO/PEMD- 92-28), July 1992.

ally is to pay the full cost of the service, the definition of full cost varies considerably from one buyer to another. In particular, a component called *unallowable costs* enters the calculation. These are costs that, although incurred by the organization, are not allowed in the reimbursable cost pool. Contracting agencies may also specify ceilings for certain items, such as the compensation of executives or the daily amount that can be spent for travel.[4]

Some of these requirements are extremely detailed. Moreover, they change frequently. As a result, managers of nonprofit organizations receiving cost-based reimbursement must be sure to be both thoroughly familiar and current with the regulations that govern their organization's reimbursement.

Example

According to OMB *Circular A-21,* travel and subsistence costs of college and university trustees are unallowable. The reasonable cost of meals served in connection with a trustee meeting is allowable, except that the cost of alcoholic beverages served at such meals is unallowable.

Market-Based Prices

Managers ordinarily apply a normal pricing policy to services that are directly (or closely) related to their organization's principal objectives. In dealing with peripheral activities, however, they usually make sure their prices correspond to market prices for similar services.

Example

Many universities believe that room and board charges should be based on full cost because students live in dormitories and eat in dining rooms as a necessary part of the educational process. For similar reasons, they believe that textbooks, laboratory supplies, and the like, should be priced at full cost. By contrast, they believe that the rental of space to outside groups, the provision of special programs requested by outside groups, or the sale of items at campus soda fountains is not closely related to the main objective of the university. Accordingly, the prices of these services are set at market levels. Similarly, many universities base tuition for graduate and undergraduate programs on full cost, whereas they use market rates for executive development programs.

In making pricing decisions, managers often have difficulty drawing the line between programs that are closely related to the organization's main mission and those that are more peripheral. For example, market rates seem appropriate for the executive development programs mentioned in the example above, but the use of market rates for university extension courses or adult

[4]See the following U.S. Office of Management and Budget (OMB) publications: *Circular A–21,* "Cost Principles for Educational Institutions"; *Circular A–87,* "Cost Principles for State and Local Governments"; *Circular A–122,* "Cost Principles for Nonprofit Organizations"; and *Circular 133,* "Audits of Institutions of Higher Education and Other Non-Profit Organizations." (Dates are not given because these circulars are revised from time to time.) United Way organizations also publish guidance on allowable costs. In most of these guidelines, even if an item is not specifically described, it must meet the general test that it be "reasonable."

education programs in municipal school systems is much less clear. Moreover, these decisions involve not only pricing issues, but legal issues as well.

Pricing Subsidized Services

Services are being subsidized when the price charged for a service to one client is lower than the price charged to another, or when the price to all clients is lower than the full cost of the services they receive. There are three basic types of subsidies: (1) for certain services, (2) for some clients, and (3) for all clients.

Subsidies for Certain Services

A nonprofit organization may decide to price a certain service at less than the normal price. Such a price is called a *subsidy price.* It may want to encourage the use of the service by clients who are unable or unwilling to pay the normal price. Or, as a matter of policy, the organization may want clients to select services on some basis other than their ability to pay. Examples are public education and low-cost housing. In most circumstances, providing a service at a subsidy price is preferable to providing it for free. This is because a price, even if low, motivates clients to give thought to the value of the service they receive. However, an organization should be careful to determine whether the price deters clients from requesting *needed* services.

Example

In a now-classic study, Milton Roemer reported that when Medicaid patients in California were charged $1 per visit for primary care, there was a sharp decline in the number of visits. Some months later, however, there was an increase in these patients' rates of hospitalization—hospitalization that could have been avoided had the individuals received timely primary care. Overall, the cost to Medicaid was higher as a result of this pricing policy.[5]

An organization may decide that its price will be the same for all services even though some services cost more than others. In this case, higher-cost services are said to be *cross-subsidized* by lower-cost services. More broadly, any difference in price that does not reflect a difference in cost results in cross-subsidization. Although cross-subsidization is frowned on in some settings, such as public utility rate regulation, there may be sound reasons for using it in other settings. For example, establishing equitable prices for narrow units of service may not be worth the cost. More importantly, the organization may not want clients to choose one service over another on the basis of price.

Example

Courses in Latin and Greek, and seminars in a college typically have small enrollments, with a resulting faculty cost per student that is two or three times the cost for more popular courses. Because the college does not

---

[5]M. Roemer et al., "Copayments for Ambulatory Care: Penny-Wise and Pound-Foolish," *Medical Care,* June 1975, pp. 457–66.

want to discourage enrollment in these courses, it charges the same tuition to all students. Thus, its low-enrollment courses are subsidized by high-enrollment courses.

Even if managers do not use cost as the basis for pricing, they may find it helpful to calculate the actual costs of the organization's services. Knowing the difference between price and full cost can help flag areas for managerial decision making. For example, if a particular service does not cover its full costs, managers have several possible courses of action:

- Accept the loss, recognizing that the service is sufficiently important to the organization's strategy to warrant subsidization.

- Reduce the variable costs or fixed costs directly associated with the service to eliminate the loss.

- Increase volume (if the service has a positive contribution margin, there is some breakeven volume at which full costs will be covered).

- Raise the price of the service to eliminate the loss.

- Phase out the service.

Example

A university discovered that the cost of operating its nuclear reactor was $50,000 per student using the reactor. The reactor probably should be phased out unless: (1) it is important to the university's strategy, (2) its operating costs can be reduced, or (3) the number of users can be increased.

The U.S. Postal Service subsidizes rural post offices because it is public policy to provide convenient mail service to everyone; this principle is rarely challenged. However, the Postal Service also subsidizes its money order service, even though commercial banks provide adequate facilities for transferring money. Some observers question whether this latter subsidy is warranted.

Subsidies as a Motivating Device

Most subsidies are intended to encourage the use of a service by clients who would not otherwise do so.

Example

Many public bathing beaches and other recreation facilities charge a lower price on weekdays to encourage off-peak use. By contrast, the Mexican government had a policy of eliminating recreational charges on Sundays. This had the effect of further crowding recreation facilities on their busiest day, which would appear to be counterproductive. The policy was judged to be sound, however, because it encouraged use of the facilities by working-class families on the only day they could do so—a purpose judged more important than reducing crowding.

Subsidies for Some Clients

A client who is not charged the same amount as other clients who receive the same or comparable services is being subsidized. The reason for this subsidy is that the organization's objective is to provide the service to all qualified clients, some of whom are unable to pay the normal price. The subsidy may be in the form of a lower price (or no charge), or the client may be charged the normal price and the subsidy treated as a deduction. The latter is often preferable because the gross revenue resulting from this method provides a better measure of the amount of service rendered by the organization than does net revenue (gross minus the subsidies). Nevertheless, net revenue is used in some situations.

Example

Colleges and universities provide subsidies to certain students in the form of scholarships and other financial aid. Many people believe that the amount of financial aid should be reported as an expense item, so tuition revenue will measure the gross amount that the college has earned in its educational programs. Tuition revenue thus would provide a sound measure of actual output.

Nonprofit hospitals are charitable organizations and, as such, are obligated to provide certain levels of care to indigent patients. At one time, to inform financial statement readers of how well they satisfied this obligation, they showed charitable care "revenue" as a deduction from the gross revenue that measured charges for all services rendered. However, according to the 1996 AICPA *Accounting and Audit Guide for Not-for-Profit Organizations,* the amount of charitable care must be excluded from the financial statements, and disclosed in a footnote to the financial statements. Hospitals that follow this recommendation will not have as sound a measure of actual output as they had under the previous practice.

Estimating Subsidies

In situations such as those described above, managers must take care to incorporate subsidies into their analyses when they are considering price increases. For example, when subsidies are present, a price increase in, say, university tuition rates or hospital charges will not necessarily result in a comparable increase in *net revenue.*

Example

Assume a college has 1,000 students who are charged $20,000 each for tuition. Gross tuition revenue is $20,000,000. Twenty percent of gross tuition is designated for financial aid. Thus, students receive financial aid in the amount of $4,000,000. An increase of 10 percent in tuition will result in an increase of $2,000,000 in gross revenue. However, if the criteria for deciding what students receive financial aid are unchanged, financial aid will also increase by 20 percent, or $400,000. Therefore, the college's net revenue will increase by only $1,600,000 (= $2,000,000 − $400,000).

Relating Subsidies to Need

Some clients are subsidized because they need the service but do not have the resources to obtain it. In some cases, this general idea is applied to a class of clients even though some members of the class have ample resources. Examples are subsidies for handicapped and elderly persons by both nonprofit organizations and for-profit companies—for transportation, movies, restaurants, drugs, and a variety of other services. Conceptually, the subsidy should be limited to those in need, but finding a practical way of applying this concept is difficult. A *means test* usually is not feasible because it is expensive and time consuming, and, more importantly, because many people resent being classified as needy. Moreover, such a subsidy is politically popular, and attempts to eliminate or modify it would encounter considerable resistance from lobbying groups.

Subsidies for All Clients

Some organizations receive contributions or appropriations intended to subsidize their services for all clients. When this happens, no client pays the normal price for services. Museums, symphony orchestras, and state universities are examples. The question then arises: Should the gross revenue resulting from the normal price of these services be reported with an offset from the contributed amount, or should only the actual amount of service revenue charged be reported? For museums and symphony orchestras, there is little reason to report the gross amount; the operating statement will show how much revenue came from clients and how much from contributions.

The case of public universities is more controversial, and relates to the reason for the existence of a subsidy in the first place. Tuition in a public university is never as high as the full cost of education (except, in some cases, for out-of-state students). The principal argument against full-cost tuition is that it would deprive some students of the opportunity for education, and educated people are valuable assets to society. The counterargument is that all students could obtain the education if they received adequate financial aid. If tuition were set at full cost, those who could afford to pay would do so, and the cost to the taxpayers would be only the amount of financial aid. Moreover, in times of financial stringency, many state governments tend to reduce appropriations to higher education, and this makes for unsettling conditions in public universities. If tuition were set at full cost, the reduced appropriation would affect only those students receiving financial aid. The university could then determine how it wished to award this aid consistent with its overall goals and objectives.

Traditions are difficult to change, and many state legislatures perceive that voters would not approve of a move to full-cost tuition. Nevertheless, there has been a recent tendency to move tuition rates upward to incorporate a higher percentage of total costs. By reporting gross revenue as the full cost of tuition, and using the state subsidy as an offset, public universities could identify more clearly the extent to which the state subsidy is serving as financial aid for needy students rather than as a benefit to all students. Few public universities do this, however.

Free Services

Some services are provided free to clients. This usually happens when public policy officials determine that it would be discriminatory to charge for a particular service, or when managers determine that attempting to collect for a service would be impossible or infeasible.

Public Goods

The most important class of services furnished without charge is that of public goods. Public goods are services provided for the benefit of the public in general, rather than for specific users. Examples are police protection (as contrasted with a police officer who is hired by the manager of a sporting event), foreign policy and its implementation (as contrasted with services rendered to an individual firm doing business overseas), and national security. In effect, public goods are products that cannot be provided through the market mechanism because (1) they are supplied to users as a group, rather than to specific individuals, and (2) there is no way of withholding the goods from users who want them but are unwilling to pay for them.

Quasi-Public Goods

Many services that superficially seem to meet the definition of public goods turn out upon analysis to be services for which prices could be charged.

Example

A classic instance of a public good is a lighthouse. It is said that one ship's "consumption" of the warning light does not leave less warning light for other ships to "consume," and there is no practical way that the lighthouse keeper can prohibit ships from consuming. Moreover, a ship cannot refuse to consume the light. However, it can be argued that shipowners, as a class, should pay for lighthouses. Then, if lighthouse costs become too high, the objections of shipowners may help bring them back in line.[6]

The lighthouse example is similar to the practice of charging users of highways for their cost via tolls or taxes on gasoline and diesel fuel, or of charging airlines and owners of private aircraft for the cost of operating the air traffic control system. In many countries, users of air waves are charged through a tax on television sets; in the United States, the air waves are regarded as a public good.

[6]In a fascinating article, Coase describes the history of British lighthouses, showing that they in fact successfully charged fees from the 17th century until the present. R. E. Coase, "The Lighthouse in Economics," *Journal of Law and Economics* 17 (October 1974), pp. 357–76.

Tuition Vouchers

A useful way to think about whether a given service should be sold or given away is to separate the question of whether a price should be charged from the question of who ultimately should pay this price. For example, it is generally agreed that all children are entitled to an education and that the community as a whole is responsible for providing this education. Education is therefore a public good—in this case, not because it is impossible to withhold the service but because it is against public policy to do so. Nevertheless, it may be possible to accept this principle and still gain the advantages of "selling the service."

This is the idea behind the *tuition voucher* plan. Parents are given vouchers that can be used to *pay* for their children's education. On the voucher is a dollar amount, which generally is the average cost per pupil in the public school system. Within certain limits, the voucher can be used at any school that the parent elects, including private schools (but perhaps not parochial schools because of constitutional prohibitions). The purpose of such a pricing mechanism is not to affect client's decisions as to whether to obtain the services, but rather to permit a consumer choice as to what school will provide the service. By using the tuition vouchers at the school of their choice, parents can express their pleasure or displeasure with individual schools and thus introduce an element of competition among schools.

There is much controversy about whether the tuition voucher idea is sound public policy. It has been used experimentally in a few locales, and yet there remains much disagreement among researchers as to whether it has improved education in those places. Proponents argue that public schools will be more effective and efficient when forced to compete with private schools for funding, and that those that cannot compete will go out of business.[7] Opponents counter that giving vouchers to students who already are attending private schools will effectively reduce funding for public schools. Moreover, they argue that vouchers constitute only part of the "price," which also includes transportation costs and, on occasion, a need to supplement the vouchers with private funds. Finally, they argue that accountability may suffer unless there is an oversight mechanism.[8]

Housing Vouchers

Vouchers also have been used in the housing field. This was done through the Experimental Housing Allowance Program (EHAP), established by the U.S. Department of Housing and Urban Development (HUD). An evaluation of

---

[7]For additional discussion of this point, see T. M. Moe and J. E. Chubb, *Politics, Markets, and America's Schools* (Washington, DC: The Brookings Institution, 1990).
[8]For additional discussion, see California Department of Education, *Analysis of Parental Choice in Education Initiative, Attachment B,* May 14, 1993; and P. Peterson, *Critique of the Witte Evaluation of Milwaukee's School Choice Program* (Cambridge, Mass.: Center for American Political Studies, Harvard University, 1995).

that program concluded that, because of relatively low income elasticities of demand for housing, the vouchers did not increase housing purchases. They did increase recipient well-being, however, presumably because they freed up rent funds for other purposes.[9]

Charges for Peripheral Services

Even when the principal service of an organization is a public good provided at no charge, managers may discover opportunities to charge for certain peripheral services rendered by the organization. For example, federal agencies charge fees for copying documents made available under the Freedom of Information Act, municipal governments charge for dog licenses, and some public school systems charge for after-school athletics.

Other Free Services

In addition to the general class of public goods, there are other situations in which prices should not normally be charged for services. These include the following situations:

• Services are provided as a public policy, but clients cannot afford to pay for them. Examples include welfare investigations and legal aid services.

• It is public policy not to ration the services on the basis of ability to pay. Examples include legislators, who do not charge fees for assisting constituents, even though a legislator's time is a valuable resource.

• A charge is politically untenable. Examples include public tours of the White House and Capitol. The public clamor over such charges could be harmful to overall organizational objectives, even though a charge would be equitable and would promote good management control.

• Client motivation is unimportant. A nominal charge to a public park or bathing beach will not measure actual output, nor will it influence a client's decision to use the facilities. A charge equal to full cost, by motivating less wealthy individuals to avoid using these facilities, may be inconsistent with public policy.

Summary

The prices that a nonprofit organization charges (or decides not to charge) for its services influence the behavior of clients, provide a measure of output, and influence the behavior of managers and service providers. The price that is usually charged is called the *normal price*. It is the sum of the full cost of a service plus a modest margin.

[9]Joseph Friedman and Daniel H. Weinberg, *The Economics of Housing Vouchers,* Studies in Urban Economics Series (New York: Harcourt Brace Jovanovich, 1982).

An important consideration in pricing is the *pricing unit*. In general, the smaller and more specific the unit of service that is priced, the better. However, for some nonprofits, unbundling pricing units can be difficult, especially if third-party payers wish to have the units bundled.

There are many situations in nonprofit organizations where prices vary from normal prices. In some instances, prices are based on costs; in others they are market based, and in still others they are prospective. Prices charged for subsidized services are less than normal prices. Subsidized prices may be charged only for certain services, only to certain clients, or to all clients. In some instances, for sound public policy purposes, a service may be provided free of charge.

Suggested Additional Readings

Andreason, Alan, and Philip Kotler. *Strategic Marketing for Nonprofit Organizations,* 5th ed. Englewood Cliffs, NJ: Prentice Hall, 1995.

Arrow, Kenneth J. *Social Choice Re-examined.* New York: St. Martin's Press, 1995.

Bryce, Herrington J. *Financial and Strategic Management for Nonprofit Organizations,* 2nd ed. Englewood Cliffs, NJ: Prentice Hall, 1992.

McKinney, Jerome B. *Effective Financial Management in Public and Nonprofit Agencies,* 2nd ed. Westport, CT: Greenwood Publishing Group Inc., 1995.

Musgrave, R. A. *Classics in the Theory of Public Finance.* New York: St. Martin's Press, 1994.

Schultze, Charles L. *The Politics and Economics of Public Spending.* Washington, DC: The Brookings Institution, 1968.

Practice Case

Job Enrichment Center[*]

Job Enrichment Center (JEC), was a small nonprofit organization, located in the southwest corner of Texas. JEC had been formed approximately two years ago, when several prominent members of the local community realized that many newly arrived immigrants were having a difficult time finding jobs due to problems with literacy and English language skills.

JEC's mission was to provide basic training in these skills. It charged local companies for each person they hired who had successfully completed one or

[*]This case was prepared by Professor David W. Young. Copyright © by David W. Young.

EXHIBIT 1
Job Enrichment
Center: Budget Data

	Basic Literacy	English as a Second Language
Number of training sessions	4	2
Length of each training session (in weeks). .	10	20
Average number trainees per session.	100	30
Number trainee-weeks	4,000	1,200
Number of trainees	400	60
Trainee-to-faculty ratio	20:1	10:1
Number of faculty needed	5	3
Average faculty salary	$20,000	$25,000
Books/workbooks per trainee	5	2
Average price per book/workbook.	$15	$20

Administrative and general costs: $92,000.

both of the center's training programs. Most companies needed employees who had a basic level of literacy in the English language, and most realized that it made economic sense to pay JEC rather than to try to train the employees themselves.

JEC conducted two types of training programs: Basic Literacy and English as a Second Language. JEC ran its programs for 40 weeks of the year, closing during the remaining weeks for breaks and vacations. Each program was run by a separate program manager, who also was a faculty member of that program. The remaining faculty were hired on a per-session basis, based on the actual number of trainees in the session and the budgeted trainee:faculty ratio.

JEC determined its prices annually based on expected enrollment, its anticipated costs, and the need for a small (5 percent) operating margin. Since not all of JEC's students needed training in both programs, each program had a separate price. Budgeted data on the two programs for the upcoming fiscal year are shown in Exhibit 1. Administrative and general costs were allocated to programs based on the number of trainees.

Questions

1. Prepare a budget for the upcoming fiscal year, and use it to determine the price per trainee for each program. What is the total operating surplus that JEC anticipates for the year?

2. What concerns, if any, should JEC's senior management have about its prices or other budgeted data?

Case 7–1

Harlan Foundation[*]

Harlan Foundation was created in 1961, under the terms of the will of Martin Harlan, a wealthy Minneapolis benefactor. His bequest was approximately $3,000,000, and its purpose was broadly stated: income from the funds was to be used for the benefit of the people of Minneapolis and nearby communities.

In the next 35 years, the trustees developed a wide variety of services. They included three infant clinics, a center for the education of special needs children, three family counselling centers, a drug abuse program, a visiting nurses program, and a large rehabilitation facility. These services were provided from nine facilities, located in Minneapolis and surrounding cities. Harlan Foundation was affiliated with several national associations whose members provided similar services.

The Foundation operated essentially on a breakeven basis. A relatively small fraction of its revenue came from income earned on the principal of the Harlan bequest. Major sources of revenue were client fees, contributions, and grants from city, state, and federal governments.

Exhibit 1 is the most recent operating statement. Program expenses included all the expenses associated with individual programs. Administration expenses included the costs of the central office, except for fund-raising expenses. Seventy percent of administration costs were for personnel. The staff members (excluding two senior officers) earned an average of $18,000 per year in salaries and fringe benefits.

In 1997, the Foundation decided to undertake two additional activities. One was a summer camp, whose clients would be children with physical disabilities. The other was a seminar for managers in social service organizations. For both of these ventures, it was necessary to establish the fee that should be charged.

Camp Harlan

The camp, which was renamed Camp Harlan, had been donated to the Foundation by a person who had owned it for many years and who decided to retire. The property consisted of 30 acres, with considerable frontage on a lake, and buildings that would house and feed some 60 campers at a time. The plan was to operate the camp for eight weeks in the summer, and to enroll campers for either one or two weeks. The policy was to charge each camper a fee sufficient to cover the cost of operating the camp. Many campers would be unable to pay this fee, and financial aid would be provided for them. The financial aid would cover a part, or in some cases all, of the fee

*This case was prepared by Professor Robert N. Anthony. Copyright © by Robert N. Anthony.

EXHIBIT 1

Operating Statement for the Year Ended June 30, 1996	
Revenues:	
Fees from clients..	$ 917,862
Grants from government agencies	1,792,968
Contributions	683,702
Investment income..	426,300
Other	24,553
Total revenues	3,845,385
Expenses:	
Program expenses:	
Rehabilitation	1,556,242
Counseling	157,621
Infant clinics	312,007
Education	426,234
Drug abuse...	345,821
Visiting nurses.......................................	267,910
Other	23,280
Total program expenses............................	3,089,115
Support:	
Administration	480,326
Dues to national associations.........................	24,603
Fund-raising	182,523
Other	47,862
Total support.......................................	735,314
Total expenses	3,824,429
Net income	$ 20,956

and would come from the general funds of the Foundation or, it was hoped, from a government grant.

As a basis for arriving at the fee, Henry Coolidge, financial vice president of the Foundation, obtained information on costs from the American Camping Association and from two camps in the vicinity. Although the camp could accommodate at least 60 children, he decided to plan on only 50 at a time in the first year, a total of 400 camper-weeks for the season. With assured financial aid, he believed there would be no difficulty in enrolling this number. His budget prepared on this basis is shown in Exhibit 2.

Coolidge discussed this budget with Sally Harris, president of the Foundation. Harris agreed that it was appropriate to plan for 400 camper-weeks, and also agreed that the budget estimates were reasonable. During this discussion, questions were raised about several items that were not in the budget.

The central office of the Foundation would continue to plan the camp, do the necessary publicity, screen applications and make decisions on financial

EXHIBIT 2
Budget for Camp Harlan

Staff salaries and benefits	$ 90,000
Food.	19,000
Operating supplies	4,000
Telephone and utilities	9,000
Insurance	15,100
Rental of equipment.	7,000
Contingency and miscellaneous (5%).	7,200
Total.	$151,300

aid, pay bills, and do other bookkeeping and accounting work. There was no good way of estimating how many resources this work would require. Ten staff members worked in administration, and as a rough guess about half a person-year might be involved in these activities. There were no plans to hire an additional employee in the central office. The workload associated with other activities usually tapered off somewhat during the summer, and it was believed that the staff could absorb the extra work.

At the camp itself, approximately four volunteers per week would help the paid staff. They would receive meals and lodging, but no pay. No allowance for the value of their services was included in the budget.

The budget did not include an amount for depreciation of the plant facilities. Lakefront property was valuable, and if the camp and its buildings were sold to a developer, perhaps as much as $500,000 could be realized.

The Seminar

The Foundation planned to hold a one-day seminar in the fall of 1997 to discuss the effect on social service organizations of some financial accounting standards that went into effect in 1996. The purposes of the seminar were partly to generate income and partly to provide a service for small welfare organizations.

In the spring of 1997, Harris approved the plans for this seminar. The following information is extracted from a memorandum prepared by Coolidge at that time:

It is estimated that there will be 30 participants in the seminar.

The seminar will be held at a local hotel, and the hotel will charge $200 for rental of the room and $20 per person for meals and refreshments.

Audiovisual equipment will be rented at a cost of $100.

There will be two instructors, and each will be paid a fee of $500.

Printing and mailing of promotional material will cost $900.

Each participant will be given a notebook containing relevant material.

Each notebook will cost $10 to prepare, and 60 copies of the notebook will be printed.

Coolidge will preside, and one Harlan staff member will be present at the seminar. The hotel will charge for their meals and for the meals of the two instructors.

Other incidental out-of-pocket expenses are estimated to be $200.

Fees charged for one-day seminars in the area ranged from $50 to $495. The $50 fee excluded meals and was charged by a brokerage firm that probably viewed the seminar as generating customer goodwill. The $495 fee was charged by several national organizations that ran hundreds of seminars annually throughout the United States. A number of one-day seminars were offered in the Minneapolis area at a fee in the range of $150 to $250, including a meal.

Except for the number of participants, the above estimates were based on reliable information and were accepted by Harris.

Questions

1. What weekly fee should be charged for campers?

2. Assuming a fee of $100, what is the breakeven point of the seminar?

3. What fee should be charged for the seminar?

Case 7–2

Town of Waterville Valley*

At the 1980 town meeting, residents of Waterville Valley, New Hampshire, would be asked to authorize a major expansion of the town's water system. Some residents believed that the supply was adequate for the foreseeable future. Others, including the area's developer, thought that the supply was inadequate and would inhibit growth in the town.

The method of paying for an expanded water system was also at issue. The capital expenditure would be financed by a municipal bond issue. Alternatives for payment of the principal and interest on this issue were: (1) a lump sum to be charged to each new housing unit, to be paid by the developer and included in the price of the unit, (2) higher water rates for all users, or (3) an annual charge made to all new water users, that is, those whose service began after the expanded system went into operation.

*This case was prepared by Professor Robert N. Anthony. Copyright © by the President and Fellows of Harvard College. Harvard Business School Case 9-179-203.

Finally, there was the question of how water was to be charged to users. At present, residential users were charged a flat monthly amount, and some people thought that the charge should be based on usage.

Background

The Town of Waterville Valley is in a valley surrounded on all sides by the White Mountain National Forest. The area of the town is about 700 acres, and it is unlikely that its area can grow because the U.S. Forest Service probably would not sell additional land to private parties. One well-paved road, 11 miles long, provides access to the valley from an interstate highway. Waterville Valley is 130 miles from Boston and 60 miles from the state capital, Concord, which is the nearest city.

The town was incorporated in 1829. In 1965 the permanent structures consisted of an inn, accommodating 60 guests, 16 homes of residents, most of whom lived in the valley year round, and a small town hall.

In 1965 the inn and 506 acres of land were purchased by the Waterville Company, a privately owned corporation. Thomas Corcoran, president, moved to Waterville Valley. He planned to develop the area as a year-round resort and to sell land to developers and individuals.

By 1979 the area had become a major ski facility, with 10 lifts, 35 miles of downhill trails, many with snowmaking facilities, and many miles of cross-country trails. About 4,000 skiers used the facilities on peak days. The ski area was leased from the Forest Service by the Waterville Company. In addition, there was a nine hole golf course, a pond for bathing and sailing, and 15 tennis courts. There were five inns with a capacity of about 200, a bunk house, 65 single-family houses, six condominium developments totaling approximately 300 units, a conference center with a capacity of 500, and a number of restaurants and stores. There were sleeping accommodations for about 2,000 persons. The ultimate capacity was estimated to be 7,000 persons. The official population, however, was 199.

Water Supply

Until 1967, property owners had provided their own water. The original inn was served by a spring, and individual homeowners used artesian wells. One consequence was that whenever a fire started, the property burned to the ground, as had happened to the inn twice before, and again in 1967.

In 1967, the Waterville Company, at its expense, drilled new wells and constructed a pumping station, a reservoir, a distribution system with an 8-inch main, and fire hydrants. At the 1968 town meeting, the voters unanimously agreed to buy this system from the Waterville Company, and voted a bond issue of $135,000 for this purpose and to finance further exploration for water.

In 1970, a bond issue of $105,000 was authorized to expand the water system, and in 1972 a third bond issue of $235,000 was authorized for this purpose. After this construction, the town had a half-million gallon storage capacity and extensive water distribution lines. However, by 1979, according to the town manager, existing wells were being used to 85 percent of capacity, and "a new source is necessary." Two pumps were used, and if one of them broke, water pressure would be seriously affected.

Sewer System

The initial sewer system consisted of collection mains and a series of lagoons for filtering wastes. These were built, owned, and maintained by the Waterville Company. By 1972 these facilities had become inadequate. The Waterville Company, however, wanted to get out of the sewer business, and it proposed the following:

1. The company would give the existing system, preliminary engineering for an expanded system, and land for a sewage treatment facility to the town, without consideration.

2. The town would set up a municipal services department to operate the water and sewer systems.

3. If in any year the operations of this system resulted in a cash loss, the town's maximum obligation from the general tax levy would be $2 per $1,000 of assessed valuation, assuming that the town would continue to assess property at full fair-market value. Any additional loss would be made up by the Waterville Company. Payments made by the Waterville Company would be repaid in future years if operations (including the $2 tax levy) produced a profit in those years.

4. Water and sewerage fees would be at an agreed-upon schedule and would increase at stated percentages thereafter (details of these fees are described subsequently).

5. The town would build a municipal sewer system, with the most modern sewage treatment facilities, to be financed with a bond issue of $1.8 million. This system would be adequate for the ultimate development of Waterville Valley to a 7,000-bed capacity.

6. The agreement would last until January 1, 1983, or until three years beyond the date of an additional bond issue to expand the water system, whichever was longer.

This proposal was approved at the 1973 town meeting, the bonds were issued, and the facilities were built. As shown in Exhibit 1, losses were experienced in 1975, 1976, and 1977; the Waterville Company reimbursed the town for these losses. In 1978, a surplus was earned.

EXHIBIT 1   Water and Sewer Calculations ($000)

	1974	1975	1976	1977	1978
Revenues:					
Operations:					
Usage charges....................	$ 59.6	$ 85.3	$ 106.1	$ 121.9	$ 139.0
Tap fees.........................	45.2	30.7	9.3	19.5	46.7
Other	5.6	3.7	1.3	2.1	2.3
Subtotal......................	110.4	119.7	116.7	143.5	188.0
State contribution (40% of debt service)...	—	59.0	57.7	56.5	55.3
Town tax revenues ($2/$1,000)	32.5	36.3	36.5	45.5	50.6
Other revenues.....................	40.4	55.6	—	—	—
Total revenues	183.3	270.6	210.9	245.5	293.9
Expenditures:					
Operating expenses	44.8	68.3	54.4	58.4	67.9
Debt service:					
Principal	27.6	100.8	100.9	100.9	102.1
Interest	89.0	110.5	106.1	100.6	95.5
Total expenditures	161.4	279.6	261.4	259.9	265.5
Excess of revenues over expenditures	$ 21.9	$ (9.0)	$ (50.5)	$ (14.4)	$ 28.4
Tax base: Assessed valuations	$16,243.0	$18,165.0	$18,261.0	$22,763.0	$25,321.0
Tax rate/$1,000	12.7	13.0	16.8	13.4	14.0
Water consumption (millions of gallons).....		19.4	22.9	25.2	27.0
Sewage treated (millions of gallons)		10.5	16.3	21.0	22.0

Source: Town records.

Water and Sewer Rates

Users were charged a one-time, fixed, "tap" fee which entitled them to tap into the town water and sewer system. The fee was determined by a point and unit system. Points were determined by the number of bedrooms, bathrooms, and other water use outlets, such as kitchens, outdoor spigots, and sinks, that were part of a unit.

Ten points comprised one water or sewer unit. For example, a half-bath was assessed at ¼ point, a sauna at ¼ point, and a full bath at 3 points. Kitchens were assessed at 2½ points; bedrooms, living rooms, hallways, and lofts at 1 point. Water coolers, ice machines, and extra sinks were assessed at ¼ point each. There was a minimum of one sewer unit and one water unit per dwelling unit. The point system was also used to establish usage rates. Exhibit 2 shows rates for the past three years.

Meters were used only for commercial establishments. The fee for installing a meter was $10, paid by the building's owner. Some town residents thought that meters should be installed in residential units as well as commercial ones. The town treasurer favored this plan because it would probably

EXHIBIT 2
Water and Sewer
Department Rate
Schedule

	1977	1978	1979
Tap fee—per water unit	$315.00	$330.00	$345.00
Tap fee—per sewer unit	525.00	550.00	575.00
Water usage—per water unit per month . .	9.45	10.00	10.50
Water usage—commercial metered per 1,000 gallons	1.90	2.00	2.10
Sewer usage—per sewer unit per month . .	12.39	13.00	13.65
Sewer usage—commercial rate	(130% of water bill)		
Turn on–turn off charge—water	20.00		

Source: Town records.

provide more revenue for the system. In addition, he felt that meters would be a more equitable way of determining charges and thus sharing expenses, and they would encourage conservation of water. This approach would become increasingly important as it became more and more difficult to find new sources of water.

He noted that the only conservation measures now being applied were mandatory installation of water-saver toilets and showers in new condominium and residential units. He felt that in the near future, there could conceivably be an outright ban on saunas and pools because of their prodigious consumption of water. He cited expense as the main reason the town had not seriously considered requiring installation of meters on residential units. It costs about $60 to install a residential water meter.

A large consumer of water was the snowmaking operations of the Waterville Company. The equipment, when operating, consumed 1,000 gallons per minute. The company had its own water supply for this purpose, which came partially from the Mad River and partially from one of the town's original wells. The company considered this "free" water.

Many experts believe that the era of an inexpensive potable water supply is over. As demand mounts, nearby sources become inadequate. In addition, the capital costs of developing new and large surface supplies of water are increasing. In many areas, the possibility of using the pricing mechanism to control demand had become a widely considered alternative to increasing supply.

In some towns, consumption and pricing decisions made by public utility managers had caused inefficient supply and demand relationships. Peak users of water who created high short-term demands requiring expensive investment in equipment were not required to pay for the added capacity. Block prices were offered to major users, thus encouraging the inefficient use of water. States and communities had subsidized local utilities by developing reservoirs at public expense and by charging less than the cost of the water. In addition, without a link between use and cost, homeowners had little incentive to install water-saving devices, even though currently available technologies could reduce residential water use by more than 30 percent. Even greater reductions could be achieved for swimming pools and lawn sprinklers with a more effective pricing mechanism. Indeed, one study had indicated that a change in price from 40 cents per 1,000 gallons (an average price) to $1 per 1,000 gallons could reduce residential demand by almost 20 percent.

Present Operations

The new sewer treatment plant was completed and operational in 1974. At that time water and sewer were combined into a Municipal Services Department with a separate budget and financial statements. All receivables and payables for the department were handled by the town's part-time bookkeeper. She estimated that she spent about five days per quarter billing and paying bills for this department. No part of her $9,095 annual salary was allocated to the department, nor were other town costs.

Similarly, the Public Safety Department was not charged for its use of water in firefighting. Although hydrants used in firefighting belonged to the town, they were paid for by the developer. The town manager estimated that each new hydrant cost $800.

The municipal services budget did not include an allowance for depreciation. The town treasurer said that the town budgets were based on a system of direct costs and that it would be confusing and arbitrary to try to allocate indirect costs. He also felt that since the town did not pay taxes, depreciation wasn't a necessary component of the budget.

Many water districts do not depreciate their capital plant and equipment for the following reasons: plants usually take a number of years to reach their full income potential although, from year one, their facilities must be adequate to serve the entire district; if depreciation were charged, the accumulating losses would have a disastrous effect on the sale of bonds; if rates were set high enough to allow for depreciation, they might not be affordable by users.

Details of the Municipal Services Department revenues and expenditures for 1978 are given in Exhibit 3. (The collection of solid waste was also a function of that department.) By comparison, total expenditures in 1970 were $22,500, of which $18,500 was for debt service.

Total revenues and expenditures for the town, as presented to the 1979 town meeting, are given in Exhibit 4.

Current Issues

The selectmen's presentation at the 1980 town meeting included a proposal to hire engineers to bore holes in a search for additional water. (A $17,000 survey in 1977 had found one additional well with an estimated flow of 80 to 100 gallons per minute. This well had not yet been developed.) The capacity of the system at that time was 400 gallons per minute.

EXHIBIT 3 Municipal Services Department 1978 Summary

	Sewer	Water	Solid Waste	Total Department
Revenues:				
Tap fees.	$ 29,029	$17,622		$ 46,651
Usage	73,904	65,069	$ 11,556	150,529
Other.	638	1,651		2,290
Revenues from operations	103,571	84,343	11,556	199,470
Additional revenues:				
State grant.	55,274			55,274
Total revenues.	158,845	84,343	11,556	254,744
Operating expenses:				
Wages	15,961	9,442	6,821	32,224
Vehicle operations	1,128	1,391	3,897	6,416
Telephone	618	126		744
Electricity.	8,912	2,806	114	11,831
Heating fuel.	6,744	502		7,245
System/plant maintenance	3,920	12,495	311	16,726
Chemicals	3,394			3,394
Disposal costs			7,991	7,991
Training and seminars	91			91
Retirement.		336	336	672
Total operating expenses	40,769	27,097	19,469	87,335
Income (loss) before debt service	118,077	57,246	(7,913)	167,409
Debt service:				
Principal.	66,080	35,999	5,102	107,181
Interest	82,040	13,503	1,055	96,598
Total debt service	148,120	49,503	6,156	203,779
Net profit (loss) of departments	$(30,043)	$ 7,743	$(14,070)	$(36,370)

Source: Annual Report.

Based on the findings of engineers, the selectmen were going to prepare a plan for expansion of the water system, which they would submit at a subsequent meeting. The cost of this plan would depend on the engineers' findings and on several alternatives for expansion. Each new well would cost from $30,000 to $40,000; and an additional storage facility would cost from $200,000 to $300,000. Engineers already had recommended some expansion of the 8-inch main distribution system, at a cost of roughly $200,000. In total, expansion of the system to accommodate the town's ultimate capacity might cost from $400,000 to $600,000, but this was a rough estimate because of the uncertainty of the exploration efforts and debate as to when ultimate capacity should be installed.

There was concern about the additional debt burden. Exhibit 5 shows the payments required by the bonds issued to date. It was customary, although

EXHIBIT 4   Income and Expenditures–1978

	1978 Estimated	1978 Actual	1979 Projected
Revenues:			
State sources:			
Interest and dividends tax	$ 27,000	$ 25,489	$ 25,500
Savings bank tax	600	558	600
Meals and rooms tax	900	999	1,000
Highway subsidy	1,285	1,271	1,552
Town road aid	1,676		2,111
Forest Service lands reimbursement	21,500	13,852	14,000
Business profits tax	350	373	400
Sewage treatment grant	55,274	55,274	54,062
Antirecession funds	–0–	224	–0–
Local sources:			
Dog licenses	60	90	100
Motor vehicle permits	6,500	7,251	7,250
Permits and filing fees	300	297	300
Interest on taxes and deposits	2,250	2,207	1,500
Cemetery	1,000	500	–0–
Public Safety Department	13,700	16,412	14,300
Municipal Services Department	180,000	199,470	215,000
Highway Department	–0–	1,011	–0–
Recreation Department	–0–	–0–	7,000
Resident taxes	1,200	1,540	1,500
Timber yield taxes	1,500	2,687	2,800
Town office	25	25	25
Revenue sharing	3,000	3,811	4,500
Short-term loans	39,250	31,200	46,575
Fire truck	72,000	72,000	–0–
Police cruiser sale	800	–0–	–0–
Proceeds—insurance claim		2,400	
Total revenues	$430,170	$438,941	$400,075

not necessary, for the town to issue bonds with a 30-year maturity, with an equal amount of principal payments each year and interest on the outstanding balance.

The state of New Hampshire had agreed to pay 40 percent of the debt service on the sewer bond issue of 1973. The selectmen hoped that the state would similarly pay part of the cost of water expansion, but this was not certain.

Because of recent improvements in the water system, the town had experienced a 12 percent reduction in insurance on private homes and a 10 percent reduction on commercial establishments. The State Insurance Commission indicated that additional water would likely result in another rate reduction.

EXHIBIT 4 (Concluded)

	1978 Appropriation	1978 Expenses	1979 Requests
Expenditures:			
Town officers salaries	$ 4,075	$ 4,148	$ 3,400
Town office expense	31,725	30,908	33,473
Town office—Public Safety			
Building maintenance	5,900	6,543	6,650
Property appraisal	1,000	1,412	1,500
Surveying and drafting	4,500	3,720	2,000
Osceola Library	800	1,247	1,100
Employees benefits	11,242	9,680	15,227
Public Safety Department	97,516	103,161	114,006
Municipal Services Department	97,894	87,335	113,360
Highway Department	20,850	22,266	24,315
Legal services.	5,945	4,304	5,000
Planning and zoning	500	4	1,200
Advertising and regional	4,275	4,275	2,025
Hospitals and health	887	877	873
Conservation Commission	800	800	1,000
Municipal recreation	2,000	3,692	20,250
Post Office.	3,000	3,000	4,000
Street lights.	1,200	1,231	1,570
Cemetery.	600	–0–	250
Insect control.	4,200	3,170	1,000
Insurance.	19,000	20,998	25,000
Capital equipment.	88,200	89,061	24,575
Capital construction	23,050	27,808	22,000
Debt service.	228,073	232,488	246,136
Contingency	5,200		6,000
Total expenditures	$662,432	$662,129	$675,911
Insurance proceeds—applied to principal		2,400	
		$664,529	

The total estimated revenues from all sources except property taxes deducted from total appropriations in the ensuing fiscal year gives estimated amount to be raised by property taxes.

One long-time resident of Waterville Valley, who considered himself a spokesman for the group who opposed further expansion of the system, expressed the concern that more water and another bond issue could not help but increase the tax rate beyond the promised $2 per thousand. He felt that future residents, if there were to be any, should bear the entire cost of any improvements that they required. He stated the concern of a number of retired residents living on fixed incomes, who were alarmed at the present 5 percent yearly increase in their taxes. He felt that the past 12 years of development

EXHIBIT 5   Debt Payments (Shown at Five-Year Intervals)

Year	Water Principal	Water Interest	Sewer Principal	Sewer Interest	Total Payments
1970	$10,000	$8,504			$18,504
1975	26,520	16,780	$65,000	$91,000	199,300
1980	26,520	9,433	65,000	75,010	175,963
1985	10,000	4,420	65,000	58,110	137,530
1990	10,000	1,820	60,000	42,120	113,940
1995			60,000	26,520	86,520
2000			60,000	10,920	70,920

Note: Approximate amounts for the years not shown can be found by interpolation, except that in 1974 the total payments were $44,878. The final bond issue matures in 2003.

were already taking their toll on the community in terms of their impact on ecology, increased traffic, and the need for additional municipal services.

The president of the Waterville Company, who was also a selectman and a resident of the town, was convinced that the town was committed to expansion of its facilities to the limits imposed by its geography, and also should be committed to expansion of its water supply. He felt that past records showed that municipal services could pay their own way from the revenues they generated. He believed that his company could work compatibly with the town. He acknowledged that his company benefited from the town's ability to borrow at favorable rates, but he also believed that the town had benefited from the company's expenditures for early water and sewer development and its help in underwriting the initial losses of the sewer system. He agreed, though, that current residents should not have to shoulder all expenses for future improvements, and felt that, through municipal borrowing, future residents, by helping to repay the debt, would share in the cost of improvements.

Questions

1. As a matter of general policy (but without attempting to arrive at specific numbers), how should the cost of an additional water system be divided between those who are now on the system, those who may subsequently become customers, and the general taxpayers (i.e., included in the tax rate)?

2. As a matter of general policy, how should the "tap charge" (i.e., the amount to amortize capital costs) and the "usage charge" be determined?

3. What is your estimate of the cost of the Municipal Services Department in 1978?

4. In calculating the cost that should be used in arriving at charges, should the capital cost be the amount of debt service (i.e., principal and interest) actually paid in the year, or is some other approach better?

5. Suggest tentative rates for each item on Exhibit 2 for a year in which expenditures are like those in 1978, with an additional capital charge of $500,000 financed by a 30-year bond issue.

6. Should meters be used to record usage by residential customers so that charges can be based on usage?

Case 7–3

Boston University Medical Center Hospital*

In early 1994 Michael Richardson, Director of Managed Care and Business Development at Boston University Medical Center Hospital (BUMCH), was notified that HealthSource New Hampshire had accepted BUMCH's proposal for specialty referrals for urology and cardiology/cardiothoracic cases. The pricing proposal for all urology cases was a per diem rate. For selective cardiology/cardiothoracic DRGs, it was a fixed fee or "bundled price" per case that included both physician and hospital services.

Mr. Richardson initially had submitted the proposal to HealthSource at the request of the cardiologists and cardiothoracic surgeons. Although New Hampshire was not considered part of BUMCH's principal service area, the cardiologists and cardiothoracic surgeons had established referral relationships with the physicians in these areas. Recently, the physicians had been unable to accept a number of referrals because the patients' insurer was HealthSource and BUMCH did not have a contract with HealthSource.

Although the initial request had come from the surgeons, they had not seen the proposal prior to its submission. Mr. Richardson now needed to meet individually with each of the key physician groups involved in the program to negotiate their fees per case. He realized that the fee per case to be offered to each of the key physician groups (i.e., cardiothoracic surgery, cardiology, radiology, and anesthesiology) was crucial to assuring the acceptability of the venture to the physicians. He also realized that the hospital's management control and reporting systems might need to be modified to monitor financial performance and clinical outcomes, so as to ensure the delivery of efficient, effective, and quality care. These changes, in his view, were critical to the financial viability of the new program.

Mr. Richardson had to work quickly as the hospital had just been notified that the first HealthSource cardiothoracic patient would be admitted next week.

*This case was prepared by Miriam G. Jost and Professor David W. Young, with the assistance of Adjunct Professor Michael D. Blaszyk and Richard A. Morse. Copyright © by David W. Young.

Background

BUMCH, the smallest of three academic medical centers in Boston, Massachusetts, was located in the southeastern portion of the inner city. The hospital's primary objective in managed care contracting was to develop relationships with as many reputable and high-profile HMOs as possible. A primary focus of the contracting efforts was to establish relationships for the provision of primary care.

A secondary focus was to obtain referrals for the hospital's specialists. When there were barriers to the development of a comprehensive relationship with a specific HMO, BUMCH developed specific product or pricing strategies that might be appealing to that HMO.

One product pricing strategy that BUMCH had developed was a bundled price per case that included both the hospital's and the physicians' fees. The hospital's management believed that a bundled price would be attractive to managed care organizations because it (*a*) was administratively simple, (*b*) offered one-stop shopping (one entity negotiated for the hospital and the physician components of patient care), and (*c*) shifted risk away from the managed care plan to the hospital.

BUMCH had approached several HMOs with bundled price proposals, but only a few had expressed an interest in pursuing the concept. The reason most HMOs stated for their lack of interest in the approach was that they did not have the administrative and accounting systems necessary to handle the billing procedures associated with bundled prices. Most managed care plans maintained separate risk pools for physicians and hospitals, and, in the words of one HMO, a bundled pricing approach would "muck up the accounting system." Thus, Mr. Richardson was extremely pleased when HealthSource had accepted the hospital's offer. Indeed, he hoped that the contract could be used to demonstrate to other HMOs the wisdom of the bundled pricing approach.

The Massachusetts HMO Market

As of June 1993, there were 2.3 million HMO members in Massachusetts, or 38.6 percent of the state's population. This was the highest HMO market penetration of any state, up from 35.4 percent in 1992 and 30.6 percent in 1991. Enrollments for the state's 16 HMOs had increased by 15.2 percent between 1991 and 1992, and by 9.5 percent between 1992 and 1993.[†]

The Boston marketplace was very competitive. Not only were most of the HMOs located in the Boston area, but Boston had seven teaching hospitals, all situated in close proximity to one another. Thus, to be competitive in bidding for managed care contracts, hospitals had to be willing to propose prices that were close to the margin, and they had to be willing to assume risk. In fact,

---

[†]Marion Merrell Dow, Inc., *Managed Care Digest, HMO Edition,* Kansas City, MO, 1993. Data were provided to Marion Merrell Dow by SMG Marketing Group, Inc., Chicago, IL.

Brandt Michaels, BUMCH's chief financial officer, was willing to consider HMO opportunities even if total costs were not covered. In his words,

> We will contract with an HMO at a price that covers only our direct costs. However, my hope is that, by going at risk, we'll be able to cover more than just our direct costs.

HealthSource New Hampshire

HealthSource, Inc., was a for-profit, publicly traded, managed care organization located in southern New Hampshire. HealthSource sponsored or managed HMOs in several states, and owned one of the largest third-party claims administrators in the region. HealthSource New Hampshire had over 200,000 people enrolled in HMOs, HMO-like services, and preferred provider organizations (PPOs). HealthSource also provided utilization review services and preferred provider networks primarily to self-insured employer plans and Blue Cross/Blue Shield of Vermont.

HealthSource had recently entered the Massachusetts market, and already had developed several contractual relationships with other Boston-area tertiary medical centers. Mr. Richardson thought that it had plans to expand its Massachusetts activities in the future, but he did not think it was actively pursuing the addition of other Boston-area teaching hospitals to its network at the time BUMCH submitted its proposal.

U.S. Health Care Financing Administration Demonstration Project

BUMCH was a participant in a Medicare Demonstration Project sponsored by the Health Care Financing Administration (HCFA). The project provided Medicare patients with coronary artery bypass graft (CABG) surgery (DRGs 106 and 107) with all financial components bundled into one negotiated payment amount for each DRG. The project, which had been initiated two years ago, had, for the first time, united three historically separate groups—the government, hospitals, and physicians—to address health care cost containment in creative ways. According to preliminary reports, the Medicare program had saved an average of some $5,300 per case with the project. The savings came mostly from shortened hospital stays, the use of generic drugs, and a reduction in the use of laboratory tests, x-rays, and disposable supplies. According to Mr. Richardson, the savings had been achieved without compromising patients' satisfaction or quality of care. Indeed, Stefan Ricardo, M.D., Chief of Cardiothoracic Surgery, claimed that there was evidence that patients in the project received better treatment, recovered faster, and were more satisfied with their care. Due to the success of the project, Mr. Richardson believed that the bundled bill could serve as a model for other contracting efforts.

Approximately 250 patients per year participated in the demonstration project. On any given day, there were approximately five to six demonstration project patients in the hospital. As a direct result of the project, the hospital

EXHIBIT 1   Changes in Clinical Practice Patterns as Result of Critical Paths

1. Decrease in ALOS for DRG 107 from 11 days to 8 days; for DRG 108 from 16 days to 9/10 days;
2. Change in intra- and perioperative anesthesia management resulting in earlier extubation, often on the same day as surgery (patients are not put back to sleep in recovery). This has also resulted in a decreased incidence of postoperative pneumonia and an increase in patient satisfaction;
3. Decreased use of ancillary services (e.g., ABGs and x-rays)—following a prospective analysis of standing orders and the number of ABGs and x-rays ordered per patient, the standing orders were rewritten;
4. Earlier removal of pacing wires;
5. Decreased utilization of ICU;
6. Elimination of Progressive Care Unit (PCU) or step-down unit. Patients are now transferred directly from ICU to the Nursing Unit.
7. Earlier referrals to social service and physical therapy;
8. Decrease in readmission rate; and
9. Increase in patient satisfaction.

Note: The critical paths were being revised to reflect a postoperative stay of five days for selected patients.

had established the Cardiovascular Center Development Program. This program brought together representatives from senior management, cardiothoracic surgery, cardiology, managed care, marketing, nursing, operations, and finance to discuss and resolve issues involving the efficient delivery of services. The program established clinical benchmarks and critical pathways that resulted in significant cost savings (see Exhibit 1). A registered nurse coordinated the implementation of critical paths and case management, from preadmission to follow-up.

The Demonstration Project's administrator, Zoe James, R.N., monitored quality and clinical outcomes. She prepared and submitted quarterly reports to HCFA that profiled patient demographics (e.g., age, sex), preoperative clinical data (e.g., cardiac catheterization report, risk factors), intraoperative data, and postoperative data (e.g., functional and clinical status one year postsurgery). Ms. James also was responsible for coordinating the bundling of physician bills for HCFA Project patients. She commented on the nature of the task:

> Identifying the physician components to be bundled is very time-consuming. The current manual system wouldn't be able to handle the volume if all contracts were bundle-priced. One of the biggest administrative problems with the bundling of patients' physician bills is identifying which patients are on the demonstration project. Since a patient's diagnosis and DRG are determined at discharge, it's not always possible to identify the project's patients until they're discharged. This is especially true for patients admitted for medical cardiology management, since we sometimes don't know whether the patient will have a CABG during the hospital stay or not.

Although Dr. Ricardo was very satisfied with the demonstration project, he noted that there was one administrative glitch associated with the DRG method of payment:

Surgery is usually performed in the early part of a patient's hospital stay, and the surgeon submits his bill shortly thereafter. Under bundled pricing, the hospital doesn't pay the physician until the patient is discharged. Since bills require a diagnosis and a DRG, and since patients are not assigned a diagnosis and DRG until they're discharged, bills cannot be submitted until the patient is discharged. In most cases this is not a problem. However, if the patient experiences complications and has a protracted hospital stay, then the bill, including the amount for the surgery, cannot be submitted as soon as the surgeon otherwise would submit it. In some outlier cases, this is a significant amount of time.

He also saw a major clinical drawback:

A physician spends a disproportionate share of time with a few very sick patients, what we call "outliers." It seems unrealistic to expect us to care for these patients for a fixed fee. The fixed fee gives us no incentive to give these patients the care and attention they require.

Despite the difficulties, Wilber Marks, M.D., Chief of Anesthesiology, reported that the anesthesiologists liked getting a fixed price per case:

Prior to the demonstration project, we [the anesthesiologists] received approximately 50 percent of our charges, and not all procedures were covered. For example, we were not paid anything for sophisticated monitoring techniques, such as trans-esophageal echocardiography and insertion of pulmonary artery catheters. Under the demonstration project, our reimbursement is more predictable and the fees we're paid are more reasonable, although they're still significantly discounted.

Dr. Marks was interested in receiving a fair and predictable price for anesthesiology, due, in part, to his department's cost structure. His department, like others in the hospital, needed an adequate flow of funds both to support the current staff and to recruit new staff for cardiac anesthesia, which required anesthesiologists with additional training to manage the complicated patients and techniques.

BUMCH Medical Staff

Unlike many other major academic medical centers, the medical staff at BUMCH was composed primarily of nonsalaried physicians. Mr. Richardson described the strategy that resulted from this arrangement:

The optimal entity for contracting with managed care entities would be a PHO [Physician Hospital Organization]. Since we don't have a PHO, however, we worked with The Evans Medical Group, a 125-physician group practice that includes the hospital's primary care physicians and our chief of surgery. The chief represents all the independent specialty group practices.

According to Dr. Marks, the medical staffs typically had some input to the managed care contracting process, even though the process generally was administratively driven:

Contracts usually are initiated and developed by the hospital's administration with clinical input from the physicians. Then, after a contract is developed by the hospital, the physicians are asked to review it for price fairness. Michael's position was created about three years ago to serve as a liaison, and to facilitate communication between the administration and the medical staff. Michael was well received by the medical staff, and we felt comfortable that he kept us informed, and that he addressed our needs as they arose.

Many BUMCH physicians were also on staff at Boston City Hospital (BCH), a large municipal hospital, located immediately adjacent to the Medical Center. The physicians at BCH were members of an independent practitioner organization (IPA). The IPA was a very active and vocal participant in BCH's managed care contracting initiatives. When comparing the physician role in managed care contracting at BUMCH and BCH, Dr. Marks saw BUMCH's approach as "loose" compared to the approach at hospitals like BCH with a strong medical staff.

BUMCH's Proposal to HealthSource, New Hampshire

Due to its satisfaction with the Medicare Demonstration Project, the hospital decided to pursue other bundled arrangements. Its proposal to HealthSource not only was a fixed bundled price for each of seven cardiology/cardiothoracic DRGs, but was automatically renewable yearly (with something called an "evergreen" clause). It also offered HealthSource stable prices for two years with no inflation-adjustment clause. The bundled rates did not include a stop-loss provision.

The individuals involved in developing the HealthSource proposal were Mr. Richardson, Ms. Carol Patterson (Contracts Manager, Managed Care and Business Development), and a reimbursement analyst from the hospital's finance department (who extracted historical data as needed).

According to Mr. Richardson, the physicians were not included in the development of the proposal for several reasons.

First, they were pleased with the Medicare Demonstration Project, and the HealthSource proposal was to be based on the same model. Second, the physicians had asked us to pursue a HealthSource contract so we assumed we had their support. Finally, I realized that there was a short "window of opportunity." If HealthSource established referral relationships elsewhere, it would be difficult, if not impossible, for us to reestablish the referral relationships at a later date. We thus did not have time to involve the physicians.

Mr. Richardson went on to describe the process that he and his staff followed to develop the pricing proposal.

We began by reviewing a lot of data from the Medicare Project, such as resource utilization per case, ALOS [average length of stay] by bed type [ICU, step-down, medical/surgical], charges for physicians, room and board, and ancillaries. We used the hospital's cost accounting system to examine costs from several different perspectives: total, average, per-discharge, fixed, variable, direct, indirect, and marginal. We also looked at cost to charge ratios, charge to reimbursement ratios, and cost to reimbursement ratios.

We used the above data, combined with data on patients in similar HMOs, to develop a model to forecast utilization, and, ultimately, costs for HealthSource patients. Obviously, cost data were an important consideration in developing the price proposal, but we also looked at other factors. We used the services of HTI [Healthshare Technology Inc.] to look at the costs and charges for six other tertiary care hospitals in the area. We then determined the discounts to charges we needed to offer to be competitive.

The results of Mr. Richardson's analysis are contained in Exhibit 2. Information from the HTI report is contained in Exhibit 3. The rates the hospital offered to HealthSource were as follows:

DRG	Rate
104	$37,260
105	24,100
106	27,442
107	17,707
112	10,463
124	4,500
125	4,500

Although HealthSource had accepted these rates, Mr. Richardson felt some uncertainty with them. He commented:

Currently, we perform a total of 15 cardiothoracic cases per week. We have two or three operating rooms available concurrently, and a fourth operating room could be made available, if necessary. Thus, we have the capacity to perform 20 cases per week. However, HealthSource has not guaranteed to deliver any minimum volume of patients. Hence, we did not include any minimum volume assumptions in developing our proposal. If the contract results in 20 admissions in the first year of the contract, I would consider it to be successful.

Questions

1. Is bundled pricing a good idea? Why or why not?

2. Under a bundled pricing contract, what can a hospital do to limit its financial risk/exposure? What risk/exposure does the managed care plan have?

3. How should Mr. Richardson handle the determination of a fee per case for the physicians, including consulting physicians and ancillary services?

4. What is your assessment of the approach Mr. Richardson followed in developing the contract? What advice would you give him about negotiating his next managed care contract?

EXHIBIT 2 Charges and Costs: Hospital and Physician Components, by DRG

	DRG(1)						
	104	*105*	*106*	*107*	*112*	*124*	*125*
Hospital Component							
Charges	$64,689	$43,820	$41,631	$30,474	$14,123	$6,697	$4,867
Costs							
Routine	23,049	14,646	17,893	10,093	4,543	3,310	1,952
Ancillary	15,850	9,626	10,660	7,614	5,641	2,196	1,677
Total	$38,899	$24,272	$28,553	$17,707	$10,184	$5,506	$3,629
Direct	$21,545	$14,807	$15,133	$9,682	$5,194	$2,753	$1,524
Indirect	17,354	9,465	13,420	8,025	4,990	2,753	2,105
Total	$38,899	$24,272	$28,553	$17,707	$10,184	$5,506	$3,629
Physician Charges							
Cardiology	$ 300	$ 300	$ 1,700	$ 250	$ 2,500	$1,300	$1,000
Cardiothoracic	8,250	8,250	6,000	6,000	NA	NA	NA
Anesthesiology and							
Radiology (2)	1,500	1,500	2,000	2,000	1,000	1,000	1,000
Total	$10,050	$10,050	$ 9,700	$ 8,250	$ 3,500	$2,300	$2,000
Combined Charges	$74,739	$53,870	$51,331	$38,724	$17,623	$8,997	$6,867

Notes: (1) 104—Valve Replacement with Catheterization; 105—Valve Replacement without Catheterization; 106—CABG with Catheterization; 107—CABG without Catheterization; 112—PTCA; 124—Catheterization, Unilateral; 125—Catheterization, Bilateral. DRGs 104, 105, 106, and 107 include Cardiology, Cardiothoracic Surgery, Anesthesiology and Radiology. DRGs 112, 124, and 125 only include Cardiology.

(2) DRGs 112, 124, and 125 do not include anesthesiology.

EXHIBIT 3

Information from Report by Healthshare Technology, Inc.[a]

Note: The HTI report was prepared using 1992 data. Medicare tapes were combined with cost and charge reports submitted to the state's Rate Setting Commission. A ratio of costs to charges (RCC) was used to convert charges to costs for different DRGs and different services provided for a given DRG.

Patient Mix

The top seven cardiac patient groups for University Hospital accounted for 1,595 or 100% of the hospital's total cardiac cases. These key patient groups were as follows:

Patient Group	DRG	No. of Cases	Pct. of Cases
PTCA	112	562	35%
Cath with complex diagnosis	124	274	17
CABG w/o cath	107	272	17
Cath w/o complex diagnosis	125	172	11
CABG with cath	106	155	10
Valve w/o cath	105	104	7
Valve with cath	104	56	4
Total cardiac		1,595	100%

[a]Healthshare Technology, Inc., is a consulting firm located in Massachusetts.

EXHIBIT 3
(Concluded)

University had an above average proportion of PTCA and an above average proportion of cath with complex diag cases among the seven hospitals in the group.

Length of Stay (DRG Mix Adjusted)

University Hospital's average length of stay per cardiac case was 7.3 days, 1.0 days or 12% lower than the average of its six major competitors of 8.3 days. Brigham and Women's Hospital had the next lowest length of stay of 7.4 days, 0.1 days or 1% higher than University's.

University's length of stay did not show a consistent pattern compared with Brigham and Women's Hospital's LOS across the key patient groups. The graph below shows a comparison of University Hospital with Brigham and Women's Hospital and the competitor average:

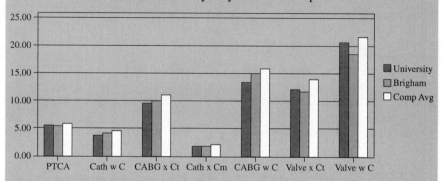

LOS Differences by Key Patient Group

Cost per Case (DRG Mix Adjusted)

University's total cost per cardiac case was $13,705. The DRG mix adjusted average total cost of its six competitors was $14,152, $447, or 3%, higher than University. University had the third lowest total cost per case. Brigham and Women's Hospital had the lowest total cost with $12,207. Specifically, the cost per case for each hospital as compared to University Hospital was as follows:

	Total Cost Per Case	% Diff than University	Direct Cost Per Case	% Diff than University
University.	$13,705		$7,265	
Brigham.	12,207	−11%	7,026	−3%
Beth Israel	16,358	+19%	8,234	+13%
New England				
Medical Center.	14,111	+3%	8,756	+21%
Deaconess	15,094	+10%	8,523	+17%
St. Elizabeth's.	13,397	−2%	7,233	0%
Mass General	13,746	0%	8,602	+11%
Average excluding				
University	14,152	+3%	8,062	+11%

Case 7–4

Atherton Medical Education Programs[*]

One of the major issues that we face going forward is how to be true to our core educational mission while at the same time meeting the needs of Bennington Hospital, the Southwestern Healthcare Network, and the broader Atherton community. This is becoming increasingly difficult with the rising number of indigent patients, our relatively recent integration into the Southwestern Network, and the constant struggle we face as a community-based program to recruit and maintain faculty. We also need to continue to enhance the partnership between Bennington and AMEP and to design systems that satisfy all the stakeholders involved.

Mary W. Bethridge, M.D., residency Program Director for Internal Medicine at Bennington Hospital, was discussing some of the issues that faced her program and the Atherton Medical Education Programs (AMEP), of which her program was a part. She continued:

One of the issues that we continue to analyze is how to distribute the various revenues streams that come into the network in a way that is fair to all parties. Between our unique relationship with the City of Atherton and the evolving relationship between Bennington and ourselves, there is some confusion about the intent of some of the revenue that comes in and, just as importantly, some disagreements around who should bear the costs of the various activities that the money is meant to cover. Right now, we have a negative bottom line, but it may appear worse than it actually is. For example, we have a lot of costs in our budget that are related to indigent care. This is problematic because it makes it seem like education is very expensive, when in fact it may have more to do with the indigent care we provide. As a program director, I worry about this and the impact it might have on my program. I know that I have to have a really good understanding of the costs of my program, as well as the benefits that it brings to Bennington and to the Southwestern Network.

Henry Byron, M.D., Medical Director of AMEP, echoed Dr. Bethridge's concerns.

I have been focusing a lot of my efforts on the business aspects of AMEP. Obviously, we're always concerned with the quality of the educational program; that is a given. As far as things beyond that, our situation is a little unusual because we have only been a part of the Southwestern network for a relatively short time and because of that we are still in the stage of getting acquainted with one another. We need to improve the financials but also continue the educational mission. Everyone is challenged financially in undergraduate and graduate education. We need to have our financial ducks in a row, so to speak, so we can convince Southwestern that we add value to them and that they're getting their money's worth.

A complication is that the education and the patient care are so inextricably linked that I find it difficult and somewhat artificial to separate the two. Nevertheless, one of the things we've been trying to do is separate the cost of education from the cost of patient care. We assume that we have to first cover the cost of our teaching program. We get money from various sources and if you were to take all the monies that flow to us simply because we have a residency program, we're pretty much financially neutral. On the books Southwestern subsidizes us, but they don't give us all the IME [indirect medical education] money from Medicare; that goes to the hospital. If you were to say that, instead of subsidizing us, they simply gave us the IME money, then I would say we're financially neutral.

Drs. Byron and Bethridge knew that in the upcoming months some key decisions were going to be made regarding how funds were allocated between Bennington and AMEP, and more broadly, there would be strategic discussions about AMEP's role in the Southwestern network. Given the importance of these issues, they saw an opportunity to present their own vision of AMEP and the most appropriate financial model. They realized that this would not be an easy task and that there would be others who might have different views. Dr. Bethridge had decided to take the lead in analyzing some of these issues as they related to the Internal Medicine Program.

Background

Atherton Medical Education Programs (AMEP) was a community-based organization that operated fully accredited medical resident training programs. Its programs included family practice, internal medicine, ob/gyn. and pediatrics. In addition, it offered integrated programs in surgery and ob/gyn in conjunction with St. Mary's Hospital in a nearby city. It also offered a transitional-year program and electives for fourth year medical school students.

AMEP's primary goal was for each of its programs to "develop educational excellence and innovation to enhance the residency training in a community setting." A related goal was that each program would "provide excellent, faculty-supervised patient care at Bennington Hospital, Atherton-Taylor County Health Department Clinics, St. David's Hospital, Blackstone Family Practice Academic Associates, and numerous private settings that provided primary care and specialty experiences for resident education."

AMEP had the following specific objectives:

- Training competent, compassionate physicians through its primary care graduate medical education programs, transitional residency, and affiliated programs in surgery and obstetrics/gynecology.

- Improving health care delivery in the greater metro area by participating as the providers of the safety net of care, and in so doing, deliver only the highest quality medical care to that segment of the population of Atherton and Taylor County.

- Developing undergraduate clerkships to enhance clinical training of State University medical students at both the junior and senior levels.

- Acting as the administrative and developmental body for regional programs in continuing medical education and research, with research concentrating on each residency program's requirements, and in the areas of clinical medicine, health care delivery, quality assurance, and education.

AMEP was established in 1972 by the Taylor County Medical Society, and had a long tradition of collaborating with Bennington Hospital, which sponsored and served as the primary site for its residency programs. In addition to its teaching and clinical care, AMEP conducted a limited amount of research related to its residency requirements.

Bennington Hospital

Bennington was an acute care hospital and outpatient facility that served as the area's only trauma center as well as the safety net hospital for the medically indigent of Taylor County. Until 1995, it was run by the City of Atherton.

In October 1995, Southwestern Healthcare Network took over management of Bennington through a 25-year lease agreement with the City of Atherton. Under the terms of the agreement Southwestern was to pay $2.2 million annually to lease the hospital from the city. The city would continue to provide reimbursement for indigent patients who received care at Bennington, including the uninsured and those enrolled in the city's Health Assistance Program. At the time of the lease, this totaled $11 million annually, with some $5.6 million dedicated to physician services for the indigent.

Southwestern Healthcare Network

The Southwestern Healthcare Network (Southwestern), a nonprofit organization, was a member of a larger health care network that spanned 16 states and had more than 87,000 employees. As the leading provider of health care services in Taylor County, Southwestern provided approximately 766,000 outpatient visits and had close to 50,000 admissions annually. As Exhibit 1 indicates, it also contributed more than $84 million in charity care and community benefits. In 2000, its facilities and programs served more than 203,000 people through charity care and community-benefit activities.

Hazel Patterson, Ph.D., Southwestern's acting CEO, commented on the importance of Southwestern's community service mission:

> As an organization, Southwestern is fully committed to caring for the uninsured and indigent of this community. We see ourselves taking a leadership role in setting up systems that allow us and other providers to better meet the needs of this population. Obviously, the need has increased since the time we entered the lease with the City. Nevertheless, caring for the poor and uninsured is a core part of our mission.

EXHIBIT 1

ATHERTON MEDICAL EDUCATION PROGRAMS: Charity Care Community Benefits 1995–2000 (In Thousands)						
	1995	1996	1997	1998	1999	2000
Actual Charity Care	$ 6,116	$11,917	$18,318	$21,204	$25,285	$32,598
Other Charity Care	$ 1,214	$ 1,702	$ 3,073	$ 3,619	$ 3,717	$ 3,713
Unreimbursed Medicaid	$ 1,183		$ 4,271	$ 1,611	$ 2,949	$ 8,252
Total Charity Care	$ 8,513	$13,619	$25,662	$26,434	$31,951	$44,563
Community Benefit	$ 878	$ 2,665	$ 7,795	$ 7,641	$ 7,955	$ 9,244
Unreimbursed Medicare	$ 5,810	$ 5,950	$10,870	$14,703	$26,426	$30,715
Total Community Benefit	$ 6,688	$ 8,615	$18,665	$22,344	$34,381	$39,959
Total Charity Care and Community Benefit	$15,201	$22,234	$44,327	$48,778	$66,332	$84,522

AMEP/Bennington Relationship

AMEP and Bennington had a long history of collaboration around Graduate Medical Education and care for the indigent. When Southwestern first took over the management of Bennington, it contracted with AMEP for physician services for the indigent. Dr. Patterson explained the rational:

> Clearly we entered into our current relationship with AMEP because of the lease with Bennington and because the physicians who serve the uninsured in our community are primarily the physicians of AMEP. Having said that, I don't think that there's any doubt here that AMEP exists with a mission that is primarily dedicated to graduate medical education and, secondarily, to indigent care. One of the worrisome things is that because of a lack of a reasonable public policy regarding care for the uninsured, we haven't grappled with the issue that the demand for care by the uninsured in this community is greater than AMEP can provide.

AMEP's Financial Condition

A related issue was the pressure to improve the financial condition of AMEP. Lyndon Jones, M.D., Senior Vice President for Medical Affairs at Southwestern, was responsible for Southwestern's relationship with AMEP. He commented:

> We want to be better partners with AMEP. Southwestern is very supportive of GME and our goal is to support the education program. There is tension at times to balance their primary goal of education with the primary function of the Southwestern network—service.
>
> Traditionally, AMEP put together a budget and the city funded it, but this approach led to increasing deficits. Right now, Southwestern provides about $7

million in direct support to AMEP. In addition, there is a budgeted deficit of about $1.4 million. However, we are proposing a change to the funding streams. We would pass through directly to AMEP the money from the city, the DME [direct medical education] money from Medicare that Bennington receives as well as some portion of the IME [indirect medical education] money that Bennington receives from Medicare. We're still studying how this should be split.

Maureen Sullivan, Administrator of Bennington Hospital, was responsible for the hospital's financial performance and also worked closely with AMEP. While she was supportive of graduate medical education (GME), and recognized the benefits that the educational programs brought to Bennington, she wanted to be sure that any changes that Southwestern might make to the financial relationship between AMEP and Bennington were fair. She shared her perspective on the AMEP–Bennington relationship:

In conjunction with the lease, Southwestern negotiated to receive the funds that the City spent for physicians' services to the indigent at Bennington. Since that time the City has given us about $5.6 million per year for indigent care physician coverage. This money was meant for indigent care. To the extent that the physicians were using a teaching model to provide this care, the $5.6 million supported teaching, but its primary goal was to fund the physician services related to indigent care at Bennington, not GME. This was enhanced each year by Bennington to bring the total to $7 million.

For AMEP's faculty, education is the most important part but we don't know whether the teaching model is always the most cost-effective model. There are other hospitals where they've found that the GME model is more expensive in some specialties, and there are situations where you could demonstrate that the GME model is less expensive. It all depends on the specialty, patient needs, residency requirements, and on how well the program is organized.

We recently compared ourselves to another Southwestern Network Hospital with about the same case mix and we have shorter lengths of stay, which I think is because of the residency program. On the other hand, there are additional costs that we incur because of the residency program. For example, the ratio of ancillary tests, such as lab and x-ray, to inpatient revenue is higher than at nonteaching hospitals; this equates to approximately $4.2 million annually. To Bennington, that is an extra cost, even though the faculty regularly challenge residents on their use of tests. In addition, there's the additional space needed to support the GME program, such as offices, sleeping rooms, conference rooms, food costs, and other things like extra scrubs and linens.

Despite these costs, the linkages between AMEP and Bennington are critical to our hospital. I can show the positive impact of GME on our quality indicators compared to other hospitals. So, I think that GME improves the quality of care. For example, we have 24-hour, in-house physician coverage for obstetrics because of the requirements to back up the residents. Also, if you look at any of the obstetrical quality indicators (C-sections, delivery rates, etc.) the patient clinical outcomes for the type of high-risk patients that we have are very good. Our outcomes are also very good for internal medicine. In general, I think having residents keeps all physicians up to date. Finally, AMEP is also committed to the population we serve—they really care about the indigent, and that is directly in line with the mission of this organization.

In addition, having residency programs means Bennington will receive a higher Medicare reimbursement rate. We also have access to the disproportionate-share dollars through the state.

Financial Benefits of GME

A Southwestern financial manager expanded on the financial benefits of GME.

The Hospital receives about $600,000 in DME funding from Medicare. This money covers the residents' salaries and benefits and is based on costs related to the 1984 cost report trended upwards for inflation. We receive $48,800 per primary care resident and $46,000 for all other residents up to a cap of 81 residents. The IME that we receive from Medicare is about $2 million. There is a somewhat complicated formula we use which ends up giving us 15.7 percent more per Medicare discharge than we would have received without residents. The BBA [The Balanced Budget Amendment of 1997] will bring this down to about 13.4 percent when it is fully phased in. In addition, there is graduate medical education money from Medicaid, which can range from approximately $500,000 to $800,000. The estimate for this year is $800,000, although this figure has not yet been audited. Of course, the residency program has costs of about $8.4 million as reported on the Medicare Cost Report. This includes direct as well as indirect or allocated expenses.

A cost report showing direct and indirect GME expenses is contained in Exhibit 2. The immediate concern to Ms. Sullivan was how the resulting revenue should be distributed. She wanted to be sure that the distribution was fair and reflected the costs that each unit incurred. She explained the way it currently worked:

The City of Atherton originally provided $5.6 million to AMEP, which now comes to the hospital for indigent care. When we contracted with AMEP, Bennington added another $1.4 million for the cost of providing indigent care. Some people think that this money is part of the GME dollar, but after talking with some involved in the negotiations, that is not what it is. At the time it was decided that the GME would remain with the hospital but the hospital agreed to pay AMEP $7 million. In addition to the revenue AMEP receives from Southwestern related to indigent care and GME, AMEP also gets the billings and collections for all the patients they see at Bennington. We are about 23 percent self-pay, and approximately 75 percent are billable, which includes Medicaid. In addition, AMEP receives another grant from the network to balance its budget. Again, that is right off the top, since the network services department has no revenue sources.

I believe we should have a formal contract to clearly identify and value what Bennington provides and to identify the value of what AMEP provides in this partnership. We look at AMEP as a very valuable partner—they need to know what we are providing them and we need to acknowledge what they are providing us. I look forward to continuing our current relationship with AMEP, and I will continue to challenge them to work with us to improve our quality of patient care and be more cost effective.

EXHIBIT 2

ATHERTON MEDICAL EDUCATION PROGRAMS:
Cost Allocation Summary from Medicare Cost Report for Bennington Hospital

	Net Expenses for Cost Allocation	New Cap Rel Costs—BLDG	New Cap Rel Costs—MVBLE	Employee Benefits	Subtotal	Admin & General	Operation of Plant	Laundry & Linen Service	House-keeping	Dietary	Cafeteria	Nursing Admin.	Central Services and Supply	Pharmacy	Medical Records & Library	Biomed Instrumentaion	I&R Services Other Prog. Costs	Total
General Services Cost Center																		
New Cap Rel Costs—BLDG	3,193,269	3,193,269																
New Cap Rel Costs—MVBLE	5,622,288		5,622,288															
Employee Benefits	2,834,392			2,834,392														
Admin & General	23,376,594				24,071,533	24,766,472												
Operation of Plant	4,299,794	206,546	363,659	124,734	5,842,486	1,166,441	7,008,927											
Laundry & Linen Service	818,118	527,003	927,878	87,811	996,749	198,999	184,377	1,380,125										
Housekeeping	2,282,932	64,706	113,925	21,759	2,381,352	475,432	35,216	34,599	2,926,599									
Dietary	1,968,633	12,259	21,759	64,302	2,269,213	453,044	240,117		103,504	3,065,878								
		84,267	148,366	67,947			90,180	18,004	93,081		40,123 1,643,780 1,885,168							
Cafeteria	-105,037		32,666	57,514	-46,159		60,363		26,020		40,224							
Nursing Admin.	2,564,758	21,184	230,869	55,519	2,982,272	595,405	373,641	8,002	161,061		68,084	13,897	4,188,465					
Central Services and Supply	4,010,020	131,126		396	4,231,364	844,783	122,075		52,622		83,214		345,052 5,679,110					
Pharmacy	1,900,922	42,841	75,429	103,074	2,048,375	403,954	106,469		45,894		48,415	2,006	106					
Medical Records & Library	1,245,476	37,364	65,786	44,303	1,341,396	267,807	80,685		34,780		13,617	2,545	36		2,658,213			
Biomed Instrumentation	7,000,000	28,316	49,855	17,749	7,000,000	1,397,536		13,742								1,738,321		
Interns & Residents— Other Program																		
Inpatient Routine Srvc Cntrs																		
Adults and Ped	13,304,172	558,090	982,612	547,134	15,392,008	3,072,928	1,590,269	697,297	685,500	1,210,495	429,684	13,897	144,925	1,123,651	242,040	98,768	3,585,831	28,287,293
ICU	5,291,975	125,284	220,584	220,333	5,858,176	1,169,573	356,995	100,589	153,896	18,875	168,862	5,138	55,274	477,090	71,647	98,768	649,045	9,184,328
CCU																		
Pedi—ICU	2,480,837	46,924	82,618	97,551	2,707,930	540,633	133,710	29,548	57,637	26,356	52,032	2,006	36,552	186,051	32,477	118,522	176,879	4,100,313
Nursery	3,046,254	61,145	107,656	134,312	3,339,367	666,698	174,231	13,037	75,104		78,675	2,545	46,014	301,584	58,761		358,144	5,111,160
Ancillary Cost Centers																		
Operating Room	7,557,537	192,630	339,158	268,029	8,297,354	1,656,550	548,897	112,468	236,606		158,862	5,138	1,117,073	109,278	297,501	217,290	901,939	13,658,956
Recovery Room	1,775,321	55,369	97,486	75,086	2,003,262	395,947	157,772	47,773	68,009		52,954	1,713	6,996	50,945	37,394	19,754		2,846,519
Delivery Room & Labor	2,705,671	40,223	70,819	99,316	2,916,029	582,179	114,613	66,306	49,405		66,571	2,153	97,875	305,691	57,807	59,261	1,211,844	5,529,734
Anesthesiology	821,096	6,963	12,260	16	840,335	167,771	19,842		8,553				245,737	54,822	52,119			1,389,179
Radiology/Diagnostic	4,825,314	129,705	228,368	155,100	5,338,487	1,065,818	369,592	35,681	159,316		111,960		55,070	52,491	156,680	809,898	48,240	8,203,233
Laboratory	4,825,859	97,932	172,426	167,614	5,203,831	1,038,934	279,056	6,726	10,289		93,805		96,339	9,586	290,127	79,015	45,316	7,263,024
Whole Blood and Packed Red	1,764,154	8,776	15,452	15,813	1,804,195	360,204	25,008		10,780		12,104				34,413			2,246,704
Respiratory Therapy	3,823,332	18,260	32,150	145,170	4,018,912	802,368	52,032		22,429		105,908		150,992	52,065	254,243	118,522		5,577,471
Physical Therapy	1,259,723	27,505	48,427	50,450	1,386,105	276,733	78,374	29,300	33,784		40,850		16,459	419,169	41,256			2,322,030
Occupational Therapy	331,406	4,437	7,812	14,262	357,917	71,457	12,643		5,450				12,583		10,889			470,939
Speech Pathology	198,505	3,588	6,317	8,677	217,087	43,341	10223		4,407		1,513		3,999		3,172			283,742
Electrocardiography	410,249	19,904	35,045	15,482	480,680	95,967	56,717		24,448		10,591		7,191	1,249	42,556	19,754		739,153
Electroencephalography	151,859	5,281	9,298	5,808	172,246	34,389	15,048		6,487		4,539		6,846		2,970			242,525
Medical Supplies Charged	8,041,703				8,041,703	1,605,510							1,474,942		105,265			11,227,420
Drugs Charged to Patients	7,088,386				7,088,36	1,415,182							1,516,283		290,994			10,310,845
Nuclear Medicine	726,042	3,751	6,604	13,211	754,608	150,656	10,689	4,607			3,026		7,631	8,724	16,621			961,485
Special Proc/Cath Lab.	2,359,044	10,878	19,152	35,649	2,424,723	484,091	30,996	4,923	13,361		24,208		80,909	17,858	65,847			3,152,058
CT Scan	724,315	5,722	10,074	13,739	759,850	151,703	16,305	10,065	7,028		13,617		42,174	4,351	138,004			1,133,032
Renal Dialysis	256,222			148	256,370	51,184							9,202	1,766	7,570			326,092
Output Service Cost Centers																		
Clinic	739,573	104,280	183,603	27,666	1,055,122	210,553	297,144	9,892	128,087		28,747	930	7,928	267,800	9,655		616,886	2,632,844
Specialty Care.	794,547	39,471	69,496	3,185	934,699	186,511	112,472	978	48,482		24,208	783	4,756	54,779	5,187			1,372,955
Emergency	5,876,226	337,514	594,250	213,502	7,021,492	1,401,327	961,740	146,498	414,566		169,453	5,481	109,231	649,358	326,042	79,015	726,522	12,011,225
Oncology	391,800	85,312	150,207	15,750	643,069	128,387	243,096	14,259	104,788		12,104	391	4,440	12,774	4,946		90,632	1,258,886
Special Purpose Cost Centers																		
Kidney Acquision	393,945	2,031	3,575	7,753	407,304	81,317	5,787	1,042	2,484		4,539			2,030		19,754		524,257
Subtotals	142,977,226	3,179,353	3,597,787	2,825,591	142,930,008	23,739,016	6,969,275	1,380,125	2,909,507	2,899,486	1,882,142	40,175	4,186,332	5,677,365	2,658,213	1,738,321	8,411,278	142,367,402
Nonreimbursed Cost Centers																		
Gift Flower, Coffee Shop.	475,947	13,916	24,501	3,540	38,417	7,760	39,652		17,092		1,513	49	442					102,831
Star Fight.	167,160				479,487	95,729												577,220
Parking	975,192				167,160	33,573												200,533
Other Nonreimbursable				5,261	980,453	195,745				166,392				1,745				1,347,539
Total	144,595,525	3,193,269	5,622,288	2,834,392	144,595,525	24,071,533	7,008,927	1,380,125	2,526,599	3,065,878	1,885,168	40,224	4,188,465	5,679,110	2,658,213	1,738,321	8,411,278	144,595,525

A complication in understanding the revenue and expenses was the difficulty in identifying which costs were related to care for the indigent and the hospital's needs, and which were related to education. Indeed, that was one of the major issues that Dr. Bethridge hoped to sort out for the internal medicine residency program.

Internal Medicine Residency Program

The internal medicine program had 30 residents and was staffed by seven full-time salaried faculty members and 35 contracted physicians. Its residents rotated through a variety of subspecialties including: gastroenterology, pulmonary/critical care, cardiology, nephrology, infectious diseases, endocrinology, rheumatology, hematology/oncology, allergy, dermatology, and neurology. While in their training program, residents received an annual salary as well as benefits. A first-year resident's salary was $34,000, second year residents received $35,300, and third year residents received $36,600. Fellows and fourth-year chief residents received $52,300.

Residents typically worked as part of a ward team that included one attending physician, one second or third-year resident, and two interns (first-year residents). There were four of these teams in addition to one overflow team to pick up the excess capacity. One of the issues that Dr. Bethridge had to manage was the set of guidelines put forth by the residency review committees that placed caps on the number of patients that residents could admit. She commented:

> In order to provide coverage for the hospital, we rely on the other programs, like family practice, to help us. Internal medicine could never provide all the coverage that is needed and meet our educational objectives. I've got to be careful not to overload our residents. One of the ways to do this would be to use hospitalists, but I would need to justify this not just on the educational merits, but also financially.

Resident Activities

Exhibit 3 contains some information on the services provided by AMEP's residents. As it indicates, internal medicine residents provided inpatient coverage for Bennington and also trained in Bennington's clinics, as well as in the clinics that were run by the City of Atherton. Dr. Byron commented on some of the issues surrounding the clinics.

> It's difficult to compare clinic coverage here with other places. The amount of space is so limited. There are a variety of subspecialty clinics in the hospital and then we have about half of the space in the professional building. However, the main sites that we use for our residency programs are the city clinics of which there are 12. These are federally qualified health centers and we have a long-standing relationship providing residents to these clinics. Since we bought AMEP, our relationship with the city clinics has been somewhat tense. I think they probably wonder if they could provide patient care for less money with private

EXHIBIT 3

ATHERTON MEDICAL EDUCATION PROGRAMS:
Highlights from Analysis of Residency Programs

- Residents provide 24 hour/7 days a week coverage at Bennington and Children's Hospital
  - **Internal Medicine:** 13 residents on General Medicine Service, 3 in ICU
  - **Pediatrics: 7–9** residents on General Pediatric Service, 5 in Pediatric and Neonatal Intensive Service, 2 in Nursery, 1 in ER,
  - **Ob/Gyn:** 7 residents
  - **Surgery:** 4 in General/trauma, 1 in pediatrics
  - **Psychiatry elective:** 1–2 residents
- **Residents Service in Clinics**
  - **Internal Medicine Clinics**
    * The Clinic at Bennington
      - Specialty care from City Clinics, People's Clinic
      - Internal Medicine Resident Continuity Clinic (38% of resident's clinic needs)
      - Multiple subspecialties—electives (2–4 residents also provide inpatient consultation.)
      - Visits per year 5,400
    * Other Continuity Clinics
      - City Clinics (50% of resident's clinic need)
      - VA Clinic (12% of resident's clinic need)
  - **Pediatric**
    * City Clinics 14,500 visits per year (35% of resident's clinic need)
    * Subspecialty electives (15% of resident's clinic need)
    * Children's Specialty Care Center (10% of resident's clinic need)
    * Continuity Clinic with private M.D.s (15% of resident's clinic need)
    * Electives (15% of resident's clinc need)
    * Adolescent, Developmental, etc. (10% or resident's clinic need)
  - **Ob/Gyn:**
    * 3,400 deliveries/year,
    * The Clinic at Bennington 7 clinics/week with 1–2 residents, 6,000 visits/year
    * City Clinics—$200,000/year contract to provide six clinics/week,
    * People's Clinic—three clinics per week with 1–2 residents
  - **Surgery**
    * The Clinic at Bennington—4,000 visits/year, three clinics/week, 4–6 residents/clinic.
  - **Family Practice**
    * 20,000 visits per year at Blackstone Family Health Center,
    * Inpatient service at St. David's Hospital,
    * Rotate at Bennington in Internal Medicine, Pediatrics, Ob/Gyn, Surgery ED, Psychiatry, Electives.

physicians. We're working with them to determine how best to work together. One of the problems on the clinic side is that they have their own scheduling system, which affects our performance. If we show up for a clinic and there are no appointments scheduled, our productivity looks bad. Nevertheless, the clinics are an integral part of the ambulatory training and continuity experience for our residents.

In addition to ward duty and clinics, residents also participated in curriculum conferences that were offered daily at noon. Some of these conferences were core didactic presentations by faculty, while others were case conferences presented by residents. In addition, there were morning reports, interactive (case based) conferences offered daily at 7:00 A.M., and grand rounds (weekly continuing medical education conferences featuring national speakers).

Financial Performance

The 2001 budget for the internal medicine residency program is contained in Exhibit 4. The budget for AMEP overall is shown in Exhibit 5. The internal medicine residency program, like all of the other residency programs in AMEP, was under pressure to improve its financial performance. This was difficult because of their poor payer mix (See Exhibit 6) and the fact that the budget contained both the training program costs and indigent care costs. Dr. Bethridge explained:

> Southwestern allows us be in a budget negative position. This is frustrating—you feel somewhat like a corporate underdog. We would rather have our services valued at x, believing the training program is worth that, rather than constantly be in a budget negative position. My budget includes the contractual costs of medical subspecialists for the hospital and for their outpatient care to the city clinics. The training program also has the "no preference contract" for all the patients who come through the ER. This can be a good thing for education, but it also means that we must be able to handle the large volume of patients in the context of education. We need a certain volume and diversity of pathology for a good educational experience. We need subspecialists to help us care for the patients, and we need a relatively high volume of patients to assure diversity. But this means we must provide the subspecialists—and, increasingly, pay them retail rates—and take the high volume to enhance education. At the same time, we are caring for a mostly indigent patient population, which cannot easily be shifted to another source of care. Most of what is in my budget is not the cost of education; it is the cost of indigent care.

Contracts with Community-Based Physicians

A key concern of Dr. Bethridge was her relationship with the community-based physicians who served as faculty for her program. These were largely subspecialists who had attending duties and supervised residents on the inpatient wards and in the clinics. Unlike full-time faculty members, however, they were not salaried. Instead, each group of subspecialists had a different

EXHIBIT 4

ATHERTON MEDICAL EDUCATION PROGRAMS:
Budget for Internal Medicine Residency Program

Patient Revenue:			
Total Charges		$3.866,365	
Less: Contracted Medical Charges		(1,594,459)	
Revenue Deductions:			
Medicare Contractuals	(181,134)		
Medicaid Contractuals	(184,294)		
HMO/PPO Write off	(71,156)		
Charity—City Maximum Allowable Payment	(202,030)		
Administrative and other write offs	(66,837)		
Charity	(616,103)	(1,321,554)	
Net Patient Care Revenue		$950,352	
Revenue from Contracts:			
University Contract	$ 4,379		
5th Floor Gastroenterology Clinic	24,000		
Bennington Hospitalists	174,055	202,434	
Revenue Contracted Medical Collections		335,501	
Reimbursed Grand Rounds		27,050	
Coordinating Board		348,864	
Total Revenue			$1,864,201
Expenses:			
Faculty Salaries	$ 868,353		
Resident Salaries	1,187,985		
Admin Salaries	73,999	$2,130,337	
Benefits		292,864	
Contract Services:			
Inpatient coverage, teaching, and some outpatient services*	$ 597,392		
Clinic attending physician stipends**	102,600		
General medical***	58,800	$ 758,792	
Grand Rounds (Honorarium and Travel, CME Consort Fee, Supplies)		27,050	
Supplies (Food, Office Supplies)		10,700	
Apparel for Residents		2,190	
Dietary (Transfer in) Resident Meals and Meals for Functions)		33,193	
Maintenance		1,450	
Equipment		9,070	
Permits and Licenses for Residents and Training Program		10,563	
Telephone and Paging		12,600	
Personal Dues and Licenses		13,490	
Books and Subscriptions (Includes $12,400 for Resident Book Funds)		18,500	
Conventions and Education		27,350	
Travel, Noneducation		1,000	
Recruitment (Includes Match Fees, Brochures, Residency Fairs etc)		8,455	
Postage		1,000	
Gifts and Entertainment		4,250	
Insurance		53,844	
Bad debt		331,743	
Total Expenses			$3,748,441
Net Profit Loss			($1,884,240)

*Includes cardiology, geriatrics, GI coverage, ICU, nephrology, neurology, hematology/oncology, and rheumatology.

**Includes allergy, cardiology, dermatology, gastroenterology, neurology, pulmonary.

***Includes weekend inpatient coverage and VA clinic coverage.

EXHIBIT 5

ATHERTON MEDICAL EDUCATION PROGRAMS
Summary Budget

	Total Programs	Trauma	Capital OB	Pediatrics	OB/GYN	Midwives	Internal Medicine	Surgery	Psychiatry	Faculty Clinic	Study Group	Family Practice	Transitional	Fac Prac FP	Coding & Comp	PFS	Admin
Gross Patient Revenue	17,312,248	979,356	899,201	811,527	6,597,600	424,162	2,271,906	1,687,794	0	830,833	0	1,619,316	—	1,190,653	—	—	—
less Contracted Medical Charges	—	—	—	—	—	—	—	—	—	—	—	—	—	—	—	—	—
Revenue Deductions:																	
Contractual Adjustments	(3,774,609)	(245,610)	(123,864)	(158,488)	(1,579,437)	(188,712)	(365,428)	(476,358)	—	(102,316)	—	(326,208)	—	(208,188)	—	—	—
HMP/PPO Writeoff	(1,703,257)	(212,164)	(266,647)	(84,009)	(118,899)	—	(71,156)	(202,458)	—	(250,288)	—	(262,157)	—	(235,479)	—	—	—
Charity – City Map	(804,358)	(56,684)	—	—	(181,164)	—	(202,030)	(267,784)	—	(593)	—	(85,354)	—	(10,749)	—	—	—
Admin & Other Writeoffs	(982,972)	(52,230)	(30,793)	(37,276)	(352,019)	(30,793)	(66,837)	(30,225)	—	(40,550)	—	(229,308)	—	(112,943)	—	—	—
Charity	(2,070,678)	(107,624)	(5,314)	(33,849)	(978,391)	(5,314)	(616,103)	(298,708)	—	(4,668)	—	(13,873)	—	(6,833)	—	—	—
Total of Revenue Deductions	(9,335,874)	(674,313)	(426,618)	(313,621)	(3,209,910)	(224,819)	(1,321,554)	(1,275,533)	—	(398,414)	—	(916,900)	—	(574,191)	—	—	—
Net Patient Revenue	7,976,474	305,043	472,583	497,905	3,387,690	199,343	950,352	412,261	—	432,419	—	702,416	—	616,462	—	—	—
Revenue-Contract	9,148,009	—	—	464,400	268,144	184,800	202,434	201,432	—	—	—	100,000	—	—	—	76,800	7,650,000
Revenue-CT Med	1,083,180	—	—	316,352	335,113	—	335,501	20,550	75,665	—	—	—	—	—	—	—	—
Revenue-Grants	38,900	—	—	10,000	—	—	27,050	—	—	—	1,850	—	—	—	—	—	—
Revenue-Grants-Coord Board	891,840	—	—	149,592	—	—	348,864	—	—	—	—	393,384	—	—	—	—	—
Total of Other Revenue	11,161,929	—	—	940,344	603,256	184,800	913,848	221,982	75,665	—	1,850	493,384	—	—	—	76,800	7,650,000
Total Operating Revenues	19,138,404	305,043	472,583	1,438,249	3,990,947	384,143	1,864,200	634,243	75,665	432,419	1,850	1,195,800	—	616,462	—	76,800	7,650,000
Total Salaries	11,490,542	200,002	326,459	2,279,580	1,800,720	258,317	2,130,337	420,832	8,200	459,929	328	1,620,356	260,412	529,638	179,086	483,422	532,923
Total Benefits	1,556,162	—	44,879	275,829	247,550	35,512	292,864	57,853	1,127	62,747	45	220,456	35,800	72,811	68,969	66,457	73,263
Total Professional Fees-Medical	2,198,478	—	—	227,766	622,000	—	758,792	325,600	205,800	—	—	78,020	—	—	—	—	—
Total Professional Fees-Other	43,440	—	—	15,390	—	—	27,050	—	—	—	—	1,000	—	—	—	—	—
Total Supplies	447,433	—	31,286	29,609	12,806	4,400	46,333	8,584	1,670	31,566	200	113,345	2,680	52,629	800	102,600	8,924
Total Depreciation/Amortization	85,286	—	—	—	—	—	—	—	—	—	—	—	—	—	—	—	85,286
Total Insurance	612,369	10,212	15,312	46,560	224,724	18,528	53,844	40,836	—	4,812	—	92,952	92,472	10,428	—	—	1,689
Total Bad Debt	1,944,373	117,631	14,046	131,036	945,934	14,046	331,743	163,033	—	27,521	—	133,586	—	65,796	—	—	—
Total Other Expenses	1,346,381	4,005	35,616	143,190	121,395	13,848	107,478	90,574	2,700	152,181	1,130	276,431	11,640	112,354	7,500	214,450	51,888
Total Utility Expenses	7,484	—	—	—	4,772	—	—	720	—	—	—	—	—	—	—	—	1,992
Network Allocation	—	—	—	—	—	—	—	—	—	—	—	—	—	—	—	—	—
Total Expenses	19,731,946	331,850	467,597	3,148,961	3,979,902	344,651	3,748,441	1,108,033	219,497	738,757	1,703	2,536,147	403,003	843,655	256,355	866,930	755,964
NET INCOME (LOSS)	(593,543)	(26,807)	4,985	(1,710,712)	11,045	39,492	(1,884,241)	(473,790)	(143,831)	(306,338)	147	(1,340,347)	(403,003)	(227,193)	(256,355)	(790,130)	6,894,036
Deduct $7.5 million from Admin for Re-allocation	—	—	—	—	—	—	—	—	—	—	—	—	—	—	—	—	(7,500,000)
Re-allocation of $7.5 million from Admin to CME Programs	—	—	—	1,619,349	846,115	—	2,458,465	524,898	—	—	—	1,223,517	368,637	—	—	—	459,019
PFS Collection Fee (8% of Net Patient Rev.)	—	(14,993.01)	(36,682.94)	(29,349.52)	(195,340.47)	(14,823.75)	(49,488.69)	(19,938.23)	—	(32,391.82)	—	(45,506.41)	—	(44,053.29)	—	482,568.13	—
Admin Fee (7% of Net Patient Rev.)	—	(13,118.88)	(32,097.57)	(25,680.83)	(170,922.91)	(12,970.78)	(43,302.60)	(17,445.95)	—	(28,342.84)	—	(39,818.11)	—	(38,546.63)	—	—	422,247.11
ADJUSTED NET INCOME (LOSS)	(593,543)	(54,919)	(63,795)	(146,393)	490,897	11,697	481,433	13,724	(143,831)	(367,072)	147	(202,154)	(34,366)	(309,793)	(256,355)	(307,562)	275,302

EXHIBIT 6

ATHERTON MEDICAL EDUCATION PROGRAMS:
Payer Mix

	2000 Actual Payer Mix	2001 Budget		2001 6-month Projection	
		Payer Mix	Collection %	Payer Mix	Collection %
Residency Program					
Self-Pay	31.4%	30.1%	5.3%	31.8%	2.8%
Medicare	29.8	27.5	47.4%	27.7	44.7%
Medicaid	17.2	13.8	26.2%	15.2	29.4%
Managed Care	14.8	10.0	60.8%	13.3	50.9%
City Health Assistance Program	6.8	18.6	0.9%	12.0	12.6%
Total	**100.0%**	**100.0%**	**24.5%**	**100.0%**	**26.0%**

	2000 Actual Payer Mix	2001 Budget		2001 6-month Projection	
		Payer Mix	Collection %	Payer Mix	Collection %
Faculty Practice					
Self-Pay	4.2%	3.9%	50.1%	3.4%	47.2%
Medicare	18.9	22.4	50.0%	24.8	48.5%
Medicaid	2.6	5.2	37.5%	2.8	32.8%
Managed Care	74.2	68.5	51.0%	68.7	49.4%
City Health Assistance Program	0.1	0.0	0.0%	0.2	0.0%
Total	**100.0%**	**100.0%**	**50.0%**	**100.0%**	**48.5%**

contract with AMEP, which usually was automatically renewed, although some were renegotiated periodically. Some of the physicians also had contacts with Bennington for other services that they provided such as trauma coverage. Gary Marks, M.D., had been hired by Southwestern to review these contracts. He commented on the challenges of this undertaking:

> My goal is to bring clarity to the cost structure. There are multiple contracts with numerous community physicians. Some are contracts with Bennington Hospital for availability, some are with Bennington for direct patient care to the medically indigent, and some are contracts with AMEP for curriculum development, GME supervision, and/or direct patient care for inpatients and clinics. These variations make it very difficult to understand the costs, relationships, and opportunities. For example, AMEP is accountable for graduate medical education but employs the primary care physicians and finances the subspecialty care for the medically indigent. Therefore, many of the AMEP contracts cover both medical education and patient care.
>
> Another issue you have with some of the physicians is the need to look at all arrangements in their entirety. A physician may be generously compensated on one

contract, but poorly on another. The more lucrative contracts subsidize the other activities that may not be well reimbursed. People are reluctant to change contracts that may be above market rates for fear that the changes will have adverse effects elsewhere. One admonishment I shared prior to my arrival was not to hire me based on any assumptions regarding the bottom line. My goal is clear and fair contracts. If the contracts and payments are not fair, the physician relationship will fall apart in the long term anyway. We must also be aware that many of the community-based physicians could walk away from Bennington and AMEP with only minor financial implications. They can easily replace the lost revenue working someplace else.

Dr. Bethridge also wanted to be sure that the contracts were appropriate. She realized that, while many of the physicians enjoyed interacting with the residents and valued their affiliation with the educational programs, they also had private practices. One such physician was Harold Davidson, M.D., a cardiologist who worked with the internal medicine program. He described his relationship:

I have worked with the training program for almost 10 years, although when I relocated to Atherton I had no intention of teaching or becoming affiliated with the GME program. I view myself as a private-practice physician as opposed to an "academic" physician, but have enjoyed all my years working with AMEP. When I moved to Atherton, the cardiologist who had previously worked with AMEP resigned to take a job in a different city, so I agreed to assume the responsibilities for cardiology. We negotiated a contract about eight years ago and it has remained the same since then. I receive a monthly stipend check and within that are the responsibilities to provide medical education for cardiology and provide cardiac care for AMEP's patients. This includes 24-hour, 365-days-a-year coverage of the ER, consultations, diagnostic tests, invasive procedures, and interventions such as angioplasty and coronary stents.

In general the monthly stipend arrangement has worked well. At one point we tried to bill and collect from the patients, but because of the poor payer mix, it wasn't worthwhile. The best we can hope for is Medicare; once in a blue moon you may have a patient insured by a managed care organization, but, overall, cardiology probably is about 50 percent unfunded. Because of that, I think the valuation of the contract is correct. We do occasionally have a slow week, but at other times we may do procedures that would generate well over $20,000 in professional fees if the patients were insured. I work with another physician to split the clinical work, but I handle almost all of the teaching duties at conferences and morning reports.

A lot of the teaching—I would say 90 percent—is at the bedside. In terms of my own productivity, I could probably go twice as fast without residents as I do with them, but that depends on how experienced the residents are. On the outpatient side, residents can help my productivity because they can do a lot of the diagnostic work. I supervise and train the residents and they are my responsibility, but given our volume it would be difficult without the residents. I also admit my private patients here. I very much encourage that and feel that it is part of the good will that flows. The training program has been very fair with me over the years and so has the hospital. Plus, the fact that I am here means it is very cost- and time-effective for me to admit my patients here. Overall, the experience has been great. The interactions with the residents keep me on my toes and I enjoy working with them.

Next Steps

As she analyzed her program, Dr. Bethridge was aware that Southwestern wanted to build a more entrepreneurial culture within AMEP and perhaps see AMEP expand its clinical activities. In the longer term there was the possibility of developing a research partnership with the State University. She also knew that there was some concern about AMEP's capacity to meet the needs of the expanding number of indigent patients. In addition, there was the possibility of some changes to the way funds were divided between AMEP and Bennington. Although she was open to the idea of change, she wanted to be sure that the approach Southwestern and AMEP took did not erode the educational mission of AMEP. She felt it was critical that she work with Dr. Byron to develop both a strong case for the internal medicine program and a solid proposal for an appropriate financial model.

Questions

1. Exhibit 2 shows $7 million on the line "Interns & Residents—Other Program." What is the source of this figure? Is it appropriate that this cost center be treated as a service center? If so, why? If not, what rationale would you use for classifying it as a production (revenue) center? Are there other options for the treatment of GME on this report?

2. How do you think the faculty salaries and contract services amounts on Exhibit 4 were determined? What kinds of activities do you think are included in these amounts?

3. How closely do you think the DME and IME payments come to the cost of graduate medical education at Southwestern? Where, if at all, do you think there might be slippages between the "real cost" of GME and the payments that are made to cover it? In answering this question, please address the relationship between GME and indigent care. Is the funding for the two activities structured appropriately? If not, how would you change it?

4. Dr. Bethridge has indicated an interest in having a good understanding of the costs and benefits of her program. Does she have it? If not, what additional information would you recommend she obtain and from where?

5. Assuming she can obtain the information you recommend in your answer to Question 4, how should Dr. Bethridge use this information to market GME to its various constituencies?

Management Control Systems

As we indicated in Chapter 1, management control systems consist of both a structure and a process. Structure describes what the system is, and process describes what it does—in much the same way that anatomy and physiology describe the human body.

In this part of the book, we discuss the important aspects of management control systems. Chapter 8 focuses on structure, placing it in the broader context of a management control environment. Understanding the management control environment is critical to understanding the management control structure, which is highly situational and governed in large measure by the organization's external and internal environments.

Chapters 9–15 describe the management control process—a set of activities encompassing a wide variety of interactions among individuals in an organization. Each phase in the management control process—strategic planning, budgeting, operating and measuring output, and reporting and evaluating performance—is the subject of at least one chapter, sometimes two. Some chapters consider specific aspects of a phase in detail. For example, Chapter 11 looks in depth at the control of operations, a part of the operations and measurement phase of the cycle. Similarly, Chapter 15 is devoted to an aspect of the management control process that is particularly important for nonprofit organizations: evaluation of program and organizational performance. In most for-profit organizations, profit is the primary means of evaluation. Most nonprofit organizations, however, do not have a corresponding means of evaluation that is as uniform or measurable. We discuss some aspects of evaluation that are useful when there is no profit measure.

Chapter 8

The Management Control Environment

The management control function is affected by many forces outside the organization. Together, these forces constitute the organization's *external environment.* In Chapter 2, we discussed some of the external forces that affect nonprofit organizations, such as tax and legal considerations, constraints on goals and strategies, professional norms, unsophisticated governance, and political influences.

Specific external environments vary greatly from one organization to the next, and these differences affect the design of the management control system. For example, management control in an entity with relatively certain revenues, almost no competition, and programs that are essentially unchanged from one year to the next, is considerably different from management control in an entity whose sources of funding are relatively uncertain, whose competitors are numerous, and whose program emphases shift rapidly. Similarly, government organizations, as well as organizations that receive substantial funds from government sources, are subject to a variety of pressures and scrutiny from legislative bodies and the general public. In these cases, the desires of the press and the public for information constitute an important design consideration for the management control system.

Organizations also have *internal environments,* and in designing the management control system, senior management must give careful consideration to the fit among a variety of elements that constitute this internal environment. These include the organizational structure, the program structure, the information structure, and a variety of administrative, behavioral, and cultural factors. Not only must these elements fit with each other, but they must fit with the external environment as well. As we discuss in this chapter, the management control system is an important tool for senior management to use in helping the organization attain these fits.

The Organizational Structure

Organizational structure refers to the *formal* reporting relationships among managers and other individuals in an entity. An entity also has an *informal* structure that is unwritten and perhaps unintended. The information structure encompasses a network of interpersonal relationships that has important implications for management. Because it is unwritten, however, the informal structure of the organization is difficult to identify and describe. For this reason, we concentrate here on the formal structure.

Senior management weighs many considerations in determining the best formal structure. These considerations involve questions such as the most appropriate division of tasks, the activities that should be carried out by specialized staff units, the activities that should be the responsibility of line managers, the decisions that should be made at or near the top of the organization, and the decisions that should be delegated to lower levels. Some of these considerations are related to individuals; that is, in part, the entity is organized to take into account the skills and personality traits of individual managers and professionals.

An organization's formal structure can take one of several forms. In a functional structure, tasks are classified according to function, and all personnel who work in the same functional area are under the direction of a manager. In a social service agency, for example, all social workers might report to a director of social work, or in a hospital all nurses might report to a director of nursing.

As organizations grow and become more diverse, many shift from a functional structure to a divisional one. In a divisional structure, functional tasks are grouped into logical clusters according to, say, clients, regions, or programs. For example, if a large home health care agency had a divisional structure, its personnel might be grouped into teams according to geographic region. If so, its home care workers would report to a team manager or regional manager, rather than to a director of home care. In a hospital with a divisional structure, nurses would report to a department head, such as the chief of surgery or chief of medicine, rather than to a director of nursing.

The most complex organizational structure is the matrix form. In this form, individuals have two supervisors—a divisional or program supervisor and a functional supervisor. Social workers might report to a team manager for their day-to-day activities, for example, and to a director of social work for their professional development and training. In a hospital, nurses might have similar dual reporting responsibilities. In some universities, faculty have dual reporting responsibilities: to both a department chair and one or more program directors.

Responsibility Centers

As we discussed in Chapter 1, the formal organizational structure for management control purposes is defined in terms of responsibility centers, with line control exercised by the managers of these responsibility centers. Although the type and degree of control exercised by a manager may be difficult to pinpoint, at some level someone in an organization has control over each resource-related decision. In some cases control is infrequent and has long-term implications, such as in the acquisition of a fixed asset or the commitment to a long-term lease. In other cases, it is of shorter duration, such as in the decision to sign a one-year supply contract. In still other cases, control is very short run, such as in the decision to ask employees to work overtime.

The key question senior management asks in defining the organization's responsibility center structure is "Who controls what resources?" Each manager's responsibility then can be aligned with the resources over which he or she exerts reasonable (although not necessarily total) control.

Types of Responsibility Centers

As the above discussion suggests, a responsibility center is an organizational unit headed by a manager who is responsible for its activities. In any organization except the smallest, there is a hierarchy of responsibility centers. At the lowest level in the organization there are responsibility centers for sections or other small organization units. At higher levels there are departments or divisions that consist of several smaller units plus overall departmental or divisional staff and management people; these larger units are also responsibility centers. From the viewpoint of senior management, trustees, or legislative oversight bodies, the whole entity is a responsibility center. In general, however, even though such large units fit the definition of a responsibility center, the term usually is used to refer to smaller, lower level units within the organization.

In Chapter 1 we described four types of responsibility centers: revenue centers, expense centers (standard and discretionary), profit centers, and investment centers. Exhibit 8–1 lists these four types and the financial responsibilities of each.

The most common responsibility centers found in nonprofit organizations are discretionary expense centers, standard expense centers, and profit centers. In a discretionary expense center the focus is on total expenses regardless of the volume and/or mix of activity. In a standard expense center the focus shifts to expenses per unit of output rather than total expenses. The budget each period (called a *flexible budget*) is adjusted based on the actual volume and mix of units of output. In a profit center, the focus is on both revenues and expenses.

Recall from discussions in earlier chapters that revenues are monetary measures of a responsibility center's output. They may be generated by sales of services both to other responsibility centers and to outside clients. To some people, the idea that profit centers exist in a nonprofit organization seems peculiar, but the profit center idea can be an important way of facilitating management control. As such, it is not at all inconsistent to have a profit center in

EXHIBIT 8–1
Types of
Responsibility
Centers

Type of Responsibility Center	Responsible For
Revenue center	Revenue earned by the center.
Expense center:	
Standard	Expenses per unit of output, but not total expenses, incurred by the center.
Discretionary	Total expenses incurred by the center.
Profit center	Total revenues and expenses of the center.
Investment center	Total revenues and expenses of the center, computed as a percentage of the assets used by the center, that is, the center's return on assets.

a nonprofit organization—the term simply refers to a manager's scope of financial responsibility.

Transfer Prices

When one responsibility center receives goods or services from another and is charged for them, the charge is called a *transfer price*. A transfer price is used exclusively for transactions *within* an organization, as contrasted with an external price, which is used for transactions between an organization and its clients.

Motivational Considerations

In all organizations—for-profit and nonprofit—transfer pricing provides a mechanism for encouraging the optimal use of an organization's resources. This is because the behavior of profit center managers (and to a lesser extent standard expense center managers) frequently is influenced considerably by the way transfer prices are structured (or by the requirement that products be furnished without charge under certain circumstances).

If a service is free, users are not motivated to consider its value. They tend to request as much of the service as they can get without considering how much it is worth to them. Resources available to most users are limited by their budgets. If a service can be obtained free, the user need not even think about how its value compares with alternative services that require resources. For example, if a motor pool provides automobiles without charge, a user who is about to take a trip need not consider whether use of a taxi, public transportation, or private automobile would be more efficient. Other things being equal, the choice is the motor pool.

Example

One organization had a motor pool that delivered freight by trucks without charging users. It found that managers were requesting trucks to deliver small quantities of freight that could be delivered less expensively by private trucking companies. The trucking company price was a charge against their budget, whereas the use of the motor pool truck was free.

When the organization started to charge for motor pool deliveries, managers gave thought to the cost of alternative methods of transportation. They were also motivated to combine shipments to a given destination to further reduce costs.

The use of transfer prices also fosters an equitable distribution of services. If a motor pool provides automobiles without charge, for example, the motor pool manager's decisions about who gets an automobile may be made on the basis of favoritism or a user's persuasive talents. With a transfer pricing system, however, the user who is willing to pay gets an automobile, just as with a car rental agency. (Of course, in periods of heavy demand, when the motor pool is operating at full capacity, favoritism or pleading capability may still be influential.)

Setting Transfer Prices

It might appear that if a responsibility center did not sell its products to outside customers, there would be no reliable way of establishing its transfer prices. But this is not so. Almost all service centers have counterparts in for-profit organizations. Motor pools are like car rental agencies; maintenance, housekeeping, laundry, and similar departments are like private contractors; computer departments are like computer service bureaus. The principles used to set prices in these organizations usually can be adapted rather easily to nonprofit organizations. Although there is no single best approach to establishing transfer prices, there are four approaches that most organizations use:

Market Price   If a valid market price exists for the product, it ordinarily is the basis for the transfer price. This price may be adjusted downward to reduce the profit component in prices charged by for-profit companies. It also may be adjusted downward to eliminate bad debts or selling expenses that do not exist with internal transactions. If, however, the market price is a distress price—that is, a price well below the one at which market transactions usually take place—it normally does not provide a valid basis for the transfer price.

Full Cost   If no valid market price exists, the transfer price ordinarily should be the product's full cost. This rule corresponds to the normal practice for arriving at normal selling prices to outside customers, except that it has at most only a small margin above costs. As with market prices, some organizations also exclude bad debts and selling expenses in a full-cost transfer price.

Standard Cost   The transfer price should be based on standard costs, rather than on actual costs. If based on actual costs, the selling unit could pass its inefficiencies to the units receiving its services.

Negotiation   In special circumstances, the buying and selling units may be permitted to negotiate the transfer price. If the selling unit is operating below capacity, for example, it may be willing to accept a lower price that will make some contribution to its overhead. Conversely, if the selling unit provides an especially high quality product or certain special services or guarantees, the manager of the buying unit may be willing to pay a somewhat higher transfer price.

Measure of Efficiency

A market price above the selling unit's full cost indicates that the unit is operating efficiently, whereas a market price below the selling unit's full cost suggests inefficiency. That is, if users can obtain needed services from either an internal responsibility center or an outside source, total revenue of the responsibility center providing the service is a good measure of its efficiency. This assumes, of course, that purchasers are motivated to seek the supplier who can furnish a service of acceptable quality at the lowest price.

If a responsibility center cannot furnish services at competitive prices, or if the revenue it earns is not equal to its costs, its operating statement will report a loss. This is an indication that something is wrong. If the responsibility center's charges are similar to those of alternative providers of the service, but its revenue is low, the center may be providing poor-quality service. If this is the case, the manager presumably will be motivated to seek quality improvements. If, by contrast, the responsibility center has comparable quality to alternative providers, but charges more than the market price, its low revenue is a sign that costs are too high. In this case, the manager will be motivated to reduce costs. If volume large enough to cover fixed costs is unattainable, senior management may decide to discontinue the service. Thus, charging for services provides senior management with information about the efficiency and quality of the service, and whether the service should be offered at all.

Need for Caution   In making decisions about efficiency and quality, managers must be cautious. Quality, service, and other considerations may mean that a responsibility center is providing a different product from the one for which a market price is available. If this is the case, the comparison between full cost and market price is invalid and potentially dysfunctional. Moreover, if the organization's full-cost accounting system is not well designed, it may be providing misleading information.[1]

| Example | Within a few years after designing a transfer pricing system based on full cost for word processing, graphics, technical publications, and secretarial services, one organization noticed some unintended consequences: researchers and engineers were spending time typing documents and making overhead slides because their departments could not afford the transfer prices. Upon investigation, the organization found that the existing cost allocation mechanisms did not measure usage of service center resources appropriately, and the people-intensive service centers were |

[1]For additional details on transfer pricing, see Robert N. Anthony and Vijay Govindarajan, *Management Control Systems* (Burr Ridge, IL: McGraw-Hill, 1998).

getting an unfair share of administrative overhead. When better measures were used to allocate overhead costs, the full cost of the people-intensive service centers fell. The transfer prices for these service centers then fell to a level that research and engineering departments were willing to pay.[2]

Criteria for Profit Centers

An important set of considerations for understanding a management control system relates to the criteria that senior management uses to decide which responsibility centers should be profit centers and which should be expense centers. Because a profit center encompasses more elements of managerial performance than an expense center, it also requires more recordkeeping. Indeed, in some circumstances the creation of a profit center may have dysfunctional consequences. For example, it may encourage managers to place too much attention on the revenue side of the equation, or to cut expenses in a given accounting period without concern for the longer-term consequences of these cuts.

Despite these potential dysfunctional consequences, a profit center generally is desirable if a manager has a reasonable amount of influence over both the outputs and the inputs of his or her responsibility center. In effect, a profit center manager behaves almost as if he or she were running a separate organization. In most organizations, managers who carry out identifiable programs, especially ones that are geographically separate, usually have their units designated as profit centers. In determining whether a responsibility center should be a profit center, senior management typically considers five criteria.

Degree of Influence

The manager of a responsibility center should be able to exert *reasonable* influence over both revenues and expenses of the center. This does not imply that the manager must have *complete* control over outputs and inputs, for few, if any, profit center managers have such authority. However, a profit center manager usually should be able to exercise some control over the volume of activity of the responsibility center, the quality of the work done, the center's variable unit costs, and its direct fixed costs. Sometimes he or she also can influence the prices charged.

Perception of Fairness

The manager should perceive that the profit reported for the center is fair as a measure of its financial performance. This does not mean that the amount of reported profit is completely accurate or that it encompasses all aspects of performance, for no profit measure does this. If a service center is designated as a profit center, for example, its usual financial objective is to break even; that

[2]Edward J. Kovac and Henry P. Troy, "Getting Transfer Prices Right: What Bellcore Did," *Harvard Business Review,* September–October 1989.

is, to provide services whose revenues approximate the costs of the center. If this is the case, both the manager and his or her superior need to agree that breakeven performance is a good financial performance.

Absence of Dysfunctional Incentives

The competitive spirit that the profit center concept fosters should not have dysfunctional consequences to the organization. For instance, in some cases when a unit is organized as a profit center, the desirable degree of cooperation with other responsibility centers does not occur. The manager of a profit center may make decisions that add to the profit of his or her own unit to the detriment of other units in the organization. For example, he or she may be reluctant to incur overtime costs even though the services may be badly needed by other responsibility centers. Senior management should attempt to avoid or minimize such dysfunctional consequences by designing the management control system so that cooperative actions have a positive impact on the profit center's reported performance (or at least do not affect it adversely).

Existence of Transfer Prices

Internal users of a responsibility center's services should be expected to pay for those services via transfer prices. If there are internal users and no transfer prices, senior management ordinarily should not designate the unit as a profit center. An internal audit organization, for example, usually provides services without charge and therefore should not be a profit center. Similarly, if senior management encourages operating units to use the services of certain staff units, these staff units probably should not be profit centers, at least not until operating units come to accept the value of the staff services and are willing to pay for them.

As discussed above, transfer prices constitute a monetary way of measuring the amount of a responsibility center's internally furnished services. As such, they measure the unit's output.

Some people believe that if a responsibility center does not sell a substantial percentage of its products to external customers, it cannot be a true profit center; it is, at most, a *pseudo profit center.* If the profit center concept is properly understood and applied, however, sales to other responsibility centers are just as real to a profit center manager as sales to outside clients.

Low Recordkeeping Costs

The benefits of having a profit center should be greater than the extra cost of recordkeeping and other administrative activities that it requires. The cost of measuring the output of most accounting departments, for example, is large enough that establishing the accounting department as a profit center probably does not make sense. If, however, an accounting department does recordkeeping for several outside organizations, as is the case in some municipalities, it may be worthwhile to incur the additional recordkeeping costs needed to make the department a profit center.

Profit Centers and Managerial Autonomy

Profit centers vary considerably as to the degree of autonomy possessed by their managers. While a profit center may operate almost as if it were an independent company, its manager will not have all the autonomy of a chief executive officer of an independent company. This is because profit centers are part of a larger organization, and their managers are subject to the policies of that organization. Profit center managers rarely are empowered to initiate new programs or commit to major capital expenditures, for example. Those decisions, like others that significantly influence the organization's overall strategy, usually are made by senior management.

Restrictions on autonomy imposed by senior management may be communicated by formal rules (described later in this chapter), by strategic planning systems, and by budgeting activities. No matter how carefully these formal devices are constructed, however, informal mechanisms constitute powerful indicators of a manager's autonomy. These mechanisms include unwritten rules concerning, for example, what decisions (*a*) are appropriately made by a profit center manager, (*b*) require approval of higher authority, or (*c*) require consultation with (but not necessarily approval of) staff offices or higher line managers. In general, chief executives tend to give more autonomy to subordinates whom they know well and whose judgment they trust. As a result, despite the presence of a variety of formal devices in an organization, some profit center managers may have considerably more decision-making latitude than others.

Subsidization among Profit Centers

Some universities have what they call an "every tub on its own bottom" philosophy, meaning that every school must operate with a surplus every year. This is relatively easy to attain for some schools, such as a business school or a law school, and quite difficult for others, such as a divinity school or a fine arts school.

Other universities engage in substantial cross subsidization. For example, a business school may generate revenue of, say, $40 million, but have a budget of only $30 million. The remaining $10 million is used to subsidize other schools that do not have an excess of revenues over expenses. Indeed, a nonprofit organization may decide to allow some of its profit centers to operate at agreed-upon deficits, with the understanding that they will be subsidized by profit centers with surpluses. In this way senior management can assure itself that strategically important organizational units are not abandoned because they cannot earn an excess of revenue over expenses.

When there is no cross subsidization, an organization's senior management must be sure that there are "teeth" in the management control system; that is, that a profit center is not allowed to slip by with a deficit.

Example	Some years ago, the School of Public Health at a university with an "every tub on its own bottom" philosophy ran a deficit. The university's central

administration informed the school's dean that any future deficits would be funded out of the school's endowment principal. The next year the dean balanced the budget.

By contrast, an organization that engages in cross subsidization must make certain that profit center managers with surpluses "buy into" the subsidies that they are providing to profit centers with deficits. In addition, senior management must develop motivation systems to assure that profit centers with agreed-upon deficits work as hard as possible to keep their deficits at or below budgeted levels.

The Program Structure

Every organization exists to carry out programs. Fixing responsibility for control over programs would be relatively easy if each program were a responsibility center and each program's resources were controllable in the same way. For example, the design of the control structure would be quite easy if: (1) each program sold its services, (2) each program were staffed by personnel who worked in no other program, and (3) each program manager had reasonable control over hiring and other personnel decisions, as well as decisions on program supply purchases. Under these circumstances, each program would be a profit center.

Most entities are not organized in a fashion that permits such tidy and well-defined control structures. Many organizations operate over large geographic areas and must consider this fact when designing their structure. For example, does a multihospital system have one director of alcoholic rehabilitation services with broad geographic responsibilities, or several area directors, each of whom has responsibility for all programs in his or her area, including the alcoholic rehabilitation program?

In other organizational settings, the program and functional lines become similarly blurred. Does the director of the summer festival program for a symphony orchestra have control over the number of personnel taking part in the festival, or their salaries? Does the director of a master's degree program in a large university control the number of applications received, the tuition charged, or the salaries of the faculty who work in the program? Moreover, while performers in the orchestra or faculty in the university may take part in a particular program, their reporting relationships within the organization generally are not to the director of one program only.

In summary, a separate program structure is needed when responsibility for the execution of programs involves more than one responsibility center. A municipality organized so that each responsibility center performs a defined type of service (e.g., public safety, highway maintenance, education) does not need a separate program structure. By contrast, a federal government agency that executes many separate programs through several regional offices does. So does a research organization that draws on the resources of several depart-ments to carry out its research projects.

In the Department of Defense (DoD) in the 1960s, the lines of organiza-tional responsibility ran to the Secretary of the Army, the Secretary of the Navy, and the Secretary of the Air Force, whereas defense programs cut across these lines. For example, the DoD had a strategic mission (or pro-gram) that was related to a possible nuclear exchange with the Soviets. Dif-ferent parts of this program were the responsibility of the army (antiballistic missiles), the navy (Polaris submarines), and the air force (strategic missiles and bombers). A mechanism that facilitated decision making about the program as a whole was necessary. The defense program structure (in which Program 1 was Strategic Forces) provided such a mechanism.

In recent years, some authors have argued that the DoD's success in ac-commodating the cutbacks it faces in the post-cold-war era will depend to a great extent on the existence of a structure such as this with transfer prices linking mission and support centers' interactions.[3]

Many organizations have found that selecting a good program structure is a difficult task. In fact, several efforts to establish programming systems in the federal government failed because the program structure was not arranged in a way that facilitated management decision making. Consequently, managers did not find the information they received useful, and paid no attention to it.

In short, the process of aligning responsibility with control and developing a responsibility center structure within an organization's broader organiza-tional structure is by no means a simple endeavor. For this reason, the selec-tion of a program structure is one of the most critical tasks facing senior management in nonprofit organizations.

Components of a Program Structure

In a large organization, the program structure usually consists of several layers. At the top are a few major programs; at the bottom are a great many program elements—the smallest units in which information is collected in program terms. A program element represents some definable activity or related group of activities that the organization carries on either directly, to accomplish an organizational objective, or indirectly, in support of other pro-gram elements.

Between programs and program elements are what we call *program cate-gories,* and, depending on how many layers are needed, *program subcate-gories.* In a relatively flat organization, there may be no need for program categories (or subcategories); program elements can be aggregated directly into programs. In a more hierarchical organization, by contrast, there may be

---

[3]See Fred Thompson, "Management Control and the Pentagon: The Organizational Strategy-Structure Mismatch," *Public Administration Review* 51, no. 1 (January–February 1991).

EXHIBIT 8–2 Programs, Program Categories, Program Subcategories, and Program Elements

Program	100. Formal Education
Program categories	101. Pre-elementary school service
	102. Elementary and secondary school service
	103. Postsecondary school education service
	104. Special education service for exceptional persons
Program subcategories (for Program Category 102)	1. Kindergarten
	2. Primary or elementary school education
	3. Secondary or high school education
	4. Vocational and/or trade high school
Program elements (for Program Subcategory 2)	.1 Language instruction
	.2 Music instruction
	.3 Art instruction
	.4 Social sciences instruction

several levels of program categories. Exhibit 8–2 contains an example of programs, program categories, and program elements.

Types of Programs

In designing the program structure, senior management focuses its attention on several different types of programs.

Mission and Support Programs   Programs can be classified as either *mission* or *support*. Mission programs relate to the organization's objectives and are usually focused on clients. Support programs provide services to other programs but usually don't work directly with clients. In making decisions about the allocation of resources, management usually focuses its attention on mission programs. Within limits, the amount of resources required for support programs is roughly dependent on the size and character of the mission programs.

Example	In a college or university, the mission programs would be those related to instruction and research. The support programs would include buildings and grounds maintenance, publications, and financial aid.

Administration

Ordinarily, there should be a separate program for administration. This support program typically includes certain miscellaneous program categories or elements that, although not strictly administrative in character, do not belong logically in other programs and are not important enough to be set up as separate program categories or elements. Alternatively, these miscellaneous program elements might be grouped in a separate program category.

The rationale for a separate program for administration is that it permits senior management to focus special attention on administrative activities. Senior management usually wishes to devote as much of the organization's total resources as possible to mission programs, and as little as possible to administration. In the absence of special attention, however, administrative activities tend to grow. A program for administration encourages senior management to direct attention to these activities.

Development

In organizations that obtain financial resources from contributors, there should be a separate program for the costs associated with development (or fund-raising). Contributors and others usually are interested in how much of the donated amounts was used for mission programs and how much was spent on development activities. Occasionally there are difficulties in drawing the line between development costs and mission program costs, but this should not deter senior management from attempting to keep track of development costs as accurately as possible. A separate program facilitates this effort.

Example	Major contributors to symphony orchestras or other arts organizations may be given special preferences, such as use of a patrons' lounge. Although conceptually these are fund-raising costs, the amounts are rarely segregated as such. As a result, the organization's reported development costs are understated.

Program Elements

If feasible, a program element should be the responsibility of a single manager. If this is not feasible, senior management should attempt to relate program elements to the responsibility of a relatively small number of persons. Items for which responsibility is widely diffused, such as long-distance telephone calls, are not satisfactory program elements. Such items should appear not as program elements but as functional categories or expense elements in the responsibility structure.

Criteria for Selecting a Program Structure

Since the primary purpose of programs is to facilitate senior management's judgment on the allocation of resources, the program structure should correspond to the principal objectives of the organization. It should be arranged so as to facilitate decisions having to do with the relative importance of these objectives; that is, it should focus on the organization's outputs (i.e., what it achieves or intends to achieve) rather than on its inputs (the types of resources it uses) or on the sources of its support. A structure that is arranged by types of resources (e.g., personnel, material, or services) or by sources of support (e.g., tuition, legislative appropriations, and gifts in a university) is not a program structure.

The optimal number of programs in an organization is approximately 10. The rationale for this limit is that senior management cannot weigh the relative importance of a large number of disparate items. There are many exceptions to this generalization, however.

The designation of major programs helps clarify the objectives of the organization. The development of the program structure may also clarify organizational purpose and, thus, suggest improvements in the overall structure of the organization. Therefore, the program structure should correspond to those areas of activity that senior management expects to use for decision-making purposes.

Matrix Organizations

Although the program structure need not match the organizational structure, there should be some person who has identifiable responsibility for each program (as well as each program category and each program element in large organizations). This need for a fit between the organizational structure and the program structure often results in a matrix organization. The matrix consists of program managers along one dimension and managers of functionally organized responsibility centers along the other. Program managers may have other responsibilities, and they may call on other parts of the organization for much of the work that is to be done on their programs, but they nevertheless are advocates for their programs, and they are held accountable for their program's performance.

Example

Faculty members of a business school typically have a home base in a subject-area department (such as organizational behavior, accounting, or marketing). They also may be assigned to one or more programs, such as undergraduate education, graduate education, or executive education. Program managers call on departments for work to be done on their programs. In these circumstances, responsibility is divided between the department head and the progam head.

An example of a matrix structure is contained in Exhibit 8–3. This is for a large state agency—a department of mental health. As this exhibit shows, the complexity in this agency exists along several dimensions, which affect both its management control structure and its budget preparation process. Some of those dimensions are as follows:

- The agency does not generate revenues. Therefore it is an expense center. Since its budget probably cannot be changed with changes in volume during the year, the agency quite likely is a discretionary expense center.

- Resource allocation is along two dimensions. One is based on field operations and facilities, which corresponds to the agency's organizational structure (the left side of the matrix). The other is based on the agency's major programs, such as community mental health (the right side of the matrix).

EXHIBIT 8–3 Matrix Structure in a Large State Agency

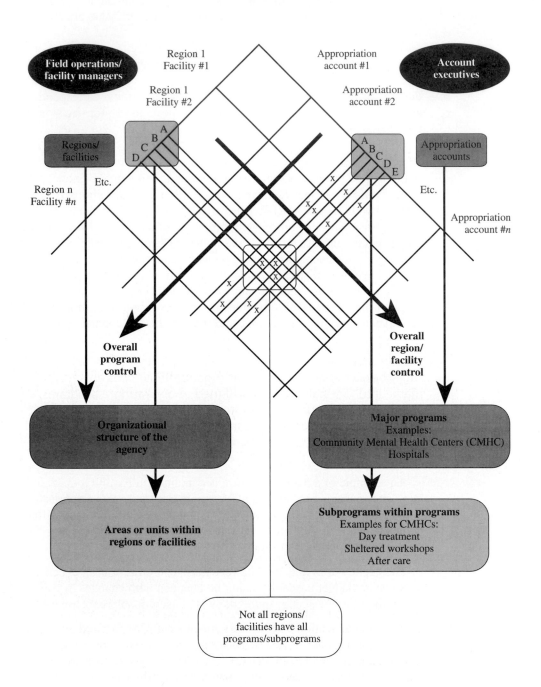

The major programs correspond to appropriation accounts in the state's budget, and are the responsibility of *account executives.*

- Both field operations and the major programs have several layers of responsibility. The field operations activity is comprised of regions at the highest level, followed by facilities, areas, and units within the facilities. The major programs are comprised of program categories (or subprograms as they are called here).

- Overall program control is the responsibility of the account executives, who presumably cannot spend more than the amount allotted to their appropriation accounts. The programs cut across all regions, although not all regions or all facilities have all programs or all subprograms. As a result, one of the jobs of an account executive is to determine which regions and facilities can most effectively serve the clients of each major program and its various subprograms.

- Control over the activities in regions and facilities is the responsibility of the field operations and facility managers. They receive budgets from the account executives and must adhere to them while striving to meet the objectives of the programs and subprograms that the budgets fund.

- Although the agency is a discretionary expense center, some units within it may be standard expense centers. This is because the managers of these units have no control over the number or mix of individuals who need their services. For these units, the account executives need to assure that increases in one region or facility are matched by decreases in other regions or facilities, since the appropriation account budgets are fixed. Nevertheless, with an appropriate flow of information to both account executives and field operations and facility managers, such a structure might provide greater motivation to the field operations and facility managers to run their operations more effectively and efficiently—each would be competing for scarce resources from the appropriations accounts.

The Information Structure

Information is needed by program planners and analysts as well as responsibility center (or operating) managers. Program planners and analysts need information both to facilitate decision making about programs and to provide a basis of comparison of the cost and output of similar programs. Responsibility center managers need information on the outputs and inputs of their organizational units, which facilitates their control of revenues and expenses.

These information needs relate to the distinction between the program structure and the organizational structure. The program structure is designed principally to meet the needs of planners and analysts, and emphasizes the full costs of carrying out programs. The responsibility structure is designed to meet the needs of operating managers, and emphasizes the controllable costs of operating responsibility centers.

In designing an information structure, senior management must be certain that the team designing (or modifying) the management control system not be dominated by people who represent the viewpoint of either program or operating managers. Ideally, systems designers should be independent of both types of users, and should weigh equally the arguments of each.

The information structure should be able to reconcile most needs. This is especially important since senior management usually is interested in summaries of information provided to all other groups. An information structure to serve these multiple purposes is complicated since the information needed for one purpose may differ from that needed for another. In some cases, compromise in designing the structure may be necessary, but in most situations, the information structure can be designed to serve both sets of needs.

| Example | The director of a Latin American studies program in a university needs information on courses, enrollment, student satisfaction, and job placement. For the most part, this information is used for operating the program and not for comparisons with other similar programs. On the other hand, the dean of the school may wish to compare the Latin American studies program with similar programs in other universities. To do this, he or she will need information on applications, standardized test scores, admission yields, and so forth. A well-designed program structure will provide information for both the program director and the dean. |

Administrative Factors

Another aspect of the internal management control environment is the set of rules, practices, guidelines, customs, standard operating procedures, and codes of ethics that exists in any organization. For brevity, we lump these together as administrative factors, or rules. Unlike the management control system, which involves continual change, administrative factors typically change infrequently. Some rules, such as those set forth in manuals, are formal; others, such as understandings about acceptable behavior, are informal. They relate to matters that range from the most trivial (e.g., paper clips will be issued only on the basis of a signed requisition) to the most important (e.g., capital expenditures of over $200,000 must be approved by the board of trustees).

Types of Rules

Some rules are guides. An organization's members are permitted to depart from them, either under specified circumstances or if the manager judges that departure is in the best interests of the organization. For example, a guideline may state that overtime is not ordinarily paid, but managers may approve overtime payments under certain circumstances, either on their own authority or after obtaining approval from their superior. Other rules are literally rules—they should never be broken. Rules that prohibit paying bribes or taking illegal drugs are examples.

Some specific types of rules, procedures, and similar actions are listed below:[4]

1. *Physical control procedures.* Security guards, locked storerooms, vaults, computer passwords, television surveillance, and other physical controls are part of the internal control environment. Most of them are associated with task control, rather than with management control.

2. *Administrative control procedures.* There are also actions specifically designed to enhance task control, such as requiring that checks for more than a specified amount be countersigned. Their enforcement frequently is the responsibility of the controller's office.

3. *Administrative rules.* These are prescribed ways of performing certain functions, such as how to use time cards or how to complete expense reports.

Role of Manuals

Much judgment is required in deciding which rules and procedures should be made formal (i.e., put in a manual), which should be guidelines rather than fixed rules, and which should be subject to managerial discretion. There are no clear-cut prescriptions for these judgments, although there are some fairly obvious patterns. Bureaucratic organizations have more detailed manuals than other organizations, large organizations have more than small ones, and centralized organizations have more than decentralized ones. Additionally, with the passage of time, some formal rules become obsolete. Manuals and other sets of rules therefore need to be reexamined periodically to ensure that they are consistent with current needs.

The Reward Structure

An important administrative factor is the reward structure. Ideally, managers should be rewarded on the basis of actual performance compared with expected performance under the prevailing circumstances. This ideal cannot be achieved, however, for two basic reasons. First, the performance of a responsibility center is influenced by many factors other than the actions of its manager, and the performance of the manager usually cannot be cleanly separated from the effects of these other factors. Second, managers are supposed to achieve both long- and short-run objectives, but the management control system usually focuses primarily on the short run. This is because the system can only report what has happened; it cannot report what will happen in the future

---

[4]This list is derived from the work of Kenneth A. Merchant, who calls them specific action controls. See Kenneth A. Merchant, *Control in Business Organizations* (Aulander, NC: Pittman Publishing, 1985), chap. 3.

as a consequence of the manager's current actions. As a result, responsibility centers and program managers are motivated to focus on achieving short-run goals. Indeed, lack of knowledge about how best to measure and reward a manager's performance on a long-term basis is probably the most serious weakness in management control systems in both for-profit and nonprofit organizations.[5]

Behavioral Factors

Management control involves interactions among human beings. The behavior of people in organizations is therefore an important environmental factor. The major issue that senior management must address here is the congruence between the *personal* goals and needs of managers and professionals, and the *organization's* goals and needs.

Personal Goals and Needs

People join an organization because they believe that by doing so they can achieve one or more personal goals. Once they have joined, their decision to contribute to the work of the organization is based on their perception that this will help them achieve their personal goals.

An individual's personal goals can be expressed as needs. Some of these needs are material and can be satisfied by the money earned on the job. Other needs are psychological. People need to have their abilities and achievements recognized; they need social acceptance as members of a group; they need to feel a sense of personal worth; they need to feel secure; they need to be able to exercise discretion; they need to feel good about themselves.

These personal needs can be classified as either extrinsic or intrinsic. Extrinsic needs are satisfied by the actions of others. Examples are money received from the organization and praise received from a superior. Intrinsic needs are satisfied by the opinions people have about themselves. Examples are feelings of achievement or competence, or a clear conscience.

The relative importance of these needs varies with different persons, and their relative importance to a given individual varies at different times. Moreover, the relative importance that people attach to their own needs is heavily influenced by the attitudes of their colleagues and superiors. For some people, earning a great deal of money is a dominant need; for others, monetary considerations are less important than serving society. Only a relatively few individuals attach much importance to the need to exercise

---

[5]For-profit organizations sometimes use stock options as away to motivate managers to think about the long-term consequences of their decisions. Some nonprofit organizations have used sabbatical leaves as a form of long-term incentive, but it is difficualt to link leave time to long-run performance.

discretion or the need for achievement, but these persons tend to be the leaders of the organization.[6]

How do people behave to satisfy their needs? One answer to this question is based on the expectancy theory model of motivation. This theory states that the motivation to engage in a given behavior is determined by (1) a person's beliefs or expectancies about what outcomes are likely to result from that behavior, and (2) the attractiveness of these outcomes; that is, their ability to satisfy needs.[7]

Individuals are influenced by both positive and negative incentives. A positive incentive, or reward, is an outcome that is expected to result in increased need satisfaction. A negative incentive, or punishment, is the reverse. Incentives need not be monetary. Praise for a job well done can be a powerful reward. Nevertheless, many people regard monetary rewards as extremely important. Such rewards may include a bonus based on a comparison between planned and actual results. As we discussed in Chapter 2, this incentive is being used increasingly by nonprofit organizations.

Example	A survey of 587 hospitals conducted by William M. Mercer-Meidinger-Hansen, Inc., found that the average target level incentive for hospital CEOs (chief executive officers) was 24 percent of salary, and 17 percent for executives reporting directly to CEOs.[8]

Goal Congruence

Since an organization does not have a mind of its own, it literally cannot have goals. Organization goals are actually the goals of the board of trustees and senior management. Senior management wants the organization to attain these goals, but the organization's goals are not always congruent with the personal goals of operating managers and professionals. Because participants tend to act in their own self-interest, the achievement of organizational goals may be frustrated.

This distinction between organizational goals and personal goals suggests a central purpose of a management control system. Wherever possible, the system should be designed so that the actions it induces participants to take in accordance with their perceived self-interest are actions that also are in the

---

[6]In a classic work, David McClelland argues that there is a relationship between the strength of the achievement need of the leaders of an organization and the success of that organization. See David McClelland, *The Achieving Society* (New York: Irvington Publishers, 1976).

[7]Texts on industrial psychology expand on these points at length. For two classic works, see Paul R. Lawrence and Jay W. Lorsch, *Organization and Environment* (Homewood, IL: Richard D. Irwin, 1969); and B. F. Skinner, *Beyond Freedom and Dignity* (New York: Appleton-Century-Crofts, 1971).

[8]Reported in "Hospitals Adopt New Strategy to Keep Top Executives," *Journal of Accountancy,* March 1988, pp. 14–17.

best interests of the organization. That is, the incentives inherent in the management control system should encourage goal congruence. If this condition exists, a decision that a manager regards as sound from a personal viewpoint also will be a sound decision for the organization as a whole.[9]

Perfect congruence between individual and organizational goals does not, and cannot, exist. For example, many individuals want as much compensation as they can get, whereas from the organization's viewpoint there is an upper limit to salaries. As a minimum, however, the management control system should not encourage individuals to act against the best interests of the organization.

Example

An organization has a goal of low-cost, high-quality services, but its management control system rewards managers exclusively for reducing costs. If some managers decrease costs by reducing the quality of service, there is an absence of goal congruence.

Given these sorts of difficulties, senior management must ask two separate questions when evaluating its management control system: (1) What action does it motivate people to take in their own perceived self-interest? (2) Is this action in the best interest of the organization?

Cooperation and Conflict

Generally, the lines connecting the boxes on an organization chart imply that organizational decisions are made in a hierarchical fashion. Senior management makes a decision, this decision is communicated down through the organizational hierarchy, and operating managers at lower levels proceed to implement it. Clearly, this military model is not the way most organizations actually function.

Operating managers react to an instruction from senior management in accordance with their perception of how it affects their personal needs. Additionally, interactions between managers affect what actually happens. For example, the manager of the maintenance department may be responsible for maintenance work in other departments. Maintenance work in one operating department may be slighted, however, if there is friction between the maintenance manager and the operating manager. Also, actions that a manager takes to achieve personal goals may adversely affect other managers. Managers may argue about which departments should get the use of limited computer capacity or other scarce resources. For these and many other reasons, conflict exists within organizations.

Clearly, an organization will not achieve its objectives unless managers work together with some degree of harmony. Thus, there also must be cooperation in an organization.

---

[9]For the classical elaboration of this idea, see Douglas McGregor. *The Human Side of Enterprise* (New York: McGraw-Hill, 1960).

Example

One response by Australian public services departments to increasing cost constraints was to create profit centers. Maintenance, information processing, telecommunications, and printing began charging consuming organizational units for their services. Some concern was expressed that the behavioral impact of this change would be to emphasize competition and negate cooperation and team building.[10]

Senior management must maintain an appropriate balance between the forces that create conflict and those that create cooperation. Some conflict is both inevitable and even desirable. It results from the competition between participants for promotion or other forms of need satisfaction; within limits, such competition is usually healthy. Conflict also arises because different members of an organization see the world differently, and believe that different actions are in the organization's best interests.

Example

Conflict arises in museums over the most suitable exhibits, in school systems over the most desirable courses, and in hospitals over the most appropriate treatment patterns for patients. To a certain extent, this sort of conflict is beneficial in that it frequently brings out the best in an organization's members. Thus, if undue emphasis is placed on fostering a cooperative attitude, the most able managers and professionals may be denied the opportunity to use their talents fully. Somehow, senior management must seek to foster the right balance.[11]

The Bureaucracy

There are many comments to the effect that in government organizations and in certain other large nonprofit organizations effective management control is inhibited by the existence of the *bureaucracy*. Bureaucracy is often used as a label for any organization that operates by complicated rules and routines, or that is characterized by delays and buck-passing, or that treats its clients impolitely. In particular, government organizations are labeled as bureaucracies with the implication that nongovernmental organizations are not bureaucracies.

In fact, any large and complex organization is necessarily a bureaucracy. The classic analysis of bureaucracy is that of Max Weber.[12] Weber described a bureaucratic organization as one in which the chief executive's authority was derived by law or through election by an authorized body, rather than by tradition or charisma. Subordinates are responsible to the chief executive through a clearly defined hierarchy and are selected on the basis of their

---

[10]Patricia Evans and Sheila Bellamy, "Performance Evaluation in the Australian Public Sector," *International Journal of Public Sector Management* 8, no. 6 (1995).

[11]For further discussion on conflict and its benefits, see Lawrence and Lorsch, *Organization and Environment.*

[12]Max Weber, *The Theory of Social and Economic Organization* (1922). See the English translation by A. M. Henderson and Talcott Parsons (New York: Oxford University Press, 1947).

technical competence, rather than by election; they are promoted according to seniority or achievement, or both; and they are subject to systematic discipline and control.

In the Weberian bureaucracy, complex problems are solved by segmenting them into a series of simpler ones, and delegating authority for solving each of the segments to specialized subunits. The subunits consist of experts who are equipped to solve problems in their area of expertise. Such technical superiority, based on increased specialization, is supposed to lead to objective and impersonal decision making at the subunit level. Weber noted that an individual who applied personal subjective values to policy or decision making could seriously lessen the effectiveness of the organization. A bureaucracy avoids this possibility by replacing the subjective judgment of individuals with routinized work tasks and by a set of rules, values and attitudes, or goals, which are approved by the individual's superior.[13]

Bureaucracy is essential in an organization where several different units perform the same function. Each office of the Internal Revenue Service (IRS) is supposed to give the same advice to a taxpayer. There would be no way of coming close to that goal without a comprehensive set of rules and regulations used by all offices.

Role of the Controller

In most organizations, the controller is the person responsible for the operation of the management control system. The controller department is a staff unit. Its responsibility is similar to that of a telephone company: it assures that messages flow through the system clearly, accurately, and promptly. It is not responsible for the content of these messages, however, or for the way managers act on them.

The controller ordinarily works with senior management to design the management control system in such a way that goal congruence is maximized. Most of this effort is associated with designing the responsibility center structure and the transfer pricing arrangements along the lines discussed earlier in the chapter. The controller also works with senior management to design the phases of the management control process, as discussed in Chapters 9 through 15. Because of the major impact that design choices can have on managers' and professionals' behavior, senior management should be extensively involved in these choices. In many organizations, senior management completely delegates these choices to the controller, which is a mistake since the controller typically does not have a sufficiently broad perspective of the organization and its goals.

---

[13]For an argument that just the opposite takes place in a bureaucracy, see Michel Crozier, *The Bureaucratic Phenomenon* (Chicago: The University of Chicago Press, 1964).

Cultural Factors

Every organization has its own culture—a climate, an atmosphere, a feeling for which attitudes are encouraged and which are discouraged. Cultural norms are derived in part from tradition, in part from external influences, such as its unions and the norms of society, and in part from the attitude of the organization's senior management and directors. Cultural norms help to explain why each of two entities may have an adequate management control system but why one has much better actual control than the other.

Cultural norms are almost never written down, and attempts to do so almost always result in platitudes. Instead, norms are transmitted partly by hiring practices and training programs. They also are conveyed by managers, professionals, and other organization members using words, deeds, and body language to indicate that some types of actions are acceptable and others are not.

Management Attitude

Perhaps the aspect of culture that has the most important impact on management control is the attitude of a manager's superior toward control. In a well-managed organization, the chief executive officer sets the tone. He or she may express this attitude in a number of ways. If performance reports typically disappear into the executive suite and no response is forthcoming, line managers soon perceive that these reports are not important. Conversely, if a report is discussed at length with a manager, there is a signal that the report is important. Conversations of this sort convey senior management's expectations about performance as powerfully as the formal budget docs.

Other Aspects of Culture

The control climate also is affected by the attitudes of a manager's peers and by staff units. The culture within a responsibility center is also important. The organization may have ways of reacting to stimuli which in some cases reflect long tradition.

Example

Despite the prestige and power of the office, a cabinet officer in the federal government may find it impossible to create the desired control climate no matter how hard he or she tries. Usually, the bureaucracy has firmly accepted certain behavioral norms and has found ways to perpetuate them. There is little that a political appointee can do in the short tenure he or she has with the organization.

Finally, the culture in the *external* environment affects the control climate within the organization. Some attitudes appear to be industrywide. For example, when times are tough, people tend to take the control process more seriously than when the economy is booming. In many nonprofit settings, the cultural norms of a professional group (e.g., physicians, nurses, social workers, artists, musicians) will have a major influence on the culture of the organization itself.

Summary

One of the most difficult aspects of designing a management control system is defining the system's structure—its network of responsibility centers. In determining what sort of responsibility center a given manager's unit will be, senior management needs to pay careful attention to the resources the manager can control. This is the driving force behind responsibility center design.

Beyond this, senior management needs to consider ways to attain goal congruence between the personal goals of each responsibility center manager and the goals of the organization as a whole. In part, a responsibility center manager's goals are determined by the incentives that senior management creates to reward certain forms of behavior. One of the major aspects of this incentive system is the organization's transfer prices, and senior management must be careful to establish the transfer pricing structure in such a way that it promotes behavior on the part of individual managers that is supportive of the organization's overall goals.

Beyond these considerations, senior management also must pay close attention to the fit between programs and responsibility centers. Programs represent the operational definition of an organization's strategy, and can be broken into program categories, subcategories, and elements. Each aspect of a program must be assigned to a responsibility center, and the management control system must be designed in such a way that it can provide information on both program and responsibility center activities. This calls for a careful design of the account structure, a task that ordinarily is carried out by the accounting staff but needs considerable guidance from senior management. Otherwise, there is a danger that the accounts will not be structured in managerially useful ways, or will be inconsistent across formats.

Senior management must constantly bear in mind that management control is fundamentally behavioral. The various control tools are effective only to the extent they influence behavior, and they will influence behavior only to the extent that the culture of the organization is conducive to their doing so. A delicate balance must be struck between cooperation and conflict so that individuals—both managers and professionals—work together toward the attainment of organizational goals and yet are able to have legitimate and healthy conflicts over the best ways to attain them.

Suggested Additional Readings

Anthony, Robert N., and Vijay Govindarajan. *Management Control Systems.* Chicago, IL: McGraw-Hill, 1998.

Cyert, R. M., and J. G. March. *A Behavioral Theory of the Firm.* Englewood Cliffs, NJ: Prentice Hall, 1963.

Lawrence, Paul R., and Jay W. Lorsch. *Organization and Environment.* Homewood, IL: Richard D. Irwin, 1969.

McGregor, Douglas. *The Human Side of Enterprise.* New York: McGraw-Hill, 1960.

Merchant, Kenneth A. *Control in Business Organizations.* Aulander, NC: Pittman Publishing, 1985.

Simon, Herbert A. *The New Science of Management Decision.* Englewood Cliffs, NJ: Prentice Hall, 1960.

Simons, Robert. *Levers of Control.* Boston, MA: Harvard Business School Press, 1995.

Practice Case

Valley Hospital*

> First they tell me that I'm a profit center, which seems to be a good idea. Then they tell me to run the department as though it were a little business, which I like. Then they tell me that I have to buy lab tests at prices much greater than what I would have to pay to Biolab, despite the fact that Biolab can give me equally fast turnaround time and equal quality. Now what do I do?

Phyllis Martin, MD, Director of the Ambulatory Care Division of Valley Hospital, had received both good and bad news. The good news, which came several months ago, was that her division, along with most other divisions in the hospital, had been reorganized into a profit center. Each profit center had been given responsibility for its own bottom line, and profit center managers and their key staff members were to be paid annual bonuses based on the surplus (or profit) of their units. The bad news was that Dr. Martin had just been told that she had to purchase all of her laboratory tests from the Laboratory Division, another profit center. She continued:

> Here's a good example. We charge our patients $11.00 for a urinalysis, which typically is required in conjunction with a diagnostic workup. The $11.00 charge covers the time spent by nurses in my division assisting the patient, the processing of paperwork by our administrative staff, the supplies needed for the urinalysis, and the time spent by our nurse, PA [physician's assistant], or physician reporting the results to the patient. However, we don't have the capability to do the actual lab work needed to analyze the patient's urine. This I must "purchase" from somewhere else. I've been using the hospital's Lab Division, but I now find out that its price is totally unreasonable.

The Laboratory Division charged all of the hospital's divisions $6.00 for an analysis. According to Joseph Goodman, the manager of the laboratory:

*This case was prepared by Professor David W. Young. Copyright © by David W. Young.

> My price for a urinalysis is very reasonable. It is based on our variable costs of $2.00, which is mainly supplies and labor, plus $3.00 of our fixed costs, and only $1.00 of profit, which is a fair amount.

Dr. Martin's concern arose because her staff had found that they could purchase analyses of comparable quality for $4.50 each from Biolab, a free-standing laboratory located nearby. She knew that, by doing so, she could improve her division's surplus considerably.

The conflict had reached the office of Sam Black, the hospital's Chief Financial Officer. According to him:

> They keep talking about what's fair and what's not fair. A fair is a summer event with cows and baked goods! We have a hospital to run. If we let Phyllis buy her lab tests from Biolab, then we have to let all our profit centers buy from Biolab. What happens to our own lab at that point? All it does are the really expensive tests that the labs-in-a-box can't or won't do. Can you imagine what would happen to our cost per test at that point, not to mention our vulnerability in the marketplace. Biolab could hold us up and we'd have no recourse. You can't have a hospital without a lab, and you can't have a lab doing only the esoteric stuff.

Although Dr. Martin was sympathetic to both Mr. Black's and Mr. Goodman's point of view, she also felt quite strongly that there had to be a better solution to the problem.

> I understand where Joe's coming from. He runs a profit center, too, and he and his staff get a bonus based on his department's bottom line. But his bonus shouldn't be at my division's expense. Each time we purchase an analysis, our profits decline by $1.50 from what they otherwise would be, and, along with that, our bonuses fall too.

Mr. Black knew that the conflict would not dissipate without some intervention from his office. He wondered what he should do, and what the implications of his decision would be for other departments in the hospital, such as radiology, that also were profit centers.

Questions

1. Complete the following table showing each profit center's financial performance under the two options shown.

	Amb Care Division	Laboratory Division	Hospital Overall
Option 1—Buy from Hospital Lab Division			
Revenue			
Variable costs			
Contribution			
Option 2— Buy from Biolab			
Revenue			
Variable cost			
Contribution			

2. What problems, if any, are illustrated by your computations? Please be as specific as you can.

3. What should Mr. Black do about the conflict between Dr. Martin and Mr. Goodman over the price of an analysis? What should he do about the prices for other lab tests and other procedures (such as *x*-rays)?

CASE 8–1

Franklin Health Associates (A)*

> We've worked through a lot of problems and I've made some changes in the organization. We're at a juncture now, and we need to think ahead. I'm concerned about whether we can shift to a more progressive and less reactive posture.

The speaker was Paul Johnson, executive director of Franklin Health Associates (FHA). Located in Farmington, Maine, FHA had been undergoing a period of rapid growth, and Mr. Johnson wondered whether the organization's existing management structure and systems were appropriate to meet its needs in the future.

Background

FHA was established in 1971 in the midst of a "hospital war" between two groups in West Central Maine. After each applied separately for Hill-Burton money and was rejected, the two groups were compelled to cooperate and compromise on the hospital's Farmington site.

At about the same time, four physicians practicing out of one of the hospitals began an affiliation with the Community Action Program, funded by the Federal Office of Economic Opportunity. They documented the need for improvement in the geographical and financial access to health care for the 30,000 residents who lived in the 27 rural townships in the nearby mountainous and heavily forested areas. FHA was set up to help fill this need, and was awarded a two-year federal grant. For the next two decades, the organization thrived in an environment of cost-based reimbursement and generous federal support for its outreach programs.

Mr. Johnson became executive director of FHA five years ago. At that time, according to him,

> . . . the organization had no logical or deliberate planning. It was separated into the three divisions of Franklin Group Practice [FGP], Franklin Area Health Plan [FAHP], and Research and Development [R&D]. The separation had occurred as a reactive stance, however. The corporation had grown unwieldy and there was infighting over the budget and public image.

*This case was prepared by Margaret B. Reber under the supervision of Professor David W. Young. It subsequently was revised by David W. Young. Copyright © by David W. Young.

Organizational Goals and Structure

FHA was chartered to develop a group practice, a prepaid health plan and minibus transportation system for the poor, and a research program. Its goals included:

1. The areawide delivery of comprehensive primary medical care with continuity and a strong preventive emphasis.

2. The recruitment of only board-certified or board-eligible physicians.

3. Peer review and audit, especially in the outpatient setting.

4. The necessity for and support of continuing education of its providers.

5. The teaching of predoctoral and postdoctoral health professions students.

6. Research and demonstration projects in clinical areas, health services delivery, health education, and nutrition.

In addition to Mr. Johnson, FHA's key staff included Ron McMahon, controller, Dave Donnelly, MD, medical director, and Jack Barber, FGP's business manager. Mr. Johnson also served as director of FAHP and R&D. In addition, there was an executive committee composed of three elected providers.

FHA had a 15-member board of directors, with eight consumers and seven providers. The board had a standing committee on goals and objectives, which Mr. Johnson had established when he became executive director. According to him:

> The committee has met off and on over the past few years, and we have another meeting next week. We need to start thinking ahead and plot where the need is going to be. For example, at the time we started FHA, there were 13 physicians in the region. Six of them are still here, but now the total is 24, 12 of whom practice at FHA. They are all young and about the same age. In fact, at age 51, I'm the oldest member of this organization. If we don't phase the MDs, they'll all be retiring at about the same time and we'll have a shortage all over again.
>
> Very few of the MDs are native "Maineiacs." There are many people who want to leave Boston and other big cities. Last week we had a husband-and-wife team from Cleveland who were interested in moving up here. Physicians get tired of the routine office work and the isolation and overload of solo practice. Some want to get away from being the 24-hour-per-day country doctor. They want to share records and coverage, and get professional stimulation.
>
> The physicians also seek challenges, and are attracted by our R&D activities and FAHP alternative delivery project. For example, I encouraged one of our physicians, who was bored with day-to-day activities, to submit a grant. Now he has funding to examine early intervention with emotionally disturbed kids. Motivation for some physicians is money; for others it's free time. In terms of quality, we don't take a back seat. In no rural setting will you find more talent. The MDs have been very well trained and are all board certified.

Franklin Group Practice

FGP was a group practice that provided medical, optometry, and dental services to about 60 percent of the people living in the service area. Its services were provided through five departments: Family Practice/Pediatrics, Internal Medicine, Surgery, Dentistry, and Optometry. There were three internal medicine specialists, three family practitioners, one pediatrician, one otolaryngologist, a general surgeon, an orthopedic surgeon, two dentists, and one optometrist. In addition, there were two physician assistants, one nurse practitioner, one dental hygienist, and one optometric assistant. An organizational chart is contained in Exhibit 1. Mr. Johnson commented:

> There are no formal or informal department heads because we are trying to maintain an overall group identity. Ideally, however, I'd like to see FGP expanded to 15 physician providers. We need two more family practitioners, who would help spread our costs over a broader base and also provide more personal care. In addition, we could have more flexible scheduling and provide better weekend coverage.
>
> Every time a new physician joins the group we have a publicity release. We take the opportunity to reiterate the hours and types of services offered. In general, we have real problems with our marketing. We can't use an objective form of marketing; we have to have a more personal form. An advertisement in the newspaper would have an impact like a sledge hammer on the head. So we try to use indirect means, like cooperation with area agencies. For example, we have a blood pressure program for the Bass Shoe Company employees, and this week I'm speaking at the Rotary Club. The physicians also contribute to the marketing of the group practice through their professional relations with various individuals and organizations.

For several years, FGP had attempted to reach many patients through the use of three satellite clinics located in secluded sections of Maine's western mountains. However, the clinics were never able to break even financially. In two cases, physicians practiced at the satellite clinic just long enough to build up a practice and then they left. As a result, only one satellite was left, located in Rangeley.

Franklin Area Health Plan

FAHP was an individual practice association (IPA) health maintenance organization, designated as a foundation. It provided comprehensive, prepaid health care to 2,700 poverty-income level and 500 commercial residents in the area. Ninety percent of each low-income enrollee's premium was paid by the state of Maine through a managed care initiative in its Medicaid program. Mr. Johnson reflected on the difficulty of marketing to the commercial segment of the market:

> FAHP had done well, so we decided to market it to local employers. Initially, all 24 physicians in the area were members of FAHP, 10 of whom were also practicing in FGP, but when we decided to market FAHP to companies on a prepayment basis,

EXHIBIT 1 Organizational Structure

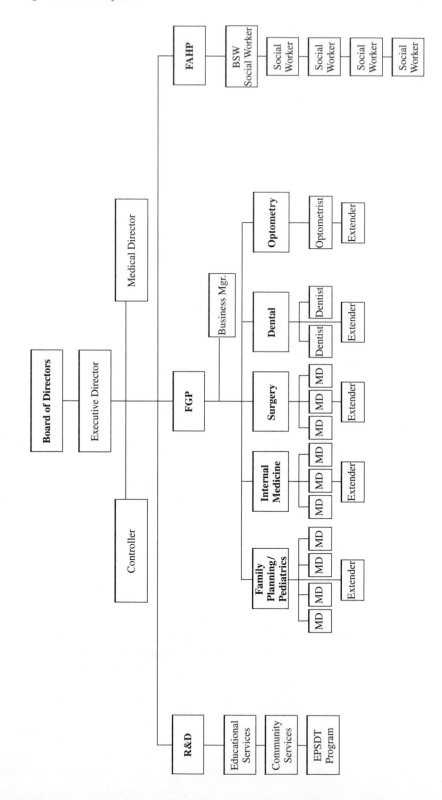

all but two of the physicians outside of FGP got out of it. They weren't willing to accept a change in philosophy from fee-for-service to prepayment. Before this, the plan was a means of getting paid for services rendered to the poor; people who couldn't otherwise pay. But the physicians weren't willing to be at risk for people who would pay anyway through the fee-for-service system.

FAHP had four full-time social workers who reported to a social worker with a Bachelor of Social Work degree. They worked with three social workers from the Community Action Program, and ran a house insulation program, a food stamp distribution program, and a parenting program. Mr. Johnson saw them as more than just providers, however:

> In general, they do a lot of outreach for FHA. People don't understand how to use the system. They won't use the facilities until they're at death's door. Attitudes are slowly changing as new people move into the area who are used to sophisticated medical systems. It takes time for patients to adjust to the less personal setup we have after being treated by an MD in a boarded-up back porch in the boondocks. To some patients we are considered the "General Electric" of health care.

Twenty percent of FHA's physician encounters were with prepaid patients from FAHP, which, in Mr. Johnson's view, wasn't enough:

> Eventually, I'd like to see 40 to 50 percent of the patients enrolled on a prepaid basis. This would help out on our seasonality problem. In the winter we have heavy usage of the facilities, whereas, in the summer, usage is the lightest. Our costs are fixed, but our fee-for-service revenues fluctuate. If more of our patients were prepaid, we could reduce our cash flow problems.
>
> I don't think there is a conflict of interest between FAHP incentives to encourage physicians to underutilize services and the FGP fee-for-service incentives to increase utilization. The physicians see the same patients over and over again so there is continuity of care. They wouldn't treat the FAHP patients differently from the fee-for-service patients just because of the patients' payment mechanism. The patients receive equal quality of care. I want FAHP and FGP to operate side by side to provide patients with a prepaid alternative to more expensive health care and a traditional fee-for-service mode where it is more appropriate.

Research and Development

R&D had many different projects, which fell into three main categories: educational services, community services, and the Early Periodic Screening and Diagnostic Treatment (EPSDT) Program. The division also did some pure research, such as testing blood pressure medicine for drug companies. The projects operated independently with each project director reporting to Mr. Johnson.

R&D supported patient education projects in areas such as blood pressure, diabetes, nutrition, and obesity. The goal was for the division to provide the financial support for these preventative health activities through grant money until such time as they were self-sufficient. Mr. Johnson commented:

> I can't conceptualize the group without the R&D component. It is a must for serving the needs of the community, for providing expanded services, and for

developing alternative delivery systems. For example, FAHP needs more patient education, and eventually we'd like to build some patient education services into the prepaid premium. We also have a pediatrician in FGP who is active in a school health program sponsored by R&D.

Additionally, EPSDT is a federally funded program for Medicaid youngsters. Unlike most of our other R&D programs, the grant pays for some overhead costs, so it eases up the financial load for R&D. The community services program provides services to employees of local industries. We have tried to keep the full-time coordinator, a half-time secretary, and several part-time nurses. It has become known as the West Central Maine Health Services, and it is financially self-sufficient. I'm considering make it a fourth division. You see, we use R&D as a means to develop programs. If they fail to develop beyond the dependency stage, we disband the program. When they become self-sufficient we try to incorporate them into another division or perhaps set them up as a separate division.

Reporting Relationships

FGP had an active medical staff, governed by an executive committee that met for lunch on Mondays and Thursdays to discuss problems that affected quality of care and physician well-being. In Mr. Johnson's view:

Unfortunately, the committee often turns out to be a discussion group, and won't arrive at decisions unless an administrator is present to provide information and act as facilitator. Even so, the physicians must have a voice in the running of the organization and a sense of control over their destiny. The administration meets with them at their beck and call.

Recently we hired Jack Barber as business manager of the group practice. He has an undergraduate degree in history with a Master's in Human Relations and 21 years in the Navy Medical Administration. Until we hired Jack, I spent 75 percent of my time in the day-to-day operation of the group practice; now it's more like 25 percent. In a setting like this, Jack doesn't have line authority. He doesn't run things; he sees that things are run.

In this regard, we adhere to the "every tub on its own bottom" philosophy for each division. So far the triadic structure has worked well. The organizational skeleton is just right. The major weakness in the system is working with the physicians. It's like a college president working with the faculty. Professionals have to have a voice in running the organization.

As executive director, I try to maintain a team with which I have rapport. I need to be kept informed. I do a lot of internal management, but about 50 percent of my job involves politics. For example, I'm beginning to develop a program with the elderly, which means negotiating a contract with Medicaid.

Budgetary Process

The budgetary process differed for each division. In R&D each project director submitted a proposed budget to Mr. Johnson showing the expected revenues and expenses for the coming year. He reviewed the budget and then met individually with each project director to firm up the figures. In FAHP, the financial director, Mr. McMahon, and Mr. Johnson developed a budget jointly. In FGP, Mr. Barber and Mr. McMahon developed the budget and then discussed it with Mr. Johnson. In all cases the final figures were examined and approved by a committee of five board members, Mr. Barber, Mr. McMahon, and Mr. Johnson. Mr. Barber commented:

> FGP is our main problem area; this is where we've had such a large discrepancy between budgeted and actual, and where we've incurred considerable deficits in the last few years in growing proportions [see Exhibit 2]. Until now, when a nursing supervisor wanted to know if she could buy a piece of equipment, she would just call up Ron and he'd tell her if there was enough money available to make the purchase. Now, we're at the point where we need a more efficient system. Here's how the process works right now:
>
> Our fiscal year runs from July to June, and we start the budgetary process in May. Ron McMahon, the FHA controller, provides me with revenue totals for the year to date. Unfortunately, the time lag for our computer information is from 30 to 45 days, so March is the most up-to-date revenue report available. The report provides us with a summary of actual revenues generated by each practitioner, including the three RN/PAs.
>
> Using the March report, we extrapolate the revenue for the three remaining months of the fiscal year. This then provides us with a baseline figure for each physician. We then make modifications to this expected revenue according to anticipated changes in physician productivity, patient volume increases, and price changes in various categories. We consider each physician separately. For example, one of our family practitioners recently came down with Hodgkins' disease, and an internist had a nervous breakdown. Obviously, the expected productivity of these providers must be modified for the new fiscal year.
>
> Last year, we factored in a 10 percent increase in volume. But what we've actually experienced was a 2 percent decrease. I'd really like to examine the trends for the area. Everybody tells me the population is going up, but some demographic information would be helpful in determining expected volume increases.
>
> If we are planning on a 5 percent charge increase for office visits, then we must adjust the expected revenue for each physician separately. For example, a charge increase in office visits will affect a family practitioner more drastically than it will a general surgeon. We use a detailed Revenue Analysis Report, which indicates the revenue generated by each physician in various charge categories.
>
> We show these figures to each individual physician and he or she tells us whether or not we're on target. For example, an MD might say, "I think that's a little high." Then I might remind the physician that he's supposed to be available for office calls, a minimum of 20 hours per week. So, we compromise and adjust the revenue accordingly.
>
> Then we aggregate the revenue for the providers and subtract 10 percent of the total to account for uncollectibles, which include bad debts and third-party disallowances. This amount is divided by 12 to get the monthly expected revenue.

Physician Compensation

Until the current fiscal year, 45 percent of projected revenue had been allocated to cover the salaries of the 13 providers, meaning that a predetermined

EXHIBIT 2 Statement of Operations and Comparisons for Franklin Group Practice

	Last Year Month May	This Year Month May	Last Year YTD May	This Year YTD May	This Year Prorated Budget
Generation:					
Medical	$219,882	$201,588	$2,115,078	$2,314,468	$2,887,634
Dental	29,022	37,370	280,862	327,388	390,272
Optometry	20,370	29,968	245,886	284,122	350,984
Pharmacy	6,436	5,556	66,014	71,898	86,828
Laboratory	22,862	24,084	205,016	234,792	269,612
X-ray	16,664	14,088	170,218	161,292	210,630
Total	$315,236	$312,654	$3,083,074	$3,393,960	$4,195,960
Grants	5,646	4,078	68,598	49,862	60,000
Other income	(58)	(16)	27,206	2,128	—
Total operating support	$320,824	$316,716	$3,178,878	$3,445,950	$4,255,960
Less uncollectibles:					
Provision for bad debts	$ 8,862	$ 8,804	$ 87,326	$ 95,928	—
Cash discount	2,946	2,734	26,266	31,004	—
Courtesy and employee					
discount	390	428	26,002	5,092	—
Disallowed charges	19,770	25,756	208,250	262,972	—
Total uncollectibles	$ 31,968	$ 37,722	$ 347,844	$ 394,996	$ 425,596
Total operating revenue	$288,856	$278,994	$2,831,034	$3,050,954	$3,830,364
Operating expenses:					
Medical	$150,448	$133,932	$1,517,492	$1,674,976	$2,044,504
Dental	17,502	19,372	203,688	234,268	267,518
Optometry	23,706	30,682	210,982	249,942	243,522
Pharmacy	5,468	6,110	61,412	73,716	76,000
Laboratory	9,020	8,594	99,832	113,008	121,200
X-ray	7,748	10,706	107,986	112,164	129,600
Medical records	3,112	3,470	37,784	38,098	43,400
Facilities	23,774	22,700	265,646	263,024	313,120
Administration	35,800	43,168	397,810	470,502	580,500
Total operating expense	$276,578	$278,734	$2,902,632	$3,229,698	$3,819,364
Interest	2,000	1,492	15,186	11,146	8,000
Total operating expense					
including interest	$278,578	$280,226	$2,917,818	$3,240,844	$3,827,364
Excess of revenue over expenses					
(expenses over revenue)	$ 10,278	$ (1,232)	$ (86,784)	$ (189,890)	$ 3,000

*Note: the fiscal year was from July to June.

amount was set aside for physician payment regardless of revenue actually generated. That practice was changed this fiscal year. As of July, the reimbursement allotment became 48 percent of the *previous year's* revenue. Out of this amount 40 percent was allocated equally to each physician for a base salary, 15 percent was distributed on the basis of the physician's contribution to the total number of encounters, 40 percent on the basis of his or her contribution to the total dollars generated, and 5 percent on the basis of the number of years he or she had been a member of FGP. Mr. Barber commented:

> Changing the payment mechanism was an unpopular move. It took us four months to resolve the issue. There is a difference between managing professionals versus nonprofessionals. For every hour that I spend with a physician, I spend 12 to 15 hours in hard work documenting the case. When I showed them the figures for expenses and revenues, they were more willing to accept it.
>
> At first all of the providers wanted to take a $2,000 pay cut. However, Paul and I just wouldn't accept this, as it wouldn't have provided a long-lasting solution, and then we would have been on the defensive. So, we provided several different formula options to the physicians to consider.
>
> Fortunately, there was an economically minded MD with a high regard for the dollar who realized what was happening. He pointed out that the higher generators were bringing in a higher percentage of what was put on the books. Essentially, they were subsidizing the low generators. Under his influence, the physicians adopted the present payment mechanism.
>
> It was rough, though, because for some of them it meant a salary cut. Some were so overpaid that it was a shock. There was a lot of turmoil. One of the physicians decided to leave, as she thought she could do better by herself.

The PA/NP salaries, as well as coverage of administrative and overhead costs, came out of the 52 percent remaining after physician compensation. The PA/NPs were each assigned to a preceptor, and Mr. Barber kept track of each one's encounters and generations separately, just as he did for the physicians. Bob Underwood, for example, worked fairly independently in Family Practice and saw many of his own patients. Maria Hennesy worked in Internal Medicine and was primarily a physician extender. She helped the physician with new patients, did initial screenings, preoperative and postoperative visits, and also visited the nursing home patients. Pat Nurse was a nurse practitioner who worked with the general surgeon doing preop and postop work. In addition, she worked with cancer patients and gave lectures to females on breast cancer. She was popular with teenage girls for physicals and family planning services. Mr. Barber pointed out that this created a problem for him:

> I guess she's straightforward, but she charges lower rates than expected. I don't know if it is right or wrong, but it causes me a problem. If the PA/NPs don't generate as much as their salary, we lose money. I spoke to a physician who worked with one of the NPs about the low generation and he said, "She's worth her weight in gold. If you get rid of my NP, you'll get rid of me." But, he isn't willing to pay her out of his salary, or even out of the physician's pot. So, I compromised in this area for now.

The remainder of the expenses were budgeted by using the previous year's actual amounts and giving each section (Medical, Dental, Optometry, Pharmacy, Laboratory, X-ray, Medical Records, Facilities, and Administration) some target amounts.

FHA's overhead costs, by contrast, were allocated to each division somewhat arbitrarily. For example, in the previous fiscal year, FGP was assigned

50 percent of all facility and administrative costs. Recently, Mr. Barber had gone through the Medical Arts Building floor plan and had calculated some figures of exclusive use areas for FGP, FAHP, R&D, and EPSDT. He figured out the exclusive and common use areas for the Surgical, Internal Medicine, Family Practice, Dental, and Optometry sections, as well as for individual physicians so that he would be better able to allocate costs on a square-foot basis.

Performance Review

Mr. Barber also had developed a monthly report on revenue generation, which he gave to each provider. It showed total office charges for each physician for the month, the average price charged per patient, the actual number of hours spent, and the average number of patients seen per hour. He compared these figures with what was possible, and showed the physician the difference between his or her potential and actual revenue for the month. He commented:

> This has really helped out. When I first started giving the physicians this report in November, I would sit down and discuss the figures with them individually. Now they know how to use them, and I just send out the reports.
>
> In general, the physicians have responded well. In fact, a few have come to my office for suggestions on ways to improve generation. One physician in particular has been very receptive to my suggestions. He was taking several unnecessary breaks during his daily schedule. When the breaks were cut out, his productivity increased drastically.

The physicians also had their own quality of care report in which Mr. Barber was not involved. At the end of each month, a patient's name was randomly picked from each of the doctor's schedules and the chart was pulled. Each doctor was assigned a chart (other than his or her own) to review. Upon completion of review, the audit was sent to the provider for his or her perusal. If there were any discrepancies, the auditor and the provider might get together to discuss them. Eventually all of the audit forms were analyzed by one person (a physician) and any problems or trends were brought up at the monthly medical staff meeting.

Questions

1. What is the strategy of FHA? Be explicit, focusing on programs, markets, personnel policies, and financing mechanisms in particular.

2. Using the organizational structure of FHA, and making assumptions where necessary, determine what kinds of responsibility centers there are at each level. Are they appropriate according to the criteria for the design of responsibility centers? Why or why not?

3. What is your assessment of the management control process at FHA? How, if at all, would you change it?

4. What should Mr. Johnson do?

Case 8–2

Piedmont University*

When Hugh Scott was inaugurated as the 12th president of Piedmont University in 1994, the university was experiencing a financial crisis. For several years enrollments had been declining and costs had been increasing. The resulting deficit had been made up by using the principal of quasi-endowment funds. (For true endowment funds, only the income could be used for operating purposes; the principal legally could not be used. Quasi-endowment funds had been accumulated out of earlier years' surpluses with the intention that only the income on these funds would be used for operating purposes; however, there was no legal prohibition on the use of the principal.) The quasi-endowment funds were nearly exhausted.

Scott immediately instituted measures to turn the financial situation around. He raised tuition, froze faculty and staff hirings, and curtailed operating costs. Although he had come from another university and was therefore viewed with some skepticism by the Piedmont faculty, Scott was a persuasive person, and the faculty and trustees generally agreed with his actions. In the year ended June 30, 1996, there was a small operating surplus.

In 1996, Scott was approached by Neil Malcolm, a Piedmont alumnus and partner of a local management consulting firm, who volunteered to examine the situation and make recommendations for permanent measures to maintain the university's financial health. Scott accepted this offer.

Malcolm worked about half time at Piedmont for the next several months and had many conversations with Scott, other administrative officers, and trustees. Early in 1997 he submitted his report. It recommended increased recruiting and fund-raising activities, but its most important and controversial recommendation was that the university be reorganized into a set of profit centers.

At that time the principal means of financial control was an annual expenditure budget submitted by the deans of each of the schools and the administrative heads of support departments. After discussion with the president and financial vice president, and usually with minor modifications, these budgets were approved. There was a general understanding that each school would live within the faculty size and salary numbers in its approved budget, but not much stress was placed on adhering to the other items.

*This case was prepared by Professor Robert N. Anthony. Copyright © by Robert N. Anthony.

EXHIBIT 1
Rough Estimates of
1996 Impact of the
Proposals ($ millions)

Profit Center	Revenue	Expenditures
Undergraduate liberal arts school.	$30.0	$29.2
Graduate liberal arts school	5.6	11.5
Business school	15.3	12.3
Engineering school	17.0	17.3
Law school	6.7	6.5
Theological school.	1.2	3.4
Unallocated revenue*	5.0	
Total, academic	80.8	80.2
Other		
Central administration	10.1	10.1
Athletic	2.6	2.6
Computer	3.4	3.4
Central maintenance	5.7	5.7
Library.	3.4	3.4

*Unrestricted gifts and endowment revenue, to be allocated by the president.

Malcolm proposed that in the future the deans and other administrators would submit budgets covering both the revenues and the expenditures for their activities. The proposal also involved some shift in responsibilities and new procedures for crediting revenues to the profit centers that earned them and charging expenditures to the profit centers responsible for them. He made rough estimates of the resulting revenues and expenditures of each profit center using 1996 numbers; these are given in Exhibit 1.

A series of discussions about the proposal were held in the University Council, which consisted of the president, academic deans, provost, and financial vice president. Although there was support for the general idea, there was disagreement on some of the specifics, as described below.

Central Administrative Costs

Currently, no universitywide administrative costs were charged to individual schools. The proposal was that these costs would be allocated to profit centers in proportion to the relative costs of each. The graduate school deans regarded this as unfair. Many costs incurred by the administration were in fact closely related to the undergraduate school. Furthermore, they did not like the idea of being held responsible for an allocated cost that they could not control.

Gifts and Endowment

The revenue from annual gifts would be reduced by the cost of fund-raising activities. The net amount of annual gifts plus endowment income (except gifts and income from endowment designated for a specified school) would be allocated by the president, according to his decision as to the needs of each school, subject to the approval of the Board of Trustees. The deans thought this was giving the president too much authority. They did not have a specific alternative, but thought that some way of reducing the president's discretionary powers should be developed.

Athletics

Piedmont's athletic teams did not generate enough revenue to cover the cost of operating the athletic department. The proposal was to make this department self-sufficient by charging fees to students who participated in intramural sports or who used the swimming pool, tennis courts, gymnasium, and other facilities as individuals. There was strong opposition, however; some felt that this would involve student dissatisfaction, as well as much new paperwork.

Maintenance

Each school had a maintenance department that was responsible for housekeeping in its section of the campus and for minor maintenance jobs. Sizable jobs were performed at the school's request by a central maintenance department. The proposal was that in future the central maintenance department would charge schools and other profit centers for the work they did at the actual cost of this work, including both direct and overhead costs. The dean of the business school said that this would be acceptable provided that profit centers were authorized to have maintenance work done by an outside contractor if its price was lower than that charged by the maintenance department. Malcolm explained that he had discussed this possibility with the head of maintenance, who opposed it on the grounds that outside contractors could not be held accountable for the high-quality standards that Piedmont required.

Computer

Currently, the principal mainframe computers and related equipment were located in and supervised by the engineering school. Students and faculty members could use them as they wished, subject to an informal check by people in the computer rooms on overuse. About one-quarter of the capacity of these computers was used for administrative work. A few departmental mainframe computers and hundreds of microcomputers and word processors were located throughout the university, but there was no central record of how many there were.

The proposal was that each user of the engineering school computers would be charged a fee based on usage. The fee would recover the full cost of the equipment, including overhead. Each school would be responsible for regulating the amount of cost that could be incurred by its faculty and students so that the total cost did not exceed the approved item in the school's budget. (The computers had software that easily attributed the cost to each user.) Several deans objected to this plan. They pointed out that neither students nor faculty understood the potential value of computers and that they wanted to encourage computer usage as a significant part of the educational and research experience. A charge would have the opposite effect, they maintained.

Library

The university library was the main repository of books and other material, and there were small libraries in each of the schools. The proposal was that each student and faculty member who used the university library would be charged a fee, either on an annual basis, or on some basis related to the time spent in the library or the number of books withdrawn. (The library had a secure entrance at which a guard was stationed, so a record of who used it could be obtained without too much difficulty.) There was some dissatisfaction with the amount of paperwork that such a plan would require, but it was not regarded as being as important as some of the other items.

Cross Registration

Currently, students enrolled at one school could take courses at another school without charge. The proposal was that the school at which a course was taken would be reimbursed by the school in which the student was enrolled. The amount charged would be the total semester tuition of the school at which the course was taken, divided by the number of courses that a student normally would take in a semester, with adjustments for variations in credit hours.

Questions

1. How should each of the issues described above be resolved?

2. Do you see other problems with the introduction of profit centers? If so, how would you deal with them?

3. What are the alternatives to a profit center approach?

4. Assuming that most of the issues could be resolved to your satisfaction, would you recommend that the profit center idea be adopted, rather than an alternative?

Case 8–3

New York City Sanitation Department*

The Bureau of Motor Equipment of the New York City Sanitation Department had about 1,200 employees and an operating budget of about $38 million. It was responsible for maintaining the department's 5,000 vehicles. It operated 75 repair garages located throughout the city and one major central repair facility.

According to a report of the New York State Financial Control Board, conditions in the Bureau of Motor Equipment in 1978 were chaotic. Over half the vehicles it was responsible for servicing were out of service on the average day, resulting in huge amounts of overtime pay for the personnel assigned to the remaining vehicles. Mr. Ronald Contino was placed in charge of the bureau in late 1978. Within two years, the bureau was supplying 100 percent of the primary vehicles needed every day. Mr. Contino estimated that $16.5 million of costs had been avoided during that period.

Mr. Contino attributed the change to two main factors: (1) a change in labor/management relations, and (2) the creation of "profit centers" as a substitute for work standards in the central repair facility.

Mr. Contino set up labor/management committees, each consisting of shop supervisors, trade people, and a shop steward. Their mandate was to investigate ways to solve problems, to improve the quality of work life, and to increase productivity. A committee was formed in each of the eight principal departments, called shops, in the central repair facility. (This case focuses only on the central repair facility.) The committees met monthly with the manager of the central repair facility.

In 1978 the central repair facility operated under negotiated work standards that covered practically every job, from rebuilding an engine to fixing a generator. Committee members were concerned that if suggestions for improving productivity were made and implemented, management would subsequently adjust the work standards upward.

After a number of discussions, the following plan was adopted: Management would no longer be interested in work standards as applied to specific jobs and individuals; individual records of time spent on jobs would no longer be required. Instead, management would be interested only in whether the shop as a whole was producing at an acceptable level. The "value" of output would be measured by what it would cost to purchase the same items or services from outside vendors, and the total value of output for a period would be compared with the total cost of operating the shop.

The output values were determined by checking outside price lists or by obtaining price quotes for specific jobs. If the electric shop repaired an

---

*This case was prepared by Professor Robert N. Anthony. Copyright © by the President and Fellows of Harvard College. Harvard Business School Case 9-184-039.

EXHIBIT 1 Profit Center Status for 1981

Profit Center	Number of Weeks Operation from Inception to End of 1981	Annualized ($000)			
		Input	Output	Profit	Productivity Factor*
Transmission.	37	$ 350	$ 716	$ 366	2.05
Unit repair	40	1,280	2,146	866	1.68
Upholstery	35	126	183	57	1.45
Radiator	36	263	438	175	1.67
Machine.	23	643	1,562	919	2.43
Passenger cars	30	494	534	40	1.08
Electric.	37	603	717	114	1.19
Motor room	43	1,272	822	(451)	.65
Total		$5,031	$7,117	$2,086	1.41

*Output ÷ Input

alternator, for example, the shop would receive a credit equal to what it would cost to buy a rebuilt alternator from a private supplier. The input costs included labor costs (salary, fringe benefits, sick pay, vacations, and jury duty), material costs, depreciation of machinery, and other overhead costs. The difference between output values and cost was called "profit," and the eight shops were therefore called profit centers.

According to Mr. Contino, the "profit center" work measurement system had a significant impact on production:

> This system provides a mechanism which measures productivity without threatening the individual worker . . . and labor has responded enthusiastically to this concept. . . . In addition, employees in individual shops can now see how well they are doing compared to the private sector (each shop has a large chart in a visible location) and a degree of competitiveness has developed, further spurring their desire to increase efficiency. The combination of the "profit motive" and the elimination of threats has worked like magic.

As evidence of progress, Mr. Contino referred to the table in Exhibit 1. He also had data showing that productivity and profits had improved with the passage of time.

As shown in Exhibit 1, all profit centers except the motor room reported a profit in 1981. The situation in the motor room illustrated the difficulty of measuring output. Initially, the shop's credit for rebuilt engines was the same as the cost to buy new motors because reliable data on the price of rebuilt motors was not available. The first reports showed that productivity was less than 1.0, meaning that the city could have purchased new engines for less than it spent rebuilding engines. As a result of decisions made by the shop's labor/management committee, the motor room subsequently doubled its productivity and appeared to be producing at a substantial "profit." However, once a data base of the outside price of rebuilt engines had been developed, all the shop's past reports were converted to the rebuilt values, the reports then showed that the shop was operating at a "loss." This led the labor/management committee to take further steps to increase productivity, including the discontinuation of unprofitable products and the transfer of personnel from support functions to line functions. By March 1982, the motor room's productivity factor hit 1.19.

The relatively low productivity in the passenger car shop had a different cause. The problem was that shop employees were required to list the actual time it took to do each job on a "job sheet," and they feared that if they consistently beat readily available industry-wide standards, sooner or later management would either require more work from individuals or would track each individual's daily performance. Thus, they tended to omit certain jobs done from their daily work sheet.

After the low productivity became apparent, meetings between the labor/management committee and the entire shop's workforce were held, and it was agreed that it would no longer be necessary for employees to list the actual time it took to do a job. The February 1982 report for the shop showed the results: productivity moved from 1.05 to 1.30.

Mr. Contino summarized his impressions of the results of the program as follows:

> I have found that the process of getting labor involved in the running of an operation is not only exciting and rewarding, but also extremely worthwhile in terms of improving productivity and service quality. BME's experience belies the common notions that the government worker cannot be productive or that the output of a government operation cannot be measured. There is no simple formula for succeeding in the change from a traditional approach to the labor/management approach, and there should be no doubt that management's commitment to the process is a critical factor. But given the effort and the true desire to see it succeed, it does work. The simple proof is what has been achieved by BME in operating in this fashion.

Questions

1. What are the strengths and weaknesses of the profit measure developed for the central repair facility? Should its use be continued? Can you suggest possibilities for improving it?

2. Records on performance by individuals or on costs for individual jobs were discontinued. Do you agree with this policy?

3. Under what circumstances, if any, should work be contracted out to the vendors whose price lists were used in measuring output?

4. The 75 garages operated by the bureau did minor repairs and maintenance. Because of the specialized nature of the department's vehicles (e.g., street cleaning trucks, solid waste collection trucks), it was estimated that output

values were available for only 20 to 30 percent of their work. Could some variation of the profit center idea nevertheless be applied to these garages?

5. Assume that adequate measures of value eventually can be developed for the 75 garages. Therefore, should the work they do be charged to the responsibility centers that own the vehicles? If so, should the charge be the output value of this work, or should it be the cost?

Case 8–4

White Hills Children's Museum*

"I'm outraged," said Jan Sweeney, director of the Urban Life Program of White Hills Children's Museum. "A few weeks ago, I asked the design and engineering (D&E) department for a bid to build the Central Artery Exhibit of my Cities and Streets project. The D&E bid was $7,000 more than a bid I got from a local construction firm, yet Mike [the museum's director] is encouraging me to use D&E anyway."

Background

White Hills Children's Museum was a medium-sized nonprofit museum located in northern California, just outside San Francisco. Its charter stipulated that it was to orient its activities and exhibits toward the environment, and it had been enormously successful in attracting a wide following of regular visitors. The museum also enjoyed a national reputation, and attracted a sizable number of visitors who were vacationing in northern California.

Recently, under the leadership of a new director, the museum had been organized into profit centers, and Ms. Sweeney's program had been designated as one of the programmatic profit centers. As such, she was encouraged, but not required, to "purchase" all design and construction services for her program from the museum's design and engineering department, a service profit center. Both managers—as well as all other profit center managers—had the possibility of earning annual bonuses based upon the profits of their profit centers.

The services of the D&E department ranged from the construction of relatively simple display cases to the design and manufacture of rather complex exhibits. Some of the recent exhibits the D&E department had developed included a miniature waterfall and an artificial windstorm.

Because of the complexity of the demands made upon it, and the resulting need for a wide variety of technical skills, the D&E department needed a rather large staff. Since the museum was too small to fully utilize its staff, however,

---

*This case was prepared by Professor David W. Young. Copyright © by David W. Young.

the department also sold its services to other organizations, including several smaller museums located within a radius of about a hundred miles from White Hills. At the moment, because it was a slow period for most museums, the department's staff was not fully utilized. This was not an unusual situation.

The Central Artery Exhibit

In planning her Cities and Streets project, Ms. Sweeney knew that she would need to have several exhibits designed and built to rather exacting specifications. One of these was the Central Artery exhibit, a large-scale illustration of the environmental impact of placing an expressway underground. Her plans called for four phases of construction, showing how the environment would be affected by each phase. The exhibits would need to be large enough to allow children to explore them from the inside, thereby allowing them to experience as well as learn about the impact of a project of this sort.

Data

Because the exhibit was a large one, Ms. Sweeney had asked John Harp, the director of the D&E department, to assist her in putting together the design and engineering specifications. The two had spent several days discussing the exhibit's objectives and constraints, and Mr. Harp had prepared some architectural and engineering drawings. At that point, Ms. Sweeney had asked him for an estimate of the cost, and, after a few days of gathering the necessary information, he had provided her with a figure of $27,000. His calculations are shown in Exhibit 1.

Shocked at the amount, Ms. Sweeney had called Mr. Harp to complain. At his suggestion, she had taken the drawings to a local construction firm and asked them for a bid. Using the drawings plus the design and engineering specifications prepared by Mr. Harp, the local firm had given Ms. Sweeney a bid of $20,000. The firm had indicated that this figure was all-inclusive and was firm; that is, it included all supplies, materials, labor, and profit, and Ms. Sweeney would be charged a flat $20,000 regardless of the actual costs the firm incurred in constructing the exhibit.

The Decision

When he heard of the situation, Mike Sampson, the museum's new director immediately had called the two managers into his office, and asked for an explanation. Mr. Harp was the first to speak:

> I simply can't do the job for less. I've been working for several months now to establish a fair pricing structure, not only for people inside the museum but for my external customers. This is the price I would use for our neighboring museums,

EXHIBIT 1
Budget Information
Prepared by the
Design and
Engineering
Department

Central Artery Project:
Materials . . . . $ 7,000
Direct labor (1).   10,000
Variable overhead (2)   2,000
Fixed overhead (3)   5,000
Total costs $24,000
Markup   3,000
Total bid. $27,000

Notes:
 1. Carpenters, plumbers, electricians, painters, and
gofers. All currently are on staff; that is, no one would be
hired especially for this project.
 2. Miscellaneous cleaning solvents, sandpaper, and other
minor materials that will not be purchased specifically for
this project but that would not be used without the project.
Also includes the cost of supervision.
 3. Allocated portion of the cost of the department head,
administrative assistant, and secretary, as well as several
other administrative costs, such as the rent charged the
department by the museum's central administration.

and it's the one I feel I should use for Jan as well. Besides, I spent all that time
helping her design the project and preparing the drawings—that must be worth
something.

Ms. Sweeney responded:

When I was in school, we were taught that the transfer price should be the market
price. I think I've pretty well established what the market price is, and I should not
be asked to pay any more than that. If I did, my profit would fall, and you've been
asking us to worry about our bottom lines. This $7,000 difference would make a
big difference at the end of the year, particularly in terms of my bonus.

Mr. Sampson's main concern at this point was with the overall surplus of
the museum. It was clear that if Ms. Sweeney used the local construction firm
to build her exhibit, the cost to her department would be less; but he felt quite
certain that the impact on the museum's surplus would be worse than if she
used Mr. Harp's department. He was not sure if he should intervene in the decision or not, and if he did, what his intervention should be.

Questions

1. What is the impact on the museum's surplus of each of the two options?

2. Should Mr. Sampson intervene in this decision? Why or why not?

3. If Mr. Sampson intervenes, what should he do? Please be specific: For example, should he tell Ms. Sweeney to purchase the work for the exhibit
   from Mr. Harp? If so, at what price?

4. If Mr. Sampson does not intervene, what do you think will happen? Is this good or bad for the museum in the short term? In the long term?

5. What other advice would you give Mr. Sampson? Ms. Sweeney? Mr. Harp?

Case 8–5

National Youth Association*

"If I were to price this conference any lower than $480 a participant," said James Brunner, manager of National Youth Association's Housing Division, "I'd be countermanding my order of last month for our marketing organization to stop shaving their bids and to bid full-cost quotations. I've been trying for weeks to improve the quality of our business, and, if I turn around now and accept this at $430 or $450 or something less than $480, I'll be tearing down this program I've been working so hard to build up. The division can't very well accomplish its objective by putting in bids that don't even cover a fair share of overhead costs, let alone give us a safety margin."

National Youth Association (NYA) was an organization with several hundred local chapters. It provided support for these chapters, published a magazine and books, held a national convention, and arranged a number of conferences. At the national headquarters were several divisions. Among them was the Conference Division, which developed and managed a number of professional development conferences for members. Another was the Housing Division, headed by Mr. Brunner, which operated a conference center in the headquarters city; its facilities were used both by NYA and by other organizations. A third was the Produce Division, which operated a cattle, poultry and produce farm, located outside the headquarters city. This property had been willed to NYA many years ago.

For several years, each division had been judged independently. The financial objective of each was to provide a margin above its costs; this margin was intended to help finance headquarters activities and to provide a cushion against unforeseen contingencies. Senior management had been working to gain effective results from a policy of decentralizing responsibility and authority for all decisions except those relating to overall association policy. The association's senior officials believed that in the past few years the concept of decentralization had been successfully applied and that the association's financial position had definitely improved.

The Conference Division had developed a three-day conference that it planned to offer several times a year. Mr. Brunner had spent many hours with the Conference Division in working on these plans.

*This case was adapted with permission from case 158-001 prepared by Wiliam Rotch under the supervision of Neil Harlan, Harvard Business School. Copyright © by the President and Fellows of Harvard College. Harvard Business School Case 9-193-152.

When all the plans were completed, the Conference Division asked for bids from the Housing Division and from two outside companies. Each division manager was normally free to buy from whatever supplier he wished; and, even on sales within the company, divisions were expected to meet the going market price if they wanted the business.

During this period, the profit margins of hotels and other conference facilities were being squeezed. Because NYA did not run conferences steadily throughout the year, many of Housing's sales were made to outside customers. If Housing got the order from the Conference Division, it probably would buy much of its raw food from the NYA Produce Division. About 70 percent of Housing's out-of-pocket cost of $400 for the conference represented the cost of raw food purchased from the Produce Division. Though the Produce Division had excess capacity, it quoted the market price, which had not noticeably weakened as a result of the oversupply. Its out-of-pocket costs were about 60 percent of the selling price.

The Conference Division received bids of $480 a participant from the Housing Division, $430 a participant from Magnolia Hotel, and $432 a participant from Golden Eagle Hotel. Golden Eagle offered to buy from the Produce Division raw food at a price equivalent to $90 a participant.

Since this situation appeared to be a little unusual, William Kenton, manager of the Conference Division, discussed the wide discrepancy of bids with NYA's executive director. He told the executive director: "We sell in a very competitive market, where higher costs cannot be passed on. How can we be expected to show a decent margin if we have to buy our accommodations at more than 10 percent over the going market?"

Knowing that Mr. Brunner had on occasion in the past few months been unable to operate the Housing Division at capacity, it seemed odd to the vice president that Mr. Brunner would add the full 20 percent overhead and margin to his out-of-pocket costs. When asked about this, Mr. Brunner's answer was the statement that appears at the beginning of the case. He went on to say that having helped in the planning for the conference, and having received no reimbursement for his time spent on that, he felt entitled to a good markup on the use of his facilities.

The executive director explored further the cost structures of the various divisions. He remembered a comment that the controller had made at a meeting the week before to the effect that costs which were variable for one division could be largely fixed for the company as a whole. He knew that in the absence of specific orders from senior management Mr. Kenton would accept the lowest bid, which was that of Magnolia Hotel for $430. However, it would be possible for senior management to order the acceptance of another bid if the situation warranted such action. And though the volume represented by the transactions in question was less than 5 percent of the volume of any of the divisions involved, other transactions could conceivably raise similar problems later.

Questions

1. Which bid should the Conference Division accept that is in the best interests of National Youth Organization?

2. Should Mr. Kenton accept this bid? Why or why not?

3. Should the NYA executive director take any action?

4. In the controversy described, how, if at all, is the transfer price system dysfunctional? Does this problem call for some change, or changes, in NYA's transfer pricing policy? If so, what specific changes do you suggest?

9

Strategic Planning and Program Analysis

In Chapter 8 we described the management control environment. We turn now to a description of the management control process. The first step in this process, called *strategic planning,* is described in this chapter. In Chapters 10 through 15 we describe the other steps: budgeting, operating, measuring output, reporting, and evaluating performance.

In the first section of this chapter, we distinguish strategic planning from strategy formulation and budgeting. We also distinguish among goals, objectives, and programs.

We then discuss the participants in the programming process, as well as several different strategic planning activities, including the development and analysis of proposed new programs. We conclude with a discussion of the techniques of program analysis.

Nature of Strategic Planning

Strategic planning is the activity that gives rise to new programs. A program is a planned course of action that involves the commitment of a significant amount of resources, large enough to warrant the attention of senior management. Presumably, the adoption of a program will have a major effect on the activities of the organization, and may even shift its strategic focus. Also, implementation of a new program usually requires several years, and the program's impact often is not apparent until some time after it has been initiated.

Strategic Planning and Budgeting

Many organizations do not make an explicit, formal distinction between strategic planning and budgeting, frequently combining the two. Since the two activities are conceptually different, however, it is useful to think about these differences even if no formal distinction is made.

Both strategic planning and budgeting involve planning, but the types of planning activities are quite different. Budgeting typically focuses on a single year, whereas strategic planning focuses on activities that extend over a period of several years. A budget is, in a sense, a one-year slice of the organization's programs, although, for reasons we will discuss in Chapter 10, this is not a complete description of a budget. Also, a budget usually is structured in terms of responsibility centers, while many programs cut across the responsibility center structure.

The budget represents a commitment by responsibility center managers to attain some specific financial and programmatic results. A program is not such a firm commitment; rather, it is an estimate or best guess as to what will happen financially over a period of several years. The numbers for the first year of the program should be close to those of the budget. In the later years, the numbers state what is likely to happen if current policies are unchanged.

Strategic Planning and Strategy Formulation

In Chapter 1 we drew a line between two management activities: strategy formulation and management control. Strategic planning, although part of management control, is close to this dividing line. While some authors use the term *long-range planning* to encompass both strategy formulation and strategic planning, we believe it is important to distinguish between them.

In the strategy formulation process, management decides on the goals of the organization and the main strategies for achieving them. The strategic planning process takes these goals and strategies as givens, and seeks to identify programs that will facilitate their implementation. In practice, there is a considerable amount of overlap. For example, studies made during the strategic planning process may indicate the desirability of changing goals or strategies. Conversely, strategy formulation often includes some consideration of the programs that will be adopted to help achieve organizational goals and strategies.

Goals, Objectives, and Programs

The nature of programs becomes clearer if they are distinguished from goals and objectives.

Goals

A goal is a statement of intended output in the broadest terms. It normally is not related to a specific time period. Goals ordinarily are not quantified, and hence cannot be used directly as a basis for a measurement system. A statement of goals has essentially two purposes: (1) to communicate senior management's aims and relative priorities, and (2) to draw rough boundaries around the areas within which senior management has decided the organization will operate.

Although thinking about goals and attempting to express them in words is often a useful exercise, it can become frustrating beyond a certain point, and not worth additional effort. For example, if a hospital has decided that it wants to be a general hospital, there may be no need to reduce to words an exact statement of the goals of a general hospital. Similarly, although many faculty committees have spent long hours attempting to find words that state the goals of a liberal arts college, the results sometimes are so vague that they have little operational impact. Nevertheless, particularly in large organizations, a clearly articulated set of goals is a prerequisite to effective strategic planning by middle-level managers.

Objectives

An objective is a specific result to be achieved in a specific time, usually one year or a few years.[1] A statement of objectives is a key element in the management control system in a nonprofit organization because an organization's effectiveness can be measured only if actual output is related to objectives.

Where feasible, an objective should be stated in measurable terms. Otherwise, performance toward achieving it cannot be evaluated with any precision. If a particular objective cannot be stated in measurable terms, management should consider modifying the objective so that it can be. Otherwise, senior management will have difficulty judging whether it has been achieved.

Example	With some effort, it is often feasible to state objectives in a measurable way. The following quotation is a vague objective for third-grade instruction in geography:

> To learn to use the vocabulary, tools, skills, and insights of the geographer in interpreting and understanding the earth and our relation to it.[2]

This objective becomes more useful if it is recast as follows:

> That 90 percent of the third-grade students attending the Booth Elementary School, by next June 30 will score between 90 and 100 percent, and the remaining 10 percent will score between 80 and 90 percent on a wide evaluative instrument and/or process which measures their ability:

---

[1] Some writers use *goal* for the idea that is here described as *objective,* and vice versa. Care must be taken to determine the intended meaning from the context.
[2] From Larry Pauline, Education Systems Consultants.

a. To understand why we have maps and why they are important.

b. To understand the importance of the globe being marked with horizontal and vertical lines which represent degrees of longitude and latitude, and that the earth consists of hemispheres, continents, and oceans.[3]

Exhibit 9–1 shows a set of goals and objectives for a church. Note that although the objectives are not stated in quantitative terms, some quantitative measures are implied. Also, the statement shows the date by which each objective is to be attained.

By contrast, consider the following:

Example

A statement of objectives from the City of Long Beach Department of Community Development reads as follows:

- Completion of the City's Community Analysis Program and development of a schedule of programs to prevent and correct blighted areas as well as predisposing and precipitating factors.

- Expansion of the federally approved low-income housing program for additional housing units.

These objectives are not stated in measurable terms, nor are the dates given by which they are supposed to be accomplished. They thus are of little help in the management control process.

EXHIBIT 9–1 Programs and Objectives, Fairfield Baptist Church, Chicago, Illinois (excerpts)

Program Goals

1. To Proclaim the Gospel to All People
   Objectives:
   a. To establish a church evangelism committee by April 15.
   b. To contact every person within the city limits (for whom we can find record) who ever attended a church function, but no longer does, with a personal visit from this church by May 1.
   c. To contact every home in our immediate census tracts by May 1.
   d. To adopt a comprehensive churchwide missionary education program by September 1.
2. To Promote Worship
   Objectives:
   a. To establish a church worship committee by April 15.
   b. To implement systemic membership participation in the church worship services by May 8.
   c. To involve all institutionalized (elderly and otherwise) members in regular church worship by June 1.

* * * * *

Source: Contributed by Dennis W. Bakke (private correspondence).

[3]Ibid.

Linking Goals, Objectives, and Programs

If program proposals are to be analyzed properly, they need to be considered in light of the objectives and goals they are designed to support. Exhibit 9–2 contains an example of these relationships. While the objectives are not specified as clearly as they might be, senior management nevertheless can see the relationship between each objective and its supporting programs. Having information of this sort, along with the approximate level of resources required to carry out each program's activities, allows senior management to make trade-offs among various program proposals. Also, program proposals related to a particular objective can be assessed in light of the existing programs designed to accomplish that objective.

Participants in the Strategic Planning Process

Five participants typically are involved in the strategic planning process: (1) the advocate, the person who wants a proposed program (or change) adopted; (2) the analyst, the person who analyzes the merits of the proposal; (3) senior management, who decides on the adoption of the proposal; (4) resource providers, who must be sold on the merits of the proposal before they will provide funds for its execution; and (5) the controller, who operates the strategic planning system. The program analyst, who usually is a member of the planning staff, is a key player. Indeed, an organization that must make many decisions about programs usually has a staff of program analysts to facilitate this

EXHIBIT 9–2   **Excerpts from a Typical Narcotics Program**

Program goals:
1.0 Reduce the abuse of narcotics and dangerous drugs in the United States.
1.1 Reduce the supply of illicit drugs.
     1.1.1 Reduce the amount of legally manufactured drugs available for abuse.
     1.1.2 Reduce domestic supply of illicit drugs.
     1.1.3 Reduce foreign supply of illicit drugs introduced into the United States.
1.2 Reduce demand for illegal use of drugs.
1.3 Expand understanding of the problem.
1.4 Improve program management and administrative support.
Operating program objectives (for Goal 1.1.3):
          1.1.3.1 Reduce smuggling into United States at ports and borders.
          1.1.3.2 Reduce foreign cultivation, production, and trafficking.
Operating program activities (for Objective 1.1.3.1):
               1.1.3.1.1 Conduct investigations of smuggling.
               1.1.3.1.2 Arrest smugglers and conspirators and seize smuggled drugs.
               1.1.3.1.3 Support prosecutions.
               1.1.3.1.4 Identify international border points vulnerable to smuggling and
                       strengthen them.
               1.1.3.1.5 Inspect carriers, cargo, persons, baggage, and mail.
               1.1.3.1.6 Develop and operate a program of mutual exchange of intelligence.

process. We refer to the program analysts as the planning staff, but other common names are programming staff, program office, or systems analysis office. The planning staff should be close to the top of the organizational hierarchy; that is, it should report directly to either the chief executive officer (CEO) or another senior manager.

If the planning staff reports to the controller, there is a danger that it will become too heavily involved in the budget preparation process, which is also the controller's responsibility. The budget preparation process necessarily has a short-range focus and is often carried out under considerable time pressure. Involving the planning staff too heavily in budgeting, or allowing the "budgeteers" in the controller organization too much influence over the strategic planning process, can stifle the long-range view that is essential to good strategic planning. Thus, if the planning staff is housed in the controller organization, it should be kept separate from the part of that organization that is involved in budget preparation.

If an appropriate separation between strategic planning and budgeting can be achieved, there may be good reasons for having the planning staff in the controller organization. This arrangement can reduce the number of staff units reporting to senior management, increase the likelihood that planners will have easy access to financial data, and possibly even out the workload in the controller organization (since the planning staff tends to be most heavily involved in strategic planning for only a few months of the year, and can assist with other controller activities during the rest of the year).

In organizations where the idea of formal strategic planning is relatively new, there may be friction between the planning staff and the operating organization, especially program advocates. The planning staff may consist of young, technically oriented, bright, but inexperienced persons who tend to be unaware of, or to minimize the importance of, the rules of the bureaucratic game. They may underestimate the value of experience and the importance of the pressures of day-to-day operations. They also tend to use jargon that is unfamiliar to operating managers. To these managers, the planning staff may represent a challenge or even a threat to the established way of doing things.

To minimize the dysfunctional effect of such conflicts, senior management may build the planning staff gradually, starting with a small group and increasing it only as it develops credibility, and as resistance from operating managers subsides. Where feasible, senior management may also try to draw some members of the initial planning staff from the existing organization.

The planning staff must never forget that it is a staff, not a line, unit; that is, it does not make decisions itself. Because of its importance in linking strategy formulation to strategic planning, however, it needs to spend considerable time communicating with line managers. It must explain its approaches to analysis and attempt to establish good working relationships. The planning staff also must gain and maintain the firm support of senior management. Line managers must perceive that the strategic planning effort is a permanent part of the management control process, not a trial or a fad. This message can only be communicated by senior management.

Role of the Controller

Whether or not the planning staff is part of the controller organization, the controller's office, as the office responsible for all information flows, should be responsible for the flow of strategic planning information. If there is a formal strategic planning system, the controller's office should oversee its operation; that is, it should set up procedures governing the flow of information through the system, and it should assure that these procedures are adhered to. In some agencies, the planning staff operates the strategic planning system, but this often leads to an unnecessary duplication of data and to a lack of coordination and consistency between strategic planning data and other data.

Process for Considering a Proposed New Program

In some organizations, the process for considering a proposed new program is quite informal; in others, there are formal procedures. In either case, essentially six steps take place: (1) initiation, (2) screening, (3) technical analysis, (4) political analysis, (5) decision, and (6) selling.

Initiation

The idea for a new program may come from anywhere—from any level—within the organization, or it may come from people outside the organization. To encourage the internal generation of ideas, senior management needs to emphasize that new ideas are welcome, and it must provide a clear mechanism for bringing them to the attention of the planning staff.

Generally, an idea becomes part of the strategic planning process only after it has attracted the favorable attention of an influential person within the organization. In many instances this is the manager of a mission or service center, who then becomes the program advocate. The program advocate may do considerable work personally in developing the idea, or he or she may submit it in rough form to the planning staff for development. Planning staffs and members of senior management also may be program advocates.

Screening

From the many ideas that come to its attention, the planning staff selects the few that seem to be worth detailed analysis. Ideas proposed by senior management are obviously in this category, unless the planning staff can demonstrate clearly that they are unsound. Ideas proposed by resource providers generally are also worth detailed analysis since funding for the endeavor is probable.

An important criterion in the screening process is whether the proposal is consistent with the goals of the organization. In their natural desire to grow or to obtain funding for their overhead costs, some organizations pursue ideas that are unrelated to their goals.

Example

Although the goal of the Port Authority of New York and New Jersey is to facilitate the movement of people and goods in metropolitan New York, it sponsored the construction of two huge office buildings in a crowded section of Manhattan. The buildings' purpose was to generate revenue for the Port Authority. Unfortunately, movement of people to and from these buildings exacerbated the city's transportation problem.

Similarly, a university that attempts to cover its overhead costs by developing research proposals for projects outside its area of competence, or by undertaking new programmatic efforts that are only marginally related to its goals, is making a screening mistake. Such projects are quite likely to be unsuccessful and thereby not only waste scarce resources but also potentially damage the institution's credibility and its ability to raise funds in the future.

The goals of the organization need to be specific if the screening process is to be effective. Without specific goals, program advocates may spend a considerable amount of time promoting new programmatic endeavors that subsequently are rejected.

Example

The stated goal of the United Nations International Children's Emergency Fund (UNICEF) is to help children in developing nations. However, there are at least 100 such nations and well over a billion children in them, with a wide variety of needs. A narrower focus is essential if program advocates are to promote programmatic ideas designed to move the organization ahead in a consistent way.

The Program Proposal

At some time in the early stages of the process, a formal program proposal is prepared. This happens after the program advocate has "tested the water" sufficiently to be assured that reducing the proposal to writing is worthwhile.

The proposal describes *what* is to be done, but ordinarily it does not contain details on *how* it is to be done. These details are the responsibility of operating management, and typically are worked out after the proposal has been approved. The program proposal should include:

1. A description of the proposed program, and evidence that it will accomplish the organization's objectives.

2. An estimate of the resources to be devoted to the program over the next several years, divided between investment costs and operating costs. Since this estimate only shows the *approximate* magnitude of the effort, the costs usually are rough amounts. Detailed cost analysis ordinarily is deferred until after the program has been approved in principle.

3. The benefits expected from the program over the same time period, expressed quantitatively if possible. One purpose of quantifying the benefits is to permit subsequent comparison of actual results with planned results.

4. A discussion of the risks and uncertainties associated with the program.

The purpose of a program proposal is to aid the decision maker. Because of this, the analysis it contains should be as thorough and objective as possible. A program proposal is quite different from a proposal designed to sell a project. This "sales" proposal is prepared after the strategic planning decision has been made. Examples of sales proposals include most environmental and economic impact statements.

Taking Account of Inflation

The monetary amounts in a program proposal can be based either on the assumption that prices will not change or on the assumption of a specified amount of inflation. Either basis will work as long as all parties understand it and act consistently. If the program proposal assumes no inflation, changes in monetary amounts reflect purely physical magnitudes, thereby facilitating calculations and making the program proposal easier to understand and evaluate. If estimates of inflation are incorporated, readers may have difficulty separating physical from inflationary changes.

On the other hand, inflation is a fact, and it may be unrealistic to disregard it. A program proposal that incorporates expected rates of inflation is particularly useful if there is good reason to believe that the several revenue and cost elements have different rates of inflation. An inflation assumption is especially important if high rates of inflation are likely to persist, or if there is a high rate of inflation in a particular sector of the economy related to the proposed program (e.g., health care technology).

Technical Analysis

Proposals that survive the initial screening process are analyzed by the planning staff. A technical analysis involves estimating the costs of a proposed program, attempting to quantify its benefits, and, if feasible, assessing alternative ways of carrying it out. The results of the technical analysis ordinarily are included in the program proposal. Techniques for carrying out technical analyses are discussed later in the chapter.

Political Analysis

The final decision on a proposed program involves political considerations (such as the predisposition of a member of Congress toward a certain policy, or the desirability of favoring a certain congressional district), as well as economic, social, and organizational considerations. Usually, the decision maker takes political considerations into account separately and subsequent to the technical analysis. The technical analysis is likely to be less lucid if it includes political considerations.

Political considerations properly are a part of some analyses, however. If, for example, several political solutions are proposed to a problem, an analysis might be able to show the lowest cost solution and the incremental cost of other solutions. The decision maker can use such an analysis as an aid in deciding whether the incremental political benefits of a higher cost solution outweigh the incremental costs.

Regardless of a proposal's technical merits, senior management may not be able to sell it to funders. Important considerations include political interference, postelection administration changes, priorities of control agencies, and demands of special interests.[4] Senior management frequently must make a difficult judgment call as to the salability of a program before developing the proposal and formally putting it forth. Much of the relationship between the president and the Congress reflects such judgment.

Decision and Selling

Following analysis, the proposal is submitted to senior management for decision; or, more frequently, tentative proposals are discussed with senior management and then sent back for further work. This process may be repeated several times, involving the program advocate and the analysts. The staff analysis may emphasize the technical aspects of the proposal, but the decision maker places considerable emphasis on the political aspects as well.

Most proposals are not submitted as "take-it-or-leave-it" propositions. Rather, they describe several alternative ways of accomplishing an objective, along with the merits and costs of each. Although the planning staff may not state formally a preference for one alternative, its views usually become clear in the discussion. At the same time, the program advocate ordinarily has a strong preference for one of the alternatives.

Since programs are important to an organization's strategy, and since they normally involve substantial resources, they usually must be sold to resource providers prior to implementation. In government organizations, resource providers are the Congress or corresponding legislative bodies at state and local levels. In other nonprofit organizations, they are the governing boards of the organization, clients, third-party payers, or outsiders who provide contributions and grants. This sales effort usually is carried out by senior management and the program advocate, often assisted by the planning staff.

Advocacy Proposals

The decision maker should consider the extent to which a proposal has been prepared by, or greatly influenced by, the program advocate. An advocacy proposal is essentially a document that is designed to sell the proposal to the decision maker, and may not contain a thorough, objective analysis. Most proposals initiated by operating managers are advocacy proposals; indeed, if the manager is not an enthusiastic supporter of the proposal, there is probably something wrong with it. Proposals initiated by a top-level planning staff presumably are more neutral, but even staff-generated proposals can incorporate an element of advocacy under certain circumstances.

[4]See Peter W. Colby and Eileen Bonner, "Managing for Productivity Improvement: Successes and Failures," *New York Case Studies in Public Management,* no. 12 (Binghamton, NY: State University of New York at Binghamton, November 1984).

Ideally, the natural tension between a program advocate and the planning staff should lead to an objective presentation of the program, but this is not always the case. In general, therefore, it is safe to assume that most proposals reflect someone's advocacy.

In this regard, a proposal may be biased in one of four ways:

1. Consequences are asserted without adequate substantiation. In a benefit/cost analysis, the proposal may estimate the program's cost and then plug in a *benefit* number, such that the resulting benefit-cost ratio looks good.

2. Technical matters beyond the comprehension of the decision maker are discussed at length. (This is one of several possible varieties of "snow jobs" that are attempted in proposals.)

3. Opposing views are omitted or not fully and accurately reported.

4. Costs and the time required to implement the proposal are underestimated.

Countering Biases

Decision makers attempt to allow for these biases and to minimize them by discouraging deliberate omissions or distortions, but they usually do not have either the knowledge or the time to detect all elements of bias embedded in a proposal. In reviewing proposals, therefore, they need ways to compensate for biases. As indicated above, the planning staff provides one important resource for this purpose. Subject to the qualification that a planning staff can develop its own biases, the staff exists to help the decision maker. In many circumstances, the staff works with the initiator of the proposal to remove unwarranted assumptions, errors in estimations or calculations, and other weaknesses before the proposal is submitted to the decision maker. The staff also may list questions for the decision maker to raise with the advocate that will shed light on the real merits of the proposal.

An outside consultant may be hired to make the same type of review. If the consultant has special expertise in the topic, his or her appraisal can be useful, but it may also be unnecessary. In many situations, the internal planning staff can do the same job as effectively. Nevertheless, a consulting firm may be used, since, by associating its prestige either for or against a proposal, it can either aid or hurt the proposal's chances for approval.

Adversarial Relationships

Another approach to the advocacy proposal is to establish an adversarial relationship. For every important proposal, there is some group that opposes it, if only because it diverts resources that the group would like to have for its own programs. If arrangements are made to identify an adversarial party and to provide for debate between it and the program advocate, the merits and weaknesses of the proposal often can be illuminated. The danger exists, however, that the adversaries will develop a "back-scratching" relationship. The presumed adversary may not argue forcefully against the proposal with the understanding, or at least the hope, that when the roles are reversed in connection with some other proposal, the other party will act with similar charity.

Making the Decision

For a variety of reasons, there is no such thing as a decision on an important proposal that is based entirely on rational, economic analysis. Instead, there is a continuum, with purely economic proposals at one extreme and purely social or political proposals at the other. Nevertheless, because resources are limited, and not all worthwhile proposals can be accepted, decisions must be made. The decision maker must determine which of the worthwhile proposals are in the best interests of the organization. Only in the rarest of occasions does a decision maker have the luxury to proceed with all desirable projects.

Example

In 1942, Dr. James Conant, the decision maker for the atomic bomb, was presented with five possible methods of producing fissionable material, each of which required enormous expenditures. He decided to proceed with all five. Two were abandoned a few months later, but the remaining three were actively pursued. There are few situations in which this luxury of adopting several competing alternatives is possible.[5]

Technical Analysis

As discussed above, technical analysis is a key step in the strategic planning process. There are two dimensions of technical analysis: (1) making estimates of those costs or benefits of proposed programs that can be stated in monetary terms, and comparing the costs with the benefits, and (2) making an overall judgment about the proposed programs, based on the idea that not all relevant costs and benefits can be expressed monetarily.

Benefit/Cost Analysis

The underlying concept of *benefit/cost analysis* is the obvious one—that a program should not be undertaken unless its benefits exceed its costs. The term *cost-effectiveness analysis* sometimes is used, incorrectly, as a synonym for benefit/cost analysis. One way to clarify the distinction between the two terms is to compare two proposals that offer approximately the same benefits. If one has lower costs, it is considered to be more cost-effective than the other.

Example

An economic analysis of education programs usually addresses two questions: (1) Does the monetary value of benefits produced by expenditures on education equal or exceed the cost of those expenditures? (2) Given their current budgets, are schools and other educational efforts producing as much learning as possible? The first question requires a benefit/cost analysis; the second a cost-effectiveness analysis.[6]

[5]See Stephane Groveff, *Manhattan Project* (Boston: Little, Brown, 1967).
[6]David Stern, "Efficiency in Human Services: The Case of Education," *Administration in Social Work* 15, no. 2 (1991), pp. 83–104.

Role of Benefit/Cost Analysis

The idea of comparing the benefits of a proposed course of action with its costs is not new. Certain government agencies, such as the Bureau of Reclamation, have made such analyses for decades; proposals to build new dams, for example, frequently were justified on the grounds that the benefits exceeded the costs. Nor are such comparisons unique to nonprofit organizations. Techniques for analyzing the profitability of proposed business investments involve essentially the same approach.

To assure useful results, decision makers relying on benefit/cost analyses should consider two essential points:

1. Benefit/cost analysis focuses on those consequences of a proposal that can be estimated in quantitative terms. Because there is no important problem where all relevant factors can be reduced to numbers, benefit/cost analysis will never provide the complete answer. Not everything can be quantified, and no one should expect a benefit/cost analysis to do so. Analyses that claim to have quantified everything are of dubious merit.

2. To the extent that managers, decision makers, or analysts can express some important factors in quantitative terms, they are better off doing so. This narrows the area where the decision maker must operate in the more judgment-based dimension of technical analysis. Thus, while the need for judgment is not eliminated, it can be reduced.

Looked at in this way, there are a variety of circumstances under which benefit/cost analysis is likely to be useful.

Example

The City of Edmonton, Alberta, decided to extend its light rail transit (LRT) system without undertaking a formal benefit/cost analysis. However, an analysis of the benefits and costs of LRT, incorporating data on population densities and air pollution, suggested that alternative transportation systems, such as express buses, were likely to achieve the city's public transit objectives at a lower cost. The authors of the benefit/cost analysis contended that the city had not produced any economic evidence that LRT was, in fact, the low-cost transit alternative. They recommended that the city's transportation program require detailed benefit/cost analyses of major transportation project proposals.[7]

In the remainder of this section, we discuss some of the factors to consider in the decision to employ benefit/cost analysis.

Clarifying Goals

The benefit in a benefit/cost analysis must be related to an organization's goals; there is no point in making a benefit/cost analysis unless all concerned

[7]John Kim and Douglas S. West, "The Edmonton LRT: An Appropriate Choice?" *Canadian Public Policy* 17, no. 2 (June 1991), pp. 173–82.

agree on these goals. That is, the purpose of benefit/cost analysis is to suggest the best alternative for reaching a goal. The formulation of goals is largely a judgmental process. Various members of management and various staff people may have different ideas of an organization's goals. Unless these groups reconcile their views, middle managers will find it difficult to formulate and implement programs to reach the goals.

It also is important to make sure that the goals are reasonable and achievable, or, stated somewhat differently, that the problem being presented is real, and that the program being proposed will help to alleviate it.

Example

In the late 1980s, locusts threatened the crops of many African nations. The U.S. Agency for International Development and other international aid agencies responded with $275 million and a fleet of aircraft that helped bomb crops with millions of liters of pesticides. A few years later, a report by the Office of Technology Assessment (OTA) said the campaign may have been a wasted effort, concluding that "massive insecticide spraying . . . tends to be inefficient in the short-term, ineffective in the medium term, and misses the roots of the problem in the longer term." The study also suggested that the entire operation may have been flawed because locusts aren't as big a threat as had been thought.[8]

Proposals Susceptible to Benefit/Cost Analysis

Benefit/cost analysis has two general principles: (1) management should not adopt a program unless its benefits exceed its costs; and (2) when there are two competing proposals, the one with the greater excess of benefits over costs is preferable.

Economic Proposals

For many proposals in nonprofit organizations, an analyst can estimate both benefits and costs in monetary terms. These economic proposals are similar to capital budgeting proposals in for-profit companies. A proposal to convert the heating plant of a high school from oil to coal involves the same type of analysis in either a for-profit or a nonprofit organization. Problems of this type are common in all organizations, and while important administratively, they frequently have little programmatic impact.

Alternative Ways of Reaching the Same Objective

Even if benefits cannot be quantified, a benefit/cost analysis is useful in situations where there is more than one way of achieving a given objective. If each alternative would achieve the objective, then management ordinarily will prefer the one with the lowest cost.

This approach has many applications because it does not require that the objective be stated in monetary terms, or even that it be quantified. We need not measure the degree to which each alternative meets the objective; we need

[8]Ann Gibbons, "Overkilling the Insect Enemy," *Science,* August 10, 1990.

only make the go-no-go judgment that any of the proposed alternatives will achieve it. Of these, we then seek the least costly.

<table>
<tr><td>

Example

</td><td>

The output of an educational program is difficult to measure. It is especially difficult to find a causal relationship between a certain teaching technique and the resulting quality of education. Nevertheless, educators can compare the costs of alternative teaching techniques, such as team teaching, computer-assisted instruction, and conventional tests and workbooks. In the absence of a judgment that one method provides better education than another, an educational manager presumably would prefer the technique with the lowest cost.

The objective of a benefit/cost analysis was to determine the optimal airport facilities and ground transportation for airline passengers arriving and departing Washington, D.C. Analysts estimated the costs of various airport locations and associated ground transport services. Senior management chose the proposal that provided adequate service with the lowest cost. There was no need to measure the benefits of "adequate service."

</td></tr>
</table>

Equal Cost Programs

If two competing proposals have the same cost but one produces more benefits than the other, it ordinarily is the preferred alternative. This conclusion can be reached without measuring the absolute levels of benefits. Analysts often use such an approach to determine the best mix of resources in a program.

<table>
<tr><td>

Example

</td><td>

Similar to the above example, we might ask, "Will $1 million spent to hire more teachers produce more educational benefits than $1 million spent on a combination of teachers and teaching machines, or $1 million spent on team teaching rather than individual teaching?" The analysis involves an estimate of the amount of resources that $1 million will buy, and a judgment of the results that will be achieved by using this amount and mix of resources. It requires only that benefits be expressed comparatively, however, not numerically.

</td></tr>
</table>

Different Objectives

A benefit/cost comparison of proposals intended to accomplish different objectives is likely to be worthless. For example, an analysis that attempted to compare funds to be spent for primary school education with funds to be spent for retraining unemployed adults is not worthwhile. Such an analysis would require assigning monetary values to the benefits of these two programs, which is an impossible task.

On the other hand, since funds are limited, policymakers must recognize that there is an opportunity cost associated with any given program. While experienced managers may have an intuitive feel for these opportunity costs *within* their organizations, relatively few managers have sufficient experience or skill to make such trade-offs *across* organizations, particularly when those organizations have disparate goals and clientele. Nor are there many managers with the *authority* to make such trade-offs. Funds used for pollution-control programs, for example, are not available for social welfare programs.[9]

Causal Connection between Cost and Benefits

Many benefit/cost analyses implicitly assume that there is a causal relationship between benefits and costs. That is, spending $X produces Y amount of benefit. Unless a causal connection such as this actually exists, a benefit/cost analysis is fallacious.

Example

An agency defended its personnel training program with an analysis indicating that the program would lead participants to get new jobs. The new jobs would increase lifetime earnings by $25,000 per person. Thus, the $5,000 average cost per trainee seemed well justified. However, the assertion that the proposed program would indeed generate these benefits was completely unsupported; it was strictly a guess. There was no plausible link between the amount requested and the projected results.

For some proposed items, the lack of benefits is so obvious that a detailed analysis is unnecessary.

Example

The superintendent of schools of Lawrence, Massachusetts, purchased 75 laptop computers, complete with carrying cases, for $202,000 for administrators (including the head custodian) and members of the School Committee. He did so with special funds that were intended to improve the quality of education in a school system in need of improvement. When asked for justification, he replied that reducing the paper that would otherwise be required in disseminating notices would save $16,000 a year, and would permit recipients to check the grades and attendance records of every student. "If they have better access to data," the superintendent boasted, "they have a better basis for their decisions."[10]

Some Analytical Techniques

The literature on benefit/cost analysis is voluminous. In the remainder of the chapter, we summarize some of the principal techniques used to conduct them, along with particularly difficult problems that arise in the application of these techniques to nonprofit organizations. More details and techniques can be found in the Suggested Additional Readings.

Capital Investment Analysis

A typical capital investment proposal is one that involves an outlay of money at the present time so as to realize a stream of benefits sometime in the future.

[9]Some insightful analyses of opportunity costs can be found in Steven E. Rhoads, *The Economist's View of the World: Government, Markets, and Public Policy* (Cambridge, England: Cambridge University Press, 1985).
[10]*Boston Globe,* October 2, 1996, Page 1.

For example, a proposal might be to install storm windows at a cost of $10,000, with an estimated savings in heating bills of $3,000 per year. In evaluating this proposal one asks: Is it worth spending $10,000 now to obtain benefits of $3,000 per year in the future? There are several approaches to answering this question.

Payback Period

One approach determines the number of years that the benefits will have to be obtained to recover the investment. This is the payback period, calculated as follows for the storm window example:

$$\text{Payback period} = \frac{\text{Initial Investment}}{\text{Annual benefits}} = \frac{\$10,000}{\$3,000} = 3.3 \text{ years}$$

If the storm windows are expected to last fewer than 3.3 years, the investment is not worthwhile. If more than 3.3 years, the storm windows will have "paid for themselves," and the benefits thereafter will contribute to the organization's surplus.

Present Value

The payback period analysis assumes that savings in the second and third years are as valuable as savings in the first year, but this is not realistic. No rational person would give up the right to receive $3,000 now for the promise to receive $3,000 two years from now. That is, if a person loans $3,000 to someone now, he or she expects to get back more than $3,000 at some time in the future. The promise of an amount to be received in the future therefore has a lower *present value* than the same amount received today.[11]

Use of the present value technique is important in the capital budgeting process. By incorporating the time value of money into the analysis, the technique recognizes that money received in the future does not have as much value as money received today.

Net Present Value

The present value, or *discounting,* technique is used in what is called the *net present value approach* to capital budgeting analysis. Net present value is the difference between the present value of a project's estimated benefits, and the amount to be invested in the project. The benefits often are called the project's *cash flows.* The approach involves the following steps:

1. Determine the estimated annual cash flows associated with the project. These may be either increased revenues or decreased costs to the organization, but they must result exclusively from the project itself and not from any activities that would have taken place without the project.

2. Estimate the economic life of the investment. This is not necessarily the investment's physical life. Rather, it is the period over which the cash flows

---

[11]The concept of present value is discussed in the Appendix at the end of this chapter.

will be received. The economic life may be shorter than the physical life because of obsolescence, change in demand, or other reasons.

3. Determine the effective amount of the investment. This is the purchase price of the new asset, plus any installation costs, plus any disposal costs for the asset it is replacing, and less the salvage value received for the asset being replaced.

4. Determine the required discount rate, or rate of return. This topic will be discussed in greater detail later in the chapter.

5. Compute the proposed project's net present value according to this formula:

$$\begin{array}{l} \text{Net present} \\ \text{value} \end{array} = \left(\begin{array}{l} \text{Cash} \\ \text{flow} \end{array} \times \begin{array}{l} \text{Present value} \\ \text{factor} \end{array} \right) - \begin{array}{l} \text{Investment} \\ \text{amount} \end{array}$$

$$\text{NPV} = \qquad (CF \times pvf) \qquad - I$$

The $(CF \times pvf)$ portion of this equation is known as *gross present value;* it becomes *net present value* when the investment amount is deducted from it.

6. If the NPV is zero or greater, the investment is financially feasible. That is, once we have determined the desired rate of return, a project that yields a net present value of zero is earning the desired rate, and therefore is acceptable from a pure financial perspective.

As discussed in the Appendix at the end of this chapter, when the cash flow is the same every year, the present value factor can be obtained from Table 9B (page 451) by looking at the intersection of the year row and the percent column selected in steps 2 and 4 above. Present value factors for one-time cash flows can be found in Table 9A.

Example

Assume we estimate that the storm windows in the above example will last five years, and that our required rate of return is 8 percent. The analysis would be performed as follows:

Step 1. Annual cash flow = $3,000

Step 2. Economic life = 5 years

Step 3. Net investment amount = $10,000

Step 4. Rate of return = 8 percent

Step 5. NPV = $(CF \times pvf) - I$
    = ($3,000 × 3.993) − $10,000
    = $11,979 − $10,000
    = $1,979

Step 6. The investment has a NPV that is greater than zero, and therefore is financially feasible.

Points to Consider

Several important points should be made about an analysis of net present value. First, the above example assumed identical cash flows in each of the years, which permits us to use Table 9B. If the cash flows were not the same in each year, we would need to calculate the term ($CF \times pvf$) for each year separately, using Table 9A, and add the results together.

Second, although an analysis of this sort appears to be quite precise, we should recognize that many of its elements are estimates or guesses, and may be quite imprecise. Specifically, cash flows projected beyond a period of two to three years ordinarily are not precise, nor are estimates of the economic life of most investments. Thus, we should be careful about attributing too much credibility to the precision that the formula seems to give us. Because of this, many managers look for the NPV to be a *comfortable margin* above zero. Of course, what is comfortable for one manager may not be so for another.

Third, inflation is a factor. It is quite likely, for instance, that potential increases in wage rates, will cause labor savings from an investment to be greater five years from now than they are today. If, however, we are to adjust our cash flow factor for the effects of inflation, we also need to adjust the required rate of return to reflect our need for a return somewhat greater than the rate of inflation. By excluding an inflation effect from both the cash flow calculations and the required rate of return, we neutralize the effect of inflation. We thus do not need to undertake the rather complex calculations that otherwise might be necessary.

Finally, the financial analysis is only one aspect of the decision-making process. As discussed above, there are many more considerations, including political analyses. Managers must be careful not to let the financial analysis dominate a decision that has political or strategic consequences that cannot be quantified. In these instances, a manager's judgment and "feel" for the situation may be as important as the quantitative factors. Indeed, if a project is *required* for nonquantitative reasons (e.g., for accreditation), its net present value is irrelevant. In short, almost all capital budgeting proposals involve a wide variety of nonquantitative considerations that will influence the final decision. The use of present value or any related techniques serves mainly to formalize the quantitative part of the analysis.

Benefit/Cost Ratio

Since most organizations do not have sufficient capital investment funds to engage in all financially feasible projects, managers must devise some method to rank projects in order of their financial desirability. One such method is to calculate their *benefit/cost ratio,* as follows:

$$\text{Benefit/cost ratio} = \frac{\text{Gross present value}}{\text{Investment}}$$

To illustrate this approach, suppose we have two proposals, one requiring an investment of $2,000 that yields a cash inflow of $2,400 one year from now, and the other requiring an investment of $3,000 that yields a cash inflow of $900 a year for five years. If the required rate of return is 10 per cent, the benefit/cost ratio indicates that the second proposal is preferable, as indicated below:

Proposal	Investment	Cash Inflow	Present Value Factors at 10 percent	Gross Present Value	Benefit/ Cost Ratio
A	$2,000	$2,400, Year 1	0.909	$2,182	1.09
B	$3,000	$900, Years 1–5	3.791	$3,412	1.14

Internal Rate of Return

Another way of ranking projects is by their *internal rate of return (IRR)*. The IRR method is similar to the net present value method, but instead of determining a required rate of return in advance, we set net present value equal to zero and calculate the *effective rate of return* on the investment. Proposed projects can then be ranked in terms of their rates of return.

To use this method, we usually assume identical cash flows in each year of a project's life.[12] Given this assumption, the IRR method begins with the net present value formula

$$NPV = (CF \times pvf) - I$$

but sets NPV equal to zero, so that

$$CF \times pvf = I$$

or

$$pvf = \frac{I}{CF}$$

Once we have determined the present value factor, we can use it in conjunction with the project's economic life to determine the effective—or *internal*—rate of return. We do this with Table 9B. For instance, in our storm window example, if we divide the $10,000 investment amount by the $3,000 annual cash flows, we get 3.33. We now find the figure 3.33 in Table 9B in the row for five years, and can see that it lies somewhere between 15 and 16 percent. This is the internal rate of return for the storm window project.

Choice of a Discount Rate

In any capital investment analysis, the choice of a discount rate is an important consideration. The approach used by many organizations, both for-profit and nonprofit, involves the calculation of an entity's weighted cost of capital, which is then adjusted as necessary to account for the riskiness of the particular proposal under consideration.

---

[12]Computer programs and some pocket calculators can solve for unequal cash flows.

Weighted Cost of Capital

As we discussed in Chapter 3, an organization's assets are financed by a combination of liabilities and equity. Some liabilities, such as accounts payable, are usually interest free, but both short- and long-term debt carry a rate of interest that the organization must pay for the use of the lender's money. Equity generally comes in two forms: (1) contributions and grants, which are called *contributed equity,* and (2) *retained surpluses* or *operating equity.*

In choosing a discount rate, we begin with the cost of each of these sources of capital and weight them by their relative amounts. For example, assume that the right side of an organization's balance sheet appears as follows, with interest rates as shown:

Item	Amount	Interest Rate
Accounts payable	$ 3,000	0.0%
Accrued salaries	2,000	0.0
Short-term note payable	10,000	12.0
Total current liabilities	15,000	
Long-term note payable	75,000	10.0
Mortgage payable	150,000	8.0
Total liabilities	240,000	
Contributed equity	150,000	0.0
Operating equity	50,000	0.0
Total liabilities and equity	$440,000	

In calculating a weighted cost of capital, we (1) determine the percentage of the total liabilities and equity that each source represents, (2) multiply this by the appropriate interest rate, and (3) add the resulting totals together. The calculations for the above situation would look as follows:

Item	Amount	Percent of Total	Interest Rate	Weighted Rate
Accounts payable	$ 3,000	0.6	0.0	0.0 %
Accrued salaries	2,000	0.5	0.0	0.0
Short-term note payable	10,000	2.3	12.0	0.28
Total current liabilities	15,000			
Long-term note payable	75,000	17.0	10.0	1.70
Mortgage payable	150,000	34.1	8.0	2.73
Total liabilities	240,000			
Contributed equity	150,000	34.1	0.0	0.0
Operating equity	50,000	11.4	0.0	0.0
Total liabilities and equity	$440,000			
Totals		100.00		4.71%

Cost of Equity

This weighted cost of capital in the above example is low because both sources of equity—contributed and operating—have been assigned a zero interest rate. An ongoing debate in many nonprofit organizations concerns the appropriate interest rates for these sources. Although some nonprofit organization managers argue that these funds are essentially free, and therefore should be assigned a zero interest rate, most managers believe there is a real cost for using their organizations' equity capital.

While managers may agree on the relevance of a cost of equity, there is considerably less agreement on how to determine the appropriate rate of interest. Some argue that contributed equity tends to be invested either in property and plant or in the entity's endowment fund. Funds tied up in property and plant obviously are not available for other investments. Endowment funds on the other hand, usually are invested in securities, real property, or other earning assets. If some of these funds are used for a particular project, the amount available for investment elsewhere is reduced by that much. The cost of using these funds on the proposed project, therefore, can be thought of as the rate they would have earned if invested in securities or other similar assets (i.e., their opportunity cost). Like all future estimates, this rate is uncertain, but most managers have a fairly good idea of what their investments can earn.

If an organization expects that it can invest its equity funds to earn a rate of 12 percent, the weighted cost of capital calculated above would change considerably, as is shown below:

Item	Amount	Percent of Total	Interest Rate	Weighted Rate
Accounts payable	$ 3,000	0.6	0.0	0.0 %
Accrued salaries	2,000	0.5	0.0	0.0
Short-term note payable	10,000	2.3	12.0	0.28
Total current liabilities	15,000			
Long-term note payable	75,000	17.0	10.0	1.70
Mortgage payable	150,000	34.1	8.0	2.73
Total liabilities	240,000			
Contributed equity	150,000	34.1	12.0	4.09
Operating equity	50,000	11.4	12.0	1.37
Total liabilities and equity	$440,000			
Totals		100.00		10.17%

Most managers would argue that this approach yields a realistic average for a nonprofit organization to use as a discount rate in its capital investment decision-making analyses. Of course, the actual amount of the weighted cost of capital will differ from one organization to the next depending on capital structure and interest rates.

Incorporating Risk into the Analysis

Capital investment proposals are not risk free. Since they all involve future cash flows, there is always the possibility that the future will not be as anticipated. This risk element should be incorporated into the analysis. If risk is not considered explicitly, then a very risky proposal might be evaluated in the same way as one that has a high probability of success.

There are a number of ways to incorporate risk into an analysis. With all of them, an increase in risk reduces the net present value of a proposal. Many organizations add percentage points to their weighted cost of capital to account for higher perceived risk. The problem with this approach is that there is no easy way to establish a meaningful risk scale. Statistical techniques are available for incorporating the relative riskiness of a project, but they require analysts to estimate the probabilities of possible outcomes. This is quite difficult to do.

Another approach, taken by many organizations, is to heavily discount any projected cash flows beyond some predetermined time period, such as 5 or 10 years. They use the weighted cost of capital as the discount rate for all cash flows in, say, the first five years of an investment. They then use a much higher rate for all subsequent years. Some even exclude all cash flows beyond a certain number of years. In all instances, the reasoning is that the future is highly uncertain, and the farther out the projections, the greater the uncertainty. While this approach tends to bias decisions in favor of projects with short payback periods, many organizations in industries experiencing rapid technological change believe that short payback periods are justified.

Finally, in considering risk, some organizations give greater weight to projections of cost savings than to projections of additional revenues. When a particular technological improvement, say, a new piece of equipment, has demonstrated its ability to produce certain cost savings in other organizations, managers reason that projections of cost savings are quite reliable. By contrast, a projection that a certain investment will result in new business and hence additional revenue is far more uncertain. Factors such as clients' willingness to use the new service, competition, third-party reimbursement changes, and so forth, will also affect a new investment's return. Some organizations incorporate this risk into the analysis by using lower discount rates for projects with cost savings and higher ones for projects that are expected to yield additional revenues.

In summary, when we consider the formula

$$\text{NPV} = (CF \times pvf) - I$$

the only element that is reasonably certain is the amount of the investment. Both cash flow estimates and economic life can be highly speculative. Organizations can include adjustments for uncertainty either by shortening economic life or by raising the required rate of return. Either approach requires managers and analysts to exercise considerable judgment.

Quantifying the Value of a Human Being

In their analyses of proposed programs, nonprofit organization managers frequently encounter a factor that rarely is relevant in proposals originating in for-profit companies: the value of a human being. This dilemma arises because some programs are designed to save or prolong human lives. Such programs include automobile safety, accident prevention, drug control, and medical research. In these programs, the value of a human life or of a workday lost to accident or illness is a relevant consideration in measuring benefits.

Analysts are often squeamish about attaching a monetary value to a human life since there is a general belief in our culture that life is priceless. Nevertheless, such a monetary amount often facilitates the analysis of certain proposals. In a world of scarce resources, it is not possible to spend unlimited amounts to save lives in general.

There are, of course, circumstances where society is willing to devote significant resources to saving a specific life, as when hundreds of people, supported by helicopters and various high-technology devices, are brought together to hunt for a child who is lost in the woods. In most situations, however, the focus is not on saving a single life, but on saving the lives of a class of people (such as motorcyclists or cancer victims) or on valuing a life that already has been lost (such as in cases of litigation for medical malpractice).

Analytical Approaches to Valuation

Analysts have advocated several approaches to estimating the value of a human life. All of them present difficulties. One approach discounts the expected future earnings of the persons affected by the program; this discounted present value presumably represents their economic value to their families or to society. A related approach subtracts the persons' food, clothing, and other costs from the earnings to find the *net* value of their lives.

These two approaches frequently are used in litigation involving "wrongful deaths." They are relevant to cases involving deceased persons, automobile accidents, industrial pollution, or the release of toxic chemicals.

Example

In a study of the costs of firearm injuries, the U.S. General Accounting Office (GAO) reported on an outside study to determine the average lifetime cost of a firearm injury. The costs used in the study included actual dollar expenditures related to illness or injury, including amounts spent for hospital and nursing home care, physician and other medical professional services, drugs and appliances, and rehabilitation. The cost estimates also included life years lost and the indirect cost associated with loss of earnings from short- and long-term disability and premature death from injury. The study's conclusion was that injuries not requiring hospitalization cost $458 per person, while those requiring hospitalization were $33,159 per person. The average lifetime cost of a firearm *fatality* was $373,520, which the GAO characterized as "the highest of any cause of injury." Using annual figures for injuries and deaths attributable to firearms, the GAO went on to conclude that the estimated lifetime costs for accidental shootings was close to $1 billion every year.[13]

Among the problems encountered in applying these approaches is the difficulty of: (*a*) estimating the amount of future earnings and related costs, (*b*) choosing an appropriate time period, and (*c*) selecting the correct discount rate. Perhaps more important, these approaches tend to discriminate against persons with relatively low expected lifetime earnings, such as elderly people, homemakers, members of minority groups, ministers, college professors, and artists.[14]

A third analytical approach computes the value of a life in terms of society's willingness to spend money to prevent deaths. One might imagine, for example, that the development and enforcement of occupational safety regulations and building codes are based on benefit/cost comparisons. This is rarely the case, however. Spending on many of these programs frequently is based on emotional arguments or political posturing, as happens, for example, when members of Congress suggest that economic costs are irrelevant for questions related to human lives.

Example	In the early 1990s, the state of Oregon planned to change its Medicaid program by covering more poor residents but offering fewer services. The state computer-ranked 1,600 medical procedures according to costs, benefits, and patients' "quality of well-being." Under the scheme, immunizations ranked higher than treatment for gallstones and depression; cosmetic surgery and sex-change operations fell in the lowest rank. Ultimately, the state drew a line through the list, with funding to be provided for procedures above the line and denied for those falling below it.[15]

The state needed a federal waiver to implement the plan since Medicaid rules required that states fund "all medically necessary" services. In 1992 (a presidential election year), the waiver was denied based, in part,

---

[13]U.S. General Accounting Office, *Accidental Shootings: Many Deaths and Injuries Caused by Firearms Could Be Prevented,* Report to the Chairman, Subcommittee on Antitrust, Monopolies, and Business Rights, Committee of the Judiciary, U.S. Senate, Washington, DC, March 1991. The study cited by the GAO was Dorothy P. Rice et al., *Cost of Injury in the United States: A Report to Congress* (San Francisco: Institute for Health and Aging, University of California, and Injury Prevention Center, The Johns Hopkins University, 1989).
[14]Ralph Estes makes an attempt to adjust for some of these factors in *Estes® Economic Loss Tables* (Wichita, KS: A.U. Publishing, 1987). He provides separate data for different educational levels, different genders, whites and nonwhites, persons with and without established earnings histories, and for persons who earn the minimum wage. In cases of wrongful death, he also provides data that adjust for terminated personal consumption.
[15]Health One® and Deloitte & Touche, *Managing Care and Costs: Strategic Choices and Issues: An Environmental Assessment of U.S. Health Care, 1991–1996* (Minneapolis: Health One Corporation, 1991).

on the argument that the plan valued some human lives higher than others, and that such a valuation was unfair.

A fourth approach seeks to measure the value people place on their own lives as indicated by, say, the amount they are willing to spend on life or disability insurance, or by risk premiums they earn in hazardous occupations. This implies that these individuals' decisions are based on economic considerations, but many other considerations may be involved.

Example	At one time the exposure standard for benzene was 10 parts per million (ppm) averaged over an eight-hour working day. At this rate, one benzene worker would die of benzene-related cancer every third year. According to the Occupational Safety and Health Administration (OSHA), a standard of one ppm would have eliminated the risk, but would have cost $100 million annually for the 30,000 workers exposed to benzene.

One analyst asked the following questions: Would each of the 30,000 benzene workers be willing to pay $3,333 a year (his or her share of the $100 million) to eliminate the risk? If not, would the $100 million be better spent in a highway-improvement or cancer-screening program that could save more than one life every third year?[16]

Merril Eisenbud, a member of the Three Mile Island Advisory Board, and former chairman, North Carolina Low-Level Radioactive Waste Management Authority, criticized some states' regulations concerning the design of low-level radioactive waste disposal sites. He argued that, in response to public pressure, some states require more protection be provided than is specified by the Nuclear Regulatory Commission. According to Mr. Eisenbud: "The additional protection involves expenditures of more than $100 million over the life of a facility, which is the equivalent to many *trillions* of dollars per premature death averted!"[17]

Alternatives to Valuation

The cost of saving lives may be a useful way of choosing among alternative proposals even when it is not possible or feasible to measure the value of a life. Specifically, the alternative that saves the most lives per dollar spent generally is considered economically preferable. The Federal Highway Administration uses this approach in ranking the attractiveness of various highway safety alternatives. Such an analysis is limited to judging whether a particular program saves more lives per dollar spent than other lifesaving or life-prolonging programs. It does not compare costs with monetary benefits.

[16]From Steven E. Rhoads, "Kind Hearts and Opportunity Costs," *Across the Board,* December 1985.
[17]Merril Eisenbud, "Disparate Costs of Risk Avoidance," *Science 9,* September 1988, pp. 1277–78.

Summary

Strategic planning provides the link between strategy formulation and management control. It accepts the goals and strategies of the organization as givens, and develops individual programs that are consistent with the strategies and are intended to help attain the goals.

Strategic planning consists of the identification, development, and analysis of proposed new programs. Every organization has a process for doing this, although in many organizations it is implicit and unstructured: when a new idea comes along, it is evaluated, and a decision is made. If there is an explicit way of dealing with proposed new programs, it should be loosely enough structured that it fosters the flow of creative ideas.

During the strategic planning process, managers frequently must choose between two or more competing programs. When this is the case, attempting to quantify both benefits and costs usually can assist in the decision-making effort.

When two or more proposals have roughly the same benefits, the comparison is relatively easy since only costs need to be calculated. Similarly, when competing proposals have the same costs but one clearly produces more benefits than the other, the decision usually is quite easy. The decision becomes complicated, however, when benefits and costs extend over several years (as is the case with almost all proposed new programs), and when competing proposals have both different benefits and different costs.

When both benefits and costs can be expressed easily in monetary terms, calculating either present values or internal rates of return can facilitate a decision. When these analyses are being used, the choice of a discount rate is a key decision; many relatively undesirable projects have been undertaken because analysts used a discount rate that was too low. Models also can assist in the decision-making effort in that they allow managers and analysts to measure the implications of changing certain key variables.

Frequently, benefits and costs cannot be expressed easily in monetary terms. This happens, for example, when managers attempt to incorporate risk into the analysis, since risk is inherently difficult to measure. It also happens when managers attempt to quantify the value of a human being, and include that in the analysis. Additionally, there are a variety of nonquantitative considerations that are part of almost every proposed program. In all these instances, although some quantitative analysis usually can be carried out, managers must be careful not to allow the quantitative factors to dominate the decision. In most program decisions, managers will need to exercise their judgment, which may override the results of the quantitative analysis.

Appendix

The Concept of Present Value

The concept of present value rests on the basic principle that money has a *time value*. That is, that $1 received one year from today is worth less than $1 received today. To illustrate the concept, consider the following situations:

> *Question.*   A colleague offers to pay you $1,000 one year from today. How much would you lend her today?

Presumably, unless you were a good friend or somewhat altruistic, you would not lend her $1,000 today. You could invest your $1,000, earn something on it over the course of the year, and have more than $1,000 a year from now. If, for example, you could earn 10 percent on your money, you could invest your $1,000 and have $1,100 in a year. Alternatively, if you had $909, and invested it at 10 percent, you would have $1,000 a year from today.

Thus, if your colleague offers to pay you $1,000 a year from today, and you are an investor expecting a 10 percent return, you would most likely lend her only $909 today. With a 10 percent interest rate, $909 is the present value of $1,000 received one year hence.

> *Question*   Under the same circumstances as the previous question, how much would you lend your colleague if she offered to pay you $1,000 two years from today?

Here we must incorporate the concept of compound interest; that is, the fact that interest is earned on the interest itself. For example, at a 10 percent rate, $826 loaned today would accumulate to roughly $1,000 in two years, as shown by the following:

Year 1 $826 × .10   − $82.60

Year 2 ($826 + $82.60) × .10   = $90.86

Total at end of Year 2 = $826 + $82.60 + $90.86 = $999.46

Thus, you would be willing to lend her $826.

> *Question.*   The previous question consisted of a promise to pay a given amount two years from today, with no intermediate payments. Another possibility to consider is the situation in which your colleague offers to pay you $1,000 a year from today, and another $1,000 two years from today. How much would you lend her now?

The answer requires combining the analyses in each of the above two examples. Specifically, for the $1,000 received two years from now, you would lend her $826, and for the $1,000 received one year from now you would lend her $909. Thus, the total you would lend would be $1,735.

Our ability to make these determinations is simplified by present value tables. Two such tables follow the Suggested Additional Readings in this chapter. Table 9A, "Present Value of $1," is used to determine the present value of a single payment received at some specified time in the future. For instance, in the first example above, we could find the answer to the problem by looking in the column for 10 percent and the row for one year; this gives us 0.909. Multiplying 0.909 by $1,000 gives us the $909 we would lend our colleague. Similarly, if we look in the row for two years and multiply the entry of 0.826 by $1,000, we arrive at the answer to the second example: $826.

Table 9B, "Present Value of $1 Received Annually for *N* Years," is used for even payments received over a given period. Looking at Table 9B, we can see that the present value of 1.736 (for a payment of $1 received each year for two years at 10 percent) multiplied by $1,000 is $1,736. With a minor rounding error, this is the amount we calculated in the third example above. We also can see that the 1.736 is the sum of the two amounts shown on Table 9A (0.909 for one year hence, and 0.826 for two years hence). Thus, Table 9B simply sums the various elements in Table 9A to facilitate calculations.

TABLE 9A Present Value of $1

Years Hence	1%	2%	4%	6%	8%	10%	12%	14%	15%	16%	18%	20%	22%	24%	25%	26%	28%
1	0.990	0.980	0.962	0.943	0.926	0.909	0.893	0.877	0.870	0.862	0.847	0.833	0.820	0.806	0.800	0.794	0.781
2	0.980	0.961	0.925	0.890	0.857	0.826	0.797	0.769	0.756	0.743	0.718	0.694	0.672	0.650	0.640	0.630	0.610
3	0.971	0.942	0.889	0.840	0.794	0.751	0.712	0.675	0.658	0.641	0.609	0.579	0.551	0.524	0.512	0.500	0.477
4	0.961	0.924	0.855	0.792	0.735	0.683	0.636	0.592	0.572	0.552	0.516	0.482	0.451	0.423	0.410	0.397	0.373
5	0.951	0.906	0.822	0.747	0.681	0.621	0.567	0.519	0.497	0.476	0.437	0.402	0.370	0.341	0.328	0.315	0.291
6	0.942	0.888	0.790	0.705	0.630	0.564	0.507	0.456	0.432	0.410	0.370	0.335	0.303	0.275	0.262	0.250	0.227
7	0.933	0.871	0.760	0.665	0.583	0.513	0.452	0.400	0.376	0.354	0.314	0.279	0.249	0.222	0.210	0.198	0.178
8	0.923	0.853	0.731	0.627	0.540	0.467	0.404	0.351	0.327	0.305	0.266	0.233	0.204	0.179	0.168	0.157	0.139
9	0.914	0.837	0.703	0.592	0.500	0.424	0.361	0.308	0.284	0.263	0.225	0.194	0.167	0.144	0.134	0.125	0.108
10	0.905	0.820	0.676	0.558	0.463	0.386	0.322	0.270	0.247	0.227	0.191	0.162	0.137	0.116	0.107	0.099	0.085
11	0.896	0.804	0.650	0.527	0.429	0.350	0.287	0.237	0.215	0.195	0.162	0.135	0.112	0.094	0.086	0.079	0.066
12	0.887	0.788	0.625	0.497	0.397	0.319	0.257	0.208	0.187	0.168	0.137	0.112	0.092	0.076	0.069	0.062	0.052
13	0.879	0.773	0.601	0.469	0.368	0.290	0.229	0.182	0.163	0.145	0.116	0.093	0.075	0.061	0.055	0.050	0.040
14	0.870	0.758	0.577	0.442	0.340	0.263	0.205	0.160	0.141	0.125	0.099	0.078	0.062	0.049	0.044	0.039	0.032
15	0.861	0.743	0.555	0.417	0.315	0.239	0.183	0.140	0.123	0.108	0.084	0.065	0.051	0.040	0.035	0.031	0.025
16	0.853	0.728	0.534	0.394	0.292	0.218	0.163	0.123	0.107	0.093	0.071	0.054	0.042	0.032	0.028	0.025	0.019
17	0.844	0.714	0.513	0.371	0.270	0.198	0.146	0.108	0.093	0.080	0.060	0.045	0.034	0.026	0.023	0.020	0.015
18	0.836	0.700	0.494	0.350	0.250	0.180	0.130	0.095	0.081	0.069	0.051	0.038	0.028	0.021	0.018	0.016	0.012
19	0.828	0.686	0.475	0.331	0.232	0.164	0.116	0.083	0.070	0.060	0.043	0.031	0.023	0.017	0.014	0.012	0.009
20	0.820	0.673	0.456	0.312	0.215	0.149	0.104	0.073	0.061	0.051	0.037	0.026	0.019	0.014	0.012	0.010	0.007
21	0.811	0.660	0.439	0.294	0.199	0.135	0.093	0.064	0.053	0.044	0.031	0.022	0.015	0.011	0.009	0.008	0.006
22	0.803	0.647	0.422	0.278	0.184	0.123	0.083	0.056	0.046	0.038	0.026	0.018	0.013	0.009	0.007	0.006	0.004
23	0.795	0.634	0.406	0.262	0.170	0.112	0.074	0.049	0.040	0.033	0.022	0.015	0.010	0.007	0.006	0.005	0.003
24	0.788	0.622	0.390	0.247	0.158	0.102	0.066	0.043	0.035	0.028	0.019	0.013	0.008	0.006	0.005	0.004	0.003
25	0.780	0.610	0.375	0.233	0.146	0.092	0.059	0.038	0.030	0.024	0.016	0.010	0.007	0.005	0.004	0.003	0.002

TABLE 9B   Present Value of $1 Received Annually for N Years

Years N	1%	2%	4%	6%	8%	10%	12%	14%	15%	16%	18%	20%	22%	24%	25%	26%	28%
1	0.990	0.980	0.962	0.943	0.926	0.909	0.893	0.877	0.870	0.862	0.847	0.833	0.820	0.806	0.800	0.794	0.781
2	1.970	1.942	1.886	1.833	1.783	1.736	1.690	1.647	1.626	1.605	1.566	1.528	1.492	1.457	1.440	1.424	1.392
3	2.941	2.884	2.775	2.673	2.577	2.487	2.402	2.322	2.283	2.246	2.174	2.106	2.042	1.981	1.952	1.923	1.868
4	3.902	3.808	3.630	3.465	3.312	3.170	3.037	2.914	2.855	2.798	2.690	2.589	2.494	2.404	2.362	2.320	2.241
5	4.853	4.713	4.452	4.212	3.993	3.791	3.605	3.433	3.352	3.274	3.127	2.991	2.864	2.745	2.689	2.635	2.532
6	5.795	5.601	5.242	4.917	4.623	4.355	4.111	3.889	3.784	3.685	3.498	3.326	3.167	3.020	2.951	2.885	2.759
7	6.728	6.472	6.002	5.582	5.206	4.868	4.564	4.288	4.160	4.039	3.812	3.605	3.416	3.242	3.161	3.083	2.937
8	7.652	7.325	6.733	6.210	5.747	5.335	4.968	4.639	4.487	4.344	4.078	3.837	3.619	3.421	3.329	3.241	3.076
9	8.566	8.162	7.435	6.802	6.247	5.759	5.328	4.946	4.772	4.607	4.303	4.031	3.786	3.566	3.463	3.366	3.184
10	9.471	8.983	8.111	7.360	6.710	6.145	5.650	5.216	5.019	4.833	4.494	4.192	3.923	3.682	3.571	3.465	3.269
11	10.368	9.787	8.760	7.887	7.139	6.495	5.937	5.453	5.234	5.029	4.656	4.327	4.035	3.776	3.656	3.544	3.335
12	11.255	10.575	9.385	8.384	7.536	6.814	6.194	5.660	5.421	5.197	4.793	4.439	4.127	3.851	3.725	3.606	3.387
13	12.134	11.343	9.986	8.853	7.904	7.103	6.424	5.842	5.583	5.342	4.910	4.533	4.203	3.912	3.780	3.656	3.427
14	13.004	12.106	10.563	9.295	8.244	7.367	6.628	6.002	5.724	5.468	5.008	4.611	4.265	3.962	3.824	3.695	3.459
15	13.865	12.849	11.118	9.712	8.559	7.606	6.811	6.142	5.847	5.575	5.092	4.675	4.315	4.001	3.859	3.726	3.483
16	14.718	13.578	11.652	10.106	8.851	7.824	6.974	6.265	5.954	5.669	5.162	4.730	4.357	4.033	3.887	3.751	3.503
17	15.562	14.292	12.166	10.477	9.122	8.022	7.120	6.373	6.047	5.749	5.222	4.775	4.391	4.059	3.910	3.771	3.518
18	16.398	14.992	12.659	10.828	9.372	8.201	7.250	6.467	6.128	5.818	5.273	4.812	4.419	4.080	3.928	3.786	3.529
19	17.226	15.678	13.134	11.158	9.604	8.365	7.366	6.550	6.198	5.877	5.316	4.844	4.442	4.097	3.942	3.799	3.539
20	18.046	16.351	13.590	11.470	9.818	8.514	7.469	6.623	6.259	5.929	5.353	4.870	4.460	4.110	3.954	3.808	3.546
21	18.857	17.011	14.029	11.764	10.017	8.649	7.562	6.687	6.312	5.973	5.384	4.891	4.476	4.121	3.963	3.816	3.551
22	19.660	17.658	14.451	12.042	10.201	8.772	7.645	6.743	6.359	6.011	5.410	4.909	4.488	4.130	3.970	3.822	3.556
23	20.456	18.292	14.857	12.303	10.371	8.883	7.718	6.792	6.399	6.044	5.432	4.925	4.499	4.137	3.976	3.827	3.559
24	21.243	18.914	15.247	12.550	10.529	8.985	7.784	6.835	6.434	6.073	5.451	4.937	4.507	4.143	3.981	3.831	3.562
25	22.023	19.523	15.622	12.783	10.675	9.077	7.843	6.873	6.464	6.097	5.467	4.948	4.514	4.147	3.985	3.834	3.564

Suggested Additional Readings

Robert N. Anthony, David F. Hawkins, and Kenneth A. Merchant, *Accounting: Text and Cases,* 10th ed. (Burr Ridge, IL: Richard D. Irwin, 1998).

Clayton, P. Gillette, and Thomas D. Hopkins. *Federal Agency Valuations of Human Life.* Washington, DC: Administrative Conference of the United States, 1988.

Gramlich, E. M. *Benefit-Cost Analysis of Governmental Programs,* 2nd ed. Englewood Cliffs, NJ: Prentice Hall, 1989.

Portney, P. R., ed. *Public Policies for Environmental Protection.* Washington, DC: Resources for the Future, 1990.

—— and Katherine Probst. *Assigning Liability for Superfund Cleanups: An Analysis of Policy Options.* Washington, DC: Resources for the Future, 1992.

Rhoads, Steven E. *The Economist's View of the World: Government Markets, and Public Policy.* Cambridge, England: Cambridge University Press, 1985.

Schultze, Charles L. *The Politics and Economics of Public Spending.* Washington, DC: The Brookings Institution, 1968.

Zeckhauser, R. J. "Procedures for Valuing Lives." *Public Policy,* Fall 1975, pp. 419–64.

Practice Case

Erie Museum[*]

Christian Larson, Executive Director of Erie Museum, was contemplating the proposal recently submitted to him by Francesca Michaels, the head of Curatorial Services at the museum. Ms. Michaels' request was for the purchase of some new equipment to perform operations currently being performed on different, less efficient equipment. The purchase price was $150,000, delivered and installed.

Background

Erie Museum was a nonprofit organization located on the shores of Lake Erie in Cleveland, Ohio; it had been in existence for some 40 years. It specialized in art from the European Renaissance, with a special focus on the Italian City States. Many of its art works were extremely fragile, and for this reason, the museum needed to regulate both the air temperature and humidity at all times. This required a rather constant upgrading of its equipment as new curatorial technology emerged. However, because of the increased financial pressures, the museum's board of trustees was taking a harder and harder look at all capital equipment proposals designated for curatorial purposes.

The Request

In the case of Ms. Michaels' request, no grant funds were available, and hence the cost would need to be financed from museum revenues. Ms. Michaels had worked closely with the equipment manufacturer to determine the potential benefits of the new equipment, however, and she estimated that it would result in annual savings of $30,000 in electricity, maintenance, and other direct costs, as compared with the present equipment. She also estimated that the proposed equipment's economic life was 10 years, with zero salvage value.

The museum had recently borrowed long-term to finance the construction for a large new exhibit. Paul Hershenson, the Vice President of Fiscal Affairs, had informed Mr. Larson that, because of this, he was certain the museum could obtain additional funds at 12 percent, although he would not plan to negotiate a loan specifically for the purchase of this equipment. He did feel, however, that an investment of this type should have a return of at least 20 percent, even though the museum paid no taxes. The museum's capital structure is shown in Exhibit 1.

---

[*]This case was prepared by Professor David W. Young. Copyright © by David W. Young.

EXHIBIT 1

Erie Museum
Weighted Cost of
Capital

	Percent of Total	Average Interest Rate	Weighted Interest Rate
Debt	40.0	12.0	4.8
Equity	60.0	0.0	0.0
Total	100.0		4.8

Complicating Factors

There were three complications. First, the present equipment was in good working order and probably would last, physically, for at least 15 more years. Second, this request was for what Ms. Michaels called "even better equipment," to replace some equipment purchased two years ago involving the same economic life and dollar amounts. Ms. Michaels had informed Mr. Larson that the new equipment would render the existing equipment completely obsolete with no resale value.

Third, at a recent board meeting, the Chairman of the museum's finance committee had discussed some inconsistencies between Erie's capital structure and the 20 percent rate of return that Mr. Hershenson was recommending. Specifically, he had pointed out that Erie's equity consisted of donations and other gifts which are essentially free. As a result, he thought the proper discount rate to use for capital investment proposals was not 20 percent, but only about 5 percent.

The Decision

Although funds could be obtained to finance the purchase of Ms. Michaels' proposed new equipment, Mr. Larson and Mr. Hershenson were both concerned about the mistake made two years ago, and wanted to be sure that a similar mistake not be made this time.

Questions

1. What is the internal rate of return of Ms. Michaels' proposal?

2. What is the proposal's net present value, using a discount rate of 20 percent? A discount rate of 5 percent? What is the appropriate discount rate to use? Why?

3. If the museum decides to purchase the new equipment for Ms. Michaels, a mistake has been made somewhere, because good equipment bought only two years ago is being scrapped. How did this mistake come about?

4. What nonquantitative factors should the museum consider in making this decision? How important are they?

Case 9–1

Suard College*

In October 1988, the management and the Trustee Budget Committee of Suard College would meet to discuss the question of whether the college should prepare a five-year program. There was disagreement as to whether such an effort was desirable, and if so, whether the results would be worth the cost.

Background

Suard College was a coeducational, residential, four-year liberal arts college of 1,800 students, of whom 1,700 lived in dormitories on the campus. Established in 1836, the original campus was small and located near the commercial center of a city. As the city grew, the environment became increasingly unattractive. Accordingly, in 1950 a new campus was started on 120 acres of land, a mile outside the city.

By 1982, the new campus was essentially completed. There were classrooms, laboratories, a library, a chapel, a museum, dormitories and cafeterias, a student center, indoor and outdoor athletic facilities, and administrative and faculty offices. The newest dormitory, accommodating 100 students, was completed in 1981; it was financed by a 30-year $4 million bond issue. A renovation of the library was completed in 1985, at a cost of $8 million. Most of the new plant had been financed from capital fund campaigns. The college had an endowment of $60 million.

Suard was invariable included in lists of "selective" liberal arts colleges, usually defined as in the top 100 or so of the 3,000 colleges and universities in the United States. As was the case with other selective colleges, its tuition was relatively high.

Generally, Suard operated with a balanced budget. Revenues had equaled or exceeded expenses in most of the past 25 years. Faculty salaries were in the top quartile of all four-year colleges, according to the survey made annually by the American Association of University Professors. The student/faculty ratio was similar to the average of competing colleges. Approximately 55 percent of the faculty had tenure, a percentage that had been fairly stable for some years. Operating statements are given in Exhibit 1.

Outlook

In the 1960s and 1970s, the total college population expanded dramatically, in part because a higher percentage of the college-age population attended col-

---

*This case was prepared by Professor Robert N. Anthony. Copyright © by the President and Fellows of Harvard College. Harvard Business School Case 9-184-010.

EXHIBIT 1

SUARD COLLEGE Operating Statements ($000)			
	1985–86 *Actual*	1986–87 *Actual*	1987–88 *Budget*
Educational and general:			
Revenues:			
Student charges	$16,697	$18,394	$20,473
Endowment	1,730	1,960	2,100
Gifts	1,089	1,230	1,450
Government grants	737	1,041	1,023
Other (principally interest)	1,006	991	959
Total	$21,259	$23,616	$26,005
Expenditures:			
Instruction	$ 7,375	$ 7,754	$ 8,917
Research	218	219	175
Academic support	2,024	2,144	2,292
Student services	2,984	3,268	3,427
Institutional support	2,923	3,123	3,625
Educational plant	2,464	2,832	3,069
Financial aid	3,388	3,712	4,402
Major renovation	–	763	537
Transfer to endowment			162
Total	$21,376	$23,815	$26,606
Net educational and general	$ (117)	$ (199)	$ (601)
Auxiliary enterprises:			
Revenue	$ 7,320	$ 8,407	$ 9,497
Expenditures	7,146	8,158	8,846
Auxiliary, net	$ 174	$ 249	$ 651
Net income	$ 57	$ 50	$ 50

lege, but primarily because the baby boom after World War II resulted in a higher college age population. By 1979, total college population reached a plateau, and forecasts were that by 1983 or 1984 it would start to decrease, reaching a low in1995 at about 75 percent of the 1983 level. In Suard's region of the United States, the percentage decline was forecast to be even greater because of the shift in population from this region to the Sun Belt of the Southwest. Although Suard's total applications had declined slightly in the past few years, the admissions office currently had no difficulty in admitting a class that was equal to those of recent years in all measureable aspects of quality.

The majority of board members and members of the administration believed that with its reputation and its new campus, Suard could maintain its enrollment at 1,800 high-quality students despite the decrease in the total population. These people believed that less selective colleges would suffer, that some of them would be forced to close (some already had closed), and that the selective colleges could maintain their enrollment by drawing students that otherwise would have gone to these colleges. Suard had increased the size and activities of its admissions and public relations offices in recent years so as to provide greater assurance of enrolling the necessary number of high-quality students. A minority thought the view of the majority was too optimistic.

Discussion of a Five-Year Plan

From time to time, most recently in 1979, committees had made studies of long-range strategy. These long-range planning committees usually had members from the faculty, administration, trustees, and the student body. Their reports had led to some changes in the curriculum, but these were generally considered to have been minor. In particular, every study concluded that the emphasis on the liberal arts should continue, and that graduate programs or vocationally oriented programs (e.g., nursing) should not be instituted. Long-range financial projections had been made from time to time, in some cases in connection with the long-range studies and in other cases as a separate exercise.

In the May 1988 meeting of the Budget Committee, a trustee suggested that the time had come to make a five-year program and financial plan, to consider its implications thoroughly, and to revise it annually thereafter. Time did not permit discussion of this proposal then, but it was decided to discuss it at the next meeting, in October 1988. In informal discussions subsequent to the May meeting, it became clear that the idea was controversial.

A programming effort obviously would be concerned with the decline in student-age population, and might develop strategies for dealing with a possible decline in Suard enrollment. Some committee members thought that the fact that such strategies were being considered would alarm the faculty unnecessarily and therefore would hurt morale. If the plan assumed faculty reductions in specified departments, the members of those departments would be upset; if it did not specifically describe departmental manning, everyone would wonder how a reduction would affect them.

Others pointed out that previous five-year financial plans had not amounted to much. These plans were primarily mechanical extrapolations of current revenues and expenditures, with assumptions as to tuition, salary, and other cost increases as a consequence of inflation. It was pointed out that tuition and other charges for a given year could not be estimated much in advance because Suard's tuition had to remain competitive with other colleges, and the decisions of these colleges were not typically made until January. Although the rate of inflation in 1988 was relatively low, no one knew what future inflation rates would be. Thus, although the annual budget was discussed thoroughly, little attention had been given to longer projections.

As an alternative to long-range planning, some believed that the college should adopt the policy of meeting a financial stringency when the need arose.

Specifically, if opening enrollment in a given year was below the budgeted amount, the college would reduce discretionary expenses by about $400,000 and absorb the remaining deficit in that year from the operating surplus of some $800,000 that had been accumulated in prior years. It would immediately plan the expenditure reductions necessary to balance the budget in the following year. An enrollment decline would affect initially only the first-year class; thus, if the entering class was, say, 8 percent below budget, total revenues should decrease by only one-fourth of this, or 2 percent below budget.

Those favoring a formal programming effort pointed out that the library renovation and other factors might have long-range expenditure implications that needed to be explicitly considered. Suard now had a software program that quickly, and at relatively low cost, would provide five-year financial projections under any specified set of assumptions.

Questions

1. Assuming that the college decided to prepare a five-year program and financial plan, how should the assumptions incorporated in it be arrived at? Should the plan be a single "best estimate," or should several alternatives be studied?

2. Should the college prepare a formal five-year program and financial plan?

Case 9–2
Yoland Research Institute*

He wants what? Or he'll do what? If we keep this up we'll all be out of a job. How can I possibly take another one of his requests to the board next week?

Brooke Russell, Executive Director of Yoland Research Institute, was reacting to a proposal that her CFO had brought to her. Submitted by Dr. Russ Roberts, Director of the Nutrition Studies Department, the request was for the purchase of some new equipment to perform operations currently being performed on similar equipment. The purchase price was $400,000 delivered and installed. Ms. Russell continued:

Correct me if I'm wrong, but this new equipment doesn't do anything from a research perspective that his existing equipment doesn't already do. And what's this about selling vitamins? We're not a pharmacy! His credibility is pretty low at this point. And now he's threatening to take his research projects to another institute where he'll get better support if we don't buy the stuff. He's got to be kidding! Maybe we'd be better off letting him go.

*This case was prepared by Professor David W. Young. Copyright © by David W. Young.

Background

Yoland Research Institute was a nonprofit, university-affiliated organization, specializing in research in a wide variety of fields. In large part, its activities were determined by a combination of the faculty affiliated with it and their research interests, although most of its projects tended to be of a basic, rather than applied, nature. As such, it was constantly involved in projects that were attempting to advance the state of the art in the particular field of investigation. One such area was nutrition, where much of the work required sophisticated equipment, and where Dr. Roberts' research had resulted in some major scientific discoveries, contributing to Yoland's growing international reputation as an institute on the leading edge of nutritional research.

Sometimes the purchase of this equipment was funded by a particular research grant or contract. Unfortunately, in the case of Dr. Roberts' request, this was not the case. Nevertheless, Dr. Roberts had worked closely with the equipment manufacturer to determine the potential benefits of the new equipment, and he had estimated that it would allow him to develop some vitamin supplements that the institute could sell for about $100,000 a year at a cost of about $40,000. He argued that the resulting $60,000 would help to cover some of the institute's overhead expenses which he knew were quite high. He also had told Yoland's CFO that if the institute bought this equipment for him, his needs would be met for the next 10 years.

Complicating Factors

There were several complications associated with Dr. Roberts' request. The first was that, although the present equipment was in good working order and would probably last, physically, for at least 10 more years, it was being depreciated at a straight-line rate of 10 percent per year. As such, it had a book value of $144,000 (cost $240,000; accumulated depreciation, $96,000). It had a very low resale value, however. Dr. Roberts commented:

> I'm pretty sure that we can find someone to remove it and pay us about $30,000 for it. There's a market for this sort of stuff in other countries, and there are always people who will buy it for pennies on the dollar and then sell if for a small profit in some other country. Maybe we could do that ourselves, but we don't have the connections, and, besides, it's a big hassle. We certainly couldn't sell it to anyone around here for more than $30,000 though.

The second complication was that the Institute had had some recent controversy on the board concerning the appropriate discount rate to use for its capital investment decision making. As one board member had put it:

> Last year's balance sheet [Exhibit 1] makes it pretty clear that well over half of our capital structure is in the form of equity. In my company [a multinational conglomerate] that equity represents our shareholders' stake in the enterprise. If we

EXHIBIT 1

YOLAND RESEARCH INSTITUTE
Balance Sheet for Most Recent Year
($000)

ASSETS

Current assets:

Cash and cash equivalents.	$10,500	
Accounts receivable (net)	400	
Inventories.	1,350	
Investments at market	9,500	$21,750

Fixed assets:

Property plant, and equipment	$83,000	
Accumulated depreciation.	(36,400)	46,600
Total assets		$68,350

LIABILITIES AND NET ASSETS

Current liabilities

Accounts payable	$ 2,050	
Salaries and wages payable	1,290	
Current portion of mortgage payable	410	$ 3,750

Long-term liabilities:

Notes payable (7.2%)	$ 8,000	
Mortgage payable (5.5%)	17,500	25,500

Net assets:

Unrestricted.	$24,400	
Temporarily restricted	6,700	
Permanently restricted.	8,000	39,100
Total liabilities and net assets		$68,350

don't give them a reasonable return, they'll sell their stock. When we make decisions like this, we use a minimum of 15 percent for our equity. In good years, when we have lots of attractive investment opportunities, we might even use a higher figure.

Another board member had been equally vociferous in his opposition:

That's the for-profit world, but this is not. We don't even call it equity here, and we certainly have no shareholders to account to. My expectation as a member of this board is that we'll do cutting edge research, and anything needed to support that is justifiable. In fact, if you look at the sources of those net assets, you'll see that most of them are unrestricted. We've been earning large surpluses over the past few years and we now have an obligation to plow those back into the Institute. The temporarily restricted are from research contracts and the permanently restricted are from donations and other gifts that were basically free. Why should we try to earn money on those? I think the donors would be outraged if we did. What I don't understand is why we don't have that $39,100 in cash. Where is it anyway?

The first board member amplified on her earlier comments:

I realize that we're nonprofit, but I don't agree that that means we can be fiscally irresponsible. If we told the donors that we were attempting to preserve the purchasing power of their gifts and donations, I think they'd be delighted. Besides, those gifts weren't free. We spent a lot of staff and board time cultivating those relationships in order to get the gifts, and that has a real cost. Even the temporarily restricted funds had an expense—grant and contract writing and such.

As far as the unrestricted funds go, plowing them back into the Institute is exactly what we're doing, but we're trying to do so in a way that lets us remain viable over the long term, and that means making wise investments. I'm not suggesting we go for huge returns, but I think an interest rate on our equity of 10 percent would be a pretty good approximation of its cost to us; that's about what we've been earning on our portfolio over the past 20 years or so. Sure, we can have some investments that don't meet the hurdle rate, but we can't have very many of those or we'll be out of business before you know it.

It was in the context of this debate that Ms. Russell needed to frame her response to Dr. Roberts' request.

Assignment

1. Where is the $39,100 of equity that the second board member wondered about? Why isn't it in cash?

2. What is the appropriate discount rate to use?

3. Is Dr. Roberts' proposal financially feasible?

4. If the Institute decides to purchase the new equipment for Dr. Roberts, what should it do with the existing equipment? What might be done to avoid similar mistakes in the future?

5. Assuming Dr. Roberts' project is financially feasible, should the Institute buy the equipment for him? Why or why not?

Case 9–3

Downtown Parking Authority*

In January a meeting was held in the office of the mayor of Oakmont to discuss a proposed municipal parking facility. The participants included the mayor, the traffic commissioner, the administrator of Oakmont's Downtown Parking Authority, the city planner, and the finance director. The purpose of the meeting was to consider a report by Richard Stockton, executive assistant

*This case was prepared by Graeme Taylor, Management Analysis Center, and Professor Richard F. Vancil, Harvard Business School.

to the Parking Authority's administrator, concerning estimated costs and revenues for the proposed facility.

Mr. Stockton's opening statement was as follows:

As you know, the mayor proposed two months ago that we construct a multilevel parking garage on the Elm Street site. At that time, he asked the Parking Authority to assemble all pertinent information for consideration at our meeting today. I would like to summarize our findings briefly for you.

The Elm Street site is owned by the city. All that stands on it now are the remains of the old Embassy Cinema, which we estimate would cost approximately $80,000 to demolish. A building contractor has estimated that a multilevel structure, with space for 800 cars, could be built on the site at a cost of about $4 million. The useful life of the garage would be around 40 years.

The city could finance construction of the garage through the sale of bonds. The finance director has informed me that we could probably float an issue of 20-year tax exempts at 5 percent interest. Redemption would commence after three years, with one-seventeenth of the original number of bonds being recalled in each succeeding year.

A parking management firm has already contacted us with a proposal to operate the garage for the city. They estimate that their costs, exclusive of the fee, would amount to $480,000 per year. Of this amount, $350,000 would be personnel costs; the remainder would include utilities, mechanical maintenance, insurance, and so forth. In addition, they would require a management fee of $60,000 per year. Any gross revenues in excess of $540,000 per year would be shared 90 percent by the city and 10 percent by the management firm. If total annual revenues are less than $540,000, the city would have to pay the difference.

I suggest we offer a management contract for bid, with renegotiations every three years.

The city would derive additional income of around $100,000 per year by renting the ground floor of the structure as retail space.

We conducted a survey at a private parking garage only three blocks from the Elm Street site to help estimate revenues from the prospective garage.

The garage, which is open every day from 7:00 A.M., until midnight, charges: $1.50 for the first hour; $1.00 for the second hour; and 50 cents for each subsequent hour, with a maximum rate of $4. Their capacity is 400 spaces. Our survey indicated that during business hours, 75 percent of their spaces were occupied by "all-day parkers"—cars whose drivers and passengers work downtown. In addition, roughly 400 cars use the garage each weekday with an average stay of three hours. We did not take a survey on Saturday or Sunday, but the proprietor indicated that the garage is usually about 75 percent utilized by short-term parkers on Saturdays until 6:00 P.M., when the department stores close; the average stay is about two hours. There's a lull until about 7:00 P.M., when the moviegoers start coming in; he says the garage is almost full from 8:00 P.M., until closing time at midnight. Sundays are usually very quiet until the evening, when he estimates that his garage is 60 percent utilized from 6:00 P.M. until midnight.

In addition, we studied a report issued by the City College Economics Department last year, which estimated that we now have approximately 50,000 cars entering the central business district (CBD) every day from Monday through Saturday. Based on correlations with other cities of comparable size, the economists calculated that we need 30,000 parking spaces in the CBD. This agrees quite well with a block-by-block estimate made by the traffic commissioner's office last year, which indicated a total parking need in the CBD of 29,000 spaces. Right now we have 22,000 spaces in the CBD. Of these, 5 percent are curb spaces (half of which are metered, with a two-hour maximum limit for 40 cents), and all the rest are in privately owned garages and open lots.

Another study indicated that 60 percent of all auto passengers entering the CBD on a weekday were on their way to work, 20 percent were shoppers, and 20 percent were business executives making calls. The average number of people per car was 1.75.

Unfortunately, we have not yet had time to use the data mentioned thus far to work up estimates of the revenues to be expected from the proposed garage.

The Elm Street site is strategically located in the heart of the CBD, near the major department stores and office buildings. It is five blocks from one of the access ramps to the new crosstown freeway, which we expect will be open to traffic next year, and only three blocks from the Music Center, which the mayor dedicated last week.

As we all know, the parking situation in that section of town has steadily worsened over the last few years, with no immediate prospect of improvement. The demand for parking is clearly there, and the Parking Authority therefore recommends that we build the garage.

The mayor thanked Mr. Stockton for his report and asked for comments. The following discussion took place:

Finance Director: I'm all in favor of relieving parking congestion downtown, but I think we have to consider alternative uses of the Elm Street site. For example, the city could sell that site to a private developer for at least $2 million. The site could support an office building from which the city would derive property taxes of around $400,000 per year at present rates. The office building would almost certainly incorporate an underground parking garage for the use of the tenants, and therefore we would not only improve our tax base and increase revenues but also increase the availability of parking at no cost to the city. Besides, an office building on that site would improve the amenity of downtown; a multilevel garage built above ground, on the other hand, would not.

Planning Director: I'm not sure I agree completely with the finance director. Within a certain range we can increase the value of downtown land by judicious provision of parking. Adequate, efficient parking facilities will encourage more intensive use of downtown traffic generators such as shops, offices, and places of entertainment, thus enhancing land values. A garage contained within an office building might, as the finance director suggests, provide more spaces, but I suspect these would be occupied almost exclusively by workers in the building and thus would not increase the total available supply.

I think long-term parking downtown should be discouraged by the city. We should attempt to encourage short-term parking—particularly among shoppers—in an effort to counteract the growth of business in the suburbs and the consequent stagnation of retail outlets downtown. The rate structure in effect at the privately operated garage quoted by Mr. Stockton clearly favors the long-term parker. I believe that if the city constructs a garage on the Elm Street site, we should devise a rate structure that favors the short-term parker. People who work downtown should be encouraged to use our mass transit system.

Finance Director: I'm glad you mentioned mass transit because this raises another issue. As you know, our subways are not now used to capacity and are running at a substantial annual deficit borne by the city. We have just spent millions of dollars on the new subway station under the Music Center. Why build a city garage only three blocks away that will still further increase the subway system's deficit? Each person who drives downtown instead of taking the subway represents a loss of $1.00 (the average round trip fare) to the subway system. I have read a report stating that approximately two-thirds of all persons entering the CBD by car would still have made the trip by *subway* if they had *not* been able to use their cars.

Mayor: On the other hand, I think shoppers prefer to drive rather than take the subway, particularly if they intend to make substantial purchases. No one likes to take the subway burdened down by packages and shopping bags. You know, the Downtown Merchants Association has informed me that they estimate that each new parking space in the CBD generates on average an additional $20,000 in annual retail sales.

That represents substantial extra profit to retailers; I think retailing aftertax profits average about 3 percent of gross sales. Besides, the city treasury benefits directly from our 3 percent sales tax.

Traffic Commissioner: But what about some of the other costs of increasing parking downtown and therefore, presumably, the number of cars entering the CBD? I'm thinking of such costs as the increased wear and tear on city streets, the additional congestion produced with consequent delays and frustration for the drivers, the impeding of the movement of city vehicles, noise, air pollution, and so on. How do we weigh these costs in coming to a decision?

Parking Administrator: I don't think we can make a decision at this meeting. I suggest that Dick Stockton be asked to prepare an analysis of the proposed garage that will answer the following questions:

Questions

1. Using the information presented at this discussion, should the city of Oakmont construct the proposed garage?

2. What rates should be charged?

3. What additional information, if any, should be obtained before making a final decision?

Case 9–4

Green Valley Medical Center*

I don't object to the priority given to medical equipment by the board of directors. At the same time, though, requests for administrative or support service capital frequently have significant cost-saving potential, and should not continue to be overlooked. There must be some way that these requests can be assessed on their merits without infringing on the hospital's ability to provide the best possible patient care.

*This case was prepared by Gregory Dorf, under the supervision of Professor David W. Young. It is based on the case *Green Valley Hospital* by H. James Graham, and is used with permission. Copyright © by David W. Young

The speaker was DeeAnne Willis, CEO of Green Valley Medical Center (GVMC). She was expressing concern that in her 12 years at the hospital both administration and support services typically had taken a back seat in the capital budgeting process.

Ms. Willis's concern was of particular importance to Allen Klein, GVMC's newly hired chief financial officer, who faced several decisions regarding the hospital's capital budgeting process. His decisions needed to be made quickly since departmental directors were just weeks away from the October 15 deadline to submit both operating budgets and capital requests.

Mr. Klein already had been approached by various senior managers in the hospital regarding their department requests for capital purchases. These managers included the Chief of Surgery, the Vice President of Operations, and the hospital's Director of Research and Residency Programs. All three had welcomed Mr. Klein with friendly greetings, followed immediately by informal presentations of their departments' proposals for new innovative capital improvements. It did not take long for Mr. Klein to realize that he needed to understand better how the capital budgeting process worked, both formally and informally.

Background

GVMC was a 330-bed nonprofit teaching hospital affiliated with a large state university in a mid-size town located several hours from the state's two urban centers. Established in the 1930s with a federal grant, Green Valley had grown with continuous support from state revenues. It also had issued municipal revenue bonds on several occasions to finance large expansions and improvements. Recent financial statements are contained in Exhibit 1.

Green Valley served a regional patient base of over one million. It was the only regional hospital, and one of only two in the state, with facilities in cardiology, oncology, and neurology. Green Valley's specialty in these fields included teaching and research as well as clinical care. It prided itself on its state-of-the-art technology as well as its overall medical expertise. In fact, the hospital was widely regarded for the innovative work and research conducted by its medical community, particularly in the neurological and oncological sciences.

The Current Capital Budgeting Process

Minimal research was enough to acquaint Mr. Klein with the current capital budgeting process at Green Valley. He was delighted to find that the hospital's available funds for capital purchases had grown at a rate of 10 to 15 percent per year during the past 5 years. How the money was distributed, however, was not so clear. The process began in each service area, where individuals submitted requests to their department head for new and replacement equipment and machinery. Capital requests included items costing $1,000 or more.

EXHIBIT 1

GREEN VALLEY MEDICAL CENTER
Financial Statements
for Most Recent Year ($000)

BALANCE SHEET

Assets

Current assets:

Cash and cash equivalents.	$11,725	
Accounts receivable (net)	5,038	
Inventories	565	
Prepaid expenses and other current assets.	1,320	$18,648

Assets whose uses are limited:

Board designated for funded depreciation (principally certificates of deposit)	$ 3,476	
Workers' compensation self-insurance fund.	227	3,703
Property, plant, and equipment (Less accumulated depreciation)		21,346
Bond issue costs (less accumulated amortization of $12)		463
Total Assets.		$44,160

Liabilities and Fund Balances

Current liabilities:

Accounts payable and accrued expenses.	$ 2,142	
Accrued compensation, payroll taxes, and related withholdings	1,163	
Amount due to third-party payers	11,711	
Current portion of long-term obligations	451	$15,467

Long-term obligations:

Bonds (net of unamortized issue discount of $28).	$ 8,300	
Mortgage note payable.	3,339	11,639

Fund balances:

Endowment fund	$ 8,550	
Unrestricted fund	8,504	17,054
Total Liabilities and Fund Balances.		$44,160

OPERATING STATEMENT

Net revenues from services to patients	$36,591	
Other operating revenues.	440	$37,031

Operating expenses:

Salaries and wages	$17,163	
Physicians' salaries and fees.	1,243	
Supplies and other expenses	12,319	
Depreciation	2,163	
Interest	1,060	
Uncompensated care	2,651	36,599
Excess of operating revenues over expenses		$ 432

Nonoperating revenues:

Investment income	$ 966	
Other nonoperating revenues	12	978
Excess of revenues over expenses		$ 1,410

Anything under $1,000 was included as an operating expense by the department. Once all new requests had been received by department heads, they were reviewed and ranked, and then ranked again incorporating all requests outstanding from the previous year. At that point, any requests not deemed necessary by the department were dropped from the list.

All additions to the list were documented with an *Equipment Request* form which contained the name of the requester, the date, price of the item, and a brief explanation of the request. Once the department head had a final list, he or she submitted it to the hospital's fiscal affairs department where it was consolidated and prioritized, along with the requests of all departments, to form one master list. The master list was reviewed and approved by the Board of Trustees at their November meeting.

At this point, it became clear to Mr. Klein why he had been pursued by so many department heads regarding their capital requests. Through his investigations, he learned that the general practice of the Board of Trustees and of the previous CFO was to give high priority to medical equipment. In fact, several department chiefs and clinical program directors did not hesitate to confirm this unwritten policy. According to the Director of Cardiology:

> Let's face it, it's no mystery that medical departments win out in head-to-head competition. We've got tradition, numbers, and the hospital's mission on our side. Of course, administration is a necessary part of the whole organization, but physicians are the ones closest to the needs of the hospital and of the patients. We're the ones who make decisions every single day.

The Chief of Medicine noted that priority assessments also differed among departments:

> Naturally certain chiefs carry more weight than others with [the CFO], and they should. Ob/Gyn, for example, would be at a disadvantage in the capital budgeting process compared to larger departments. If surgery, for example, fills 200 beds and Ob/Gyn only 20, then, all things equal, the Chief of Surgery is more likely to get what he wants than the Chief of Ob/Gyn.

Historically, although capital requests tended to be presented subjectively, their financial consequences usually were taken into consideration as well. The financial data presented, however, tended to be unreliable and often unfounded. In an attempt to be fair, the previous CFO tried to ensure that each medical department received at least one high-priority spot on the master list.

Mr. Klein also realized why he received so many capital requests from administration and support services, and he now understood why the CEO had voiced such strong concern about the process. In a follow-up conversation with Ms. Willis, she elaborated:

> The argument of efficient services and financial contribution to the hospital must be given foremost consideration by the Board of Trustees. However, physicians also should be concerned that conditions in certain administrative service areas could deteriorate to the point that we're unable to contain costs for the hospital, or

that we're unable to maintain quality. Everyone associated with the medical center is affected then.

Thus, Mr. Klein realized he needed to somehow measure all capital requests with a system that would be much more objective than what had been typical at Green Valley until now. Although he was not entirely familiar with modern capital budgeting systems used by hospitals, he was quite familiar with common practices in the private sector. He was certain that the techniques were similar. He decided to dig out his files on capital budgeting.

Two Techniques for Capital Budgeting

Upon examining his files, he discovered two techniques that pertained directly to hospitals. He found that the most critical aspect of a capital budgeting system for a hospital was to achieve a proper balance between the quantitative and qualitative analyses. Furthermore, he felt that the capital evaluation process itself should guide the acceptance of requests. Similarly, capital projects needed to be consistent with the hospital's overall goals.

Before experimenting with his new methods, Mr. Klein asked his assistant to compare the two techniques with more modern methods employed by hospitals. His assistant found that modern techniques for capital budgeting had changed very little, and that any differences were trivial or pertained to specific circumstances of a given hospital. That being the case, Mr. Klein and his assistant modified each of the two techniques to fit the needs of Green Valley.

Each technique consisted of both quantitative and qualitative evaluation. Mr. Klein believed that either technique would help to achieve a better balance of information for a consistent decision-making process, and decided to use this year as a test to see which technique he would adopt on an ongoing basis.

Technique #1

Technique #1 required four steps in evaluating a request for capital funds. These included a description of the project or equipment, verification of information, evaluation of the request, and a final decision. The technique used net present value as the quantitative evaluator, and a medical staff review as the qualitative evaluation. The data form is shown in Exhibit 2.

Technique #2

Technique #2 also used a net present value approach to quantitative analysis. It further required an investment to produce sufficient positive cash flows during a specified period to pay back the original capital expenditure plus any accumulated interest. The project also would have to provide a return on investment at the specified rate set for the payback period. Exhibit 3 contains the formal scoring sheet that was used to rank investments according to the financial and subjective evaluations.

EXHIBIT 2   Technique #1. Capital Asset Planning Form

1. date _____
A. of request _____
B. when item is needed _____

2. department/division _____

3. cost center _____

4. Briefly describe item desired location, and how its funding would be consistent with the stated goals of the department and the hospital.

5. classification (check only one)
A. Necessary to maintain present level of services including legally necessary items and new equipment and space to meet volume growth. _____
B. Results in direct cost savings and/or additional revenue without reduction (or with improvement) in the quality of present services offered. _____
C. Improves the quality of present services (no material cost savings or additional revenue). _____
D. Expands the scope of present services (new programs). _____

6. cost   Cost   verified by:
A. purchase cost _____
B. lease/rent cost _____
C. installation cost _____
D. annual operating and support costs
    1. Manpower costs _____
    2. Supplies and maintenance costs
E. interest expense (to be completed by the budget officer) _____
F. disposal cost of equipment to be replaced (less salvage value if any) _____
G. Can any necessary installation not included in the purchase price be performed by the physical facilities department?   yes_____ no_____
H. Can maintenance be performed by the physical facilities department?   yes_____ no_____
I. Can construction be performed by the physical facilities department?   yes_____ no_____

7. utilization
A. expected hours of use per day _____
B. expected days of use per week _____
C. estimated % utilization (assume 100% utilization is equal to 24 hours per day, 7 days per week) _____

8. service availability
Will the proposed investment provide a service to the hospital's patients which is presently not available or not available in sufficient quantity?
A. service presently available   yes_____ no_____

B. service presently available in sufficient quantity (if "no" give support, e.g., delays, comments of other departments, etc.)   yes_____ no_____

9. qualitative benefit
A. Number of patients benefiting (select either #1 or #2):
    1. Number of patients directly benefiting from this investment per year, if any (for investments which are used directly in patient care).
        A. maximum _____
        B. most likely _____
        C. minimum _____
    2. Number of patients *indirectly* benefiting from this investment per year, if any (for investments which are not used directly in patient care).
        % of Average Daily Inpatient Census _____
        % of Average Daily Outpatient Visits _____
B. Number of other departments which will directly benefit from this investment. _____
Briefly describe how these departments will make use of the proposed investment
C. Primary contribution to patient welfare (check one or give approximate percentage of the number of patients in each group)
    1. lifesaving or life-extending therapy _____
    2. restorative benefits or rehabilitation therapy _____
    3. preventive _____
    4. diagnostic _____
    5. patient service or convenience _____
D. Nature of other contribution (check one or more).
    1. staff and employee service or convenience _____
    2. research _____
    3. education _____
    4. other (describe briefly) _____
E. expected useful life of the service or program _____
F. Briefly describe the consequences if this investment is not made this year.

10.	quantitative benefit	department estimate	financial analysis estimate
A. number of years that economic benefits will be received		_____	_____
B. expected annual cost savings (explain briefly)		_____	_____
C. annual revenue resulting from this investment (explain briefly)		_____	_____

11. comments (add any information that may be useful in the decision-making process)

12. Net Present Value (to be completed by the financial analysis department) _____

13. medical review committee ranking (to be completed by the medical review committee) _____

Source: Reprinted from the article "4-step Capital Budgeting," *Hospital Financial Management*, June 1976, p. 51, with the permission of the author, R. Neal Gilbert.

EXHIBIT 3

TECHNIQUE #2. THE DEVELOPMENT MODEL:
A Standard Summary and Analysis of Development Expenditures

PURPOSE: To summarize the essential information required to evaluate the relative contribution to hospital operation of any addition to patient services or adjustment or extension of any support or administrative department

SECTION I: Background

A. Describe the proposed development expenditures

B. Does this development expenditure duplicate a patient service provided by another hospital in the area? Yes_____ No_____
If yes, what hospital(s)?

C. Does this proposed development expenditure require approval by comprehensive health planning? Yes_____ No_____
If no, explain why not.

D. Is there evidence to believe that the development expenditure will favorably affect any hospital service or department other than that most directly affected? Yes_____ No_____
If yes, explain.

SECTION II: Incremental Economic Analysis

PURPOSE: To provide the information required to determine the economic benefits of the development expenditure in relation to other proposed expenditures.

A. Required Initial Investment

	Cost	Depreciable Life (years)	Annual Depreciation
Capital expenditures attach support including installation cost			
Special training cost			
Initial expenditure			

B. Expected Additional (Incremental) Revenue

Unit of Service	Projected Annual Volume Inpatient	Outpatient	Suggested Patient charge
a.			
b.			
c.			
d.			

Annual Incremental Revenue		
Inpatient	Outpatient	Total

C. Expected Annual Incremental Operating Cost Increases (Decreases)—attach detail in support of each factor.

	Incremental	Annual	Cost
Personnel	$		
Employee benefits @ 12%			
Physician cost			
Materials and supplies			
Maintenance contracts			
Insurance			
Other			
Total Incremental annual cost	$		

D. Incremental Financial Analysis (to be completed by treasurer)

Let X = Total annual revenue = _____(B)
$\quad X_1$ = Annual inpatient revenue = _____(B)
$\quad X_2$ = Annual outpatient revenue = _____(B)
$\quad Y$ = Total operating cost = _____(C)
$\quad Z$ = Allowable depreciation = _____(A)

$\frac{X_1}{X} \times (Y+Z) = Y_1$ = Inpatient operating cost* = ___

$\frac{X_2}{X} \times (Y+Z) = Y_2$ = Outpatient operating cost** = ___

$\quad E$ = Total initial expenditure = ___
Present value = Present value of $1 received each year for 5 years @ 6% interest** = <u>4.212</u>

68.50 = % cost reimbursers inpatient
.03 = % bad debts inpatient
.20 = % contractual allowances & bad debts outpatient

Formulation:

Gross revenue	X
Less	
Contractual allowances inpatient	$-.685\,X_1 + .685\,Y_1$
Bad debts inpatient	$-.03\,X_1$
Contractual allowances and bad debts outpatient	$-.20\,X_2$
Net patient revenue	$X - .715\,X_1 - .20\,X_2 + .685\,Y_1$
Operating cost	Y
Net incremental revenue (NIR)	$= X - .715\,X_1 - .20\,X_2 + .685\,Y_1 - Y$

Net present value of project:
4.212 (NIR)$-E=$ net present value$= \$$(attach calculations)

*If the project or expenditure does not result in new revenue but does affect operating cost, use 12 percent as outpatient and 88 percent as inpatient cost.
**In order to properly analyze the return from investment, it is important to realize that the hospital could invest its funds in other investments and make a return. That being the case, a dollar received one year from now is worth only $.94 as compared to a dollar received now. An initial expenditure made now would be made in current dollars while the payback will be in dollars which, when compared to current dollars, are worth less. Five years is used as a standard payback period.

EXHIBIT 3 (Continued)

SECTION III: Subjective Evaluations

A. Physician Impact

1. Will this expenditure or project result in a change in physician attitude toward the hospital?
   Yes _____ No _____
   If no, ignore the remainder of A and proceed to B.
2. What is the scope of the physician attitude change? (check one)
   ___ a. One or two physicians will be affected.
   ___ b. The majority of the physicians in a hospital service will be affected.
   ___ c. A substantial portion of the medical staff will be affected.

Explain your answers (attach memorandum).

3. What is the intensity of the effect on physician attitude? (Check two answers—one for acceptance and one for nonacceptance.)

Not Accepted

☐ –4 The physicians affected will move their practices to other hospitals.

☐ –3 The physicians affected will tend to reduce their practices at the hospital.

☐ –2 The physicians affected, at the very least, will be disgruntled and will tend to discuss the lack of the expenditure or project in the community and with other physicians.

☐ –1 The physicians will be aware of the lack of support for the project and expenditure and will be less likely to believe that the hospital is maintaining a proper level of patient care.

☐ 0 No effect

Accepted

☐ 1 The physicians affected will be aware of the expenditure or project and will be satisfied that the hospital is maintaining a high level of patient care.

☐ 2 The physicians affected will be very impressed and will tend to discuss the expenditure or project favorably in the community and with other physicians.

☐ 3 The physicians affected will tend to moderately increase their practices at the hospital.

☐ 4 The physicians affected will move their practices to the hospital.

Explain these answers.

B. Community Impact

1. Will this expenditure or project have an effect on community attitude toward this hospital?
   Yes _____ No _____
   If no, proceed to C.
2. If yes, check the answers below which best describe the expected community Impact. (Check one for acceptance and one for nonacceptance.)

Not Accepted

☐ –4 Intense and widespread negative reaction in the community will result in a severe blow to the hospital's image.

☐ –3 A widespread negative effect on the hospital's general image and reputation will result.

☐ –2 The hospital's image will be damaged among certain groups in the community.

☐ –1 The attitudes of a relatively few people will be negatively affected.

☐ 0 No effect.

Accepted

☐ 1 Relatively few people will be positively affected.

☐ 2 Certain groups in the community will be favorably impressed.

☐ 3 A widespread positive effect on the hospital's image and reputation will result.

☐ 4 Significant and widespread positive community reaction will contribute significantly to the hospital's general image and reputation.

Explain these answers.

C. Employee Impact

1. Will this expenditure or project have an effect on the attitude of the hospital's personnel?
   Yes _____ No _____

2. If yes, check the answers which best describe the expected employee impact. (Check one for acceptance and one for nonacceptance.)

Not Accepted

☐ –4 Major and widespread negative impact on employee morale and attitude toward the hospital will result.

☐ –3 Widespread disappointment with the hospital and some general negative effect on the hospital's image among employees will result.

☐ –2 A limited group of employees (one or two departments) will react negatively.

☐ –1 Relatively few employees will be disturbed.

☐ 0 No effect.

Accepted

☐ 1 Relatively few employees will know about the decision, but they will be pleased.

☐ 2 A limited group (one or two departments) will be very pleased.

☐ 3 Nearly all employees will be pleased.

☐ 4 Major and widespread positive impact with long-term effect on employee attitude toward the hospital will result.

Explain these answers.

EXHIBIT 3 *(Concluded)* **Development Analysis Score Sheet**

	Item No.	Instruction	Value to Be Assigned	Raw Score	Instructions	Priority Score
Economic Evaluation						
	Section II					
	A3	If total initial expenditure is less than $25,000	1			
		If total initial expenditure is more than $25,000	−1			
	C4	If total annual incremental cost increase is less than $50,000	1			
		If total annual incremental cost increase is greater than $50,000	−1			
	D	If present value is equal to or greater than zero	2			
		If present value is less than zero	−2			
			Total economic score		If total economic raw score is greater than zero, enter raw score in priority score column	
Subjective Evaluation						
	Section III					
	A2a		1		Not applicable	
	A2b		2		If A3 is less than 4, the priority score is 1	
	A2c		3		If A3 is greater than 4, the priority score is 3	
	A3	Add positive and negative answers	1–8		If raw score exceeds 4, the excess is priority score	
	B	Add positive and negative answers	1–8		If raw score exceeds 4, the excess is priority score	
	C	Add positive and negative answers	1–8		If raw score exceeds 4, the excess is priority score	
			Total subjective score			
		Total Score				

Notes: 1. The score sheet is weighed towards the small, profitable project. This concept is based on the limited resources of the hospital and the broader impact a group of smaller projects will have on the hospital and community than a single, costly project.

2. Reprinted with permission from *Hospital Progress,* December 1975, Copyright 1975 by The Catholic Hospital Association.

The Decision-Making Process

By the October 15th deadline for departmental budgets, Mr. Klein had received a total of 130 capital requests ranging from $1,000 to $5.8 million. He felt that it was impractical to treat all capital requests as homogeneous. Rather, he thought they should be divided into several broad groupings to make it easier to compare projects of similar nature and costs. He developed four categories:

Group I   Essential items to maintain operations

Group II   Revenue producing or cost saving equipment

Group III   Optional items for improvement

Group IV   Miscellaneous items

Within each major category, all requests would then be classified by cost groupings, not as a means of prioritization, however, but only to organize them for evaluation. After checking the 130 requests for complete information, he and his assistant sorted them into the four main categories, and into cost groupings within each.

Sample Comparisons

To compare the two techniques, Mr. Klein decided to assess two very different capital requests. He chose the largest administrative support request and the most expensive request for medical equipment, assuming that there would be funds to support only one of the two. The cardiology, neurology, and oncology programs had jointly requested a Positron Emission Tomography (PET) facility for a total investment of $5.8 million. The nonmedical request was for an entirely new in house laundry facility costing approximately $1 million.

The PET Proposal

Positron Emission Tomography (PET) was an imaging technique that permitted examination of the chemistry of the brain and other organs. Unlike MRI and CT scanners, which provided images and details about organs and tissues, PET could noninvasively measure biological and physiological activity. This application was most powerful in the areas of cardiology, oncology, and neurology/psychiatry. PET was used to detect diseases, to evaluate tissue viability, to measure tumors and the degree of malignancy, to pinpoint specific sources of neurological disorders, and to assist in the planning of various treatments.

Financially, many observers believed that PET would save the health care system considerable resources by helping to avoid unnecessary procedures.

The savings were to come from the technology that would replace other procedures and improve the medical community's ability to diagnose and treat patients.

The short- and long-term need for PET scans nationally had been determined by the American Hospital Association. In February 1992 the AHA predicted an annual need for 1.1 million scans in the short term and 1.7 million scans in the long term. Currently, there were only 64 PET centers in the U.S. and Canada, roughly half of which were in research centers.

There were no PET centers within 600 miles of Green Valley. Yet, the AHA's prediction, combined with a patient base of 1 million, translated into a regional demand for 2,750 scans per year: 300 epilepsy, 200 brain, and 2,250 cardiac. The hospital expected to provide a maximum of 2,300 scans, however: 1,600 scans for clinical use and 700 for research.

The total capital investment included $1.4 million for the cyclotron, $2 million for each of two cameras (one for the head and one for the body), and $400,000 for facility renovations to accommodate the equipment. The anticipated operating expenses (other than depreciation) were $1.7 million for each of the ten years of the depreciable life of the equipment.

According to a study prepared for the Institute for Clinical PET (a trade association), the scans would be reimbursable at an average rate of $1,700. Although the 700 scans each year for research purposes would be charged at $1,700 each to research grants, Mr. Klein was concerned about reimbursement for the 1,600 clinical scans billed directly to patients and third-party payers. The PET imaging process used several radiopharmaceutical drugs. The most important of these was a drug called FDG, which had to be produced on site or close by due to the drug's short half-life. For this reason, the Food and Drug Administration had not yet approved FDG. While it was still under review, however, the FDA permitted the hospitals to continue using it. Although some third-party reimbursement was already available, several of the large national insurance companies were not covering some or all of the PET scans. Mr. Klein estimated that Green Valley would be reimbursed for roughly half of the 1,600 clinical scans as long as FDG remained FDA unapproved.

The medical staff at Green Valley believed that the PET project would not only greatly contribute to the quality of the hospital's clinical care and research, but once FDG was approved, PET would be a big moneymaker for the hospital. Furthermore, the medical staff was convinced that PET's contribution to the medical needs of the hospital's patient base, and to society as a whole through teaching and research, far outweighed any potential losses in the short term.

The Laundry Proposal

Unlike most urban hospitals that subcontract out for laundry services, Green Valley provided all of its laundry services in-house. This was mainly because there were no available subcontractors in the vicinity. As the hospital grew, laundry facilities had struggled to keep up with the demand. The current process was quite labor intensive due to relatively small capacity washer and dryer machines that the hospital had owned for many years. Furthermore, the machines required a great deal of servicing. Nevertheless, the department's request for capital had been turned down in each of the past two years.

The Laundry Department Manager had carefully researched the most cost-efficient equipment available. The request was for a Continuous Batch Washer (CBW) with a single capacity of 3,000 pounds per hour, which would accommodate the needs of the hospital. A CBW cost $500,000. In addition, the request included three 220-pound-capacity dryers costing $75,000 each and a $100,000 press which would be used to squeeze out excess water before drying. There was an additional $200,000 cost of installation, which included training and maintenance for the 15-year depreciable life of the equipment.

In addition to improving the quality and capacity of the hospital's laundry services, the new facility would operate more efficiently than the current system, with large cost savings for the hospital. Currently, the hospital employed 12 full-time workers in addition to the supervisor to operate the laundry services. The full cost of the 12 employees was $393,120. The new laundry facility would require a total of six full-time employees plus the supervisor.

Because of varying salary levels, Mr. Klein calculated that the labor savings would be approximately $197,000 per year. In addition to labor savings, the new equipment would save about $50,000 per year due to reduced utilities and maintenance costs. The current equipment was not resalable, but a local scrap dealer had offered to remove it at no cost to the hospital.

The Discount Rate

Mr. Klein evaluated each of the proposals using the two capital budgeting techniques. Since both techniques used net present value approaches, Mr. Klein had to determine the appropriate discount rate to use. This in itself presented the problem of deriving the hospital's cost of capital and return on its assets. The hospital's liabilities entailed several different rates of interest. Long-term debt included payments on its municipal bonds averaging 6 percent and fixed mortgage payments at 8 percent.

Equity capital, on the other hand, was divided between donor-restricted funds (mainly restricted to property and plant investments) and unrestricted funds (which could be used for any purpose). Mr. Klein believed that the appropriate discount rate should take all of the debt interest rates into account, but he was not sure how to assign a rate to the fund balances, or whether any rate should be used for them at all. He also thought that the discount rate should be adjusted to reflect the risk and uncertainty associated with each project.

The Decision

Mr. Klein was confident that at least one of the two techniques would be a vast improvement for the hospital. He was optimistic about the prospects of developing a system for Green Valley that finally had a rational, systematic approach to evaluating capital requests. By including the subjective analyses, he believed it would be possible to quantify some of the hospital's returns that did not always translate into dollars. At the same time, however, he realized that someone would still lose out in the end. For this reason, presenting his findings to his colleagues would not be an easy task.

Questions

1. What are the key elements of the existing capital budgeting system? Why does Mr. Klein want to change it?

2. How would the two projects fare under each of the proposed techniques? As part of your assessment, be sure to calculate each project's NPV.

3. What are the key differences between the two techniques? Which is the better technique? Please be as specific as you can in making this assessment: what kinds of projects would be given high rankings in each system and why?

4. Assuming both proposals cannot be accepted, which one would you choose?

Case 9–5

Disease Control Programs*

In February 1967 Mr. Harley Davidson, an analyst in the office of the Injury Control Program, Public Health Service (Department of Health, Education and Welfare) was reviewing DHEW's recently published Program Analysis 1966–1 titled *Disease Control Programs–Motor Vehicle Injury Prevention Program.* Included therein were nine program units. Mr. Davidson was a member of a task force established within DHEW to evaluate a series of benefit/cost analyses of various proposed disease control programs. In addition to motor vehicle injury prevention, benefit/cost studies had been made of programs dealing with control of arthritis, cancer, tuberculosis, and syphilis. Mr. Davidson's specific responsibility was to review Program Unit No. 8 of the Motor Vehicle Injury Prevention Program (Increase Use of Improved Safety Devices by Motorcyclists) in order to (*a*) evaluate the methodology

*This case was prepared by Professor Charles J. Christenson, Harvard Business School.

and results of the benefit/cost analysis of Program Unit No. 8, and (b) recommend whether or not the analysis justified the level of funding contemplated in the program unit.

The Motorcycle Program

The following is the description of Program Unit No. 8, which appeared in Program Analysis 1966–1:

Increase Use of Improved Safety Devices by Motorcyclists

To prevent accidental deaths due to head injuries of motorcycle riders through appropriate health activity at the national, state, and local levels.

Approach.   The Public Health Service approach to solving the motorcycle injury problem will involve four phases. Although each of the four phases of activity is identified separately, all will be closely coordinated and carried out simultaneously. The four phases of activity are:

1. A national education program on use of protective head gear aimed primarily at motorcycle users. It will also include efforts to prepare operators of other motor vehicles to share the road with motorcycles.

2. A cooperative program with other national organizations and the motorcycle industry to improve protective and safety devices.

3. Involvement of state and local health departments and medical organizations in programs and activities designed to minimize accidental injury in motorcycle accidents.

4. Conduct surveillance activity on appropriate aspects of the motorcycle accident and injury problem.

The program unit was estimated to require the following level of new funding during the five-year planning period 1968–72:

	Estimated Program Level (millions of dollars)
1968	$1.679
1969	1.609
1970	1.574
1971	1.569
1972	1.569

Exhibit 1 gives a summary of the way in which the proposed funds would be spent.

The benefit/cost study estimated that the above program would result in the saving of 4,006 lives over the five-year period 1968–72 (no reduction in injuries was considered). The cost of the program discounted at 4 percent was

EXHIBIT 1   Proposed Budget for Program to Increase Use of Protective Devices by Motorcyclists (1968–1972; $000)

	1968	1969	1970	1971	1972
Total number of persons	42	42	42	42	42
Total costs	$1,679	$1,609	$1,574	$1,569	$1,569
Personnel	504	504	504	504	504
Program	1,175	1,105	1,070	1,065	1,065
Staff:					
Central office.	13	13	13	13	13
Regional office.	9	9	9	9	9
State assignees	20	20	20	20	20
Personnel	$ 504	$ 504	$ 504	$ 504	$ 504
Evaluation and surveillance	300	300	300	300	300
State projects*	500*	500	500	500	500
National TV spots	60	60	60	60	60
Educational TV series.	100	100	100	100	100
Safety films	40	40	20	20	20
Publications	100	30	30	30	30
Exhibits.	30	30	15	15	15
Community projects	25	25	25	25	25
Campus projects.	20	20	20	15	15

*Ten projects at $50,000 per project.

$7,419,000; the benefits of the program, based on the lifetime earnings discounted at 3 percent of those whose deaths would be averted, were estimated at $412,754,000. Hence, the benefit/cost ratio equaled 55.6:1. Another measure of program effectiveness was the cost per death averted, $1,852. Exhibit 2 summarizes the benefit/cost ratios and the costs per death averted for all nine motor vehicle injury prevention program units and for the arthritis, cancer, tuberculosis, and syphilis programs. Exhibit 3 presents, for all programs, the estimated five-year reduction in numbers of injuries and deaths and the estimated discounted five-year program dollar costs and benefits.

Overall Methodology

In this effort to apply benefit/cost analysis to the domain of vehicular accidents, three major constraints were laid down:

1. The problem of motor vehicle accidents is examined exclusively in terms of public health concerns. This mandate focused on the role of human factors in vehicular accidents and the amelioration of injury caused by vehicular accidents. In adopting this posture, three major factors in the vehicular accident complex—law enforcement, road design, and traffic engineering—were, for the most part, excluded. This constraint had the effect of limiting the problem to considerations traditionally within the purview of

EXHIBIT 2

Costs per Death
Averted and
Benefit/Cost Ratios
for All Program Units
Studied

Program Unit	Program Cost per Death Averted	Benefit/Cost Ratio
Motor vehicle injury prevention programs:		
Increase seat belt use	$ 87	1,351.4:1
Use of improved restraint devices	100	1,117.1:1
Reduce pedestrian injury	600	144.3:1
Increase use of protective devices by motorcyclists	1,852	55.6:1
Improve driving environment	2,330	49.4:1
Reduce driver drinking	5,330	21.5:1
Improve driver licensing	13,800	3.8:1
Improve emergency medical services . . .	45,000	2.4:1
Improve driver training	88,000	1.7:1
Other disease control programs studied:		
Arthritis	n.a.	42.5:1
Syphilis	22,252	16.7:1
Uterine cervix cancer	3,470	9.0:1
Lung cancer	6,400	5.7:1
Breast cancer	7,663	4.5:1
Tuberculosis	22,807	4.4:1
Head and neck cancer	29,100	1.1:1
Colon-rectum cancer	42,944	0.5:1

n.a. = Not available.

DHEW, while excluding those elements which are traditionally handled by the Department of Commerce and other government agencies.

2. The problem of motor vehicle accidents is handled by nine programs which, in the opinion of committee members, were feasible and realistic. Criteria for determining "feasible and realistic" were not made explicit. However, program proposals which were rejected, such as no person under 21 being allowed to drive, reduction of maximum speeds on all roads by 20 percent, the federal government paying for the installation of $100 worth of safety devices on all automobiles, indicate the cultural values and assumed cost factors, which were two issues involved in judging "feasible and realistic."

3. The problem of motor vehicle accidents is handled by programs based on what is known today. This constraint ruled out dependence on new findings based on future research. Unlike the other constraints, this ruling, in the minds of the committee members, constituted a basic condition for undertaking a benefit/cost analysis of alternative program strategies. Unless the analysis was restricted to "what is known," the "need for more research" would allow one partner in the dialogue to withdraw from the struggle without even having been engaged.

EXHIBIT 3 Reduction in Injuries and Deaths and Total Discounted Program Costs and Savings for All Program Units Studied (1968–1972)

Program Unit	Discounted Program Costs ($000)	Discounted Program Savings ($000)	Reduction in Injuries	Reduction in Deaths
Motor vehicle injury prevention programs:				
Seat belts.............................	2,019	2,728,374	1,904,000	22,930
Restraint devices	610	681,452	471,600	5,811
Pedestrian injury	1,061	153,110	142,700	1,650
Motorcyclists.........................	7,419	412,754	—	4,006
Driving environment	28,545	1,409,891	1,015,500	12,250
Driver drinking........................	28,545	612,970	440,630	5,340
Driver licensing	6,113	22,938	23,200	442
Emergency medical services.............	721,478*	1,726,000	†	16,000
Driver training........................	750,550	1,287,022	665,300	8,515
Other disease control programs studied:				
Arthritis	35,000	1,489,000	n.a.	n.a.
Syphilis	179,300‡	2,993,000	n.a.	11,590
Uterine cervix cancer...................	118,100‡	1,071,000	n.a.	34,200
Lung cancer...........................	47,000‡	268,000	n.a.	7,000
Breast cancer.........................	22,400	101,000	n.a.	2,396
Tuberculosis..........................	130,000	573,000	n.a.	5,700
Head and neck cancer..................	7,800	9,000	n.a.	268
Colon-rectum cancer...................	7,300	4,000	n.a.	170

n.a. = Not available.
*Includes $300 million state matching funds.
†This program does not reduce injury; however, it is estimated to reduce hospital bed/days by 2,401,000 and work loss days by 8,180,000.
‡Funding shown used as basis for analysis—includes funds estimated to come from sources other than DHEW.

The report then went on to describe the rationale behind benefit/cost analysis:

> The reasoning behind the benefit/cost analysis is quite straightforward. The idea is to allow for a meaningful comparison of the change which results in a given situation as a result of applying alternative programs. In order to bring about this state of affairs, a measurable common denominator is useful for rating program outcome and program costs. This common denominator is dollars. Granting the existence of the common denominator, there must, in addition, be a point on which to take a "fix" in order to support the contention that change has, in fact, taken place. This point for fixing position and shifts in relation to change wrought by program is the baseline.
>
> In this exercise the baseline was created by assessing past rates for motor vehicle and pedestrian deaths and injuries. The assumption was made that the current level of program effort in DHEW would remain constant through 1972

with the exception of increases for obligated administrative costs. The observed trend was then projected and applied to the anticipated population distribution for the years 1967–72. Program costs and savings due to the introduction of the program were limited to the five-year period 1968–72, although certain programs were just gathering momentum by the end of this period. . . . The required common denominator was incorporated into the baseline by converting fatalities into lost earnings and by translating lost work days, bed disability days, length of hospitalization, physician visits, and other medical services resulting from injuries into the direct and indirect costs represented by these statistical measures. . . . Throughout this analysis, the total dollar costs and benefit for the five-year period are discounted to 1968, the base year, to convert the stream of costs and benefits into its worth in the base year. . . .

With the baseline and common denominator established, the Committee was able to examine the potential payoff for a variety of program units even though these units differed with respect to such factors as cost of implementation, target group to be reached, method to be employed, and facet of the total program addressed by the proposed program.

With the establishment of the baseline and the development of techniques to convert all elements of the equation to a common denominator, the energies of the Committee were given over to the creation of program units. There are a number of variables which may contribute to the occurrence of a vehicular accident and its resultant injury or death. The skill of the driver, the condition of the road, the speed of the vehicle, the condition of the car, the failure to have or to use safety devices incorporated in the car are just a few of many that are mentioned in the literature. What we know about vehicular accidents is expressed in terms of these variables and, as a consequence, program formulations are generally placed in the context of managing these variables, either singly or in combination. A program unit, as developed by the Committee, usually addressed a single variable.

There are two links needed to effect the benefit/cost analysis in vehicular accidents. The first link is associated with the estimate of reduction that could be realized if a given variable were addressed by a program of some sort. This link is supplied in vehicular accidents by the expertise of the Committee members and recourse to studies on the particular variable in question. The second link is associated with the effectiveness of the program proposed to bring about the estimated reduction. In vehicular accidents this is supplied by the experience with programs of the Committee members and the success in the past of programs, similar in content, devoted to public health problems.

Estimate of Benefits

The benefit/cost studies of the motor vehicle injury prevention programs began with a stipulation of a "base line," or the number of deaths and injuries to be expected if the level of DHEW effort remained constant. Next, an estimate was made of the number of deaths and injuries which would be avoided if the proposed program unit were adopted. Finally, the reduction in deaths and injuries was translated into dollar terms. These three steps will now be described as they applied to Program Unit No. 8.

Year	Total Number of Registered Motorcycles in the U.S.	Number of Deaths from Motorcycle Accidents	Rate of Deaths per 100,000 Motorcycles
1959	565,352	752	133.0
1960	569,691	730	128.1
1961	595,669	697	117.0
1962	660,400	759	114.9
1963	786,318	882	112.2
1964	984,760	1,118	113.5

The Baseline

The team working on the motorcycle unit had available the information given in Table 1.

The team estimated that (1) the number of registered motorcycles would continue to increase at an increasing rate, and (2) the death rate would decline, in the absence of new safety programs, to a level of 110 deaths per 100,000 registered motorcycles. Accordingly, the number of motorcycle accident deaths to be expected without the safety program was projected as shown in Table 2.

Effectiveness of the Program Unit

Calculation of the anticipated reduction in the number of deaths resulting from the proposed program unit involved two separate estimates: (1) the effectiveness of the program in persuading motorcyclists to wear helmets and protective eyeshields; and (2) the effectiveness of these devices in reducing deaths (injuries were not considered in the analysis of this program unit). The team's judgment was that the program would result in use of helmets and eyeshields to the degree shown in Table 3.

Regarding the second factor, the effectiveness of protective devices in reducing deaths, the team relied on a study entitled "Effect of Compulsory Safety Helmets on Motorcycle Accident Fatalities" which appeared in *Australian*

Year	Projected Total Number of Registered Motorcycles in the U.S.	Projected Number of Deaths from Motorcycle Accidents without Program (based on 110 deaths per 100,000 registered motorcycles)
1968	2,900,000	3,190
1969	3,500,000	3,850
1970	4,200,000	4,620
1971	5,000,000	5,500
1972	6,000,000	6,600

TABLE 3

Estimated
Effectiveness of
Program in
Encouraging
Protective Devices

Year	Estimated Percentage of Motorcyclists Using Helmets and Eyeshields
1968	20
1969	30
1970	40
1971	50
1972	55

Road Research, vol. 2, no. 1, September 1964. This study reported that the number of motorcycle fatalities occurring in the Australian state of Victoria in the two years following the effective date of a law requiring the wearing of helmets was only 31 while the number of fatalities projected on the basis of the experience of the two preceding years was 62.5, for a reduction of about 50 percent. Other states, which did not have such a law, had shown a reduction of about 12 percent in the same period, a difference of 38 percent. The committee concluded that 100 percent usage of helmets and eyeshields by American motorcyclists would reduce the number of deaths by about 40 percent.

Multiplication of the figures for projected usage of protective devices given in Table 3 by 40 percent gave the estimated percentage reduction in deaths, and application of these percentages to the baseline data of Table 2 gave the estimated reduction in number of deaths. The results are summarized in Table 4.

Conversion to Economic Benefits

For the purpose of calculating the lifetime earnings lost in the event of a motorcycle fatality, it was necessary to estimate the distribution of fatalities by age and sex. In 1964, approximately 90 percent of the victims of motorcycle accidents had been male and 10 percent female; similarly, about 90 percent had been in the age group 15–24 and 10 percent in the age group 25–34. The data were not cross-classified, so it was considered necessary to assume

TABLE 4 Estimated Reduction in Deaths from Proposed Program

Year	Projected Number of Deaths from Motorcycle Accidents without Program	Estimated Percentage Reduction in Deaths with Program	Estimated Reduction in Number of Deaths with Program
1968	3,190	8	255
1969	3,850	12	462
1970	4,620	16	739
1971	5,500	20	1,100
1972	6,600	22	1,450
5-year total	23,760	—	4,006

TABLE 5 Estimated Reduction in Deaths by Age and Sex

Year	Age 15–24		Age 25–34		
	Males	Females	Males	Females	Total
1968	207	23	22	3	255
1969	374	42	41	5	462
1970	598	67	67	7	739
1971	891	99	99	11	1,100
1972	1,174	131	130	15	1,450
Total	3,244	362	359	41	4,006

that the sex distribution of fatalities in each age group was the same as the overall distribution, i.e., 90:10. Projecting these percentages into the future, it was calculated that, of the 255 fatalities which the proposed program was expected to avoid in 1968, 207 would be males between 15 and 24 inclusive (i.e., .9 × .9 × 255). Combining this procedure for all categories and years resulted in the estimates of the distribution of death reductions over the five-year period shown in Table 5.

The final step in calculating the expected benefits of the proposed program was to assign the appropriate dollar benefits to the above estimates of decreases in deaths by age group and sex. This was done by multiplying the decrease in deaths in each sex-age group "cell" in the above table by the applicable discounted lifetime earnings figure for that particular cell.

Table 6 shows lifetime earnings by age and sex, discounted at 3 percent used in computing the dollar benefits of reducing motorcycle accident fatalities. (The report contained a detailed description of the methodology used in deriving these amounts.)

The number of deaths saved in each cell of Table 5 was multiplied by the appropriate earnings figure from Table 6, and discounted at 3 percent to the base year, 1968. For example, Table 5 indicates that it was estimated that, in 1968, the lives of three females between the ages of 25 and 34 would be saved. The discounted lifetime earnings of females in this age group was found from Table 6 by averaging the discounted lifetime earnings for females

TABLE 6
Discounted Lifetime Earnings by Age and Sex

Age	Males	Females
Under 1	$ 84,371	$50,842
1–4	98,986	54,636
5–9	105,836	63,494
10–14	122,933	73,719
15–19	139,729	81,929
20–24	150,536	84,152
25–29	150,512	81,702
30–34	141,356	77,888

TABLE 7 Discounted Savings Resulting from Program to Promote Use of Protective Devices by
Motorcyclists (000s)

| Year | Total | Age 15–24 | | Age 25–34 | |
		Males	Females	Males	Females
Total	$412,754	$334,002	$27,164	$48,714	$2,874
1968	36,140	30,347	1,976	3,578	239
1969	61,972	52,423	3,282	5,895	372
1970	97,152	82,363	5,059	9,248	482
1971	39,547	17,928	7,408	13,393	818
1972	177,943	150,941	9,439	16,600	963

25–29 and 30–34, the average of $81,702 and $77,888 being $79,795. This
was multiplied by 3 to give $239,385; using a present value factor of 1 (since
1968 was the base year), the figure derived was $239,385. Similarly, dis-
counted figures were obtained for each year by age group and sex; the results
are shown in Table 7.

Thus, over the five-year program period, 1968–72, it was estimated that
4,006 deaths could be averted (Table 5), at a present-value cost of $7,419,000.
The present value of the lifetime earnings of the 4,006 persons whose lives
would be saved during this period was shown in Table 7 to be $412,754,000.

These data were summarized in the form of two measures of program
effectiveness:

$$\text{Program cost per death averted} = \frac{\$7,419,000}{4,006} = \underline{\underline{\$1,852}}$$

$$\text{Benefit/cost ratio} = \frac{\$412,754,000}{\$7,419,000} = \underline{\underline{55.6}}$$

Questions

1. As Mr. Davidson, prepare a critique of the methodology and findings of the
   benefit/cost analysis of Program Unit No. 8.

2. Based on your evaluation of the analysis, would you recommend the level
   of funding proposed?

Chapter 10

Budgeting

A budget is a plan expressed in monetary terms. There are essentially three types of budgets: (1) the *capital budget,* which lists and describes planned capital acquisitions, (2) the *cash budget,* which summarizes planned cash receipts and disbursements, and (3) the *operating budget,* which describes planned operating activities.

The general character of the budgeting process in a nonprofit organization is similar to that in a for-profit one. There are significant differences in emphasis, however. This chapter focuses on both the similarities and the differences. We put most of our emphasis on the operating budget. The capital budget is derived more or less automatically from decisions made during the strategic planning process, as described in Chapter 9; we discuss it briefly to show its link to both strategic planning and the operating budget. The cash budget is derived from the operating budget, and forecasts planned cash flows on a monthly (or sometimes more frequent) basis during the operating year. We do not discuss the cash budget in this chapter.[1]

The Capital Budget

The capital budget contains a list of capital projects that are proposed for financing during the coming year. In effect, the capital budget includes all acquisitions of long-lived assets planned for the year.

In most organizations, items to be included in the capital budget emerge from decisions made during the strategic planning process. If the total approved capital expenditures are larger than can be financed, senior management must reduce the capital budget. Since capital projects affect program execution for years to come, such reductions require careful consideration.

---

[1]"The Menotomy Home Health Services" case in Chapter 4 required the preparation of a cash budget.

Capital expenditures ordinarily have an impact on operating costs. For this reason, there is an important link between the capital budget and the operating budget. For example, if a capital expenditure was approved because it would lead to some labor savings, senior management must be certain that line managers include those labor savings in their operating budgets. Similarly, if the capital budget includes some expenditures for new equipment as part of a new program, there no doubt will be new operating costs and new revenues associated with the new program. Senior management should expect these to be included in the operating budget.

General Nature of the Operating Budget

The operating budget is always for a specified period, usually one year, although some organizations use a different time frame.[2] For example, some states, such as Nevada, prepare a biennial (once every two years) budget. By contrast, some theaters have semiannual budgets: one for the winter season and one for the summer season.

Relationship between Strategic Planning and Budgeting

In concept, operational budgeting follows, but is separate from, strategic planning. The budget is supposed to be a "fine tuning" of an organization's programs for a given year. It incorporates the final decisions on the amounts to be spent for each program, and specifies the organizational unit that is responsible for carrying out each program. In some organizations, these decisions take place within the context of basic decisions made during the strategic planning process. In most organizations, however, no such clean separation between strategic planning and budgeting exists. Even organizations that have a well-developed strategic planning process frequently discover circumstances during budgeting that require revisions of program decisions. In organizations that have no recognizable or separate strategic planning activity, program decisions are made as part of budgeting.

Despite this overlap, it is useful to think about the two activities separately because they have different characteristics. As discussed in Chapter 9, strategic planning decisions typically have multiyear consequences. The purpose of budgeting, by contrast, is to decide on the details of the actual operating plan for a year. Budgeting requires careful estimates of expenses and revenues, using the most current information on prices of both outputs and inputs. Moreover, a budget usually is formulated within a ceiling of estimated available resources.

[2]Budget (or fiscal) years end in different months of the calendar year. In colleges and universities, for example, the fiscal year usually ends June 30, July 31, or August 31. In nongovernment organizations, the budget year is usually the calendar year. In the federal government, the fiscal year ends September 30. In many state and local governments the fiscal year ends June 30.

Since a budget is a plan against which actual performance is compared, senior management must be certain that it corresponds to individual responsibility centers. As such, the budget provides a basis for measuring the performance of responsibility center managers. If a program is to be used as a basis for performance measurement, senior management generally must designate it as a responsibility center. Otherwise, responsibility for many of a program's elements may be too diffused throughout the organization to permit the measurement of the performance of any given manager.

Two-Stage Budgets

This chapter refers to the operating budget as if there were only one. In government organizations and some other nonprofit organizations, there actually are two budgets.

1. The *legislative budget* is essentially a request for funds. It does not correspond to the budget that is prepared in a for-profit company. Its closest counterpart is the prospectus that a company prepares when it seeks to raise money. Most media reports about government budgets relate to the legislative budget, and many textbook descriptions of government budgeting focus on this budget.

2. The *management budget* is prepared after the legislature has decided on the amount of funds that is to be provided (or, if the legislature is dilatory, it is prepared as soon as the executive branch can make a good estimate of what the legislature eventually will approve). This budget corresponds to the budget prepared in a for-profit company; that is, it is a plan showing the amount of authorized spending for each responsibility center. If the amount of revenue is known within reasonable limits, the management budget can be an accurate reflection of the organization's plans for the year. Our discussion concerning the operating budget focuses almost exclusively on this management budget.

Contrast with For-Profit Companies

Budgeting is an important part of the management control process in any organization. It is even more important in a nonprofit organization than in a for-profit company, however, for two reasons—cost structure and spending flexibility.

Cost Structure

In a for-profit company, particularly a manufacturing company, many costs are engineered. The amount of labor and the quantity of material required to manufacture products are determined within close limits by design and engineering specifications. Consequently, little can be done to affect these costs during the budgeting process. By contrast, in most nonprofit organizations many costs are discretionary; that is, the amount to be spent can vary widely depending on management's decisions. Many of these decisions are made during the budget formulation process.

Spending Flexibility

In a for-profit company, a budget is a fairly tentative statement of plans. It is subject to change as conditions change, and such changes, particularly in the volume and mix of sales, can occur frequently during the year. Furthermore, there is general agreement on the way managers should react to such changes; they should make revised plans that are consistent with the overall objective of profitability.

In many nonprofit organizations, conditions are more stable and predictable. In a university, the number of students enrolled in September governs the pattern of spending for the whole year. A hospital gears up for a certain number of beds, and, although there may be temporary fluctuations in demand, these ordinarily do not cause major changes in spending patterns. A federal agency or a public school system has a certain authorized program or set of programs for the year that it must carry out. Under these circumstances, the budget is a fairly accurate statement of both its activities and the resources to be used. It is therefore important to prepare the budget carefully. Much time, including much senior-management time, should be devoted to it.

Components of the Operating Budget

The numerical part of the operating budget (which is often supplemented by explanatory text) consists of three components: (1) revenues, (2) expenses and expenditures, and (3) output measures.

Revenues

As we discussed in Chapter 2, the general purpose of a nonprofit organization is to provide as much service as it can with available resources. In many nonprofit organizations, the total amount of resources (revenue) in any given budget year is, for all practical purposes, confined within quite narrow limits. The approach to budgeting, therefore, is to decide how best to spend it. This suggests that the basic approach to budgeting should be, first, to estimate the available resources—that is, revenues—and, second, to plan spending to match those resources.

Most managers would agree that the policy of anticipating revenues first, and then budgeting expenses below or equal to them, is fiscally sound. The policy also provides a bulwark against arguments, often made by highly articulate and persuasive people, that an organization should undertake a program even though it cannot afford to do so.

In federal or state governments, application of this principle requires that public managers make careful estimates of the level of funds that the legislature is likely to appropriate. In state and municipal governments, it requires judgment as to feasible taxation and other revenues. In other organizations, it requires estimating the revenues to be derived from fees charged to clients, gifts and grants, endowment earnings, and other sources.

Discipline Required for a Revenue-First Policy

Carrying out a revenue-first policy requires considerable discipline in two respects. First, it requires a careful and prudent estimate of total revenues from all sources, including clients, grants, contracts, third-party payers, and endowment earnings. Once this figure has been established, it is "locked in."

Second, it requires a commitment to engage in cost cutting if necessary. That is, if the first approximation to the budget indicates a deficit, the least painful course of action is to anticipate additional sources of revenue that will eliminate it. This is a highly dangerous course of action. If the original revenue estimates have been made carefully, all feasible sources of revenue were included. New ideas that arise subsequently may produce additional revenue, but the evidence that they will do so usually is not strong. If they do not produce the additional revenue, operations may proceed without taking the steps needed to balance revenues and expenses. The safer course of action is to take whatever steps are necessary to bring expenses into balance with revenues.

Example

Some churches and religious organizations adopt a "God will provide" approach to budgeting. Many have discovered, much to their dismay, that the Lord works in mysterious ways.

During one fiscal year, the Baltimore Ballet budgeted its expenses first, and then compared them with estimates of earned revenue. The excess of expenses over earned revenue was deemed "to be raised" through contributors. This sum was overly optimistic as were estimates of earned revenue. Although monthly statements indicated unfavorable revenue and expense variances, no corrective action was taken by the board for eight months. The result was a deficit of several hundred thousand dollars.[3]

Preliminary versus Final Budgets

Some college and private school boards approve a *preliminary* budget in early summer, just prior to the beginning of their fiscal year. This gives department heads the spending authority needed to prepare for fall classes. In September, once actual enrollments are known with almost total certainty, they prepare a final budget. This final budget uses total revenue as the ceiling for total expenses. Such a process works if the total revenue is known with considerable certainty early in the fiscal year, and if line managers have enough discretionary items in their budgets (such as part-time faculty) so they can make cuts if necessary.

Hard and Soft Money

A college with a reasonable expectation of meeting its enrollment quota can count on a certain amount of tuition revenue; this is *hard money*. Income from endowment is also hard money. It is prudent to make long-term commitments,

---

[3]From a report by Rosemary Dougherty (personal correspondence).

such as tenured faculty appointments, when they will be financed by hard money. By contrast, revenue from annual gifts or short-lived grants for research projects is *soft money*. In a recession, gifts may drop drastically and grantors may decide not to renew their grants. Managers must be careful about making long-term commitments that are financed with soft money.

Exceptions to the Revenue-First Policy

The policy that budgeted revenue sets the limit on expenses is not applicable under certain conditions. Some of these are discussed below.

The Federal Budget   The considerations mentioned above do not apply to the federal budget. This budget may be either a surplus or a deficit. The amount of either is determined by the administration's conclusion (with the concurrence of the Congress) as to the proper fiscal policy in a given year. The federal government rarely plans for a balanced budget.

Discretionary Revenue   In some organizations, management has an ability to increase revenues. For example, it may be able to increase revenues from current gifts by an intensified fund-raising effort. This idea of "spending money to make money" is the nonprofit counterpart of a for-profit company's marketing budget. To the extent that this argument is valid, it is appropriate to speak of discretionary revenue as well as discretionary expenses. Ordinarily such opportunities are not of major significance, however. In most situations, the organization has already used all the fund-raising devices that it can think of, and managers must take the probable revenues from such efforts as a given, not subject to major upward revision.

Anticipated Revenue   Some organizations such as universities, research institutes, and social service agencies include anticipated grant revenues in their budgets. This is because they frequently apply for grants, but do not learn whether the funds will be approved until well into the fiscal year. If the budget were prepared only on the basis of *known* revenues, key professional staff might be laid off, obtain employment elsewhere, and not be available if the grant is awarded. Thus, some organizations decide to incur deficits in anticipation of receiving grant awards. Such a strategy is risky and clearly can be sustained only if grants of sufficient magnitude are received.

Example

Some years ago, New York University embarked on a major expansion program. Substantial amounts of additional revenue were obtained from additional enrollments, fund-raising campaigns, and government grants. Several years later, funds from all these sources began to shrink. Instead of cutting costs to meet the lower level of revenues, however, deficits were permitted, which reached a peak of $14 million. Drastic steps were finally taken to bring costs in line with revenue, but by then a considerable portion of the university's capital had been dissipated.[4]

[4]Condensed from a report in *Science,* December 8, 1972, pp. 1072–75.

Short-Run Fluctuations   When managers expect short-term revenue fluctuations around an average, it is appropriate to budget for the average revenue, rather than for the specific level of revenue in a given year; that is, in some years expenses may exceed revenue if in other years revenues exceed expenses by a corresponding amount. Indeed, some nonprofit organizations consciously adopt a "countercyclical" fiscal policy as a strategy. They reason that when the economy is in a downswing, more clients who cannot pay will need their services, with the opposite effect taking place during economic expansion. They thus plan to incur deficits in bad times and surpluses during good times. This strategy must be carefully managed. If, for example, the policy is overly conservative, it deprives current clients of services. Conversely, as is the case with uncertain revenue, if management assumes that next year will be better, and when this doesn't happen, that the following year surely will be better, the institution may be headed for disaster.

The Promoter   Occasionally, the amount of resources available can be increased by a dynamic individual. The governing board thereupon authorizes an operating budget in excess of current revenues in anticipation of the new resources that the promoter will provide. Such a decision is obviously a gamble. If it works, the institution may be elevated to a permanently higher plateau. If it doesn't work, painful cutbacks may be necessary to bring expenses back in line with revenues.

Deliberate Capital Erosion   There are situations where the current revenue is deliberately not regarded as a ceiling, and part of the organization's permanent capital is used for current operations. This may represent a gamble in anticipation of new resources as described above, or it may reflect a conscious policy to go out of existence after the capital has been consumed.

In effect, any budget with a deficit is consuming permanent capital. Thus, decisions to use permanent capital for current operations should be made with great care. No organization can live beyond its means indefinitely.

Example

One university had its schools organized as profit centers. Each school was responsible for achieving a balanced budget every year. One year, when a school was facing its third substantial deficit in three years, the university's central administration informed the school's dean that the deficit would be financed with the principal from the school's endowment fund. Faced with the prospect of capital erosion, the dean balanced the budget.

Expenses and Expenditures

There are two general formats for the spending portion of the budget. The traditional format is called the *line-item budget,* although this term is not descriptive because every budget has items arranged in lines. A line-item budget focuses on expense elements; that is, wages, fringe benefits, supplies, and other types of resources. The other format is called a *program budget.* It

EXHIBIT 10–1

Examples of Types of Budgets—Municipal Public Safety Activities ($000)

	Estimated Actual 2001	Budget 2002
A. Line-Item Budget		
Wages and salaries	$4,232	$4,655
Overtime	217	72
Fringe benefits	783	861
Retirement plan	720	792
Operating supplies	216	220
Fuel	338	410
Uniforms	68	70
Repairs and maintenance	340	392
Professional services	71	0
Communications	226	236
Vehicles	482	450
Printing and publications	61	65
Building rental	447	450
Other	396	478
Total	$8,597	$9,151
B. Program Budget		
Crime control and investigation	$2,677	$2,845
Traffic control	1,610	1,771
Correctional institutions	470	482
Inspections and licenses	320	347
Police training	182	180
Police administration	680	704
Fire fighting	1,427	1,530
Fire prevention	86	92
Fire training	64	70
Fire administration	236	260
Other protection	563	560
General administration	282	310
Total	$8,597	$9,151

focuses on programs and program elements that represent the activities for which the funds are to be spent. Examples of each type for the public safety department of a municipality are shown in Exhibit 10–1. Although the focus of a program budget is on programs, condensed element information—such as the amount of personnel costs, supplies, and other operating costs—is usually shown for each program as well.

The program budget permits a decision maker to judge the appropriate amount of resources for each activity, and hence the emphasis to be given to that activity. It also permits senior management to match spending with measures of each activity's planned outputs. These are important advantages of the program budget format.

Link to the Capital Budget

If the operating budget is prepared on an expenditure (rather than expense) basis, it may include amounts for equipment and other long-lived assets. When this is the case, only buildings and major capital acquisitions will be included in the capital budget.

When the operating budget is prepared on an expenditure basis, senior management should make a clear distinction between the types of items included in these two budgets. Otherwise, there is a temptation to balance the operating budget by moving some items from it into the capital budget.

Example	Some years ago, officials in New York City made many maneuvers to hide the true operating deficit. One was to shift operating items to the capital budget where they presumably would be financed by bonds rather than by current revenues. An extreme example was vocational education expenses, which were shifted to the capital budget on the grounds that students would enjoy the benefits for many years to come and that vocational education was therefore a long-lived asset!

Output Measures

The third component of a budget is information about planned outputs. As we describe in Chapter 12, output information usually consists of process (or workload) measures and results measures. Some organizations commit themselves to specific results measures as part of the budgetary process.

Example	In one public school system, principals' budgets were determined in part by a combination of expected enrollments and centrally mandated student-teacher ratios; these ratios are process or workload measures. The principals also committed themselves to achieving certain levels of reading scores for students completing different grades. Senior management believed that these results measures indicated how well teachers achieved the school system's objectives.
	An article on university budgeting lists several output criteria that can be used to determine merit salary increments for faculty: dollar amounts of research grants generated, number of Ph.D.s graduated, number of journal publications, and teaching quality.[5] These criteria help to link the budget to a university's objectives.

Steps in the Operations Budgeting Process

The principal steps involved in the operations budgeting process are: (1) dissemination of guidelines, (2) preparation of the budget estimates, (3) review of

---

[5]Allen G. Schick, "University Budgeting: Administrative Perspective, Budget Structure, and Budget Process," *Academy of Management Review* 10, no. 4 (1985), pp. 794–802.

these estimates, and (4) approval of the budget. The review process may lead to revision of the original estimates, so the proposed budget may be recycled several times before being approved. In this regard, timing is an important consideration. If the budget is prepared too far in advance, it will not be based on the most current information. If, on the other hand, not enough time is allowed, the process may be rushed and incomplete. In the federal government, for example, the budgeting process starts about six months before the budget is submitted to the Congress, and well over a year before the budget year begins. In less complex organizations, the period is considerably shorter.

Dissemination of Guidelines

Senior management usually begins the budgetary process by formulating the budget guidelines and disseminating them to operating managers. Senior management needs to give considerable attention to these guidelines; if the budget is formulated on the basis of unrealistic assumptions, it may have to be redone with consequent wasted effort.

If approved programs exist, one guideline is that the budget should be consistent with them. This does not necessarily mean that the budget should consist only of approved programs, since this can be frustrating for operating managers. Moreover, desirable innovations may come to light if managers are permitted to propose activities that are not part of approved programs. These unapproved activities should be clearly distinguished from those in the approved programs, however, and operating managers should understand that the chances for approval of new programs during budget formulation are slight. Any other impression downgrades the importance of strategic planning.

Even if there are no formal programs, senior management should make operating managers aware of the constraints within which the budget is prepared. These constraints can be expressed in an overall statement such as "budget for not more than 105 percent of the amount spent this year," or they can be stated in much more detail. These details might include:

- Planned changes in the activities of the organization.
- Assumptions about wage rates and other prices.
- Conditions under which additional personnel can be requested.
- Number of personnel who may be promoted.
- Services to be provided by support responsibility centers.
- Planned productivity gains.

In the absence of guidance to the contrary, the usual assumption is that next year's activities will be similar to this year's.

In addition to the substantive guidelines, there are also guidelines about the format and content of the proposed budget. These are intended to ensure that the budget estimates are submitted in a fashion that both facilitates analysis and permits their subsequent use in comparing actual performance with planned performance.

Preparation of Budget Estimates

In many organizations, managers at the lowest levels are responsible for preparing a budget for their activities. This "participatory" budgeting approach contrasts with the practice of "imposed" budgeting in which budgets are prepared by top-level staffs and then imposed on operating managers. Under participatory budgeting staff assistants may help managers by making calculations and filling out the forms, but the basic decisions that are reflected in the proposed budget are made by operating managers, not by staff.

Relation to Programs

If an approved program exists, the expense budget usually is constructed by fine-tuning the estimated program costs. For new programs, this involves assigning program responsibility to responsibility centers and constructing careful cost estimates in each responsibility center. For example, a research-and-development program may be budgeted at $400,000 simply by estimating that it will require four professional work years at $100,000 a work year. In constructing the budget, the salaries of professionals and the other support costs that make up the overall estimate of $100,000 per work year will be stated. The resulting total will approximate $400,000 but will vary somewhat from this estimate as the costs are examined in more detail.

Arriving at Budget Amounts

If the current level of spending is used as a starting point, the budget can be constructed by adjusting for:

• Changes in wage rates and prices.

• Elimination of unusual factors that may have affected current spending.

• Changes in programs.

• Possible adjustments in certain discretionary items (such as expenses for attendance at conventions) that may have been mandated in the guidelines.

Variable Budgets

If the workload for the budget year can be estimated and if unit costs are available, the budget can be constructed so as to include this estimate. In a welfare office, for example, if the number of cases can be predicted, the number of budgeted social workers can be found by using a standard number of cases per social worker. Other elements of cost can be estimated as a function of the number of social workers.

If revenues and expenses vary with volume, as happens with, say, food service costs, the expense budget may be stated in terms of a fixed amount plus a variable rate per unit of volume (e.g., $300,000 + $5 per meal). It is appropriate to budget, say, food service in a hospital or a private school in this fashion because the revenue from patient care or student board varies with volume. (The amount reported in the budget would be the total cost of food service at the estimated number of meals served.)

Despite the logic of developing the budget from workload estimates and unit costs, the budget guidelines may prohibit increases above a certain amount, regardless of the workload. This requirement overrides the workload calculations. The manager may point out, however, that the budgeted amounts are inadequate to carry out the planned workload so that trade-off decisions can be made.

Advanced Techniques

Various analytical techniques, such as the use of subjective probabilities, preference theory, multiple regression analysis, and models, have been advocated as an aid to budget formulation. For a variety of reasons, few of these are used in practice.

Budget Detail

Many dollar amounts in the budget are the product of a physical quantity times a cost per unit. For example, personnel costs are a product of the number of staff times average compensation. These amounts should be shown separately because of a breakdown of quantities and unit costs both facilitates review of the budget and also is useful in subsequently analyzing differences between budgeted and actual expenses.

In addition to the numbers, the proposed budget usually includes explanatory material. In particular, if additional personnel are requested, a justification may be required.

Review of Budget Estimates

The budget review and approval process has both a technical and a behavioral dimension. Although the two are closely related, we discuss them separately to illustrate the important distinctions.

Technical Aspects

The technical aspects of the process usually are carried out by budget analysts, who are quite different in makeup from the program analysts discussed in Chapter 9. A program analyst usually does not work under tight time constraints, and is less interested in accuracy than a budget analyst. He or she is more interested in judging, even in a rough way, the relation between costs and benefits of a proposed program. A budget analyst, by contrast, must be concerned with accuracy, but also must work under great time constraints, possess a feel for what is the right amount of cost, and be able and willing to get to the essence of the calculations quickly.

Time Constraints   An important, but sometimes overlooked, fact about the review process is that not much time is available for it. The proposed budgets for every responsibility center must be examined in the space of, at most, a few weeks. This is in contrast with the strategic planning process in which one program, covering only a small fraction of the organization's activities, can be examined in depth. Because there is not enough time to do otherwise, managers typically take the level of current spending as the starting point in examining the proposed budget. Although the burden of proof to justify amounts above that level is on the budgetee, there is an implication that budgetees are "entitled" to the current level. This practice is widely criticized (it sometimes is called the *blight of incrementalism*), but there is little that can be done about it as a practical matter, simply because of time pressure. The place for a more thorough analysis of spending needs is the strategic planning process.

Methods of Analysis Frequently, proposed budgets are first reviewed by the budget staff, which then makes recommendations to line managers. This review has two aspects, one relating to mission programs, and another to support programs.

If a mission program is new, little can be done to change the revenue and expense estimates during the budget review process. Not only has a rough budget ordinarily been agreed to during the strategic planning phase, but there is no experience with actual operations of the program that can be used as a basis for assessing the adequacy of the budget.

If a mission program is ongoing, the appropriateness of actual and proposed expenses can be analyzed. Many budget analysts develop unit cost guidelines that assist them in judging proposed increases in items such as staffing and supplies for a program. For example, a budget analyst, whose programs include restaurant inspections for a state department of public health, knows that each inspector should cover a certain number of restaurants in a year. By obtaining information on the number of new and closed restaurants, the analyst can judge the adequacy of proposed staffing levels.

The budget analyst also focuses on support programs. If the entity's size will change because of mission program decisions, corresponding adjustments must be made in the current level of spending for support activities. After making adjustments for changes in size, a budget analyst also can make a careful review of the details of support activities, using the adjusted current levels of spending as a starting point.

There is a tendency for support costs to creep upward, especially in affluent organizations. Because of this, analysts make special efforts to detect and eliminate unnecessary increases in these costs. If unit costs or ratios can be calculated, a comparison of these with similar numbers in other responsibility centers, or with published data for other organizations, may be helpful. In the absence of such a basis for comparison, reviewers frequently rely on their feel for the appropriateness of the requested amounts.

Finally, the analyst makes comparisons among the unit costs of similar activities within the organization. The budget is checked for consistency with the guidelines; wage rates and costs of significant materials are checked for reasonableness; and other checks—including the simple but essential check of arithmetic accuracy—are made.

Behavioral Aspects

In estimating the labor cost of making shoes, there is little ground for disagreement on the part of well-informed people: the cost of each operation can be estimated within close limits, and the total labor cost can be found by adding the costs of each operation and multiplying by the number of pairs of shoes. As noted above, such engineered costs constitute a relatively large fraction of the costs of an industrial company. By contrast, discretionary costs—costs for which the optimal amount is not known, and often is unknowable—constitute a relatively large percent of the budget of a nonprofit organization. Since there is no scientific way to estimate the amount of discretionary costs, these costs do not lend themselves to analysis by the budget staff. Rather, the budget amounts must be determined through negotiation. Negotiation is also required because there is no objective way to decide which requests for funds have the highest priority.

On one level, this negotiation process can be thought of as a *zero-sum game*. Specifically, in many organizations, each budgetee negotiating with a particular supervisor is competing with all other budgetees who report to that supervisor for a share of the resources the supervisor controls. In instances where resources are not abundant, such an arrangement generally produces a great deal of conflict and game-playing by budgetees in order to obtain as large a share of resources as possible.

Senior management can eliminate the zero-sum aspect of this process, and potentially lessen conflict, by decentralizing the budgetary process and increasing the number of budgetary decisions to be made. Doing so tends to reduce the stakes in such a way that each budgetee can gain something.[6]

On another level, the process of negotiation in a decentralized budgetary process has been described as a two-person, nonzero-sum game.[7] The players are the budgetee, who is advocating a proposed budget, and the supervisor, who must approve, modify, or deny the request. Except for the lowest echelon, all managers are supervisors at one stage in the budget process, and they become budgetees in the next stage. Even senior management becomes a budgetee in presenting the budget to the outside agency or board that is responsible for providing the funds. Although in one sense a new game is played each year, there are important carryover consequences from one year to the next. The judgment that each party develops in one year about the ability, integrity, and forthrightness of the other party affects attitudes in subsequent years.

As in any negotiation, the two parties have a common interest in reaching a satisfactory outcome, but they usually have conflicting interests in what that outcome should be. The essence of this conflict is that budgetees generally want as large a budget as possible, and supervisors usually want to cut the proposed budget as much as they safely can.

---

[6]Schick, "University Budgeting," pp. 794–802.
[7]See G. H. Hofstede, *The Game of Budget Control* (Assen, Neth.: Van Gorcum & Co., N.V., 1967). This book is a classic in the management literature.

A budgetee's desire for resources is particularly troublesome in responsibility centers whose output cannot be reliably measured. Under these circumstances, not only are budgetees motivated to acquire as many resources as they can, but it is extremely difficult for supervisors to measure the effectiveness of their use of the resources. This phenomenon has been analyzed by economists in socialist countries where it is crucial to understanding the budget preparation process.

Example

The following factors were considered particularly significant in the budget preparation process in Hungary: (1) a good manager wants to do the job properly and therefore wants all the resources that may be needed to accomplish it; (2) the manager wants the operation to run smoothly and for this purpose needs slack in order to meet peaks in demand; (3) the manager wants the unit to be viewed favorably in comparison with other units and therefore wants the resources to be up to date; (4) the manager's power and prestige is perceived as being related to the size of the responsibility center, and, in contrast with profit centers, there is no penalty in having too many resources in a discretionary expense center.

For these reasons, the manager's desire for resources is insatiable. Moreover, if supervisors grant all the budget requests this year, it is likely that the requests next year will be even larger.[8]

Role of Professionals The attitude of professionals is also an important factor. For example, in a hospital, the budgetee may be a physician and the supervisor a hospital administrator. Physicians are primarily interested in improving the quality of patient care, improving the status of the hospital as perceived by their peers, and increasing their own prestige. Their interest in the amount of costs involved generally is secondary. By contrast, hospital administrators are primarily interested in costs, although they realize that costs must not be so low that the quality of care or the status of the hospital is impaired. Thus, the two parties weigh the relevant factors considerably differently.

Role of Norms The budget process is most effective when the two parties conform to certain norms. In general, effective behavior by supervisors includes:

- Trusting their subordinates.

- Assuming their subordinates are competent and have goodwill and honesty.

- Allowing subordinates to develop their own solutions to budget-related problems.

- Not feeling threatened if a subordinate does not agree with them.

- Sharing information with subordinates.

- Not forcing their personal goals onto subordinates.

[8]See Janos Kornai, *Economics of Shortage* (Amsterdam, Neth.: North-Holland Publishing, 1980), especially pp. 62–64 and 191–95.

Similarly, budgetees need to be able to also trust their superiors. A budget ordinarily is based on certain assumptions about the external world; these assumptions often prove to be wrong. If budgetees do not trust their supervisors to recognize this fact, they will be reluctant to make realistic estimates. Indeed, they may be so afraid of their supervisors that they cannot enter into a give-and-take collaboration with them.

Role of the Analyst In general, both senior management and lower level line managers must trust the budget analysts' recommendations as to the details of the budget. If the analysts' calculations indicate that four, not five, new employees are needed for a new function, these calculations ordinarily must be accepted. If each of these detailed decisions is challenged, the whole process will bog down. Moreover, as the budget goes up the chain of command, decision makers may have difficulty identifying and concentrating on key issues. In short, the budget process will work smoothly only if line management has confidence in the judgment of the budget analysts. The solution, if such confidence is lacking, is to reeducate, or in the extreme, replace the analysts.

Rules of the Game and Budget Ploys As in any game, rules exist for the budget process; many of these rules are unwritten. Moreover, they vary considerably from organization to organization. They also depend in large part upon the size of the organization and the relationships between supervisors and budgetees.

Example

One study of budget games that managers play in manufacturing organizations identified five major activities: (1) understating volume estimates, (2) undeclared (or understated) prices increases, (3) undeclared (or understated) cost reduction programs, (4) overstated expenses (such as for research), and (5) undeclared extensions of a product line. A principal reason given by one manager was "senior management just doesn't have the time for checking every number you put into your plans . . . so one strategy is to 'pad' everything. If you're lucky, you'll still have 50% of your cushions after the plan reviews."[9] Similar, sometimes identical, games are played in many nonprofit organizations.

Even when the formal rules are clear, the budget game frequently is characterized by certain ploys. To play the budget game well, each party should be familiar with these ploys and the appropriate responses to them.

Ploys can be divided into two main categories: (1) *internal*—those used primarily within an organization, and (2) *external*—those used between the head of the organization and the legislative body or governing board that authorizes funds for the organization. External ploys are well described in

---

[9]Christopher K. Bart, "Budgeting Gamesmanship," *The Academy of Management Executive* 2, no. 4 (1988), pp. 285–94.

Wildavsky's *The Politics of the Budgeting Process.*[10] Some internal ploys are given in the Appendix at the end of this chapter.

The Commitment   The end product of the negotiation process is an agreed-upon budget that represents a commitment by both the budgetee and the supervisor. Some organizations go so far as to state this commitment in the form of a formal contract, in which the budgetee agrees to deliver specified services for an agreed-upon sum of money. This becomes the amount in the approved budget.

By agreeing to the budget estimates, the budgetee says, in effect: "I can and will operate my responsibility center in accordance with the plan described in this budget." By approving the budget estimates, the superior in effect says, "If you operate your responsibility center in accordance with this plan, you will be doing what we consider to be a good job." Both statements contain the implicit qualification, "subject to adjustment for unanticipated changes in circumstances."

Example	In the one and one-half months that elapsed following its submission on May 10, 1985, the fiscal year 1986–87 budget for New York City became obsolete because of changes in circumstances. Among the changes were: (1) a tentative union agreement covering the city's uniformed employees, which necessitated wage increases of 6 percent; (2) receipt of notice from the state of New York that the city's estimates of state aid were unrealistic; (3) a refinancing of the city's general obligation bonds; (4) an agreement between the state and the city to jointly finance a housing program; (5) a budget resolution passed by the U.S. Congress, which, among other things, made it clear that the Federal General Revenue Sharing Program would likely be terminated; and (6) the city received two additional months of revenue collection information as well as indications of final real property assessments, that resulted in changes in its local revenue estimates for the budget year. As a result, the city submitted a revised financial plan on June 26, 1985.

To reinforce this commitment, some nonprofits "reward" programs for beating their budgets with a sharing of the savings. The program managers can use the savings for activities such as purchasing extra equipment, paying for training, or hiring a part-time person to carry out a discretionary task. They claim that the reward system provides staff with an incentive to cut costs.[11] Clearly, senior management must be careful not to put such a heavy focus on budgetary savings that insufficient attention is given to quality. We discuss this matter in greater detail in Chapter 11.

---

[10]Aaron Wildavsky, *The Politics of the Budgetary Process,* 2nd ed. (New York: Harper Collins, 1992).
[11]Peter C. Brinckerhoff, "How to Save Money Through Bottoms-Up Budgeting," *Nonprofit World* 14, no. 1 (1996).

Budget Approval

The final set of discussions is held between senior management and whatever body has ultimate authority for approving the organization's plans—trustees or similar groups for private nonprofit organizations, or legislatures for public ones. After approval, the budget is disseminated throughout the organization and becomes the authorized plan to which managers are expected to adhere unless compelling circumstances warrant a change.[12]

Use of Models

Many budgetary analyses can benefit from a model that describes both the essential variables in the situation being studied and the relationships among them. Such a model need not be complicated; indeed, the use of models has been greatly facilitated by the use of spreadsheet software.

Example

Exhibit 10–2 shows a simple financial model that focuses on the relationships of important variables for the instructional program of a college. All the "initial values" are entered except one: tuition per student. The *equations* in the spreadsheet are established in accordance with the college's policies concerning section sizes, faculty workloads, faculty salaries, the number of nonteaching faculty, and other expenses.

With this information, the college can solve for the amount of tuition per student necessary to put the model into "equilibrium." It is in equilibrium in the sense that the revenues available for instruction equal the costs of instruction. The first *management decision equation* does this, indicating that the tuition and fee figure would need to be $10,174.

Alternatively, tuition could be entered into the model at the level set by senior management and the trustees, and the model could be used to solve for the number of students needed to reach equilibrium (i.e., to break even). The second management-decision equation does this, using a tuition and fee figure of $9,800. The number of students needed for equilibrium is 1,632.

By changing the unknown in a management-decision equation, or by changing the college's policy concerning section sizes, faculty workloads, or salaries, this model could be used to answer many questions: By how much, for example, could we increase average faculty compensation if we reduced (*a*) the number of sections by *X*, (*b*) the number of nonteaching faculty by *Y*, or (*c*) nonfaculty instruction costs by *Z*? If we increased the course offerings, by how much would tuition have to be increased? What

---

[12]Some people refer to actual operations as "executing the budget." This is an unfortunate term because it implies that the operating manager's job is to spend whatever the budget says can be spent. A better term is *executing the program*. This implies that the manager's primary job is to accomplish program objectives. The budget simply shows the resources available for this purpose.

EXHIBIT 10–2 College Financial Model

Line I.D. Formula	Name of Variable	Value
a	Number of students	1,572
b	Number of courses (or sections) per student per year	10
c	Average number of students per section	24
d=(a*b)÷c	Number of sections offered per year	655
e	Number of FTE faculty	120
f	Number of sections per FTE teaching faculty per year	6
g=d÷f	Number of FTE teaching faculty needed per year	109.2
h=f−g	Number of FTE nonteaching faculty per year (sabbaticals, department head buyout, slippage)	10.8
i	Average compensation per faculty	$ 70,000
j=e*i	Total faculty compensation	$ 8,400,000
k	Instruction cost other than faculty compensation (e.g., faculty support staff, admissions, registrar, career center)	$ 7,993,000
l=j+k	Total instruction cost	$16,393,000
m	Nontuition revenue available for instruction (e.g., from endowment)	$ 400,000
n=l−m	Tuition revenue needed	$15,993,000

Management Decisions

Option #1	Tuition is dependent variable	
	Tuition per student = n ÷ a	$ 10,174
Option #2	Tuition fixed at $9,800 per student; number of students is dependent variable	
	Number of students needed = n ÷ $9,800	1,632

would happen if we increased the number of students by 10 percent?

Moreover, beginning with this simple model, we can refine the analysis by substituting a frequency distribution of section sizes for the average section size, by substituting a distribution of faculty compensation by rank for the overall average, by bringing in noninstruction costs, or by being more specific about any of several other variables.

Computer models such as this are available for many types of nonprofit organizations, and spreadsheet packages can be adapted to meet managers' needs in a wide variety of circumstances. Frequently these models serve to quantify an organization's policy decisions, and require analysts, senior management, and governing bodies to determine which variables are policy driven and which can be formula driven. In so doing, the models help to bring considerable discipline to an organization's financial analyses, and add a great deal of power to the decision-making processes undertaken by senior management and the board.

Example

The operating budget for a hospital or health maintenance organization could be determined by a model that incorporates morbidity estimates (types and number of cases expected), physician treatment protocols for each diagnosis, expected efficiency measures and factor prices for physician-ordered services, and fixed facility costs. Such a model would permit decision makers to determine where and how expenditures might be reduced by focusing on specific "cost drivers." Reductions could take place, for example, by avoiding the treatment of certain types of cases, by changing physician treatment protocols, by seeking improved administrative efficiency, or by guaranteeing certain factor prices. The model could permit analysts to test the impact of each of these options, as well as combinations of options, on total costs. Such an approach is being used in some hospitals.

Summary

Many aspects of operations budgeting in nonprofit organizations are similar to those in for-profit companies. Perhaps the most important difference is on the revenue side of the budget. Many nonprofit organizations are not "self-financing." Because of this, they must be careful to forecast their revenues accurately, and to assure themselves that expenses will not exceed revenues. Although there are some exceptions to this rule, and most organizations can have a year or two where expenses exceed revenues, the effective result of such a policy is to erode the organization's capital.

Some other differences between nonprofit and for-profit organizations are (1) the presence of two-stage budgets in some nonprofit organizations, (2) the existence of soft money and the uncertainty about grant revenue in some nonprofits, (3) the need for output measures as well as measures of revenue and expenses, and (4) the role of professionals.

In all organizations, the budget frequently has a "gamelike" quality to it. Because of this, the players have developed many ploys to assure their success in the game. These ploys are described in some detail in the Appendix.

Appendix

Some Budget Ploys

Internal ploys used in the budget game can be divided into roughly four categories:

1. Ploys for new programs.

2. Ploys for maintaining or increasing ongoing programs.

3. Ploys to resist cuts.

4. Ploys primarily for supervisors.

There is some overlap among the categories, with some relating to strategic planning as well as to budgeting. Each ploy is described briefly, and an appropriate response is given

Ploys for New Programs

1. Foot in the Door

Description

Sell a modest program initially, with the idea of concealing its real magnitude until after it has gotten under way and has built a constituency.

Example In a certain state, the legislature was sold on a program to educate handicapped children in regular schools rather than in the special schools then used. The costs were said to be transportation costs and a few additional teachers. Within five years, the definition of handicapped had been greatly broadened, and the resources devoted to the program were four times the amount originally estimated.

Response

This ploy can elicit either of two responses: (*a*) detect the ploy when it is proposed, consider that it is merely a foot in the door and that actual costs eventually will exceed estimates by a wide margin, and therefore disapprove the project (difficult to do); or (*b*) hold to the original decision, limiting spending to the original cost estimate despite pleas for more funds (effective only if the ploy is detected in time).

Variations

One variation of this ploy is *buying in;* that is, underestimating the real cost of a program. An example is the B-1 bomber program. In the early 1980s, this program was estimated to cost $11.9 billion. The Air Force submission for the B-1 bomber for FY 1983 "certified" that the cost of the program was $20.5 billion. However, two independent audit groups within the Pentagon estimated its cost as $23.6 billion and $26.7 billion, respectively. The Congressional Budget Office estimated the cost at $40 billion.

Another variation is bait and switch; that is, initially requesting an inexpensive program but increasing its scope (and cost) after initial approval has been obtained. This differs from the "foot in the door" ploy in that the changes in the program take place before the program begins rather than after it has been operating for a while.

2. Hidden Ball

Description

Conceal the nature of a politically unattractive program by hiding it within an attractive program.

Example Some years ago the Air Force had difficulty in obtaining funds for general-purpose buildings but found it easy to get funds for intercontinental ballistic missiles, so there was included in the budget for the missile program an amount to provide for construction of a new office building. Initially this building was used by a contractor in the missile program, but eventually it became a general-purpose Air Force office building.

Response

Break down programs so that such items become visible.

3. Divide and Conquer

Description

Seek approval of a budget request from more than one supervisor.

Example   The City Planning Commission in New York City was organized so that each member was supposed to be responsible for certain specified areas. The distinctions were not clear, however, so budgetees would deal with more than one supervisor, hoping that one of them would react favorably.

Response

Responsibilities should be clearly defined (easier said than done).

Caution

In some situations, especially in research, it is dangerous to have a single decision point. It is often desirable to have two places in which a person with a new idea for research may obtain a hearing. New ideas are extremely difficult to evaluate, and a divided authority, even though superficially inefficient, lessens the chance that a good idea will be rejected.

4. Distraction

Description

Base a specific request on the premise that an overall program has been approved when this is not in fact the case (difficult, but not impossible, to use successfully).

Example   At a legislative committee, a university presented arguments to replace buildings prior to implementing an approved plan for doubling the capacity of a certain professional school. The argument was that newer buildings would be more useful and efficient than the existing buildings. The merits were discussed in terms of the return on investment arising from the greater efficiency of the new buildings. This discussion went on for some time until a committee member asked who had approved the plan for expansion of the school in the first place. It turned out that the expansion had never been approved; approval of the new buildings would have de facto approved the expansion.

Response

Expose the hidden aims, but this is sometimes very difficult.

5. Shell Game

Description

Use the statistics to mislead supervisors as to the true state of affairs.

Example   The budgetee was head of the Model Cities program for a certain city. He wanted available funds to be used primarily for health and education programs but knew that his superiors were more interested in "economic" programs (new businesses and housing). He drew up the following table:

	Source		
Purpose	*Federal*	*Other*	*Total*
Health and education	$2,000,000	$ 15,000	$2,015,000
Economic	50,000	2,300,000	2,350,000

The budgetee emphasized to the mayor and interested groups that over half the funds were intended for economic purposes. The catch was that the source of "other" funds was not known, and there were no firm plans for obtaining such funds. This was not discovered by the supervisor until just prior to the deadline for submitting the request for federal Model Cities funding, at which time the budgetee successfully used the delayed buck ploy (No. 17).

Response

Careful analysis.

6. It's Free

Description

Argue that someone else will pay for the project so the organization might as well approve it.

Example   States often decide to build highways, reckoning the cost is low since the federal government reimburses 95 percent of the cost. These states overlook the fact that maintenance of the highway is 100 percent a state cost.

Response

Require analysis of the long-run costs, not merely the costs for next year. This technique, called *life-cycle costing,* is becoming increasingly popular.

7. Implied Top-Level Support

Description

The budgetee says that, although the request is not something that he personally is enthusiastic about, it is for a program that someone higher up in the organization asked to be included in the budget (preferably this person is not
well known to, and more prestigious than, the budgetee's superior). The budgetee hopes that the supervisor will not take the time to bring this third party
into the discussion.

Response

Examine the documentation. If it is vague, not well justified, or nonexistent,
check with the alleged sponsor.

Note

In a related ploy, the end run, the budgetee actually goes to the supervisor's
boss without discussing the matter with the supervisor first. This tactic should
not be tolerated.

8. You're to Blame

Description

Imply that the supervisor is at fault, and that defects in the budget submission
therefore should be overlooked.

Example It is alleged that the supervisor was late in transmitting budget
instructions or that the instructions were not clear, and that this accounts
for inadequacies in the justifications furnished.

Response

If the assertion is valid, this is a difficult ploy to counter. It may be necessary
to be contrite, but arbitrary, in order to hold the budget within the guidelines.
(It also may be necessary to reexamine one's management style.)

9. Nothing Too Good for Our People

Description

Used, whether warranted or not, to justify items for the personal comfort and
safety of military personnel, for new cemeteries, for new hospital equipment,
for research laboratory equipment (especially computers), and for various facilities in public schools and colleges.

Response

Attempt to shift the discussion from emotional grounds to logical grounds by
analyzing the request to see if the benefits are even remotely related to their

cost. Emphasize that in a world of scarce resources, not everyone can get all that is deserved.

10. Keeping Up with the Joneses

Example   Minneapolis must have new street lights because St. Paul has them.

Response
Analyze the proposal on its own merits.

11. We Must Be Up to Date

Description
This differs from Ploy No. 10 in that it does not require that a "Jones" be found and cited. The argument is that the organization must be a leader and must therefore adopt the newest technology. Currently, this is a fashionable ploy for computers and related equipment, for hospital equipment, and for laboratory equipment.

Response
Require that a benefit be shown that exceeds the cost of adopting the new technology.

Caution
Sometimes the state of the art is such that benefits cannot be conclusively demonstrated. If this leads to a deferral of proposals year after year, opportunities may be missed.

12. If We Don't, Someone Else Will

Description
Appeal to people's innate desire to be at least as good as the competition.

Example   A university budgetee argued that a proposed new program was breaking new ground, and was important to the national interest. She stated that if her university didn't initiate the program, some other university would. Moreover, the other university would obtain funds from the appropriate government agency, and thus make it more difficult for her university to start the program later on.

Response
Point out that a long list of possible programs have this characteristic, and the university must select those few that are within its capabilities.

13. Call It a Rose

Description

Use misleading, but appealing, labels.

Example   The National Institutes of Health were unable to obtain approval for the construction of new buildings but were able to build annexes. It is said that Building 12A (the annex) is at least double the size of Building 12.

Response

Look behind the euphemism to the real function. If the disguise is intentional, deny the request and discourage recurrence.

14. Outside Experts

Description

The agency hires outside experts to support its request, either formally in hearings, or informally in the press.

Response

Determine whether these experts are biased, either because they have connections with the agency or because they are likely to benefit if the request is approved. Seek other experts with contrasting views.

Ploys for Maintaining or Increasing Ongoing Programs

15. Show of Strength

Description

Arrange demonstrations in support of a request; occasionally, threaten violence, work stoppages, or other unpleasant consequences if the request is not approved.

Response

Have fair criteria for selecting programs, and have the conviction to stand by your decision.

16. Razzle-Dazzle

Description

Support the request with voluminous data, arranged in such a way that their significance is not clear. The data need not be valid.

Example   A public works department submitted a 20-page list of repairs to municipal buildings that were said to be vitally needed, couched in highly technical language. This was actually a "wish list," prepared without a detailed analysis.

Response

(*a*) Ask why the repair budget should be greater next year than in the current year. (*b*) Find a single soft spot in the original request and use it to discredit the whole analysis.

17. Delayed Buck

Description

Submit the data late, arguing that the budget guidelines required so much detailed calculation that the job could not be done on time.

Example   The budget guidelines requested a "complete justification" of requested additions to inventory. The motor vehicle repair shop of a state did not submit its budget on time. At the last minute, it submitted an itemized list of parts to be ordered, based on a newly installed system of calculating economic order quantities. It argued that its tardiness was a consequence of getting the bugs out of the new system (which was installed at the controller's instigation), but that it was generally agreed that the economic order quantity formula was the best way of justifying the amount of parts to be purchased.

Response

This is a difficult ploy to counter. Complaining about the delay may make the supervisor feel better but will not produce the data. One possible response, designed to prevent recurrence, is to penalize the delay by making an entirely arbitrary cut in the amount requested, although this runs this risk that needed funds will be denied.

18. Reverence for the Past

Description

Whatever was spent last year must have been necessary to carry out last year's program; therefore, the only matters to be negotiated are the proposed increments above this sacred base.

Response

As a practical matter, this attitude must be accepted for a great many programs because there is not time to challenge this statement. For selected programs, there can be a zero-base review (see Chapter 15).

19. Sprinkling

Description

"Watering" was a device used in the early 20th century to make assets and profits in prospectuses for new stock offerings look substantially higher than they really were. "Sprinkling" is a more subtle ploy, which increases budget estimates by only a few percent, either across-the-board or in hard-to-detect areas. Often it is done in anticipation that the supervisor will make arbitrary reductions, so that the final budget will be what it would have been if neither the sprinkling nor the arbitrary cuts had been made.

Response

Since this ploy, when done by an expert, is extremely difficult to detect, the best response is to remove the need for doing it; that is, create an atmosphere in which the budgetees trust the supervisor not to make arbitrary cuts.

Ploys to Resist Cuts

20. Make a Study

Description

The budget guidelines contain a statement that a certain program is to be curtailed or discontinued. The budgetee responds that the proposed action should not be taken until its consequences have been studied thoroughly.

Response

Make the study; be persistent; supplement with other ploys.

21. Gold Watch

Description

When asked in general terms to cut the budget, propose specific actions that do more harm than good.

Example   This well-known ploy derives its name from an incident that occurred when Robert McNamara was with the Ford Motor Company. In a period of stringency, all division heads were asked to make a special effort to cut costs. Most responded with genuine belt tightening. However, one division manager, with $100 million sales, reported that the only cost reduction opportunity he had found was to eliminate the gold watches that were customarily given to employees retiring with 30 or more years of satisfactory service.

Response

Reject the proposal. (In the example, disciplinary action was also taken with respect to the division manager.)

22. Arouse Client Antagonism

Description

When a budget cut is ordered, cut a popular program, hoping to provoke complaints from clients that will pressure the supervisor to restore the program. A classic case is known as the "Washington Monument elevator ploy," where the manager of the Washington Monument proposes to cut the monument's budget by eliminating its elevator service, knowing that doing so will arouse considerable antagonism from hundreds of thousands of visitors each year.

Example   When Mayor Abraham Beame was asked in 1975 by the federal government to reduce spending in New York City to avoid bankruptcy, he responded by dismissing 7,000 police officers and firefighters and closing 26 fire houses. Many people believe he did this to inflame public opinion against budget cuts. It did have this effect, and the order was reversed.

Response

Try to redirect client attention by publicizing areas where cuts are feasible.

23. Witches and Goblins

Description

The budgetee asserts that if the request is not approved, dire consequences will occur. It is used often by the House Armed Services Committee in its reports to Congress. For example, an antiballistic missile system was recommended as a counterdefense to the "Talinin System" that the Soviets were alleged to be building. In fact, the Soviets were not building such a system.

Response

Analysis based on evidence rather than on emotion.

24. We Are the Experts

Description

The budgetee asserts that the proposal must be accepted because he or she has expert knowledge that the supervisor cannot possibly match. This ploy is used by professionals of all types: military officers, scientists, professors, physicians, and clergy.

Response

If the basic premise is accepted, the budget process cannot proceed rationally, for the supervisor tends to be a generalist and the budgetee a specialist. The supervisor should insist that the expert express the basis for his or her judgment in terms that are comprehensible to the generalist.

25. End Run

Description

Go outside normal channels to obtain reversal of a decision.

Example   In Massachusetts in the early 1980s, many hospitals that had been denied a certificate of need (CON) to engage in capital building projects asked their state legislators to introduce a bill overriding the decision by the public health council (an executive branch agency) and permitting the project to proceed. Other legislators, knowing that the next CON denial might be in their district, supported their colleagues, and the entire CON process was weakened.

Response

If the end run is made to the legislature or an equivalent powerful body, the executive probably has no choice except to grin and bear it (pressures for a veto frequently are hard to muster). In other cases, anyone who attempts an end run should be reprimanded and the request denied, because attempts to go outside proper channels upset the authority of the whole budgetary process.

Ploys Primarily for Supervisors

26. Keep Them Lean and Hungry

Description

The supervisor tells the budgetee that the latter's organization will work harder and possibly more effectively if it doesn't carry so much fat.

Response

Show that the analogy with human biology is false, or go along with the analogy and show that the cuts represent muscle rather than fat.

27. Productivity Cuts

Description

It is assumed that many capital expenditures are made with the intention of cutting operating costs. Although few systems permit individual cost reductions to be identified, it is reasonable to assume that they, together with continuing management improvements, should lead to lower operating costs in the aggregate. Some organizations therefore reduce personnel-related costs by about 1.5 percent from the previous year's level. In the entire economy, productivity increases by about 3 percent annually. The lower percentage assumes that nonprofit organizations are only half as susceptible to productivity gains as the economy as a whole.

In some organizations the cost reductions can be specifically traced. When an organization makes a large capital expenditure to convert its recordkeeping to computers, this presumably results in lower operating costs, and the planned savings should be specifically identified. If an approved program for, say, 1991 contains an item for the installation of a new computer system that is designed, in part, to reduce clerical expenses beginning in 1993, the budgeted clerical expenses in 1993 should reflect the promised reduction.

Response

Point out that dismissals are politically expedient, and retirements and resignations may not be rapid enough to permit costs to be reduced to the desired level.

28. Arbitrary Cuts

Example   The supervisor, who was director of research of a large company, followed the practice of reducing the budget for certain discretionary items (travel, publications, professional dues) in certain departments by approximately 10 percent. Although the supervisor did this on a purely random basis, he achieved a reputation for astute analysis.

Response

Challenge the reason for the cuts (but the items tend to be so unimportant and difficult to defend that such challenges may consume more time than they are worth.)

29. I Only Work Here

Description

The supervisor says she cannot grant the budgetee's request because it is not within the scope of ground rules that her superiors have laid down.

Response

Ask that the issue be brought to the appropriate decision-making authority. This, of course, relies on a good relationship (trust) between the budgetee and the supervisor.

30. Closing Gambits

Description

The supervisor uses various tactics to bring the negotiation to a close. A simple one is simply to glance at his or her watch, indicating that time is valuable. Another is to "split the difference" between the amount requested and the amount the supervisor initially wanted to approve. Still another is the proposal to settle on a small amount now, with an indication that a larger amount will be considered later on.

Response

Suggest that another meeting be scheduled to complete the negotiation. If this is not possible, be sure to clarify in writing those decisions that have been made.

31. Program Elimination

Description

The dean of a business school was not in favor of a small program that had been developed by the school's department of accounting. However, the program had considerable support both from the school's faculty and from the local accounting community. It also produced an annual contribution of several hundred thousand dollars for the university. To eliminate the program formally would have required obtaining faculty approval, which the dean knew he could not obtain. Thus, when asked by the university's central administration to cut the school's budget, the dean cut the budget of this program to such an extent that it could not survive. One year later, the program was no longer in existence.

Response

Initiate a process for budget reductions that requires faculty approval for any amount greater than some small percentage in any given program.

Suggested Additional Readings

Anthony, Robert N. "Zero-Base Budgeting: A Useful Fraud?" *The Government Accountant,* Summer 1977, p. 7.

Harmer, W. Gary. "Bridging the GAAP between Budgeting and Accounting." *Governmental Finance,* March 1981, pp. 19–24.

Lynch, T. D. *Public Budgeting in America,* 5th ed. Englewood Cliffs, NJ: Prentice Hall, 1995.

McLeod, R. K. "Program Budgeting Works in Nonprofit Organizations." *Harvard Business Review,* September–October 1971.

Rabin, J., ed. *Handbook of Public Budgeting.* New York: Marcel Drekker, 1992.

Rachlin, Robert, and H. W. Allen Sweeny, eds. *Handbook of Budgeting.* Somerset, New York: John Wiley & Sons, 1993.

Wildavsky, Aaron. *The Politics of the Budgetary Process,* 2nd ed. New York: Harper Collins, 1992.

Practice Case

Bandon Medical Associates (A)*

> Preparing this budget requires a lot of assumptions, and I'm not even sure that we're using the right approach. But if the group is to have something that's realistic, and if we're going to survive within the IDS [integrated delivery system], we've got to push ahead.

Mark Desautels, MD, the senior physician member of Bandon Medical Associates (BMA), a small physician group practice located in Oregon, was commenting on the frustration he felt in trying to prepare the group's budget for the upcoming fiscal year. He realized that, although BMA's budget process had come a long way in just a few months, much remained to be done.

Background

Bandon Medical Associates (BMA) had been established about 20 years ago by Dr. Desautels and a colleague he had met during his residency. Over the years, the group had grown, and currently comprised six physicians and two medical assistants, who functioned as "extenders" for the physicians. The extenders assisted the physicians by completing a variety of tasks such as taking patients' blood pressure, drawing blood samples, and so forth. They did not bill for their time.

Two years ago, BMA had joined Coos Bay Health System, a large IDS that included several primary care and multispecialty group practices, a free-standing laboratory, a free-standing radiology unit, two acute care hospitals, a nursing home, a home health agency, and a hospice. Coos Bay coordinated care, negotiated contracts with third-party payers, and provided some central services, such as information systems support.

Financial Matters

Recently, Coos Bay's chief financial officer had told Dr. Desautels that BMA along with the other physician practices in the IDS were going to be treated as

*This case was prepared by Professor David W. Young. Copyright © by David W. Young.

"profit centers." She had emphasized that, even though Coos Bay was a nonprofit organization, each provider entity nevertheless would be required to generate sufficient revenue from its outpatient activities to cover its own expenses plus the costs of the Coos Bay central services that would be allocated to it. Each entity also would need to generate an operating surplus to provide the cash required for any capital purchases (such as office and testing equipment) that it wished to make to support its outpatient activities.

The CFO also pointed out that, in accordance with the contracts signed with the various provider entities at the time they had been purchased by Coos Bay, all inpatient revenue—from both hospital and physician billings—would be retained by the hospital, and a portion distributed to physicians in accordance with the compensation formulas negotiated with them as part of Coos Bay's bundled-pricing and subcapitation arrangements with its payers.

Additionally, the CFO had reminded Dr. Desautels that, as had been the practice for the past two years, revenue from all outpatient laboratory and radiological testing would be retained by the free-standing facilities. Thus, all of the physician groups would need to earn a surplus on the basis of the revenue generated from their outpatient visits only.

Stunned by this news, Dr. Desautels had held a retreat for the group's physicians and extenders at which they had discussed a wide variety of matters related to the new financial arrangements. After considerable debate, some of it acrimonious, they had reached the following conclusions:

1. Different visit types required different levels of physician intensity, and although there were several different approaches to measuring productivity, revenue generation would be the best method. Everyone had agreed that, since the payment for each visit type was a rough reflection of its intensity, revenue generation was not only a good way to measure each physician's productivity, but a simple one as well.

2. While most third-party payers classified visits by precise codes, the BMA physicians had agreed that four visit types (initial consultation, routine physical, intensive visit, and routine visit) were sufficient for budgeting purposes.

3. Physicians would be available to see outpatients for 32 hours a week (eight 4-hour sessions). They also had agreed that, with time off for continuing medical education and vacations, they would be available for a total of 1,500 hours a year (about 47 weeks).

4. The extenders would be expected to see patients for 1,400 hours a year—less than the physicians since they had some other responsibilities in the group.

5. Physicians would be paid by a combination of base salary and bonus. The extenders would be on a straight salary with no bonus, although physicians could share their bonuses with one or more extenders who they thought were especially helpful.

6. Each physician's base salary would be set at 42 percent of his or her expected revenue generation. Ten percent of that amount would be kept in reserve until the end of the year, and paid out as a year-end bonus if the group reached at least 95 percent of its total revenue target.

7. The remaining revenue would be used to cover the group's operating expenses and to provide the surplus needed to fund office renovations, equipment purchases, and other similar items.

With these decisions in mind, Dr. Desautels had met with each physician to discuss his or her plans for the upcoming year, and to arrive at a forecast for the different visit types. He and BMA's administrator, Alvin Hanson, had then summed the individual physician forecasts to get the group's total volume forecast.

Dr. Desautels and Mr. Hanson next developed expense estimates. To do this, they decided to treat physicians, extenders, and the group's medical supplies as "variable expenses." Dr. Desautels commented:

> Clearly, the only truly variable expenses are the medical supplies, but if we're to find out how we're doing, we need to know both physician and extender costs for the different visit types. If we use straight salaries, and essentially treat the providers as fixed costs, we won't be able to do that. So I need to compute per-minute rates for both physicians and extenders, and then multiply those rates by the number of minutes that each provider type spends for each visit type. As I look at this, it all seems pretty daunting, and it's not something that Alvin has done before either, so we're both struggling a little.
>
> Medical supplies, on the other hand, are pretty easy. They include a wide variety of disposable items that we use in conjunction with a visit. To keep the budget simple, we've decided to measure them in terms of "units," and Alvin has computed an average cost per unit. We just need to multiply those out to get the budget for each visit type.

The group's fixed expenses included rent, cleaning, administrative staff, receptionists, office supplies, and similar items, which Dr. Desautels expected to total $300,000 for the year. Allocated overhead was for a variety of administrative services provided by Coos Bay, such as billing, collections, and information services. Coos Bay's CFO had told Dr. Desautels that she thought the allocations would total about $250,000, but since they were based on the formulas from Coos Bay's full cost allocation system, she could not be completely certain.

The Current Year's Budget

The elements of the current year's budget that Dr. Desautels and Mr. Hanson had developed are shown in Exhibit 1. This exhibit contains the anticipated revenue for each visit type, the anticipated provider time and medical

EXHIBIT 1

	BANDON MEDICAL ASSOCIATES (A): Budget Data				
Type of Visit	Expected Number of Visits	Expected Revenue per Visit	Expected Physician Time per Visit (1)	Expected Extender Time per Visit (2)	Expected Medical Supplies per Visit (3)
Initial consultation	3,000	$150	60	15	3
Routine physical.	4,000	$110	45	10	2
Intensive visit	6,000	$ 80	20	10	2
Routine Visit.	6,000	$ 60	10	15	1

Notes:
1. In minutes at $1.35 per minute.
2. In minutes at $0.90 per minute.
3. In units at $4.00 per unit.

supply units per visit, and the corresponding unit variable expense figures. Dr. Desautels commented:

> I think we're almost there. We now need to calculate the total variable expense per visit for each visit type, multiply the revenue and total variable expense per visit by the anticipated number of visits to give total revenue and total variable expenses by visit type, deduct the latter from the former to get the contribution to fixed expenses from each visit type, and finally, deduct our anticipated fixed expenses and allocated overhead from the total contribution to give our total budgeted surplus for the year.

Questions

1. Using the information contained in the case and Exhibit 1, prepare a budget for BMA for the four visit types shown. Use the approach suggested by Dr. Desautels at the end of the case, and organize your figures so that he will find them understandable and useful.*

2. Assuming Dr. Desautels is unhappy with the "bottom line" of this budget, what options are available to change it? Which options seem the most feasible to implement?

3. What problems do you think Dr. Desautels will encounter in attempting to implement this budget? What should be done about those problems?

*If you set the budget up a spreadsheet, and make it as formula-driven as possible, you you will find it relatively easy to test assumptions in answering Question 2.

Case 10–1

Moray Junior High School*

This budget cut is a serious problem for us. I don't know quite how to reduce our costs because there really wasn't much flexibility in the budget to begin with. However, we're all in the same situation; we expect to have only $2.2 million to spend on Moray and we have to find some way to live with that.

Ms. Hilda Cook, principal of Moray Junior High School, had just returned from the March 2001 meeting of the Moray Public School System's School Committee, where she had agreed to attempt to cut her school's budget by almost 12 percent. Although Ms. Cook did not consider her projected costs to be excessive, neither did several of the other principals, who also had agreed to attempt to reduce their budgets.

Background

Moray Junior High School was one of three junior high schools in the town of San Pedro, Arizona. It was in excellent physical condition, and had an enrollment of approximately 700 students a year. The quality of education was considered extremely high, and a student-teacher ratio of no more than 15:1 had always been maintained. Among the school's special programs were a highly-regarded Drug and Alcohol Awareness Program, and an Understanding Handicaps Program, in which trained parents and handicapped speakers provided a course of instruction to both students and teachers to acquaint them with the various handicapping conditions, such as epilepsy, blindness, physical handicaps, retardation, and deafness.

Moray was best known, however, for its Spanish Language Program, which used native speakers of Spanish to teach courses that began in the 7th grade and continued through the 9th grade. A special language laboratory with 30 student "stations" and three instructor stations was equipped with the latest in audio technology, including an "interrupt" feature that allowed an instructor to listen in on a student practicing with a cassette tape and to intervene electronically, when necessary, to correct the student's pronunciation or grammar. Students successfully completing the program were considered to be extremely proficient in the Spanish language, and a special field trip to a "sister" junior high school in Anguila, Mexico, was organized each year for the 9th graders. The students lived with local families for an entire week while actively participating in the Anguila school system's activities.

As principal of Moray since 1995, Ms. Cook had witnessed numerous changes in the school. For over 40 years, Moray had been the only junior high

---

*This case was prepared by Professor David W. Young. Copyright © by David W. Young.

school in San Pedro; however, in the late 1980s, when migration from the northern United States had led to a large influx of new residents, additional demands had been placed on the school system. As a result, Moray had been expanded and two new junior high schools had been built.

With such a dramatic increase in services, the School Committee had become increasingly concerned with budgeting, cost control, and accountability. Accordingly, in the past few years, Ms. Cook had become more actively involved in the financial management of Moray. By 2001, she, along with other principals in the San Pedro system, had assumed responsibility for constructing her school's annual budget. Moray's proposed budget for 2001–02 is contained in Exhibit 1.

Budget Data

San Pedro's budget process began in January. At that time, the Central Office made enrollment projections, and, using these figures, all school principals held conferences with their teachers and program heads to determine their school's requirements for staffing, supplies, and other cost items. In 2001, all budget needs for Moray were calculated on the basis of a projected enrollment of 690 students, although not all programs served all 690 students. In particular, as Exhibit 1 shows, Regular Instruction was scheduled to serve 615 students, Special Education 75 students, and the Spanish Language Program 180 students. (As Exhibit 1 indicates, some students were enrolled in more than one program.) The student-teacher ratio in Regular Instruction was scheduled to be 15:1, while in the Special Education Program it was only 6:1.

Shortly before the budget was completed, Ms. Cook and other principals met with the Director of Finance and Administration to discuss the Central Office costs. These indirect costs were allocated to individual schools based on measures such as salary expenses and student enrollments. The specific allocation bases for 2001–02 are shown in Exhibit 2.

In reviewing her budget for Fiscal Year 2001–02 (which ran from July 1, 2001, to June 30, 2002), Ms. Cook realized that the nature of the costs varied. She quickly ascertained that the budget contained no superfluous costs that simply could be cut; indeed, the instructional and administrative supply costs reflected only higher supply prices, and the teacher and administrative salaries were based on a very small increase in the wage rate. It appeared that if Ms. Cook wanted to reduce the budget by 20 percent, she would have to analyze the behavior of each cost, and adjust those that were flexible. If necessary, she also was prepared to alter Moray's operations to comply with the School Committee's budget ceiling.

To prepare a modified budget for the School Committee, Ms. Cook decided to meet with some of Moray's teachers and program heads, who she thought could provide information concerning some of the budgeted expenses. Her first meeting was with Mr. Steven Hartman, the teacher with the

EXHIBIT 1 Budgeted Statistics and Expenses 2001–2002

	Regular Instruction Program	Special Education Program	Spanish Language Program	Other Programs	Total*
Statistics:					
Number of registered students......	615	75	180	450	690
Number of days in academic year ...					170
Number of potential student days ...					117,300
Expected number of student days ...					110,497
Attendance rate					94.20%
Direct costs—instruction:					
Regular teacher salaries	$1,119,300	$376,875	$85,000	$15,000	$1,596,175
Substitute teacher salaries.........	37,200	12,500	0	0	49,700
Aide salaries	20,300	9,100	6,500	3,000	38,900
Instructional supplies and library	84,870	37,275	8,280	1,100	131,525
Travel and lodging	0	0	3,000	0	3,000
Depreciation	12,300	8,000	40,000	0	60,300
Total	$1,273,970	$443,750	$142,780	$19,100	$1,879,600
Direct costs—administration[†]:					
Administrative salaries (regular teacher salaries).........	$ 87,655	$ 29,514	$ 6,657	$ 1,175	$ 125,001
Administrative supplies (regular teacher salaries).........	10,869	3,660	825	146	15,500
Operations and maintenance (square feet).................	175,500	40,500	27,000	27,000	270,000
Other (regular teacher salaries)......	5,259	1,771	399	70	7,499
Total	$ 279,283	$ 75,445	$ 34,881	$28,391	$ 418,000
Total direct costs	$1,553,253	$519,195	$177,661	$47,491	$2,297,600
Indirect costs—allocated from Central Office:					
School Committee	$ 2,419	$ 815	$ 184	$ 32	$ 3,450
Administration	30,362	10,223	2,306	407	43,298
Health/life insurance.............	94,514	31,824	7,177	1,267	134,782
Operations and maintenance	4,739	1,093	729	729	7,290
Rent and depreciation	2,243	518	345	345	3,450
Contract services	1,048	128	307	767	2,250
Travel	581	195	44	8	828
Total	$ 135,905	$ 44,796	$ 11,092	$ 3,555	$ 195,348
Total direct and indirect costs	$1,689,158	$563,991	$188,753	$51,046	$2,492,948
Average cost per registered student....					$3,613

* Registered students do not crossfoot, since students are enrolled in more than one program.
[†] Basis for allocations to programs shown in parentheses ( )

EXHIBIT 2   Allocation Bases 2001–02

Indirect Cost	*Basis for Allocation to Moray*
School committee..................	$5.00 per registered student
Administration	$62.75 per registered student
Health/life insurance	$0.08 per teacher salary dollar (regular teachers, substitute teachers, and aides)
Operations and maintenance	$0.027 per Operations and Maintenance dollar in the school
Rent and depreciation...............	$5.00 per registered student
Contract services..................	$0.018 per administrative salary dollar
Travel	$1.20 per registered student

Indirect Cost	*Basis for Allocation to Programs within Moray*
School committee..................	Proportion of regular teacher salaries
Administration	Proportion of regular teacher salaries
Health/life insurance.................	Proportion of regular teacher salaries
Operations and maintenance	Proportion of floor space: 65% to Regular Instruction; 15% to Special Education; 10% to Spanish Language Program; 10% to Other Programs
Rent and depreciation...............	Same as Operations and Maintenance
Contract services..................	Proportion of registered students
Travel	Proportion of regular teacher salaries

Examples of Calculations for Allocation to Programs within Moray

School committee	Regular teacher salaries = $1,119,300; Total salaries = $1,596,175. Proportion = .7012. Therefore Regular Instruction share = .7012 × $3,450 = $2,419.
Administration	Regular Instruction share = .7012 × $43,298 = $30,362
Health/life insurance	Regular Instruction share = .7012 × $134,782 = $94,514
Operations and maintenance	Regular Instruction share = .65 × $7,290 = $4,739
Rent and depreciation...............	Regular Instruction share = .65 × $3,450 = $2,243
Contract services	Regular Instruction share = [615/(615 + 75 + 180 + 450)] × $2,250 = $1,048
Travel	Regular Instruction share = .7012 × $828 = $581

greatest seniority in the school, and the designated representative of the teachers' union, to discuss the teachers' salary expense. Ms. Cook hoped to make substantial cuts in the teacher salary expense item by increasing the average class size from 15 to 20 students. Mr. Hartman's response was not particularly encouraging:

> We can't possibly cut teachers' salaries in the way you envision because the teachers are already overworked. We have to cover lunch and recess periods, and most of us substitute regularly during our break periods for teachers who are out

sick. So we need a minimum of one teacher for every 15 students. Unless we cut down on students, we can't possibly reduce the number of teachers.

Next, Ms. Cook met with Dr. Mariana Olivera, the lead teacher for the Special Education Program, and Ms. Lillian Higgins, the librarian. Ms. Higgins, the most senior of the two, discussed the use of books and other instructional supplies, and her ideas for reducing costs:

> The instructional supplies and library item does appear to be a large amount, but there is really nothing included in it that's excessive. I think we're already quite frugal in our supply use, and we can't just stop ordering pencils, paper, books, or anything else we need for instructional purposes.
>
> I do see one problem with the budget, however; we're budgeting for a full 690 students when, in fact, due to absences, we probably have only about 650 students in school at any one time. If we adjust the budget to reflect our actual attendance, we can cut costs by at least 5 percent.

Dr. Olivera also had an idea for cutting costs. She suggested that the school reduce or eliminate the Spanish Language Program, thereby reducing the budget by almost $189,000. In considering Dr. Olivera's suggestion, Ms. Cook called the audio equipment manufacturer to discuss the resale value of some of the school's equipment. The company informed her that machines used for four years or more could not be sold, even for scrap. All of the equipment in Moray's language laboratory had been purchased prior to 1997.

Ms. Cook also reviewed the salaries for the Spanish Language Program and found that $35,000 was for a lead teacher, with the remaining $50,000 designated for two regular teachers, at $25,000 each. No substitutes were budgeted since, in the case of a teacher absence, the aide could cover. She also noted that the program's size was limited by the number of teachers. That is, since a strict 10:1 student-teacher ratio was maintained, and the students attended the lab daily, the maximum number of students the program could accept was 180 (30 per class period with six class periods in a day). This did not mean that the lab equipment was fully utilized, however, since the nature of the instructional process was such that some days the students would not use the lab at all.

As she reflected on the nature of the task before her, Ms. Cook realized that she had to consider the interactive effects of several factors. First, there was the question of the nature of the direct costs in her budget. Although Mr. Hartman had given her a good indication of how teachers' costs might change with changes in enrollment, the behavior of the other costs was less clear. Administrative salaries and supplies, she reasoned, would remain about the same regardless of the number of students. This would probably be true for operations and maintenance expenses as well. Instructional supplies and library expenses, on the other hand, would probably change in direct proportion to the number of students.

A second consideration of Ms. Cook's was the level of indirect costs. When she called the Central Office to learn more about the allocation process, she was told that the distribution of indirect costs among programs within Moray used a different set of allocation bases from those used to allocate the costs to the school; these are shown in Exhibit 2. She also realized that at least some of the indirect costs allocated to Moray from the Central Office would change as both student enrollment and the level of Moray's direct costs changed. Nevertheless, she felt quite certain that the School Committee would hold her responsible for whatever amount was allocated. But then, if she was responsible for these costs, she wondered about the extent to which she could control or reduce them.

Finally, Ms. Cook mused about Dr. Olivera's suggestion. Reducing or eliminating services did not seem appropriate, yet it might be the only way to meet the targeted budget reduction. If she were to cut the Spanish Language Program in half, she thought she might be able to reduce some of the Program's costs, but she was not at all sure. She also noted that approximately two-thirds of the depreciation in her budget was for language laboratory equipment.

As she began to prepare her budgetary modifications, Ms. Cook realized that Dr. Olivera's suggestion posed some very difficult issues. She decided to revise her budget first by making the appropriate changes in costs associated with an average attendance of 650 students. Only if this failed to produce the requisite reduction, would she consider cutting back the Spanish Language Program. However, in order to demonstrate to the School Committee the true impact of its request, she also decided to calculate what her average attendance in the Regular Instruction Program would have to be in order to meet the Committee's requested cut without curtailing the Spanish Language Program. Since several teachers were expected to retire at the end of the current fiscal year (FY2000–01), she realized that if attendance levels were cut on a permanent basis, she might be able to get by without hiring replacements.

Since Ms. Cook would soon be required to make employment offers for any new or replacement teachers, she realized that preparing revised budgetary projections and gaining School Committee approval for them was of the utmost priority.

Questions

1. What is the average teacher salary for the Regular Instruction and Special Education Programs?

2. Please analyze the costs in the category "Direct Costs-Instruction," and classify each line item as either fixed, variable, semivariable, or step-function. If variable, semivariable, or step-function, please indicate specifically how the cost behaves. How, if at all, is this analysis useful to Ms. Cook?

3. What are the budgetary options open to Ms. Cook? What are the cost savings associated with each?

4. What should Ms. Cook do?

Case 10–2

Urban Arts Institute*

In May 2002, Tim Stanley, president of the Urban Arts Institute (UAI), had just received some good news and some bad news. The good news was that the Institute's bank had approved the conversion of a portion of a long-term note (secured by a second mortgage on the Institute's property and building) to an increase in its short-term line of credit. The increase had allowed the Institute to close its budget gap for the fiscal year ending June 30, 2002. The bad news was that the bank also had informed Mr. Stanley that the additional drawings on the line of credit needed to close the budget gap had taken the line of credit up to its maximum. Since the Institute had virtually no endowments or other reserves, there was no margin for error left for the upcoming fiscal year.

Mr. Stanley realized that unless he took some immediate steps to improve UAI's budgeting system, the Institute was headed toward financial disaster. With the budget formulation process for fiscal year 2003 (July 2002 to June 2003) almost complete, he turned his attention to UAI's fiscal operations with the following questions:

1. With no reserves to fall back on, the Institute needed a balanced budget in FY 2003. What measures should he put in place to assure himself that this would happen?

2. How could the overall budget formulation process be changed to reflect his management style and support some of his other strategic goals, such as improved communications among faculty, administration, and the board?

Background

UAI was founded in 1911 as a private for-profit enterprise with a mission to provide training for business and commercial applications of art skills. In 1965, to permit it to tap into additional revenue sources (e.g., government grants, scholarships, and so on), the UAI changed its legal status to private nonprofit. Despite this change, the management of the Institute retained its for-profit flavor, operating as a family-owned business. Until 2000, it was run by the same family that had founded it, with decision-making authority vested in a small circle, and board members comprised of friends of the family.

Historically, the school always had been highly tuition-dependent, with almost no endowment to contribute toward operating expenses. In 1995, the UAI financed about $2 million in building renovations entirely through

*This case was prepared by William Wubbenhorst, under the supervision of Professor David W. Young. Copyright © by David W. Young.

bonds issued by the Massachusetts Health and Education Financing Authority (HEFA). In 1999, the UAI became accredited as a four-year institution, having previously offered only a three-year diploma to its students. To receive accreditation, the UAI needed to increase its curriculum to include the requisite number of liberal arts credits for its students.

In mid-2000, the Institute's president of 11 years resigned. In the ensuing weeks, several board members also resigned, marking an end to the founding family's control over the Institute. Steven Roberts, Dean of Academic and Faculty Affairs, stepped in as interim president until a new president could be recruited. Mr. Stanley assumed the position in August 2001.

Organizational Structure

The Institute's president reported to the Board of Trustees. The current board chair, Henry Hunter, was elected in May 2000, while the Institute was still under the leadership of the previous president. The turnover of trustees following in the wake of the president's resignation marked a period of awakening for the board. Mr. Hunter took the opportunity to recruit new board members who were committed to playing a much more active role in the Institute's affairs than had been expected previously.

Three administrative deans (for Academic/Faculty Affairs, Student Affairs, and Admissions) reported directly to the president. Also reporting to the president were the directors for public relations, financial aid, development, and the business manager. The bulk of the Institute's professional staff, mainly faculty, reported to Dean Roberts.

The instructional side of UAI consisted of six academic departments, each with its own chair. The six chairs also reported to Dean Roberts. The Fine Arts, Liberal Arts, and Foundation departments comprised the institute's "core" curriculum through which students received a common grounding in art skills. In the case of Liberal Arts, this curriculum was also required as part of the school's authority in granting bachelor's degrees. As described by Mr. Hunter:

> All of our students, regardless of concentration, receive a grounding in Fine Arts and Foundation. This integrated approach to our curriculum is one aspect of the school that makes us different and unique from other art schools.

The other three departments (Design, Illustration, and Photography) were the principal areas of concentration students pursued after completing the core curriculum. Each year, a small number (four to five students) chose a concentration in Fine Arts.

Tim Stanley

Prior to assuming his role as president, Mr. Stanley had served as director of a nearby university-affiliated arts center, a position he held for 11 years. Previously, he had earned Master's degrees in both Business Administration (with concentration in international banking) and Fine Arts (concentrating in arts management).

Mr. Stanley's first few months at UAI were spent acclimating himself to the school through both informal conversations as well as a formal survey of staff, faculty, and trustees. He reflected on his key findings:

> One of the first things I discovered at the UAI was that previously, the school's affairs had been managed by a very tight circle of decision-makers, especially as it applied to fiscal and budget matters. As a result, I found many of the staff and faculty surprisingly ill-informed about the fiscal condition we were in. The previous leadership clearly had left a management legacy characterized by extremely poor communication and coordination with the instructional and programmatic side of the school.
>
> There was also an atmosphere of annual crisis management, with severe cash flow problems arising from unanticipated budgetary shortfalls on a regular basis. Furthermore, the MIS in place was unable to give critical and timely answers to questions concerning enrollment and the budget.

In response to these findings, Mr. Stanley and Mr. Hunter (who shared many of Mr. Stanley's concerns and observations about the school's condition) organized a two-day retreat with staff, faculty, and trustees. The primary purpose of the retreat was to communicate their findings and to begin to forge a common understanding of the problems and challenges facing the school in the future.

The retreat, according to Mr. Stanley:

> . . . was a great success. People had been left in the dark for so long, they were very receptive and attentive to what Henry and I had to say. The retreat got people enthusiastic and they welcomed the opportunity to share more responsibility in the change process. Our message to all of them was: "You are an active partner," and they heard that.
>
> The retreat was also successful in developing some common agreement and discussion around such critical issues as student enrollment, recruitment and retention, as well as ideas for new program delivery systems.

As he reflected on the retreat and looked toward the future, Mr. Stanley saw a number of challenges:

> In a sense, everything I had done to date, in terms of the interviews and the retreat, was the easy part. Now, I had to figure out how to change the fiscal, and especially the budgetary, decision-making and communication processes in a way that would support my participatory management style. Now that I had gotten everybody excited about being a part of the school, I needed to figure out how to channel the energy and efforts of the staff, faculty, and trustees toward solving the school's critical financial problems.

The Budgetary System

The Institute's budgeting system had gone largely unchanged in recent years. As described by one of the school's administrators, the system was a reflection of the school's history of management:

It was a very closed process, with almost all of the decisions being made by the president, the Dean of Student Affairs [who had since left the school], and a couple of the trustees, including the chairman [who also had left]. The budget process itself wasn't really very rigorous, and we were constantly having to make mid-fiscal year reductions because of unanticipated cash flow problems.

Budget Structure

Revenues were recorded in 14 different accounts. Expenses were tracked through approximately 140 different accounts. These accounts and the relevant amounts for fiscal years 2002 (as of 4/30/02) and 2003 (budget) are shown in Exhibit 1 (Revenues) and Exhibit 2 (Expenses). (Exhibit 2 has been abbreviated somewhat due to length considerations.) The original FY 2002 budget, which was approved by the board in October 2001, contained a surplus of $2,062, up from a loss in FY 2001 of $28,350.

The largest expense, accounting for over half of the Institute's expenses in FY 2002, was personnel. For budget planning purposes, these costs were determined centrally, based on department heads' estimates of the number of classes they would be providing. The academic heads generally used historical

EXHIBIT 1

URBAN ARTS INSTITUTE				
Revenues				
FY 2003 Budget	FY 2003 Proposed	% Revenue	FY 2002 (Revised 2/13)	% Revenue
1. Federal work study	$ 45,000	1.5%	$ 45,000	1.62%
2. Tuition—day students	2,514,700	83.6	2,370,990	85.30
3. Registration—day students	9,600	0.3	8,000	0.29
4. General fees—day students	160,400	5.3	133,530	4.80
Day students (subtotal).	2,729,700	90.7	2,557,520	92.01
5. Continuing education	107,300	3.6	101,500	3.65
6. Registration—continuing education	6,900	0.2	5,750	0.21
7. Summer	65,075	2.2	64,575	2.32
8. Application fee	9,000	0.3	9,000	0.32
9. Pre-college	37,125	1.2		0.00
Other tuitions/fees (subtotal)	225,400	7.5	180,825	6.5
10. Miscellaneous	2,500	0.1	6,100	0.22
11. Interest	0	0.0	12,000	0.43
Earned income (subtotal)	2,500	0.1	18,100	0.7
12. Gifts—unrestricted	25,000	0.8	15,000	0.54
13. Gifts—restricted	25,000	0.8	5,000	0.18
14. HGCC/bazaar	0	0.0	3,000	0.11
Contributed income (subtotal)	50,000	1.6	23,000	0.8
Total revenue.	$3,007,600		$2,779,445	

EXHIBIT 2

				URBAN ARTS INSTITUTE		
				Expense Accounts		
				FY 2003 Proposed Budget		

Expenses	Account Number	FY 2003 Proposed	% Expense	FY 2002 (Revised 2/13)	% Expense
Personnel:					
Instruction....................	4001	$ 700,000	23.0%	$ 698,134	25.2%
Department heads.............	4002	81,120	2.7	81,120	2.9
Department staff...............	4003	3,000	0.1	2,000	0.1
Administration heads...........	4004	215,280	7.1	215,280	7.8
Administration staff............	4005	400,000	13.1	384,344	13.9
Nonpersonnel:					
Foundation:					
Materials..................	5030	600	0.0	650	0.0
Models	5050	7,000	0.2	8,200	0.3
Equipment..................	5070	600	0.0	0	0.0
Fine Arts:					
Materials—General	5130	200	0.0	2,220	0.1
Print materials	5131	2,000	0.1	0	0.0
Sculpture..................	5132	2,000	0.1	0	0.0
Speaker	5140	1,000	0.0	500	0.0
Models	5150	14,000	0.5	13,280	0.5
Equipment..................	5170	1,800	0.1	1,720	0.1
Design:					
Materials..................	5230	1,500	0.0	1,500	0.1
Speaker	5240	500	0.0	300	0.0
Models	5250	0	0.0	900	0.0
Equipment..................	5270	0	0.0	0	0.0
Illustration:					
Materials..................	5330	500	0.0	200	0.0
Speaker	5340	1,000	0.0	500	0.0
Models	5350	2,800	0.1	3,800	0.1
Equipment..................	5370	240	0.0		
Photo:					
Materials..................	5430	4,000	0.1	2,050	0.1
Speakers	5440	1,500	0.0	1,200	0.0
Models	5450	900	0.0	600	0.0
Video.....................	5455	0	0.0	0	0.0
Equipment..................	5470	2,000	0.1	1,020	0.0
Liberal Arts:					
Materials..................	5530	500	0.0	600	0.0
Speaker	5540	1,100	0.0	900	0.0
Equipment..................	5570	600	0.0	200	0.0

EXHIBIT 2   *(Continued)*

Expenses	Account Number	FY 2003 Proposed	% Expense	FY 2002 (Revised 2/13)	% Expense
Continuing education:					
Materials	5630	$ 850	0.0%	$ 200	0.0%
Models	5650	1,500	0.0	1,000	0.0
Summer:					
Materials	5730	250	0.0	150	0.0
Models	5750	1,500	0.0	1,500	0.1
High school:					
Materials	5830	2,500	0.1	500	0.0
Models	5850	600	0.0	600	0.0
Production room:					
Materials	5911	5,000	0.2	9,800	0.4
Equipment	5912	2,000	0.1	700	0.0
Photo lab:					
Materials	5921	20,500	0.7	23,950	0.9
Equipment	5922	9,000	0.3	7,280	0.3
Repair	5923	3,000	0.1	1,000	0.0
Computer lab:					
Materials	5931	2,500	0.1	2,000	0.1
Equipment	5932	11,816	0.4	16,900	0.6
Video lab:					
Materials	5940	75	0.0	0	0.0
Equipment	5941	2,500	0.1	3,700	0.1
Repair	5942	1,500	0.0	0	0.0
Student affairs (8 accounts)		26,500	0.9	19,380	0.7
Admissions (6 accounts)		34,800	1.1	29,335	1.1
Gallery (4 accounts)		11,100	0.4	9,400	0.3
Library (7 accounts)		21,100	0.7	16,200	0.6
Dean of faculty (1 account).		0	0.0	0	0.0
Front desk (1 account)		33,408	1.1	40,240	1.5
Institutional:					
Professional fees	8125	52,500	1.7	43,000	1.6
Insurance	8130	20,000	0.7	20,000	0.7
Postage/delivery	8160	32,000	1.0	27,000	1.0
Reserve	8165	100,000	3.3	25,000	0.9
Phone	8180	30,800	1.0	7,500	0.3
Health	8230	44,084	1.4	10,900	0.4
Social Security	8240	114,582	3.8	6,500	0.1
State health	8235	1,400	0.0	36,400	1.3
Tuition reimbursement	8250	3,000	0.1	108,716	3.9
All other		141,065	4.8	136,865	4.9
President (4 accounts)		7,500	0.2	12,500	0.5

EXHIBIT 2 *(Concluded)*

Expenses	Account Number	FY 2003 Proposed	% Expense	FY 2002 (Revised 2/13)	% Expense
Publicity (9 accounts)		$ 166,000	5.4%	$ 158,400	5.8%
Development (4 accounts)		29,000	1.0	10,300	0.4
Building maintenance 4 accounts) . . .		35,075	1.2	35,350	1.3
Utilities (4 accounts)		59,000	1.9	56,200	2.0
Building renovation (2 accounts)		0	0.0	0	0.0
Finance:					
HEFA interest	9700	118,000	3.9	118,000	4.3
HEFA principal	9750	87,000	2.9	87,000	3.1
Bank interest	9762	60,000	2.0	83,000	3.0
Bank principal	9763	20,000	0.7	13,000	0.5
Scholarships (5 accounts)		288,800	9.6	169,704	6.1
Total Expenses		$3,048,145		$2,765,388	

information, along with their own projections of enrollments, to estimate their staffing needs for the coming semester. These projections then were collected and added to the administrative staffing costs to determine the total projected personnel budget. Exhibit 3 provides a breakout of full- and part-time faculty by academic department, along with actual enrollment figures (credit hours).

Most department heads controlled only a very small discretionary budget to pay for models, speakers, supplies, and equipment. The exceptions to this were the heads of the Design and Photography departments, who controlled considerably larger budgets for operating two labs each. The Design Department operated the production room and the computer lab; the Photography Department operated the photo lab and the video lab.

The Budget Formulation Process

UAI's budget formulation process typically began in early March and was completed in mid-October, when the board of trustees formally adopted the budget. Exhibit 4 contains a memo prepared by the school's business manager, Edward Carlton, outlining the timetable for the FY 2003 budget.

Dean Roberts described one of his main frustrations surrounding the budget formulation development process:

> Because the school is so highly dependent on tuition revenues, the information around the number of enrolled students is a critical element in preparing the budget. However, due to the school's "open" admissions policy, which permits students to register for courses up to one week before fall semester classes are scheduled to begin, both revenue projections and course planning are subject to last minute revisions. These revisions sometimes take place as late as two months into the fiscal year.

EXHIBIT 3 Faculty and Enrollments by Department (faculty figures are from the 2002–03 Budget)

	No. of Full-Time Teaching Faculty*	Average Salary†	No. of Part-Time Teaching Faculty	Average Salary	Enrollment (Number of Credit Hours)		
					Fall 2001	Winter 2002	Fall 2002
Fine Arts	4	$26,250	5	$10,215	608.0	484.5	642.0
Foundation	4	28,593	2	12,913	593.5	595.0	721.0
Liberal Arts.	3	30,000	5	6,025	1,155.0	1,317.0	1,236.0
Design‡	1½	25,000	12	4,898	756.0	475.5	715.0
Illustration‡	¾	26,667	6	4,583	541.0	632.5	426.5
Photography	4	28,750	7	3,571	514.0	602.0	603.0
	17¼		37				

*Some faculty have part-time administrative responsibilities. Their time in administrative activities is not counted here. Also, some faculty who reside in one department actually spend some of their time teaching in another department. These shifts are not shown here.
†Includes chair's salary.
‡Chair is part-time.

Budget Monitoring

Once the preliminary budget was finalized at the beginning of the fiscal year, Mr. Carlton began monitoring budget-to-actual expenditures on a monthly basis, beginning with the end of August. Exhibit 5 shows a portion of this report for April 2002. Mr. Carlton commented:

> Since Tim arrived, I have continued to do essentially the same things that I did before. I look at the budgeted versus actual year-to-date spending for each account and send the information out to each academic head and administrative dean and director. If there is a small variance, I'll usually just have a quick informal chat with the person responsible for that account. If it's a big variance, I generally communicate those accounts directly to the president.

Perspectives on the Budget Process

Different members of the organization had different perspectives on the budget process. For example, most academic department heads considered themselves outside of the budget decision-making process. As Sally Ames, the chair of the Fine Arts Department, explained:

> At UAI, the budget is run kind of like a shopping mall. All of us operate in our own little world without much knowledge about how each department or the school as a whole is doing. The budget process here has always been shrouded in mystery to me. I don't really know if and when budget decisions are made. In the past few years, we've been sent back mid-semester on several occasions to reassess our budget, and to make more cuts. It becomes very difficult to do any kind of long-term planning or to try to administer new ideas or course expansion because of the uncertainty over whether you'll actually get to spend what you think you're budgeted for.

EXHIBIT 4   **The Budget Preparation Schedule**

February 21, 2002

To: Department Heads
From: Edward Carlton
Re: FY 03 budget process

This year's budget process will be essentially the same as it has been in prior years. We will use the following schedule:

March 9	Proposals for new programs, courses, building projects, and major purchases due to Carlton (use attached form).
During March	Academic Dept. heads meet with Frank Angelo for proposals for classes and programs and with Steven Roberts for all other proposals. Dept. heads responsible for setting appointments.
	All Dept. heads meet with Tim Stanley, Roberts, Carlton, and Angelo regarding general plans for the depts. for FY 03.
April 1	Carlton announces decisions on proposals if the decision has not been given before.
During April	Dept. heads prepare detailed budgets on the basis of FY 02 and the approved proposals. Carlton will supply basic information for FY 02.
April 24	Detailed budgets due to Carlton, including faculty hours.*
May	Dept. heads individually meet with Stanley, Carlton, and Angelo.
June 1	Carlton announces proposed budget.
June 15	Dept. heads submit revised budgets to Carlton if desired.
June 30	Stanley and Carlton announce Preliminary Budget for FY 03.
During Sept.	Stanley and Carlton review Preliminary Budget in light of enrollments.
Sept. 30	Carlton announces proposed changes in Preliminary Budget.
Oct. 7	Dept. heads submit revised budgets to Carlton if desired.
Oct. 15	Board of Trustees adopts budget.

*This projection was based on the department head's estimate of students and classes to be taught for the fall semester.

EXHIBIT 5

URBAN ARTS INSTITUTE
Monthly Financial Report
Sample Pages from Report Dated May 21, 2002

CODES:

A	12-month expense	83%	
B	12-month salary	85%	22
C	9-month expense	89%	
D	9-month salary	94%	17

FY 02 Revised per 2/13

Account Name	Account Number	Year to Date April 30	FY02 Revised	FY02 Original	Year to Date FY02 Revised (percent)	CODE
Net total		$ 90,054	$ 14,057	$ 2,062		
Revenue:						
Federal work study	1910	$ 28,731	$ 45,000	$ 45,000	63.85%	
Tuition day	3105	2,312,345	2,370,990	2,370,990	97.53	
Registration day	3110	5,240	8,000	8,000	65.50	
Day general fee	3150	132,255	133,530	133,530	99.05	
Student health						
Continuing education						
(Coned)		93,776	101,500	101,500	92.39	
Registration, Coned . .	3210	4,350	5,750	5,750	75.65	
Summer		3,127	64,575	64,575	4.84	
Application fee	3015	8,176	9,000	9,000	90.84	
Miscellaneous	3440	15,030	6,100	6,100	246.39	
Interest	3410	1,453	12,000	12,000	12.11	
Art kits	3610					
Gifts, unrestricted	3800	7,446	15,000	15,000	49.64	
Gifts, restricted	3830	0	5,000	5,000	0.00	
HGCC/Bazaar	3920	2,377	3,000	3,000	79.23	
Total revenue		$2,614,306	$2,779,445	$2,779,445	94.06	
Expenses:						
Instruction	4001	$ 693,263	$ 698,134	$ 698,134	99.30	
Department heads	4002	70,027	81,120	81,120	86.33	
Department staff	4003	0	2,000	2,000	0.00	B
Administration heads	4004	194,764	215,280	215,280	90.47	B
Administration staff	4005	314,498	384,344	384,344	81.83	
Payroll adjustment				(20,713)		
Foundation:						C
Materials	5030	175	650	650	26.92	C
Models	5050	7,750	8,200	8,200	94.51	
Equipment	5070		0	500		

EXHIBIT 5   *(Continued)*

Account Name	Account Number	Year to Date April 30	FY02 Revised	FY02 Original	Year to Date FY02 Revised (percent)	CODE
Fine arts:						C
Materials	5130	$ 3,427	$ 2,220	$ 2,220	154.37%	C
Speaker	5140	400	500	500	80.00	C
Models	5150	14,396	13,280	13,280	108.40	C
Equipment	5170	596	1,720	1,720	34.65	
Design:						C
Materials	5230	488	1,500	1,500	32.53	C
Speakers	5240	374	300	300	124.67	C
Models	5250	0	900	900	0.00	
Equipment	5270	0				
Illustration:						C
Materials	5330	220	200	200	110.00	
Speaker	5340	460	500	500	92.00	C
Models	5350	2,335	3,800	3,800	61.45	C
Equipment	5370					
Photo:						
Materials	5430	2,345	2,050	2,050	114.39	C
Speakers	5440	570	1,200	1,200	47.50	C
Models	5450	495	600	600	82.50	C
Video	5455	0				
Equipment	5470	104	1,020	1,020	10.20	C
Liberal arts:						
Materials	5530	618	600	600	103.00	C
Speaker	5540	1,130	900	900	125.56	C
Equipment	5570		200	200		
Continuing education:						
Materials	5630	757	200	200	378.50	C
Models	5650	1,511	1,000	800	151.10	C
Summer:						
Materials	5730	175	150	150	116.67	
Models	5750	1,510	1,500	1,500	100.67	
High school:						
Materials	5830	189	500	500	37.80	C
Models	5850	270	600	600	45.00	C
Production room:						
Materials	5911	5,681	9,800	9,800	57.97	A
Equipment	5912	256	700	700	36.57	A

EXHIBIT 5   *(Concluded)*

Account Name	Account Number	Year to Date April 30	FY02 Revised	FY02 Original	Year to Date FY02 Revised (percent)	CODE
Photo lab:						
Materials	5921	$ 15,632	$ 23,950	$ 23,950	65.27%	A
Equipment	5922	10,986	7,280	7,280	150.91	A
Repair	5923	2,385	1,000	1,000	238.50	A
Computer lab:						
Materials	5931	2,038	2,000		101.90	A
Equipment	5932	15,373	16,900	21,438	90.96	A
Video lab:						
Materials	5940	41				
Equipment	5941	3,081	3,700	3,700	83.27	
Also included were expenses for:						
Student affairs (8 accounts)						
Admissions (6 accounts)						
Gallery (4 accounts)						
Library (7 accounts)						
Dean of faculty (1 account)						
Front desk (1 account)						
Institutional (26 accounts)						
President (4 accounts)						
Publicity (12 accounts)						
Development (4 accounts)						
Building maintenance (4 accounts)						
Utilities (4 accounts)						
Building renovation (2 accounts)						
Finance (4 accounts)						
Scholarship (4 accounts) . .						
Total expenses		$2,524,252	$2,765,388	$2,777,383	91.28%	

John Christopher, chair of the Photography Department, also cited the poor communication associated with department budgets:

After I sat down and negotiated my budget with the business manager and Steve [Dean Roberts] back last May, I assumed that the result of that conversation led to my final budget, since I didn't hear anything back from either of them. So, when the new fiscal year started, I began making needed equipment and supply purchases based on that budget. Then, at the end of August, I received the first end-of-month summary report, only to find out that my final budget was less than I thought. If I knew then what I did at the end of August, I would have spent my budget differently during the first two months, but it's too late now.

Walter Robertson, chair of the Liberal Arts Department, added:

The uncertainty on what my budget really is causes me to make purchases in a more cautious, and expensive, piece-meal fashion. Furthermore, I feel the budget categories are not really relevant for me. I know what my total budget is, and I'll stay within that bottom line, but I might overspend and underspend in certain accounts.

Others, such as Mary Susans (the chair of the Design Department) and Scott Davidson (the chair of the Illustration Department) were frustrated with the lack of full-time faculty in their departments. Mr. Christopher also noted how the poor communication with management had made staff indifferent in responding to administrative tasks:

In past years, we've received various directives from the administration around certain planned purchases for the school. One year, they told us they were going to make a major purchase of new books for the library, so a bunch of us, including faculty, spent a number of months researching and compiling a list of books. By the time we were about done, we found out there was no money to buy the books after all. After a few of these wasted exercises, we and the involved faculty have become somewhat wary and indifferent to these types of requests from the administration.

These problems around budget uncertainty and communication also made it difficult for the department heads to manage their faculty, especially the part-time teachers. Because of the open admissions policy, teachers often did not know if they were going to teach a particular section until a week before the first class. The school also had a policy whereby full-time faculty were guaranteed a certain number of classes before determining whether classes were available to be taught by part-time faculty.

According to Ms. Ames, this class scheduling and faculty selection process was seen by many teachers as having political dimensions:

The whole process by which the administrative deans plan classes and sections is seen by many faculty as a process driven by political considerations, in which teachers had a "favored" or "unfavored" status in the eyes of UAI administrators.

The administrative staff faced the difficult task of managing a budget process with high tuition-dependency. The Institute's open admissions policy meant that enrollments, and therefore tuition revenues, were not certain until the fall, but the summer was often the best time for discretionary spending projects like restocking supplies and fixing the building. As Mr. Carlton explained:

> In past years, we have gotten ourselves into a jam because we spent our discretionary funds during the summer, only to find enrollments, and thus revenues, coming in lower than expected. By that time, we have essentially lost any flexibility in terms of our spending, and are forced to lay people off and cancel classes at the 11th hour, which is very disruptive to the school's instructional operations.

Amy Danielson, the Dean of Admissions, had a similar concern:

> For my office, the summer is a critical time for outreach, both through printing and mass mailings of UAI course catalogs as well as travel and attendance at portfolio days [recruitment conventions for prospective art students to learn more about various art school programs and offerings] and other recruitment efforts.

She also had some concerns over how the school set enrollment goals for budgetary purposes:

> Over the past few years I've been here, I've detected a distinct and recurring sense of eternal optimism around the numbers of students, and subsequently the revenues, that will be coming through the door on a given year. The question around setting admissions goals seems to be framed around the question: "How many students do we need in order to cover the school's expenses?" I think, perhaps, that we've been putting the cart before the horse on this matter.

The board of directors also had some concerns not only about the budget process, but about the kind of information it was receiving on the Institute's financial situation. The critical need from Mr. Hunter's perspective was related to the quality of cost information and reporting:

> For many years, the UAI had been run more like a family-owned business than a nonprofit corporation. As the UAI's fiscal condition worsened in recent years, this small circle of decision-makers, consisting primarily of a handful of trustees and the president, became more and more defensive and secretive of the school's fiscal operations. During that time, the remainder of the board served effectively a rubber-stamp function, approving decisions with little or no inquiry or involvement.
>
> Consequently, there is no MIS in place to answer critical questions, such as: "How much are the instructional costs related to this department?" or "What does it cost us to operate the public art gallery?"

One reason why Mr. Hunter wanted to have more detailed information about the Institute's expenses was reflected in his broad definition of what he saw as the Institute's mission:

> I feel that a part of our mission is not just to teach art, but also to serve a role of supporting the local artist community through our part-time teaching positions.

Many of these teacher/artists are in great need of the steady income that teaching provides to support them while they pursue their creative aspirations.

When Mr. Hunter took the helm, he recruited new members onto the board who wanted to know more about the school's finances and operations. Both he and the new board members felt it necessary for the school to take a "leave no stone unturned" approach to revamping the school's fiscal operations, with special attention to the budgeting and information systems. From his perspective, there were three key ingredients needed in an improved MIS:

We need to develop specific guidelines on reporting. For example, I think we need to know how much each academic department generates in revenue, and how much it costs to operate. In addition, we should know the administrative overhead costs on a per student basis. Secondly, reports should be generated on at least a weekly basis. These reports should pay close attention to the bottom line and anticipate any cash flow problems. Finally, we need to establish specific conditions under which a particular department or administrative office should be permitted to exceed its budget.

I also want the information in these reports to focus on two key policy objectives for the school: (1) To increase the school's "standard of living" through a more efficient allocation of the existing revenue base; and (2) To provide detailed cost information on each of the school's academic departments to help ascertain "what we do best" and, presumably, concentrate resources in those areas.

In considering these and other issues relating to the budget process, Mr. Stanley categorized the problems into three main areas: information/reporting, timeliness, and communication. He commented on the first area:

My initial frustration in the area of MIS was with the lack of comparable historical data for multi-year trend analyses of the school's finances. I was also frustrated, as was Henry, with our inability to retrieve needed current budget information in a timely manner. For example, there was no ability to even provide a projected cash flow report to anticipate possible short-term borrowing needs during the course of the year. In addition, data on enrollment, both past and current, were difficult to retrieve and analyze.

The second area, timeliness, appeared to be somewhat less complicated. Although the preliminary budget was put into place in July, final enrollment figures were not available until early September. Furthermore, the board didn't officially adopt the budget until mid-October, more than one quarter into the fiscal year. If changes needed to be made at that time, they would likely have to occur in the middle of the fall semester, often causing disruptions in academic scheduling.

The last area for Mr. Stanley was communication. He commented:

Years of being excluded from the school's financial decision-making has left most staff, faculty, and department heads largely ignorant of budget issues and concerns. In fact, prior to the retreat, most of the staff, faculty, and trustees were largely unaware of the extent of the school's financial difficulties.

Furthermore, because the budget had been subjected to so many revisions during the course of the year, there was widespread confusion over what the actual budget was. In FY 2002, this confusion led the director of the Financial Aid office to significantly overspend her budget. This meant we had to approach the bank to increase our long-term debt.

To avoid these and other problems, Mr. Stanley knew that improved communication of budgetary information would be essential if the school were to successfully navigate itself through the coming years. With the mixed news from the bank, Mr. Stanley came to understand that UAI had perhaps escaped the frying pan only to face falling into the fire. With no financing options to fall back on, the school would now survive based solely upon its ability to live within its tuition revenue base. With this in mind, he set out to change the budgeting process. He had four objectives:

> First, I want to involve faculty and staff in UAI operations through the budget decision-making process. Second, I want to be able to provide budget information by department. Everyone should know how much they're spending, including salaries. Third, I think Trustees should have cost and budget information, but on a programmatic basis, not on a line-item basis. Finally, all of this must help us to keep the school within the bottom line. We simply cannot have any more deficits.

Questions

1. What is your forecast of the surplus for FY 2002? What assumptions did you make in your analysis?

2. What measures should Mr. Stanley put in place to assure himself of a balanced budget in FY 2003?

3. How, if at all, should the budget formulation process be changed to reflect Mr. Stanley's management style and his goals for the organization?

Case 10–3

Lomita Hospital*

> Professionals must become aware of the necessity of using quantitative data in budgetary justifications. Very often I will get four or five justifications before one is finally written in terms of numbers that I can then relate to the administration. If the request cannot be put in terms of generating income or increasing productivity, the justification must be even more convincing. These statements can be in terms of loss of time, ease in handling, or better service. But none of these justifications can be emotional.

Charles Russell, MD, Chief of Pathology at Lomita Hospital, was in the process of formulating his budget for fiscal year 1997. He had just received statistics from the Fiscal Affairs Department detailing the number of patient days

*This case was prepared originally by Pamela A. Sytkowski, Ph.D., under the supervision of Professor David W. Young. It subsequently was modified and updated by David W. Young. Copyright © by David W. Young.

and ancillary services used in the past two years and estimating the figures for FY 1997 (see Exhibit 1). One of Dr. Russell's responsibilities was to review the FY 1997 estimates and make whatever revisions he deemed appropriate. Once he and the other department heads had completed this process, the Fiscal Affairs Department could aggregate the totals and make overall hospital volume projections. The volume projections then were used to estimate hospital revenue which, in turn, determined the costs that the Fiscal Affairs Department allowed each department within the hospital. Since the beginning of intensified cost control measures by Lomita in 1993, a tight rein had been put on departmental costs. Therefore, these statistics became highly meaningful to Dr. Russell as well as other service chiefs in the hospital. Each service chief had his or her own set of statistics which had to be analyzed in light of the hospital as a whole.

Dr. Russell's primary objection to the accounting statistics was that they were aggregated figures and, therefore, did not show the distribution of procedures undertaken by the various sections within his department. As a result, fluctuations within these sections were concealed. Since he felt that realistic projections of future volume could only be made on the basis of statistics for each section, he kept his own record of numbers of procedures, broken down according to section and specific laboratory process (Exhibit 2).

Dr. Russell was especially concerned with the projections of expenses insofar as they related to the cytology section of his department. There was a quite reliable rumor that the staff of the Gynecology Department would be leaving Lomita to set up their own clinic. If this should happen, it was by no means clear that the new, perhaps lesser known, staff would have the same volume of patients so as to generate the cytology work which the present staff gave to the Pathology Department.

Besides contemplating these issues and their effects on his budget proposal for the coming year, Dr. Russell was concerned about the request of one of his section heads, Dr. Pamela Gordon. She and Dr. Cornell Johnson were responsible for the major portion of the surgical service pathology done in the department, and Dr. Gordon was directly responsible for the administration of the histology lab (see Exhibit 3). Over the past few years Dr. Gordon had indicated that her lab was understaffed, and once again this year she had requested that a new technician be hired. She felt that the pressure put on the technicians as well as that put on herself was creating an unbearable situation in which both the quantity and quality of work in her lab were suffering. A new technician had not entered into Dr. Russell's initial calculation of expenses, and although the projected volume seemed to warrant the addition, these projections had not been available to him in January when he had made an emergency appeal for extra help. At that time, his request for an additional technician had been approved by Mr. Malcolm Gunderson, the Laboratory Administrator of the hospital, only after a detailed analysis of the pathology logs had been prepared. Dr. Russell knew that the histology lab technicians were still overworked—he *personally* was taking their overtime pay directly

EXHIBIT 1   Ancillary Service Statistics—Pathology and Laboratories

		Inpatient				Outpatient (OPD)				Totals			
Patient days		110,579	111,000	110,500									
Patient visits						134,119	130,000	126,000					
Expense Code	Department/ Laboratory	Fiscal 1995	Projected 1996	Estimated 1997	Percent +(−)	Fiscal 1995	Projected 1996	Estimated 1997	Percent +(−)	Fiscal 1995	Projected 1996	Estimated 1997	Percent +(−)
212	Cytoscopy lab	602	612	600	(2.0)	803	726	725	—	1,402	1,338	1,325	(1.0)
213	Blood gas lab	20,465	23,296	25,000	7.3	993	1,378	1,600	16.1	21,463	24,674	26,600	7.8
220	Chemistry lab	214,824	205,888	206,000	0.1	104,593	70,327	70,000	(0.5)	319,417	276,215	276,000	—
221	Bacteriology lab	69,769	70,250	72,000	2.5	31,893	32,987	33,000	0.2	101,662	103,187	105,000	1.8
222	Hematology lab	154,312	162,234	162,000	(0.1)	86,655	84,049	85,000	1.1	240,967	246,283	247,000	0.3
228	Coagulation lab	433	894	900	0.7	899	857	970	13.2	1,332	1,751	1,870	6.8
229	Outside lab	14,673	16,028	17,000	6.1	10,239	9,323	9,300	(0.2)	24,912	25,351	26,000	3.7
230	Blood tests	93,004	98,894	108,600	9.3	21,875	22,305	24,200	8.5	114,879	121,199	132,800	9.6
233	Tissue typing	100	76	90	18.4	975	720	990	37.5	1,075	796	1,080	35.7
235	EKG lab	18,552	18,472	18,400	(0.4)	7,493	7,376	7,575	2.7	26,045	25,848	25,975	0.5
236	Cardiac cath lab	2,187	2,974	3,900	31.1	952	1,278	2,190	71.4	3,139	4,252	6,090	43.2
240	EEG lab	2,140	1,292	1,450	12.2	2,585	1,096	1,200	9.5	4,725	2,388	2,650	10.8
242	Tissue typing–IHOB	110	94	90	(5.3)	1,339	826	1,340	62.2	1,499	920	1,430	55.4
245	Pathology	4,618	4,524	4,700	3.9	3,705	3,513	3,820	8.7	8,323	8,037	8,520	6.0
246	Cytology lab	1,907	1,830	1,860	1.6	7,752	6,290	6,506	3.4	9,659	8,120	8,366	3.0
247	Frozen sections	538	654	770	17.7	337	511	605	18.4	975	1,165	1,375	18.0
257	Vascular lab	—	130	750	576.9	—	35	500	1,428.6	—	165	1,250	757.6
264	Blood preservation lab	50	44	50	13.6	22	10	10	—	72	54	60	11.1

EXHIBIT 2 Review of Test Statistics

	1996–1989 Differences									
	Percent	Total over (under)	Est. 1996	1995	1994	1993	1992	1991	1990	1989
Surgicals	68.5	3,820	9,396	8,546	8,490	7,791	7,461	6,810	6,109	5,576
Autopsies	13.77	46	380	327	324	363	358	340	339	334
Cytology	(20.29)	(1,935)	7,600	9,358	10,579	10,457	13,676	12,426	12,097	9,535
		(1996–1990)								
Specials:										
Electron microscopy	94.33	77	130	117	119	110	82	85	53	—
Fluorescence microscopy	594.44	107	125	118	97	84	31	62	18	—

Comparison of Fiscal Years, by Quarters

	Q1	Q2	Q3	Subtotal	Q4	Total
Surgical pathology 1994–95	2,141	2,126	2,173	6,440	2,025	8,465
1995–96	2,156	2,188	2,385	6,729	2,085	8,814
Difference/% increase	15	62	212	289	60	349
Autopsies 1994–95	87	89	67	243	79	322
1995–96	92	95	98	285	101 (est.)	386
Difference/% increase	5	6	31	42	22	64
Cytology 1994–95	2,501	2,401	2,361	7,263	2,361	9,624
1995–96	2,239	1,910	2,014	6,163	2,201 (est.)	8,364
Difference/% increase	(262)	(491)	(347)	(1,100)	(160)	(1,260)
Electron microscopy 1994–95	30	37	33	100	21	121
1995–96	27	21	25	73	25 (est.)	98
Difference/% increase	(3)	(16)	(8)	(27)	4	(23)
Fluorescence microscopy 1994–95	17	26	23	66	15	81
1995–96	15	20	24	59	22 (est.)	81
Difference/% increase	(2)	(6)	1	(7)	7	—

EXHIBIT 3
Pathology
Organization Chart

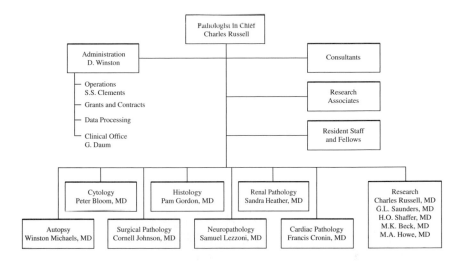

out of his Pathologist-in-Chief funds—yet administration had not been convinced in the past by overall hospital statistics, and it was now necessary to attempt again to justify this need. Dr. Russell, therefore, had asked Dr. Gordon and Dr. Johnson to prepare a detailed quantitative justification. Dr. Russell explained his problems in this regard:

> I ask my people to prepare a justification for all requests since I do not feel a hospital is any different from industry in this respect. In industry, expenses and budgets must routinely be justified either to the board of trustees or to the stockholders. A service chief and section heads must learn to do the same thing within the hospital setting. The problem is that my staff most often gives me emotionally charged justifications. There is never a justification in terms of numbers.

Background

Lomita Hospital was a 325-bed teaching hospital located in the heart of a large metropolitan area and affiliated with a local medical school. It employed some 2,000 persons and delivered well over 100,000 patient days of service a year. It admitted over 10,000 patients a year, had an average daily census of approximately 300, and an average occupancy rate of 92 percent. Its outpatient department handled over 100,000 patient visits a year. Exhibit 4 contains an organizational chart for Lomita Hospital.

The Budgetary Process

Budgeting at Lomita depended on a justification procedure that took place at various levels in the line of management. Projected expenses for the Pathology Department and other ancillary service departments were based on the

EXHIBIT 4 Administrative Organization Chart

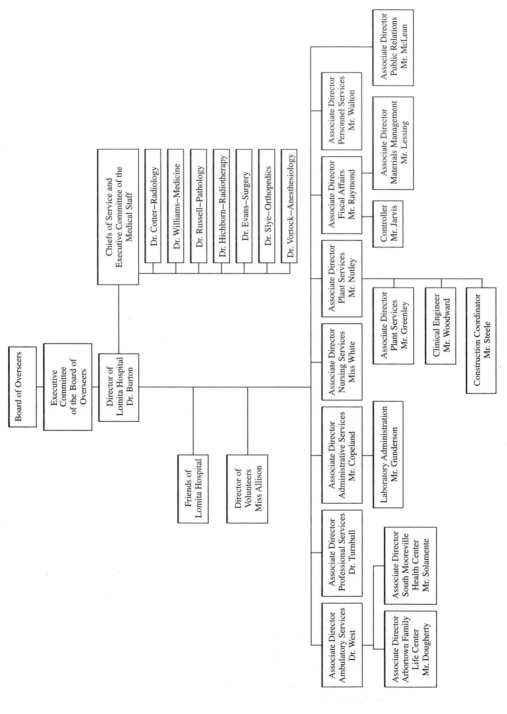

projected number of patient days and the related service units (e.g., number of tests) as determined by the accounting unit, using historical data as well as trend analysis and simulation modeling. These projections were open to revision by the service departments if they were able to show that their numbers were more realistic. Each department chief, his or her administrator, and, if appropriate, the Laboratory Administrator weighed the accounting unit projections against the department's own projections. When the department and the accounting unit agreed upon a projected volume, the accounting unit calculated a projected expense figure. Following this, the department and the Laboratory Administrator could contest the numbers on the basis of previous years' experience. In this respect, both past experience and the distribution of specific procedure projections were relevant since the accounting unit based its projected expense figure on a "weighted average cost" which was not always consistent with the department's evaluation of the distribution of procedures. These projections were extremely important since the department was held responsible for both projected expenses and projected volume.

Dr. Russell indicated that the projected expense figures for FY 1997 were more than simply a matter of estimating volume:

> The problem of cost accounting becomes especially acute when an increase in cost is seen as not merely due to an increase in volume but rather due to differences in efficiencies. The only increase the hospital will accept as a justifiable increase is one in terms of workload. For example, because of the advances in science, it has become easier but more time-consuming to classify lymphomas according to their types. There are many tests that can be performed before the exact classification of the lymphoma is agreed upon. To the administration or to Malcolm Gunderson, a lymph node is a lymph node. We must try to explain the difficulty in classification in terms of the number of slides which are necessary to thoroughly classify it. But when the number of slides hasn't changed, the argument becomes more and more difficult.

Dr. Cornell Johnson, Chief of Surgical Pathology, amplified on this:

> Arguments based on cost can cut both ways. For example, if the pressure to cut costs becomes too strong, one may undersample specimens in order to lower the cost of processing the specimens. This may result in extra hospital days for the patient because of the need to return and take another sample of the specimen, or even because of an error in diagnosis. Although I do not see this as a problem now, I believe one must bear in mind the potential hazards of undersampling as efforts are made to cut costs.

Dr. Russell also realized that any modifications he made to the budget for FY 1997 or any additional staff he wished to hire had to be justified not only to the Fiscal Affairs Department but to Mr. Gunderson as well. Mr. Gunderson reported directly to the Associate Director for Administrative Services of the hospital, and as such was required to approve every change in status and every requisition for each clinical laboratory in the hospital.

According to Mr. Gunderson, the main concern in the budgetary process was to see that each department had the resources necessary to be run efficiently. However, he also felt that he had an obligation to justify any increase in resources. He commented:

I help the labs to obtain budgetary approval for all of their needed personnel, supplies, services, and capital equipment. My job is to make sure that no major need or expense has been omitted from the budget. The budget workpapers are based on seven months actual expense extrapolated to twelve months. It is, therefore, imperative to identify any continuing expense commitments made part way through the fiscal year or to be made subsequent to the preparation of the budget projection. I also work with the departments to identify anticipated new needs for the coming fiscal year and to develop justifications for the requests. For proposed new clinical tests I assist in the development of a need analysis, a revenue and expense projection, and a cost/price analysis.

I try to remain unbiased and truly evaluate the necessity of new projects and equipment requested in the budget. Then I call it as I see it. If the analysis supports the request, I will recommend approval; if not, I will recommend disapproval.

With respect to personnel, the Budget Worksheet provided by the Fiscal Affairs Department is not always complete, due to the time interval between the data processing run and actual budget preparation. Any positions vacant on the date the worksheet is run are automatically deleted and justification for continuing the availability of any such position, along with an indication of the length of time the position has been vacant, must be provided. The rationale for this is that if a department has been able to get along for a number of weeks without a position being filled it may be that the position is not essential.

Another part of my job is to carefully review each department's personnel worksheet to be sure that: (1) all of the hours for which they have received prior authorization, and which are demonstrably necessary, are reentered on the worksheet and the required justification submitted; and (2) that all anticipated position upgradings and new position requests have been included, also along with the required justification. If necessary, I provide them with assistance in developing the justifications.

If, by reviewing the laboratory test volume statistics, annual trends, and technical staff productivity—when possible employing the College of American Pathologists' [CAP] "Laboratory Workload Recording Method"—I conclude that a position should not be filled, I will so advise the laboratory director and the Associate Director for Administrative Services. He will either act on the recommendation or, in some circumstances, review it with the Director of the Hospital. In some instances a recommendation will be made for a complete study by the Management Engineering Department.

I did not approve a request for a new technician in the Pathology Department when it was initially requested in January of 1996. This was between budgetary periods. Our fiscal year runs from October 1 to September 30. Since the position had been vacant for a long time, there was a question as to whether it was necessary. Moreover, an examination of the Fiscal Affairs Department's Expense Distribution Report revealed that the overall test volume in Pathology had declined 6 percent between calendar year 1994 and calendar year 1995. Excluding Cytology, test volume was nearly stable over the two years, having only a 1 percent increase. Useful as these data were as a very broad measure or indicator, I felt that a detailed count of the historical workload taken from the laboratory logs for at least the period covering the preceding two years (perhaps on a sampling basis) was needed to make a valid evaluation. The logs indicate the number of blocks, slides, routine and special stains prepared for each accession number. CAP workload units could then have been applied so as to approximate total workload. I asked Debbie Winston, the Pathology Administrator, to provide this summary, offering to supply clerical assistance if it was necessary.

Debbie did not compile this detailed summary from the logs, which I needed for a workload computation. Instead, she provided summary data, comparing the total number of surgicals and autopsy slides prepared in 1995 with 1985 and providing a calculation of the average number of slides per "surgical" and per autopsy case. Lacking the detailed summary, the position was disapproved again when it was requested in the budget in May.

Later, in the summer of 1996, Pathology again requested approval for this position. Data taken from lab records were submitted indicating that the number of surgicals and autopsies in total had increased about 9 percent over the two-year period despite the fact that accounting data revealed almost no increase. A small part of this increase was represented by autopsies. However, a surgical represents a workload of 5.27 slides while an autopsy represents a workload of 28.6 slides. Therefore, to produce a meaningful basis of comparison, I converted both surgical and autopsies to "slides prepared" and compared the total slides prepared for fiscal 94 with fiscal 95. This showed an increase of only 3 percent, which did not appear to represent a significant increase in workload.

I presented this analysis to Dr. Russell, who then directed his senior staff physician in charge of histology to carry out a tally of the pathology logs, summarizing the total number of slides stained, categorized by the type of stain. This showed an actual annual increase of 10,032 H&E[1] stained slides over the most recent two-year period, while the number of special stains rose by 2,614 slides. Since the CAP workload allocation for these two staining procedures is six and 23 man-minutes per slide, respectively, there apparently had been an increase in histology workload of 120,314 man-minutes which represents an increase in workload in excess of one full-time equivalent. On the basis of this analysis, approval of the position was granted and a budget addendum obtained.

I also try to distinguish the uses for which the money is budgeted. If I determine that the operating budget is being inflated with research-related supplies or services, research employees, or other expenses, I delete them from the lab budget. I look at every increase and expenditure which is above the allowable inflationary increase and make sure there is a justification, in quantitative terms whenever possible, which Fiscal Affairs and the Director will require. If an additional employee is requested in the budget, I will assist the department, to the extent necessary, in preparing a justification which should include an explanation of the medical or other necessity of the work to be performed—including quantification of demand by diagnosis for proposed new tests, a workload analysis, a revenue and expense analysis showing (when possible) that the expense will be recovered through additional revenue generated, and also, for proposed new tests, a cost-price analysis.

---

[1] Hematoxylin and Eosin.

Similar justification is often required for capital requests. However, there may be other justifications for a capital purchase; for example, the age of an instrument, poor instrument repair record and high repair expense, equipment obsolescence, unsafe equipment, improved method, all of which cannot or need not be justified with a revenue and expense analysis. Here documentation of the problem with records and other factual material greatly facilitates obtaining approval. Although quality of care is an important argument in any justification, it must be factually supported. Frequently a cost-benefit analysis is required to properly evaluate such a request. A request based on "quality of care" need without supporting justification will not hold.

Dr. Johnson, who was also an adviser to Dr. Russell on capital budget items for the Pathology Department, indicated that responding to the administration's needs was no simple matter:

> The hospital doesn't increase costs without justification, and the review process is necessary. Administration will always ask the question whether the needed item will reduce costs or increase quality of care. Therefore, a cost-benefit analysis always colors our perception of needs. This analysis takes into consideration the requirements of service, efficiency, and quality of care.

Others in the hospital pointed out the difficulties inherent in the interrelationship among the three activities of patient care, teaching, and research. Frequently, equipment as well as personnel cut across all three areas and the costs incurred for various items could not easily be separated. Most purchasers, which increasingly included managed care companies, had indicated they would not pay Lomita for the research and teaching portions of a particular item, thereby posing a difficult dilemma for a chief attempting to cost-justify a request.

An additional concern of Dr. Russell's was the need to defend his budget not only to the Laboratory Administrator, but to several other levels in the hospital's hierarchy. He commented:

> At each level, attempts will be made to cut the budget. Whether the cut is successful or not depends on the strength of your justification and the availability of funds. The checks and balances within the Lomita system are very good. Everyone operates under the impression that people under them inflate their needs—I know I do. Sometimes needs *are* inflated; sometimes not. The problem is that at times administration can be very capricious about matters.

The Fiscal Affairs Department

The Fiscal Affairs Department of Lomita had the role of coordinating the budget preparation process. Once the data on volume and expenses had been submitted by each department, the Fiscal Affairs Department prepared a pro forma budget. This budget had both revenue and expenses, with revenue determined in accordance with the hospital's payer mix. Mr. Kenneth Javits, the hospital controller, pointed out the value of the pro forma:

This is termed our "Expense Budget before Adjustment." From this, we are able to deduce what the net income will be before the need for an expense reduction. The next problem is where to look when a cut is necessary. We usually do this in terms of measuring increases in productivity. We generally can judge where the budget looks spongy and where it looks quite hard. We look for excessive increases to be tied to the volume of business. We then look at new programs and determine whether a commitment has been made, whether the program appears necessary for the standing of the hospital, or if an impact is questionable in terms of any goal or policy of the hospital. This part of the budget is somewhat subjective and is the initial stage of the budget reduction process.

If Fiscal Affairs determined that the budget contained any "soft areas," it would request the Chief of Service to cut expenses. After as many cuts as possible had been negotiated, the budget was turned over to the hospital's Director, Dr. Henry Burton. According to Mr. Javits, the Fiscal Affairs Department played a coordinating role in this process but did not impose decisions on the various departments:

Fiscal Affairs "proposes" expenses and "requests" cuts. We do not "cut." The Chiefs and Dr. Burton do that. After the budget has been negotiated as far as possible, we provide data and recommendations for the budget *we* propose to Dr. Burton. He must decide which items among the departments should be pushed and which should not. He must make an indirect evaluation of the contribution of each item on the budget to the hospital's final goal. At times, there is need for clinical judgment. In these instances, the Associate Directors, or "Administrative Physicians," as they are termed, will be called in to give judgment of clinical value. Dr. Burton will notify the Chief of Service that he has received specific budget recommendations from the budget unit which are contrary to the Chief's. The Chief is then allowed to decide whether he will push or not push for his decision over that of Fiscal Affairs. Ultimately, Henry Burton is able to negotiate through this process very well. If the Chief of Service does not feel that he is heard, he may request that the Board of Overseers intervene and make a judgment, but normally this does not occur.

The budget, as recommended by the budgeting unit and revised by Dr. Burton, then went to the Budget Finance Committee (a Board of Overseers Committee) which was composed of Dr. Burton, Mr. Colin Raymond (the Associate Director for Fiscal Affairs), and various board members. The chief of each service could address this group also if he specifically felt that his program needs were not being met.

According to one observer:

Uppermost in the minds of both Mr. Raymond and Dr. Burton is the hospital's "Fiscal Status Report," which reflects last year's costs and is the basis for the projection of the expected costs for the following year. This report governs the budget from the beginning to the end, since administration is very concerned with the impact of the budget on the image of Lomita Hospital. Therefore, they are interested in working from the *bottom line* and fitting their costs and income in order to meet *this* objective.

The question now facing Dr. Russell was whether it would be possible for him to build an additional technician into his new budget. He did not feel, however, that this decision could be considered independently of the other decisions confronting him, namely the department's projected volume and expenses, and the volume projections for the cytology section, considering the change in the staffing of the Gynecology group. He knew that whatever changes and projections he made would have to be justified in a highly convincing manner.

Questions

1. Trace through the steps in the budgetary process at Lomita. Who are the key actors in this process and how can/do they influence the final budget?

2. What is your assessment of the way in which the request for an additional technician was handled? How, if at all, would you have changed the role that Mr. Gunderson played?

3. What kinds of responsibility centers have been established at Lomita? How do they influence the budgetary process?

4. What changes, if any, would you make to the budgetary process at Lomita? The responsibility center structure?

Case 10–4

New England Medical Center*

> If our 1989 volume and mix of patients stays the same as 1988, the hospital will face an operating loss of $13 million out of a $200 million budget. Our investments and interest from endowments would cover $2.5 million of this, so we need a plan to come up with the remaining $10.5 million.

The speaker was Peter Van Etten, Executive Vice President and Chief Financial Officer of New England Medical Center (NEMC). Mr. Van Etten was hoping that the new budget process implemented by the hospital would bring about the changes needed to correct the looming deficit. He knew that the hospital could not increase its prices by more than 5 percent, yet expenditures were up 11–12 percent, and nursing expenses alone had increased by 18 percent.

Background

New England Medical Center was a 480-bed Boston-based teaching hospital, affiliated with Tufts University. Located in downtown Boston, near Chinatown and the city's dwindling but infamous "combat zone," the hospital had undergone dramatic changes over the past 10 years. Under the leadership of Jerome Grossman, a specialist in Internal Medicine, the hospital had seen its revenues double since 1980 and had incurred operating surpluses every year from 1981 to 1987. In 1988 it had incurred an operating loss of just over $2.3 million.

Over the past five years, the hospital also had established a reputation as a leading clinical care and research institution, enabling it to join the ranks of Boston's top teaching hospitals. The hospital especially prided itself on innovative approaches to tertiary care, and it ranked 6th in the nation among teaching hospitals receiving funding from the National Institutes of Health. It was one of six sites nationally where experimental Interleukin-2 cancer trials were being conducted.

In addition to its clinical image, NEMC had become particularly well known for its budgeting and control system. The system, unlike those in most hospitals, required physicians—particularly department chairs—to play key roles in planning and controlling the use of clinical resources. The system had been so successful that the hospital had created a for-profit entity, called Transitions Systems, Inc. (TSI), to market and distribute the software to other interested hospitals. TSI was enjoying remarkable growth.

In large part, the hospital's budgeting and control system had been developed in response to the Massachusetts hospital reimbursement environment. This environment had turned progressively more constraining since 1983, when the Commonwealth of Massachusetts, in return for receiving a three-year federal Medicare waiver, had enacted Chapter 372. Chapter 372 was the first in a series of several health care cost containment laws; it included a six-year plan that established a maximum allowable cost (MAC) for hospitals each year. A hospital's MAC was based on the actual costs it experienced in 1982, rolled forward and adjusted for inflation and volume, and allowing for various pass-throughs (costs reimbursed outside the MAC) each year. In 1986 when the Medicare waiver expired, the state amended Chapter 372 with Chapter 574. At this time it also created an "uncompensated care pool" which provided for hospitals to be reimbursed for free care services to patients. In 1988 Chapter 574 was replaced with Chapter 23, which would affect hospitals through 1992.

The key elements of all three laws were the incentives to control costs. There was an increase in costs allowed to compensate for inflation each year, and hospitals were expected to keep their own price increases below this ceiling. Additionally, hospitals were expected to control the use of inpatient ancillaries, reduce average lengths of stay, and increase patient volume, both for inpatient and outpatient services. Increases in volume increased the MAC.

Chapter 23 was the first law to stipulate that allowable revenue increases for in-patient care were to be measured by case–mix–adjusted discharges. Diagnosis Related Groups (DRGs), a patient classification scheme for reimbursement of patients with similar clinical diagnoses and similar patterns of resource use, were part of the reimbursement scheme for the hospitals. Each DRG was reimbursed at a different predetermined amount. A hospital, therefore, could increase its revenue by either (a) increasing its volume, or (b) shifting its case mix toward better-reimbursed DRGs.

Additionally, for outpatient care, a hospital's MAC would be adjusted upward if clinic, emergency room visits, and outpatient surgery cases were increased. Each incremental visit above the 1982 volume would add to the MAC, while each visit below the 1982 volume would decrease the MAC.

Organization

Dr. Grossman had built a team of highly professional physicians, nurses, and administrators to work with him. Since he did not believe in organization charts, none was available for the hospital as a whole. A rough schematic showing key managers, their titles, and their reporting relationships is contained in Exhibit 1, however.

This schematic reflects an important change that had taken place in 1988: the formation of operating division management matrix teams. The leadership of each of the hospital's three main divisions—surgery, medicine, and pediatrics—had been given to a 3-person team, consisting of a physician, a nurse, and an administrator. In medicine and surgery the physicians were the vice-chairs of their departments; in pediatrics the physician was the department chair.

Despite the presence of physician-managers on the teams, each team member had an equal voice in the running of his or her division. The profitability-improvement exercise was to be one of the first tests of each team's ability to collaborate toward the achievement of a common end.

Data

NEMC's budgeting and control system allowed it to model its costs and revenues based on changes in case mix, volume, physician clinical orders, administrative efficiency in delivering physician-ordered services, and changes in wages and prices. The first pass for fiscal year 1989 made changes in wages and prices only, and assumed that everything else would be the same as fiscal 1988. It was this assumption, in conjunction with Chapter 23's limit of 5 percent on price increases, that led to the projected $13 million operating deficit.

EXHIBIT 1
Organizational
Structure

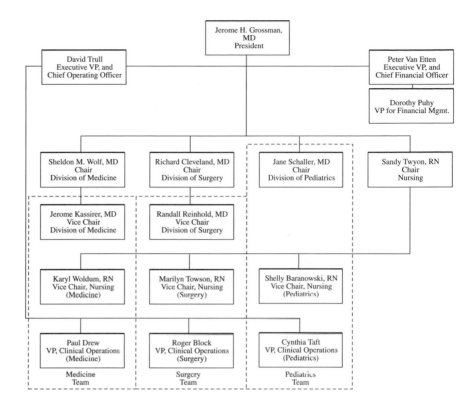

According to Mr. Van Etten, the hospital's plan to come up with the $10.5 million needed after endowment earnings was to earn $4 million in revenue from increased activity and to reduce expenses by $6.5 million, or 5 percent. He commented:

> In order to earn $4 million from increased activity, we needed a 5 percent increase in admissions and a 3 percent improvement through case mix changes. This would increase our revenue by $7 million but would cost an additional $3 million to achieve.
>
> We knew that the $4 million in increased volume and case mix improvements would have to come from the three major operating divisions of the hospital. These three divisions would also need to bear the brunt of at least $3 million of the $6.5 million in cost cuts. So, we decided to hold the new organized operating division management matrix teams responsible for arriving at $7 million of the $10.5 million needed.
>
> The distribution of the $7 million among the three divisions was based in each division's ability to contribute. The Finance Officer worked with the divisions to establish the assignment of each division's share of the $7 million. Once the contribution amount had been agreed upon, the teams were responsible for arriving at the established bottom line. They could reach this contribution target through increases in revenue or decreases in expenses. It was up to them.

The variables they had for revenue were case mix and volume. The variables they had for expenses were direct expenses such as nursing, supplies, and standard costs for other services such as pharmacy and radiology. The standard cost amount had been determined as the direct variable costs of the support service. Overhead (space and support) and indirect expenses (administration and medical records) were to come out of the contribution.

The volume increase needed to come from shorter lengths of stay and more beds. Three or four beds came from the new intensive care unit; others came from consolidating some of the smaller services such as combining the Rehabilitation and Psychiatry Units. Some examination of case mix changes (classification of discharge and diagnosis) also occurred.

The incentives of the teams to arrive at the budget contribution varied. For the administrators and nurses on the team, their year-end bonuses were on the line. The successful development and implementation of the budget was part of their job description. This was not the case for the physicians. They were very carefully selected as team players, but there was no direct, immediate threat to their positions. Also, there was no financial incentive. The physicians were salaried through their own physician corporations. They received an explicit $7 million for administration and training as the hospital's payment to the corporations. There was no agreed upon increase or decrease in this amount based upon the negotiated profit. There was a top down message in terms of growth, however. Jerry Grossman said, "We need a thousand more cases next year. How are you going to do this?"

The Budgeting Process

To begin the budgeting process, the divisions were supplied with "Clinical Financial Planner" reports (Exhibits 2–7) containing information on revenue and expenses by service. These reports calculated revenue and costs of each service, by DRGs, in varying levels of detail. For example, Exhibit 2, Profitability Report, provided revenue information on the various types of pediatric cardiology cases. Exhibit 3, Utilization History—Summary, provided a breakdown of information on resources used to provide care to patients falling under the DRG 241/137 category of pediatric cardiology. Exhibit 4, Activity Modeling Utilization Report, was a detail report that broke down all of the Chemistry Lab work summarized as one line item on Exhibit 3. Looking at data from the Pediatric Department as a whole, Exhibit 5 was another Activity Modeling Utilization Report that provided information on the Pediatric Department's use of the Chemistry Lab. Exhibit 6, Department Cost Comparison Report, provided the Chemistry Lab with a breakdown of its variable and fixed costs. Exhibit 7, Profitability Report at the Corporate Level, provided inpatient information on revenue by department.

Dorothy Puhy, Vice President for Financial Management, explained the concepts underlying the Clinical Financial Planner:

> We have case mix flexible managing systems which are part of the planning package. The administrator of the division meets with the physician and nurse and

EXHIBIT 2   **Clinical Financial Planner Profitability Report (Revised)**

Level 2: Pediatric Cardiology

Inpatient

	Inpatient Cases	Gross Revenue	Deductions	Net Revenue	Variable Direct Cost	Variable Contribution Margin	Fixed Direct Cost	Direct Contribution Margin	Indirect Cost	Net Margin
DRG 108	10	286,019	7,217	278,802	131,454	147,348	40,808	106,540	112,096	−5,556
DRG 125	35	159,178	37,409	121,769	66,926	54,843	29,464	25,379	56,967	−31,588
DRG 241/137	35	128,067	27,910	100,157	37,042	63,115	28,201	34,914	33,611	1,303
Other	107	615,137	121,250	493,887	210,608	283,279	115,051	168,228	142,206	26,022
OUTL540	8	979,744	206,811	772,933	377,221	395,712	127,274	268,438	274,325	−5,887
Pediatric cardiology . .	195	2,168,145	400,597	1,767,548	823,251	944,297	340,798	603,499	619,205	−15,706

EXHIBIT 3 Clinical Cost Manager Utilization History—Summary

Current Period: 1988

Pediatric Cardiology
Case Type: DRG 241/137

Inpatient

Discharges				
			FY89 Budget	
FY86	FY87	FY88 Proj	Orig	Revised
23.00	12.00	32.12	32	35

	Units Per Case					Changes in Unit/Case			Total Var Cost FY88 Proj
				FY89 Budget					
	FY86	FY87	FY88 Proj	Orig	Revised	FY86-87	FY87-88	FY88-89 Bud	
12110—Nursing Floating 7 North	1.61	1.75	2.05			9%	17%		$8,320
12120—Nursing Floating 7 West	0.61	1.58	0.95			159%	−40%		$1,939
12130—Nursing Floating 7 South	0.00	0.17	0.00				−100%		$0
12210—Nursing Pediatric ICU	0.00	0.00	0.10						$1,119
12220—Nursing Neonatal ICU	0.04	0.00	0.19			−100%			$1,628
12230—Nursing Special Care Nur	1.61	0.42	0.86			−74%	105%		$4,107
15110—IV Therapy	1.30	0.98	1.01			−25%	3%		$95
15120—IV Solutions	1.30	0.98	1.01			−25%	3%		$109
19110—CCM Nursing—Volume Onl	3.87	1.08	0.00			−72%	−100%		$0
19120—Length of Stay	3.87	3.08	3.33			−20%	8%		N/A
19130—Actual Nursing Hours—CCM	0.00	20.22	21.25				5%		N/A
30010—Hematology Lab	6.91	7.42	9.90			7%	33%		$937
31110—Chemistry Lab	8.87	7.58	11.38	12.254	10.799	−15%	50%		$962
31130—Microbiology	1.09	1.25	2.05			15%	64%		$503
32120—Immunology	1.83	1.00	0.00			−45%	−100%		$0
32130—Cytology	0.00	0.00	0.05						$31
41120—Ped Diagnostic Radiology	0.52	0.33	0.86			−37%	161%		$429
41160—ER Radiology	0.00	0.08	0.05				−38%		$23
51110—Pharmacy Inpatient Drugs	29.17	23.50	45.19			−19%	92%		$324
51120—Pharmacy Dosage Forms	29.17	23.50	45.19			−19%	92%		$237

EXHIBIT 4   Clinical Financial Planner Activity Modeling Utilization Report—FY 1989 Budget

Level 3: DRG 241/137   Inpatient
    Original Cases: 32
    Revised Cases: 35 (9.4% A)

	A Original Qty per Case	B Original Quantity	C Revised Qty per Case	D Revised Quantity	E % Change Qty per Case	F % Change Quantity
Department/Product						
31110 Chemistry Lab						
Blood Gas Analysis	0.500	16	0.441	15	−11.8	−6.3
Glucose Serum.	0.375	12	0.331	12	−11.7	0.0
Urea Nitrogen Ser	1.813	58	1.598	56	−11.9	−3.4
Creatine Serum	1.000	32	0.882	31	−11.8	−3.1
Digoxin, Serum	0.063	2	0.055	2	−12.7	0.0
Transaminase, Aspart	0.250	8	0.220	8	−12.0	0.0
Transaminase, Alanin	1.313	42	1.157	41	−11.9	−2.4
Phosphatase, Alk, To	0.188	6	0.165	6	−12.2	0.0
Calcium, Total, Seru	0.125	4	0.110	4	−12.0	0.0
Bilirubin, Total, Se	1.250	40	1.102	39	−11.8	−2.5
Albumin, Quantitative . . .	1.188	38	1.047	37	−11.9	−2.6
LDH, Tot	0.063	2	0.055	2	−12.7	0.0
Protein, Tot, Serum	0.875	28	0.771	27	−11.9	−3.6
Protein, Tot, CSF	0.125	4	0.110	4	−12.0	0.0
Glucose, CSF	0.125	4	0.110	4	−12.0	0.0
Sodium, Serum	0.063	2	0.055	2	−12.7	0.0
Hepatitis, BS Antibody . . .	0.625	20	0.551	19	−11.8	−5.0
Hepatitis, BS Antigen	0.625	20	0.551	19	−11.8	−5.0
Electrolytes Prof	1.125	36	0.992	35	−11.8	−2.8
CO_2	0.063	2	0.055	2	−12.7	0.0
Other.	0.500	16	0.441	15	−11.8	−6.3
Department Total.	12.254	392	10.799	380	−11.9	−3.1

completes this budget package. The standard costs for each service can be used as a tool to help managers determine their targets. In the past, product line management had no cost center responsibility. What it actually cost to produce a minute of OR time was someone else's responsibility. This is not true in the new budget system. The Surgery Division, for example, controls operating rooms, anesthesia, and surgical floors, and is responsible for these costs.

Results

One important result of the new budgeting process was that there was an increase in productivity. Mr. Van Etten explained:

> The most exciting productivity savings came in a 5 percent cut in floor nurses. Unionized nursing committed that they would not add nurses to service the 9.6 percent increase in volume. All of this occurred within the context of a 6 percent increase in admissions and a one day decrease in length of stay in Surgery during last year.

EXHIBIT 5 Clinical Financial Planner Activity Modeling Utilization Report

Level 0: Corporate Level   Inpatient
Level 1: Pediatrics
       Original Cases: 2274
       Revised Cases: 2450 (7.7% O)

Department/Product	Original Qty per Case	Original Quantity	Revised Qty per Case	Revised Quantity	% Change Qty per Case	% Change Quantity
31110 Chemistry Lab						
Blood Gas Analysis	6.205	14110	5.836	14299	−5.9	1.3
Glucose Serum.	2.036	4630	2.001	4902	−1.7	5.9
Urea Nitrogen Ser	4.219	9594	4.107	10062	−2.7	4.9
Creatinine Serum	4.024	9150	3.914	9590	−2.7	4.8
Serum Amylase	0.160	364	0.157	384	−1.9	5.5
CK-Muscle/Brain	0.026	58	0.025	62	−3.8	6.9
Thyroid Screen.	0.044	100	0.044	109	0.0	9.0
Theophylline, Serum	0.766	1742	0.755	1850	−1.4	6.2
Digoxin, Serum	0.033	74	0.038	92	15.2	24.3
Transaminase, Aspart	0.853	1940	0.838	2052	−1.8	5.8
Transaminase, Alanin	0.877	1994	0.861	2109	−1.8	5.8
Phosphatase, Alk, To	0.732	1664	0.717	1757	−2.0	5.6
Calcium, Total, Serum . . .	1.680	3820	1.628	3989	−3.1	4.4
Bilirubin, Total, Serum . . .	1.686	3834	1.588	3892	−5.8	1.5
LDH, ISO	0.010	22	0.010	24	0.0	9.1
Albumin, Quantitative . . .	0.743	1690	0.719	1762	−3.2	4.3
LDH, Total	0.493	1120	0.482	1180	−2.2	5.4
Magnesium, Serum	0.624	1420	0.614	1505	−1.6	6.0
Protein, Total, Serum	0.702	1596	0.670	1642	−4.6	2.9
Thyroxin (T-4), Total.	0.022	50	0.024	58	9.1	16.0
Phosphorous Serum	0.649	1476	0.646	1582	−0.5	7.2
Potassium, Serum.	1.010	2296	0.952	2331	−5.7	1.5
Uric Acid, Serum/Other . .	0.218	496	0.218	534	0.0	7.7
Creatine Kinase (CPK) . . .	0.139	316	0.137	334	−1.4	5.7
Protein, Total, CSF	0.236	536	0.233	571	−1.3	6.5
Glucose CSF.	0.237	538	0.234	574	−1.3	6.7
Sodium, Serum	0.112	254	0.109	268	−2.7	5.5
Carbamazepine	0.028	64	0.029	72	3.6	12.5
Cholesterol, Total	0.077	176	0.077	188	0.0	6.8
Carcinoemryonic Antigen.	0.001	2	0.001	2	0.0	0.0
Folates	0.016	36	0.015	38	−6.3	5.6
Hepatitis, BS Antibody . . .	0.053	120	0.052	128	−1.9	6.7
Hepatitis, BS Antigen	0.057	130	0.056	137	−1.8	5.4
Lipid Profile & Screen. . . .	0.009	20	0.008	20	−11.1	0.0
Phenytoin	0.077	174	0.075	185	−2.6	6.3
Protein, Ur/Other	0.044	100	0.042	104	−4.5	4.0
Quinidine, Serum	0.007	16	0.011	26	57.1	62.5

EXHIBIT 6 Clinical Financial Planner Department Cost Comparison Report

Department: 31110 Chemistry Lab

		Original		Revised	Change
Total Units		733,022		809,668	76,646
	$/Unit	*Total $*	*$/Unit*	*Total $*	*$/Unit*
Direct Costs					
Variable					
Labor	$1.46	$1,072,489	$1.49	$1,205,356	$0.03
Supplies	0.69	504,205	0.72	580,361	0.03
Other	0.28	203,160	0.28	223,414	0.00
Total Variable.	$2.43	$1,779,854	$2.49	$2,009,131	$0.06
Fixed					
Labor	$0.25	$ 182,615	$0.23	$ 186,632	($0.02)
Equipment	0.00	0	0.00	0	0.00
Facilities	0.00	0	0.00	0	0.00
Other	0.13	98,150	0.12	98,150	(0.01)
Total Fixed Cost.	$0.38	$ 280,765	$0.35	$ 284,782	($0.03)
Total Direct Cost.	$2.81	$2,060,619	$2.84	$2,293,913	$0.03

Beyond this, each team took a different approach to arriving at its contribution objective. Dr. Randolph Reinhold, Vice Chair of Surgery, explained the process that his team followed:

> We began with an assessment of the operating room. The team thought we could do more services and increase our surgical activity given our FTEs [full-time equivalents]. We looked at our staff individually, discounted other activities such as bench research, and determined a reasonable workload for clinical surgery. Jerry Grossman assigned goals for each individual. We've been working on improving efficiency for some time and we're reaping the rewards. Surgery has had a 4.7 percent average growth rate in cases for three or five years. We've done more same day surgery and had shorter lengths of stay. When we did more outpatient surgery, we had to increase our inpatient admissions referrals. Our length of stay dropped. Acuity of the inpatient population is going up. Our average length of stay [ALOS] in FY 88 dropped one day in Surgery. Our base is already low. In part, this change in Surgery has come from third party payers' pressure with preadmission screenings.

The process in Pediatrics was viewed with a different perspective. Ms. Cynthia Taft, Vice President of Clinical Operations in Pediatrics, described the approach:

> Pediatrics is not a money maker for the hospital. The way the reimbursement system works now is based on DRG case weights, and because pediatric case weights are significantly less than for Surgery or Medicine, we were glad that the

EXHIBIT 7   Clinical Financial Planner Profitability Report (Revised)

Level: Corporate Level

Inpatient

	No. of Cases	Gross Revenue	Deductions	Net Revenue	Variable Direct Cost	Variable Contrib Margin	Fixed Direct Cost	Direct Contrib Margin
Other...................	0	0	0	0	0	0	0	0
Medicine (Adult).......	5,303	48,282,164	12,099,075	36,183,089	17,763,768	18,419,321	7,688,391	10,730,930
Mixed Cardiac..........	477	14,091,721	1,732,311	12,359,410	5,729,267	6,630,143	1,528,682	5,101,461
Surgery...............	7,887	81,670,354	21,759,763	59,910,591	29,447,521	30,463,070	12,079,988	18,383,082
Pediatrics............	2,450	25,736,188	4,994,341	20,741,847	10,539,858	10,201,989	4,543,527	5,658,462
Rehab................	190	3,797,353	333,522	3,463,831	1,536,508	1,927,323	925,649	1,001,674
Psychiatry............	432	6,014,559	606,152	5,408,407	2,649,369	2,759,038	1,787,606	971,432
Neurology............	555	5,514,161	1,372,450	4,141,711	1,934,439	2,207,272	1,197,634	1,009,638
Other (Der, Therapeu)...	16	78,481	6,909	71,572	24,024	47,548	16,959	30,589
Emergency Rm Visits....	0	0	0	0	0	0	0	0
Day Surgery—Amb......	0	0	0	0	0	0	0	0
Day Surgery—1B.......	0	0	0	0	0	0	0	0
Non-Visit Ambulatory...	0	0	0	0	0	0	0	0
999..................	0	0	0	0	0	0	0	0
Corporate Level........	17,310	185,184,981	42,904,523	142,280,458	69,624,754	72,655,704	29,768,436	42,887,268

hospital administration chose not to allocate our share of the contribution strictly on a case weight basis. So Pediatrics came out lower in required budgeted contribution.

Ms. Shelley Baranowski, Vice Chair for Nursing in Pediatrics, provided an assessment of the approach from her perspective:

We have managed to decrease our ALOS in some areas yet maintain the nursing staff level. We want to provide services as quickly, safely, and efficiently as possible. Nurse managers meet with chiefs and say, "If we add these patients, what can we do?" We have been increasing admissions cautiously and reducing length of stay. We have a higher acuity and therefore higher nursing care requirements. If we improved other programs, it was through nursing only being involved in nursing care, not doing secretarial, clerical, or transport work. We worked with other departments such as Radiology and Pharmacy and said we can't do your work. We can't accompany a patient to Radiology in the middle of the night. We eliminated some of the nonnursing functions so we could do more with less staff while we also increased nursing salaries 18 percent.

In the Division of Medicine, there were some different issues. Dr. Jerome Kassirer, the Vice Chair of Medicine, commented:

When we thought about what we could do, we weren't eager to cut expenses. We decided to grow. NEMC is a referral hospital. We depend on docs in the community. If their referrals increase, then our business increases. There is no magic spigot. We can encourage physicians to refer by being as good as possible. We've reconstituted some of our medical services. We've added staff and changed the leadership, especially in Cardiology. We've also changed patient care.

We now have a more aggressive referring MD group. We do have control over our lengths of stay. Our ALOS has decreased three days in three years. Two years ago, our ALOS was 10.5 days and now it's 8.5 days. Our business has increased and so we needed to free up beds. We had a wealth of information from historical data about the major types of cases seen. We worked with nurses. We looked at the length of stay and we coordinated services. We decreased the length of stay and decreased costs.

Ms. Karyl Woldum, the Vice Chair for Nursing in the Medicine Division, continued:

To help us reach our targeted increase in productivity, we changed the focus of our medical management teams. Three years ago the goals were more concrete, like getting a conference room, or moving a medication room. We reoriented the goals to look at case types. The nurses became interested in coding and length of stay. We meet with the teams on each unit quarterly. They present management reports at each meeting. With the present regulations, it is easy to feel "done to," so the more information you have, the less knee jerking response you have. We have more control in our day-to-day lives, a more quantifiable way of what we do. We can put our hands around our work. The MIS is providing us with clinical outcome data and it's satisfying to see that we're not just putting patients through faster. The ICU [intensive care unit] days have decreased and we're more efficiently managing these services.

We did a study of inpatient services under a grant from the Hartford Fund which will be published by the *Journal of Medical Care* which explores delay days. We identified why patients stay in the hospital unnecessarily. The number of delay days has fallen due to the budget crunch. We do a lot to avoid delay days. We are getting a lot of information on LOS, costs, and case mix.

Current Issues

Although the budget-cutting process had led to the required reductions, there were several issues about the new structure and process that concerned Mr. Van Etten. First, he was worried about physician incentives. Since only the physician manager of each service had participated in making the budget reductions, Mr. Van Etten wondered about the extent to which the other physicians in each division really were committed to the agreed-upon changes. Since their personal financial incentives were unrelated to the hospital's financial condition, he wondered what motivation they would have to actually attempt to reach the budget targets. Moreover, he wondered if anything could be done to give them a greater financial stake in the hospital's bottom line.

Second, he was concerned about the incentives of the ancillary departments, such as the laboratory, to participate in the process. The budget had been built around standard costs in each ancillary department, and these standards accounted for a sizable portion of the needed cuts. Was this reasonable? How, if at all, could the standards be enforced?

Finally, he was concerned about holding the divisions responsible for both revenue and expenses. Was this reasonable? Did it produce the right incentives? From the divisions' perspective, the new system was preferred over the prior one that had held them responsible only for expenses. This was because the teams felt they were able to exercise more control over how the contribution objective was to be met. Ms. Taft commented:

> The new budgeting and accountability system was preferred because the teams were able to exercise more control over how the contribution objective was to be met. We like the decentralized approach. It lets people closest to areas of concern come up with ways to meet these targets. It's a much better way to do it. We have worked with the nurse managers and introduced financial management courses. People have received reports. They are held accountable and must look at their budgets, both projections and actuals. We have more expense control, analysis of expenses, patient/staff ratios, overtime, and average length of stay by case type, specialty groups and group activities.

Dr. Kassirer added his support:

> By participating in this process, we were able to control our services. Certain programs residing in the Department of Medicine are money losers like bone marrow transplant, and kidney and liver transplants, which we could bag but we won't because we think they are important. It is crucial to have a full-service bank for the referral of patients. If we don't, the referring MD might not send us the next

patient. Also, it is important to be on the cutting edge, the forefront of medicine. We do hope that we can continue these services by effectively managing our other services and meeting the financial demands of the hospital.

Thus, as he contemplated the financial future of the hospital, Mr. Van Etten realized that, in addition to worrying about the $10.5 million in cuts for FY 1989, and whether the divisions could actually meet their budgeted reductions, he needed to be concerned about the new system that had been developed and the incentives it created. It was easy to cut a budget—anyone could do that. But it was far more difficult to actually *achieve* the budgeted targets. Doing so would require that managers, nurses, and physicians alike would have not only the ability but the motivation to do so.

Questions

1. How does the Department of Pediatrics at NEMC build its budget? Please be specific, using the appropriate exhibits as references.

2. How does the Chemistry Lab build its budget? How does its budget relate to the budgets prepared by the divisions?

3. What kinds of responsibility centers are the divisions? The support departments? What other options are possible?

4. What options are available to a responsibility center in NEMC to reach its contribution objectives? How do these options differ between a clinical department (such as Pediatrics) and a support department (such as the Chemistry Lab)? How does the choice of responsibility centers affect these choices?

5. What changes are possible to deal with the concerns Mr. Van Etten has expressed about the new system? What changes should he make?

Chapter

11

Control of Operations

The third phase in the management control cycle is that of operations and measurement. Although described as a single phase, it actually consists of two separate but related activities: control of operations and measurement of inputs and outputs. Chapters 3, 4, 5, and 6 discussed the measurement of inputs. This chapter describes tools and techniques that are useful in the control of operations. Chapter 12 looks at the measurement of outputs.

Control of operations encompasses two quite distinct activities: financial control and performance control. The former, as the name implies, is related to spending activities. Financial control systems are designed to assure that proper steps are taken, and appropriate records are maintained, to preserve the financial integrity of the organization's activities.

Performance control focuses on the activities of line managers, professional staff, technical support staff, clerical employees, and other members of the organization. Its goal is to assure that performance is in accordance with the organization's objectives. It concentrates on matters of productivity, and on managers' motivations to operate their programs and projects effectively and efficiently.

Since many of their programs are not subject to market forces, nonprofit organizations must be especially concerned with performance control activities. Performance control can help to assure clients and other constituents that the organization's resources are being used as efficiently as possible in carrying out ongoing operations.

The first half of this chapter is devoted to financial control, where we focus on matters such as accounting systems and auditing. In the second half we discuss performance control, including both technical and behavioral matters.

Financial Control in General

The approved operating budget, consisting of both planned expenses and expected outputs, is the principal financial guideline for operations. Presumably, management wants the organization to operate in a way that is consistent with this plan unless there is good reason to depart from it. This qualification is important, for it means that the control process is more complicated than simply insisting that the organization do what the budget prescribes. One of the principal purposes of management control is to assure that objectives are accomplished as efficiently as possible. If changed conditions suggest that a different course of action than that specified in the budget will do a better job of attaining the objectives, that course of action should be followed. Thus, the financial control activity should have two aspects: (1) to assure that, in the absence of reasons to do otherwise, the plan set forth in the budget is adhered to, and (2) to provide a way to change the plan if conditions warrant.

Types of Financial Control

The total amount in the approved budget ordinarily is a ceiling that should not be exceeded. Indeed, as discussed below, if funds are received from a legislative appropriation, it is a ceiling that legally *cannot* be exceeded. Within this ceiling, there are more detailed controls. These usually take the form of ceilings for specific activities or programs, but in some cases they may be floors.

Example

In a social work agency, each program manager has a budget ceiling. However, senior management also requires that a minimum amount of resources (a floor) be spent on each family.

Although the budget may contain a detailed listing of amounts for expense elements (e.g., wages, supplies, travel, utilities), these amounts are normally guides rather than ceilings. The primary focus should be on programs and responsibility centers, not on expense elements. Some years ago, financial control focused on individual line items of expense. Although some nonprofit organizations persist in using line-item controls, most have shifted their focus to programs and responsibility centers.

Need for Some Line-Item Restrictions

Despite the shift to a focus on programs and responsibility centers, most organizations also require line managers to obtain approval for shifts among line items above a certain amount or percentage. Although this policy may seem inconsistent with shift to program control, there are several reasons that justify its existence.

Lack of Experience   Many line managers are professionals (such as artists, teachers, or social workers), and have not had much experience with budgets. Overspending one line item by a large amount early in the fiscal year (such as for travel to professional meetings) may use up funds that are needed later in the year for ongoing program operations.

In a college of arts, one department head gave out considerably more financial aid early in the fiscal year than he had in his budget. Later in the fiscal year, he informed management that there were no funds left in his budget to pay for models for art classes. Since models were essential for art classes, the department head was allowed to overrun his budget. The next year the CEO told the department head that all his budget expenditures needed to be approved in advance by the college's CFO.

Potential Changes in Objectives   When the budget was agreed upon, it represented a commitment between the line manager and senior management that it was the most appropriate way to use the organization's resources to accomplish certain objectives. A large change in the use of resources suggests a change in the activities of a program or responsibility center and, hence, may inhibit the attainment of certain objectives. Senior management needs to be a party to this sort of decision.

Long-Run Implications   Some expenses represent long-term commitments. If personnel are added to the organization, for example, the corresponding increase in costs tends to be relatively permanent. This is especially true if the newly hired person occupies a union or civil service position, or otherwise assumes a position with some sort of tenure commitment. Therefore, the number of personnel (i.e., a "head count"), frequently constitutes a ceiling that cannot be exceeded without senior-management approval.

Potential for Duplication   Since line managers do not have a complete view of the organization, senior management needs a way to avoid duplication in the use of resources. This was an important aspect of the budget preparation process. If line managers are permitted to make large changes in their operating budgets without the review and approval of senior management, they may be undertaking activities that overlap or conflict with activities of other programs or responsibility centers.

For these reasons, most organizations require program and responsibility center managers to obtain approval from higher levels of authority for major deviations from their budgets. Depending on the size of the organization and the dollar amounts involved, this approval may be required from several higher levels of authority. Despite this approval process, line managers usually have sufficient flexibility to carry out their programs as planned if two conditions are in place: (1) they are allowed to make minor shifts among line items in their budgets without higher level approval, and (2) there is an efficient and noncapricious approval process in place that will allow them to make larger shifts if necessary to attain programmatic objectives more efficiently.

Flow of Spending Authority

The flow of spending authority within an organization generally should follow the lines of operating management responsibility; that is, spending should be authorized from higher levels to lower levels according to the formal organizational hierarchy. Difficulties arise when funds are received directly by organizational units, rather than through the organizational hierarchy. If it does not control the distribution of spending authority, senior management often cannot exercise appropriate control over subordinate elements because it does not have "the power of the purse."

Example

In one city, mental health services were provided to the public on a contractual basis by private institutions. These institutions were supposed to be accountable to the city's Department of Mental Health; however, operating funds for these institutions were provided directly by the state, and the institutions therefore tended to disregard the city agency.

There are two types of difficulties that senior management encounters in attempting to control the flow of spending authority: compartmentalized funds and funds from several sources. Each constrains senior management's ability to exercise spending authority.

Compartmentalized Funds

If a legislature or other source of funds specifies in great detail the way the funds can be spent, managers can be inhibited from making sound decisions on the best use of operating resources. This is because some activities may turn out to be overfunded while others are underfunded. Without the ability to shift funds from one "compartment" to another, senior management's ability to coordinate the various activities of the organization is impeded.

Example

In the Navy, ships have been known to steam on unneeded missions, even though they lacked vital parts for radar, because they had ample funds for fuel, but no funds for radar parts. The overall effectiveness of the ship would have been enhanced if some of the money budgeted for steaming had been shifted to radar repair, but there was no mechanism that permitted the easy shifting of funds among line items.

Funds from Several Sources

If program managers have funding from several sources, they frequently play off one funding source against another. Thus, while senior management may desire that the overall level of spending be reduced, a program manager can sometimes defeat this desire by finding one source, among the several available, to provide the additional funds.

Example

The manager of a program in a university wanted to purchase an expensive computer with funds from her operating budget, but was denied permission by the dean, who was attempting to control overall spending. The manager then used grant funds to purchase the computer, and operating funds to pay for a research assistant who otherwise would have been paid with funds from the grant.

The University of Minnesota spent $1.7 million for the renovation of the campus office and official residence of the president. The money came from a $55 million reserve fund of "unrestricted private donations, interest on university investments, and surpluses from the campus food and housing services and bookstores." Neither the Board of Regents nor legislators were fully aware of the existence of this fund. Further, although the Board of Regents was required to approve all capital expenditures in excess of $100,000, this project was carried out "through a series of smaller projects costing less than $100,000 each."[1]

Dan Wiant, former chief administrative officer for the Ohio chapter of the American Cancer Society, reportedly faxed a letter to the Society's bank stating that he wanted to transfer $6.9 million to a law firm in Austria to be disbursed for research purposes. The money was among funds raised by volunteers to support cancer research, education, and prevention programs.

Wiant was arrested after returning to the United States from Zurich and accused of bank fraud. Of concern to at least some observers was the ease with which he allegedly moved almost half of the chapter's $15 million budget out of the country.[2]

In addition, if funds are received from several sources, performance measurement may be difficult. This is because each funding source tends to focus on a different aspect of operations, rather than evaluating the organization's activities as a whole.

Budget Adjustments

In many nonprofit organizations, the total annual budget constitutes an absolute ceiling that cannot be exceeded except under highly unusual circumstances. Nevertheless, changed circumstances may call for modifications in detailed spending requirements. This raises the problem of accommodating these modifications within the prescribed ceiling. There are two general techniques for solving this problem: contingency allowances and revisions. The choice between the two is largely a matter of management preference.

Contingency Allowances

In this approach, amounts are set aside at various levels in the organization for unforeseen circumstances. Thus, the budgeted expenses for each responsibility

---

[1] *Chronicle of Higher Education,* March 21, 1988, p. 1.
[2] Anonymous, "American Cancer Society Executive Accused of Embezzling," *Fund Raising Management,* August 2000, p. 8.

center and program are targets that can be exceeded, if necessary, with the excess being absorbed by the contingency allowance. Ordinarily, a contingency allowance is not more than 5 percent of the budget for each organizational level.

An advantage of contingency allowances is that increases in spending can be accommodated without the sometimes painful task of finding an offsetting decrease. A risk is that if there is a 5 percent contingency allowance, there may be a tendency to regard the actual ceiling as 105 percent of the target in all responsibility centers. This defeats the purpose of the contingency allowances.

A variation of the contingency allowance is the practice of releasing somewhat less than the proportionate amount of funds in the early part of the year. For example, in an agency whose spending is expected to be spread evenly throughout the year, only 22 percent of the funds, rather than 25 percent, might be released in the first quarter. As the year progresses and spending needs become clearer, subsequent releases of the contingency allowance are allocated to those responsibility centers that need them the most.

Revisions

In this approach, 100 percent of the authorized amount is divided among responsibility centers. Changed circumstances are accommodated by increasing the budget of one responsibility center and making a corresponding reduction in the budget of one or more other responsibility centers. Under this plan the budget for each responsibility center cannot be exceeded without specific approval. Moreover, some responsibility centers will be asked to spend less than their budget to accommodate the needs of other responsibility centers.

When the revision approach is used, operating managers frequently will create an informal contingency allowance to avoid having to seek formal approval for changed spending needs. Thus, allowances exist in both approaches, even though they are not visible in the second type.

Whichever approach is used, senior management should recognize the likelihood that changes will be necessary. It therefore should be certain that the mechanism for making these changes is well understood. Otherwise, the budget may not conform to the demands managers face, and thus will not serve as a reliable instrument for measuring their performance.

Example

Some states have three budgets: the originally approved one, a supplemental budget, and a deficiency budget. The supplemental and deficiency budgets are submitted to the legislature by the governor during the course of the fiscal year. The supplemental budget is a request for a budget increase. The deficiency budget, by contrast, is submitted after the state incurs obligations that exceed the funds provided in either the original or the supplemental budget. This process calls the legislature's attention to the situation, and permits it to: (a) approve the proposal as warranted, (b) disapprove it, or (c) approve it but criticize the governor's performance.

Financial Control via the Accounting System

The central device for reporting internal operating information is the accounting system. It is central because accounting deals with monetary amounts, and money provides the best way to aggregate and summarize information about a wide variety of inputs, including labor, supplies, and purchased services.

General Characteristics

In Chapter 3 we described the nature of accounting systems in nonprofit organizations. Several important aspects of these systems are relevant for financial control purposes: donor restrictions, double entry, consistency with the budget, and the need for integrated systems.

Donor Restrictions

The accounting system must assure that restrictions placed on contributions are observed. If a donor specifies that a scholarship may be used only for residents of a particular state or community, for example, this restriction must be honored. Many organizations set up a separate account for each type of restriction as a device for exercising this control, even though there is no need to report the details of the restrictions in the financial statements. The result often is considerably more detail in the accounting system than one typically would find in a for-profit setting.[3] The principal purpose of this detail is to assure donors that their funds were used only for the specified purposes. Since the auditor can provide this assurance (or identify the rare instance where restrictions were not observed), there is no need to report the detail.

Consistency with the Budget

The accounting system should be consistent with the budget. The budget states the approved plan for spending, and the accounting system reports actual spending. Unless the two are consistent, there is no reliable way of determining if actual spending occurred according to plan. This does not mean that the accounting system should contain only the accounts that appear in the budget, however. Management usually needs more accounting detail than is suggested by the budget items, and it needs rearrangements of the basic data for various purposes. Nevertheless, as a minimum, the accounting system should contain accounts that match each item on the budget.[4]

---

[3]Some colleges and universities, where the number of separate funds typically is quite large, will not accept restricted contributions unless they exceed a given amount. They reason that the extra cost of controlling for the restrictions is only warranted for large contributions.

[4]If accounts do not match the budget, it generally is possible to develop a mechanism for reconciling the two. This mechanism, called a *crosswalk,* is a rearrangement of the accounts to match the budget categories. A crosswalk is not as reliable as recording amounts in the proper accounts in the first place.

Need for Integrated Systems

Not only should budget and accounting data be consistent with one another, but the accounting system should be an integral part of a total information system for reporting on both inputs and outputs. In the federal government, for example, *Circular No. A-123* from the Office of Management and Budget (OMB) defines management accountability as "the expectation that managers are responsible for the quality and timeliness of program performance, increasing productivity, controlling costs and mitigating adverse aspects of agency operations, and assuring that programs are managed with integrity and in compliance with applicable law."[5] Clearly, an integrated system is needed to report on both the inputs and outputs.

Encumbrance Accounting

An *encumbrance* occurs when an organization becomes obligated to pay for goods or services. This happens when a contract is entered into or when personnel work. (At the time they work, they become entitled to salaries and related benefits.) An appropriation by a state or local government usually is an authority to encumber (a federal appropriation is an authority to *obligate*, which means the same thing).

In federal government organizations, amounts appropriated in accordance with the budget cannot legally be exceeded, and violators are subject to criminal penalties under the federal Anti-Deficiency Act (R.S. Sec. 3679). Most states have similar legislation.[6]

Appropriations for operating purposes usually cannot be encumbered after the end of the fiscal year; that is, they lapse. There is therefore a natural tendency to fully encumber all appropriated funds. Thus, while an encumbrance accounting system is designed to avoid spending more than the amount appropriated, it also discourages spending less than the amount appropriated. The accounting process for encumbrances is described in the Appendix at the end of this chapter.

Financial Control via Auditing

No matter how well an accounting system has been designed, there is always the possibility of error or fraud. To detect such irregularities, many nonprofit organizations have an internal audit function called *compliance auditing*. In addition, most nonprofits have their financial statements and financial control

[5]Alice M. Rivlin, "Management Accountability and Control," OMP *Circular No. A-123,* Revised June 21, 1995.

[6]As a practical matter, punishment under these acts is rare. In the Department of Defense there are only a few dozen violations per year, most of them for trivial amounts. Some years ago, because of a breakdown in its control system , the Army spent $225 million more than was appropriated, but no one went to jail, much less paid back the $225 million. Nevertheless, the possibility of legal action is a deterrent.

systems audited by an external body, usually an independent public accountant. This latter function is called an *external audit.*

Compliance Auditing

A well-designed management control system contains its own financial controls. When there is an internal audit staff, its responsibility is to ensure that these controls are effective. Internal financial controls have three general purposes: (1) to minimize the possibility of financial loss by theft, fraud, or embezzlement; (2) to ensure adherence to senior management's rules governing the receipt and spending of money, and the use of other resources; and (3) to ensure that information flowing through the system is accurate.

Some organizations, including many state and municipal governments, do not have even minimal controls. This problem is revealed by frequent newspaper exposés of contracts let in an unauthorized manner, persons on the public payroll who do not actually work, or welfare payments made to persons not entitled to receive them.

Example

For 11 years, John T. Glennon was purchasing agent at the University of California, San Francisco. He was considered to be an "extremely valuable employee" until three months after he left the university, when it was discovered that during the preceding four years he had embezzled $310,000 by billing fake purchases to a dummy corporation. He was in complete charge of placing orders, receiving the goods, and paying for them.[7]

Internal controls are never perfect. Their limitations are well described in the AICPA's *Statement of Auditing Standards No. 30,* a document that describes the objectives and difficulties of compliance auditing.

> The objective of internal accounting control is to provide reasonable, but not absolute, assurance as to the safeguarding of assets against loss from unauthorized use or disposition, and the reliability of financial records for preparing financial statements and maintaining accountability for assets. The concept of reasonable assurance recognizes that the cost of a system of internal control should not exceed the benefits derived and also recognizes that the evaluation of these factors necessarily requires estimates and judgments by management.
>
> There are inherent limitations that should be recognized in considering the potential effectiveness of any system of internal control. In the performance of most control procedures, errors can result from misunderstanding of instructions, mistakes of judgment, carelessness, or other personal factors. Control procedures whose effectiveness depends upon segregation of duties can be circumvented by collusion. Similarly, control procedures can be circumvented intentionally or with respect to the estimates and judgments required in the preparation of financial statements. Further, projection of any evaluation of internal control to future periods is subject to the risk that the procedures may become inadequate because

---

[7]*Chronicle of Higher Education,* April 10, 1991.

of changes in conditions, and that the degree of compliance with the procedures may deteriorate.[8]

Resources devoted to internal auditing in government agencies have increased greatly in recent years. In most agencies, this additional effort has resulted in the detection of fraud and waste many times larger that the additional cost, but there is still a long way to go.

Example

In one study of 77,000 cases, only 2.5 percent of fraud exposed was uncovered through audit effort. Much of the rest was uncovered by chance or by scheduled compliance and eligibility reviews by program units. Additionally, reports by alleged victims and gratuitous reports by private individuals helped uncover some of the fraud.[9]

Since both chance discoveries and discoveries associated with scheduled reviews revealed deficiencies in the internal control systems in use, one conclusion is that more attention needs to be devoted to designing good control systems.

Example

In April 1997 federal prosecutors charged New York University Medical Center with overcharging the Federal Government for research costs, and announced that they had reached a $15.5 million settlement, by far the largest amount ever in any case involving research overhead at a university. While denying it did anything wrong, the university acknowledged that it had made some "administrative and accounting mistakes with respect to certain cost items from 1982 to 1993." It insisted that none of the errors was intentional.[10]

Incorrect Charges

One possible reason for the relative ineffectiveness of internal auditing is its focus. Many nonprofit organizations spend considerable effort assuring that certain rules are obeyed precisely (for instance, checking every travel voucher to ensure that per diem calculations are accurate and that mileage between points is stated correctly). They also have voucher systems, locked petty cash boxes, and other devices that inhibit obvious possibilities for theft or losses by individuals. By contrast, the same organizations may pay little attention to procedures for assuring that expenditures are charged to the proper accounts; that is, to projects or other items that correspond to those for which the costs

---

[8]American Institute of Certified Public Accountants, *Statement of Auditing Standards (SAS) No. 30*. Subsequent *SASs* have expanded upon this basic definition. See, for example, *SAS* numbers 53, 54, and 55. See also Mary Lou Epperly, "Audits of Academic Programs," *Internal Auditing* 5, no. 4 (Spring 1990); and Robert Forrester, "Are Your Not-for-Profit Clients Ready for Compliance Auditing?" *Journal of Accountancy* 170, no. 1 (July 1990).
[9]Mortimer A. Dittenhofer, "Internal Control and Auditing for Fraud," *The Government Accounts' Journal,* Winter 1983–84.
[10]Elisabeth Rusenthal, "N.Y.U. Hospital Settles Case on Research Billing Charges," *New York Times,* April 8, 1997.

actually were incurred. If the amounts charged to accounts are used as a basis for reimbursement by a client, as is often the case, deliberate mischarging amounts to stealing. The situation is even more flagrant when the persons responsible sign their names to a certificate that states that costs are recorded correctly, knowing full well that they are not.

In addition to the illegality of this practice, one obvious consequence is that recorded data are inaccurate. Reports prepared from such data give management an incorrect impression about current performance, and a misleading basis for future plans. In general, internal auditors do not pay enough attention to the prevention and detection of incorrect charges.[11]

Example

Some years ago, auditors at one university found that 7 percent of faculty members charged more of their time to research projects than they actually spent. Over a 2½-year period, this amounted to $100,000 of excess charges. Recent disclosures are much larger.

An interesting ethical question arises when the rules under which an agency is forced to operate are such that efficient operations are inhibited. Should managers get the job done and cover up the fact that, to do so, they had to break rules, or should they use the existence of the rules as an excuse for not getting the job done? Managers with different temperaments answer this question in different ways.

Example

A certain state legislature set maximum payment rates for part-time psychiatrists employed by the state mental health institutions. These rates were about half the going rate for psychiatrists. At these rates, few psychiatrists would work for the state. Consequently, administrators hired psychiatrists for half a day and paid them for a full day. They said that this was the only way they could hire a sufficient number of psychiatrists. On balance, was this wrong? Whether or not it was wrong, the records showed that twice as many psychiatrist work-hours were provided as actually was the case.

External Auditing

In many states, the Office of the Attorney General requires most tax-exempt organizations to submit financial statements annually. For large organizations, they require that these statements be audited. Moreover, any state or local government unit receiving more than $25,000 annually in federal assistance is subject to audit at least once every two years, and organizations that receive grants from government agencies are also subject to audit.[12] Although gov-

---

[11]For additional discussion of this point in a hospital context, see Gouranaga Ganguli and Sue Winfrey, "Auditing Medical Records Helps Reduce Liability," *Healthcare Financial Management* 44, no. 10 (October 1990). For discussion in a religious context, see L. Murphy Smith and Jeffrey R. Miller, "An Audit of a Church," *Internal Auditing* 5, no. 1.

[12]Because the requirements for conducting a government audit generally are somewhat different from those for a nongovernment audit, special training is needed. See American Institute of Certified Public Accountants, *Report of the Task Force of the Quality of Audits of Governmental Units,* March 1987.

ernment auditors conduct many of these audits, outside independent public accountants increasingly are engaged to perform them.[13]

Even where audits are not required by law or by grantors, there is a general recognition that, for purposes of reliability and continuity, such reports should be prepared by an outside auditor. These audits determine whether: (*a*) financial operations were conducted properly, (*b*) the financial reports of an audited entity were presented fairly, and (*c*) the entity complied with applicable laws and regulations.[14] When defects in an organization's financial control system prevent the auditors from undertaking a thorough analysis of compliance, the organization may have to spend a considerable sum upgrading its system.

Example

According to one study, auditors of the Department of Health and Human Services found it impossible to resolve salary and related charges claimed by large universities under research contracts when the universities did not maintain or properly supervise the after-the-fact (i.e., after the budget) time and effort reports required by governmentwide standards. Ultimately, the auditors identified a need for universities to upgrade their payroll distribution and support systems.[15] For many universities this was an expensive endeavor.

Performance Control

Apart from establishing financial control systems to assure that funds are spent as intended, nonprofit managers also must be concerned about assuring the effective and efficient performance of their organizations. Chapters 12, 13, and 14 discuss the process of measuring and reporting performance. In the remainder of this chapter we address several issues related to managers' need to exert control over the *day-to-day operations* of their organizations.

Relationship to Task Control

In many respects, performance control is concerned with the processes that we defined in Chapter 1 as task control: the rules, procedures, forms, and other devices that govern the performance of specific tasks to assure that they are carried out effectively and efficiently. For example, professionals in a research organization must report the time they spend on various projects; payroll checks must be issued in a timely way; inventories must be replenished before

---

[13]For details on the various audit requirements, see Office of Management and Budget, *Circular A-102* (for state and local governments), OMP *Circular A-110* (for other nonprofit organizations), and U.S. Office of Revenue Sharing, *Audit Guide and Standards for Revenue Sharing and Antirecession Fiscal Assistance Receipts.*

[14]Comptroller General of the United States, *Standards for Audit of Governmental Organizations, Programs, Activities, and Functions* (Washington, DC: Government Printing Office), p. 2.

[15]Edward W. Stepnick, "Accountability for Government-Sponsored University Research: A Lesson from the Behavioral Sciences," *The Government Accountants' Journal,* Winter 1985–86.

they are depleted, but must not be maintained at excessively high levels; and accounts receivable must be monitored and steps taken to collect delinquent accounts. The larger and more complex the organization, the larger the number of these rules. Also, a mature organization tends to have more formal rules and procedures than a young organization.

Although most managers dislike rules, they also recognize that many rules are necessary to assure that members of the organization handle similar situations in a similar manner. Some rules, however, may have been devised to deal with situations that no longer exist, or they may unduly restrict the ability of managers to use good judgment. Because of this, an organization needs to review its rules from time to time, and eliminate those that no longer serve a useful purpose.

Example

In the Department of Labor, a committee of OSHA employees and managers reviewed the agency's 400-page field operations manual. The new manual was fewer than 100 pages long, and, according to one manager "should help people spend less time on documentation and more time doing what they were hired to do."[16]

Without revisions of this sort from time to time, frustrations such as those implicit in the following apocryphal description of procurement procedures may impede the smooth functioning of the organization:

> . . . If you want to buy a short length of coaxial cable, please fill out a requisition sheet, university budget form 16-j. (Use the orange form if the money is to come from operating funds, and blue if the money is to come from capital funds.) Never indent on any line more than five spaces or the form will be returned. Submit in triplicate to the Office of Budget Approval, Administration Building, Room 1619, attention Mrs. Bagley. After Mrs. Bagley initials the form signifying that you have the $38 in your budget, the form is sent to the Technical Buyer, located in Room 1823. There Mr. Ted Rosler puts out a request for bids. If there is only one coaxial cable distributor in the region, it presents difficulties, but they can be surmounted with a special Sole Source form, which should be approved by the Comptroller's Council of Purchases and Services. The Council meets bimonthly. To get on their agenda, you must submit, in duplicate. . . .[17]

In many organizations, the use of information technology and the development of intranets can help to keep information updated on something close to a real-time basis.

Example

The internal Red Cross intranet, *ARC Online,* connects each of the 1,500 Red Cross offices across the United States so that information and updates can be passed along quickly and effectively.[18]

---

[16]Bruce G. Posner, "Sowing the Seeds of Change at the Department of Labor," *Harvard Business Review,* May–June 1994.
[17]By Frederick Brientenfeld, Jr., executive director, the Maryland Center for Public Broadcasting (personal correspondence).
[18]Steward Deck, "Net Aids Red Cross," *Computerworld* 30, no. 37 (1996).

While this approach does not prevent excessive information, it can help to avoid the existence of *outdated* information, and thus represents a step in the right direction.

Relationship to Productivity

Many nonprofit organizations have instituted measures designed to improve employee productivity.[19] These include attempts to classify costs into controllable and noncontrollable categories so managers can focus on costs that might be reduced without affecting the organization's programmatic outcomes. They also include investment in equipment that will reduce operating expenditures, principally labor.

In some instances these measures call for consolidation of activities across two or more organizational units. In others, they attempt to assure that the time of professionals is being used as much as possible in the activities for which they were hired.

Example

Many colleges and universities have undertaken a variety of measures to improve productivity. These include: renegotiating banking relationships to obtain less expensive transaction processing and credit services, consolidating purchasing for five science labs in one large university, and conducting on-site surveys of facilities maintenance to determine the average time for completion of certain activities so that standards can be established.[20]

In one public school system, managers found that significant savings could be achieved by consolidating certain functions, such as that of a registrar. Since the optimum-size school was determined to be one with about 1,500 students, principals of schools with fewer than 800 students were encouraged to share registrars with similarly small nearby schools.

A rural health clinic found that it could significantly improve the productivity of its physicians by using a nurse practitioner (NP). The NP was able to screen patients, treat those who did not require a physician, and conduct many tests and procedures that physicians formerly conducted. As a result, the clinic greatly increased productivity of its physicians with consequent reduction in the cost of a patient visit and a higher volume of patients seen.

Selection of a Measure

Efforts to improve productivity require measures that managers can use to judge their success. The major difficulty in selecting a measure of productivity

---

[19]See, for example, Henry M. Levin, "Raising Productivity in Higher Education," *Journal of Higher Education* 62, no. 3 (May/June 1991).
[20]See Clark L. Bernard and Douglas Beaven, "Containing the Costs of Higher Education," *Journal of Accountancy,* October 1985.

is choosing a unit that is sufficiently homogeneous to provide a reliable indicator of improved (or worsened) performance. In a membership organization, for example, clerical staff might be evaluated according to the number of applications processed per hour. Since each application is about the same as all others, this can be a reliable measure. In an ambulatory care clinic, on the other hand, there are many different types of visits and levels of severity associated with different patients. Therefore, a patient visit is at best only a rough measure of productivity.

Operational Auditing

Compliance auditing, as described above, is used to determine whether financial data are being recorded properly and whether financial rules (such as those concerning spending authorizations) are being followed. Another type of auditing, called *operational auditing,* has become increasingly important in recent years.[21] Its development was fostered by the U.S. Comptroller General's 1973 publication *Standards for Audit of Governmental Organizations, Programs, Activities and Functions.* According to this booklet, operational auditing

> determines whether the entity is managing or utilizing its resources (personnel, property, space, and so forth) in an economical and efficient manner and [attempts to identify] the causes of any inefficiencies or uneconomical practices, including inadequacies in management information systems, administrative procedures, or organizational structure.[22]

By showing where changes in policies or procedures are desirable, operational auditing can help an organization improve both its effectiveness and efficiency. If properly conducted, it can be a valuable tool in the management of a nonprofit organization. If not properly conducted, however, it can be a source of friction and frustration, with no constructive results.

Example

James Watkins, head of the Department of Energy, created "tiger teams" in 1989 to serve as a special inspection force to enforce compliance with federal rules on environmental purity, worker safety, and public health. While some of the teams identified serious problems, others focused on the trivial. In one reported instance, a team member discovered a paint

---

[21] For a description of operational auditing in health care, see Charles Holley and Ross McDonald, "Operational Auditing of Health Care Ancillary Departments," *Internal Auditing* 6, no. 1. For a description of its use in higher education, see John Krallman and Wayland Winstead, "Operational Audits in a University Environment," *Internal Auditing* 5, no. 2. For a description of its use in a municipality, see John D. Heaton, Linda J. Savage, and Judith K. Welch, "Performance Auditing in Municipal Governments," *Government Accountants Journal,* Summer 1993.

[22] Comptroller General of the United States, *Standards for Audit of Governmental Organizations, Programs, Activities, and Functions* (Washington, DC: Government Printing Office), pp. 1–2. This document, called "The Yellow Book," was updated in 1988 and published as *Government Auditing Standards.*

brush left under a fume hood in a laboratory. Someone in the lab had used it to apply ordinary paint to a piece of equipment, setting it down to dry so that it could be disposed of safely in the trash later. The tiger team threatened to cite the lab for a violation. As a result, the lab staffer was forced to wrap the brush in two layers of plastic, and dispose of it as costly hazardous waste.[23]

The operational auditor must recognize that all managers make mistakes, and that hindsight permits identification of decisions that should have been made differently. There is no point, however, in publicizing such decisions if they were made in good faith, given the information available at the time. Operational auditing serves a useful purpose if, and only if, it shows how future decisions can be made in a better way.

Skills Required

Because of the above needs, operational auditing requires a quite different approach and a quite different type of auditor than does compliance auditing. This is evidenced by the fact that the General Accounting Office hires approximately equal numbers of accountants and nonaccountants. Operations analysts, economists, and social psychologists are well represented among the nonaccountants.[24]

Process Flow Analysis One technique that has proven quite effective in operational auditing is process flow analysis. Such an analysis can map levels of decision making for a particular activity, thereby assisting managers to focus on potential problem areas or gaps in the way clients are handled by the organization's employees. While a process flow analysis can become highly complex, depending on the activity being analyzed, the technique itself is quite simple, identifying key decision points in a process, and analyzing the consequences of each.[25]

Once process analysis has laid out all tasks, decision points, and documents generated in conjunction with a particular activity, managers can then determine if all possible tasks have been considered, and where, if at all, tasks should be monitored to compare performance with expectations.

The value of process analysis is that it identifies in a very specific way the decisions that are made in conjunction with a particular activity. Since there can be no loose ends (i.e., paths that are left undefined), managers can view the

[23]Eliot Marshall, "Tiger Teams Draw Researchers' Snarls," *Science* 252 (April 19, 1991), pp. 366–69.

[24]This is true outside government as well. See Ali N. Azad and Ted D. Skekel, "Personal Attributes and Effective Operational Auditing: Perceptions of College and University Internal Auditors," *Governmental Accountants Journal* 39, no. 3.

[25]For a brief but very useful description of process analysis in a nonprofit context, see Janelle Heineke, *Note on Process Analysis in Health Care* (Boston: Boston University School of Management, February 1996).

decision-making process in its entirety and identify potential problem areas. Managers can monitor these areas, and take corrective action when necessary.

Process analysis has become increasingly important in organizations implementing continuous quality improvement (CQI) and total quality management (TQM). These organizations effectively ask line managers to engage in operational auditing. If senior management fosters an organizational environment that supports such an effort, line managers will be able to undertake operational analyses on their own. They do not have to wait for, or rely on, operational auditors to conduct them.[26]

Controls on Effectiveness

Some management control systems omit effectiveness considerations, that is, comparisons of actual versus planned outputs. Indeed, the absence of information on effectiveness frequently is used as a reason for not giving appropriate attention to information that *is* provided by the system. For example, in a hospital there may be no adequate formal mechanism for measuring the quality of care, and this fact leads some people to conclude that little attention should be given to the control of costs because of the danger that such attention might lead to a lowering of quality.

Notwithstanding the absence of good data, there actually are powerful forces at work in hospitals and other nonprofit organizations where professionals deliver services, to ensure that the quality of service is adequate. If it becomes inadequate, this fact usually is brought to senior management's attention. Physicians, nurses, and other hospital professionals are vitally interested in patient welfare, and usually will not tolerate reductions in quality. Some hospitals also use patient care representatives to question patients about the quality of care they receive, and to bring patient complaints to the attention of management. Additionally, if there are problems with nonclinical quality, patients may complain directly. When these complaints are about poor food, dirty floors, or other matters within the patient's competence, they are relevant. They may even come to the attention of the general public or the trustees, which is an outcome senior management certainly wants to avoid.

The presence of competition also may affect quality, for if quality levels deteriorate in one hospital, physicians may threaten to use (or actually use) another. Accrediting and licensing agencies also make periodic inspections and check actual conditions against prescribed standards. Thus, physicians, nurses, patient representatives, patients, trustees, competition, and outside agencies are all of some help in assuring adequate quality levels, even in the absence of a formal method of measurement.

---

[26]For additional discussion of TQM and CQI in nonprofit settings, see Barbara Bordelon and Elizabeth Clemmer, "Customer Service, Partnership, Leadership: Three Strategies that Work," *The G.A.O. Journal,* Winter 1990/91; and Edwin L. Coate, "TQM on Campus: Implementing Total Quality Management in a University Setting," *NACUBO Business Officer,* November 1990.

Example

In one large medical center, a volunteer interviewed eight patients a month, following a printed interview guide. Serious problems, if any, were brought to the attention of management immediately. A summary report was discussed monthly at a meeting of management and the volunteer team.

Peer Review   Several professions have devised methods to ensure a satisfactory quality of service. Although the movements have different labels, they share in common the concept that a professional's work should be subject to review by his or her peers. For example, hospitals have medical records committees, tissue committees, and utilization review committees. These committees review the accuracy and completeness of records, the accuracy of surgical diagnoses, and the clinical treatments and lengths of patient stay.

Peer review also exists in other organizations in which professional decision making is a critical activity. Colleges and universities have mechanisms for reviewing the performance of faculty members, and the schools are themselves subject to review by accrediting agencies. In research organizations, work done by one group is reviewed by other groups.

In general, when the principal output of an organization is the work of professionals, the quality of that output is best judged by other professionals. Professionals tend to resist peer review activities, however, and there is a strong possibility of back scratching, so the mechanism needs senior management attention if it is to be effective.[27]

Results of Operational Auditing

Despite 25 years of emphasis on operational auditing, little in the way of management reform has taken place in the federal government. For example, the President's Private Sector Survey on Cost Control (the Grace Commission) in 1984 identified programs where it claimed that waste reduction and improved management could result in savings of $424.6 billion in five years.[28] Relatively few of its proposals were implemented.

By contrast, a detailed follow-up process was instituted for Vice President Gore's 1993 National Performance Review. Responsibility for implementing each of the Review's 1,250 recommendations was assigned to an agency or office, and each of these units was instructed to make annual reports to the Congress. By 1995, according to Vice President Gore, 244,000 jobs had been

---

[27]It should be noted that peer review focuses on the effectiveness of an organization's *professionals* and not on the broader question of the effectiveness of its *programs*. It may be, for example, that individual teachers in a bilingual education program are all extremely well qualified and carry out their responsibilities in a highly effective manner, but that the nature of the student population has changed such that the program no longer is needed. Questions such as these are part of an evaluation review, discussed in Chapter 15.

[28]President's Private Sector Survey on Cost Control, *War on Waste*, 1984. For current efforts to improve performance in the federal government, see *Management of the United States Government*, a report prepared annually by the Office of Management and Budget.

eliminated, 2,000 obsolete field offices had been closed, and 200 programs and agencies had been eliminated. The result was savings of $118 billion.[29]

Confusion with Compliance Auditing Some organizations have not been successful at operational auditing because they do not appear to be aware of the differences between operational auditing and compliance auditing. As a result, they use persons with an accounting background for operational auditing, simply because the current auditing organization consists exclusively of accountants. When accountants imply that they know how to run a school, hospital, or any other organization better than the professionals who have spent their careers working in and managing such organizations, or when they attempt to recommend changes that are outside their areas of competence, their work is resented and frequently disregarded.

Project Control

The foregoing description has focused on the control of individual responsibility centers. Somewhat different techniques are appropriate for the control of projects, such as individual research projects or the building of a major capital asset. Specifically, in controlling a responsibility center, the focus is on work done in a specified period, such as a month or a quarter. In project control, by contrast, the focus is on the accomplishment of a project that, in many instances, may extend over a period of several years.

A project control system must consider three aspects of the project: cost, quality, and time requirements. The essentials of the system for controlling these items are work packages, budgets, cost and output reporting, and plan revisions.

Senior management begins the effort by specifying the responsibility centers that will do the work. Responsibility center managers then estimate the activities to be done and the resources and time required to complete them. These estimates should be made as near to the inception of the project as possible and organized in terms of *work packages*—relatively small, measurable increments of work that can be related to a physical product, milestone, or other measurable indicator of progress. These units should be of short duration, with discrete starting and completion points, and should be the responsibility of a single organizational unit.

Based on the work packages, responsibility center managers prepare a work schedule and a budget showing (*a*) physical products, milestones, technical performance goals, or other indicators that will be used to measure output, (*b*) budgets for costs expected to be incurred for each work package and

---

[29]Al Gore, *The Best Kept Services in Government* (Washington, DC: U.S. Government Printing Office, 1996). For a critical appraisal of the National Performance Review, see Barbara A. Coe, "How Structural Conflicts Stymie Reinvention," *Public Administration Review,* March–April 1997.

for overhead costs, (*c*) starting and completion time for each work package, (*d*) the organizational unit responsible for the work, and (*e*) any interdependencies among work packages.

During the project, the accounting staff maintains records of actual outputs and actual costs incurred. At frequent intervals, it prepares reports from these records showing, both for the interval and cumulatively, significant differences between budgeted and actual direct costs, overhead costs, work performed, and performance.

Based on these reports, managers make revisions to the project plan and budget to reflect current estimates of the work schedule, the expected level of technical performance, and costs. Once they have revised plans and budgets, subsequent management reports should show comparisons both with the original (i.e., baseline) budget and with the current budget. The reasons for significant revisions should be readily identifiable in these reports.[30]

Behavioral Considerations

Thus far we have focused mainly on the technical aspects of performance control systems. While these matters are important, so too are the attitudes of those who use, and are affected by, the information from these systems. In this section, we discuss several matters related to the use of performance control information.

Senior Management Involvement

A management control system is likely to be ineffective unless operating managers and professionals perceive that it is considered important by their supervisors. This requires that both senior management and line managers use information from the system in decision making, in appraising the results of performance, and as a basis for salary adjustments, promotions, and other personnel actions. It also requires that superiors at all levels discuss the results of operations with their subordinates.

Some managers convene regular meetings at which performance of the entire organization is discussed. Others prefer individual discussions with responsibility center heads. Still others prefer to make comments in writing, holding only infrequent meetings.

In discussions of performance, subordinates should be given an opportunity to explain circumstances not revealed in the reports. If corrective action seems called for, constructive suggestions for such action should be put forth and agreed upon. If the performance is good, managers should convey appropriate recognition of this.

Sometimes it is difficult for management to convey the correct impression about the importance of quantitative information, especially the comparison

---

[30]For a more complete description of project control, see Robert N. Anthony and Vijay Govindarajan, *Management Control Systems,* 7th ed. (Chicago: McGraw-Hill, 1998).

of budgeted and actual revenues and expenses. Inadequate attention leads to a common disregard of these numbers. On the other hand, if senior management places too much emphasis on numerical measures of performance, operating managers may act in such a way that their performance looks good according to the measures that are emphasized, but to the detriment of the real objectives of the organization. These actions are called *playing the numbers game.* They can be avoided only by convincing operating managers that they should concentrate on accomplishing the real objectives of the organization and that they will not be penalized if such efforts do not show up in numerical measures of performance.[31]

Importance of Adequate Staffs

Quantitative information for appraising performance cannot be used unless qualified people are available to make the calculations. Except in very small organizations, managers do not have time to make the calculations themselves. Unfortunately, a great many nonprofit organizations, including some very large ones, do not have staffs large enough to undertake such analyses in a thorough and systematic way. For example, one state government agency with a multibillion dollar budget has only six professionals who are engaged in the regular analysis of operating reports. Some states have none at all.

Balance between Freedom and Restraint

In any organization, for-profit or nonprofit, the right balance has to be struck between freedom and restraint. *Freedom* is needed to take advantage of the ability and knowledge of the person on the firing line. *Restraint* is needed to ensure that management policies are followed and to reduce the effect of poor judgments or counterproductive decisions by lower-level managers.

In nonprofit organizations, there are two complications to attaining an appropriate balance between freedom and restraint. First, the absence of profit as an overall basis for measuring performance usually calls for somewhat less freedom and somewhat more restraint than in a for-profit organization. Second, the presence of professionals in many nonprofits introduces a level of knowledge about client needs that senior management must consider carefully.

This is a matter of degree. Many nonprofit organizations, particularly government organizations, impose far too many and too detailed restraints on first-line managers. Sometimes this is caused by the *goldfish bowl problem.* Errors are likely to be played up in the newspapers, and, as a protective device, managers prescribe rules, which they can point to when errors come to light: "I am not to blame; he (the sinner) broke my rule." The detailed restraints also result from encrustation: a sin is committed, and a rule is promulgated to avoid that sin in the future; but the rule continues even after the

[31]For a good discussion of some of the important aspects of performance review, see Berkley Rice, "Performance Review: Examining the Eye of the Beholder," *Across the Board,* December 1985.

need for it has disappeared. No one considers whether the likelihood and seriousness of error is great enough to warrant continuation of the rule.

Motivation

A central purpose of any control system is to motivate operating managers to take actions that help accomplish the organization's objectives efficiently and effectively. As discussed in Chapter 8, the problem of inducing the desired degree and direction of motivation is a difficult one in any organization, but it is particularly difficult in a nonprofit organization. In a school system, for example, all groups are interested in better education, but teachers as individuals also are concerned with salary, educational advancement, and professional status.

The Problem of Budget Conformance

The fact that performance in a nonprofit organization is measured in part by how well managers conform to their budgets can have dysfunctional consequences. Suppose a manager has a $1 million budget, and by careful, hard work performs the required job, but spends only $990,000. In many organizations, the budget for the following year, other things equal, will be $990,000. In effect, the manager is punished, rather than rewarded, for reducing costs— his or her department now has less money to work with than would have been the case if the entire $1 million had been spent.

It is a difficult matter to create the right attitude in these circumstances. On the one hand, if the program can be run more efficiently or if demand for it has fallen, its budget should be less than before. On the other hand, managers need incentives to be efficient this year that do not penalize them in future years. There are several possible ways to do this.

One possibility is to guarantee managers that their budgets will not be reduced for the current year or the succeeding year, even if the job can be done at less than the amount budgeted. To make this policy work, senior management may need to expand the definition of operating expenses to include minor capital expenditures, for it is on items of this type that managers tend to spend the extra money.

A second possibility is to convince operating managers that a budget reduction per se should not be viewed as a punishment, and that senior management recognizes and rewards cost reductions. An effective and efficient manager is rewarded with a combination of promotion, salary, and the respect of peers, superiors, and subordinates. If senior management successfully stresses the importance of cost reduction and provides appropriate rewards, it may be able to avoid negative reactions to reducing the budget.

The third possibility is to release substantially less (say, 20 percent less) than the funds managers need. They know that additional funds are available, but they can never be sure of getting them. This may make them more than ordinarily careful in spending available funds. There is a risk, of course, that this practice will stifle their initiative, resulting in a reluctance to both introduce new programs and maintain existing facilities.

A fourth possibility is to hold next year's budget constant, but expect managers to accomplish more work with the same amount of resources. This approach increases efficiency just as much as a policy of expecting a unit to do the same amount of work with fewer resources. It also assumes that the organizational unit can, in fact, accomplish more work with the same amount of resources.

Use of Monetary Incentives

For-profit organizations often pay cash bonuses or give stock options when savings are realized or profits are high. Increasingly, as we discussed in Chapters 2 and 8, nonprofit organizations are paying bonuses; frequently the bonuses are related to nonfinancial as well as financial performance.

Example

A survey of hospitals found that, in many instances, bonuses paid to executives were related to both net operating income and at least one measure concerning quality of care or improvement of services delivered.[32]

The state of Tennessee permitted a college or university to earn a bonus of up to 2 percent of its budget based on its performance with regard to five variables:

- Number of academic programs accredited.
- Performance of graduates on outcomes related to general education, as measured by tests administered to alumni.
- Performance of graduates on tests in their major fields.
- Evaluation of programs by students, alumni, and community representatives, by questionnaires.
- Evaluation by peers at other institutions.[33]

Some organizations also emphasize the importance of collaboration and teamwork in their incentive systems.

Example

One nonprofit organization had an incentive system in which a portion of each manager's salary was withheld monthly with the understanding that it might not be paid at all. Depending on the extent to which the organization as a whole achieved its financial and programmatic objectives for the year, all or a portion of this withheld salary would then be paid out as a bonus. Since all managers received the same proportion of the amount withheld, and since the proportion was based on the performance of the

---

[32]"Hospitals Adopt New Strategy to Keep Top Executives," *Journal of Accountancy,* March 1988, pp. 14–17.
[33]E. Grady Bogue and Wayne Brown, "Performance Incentives for State Colleges," *Harvard Business Review,* November–December 1981, p. 123–28.

entire organization, managers had a major incentive to collaborate, which was essential activity for the success of the organization.

All of the above bonus arrangements relate to performance in the short term. In general, nonprofit organizations have not been successful in designing incentive compensation plans that motivate managers to consider the long-term consequences of their decisions. One important reason is that they cannot use stock options, which frequently are used by for-profit companies to motivate managers to think in terms of the long run.

Some nonprofit organizations have attempted to design incentive plans that encourage managers to adopt a long-term perspective. The accumulation of extra vacation days is one such approach, with the possibility of an extended sabbatical leave at some point in the future. If the system is designed in such a way that these days are not paid if the employee leaves the organization voluntarily, there is an incentive for the employee to remain with the organization.

Gainsharing

Increasingly, nonprofit organizations are incorporating financial rewards into productivity improvement programs. Sometimes called *gainsharing,* these programs allow the savings generated by increases in productivity to be shared between the employee and the organization. At the federal level, the major barriers to gainsharing programs are the lack of legislation authorizing such programs, the presence of existing regulations that limit managers' flexibility in designing and operating the programs, and the absence of specific policies and guidelines from the Office of Personnel Management. Nevertheless, several instances have been reported in the Department of Defense of successful efforts, including elimination of work backlogs, decreased equipment downtime, reduction in time lost from on-the-job injuries, and substantial reductions in overtime and sick leave.[34]

There are also gainsharing successes outside the federal government. For example, one hospital paid bonuses to employees of departments where productivity exceeded historical standards. The result was an increase of productivity of 8 percent, producing $2 million in savings; employee bonuses averaged 4.3 percent of base salaries.[35]

If properly designed, a gainsharing program takes advantage of the knowledge of possible improvements that usually exists in the lower levels of an organization. While there can be problems with gainsharing, such as a tendency to hold back some ideas for next year so that there will be constant evidence

---

[34]U.S. General Accounting Office, *Gainsharing: DOD Efforts Highlight an Effective Tool for Enhancing Federal Productivity,* Briefing Report to the Chairman, Subcommittee on Defense, Committee on Appropriations, House of Representatives, GAO/GGD86-143BR, September 1986.
[35]Ibid.

of effort, the program nevertheless provides managers with a financial incentive to reduce costs.

Summary

Control of operations consists of both financial control and performance control. The former focuses on assuring that the spending limitations of the budget are adhered to. The latter is concerned with effective and efficient managerial performance. The distinction between the two types of control is highlighted by the kind of auditing that takes place in each. Financial control uses the compliance audit, an audit that is relatively narrow in scope, and is concerned with safeguarding the organization's assets against loss from unauthorized use or disposition. It also verifies the reliability of the records used for preparing financial statements. Its main focus is on the accounting system.

Performance control uses the operational audit, which is relatively broad in its scope, and focuses on how an organization is managing its resources. It attempts to identify the causes of any inefficiencies or uneconomical practices. The operational audit's main units of analysis are the management information system, administrative procedures, and the organizational structure.

Behavioral considerations are important in the control of operations. In particular, senior management should seek an appropriate balance between freedom and restraint. That is, they should give program heads and responsibility center managers the freedom to exercise judgment in their operating activities, but they also must ensure that overall management policies are followed, and that the possibilities for poor judgment or counterproductive decisions by lower level managers are minimized. One tool to help attain this balance is a system of monetary incentives that is used to reward managers for attaining superior financial and programmatic operating results.

Rewarding managers for good performance is more difficult in a nonprofit organization than in a for-profit one, largely because the "bottom line" doesn't measure effectiveness or efficiency in the same way it does in a for-profit company. Thus, senior management must seek ways to reward managers for the programmatic results they attain. This requires measuring output, which is the subject of Chapter 12.

Appendix

The Encumbrance Accounting Process

Encumbrance accounting is used when an organization wishes to maintain accounting records of *obligations* to pay for goods or services. An encumbrance arises when such an obligation is made. Usually, encumbrance accounting takes place when a state or local authority is appropriated funds by its legislative body, thereby giving it the authority to encumber. Accordingly, the first step in an encumbrance accounting is to record the amount appropriated for each fund. The next step is to charge the appropriated amount for encumbrances.

Example

If the legislature appropriates $10 million for a certain activity in 1997, this amount is set up in the accounts, and it is reduced as contracts are entered into, so the accounts show at all times how much of the $10 million has not yet been encumbered. The organization has complied with the law if, by the end of 1997, it has not encumbered more than $10 million, whether or not goods or services contracted for have been received, and whether or not cash disbursements to vendors or employees have been made.

A formal business accounting system starts when goods or services are received; it does not record purchase orders. From this point on, the accounting process is the same in many nonprofit organizations as in a business; that is, resources are held in asset accounts until they are used, at which time they are charged as expenses to responsibility centers and programs.

Some nonprofit organizations charge responsibility centers and programs as soon as the amounts are encumbered; others make these charges when the goods or services are acquired, rather than when they are consumed. (The latter is called the *expenditure basis* of accounting.) Alternatively, the charge may be made to the responsibility center that *incurs* the encumbrance or the expenditure, which is not necessarily the same as the responsibility center that *uses* the resources.

Example

Consider $1,000 of supplies to be used by an operating agency but purchased by a central supply office. The supplies are purchased in March and consumed in April. Under encumbrance accounting, the $1,000 is recorded as a charge to the central supply office in the month of March; it may never be recorded as an expense of the operating agency. Under accrual accounting, it is recorded as an expense of the operating agency in the month of April.

As explained in Chapter 3, these differences can have a significant effect on the amount of resources reported as consumed by a given responsibility center.

Reconciling Encumbrance and Expense Accounting

It is feasible to design an accounting system that keeps track of encumbrances, expenditures, and expenses. This is accomplished by the use of working capital accounts that hold costs in suspense until the resources are consumed. The inventory account in a business accounting system serves this purpose, and inventory accounts can be used for the same purpose in organizations that record encumbrances. In addition, such organizations need an account called *Undelivered Orders* that holds items in suspense between the time a contract is placed and the time goods are received.

The procedure for doing this is illustrated in Exhibit 11–1. As it indicates, in the month of April, labor services of $100,000 were used, and orders were placed for $80,000 of material and $60,000 of other services (e.g., a contract was let for painting buildings). Total encumbrances for the agency in April (shown in Account A) were therefore $240,000.

Labor is accounted for essentially the same on an encumbrance basis as on an expense basis, so labor expense is here assumed to be equal to the encumbered $100,000. This is shown in Account C. To record material expense and services expense, however, two types of working capital accounts are necessary. One is Undelivered Orders (Account B); the other is Inventory (Account D). Inventory is of the same nature in a nonprofit organization as in a for-profit business; namely, it records the amount of material that is on hand at any time (which, by definition, is an asset). Thus, it holds the cost of material between the time of acquisition and the time of consumption.

As orders are placed, Account B is debited, and Account A is credited. As the services are rendered, Account B is credited and Account C is debited. Thus, for $70,000 of services performed in April (e.g., the buildings were painted and $10,000 of work was done under contracts let in earlier months), a credit is made to Undelivered Orders (Account B), with a corresponding debit to an expense account (Account C). The Undelivered Orders account has no counterpart in a for-profit company.

As material is received, Undelivered Orders (Account B) is credited and Inventory (Account D) is debited. When the inventory is used, Account D is credited and an expense account (Account C) is debited. To illustrate, in the above example, $50,000 of material was received in April, reducing Undeliv-

EXHIBIT 11–1 Reconciliation of Encumbrance and Expense Accounting Transactions for April ($000)

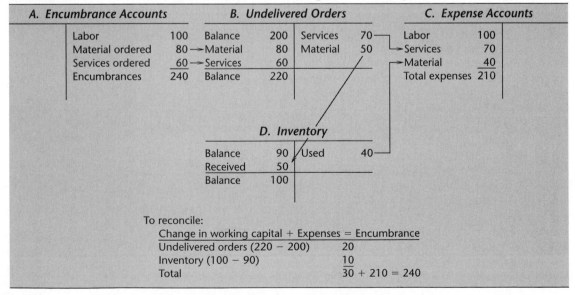

ered Orders by $50,000 and increasing Inventory by the same amount. In April, $40,000 of material was issued from inventory for use in current operations, so Inventory was credited $40,000, with a corresponding debit to an expense account.

As Exhibit 11–1 shows, total expenses and total encumbrances for April can be reconciled by measuring the changes in the two working capital accounts. Undelivered orders increased by $20,000 (from $200,000 to $220,000) and Inventory increased by $10,000 (from $90,000 to $100,000). The sum of these two changes ($30,000), plus the expenses for the month of $210,000 is the same as total encumbrances.

If senior management wishes, a manager's budget can include these working capital accounts. The budget report can show the amount of expenses authorized for each program, and also the amounts authorized for changes in working capital (which may be either positive or negative). As a result, the total amount budgeted is the sum of these amounts.

The mechanism described above provides a way of holding charges in suspense between the time an asset is acquired and the time it is consumed. Working capital accounts also hold items in suspense so as to differentiate between the organizational unit acquiring the asset, and the unit consuming it. Again, this is a function that inventory accounts serve in a business. In a manufacturing company, all the costs of manufacturing goods are accumulated in Work-in-Process Inventory accounts until the manufacturing process is completed. At that time, the costs are moved from Work-in-Process Inventory to Finished Goods Inventory, effectively shifting *responsibility* for the goods from the manufacturing department to the marketing department. Similarly, the costs incurred by service centers in nonprofit organizations can be held in suspense in working capital and inventory accounts until the goods or services are consumed. At that point, the expense account of the responsibility center that benefits from the goods or services can be debited, reflecting their consumption.

Suggested Additional Readings

Azad, Ali N., and Ted D. Skekel. "Personal Attributes and Effective Operational Auditing: Perceptions of College and University Internal Auditors." *Governmental Accountants Journal* 39, no. 3 (Fall 1990).

Barzelay, Michael, and Babak J. Armajani. *Breaking through Bureaucracy: A New Vision for Managing in Government.* Berkeley: University of California Press, 1992.

Bowsher, Charles A. *Improving Operations of Federal Departments and Agencies, Annual Report to the Chairmen and Ranking Minority Members, House and Senate Committees on Appropriations.* General Accounting Office, GAO/OP-96-1, 1996.

Brizius, Jack A., and Michael D. Campbell. *Getting Results.* Washington, DC: Council of Governor's Policy Advisors, 1991.

Carr, David K., and Ian D. Littman. *Excellence in Government: Total Quality Management in the 1990s.* Arlington, VA: Coopers and Lybrand, 1990.

Davenport, T. H. *Process Innovation: Reengineering Work through Information Technology.* Boston: Harvard Business School Press, 1994.

Gabor, Andrea. *The Man Who Discovered Quality: How W. Edwards Deming Brought the Quality Revolution to America—The Stories of Ford, Xerox, and GM.* New York: Times Books (Division of Random House), 1990.

Gore, Al. *Creating a Government That Works Better and Costs Less. Report of the National Performance Review.* Washington, DC: Government Printing Office, 1993.

Hammer, Michael, and Steven A. Stanton. *The Reengineering Revolution.* New York: Harper Business, 1995.

Kettl, Donald F. *Improving Government Performance: An Owner's Manual.* Washington, DC: The Brookings Institution, 1993.

———. *Reinventing Government? Appraising the National Performance Review.* Washington, DC: The Brookings Institution, 1994.

Linden, R. M. *Seamless Government: A Practical Guide to Reengineering in the Public Sector.* San Francisco: Jossey-Bass, 1994.

Osborne, D., and T. Gaebler. *Reinventing Government.* Reading, MA: Addison Wesley, 1992.

Pappas, Alceste T. *Reengineering Your Nonprofit Organization: A Guide to Strategic Transformation.* New York: John Wiley & Sons, 1996.

Swiss, James E. "Adapting Total Quality Management (TQM) to Government." *Public Administration Review* 52, July/August 1992.

Wilson, James Q. *Bureaucracy: What Government Agencies Do and Why They Do It.* New York: Basic Books, 1989.

Case 11–1

Hospital San Pedro[*]

Sr. Julio Rivera, Director General of Health of the Social Security Administration of the country of Ilobasco, sat down at his desk one morning late in

*This case was prepared by Antoni Garcia Prat, Instituto de Estudios Superiores de la Empresa, Barcelona, Spain. It was translated and modified slightly by Professor David W. Young. Copyright © by Antoni Garcia Prat and David W. Young.

September, and began to open his mail. One of the first items he came to was a letter from Sr. Fidel Sanchez Hernandez. The letter read as follows:

Sonsonate
September 20

Sr. Director General of Health
San Miguel

Dear Sir,

In a routine examination which took place last April 3, Dr. Magaña, the primary care doctor for my community, discovered that my son, Gabriel, suffered from a visual defect. Since it was necessary for him to be treated by an eye specialist, Dr. Magaña gave me a referral to go to the ambulatory care center in our county capital, Santa Ana, where all the medical specialists are located.

The 8th of that month, at noon, the hour specified for ophthalmology consultations, my son and I were in the clinic waiting to be seen by Dr. Duarte, the center's ophthalmologist. You can't imagine my surprise when, after a MINIMAL examination, the doctor gave me a referral so that my son could be seen in Hospital San Pedro, in Santa Telca, since, as was patently clear, the center at Santa Ana DOESN'T HAVE THE MINIMUM REQUIRED FACILITIES NECESSARY TO CONDUCT AN EYE EXAMINATION

That was the beginning of the Odyssey of a patient seeking to find and obtain a diagnosis.

On April 13, in the afternoon, I had to return to the center at Santa Ana so that the Inspector[1] could authorize the referral, so that I could go to the Hospital San Pedro, as we had been directed.

I was informed by his office that in San Pedro, specialist visits begin at 8:30 A.M. daily.

The following day, April 14, at 8:30 in the morning, accompanied by my son, I arrived at the facilities of Hospital San Pedro, and completed the administrative transactions related to my son's case. After ONE HOUR in line, they gave me a visit for the 4th of June (ALMOST TWO MONTHS!), telling us that we should arrive at 8:30 in the morning.

On June 4th, at 8:30 in the morning, my son and I were in front of the door of the ophthalmology clinic of San Pedro, awaiting our turn. After waiting TWO HOURS, my son was seen in one of the offices, where we were asked to go to another room for the next step . . . and to wait some more.

At last, we entered the clinic. After conducting various tests, the doctor indicated to us that it was necessary to dilate the pupils in order to complete the exam thoroughly, and that therefore we should return another day, telling us that we should put in some drops a few hours before the consultation. Returning to the reception desk, after waiting A HALF HOUR we were given a new visit time on the 5th of August (TWO MORE MONTHS). At the same time, the clerk requested from us a new referral form, P–10, from the Inspector in which he should ask the Hospital to conduct the test that the specialist at San Pedro already had told me they would give to my son.

---

[1]An Inspector is a Social Security Officer, always a physician, who, among other duties, is responsible for authorizing patients to be treated in contracted (i.e., non-Social Security) hospitals.

The same day, the 4th, I had to make another trip to Santa Ana in order to obtain Form P–10 from the Inspector, and, in the afternoon I had to go to San Miguel, to the Chaparestique Clinic on Madrazo Street, so that the Inspector there could authorize the referral since the Inspector at Santa Ana was on vacation (ARE THERE NO SUBSTITUTES?).

The 5th of August. 8:30 in the morning. We arrive at San Pedro. My son with drops in his eyes. We enter the clinic at TEN O'CLOCK. After the visit, the doctor tells me that we have to return another day since the results of the exams conducted on June 4th have been lost (!!??!!) and it was impossible to repeat them now with the pupils dilated. Because of the expression on my face and because of what I had on the tip of my tongue to spit out at him, the doctor understood my justified indignation, and he himself gave us a new date, for the 12th of August, eight days later, without any type of referral.

On the 12th, at 8:30 in the morning, once again in the clinic of San Pedro. My son was not seen until ELEVEN O'CLOCK. The doctor diagnosed strabismus.

That's the story until now. Now, I request that you, as the person responsible for health in Ilobasco, answer the following questions for me.

1. Is it necessary to pass FOUR MONTHS, visit after visit, from clinic to clinic, in order to be seen and learn what type of illness a person suffers from, especially in the case of my son, in which the diagnosis of the specialist of San Pedro coincides exactly with that given to me on the 14th of April, free and in half an hour, by an optometrist?
2. Who will reimburse me for the costs that I have been obliged to incur for travel and lost working hours?
3. Of what use is an ophthalmology consultation at Santa Ana if they don't know how or can't diagnose a basic defect such as astigmatism?
4. Why is there the confusion such as exists at San Pedro, and why is it tolerated, where patients gather at 8:30 A.M., the physicians arrive at 9:00, and visits are conducted until 1:00 P.M.?
5. Why were we sent to San Pedro, when there is a Social Security Hospital in my own service area which has an ophthalmology service?

Awaiting your answer, I would like to take this opportunity to give you my best wishes.

Signed

Fidel Sanchez Hernandez

Background

Hospital San Pedro was a private general hospital with some 300 beds, reimbursed in part by the Social Security Administration (SSA) in order to alleviate the deficit of beds in the densely-populated area of Santa Tecla. The reimbursement system established a method with a monthly payment based on the services delivered to SSA patients. Units of payment for ambulatory consultation distinguished among first visits, subsequent visits, and emergency visits. Separate payment units existed for inpatient care. The rates for each one of these visit types were determined by the SSA, and, without exception, each hospital received rates that corresponded to the group and level in which it had been classified. Traditionally, Hospital San Pedro had been incurring significant losses owing to the fact that the SSA's rates were below its costs. Even so, the hospital had begun, in the last few years, some new services and programs.

The new investments, small in comparison with the requests of the medical staff, served to give the hospital a greater base of facilities and equipment. With these it had an opportunity to move to a higher reimbursement group and level, and therefore an ability to increase its rates by 10 percent.

Another concern of the hospital had been to widen its geographic service area and broaden its scope of services. This was due to the fact that management feared, because a Social Security Hospital existed in the same area, the SSA authorities would prefer to fill their own hospital, thereby saving reimbursement monies.

On the other hand, the hospital faced a serious problem of waiting lists in its clinics, owing to the traditional inadequacy of primary care in SSA facilities. This was quite serious since long waiting lists of SSA patients could threaten the portion of utilization that was made up of patients affiliated with private insurance companies, or who were self-pay. Both of these groups not only paid more for a clinic visit, but also could decide to utilize the services of other clinics or private centers if they were dissatisfied with their care at Hospital San Pedro.

Next Steps

Sr. Rivera realized that a nicely written letter of apology probably would pacify Sr. Sanchez Hernandez, but he also knew that the case presented in the letter was not an unusual one. In part, it indicated some serious deficiencies in the patient referral system, but it also called into question the government's newly formulated policy of decentralization with an emphasis on primary care, and the role of private hospitals in that effort. It was because of these latter matters that he decided to convene a meeting of the Director of Hospital San Pedro, the SSA's Director of Reimbursement, and the Director of Primary Care Services for the Ministry of Health. He then set about preparing for the meeting.

Questions

1. Based on the information in Sr. Sanchez Hernandez's letter, prepare a process flow analysis for a patient in Ilobasco seeking a diagnosis for a medical problem. Make assumptions where necessary.

2. How, if at all, does this assist you in suggesting ways to improve the country's health care delivery system?

3. What should Sr. Rivera do?

Case 11–2

WIC Program*

In late October, Emily Foster, the Assistant Director for Food Delivery at the Women, Infants, and Children Program (WIC), was pressing National Bank for its monthly report, which provided essential information for monitoring most aspects of the supplemental food program. Bank officers were responding that it was impossible to produce a timely report when WIC was responsible for the delay. A tense situation threatened to impair an otherwise good relationship.

As part of its contract with the food program, the National Bank provided space for three WIC Voucher Monitors, whose job it was to screen WIC's food and infant formula vouchers deposited by store owners in their bank accounts, and to reject violative vouchers. WIC routinely rejected 3,500 to 4,500 vouchers a month for violations, at an average voucher price of $7.60.

Data on valid payments and bounces (as rejections were called) were keyed into the bank's computer system and became part of a comprehensive monthly report of food delivery activity in the WIC Program. The bank's contract called for it to file the report for each month at WIC on or before the 21st day of the following month.

Vouchers were similar to checks. Issued to participants in the WIC Program, they were redeemed at authorized food stores, which deposited them directly in their bank accounts. Like regular checks they were cleared through the Federal Reserve System and were subject to a state law requiring payment within 24 hours. In fact, since the WIC Program was liable for payment of any voucher that was not cleared within the required 24 hours, they were assumed to be paid unless rejected by the WIC Voucher Monitors within the 24-hour period.

At one point that fall, WIC screening activity was 21 workdays behind schedule; and, therefore, vouchers that were found to be in violation of WIC redemption regulations were being rejected by the monitors as much as a month after the vendors had deposited them.

Background

The Special Supplemental Food Program for Women, Infants, and Children was established in 1972 (with an amendment to the federal Child Nutrition

*This case was prepared by Nancy E. Fiske under the supervision of Professor David W. Young. Copyright © by David W. Young.

Act of 1966) to provide supplemental foods to low-income, pregnant, post-partum, and nursing mothers, and to infants and children up to age 5 who were diagnosed to be at *nutritional* risk. (Standards for determining *nutritional risk* were defined by the United States Department of Agriculture and further refined by each state administering a program.) In addition to specially prescribed foods, WIC also provided nutrition counseling, education, and access to health care.

WIC enjoyed strong bipartisan support in Congress. In fact, when funding for other nutrition programs was being cut in the early years of the first Reagan administration, WIC received a substantial increase. In hearings before the Senate Subcommittee on Nutrition, the Assistant Secretary of Agriculture testified:

> [WIC] is amazingly cost-effective. Our 1982 budget contains a substantial increase for the program, primarily because several recent studies have demonstrated the value of the WIC Program. One study . . . found that the incidence of low birthweight among infants whose mothers participated in the WIC Program during the prenatal period was markedly less than among infants whose mothers, although eligible for the Program, did not participate.
>
> The reduction in incidence of low birthweight babies led to much lower hospitalization costs. The study estimated that each dollar spent in the prenatal components of the WIC Program resulted in a $3 reduction in hospitalization costs, since the number of low birthweight infants who had to be hospitalized was significantly reduced.[1]

Other national evaluations and studies linked WIC with increasing weight gain among low-income pregnant women, reduced late fetal deaths, improved cognitive development among children, and increased head circumference at birth.

The Local WIC

"I like WIC. It's a good, essential program," began Jack Mason, the National Bank calling officer assigned to manage the WIC account in the Governmental Services Division of the bank. As a former staff person in the state legislature and manager of a number of low-income advocacy and planning agencies, Mason understood the issues posed by publicly funded human services programs.

> I'm spending much more time with WIC now—and I like that. WIC represents to me where I come from—it's a movement type of organization. People there are absolutely dedicated to the reason WIC exists, and you can feel it when you go there. Working with WIC gives me a chance to do good things for people.

---

[1]Carol Tucker Foreman, in hearing before Senate Subcommittee on Nutrition, April 1980; as quoted in *Performance and Credibility*, Joseph S. Wholey, ed. (Lexington, MA: Lexington Books, 1986), p. 277.

There are two things that WIC needs to be concerned about. First, WIC should be primarily concerned with providing food to low-income women and children. Secondarily WIC needs to be concerned about the business aspects of the program—but not at the expense of the first goal.

My superiors here don't necessarily have a strong love for human service clients, but they'll work on the issue if the contract can earn a profit. And WIC is a good contract for this bank. We reconcile about three million vouchers annually, and the profit is considerable. It's good public policy and it's good business for the bank to support WIC.

The philosophy here is one of relationship banking. It's important not only to earn the client's faith and confidence, but also to give a high-quality product. This is probably the only bank in town that the WIC director could call up if funding were in trouble, and our lobbyist would be down at the capital in a minute speaking to the Senate President.

Program Organization

Eighty percent of the WIC Program funding was through a cash grant from the Food and Nutrition Service of the United States Department of Agriculture. The remaining 20 percent was from supplemental funding by the state legislature. The WIC budget was $34.3 million, which was intended to service a projected monthly caseload of 68,500 participants. Eighty percent of that budget, or $27.4 million, was designated for food costs; the remaining 20 percent was budgeted for administration.

The WIC Program had experienced significant growth since its inception in 1975. During the three most recent fiscal years, the actual caseload had grown by 40 percent from a monthly average of 46,000 participants to 64,200, but a recent needs assessment put the eligible population at 145,000.

The WIC Program was administered by the State Department of Public Health. The WIC unit was located in the Maternal and Child Health Section of the Division of Family Health Services. It was a relatively small unit, with approximately 30 employees. The WIC unit administered the program through contracts awarded to local agencies—usually either a health agency or a Community Action Program—in 35 different catchment areas in the state. Local agencies in turn established local WIC programs, which then received programmatic direction from the state agency.

The local programs determined the nutritional needs of their participants, and prescribed packages of vouchers which could be redeemed for the foods designated on the face of each voucher. "Food messages" contained on each voucher stipulated the kinds of foods for which the voucher could be exchanged, and included infant formula, milk, cheese, cereal, juice, peanut butter, beans, and eggs, in specified amounts. Participants could purchase up to the entire amount of the food message within 30 days from the issuance date on the voucher; they were required to use a WIC-authorized food vendor or pharmacy, that is, a vendor who contracted with the local program.

A sample voucher is shown in Exhibit 1. There were 66 different voucher types, each with a different maximum redemption price determined by the

EXHIBIT 1
Sample WIC Voucher

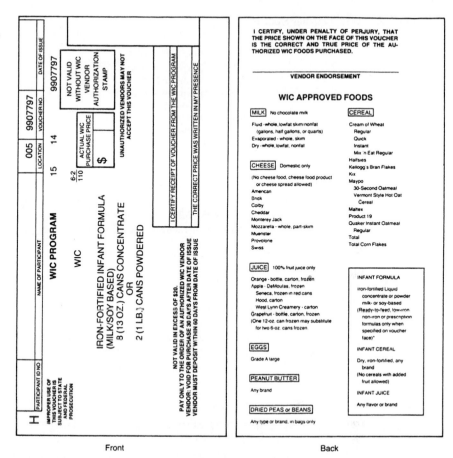

Front

Back

shelf prices submitted competitively by vendors, initially as part of their application, and quarterly thereafter.

At the time a participant picked up vouchers, he or she was required to sign both a register and the vouchers. At the time of purchase the participant was required to sign the voucher again as certification that the price written on the voucher by the vendor was correct. Signatures had to match. The vendor would later stamp the voucher with an authorizing vendor identification stamp, endorse the voucher, and submit it to his or her bank for deposit like any other check. This voucher system is shown schematically in Exhibit 2 on page 604.

Vendor Controls

In order to become WIC-authorized, a vendor had to sign a five-page agreement containing a total of 58 requirements for the proper acceptance of vouchers. Incorporated into the agreement was a sanction policy which described the method of disqualifying vendors, and itemized sanction points

EXHIBIT 2 WIC Voucher System

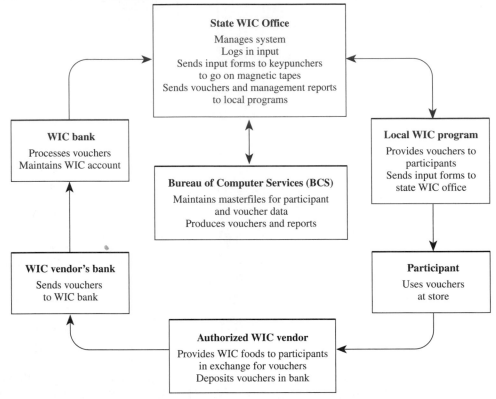

applicable for each type of violation. Point values ranged from 0 to 10, and accumulation of 10 or more points was a basis for disqualification.

The state agency and local programs shared the responsibility for monitoring vendors for compliance with WIC regulations. Local programs were authorized to perform on-site reviews of the business as well as to respond to participant complaints about vendor abuse. The state agency monitored vendors through visual screening of vouchers and through investigative "compliance buys," which were often initiated because of a suspected violation.

An important component of vendor monitoring was the local programs' education of participants in the proper use of WIC vouchers: certification that the correct price had been entered *before* countersigning the voucher, selection of only WIC-authorized foods, not using the voucher before the issuance date noted on the front, etc. A typical complaint from a vendor was that many of the redemption violations were due to participant abuse and that the local program was not doing an adequate job of preparing participants to use the program properly.

Sanctioning of vendors involved warnings, application of sanction points, denial of payment, disqualification, and recoupment of payment. Much of the sanctioning activity depended on the availability of WIC Voucher Monitors stationed at the bank for locating and screening either current or previously paid vouchers for abuse.

Voucher Processing

Vouchers were drawn on the WIC food account at the National Bank. Two part-time WIC Voucher Monitors worked in the space provided by the bank, and visually screened the vouchers for violations of the redemption procedure. Reasons for violations included missing or nonmatching signatures, missing or invalid vendor identification stamp, missing or invalid local WIC program stamp, submission after the expiration date, missing or invalid vendor endorsement, the price written in pencil, overcharging, and charging a fixed price for a voucher with combinations of foods.

The WIC Voucher Monitors screened approximately 12,000 to 15,000 vouchers a day. When a violation was found, the monitor recorded the serial number, vendor code, reason for rejection, and voucher price on both a purge sheet and a credit slip. The data were then given to the bank's bookkeeping department so that the payment could be removed from the list of checks paid on that day.

When the payment activity for the month was completed, the bank had 10 days to submit three magnetic tapes to the state agency. These tapes reflected vouchers paid, vouchers bounced, and vouchers remaining undistributed to participants that month. The contents of each tape are shown in Exhibit 3.

Information on the tapes was then reconciled against master files of vouchers issued. From this reconciliation, the WIC Program could obtain information about average voucher prices, value and proportion of vouchers bounced, and the cost of errors due to mismatches of the MICR (Magnetic Ink Character Recognition) data with voucher masterfile data. Exhibit 4 contains an excerpt from the National Bank's September monthly report.

Payment for some bounced vouchers could be arranged if the vouchers were submitted directly to the state agency. There were several reasons for exceptions of this sort, including instances where the price written on the voucher had been altered because of a cashier error or where the price of special infant formulas exceeded $20. In these cases, the WIC Unit's Vendor Compliance Assistant manually authorized the National Bank's Office of Government Services to pay whatever amount of the voucher was *undisputed* out of a separate reimbursement account. Vendors who thought their vouchers might be bounced inappropriately, and who wished to avoid bounced check fees, submitted their vouchers directly to the state agency, thereby bypassing their checking account. Additionally, vendors who thought a voucher *had been* bounced inappropriately, could resubmit it directly to the state agency.

When the contract for services was originally signed with National Bank, these manual authorizations were projected to be approximately 10 to 15 per

EXHIBIT 3 **Contents of Magnetic Tape Files**

Paid Vouchers File

An itemized listing of all food vouchers paid from the Food Voucher Payment Accounting during the month's transactions. Voucher serial number, amount paid, and date paid are listed for each item. Items are sorted by sequential serial number in ascending order. Standard information for bank number, account number, and transaction type are also included for each item. A trailer record is included at the end of the file, identifying the total number of items and total dollar amounts.

Bounced Vouchers File

An itemized listing of all food vouchers presented for payment and rejected (returned to the depositor) during the month's transactions. Voucher serial number, dollar amount, and date rejected are listed for each item. Items are sorted by sequential serial number in ascending order. Standard information for bank number, account number, and transaction type are also included for each item. A trailer record is included at the end of the file, identifying the total number of items and total dollar amount.

Undistributed Vouchers File

An itemized listing of items identified and processed as undistributed vouchers. The voucher serial number is listed for each item, and dollar amounts are zero filled. Standard information for bank number, account number, transaction type, and date processed are also included for each item. A trailer record is included at the end of the file, identifying the total number of items.

month. In recent months, the average monthly manual reimbursement activity had reached 300 authorizations, covering approximately 1,400 vouchers.

Copies of the authorization (or letter of denial) and the vouchers in question were filed by date of authorization. These payments and denials were not reconciled with the voucher masterfile, and data were neither tallied nor reported. The entire automated system is shown schematically in Exhibit 5.

Evaluation of the WIC Control System

In April, an external evaluation of the WIC computer system focused almost entirely on the voucher distribution system. Among other things, the evaluators noted that the system was antiquated and expensive, and that, while it supported minimum operational requirements, it was deficient in its provision of information for management purposes. The current system had been operational for nine years, whereas the expected life span of such systems was typically five years. Moreover, the inability of the bank to capture the vendor code for vouchers that were paid rendered impossible the timely gathering of vendor-specific payment data.

The result, according to the evaluators, was that vendor monitoring strategies were extraordinarily labor intensive. The evaluators noted the lack of reliable national data concerning retailer fraud, but cited case study estimates in other states of 5 to 15 percent of total food costs. A more conservative esti-

EXHIBIT 4   Summary of Activity by Voucher Code, Report–1

Voucher Status	June Vouchers	June Amount	July Vouchers	July Amount	August Vouchers	August Amount	September Vouchers	September Amount
Valid	241413	$1,845,561.57	261259	$2,001,459.21	229168	$1,762,605.24	248106	$1,907,695.52
Resubmitted and paid	000000	$ 0.00	000000	$ 0.00	000000	$ 0.00	000000	$ 0.00
Valid: 61-89 days	000257	$ 2,009.59	000245	$ 1,852.24	000283	$ 2,159.61	000492	$ 3,699.49
Expired	000024	$ 183.99	000047	$ 409.93	000046	$ 362.95	000092	$ 671.78
Future dated	001932	$ 16,207.37	001448	$ 12,268.84	001657	$ 13,731.17	001509	$ 12,605.41
Excessive amount	000006	$ 90,807.48	000005	$ 3,778.37	000003	$ 609.11	000003	$ 64.59
Subtotal	243632	$1,954,770.10	263004	$2,019,768.59	231157	$1,779,468.08	250202	$1,924,736.79
Cash error	001227	$ 10,127.51	001422	$ 11,580.49	001598	$ 13,606.05	001439	$ 11,876.78
Subtotal main acct	244859	$1,964,897.61	264426	$2,031,349.08	232755	$1,793,074.13	251641	$1,936,613.57
Reimbursement acct	000000	$ 0.00	000000	$ 0.00	000000	$ 0.00	000000	$ 0.00
Reimbursement error	000000	$ 0.00	000000	$ 0.00	000000	$ 0.00	000000	$ 0.00
Total paid	244859	$1,964,897.61	264426	$2,031,349.08	232755	$1,793,074.13	251641	$1,936,613.57
Bounced	001727	$ 13,273.11	003508	$ 27,283.66	004240	$ 34,264.53	003317	$ 25,605.70
Bounced error	000967	$ 7,478.19	000892	$ 6,695.57	000332	$ 2,767.34	000192	$ 1,520.01
Total used—not paid	002694	$ 20,751.30	004400	$ 33,979.23	004572	$ 37,031.87	003509	$ 27,125.71

EXHIBIT 5 WIC Automated System for Food Delivery

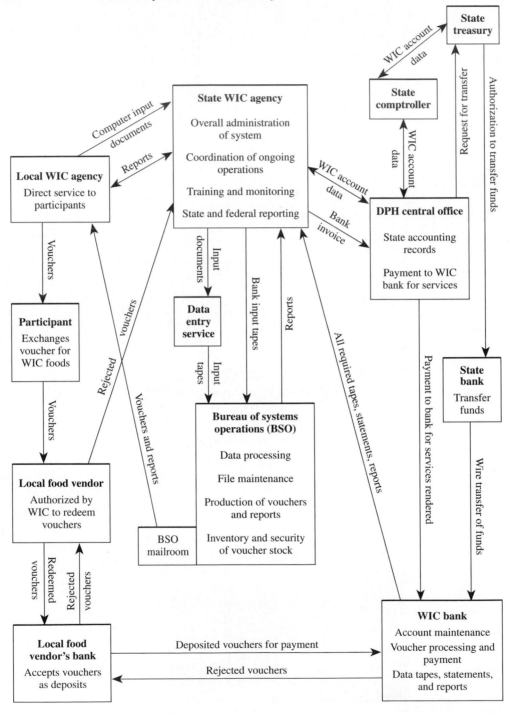

mate by a National Bank official put the statewide loss from fraud at a minimum of $1 million.

The report mentioned the voucher reimbursement system, indicating that a major problem of that system was the failure to include manual reimbursements in the monthly reconciliation report as items paid, thus violating the agency's financial integrity. It criticized the method of estimating food cost obligations outstanding, the lack of vendor identification in redemption data, the high labor-intensiveness of monitoring strategies, and the lack of meaningful vendor reports. The evaluators noted that the present system was functional only to the degree that it was supported by manual intervention and data manipulations, and warned of the increasing potential for system breakdowns. None of the recommendations specifically addressed reimbursement controls.

Dilemma at the Bank

Prompted by staff turnover the previous summer, Ms. Foster made several visits to the National Bank operations offices where the WIC vouchers were screened. While there, she discovered that, contrary to her instructions, the voucher monitors were using a less-than-100 percent method of review.

Asked by Foster to screen *all* vouchers for all possible violations, the monitors' workload doubled immediately. At the same time WIC management requested that monitors spot and pull vouchers submitted by certain suspect vendors. This job entailed identifying the payment date through the computer and microfiche, then retrieving the actual voucher from the storage area. Old vouchers were stored for up to three months in boxes labeled by the pay date, with approximately 3,500 in a box, filed sequentially by the last two digits of the serial number. Retrieval of one voucher could take up to an hour. The increased screening activity was adding to the workload.

Concurrent with additional work demands, the regular staff were taking vacations, uninspired temporary help was being trained, and supervision was changing. Over the course of the summer and fall months, the boxes of vouchers had piled up. One worker sympathized with the temps in admitting that the work was boring and difficult on the eyes. She noted that the slightest irregularity or required variation in the work was enough to slow them down to the point of getting further behind. One temp had complained of headaches and had joined the Army.

A bank official warned that the problem was exacerbated by an increase in the number of vouchers being processed, and that when the food budget was increased, the number of vouchers would increase still further, and WIC would fall even further behind in screening them.

Another bank official commented that WIC needed to figure out how it wanted to handle staffing, and speculated that perhaps it wouldn't be such a bad idea to make National Bank responsible for the screening and staffing. He suggested that with being responsible for screening, the bank would be better able to control its ability to deliver its monthly reports on time. Recognizing that a long-term plan was being shaped that would include the capture of vendor identification, he predicted that in the intervening two or more years, paralysis in problem solving might set in at WIC.

Ms. Foster summed up her view of the problem:

> There are ways to save money, but you have to spend money in order to save it. The resources are hard to get on a tight budget so that you can set up the systems to ultimately save the money, and also to draw the connections to be able to show that if we spend money here, we can save money there. I have to lobby for resources for such things, and it's difficult to show that there would be a savings. It takes time to get decisions made. And when it comes to hiring staff, the constraints of the state personnel system are enormous.

Questions

1. Prepare a process flow analysis for the voucher processing activity of the WIC Program. What problems, if any, does it reveal? What is the cost of these problems?

2. What other operational problems does the WIC Program have? What must it do well if it is to be successful?

3. What recommendations would you make to Ms. Foster?

Case 11–3

Haas School of Business*

> . . . The most serious finding of the audit confirmed that the HSB paid approximately $648,000 in unauthorized supplemental compensation to selected faculty members. [Of that total,] $323,000 represented additional salary to 17 faculty members for which no services were performed. . . .
>
> While the goal of the Haas School in terms of addressing an identified salary parity problem was honorable, the mechanism used was in violation of existing policy. . . . With respect to the Dean, we have agreed that he will step down on June 30, 1998. . . . Further, the campus is addressing audit recommendations to ensure policy compliance and to strengthen internal controls.
>
> > Letter from Chang-Lin Tien, Chancellor of the University of California-Berkeley, to Richard C. Atkinson, President of the University of California, reproduced in the December 11, 1996 California edition of *The Wall Street Journal.*

*Portions of this case were adapted with permission from the following article: Marc Lifsher, "Audit Finds Financial Irregularities at UC-Berkeley Business School," *The Wall Street Journal,* California Edition, December 11, 1996. Additional information from public documents was provided by Dean William Hasler of the Haas School of Business. Copyright © by David W. Young.

On December 11, 1996, the California edition of *The Wall Street Journal* contained an article by Marc Lifsher entitled "Audit Finds Financial Irregularities at UC-Berkeley Business School." The article was followed at 11:00 A.M. on the same day by an e-mail from William A. Hasler, the Dean of the Haas School, to the school's students, faculty, and staff. On December 12, the Public Relations Office of the University issued a statement concerning the audit. On December 16, the elected faculty representatives of the Haas School sent a letter to "Friends of the Haas School of Business." And on February 5, 1997, a Letter to the Editor from Chang-Lin Tien was published in the California edition of *The Wall Street Journal*. Excerpts from these documents follow:

Lifsher Article

The dean of the University of California-Berkeley's prestigious Haas School of Business violated university rules by funneling nearly $650,000 in unauthorized faculty pay through an executive-training program, according to a confidential internal audit.

The audit, which was obtained by *The Wall Street Journal,* found that some $323,000 in payments over a two-year period were used to boost salaries for 17 professors who didn't teach extra classes or perform any other special duties for their enhanced pay. An additional 18 faculty members received pay increases totaling $325,000 for providing loosely defined "program and curriculum development" services from the fall of 1993 through the fall of last year, the May 28 auditor's report to Berkeley Vice Chancellor Carol Christ shows.

In all, supplementary payments for which no extra work was performed averaged $17,950 per teacher. Checks to the faculty—who weren't identified in the report—were processed through a university extension program for the Berkeley Center for Executive Development, which offers evening courses for mid-career professionals.

The dean of the Haas School, William A. Hasler, wasn't accused of benefiting personally, and, after reviewing the matter, the Berkeley campus police declined to refer the case to the district attorney for possible criminal prosecution. The 55-year-old Mr. Hasler, former vice chairman and director of the accounting and management-consultant firm KPMG Peat Marwick, has run the school since 1991. He says he plans to step down in 1998.

Additional Excerpts from Mr. Lifsher's Story Follow

In Defense

In a May 22 letter to Vice Chancellor Christ in response to the audit, as well as in a subsequent interview, Dean Hasler defends his decision to raise faculty pay as a way to bolster Haas's stature and attract and retain topnotch professors inclined to leave for better-paying institutions such as Stanford and Harvard. He calls the dispute "an unhappy disagreement" that turned out fine in the end because the administration has approved a permanent salary increase for business-school faculty.

"We cannot sustain a great business school at Berkeley without a top, research-based business faculty," Mr. Hasler wrote in his May 22 letter, "and we cannot retain and recruit this type of faculty at a 26 percent discount from market." The extra payments, Mr. Hasler argued, allowed him to cut that pay gap to only 10 percent.

Still, outside ethics experts were sharply critical when told of what the audit report found the dean had done. They say his actions set a particularly poor example for Berkeley students who may be running major corporations someday.

'Patently Dishonest'

"The best way to teach ethics is by example," says John E. Fleming, professor emeritus of business ethics at the University of Southern California. "You can talk forever and people may or may not listen, but when the leader of a school acts unethically he is setting a very dangerous example."

Funneling funds through a series of irregular payroll accounts undermines the integrity of established financial-control systems, adds Michael Josephson, director of the Josephson Institute of Ethics, a Los Angeles-based nonprofit organization that provides training and consulting to private companies and government agencies.

"This work-around reasoning is just patently dishonest," Mr. Josephson says.

Of course, experts say, in the corporate world it's probably not all that uncommon to find managers moving money around between line items on a budget. So long as a manager meets his or her overall budget—and acts with the approval of higher-ups—it may be prudent to find extra cash in one spending category and move it over to a more pressing area to help make up for a shortfall.

But Dean Hasler's critics say that such a balancing act doesn't mesh with the centralized management needs of a large public university. And despite the dean's contention that his salary-enhancement plan was carried out with the knowledge and approval of his superiors, some on U.C.'s independent governing Board of Regents say they believe he acted on his own.

"What happened at the Haas School was very unfortunate," says Howard Leach, chairman of the board's Audit Committee. "I think Dean Hasler's intentions were good, but you can't have every dean making his own policy on salaries, and you can't have [payroll] records that are not accurately kept."

Such haphazard oversight, adds Regent Jess Bravin, a Berkeley law student, is typical of the university's lack of accountability during a series of recent financial scandals.

"Whatever the policies we have apply across the board," he says. "But we are currently under tremendous pressure to loosen the sort of minimum bounds of public accountability to allow this sort of swashbuckling approach to public administration. . . . Deans are allowed to cut whatever deals they can cut with private entities and move money around to make their enterprises as wealthy as possible."

Top versus Bottom

The Haas School's attitude, says Mr. Bravin, exemplifies the university's insistence on raising compensation for top administrators and professors while slashing pay for low-level teaching assistants and fighting off unionization efforts.

"They're doing everything possible to pay people at the top as much as they can by fudging rules and looking for every single income source," he says, "while at the same time, they're telling people at the bottom to enjoy their suffering because it's good for their development as scholars."

Mr. Josephson says that university officials deserve praise for uncovering the financial irregularities at Haas—the supplemental salary payments were stopped on March 1—but says that credit should be tempered by the administration's decision to keep the problems under wraps.

"They, in fact, dealt with the problem, but they are still not comfortable being accountable," he says.

Blow to Reputation?

Indeed, the reported mismanagement could well prove a blow to the Haas School's growing national reputation. In surveys, the institution consistently ranks among the top 20 business schools in the country. And in August 1995 it moved into a $55 million building endowed by the Haas family, which controls Levi Strauss & Co., the San Francisco apparel giant. Applicants to the master's program for 1996 jumped nearly 40 percent from the previous year.

The mishandling of funds at Haas, reported in September to the Audit Committee of the Board of Regents by University of California President Richard Atkinson, is the latest in a series of financial irregularities that have plagued the 10-campus U.C. system during the past two years. . . .

In his written response, Dean Hasler argued that his superiors had authorized "equity adjustments where faculty salaries were substantially behind demonstrated competitive levels."

But Berkeley Chancellor Chang-Lin Tien wrote to President Atkinson on Aug. 22 that, while Mr. Hasler "believed there to be an agreement with former campus management to use this approach to pay supplemental faculty payments," the "former campus officials cited by Dean Hasler have denied the existence of such an agreement.

In an interview, Vice Chancellor Christ says that while there was nothing wrong with giving salary increases, they must be approved by the central administration. "What the dean did was use his internal process, but he did not consult with me," she says.

Long-Established Rules

Ms. Christ and other university officials make clear that the dean broke long-established U.C. pay practices. "While the goal of the Haas School in terms of addressing an identified salary parity problem was honorable, the mechanism used was in violation of existing policy," Mr. Tien wrote.

Despite the violation, Mr. Tien noted, the 35 Haas faculty members who received the extra pay—more than half of Haas's total faculty of 63—haven't been required to return the money.

"The campus is persuaded that the faculty members accepted these payments in good faith, believing that such payments had received appropriate authorization," he wrote.

"With respect to the dean," he added, "we have agreed that he will step down on June 30, 1998."

Both Mr. Hasler and Ms. Christ maintain that the dean's departure date isn't linked to the supplementary-pay issue. Rather, Mr. Hasler says that seven years is a normal tenure for someone in his position and, now that the pay increase has been approved, he feels he has accomplished his goal of making the Haas School "a crown jewel of U.C."

Though the audit results were kept confidential, they have raised red flags in the university president's office. In a letter to the Board of Regents, Mr. Atkinson wrote that the university is "taking steps" to make sure that the problems at Haas "do not represent problems of a similar nature at other campus locations."

"In addition," he wrote, "the appropriate offices . . . are reviewing the sufficiency of policy guidance in regard to issues raised, as well as the state of awareness of existing policy."

The staff payments were the most serious but not the only violation of university policies and procedures found by the May 28 audit and a June 19 follow-up. Auditors identified five instances in which faculty, teaching extension courses at the Berkeley Center for Executive Development, were paid in excess of a systemwide cap of 20 percent over their base salary. In his response, Dean Hasler maintained that he understood that the 20-percent limit is only a general guideline to be used at administrators' discretion. . . .

Meanwhile, the increase in business-faculty pay, if not linked to overall instructor raises, could exacerbate an already growing chasm between what the University of California now pays its business and engineering professors and what it pays all other teachers. According to the state's California Post-secondary Education Commission, business and engineering professors currently make 9.8 percent to 31.6 percent more than their colleagues in other departments.

In the end, the threat that teachers will flee Haas and other U.C. schools because of low pay may be overblown, suggests Paul Warren, director of the education unit at the nonpartisan Legislative Analyst's Office in Sacramento.

"U.C. is the best-funded public university in the country," says Mr. Warren. "We may be losing some people to big private schools, but it can't be in great numbers."

Dean Hasler's E-Mail

Today's California edition of *The Wall Street Journal* contains an unfortunate and largely inaccurate article about Haas School efforts to adequately compensate its key scholars and teachers for critical faculty recruitment and retention reasons. The article is correct in its discussion of the average 26 percent shortfall in salaries vs. peer business schools and the general approach used to attempt to close this gap.

It incorrectly implies that the additional compensation was made without campus authorization. At the time of the referenced audit, the school very strongly asserted that they were authorized and paid openly, but subsequently agreed to discontinue them in return for their inclusion in regular salary. The faculty was not asked to return any of the compensation payments, and no one was sanctioned. Certainly my own decision to step down in 1998 was made entirely separately from this disagreement and its successful resolution.

With the campus, we are preparing appropriate press releases and communications to the friends and alumni of the Haas School to attempt to mitigate any negative reaction. As to the article's recommendation that this serve as "an ethics case study," I plan to offer it and myself up for a case discussion in our ethics course. I am confident that the students in the course will find that the administration and faculty acted honorably, in good faith and ethically. More importantly, perhaps, we all need further education in press relations!

Public Relations Statement

The campus recently completed an internal audit at the Haas School of Business on the UC Berkeley campus, which focused on the payment of salary supplements to a number of faculty for the period from May 1993 to February 1996.

The audit determined that some of the salary supplements were in violation of university policies. The report of the audit was presented to the UC Regents in September. The Haas School response disagreeing with these findings was appended to the audit report. The issue has subsequently been resolved to the satisfaction of the campus and the Haas School.

William Hasler, Dean of the Haas School of Business, terminated all payment of these salary supplements on March 1, 1996 even before the audit was finished. Hasler had initiated this salary supplement program as an attempt to deal with the fact that the School's faculty salaries were lagging 20 to 30 percent behind comparison institutions.

The funds used for the salary payments were generated by the Haas School of Business from non-state sources. The funds were paid through the Berkeley Center for Executive Development, which is a joint program between the Haas School of Business and University Extension.

The campus did not seek recovery of the supplements in question because the Haas School of Business faculty members accepted these payments in good faith. They believed that these payments had been approved through the proper channels.

Furthermore, Dean Hasler also acted in good faith, believing that he had received permission from a prior administrator to deal with the faculty compensation parity issue.

The Vice Chancellor and Provost Carol T. Christ said the campus acknowledged that, in fact, the faculty salaries were substantially lower than those in comparable institutions. She chaired a task force that developed a plan to address those inequities. Under the new plan, the faculty salaries will be adjusted after appropriate review and through established university procedures.

Chancellor Chang-Lin Tien added that my implication that Hasler's notification of his intention to step down in 1998 after seven years of service was motivated by or linked to this audit is incorrect. It was a decision reached by the Dean and accepted by Chancellor Chang-Lin Tien based on normal career succession planning.

The complete audit can be acquired from the Public Information Office at UC Berkeley.

Letter from Elected Faculty Representatives

Dear Friends of the Haas School of Business:

A recent *Wall Street Journal* article (California section) implied that Dean Hasler had behaved unethically with regard to the payment of supplemental compensation to some members of the faculty. As elected representatives of the faculty, we want you to know that the faculty has full faith in Bill Hasler. From our many dealings with him, we know him to be an honorable person. As the campus itself made clear in its press release on the matter, Bill acted in good faith in making these payments, believing that he had received campus permission to do so to retain and recruit outstanding faculty for Haas. Moreover, despite the article's allusions to the contrary, Bill was not acting alone in this. The general policy of salary supplements was approved at an open meeting of the faculty and a specific policy governing how the payments were to be made was developed by a faculty committee. Nor was there any secrecy to this. There was never any instruction, nor suggestion that we keep quiet about this. Indeed, to the contrary, explicit mention of the policy was made in documents such as recruitment letters. Dark hints of scandal unhappily sell more newspapers than reporting on an unfortunate misunderstanding between the Dean and central campus administrators. Yet, in the end, that is all there is to the story.

By any metric, Bill has done a wonderful job here at Haas. He oversaw the building of our magnificent new home. In various ways, he has greatly improved the quality of education that we provide—to which our recent jump up in the *Business Week* rankings of MBA programs and our number one ranking for our undergraduate program attest. Staff and faculty morale is high. The School and, indeed, the campus as a whole owe Bill a giant debt of gratitude. All of which makes this unfair attack so upsetting to those of us who know Bill and have seen what he has accomplished here.

We believe that you can remain proud of your association with Haas and confident in its administration's ethics and abilities. With your continued support, we can easily overcome this minor setback, as we jointly work to further enhance the world class reputation of the Haas School of Business.

Sincerely,

Jennifer Chatman, Member of the Policy & Planning Committee and Associate Professor of Business

Benjamin E. Hermalin, Member of the Policy & Planning Committee and the Harold Furst Associate Professor of Management Philosophy & Values

Richard Lyons, Chair of the Policy & Planning Committee and Associate Professor of Business

Matthew Spiegel, Member of the Policy & Planning Committee and Associate Professor of Business

Nancy E. Wallace, Member of the Policy & Planning Committee and Associate Professor of Business

Chang-Lin Tien Letter to the Editor

Contrary to the implication in your Dec. 11 article "Audit Finds Financial Irregularities at UC-Berkeley Business School," Dean William Hasler acted in good faith, believing that he had received permission from a prior campus administrator to deal with the faculty compensation-parity issue.

Also, any implication that the dean's decision to step down in 1998 after seven years of service was motivated by or linked to this audit is incorrect. This was a decision reached by the dean and accepted by me based on normal career and succession planning.

Finally, the campus acknowledges that, in fact, business-school faculty salaries are substantially lower than those in comparable institutions. A UC Berkeley task force has developed a plan to address these inequities, and under that business plan faculty salaries will be adjusted after appropriate review and through established university procedures.

> Chancellor
> University of California-Berkeley
> Berkeley

Dean Hasler's Reflections

On October 31, 1997, in reflecting on the issues, Dean Hasler wrote:

The Haas School faculty and administration *did* act in good faith, believing we had campus authorization to proceed with the supplemental faculty payments. Our response to the audit report clearly documented the openness and good faith in the process in four ways:

- The Haas School faculty debated and voted on the School review process to be used for these payments during an open department meeting attended not only by Haas faculty but also faculty with joint appointments in other schools and departments.
- The supplemental payments were processed openly through the correct channel for any such authorized payments (i.e., University Extension, a campus unit that is separate from the Haas School and is under the supervision of central campus administration).
- Faculty receiving the payments got letters detailing the reason and mechanisms for the payment and were never in any way asked or expected to keep them confidential.
- The supplemental payments were openly referred to by Haas administrators and faculty at a number of campus forums over many months.

How then could the issue of lack of campus authorization become the subject of any audit? I believe we all came to realize that there was a genuine misunderstanding and miscommunication. In addition, one cannot overlook the fact that this question of adequate faculty compensation at Haas vs. its peer group relative to Haas compensation vs. internal campus compensation levels was an intensely debated and highly political one on campus.

In any case, the reason no one was censured by the audit report and the faculty was allowed to retain the payments was that all parties agreed that the misunderstanding was not intentional and that everyone had acted in good faith. Certainly my decision to step down at the end of seven years as dean was not linked to the audit as clearly stated in the Chancellor's subsequent letter to the editor. Could anyone really imagine that my giving two years and four months notice of my intention to step down as dean was the result of a sanction for actions such as those inaccurately portrayed by the *Journal?*

Given the clear campus position that the issue was not as portrayed by the *Journal,* other media following up on the *Journal* article generally provided more balanced coverage because they took the time to interview campus personnel and consider facts presented in opposition to the *Journal* theory of unethical behavior. Unfortunately, the *Journal* reporter did not do these things. He only called Vice Chancellor Christ and myself the evening of his deadline.

Questions

1. Do you agree with Dean Hasler's decision?

2. Do you agree with the reaction of Professor Fleming, Mr. Josephson, Mr. Leach, and Mr. Branin? How would you respond to each of them?

3. What is your assessment of the manner in which the University's administration dealt with this situation?

# Chapter 2

Measurement of Output

No single overall measure of the performance of a nonprofit organization is analogous to the profit measure in a for-profit company. The goals of non profit organizations arc usually complex and often intangible. The outputs of such organizations frequently arc difficult or impossible to measure.

In general, output information is needed for two purposes: (1) to measure efficiency, which is the ratio of outputs to inputs (i.e., expenses), and (2) to measure effectiveness, which is the extent to which actual output corresponds to the organization's goals and objectives. In a for-profit organization, gross margin or net income are useful measures for both these purposes. In a nonprofit organization, no such monetary measure exists because, as we discussed in Chapter 2, revenues do not approximate true output as they may in a for-profit company. This chapter looks at alternative ways of measuring output in nonprofit organizations.

In the absence of a profit measure, analyses of efficiency and effectiveness require adequate substitute measures of output. Despite the importance of devising such alternatives, current nonprofit management control systems tend to be deficient in this respect. Few nonprofits have specific, written criteria for measuring their effectiveness.

The problem of measuring output in nonmonetary terms is not unique to nonprofit organizations. The same problem exists in responsibility centers in for-profit organizations in which discretionary costs predominate (e.g., research, law, personnel). Conversely, the output of many individual activities in nonprofit organizations can be measured as readily as can that of corresponding activities in for-profit ones (e.g., food service, vehicle maintenance, clerical work).

| Example | A library estimated that it should take two minutes to reshelve a book (including an allowance for personal time). One hundred books were replaced by a staff person who took four hours to complete the task. |

The output (100 books replaced) multiplied by the standard time per book (2 minutes) gave a total expected time of 200 minutes, or 3.3 hours (200 ÷ 60 minutes per hour). This can be compared with the actual total of four hours to measure productivity. This sort of analysis could be performed in a library of any sort, whether in a for-profit company or a city government.

Basic Measurement Categories

Many different terms are used to classify output measures according to what they purport to measure. For our purposes, there are three: social indicators, results measures, and process measures.

Social Indicators

A social indicator is a broad measure of output that reflects the impact of an organization's work on society at large. Unfortunately, few social indicators can be related to the work of a single organization because in almost all cases they are affected by forces other than those of the organization being measured. The crime rate in a city may reflect the activities of the police department and the court system, but it is also affected by unemployment, housing conditions, and other factors unrelated to the effectiveness of these organizations. Similarly, life expectancy (or its converse, mortality) is partly influenced by the quality of health care, but it is also affected by nutrition, environment, heredity, and other factors.

Example　　The Peace Corps sponsored an attempt to measure the effectiveness of its program in Peru, using measures that purported to show the change in the well-being of Peruvians during a two-year period. Since there was no plausible way of relating the measures of well-being to the efforts of Peace Corps workers, the effort to measure output was probably a waste of time and money.

Valid social indicators are difficult to collect. They also are difficult to use properly because there ordinarily is no demonstrable cause-and-effect relationship between what an organization does and the change in a social indicator. Likewise, proxy indicators for intangible factors, such as percentage of registered citizens voting as an indicator of citizenship, or crime and disturbance statistics as an indicator of social unrest, may be collected fairly easily, but frequently are of limited reliability. Indeed, any social indicator that can be collected fairly easily is likely to be of dubious validity.

In short, social indicators are nebulous, difficult to obtain on a current basis, little affected by an organization's current programmatic efforts, and much affected by external forces. As a result, they are, at best, a rough indication of what an organization has accomplished, and therefore are of limited usefulness for management control purposes.

Social indicators can be useful in strategic planning, however, in that they can help guide senior management's decisions about the overall directions the organization should take. Because of this, social indicators are often stated in broad terms (e.g., "the expectation of healthy life free of serious disability and institutionalization"). For management control purposes, output objectives need to be expressed in more specific, preferably measurable, terms (e.g., infant mortality rates).

Example

The American Cancer Society, (ACS) has avoided this problem by ignoring it. That is, the ACS allocates its resources to activities that it knows have an impact on reducing morbidity and mortality: screening, education, and advocacy. One of its goals is a 50 percent reduction in cancer mortality rates and a 25 percent reduction in overall cancer incidence by 2015. It knows that other organizations will contribute to this societal goal but has decided that it nevertheless needs the goal as a rallying point for its programs.[1]

The Boy Scouts of America (BSA) commissioned a large-scale outcome survey to establish that "Scouting works," that is, that Boy Scouts were "more successful and more responsible citizens than people who had not been Scouts." Regardless of the underlying causality (e.g., that Scouts' families both encouraged their sons to join Scouting and helped them become more successful and more responsible citizens), the BSA no longer worried about its societal impact. It was able to shift its focus to a results measure: the percentage of eligible youth participating in Scouting.[2]

Results Measures

Results measures attempt to express output in terms that are related to an organization's objectives. As such, they tend to avoid many of the difficulties inherent in social indicators. Ideally, objectives are stated in measurable terms, and output measures are stated in these same terms. When it is not feasible to express objectives in measurable terms, as is often the case, the results measure represents the closest feasible way management has to both specify the objectives and measure the organization's progress toward them.

Properly designed, a results measure relates to an organization's success in attaining its goals. If the organization is client oriented, its results measures should relate to what it did for its clients. Organizations that render services to a class of clients, such as alcoholics or unemployed persons, often measure output in terms of results for the whole class or a target group.

---

[1] John C. Sawhill and David Williamson, "Mission Impossible: Measuring Success in Nonprofit Organizations," *Nonprofit Management and Leadership,* Spring 2001.
[2] Ibid.

Example

Executive Order 12862, "Setting Customer Service Standards," requires federal agencies to be customer driven with "best in the business" customer service standards. Under this executive order, federal agencies must, among other things, determine their service standards and measure performance against them. Some examples of these standards are serving customers within 10 minutes of a scheduled appointment time (Social Security Administration), informing individuals of their eligibility for food stamps within 30 days of the date of an application (Department of Agriculture Food Stamp Program), delivering first class mail anywhere in the United States within three days, and local first class mail overnight (U.S. Postal Service), and responding to telephone or written requests within five business days (The Department of Interior's Information Access Centers).[3]

Although results measures usually are easier to collect and use than social indicators, they still can pose difficulties. Indeed, the closer a results measure comes to indicating an organization's impact on society, the more difficult it is to establish valid cause and effect relationships.

Example

A program to rehabilitate alcoholics might measure results in terms of either the percent of enrollees successfully completing the program or the rate of recidivism. While the latter is a more accurate results measure, it is complicated by three factors: (1) the choice of an appropriate time period, (2) the difficulty of identifying clients who resume drinking but do not notify the program of this fact, and (3) the influence of forces outside the organization's control on an individual's decision to resume drinking. The third complication is similar to a complication associated with social indicators.

Process Measures

A process measure (also called a *productivity* measure) relates to an activity carried on by the organization. Examples are the number of livestock inspected in a week, the number of lines typed in an hour, the number of requisitions filled in a month, or the number of purchase orders written in a day. The essential difference between a results measure and a process measure is that the former *is ends oriented,* while the latter is *means oriented* (the terms *performance oriented* and *work oriented* are other names for the same distinction).

A process measure relates to what a responsibility center or an individual does to help an organization achieve its objectives. Thus, process measures help managers gauge efficiency. Since they do not measure effectiveness, however, they ordinarily are only remotely related to the organization's goals and objectives. Because of this, senior management should be careful not to

---

[3]James J. Kline, "Local Government Outcome Based Performance Measures and Customer Service Standards: Has Their Time Come?" *The Government Accountants Journal,* Winter 1997.

put too much emphasis on process measures, especially if they are unrelated or only tenuously related to results measures.

Example

A U.S. Air Force Command measured performance of its squadrons by the number of hours flown, which is a process measure. As a consequence, squadrons sometimes would build up a record of performance simply by flying for many hours in large circles around a base, without any real accomplishments.

Need for Cause-and-Effect Relationships

In developing process measures, management must be careful to assure itself of a cause-and-effect relationship between the processes it wants employees to engage in, and the results it wants to accomplish. There frequently is an implicit assumption that a responsibility center's work helps the organization achieve its objectives, but this is not always the case.

Example

In an air pollution program, the change in the amount of ozone in the atmosphere is a results measure, while the number of inspections made of possible violators is a process measure. The implication of a causal relationship between the number of inspections made and the amount of air pollution may or may not be valid.

Process measures are most useful in the measurement of current, short-run performance, and are particularly helpful in the control of lower level responsibility centers. They are the easiest type of output measure to interpret, presumably because there is a close causal relationship between them and inputs. Indeed, for those activities whose costs are related to inputs, process measures can be useful in constructing relevant parts of a budget.

Example

In a department of public health, restaurant inspections are considered an important process measure. If each restaurant inspection (including travel time, office time, and other factors) should take approximately one hour and 15 minutes (a measure of efficiency), and there are 10,000 restaurant inspections to be made, there is a need for 12,500 inspector hours (10,000 restaurants × 1.25 hours per restaurant). This can be converted into the number of inspectors needed, which can be multiplied by the average inspector compensation to arrive at a budget.

Development of Standards

As the above example suggests, process measures require (*a*) identification of the activities of a person or a responsibility center, and (*b*) development of a *unit standard*. A unit standard is the amount of time needed to complete a single activity. For instance, in the above example, a unit standard is the amount of time needed to inspect a single restaurant. When the total activity count is multiplied by the unit standard, the resulting amount can be compared with the actual time spent, and can be used to evaluate performance.

Example

In the above example, if 3,000 restaurants were actually inspected during a given period of time, the 3,000 could be multiplied by the unit standard of 1.25 hours to give a total of 3,750 hours. This amount could be compared with the actual number of inspector hours used during the same period to obtain a measure of the efficiency of the inspectors. For example, if the inspectors did the job in 3,500 hours, they would be considered more efficient than anticipated.

In an office or clerical setting, there are three approaches to arriving at unit standards:

1. Using time standards for individual office operations developed by standard-setting organizations.

2. Having employees keep detailed records of the time taken to perform specific activities, and using averages of these records.

3. Having external observers record the time required to perform activities and the amount of idle time, according to a random plan of observations, and using averages of these records. (This procedure is called *work sampling.*)

Example

The National Institutes of Health established productivity measurement systems for many of its support activities. One is the Accounts Payable section, whose function was to examine about 30,000 vouchers monthly to determine whether they were a proper basis for payment.

Various types of vouchers required different amounts of examination time, and standard times were established by engineering studies. For convenience in calculating, these unit standards were expressed as *equivalent units.* The simplest voucher, a transportation request, had a standard time of 7.37 minutes, and this was designated as one equivalent unit. Equivalent units for the 14 other types of documents were determined based on the ratio of their standard time to 7.37. For example, a purchase order accompanied by a record of the call (ROC) had a standard time of 16.68 minutes, which was 2.3 standard units (16.68 ÷ 7.37).

Exhibit 12–1 shows how these measures were used to calculate one person's productivity for a four-week period. Employee F worked 125 productive hours during this period and produced 2,163 equivalent units or 17.31 per productive hour. The standard per productive hour was 8.14 units (60 minutes ÷ 7.37). Employee F therefore performed at 213 percent of standard.[4]

Definitional Problems

Productivity *should* mean output per unit of input. The inputs in the ratio should include labor, energy, equipment, and all the other resources used to

---

[4]From *Measuring Productivity in Accounting and Finance Offices* (Washington, DC: Joint Financial Management Improvement Program, September 1981), pp. 4–12.

EXHIBIT 12–1
Productivity
Calculation

Name: Team 02   Employee: F
Workstation: 15
Period Reported: June 2 to June 28

Type of Vouchers Processed	Equivalent Units	Invoices Quantity	Processed Equivalent Units
Telephone charge order	1.20	170	204.00
Purchase order—No ROC	2.10	197	413.70
Purchase order—ROC	2.30	237	545.10
Research contract	2.80	2	5.60
Contract—ROC	2.30	341	784.30
Contract—No ROC	2.20	51	112.20
Library MOD	2.10	47	98.70
Total invoices processed		1,045	2,163.60

	Hours
Total available hours	160
Less annual leave	
Less sick leave	8
Less others	
Total regular hours	152
Plus overtime hours	40
Total hours worked	192
Less nonproductive hours	67
Total productive hours	125
Equivalent units produced per productive hour (2,163.60 ÷ 125)	17.31
Performance rating (17.31 ÷ 8.14)	213%
Total treasury rejections charged to the individual	2

achieve the output. In practice, however, productivity usually has a much narrower definition. Specifically, because labor is the critical resource in most nonprofits, the term usually means output per person-hour or person-year. However, an increase in output per person-hour is equivalent to an increase in efficiency *only if* all input factors other than personnel remain constant.

Terminology Problems

Not all writers use the terms in the same way we have. In the work done by the Governmental Accounting Standards Board (GASB) to develop service effort and accomplishment (SEA) measures, a slightly different set of terms is used from what we have described above. The overall thrust is the same, however. The GASB distinguishes among inputs, outputs, and outcomes. Inputs are expenditures, outputs are what we call process measures (e.g., number of visits per month in a clinic, number of student-days in a school), and outcomes are what we call results measures (e.g., infant mortality rates in a clinic, academic test scores in a school). The GASB's work also measures efficiency as a cost per unit (e.g., cost per immunization in a clinic, average cost per student-day in a school). Efficiency measures are computed for both outputs and outcomes. Exhibit 12–2 shows these measures for public health agencies. Several of the readings at the end of this chapter refer to publications emerging from the GASB's efforts.[5]

Example

For many years, The Nature Conservancy, a nonprofit organization dedicated to conserving biodiversity by protecting the lands and waters that rare species need to survive, used two measures of success: bucks and acres. Bucks referred to total revenue and its annual growth rate; acres referred to referred to acres under protection in the Untied States. Despite growth in both measures, species extinction continued to grow at alarming rates. Even endangered species that had once lived on the acreage under the Conservancy's control had, over time, vanished from its properties.

As a result, the Conservancy began to develop new performance measures. Its first redesign resulted in a list of 98 separate measures, which posed insurmountable problems in both record-keeping and priority selection. The Conservancy then more clearly articulated its vision, goals, strategies, and programs, so that it could develop measures appropriate to its focus. The final result was a "family of measures" that focused on three areas: impact, activity, and capacity. Impact measures focused on the organization's mission; activity measures focused on goals and strategies; and capacity measures were oriented toward obtaining the required resources. These categories are quite similar to social indicators, results indicators, and process measures.[6]

Measurement Problems

Beyond problems with definition and terminology, there also are problems occasionally in reaching agreement on the adequacy of a measure. That is, whether the measurement device actually gives useful information on the item in question.

Example

One study has questioned the Governmental Accounting Standard Board's (GASB) measures of efficiency in education.[7] Using a technique called "data envelopment analysis" (DEA) as the "gold standard," the study compared the GASB's measures to relative efficiency as determined through the use of DEA. The study concluded that the GASB's measures may be unable to provide reliable information for distinguishing between relatively efficient and inefficient school districts.[8]

[5]For additional details, see Vivian L. Carpenter, "Improving Accountability: Evaluating the Performance of Public Health Agencies," *Association of Government Accountants Journal,* Fall Quarter 1990. Carpenter considers the usefulness of GASB's recommended performance indicators for assessing the performance of public health agencies.
[6]John C. Sawhill and David Williamson, "Mission Impossible: Measuring Success in Nonprofit Organizations," *Nonprofit Management and Leadership,* Spring 2001.
[7]See Governmental Accounting Standards Board, *Concepts Statement No. 2,* "Service Efforts and Accomplishments," 1994.
[8]Frank Engert, "The Reporting of School District Efficiency: The Adequacy of Ratio Measures," *Public Budgeting and Financial Management,* Summer 1996. For a discussion of DEA, see R. Silkman (ed.), *Measuring Efficiency: An Assessment of Data Envelopment Analysis, New Directions for Program Evaluation* (San Francisco: Jossey-Bass, 1986).

EXHIBIT 12–2 Recommended SEA Measures for Public Health Agencies

Indicator	Rationale for Selecting Indicator
Maternal and Child Health (MCH) Care	
Inputs:	
Expenditures (may be broken out by program or activity) in current and constant dollars	Measure of resources used to provide services.
Output:	
Number of clients admitted to MCH program	
Number of clinic visits per month	Widely reported measures that provide an
Number of prenatal and postnatal mothers contacted	indication of MCH program outputs.
Outcome:	
Infant mortality rate.	
Low-birth-weight rates	
Teenage pregnancy rate	Widely accepted measures used by public health
Rate of lead poisoning cases	officials to measure MCH program outcomes.
Reported cases of preventable diseases in children. . .	
Number of clients authorized to be served and actually served by WIC program	
Percentage of low-birth-weight babies in target population.	Widely reported measures by MCH program to provide indicators of the accomplishment of
Projected low-birth-weight births prevented	short-term MCH program objectives.
Projected infant deaths prevented.	
Cases of measles prevented.	
Efficiency:	
Cost per immunization	Indication of the agency's efficiency in purchasing immunizations.
Cost of WIC supplements per unit.	Indication of the agency's efficiency in purchasing WIC supplements.
Number of premature births/number of patients	Indication of the agency's efficiency in reducing premature births.
Projected health care costs saved through routine checkups/costs of routine checkups.	Indication of the agency's efficiency in reducing future health care costs.

Source: Governmental Accounting Standards Board.

Linkages among Measures

Some organizations have had success in linking process measures to results measures, and even in suggesting a link between results measures and social indicators. For reasons discussed earlier, the latter linkage is difficult to identify with any certainty, but the former is quite feasible. Specifically, for many activities, once an organization has determined its objectives, management can specify the corresponding results measures, and can link those measures to the process measures required to achieve them. The process measures also can be linked to the productivity of the organization's employees. Then, if objectives are not achieved, or if the cost of achieving certain objectives is higher than anticipated, the measurement system can help to pinpoint the reasons.

Example

A social service agency undertook a special program to operate a group home for delinquent adolescent girls. In an effort to measure the program's success, the agency worked with each girl entering the program to determine: *(a)* vocational and living goals, *(b)* related objectives for each goal, and *(c)* service needs for each objective. For example, if a girl wished to become a beautician, this was established as a vocational goal. The related objectives might have been obtaining a high school diploma, completing beauticians' school, improving the girl's relationships with adults, and developing her ability to manage personal finances. The associated service needs might then be 10 hours per week of tutoring, tuition for beauticians' school, three hours a week of psychotherapy, structured summer employment in a job entailing interaction with adults, and so forth.

The entire structure of goals, objectives, and service needs was then time phased, and the progress of each girl was assessed every three months. During the quarterly assessments, program managers asked the following questions:

1. Were service needs delivered as anticipated? If not, what changes were made and why?
2. Were the service needs delivered at the cost anticipated? If not, why not?
3. If an objective was scheduled to be accomplished, was it? If not, why not? Was it because designated service needs were not delivered, because needed services were not designated as such, or for some other reason?
4. If the objective was accomplished, did it have its anticipated effect? If not, why not?
5. Do any new objectives need to be established?
6. Is the goal still desired by the girl, and is it realistically attainable? If not, what new goal, objectives, and service needs are required?

Over several years, the program was able to develop a results measure that focused on the target population: percent of girls who achieved their goal. In addition, managers developed a number of process measures, such as percent of objectives accomplished, percent of services delivered as anticipated, and actual expenditures per girl as compared to budget.

In some instances, linkages are not always easy to establish. As a result, the connection between process and results measures can become blurred.

Example

For its field collection activities, the IRS identified four process measures: (1) total time taxpayer cases are open, (2) percent of cases resolved, (3) compliance contracts completed, and (4) percent of seizures sold without filing bankruptcy. Its results measures included (1) total dollars collected, (2) taxpayer delinquent accounts closed with full payment, and (3) percent of delinquent returns incurred.[9] Although the distinction between process and results measures seems to have been clearly delineated, there does not seem to be a well-established causal linkage between the two.

In other instances, results measures and process measures can become confused:

Example

Senior managers at the Department of Labor were required to develop performance goals for the upcoming year. As part of this effort, the Occupational Safety and Health Administration (OSHA) claimed that it was moving beyond its traditional process measures, such as number of workplace inspections, to goals like revising recognition and reward systems for employees and introducing an e-mail system to enhance communication.[10] Neither of these goals would seem to be a results measure, however; indeed, both would appear to be a different sort of process measure than had been used previously.

Clearly, in both of the above situations, it would have been helpful if the organizations had given some greater thought to (*a*) the distinction between process and results measures, and (*b*) the causal linkages between the two.

Issues in Selecting Output Measures

In selecting output measures, senior management makes several choices, all of which affect the kind of output information that managers will see, and consequently how they and others will view the effectiveness and efficiency of the organization. It therefore is important for senior management to think through these choices carefully.

Subjective versus Objective

An output measure may result from the subjective judgment of a person or a group of persons, or it may be derived from data that (unless consciously manipulated) are not dependent on human judgment. In many instances, a judgment made by a qualified person can be a better measure of the quality of performance than any objective measure. This is because humans incorporate the effects of circumstances and nuances of performance into their judgment. No set of objective measures can take all of these factors into account.

Example

Hospitals are usually reluctant to measure the performance of physicians by any means other than peer review. Professors also prefer peer review judgments but will increasingly accept ratings made by students. Many

[9]John B. MacArthur, "Cost Management at the IRS," *Management Accounting,* November 1996.
[10]Bruce G. Posner, "Sowing the Seeds of Change at the Department of Labor," *Harvard Business Review,* May–June 1994.

will not accept the number of students electing a course or the number of articles published as valid measures of performance, however.

On the other hand, subjective judgments necessarily depend on the person making the judgment, and thus may be affected by the prejudices, attitudes, and even the person's emotional and physical state at the time the judgment is formed. Objective measures, if properly obtained, do not have these defects. Ideally, an organization's output measures should include both.

Quantitative versus Nonquantitative

Information in a measurement system is usually quantitative so that it can be summarized and compared. Even some subjective information can be measured quantitatively. However, nonquantitative information also can be valuable in some instances.

Examples

Subjective Judgments Expressed in Quantitative Terms. Grades in schools, even though numerical, are an expression of the instructor's judgment as to where a student's performance is located along some scale. Performance in figure skating contests, gymnastics, and certain other athletic events is measured by the subjective judgments of the judges; however, the performer is ranked along a numerical scale by each judge, and these ranks are then averaged to give a quantitative measure.

Subjective Judgments Expressed in Nonquantitative Terms. Most case files in a social service agency contain narrative statements of the social workers' assessments of clients. In many instances, these statements contain judgments about the kind of progress the client is making. While these statements frequently do a good job of measuring results of each case, they ordinarily cannot be summarized and reported to management in a quantitative way. Unless it reviews each case file, which is an impossible task, senior management has considerable difficulty measuring overall performance of the agency's social work professionals.

Discrete versus Scalar

A measure of performance may be either discrete, that is, a dichotomy ("satisfactory/unsatisfactory" or "go-no-go"), or it may be measured along a scale. For example, to measure performance of a reading program in a school, a target could be established, such as "80 percent of students should read at or above grade level on a standardized test." If the measure were discrete, any performance of 80 percent or higher would be counted as success, and any performance below 80 percent would be counted as failure. If the measure were scalar, the percentage of students reading at each grade level on a standardized test would be used as the measure of output.

In general, scalar measures are preferable to discrete ones. However, there are many situations where discrete measures are appropriate. For example, most colleges do not measure how close their applicants came to being admitted; they simply use a discrete measure: x percent of all applicants met the admission criteria.

Actual versus Surrogate Measures

Whenever actual output can be measured, an organization should do so. If actual output cannot be measured, a surrogate measure may be used instead. In this case, the surrogate measure should be closely related to an objective. By definition, however, a surrogate does not correspond exactly to an objective, and managers should keep this limitation in mind. If this limitation is not recognized, the organization may focus too much attention on the surrogate, which may be dysfunctional. Achieving the surrogate should not be permitted to become more important than achieving the objective.

Example

A city used "number of complaints" as a surrogate measure for the performance of the agency that managed low-cost rental housing units. It was later discovered that after this measure was introduced, the agency put considerable pressure on tenants not to make complaints. This made performance, as measured by the surrogate, appear to improve, whereas service to tenants actually had deteriorated.

When "effectiveness" of a Job Corps training program was being calculated by the contractor, "completions" were the mark of success; "dropouts" were the failures. When the latter appeared to be on the increase, "certificates of completion" were issued every other Saturday instead of the diploma originally given at the end of six months. Immediately, the number of completions rose, and the proportion of dropouts declined. As a result, the effectiveness of the enterprise was assured, and so was its continued funding.

The success of some U.S. Department of Labor employment programs was measured by the proportion of people placed in jobs. This led to the practice known as *cream skimming:* accepting as job applicants the cream of the unemployed (persons temporarily unemployed and with a high probability of being placed).

Performance of Veterans Administration hospitals was measured in part by the percentage of beds occupied. Because many hospital costs were fixed, a high occupancy rate resulted in a low cost per patient day. Studies showed that some veterans hospitals tended to keep patients longer than their legitimate need for hospitalization. The result was a low cost per patient day, but a higher than necessary *total* cost.

The inappropriateness of a surrogate output measure may cause the discontinuance of a useful program, but more likely it will support the continuance of a marginally useful one, with a corresponding waste of resources. Inappropriate surrogate measures also may cause agencies to be complacent even though they are not reaching their objectives.

Quantity versus Quality

Although performance has both a quantity and a quality dimension, it usually is more feasible to measure quantity than quality. Despite this difficulty, the quality dimension should not be overlooked.

Frequently, the indicator that is chosen to measure quantity implies some standard of quality, "Number of lines typed per hour" usually carries with it the implication that the lines were typed satisfactorily; there may even be an explicit statement of what constitutes a satisfactory line of typing, such as the requirement that it be free of errors. Similarly, the measure "number of students graduated" implies that the students have met the standards of quality that are prescribed for graduation.

In some situations, judgments about quality are limited to discrete measures such as those given above: either a line of typing was error-free or it was not; either students met the requirements for graduation or they did not. In these situations, it is not feasible to measure quality along a scale, and this precludes a determination of, say, whether this year's graduates received a better education than last year's.

Importance of Quality

During the past 15 years or so, many nonprofit organizations have begun programs in total quality management (TQM) or continuous quality improvement (CQI). One of the dilemmas faced by these organizations is measuring improvements in quality, which is inherently subjective. Moreover, in nonprofit organizations, measures of quality tend to be more important than in for-profit companies, where the market mechanism provides an automatic quality check. If a pair of shoes is shoddy, people will not buy it. The company will then have to raise quality to stay in business. If the company does not raise quality, other companies will take its customers away.

Similar market mechanisms exist for some nonprofit organizations. For example, a university that gives poor quality education most likely will lose students to other universities. A museum that has poor quality exhibitions will not have as many visitors as otherwise. However, in some nonprofits, there is no such mechanism for consumer reaction to output. Hospital patients generally are not competent to judge the quality of their care, and, even if they are dissatisfied, there may be little they can do. Clients of welfare departments, courts, public safety departments, license bureaus, and other government offices cannot "vote with their feet" as customers of commercial businesses can; they have nowhere else to go. Because of the absence of market-oriented client checks on quality in nonprofit organizations, it is usually worthwhile for an organization to devote considerable effort to developing quality measures. If possible, these measures should be linked to the individuals responsible for attaining them.

Example

In Kentucky, each of the state's 1,300 schools was given a benchmark grade, based on tests of 4th, 8th, and 11th graders, and ordered to improve its rating each year until 2012. If a school improved, its teachers could earn bonuses of up to $2,300 each. As of 1997, 53 percent of the schools had improved their ratings.[11]

Further, in some programs where a market mechanism might provide a measure of quality, an individual's personal motive for participating in the program may diverge from the social motive for sponsoring it, so that personal and social measures of quality differ. For example, even if a preschool program produces indifferent results, parents may still send their children to the program just to get them out of the home. Similarly, if a job training program neither trains nor places its clients well, unemployed people may still participate in it out of boredom, or out of hope it will assist them, or because they receive a stipend for participation. In such circumstances, unless there are adequate measures of quality, management may be misled about the value of the program's services.

Measuring Quality

Unless management can find some way to measure quality changes in a relatively objective fashion, the claim that quality has improved will have little credibility. There are three approaches that managers generally take to measure quality: crude measures, estimates, and surrogates.

Crude Measures of Quality   The absence of quality measures may lead to an emphasis on quantity. For example, people may be pushed rapidly through an education program, or inspectors may make a large number of quick and careless pollution inspections; or construction jobs may be done in a quick and shoddy manner. Thus, managers should make every effort to find acceptable quality measures, even if they are crude ones.

Example

In preschool programs, one can measure a child's degree of literacy, social acclimation, and so forth, before and after the program. In personnel training, one can ask employers to rate graduates. In construction, one can test fulfillment of construction standards.

Even though some measures are crude, and even though they may not even contain the "proper" attribute of quality, they may, if nothing else, serve as good motivators for the program's management and service delivery personnel. This assumes, of course, that there is a clear relationship between inputs and quality. If there is no demonstrable relationship between the two, senior management may not find it worthwhile to attempt to measure quality.

Estimates of Quality   In the absence of objective data, estimates of quality may be useful. For example, in a university, comparisons can be made between

---

[11]Peter Galuszka, "Kentucky's Class Act," *Business Week,* April 7, 1997.

the standing of a college or department within its professional discipline, or its position currently with its position in the past. Similar judgments can be made about the kinds of positions graduates hold and the kinds of organizations that employ them.

Surrogates for Quality In some nonprofit organizations, surrogates for the quality of services provided, such as accuracy and response time, are important indicators of quality. Often, objective measures of such surrogates are readily obtainable. Examples are the backlog of information requests, the number of checks returned because of error, average time taken to process an application, and the number of applications completed within seven days after their receipt. In using surrogates, managers must be cautious to avoid some of the problems discussed above, however.

Implementing Output Measures: Some General Principles

As the foregoing discussion has suggested, the selection and implementation of output measures for a management control system is an extremely complex task. It also is highly situational; that is, what works for one organization quite likely will not work for another. This is certainly true if two organizations have contrasting missions and clientele, but it also may be the case even if the two have similar missions and clientele.

Despite dissimilarities among organizations, we can state some general principles that are relevant in selecting and implementing the output measures for an organization's management control system. These principles are very general; there no doubt are exceptions to each rule. Nevertheless, they provide some useful guidance to managers concerned with measuring their organizations' output.

Principle 1: Some Measure of Output Is Usually Better than None

Valid criticism can be made about almost every output measure, since few measures, if any, are perfect. There is a tendency on the part of some managers to magnify the imperfections and thus downgrade the attempt to collect and use any output information. In most situations a sounder approach is to take account of the imperfections and to qualify the results accordingly. In general, some output data, however crude, are of more use to a manager than none at all.

Although several caveats were expressed earlier concerning the use of inappropriate output measures, most organizations can develop reasonable, albeit imprecise, indicators of output. Rather than using such indicators as absolute bases for judgment, managers can use them as the means for asking questions to determine if a significant problem really exists. Moreover, the whole idea of benefit/cost analysis, which was discussed in Chapter 9, rests on the foundation of some measure of benefits, which means output. It follows that a considerable expenditure of effort in finding and developing output measures generally is worthwhile.

Example

The Income Maintenance Program of Canada administers many social programs. Its ultimate output is the well-being it provides to the families it serves. Its management believes that the following are satisfactory measures of this output:

- Number of accounts administered per employee-year.
- Units of service performed for clients per employee-year.
- Processing error rates.
- Average waiting time for client interviews.
- Percentage of checks returned.

Inputs as a Measure of Outputs

Although generally less desirable than a true output measure, inputs are often a better measure of output than no measure at all. For example, it may not be feasible to construct output measures for research projects. In the absence of such measures, the amount spent on a research project may provide a useful clue to output. In the extreme, if no money was spent, it is apparent that nothing was accomplished. (This assumes that the accounting records show what actually was spent, which sometimes is not the case.)

Example

The New Communities Program offered assistance to private and public developers of new communities. Although funds were available, no new projects were financed for 10 years. This was conclusive evidence that the program was not generating outputs.

As with other surrogates, when inputs are used as surrogate output measures, managers must be careful to avoid undue reliance on them. An organization should continually try to develop usable measures of output.

Principle 2: If Feasible, Compare Output Measures to Measures Available from Outside Sources

Several professional associations, including those for hospitals, schools, colleges and universities, and welfare organizations, collect information from their members, and compile averages and other statistics. These statistics may provide a valuable starting point in analyzing the performance of an organization. Similar data are available from government sources, such as the Office of Productivity and Technology of the Bureau of Labor Statistics (although not much for nonprofit organizations), the U.S. Department of Health and Human Services, and various state agencies. In some cases the measures reported are too detailed or not well suited to management needs, but some of the available statistics may nevertheless be useful.

Example

The Hospital Performance Report, developed by the Joint Commission on Accreditation of Healthcare Organizations, lists 45 performance areas. The report shows a hospital's score for each area and compares this score to other hospitals. The areas are classified into categories such as patient rights and organizational ethics (e.g., protection of patient confidentiality), use of medications (e.g., processes to ensure the right medication is given to the right patient), education (e.g., assessing what patients need to know and their ability to learn it), continuity of care (e.g., how well services are coordinated to ensure that the patient receives appropriate care from entry through discharge), design of new services (e.g., collecting outcome data and assessing opportunities for improvement), leadership (e.g., responsiveness to the needs of the community), and social environment (e.g., assessing how space, furnishing, equipment, and patient clothing contribute to patient dignity).[12]

Problems with Comparability

When one organization's output information is being compared with averages of other organizations, the data must be comparable. This requires that the detailed definitions used in compiling the averages be studied carefully; the user should not rely on the brief titles given in the tables themselves. Moreover, in using published statistics, an organization must be sure that its data are prepared according to the same definitions and ground rules as those used by the compiling organization.

Example

The reporting system of the Department of Health of the state of New York defined hospital bed three different ways: certified beds, bed complement, and total beds. Unless users knew which of these definitions corresponded to the meaning of beds to which they were accustomed, they could not make valid comparisons.

Comparability is especially important when data are reported for costs per unit of output. If the organization's definitions do not correspond to those used for both the numerator and the denominator of this ratio, the comparison is invalid. "Cost per FTE (full-time equivalent) student" can be a valuable statistic, but there are several different ways of defining the denominator of this ratio, and innumerable ways of defining the elements of cost that make up the numerator.

Problems with Reliability

Managers also should ensure that reliable data underlie the statistics. For example, many people believe that certain statistics on education published by

---

[12]Joint Commission on Accreditation of Healthcare Organizations, *The Health Care Organization Performance Report,* 1995.

the Department of Education were compiled from data of dubious validity. Obviously, one cannot expect to obtain valid comparative information from poor raw data.

Within an organization, if costs per unit of output are desired, output measures must be comparable with expense measures. In some organizations, the output measurement system is developed by one group and the expense reporting system by another; under such circumstances comparability is unlikely. Furthermore, if the cost-per-unit ratio is for responsibility centers, the responsibility center must be defined in the same way in measuring outputs as it is in measuring inputs (expenses); this is also the case for program elements or for other cost objects.

Principle 3: Use Measures That Can Be Reported in a Timely Manner

There is no point in furnishing information after the need for it has passed. If managers need information quickly as a basis for action, the controller's staff must develop some way of compiling the information quickly. Timeliness requirements are different for different types of information, however. Moreover, for management control purposes a timely, but less accurate, output measure is usually preferable to an accurate, but less timely, one. Timeliness is not equivalent to speed in this context, but rather is related to the time span of the task.

Example

Mortality from emphysema, which can be measured only years after the occurrence of the cause of the disease, is less useful for control of air pollution programs than less accurate but more timely measures, such as the number of persons with eye/ear/nose/throat irritations, the number of persons who are advised by physicians to move to another locality, or the amount of effluents in the air.

Reasons for Timeliness Problems

The problem of timeliness is different in nonprofit organizations (especially government) than it is in for-profit organizations for several reasons.

Lack of Prompt Feedback Output often cannot be measured immediately after a program's efforts have taken place. The results of funds invested in a school program in September may not be measurable until the following June, for example. The effect of interest rate subsidies on the supply of low-income housing may not be measurable for two or three years after the program is initiated because of the time necessary to design and construct buildings. The impact of reforestation programs may take a decade or two to measure.

Organizational Hierarchy Reports on a program may have to work their way through several organizational layers and thus become too old to be of use.

Example

Title I, an educational program, provides grants through a state educational agency, then through a local educational agency, and ultimately to the local Title I administrator. The data that work their way back through this chain could well be several months old by the time they reach program analysts in Washington.

Slowly Changing Circumstances   Some data, although not timely, may describe a situation that is not likely to have changed since the time of measurement. Thus, old data are as accurate as if they were current. School desegregation programs are examples of programs for which data need not be collected frequently or processed quickly.

Principle 4: Develop a Variety of Measures

There is no such thing as a general-purpose report on output that is analogous to a general-purpose financial statement. Just as management accounting information must be tailor-made to the needs of individual managers, so too must output measures.

For most responsibility centers, and for an organization as a whole, there are usually a few *key result measures* that are the important indicators of the quality and quantity of performance. In a given situation, opinions may differ as to what these are, but it is usually worthwhile to give careful thought to identifying them.

When there are several measures, each tends to be used for a different purpose. For example, with respect to health care in a community:

1. There can be a measure of the total cost of the health care system as a basis for comparison with the cost of other community services; this measures the relative emphasis given to each service. Expressed as a cost per person in the community, this can be compared with costs per person in other communities as another expression of relative emphasis.

2. There can be a measure of the cost per episode of illness, or cost per discharge, perhaps classified by diagnosis.

3. At a lower level, information can be collected on the overall cost per patient day in each hospital as a basis for detecting gross differences in the operating characteristics of each hospital. Patient-day costs for each service (medicine, surgery, pediatrics, psychiatry, and so forth) are useful for similar reasons.

4. At a still lower level, one can measure the cost per unit of service rendered, such as cost per meal served, or cost per nursing hour.

A Continuum of Output Measures

When several types of output measures are used in a given organization, they tend to be arranged along a continuum. At one end are rough social indicators that are closely related to the goals of the organization, and at the other end are precisely stated process measures that are only remotely related to the goals of the organization.

Example

At one extreme, the U.S. Information Agency measures the degree to which the agency influences international behavior through its activities. This might be called a *social indicator.* A second level measures the extent to which specific attitudes and opinions of the governing members of other nations have been changed by the agency's work. A third level represents a measurement of the increase of understanding of people overseas in regard to specific issues. A fourth level counts the number of times people have been reached by media of different kinds. A fifth and the lowest level counts the number of "media products" produced by the agency; this clearly is a process measure.

It is useful to think of output measures in terms of this continuum for two reasons. First, higher level output measures generally are better indicators of program effectiveness than lower level measures, which often are not closely related to program goals. Second, lower level indicators are easier to specify and quantify than are higher level indicators. This fact explains the prevalence of measures of personnel efficiency in situations where personnel efficiency is only marginally related to overall program goals.

The continuum also corresponds to the relative usefulness of particular types of output indicators at various levels in the organization's hierarchy. Social indicators and results measures are most useful to senior management, governing bodies, and funding sources, whereas process measures are most useful to first-line supervisors.

Example

A regional Air Pollution Control Administration headquarters has a wide variety of measures. It is concerned with its own efficient functioning; that is, it has its own process measures (how fast a request is considered, how quickly budget and project requests can be handled, and so on). At the other end of the spectrum, it has objectives for air quality in each region. The progress toward these objectives can be measured by the appropriate instrumentation.

Between these process measures and results measures are several measures related to the functioning of the regional administrator and the state programs within a region. For example, the agency may establish as an objective the improvement of air quality in the New England region by more vigorous antipollution efforts on the part of the Commonwealth of Massachusetts.

Combined Output Measures

Sometimes it is feasible to combine several output indicators into an aggregate that provides an indication of output quality and organizational performance. This sometimes is called a *combined output measure.*

The weights placed on each component of a combined output measure should reflect the values of the policymakers who govern the organization, not of the systems analysts or accountants who staff its programs. The output of many programs conceivably could be described by such a measure if enough work were devoted to constructing it. The question for management is whether the effort is worthwhile.

Example

For many years, the Strategic Air Command evaluated its wings by a combined output measure that was computed by weighting scores for each of several dozen measures of performance. Some observers judged this system to be highly valuable; others doubted it was worth its cost.

In general, many managers decide that developing a combined output measure is more time-consuming than the results justify, but simplified versions of this general approach may be eminently worthwhile.

The Balanced Scorecard   One such simplification is the "balanced scorecard," an approach that entails combining several different categories of output measures and linking them to each other.[13]

Nonprofits tend to have difficulty implementing the balanced scorecard because of its emphasis on financial performance as the end result. In part, the difficulty arises because adequate financial performance generally is seen as a constraining variable for a nonprofit organization rather than a strategic objective. It also comes about because in a for-profit organization the same person (a customer) usually is both paying for and receiving the goods or services, whereas in a nonprofit the funders and the recipients frequently are different people.

To overcome this dilemma, Robert Kaplan and David Norton have suggested placing both donor and recipient perspectives at the top of the balanced scorecard. Nonprofits then can develop objectives for both groups as well as the internal processes needed to appropriately serve the two categories of customers. They also suggest, however, that placing a social indicator at the top of the scorecard may serve the purpose equally well. Social indicators such as a reduction in poverty or illiteracy, or improvements in the environment may provide a sufficiently broad focus that the remaining categories of the balanced scorecard can be developed to reinforce the social indicator.[14]

Example

The city of Charlotte selected five themes of strategic priority: community safety, transportation, preservation of older urban neighborhoods, restructuring government, and economic development. A core project team translated these five themes into strategic objectives for a balanced scorecard. The customer (citizen) was placed at the top of the scorecard, and the team identified the elements needed to address the themes from a customer perspective. When the team moved to the other aspects of the

[13]See Robert S. Kaplan and David P. Norton, "The Balanced Scorecard–Measures that Drive Performance," *Harvard Business Review,* January–February 1992.
[14]Robert S Kaplan and David P. Norton, "Balance Without Profit," *Financial Management,* January 2001, pp. 23–26.

balanced scorecard, it found that the financial, internal process, and learning and growth objectives were quite similar for all five themes.[15]

Example

Henry Ford Health System's balanced scorecard divides measures into four general categories: financial performance, customer service, growth, and system integration. Within each category, there are five items that are measured. For example, in the financial performance category, one measure is cost per unit of service; in customer service, a measure is HMO turnover rate; in growth, a measure is HMO enrollment; in system integration, a measure is employee satisfaction. Henry Ford's senior management has developed specific measures and targets for each item, and presents the information to its board each month in the form of a "spidergram," as shown at top on page 642.[16]

There are many possible variations on the balanced scorecard. For example, Regina Herzlinger has suggested the use of a Four-by-Four Report. The report addresses four questions of particular importance to the four constituencies of nonprofit organizations and government agencies. The four constituencies are clients, donors, staff, and society. The four questions are (1) Have we achieved our goals effectively, efficiently, and in relationship to our resources? (2) Have we been fair to different generations and types of people or have we favored one group at the expense of another? (3) Have we appropriately matched the organization's activities and the resources they use? (4) Have we diversified sufficiently to sustain our activities?[17]

Principle 5: Don't Report More Information than Is Likely to Be Used

Although a variety of output measures may be feasible, managers should avoid receiving too much information. In part, this problem arises because there is a reluctance in many organizations to discontinue the use of certain output measures when they no longer serve an important managerial purpose. This reluctance must be overcome if the measurement system is to remain valuable and cost effective.

Example

In response to a request from a manager, the Information Services Department in a social service agency developed a report that classified clients according to race and age. This was valuable output information to the manager at the time. Several years later, after that manager had left the agency, and the kinds of problems and issues the agency faced had changed, the Information Services Department continued to prepare the report, even though no one now used it.

---

[15]Ibid. See also Robert S. Kaplan, "City of Charlotte," Harvard Business School Case 9-199-036, 1998.
[16]See the conference proceedings of the Medical Group Management Association, 69th Annual Conference.
[17]Regina Herzlinger, "The Outsiders," *Management Accounting,* June 2000.

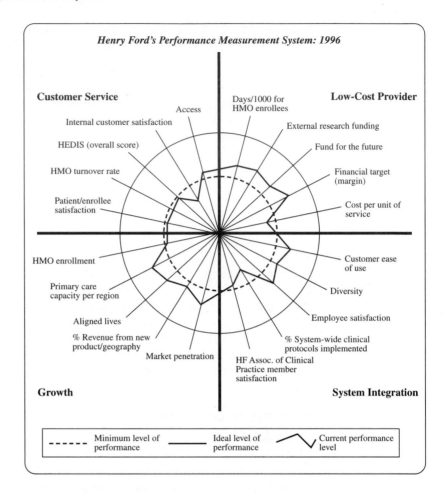

Henry Ford's Performance Measurement System: 1996

A similar problem also arises when output measurement systems are being designed initially. In developing a new system, system designers have a tendency to collect a great mass of data so that somewhere within the mass are data that will meet everyone's desires. Too much data swamp the system, increase its "noise level," draw attention away from important information, and lessen the credibility of the system as a whole.

Principle 6: Don't Give More Credence to Surrogates than Is Warranted

As discussed previously, a surrogate can be a useful approximation of actual output, but it never should be interpreted as representing actual output. Its limitations must be kept in mind.

Comparison of Output Measures for Strategy Formulation and Management Control

The management control system should provide output information that is useful for both strategy formulation and management control. Managers should recognize, however, that the criteria governing the output measures used for strategy formulation tend to differ from those used for management control in the following ways.

Precision

For strategy formulation, rough estimates of output generally are satisfactory. For management control, the measure must be more precise to be credible (although, as indicated above, timeliness considerations sometimes outweigh the desire for precision).

Example

One hospital's strategy formulation activities included the purchase of a magnetic tape from the local telephone company; the tape contained information on new telephone installations. This information was used to analyze rough changes in the number of potential new patients in the hospital's service area. The fact that the tape contained data on people who had moved within the service area, and thus did not indicate precisely how many new residents there were, was not considered a serious limitation.

Causality

For management control, there should be a plausible link between the effort (i.e., inputs) of the organization and the output measure. For strategy formulation, the connection can be more tenuous. If output measures are to be used in analyzing a proposal for a specific program, however, there should be some connection between inputs and outputs. To include correlating but noncausal output numbers in an analysis is not only a waste of time, but may do more harm than good if it leads people to believe erroneously that a causal connection exists.

Example

In one rural community there was a high positive correlation between the number of storks observed in the spring and the number of babies born in the following winter. If health planners wish to determine the demand for maternity services, a model that used the number of storks as a predictive indicator probably would suffice. If, however, health planners wish to lower the birthrate, the systematic extermination of storks would not work, since the causal factor for both storks and babies was something entirely different: the richness of spring crops. Rich crops caused the storks to come in the spring because there was plenty of food for them; the rich crops also were a cause for optimism among the farmers and their wives, resulting in higher birthrates.[18]

The absence of a demonstrated causal connection is no reason to avoid analyzing *plausible* connections to assess the impact of a certain program. When there is no causal connection, decisions must be based on judgments unaided by quantitative information. For example, it seems obviously desirable to spend money on a judiciary system even though no good measurement of output is available.

Responsibility

For management control, the output measure must be related to the responsibility of a specific person or organization unit. For strategy formulation, this is unnecessary. Thus, strategic considerations may require operating personnel to collect data for which they themselves have no use.

Example

Title I education programs are intended to provide funds for improvement of education of low-income and disadvantaged children. In connection with these programs, planners in Washington require the collection of data (e.g., test scores) that will be of no use to operating managers. They are nevertheless necessary for reformulating program goals and strategies.

Timeliness

For management control purposes, data on output must be available shortly after the event. For strategy formulation, this is less important.

Example

Measures of the high school and college performance of students who attended particular elementary schools are useful for strategy formulation, but they cannot be part of a management control system.

Cost

For both strategy formulation and management control, the benefits of obtaining information about inputs and outputs must exceed the costs of obtaining the information. For strategy formulation, it may be possible to obtain certain data on an ad hoc or sampling basis to keep the cost low, whereas the continuous collection of the same data for management control would be prohibitively expensive.

Relation to Program Elements

If output measures are to be useful for strategy formulation, they must be related to overall goals and objectives. If it is not feasible to do this directly, it

---

[18]Richard Normann, *A Personal Quest for Methodology, SIAR Dokumentation AB* (Stockholm, Sweden: Scandinavian Institutes for Administrative Research, 1975), pp. 7-9.

may be necessary to relate the measures to program categories or even to individual program elements. Ideally, they should be related to all three.

Example

In a study of quality assurance and measurement in home- and community-based services, the United States General Accounting Office (GAO) found that quality assurance strategies were insufficient to assure the delivery of high-quality services, in part because of the undeveloped state of program and outcome measurement. Without better measurement, the GAO felt that it could not establish a relationship between the quality assurance strategies and the quality of services rendered.[19]

Summary

Just as the economy has many indicators of prosperity that various people interpret differently, nonprofit organizations have numerous ways of looking at their complex outputs. Several output measures, including a number of surrogates, often are necessary for a valid impression of the effectiveness of a nonprofit organization or one of its programs.

In selecting a set of output measures, management must give consideration to three separate but related matters. First, it must look at measures that strike a balance between (*a*) subjective and objective, (*b*) quantitative and nonquantitative, (*c*) discrete and scalar, (*d*) actual and surrogates, and (*e*) quantity and quality. Second it must determine how it will respond to six principles concerning the implementation of output measures: (*a*) the need for some measurement, (*b*) the ability to make comparisons, (*c*) the need for timely information, (*d*) the importance of having a variety of measures, (*e*) the avoidance of an excessive quantity of information reported, and (*f*) the role of surrogates. Finally, it must recognize that the demands for management control purposes are quite different from those for strategy formulation. It therefore must be careful to choose output measures that are appropriate for the purposes to which they will be put.

[19]Eleanor Chelimsky, *Long-Term Care: Status of Quality Assurance and Measurement in Home and Community-Based Services,* United States General Accounting Office, March 1994.

Suggested Additional Readings

American Society for Public Administration. *Resolution Encouraging the Use of Performance Measurement and Reporting by Government Organizations.* Washington, DC: 1992.

Barnow, Burt S. "Performance Standards in State and Local Programs." In F. Manski and I. Garfinkel, eds., *Evaluating Welfare and Training Programs.* Boston: Harvard University Press, 1992.

Cave, M., M. Kogan, and R. Smith, eds. *Output and Performance Measurement in Government: The State of the Art.* London: Jessica Kingsley, 1990.

Comptroller General of the United States. *Government Auditing Standards.* Washington, DC: U.S. Government Printing Office, 1994.

Cutt, James, et al. "Nonprofits Accommodate the Information Demands of Public and Private Funders." *Nonprofit Management and Leadership* 7, no. 1 (Fall 1996).

Epstein, Paul D. *Using Performance Measurement in Local Government.* New York: National Civic League Press, 1988.

Governmental Accounting Standards Board. *Concepts Statement No.* 2. "Service Efforts and Accomplishments." Norwalk, CT: April 1994.

Harr, David J., and James T. Godfrey. *Private Sector Financial Performance Measures and Their Applicability to Government Organizations.* Montvale, NJ: National Association of Accountants, 1991.

Hatry, Harry P., et al. *Service Efforts and Accomplishments Reporting: Its Time Has Come. An Overview.* Norwalk, CT: Governmental Accounting Standards Board, 1990.

Hodgkinson, V. A., and R. A. Wyman, eds. *The Future of the Nonprofit Sector.* San Francisco: Jossey Bass Publishers, 1989.

Kamensky, John M. "Program Performance Measures: Designing a System to Manage for Results." *Public Productivity and Management Review* 16, no. 4 (1993), pp. 395–402.

National Academy of Public Administration. *Toward Useful Performance Measurement: Lessons Learned from Initial Pilot Performance Plans Prepared under the Government Performance and Results Act.* Washington, DC: November 1994.

United States Congress. *Government Performance and Results Act of 1993.* Public Law 103–62 (August 3). 107 STAT. 285, 1993.

United States Executive Office of the President. *Executive Order 12862: Setting Customer Service Standards.* Washington, DC: 1993.

United States General Accounting Office. *Pay-for-Performance: State and International Public Sector Pay-for-Performance Systems.* GAO/GGD-91-1, October 1990.

———. *Tax Administration: IRS Needs to Improve Certain Measures of Service Center Quality.* GAO/GGD-91-66, March 1991.

———. *Program Performance Measures: Federal Agency Collection and Use of Performance Data.* Washington, DC: 1992.

———. *Long-Term Care: Status of Quality Assurance and Measurement in Home and Community-Based Services.* Washington, DC: 1994.

————. *Managing for Results: State Experiences Provide Insights for Federal Management Reforms.* 1994.

Wallace, Wanda A. *Service Efforts and Accomplishments Reporting: Mass Transit.* Norwalk, CT: Governmental Accounting Standards Board, 1991.

————. *Performance Measurement and Risk Monitoring,* RIA/Warren Gorham & Lamont, 1997.

Case 12–1

Charlottesville Fire Department*

In December 1976, the Research Triangle Institute (RTI), in collaboration with the National Fire Protection Association (NFPA) and the International City Management Association (ICMA), issued preliminary findings of an 18-month evaluation of fire protection delivery arrangements in a nationwide sample of 1,400 fire departments. Charlottesville Fire Chief Julian Taliaferro immediately began using the RTI criteria to measure the effectiveness and productivity of the Charlottesville Fire Department, in relation to similarly constructed fire departments in cities of comparable size nationwide.

Background

The Charlottesville Fire Department protected both the City of Charlottesville and part of Albemarle County. The city itself included some 10.4 square miles, a population of approximately 56,000, and property valued at $766,143,984 (true market value).

Fire department resources included 5 engine companies, 1 aerial ladder, 68 paid personnel, and a volunteer force that functioned in an auxiliary capacity.

Albemarle County itself had no paid fire department. Protection was maintained through a network of 6 volunteer companies numbering 250 persons. The county also had, for a number of years, a verbal agreement with the city that the latter would automatically respond to fire alarms originating within a specified 30-square-mile area of the county, comprised mostly of that urbanized portion surrounding the city. This area had a population of approximately 19,800 and property valued at $202,365,670. While there were no county volunteers located within this area, those in close proximity would respond to fire alarms there.

*This case was prepared by S. Y. Young and C. J. Tompkins; revised by C. J. Tompkins, Michigan Technology University. Copyright © by C. J. Tompkins.

The county contributed to the annual budget of the city fire department in proportion to the services it was rendered. In fiscal year 1977 this amounted to $163,303 of a total budget of $831,629. The county also maintained one engine company located at the main fire station, this being the engine the city normally used to respond to county fires. Therefore, it can be seen that the city fire department served two distinct regions: the city itself and a portion of Albemarle County. Chief Taliaferro's study attempts to evaluate and compare levels of fire protection provided by the city fire department to each area.

Measurement Criteria

RTI reduced all departments studied to 4 categories: fully volunteer, mostly volunteer (50 to 90 percent), mostly paid (50 to 90 percent), and fully paid departments. The departments were then further divided by size of population and type of community protected, whether center, ring, or fringe. A center city was described as an urban area with a population greater than 25,000 having considerable fire hazard and a paid fire department. A ring city was defined as a suburban community with a population of less than 100,000, and with a fire department composed of some volunteer personnel. A rural, low-density community on the edge of an urbanized or suburban area was considered to be a fringe city.

The city of Charlottesville was classified as a center city of population between 25,000 and 100,000 with a fully paid fire department. It may be noted that RTI offered no category for a center city with a mostly paid force. This is ideally what Charlottesville would be considered, but since that classification did not exist, the next most accurate one was chosen. Chief Taliaferro felt the fully paid description to be closest to the true situation as over 90 percent of all fire alarms were handled with available paid personnel.

The 30 square miles of Albemarle County protected by the city was classified as a ring city of a population between 5,001 and 25,000 with a mostly volunteer force. The force was considered mostly volunteer because, while the city did respond to fire alarms in the area, its function was considered to be auxiliary to county volunteer companies that also responded to alarms in the area. Criticality of city response depended upon response time for county units and the seriousness of the fire. The city would normally respond to alarms with one engine company and three firefighters, but would usually be outnumbered by volunteer equipment and personnel.

RTI evaluated all departments as related to measures of effectiveness and productivity, using information gathered from years 1973, 1974, and 1975. Most of the figures used are averages for the three-year period and all are corrected for inflation.

Effectiveness was described as the extent to which the incidence of fire, loss of life, personal injury, and property loss was minimized. The seven measures used to operationalize the concept were:

1. Number of fires per 1,000 of population protected.

2. Dollars of property loss per capita.

3. Dollars of property loss per $1,000 of market value of property.

4. Dollars of property loss per fire.

5. Number of civilian injuries and deaths per 100,000 of population protected.

6. Number of civilian injuries and deaths per 100 fires.

7. Number of firefighter injuries and deaths per 100 fires.

Productivity was defined by RTI as the measure of the relationship between results obtained and resources utilized. Rather than rely strictly on levels of effort (expenditures) to measure fire department costs, RTI preferred to speak of *total cost,* defined as the sum of expenditures and dollar property losses.

Indicators used to reflect productivity were:

1. Expenditures per capita.

2. Expenditures per $1,000 of market value of property.

3. Total cost per capita.

4. Total cost per $1,000 of market value of property.

5. Total cost per fire.

After obtaining all measurement figures for each fire department, an average of each was computed for those departments considered to be in the lower quartile of service delivery (more effective), those at the median or average level of delivery, and those in the upper quartile, or less effective level, of service delivery. Those were the figures used for comparison in this study, target figures being those in the lower quartile.

Charlottesville's Performance

As shown in Exhibit 1, the number of fires per 1,000 of population protected in the city averaged 10.68 for the 1973–1975 period; this pushes the city above the lower quartile figure of 7.24. Chief Taliaferro believed the difference might be attributed to the fact that Charlottesville did not have a well-developed fire prevention program. In 1977 there was only one fire prevention officer, and, therefore, the program was conducted on a somewhat hit-and-miss basis. The Chief felt more time spent on public education and prevention programs would decrease the figure substantially.

The county figure of 2.98 compared favorably with the more effective target 6.63. This would be due to the low population density in the county, which provided for less fire hazard than a high-density area such as the city. The Chief expected this figure to rise as population and age of structures in the county increased.

EXHIBIT 1 Effectiveness Measures

Effectiveness Measures	Albemarle County Charlottesville	Target More Effective (Lower 25%)	Median	Less Effective (Upper 25%)
Prevention:				
Number of fires/1000 of	2.98	6.63	9.43	15.95
population protected	10.68	7.24	12.78	19.23
Suppression:				
Dollar property loss	27.47	5.10	7.69	11.98
per capita	10.90	5.39	10.40	14.96
Dollar property loss per	2.69	.34	.50	.75
$1,000 of market value	1.25	.31	.54	2.10
Dollar property loss	9,219.00	438.51	938.21	1,647.40
per fire	1,021.00	393.94	1,111.97	2,210.82
Civilian injuries and				
deaths per 100,000	5.05	0.00	7.93	21.73
population.	35.71	13.84	19.09	28.48
Civilian injuries and	1.70	0.00	.85	1.79
deaths per 100 fires.	3.34	.86	1.66	2.23
Firefighters injuries and	1.70	0.00	.58	2.65
deaths per 100 fires.	.84	1.07	2.51	4.14
Levels of effort:				
Expenditures per	5.28	8.08	15.02	21.02
capita	8.61	20.92	24.77	31.75
Expenditures per $1,000				
market value of	.52	.51	.98	1.44
property	.62	.86	1.84	3.22
Productivity measures:				
Total cost per	32.76	18.36	28.75	30.77
capita	19.51	23.12	33.10	44.17
Total cost per $1,000				
market value of	3.20	.96	1.38	2.05
property	1.42	1.01	1.66	5.99
Total cost per	10,993.00	1,467.00	2,635.00	3,638.00
fire.	1,827.00	2,373.00	3,041.00	4,134.00

Property loss per capita and per $1,000 of market value of property for the city are both higher than the median figures. This is in part due to the relatively low average manning of 2.6 firefighters per engine company. The number of firefighters immediately present at a fire would help determine the number and type of suppression activities that could be initiated. The longer certain activities must be delayed, the greater the chance of increased property loss.

In contrast, the property loss per fire for the city was below the median. This was in part due to the fact that Charlottesville had relatively little industry as compared to other cities of the same size. More industry would increase the risk of industrial fires, where property loss is normally greater than in dwelling fires (the type with the greatest frequency in Charlottesville).

A comparison of property loss per capita and per $1,000 of market value of property would indicate the county to be high above the less effective range. But these figures are somewhat misleading. The property loss totals used here are averaged for the three-year period 1973–1975. In 1973 and 1974 there were two large industrial fires in the county, one where loss was estimated at $270,000, the other at $750,000. Without these two fires, property loss would have been substantially less for both years. For example, in 1973 loss was actually $97,000. Chief Taliaferro believed these two catastrophic fires inflated what property loss might routinely have been. Calculations with these two fires deleted showed property loss indicators to fall, although they still hovered in the less effective range (i.e., per capita, $9.38 and per fire, $3,102).

Also, when using property loss figures in terms of per capita and per fire, Chief Taliaferro believed it was important to keep in mind the low population density of the county area (19,800 total) and also the low number of fires occurring in the county (i.e., 59 in 1975 as opposed to 598 for the city). Another contributing factor to higher property losses in the county was the longer response time experienced, meaning the fire was already somewhat advanced by the time the engine company arrived.

Civilian injuries and deaths per 100 fires were very high for Charlottesville as compared to other cities of its size. One reason may be the way in which injuries and deaths were reported in Charlottesville and other cities, a factor for which the RTI survey makes no allowance. Chief Taliaferro indicated that the Charlottesville Fire Department reported any civilian injury at the scene of a fire, however slight. Other cities may have reported the same way, or they may report only those injuries of a more serious nature. Those departments who follow the latter policy would compare more favorably in this measure than the former.

Grouping together injuries and deaths may also have distorted the meaning of the rating. Charlottesville averaged one death due to fire per year. The year 1975 saw 19 injuries and one death. Considering some injuries were probably slight, do those figures carry the same meaning as do 19 deaths and one injury?

Civilian injuries and deaths were also relatively high in the county. This again may be due to the reporting procedure. Also involved may be longer response time averaged for county alarms. Chief Taliaferro felt that possibly 25 percent of injuries could be related to this last factor.

The fighter injuries and deaths per 100 fires for the city were extremely low —well below the lower 25th percentile figure. This was due in part to mandatory protective clothing and required training for the firefighters. Also fewer injuries were reported in this fire department than may be the case in others.

Those explanations would also apply to firefighter injuries and deaths in the county as related to city firefighters. But the county figure was high as compared to the city figure probably due to the county volunteers that would respond to these fires. Volunteer firefighters normally wore less protective clothing and had fewer training hours, two factors that would increase chances of firefighter injuries.

Fire department expenditures per capita and per $1,000 of market value of property were low for both the city and county. But low expenditures do not automatically indicate efficiency. For a comparison with the target figures it must be kept in mind that while expenditures were lower than the 25th percentile, property loss figures were higher. This would indicate that the fire department was not as effective in the provision of fire protection as it might have been—whether this be due to resource misallocation or underfunding, a more likely factor in this case.

The extremely low expenditure per capita for the city might also relate to an additional factor. It must be kept in mind that the target figure for Charlottesville corresponds to that for a fully paid department and that Charlottesville was not strictly all paid, as there was an auxiliary force available. It seems probable that if Charlottesville had not had this auxiliary force, the city would have had to hire additional personnel at added cost.

Total Cost

The concept of total cost, while more informative than that of expenditures alone, may be somewhat misleading in its implications. As a combination of property losses and expenditures, it purports to be a productivity measure of effectiveness and efficiency where maximum productivity is achieved when total cost is minimized. RTI admitted that the calculation is indifferent to trade-offs between property loss and fire department expenditures.

For example, the same total cost could be achieved both by a department with low expenditures and high property losses and by one with higher expenditures and lower property losses. Chief Taliaferro believed that a service-oriented agency such as a fire department cannot be indifferent to these trade-offs. The departmental goal of minimizing property loss due to fire must be part of any productivity measure. Chief Taliaferro was not certain that equal total costs reflect equal productivity when one department may spend more money, but have a good suppression record, and another may spend a minimal amount, but have a history of high property loss.

Chief Taliaferro thought the productivity concept would be more useful if property loss and expenditure could be weighted in a manner to reflect departmental goals and objectives.

For the city, total cost per capita was low, a commendable figure upon first inspection. But closer examination shows that this figure was a combination of extremely low expenditures per capita and higher than average property losses.

Total cost per $1,000 of market value of property for the city was below the median for comparable fire departments. This again was the result of low expenditures and high property loss in this category.

Total cost per fire for the city was below the target figure mostly as a result of low expenditures as property loss per fire was closer to the median level.

In contrast to the city, total cost per capita and per $1,000 of market value of property for the county was above the median level. This was due to extremely high property loss in the county as discussed earlier.

Questions

1. Assume that the information furnished by Research Triangle Institute was the only information available as a basis of comparison. What is your judgment as to the performance of the Charlottesville Fire Department?

2. What additional information, if any, would you like to have, if it could be obtained at a reasonable cost, in order to improve your judgment of performance?

Case 12–2

Barrington High School*

It's a ridiculous request. Let's just fill out something and send it back. I don't want to spend a lot of time on this.

A 10th Grade Science Teacher

I disagree It makes a lot of sense. How are we going to argue that we're doing a good job unless we can prove it with some concrete data?

A 12th Grade Math Teacher

Using concrete data is a good idea in the cement industry, but we're educators. You can't measure what we do in any way that's meaningful, and I don't think we should even try.

An 11th Grade English Teacher

It was clear to Carol Kohn, Principal of Barrington High School, that responding to her new superintendent's request to develop and monitor

*This case was prepared by Carol Elder under the supervision of Professors David W. Young, Helen Long, and Gerald Leader. Partial funding for its preparation was provided by the BEST Program, Boston University School of Management. Copyright © by David W. Young and the BEST Program at Boston University.

performance measures for the 1,500-student high school would be a challenge. The school's faculty had mixed views of the value of the undertaking, and even if she could garner support, the actual task would take a lot of time and effort—scarce commodities in public education. Nevertheless, she was committed to developing some measures that would be both responsive to the superintendent's request and, most importantly, useful to her in the ongoing management of the high school.

Background

Barrington High School was part of a large urban school district and faced most of the challenges commonly found in large urban schools. It had a 15 percent annual dropout rate, among the highest in the district. Its attendance rate of 80 percent was about average for the district. A total of 60 percent of the students received reduced-price lunches. It had a diverse student body, with 35 percent black students, 25 percent Asian, 25 percent Latino, and 15 percent white. Barrington offered bilingual education programs in Chinese and Spanish to 25 percent of its students, and another 15 percent participated in special education programs. Only 40 percent of the students planned to attend college after graduating.

The school had experimented with a variety of improvement efforts in recent years, including schools-within-a-school clusters, site-based management, and revamping student assessment. Barrington also had developed relationships with several local businesses to provide internships, mentoring programs, and other real-world opportunities to its students. The history of these efforts was generally the same: first, enthusiasm and a flurry of work, followed by gradual disillusionment as faculty and staff were faced with uncertain results. Some efforts still lumbered on in name only, while others had withered away entirely. At the same time, there was a growing sense of urgency, both within the school and within the local community. The last administration of the MEAP test showed the school well below the state average, and, more seriously, below its comparison group.

A School "Scoreboard"

The Superintendent had sent out materials explaining the genesis of the "school scorecard" she was asking her principals to put together. The ideas originated in a new performance measurement tool that was being used increasingly in the private sector, known as the Balanced Scorecard (BSC). First presented in a 1992 *Harvard Business Review (HBR)* article,[1] the BSC

---

[1] Robert S. Kaplan and David P. Norton, "The Balanced Scorecard: Measures That Drive Performance," *Harvard Business Review,* January–February 1992. See also Kaplan and Norton, "Putting the Balanced Scorecard to Work," *Harvard Business Review,* September–October 1993.

allowed managers of for-profit enterprises to see results along several dimensions that affected their firm's profit.

According to the *HBR* article, which the Superintendent had included in his memo to the schools, the process of creating a BSC can help an organization to focus on its mission and define the intermediate steps it needs to take to achieve it. In addition, because "what is measured is what is done," many managers believe that, by tracking performance against goals, they can use a BSC to motivate employees to meet the targeted levels of each goal. Moreover, since its measures are closely linked to the organization's mission, a BSC can be a powerful tool for channeling employee energy into improved performance.

The BSC is based on the idea that no single measure, not even profit, can adequately capture the performance of an entire organization. At the same time, it would be a waste of resources to track all measurable activities and outputs. A typical BSC contains a limited set of measures that focus management's attention on the key activities that an organization must do well to succeed.

The *HBR* article outlined four performance-measurement perspectives: customers, internal processes, innovation and learning, and financial (see Exhibit 1). To develop a BSC, a for-profit organization needed to choose a set of measures that served as indicators of profitability. In other words, if the organization performed a BSC activity well, it likely would be profitable.[2]

After deciding what to measure, an organization must set targets for each item to make the BSC a true "scorecard" on which performance is compared to goals. Because the BSC is a "living document," management needs to periodically reevaluate both the target levels and the measured activities themselves to ensure that the indicators are still aligned with the organization's mission, and responsive to its environment.

The BSC in Nonprofit Organizations

Ms. Kohn reflected on these advantages:

> I know the BSC could help me to track how things are going with intermediate measures that should be linked to performance. In fact, one of the failings of our previous reform efforts here is that it simply took too long to find out whether things were working. Measures such as standardized tests, dropout rates, or college matriculation rates take three to five years to show changes, and by then it may be

---

[2]For example, a toy company might evaluate performance from the customer perspective by measuring the percent of each type of toy returned unsold by retailers to determine if it is producing what customers want. It could measure the number of defective toys to evaluate its internal manufacturing processes. The length of time required to turn a new idea into a product would indicate its performance from an innovation perspective. Finally, the return that shareholders earn on their investment in the company would measure financial performance.

EXHIBIT 1   **The Balanced Scorecard**

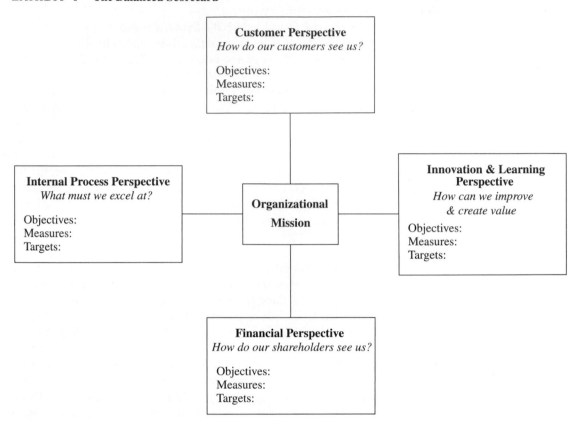

hard to know what caused the changes. If the BSC can help me sort through how and where we could improve, it would be worth the effort.

Knowing that there were bound to be disadvantages to the BSC, Ms. Kohn decided to to do some research. As part of her investigation, she discovered that the local United Way had tried the approach. The United Way's Director had been candid in his assessment:

I think it's a great tool but I guess you could say our results were mixed. If I had to do it over again, I would do things differently. There were some real pluses. Many of our employees said they felt more connected to the organization and had a better understanding of the link between their work and our mission. It's hard to get that kind of commitment. On the other hand, there was some frustration and disappointment about the process. One source of tension was the level of employee participation. Some were skeptical that the BSC was simply the latest management fad, but many were enthusiastic about the opportunity to voice their opinions on the kinds of activities that drive our success. Employee teams spent hours working with an outside facilitator to develop measures for the four BSC perspectives we chose. Problems came up, though, when we in senior management decided to make all the final decisions ourselves. As a result, employees felt their efforts weren't valued. I would definitely reconsider that approach.

Interesting philosophical differences emerged also. One of our quadrants was the "customer perspective," and there was a lot of disagreement about who that was. Was it donors? The community? Recipient agencies? The people served? After a long debate, we decided to focus on donors, but some folks thought this was fundamentally wrong. A final problem was the lack of systems for collecting data to measure the outcomes of our activities. Employee teams debated whether an activity should be included on the BSC if no measurement system existed for it. They resolved the issue by deciding to develop measures for key activities and making "data measurement" a BSC goal. Unfortunately they did not prescribe how these programs would be developed, so there were no bench-marks. We ended up stalled in this area.

The Spidergram

The United Way was not the only nonprofit organization to implement a BSC. The superintendent had included with his memo a Spidergram based on a BSC developed by a nearby hospital (see Exhibit 2). This hospital was pleased with its BSC results, and felt that the Spidergram provided a power-ful visual representation of its performance compared to target levels in the areas of system performance, resource utilization, medical outcomes, and customer satisfaction.

As the Superintendent had explained, the Spidergram's inner circle repre-sented the minimum acceptable level for each category, while the outer circle indicated the target level. The irregular line charted actual performance, so anyone could see at a glance where the hospital had exceeded expectations (outside the outer circle) and where it failed to meet minimum standards (in-side the inner circle). With this tool, it was easy for the hospital to demonstrate to even a casual observer how it was doing relative to its self-selected goals.

The hospital's successful effort convinced Ms. Kohn that the process could work. If she could be similarly successful, she might be able to document how Barrington was doing, and perhaps better manage the school as well.

The Challenge

The Superintendent had indicated that he would like to see a Spidergram for Barrington High, and that he hoped to obtain similar Spidergrams from all schools in the district. He planned to standardize some measures, such that all schools reported on some common indicators, but he recognized that some measures would differ among schools.

Other than providing a sample Spidergram, the Superintendent's request had been vague. He had indicated that he wanted to see performance mea-sures broken into four general categories that would form quadrants on the

EXHIBIT 2   **Balanced Scorecard Spidergram for a Hospital**

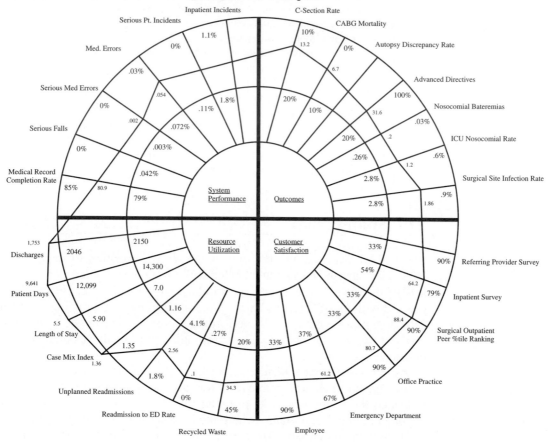

Spidergram. In addition, he was convinced that the quadrants used in the for-profit world were not appropriate for nonprofit organizations in general, and certainly not for educational institutions. As he wrote in his memo:

> I don't know what the appropriate quadrants should be, and I'm looking to the principals for some guidance in this respect. In addition, of course, I would like the principals to develop a set of measures for each quadrant, along with some minimum levels and goals.

He also had said that he realized implementation of the effort would be difficult, and he wanted the principals to share with him their views on what steps were needed to make the BSC a reality in the district's schools.

Ms. Kohn's Thoughts

As she reflected on the Superintendent's request, Ms. Kohn had several thoughts.

If a BSC focuses an organization on its mission, then it seems like our BSC should start with student performance. But we don't have an agreement on the measures of performance. Test scores are one measure but what about matriculation rates, or job placement? What should the other quadrants be? We will have to decide what factors contribute to student performance. Instruction is certainly important. I am convinced that "chalk and talk" results in lower student performance, so we need to motivate teachers to use more project-based and cooperative learning techniques. Maybe we could measure things like teachers trying new practices, or teachers visiting each others classrooms, or students working independently and together in classrooms.

Also, how can I get teachers' buy-in for this effort and make it less threatening to them? I'm afraid that a lot of our teachers won't want to get involved in developing a BSC. In fact, it's likely that that the union will oppose any effort to measure individual teacher performance as part of a BSC. Maybe we should develop measures that aren't related to individual faculty. We could measure student performance by grade, subject, or type of student, such as Advanced Placement and Special Education. But if you can't link a measure to the person responsible for achieving it, why have it at all?

Similarly, where do parents and the community fit into the BSC? Should they be involved in its development? Should we try to measure their participation in the educational system? And what about the students? What should we do to get their buy-in? Or, do we even need it? Maybe they shouldn't even know we're doing this.

And then there's the question of what we can measure. We already collect a lot of data [See Exhibit 3], but how much of it is actually relevant to student performance? For example, do we really know that lower student/teacher ratios increase student performance? Or that teachers with a masters degree are more effective? Even if we assume that some of these data are relevant, how do we choose what is really important?

Finally, even if we can agree on what to measure, then how do we set targets for each measure? The minimum acceptable levels should be high enough to be meaningful, yet if our target goals are unrealistic, people will become demoralized. I'm not sure who should set the targets and how we should assign responsibility for achieving them, but if no one feels accountable for the goals, we'll never reach them.

Next Steps

Ms. Kohn had discussed the superintendent's request with the school's department heads and had received the mixed reactions shown at the beginning of the case. Her own belief was that the BSC could bring the school together and advance the district's ongoing school reform process. However, there was

EXHIBIT 3
Data collected at
Barrington High
School

Student Data

Standardized reading test scores, by grade
    % of students in top quartile
    % of students in middle quartiles
    % of students in lower quartile
% improvement in median reading scores over previous year
Standardized math test scores, by grade
    % of students in top quartile
    % of students in middle quartiles
    % of students in lower quartile
% improvement in median math scores over previous year
# students in summer classes
Average # years spent m bilingual classes
% of students in mainstream classes
% of students in bilingual classes
% of students in special education classes
% of students in Advanced Placement classes
Student absence rate
Student tardy rate
Student suspension rate
Student dropout rate
Number of college acceptances

Teacher and Staff Data

Student/teacher ratio, overall school
Student/teacher ratio, regular classes
Student/teacher ratio, special education classes
Student/teacher ratio, bilingual classes
Grade distribution, by teacher
Grade distribution, by course
Teacher absence rate
% of teachers with Bachelor's degree
% of teachers with Master's degree
% of teachers with doctorate
education level of administrators and staff
professional development days for teachers

Financial Data

Total cost per student
% budget spent on teacher salaries
% budget spent on administration
% budget spent on books and supplies
% budget spent on operations and maintenance

a risk that the benefits would not justify the use of the school's scarce resources, since developing a BSC would be a time-consuming and potentially controversial process. It would be easier, she thought, if she just developed the BSC herself and asked teachers to use it, but she wasn't sure what that would really accomplish besides token compliance with the superintendent's request.

Questions

1. What is the value of the BSC? Why would a for-profit business firm want to develop one?

2. Do you agree with Ms. Kohn that student performance is the educational equivalent of financial performance in a for-profit enterprise? If not, what is the educational equivalent?

3. Assuming that student performance is the equivalent of financial performance, what are the educational equivalents of the other three areas shown in the Kaplan/Norton article. What criteria did you use to reach your conclusions?

4. What role should teachers play in the development of a BSC? How would you respond to Ms. Kohn's other concerns?

5. How should Ms. Kohn respond to the superintendent's request to develop a BSC for Barrington High? What steps should she take next?

Chapter **13**

Reporting on Performance: Technical Aspects

Senior management generally reviews a nonprofit organization's performance in two somewhat different ways. First, it monitors current operations on a regular basis, using a set of reports designed for this purpose, together with other information. This type of review is discussed in this chapter and the next. Second, it reviews programs at infrequent intervals, using information that is developed specifically for each program. These reviews, called *program evaluations,* are discussed in Chapter 15.

Reports concerning the performance of current operations customarily are called *management control reports* since their purpose is to aid in the management control process. The dissemination of such reports, coupled with an analysis of the information they contain, is only one facet of this process, however. The whole process consists of several activities as well as a variety of formal and informal devices. Many of these activities and devices were discussed in Chapter 8.

This chapter discusses the technical aspects of the management control reports. We focus, in particular, on variance analysis, a technique that allows managers to determine in some considerable detail why actual revenues and expenses diverged from budgeted ones. In Chapter 14, we look at how the reports themselves can be structured, and how variance analysis can be combined with other information to facilitate managerial action to improve organizational performance.

Types of Information

In monitoring performance, managers typically rely on both quantitative and nonquantitative information. Quantitative information can be either financial or nonfinancial. For example, as we will see in this chapter, variance analysis uses financial information. By contrast, as we discussed in Chapter 12, output information, while frequently quantitative, is not usually financial.

Example
A school system can measure output at each school by a combination of: (1) attendance figures, (2) extracurricular activity participation, (3) number of diplomas, (4) number of scholarships, (5) percent of pupils with five or more major subjects, (6) percent of pupils with an 85 percent grade average or above, and (7) standard test results.

Quantitative information also can include nonmonetary information on inputs, such as the number of employees or the number of hours of service, which supplements the financial information on expenses. Output and input information frequently is shown on the same page as financial information, and the two types are related by reporting, say, cost per unit of output.

Quantitative information usually is included on reports that are prepared according to a regular schedule. The reports may arrive weekly, monthly, quarterly, or according to some other schedule that provides the information to managers in a timely way. As we discussed in Chapter 12, timely means that the information arrives soon enough to help managers make needed decisions.

In addition to receiving these routine reports, which tend to have the same format and content month after month, managers also can receive a variety of nonroutine, unsystematic, and generally nonquantitative performance information. Some of it comes from trade publications, newspapers, and other outside sources. Some of it comes from conversations within the organization, from memoranda, or from managers' personal observations as they visit responsibility centers and talk with people there.

Although the routine reports serve as a useful starting point in monitoring performance, additional information obtained from these other sources is essential to understanding how organizational units are performing and what factors are affecting them. Indeed, this nonquantitative information often is more important than that contained in the routine reports.

Types of Organizations

Some nonprofit organizations, or parts of such organizations, have activities that are quite similar to those in for-profit businesses. Analysis of management performance in these *businesslike* organizations is essentially the same as it is in a for-profit company. Other nonprofit organizations are unlike a business in that they are not self-financing. Instead, the amount of resources they have available for operation in a given year is fixed in advance. We call these *fixed-resource* organizations. Still other nonprofit organizations are required to do a job that is relatively fixed, regardless of the amount of resources planned. We call these *fixed-job* organizations.

Businesslike Organizations

A *businesslike organization* obtains a substantial fraction of its revenues from fees charged to clients, either directly or through third parties (such as Medicare for hospitals, state governments for some mental health agencies, or city governments for some foster care agencies). A businesslike organization ordinarily can exert a significant amount of influence over either the amount of revenues earned, the amount of expenses incurred, or both. Analysis of its operating performance, thus, is similar to analysis of the performance of a for-profit company.

Example

A hospital cannot influence the number of individuals in its community who need hospital care, but it can—through a variety of techniques—influence the number of individuals who are admitted to its facility. Moreover, although management cannot directly influence physician-ordering patterns, it can have a direct effect on unit costs in terms of efficiency of personnel, wage rates, and unit prices for supplies and materials.

A museum or symphony orchestra can engage in a wide array of marketing activities in an attempt to increase the number of clients using its services. Choices about programming, prices, promotional activities, and the like, are all comparable in nature to those of a for-profit company. Furthermore, cost analysis and control are of equally great significance.

Fixed-Resource Organizations

In many nonprofit organizations, the amount of resources available for operations in a given year is essentially fixed. This is the case with many religious organizations and other membership organizations whose resources are fixed by the amount of pledges or dues. Colleges with a fixed enrollment know their available resources, within narrow limits, as soon as the students enter. Health maintenance organizations (HMOs) know their resources based on annual enrollments.

Fixed-resource organizations must carefully monitor their spending to assure that they spend no more than the amount of available resources. Moreover, their success is measured by how much service they provide with these resources. In such organizations, spending more than the budget could portend financial disaster, and spending too far below the budget may be the first sign of impending client dissatisfaction.

In some fixed-resource organizations, the amount of service provided is a subjective judgment rather than a measured quantity. When this is the case, the reporting system cannot express the output for the whole organization in quantitative terms, and overall measures of effectiveness and efficiency therefore cannot be developed. Nevertheless, within such an organization there may well be service units whose output can be measured, and it may be possible to develop output and efficiency measures for these units. It also may be possible for managers to use quantitative information to help them determine when and where they need to take corrective action.

Fixed-Job Organizations

A fire department has a specific job to do; it must be ready to fight all fires that occur in its service area. Differences between the budget and actual amounts of spending may exist in either direction because of the nature of the job that had to be done. Similarly, if there are many snowstorms, the budget for snowplowing may need to be exceeded. Judgments about the performance of such organizations therefore must be in terms of how well they did whatever they were supposed to do, and whether an appropriate amount of resources was used in doing whatever they did. It is more important, for example, to consider the cost of snow removal per snowstorm or per inch of snow than the total snow removal cost of the year.

In fixed-job organizations, there is a tendency to ascribe differences between actual and budgeted amounts in a general way to the requirements of the job, whereas a detailed analysis may reveal inefficiencies. It is not sufficient to explain away a budget overrun in the highway maintenance department on the grounds that the winter was severe. Analysis of the variable costs that are caused by snowstorms of varying depths may indicate that the overrun was greater than it should have been. Thus, in almost all of these situations, a quantitative analysis of the reasons why actual results diverged from the budget is an essential management tool.

Role of Responsibility Centers

All three types of organizations can use both quantitative and nonquantitative information. In all but the smallest, the information usually is organized in terms of responsibility centers. This is because senior management usually acts by communicating with heads of responsibility centers. For ease of comparison, the same format usually is used for all responsibility centers. Most of the examples in our discussion of variance analysis assume that the computations are being made for a single responsibility center within a larger organization.

Variance Analysis

In most types of organizations, the difference, or *variance,* between budgeted and actual performance can be explained by five factors:

1. Volume (number of units of service).

2. Mix of units of service.

3. Revenue per unit of service (or selling price).

4. Rates paid for inputs (such as labor wages and cost per unit of raw materials).

5. Usage and efficiency of inputs (usage of raw materials and efficiency of labor).

Ordinarily, these variances are considered separately. There are three reasons for the separation: (1) they have different causes, (2) they usually involve different responsibility center managers, and (3) they require different types of corrective action.

Basic techniques for calculating these variances are given in the Appendix at the end of this chapter; more complex techniques are described in cost accounting textbooks. Computer programs, such as spreadsheets, can perform the actual calculations.

Volume Variances

If the actual quantity of services rendered differs from the quantity assumed in the budget, both revenue and certain expense items will be different from the budgeted amounts. For this reason, there are several different volume variances. The *revenue volume variance* shows the amount of change in revenue due exclusively to a change in volume (assuming that selling price remained constant). Similarly, the *expense volume variance* shows the change in variable expenses due exclusively to a change in volume (assuming that the variable expense per unit of volume remained constant). The sum of these two is the *contribution margin variance*.

Revenue Volume Variance

The revenue volume variance is the difference between the actual volume and the budgeted volume multiplied by the budgeted unit price:

$$\text{RVV} = (V_a - V_b) \times P_b$$

Example

If a museum budgets 10,000 visitors per month at $6 per visitor, its budgeted monthly revenue is $60,000. If in April it had 11,000 visitors, its revenue volume variance would be a favorable $6,000 [= (11,000 − 10,000) × $6].

Expense Volume Variance

The expense volume variance is the difference between the budgeted volume and the actual volume multiplied by the budgeted variable expense per unit:

$$\text{EVV} = (V_b - V_a) \times E_b$$

The calculation of the expense volume variance therefore requires classifying expense items as either fixed or variable. Recall from Chapter 5 that fixed expenses do not vary at all with volume, while variable items vary directly with volume.

Fixed versus Flexible Budgets   A budget that has no variable expense component is called a *fixed budget.* A fixed budget typically is used in a discretionary expense center. In a discretionary expense center, the manager is held responsible for spending no more than the budgeted, fixed amount each month (or other reporting period).

A budget developed from a classification of expenses into their fixed and variable elements is called a *flexible budget.* Rather than being a fixed amount, a flexible budget is expressed as a cost formula using agreed-upon fixed expenses and agreed-upon variable expenses per unit. An expected level of volume is specified to make sure that the fixed expenses are within their relevant range. This budget is then "flexed" each month (or other reporting period) by applying the actual volume of activity to the cost formula. The difference between the budget using the original estimate of volume and the budget using actual volume is the expense volume variance.

| **Example** | Assume that the budget for the kitchen of a shelter for the homeless consists of $12,000 per month of salaries and benefits, occupancy costs, and other costs that are unaffected by the number of meals served. The cost of ingredients, supplies, utilities, and other costs that vary with the number of meals served is expected to be $4 per meal. The cost formula for the kitchen therefore is $12,000 + $4x. The kitchen expects to serve 900 meals a month. Its monthly costs therefore should be $15,600 [= $12,000 + ($4 × 900)].

If, in April, the kitchen served 1,000 meals, the flexible budget would be $16,000 [= $12,000 + ($4 × 1,000)]. The expense volume variance would be an unfavorable $400 (= $15,600 − $16,000). It is unfavorable because the increase in meals, other things equal, would cause higher expenses and thus a lower surplus of revenues over expenses. As indicated above, the expense volume variance also can be computed by multiplying the difference between actual and budgeted volume by the budgeted variable expense per unit; this results in the same unfavorable $400 [=(900 − 1,000) × $4]. |

A flexible budget typically is used in a standard expense center. In this sort of responsibility center, the manager is not expected to exert any control over volume, but he or she is expected to adhere to the amount determined by the flexible budget. Thus, for the manager of the kitchen in the above example, actual expenses for the month of April would be compared to a flexed budget of $16,000 to measure the kitchen's financial performance.

Contribution Margin Variance

Differences in volume affect a nonprofit's surplus by the difference between revenue per unit of volume and variable expenses per unit of volume. As we discussed in Chapter 5, this difference is called the *contribution margin.* The contribution margin variance is the sum of the revenue volume variance and the expense volume variance:

$$CMV = RVV + EVV$$

Example

Assume that a food and wine association charges $50 per year for a membership, and expects that member service activities will cost $30 per year. The association has $380,000 in fixed costs. Assume that the management anticipated 20,000 members, but that only 15,000 joined. The revenue volume variance would be an unfavorable $250,000 [= (15,000 − 20,000) × $50]. The expense volume variance would be a favorable $150,000 [= (20,000 − 15,000) × $30]. The contribution margin variance would be an unfavorable $100,000 (= $150,000 − $250,000). Alternatively, the association thought it would have $400,000 [= ($50 − $30) × 20,000] of contribution to its fixed costs, but it had only $300,000 [= ($50 − $30) × 15,000], a $100,000 unfavorable variance.

Mix Variances

The volume variance computed above assumes that every unit of volume has the same selling price and unit variable expense. In many organizations, different types of services have different selling prices and different unit variable expense amounts. When this is the case, the volume variances are calculated using weighted averages of the selling price and variable expense amounts. If there is a change in the budgeted proportions of the different service types, a *mix variance* develops.

Many organizations do not calculate mix variances. In these organizations, the mix variance is automatically a part of the volume variance.[1] This can be misleading, however. In a hospital, for example, a mix variance can result from a change in the hospital's case types (e.g., relatively more coronary artery bypass surgery cases than influenza cases). Thus, even though volume may have remained at budget, the change in mix could have a substantial impact on the contribution margin variance.

Selling Price Variances

The selling price variance is the difference between the budgeted and actual selling prices, multiplied by the actual level of volume:

$$SPV = (P_a − P_b) \times V_a$$

[1]For an explanation of the process of calculating mix variances, see Anthony, Hawkins, and Merchant, *Accounting: Text and Cases,* 10th ed. (Burr Ridge, IL: McGraw-Hill, 1998). For an application to health care see Thomas R. Miller and Ryan J. Bruce, "Analyzing Cost Variance in Capitated Contracts," *Healthcare Financial Management* 49, no. 2 (February 1995).

If, for example, a day care center changed its fees during the year, there is a selling price variance. The computations for a selling price variance are shown in the revenue portion of the section "Making the Computations" in the Appendix at the end of this chapter.

Rate Variances

If the actual rates an organization pays for its material and labor inputs change from their budgeted levels, there is a rate variance. Rate variances usually are for either raw materials or labor. To compute them, we must know the unit amounts (raw material prices or wage rates) that were used in developing the budget (this is why we suggested in Chapter 10 that the budget show both quantity and unit price components).

Raw Material Rate Variances

If the prices (rates) an organization pays for its raw materials change from what was budgeted, there is a raw material rate variance. The raw material rate variance is the difference between the budget rate and the actual rate, multiplied by the actual quantity of raw materials purchased:

$$MRV = (R_b - R_a) \times Q_a$$

Example

If an association planned to purchase paper for its newsletters for $10 a ream, and paid $8 instead, there is a material rate variance. If the association purchased 500 reams, the total material rate variance is a favorable $1,000 [= ($10 − $8) × 500].

Wage Rate Variances

If the wages we pay our staff change from the budgeted levels, there is a wage rate variance. The wage rate variance is the difference between the budget rate and the actual rate, multiplied by the actual hours worked:

$$WRV = (R_b - R_a) \times H_a$$

Computations for a wage rate variance are shown in the Appendix.

Example

If a laboratory planned to pay its technicians $12 an hour, but paid them $14 instead, there is a wage rate variance. If the technicians worked 600 hours, the total wage rate variance is an unfavorable $1,200 [= ($12 − $14) × 600].

Usage/Efficiency Variances

Usage and efficiency variances measure, respectively, the actual use of raw materials and productivity of labor as compared to budgeted levels. Organizations typically use the terms *material usage variance* (for raw materials) and *labor efficiency variance* (for labor).

Material Usage Variance

The material usage variance is the difference between the budgeted and actual usage of raw materials per unit of output, multiplied by the budgeted rate, multiplied by the actual volume of output:

$$\text{MUV} = (U_b - U_a) \times R_b \times V_a$$

The computation for a material usage variance is the same as the computation for a labor volume variance, as shown in the Appendix.

Example

A free-standing radiology laboratory budgeted an average of 1.3 films per chest X-ray, but actually used 1.6 films. The raw materials in each film had a budgeted cost of $12 each. The lab performed 2,000 chest X-rays during the most recent month. The material usage variance is an unfavorable $7,200 [= (1.3 − 1.6) × $12 × 2,000].

Labor Efficiency Variances

The labor efficiency variance is the difference between the budgeted and actual time needed to produce a unit of output, multiplied by the budgeted rate, multiplied by the actual volume of output:

$$\text{LEV} = (T_b - T_a) \times R_b \times V_a$$

Example

A welfare department's social workers were budgeted to spend an average of one-half hour per interview with potential clients, but actually spent an average of one-third hour. The social workers were paid $18 an hour. They interviewed a total of 300 clients during the most recent month. The efficiency variance is a favorable $900 [= ($3/6$ hours − $2/6$ hours) × $18 × 300].

Use of Variance Analysis

An important feature of variance analysis is the ability it gives senior management to link managerial responsibility to changes in revenues and expenses. By way of summary, Exhibit 13–1 lists each variance, and identifies, in a general sense, the department or responsibility center that most likely controls it. Although Exhibit 13–1 is most applicable to a businesslike organization, it also has validity for fixed-resource and fixed-job organizations. The principal difference is that certain fixed-resource and fixed-job organizations will not be concerned with some of the variances. For example, a fixed-resource organization ordinarily will not be concerned with selling price variances.

In many organizations, operating managers do not control the volume or mix of services supplied, nor do they set wage rates for employees, or control the rates paid for raw materials and other items of expense. Consequently, the principal reason for identifying the volume, mix, selling price, and rate variances is to isolate them so that management can focus attention on efficiency variances (and, therefore, the individual managers responsible for these variances). This is the principal reason for preparing a flexible budget.

EXHIBIT 13–1   Types of Variances and Controlling Agents

Variance	Controlling Agent
Volume variance	Marketing department/senior management/the environment (depending on the organization).
Mix variances	Same as above.
Selling price variances	Senior management/marketing department/ program managers (depending on the organization).
Raw material price variances	Purchasing department/program managers.
Wage rate variances	Senior management (who negotiate union contracts)/program managers (who make job offers).
Usage variances	Program managers/department heads.
Efficiency variances	Program managers/department heads.

In any event, senior management needs to have an adequate explanation of the reasons underlying efficiency variances, and it especially needs to know whether unfavorable variances are likely to persist or whether steps are under way to correct them. By distinguishing between efficiency variances and all other variances, senior management is in a better position to discuss these steps with operating managers.

An Illustration of Variances in a Hospital Setting

To illustrate how the above variances can be used, assume that Nucio Hospital has prepared the somewhat simplified budget shown in Exhibit 13–2. As this budget shows, the hospital anticipates four different kinds of cases: acute myocardial infarction (heart attack), influenza, pneumonia, and phlebitis. Its budgeted variable expenses per case are based on four different services: routine care (i.e., the hospital stay itself), radiology films, laboratory tests, and pharmacy units (such as prescriptions). (Obviously, there are many more services and many more case types in a hospital than this, so the overall totals may not be completely realistic. Nevertheless, the numbers are sufficient for illustrative purposes.)

Operating under a diagnosis-based form of reimbursement, the hospital is paid on a per-case basis. For each case type, the anticipated "selling price" is shown, along with the anticipated utilization and variable expense per unit for each service. The total variable expense per case for each case type is then calculated, and the revenue and total variable expense per case are multiplied by the anticipated number of cases to give total revenue and total variable expenses by case type. The latter is deducted from total revenue to give the contribution to fixed expenses from each case type. The fixed expenses are then

EXHIBIT 13-2 Original Budget

	Acute MI	Influenza	Pneumonia	Phlebitis	Total
Overall budget:					
Number of cases	300	200	100	50	650
Revenue per case. . . . . $	6,000	$ 1,000	$ 1,500	$ 3,000	
Total revenue.	1,800,000	200,000	150,000	150,000	2,300,000
Variable expenses per case. . . .	3,590	910	1,031	1,218	
Total variable expenses	1,077,000	182,000	103,100	60,900	1,423,000
Contribution . . . . $	723,000	$ 18,000	$ 46,900	$ 89,100	$ 877,000
Total fixed expenses					800,000
Surplus					$ 77,000
Variable expense detail:					
Routine care:					
Number of days per case . . .	21	5	6	7	
Expense per day. . . . . $	150	$ 150	$ 150	$ 150	
Total expense per case . . . . . $	3,150	$ 750	$ 900	$ 1,050	
Radiology:					
Number of films per case . . .	5	1	2	0	
Expense per film . . . . $	25	$ 25	$ 25	$ 25	
Total expense per case . . . . . $	125	$ 25	$ 50	$ 0	
Laboratory:					
Number of tests per case . . .	10	5	3	7	
Expense per test. . . . . $	15	$ 15	$ 15	$ 15	
Total expense per case . . . . . $	150	$ 75	$ 45	$ 105	
Pharmacy:					
Number of units per case. . .	55	20	12	21	
Expense per unit . . . . $	3	$ 3	$ 3	$ 3	
Total expense per case . . . . . $	165	$ 60	$ 36	$ 63	
Total variable expense per case . . $	3,590	$ 910	$ 1,031	$ 1,218	

deducted from the total contribution to give a total budgeted income of $77,000 for the accounting period.

Exhibit 13–3 is a flexible budget based on the actual volume and mix of cases served. The flexible budget shows what the surplus *would have been* if everything remained the same as the original budget except volume and mix. That is, the calculations use budgeted figures for both revenue per case and variable expense per case. Fixed expenses are shown as budgeted based on the assumption that change in mix and the volume did not affect them. The result is that there would have been a surplus of $43,450 instead of the original $77,000.

The flexible budget is followed by revenue and expense volume variances, and a contribution margin variance. There are several items worth noting in these computations. First, as discussed in the Appendix, in computing the revenue variance, budgeted cases are subtracted from actual cases, whereas in computing the expense variance the reverse is true. Second, when the unfavorable $33,550 contribution margin variance is added to the original budget

EXHIBIT 13–3 Flexible Budget and Variances

	Acute MI	Influenza	Pneumonia	Phlebitis	Total
Overall budget:					
Actual number of cases	250	150	200	75	675
Revenue per case	$ 6,000	$ 1,000	$ 1,500	$ 3,000	
Total revenue	1,500,000	150,000	300,000	225,000	2,175,000
Variable expenses per case . .	3,590	910	1,031	1,218	
Total variable expenses	897,500	136,500	206,200	91,350	1,331,550
Contribution	$ 602,500	$ 13,500	$ 93,800	$133,650	$ 843,450
Total fixed expenses					800,000
Surplus					$ 43,450
Revenue volume variance:					
Actual budgeted cases	−50	50	100	25	
Budgeted unit revenue	$ 6,000	$ 1,000	$ 1,500	$ 3,000	
Variance	$ (300,000)	$ (50,000)	$ 150,000	$ 75,000	$ (125,000)
Expense volume variance:					
Budgeted—actual cases	50	50	−100	−25	
Budgeted expense per case . .	$ 3,590	$ 910	$ 1,031	$ 1,218	
Variance	$ 179,500	$ 45,500	$(103,100)	$ (30,450)	$ 91,450
Contribution margin variance:					
Revenue volume variance +					
Expense volume variance . .	$ (120,500)	$ (4,500)	$ 46,900	$ 44,550	$ (33,550)

of $77,000, the result is $43,450, the same amount as the flexible budget. Third, when we disaggregate the contribution margin variance, we see that the hospital lost $125,000 in revenue that it had anticipated receiving, but saved $91,450 in expenses that it had anticipated incurring.

Finally, note that the actual number of cases was 675, compared to 650 in the original budget. The fact that volume has increased but the surplus under the flexible budget declined by $33,550 indicates that there was a fairly significant mix variance. Indeed, the reason for the decline is that the mix shifted away from high-margin cases to low-margin ones. Had the mix (the proportion of each case type) remained the same as budgeted, the flexible budget surplus would have increased with the increase in volume.

Exhibit 13–4 shows the actual results for the 675 cases that were served during the accounting period. Although revenue per case remained as budgeted, there were several changes in expenses between the original and flexible budgets: the average length of stay (i.e., number of patient days) was different for three of the four diagnoses and the average variable expense per day was $10 more than budgeted; the average number of radiological films was different for three of the four case types, and the average expense per film was $2 less than budgeted; the average number of laboratory tests differed, and the average expense per test was $5 more than budgeted; the average number of pharmacy units was different, although the average expense per unit remained as budgeted.

EXHIBIT 13–4 Actual Results

	Acute MI	Influenza	Pneumonia	Phlebitis	Total
Overall results:					
Actual number of cases.....	250	150	200	75	675
Revenue per case .... $	6,000	$ 1,000	$ 1,500	$ 3,000	
Total revenue	1,500,000	150,000	300,000	225,000	2,175,000
Variable expenses per case ..	3,491	1,126	991	1,252	
Total variable expenses	872,750	168,900	198,200	93,900	1,333,750
Contribution.............	627,250	(18,900)	101,800	131,100	$ 841,250
Total fixed expenses					800,000
Surplus					$ 41,250
Variable expense detail:					
Routine care:					
Average number of days					
per case.............	19	6	5	7	
Average expense per day.. $	160	$ 160	$ 160	$ 160	
Total average expense					
per case............. $	3,040	$ 960	$ 800	$ 1,120	
Radiology:					
Average number of films					
per case.............	4	2	2	0	
Average expense per film.. $	23	$ 23	$ 23	$ 23	
Total average expense					
per case............. $	92	$ 46	$ 46	$ 0	
Laboratory:					
Average number of tests					
per case.............	10	3	5	3	
Average expense per test.. $	20	$ 20	$ 20	$ 20	
Total average expense					
per case............. $	200	$ 60	$ 100	$ 60	
Pharmacy:					
Average number of units					
per case.............	53	20	15	24	
Average expense per unit . $	3	$ 3	$ 3	$ 3	
Total average expense					
per case............. $	159	$ 60	$ 45	$ 72	
Total average variable expense					
per case .... $	3,491	$ 1,126	$ 991	$ 1,252	

The result is an actual average variable expense per case that differs from the budgeted average variable expense per case. This total is multiplied by the actual number of cases served to give total variable expenses per case. As is shown in the totals at the top of Exhibit 13–4, the resulting actual surplus is $41,250, which is $2,200 below the $43,450 surplus in the flexible budget.

Exhibit 13–5 shows the calculation of the variances resulting from changes in the use of resources per case (e.g., length of stay, radiology films). By

EXHIBIT 13–5 Resource Use Variances

Type of Resource	Acute MI	Influenza	Pneumonia	Phlebitis	Total
Routine care:					
Budgeted—actual days per case	2	−1	1	0	
Budgeted expense per day	$ 150	$ 150	$ 150	$ 150	
Use variance	$ 300	$ (150)	$ 150	$ 0	
Radiology:					
Budgeted—actual films per case	1	−1	0	0	
Budgeted expense per film	$ 25	$ 25	$ 25	$ 25	
Use variance	$ 25	$ (25)	$ 0	$ 0	
Laboratory:					
Budgeted—actual tests per case	0	2	−2	4	
Budgeted expense per test	$ 15	$ 15	$ 15	$ 15	
Use variance	$ 0	$ 30	$ (30)	$ 60	
Pharmacy:					
Budgeted—actual units per case	2	0	−3	−3	
Budgeted expense per unit	$ 3	$ 3	$ 3	$ 3	
Use variance	$ 6	$ 0	$ (9)	$ (9)	
Total resource use variances per case . .	$ 331	$ (145)	$ 111	$ 51	
Actual number of cases.	250	150	200	75	
Total resource use variances	$82,750	$(21,750)	$22,200	$3,825	$87,025

multiplying the change in resource units per case by the budgeted unit expense figure, we isolate the impact on the budget of changes in the use of each resource. The total dollar effect for each case type is the sum of the use variances multiplied by the actual number of cases. It is shown at the bottom of the exhibit. Acute MI cases, with a total of $82,750, had the biggest reduction in resource use, while influenza had somewhat higher resource use (an unfavorable variance of $21,750). Overall, the hospital saved a total of $87,025 from reduced resource use.

Exhibit 13–6 isolates the effect of the changes in expense per unit, or what can be called *rate/efficiency variances*. The reason this is both rate and efficiency is that the expense per resource (e.g., a lab test) actually is the result of two separate elements: the rate paid per unit for each resource (e.g., the laboratory technician wage rate) and the efficiency with which the service is provided (e.g., the number of tests that the laboratory technician completes in an hour). Thus, in the laboratory, a change in expense per test could be the result of a change in the wage rate of the lab technicians performing tests, a change in their efficiency in conducting tests, or some combination of the two.

The rate/efficiency variance per case can be multiplied by the actual number of cases served of each type to give a total rate/efficiency variance for each resource type. This figure consists of variable expenses only. Thus, given the *actual* number and mix of cases served, and the number of resource units *actually* ordered, the rate/efficiency variance shows how well the department

EXHIBIT 13–6 Rate/Efficiency Variances

Type of Resource	Acute MI	Influenza	Pneumonia	Phlebitis	Total
Actual number of cases.............	250	150	200	75	
Routine care:					
Budgeted—actual expense per day . . $	(10)	$ (10)	$ (10)	$ (10)	
Actual number of days per case.....	19	6	5	7	
Rate/efficiency variance per case . . . . $	(190)	$ (60)	$ (50)	$ (70)	
Total rate/efficiency variance....... $	(47,500)	$(9,000)	$(10,000)	$(5,250)	$(71,750)
Radiology:					
Budgeted—actual expense per film . . $	2	$ 2	$ 2	$ 2	
Actual number of films	4	2	2	0	
Rate/efficiency variance per case . . . . $	8	$ 4	$ 4	$ 0	
Total rate/efficiency variance....... $	2,000	$ 600	$ 800	$ 0	$ 3,400
Laboratory:					
Budgeted—actual expense per test . . $	(5)	$ (5)	$ (5)	$ (5)	
Actual number of tests	10	3	5	3	
Rate/efficiency variance per case . . . . $	(50)	$ (15)	$ (25)	$ (15)	
Total rate/efficiency variance....... $	(12,500)	$(2,250)	$ (5,000)	$(1,125)	$(20,875)
Pharmacy:					
Budgeted—actual expense per unit. . $	0	$ 0	$ 0	$ 0	
Actual number of units	53	20	15	24	
Rate/efficiency variance per case . . . . $	0	$ 0	$ 0	$ 0	
Total rate/efficiency variance....... $	0	$ 0	$ 0	$ 0	$ 0
Total rate/efficiency variances					$(89,225)

performed in meeting its budget. As can be seen, routine care, with an unfavorable variance of $71,750, performed considerably worse than budgeted; the laboratory also had an unfavorable variance ($20,875). The radiology department performed slightly better than budgeted, and pharmacy was right on budget.

The rate and efficiency effects are combined in this illustration. However, managers of routine care, the laboratory, and the other service departments most likely would want to undertake a more detailed variance analysis to isolate the individual effects of rate and efficiency. The approach to doing this would be similar to that for calculating all other variances; that is, the effect of each item would be determined by holding everything else constant and calculating the impact of that item alone.

To illustrate, assume that the following data are available for the laboratory:

	Time per Test (Minutes)	Wage Rate $ per minute	Total Expense per Test
Budget	75	$0.20	$15.00
Actual	80	0.25	20.00

To perform the calculations, we look first at the change in wage rate:

(Budgeted rate − Actual rate) × Actual efficiency = Wage rate variance

or

($0.20 − $0.25) × 80 minutes = ($0.05) × 80 minutes = $4.00 unfavorable

Next, we look at the change in efficiency:

(Budgeted time − Actual time) × Budgeted wage = Efficiency variance

or

$$(75 \text{ minutes} - 80 \text{ minutes}) \times \$0.20 = (5 \text{ minutes}) \times \$0.20$$
$$= \$1.00 \text{ unfavorable}$$

These per-test variances can be applied to the total number of tests to obtain the total variances. The computations are as follows:

Case Type	Actual Number of Cases	Tests per Case	Total Tests	Wage Rate Variance $(4.00)/test	Efficiency Variance $(1.00)/test	Total
Acute MI	250	10	2,500	$(10,000)	$(2,500)	
Influenza	150	3	450	(1,800)	(450)	
Pneumonia. . .	200	5	1,000	(4,000)	(1,000)	
Phlebitis	75	3	225	(900)	(225)	
Total.			4,175	$(16,700)	$(4,175)	$(20,875)

Note that the total variance for the laboratory shown here is the same as the total shown on Exhibit 13–6. With this additional information, however, the laboratory manager can now see that the total is divided between $16,700 that is due to a change in the average wage rate of technicians, and $4,175 that is the result of lower than expected technician efficiency (minutes per test).

Variance Analysis and Management Control

The principal purpose of variance analysis is to facilitate the management control process. In this regard, it is important to structure the variance calculations so that managers find them useful for taking corrective action. In the case of Nucio Hospital, for example, we might decide that the $33,550 unfavorable contribution margin variance is due largely to factors outside the control of the hospital, namely, a reduction in acute MI and influenza cases. (Some might argue that this variance is senior management's responsibility, since senior management is charged with improving the hospital's competitive position vis-à-vis other hospitals in the area.)

The $33,550 negative contribution margin variance reduces the originally budgeted surplus of $77,000 to a flexible budget surplus of $43,450. However, as discussed above, the actual surplus was $41,250, or $2,200 less. This rather small difference is somewhat misleading, since it is due to the combination of a favorable variance of $87,025 in resources per case and an unfavorable variance of $89,225 in the rate/efficiency of the delivery of those resources ($87,025 − $89,225 = −$2,200).

Since physicians tend to control resources per case, they would appear to be responsible for the former variance. By contrast, cost center or department managers, who are responsible for the efficient delivery of physician-ordered resources, would appear to be responsible for the latter variance. It is for this reason that department managers most likely would want to compute the separate rate and efficiency variances associated with their activities. Most no doubt would argue that they have greater control over efficiency than wage rates.

Example

Sometimes, a change in cost per resource unit can have a big impact. For example, radiologists can choose between two types of contrast media to diagnose diseases of the kidneys and other organs: low osmolar contrast agents (LOCAs) or high osmolar contrast agents (HOCAs). LOCAs produce fewer adverse side effects and less patient discomfort than HOCAs; however, they cost 10 to 20 times more per dose than HOCAs.

Although there is a favorable variance in resources per case, the medical director of the hospital might still have some concern, since, as Exhibit 13–5 indicates, the $87,025 favorable variance is the result of both favorable and unfavorable variances for individual case types. Specifically, the mix of services was $21,750 unfavorable for the influenza cases, and the large favorable variance for the acute MI cases might suggest potential problems with the quality of care.

From a management control perspective, discussions with the medical staff about these matters are greatly facilitated by variance analysis. For example, all of the variances in Exhibit 13–5 are due exclusively to changes in the use of resources per case; that is, they reflect only the cases actually treated (not those that were budgeted to be treated), and both rate and efficiency have been held constant by using the budgeted expense per unit (e.g., day, film).

More generally, with information on variances, senior management can discuss the reasons underlying each variance with the managers who are involved, and who can take corrective action, if appropriate. Managers should note, however, that a variance is not designed to be used as a "club;" rather, it is intended as a tool to assist in understanding why actual costs diverged from budget and for exploring these reasons with the appropriate managers so that, if possible, action can be taken to bring costs back in line.

Other Measures

As discussed in Chapter 12, in addition to a concern with inputs, many nonprofit organizations attempt to report on outputs. As Chapter 12 suggested, most nonprofits use two broad types of output measures: results and process.

Variance analysis is concerned principally with process measures. As such, it says little about results, and whether the organization is *effective,* that is, whether it is moving toward the attainment of its objectives.

By definition, effectiveness in a nonprofit organization cannot be measured by financial data alone. If reliable measures of the organization's accomplishments can be found, a comparison of planned and actual output provides a numerical measure of effectiveness. As discussed in Chapter 12, however, in many situations the most that quantitative measures can do is give clues to the organization's effectiveness. Nevertheless, in designing its reporting system, senior management should make an effort to provide quantitative reports on effectiveness as well as efficiency.

Summary	In this chapter we have discussed some of the technical aspects of the management control reports, focusing on variance analysis. Variance analysis allows managers to determine in some considerable detail why actual revenues and expenses diverged from budgeted ones. In particular, it disaggregates differences between budget and actual data into five general categories:

1. Volume and mix of outputs.

2. Selling price per output unit.

3. Usage and mix of resources per unit of output (e.g., a case).

4. Rates paid for inputs.

5. Efficiency in the provision of inputs.

Variance analysis can be used in any of three types of organizations: businesslike, fixed-resource, or fixed-job. Although it is more limited in the latter two than in the first, it nevertheless can help management focus on questions like why actual expenses exceeded the fixed resources, or why a particular job cost more than anticipated. In this regard, managers must bear in mind that variance analysis does not *answer* questions, as such; rather, it directs management's attention to areas where problems appear to exist. As such, it is not a substitute for, but rather an aid to, conversations with managers to decide what action, if any, is needed to improve operations.

Appendix

Computing Variances

The concept of variance analysis can be illustrated graphically, using an example of labor costs. Total labor costs are the product of the number of hours worked and the wage rate per hour. Assume that the labor budget for a particular activity is 100 hours of work at $8 per hour, for a total of $800. Graphically, this can be represented by a rectangle, with the vertical axis indicating the wage rate and the horizontal axis the number of hours, as shown in Diagram 1.

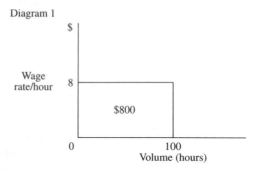

Diagram 1

Now, assume that actual labor costs for the period are $1,200. A typical budget report might indicate the variance as:

Item	Budget	Actual	Variance
Labor cost	$800	$1,200	$(400)

The parentheses indicate an unfavorable variance, that is, one that reduces the organization's surplus. In this instance, the variance is negative because actual expenses were greater than budget.

While this information may be useful to managers, it does not indicate why the variance occurred. Specifically, in this instance, we cannot tell whether it was the result of a higher wage than anticipated, more hours than anticipated, or some combination of the two. If the variance were solely the result of a higher wage, it could be viewed graphically shown in Diagram 2.

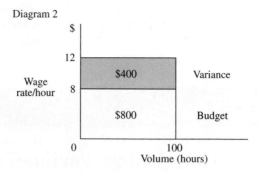

Diagram 2

If, on the other hand, it were the result solely of more hours, it could be viewed as depicted in Diagram 3.

Diagram 3

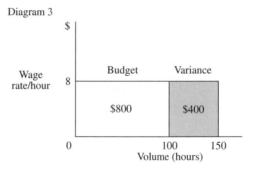

If the variance resulted from a combination of a higher wage *and* more hours, it could be depicted by a variety of wage/hour combinations; Diagram 4 is one possibility.

Diagram 4

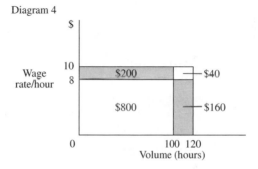

Note that, in this last instance, we have a problem because the $40 rectangle in the upper right portion of the graph is the result of a combination of *both* the wage variance *and* the hour (or volume) variance. The combination variance is referred to as the gray area, because it cannot reasonably be assigned to either the higher price or the higher volume; rather it is caused by the *combined effect* of the two. In this instance, $200 of the total variance can be attributed to the higher wage rate, $160 to the higher number of hours (volume), and $40 to the combination effect.

For ease of calculation, the gray area typically is assigned to the factor represented on the vertical axis, which usually is the factor that measures the rate. In this case, it would be assigned to the wage variance, such that, graphically, the analysis would look as shown in Diagram 5.

This type of information makes the budget report much more useful to management. The resulting report might look something like the one shown below. This report is useful because, in most organizations, different managers are responsible for different elements of a total variance, and, for management control purposes, it is important to identify the variance that is attributable to each individual manager.

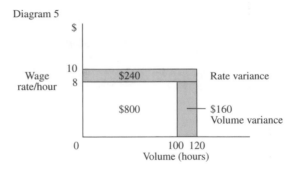

Diagram 5

Item	Budget	Actual	Variance
Labor costs	$800	$1,200	$(240)
Wage-rate variance			(240)
Volume variance.			(160)
Total variance			$(400)

Making the Computations

The technique used to calculate a variance isolates the change between budget and actual for each item and calculates its effect independently of other changes. The calculations for expense variances differ slightly from those for revenue variances.

Expense Variances

An expense variance is calculated by subtracting the *actual* amount from the *budgeted* amount. For a rate variance, the result is multiplied by the actual volume amount. For a volume variance, the result is multiplied by the budgeted rate amount.

Let's return to the above example and perform the calculations:

$$\frac{\text{Wage rate}}{\text{variance}} = \left(\frac{\text{Budgeted}}{\text{wage rate}} - \frac{\text{Actual}}{\text{rate wage}}\right) \times \frac{\text{Actual}}{\text{hours}} = \text{Variance}$$

$$(\$8 \quad - \quad \$10) \quad \times \quad 120 \quad = \quad \$(240)$$

$$\frac{\text{Volume}}{\text{variance}} = \left(\frac{\text{Budgeted}}{\text{hours}} - \frac{\text{Actual}}{\text{hours}}\right) \times \frac{\text{Budgeted}}{\text{wage rate}} = \text{Variance}$$

$$(\$100 \quad - \quad \$120) \quad \times \quad \$8 \quad = \quad \$(160)$$

Revenue Variances

For a revenue variance, the process is the same with one exception: we subtract the *budgeted* amount from the *actual* amount. When this is done, a negative result of the computation will indicate an unfavorable variance; that is, a variance that, other things being equal, reduces the organization's surplus.

To illustrate, if, in the above example, we had budgeted a selling price of $20 per hour, and actually had earned $25 per hour, our total variance would have been the difference between the budget of $2,000 [= $20/hour × 100 hours] and $3,000 [= $25/hour × 120 hours]. This has a $1,000 favorable effect on income. The computations would be as follows:

$$\begin{array}{c}\text{Selling price/} \\ \text{hour variance}\end{array} = \left(\begin{array}{c}\text{Actual} \\ \text{rate}\end{array} - \begin{array}{c}\text{Budgeted} \\ \text{rate}\end{array}\right) \times \begin{array}{c}\text{Actual} \\ \text{hours}\end{array} = \text{Variance}$$

$$(\$25 \quad - \quad \$20) \quad \times \quad 120 \quad = \quad \$600$$

$$\begin{array}{c}\text{Volume} \\ \text{variance}\end{array} = \left(\begin{array}{c}\text{Actual} \\ \text{hours}\end{array} - \begin{array}{c}\text{Budgeted} \\ \text{hours}\end{array}\right) \times \begin{array}{c}\text{Budgeted} \\ \text{revenue/hour}\end{array} = \text{Variance}$$

$$(\$120 \quad - \quad \$100) \quad \times \quad \$20 \quad = \quad \$400$$

Note that, although this technique was performed in a situation involving only two variances (wage rate and volume), it could be performed equally well with several variances. The only difference is that the multiplication would involve more than just two factors. Indeed, a complete explanation of the divergence from budget in most organizations usually calls for an analysis of mix and efficiency variances as well as volume and prices (or wages). We discuss variances involving these four factors in the text.

Suggested Additional Readings

Anthony, Robert N., David F. Hawkins, and Kenneth A. Merchant. *Accounting: Text and Cases*, 10th ed. Burr Ridge, IL: McGraw-Hill, 1998.

Finkler, Steven A. *Financial Management for Public Health and Not-for-Profit Organizations*. Englewood Cliffs, NJ: Prentice Hall, 2000.

Horngren, Charles T., George Foster, and Srikant M. Datar. *Cost Accounting: A Managerial Emphasis*. Englewood Cliffs, NJ: Prentice Hall, 2000.

Practice Case

El Conejo Family Planning Clinic*

Rosa Ruiz, the Director of Finance of El Conejo Family Planning Clinic, recently had received a memorandum from the Chairman of the Finance Committee of the Clinic's Board of Trustees. The memorandum also had been

*This case was prepared by Professor David W. Young. Copyright © by David W. Young.

sent to all department heads, and had expressed concern that the results of the year's operations were considerably worse than budgeted. One reason for this problem was that third parties had lowered their rate for one of the Clinic's most significant visit types, but there appeared to be some other explanations as well. Ms. Ruiz had been asked to analyze the reasons for the poor performance, meet with the relevant department heads, and make a presentation at the next board meeting concerning the Clinic's performance.

In reviewing the budgeted and actual results, Ms. Ruiz discovered that almost all of the Clinic's variation from its budget could be attributed to four visit types and four services. For reasons of simplicity, she decided to base her presentation on these only.

Exhibit 1 contains the original budget for these four visit types: IUD, first visit; oral contraceptive, first visit; special follow-up visits (when problems existed with the contraceptive or contraceptive method); and routine follow-up. It also shows the budgeted variable expenses per visit for the four services: physician care, nursing care, medical supplies, and laboratory tests.

As Exhibit 1 indicates, the Clinic was paid on a per-visit basis. Its anticipated revenue for each visit type is shown in Exhibit 1, as is the anticipated utilization of services and the variable expense per unit for each service for each visit type. These estimates were used to calculate the total variable expense per visit for each visit type. The revenue and total variable expense per visit were then multiplied by the anticipated number of visits to give total revenue and total variable expenses by visit type. The latter was deducted from total revenue to give the contribution to fixed expenses from each visit type. The fixed expenses were then deducted from the total contribution to give a total budgeted surplus of $85,000 for the accounting period.

Ms. Ruiz asked her staff assistant, Anthony Hourihan, to use the actual data for the period, shown in Exhibit 2, as the basis for a report on results for the year. This report was to contain a complete breakdown of the reasons why the Clinic's actual surplus diverged from the budgeted one. The report would be submitted to the Clinic's chief executive officer, and would be used by Ms. Ruiz for her presentation to the Board of Trustees.

Mr. Hourihan began by using the data from Exhibit 2 to compute the actual financial results for the period (Exhibit 3), which showed that, instead of earning a surplus, the Clinic actually had incurred a deficit of $218,300. Then, reasoning that the Clinic had essentially no control over the number or type of visits seen, he also prepared a flexible budget (Exhibit 4), which showed that $750 of the difference was due exclusively to the change in the number of visits seen in the Clinic. Using similar reasoning, he prepared an analysis of the variance due to the changes in the third-party reimbursement rates (shown at the bottom of Exhibit 4), which showed that $17,000 of the difference was a result of these rate changes.

Having analyzed and explained only $17,750 of the $303,300 total difference between budgeted and actual performance, Mr. Hourihan met with Ms. Ruiz to show her the results of his work. Ms. Ruiz explained to Mr. Hourihan that he

EXHIBIT 1   Original Budget

	IUD 1st Visit	Oral Conc 1st Visit	Special Follow-Up	Routine Follow-Up	Total
Overall budget:					
Number of visits.............	3,000	2,000	1,000	500	6,500
Price per visit	$ 200.00	$ 100.00	$ 125.00	$ 40.00	
Total revenue	$600,000	$200,000	$125,000	$20,000	$945,000
Variable expenses per visit	$ 165.00	$ 75.00	$ 110.00	$ 10.00	
Total variable expenses........	$495,000	$150,000	$110,000	$ 5,000	760,000
Contribution	$105,000	$ 50,000	$ 15,000	$15,000	$185,000
Total fixed expenses..........					100,000
Surplus...................					$ 85,000
Variable expense detail:					
Physician care:					
Average # minutes per visit...	30	10	15	5	
Average wage per minute....	$ 1.00	$ 1.00	$ 1.00	$ 1.00	
Total expense per visit	$ 30.00	$ 10.00	$ 15.00	$ 5.00	
Nursing care:					
Average # minutes per visit...	30	20	30	10	
Average wage per minute....	$ 0.50	$ 0.50	$ 0.50	$ 0.50	
Total expense per visit	$ 15.00	$ 10.00	$ 15.00	$ 5.00	
Medical supplies:					
Average # units per visit	3	1	2	0	
Average expense per unit	$ 25.00	$ 25.00	$ 25.00	$ 25.00	
Total expense per visit	$ 75.00	$ 25.00	$ 50.00	$ 0.00	
Laboratory:					
Average # tests per visit	3	2	2	0	
Average expense per test	$ 15.00	$ 15.00	$ 15.00	$ 15.00	
Total expense per visit	$ 45.00	$ 30.00	$ 30.00	$ 0.00	
Total average variable					
expense per visit............	$ 165.00	$ 75.00	$ 110.00	$ 10.00	

EXHIBIT 2 Actual Results

	IUD 1st Visit	Oral Conc 1st Visit	Special Follow-Up	Follow-Up	Total
Overall results:					
Actual number of visits	2,750	2,200	1,000	600	6,550
Actual price per visit	$200.00	$90.00	$130.00	$40.00	
Total fixed expenses.					100,000
Variable expense detail:					
Physician care:					
Average # minutes per visit	25	5	20	10	
Average wage per minute	$ 1.20	$ 1.20	$ 1.20	$ 1.20	
Nursing care:					
Average # minutes per visit	40	30	25	5	
Average wage per minute	$ 0.60	$ 0.60	$ 0.60	$ 0.60	
Medical supplies:					
Average # units per visit	4	2	2	0	
Average expense per unit.	$ 21.00	$21.00	$ 21.00	$21.00	
Laboratory:					
Average # tests per visit	5	3	5	0	
Average expense per test	$ 16.00	$16.00	$ 16.00	$16.00	

EXHIBIT 3   Actual Results with Calculations

	IUD 1st Visit	Oral Conc 1st Visit	Special Follow-Up	Follow-Up	Total
Overall results:					
Actual number of visits	2,750	2,200	1,000	600	6,550
Actual price per visit	$ 200.00	$ 90.00	$ 130.00	$ 40.00	
Total revenue.	$550,000	$198,000	$130,000	$24,000	$902,000
Actual variable expenses per visit	$ 218.00	$ 114.00	$ 161.00	$ 15.00	
Total variable expenses	$599,500	$250,800	$161,000	$ 9,000	1,020,300
Contribution	($ 49,500)	($ 52,800)	($ 31,000)	$15,000	($118,300)
Total fixed expenses					100,000
Surplus					($218,300)
Variable expense detail:					
Physician care:					
Average # minutes per visit .	25	5	20	10	
Average wage per minute . .	$ 1.20	$ 1.20	$ 1.20	$ 1.20	
Total expense per visit	$ 30.00	$ 6.00	$ 24.00	$ 12.00	
Nursing care:					
Average # minutes per visit .	40	30	25	5	
Average wage per minute . .	$ 0.60	$ 0.60	$ 0.60	$ 0.60	
Total expense per visit	$ 24.00	$ 18.00	$ 15.00	$ 3.00	
Medical supplies:					
Average # units per visit	4	2	2	0	
Average expense per unit. . .	$ 21.00	$ 21.00	$ 21.00	$ 21.00	
Total expense per visit	$ 84.00	$ 42.00	$ 42.00	$ 0.00	
Laboratory:					
Average # tests per visit	5	3	5	0	
Average expense per test . . .	$ 16.00	$ 16.00	$ 16.00	$ 16.00	
Total expense per visit	$ 80.00	$ 48.00	$ 80.00	$ 0.00	
Total average variable expense per visit	$ 218.00	$ 114.00	$ 161.00	$ 15.00	

EXHIBIT 4 Flexible Budget and Related Variances

	IUD 1st Visit	Oral Conc 1st Visit	Special Follow-Up	Follow-Up	Total
Overall budget:					
Actual number of visits	2,750	2,200	1,000	600	6,550
Budgeted price per visit.	$ 200.00	$ 100.00	$ 125.00	$ 40.00	
Total revenue.	$550,000	$220,000	$125,000	$24,000	$919,000
Budgeted variable expenses per visit	$ 165.00	$ 75.00	$ 110.00	$ 10.00	
Total variable expenses	$453,750	$165,000	$110,000	$ 6,000	734,750
Contribution	$ 96,250	$ 55,000	$ 15,000	$18,000	$184,250
Total fixed expenses					100,000
Surplus					$ 84,250
Revenue volume variance:					
Actual-budgeted visits	−250	200	0	100	
Budgeted price per visit.	$ 200.00	$ 100.00	$ 125.00	$ 40.00	
Variance	($ 50,000)	$ 20,000	$ 0	$ 4,000	($ 26,000)
Expense volume variance:					
Budgeted-actual visits	250	−200	0	−100	
Budgeted expense per visit . . .	$ 165.00	$ 75.00	$ 110.00	$ 10.00	
Variance	$ 41,250	($ 15,000)	$ 0	($ 1,000)	$ 25,250
Contribution margin variance:					
Revenue volume variance + Expense volume variance.	($ 8,750)	$ 5,000	$ 0	$ 3,000	($ 750)
Revenue price variances:					
Actual-budgeted price per visit	$ 0.00	($ 10.00)	$ 5.00	$ 0.00	
Actual number visits	2,750	2,200	1,000	600	
Revenue price variance	$ 0	($ 22,000)	$ 5,000	$ 0	($ 17,000)

needed to look into matters such as physician and nursing productivity and wage rates, medical supply costs, and laboratory costs. She asked Mr. Hourihan to assess these other reasons why actual results might have diverged from the budget, and to prepare a variance analysis that would explain each of them.

Assignment

1. Be sure you understand how Exhibits 3 and 4 were prepared. Do you agree with Mr. Hourihan's analyses so far?

2 Besides changes in the number of visits and the reimbursement rate per visit, what are the other reasons why actual results might have diverged from budget?

3. Calculate the variance associated with each of the reasons you gave in Question 2. How, if at all, might this information be used in managing the Clinic?

Case 13–1

Huntington Beach*

In late October, Mr. Matthew Cohan, Assistant Commissioner of the Department of Public Works of Huntington Beach, South Carolina, was reviewing the results of a recently completed construction project on Huntington Avenue, a beachfront road. The project, which had been completed under a contract with a private developer, had run considerably over budget, and Mr. Cohan wished to determine the reasons for the excessive expenditures.

Because the actual length of the road had exceeded the City's original estimate, Mr. Cohan knew that the contractor would be entitled to some additional compensation from the City. However, he also realized that not all of the extra costs could be attributed to the additional length and had, therefore, asked his accountant to prepare a summary of the reasons for the deviation from the budget.

While the accountant's summary (Exhibit 1) shed some light on the reasons for the variance, Mr. Cohan was convinced that it did not tell the full story. He knew, for example, that the city had asked the contractor to extend the length of the road by a half mile (880 yards). He also knew that, because of material wastage, the road had required 21 rather than 20 square yards of asphalt per linear yard. Further, in his discussions with the contractor, he had learned that the efficiency of the paving crew had increased by a factor of 20 percent, resulting in some apparent savings which did not show up on the accountant's

*This case was prepared by Professor David W. Young. Copyright © by David W. Young.

EXHIBIT 1
Summary of Budget
Variations

	Rate	Quantity	Cost
Grading			
Actual	$15 per linear yard	5,280 linear yards	$ 79,200
Budget	$12 per linear yard	4,400 linear yards	52,800
Variance			($ 26,400)
Paving.			
Actual	$8 per square yard	110,880 square yards	$887,040
Budget	$10 per square yard	88,000 square yards	880,000
Variance			($ 7,040)
Overhead			
Actual	$3 per linear yard	5,280 linear yards	$ 15,840
Budget	$3 per linear yard	4,400 linear yards	13,200
Variance			($ 2,640)
Total Variance . .			($ 36,080)

report. Finally, since the contractor had given his grading crew a wage in-crease, the cost per linear yard of grading had increased from $12 to $15.

Mr. Cohan had a meeting the next day with the contractor to determine the additional amount the city would owe. He commented on the issues that needed to be addressed at that meeting:

> This was a fixed-price, not a cost-based, contract, but we then changed the length of the road. Our mistake was not to have prepared an amended contract, but we've worked with this contractor before, and we trust him. Nevertheless, fair is fair, and we need to determine how much of the cost overrun each of us should bear. Sometime before tomorrow, I need to prepare a more thorough analysis of the reasons for the variance.

Questions

1. Compute the relevant variances. What do they show that the accountant's report does not?

2. What additional information would you suggest Mr. Cohan obtain about this project? Why?

3. How much more should the city pay? How much should the contractor be asked to absorb?

Case 13–2

Pacific Park School*

Ms. Audrey Hollingsworth, director of the Pacific Park School (PPS), was reviewing the results of the school's Summer Camp Program in preparation for the upcoming academic year. On her desk was a report (Exhibit 1) showing that instead of the $6,000 surplus she had budgeted, the Summer Camp Program had operated at a $50 loss. While the loss was not great, she had been planning to use the surplus to make some much needed improvements in the school's playground facilities. She now would need to either postpone these plans or find alternate sources of financing. Unhappy with this prospect, she resolved to determine exactly why the $6,000 surplus had evaporated.

Background

Pacific Park School was established in 1991 as an alternative to the many custodial daycare programs that operated in the city and its nearby suburbs. It accepted children as young as two years of age and worked with them until they reached the age of five, when they enrolled in a regular school.

Located in the annex of a church, the school had five classrooms and a playground. Enrollment during the academic year was limited to 50, and admission was extremely competitive. PPS enjoyed an excellent reputation in the community, and its graduates were virtually assured of admission to one of the city's prestigious private schools.

Parents could enroll their children on either a half-day or a full-day schedule. In either case, a wide variety of activities was available, and children could choose among them in a relatively unstructured way. Classrooms resembled those of a well-run elementary school, with amenities such as books, paints, blocks, toys, an aquarium, and small animals, such as turtles. Since most of the children could not read, each child had his or her own symbol

EXHIBIT 1
Summer Camp Program: Budgeted and Actual Revenues and Expenses

	Budget	Actual	Variance
Revenue	$65,000	$60,750	$(4,250)
Expenses:			
Teachers and aides	40,000	40,250	(250)
Supplies	2,500	2,700	(200)
Administration	12,000	13,500	(1,500)
Rent and utilities	4,500	4,350	150
Total	$59,000	$60,800	$(1,800)
Surplus (deficit)	$ 6,000	$ (50)	$(6,050)

*This case was prepared by Professor David W. Young. Copyright © by David W. Young.

EXHIBIT 2

Summer Camp
Program: Budget
and Actual Statistics

	Budget	Actual
Number of child-weeks.	500	450
Tuition (per week).	$ 130	$ 135
Teacher and aide average salary (per week)	500	575
Supplies (per child-week)	5	6
Administration and clerical total (per week)	1,200	1,350
Rent and utilities (per month).	1,500	1,450

(such as a triangle) that was used to indicate certain responsibilities (such as feeding the turtle). In all of their activities, the children were supervised by certified teachers and aides, who interacted with them constantly. Low child-teacher ratios were carefully maintained.

Summer Camp Program

The Summer Camp Program was almost identical to the program during the regular academic year. The only differences were that, with summer camp, children could enroll for as little as 1 week or as long as 10 weeks, outdoor activities were somewhat more prevalent, and the term *camp* was used to make the program more appealing to children who might have grown tired of *school*.

Because the amount of time a child could spend in camp ranged from 1 to 10 weeks, and because parents did not need to commit themselves in advance to more than 1 week, budgeting was a little tricky. Instead of basing the budget on the number of children, Ms. Hollingsworth used *child-weeks* as the basic building block. As Exhibit 2 indicates, the budget had been based on 500 child-weeks, whereas only 450 actually materialized. In addition, qualified teachers and aides were in short supply, and instead of paying an average of $500 per week as she had anticipated, Ms. Hollingsworth had been obliged to pay an average of $575. She had, however, been able to operate with one fewer teacher than budgeted due to the reduced enrollment.

A similar salary problem had arisen on the administrative side, and in order to remain competitive, she had had to pay $1,350 a week in administrative salaries, rather than the $1,200 she had budgeted. At $6.00 per week per child instead of $5.00, curriculum supplies also had turned out to be more expensive than anticipated. Finally, she had managed to cut back a bit on telephone and electricity usage, thereby lowering her rent and utilities from the $1,500 per month budgeted to $1,450.

Because she had seen some of these problems coming, Ms. Hollingsworth had been able to send out a special notice to parents, informing them of a small increase in tuition of $5.00 per student week. At the time, she had thought this would defray the additional costs; obviously it had not.

With all of this in mind, Ms. Hollingsworth set about determining exactly why her budgeted surplus had not materialized. She also knew that she owed her board of directors an explanation, since it was at their insistence that she had planned to undertake the improvements to the school's facilities.

Questions

1. Calculate all relevant variances.

2. Prepare a nontechnical memorandum to the board of directors, explaining why the $6,000 budgeted surplus turned into a $50 loss.

3. What should Ms. Hollingsworth do to avoid similar problems in the future?

Case 13–3

Spruce Street Inn*

Sam Donaldson, the laundry supervisor of the Spruce Street Inn, stared at the memo that had just reached his desk:

> The Inn has adopted a responsibility accounting system. From now on you will receive quarterly reports comparing the costs of operating your department with budgeted costs. The reports will highlight the differences (variances) so that you can zero in on the departure from budgeted costs. (This is called *management by exception.*) Responsibility accounting means you are accountable for keeping the costs in your department within the budget. The variances from the budget will help you identify which costs are out of line, and the sizes of the variances will indicate the most important ones. Your first such report accompanies this announcement.
>
> As this report indicates, your costs are significantly above budget for the quarter. You need to pay particular attention to labor, supplies, and maintenance. Please get back to me by the end of next week with a plan for making the needed reductions.

Mr. Donaldson knew he needed a plan, yet midwinter was the busiest time of the year at the inn, and the laundry was piling up faster than his staff could wash it.

Background

Spruce Street Inn was located in the heart of a large metropolitan area in the north-central United States. Founded in the late 1800s, it had been serving the homeless ever since, providing hot meals, shelter, and companionship. Situated on a busy urban thoroughfare, it was a haven of last resort for many of the city's indigent, and "home" for many others. As might be expected, the demand for its services was especially high in the winter, when temperatures frequently dropped to below zero, and life "on the street" became unbearable.

*This case was prepared by Professor David W. Young. Copyright © by David W. Young.

The inn provided three types of services. By far, its most significant activity was the Hot Meal Program, in which it served hundreds of meals a day. A meal of hot soup and a sandwich was available to anyone who arrived between the hours of 12:00 and 2:00 in the afternoon and 5:00 to 7:00 in the evening. Its second program was its Overnight Hostel, in which it made available 150 beds on a first-come, first-served basis. The linen was changed daily, and fresh towels were always available, so that its clients could look forward to "clean sheets and a hot shower." Finally, it had a counseling program, in which a staff of three full-time social workers assisted the inn's clients in coping with the difficulties that had brought them to the inn, and in establishing themselves in a more self-sufficient lifestyle.

In March 1993, the inn had hired a new administrator to improve its business activities. A business school graduate with prior experience in manufacturing and service companies in the private sector, he had introduced as one of his first steps what he called "responsibility accounting." He also had instituted a new budgeting system, along with the provision of quarterly cost reports to the inn's department heads. (Previously, cost data had been presented to department heads only infrequently.)

The annual budget for fiscal year 1994 (October 1993–September 1994) had been constructed by the new administrator. Quarterly budgets were computed as one-fourth of the annual budget. The administrator compiled the budget from an analysis of the prior three years' costs. The analysis showed that all costs increased each year, with more rapid increases between the second and third year. He considered establishing the budget at an average of the prior three years' costs, hoping that the installation of the system would reduce costs to this level. However, in view of the rapidly increasing prices, he finally chose fiscal year (FY) 1993 costs less 3 percent for the FY 1994 budget. He decided to measure activity by client nights, and to set the budget for pounds of laundry processed at the FY1993 level, which was approximately equal to the volume of each of the past three years.

Mr. Donaldson had received his first report (Exhibit 1) in mid-January 1994. He reflected on its content:

> A lot of my costs don't change, even if the number of pounds of laundry changes. I suppose laundry labor, supplies, water-related items, and maintenance vary with changes in pounds, but that's about all. Nevertheless, shouldn't my budget reflect those changes? Also, I hadn't planned for the fact that I was given a salary increase as of October 1—was I supposed to refuse it to help keep my budget in balance?
>
> Finally, I think it's important to note that I had to pay overtime to the staff because the department became inundated with laundry during the cold snap we had back in mid-December. Because of this, my average hourly rate for the whole three months was $10.20 instead of the $9.00 that was in my budget. In fact, and maybe this is a little picky, the average number of minutes it took my staff to wash a pound of laundry actually dropped from .48, which was my budget target, to .47 for the quarter. Somehow, even though it's pretty small, I think that should be taken into consideration.

EXHIBIT 1   **Performance Report—Laundry Department, October–December 1993**

	Budget	Actual	(Over) Under Budget	Percent (Over) Under Budget
Client nights.	9,500	11,900	(2,400)	(25)
Pounds of laundry processed	125,000	156,600	(31,600)	(25)
Costs:				
Laundry labor	$ 9,000	$ 12,512	$ (3,512)	(39)
Supplies	1,125	1,875	(750)	(67)
Water and water heating and softening.	1,750	2,500	(750)	(43)
Maintenance.	1,375	2,200	(825)	(60)
Supervisor's salary	3,125	3,750	(625)	(20)
Allocated administrative costs	4,000	5,000	(1,000)	(25)
Equipment depreciation	1,250	1,250	—	0
Total	$ 21,625	$ 29,087	$ (7,462)	(35)

Questions

1. What is your assessment of the method the administrator used to construct the budget?

2. Prepare a flexible budget for the laundry department. What does it tell you?

3. Compute the appropriate labor variances. What do thcy tell you?

4. What should Mr. Donaldson tell the administrator about his budget variances?

Case 13–4

Los Reyes Hospital*

I'm very concerned about your department's financial performance. We'd been planning on a surplus of about $74,000 from you, and you've run a deficit of over $125,000. Unless something is done to turn this trend around, the hospital will have to begin a series of layoffs that will affect all departments.

Maria Delgado, Chief of Medicine of Los Reyes Hospital, stared at the memorandum from the hospital's Vice President for Medical Affairs. A similar memorandum had been sent to all chiefs of service, expressing concern that the results of the most recent quarter's operations were considerably worse than budgeted.

*This case was prepared by Professor David W. Young. Copyright © by David W. Young.

Dr. Delgado knew she had some explaining to do. In fact, she, along with several other chiefs, had been asked to make a presentation at the next Executive Committee meeting of the hospital concerning the role that their departments had played in the hospital's poor performance, and their plans for corrective action.

In reviewing the budgeted and actual results, Dr. Delgado discovered that all of her department's variation could be attributed to four case types and four hospital services. Exhibit 1 contains the original quarterly budget for these four case types: DRG 089 (Simple pneumonia & pleurisy, age greater than 17), DRG 014 (Specific cerebral vascular disorders except transient ischemic attack), DRG 096 (Bronchitis & asthma, age greater than 17), and DRG 140 (Angina pectoris). It also shows the budgeted variable expenses per case for the four hospital services: routine care (i.e., the hospital stay itself), radiology films, laboratory tests, and pharmacy units (such as prescriptions).

Since the hospital negotiated all of its managed care contracts on the basis of diagnosis, it was paid on a per-case basis. Its anticipated revenue for each

EXHIBIT 1 **Original Budget**

	DRG 089	DRG 014	DRG 096	DRG 140	Total
Overall budget:					
Number of cases	300	200	100	50	650
Revenue per case . . . . $	6,000	$ 6,500	$ 5,000	$ 3,000	
Total revenue . . . . $	$1,800,000	$1,300,000	$500,000	$150,000	$3,750,000
Variable expenses per case . . . $	2,800	$ 3,150	$ 1,955	$ 1,205	
Total variable expenses . . . . . $	840,000	$ 630,000	$195,500	$ 60,250	$1,725,750
Contribution . . . . $	960,000	$ 670,000	$304,500	$ 89,750	$2,024,250
Total fixed expenses					1,950,600
Surplus (deficit)					$ 73,650
Variable expense detail:					
Routine care:					
# days per case	9	11	7	4	
Expense per day . . . . $	250	$ 250	$ 250	$ 250	
Total expense per case . . . . $	2,250	$ 2,750	$ 1,750	$ 1,000	
Radiology:					
# films per case	5	6	4	1	
Expense per film . . . . $	25	$ 25	$ 25	$ 25	
Total expense per case . . . . $	125	$ 150	$ 100	$ 25	
Laboratory:					
# tests per case	10	10	3	5	
Expense per test . . . . $	15	$ 15	$ 15	$ 15	
Total expense per case . . . . $	150	$ 150	$ 45	$ 75	
Pharmacy:					
# units per case	55	20	12	21	
Expense per unit . . . . $	5.00	$ 5.00	$ 5.00	$ 5.00	
Total expense per case . . . . $	275	$ 100	$ 60	$ 105	
Total variable expense					
per case . . . . $	2,800	$ 3,150	$ 1,955	$ 1,205	

DRG is shown in Exhibit 1, as is the anticipated utilization of services and the variable expense per unit for each service for each DRG.

Using these estimates, the hospital's fiscal affairs department had calculated total variable expense per case for each DRG. The revenue and total variable expense per case then had been multiplied by the anticipated number of cases to give total revenue and total variable expenses by DRG. The latter was deducted from total revenue to give the contribution to fixed expenses from each DRG. The department's fixed expenses (including its allocated overhead) were then deducted from the total contribution to give a total budgeted surplus of $73,650 for the quarter.

Exhibit 2 is similar to Exhibit 1, except that it shows actual results. As it indicates, instead of a surplus, the department incurred a deficit of $125,475. It

EXHIBIT 2   **Computation of Actual Surplus**

	DRG 089	DRG 014	DRG 096	DRG 140	Total
Overall results:					
Actual number of cases	275	250	100	75	700
Revenue per case .... $	5,500	$ 6,400	$ 4,900	$ 3,300	
Total revenue	$1,512,500	$1,600,000	$490,000	$247,500	$3,850,000
Variable expenses per case ... $	2,952	$ 3,346	$ 2,166	$ 1,673	
Total variable expenses ... $	811,800	$ 836,500	$216,600	$125,475	$1,990,375
Contribution .... $	700,700	$ 763,500	$273,400	$122,025	$1,859,625
Total fixed expenses					1,985,100
Surplus (deficit)					($ 125,475)
Variable expense detail:					
Routine care:					
Average # days per case ...	10	12	8	6	
Average expense per day .. $	240	$ 240	$ 240	$ 240	
Total average expense					
per case .... $	2,400	$ 2,880	$ 1,920	$ 1,440	
Radiology:					
Average # films per case ...	6	7	3	2	
Average expense per film .. $	24	$ 24	$ 24	$ 24	
Total average expense					
per case .... $	144	$ 168	$ 72	$ 48	
Laboratory:					
Average # tests per case ...	8	10	6	5	
Average expense per test .. $	21	$ 21	$ 21	$ 21	
Total average expense					
per case .... $	168	$ 210	$ 126	$ 105	
Pharmacy:					
Average # units per case ..	60	22	12	20	
Average expense per unit .. $	4	$ 4	$ 4	$ 4	
Total average expense					
per case .... $	240	$ 88	$ 48	$ 80	
Total average variable expense					
per case .... $	2,952	$ 3,346	$ 2,166	$ 1,673	

was this that led to the concern expressed in the memorandum from the hospital's Vice President for Medical Affairs.

Dr. Delgado outlined some of her thinking about the deficit:

> Our budget is a little tricky to understand. The average-expense-per-day figures all use what the hospital calls "variable expenses." I think this is right, since our fixed expenses shouldn't change with small changes in the number of patients, but it makes the amounts look awfully low.
>
> Apart from the expenses, one reason for the deficit is that the hospital renegotiated payment rates with HealthStop [a local managed care provider], and the result was lower payment rates for several of our DRGs. But I don't think that's the whole story. We overspent our fixed expenses a bit, for example, but I think that's okay since we had about an 8 percent increase over budget in the number of patients we treated during the quarter, and I remember having to bring in some agency nurses to cover the extra workload.

In preparation for her presentation to the Executive Committee, Dr. Delgado asked her staff assistant, Asher Hawkins, to prepare a report containing a complete breakdown of the reasons behind the deficit.

EXHIBIT 3 Flexible Budget and Related Variances

	DRG 089	DRG 014	DRG 096	DRG 140	Total
Overall budget:					
Actual number of cases	275	250	100	75	700
Revenue per case	$ 6,000	$ 6,500	$ 5,000	$ 3,000	
Total revenue	$1,650,000	$1,625,000	$500,000	$225,000	$4,000,000
Variable expenses per case ..	$ 2,800	$ 3,150	$ 1,955	$ 1,205	
Total variable expenses	$ 770,000	$ 787,500	$195,500	$ 90,375	1,843,375
Contribution	$ 880,000	$ 837,500	$304,500	$134,625	$2,156,625
Total fixed expenses					1,950,600
Surplus					$ 206,025
Revenue volume variance:					
Actual-Budgeted cases	−25	50	0	25	
Budgeted Unit revenue	$ 6,000	$ 6,500	$ 5,000	$ 3,000	
Variance	($ 150,000)	$ 325,000	$ 0	$ 75,000	$ 250,000
Expense volume variance:					
Budgeted-Actual cases	25	−50	0	−25	
Budgeted expense per case .	$ 2,800	$ 3,150	$ 1,955	$ 1,205	
Variance	$ 70,000	($ 157,500)	$ 0	($ 30,125)	($ 117,625)
Contribution margin variance:					
Revenue Volume Variance +					
Expense Volume Variance .	($ 80,000)	$ 167,500	$ 0	$ 44,875	$ 132,375
Revenue price variances:					
Actual-Budgeted revenue					
per case	($ 500)	($ 100)	($ 100)	$ 300	
Actual number cases	275	250	100	75	
Revenue price variance	($ 137,500)	($ 25,000)	($ 10,000)	$ 22,500	($ 150,000)

Mr. Hawkins began by reasoning that the department had essentially no control over the number or mix of cases seen. He thus prepared a flexible budget (Exhibit 3), which showed that the change in the number and mix of cases seen in the department should have led to a surplus of $206,025.

Using similar reasoning, he prepared an analysis of the variance due to the lower prices that had been negotiated with the managed care providers. This analysis is contained at the bottom of Exhibit 3, and shows that $150,000 was a result of the price changes. Since the department had had almost nothing to do with these negotiations, this finding made him feel quite good.

At this point, Mr. Hawkins felt that he had accomplished the majority of his task. He had found $132,375 in positive variances due to the changes in volume and mix, and $150,000 in negative variances due to changes in prices. Since he felt that the department could control neither, and since the two almost offset each other, he felt that there was little left to explain.

Mr. Hawkins then met with Dr. Delgado to show her the results of his work. At the meeting, it became clear that Dr. Delgado was not satisfied.

> This is not good enough. First of all, the two don't really offset each other, so that's an issue. Secondly, though, there's something else going on here. It's clear from your analysis that the situation is even worse than I had originally thought. This [Exhibit 3] suggests that we should have had a surplus of slightly over $206,000 instead of $73,000. That makes our deficit look really bad. I've got more explaining to do than I had thought. You're going to need to dig a little more deeply into the issues here, and I'm going to need to see your analysis soon, since the meeting is early next week.

Questions

1. Be sure you understand how Exhibit 3 was prepared. Do you agree with the approach Mr. Hawkins used to prepare it?

2. Besides changes in the number of cases and the payment rate per case, what are the other reasons why actual results might have diverged from budget?

3. Calculate the variance associated with each of the reasons you gave in Question 2. How, if at all, might this information be used by Dr. Delgado in managing the department? How might it be used by the hospital's administration?

4. What information concerning cases, costs, and revenues would you suggest Dr. Delgado see on a regular basis? How might your answer be affected by the hospital's decision about the types of responsibility centers in its management control system?

Case 13–5

Bandon Medical Associates (B)*

We've got a budget crisis! Instead of a surplus of almost $100,000, we're looking at a potential deficit of over $145,000. Not only won't we be able to buy the new equipment that everyone's been screaming for, but I don't see how we can pay physicians the bonuses they're counting on.

Mark Desautels, MD, the senior physician member of Bandon Medical Associates, a small physician group practice located in Oregon, was expressing his concern about the results of the year's operations. One reason for the problem was that third-party payers had lowered the rate for one of the group's visit types, but there appeared to be some other, perhaps more important, explanations as well. Dr. Desautels decided to analyze the reasons for the poor performance and present his findings at the group's annual strategic planning retreat, which was about 10 days away.

Background

Bandon Medical Associates (BMA) had been established about 20 years ago by Dr. Desautels and a colleague he had met during his residency. Over the years, the group had grown, and currently comprised six physicians. In addition, the group used medical assistants as extenders for the physicians. Last year there were two extenders, but during the most recent year, at the insistence of several of the newer physicians, four additional extenders had been hired to meet the increased demand for services.

Three years ago, BMA had joined Coos Bay Health System, a large integrated delivery system (IDS) with several primary care and multispecialty group practices, a free-standing laboratory, a free-standing radiology unit, two acute care hospitals, a nursing home, a home health agency, and a hospice. Coos Bay coordinated care, negotiated contracts with third-party payers, and provided some central services, such as information systems support.

The costs of Coos Bay's central services were allocated to each provider entity in the IDS according to some prearranged formulas. *(Bandon Medical Associates (A),* the practice case for Chapter 10, contains details on these formulas and several other financial arrangements that had been agreed to at the time BMA was purchased by Coos Bay. Knowledge of these financial arrangements is not needed for the analysis of this case, however.)

Financial Matters

BMA's physicians were paid according to a combination of a base salary and a bonus. Because different visit types required different levels of physician

*This case was prepared by Professor David W. Young. Copyright © by David W. Young.

intensity, Dr. Desautels and his colleagues had had a lengthy discussion at last year's retreat about different approaches to measuring productivity. They had finally settled on revenue as the best method. Everyone had agreed that, since the payment for each visit type was a rough reflection of its intensity, revenue generation was not only a good way to measure each physician's productivity, but a simple one as well.

BMA's physicians and extenders also had agreed upon the following principles to guide their budgeting activities and compensation arrangements"[1]

1. While most third-party payers classified visits by precise codes, four visit types (initial visit, routine physical, intensive follow-up, and routine follow-up) were sufficient for budgeting purposes.

2. Physicians would be available to see outpatients for 32 hours a week (eight 4-hour sessions). They also had agreed that, with time off for continuing medical education and vacations, they would be available for a total of 1,500 hours a year (about 47 weeks).

3. Physicians also would see their patients in the hospital, when necessary, and would make the occasional house call for patients who were home-bound. Revenue from, and compensation for, their inpatient activities was accounted for and paid separately from the BMA budget.

4. The extenders would be expected to see patients for 1,400 hours a year—less than the physicians since they had some other responsibilities in the group.

5. Although physicians were paid by a combination of base salary and bonus, the extenders would be on a straight salary with no bonus. Physicians could share their bonuses with one or more extenders who they thought were especially helpful, however.

6. Each physician's base salary would be set at 42 percent of his or her expected revenue generation. Ten percent of that amount would be kept in reserve until the end of the year, and paid out as a year-end bonus if the group reached at least 95 percent of its total revenue target.

7. The remaining revenue would be used to cover the group's operating expenses and to provide the surplus needed to fund office renovations, equipment purchases, and other similar items.

This Current Year's Budget

In preparing the current year's budget, Dr. Desautels had met with each physician individually to arrive at a his or her visit forecast, broken down by the four

[1]Some of the details that underlie these principles and other elements of BMA's budget formulation process are contained in *Bandon Medical Associates (A)*. These details are not needed for an analysis of this case.

visit types. He and BMA's administrator, Alvin Hanson, had then summed the individual physician forecasts to obtain a total for the entire group.

Dr. Desautels had asked Mr. Hanson to treat physicians, extenders. and medical supplies as "variable expenses" for budgeting purposes, in that they were expected to increase or decrease in rough proportion to the number of visits. While this was not completely precise, Dr. Desautels found the approach a useful way to "attach" costs to each visit type.

Medical supplies included a wide variety of disposable items needed in conjunction with a visit. To keep the budget simple, Dr. Desautels had asked Mr. Hanson to measure medical supplies in terms of "units," and to use an average cost per unit.

The budget's fixed expenses included rent, cleaning, administrative staff, receptionists, office supplies, and similar items. Allocated overhead was for a variety of administrative services provided by Coos Bay, such as billing, collections, and information services.

Using estimates prepared by Dr. Desautels for the above items, Mr. Hanson had calculated the total variable expense per visit for each visit type. He next

EXHIBIT 1 Original Budget

	Initial Consult	Routine Physical	Intensive Visit	Routine Visit	Total
Overall budget:					
Number of visits.	3,000	4,000	6,000	6,000	19,000
Price per visit	$ 150.00	$ 110.00	$ 80.00	$ 60.00	
Total revenue	$450,000	$440,000	$480,000	$360,000	$1,730,000
Variable expenses per visit	$ 106.50	$ 77.75	$ 44.00	$ 31.00	
Total variable expenses.	$319,500	$311,000	$264,000	$186,000	1,080,500
Contribution	$130,500	$129,000	$216,000	$174,000	$ 649,500
Total fixed expenses					300,000
Allocated overhead					250,000
Surplus.					$ 99,500
Variable expense detail:					
Physician care:					
Average # minutes per visit. . . .	60	45	20	10	
Average wage per minute.	$ 1.35	$ 1.35	$ 1.35	$ 1.35	
Total expense per visit	$ 81.00	$ 60.75	$ 27.00	$ 13.50	
Extender care:					
Average # minutes per visit. . . .	15	10	10	15	
Average wage per minute.	$ 0.90	$ 0.90	$ 0.90	$ 0.90	
Total expense per visit	$ 13.50	$ 9.00	$ 9.00	$ 13.50	
Medical supplies:					
Average # units per visit	3	2	2	1	
Average expense per unit	$ 4.00	$ 4.00	$ 4.00	$ 4.00	
Total expense per visit	$ 12.00	$ 8.00	$ 8.00	$ 4.00	
Total average variable					
expense per visit	$ 106.50	$ 77.75	$ 44.00	$ 31.00	

multiplied the revenue and total variable expense per visit by the anticipated number of visits to give total revenue and total variable expenses by visit type. He deducted the latter from the former to give the contribution to fixed expenses from each visit type. Finally, he deducted the anticipated fixed expenses and allocated overhead from the total contribution to give a total budgeted surplus for the year. Details of his work are shown in Exhibit 1.

The Budget Crisis

Dr. Desautels' "budget crisis" is indicated in Exhibit 2. About $125,000 was in the bonus pool. Since the group had achieved its revenue target, the physicians were expecting to be paid the full $125,000. However, doing so would create a deficit for the year of over $145,000. As Dr. Desautels said:

> This is an even bigger problem than it first appears to be. Although revenue generation exceeded the target, the physicians worked an average of only about 1,100 hours each for the year. The rate of $1.35 per minute that we used in the budget assumed they would work 1,500 hours each during the year, for a total of

EXHIBIT 2 Actual Results

	Initial Consult	Routine Physical	Intensive Visit	Routine Visit	Total
Overall results:					
Actual number of visits.........	2,500	5,500	5,600	7,000	20,600
Actual price per visit..........	$ 150.00	$ 110.00	$ 75.00	$ 65.00	
Total revenue.................	$375,000	$605,000	$420,000	$455,000	$1,855,000
Total variable expenses.........	$303,250	$622,600	$288,960	$235,900	1,450,710
Contribution	$ 71,750	($ 17,600)	$131,040	$219,100	$ 404,290
Total fixed expenses...........					300,000
Allocated overhead					250,000
Surplus......................					($ 145,710)
Variable expense detail:					
Physician care:					
Average # minutes per visit....	45	30	15	5	
Average wage per minute.....	$ 1.84	$ 1.84	$ 1.84	$ 1.84	
Total expense per visit	$ 82.80	$ 55.20	$ 27.60	$ 9.20	
Extender care:					
Average # minutes per visit....	25	40	15	20	
Average wage per minute.....	$ 1.00	$ 1.00	$ 1.00	$ 1.00	
Total expense per visit	$ 25.00	$ 40.00	$ 15.00	$ 20.00	
Medical supplies:					
Average # units per visit	3	4	2	1	
Average expense per unit.....	$ 4.50	$ 4.50	$ 4.50	$ 4.50	
Total expense per visit	$ 13.50	$ 18.00	$ 9.00	$ 4.50	
**Total average variable expense per visit...........	$ 121.30	$ 113.20	$ 51.60	$ 33.70	

9,000 hours. With only 6,600 hours of work, their effective rate per minute has increased to $1.84.

To better understand the reasons for the shift in financial performance, Dr. Desautels had asked Mr. Hanson to use the data in Exhibits 1 and 2 as the basis for a report on results for the year. His report was to contain a complete breakdown of the reasons why BMA's actual surplus had diverged from the budgeted one. The report would be used by Dr. Desautels for his presentation at the retreat.

The Analysis

Reasoning that BMA had essentially no control over the number or type of visits, Mr. Hanson began his analysis with a flexible budget (Exhibit 3). This showed that with the increased volume of business (20,600 visits versus

EXHIBIT 3   Flexible Budget and Related Variances

	Initial Consult	Routine Physical	Intensive Visit	Routine Visit	Total
Overall budget:					
Actual number of visits.........	2,500	5,500	5,600	7,000	20,600
Budgeted price per visit........	$ 150.00	$ 110.00	$ 80.00	$ 60.00	
Total revenue................	$375,000	$605,000	$448,000	$420,000	$1,848,000
Budgeted variable expenses per visit	$ 106.50	$ 77.75	$ 44.00	$ 31.00	
Total variable expenses.........	$266,250	$427,625	$246,400	$217,000	1,157,275
Contribution	$108,750	$177,375	$201,600	$203,000	$ 690,725
Total fixed expenses...........					300,000
Allocated overhead					250,000
Surplus.....................					$ 140,725
Revenue volume variance:					
Actual-budged visits...........	−500	1500	−400	1000	
Budgeted price per visit........	$ 150.00	$ 110.00	$ 80.00	$ 60.00	
Variance....................	($ 75,000)	$165,000	($ 32,000)	$ 60,000	$ 118,000
Expense volume variance:					
Budgeted-actual visits	500	−1500	400	−1000	
Budgeted expense per visit	$ 106.50	$ 77.75	$ 44.00	$ 31.00	
Variance....................	$ 53,250	($116,625)	$ 17,600	($ 31,000)	($ 76,775)
Contribution margin variance:					
Revenue volume variance + Expense volume variance	($ 21,750)	$ 48,375	($ 14,400)	$ 29,000	$ 41,225
Revenue price variances:					
Actual-budgeted price per visit...	$ 0.00	$ 0.00	($ 5.00)	$ 5.00	
Actual number visits...........	2,500	5,500	5,600	7,000	
Revenue price variance.........	$ 0	$ 0	($ 28,000)	$ 35,000	$ 7,000

19,000 in the budget) and a change in the mix of visits, the "flexed surplus" was $140,725—an increase of $41,225 over the original surplus.

Using similar reasoning, Mr. Hanson prepared an analysis of the variance due to the changes in third-party payer rates. This analysis (contained at the bottom of Exhibit 3) showed that an additional $7,000 in surplus should have resulted from the changes in payment rates.

Mr. Hanson next met with Dr. Desautels to show him the results of his work. Dr. Desautels explained to him that he needed to look into matters such as physician and extender productivity and wage rates, and medical supply usage and costs. He asked him to analyze these other reasons why actual results might have diverged from the budget, and to prepare a variance analysis that would explain how each of them had affected the difference.

Assignment

1. Be sure you understand how Exhibits 2 and 3 were prepared. Do you agree with Mr. Hanson's analyses so far?

2 Besides changes in the number of visits and the payment rate per visit, what are the other reasons why actual results might have diverged from budget?

3. Calculate the variance associated with each of the reasons you gave in Question 2. How, if at all, might this informafion be used in managing the group practice?

4. How might BMA's approach to physician compensation have affected the group's financial performance for the year?

5. What should Dr. Desautels do about the bonuses? What changes, if any, should he make to the group's budgeting and control system?

14

Reporting on Performance: Management Control Reports

In all organizations—nonprofit and for-profit—managers need an ongoing flow of information to assist them in carrying out the management control process. As we have discussed previously, much of this information comes from talking with people and observing performance directly, but much also comes from formal reports. This chapter discusses the types of formal reports that can be used by nonprofit organizations, the contents of the reports used for management control purposes, the technical criteria for control reports, and some of the issues managers face in using these reports.

Types of Reports

There are essentially two types of formal reports: information reports and performance reports. Our primary interest in this chapter is performance reports, but first we shall briefly discuss information reports.

Information Reports

Information reports are designed to tell management "what is going on." Such reports do not always lead to action. Each reader studies these reports to detect whether or not something has happened that requires investigation. If nothing of significance is noted in an information report, which is often the case, the report is put aside without action. If something does strike the reader's attention, an inquiry or other action is initiated.

The information contained in such reports may come from the accounting system or from a variety of other sources. Information reports derived from accounting records include income statements, balance sheets, cash flow statements, and details on such items as cash balances, the status of accounts receivable and inventories, and lists of accounts payable that are coming due.

A list of nonaccounting information reports could easily be quite long. These reports might include internal information such as the number of new clients or patients, the number of discharges, the incidence of service delivery that did not meet quality standards, rates of absenteeism, admission applications, yield rates (the percentage of accepted applicants who decide to attend a college or university), number of failing grades, or the position titles of members of an association who did not renew. Information reports might also include external information, such as general news summaries, legislative updates, new regulations, information on the industry from trade associations, and general economic information published by the government.

Performance Reports

Performance reports look at two general types of output: economic performance and management performance. A conventional income statement can be prepared for a separate program, a profit center, or an entire organization. When this is done, the surplus shown at the bottom of the income statement is a basic measure of the unit's *economic performance.*

A *management performance report* focuses on the performance of a manager of a responsibility center. This report also is called a *control report.* A control report may show that a manager is doing an excellent job. If, however, an economic performance report shows that the responsibility center is operating at a loss, or is not producing a satisfactory surplus, action may be required despite the good performance of the manager.

Example

An economic performance report showed that the nursing school in a private university was operating at a loss. This continuing loss was explained by the fact that a state university nearby had opened a nursing school and was charging much lower tuition rates. The dean of the nursing school was not responsible for this environmental trend, and, indeed, the control reports showed the dean's performance to be quite good. Nevertheless, a thorough analysis revealed no way to eliminate the ongoing loss in the nursing school, that is, to make it a sound economic entity. The decision therefore was made to close the nursing school and devote the university's resources to other activities.

In sum, there are two quite different ways to judge the performance of a responsibility center. First, there is the analysis of the responsibility center as an economic entity; in such an analysis, economic considerations are dominant. Second, there is the analysis of the performance of the responsibility center manager vis-à-vis the commitments made during the budget preparation process; the principal consideration in this analysis is behavioral. It is this latter analysis that is carried out in part by control reports.

Sources of Information

Information on economic performance typically is derived from conventional accounting information, including the full-cost accounting system. Control reports are prepared from responsibility accounting information, and attempt to distinguish between controllable and noncontrollable costs.

Contents of Control Reports

Each responsibility center in an organization is expected to do its part in helping the organization achieve its objectives. To the extent that at least some of these expectations consist of achieving targeted revenues, controlling costs, or both, they are set forth in the budget for the responsibility center. The purpose of control reports is to communicate how well managers of responsibility centers performed in comparison with the budget as well as any other standard of performance.

If the budget is a valid statement of expected performance, the control report simply calculates the difference between budgeted and actual performance. Positive differences represent good performance and negative differences represent poor performance. However, such labels are valid only if there has been no change in the circumstances that were assumed when the budget was prepared. This is rarely, if ever, the case.

The purpose of a control report, then, is to compare actual performance with what performance should have been considering the actual circumstances. If inflation is greater than expected, if volume is down for uncontrollable reasons, or if any of a number of other circumstances has altered original assumptions, a negative variance does not necessarily represent poor performance.

Good control reports have three essential characteristics:

1. They are related to personal responsibility.

2. They compare actual performance to the best available standard.

3. They focus on significant information.

We will discuss each characteristic separately, using the sample set of control reports shown in Exhibit 14–1.

Relationship to Personal Responsibility

As described earlier, responsibility accounting classifies the costs assigned to each responsibility center according to whether they are controllable or noncontrollable. Many control reports show only controllable costs, but some control reports also show a separate category of noncontrollable costs for information purposes. In Exhibit 14–1 the majority of costs are controllable, but some noncontrollable costs, such as rate variances (on the third- and fourth-level reports) also are shown for completeness.

Levels of Reports

To facilitate analysis and appropriate action, the total amount of controllable costs is classified by program, as shown in the first-level report. On this report,

EXHIBIT 14–1
State Human Service Agency ($000)

A First-Level Report

Program Summary (Agency Director)	Actual		(Over) or Under Budget	
	June	Year to Date	June	Year to Date
Direct costs:				
Family planning................	$ 2,110	$ 12,030	$ (315)	$ 35
Maternal/Infant Nutrition.......	**24,525**	**147,280**	**(710)**	**(2,590)**
Early childhood screening........	1,235	7,570	(125)	(210)
Remedial reading...............	1,180	7,045	95	75
Adolescent drug counseling.......	3,590	18,960	(235)	245
Job training...................	4,120	25,175	160	(320)
Senior citizen drop in...........	2,245	13,680	180	(160)
Hospice......................	3,630	22,965	(70)	(730)
Total direct	$42,635	$254,705	$(1,020)	$(3,655)
Controllable overhead............	$27,120	$161,970	$ 3,020	$ 5,130
Total.........................	$69,755	$416,675	$ 2,000	$ 1,475

B Second-Level Report

Maternal/Infant Nutrition Program Direct Cost Summary (Program Director)	Actual		(Over) or Under Budget	
	June	Year to Date	June	Year to Date
Direct labor:				
Counselors	$ 5,340	$ 35,845	$ (625)	$(1,380)
Nutritionists.................	**3,310**	**19,605**	**(30)**	**(620)**
Physicians	3,115	18,085	90	(135)
Supplies and materials:				
Food and beverages	5,740	33,635	(65)	(640)
Stationery	1,865	9,795	(175)	825
Contract services:				
Computer expense	3,195	18,015	210	35
Housekeeping	1,960	12,300	(115)	(675)
Total direct	$24,525	$147,280	$ (710)	$(2,590)

(from next page)

EXHIBIT 14–1
(Concluded)

C Third-Level Report

Nutritionists (Supervisor)	Actual		(Over) or Under Budget	
	June	Year to Date	June	Year to Date
Output:				
Standard direct labor-hours (000)	135	906	85	401
Direct-contact time cost:				
Amount	$ 2,187	$ 12,524	$ (265)	$ 90
Efficiency variance			(115)	515
Rate variance			(150)	(425)
Noncontact time cost:				
Meetings	420	1,916	180	91
Community/collateral work	284	1,748	(75)	(530)
Professional development	115	808	(121)	(384)
Administrative activities	60	721	160	(82)
Sick and vacation time.	244	1,888	91	195
Total noncontact time cost	$ 1,123	$ 7,081	$ 235	$ (710)
Total direct labor cost	$ 3,310	$ 19,605	$ (30)	$ (620)

D Fourth-Level Report

Regional Summary of Nutritionists Direct-Contact Time (Regional Supervisors)	Actual		(Over) or Under Budget	
	June	Year to Date	June	Year to Date
Output:				
Standard direct labor-hours (000)				
Region 1	50	342	20	120
Region 2	45	340	35	165
Region 3	40	224	30	116
Total	135	906	85	401
Direct contact time cost:				
Amount				
Region 1	$ 750	$ 4,140	$ (85)	$ 27
Region 2	795	3,890	(70)	30
Region 3	642	4,494	(110)	33
Total	$ 2,187	$ 12,524	$ (265)	$ 90
Efficiency variance				
Region 1			$ (15)	$ 120
Region 2			(25)	155
Region 3			(75)	240
Total			$ (115)	$ 515
Rate variance				
Region 1			$ (70)	$ (93)
Region 2			(65)	(120)
Region 3			(15)	(212)
Total			$ (150)	$ (425)

controllable overhead is reported separately from direct costs, but noncontrollable costs are excluded.

Direct costs for each program are broken down by item (also called *object, line item,* or *cost element*) in the second-level report. Direct costs in this organization include not only direct labor, but also supplies and materials and contract services.

On the third-level report, the direct labor cost for each job category, such as nutritionists, is divided into direct-contact time and noncontact time for purposes of analyzing the activities of employees and the associated costs. Efficiency and rate variances are calculated for direct-contact time; noncontact time is divided into as many categories as are meaningful for the responsible supervisor.

Finally, on the fourth-level report, the costs and variances for direct-contact time are broken down by region. This allows responsibility to be decentralized to a very low level in the organization: in this instance, a regional supervisor of nutritionists.

Essentially, then, responsibility accounting requires that: (1) costs be classified by responsibility center (e.g., Maternal/Infant Nutrition Program), (2) costs within each responsibility center be classified according to whether they are controllable or noncontrollable, and (3) controllable costs be broken down into cost elements of sufficient detail to provide a useful basis for analysis and action. If it is not possible to give a positive answer to the question "Is there any conceivable action a manager could take on the basis of this report?" the report is a candidate for either revision or elimination.

Comparison with a Standard

A report that contains information on actual performance only is virtually useless for control purposes. To be useful, control reports must compare actual performance with a standard. There are three types of standards: budgeted, historical, and external.

Budgeted Standards

If carefully prepared, a budget is the best standard. It takes into account the conditions that are expected to exist in the budget year, and the revenue and expense items show the expected monetary effect of these conditions. Although budgeted amounts are not shown in Exhibit 14–1, it is clear that they exist, since the last two columns are labeled "(Over) or Under Budget."

Historical Standards

Some organizations compare current performance with past performance. Results for the second quarter of 2002, for example, could be compared with those of the first quarter of 2002 or the second quarter of 2001. Ordinarily, a historical standard is not as good as a well-prepared budget for at least two reasons: (1) conditions in the current period are probably different from those of the prior period, which lessens the validity of the comparison, and (2) performance in the prior period may not have represented good performance.

Despite these limitations, historical data are better than those in a sloppily prepared budget. Since they are drawn directly from the accounting records, they are not influenced by the judgments and persuasive arguments that sometimes affect the budget numbers. Furthermore, if the environment in which the organization operates is relatively stable from one year to the next, a historical standard may be practically as good as a budget.

External Standards

The standard for analyzing performance in a given responsibility center may be the average performance in similar responsibility centers in the same organization or performance in similar outside organizations. The performance of one hospital in a multi-institutional chain can be compared with all other hospitals in the chain, for example. If the conditions in each hospital are reasonably similar, a comparison of this sort can provide a reasonable basis for judging the performance of hospital managers.

In practice, even reasonably similar conditions may not exist. A hospital's size, demographic and epidemiological environment, labor market, supply market, and other factors all affect its performance in some way. Senior management must decide if these conditions are sufficiently different to invalidate any sort of meaningful comparison.

Many industry associations compile and distribute useful information about changes in the general environment of their member institutions, and about current data on average costs and other statistics. Management can use such data for comparative analyses that may provide helpful indicators of whether the organization is drifting out of line with its peers.

Example

The Healthcare Financial Management Association publishes detailed data on hospitals in its *Hospital Industry Analysis Report.* A typical report contains 29 financial ratios based on information supplied by 675 hospitals, with hospitals classified by type and bed size. Medians, upper quartiles, and lower quartiles are published.

As pointed out in Chapter 12, external data are of little use unless they are prepared in accordance with carefully worked out and well-understood definitions.

Example

State governments publish data on cost per mile of highway maintained. Some states define this amount as "trunkline miles" (i.e., linear miles of main highways). Other states use miles adjusted for number of lanes; still others use "equivalent trunkline miles." In the absence of an agreed-upon definition of "mile of highway," these data are useless for comparison purposes.

Comparative measures are especially useful for control in situations involving a large number of moderately small, discrete, and independent entities with similar clientele, operations, and cost structures, such as daycare centers, urban schools, suburban schools, community hospitals, and inner-city job placement programs. In these cases the indicators measuring similar aspects of performance (such as pupil-teacher ratio, cost of instruction, cost of supervisory personnel, and cost of maintenance and construction) may be valid indicators of *relative performance* even in the absence of an absolute measure of performance.

Focus on Significant Information

The problem of designing reports is, in part, one of deciding on the right type of information to give to management. Clearly, whenever feasible, managers should be given all the information they request. At the same time, to swamp managers with more information than they can assimilate (called *information overload*) is not helpful. Indeed, experiments have shown that if information overload exists, there is a tendency to disregard the whole reporting mechanism.

Example

A high school in Sacramento, California, installed a computerized attendance system at a cost of $100,000. It electronically transmitted to the accounting office the attendance of each pupil in each class period. One full-time person was required to operate the system. It provided instantaneous data, but data that no one needed instantaneously.[1]

A reporting system installed in naval shipyards some years ago produced 5,000 pages per month in each shipyard. This was far more than managers could use.

Because of these sorts of problems, the controller should assure that line managers are receiving only the information they need. Periodic discussions with line managers to ascertain what information is being used for what sorts of purposes can facilitate this process. Clearly, a similar review process should take place for the information senior management itself receives.

Role of Personal Computers

In the past, because control reports in most organizations were prepared centrally, it usually was difficult to tailor them to the needs of each individual manager. Now, however, it is possible for managers to have information downloaded from a central computer to their personal computer, and then to structure and present the information in ways that best suit their individual needs.

Even under these circumstances, there can be a tendency to report too much information, or to design reports in too complex a fashion. Senior managers generally need highly aggregated output data, while operating personnel or individuals responsible for program elements need more detailed data at more frequent intervals. Moreover, if their level of sophistication is low, operating personnel will require information that is both simple and displayed in a format that is easy to understand.

[1] Ida Hoos, *Systems Analysis in Public Policy* (Berkeley: University of California Press, 1972), p. 153.

Definition of Significant

Clearly, what is significant for one type of manager may not be significant for another. In general, significant items are those that can make a difference in the way a manager acts. There is no way of specifying exactly what such items are; they vary depending on the situation and on the wishes of individual managers. Nevertheless, some generalizations can be made:

- The significance of an item is not necessarily proportional to its size. In particular, certain discretionary cost items, such as travel, or dues and subscriptions, may be significant even though they are relatively small.

- Minor items should be aggregated. For example, costs for heating, air-conditioning, electric lighting, and perhaps telephone can be reported as utilities. Indeed, reporting a long list of cost items, many of which are relatively minor, can tend to obscure the few relatively significant items.

- The higher the management level using a report, the more aggregated it should be. Exhibit 14–1 illustrates this point. The report for each of the four successively higher levels contains less detail than the one below it. (Despite this aggregation, higher level managers may want access to reports prepared for lower levels so they can follow up on the details of items that appeared problematic on a summary report.)

- Managers do not care about the calculations. Note that Exhibit 14–1 does not show the budgeted amounts, but only the difference between actual and budget; the budget amount could be included to show how the difference was calculated, but it is omitted because the manager does not need to make this calculation. Similarly, calculations for the variances also are omitted.

Key Indicators

In most organizations and the responsibility centers within them, there are a few factors that must be watched closely. In Chapter 12, we called these *key results measures;* they also can be called *key success factors* or, in some instances, *danger signals.* The quantitative measures that allow managers to focus on them are called *key indicators.* These indicators often can signal upcoming problems, particularly financial ones. For example, in many nonprofit organizations, the number of new clients or client inquiries is a key indicator; in a hospital average length of stay, classified by diagnosis, may play this role.

Example	In a college, management needs to be alert to such danger signals as:

- A decrease in the number of inquiries.
- A decrease in the number of applications.
- A decrease in the quality of applicants.

- A decrease in yield (i.e., percentage of admitted applicants who enroll).
- A shift in enrollment among majors.
- An increase in student aid needs.
- An unplanned change in sections per faculty member.
- An increase in student attrition rates.
- An increase in administrative and support personnel.
- A decrease in gifts.

These danger signals are associated with several different responsibility centers within the college.

The number of key indicators typically is small, perhaps only numbering five or so for each responsibility center, but the reporting system must be designed so that managers can focus on them.

Example

The director of a mental health clinic states that in order to know how well the clinic is doing financially, she needs to focus on three items: (1) billed hours (i.e., the number of hours spent with clients), (2) accounts receivable as a percent of monthly billings (an indication of how promptly clients are paying their bills), and (3) the ratio of expenses to revenues.

Technical Criteria for Control Reports

In addition to the basic characteristics listed above concerning their content, control reports also must satisfy certain technical criteria. While the satisfaction of these criteria is largely the controller's responsibility, senior management needs to be aware of the criteria so it can guide the controller in the design effort, and so that it can diagnose problems when they arise.

The Control Period

The period of time covered by one report should be the shortest period in which management can usefully take action, and in which significant changes in performance are likely. If a serious situation develops, management needs to know immediately; otherwise substantial losses can occur. By contrast, reports on overall performance are usually made monthly or quarterly, because management does not need to act sooner.

Of particular importance is the fact that key indicators usually need to be reported separately from revenues, expenses, and variances. They also need to be distributed more frequently than financial information so as to facilitate timely intervention.

Example

The principal of a junior high school receives a report that shows the cumulative number of days of absence in the school year for each student. Since there is a strong correlation between attendance and performance, and since 10 days of absences mean that the student must repeat the school year, a growing number of absences for any given student is an important danger signal. Frequently, the only action necessary is for the principal to express concern to the student the next time they see one another; the fact that the principal knows—and the student knows that the principal knows—often provides the proper motivation. To be useful, such a report must be prepared on a daily basis.

Bases for Comparison

A control report should compare actual year-to-date amounts with budgeted amounts for the same time period. That is, unless revenues and expenses flow evenly during the fiscal year, budgeted amounts for, say, a quarterly report should not be obtained by taking one-quarter of the annual budget, but, rather, should be constructed by estimating the correct proportion of the annual budget that is applicable to the quarter. This is extremely important. Some organizations compare actual spending for a quarter with one-fourth of the annual budget. Others compare actual spending for the quarter with the total annual budget. Neither comparison is of much use to management.

Similarly, comparisons ordinarily should be made with the budget, not with the corresponding period from the prior year. Historical comparisons represent a holdover from the days when budgets were generally nonexistent or unreliable. A good budget provides a much better basis for comparison than last year's performance because the budget presumably incorporates the significant changes that have occurred since last year.

Timeliness

In all instances, it is important that reports be made available in a timely fashion; that is, soon enough to facilitate whatever action might be called for. A good rule of thumb is that an organization should make monthly reports available to its managers within a few days after the end of the month, certainly not more than a week. Indeed, one large multinational for-profit company invested several hundred thousand dollars in modifications to its computerized reporting system so that the waiting period for monthly financial statements could be shortened by *one day!*

Generally, obtaining a short reporting interval means that some accuracy is sacrificed in the interest of speed. However, approximately accurate reports available soon enough to provide a basis for action are far preferable to precisely accurate reports unavailable until so long after the event that nothing can be done about the problems they reveal.

Clarity

A control report is a communication device, and it is not doing its job unless it communicates its intended message clearly. This is much easier said than done. Those who design control reports, therefore, spend much time carefully choosing terminology that conveys the intended meaning and arranging the numbers in a way that emphasizes the intended relationships.

Clarity may also be enhanced if the variances are expressed as percentages of budget as well as in absolute dollars. The percentage gives a quick impression of how important the variance is relative to the budget. Particularly in reports for profit centers, clarity may be enhanced if ratios are used to call attention to important relationships.

Depending on the audience, even greater clarity can be achieved by using graphs and narrative explanations. Computers and their associated software make graphical presentations easy to prepare, and many managers find them quite helpful in explaining trends or other changes to their superiors.

Example

The reporting system for the finance operation of the Town of Concord, Massachusetts, includes: (1) a statement of results for the period, (2) a comparison of the results with an acceptable benchmark, (3) comparisons of the town's cash position to prior periods, (4) a comment on market conditions, (5) a summary of performance results, (6) a log of investments, and (7) a graphical depiction of the results. The report is useful not only to the town treasurer but also to the elected officials and the citizenry.[2]

Narrative explanations often are used to clarify the quantitative information in a report. A good narrative explanation needs to go beyond restating what a report already says. In general, such explanations are used to describe the reasons underlying a variance.

Example

In Exhibit 14–1, a narrative explanation might say: "The unfavorable rate variance was the result of the use of three nutritionists in Pay Grade 14, whereas the job called for Grade 12. This condition has existed since April because no Grade 12 employees were available. We are actively working to recruit Grade 12 people, and hope to have the situation corrected by July."

Rounding

To help focus managers' attention on significant information, the accounting staff should round the numbers in control reports, rather than calculate them to the last penny. Most managers care little about cents; some, depending on the magnitude of the budget, may not care about the last thousand dollars. An amount of $433,876 might just as easily be reported for control purposes as $434, with the report headed "Dollar Amounts in Thousands" or "$000."

As a rule of thumb, most control reports do not need dollar amounts reported with more than three digits, although decimal points might be used to make a column easier to understand or add. For example, the above amount

---

[2]Anthony T. Logalbo, "Spotlighting Small Governments: Performance Reporting—The Forgotten Element in Cash Management," *Government Finance Review* 3, no. 4 (April 1987), pp. 41–43.

might be reported as $433.9. In general, the amount of rounding depends on the size of the responsibility center and what makes most sense for the managers charged with controlling costs.

Integration

Ordinarily, control reports should consist of an integrated package. Specifically, reports for lower-level responsibility centers should be consistent with, and easily relatable to, summary reports prepared for higher-level responsibility centers.

Exhibit 14–1 illustrates this process of integration. The third-level report is for the supervisor of nutritionists, who is on the next higher level in the organization hierarchy above the regional supervisors (fourth-level report). Data for the regions for which the supervisor is responsible appear in summary form in the third level. Note that the amounts reported on a single line in Level 3 for the nutritionists' direct-contact time are the same as the totals on the Level 4 control report.

The second-level report is for an even higher level of management, the Maternal/Infant Nutrition Program. It includes the nutritionists as reported in detail in Level 3, plus the other professionals who are affiliated with the program. It also includes the other direct expenses of the program (supplies and materials, contract services). Note that the total direct labor cost figures for nutritionists at the bottom of Level 3 appear as a single line on the Level 2 report.

Level 1 is the most highly summarized report and is used by the agency director or governing body to review financial results of all the agency's programs. Note that the total direct costs of the Maternal/Infant Nutrition Program at the bottom of Level 2 appear as a single line in Level 1.

Benefit/Cost

A reporting system, like anything else, should not cost more than it is worth. Unfortunately, there are great difficulties in applying this obvious statement to practical situations. For one thing, it is difficult to measure the cost of a given report. This is partly because most preparation costs are joint costs with other reports, and partly because the real cost includes not only the preparation cost, but also the opportunity cost of the hours that managers spend reading reports when they might be doing something else.

Because of the difficulty in assessing the benefit/cost ratio of reports, it is worthwhile to review an organization's management control reports periodically and eliminate those that no longer are needed. Useless reports are not uncommon. Frequently they exist because a new problem area created a need for a report at some earlier time, and the report continues to be prepared even though the problem no longer exists. A report structure, like a tree, is often better if it is pruned regularly.

An Illustration

Not all control reports follow the above criteria. Many organizations, for sound management reasons, diverge from these criteria. The control report shown in Exhibit 14–2 is an example of how a report might depart from some of the above criteria, and yet serve management's purposes well. The report is the operating statement for a college.[3] It summarizes results for the fiscal year to date, that is, from July through December. It was prepared for a January meeting of the board of trustees. Some comments about it follow.

Numbers Are Rounded

The report is short, and the numbers are rounded so that a maximum of four digits is shown. It nevertheless conveys the significant information the board needs so that it can understand what has happened and what is likely to happen.

Management's Current Estimates Are Included

In a departure from the criteria discussed above, the report does not compare actual expenses for the year to date with the year-to-date budget; rather it compares the budget for the *entire year* with management's current *estimate* of revenues and expenses for the *entire year.* In the board's view, this is one of the most important parts of the report. Management must explain each significant difference, then seek board approval of controllable differences *before* the expenses actually are incurred.

Auxiliary Enterprises Are Shown Separately

The report is structured so that revenues and expenses of auxiliary enterprises are shown separately from educational revenues and expenses, and so that the net income of these activities is shown. (It may be desirable to show separately the revenues and expenses of each important auxiliary activity, such as dormitory, food service, bookstore, and varsity athletics.) In some reports all revenues are presented first, and then all expenses, so that important programmatic relationships are difficult to determine. This report is structured so that attention is focused on the revenues and expenses of the primary program, education, and then on the revenues and expenses of the auxiliary programs.

Approved Variances Are Separated

The variances that the board has considered and approved at earlier meetings are listed separately, so that attention is focused on variances that have developed since the last meeting. (A separate, two-page memorandum explains the important new variances.)

---

[3]Additional examples of operating statements can be found in Leon E. Hay, *Accounting for Governmental and Nonprofit Entities* (Homewood, IL: Richard D. Irwin, 1988); Malvern J. Gross, Jr., Richard F. Larkin, Roger S. Bruttomesso, and John J. McNally, *Financial and Accounting Guide for Nonprofit Organizations,* 5th edition (New York: John Wiley & Sons, Inc., 1995).

EXHIBIT 14–2

ILLUSTRATIVE COLLEGE BUDGET REPORT
For the Period July 1, 2001 to March 31, 2002
(Dollar Amounts in Thousands)

	Fiscal 2001–02 Budget	Fiscal 2001–02 Estimated	Variance Total	Variance Previously Reported	Variance New This Quarter
Audited student enrollment	1,670	1,766	96	91	5
Educational and general					
Revenues					
Student charges—tuition	$33,517	$35,435	$1,918	$1,826	$ 92
—fees.	4,683	4,679	(4)	(20)	16
Endowment utilized for operations	4,915	4,939	24	24	0
Gifts—unrestricted	1,900	1,950	50	50	0
—restricted	1,024	1,354	330	330	0
Government grants.	886	904	18	18	0
Other revenues	1,603	1,760	157	(42)	199
Total revenues	$48,528	$51,021	$2,493	$2,186	$307
Expenses					
Instruction and research					
On-campus programs	$14,455	$14,586	$ (131)	$ (176)	$ 45
Off-campus programs	2,514	2,549	(35)	(40)	5
Academic support.	4,261	4,238	23	23	0
Student services	5,970	6,226	(256)	(221)	(35)
Institutional support	6,718	6,866	(148)	(48)	(100)
Educational plant	4,078	4,226	(148)	(88)	(60)
Student aid.	8,533	8,614	(81)	(113)	32
Contingency.	1,048	262	786	524	262
Total expenses.	$47,577	$47,567	$ 10	$ (139)	$149
Educational and general income	$ 951	$ 3,454	$2,503	$2,047	$456
Auxiliary enterprises:					
Revenues	$13,097	$13,502	$ 405	$ 378	$ 27
Expenses.	11,766	12,159	393	309	84
Income (loss).	$ 1,331	$ 1,343	$ 12	$ 69	$ (57)
Total net income (loss).	$ 2,282	$ 4,797	$2,515	$2,116	$399

	Fall Term 2002	Fall Term 2001	Fall Term 2000
Admissions data:			
Average SAT scores.	945	952	958
Percent requesting financial aid	25%	22%	21%
Percent minority applications	18%	16%	15%
Percent applicants below 20 years old	96%	97%	97%
Full-time students to part-time	17:1	15:1	14:1
Applicants admitted	87%	82%	64%
Admits enrolled	54%	55%	59%

Unfavorable Variances Are Highlighted

"Unfavorable" variances, that is, those that reduce income, are enclosed in parentheses. These are revenue items for which the estimated actual is less than budget, and expense items for which the estimated actual is more than budget.

Use of Control Reports

If control reports are to have any value, they must be used; that is, managers must rely on them as an important resource. In this regard, an issue that frequently arises concerns the value of a comparison between expected and actual performance after the performance already has taken place. Since the work has been completed, and the past cannot be changed, of what value is such a report? There are two answers to this question.

First, if a manager understands that his or her performance is being measured, reported, and evaluated, there is at least some tendency to attempt to influence the results so as to obtain a good report. Assuming that the reporting system is fair—so that a "good" action (one that benefits the organization) on the part of a manager will be reflected accordingly on the control reports—a manager ordinarily will tend to act in ways that benefit the organization.

Second, although the past cannot be changed, analysis of the past can be extremely helpful. Among other things, it may help to identify ways that performance can be improved in the future. Specifically, a good set of control reports can help managers to take whatever corrective action appears appropriate. Clearly, an important aspect of this process is the involvement of the manager's superior, who can praise, constructively criticize, or otherwise suggest ways to improve performance. At the extreme, a good reporting system can assist a manager to determine whether a subordinate should be promoted or terminated.

Feedback

Viewed in the above way, a good set of control reports functions as a *feedback mechanism*. In engineering, feedback refers to electrical circuits that are arranged so that information about a machine's performance is fed back to a control mechanism that can make adjustments. A thermostat is a feedback device. If the temperature in a room falls below a certain level, a thermostat will activate a furnace that will return the room to its prescribed temperature.

Control reports are feedback mechanisms, but they are only one part of the process. Unlike the mechanical cause-and-effect pattern of a thermostat, the feedback process associated with a set of control reports is not automatic. A control report by itself does not lead to a change in performance; this happens only when a manager gets involved and takes action. For a manager to take action, a three-step process must occur:

1. A *review* must take place, and one or more areas must be *identified* as candidates for action.

2. Each area must be investigated to determine whether action is warranted.

3. When necessary, some sort of *action* must take place.

We discuss each of these steps separately.

Review and Identification

A good control report will suggest areas that require investigation. An investigation sometimes, although not always, may come about because of a significant variance between budgeted and actual performance. Large unfavorable variances are not necessarily a reason for investigation, however, nor are large favorable variances a reason for complacency. Good managers will interpret the information on a control report in light of their own knowledge about conditions in the responsibility center and their "feel" for what is right.

| Example | If a manager has learned from conversations and personal observations that, because of personnel shortages, there was need for considerable overtime (and therefore the payment of premium wage rates) in a particular responsibility center, there is little need to investigate a large wage rate variance. On the other hand, a large favorable price variance in the purchase of medical supplies in a hospital may indicate that low-quality supplies were purchased, perhaps implying problems later on when those supplies are used. |

Some managers argue that an essential characteristic of a good management control system is that the reports contain no surprises. They expect their subordinates to inform them when significant events occur so that appropriate action can be taken immediately. When the control report subsequently appears, the manager will not be surprised by a particular variance, since the factors leading up to it were known and corrective action was taken.

The Exception Principle

Problem identification is facilitated if the control system operates on the exception principle. According to this principle, a control report focuses a manager's attention on that limited number of items where performance differs significantly from the standard. Little or no attention is given to the rather large number of situations where performance was satisfactory.

Obviously, no control system can make this sort of distinction perfectly. Sometimes, as mentioned above, a large positive variance can be as much of a red flag as a large negative one. Sometimes a negligible variance masks underlying factors that a manager needs to address.

| Example | When the program director reads the Program Direct Cost Summary second-level report in Exhibit 14–1, his or her attention is not called to the performance of the nutritionists in June, because actual costs were only |

$30,000 in excess of budget, an insignificant amount. We can observe from the details of nutritionists' performance in Level 3, however, that costs for direct-contact time, community collateral work, and professional development are considerably in excess of budget, and these excesses may indicate that problems exist.

The exception principle is tricky to apply in practice because it requires that significant items be identified, and significance is a matter of judgment. Nevertheless, a good set of control reports will at least attempt to highlight problem areas so as to save managers as much time as possible in the process of review and problem identification.

Engineered and Discretionary Costs

In reviewing a set of control reports, a manager must distinguish between items of engineered cost and items of discretionary cost. In general, managers are looking for engineered costs to be as low as possible vis-à-vis the standard (consistent, of course, with quality and safety standards). Discretionary costs, on the other hand, are somewhat more complicated, since optimal performance frequently consists of spending the amount agreed upon in the budget. Spending too little may be as problematic as spending too much.

Example

To reduce expenses, a manager in a research organization can easily skimp on maintenance or on training; the manager of the information services department can turn down requests for special computer runs; senior management can cancel an unfunded research project. All of these actions result in lower costs during the current budget year, but none may be in the long-run best interest of the organization.

Limitations of the Standard

No standard is perfect. Sometimes standards are derived in ways that are not methodologically sound. Even if a standard cost is carefully prepared, it may not be an accurate estimate of what costs should have been under the particular set of circumstances a manager faced during a reporting period.

Example

The standard direct labor cost for a particular procedure is $13.72. This may not be accurate if the engineering analysis that led to the standard was conducted improperly. Even if the engineering analysis was methodologically sound, the rate may not be an accurate estimate of current direct labor costs because of methods changes, changes in technology, changes in wage rates, or changes in the kind of personnel conducting the procedure.

In short, even with a valid budget, managers should exercise caution in using variances as indicators of performance. A variance may have a combination of causes, some of which were controllable, some not. At best, a good variance analysis provides the starting point for evaluating performance and discovering the underlying causes of deviations from the budget. Therefore, in deciding what action to take, managers should use not only the control reports, but also whatever information they obtain through other channels, and their intuitive judgment regarding areas that need attention.

Investigation

Ordinarily, an investigation consists of a conversation between the manager of a responsibility center and his or her superiors and subordinates. In these conversations, the superior typically probes to determine whether corrective action of some sort is needed. Frequently, it turns out that special circumstances gave rise to the variance; that is, the assumptions that underlay the budget did not hold. If these changes were not controllable by the subordinate, there is little that can be done. Certainly there is no cause to criticize the subordinate. This does not mean that no corrective action can be taken, however; rather, it suggests that corrective action must be taken at some level other than the subordinate's.

It also is possible that the variance resulted from a random occurrence that probably will not repeat itself, such as an equipment breakdown or a strike. In this case, about all that can be done is to accept the variance and hope that it will not recur.

Finally, it is possible that the variance came about from performance that needs to be modified. In this case, the superior wants to determine the underlying causes of the deviation from budget, and assist the subordinate in taking corrective action to reverse the trend.

Action

Usually, a course of action comes about as a result of a meeting between a superior and a subordinate; the meeting generally revolves around a particular variance. If the variance is negative, the two individuals agree on the steps that must be taken to remedy the situation. If a favorable variance is the result of good performance, praise is appropriate.

In all respects, it is important for superiors to weigh the trade-offs between current performance and the long-run interests of the organization. An inherent weakness of management control systems is that they tend to focus on short-run rather than long-run performance. They measure current revenues and expenses, rather than the effect of current actions on the future financial health of the organization or the quality of services provided. Thus, if too much emphasis is placed on financial results as they are depicted in current control reports, long-run performance may be affected. We explore this dilemma more fully in the next chapter.

Summary

Performance reports, as distinct from information reports, typically focus on two types of output: economic performance and management performance. Most of our attention in this chapter was directed toward management performance, which is the subject of the management control reports.

Good control reports have three essential characteristics: (1) they are related to personal responsibility, which typically calls for several levels of reports; (2) they compare actual performance to a standard, usually the budget; and (3) they focus on significant information, which frequently includes key indicators (many of which are nonfinancial in nature). By focusing on key indicators, managers frequently can see a problem developing and take action to avert it before it becomes serious.

Good control reports also must satisfy certain technical criteria. They must (1) cover a period of time that facilitates management action; (2) be timely enough to allow management's actions to have an effect; (3) clarify important relationships, which frequently requires using graphs and narrative explanations, and rounding numbers; (4) consist of an integrated package in which the reports for lower-level responsibility centers are consistent with and easily relatable to the reports for higher-level responsibility centers; and (5) be worth more than they cost.

A good set of control reports functions as a feedback mechanism that guides managers in identifying and investigating areas for possible action. To do this, the reports should function on the exception principle, which typically allows managers to focus their attention on a few areas where investigation is required. In so doing, managers need to bear in mind that a standard, no matter how carefully prepared, may not be an accurate estimate of what costs or revenues should have been under actual circumstances. Therefore, variances should be used with caution; they are a means to guide a manager's investigation and subsequent action, but not necessarily a reason for criticism of subordinates.

Suggested Additional Readings

Anthony, Robert N., David F. Hawkins, and Kenneth A. Merchant. *Accounting: Text and Cases,* 10th ed. Burr Ridge, IL: McGraw-Hill, 1998, chap. 26.

Anthony, Robert N., and Vijay Govindarajan. *Management Control Systems,* 10th edition. Burr Ridge, IL: McGraw-Hill, 2000.

Institute of Management Accounting. *Statement on Management Accounting 5-B: Fundamentals of Reporting Information to Managers.* Montvale, NJ: 1992.

Case 14–1

Franklin Health Associates (B)*

> When I came here in November, I looked at the physicians' generation of revenue
> and the corresponding expenses, and I knew something was wrong. The generation
> figures in all categories were less than budgeted, but the expenses were not
> proportionally less, so we were heading for a big deficit.

The speaker was Jack Barber, manager of Franklin Group Practice (FGP).
FGP was a division of Franklin Health Associates, a large health care organization located in Farmington, Maine (see Franklin Health Associates (A) for a
description). Mr. Barber had been working at FGP for eight months, and had
already instituted some changes in the group practice. He continued.

> At the time I arrived, the physicians didn't care whether or not they met budgeted
> amounts. They had no incentives to do so, as they were paid prospectively based
> on anticipated revenue for the budget year. They eventually became concerned
> when they realized the group practice would go under if we didn't reverse the
> deficit trend. Then I had their support.

To approach the problem, Mr. Barber decided to analyze why actual revenue was lower than budgeted. He focused on each individual provider. Although the year's budgeted values for physician generation were derived
somewhat subjectively from discussions with individual physicians and examination of past trends, there were some standards that he thought he could
use to find the revenue that FGP could expect from each physician.

He first identified each physician's specialty area and used the fee guidelines to determine the typical fee per visit for each provider (Exhibit 1). Next,
he talked to the physicians to determine how many hours per week they were
scheduled to be in the office (Exhibit 1). Although all of FGP's providers were
full time, some of them spent a greater percentage of their working time at
FGP. For example, Dr. Sewall, a dentist, was available for office visits 40
hours per week, whereas Dr. Dixon, a general surgeon, spent a good deal of
time at the hospital.

Using some general guidelines, Mr. Barber worked with each provider to
determine how many patients she or he could see in an hour's time based on
the length of an average office visit (Exhibit 1). Then he multiplied the expected number of hours worked per week by the expected number of patients
in a week. To give the physician some leeway for telephone calls and paperwork, he used a 4.5-day workweek. He multiplied this amount by the expected
number of provider days in the month, which he determined by subtracting all
legitimate sick and vacation days for the particular month (Exhibit 1). This

*This case was prepared by Margaret B. Reber under the supervision of Professor David W.
Young. It subsequently was revised by David W. Young. Copyright © by David W. Young.

EXHIBIT 1   Expected Provider Charges, Office Hours, Visits, and Workdays

Provider	Specialty	Average Fee per Visit	Expected Number of Office Hours/Week	Expected Number of Office Visits/Hour	Expected Number of Workdays in May
Bitterauf	Orthopedic Surgery	$40	16	4	16
Condit	Family Practice	$34	32	4	20
Dixon	General Surgery	$36	16	4	15
Fuson	Family Practice	$34	32	4	15
Haeger	Dentistry	$60	40	2	20
Hurst	Otolaryngology (ENT)	$40	16	4	16
MacMahon	Pediatrics/Family Practice	$34	32	6	10
Prior	Internal Medicine	$34	23	4	18
Record	Internal Medicine	$34	23	4	16
Sewall	Dentistry	$60	40	2	20

gave him the expected number of patients per month. Finally, he multiplied this number by 0.80. He commented on this last computation:

I provided physicians with this additional leeway to get a more realistic number of patients a physician is expected to see in a month. The physicians engage in many nonincome-generating activities and they thought some allowance should be used to account for the time they spend in the reexamination of patients, delivery of medication and shots, and public relations activities for which there is a minimal charge or perhaps no charge at all.

Finally, he multiplied this adjusted figure by the average fee per visit to get the revenue which he could expect each provider to generate. To compare the expected amount with the actual, he used the physicians' schedule books. His secretary tallied up office visits, office surgery, and injection charges for the month for each physician to get the actual office visit generation. She also computed the number of patients seen, the total hours worked, the number of appointments rescheduled or canceled, and the number of no shows.

Mr. Barber's secretary spent about six hours each month tabulating this information. She gave it to him (Exhibit 2) and he then subtracted the actual from the expected and prepared a report for each physician comparing expected and actual values. Exhibit 3 is a sample of a report showing performance for Dr. Bitterauf for the month of May. Exhibit 4 shows the totals for all departments for May. He commented on what he had learned from the reports:

I've been doing this for about six months. As might be imagined, the revenue of some providers was way below expected. In certain cases, it was due to low productivity; in others, it was because the physicians weren't charging enough or they weren't spending enough time in the office. So I decided to talk to them.

The first time I produced the report, I sat down with each physician individually and explained the figures. I had to convince them that I was right. I had to be able to back up my words with figures. For every hour I spent with a

EXHIBIT 2
Actual Provider
Visits, Hours
Worked, and
Generation

Provider	Actual Number of Visits in May	Actual Number of Hours Worked in May	Actual Revenue Generation in May
Bitterauf	208	44	$ 7,634
Condit	413	107	13,778
Dixon	88	30	4,796
Fuson	242	87	8,543
Haeger	218	130	14,985
Hurst	203	61	13,406
MacMahon	191	43	7,518
Prior	207	70	7,721
Record	182	56	7,433
Sewall	211	133	20,201
Totals	2,163	761	$106,014

EXHIBIT 3
Sample Physician's
Report

Dr. Bitterauf   May 2000

$$16 \text{ hrs/wk} \times 4 \text{ pts/hr} = 64 \text{ pts/wk}$$

No. of patients	No. of hours	Generation
208	44	$7,634
$36.70	$173.49	4.7 pt/hr

$$64 \text{ pt/wk} \div 4.5 \text{ days/wk} = 14.2 \text{ pt/day}$$
$$14.2 \text{ pt/day} \times 16 \text{ provider days} = 227 \text{ pt/mo (max)}$$
$$227 \text{ pt/mo} \times .80 = 182$$
$$182 \times \$40.00 = \$7,280$$
$$\underline{\$7,634 - \$7,280 = \$354}$$

physician, I spent 12 to 15 hours documenting what I was talking about. When I showed them all the data, they accepted my conclusions.

Let me give you an example of a conversation I had with one of our physicians who was undercharging patients. I said, "Roger, I've been studying the way you've been practicing, and I'd like to talk to you about it. Although you see a lot of patients, your total generation is under what we expected." Then Roger said, "How do you know?" After I showed him the numbers, we progressed to a discussion of his pattern of undercharging. Roger told me that some people didn't have much money, so he didn't charge as much. Then I told him, "You can't do that. You can't charge one patient less than another for the same service. That's discrimination." Now, we're gradually getting Roger's fees up to what they should be. But I couldn't do it without this report.

Overall, Mr. Barber felt that the physician's report had been a useful tool for controlling revenue:

EXHIBIT 4   Statement of Operations and Comparisons for Franklin Group Practice

	1999 Month May	2000 Month May	1999–2000 YTD 05/31/99	2000–01 YTD 05/31/00	2000–01 Prorated Budget
Generation:					
Medical	$219,882	$201,588	$2,115,078	$2,314,468	$2,887,634
Dental	29,022	37,370	280,862	327,388	390,272
Optometry	20,370	29,968	245,886	284,122	350,984
Pharmacy	6,436	5,556	66,014	71,898	86,828
Laboratory	22,862	24,084	205,016	234,792	269,612
X-ray	16,664	14,088	170,218	161,292	210,630
Total	$315,236	$312,654	$3,083,074	$3,393,960	$4,195,960
Grants	5,646	4,078	68,598	49,862	60,000
Other income	(58)	(16)	27,206	2,128	
Total operating support	$320,824	$316,716	$3,178,878	$3,445,950	$4,255,960
Less uncollectibles:					
Provision for bad debts	$ 8,862	$ 8,804	$ 87,326	$ 95,928	—
Cash discount	2,946	2,734	26,266	31,004	—
Courtesy and employee discount	390	428	26,002	5,092	—
Disallowed charges	19,770	25,756	208,250	262,972	—
Total uncollectibles	$ 31,968	$ 37,722	$ 347,844	$ 394,996	$ 425,596
Total operating revenue	$288,856	$278,994	$2,831,034	$3,050,954	$3,830,364
Operating expenses:					
Medical	$150,448	$133,932	$1,517,492	$1,674,976	$2,044,504
Dental	17,502	19,372	203,688	234,268	267,518
Optometry	23,706	30,682	210,982	249,942	243,522
Pharmacy	5,468	6,110	61,412	73,716	76,000
Laboratory	9,020	8,594	99,832	113,008	121,200
X-ray	7,748	10,706	107,986	112,164	129,600
Medical records	3,112	3,470	37,784	38,098	43,400
Facilities	23,774	22,700	265,646	263,024	313,120
Administration	35,800	43,168	397,810	470,502	580,500
Total operating expense	$276,578	$278,734	$2,902,632	$3,229,698	$3,819,364
Interest	2,000	1,492	15,186	11,146	8,000
Total operating expense including interest	$278,578	$280,226	$2,917,818	$3,240,844	$3,827,364
Excess of revenue over expenses (expenses over revenue)	$ 10,278	$ (1,232)	$ (86,784)	$ (189,890)	$ 3,000

Note: The fiscal year was from July–June. FY 2001 began on July 1, 2000.

The report has enabled me to pinpoint the sources of our low-revenue-generation problem, and it's given me the backup I need to discuss problems with the providers. We've seen some dramatic increases in certain physicians' office visit revenue since we instituted the report. We have a ways to go, but this report is helping us to get our feet back on the ground.

The most important thing to do now is to be able to give the providers a breakdown of why they are not achieving their budgeted levels of performance. This is going to require designing a somewhat more sophisticated report than we have right now.

Questions

1. Prepare a variance analysis for Dr. Bitterauf. How would you report this information to him/her?

2. Design a set of reports for FHA that more adequately addresses the needs of management and the physicians.

Case 14–2

Union Medical Center*

Your system can't supply us with any information that we couldn't easily put together ourselves. Look at that wall. Those stacks of printouts represent six different approaches to care monitoring and illness classification that I'm in the process of evaluating.

Harriet Bingley, MD, Manager of Clinical and Financial Systems at Union Medical Center (UMC), was discussing the theoretical underpinnings of the Diagnosis Related Group (DRG) system with one of her assistants and a representative of a western data analysis firm. The representative was at UMC to present a classification system and to explain its usefulness in comparison to other monitoring systems. Dr. Bingley was not especially impressed, however. She was much more concerned with how she would get physicians to buy into the new system—whichever one she chose.

Background

UMC was a 400-bed acute care teaching hospital located in an old downtown neighborhood undergoing considerable reconstruction. The physician staff was predominantly salaried under a contract with the hospital. Several years ago, the Chief Financial Officer, Richard Veller, had joined UMC, bringing with him a strong interest in case mix, DRGs, and the belief that management of a hospital must revolve around its products, which are its cases. He intended to take an industrial model of management and apply it to the hospital.

Part of Mr. Veller's plan was to make those who manage the products responsible for resources used to produce them. This new structure thus required that a management team composed of a physician, nurse, and lay administrator be responsible for specific hospital products or case types. Another part of the plan was to merge clinical with financial data. This required changing the

---

*This case was prepared by Jill Piatek under the direction of Professor Nancy M. Kane, with support from the Massachusetts Health Data Consortium. It subsequently was revised by Professor David W. Young. Copyright © by Nancy M. Kane, David W. Young, and the Massachusetts Health Data Consortium.

accounting system to track product costs in addition to departmental costs, the traditional focus of hospital cost accounting. To date, substantial progress had been made on the accounting system aspect of the plan.

Dr. Bingley had begun working with Mr. Veller to implement these plans. Besides her MD, she had an MBA, which she felt gave her a better appreciation of the administrative aspects of clinical information. Her job entailed (1) defining a care monitoring system; (2) refining the definitions of the hospital's products (case types); (3) development of standards of patient care by which future performance could be measured and goals set; (4) design of incentives for the departments and/or physicians to reach these goals; and (5) development of fixed prices for certain case types to bid for HMO business. Dr. Bingley reported to the vice president of finance and to the assistant director and administrator of the department of surgery.

Physician Relationships

As a first step toward implementation of the care monitoring system, Dr. Bingley launched an educational campaign for physicians. She began with the surgical department. With the backing of her superiors, she was given one physician from each surgical specialty with whom she discussed the care monitoring system development. The other departments would be undertaken in the future. Dr. Bingley planned four visits to each of the surgical specialty physicians. The first round, already completed, had been to introduce the physicians to the case concept, explain the types of information available about cases, and discuss the implications of a management control system based on DRGs. The second visit, which Dr. Bingley was about to make, was to show them reports on their department and their own practice patterns, in terms of their Diagnosis Related Groups. In a future visit, Dr. Bingley expected to compare cases categorized by two other medically meaningful case classification systems which addressed severity of illness. In the last visit, she hoped to sum up her analyses of the monitoring systems and methods used to estimate product costs.

The purposes of the physician interviews were to familiarize and educate physicians on product-based management information systems, to create a dialogue in which the physicians expressed their opinions on the utility of each system, and to lay the groundwork for their assuming accountability in the future for resources used for their patients. Dr. Bingley expected to employ their suggestions to modify the data in ways that would be most useful for the medical staff.

The Second Round of Meetings

In November Dr. Bingley began her second round of visits. She began each interview by reiterating that DRGs were based on the principal diagnosis listed on the discharge summary, and that they were the basis by which

Medicare and several managed care plans reimbursed the hospital. For each interview, she had prepared four different sets of summary statistics (see Exhibits 1–4). Exhibit 1 showed a case summary for an individual patient classified into Diagnosis Related Group (DRG) number 198, total cholecystectomy without common bile duct exploration, age under 70 years, without complications and comorbidities. The nature of information collected by the information system for each patient is shown.

Exhibit 2 described, for the same DRG, total costs incurred by the general surgery service in the base and current year, and the "variance" between years due to the changes in volume (number of patients), utilization (units; e.g., LOS per case), and cost per unit. In Exhibit 3 each ancillary service used by the general surgery service in treating DRG 198 was broken out and the number of patients and units per patient were shown in the base and current years. Finally, in Exhibit 4 the specific units used in one ancillary service, the clinical pathology lab, were broken down for the same DRG, for the general surgery department in the base and current years.

The first physician she visited was Dr. Gerald Farr in orthopedic surgery. Dr. Bingley pointed out the concern for efficiently managing cases under both Medicare's prospective reimbursement system and some of the hospital's managed care contracts, and suggested that cutting the quantity of lab tests might result in both lower costs and higher-quality care. She also emphasized the excellent potential these data had as a research tool since all procedures, lab tests, and so on, were documented for each case. Dr. Farr expressed interest in using the data to justify purchasing new equipment. He also could see that it might be possible to cost out the possibility of trading off lower lengths of stay against higher ancillary costs. His final comment was, "That's interesting. It's nice that you can go into such detail to know what's going on."

Dr. Bingley's second interview was with Dr. Richard Rair, who was Chief of General Surgery. During her first interview with Dr. Rair, he had told her that he didn't need anyone to tell him about his patients, since he already knew everything about them. For the second interview he started with a similar position.

> The groupings are terrible. I also question several length-of-stay measures. I certainly wouldn't point to those numbers and say anything, since something's clearly wrong with the system. I also can't recognize some of the cases, which is probably because the residents and physician assistants actually fill out the discharge summaries, and I usually only scan them before signing. In fact, I'd go as far as to say that the number of people filling out the summaries and their carelessness compromise the accuracy of the whole database.

Dr. Bingley commented that she had done a review of the primary diagnoses listed on the summaries and found an error rate of only 2–4 percent in coder interpretations of medical record data, but close to a 12 percent error rate in terms of the content expressed in the records.

EXHIBIT 1
Clinical Case
Summary

Department Surgery	
198 Total Cholecystectomy w/o C.D.E.	
Age <70 w/o c.c.	
Patient Name	
Patient Number	
Admit-Date, Time	05-27-01 11 a.m.
Disch-Date, Time.	06-04-01 11 a.m.
Admission Source	Physician
Days Since Last Hospital Stay.	No Previous Stay
Patient Age	61 years
Admit Weight	Unknown
Diagnosis	
Principal Diagnosis 57420	Cholelithiasis NOS
Admitting Diagnosis 57420.	Cholelithiasis NOS
Total Secondary DXS.	00
Infection/Complications	None
Operative Procedures	
Principal Proc (Hour 24)	Total Cholecystectomy
Associated Proc	Intraoper Cholangiogram
Associated Proc	Incidental Appendectomy
Associated Proc	Whole Blood Transfus NEC
Total Operative Episodes	01
Other Procedures	
Total Other Procedures	0
Physicians/Consultations	
Attend.	Dr. Rair
Resident	Dr. Training
Surg Res	Dr. Intern
Total Consultations	Unknown
Discharge Disposition	
Deceased	
Nursing Home or Other Hospital	
Home, Home Care or Other	Home
Discharge Condition	
Afebrile	Unknown
Normal GI Function.	Unknown
Ambulatory	Unknown
Physician Appointment	Unknown
Progress Satisfactory	Unknown
Instructions Understood	Unknown
Length of Stay.	8 days
LOS Excluding Deaths, etc.	
LOS vs. Region Median	Not Available
UR Uncertified Days.	0 Days
Special Care Days	0 Days
Costs	
Routine Services.	$2,152
Diagnostic Services	827
Therapeutic Services	2,134
Physician Services	0
Total costs	$5,113
Medicare Reimbursement Rate	$4,300

EXHIBIT 2 Costs for the General Surgery Service for DRG 198
(Cholecystectomy w/o C.D.E.; Age<70 w/o c.c.)

1	2	3	4	5	6	7	8	9	10	11	12
Base Period YTD				Current YTD			YTD Change		Change Due to		
No. of Pts.	Cost per Patient	Total Costs	Diagnostic Group	No. of Pts.	Cost per Patient	Total Costs	Costs	%	Volume/ Mix	Util.	Cost/ Unit
18	6,000	108,000	Cholecystectomy without common duct exploration age less than 70 without CC	20	5,934	118,680	(10,680)	(10)%	(12,000)	9,259	(7,939)

EXHIBIT 3 Costs for the General Surgery Service for DRG 198 (By Intermediate Cost Object)

1	2	3	4	5	6	7	8	9	10	11	12
Base Period YTD				Current YTD			YTD Change		Change Due to		
% of Pts.	Units/ Pts. Receiving	Costs/ Pt. in Dx Grp	Dep. Description	% of Pts.	Units/ Pts. Receiving	Costs/ Pt. in Dx Grp	Costs		Volume/ Mix	Util.	Cost/ Unit
100	20	250	Pharmacy	100	20	272	(940)		(500)	0	(440)
100	2	25	CSR	100	2	27	(90)		(50)	0	(40)
100	4	50	P. Care Eq.	100	4	54	(180)		(100)	0	(80)
100	1	15	SDS	100	1	16	(50)		(30)	0	(20)
100	1.5	20	SDS-P4	100	1.5	22	(80)		(40)	0	(40)
100	7	1,750	P4 Room	100	7	1,907	(6,640)		(3,500)	0	(3,140)
100	2	40	Bati Lab	100	1	24	240		(80)	400	(80)
100	17	160	Clin. Path	100	14	124	400		(320)	780	(60)
100	60	480	Chem. Lab	100	40	363	1,380		(960)	3,200	(860)
100	1	50	Path. Lab	100	1	54	(180)		(100)	0	(80)
100	2.5	250	Ad. Rad-Diag.	100	1.8	272	(940)		(500)	1,400	(1,840)
40	1	50	Rad-Nuclear Med	10	1	42	60		(100)	0	160
50	1	75	Rad-UltraSnd	50	1	81	(270)		(150)	0	(120)
100	1	60	OR Monitoring	100	1	65	(220)		(120)	0	(100)
100	1	50	AD. Card.	100	1	54	(180)		(100)	0	(80)
100	3	1,700	Oper. Rm	100	3	1,653	(2,460)		(3,400)	0	940
100	14	200	OR Med. Sup.	100	14	218	(760)		(400)	0	(360)
100	1	65	OR Drgs	100	1	71	(250)		(130)	0	(120)
100	1	200	Rec. Rm.	100	1	218	(760)		(400)	0	(360)
100	55	350	IV Solutions	100	35	281	680		(700)	2,545	(1,165)
100	3	110	Blood Bank	80	2	87	240		(220)	733	(273)
100	5	50	Resp. Ther.	80	4	29	320		(100)	200	220
		6,000	Total			5,934	(10,680)		(12,000)	9,259	(7,939)

EXHIBIT 4   Costs for the General Surgery Service for DRG 198 for the Clinical Pathology Lab

1	2	3	4	5	6	7	8	9	10	11	12
	Base Period YTD				Current YTD		YTD Change		Change Due to		
% of Pts.	Units/ Pts. Receiving	Costs/ Pt. in Dx Grp	Dep. Description	% of Pts.	Units/ Pts. Receiving	Costs/ Pt. in Dx Grp	Costs		Volume/ Mix	Util.	Cost/ Unit
100	5	65	CBC	100	2	29	590)		(130)	780	(60)
100	3	40	Differential	100	3	40	(80)		(80)	0	0
100	2	6	Routine urinalysis	100	2	6	(12)		(12)	0	0
100	1	13	PT	100	1	13	(26)		(26)	0	0
100	1	14	PTT	100	1	14	(28)		(28)	0	0
100	1	6	Platelet count	100	1	6	(12)		(12)	0	0
100	4	16	Stat Test	100	4	16	(32)		(32)	0	0
	17	160	Total		14	124	400		(320)	780	(60)

Calming down a bit, Dr. Rair agreed that overuse of lab tests probably was a large problem. However, he went on to say that he didn't know if it could be stopped in a teaching hospital or if the administration would want to cut back since equipment like CT scans wouldn't pay for themselves. However, he primarily faulted the students: "Students are so into numbers, they can't practice medicine anymore. Residents, too. But if I told my residents to get a crit once a week and that's all, do you think that they're going to?"

Dr. Rair told Dr. Bingley that he applauded her efforts to combat these cost problems and wished her luck.

Dr. Bingley then visited Dr. Herbert Rand, the assistant chief of surgery at UMC. He was concerned with statistical meaningfulness of the data, and said that he preferred the use of medians instead of means so that outliers wouldn't bias the data, and was concerned that the comparison of quarterly data should be to quarters having similar numbers of days. He also thought that a severity index would be more useful in terms of similarity of case costs. When Dr. Bingley pointed out that severity indices weren't clinically meaningful, his response was not very encouraging:

DRGs are worthwhile for year-to-year practice pattern changes but once the patterns are established, then severity is more important. You can't compare one of these with one of these with one of thats. Moreover, many of the DRG groupings in the department and physician profiles are anecdotal since they only contain one or a few cases.

Dr. Bingley also spoke with Dr. Sandra Bahr, a pediatric surgeon. It was apparent that the pediatric DRGs weren't very precise since actual pediatric cases were subsets of the categories. Dr. Bahr also was concerned about the lack of severity indices, especially for a tertiary referral hospital. Finally, she felt that the accuracy of the data was questionable since older physicians were less specific on the discharge summaries, writing comments such as "see old chart" or "multiple congenital anomalies" instead of listing each one.

The two discussed lab tests, and Dr. Bahr voiced a familiar opinion:

DRGs give us something to beat residents over the head with when they order too many electrolytes. Residents at UMC order 3–4 times too many tests, partly because it's a training institution. But even so, twice as many tests are ordered than a good training institution needs.

Pediatrics is different from the rest of the hospital in that we have fewer residents, so there is more consistency in test ordering and lower numbers of "stats." But for less efficient departments and for people who don't practice good medicine, DRGs are threatening. In fact, there are two defects in the health care system: the second is that doctors control everything, and the first is that incentives are lacking for them to change.

Dr. Bingley had several more interviews before completing her second round. She wondered whether the third round, with the severity data, would be more popular with the doctors; she certainly hoped so. She also pondered Dr. Bahr's last comment about incentives. Would severity information alone provide an incentive on the part of the doctors to change their behavior? Or should the administration develop additional incentives? What might those be? Before going on, she decided to have another chat with Mr. Veller about these issues.

Questions

1. What are the physicians' concerns with respect to management uses of case mix information? How might management address those concerns?

2. What do the exhibits suggest about the kinds of responsibility centers the UMC has established? Are they appropriate according to the criteria for the design of responsibility centers? Why or why not?

3. What is your assessment of the reports? To answer this question you will need to focus on the ways the reports relate to each other, and on the ways the chief of surgery (or any other chief) might use one or more of the reports. Specifically, if you were the chief of surgery, how would you decide which reports to review first each reporting period?

4. What changes, if any, would you make to the management control system?

Case 14–3

University Daycare Center*

Susan Brooks, Director of the University Daycare Center, was reviewing the year-to-date Budget Performance Report from the Finance Department of the university. As she tried to analyze the components of the report, she realized that

*This case was prepared by Emily Hayden, RN, MBA, under the direction of Professor David W. Young. Copyright © by David W. Young.

EXHIBIT 1   Variances from Budget Based on Actual Enrollment and Estimated Annualized Expenses

	FTES*			Budget	Actual Expenses	Variance
	Budget	Actual				
Revenues:						
Enrollee tuition				$ 329,194	$ 141,926	$(187,268)
Expenses:						
Salaries:						
Director	1	1		$ 32,000	$ 31,990	$ 10
Instructors	3	3		66,000	66,500	(500)
Teachers.	6	6		120,000	114,108	5,892
Aides	5	1.5		83,200	27,140	56,060
Clerical.	0.5	0.5		9,000	9,000	0
Subtotals	15.5	12		$ 310,200	$ 248,738	$ 61,462
Fringe benefits.				68,244	54,722	13,522
Supplies:						
Training				4,000	2,190	1,810
Conference				1,650	904	746
Food				16,000	8,762	7,238
Disposables				4,200	2,300	1,900
Classroom supplies.				4,800	2,629	2,171
Field trips.				1,100	602	498
Equipment.				1,000	548	452
Laundry.				500	274	226
Contingency				4,000	2,190	1,810
Maintenance				13,000	7,119	5,881
Telephone				500	274	226
Supplies subtotals				$ 50,750	$ 27,792	$ 22,958
Rent				60,000	60,000	0
Total expenses.				$ 489,194	$ 391,252	$ 97,942
Total revenues less expenses				$(160,000)	$(249,326)	$ (89,326)
Plus budgeted deficit				$ 160,000	$ 160,000	
Variance from budgeted deficit					$ (89,326)	

*Full-time equivalents.

something needed to be done about the Center's financial status. The variance analysis for the Daycare Center showed a shortfall of over $89,000 (Exhibit 1).

Background

University Daycare Center (UDC) was affiliated with a large urban university and maintained a facility located two miles from the main campus. It had passed state inspection in April, and had opened in July, just in time for the beginning of the fiscal year. The building in which the UDC was located had formerly been an elementary school, and the Center occupied one corridor, with four large classrooms on each side. Two other corridors in the same building were unoccupied and had not been renovated. At the end of the hallway was the director's office and a small reception area where parents arrived with their children, usually by eight o'clock in the morning.

The rooms had been carpeted and all of their doors had been removed to decrease the possibility of injuries. Additionally, the walls had been remodeled so that glass panels occupied the upper half of each wall on the corridor side. This made it possible for teachers and aides to observe children directly from the hallway. Each room was supplied with furniture, supplies, and toys appropriate to different age-groups of children. The infant room, for example, had cribs and bassinets and was stocked with various sizes of disposable diapers. The facility was cleaned and maintained, respectively, by the housekeeping and maintenance departments of the university.

In December of the previous year, the university's Department of Human Resources had surveyed 300 of the 1,250 university employees, including professors, administrative personnel, laboratory workers, and office assistants, to determine whether they would utilize a day care center. The survey included questions regarding fees, hours of operation, and coverage for emergencies. The response was overwhelmingly in favor of providing such a service. The Human Resources director, therefore, had drafted a proposal for the following year's budget and received approval for a one-year $160,000 subsidy for the operation of a day care center. Funds for the remodeling and furnishing of the Center were to be obtained from the Capital Improvement Fund and the building was to be rented at a cost of $60,000 a year, with a one-year renewable lease.

The Department of Human Resources began promoting the Center two months prior to its opening. Flyers were posted throughout the university and were placed in the mailboxes of virtually every permanent employee. A Human Resources representative attended orientation sessions for new employees and answered questions regarding the Center's services. The promotion approach emphasized the presence of the Center as an employee benefit, despite the fact that employees would pay for most of the operating expenses in the form of tuition fees. No fees were printed on the promotional literature, and all tuition discussions between potential enrollees and the UDC director were to be held confidential.

The proposal stated that the Center intended to provide day care at reasonable rates (based on parental income) for any permanent university employee. A sliding fee scale would guarantee access for employees of all income levels. The Department of Human Resources hoped that the UDC would become a permanent service and envisioned that its implementation and operation would become a model for other university-affiliated day care centers. Additionally, its presence could be an attractive incentive for employees to stay with the university or to choose employment there in the first place.

EXHIBIT 2 Sliding Fee Scale

Annual Family Income Range	Total Annual Tuition		
	Infant	Toddler	Preschool
$0–19,999	$ 5,980	$4,680	$3,900
20,000–24,999	6,644	5,200	4,333
25,000–29,999	7,309	5,720	4,767
30,000–34,999	7,973	6,240	5,200
35,000–39,999	8,638	6,760	5,633
40,000–44,999	9,302	7,280	6,067
45,000–49,999	9,967	7,800	6,500
50,000–59,999	10,631	8,320	6,933
60,000–69,999	11,296	8,840	7,367
70,000—Above	11,960	9,360	7,800

Fees and Enrollees

After considerable market research and consideration of various fee structures, a sliding fee scale had been developed. It incorporated not only income
measures, but also intensity of care. Thus, the tuition charged for infants was
generally higher, since they required closer supervision (Exhibit 2).

The UDC was licensed to have seven spaces for infants (2 to 18 months old),
18 spaces for toddlers (18 months to 2 years old), and 17 for preschoolers (2
to 5 years old). In October, the enrolled population consisted of 4 infants, 10
toddlers, and 9 preschoolers (Exhibit 3). Some of the children did not attend
every day because their parents were part-time employees or had other child
care arrangements for the remaining days of the week. All parents were required to submit documentation of immunizations, as well as a physician
statement attesting to the health of each child.

Staffing

The original budget allowed for staffing consisting of the director, three instructors, six teachers, five aides, and a half-time clerical worker. The Center
was not fully staffed in some of these categories, but, since the staffing budget
had assumed full enrollment, some positions were, in fact, overstaffed (Exhibit
4). In anticipation of high demand for the service, Ms. Brooks had hired all of
the instructors and teachers one month before the Center's opening, both to accommodate an immediate full enrollment, as well as to comply with state requirements concerning child-to-teacher ratios. All instructors and teachers were
certified in child care. Aides were trained and supervised by the instructors.

EXHIBIT 3 Annual Individual Tuition Contributions (revenues) Based on Present Enrollment

	Infants	Toddlers	Preschoolers	Totals
Number of full-time slots	7	18	17	42
Tuition payments	$11,296	$ 4,680	$ 3,900	
	11,960	8,320	3,900	
	3,588*	7,800	4,767	
	10,631	7,800	7,367	
		8,320	3,120	
		5,720	6,500	
		5,720	5,633	
		4,680	2,340*	
		3,744*	2,340*	
		7,800		
Revenue subtotals	$37,475	$ 64,584	$39,867	$ 141,926
Budgeted revenue	$73,694	$156,048	$99,452	$ 329,194
Variance from budgeted revenue				$(187,268)
Average tuition per enrollee	$ 9,369	$ 6,458	$ 4,430	
Budgeted average tuition per enrollee	$10,528	$ 8,669	$ 5,850	

*Part-time enrollees.

Budgeting Problems

The university's $160,000 subsidy was to be used to finance the deficit at full enrollment; that is, at full enrollment, tuition fees were expected to contribute a total of $329,194; and expenses were expected to total $489,194. Since expenses had not fallen proportionately to revenue, the university was facing a subsidy of $249,326 (Exhibit 1).

Ms. Brooks believed that the Center should remain an integral part of the university community; however, she also recognized the need to maintain financial viability. She knew that if she did not make the necessary adjustments in expenses, revenues, or both, that these decisions would simply be made by someone from the Department of Human Resources. This would reflect poorly on her ability to manage the budget and might also make the Center a target for elimination if budget cuts became necessary.

As she reviewed the set of reports generated by the Finance Department, a number of items remained unclear as to what impact they would have on the continuing operation of the Center. For example, adjustments made for the actual enrollment showed a variance of almost $65,000 for staff positions alone (Exhibit 4).

Supply expenses, by contrast, included many start-up items. Some of these were relatively long-lasting objects, such as toys and linens. Others, including disposable diapers and snack foods, were consumables. Many of the invoices for various classroom items had not yet been received. Additionally, charges for various services provided by the university, such as maintenance

EXHIBIT 4   Salary Variances Based on Actual Enrollment

A:

Salary Category	Budgeted FTEs at Full Capacity	Budgeted FTEs Needed for Current Enrollment*	Budgeted Salaries at Full Capacity	Budgeted Salaries Adjusted for Current Enrollment	Variances
Director	1.0	1.0	$ 32,000	$ 32,000	0
Instructors	3.0	1.5	66,000	33,000	$ 33,000
Teachers	6.0	3.0	120,000	60,000	60,000
Aides	5.0	3.0	83,200	49,920	33,280
Clerical	0.5	0.5	9,000	9,000	0
Totals	15.5	9.0	$310,200	$183,920	$126,280

B:

Salary Category	Budgeted FTEs Needed for Current Enrollment*	Actual FTEs	Budgeted Salaries Adjusted for Current Enrollment	Actual Salaries	Variance
Director	1.0	1.0	$ 32,000	$ 31,990	$ 10
Instructors	1.5	3.0	33,000	66,500	(33,500)
Teachers	3.0	6.0	60,000	114,108	(54,108)
Aides	3.0	1.5	49,920	27,140	22,780
Clerical	0.5	0.5	9,000	9,000	0
Totals	9.0	12.0	$183,920	$248,738	$ (64,818)

*Budgeted positions have been adjusted here to account for the current staffing needs of the Center. Amounts are budgeted to nearest half FTE (full-time equivalent) except director.

and laundry, were only generated every two to three months. Since this was the Center's first year of operation, however, the clerk had been instructed to carefully record the nature and the amount of each purchase, so that a better estimate could be submitted for the following year's budget. As a result, Ms. Brooks believed that the expenses shown in Exhibit 1 accurately reflected the results of the Center's activities.

As of November, the UDC had increased its enrollment to over 50 percent of capacity in each category. Still, total revenues from all contributions were far below what had been projected (Exhibit 3). Ms. Brooks knew that part of this was due to the empty slots as well as the partial attendance by some children; however, even if adjustments were made for full enrollment by the end of the year, there would still be a revenue shortfall of approximately $67,000, assuming that average tuition in each category remained unchanged (Exhibit 5). It was clear that revenue could probably be increased if enrollment were limited to those in the highest paying scales. One of the goals of the UDC, however, was to provide access to all employees, and charging the maximum tuition for the remaining slots would effectively limit the service

EXHIBIT 5 Annual Individual Tuition Contributions (revenues) Based on Full Enrollment

	Infants	Toddlers	Preschoolers	Totals
Number of full-time slots	7	18	17	42
Tuition payments	$11,296	$ 4,680	$ 3,900	
	11,960	8,320	3,900	
	3,588*	7,800	4,767	
	10,631	7,800	7,367	
	9,369†	8,320	3,120*	
	9,369†	5,720	6,500	
	9,369†	5,720	5,633	
		4,680	2,340*	
		3,744*	2,340*	
		7,800	4,430†	
		6,458†	4,430†	
		6,458†	4,430†	
		6,458†	4,430†	
		6,458†	4,430†	
		6,458†	4,430†	
		6,458†	4,430†	
		6,458†	4,430†	
		6,458†	4,430†	
Revenue subtotals	$65,582	$116,248	$79,737	$261,567
Budgeted revenue	$73,694	$156,048	$99,452	$329,194
Variance from budgeted revenue				$ (67,627)

*Part-time enrollees.
†Assume future enrollees pay the current average tuition and attend full-time.

to high-income applicants. Also, since the Center was not at full capacity upon opening, Ms. Brooks had seen no reason to exclude part-time attendance by some children. She had assumed that the revenue provided by part-time enrollees would offset at least some of the losses from the empty slots.

Decisions

Complicating all of these considerations was the fact that even though future revenues and expenses were uncertain, both could be substantially manipulated. For example, decisions concerning the hiring or firing of staff could have a large impact on salary expenditures. Ms. Brooks was reluctant to make these decisions too quickly. If teachers were laid off and then enrollment suddenly increased, she would have to rehire them in order to maintain the required child-to-teacher ratios. By contrast, discretion in the use of supplies was limited, but she wondered if it might be worthwhile to investigate different vendors for expensive items like disposable diapers.

With only four months of operation as a basis for making predictions, Ms. Brooks was uncertain as to how soon, if ever, the Center would be at full capacity. She also did not know what type of enrollee mix would best fit the mission of the Center and, at the same time, generate enough revenue to ensure its survival. The sliding fee scale might be flawed, but the university's budget department was reluctant to do any more research on this item. They maintained that day care centers throughout the city had comparable fee schedules. Ms. Brooks doubted that she could duplicate the efforts of the research by herself and, therefore, decided to accept the fee scale, and perhaps make minor adjustments for individual applicants.

Whether to encourage the presence of more part-time enrollees presented another dilemma. The child-to-teacher ratio on any given day could be compromised by the presence of too many part-time children attending on the same days. The Center might be overstaffed on other days due to such uneven attendance. This not only created problems in the scheduling and hiring of staff, but also meant that the partial slots occupied by part-time enrollees could no longer be used by potential full-time enrollees. Ms. Brooks had wanted to make the service available to all employees, but wondered if she should limit attendance to full-time children. On the other hand, if additional full-time applicants never materialized, the part-time attendees were needed, even if they did create staffing problems.

Although much of the promotional effort was ongoing, Ms. Brooks was unclear as to whether there were better ways of advertising the service to employees. The option of promoting to potential applicants outside the university community had occurred to her, although she doubted if the university's trustees would approve of funding for this. In addition to questions of how to increase enrollment, she wondered if the Center should instead opt to simply maintain the present enrollment or even to decrease it (by attrition). This would make the task of laying off teachers easier, since fewer children would provide a suitable justification for terminating the teachers' employment. If the Center could run at less than full capacity, but not run a deficit, then she might be in a better position to bargain for a larger subsidy in next year's budget proposal.

She also questioned the $160,000 subsidy amount. Was this just a token gesture to demonstrate to the community how progressive the university was, but one without real support from those who controlled the budget? The amount had seemed generous at first, but clearly there were problems in complying with the revenue and expenditure targets on which the subsidy was based.

Although Ms. Brooks did not expect the university to subsidize any shortfalls in enrollment completely, she realized that she would need to make a convincing argument for the continued operation of the Center. Unless she could do this by the time budget negotiations began in February, the closure of the UDC would no doubt become a subject for discussion at the annual trustees' meeting in March.

Questions

1. What is the source of the financial problems at the UDC? Please be as specific as you can, explaining all the reasons why actual results differ from budgeted ones.

2. What additional reports, if any, does Ms. Brooks need to see on a regular basis?

3. What might Ms. Brooks do to correct the financial problems? Please be as specific as you can in outlining a course of action that you believe she should follow.

4. What action would you recommend the trustees take at their March meeting?

15

Operations Analysis and Program Evaluation

In Chapters 11–14 we described the regular, recurring process of monitoring the current activities of an organization. In this chapter we describe two other processes for analyzing and evaluating the performance of an organization and the effectiveness of its programs. One of these examines the operations of the organization as a whole, with the objective of assessing whether its efficiency and effectiveness can be improved. We call this *operations analysis*. The other focuses on individual programs, with the objective of recommending whether a program should be expanded, contracted, redirected, or discontinued. We call this *program evaluation*.

Basic Distinctions

The operations analysis and program evaluation processes described in this chapter differ from the monitoring processes described in Chapters 13 and 14 in several respects. Specifically, an operations analysis or program evaluation usually: (1) is made at irregular intervals, usually every five years or so, rather than on a monthly or quarterly basis; (2) is much more thorough and time-consuming than routine performance monitoring; (3) is conducted by an outside individual or team, or by a headquarters staff unit, rather than by an operating manager; and (4) uses different techniques than routine performance monitoring.

Differences between Operations Analysis and Program Evaluation

The essential difference between operations analysis and program evaluation is that the former is an evaluation of *process* and the latter an evaluation of *results*.[1] Because of this, operations analysis accepts the objectives of a responsibility center as given. Although there may be problems in finding out what these objectives are, once they have been identified, they are not challenged. Operations analysis assumes that a unit will continue its activities in achieving the overall goals of the organization (although occasionally the analysis may lead to the conclusion that an activity should be discontinued). The purpose of the analysis is to find more effective and efficient ways of carrying out these activities, whatever they are.

Program evaluation, by contrast, asks whether the objectives of a program are appropriate and whether the organization is attaining these objectives in the most effective and efficient way.

Example

An operations analysis of a job training program would accept the fact that the responsibility center is supposed to train a certain target group for certain types of jobs and would examine ways of improving the efficiency and effectiveness of the training process. A program evaluation would attempt to determine whether the training in fact results in personnel who have acquired the desired skills, whether the benefits exceed the costs, and perhaps also whether society needs persons with these skills.

Essentially, then, the objective of operations analysis is reasonably clear-cut; it is to improve performance. The nature of a program evaluation is much more vague. The vagueness starts with the objectives of the program and continues through each step in the process. For this reason program evaluators usually prepare a careful plan and obtain the assent of the parties to this plan before undertaking the evaluation. Operations analysts can proceed with much less debate about what they are trying to do.

Skills Required

The skills desirable in a program evaluation team differ considerably from those desirable for an operations analysis team. Operations analysis requires knowledge of management processes, principles of human behavior, efficient work methods, and other techniques. These principles and techniques are similar for most types of organizations. By contrast, a program evaluator must be knowledgeable about the specific type of program being evaluated. An expert in education, for example, is not likely to make a sound assessment of a health care program. Moreover, at least one member of the evaluation team should

---

[1] Sometimes, the terminology can be confusing. For example, the United States General Accounting Office uses the term *economy and efficiency audit* for what is labeled here *operations analysis* and the term *program results audit* for what is labeled *program evaluation.*

be an expert in statistical and experimental methods if the evaluation method involves them, whereas operations analysis usually requires only rudimentary statistics.

Operations Analysis

Although the techniques used in an operations analysis (which some people call a *management audit*) can be applied to any type of ongoing activity, they are especially applicable to service, support, and administration activities, to ongoing mission activities, such as police and fire protection, and to the regular activities of a hospital or educational institution. The need for continuing these activities in some form usually is not debatable. With respect to mission activities—where there may be questions about the appropriateness of the objectives or the continuation of the activity itself—an operations analysis is sometimes combined with a program evaluation.

Need for Operations Analysis

In many organization units, fat tends to accumulate with the passage of time. Senior management attempts to slow this accumulation by carefully examining budgets and monitoring current performance. However, adequate time for thorough analysis by these means often is not available. New technology and new production or service methods continually develop and tend to make current ways of doing things obsolete, but management, because of time limitations, often cannot consider the effect of these developments when reviewing the budget. Consequently, management usually relies on the current performance of the unit as a guide to what future performance should be.

To avoid the accumulation of fat, senior management in many organizations undertakes an occasional, basic review of activities. Such a review is often called a *zero-base review,* a term indicating that the analysis does not assume that any of the current ways of doing things are accepted as given; all are open to scrutiny. When people use the term *zero-base budgeting,* they usually mean zero-base review because there simply is not enough time in the annual budgeting process to conduct the thorough analysis that is implied by the term *zero base.*

Impetus for Operations Analysis

In some large organizations, operations analysis is conducted on a more-or-less regular cycle that covers all responsibility centers once every five to eight years. The results of this analysis are used to establish a new benchmark for the responsibility center. In subsequent budget reviews senior management attempts to maintain this benchmark, recognizing that it is likely to become gradually eroded over time until the next evaluation takes place.

In some organizations, an operations analysis is initiated because of a financial crisis. The citizens' revolt against increased property taxation in the late 1970s and 1980s led to operations analyses in many municipalities. A decrease in the inflow of financial resources, or, indeed, any situation in which expenses seem to be chronically in excess of revenues, is usually a signal that an operations analysis is warranted. Allegations, or even rumors, of fraud or gross inefficiency emanating from either inside or outside the organization also may touch off a crisis that calls for analysis. For example, spying scandals in the late 1980s led to the initiation of operations analyses in many U.S. embassies.

Example

Between 1990 and 1995, federal support for the National Railroad Passenger Corporation (Amtrak) increased from $640 million to almost $1 billion. Nevertheless, Amtrak continued to run deficits. In addition, Amtrak's requirements for capital investment continued to grow. In 1995, although it had an aggressive plan to reduce its deficit, its unmet needs for new equipment and improvements to facilities and track totaled several billion dollars ($4 billion for the Northeast corridor alone). It also was faced with increased fare competition from airlines, a need to negotiate new labor agreements, and the possibility of substantial additional costs for a new agreement with freight railroads to use their track. As a result, the U.S. General Accounting Office undertook an assessment of Amtrak's financial and operating conditions and presented several alternative courses of action for consideration by the Congress.[2]

Who Conducts the Operations Analysis?

It is neither reasonable nor prudent to expect an operating manager to conduct an unbiased review of the activities of his or her own responsibility center or program. Presumably the manager is satisfied with the way these activities currently are carried out and will defend these practices in discussions with superiors. Occasionally, a cost-reduction program with adequate incentives can result in objective self-appraisals, but this is an exception to the rule. Most analyses must be conducted by a person or group not associated with the responsibility center being studied.

In organizations that have systematic review process, operations analysis may be conducted by a staff unit whose full-time responsibility is to conduct such reviews. This unit may be designated as internal audit, industrial engineering, or, more recently, inspector general.

Outside consultants often are used for operations analysis. Although their hourly fees tend to be higher than the cost of internal personnel, they may be able to complete the analysis in fewer hours because of greater expertise and knowledge accumulated about how other organizations conduct the activities being reviewed.

[2]Keith O. Fultz, Assistant Comptroller General, *Intercity Passenger Rail: Financial and Operating Conditions Threaten Amtrak's Long-Term Viability,* United States General Accounting Office, February 1995.

Occasionally, a government agency may create a "blue ribbon commission" of qualified citizens to conduct an operations analysis. The largest such undertaking was the President's Private Sector Cost Survey, under the leadership of J. Peter Grace, in 1982–83. This survey covered most activities of the federal government. Its volunteer staff, recruited mostly from private business, numbered approximately 1,500.

Unless properly led, such evaluations by business executives can be unproductive, or even counterproductive. The group must understand the differences between the management of a government entity and the management of a for-profit business. As one city manager said: "All the Commission did was to describe the problems that we already knew about; they didn't help us find and implement solutions to them."

Colleges, universities, and hospitals have a type of operations analysis that is conducted by the agencies that accredit them. Typically, such reviews focus on the organization's effectiveness, especially on the quality of the services it provides.

The Operations Analysis Process

Depending on the size and complexity of the activity, an operations analysis may take anywhere from a few days to a year, or even longer. The U.S. General Accounting Office makes operations analyses of federal agencies on a regular basis, which it calls *economy and efficiency audits,* or, sometimes, *general management reviews.* As an indication of their magnitude, the following information is taken from a GAO internal planning document:

> The elapsed time, start to finish, should be estimated to be 12 months: 2 months for planning, scoping and assembling the team; 6 months for collecting information; 3 months for developing the report; and 1 month for briefing the agency.
>
> One review should involve approximately 2,200 staff days. The team should consist of not more than 10 persons, headed by an associate director.

There are seven principal steps in the operations analysis process. They are arranged in the order in which they usually are carried out:

1. Obtain a mandate.

2. Identify the organization's objectives.

3. Identify fruitful areas of investigation.

4. Decide how output is to be expressed.

5. Conduct the analysis.

6. Make recommendations and sell them.

7. Follow up on implementation.

Step 1. Obtain a Mandate

Before work begins, the operations analysis team should obtain a clear mandate from senior management, the governing board, or whatever body has the power to ensure that recommendations are implemented. There must be a mutual understanding of the boundaries of the activities the analysis will encompass, freedom for the team to investigate within these boundaries, and assurance that the sponsoring body will provide support to the team conducting the analysis and be prepared to see that the recommendations are implemented. In some cases an analysis is instituted as a delaying action in response to public criticism, with the expectation that the furor—and the pressure for change—will eventually fade. Obviously, the analysis team is wasting time if it undertakes work sponsored for this purpose. Unfortunately, identifying such a motive may be difficult.

An operations analysis can be stressful to the operating managers of the unit being examined. As a minimum, the analysts' interviews take time that the manager could be using in day-to-day activities. More common is the manager's fear that the recommendations may lead to criticism or, in the extreme, dismissal. Consequently, the mandate from senior management or the outside body that sponsors the audit must be strong enough to assure full cooperation by operating managers. In fact, W. Edwards Deming, considered by many to be the founder of the total quality management (TQM) movement, emphasizes that *true cooperation*—and therefore a more successful analysis—can be gained only by establishing a trusting environment, that is, one where the unit managers are not threatened or (barring gross misconduct) punished. Not only does this environment foster cooperation, but it makes the whole analysis go faster.[3]

In organizations that must undergo an operations analysis to maintain accreditation, the accrediting body provides the mandate. Some government agencies are required by the legislature or a high-level body to have a periodic operations analysis; such requirements are not common, however. Many organizations do not have regularly scheduled operations analyses, and conduct them only when a crisis makes it necessary. Clearly, some crises could be averted if operations analyses were conducted at regular intervals. In many respects, this is the focus of the TQM efforts under way in some nonprofit organizations.

Example

In a physician's office, a variety of questions can be asked that eventually will lead to an improvement in quality. When quality fails in your own work, why does it fail? Do you ever waste time waiting, when you should not have to? Do you ever redo your work because something failed the first time? Do the procedures you use waste steps, duplicate efforts, or frustrate you through their unpredictability? Is information you need ever lost? Does communication ever fail? If the answer to any of these is yes,

---

[3]W. Edwards Deming, *Out of Crisis* (Cambridge, Mass.: MIT Press, 1986).

then ask why. How can it be changed? What can be improved and how? Must you be a mere observer of problems, or can you lead toward their solution?[4]

Step 2. Identify Objectives

To improve operations, the analysis team begins by identifying the objectives of the organization. In many organizations, such as most health care or religious organizations, the objectives are fairly obvious. In other cases, such as certain charitable organizations, the objectives may be quite ambiguous. Furthermore, the work that the organization is actually doing may be different from what its sponsor, authorizing body, or governing board intended. For example, a charitable organization may undertake a campaign to achieve a political or social goal although this was not intended by its sponsors. Nevertheless, once the legitimate objectives are understood by the analysts, they are accepted. The purpose of the study is not to challenge the appropriateness of these objectives, but rather to analyze how well they are being achieved.

Step 3. Identify Fruitful Areas

Operations analysis teams and consulting firms often have a checklist of possible topics that might be investigated, a list that includes every conceivable aspect of activities, organizational relationships, systems, personnel and other policies, communication devices, and the like. It is not worthwhile to analyze every topic on this list. Rather, the team uses it as a basis for identifying those areas where the opportunity for a significant payoff seems to exist.

Example

A public accounting firm has developed a long checklist as a starting point in making an operations analysis of a hospital. It includes such questions as: Is the average age of physicians over 48 years? Is there difficulty in recruiting qualified specialist physicians? Is the amount of accounts receivable more than 75 days of revenues? Is there a backlog of incomplete medical record charts in excess of 14 days of discharges? Is the number of employees per occupied bed greater than 3.3? Is debt service more than 8 percent of revenue?

Experienced reviewers often can spot significant opportunities for improvement simply by visual inspection and by asking appropriate questions.

Example

The following is the reminiscence of a member of the team that examined the operations of the Louisville, Kentucky, police court:
"You remember one clerk, in particular, who was industriously banging away at a typewriter. You asked her what she was doing. She looked up briefly from her keyboard to explain that she was typing case dispositions. 'What happens to them when they're typed?' you asked. 'Why,' she

---

[4]Donald M. Berwick, "Continuous Improvement as an Ideal in Health Care," *New England Journal of Medicine* 320, no. 1 (January 5, 1989).

answered, 'they go into the judge's order book.' 'What's the book used for?' you asked. She didn't know. So you went to her superior. 'Why is this done?' you asked. You learned why. It's done because a city ordinance says it must be done. But nobody ever uses the book. The same information is available in other records that are easier to use."

Step 4. Decide on Output Measures

Many operations analyses involve comparisons of inputs and outputs, either explicitly or implicitly. As emphasized in earlier chapters, inputs are measured by costs. Although many organizations do not have good cost accounting systems, the nature of the information that is needed is fairly clear-cut. As we discussed in Chapter 12, the measurement of outputs is much more difficult. The team needs to decide on the most feasible way to measure what the organization is accomplishing. In many cases, no good quantitative measure exists, and judgment as to the quantity and quality of outputs is based strictly on the opinions of the analysis team.

Example

Some years ago, the Standards Committee of the American Assembly of Collegiate Schools of Business voted to "look at the question of validation of current accreditation standards with special reference to performance and outcomes." Twenty years later, after spending half a million dollars and "countless hours of volunteer and staff time," no measurements had been agreed on.[5]

The Government Performance and Results Act (often referred to as the Results Act, or GPRA) is aimed at improving the efficiency and effectiveness of the federal government. The General Accounting Office studied the implementation plans of six agencies in the science and technology area, and, according to Susan Kladiva, Associate Director, Energy, Resources, and Science Issues of the GAO, only one plan contained all six of the Act's critical elements. Moreover, although the goals and objectives were frequently results-oriented, it was unclear in all of the plans how some of the goals would be measured.[6]

Step 5. Conduct the Analysis

Once it has a tentative list of areas to be investigated, the team discusses it with operating managers and senior management. After their concurrence, the team makes a detailed analysis of these areas. This may include an analysis of work flows, methods, and organizational relationships, using formal techniques developed for each area. Occasionally, it may involve sophisticated

---

[5]Quoted from a report of the Academy of Management.
[6]Susan Kladiva, "GAO Testimony on Federal Science Agencies," *Federal Document Clearing House: Congressional Testimony,* July 30, 1997.

operations research techniques. Often the principal tools are an inquiring mind and common sense.

<table>
<tr><td>

Example
</td><td>

Ishikawa's seven tools for quality control are relatively simple techniques that can be used to analyze numerical and categorical data. Ishikawa contends that the vast majority of quality problems can be solved with their use alone. The seven tools include such relatively common-sense techniques as cause-and-effect diagrams, checksheets, histograms, graphs and control charts, and scatter diagrams.[7]
</td></tr>
</table>

To the extent feasible, an operations analysis draws on information about similar processes in other organizations. Three types of information are described briefly below: (1) best practice, (2) industry data, and (3) intraorganization data.

Best Practice The team may learn from journal articles or conversations about an organization that is judged to be outstanding in performing the process. Visiting such an organization can provide useful ideas. Because such a visit is distracting to the organization, arranging it may be difficult. Often, the door is opened only on the basis of friendship or on a promise to reciprocate with ideas or comments. The articles, by themselves, usually are inadequate.

<table>
<tr><td>

Example
</td><td>

In Minnesota, a best practices review of snow and ice control on local roads concluded that effective winter maintenance shops typically embraced 12 actions, including everything from adopting written snow policies to storing road sand in appropriate facilities. The review described more than 80 examples in Minnesota local government, explaining what the practice was, describing the circumstances under which it worked best, and listing the names and telephone numbers of resource people whom other local governments could contact to learn more about the practice.
</td></tr>
</table>

Industry Data Several industries collect and publish data on costs and performance, including comparisons of unit costs for similar activities. The process of making such comparisons is now called *benchmarking*.[8] Benchmarking seeks to measure an organization's performance by comparing it against other organizations in the same industry. It has been used for strategic and performance analysis, as well as for operations analysis. In the strategic area, benchmarking may lead to budget shifts by showing how other organizations allocate their

---

[7]Masao Akiba, Shane J. Schvaneveldt, and Takao Enkawa, "Service Quality: Methodology and Japanese Perspectives," in G. Salvendy, *Handbook of Industrial Engineering,* 2nd ed. (New York: John Wiley & Sons, 1992). The authors cite K. Ishikawa, *Guide to Quality Control,* 2nd rev. ed. (Tokyo: Asian Productivity Organization, 1976).

[8]When first used in the literature, *benchmarking* referred to studies of best practice. Currently the word is used for all types of comparison, even though these are not literally benchmarks.

resources. In the performance area, it permits comparisons among like entities. In the operations area, it frequently is concerned with service delivery activities and processes.[9] As a result of these sorts of activities, a relatively large literature on benchmarking has evolved during the past few years that can be of considerable use to many nonprofits.[10]

Benchmarking can be useful even though there are problems in achieving comparability and finding a "correct" relationship between cost and output. Such comparisons may identify costs that appear out of line, and thus lead to a more thorough examination of certain activities. They often lead to the following interesting question: If other organizations get the job done for X, why can't this one?

Good cost data for such comparisons exist on a national basis for only a few types of nonprofit organizations, principally hospitals and certain municipalities. Nevertheless, it may be possible to find data for activities within a state, or it may be feasible to compare units performing similar functions within a single organization, as in the case of local housing offices. The Charlottesville Fire Department case (Case 12–1) describes an example of the use of this kind of information.[11]

| Example | In his 1988–89 President's Report, Derek Bok, then president of Harvard University, noted the difficulty with cost comparisons in universities: "It is [hard] to awaken a . . . zeal for finding ways to reduce administrative costs. After trying a number of conventional methods unsuccessfully, I eventually decided on a flat rule that the rate of increase in Central Administration expenses must be kept below that of the several faculties so that administrative costs would make up a gradually decreasing share of the University budget."[12] |

The comparisons in most cases are simple, such as the average cost per student in one school compared with the average cost per student in similar schools. In some circumstances, more sophisticated approaches are illuminating. For example, algorithms incorporating a number of interrelated variables have been developed for hospital costs.

Intraorganization Data   An organization that has several geographically dispersed units, such as regional organizations at the federal level, and community

---

[9]For a good discussion of benchmarking and its role in nonprofit organizations, see Anthony H. Rainey, "Benchmarking to Become Best in Class: Guiding Principles in Gresham, Oregon," *Government Finance Review,* February 1997.

[10]See, for example, U.S. General Accounting Office, *Best Practices Methodology: A New Approach for Improving Government Operations,* Washington, DC, 1995. See also U.S. Department of Labor, Best Practices Clearinghouse, Office of the American Workplace, 1995.

[11]For additional discussion, see Governmental Accounting Standards Board, *Concepts Statement No. 2: Service Efforts and Accomplishments* (1994). Federal Accounting Standards Advisory Board, *Exposure Draft: Supplementary Stewardship Reporting* (1995).

[12]Derek Bok, *The President's Report 1988–89* (Cambridge, MA: Harvard University).

or county organizations at the state level, can make similar comparisons of the costs and outputs of these units. Because all its units presumably used the same accounting rules, the problems of comparability are probably less than in industrywide data. On the other hand, the performance of these units may be constrained by overall policy, which can inhibit innovations.

Judging the Appropriate Level of Activity   At some stage, possibly in the preliminary investigation, the analysis team should give some thought to the appropriate amount of service that the unit being evaluated should be furnishing. Although the overall objectives are accepted as given, the level of activity in attaining these objectives is a proper subject for analysis. In some situations, the services provided may be inadequate. More commonly, the question is: Is the unit doing more than really needs to be done for the overall good of the organization? The addition of functions of questionable value is often found in administrative units.

Example

Over a period of five years, the budget of a certain personnel department tripled, although the number of employees in the whole organization increased only slightly. The personnel department had instituted two in-house newsletters (one for professionals, the other for the entire staff); it had set up an elaborate computerized system of personnel records; it had started a clipping service which found and circulated published information about people in the organization; it conducted management training programs, clerical training programs, and interpersonal relations training programs; it had instituted psychological testing and counseling; its members went to and delivered papers at many professional meetings. There was general agreement that people in the personnel department worked diligently. The question was whether all this work was necessary.

Privatization   As we discussed in Chapter 6, one possible approach to the improvement of efficiency in a nonprofit organization is to have certain activities performed by an outside organization, generally a for-profit one. The expectation is that the spur of competition that presumably exists in such organizations will result in lower costs. Possibilities for doing this are often explored in an operations analysis. Opportunities range from such specialized activities as building cleaning and maintenance to those that are usually thought of as belonging exclusively to the public sector, such as fire protection and other municipal services.

Managers of organization units whose functions might be taken over by an outside company naturally resist such threats to their continued existence. They frequently point out, quite correctly, that it should not be assumed that a for-profit company will perform a particular function more efficiently than their unit. The proper approach is, of course, to make a careful analysis of the cost of the alternative ways of performing the function. *Circular No. A-76* of the U.S. Office of Management and Budget, *Policies for Acquiring Commercial or*

Industrial Type Products and Services Needed by the Government, provides excellent guidelines for making such comparisons. Even if such analyses lead to the conclusion that the function should continue to be performed by the organization itself, the fact that such comparisons are being made tends to keep managers on their toes.

Step 6. Make and Sell Recommendations

In some cases, recommendations for improvements can be made, accepted, and implemented while the operations analysis is in process. To the extent that this can be done on a cooperative basis with the operating manager, the changes are likely to have longer lasting effects than those that are imposed by a higher authority. Thus, the team should forgo public recognition of its own role in obtaining such changes and give credit to the operating manager.

The team cannot always count on a favorable reaction to its suggestions, however. Challenges to the established way of doing things are often not well received. Recommendations are subject to all the ploys used in the annual budget review, described in the Appendix to Chapter 10, but the game is usually played with much more gusto because more is at stake. Managers under scrutiny can be expected to do their best to justify their current level of spending. Moreover, unless an atmosphere of trust is developed, they may attempt to undermine the entire effort. They consider the annual budget review as a necessary evil, but an operations analysis as something to be put off indefinitely in favor of "more pressing business." If all else fails, they may attempt to create enough doubts about the competence of the analysis team that the findings are inconclusive and the status quo prevails.[13]

A team that writes a report and then leaves is therefore not likely to accomplish much, if anything, of enduring value. In most cases, the team must devote a considerable amount of time to planning how its recommendations will be sold to those in a position to act, and to laying out a program of implementation and follow-up. If it turns out that the commitment to action obtained in the first stage of the process has, for some reason, disappeared, the team may decide to attempt a new approach to action, perhaps through publicity. This step is sometimes necessary with the blue-ribbon commission type of effort mentioned earlier.

Caution against Overselling Having worked hard to develop good recommendations, there is a tendency for the analysts to attribute more validity to the results than is warranted. For example, the Grace Commission reported that the federal government would save $424 billion over three years if its recommendations were adopted, but an analysis of its report by the U.S. Gen-

---

[13]The General Accounting Office, although conducting operations analyses with statutory authority and with the full backing of the Congress, has difficulty in getting agencies to implement its recommendations, even those recommendations that the agency explicitly agreed were sound. See the GAO Report, *Disappointing Progress in Improving Systems for Resolving Billions in Audit Findings,* January 23, 1981.

eral Accounting Office concluded that the possible savings would be a small fraction of this amount. Such exaggeration casts doubt on the soundness of the whole effort. Indeed, a sound report should frankly reveal the limitations of the study.

Step 7. Follow up on Implementation

The analysts' report presumably contains a list of recommended actions. Acceptance of the report by senior management by no means assures that these actions will be taken. The report itself should state who will be responsible for acting on each recommendation, specify how progress toward implementation will be measured, and, if feasible, establish a timetable. Senior management should be counseled to establish a mechanism for overseeing progress. This mechanism is a form of project control (discussed in Chapter 11).

Program Evaluation

Programs tend to go on forever unless they are subject to periodic, hardheaded reexamination.[14] There is a need to look at operations in program terms to ascertain whether the benefits of each program continue to exceed their cost and whether there are ways to improve effectiveness. Although opportunities for improvement exist in every organization, there is a general feeling that these opportunities are especially significant in nonprofit organizations, primarily because the semiautomatic measure of efficiency provided by the bottom line on a business income statement does not exist in nonprofit organizations.

Evaluations of some type have been going on ever since there have been programs. It has been estimated that a moderately large metropolitan hospital is periodically evaluated by 100 or more agencies, ranging from fire inspection to the Joint Commission on Accreditation of Healthcare Organizations, without whose certificate the hospital cannot continue to operate. We are here concerned not with evaluation of specific aspects of a program, but rather with the broad evaluation of a program as a whole, particularly those programs whose continued existence is optional.

Impetus for Program Evaluation

The legislative or other governing body that initially authorized and funded a program ordinarily wants to find out how well it is proceeding, as a basis for continuing, changing, or ending it. The public and the media become interested in certain programs, particularly those that they believe to be ineffective. Users or potential users of the program, such as prospective students of a university or physicians considering the referral of patients to a hospital, want

---

[14]For a discussion of this issue, see Larry B. Hill, "Is American Bureaucracy an Immobilized Gulliver or a Regenerative Phoenix?" *Administration and Society,* November 1995. See also Herbert Kaufman, *Are Government Organizations Immortal?* (Washington, DC: The Brookings Institution, 1976), p. 35.

information about the program's quality. Donors or other fund providers to arts organizations, charities, museums, and the like, want to know how well the funds were spent.

The federal government carries out some 6,000 identifiable programs. Legislation requiring regular review of these programs was first enacted in the early 1970s when the federal government delegated to the states the task of providing many social services, and required, as a condition of funding these programs, that a formal means of evaluating them be established. At about the same time there was widespread interest in sunset legislation—laws that provided for the automatic discontinuance of a program unless it was evaluated every six to eight years and found to be effective. The majority of states now have such sunset laws. Usually, the evaluation is conducted under the direction of a committee of the legislature.

As a result of these developments, program evaluation has become a growth industry.[15] Hundreds of evaluations are conducted annually at both the state and federal levels. Professional journals, such as *Evaluation Quarterly, Evaluation and Program Planning,* and *Journal of Evaluation Research,* are now well established, along with a professional organization, the American Evaluation Association. Indeed, according to Eleanor Chelimsky, then-assistant comptroller general for Program Evaluation and Methodology of the U.S. General Accounting Office:

> Today, program evaluations are a familiar adjunct of congressional policymaking; they now figure notably in program reauthorizations, legislative decisions and markups, oversight, and an informed public debate. One PEMD [Program Evaluation and Methodology Division] evaluation caused working mothers leaving AFDC to receive Medicaid health insurance for their children over longer periods; another set of studies held up production of the inadequately tested Bigeye bomb; another evaluation led to doubled funding for the high-quality Runaway and Homeless Youth program, whose appropriations the relevant executive agency had proposed halving; another (on employee stock ownership plans) was responsible for a reduction of nearly $2 billion in tax expenditures; still another—showing that an increase in the drinking age from 18 to 21 unambiguously reduces traffic fatalities—spurred legislation to this effect in 16 states, resulting in the estimated saving of 1,000 young lives.[16]

Problems in Program Evaluation

A program evaluation seeks to answer broad, fundamental questions: Is the program being carried out according to the intent of those who authorized it? If not, why not? What would have happened if there had been no program? Answering these questions is an extraordinarily difficult task. Among the more important problems are these:

[15]U.S. General Accounting Office, *Federal Evaluation.* GAO/PEMD-87-9, January 1987, p. 22.
[16]Eleanor Chelimsky, "Expanding GAO's Capabilities in Program Evaluation," *The GAO Journal,* Winter/Spring 1990, p. 48.

- Objectives are often difficult to define.

- Output is often difficult to measure.

- The relationship between cause and effect is often obscure.

- The effort required to make a valid judgment may cost more than it is worth.

- Appropriate action may not be forthcoming.

These problems are discussed below.

Problems in Defining Objectives

In general, those who initially approved a program had in mind one or more objectives that they hoped the program would accomplish. In a program enacted by legislation, these objectives are supposed to be stated in the authorizing act. The fact is, however, that various supporters of a program may differ in their ideas about the program's objectives. Additionally, the stated objectives may be worded ambiguously to accommodate various points of view, and the objectives, either stated or unstated, may be numerous and possibly contradictory.

Example

Some people viewed the purpose of the Comprehensive Employment and Training Act (CETA) as primarily to remove people from the unemployment rolls, others as a way of training unskilled persons so that they would qualify for better jobs, others as a device for channeling federal funds to reduce the tax burden of hard-pressed municipalities, others as a way of providing welfare payments, and still others as a device for reducing crime by taking youths off the street. Most advocates had more than one of these objectives in mind, but they differed as to the relative importance of each.

For some programs the objectives may be even more murky. Scholars have made many attempts to define the objectives of a liberal arts college in a way that permits evaluation, but with no success. A charitable organization may start out with a well-defined objective, such as providing a shelter for homeless people, but the objective may change over the years into providing other types of support. Sometimes this happens without an explicit decision by the governing body.

The evaluators must make every attempt to discern the real objectives and the relative importance of each. If they begin with the wrong objectives, the whole evaluation may be discredited on the grounds that it is based on a false premise.

Problems of Results Measures

In Chapter 12 we discussed problems in measuring a program's output and the limitations of various output measures. For many programs there are no valid techniques for measuring what actually happened as a consequence of undertaking the program. In educational programs, for example, there are no reliable ways of measuring how much additional education a given program produces, except in the case of certain basic skills such as reading and arithmetic. Therefore, a comparison of some new educational effort, such as computer-assisted instruction, team teaching, or programmed learning, is unlikely to reveal any significant difference between those who learned in the new way and those who learned by conventional methods. Indeed, it is said, with considerable truth, that the best way to kill an educational experiment is to evaluate it. One can be almost certain in advance that the measurable results will not show a significant improvement.

Example

The United States General Accounting Office reported that despite increased attention to removing the barriers that prevented the full involvement of persons with disabilities in work and other activities, the Department of Education had not evaluated the effectiveness of its $1.8-billion-per-year program of vocational rehabilitation. The GAO's evaluation showed only modest gains in earned income, in contrast to the dramatic short-term employment effects often cited by the program.[17]

Problems of Cause-and-Effect Relationships

If the results of a program are favorable, there is a tendency to conclude that the program efforts caused this result, but this conclusion may be erroneous. In education, reference is often made to the *Coleman effect,* a term derived from a report by James S. Coleman and his colleagues,[18] which gave an impressive body of evidence to support the conclusion that no important quantifiable correlation exists between the cost of education and its quality, and specifically between pupil learning and class size, teachers' salary, teachers' experience, age of plant, or type of plant. The effects of these variables were swamped by the influence of the pupil's family environment. Although not everyone agrees with Coleman's conclusions, most people agree that it is extremely difficult to devise experiments that demonstrate quantitatively that one teaching tool or technique is more effective than another.

Even if the evaluation team recognizes that extraneous variables may have an effect, their importance in explaining program results may not be measurable.

Example

At the request of Representatives John R. Kasich and James H. Quillen of the House Committee on the Budget, the U.S. General Accounting Office (GAO) compiled information on the effectiveness of three federal agencies whose programs provided economic development assistance: the Appalachian Regional Commission (ARC), the Department of Commerce's

[17]United States General Accounting Office, *Program Evaluation Issues* (Washington, DC: December 1992).
[18]James S. Coleman et al., *Equality of Educational Opportunity,* OE-38001 (Washington, DC: U.S. Department of HEW, 1966).

Economic Development Administration (EDA), and the Tennessee Valley Authority (TVA). The GAO was unable to find any study that established a strong causal linkage between a positive economic effect and an agency's economic development assistance. According to the GAO, this finding was not surprising because "conducting a persuasive study of impact— one that documents an improvement, links it to an agency's programs, and rules out alternative causes—would be extremely difficult." In the case of the ARC, for example, it was impossible to say with certainty whether Appalachia's economy grew because of the ARC or whether much of the measured growth was caused by the rising price of coal.[19]

The use of any quantitative basis or comparison causes concern to some people. For example, Sol M. Linowitz, a highly respected business leader and university trustee, wrote:

> As to a numerical ratio of students per teacher, I am deeply disquieted—not because I am nurturing a romantic kind of Mark Hopkins hangover, but simply because I think this is the result of regarding a college as first a business operation and only secondarily as an educational institution trying to turn out the right kind of men and women.[20]

Although the faculty-student ratio can be misused, its proper use does not imply that a college is primarily a business operation and only secondarily an educational institution. A college is, in fact, both; neither aspect can be slighted.

A similarly difficult problem is that of measuring the *impact* of a program as contrasted with its output. For example, the Clean Air Act limits the amount of pollutants that industrial plants may release into the air, and the results of the Environmental Protection Agency's programs can be assessed by measuring the pollutants in the atmosphere. However, if the objective of these limitations is to reduce to tolerable limits the amount of acid rain that is damaging forests and water supplies, it is much more difficult to determine whether this objective has been achieved. In particular, the impact of such programs may not be measurable for many years after the presumed corrective action has occurred.

Example

The Head Start Program, which was begun in the 1960s, was based on the assumption that a brief intervention in the formative years could raise children's IQs. This was considered important, since IQ correlates with school achievement, persistence, motivation, social skills, and self-confidence. A 1969 report on Head Start performed by the Westinghouse Learning Corporation revealed that the IQ gains by children in preschool programs dissipated by the time they reached the third grade. Now, almost 25 years later, the Head Start Program still exists, not

---

[19]Judy A. England-Joseph, *Economic Development—Limited Information Exists on the Impact of Assistance Provided by Three Agencies* (Washington, DC: U.S. General Accounting Office, April, 1996).
[20]Sol M. Linowitz, "A Liberal Arts College Isn't a Railroad," *The Chronicle of Higher Education,* February 26, 1973, p. 12.

because it raises IQs, but because it enhances school readiness, improves health services for young children, educates parents about community services, and gets some parents involved in their children's education. In addition, it produces several important side effects, including employment for many low-income people.[21]

Problems with the Scope of the Analysis

As is the case with any activity, the results of an evaluation should be worth more than the cost of obtaining them. Analyses range in complexity, cost, and time required; they vary from a simple observation to an elaborate experiment involving thousands of people and lasting several years. Before an evaluation is undertaken, the agency that authorizes it should give considerable thought to the likelihood of obtaining useful results within the available time and cost constraints.

Example

In a statement before the House Education and Work Force Committee on the subject of Federal Compensatory Education Programs, Professor Maris A. Vinovskis of the University of Michigan concluded that while there have been some useful national assessments of the overall impact of Head Start and Title I, usually these evaluations have not even attempted to ascertain in a rigorous and systemic manner which components of their programs have been successful. He gave four major reasons for this: (1) the limited funds available for educational research and development during the past three decades, (2) the misallocation of research and development funds to small, short-term projects that often have limited scientific validity and little practical usefulness, (3) constraints established by the Department of Education on the ability of its agencies to design and monitor high-quality research and development, and (4) the relatively low priority that has been assigned over the years by educators and policy makers to the design and rigorous testing of compensatory education interventions to find out which are most effective with at-risk populations in different settings.[22]

Problems in Obtaining Action

Some groups that evaluate programs view the evaluation as a challenging research effort and lose interest when the research has been completed. They do not plan, or care about, how the results can be used as a basis for action. In other cases, the evaluation effort is undertaken by a program's manager to prove that the program is beneficial; if the evaluation comes to a contrary conclusion, it is buried. An unused program evaluation is just as wasteful as a useless program.

[21]Constance Holden, "Head Start Enters Adulthood," *Science* 247, no. 22 (March 23, 1990), pp. 1400–1402.
[22]Maris A. Vinovskis, "Prepared Statement before the House Education and Work Force Committee," *Federal News Service,* July 31, 1997.

Furthermore, the conclusion that a program is worthwhile is a necessary but not sufficient reason for continuing it. In a world of finite resources, worthwhile programs must compete with other programs that may be even more worthwhile. The legislative body or other group that decides how best to use limited resources has a more complicated task than does the team that evaluates a single program; it must decide which of many worthwhile programs should continue to be supported and at what level.

Example

A survey of 91 human service agencies in the Dallas Metropolitan area, found that although 96 percent of the agencies indicated that they planned to use the results of an evaluation to make improvements in a program's operations, only 16 percent indicated that they planned to use the results to shift funding *toward* successful programs. No respondents planned to shift funding *away from* an unsuccessful program. Most planned to use the results to advocate for increased funding.[23]

Types of Program Evaluations

Before a full-scale evaluation is undertaken, the evaluators ordinarily make a preliminary analysis to settle on the evaluation type(s) to be used, and work out a plan for the evaluation effort. In this section, we list the principal types of evaluations and briefly describe the advantages and limitations of each. A more thorough description can be found in the references at the end of the chapter, particularly those of the U.S. General Accounting Office, the largest and most sophisticated evaluation organization in the United States. (Despite its name, the General Accounting Office is not primarily an accounting organization. Most of its more than 4,000 professionals are called evaluators; they include attorneys, actuaries, economists, engineers, computer specialists, management analysts, and personnel specialists, as well as accountants.)

Subjective Evaluations

The majority of program evaluations are subjective; that is, they are characterized by judgments arrived at by personal observations of an individual or a small committee. The validity of such evaluations depends heavily on the expertise of those involved. Judgments also are influenced by the situations that the evaluators happen to observe; that is, they may be unduly impressed by what appear to be either excellent or poor results in particular cases.

Because support for the conclusions from such an evaluation is based on unsubstantiated evidence, decision makers may be unconvinced. For this reason, the evaluators may develop statistical or other data as a means for adding credence to their opinion.

In some situations the evaluation is subjective simply because a more elaborate approach is not warranted. If a team visits a vocational education school

[23]Richard Hoefer, "Accountability in Action? Program Evaluation in Nonprofit Human Service Agencies," *Nonprofit Management and Leadership,* Winter 2000.

and observes that only half the students regularly attend class and that those who do attend are taught by incompetent teachers using ineffective methods, there is little need to collect data on the effectiveness of the school.

Peer Review Evaluation

As noted above, colleges, universities, and hospitals are regularly evaluated by accrediting organizations. The evaluation is conducted by a team of colleagues; that is, peers, who work at similar organizations. The team is guided in part by specified minimum standards (e.g., for a college, the number of books in the library, the proportion of faculty with advanced degrees) and, in part, by observation and discussion. This is a relatively inexpensive approach. A favorable conclusion means that the institution meets certain minimum requirements, but there is no attempt to rank the institution on a scale of excellence. In general, as we discussed above, these reviews are operations analyses rather than program evaluations. Sometimes they take on characteristics of a program evaluation, however. This happens when they question the appropriateness of the organization's goals, or when they suggest that certain programs' objectives do not fit well with the organization's goals.

Case Study Evaluations

In a case study, the evaluation team identifies a few situations that it believes to be typical and examines each in depth. Although statistically valid conclusions cannot be based on a small sample, the results may be informative. This approach is often used as a preliminary step in an evaluation; it gives the evaluators a feel for the situation. Based on what they uncover, the evaluators may decide not to proceed further; or, if they decide to proceed, the case studies help them select the appropriate research design.

Example

Some years ago, the Deputy Secretary of Defense directed the armed services to develop procedures for quantifying the effect of "technological risk" on the cost of weapons systems development projects. Two years later, the General Accounting Office was asked to evaluate this effort. It made a preliminary study of six weapons systems, two each from the Army, Navy, and Air Force, and did not find any case of quantified technological risk. It therefore decided to describe what *might* be done, rather than to evaluate what had been done.[24]

Statistical Evaluation

An evaluation may be based at least in part on data about the program that have been collected routinely, or on data that have been collected for another purpose but can be recast to provide information relevant to the evaluation. There are four possible approaches, each of which has merit. The one or ones

[24]U.S.General Accounting Office, *Designing Evaluations: A Workbook*, February 1986, pp. 73–128.

chosen will depend to a great extent upon the kinds of data that are available and the needs of the agency sponsoring the evaluation.

1. Compare Current Results with Performance Data Gathered Some Time Prior to the Initiation of the Program   This approach allows the sponsoring agency to determine if the program has had some impact over a baseline situation.

Example

After two sociology professors published the results of a rigorous study, concluding that exposure to the Drug Abuse Resistance Education (D.A.R.E.) Program did not produce any long-term effects on adolescent drug use rates, D.A.R.E. officials continued to claim that an earlier study showed that kids who went through the program accepted drugs less often than kids who had not gone through the program. The earlier study did not ring true to many researchers, however, because it had no pretest. In other words, students were only surveyed after graduating from D.A.R.E. Without measuring drug use before D.A.R.E., it was difficult to know if the students' behavior had changed. According to a biologist who examined the methodology of the earlier study, "If you don't know where your base is you really don't know anything."[25]

2. Compare Current Results with Historical Trends   This approach allows the sponsoring agency to observe how well the program is performing over time.

Example

If a job training program placed 25 percent of its graduates during its first year, 30 percent during its second year, 40 percent during its third year, and 50 percent during its fourth year, there is some indication that the program is improving. Clearly, however, the evaluators would need to look for other factors, such as a change in the program's selection criteria.

3. Compare Current Results of the Program with the Results of Other, Presumably Similar, Programs   Using this approach assumes that a sufficiently similar program can be found, and that the available data will be comparable to those for the program being evaluated.

Example

A federally funded program to increase the quantity of low- or moderate-income housing in one city can be compared with the same program in another city. If the two cities are reasonably similar in terms of the difficulty of constructing new housing, the comparative results should allow the sponsoring agency to determine which is the more successful.

4. Compare Current Results with the Results That Were Anticipated When the Program Was Initiated   The validity of this comparison obviously depends on the soundness of the original estimates of results.

[25]Stephen Glass, "Don't You D.A.R.E.: An Anti-Drug Program Strong-Arms Its Critics," *The New Republic,* March 3, 1997.

Example

A program to provide literacy training projected that 3,000 people a year would become literate as a result of the training activities. This number can be compared with the actual number. If the actual is less than anticipated, the program's manager can be asked to explain why. The results can be used to set an objective either for the subsequent year or for similar programs in other locales.

Problems with Statistical Evaluations   Many problems are encountered in statistical evaluations. It may be difficult to:

1. Define the measures to be used.

2. Assure that data from different data bases are comparable.

3. Determine that the data are reliable.

4. Allow for extraneous factors.

5. Decide whether trends or comparisons are significant.

Evaluators need to determine in advance whether these problems are sufficiently manageable to make the results of the statistical analysis worth the considerable cost that may be involved in gathering and analyzing the data.

Sample Survey Evaluations

A survey of a sample of the target group (i.e., the individuals the program is intended to benefit) or of others who may be knowledgeable about the program may provide highly useful information. The survey may be either in the form of a written questionnaire or an interview. The latter technique is much more expensive, but permits more probing than is feasible with a questionnaire. Occasionally, some combination of the two may be feasible. To assure valid results, evaluators must word survey questions so that respondents' answers are unambiguous. They must also take care to select a sample so that the responses approximate those that would be given if the whole population were surveyed, and they must take steps to avoid any biases in administering the survey. Sampling theory is a complex topic; unless proper techniques are used, the results are likely to be questionable.

Field Experiments

In evaluating the efficacy of a new drug or a new medical or surgical procedure, medical researchers have a well-developed protocol. Two groups of subjects (animals or humans) are created: an experimental group and a control group. Individual subjects are assigned to one of these groups either randomly or in such a way that the factors that may affect the outcome of the experiment (e.g., age, sex, weight, health) are similar for each group. The experimental treatment is administered to the experimental group. (In a double-blind experiment, the experimenter does not know to which group an individual subject belongs nor whether the chemical administered is the test drug or a placebo.)

Factors other than the experimental treatment that might affect the outcome either are insulated from the experiment or are observed and allowed for when results are analyzed. After results are measured, statistical tests are applied to determine if there is a significant difference (associated with the treatment) between the experimental group and the control group. If there is, the treatment is judged to be successful.

Much of the literature on program evaluation discusses ways of applying analogous experimental methods to social programs; such efforts frequently are called *social experiments*. Success has been minimal, however. In many cases, the analysis did not show a significant difference between the two groups. And in most cases with a statistically significant difference, critics maintained that the experiment did not satisfactorily answer the key question: Were the results caused by the treatment, or were they caused by something else?

Example	Some of the largest social experiments have been related to income maintenance. Most experiments were designed to find out whether cash payments to low-income people (the negative income tax) were preferable to welfare programs. The first effort was in New Jersey, begun in the late 1960s, followed by experiments in six other states, with those in Denver and Seattle being the most comprehensive. These experiments involved 8,500 families at a cost of $112 million. Despite the wealth of data, there is no consensus on whether a negative income tax works better than a traditional welfare program.

Problems with Social Experiments Social experiments carry special problems that do not exist for medical experiments. For one thing, most people do not like to be subjects. Guinea pigs can't object, and medical patients usually do not object because they see possible benefits to themselves. But subjects of social experiments often see no benefit in being treated like guinea pigs. In particular, control groups usually know from the beginning that they are not going to benefit, and dropout rates among these groups consequently are high. This compromises the statistical database. Furthermore, to measure results, the experimenters usually must ask personal questions of the subjects, and despite pledges of confidentiality these are often regarded as an invasion of privacy. It therefore is difficult to determine whether the answers are honest. Even if they are honest, many answers depend on fallible memory.

Although field experiments have these limitations and although they are expensive, they can, if properly done, provide the best information on the results attributable to *the program;* that is, the relationship between cause and effect.

Steps in Making an Evaluation

There is no clear consensus among evaluators on the exact procedure an evaluation team should follow. Nevertheless, the following eight steps seem to take place in most evaluations.

1. Decide on the Purpose of the Evaluation   Is it to appraise the success of the program as a basis for deciding its future? Is it to provide recommendations for improvement? Specifically, what questions is the evaluation intended to answer? Presumably, the body that requested the evaluation should state these questions. As a practical matter, however, the charge from that body may be vague, and the evaluation team may need to identify the most useful questions to address. These questions need to be carefully thought out and specifically stated; otherwise, the evaluation may proceed down the wrong road, with a waste of time and resources. The questions are subject to change, of course, if the team finds that the answers cannot feasibly be obtained, or if it uncovers better questions.

2. Examine the Available Information   In some cases, information that is already available, either within the organization or from other researchers, may provide an adequate basis for evaluation. Alternatively, such information may provide a useful starting point.

3. Select a Tentative Strategy   Which of the various types of evaluations is the most appropriate, considering the limitations of time, expertise, and money available for the study? What research design best suits the approach selected? In answering these questions, the evaluation team may assemble a panel of experts to provide guidance. The panel may use the *Delphi Technique;* that is, it may arrive at a conclusion by several iterations of proposed approaches. If the evaluation involves the use of quantitative data, a model showing how these data are to be analyzed should be constructed and examined for feasibility and for relevance to the evaluation questions. The team also should develop a project plan, showing personnel assigned to the project and a timetable.

The evaluation strategy should be presented to the body requesting the study, and that body should sign off on the strategy. If the resources initially available are inadequate, or if the completion time originally expected is too short, additional money or time should be negotiated with the requesting body. If additional money or time is not forthcoming, the scope of the project should be narrowed or, in the extreme case, discontinued. All of these decisions need to be agreed to by the requesting body before the evaluation commences.

4. Test the Proposed Design   Some sort of testing usually is feasible, and tests should be made before major resources are committed to the project. A pretest of questionnaires or interview questions, collection and tabulation of a sample of statistical data, or (if the evaluation is to be conducted at many sites) a complete test at one site may lead to a revision of the evaluation design—and significant cost savings.

5. Carry Out the Evaluation   In carrying out the evaluation, the evaluation team should pay attention to both the agreed-upon timetable and the allowed budget. Exceeding either without prior approval, and usually without sound justification, can cost the team some of its credibility, even though the loss of credibility may have nothing to do with the quality of the evaluation itself. As Chelimsky notes:

> Evaluators working for the legislative branch much be extremely concerned about the timing of the final product and how it dovetails with congressional policy cycles and plans for use. We've learned that what is most important sometimes is not having the best design, but having an adequate design that will bring the findings in at the time they were promised.[26]

6. *Draft a Tentative Report* In doing so, the evaluation team should think about the best way of "selling" the results to those who are expected to act on them. Does the audience prefer a written report? An oral presentation? Both? Are there different audiences, with different desires? Initial response to the tentative report may, for example, lead the team to issue a formal report with wide circulation and an oral report of more sensitive findings.

7. *Obtain Informal Feedback* Within the organization conducting the evaluation, someone other than a member of the evaluation team should carefully examine the draft report. This quality control check should range from such details as arithmetic accuracy and proper grammar to the broad question of whether the conclusions are substantiated by the underlying data. In addition, the draft should be submitted for comment to the agency being evaluated. These comments may lead to changes in the report. Even if the evaluating team disagrees with the agency's comments, these comments should be noted in the report, together with the reasons for disagreement. It is much better to find out about errors or disagreements before the final report is submitted than to have it shot down after it has been formally submitted.

Example

A study of 140 nonprofit organizations that had completed at least one program evaluation in the prior three years found that stakeholder involvement in an evaluation increased the likelihood that the evaluation results would be used, and that the evaluation processes would continue. In particular, in those evaluations with high stakeholder involvement 58 percent led to changes in resource allocation within the organization, compared to only 22 percent of the evaluations with low stakeholder involvement.[27]

8. *Sell the Findings* By the time it has completed its final report, the evaluation team frequently has considerably more knowledge about the program than perhaps even the program's managers. When this is the case, there is a tendency to present too much information without appropriate summaries. The team must think about a reader with limited time, and present the information

[26]Eleanor Chelimsky, "What Have We Learned about the Politics of Program Evaluation?" *Evaluation Practice* 8, no. 1 (February 1987).
[27]Allison H. Fine, Colette E. Thayer, and Anne T. Coghlan, "Program Evaluation Practice in the Nonprofit Sector," *Nonprofit Management and Leadership,* Spring 2000.

in such a way that it is both succinct and compelling. Key points should be highlighted in an executive summary, and most of the statistical computations should be relegated to appendices, no matter how elegant the team thinks they are. As Chelimsky puts it:

> We have learned that telling all is tantamount to telling nothing. The important thing is to answer the policy question as clearly and simply as possible, to emphasize a few critical and striking numbers, and to do all that in such a way as to highlight those findings that give rise to policy action.[28]

In sum, the program evaluation process is as much political as it is scientific. The recommendations will not be implemented unless those who have the authority to do so are convinced that implementation is desirable. The decision maker is often influenced by factors other than those set forth in the report, no matter how scientifically sound the analysis may be. The evaluation team should attempt to identify and deal with these political factors, even though they may be regarded as being illogical.

Summary

In many respects, the process followed in an operations analysis parallels that in a program evaluation. In both activities, the team needs to: (1) obtain a mandate from a body that is prepared to act on its recommendations, (2) identify objectives, (3) determine a strategy for conducting the activity, (4) carry out the activity, and (5) make and sell recommendations.

Despite these similarities, there are some important differences. An operations analysis tends to be much more constrained than a program evaluation. Since the analysis team is focusing on *process* rather than *results,* it has a relatively easy time defining objectives, measuring output, and identifying areas where improvements might be made. Operations analysis is needed principally because fat tends to accumulate in any program, and a fat-trimming effort occasionally is necessary.

Program evaluation tends to be much more complicated than operations analysis. The objectives frequently are difficult to define, output frequently is tricky to measure, and cause-and-effect relationships can be elusive. Moreover, the choice of the most appropriate type of program evaluation frequently is highly debatable. Subjective, peer review, case study, statistical, sample survey, and field experiments are all candidates, and it frequently is not clear which will provide the best information for assessing whether a program should continue as is, be modified, or be discontinued.

Despite these difficulties, governing bodies need to undertake program evaluations. In a world of scarce resources, they provide essential information for the difficult task of making trade-offs among a variety of possible programmatic endeavors. Indeed, without undertaking both operations analysis and program evaluation, a governing body cannot be certain that it is using resources in the most appropriate way to achieve the organization's goals.

[28]Chelimsky, "What Have We Larned?"

Suggested Additional Readings

Bowsher, Charles. *Program Evaluation Issues.* Transition series, U.S. General Accounting Office, December 1992.

Chelimsky, Eleanor. "The politics of program evaluation." *Social Science in Modern Society* 25, no. 1 (1987), pp. 24–32.

———. *Partnership Projects: A Framework for Evaluating Public-Private Housing and Development Efforts.* U.S. General Accounting Office, May 1990.

———. "Expanding GAO's Evaluation Capabilities." *The Bureaucrat* 20, no. 1 (March 22, 1991), p. 29.

———. "On the Social Science Contribution to Governmental Decision-making." *Science* 254, no. 502 (October 11, 1991), p. 226.

Cutt, James, Vic Murray, and Victor V. Murray. *Accountability and Effectiveness Evaluation in Nonprofit Organizations.* New York: Reutledge, 2000.

Deming, W. Edwards. *Out of Crisis.* Cambridge, MA: MIT Press, 1986.

Fried, H. O., C. A. K. Lovell, and S. S. Schmidt. *The Measurement of Productive Efficiency—Techniques and Applications.* Oxford, Eng.: Oxford University Press, 1993.

Ganley, J. A., and J. S. Cubbins. *Public Sector Efficiency Measurement—Applications of Data Envelopment Analysis.* Amsterdam, Neth.: North Holland, 1992.

Gronbach, L. J. *Designing Evaluations of Educational and Social Programs.* San Francisco: Jossey-Bass Publishers, 1982.

Institute of Management Accounting. *Statement of Management Accounting 4V: Effective Benchmarking.* Montvale, NJ: 1995.

Ishikawa, K., ed. *Guide to Quality Control.* White Plains, NY: Kraus International Publications, 1986.

Judd, C. M., and D. A. Kenny. *Estimating the Effects of Social Interventions.* Cambridge, Eng.: Cambridge University Press, 1981.

Juran, J. M. *Juran on Planning for Quality.* New York: The Free Press, 1989.

Keppel, G. *Design and Analysis: A Researcher's Handbook,* 3rd ed. Englewood Cliffs, NJ: Prentice Hall, 1991.

Kidder, L. H., and R. Judd. *Research Methods in Social Relations,* 4th ed. Fort Worth, TX: Holt, Rinehart & Winston, 1991.

Light, Richard, and David Pillemer. *Summing Up: The Science of Reviewing Research.* Cambridge, MA: Harvard University Press, 1984.

———, Judith Singer, and John Willett. *By Design.* Cambridge, MA: Harvard University Press, 1990.

Manski, F., and I. Garfinkel, eds. *Evaluating Welfare and Training Programs.* London: Harvard University Press, 1992.

Perry, James L., ed. *Handbook of Public Administration,* 2nd ed. San Francisco: Jossey-Bass Publishers, 1996.

Pesieau, P., and H. Tulkens. *Assessing the Performance of Public Sector Activities: Some Recent Evidence from the Productive Efficiency Viewpoint.* CORE Discussion Paper no. 9060, Centre for Operations Research and Econometrics, Université Catholique de Louvain, November 1990.

Senge, Peter. The Fifth Discipline: *The Art and Practice of the Learning Organization.* New York: Currency Doubleday, 1990.

Shadish, W. R., T. D. Cook, and L. C. Leviton. *Foundations of Program Evaluation.* Newbury Park, CA: Sage, 1991.

Silkman, R., ed. *Measuring Efficiency: An Assessment of Data Envelopment Analysis, New Directions for Program Evaluation.* San Francisco: Jossey-Bass Publishers, 1996.

U.S. General Accounting Office, Program Evaluation and Methodology Division. Methodology Transfer Papers. Washington, DC. (A series of papers on aspects of program evaluation. See especially "Designing Evaluations," *Paper No. 4,* 1984; "Using Statistical Sampling," *Paper No. 6;* and *Designing Evaluations: A Workbook,* February 1986.)

U.S. General Accounting Office. *Improving Program Evaluation in the Executive Branch.* GAO/PEMD-90-19, May 1990.

————. *Program Evaluation Issues.* GAO/OCG-936TR, December 1992.

Wholey, Joseph, Harry P. Hatry, and Kathryn E. Newcomer, eds. *Handbook of Practical Program Evaluation.* San Francisco: Jossey-Bass Publishers, 1994.

Case 15–1
Bureau of Child Welfare[*]

The number of adoptions has been declining over the past two years, and represents an increasingly smaller percentage of children in foster care. We've been emphasizing the importance of placing children in adoptive homes when the situation warrants such a move, so I'm uncertain as to why the private agencies, with which we contracted for the delivery of social services, are not making a greater effort to do so.

*This case was prepared by Professor David W. Young. Copyright © by David W. Young.

EXHIBIT 1
Number of Legal
Adoptions,
1992–1996

	1992	1993	1994	1995	1996
Legal adoptions	1,000	993	1,166	1,032	807
Children in foster care	24,973	25,934	27,115	27,900	28,625
Percent adopted	4.0	3.8	4.3	3.7	2.8

The speaker was Henry Brown, Special Assistant to the Director of the Bureau of Child Welfare, who was evaluating the results of the Bureau's activities in its Adoption Program. As indicated in Exhibit 1, the city's child welfare system provided care and delivered services to some 29,000 children at any given time. Approximately 8,000–10,000 children entered the system during the course of a year and slightly fewer were discharged, so that the total population increased gradually each year.

Background

Although the city was legally responsible for all children in its care, it had few programs and facilities of its own. Thus, the vast majority of children actually were under the direct supervision of some 80 private (or *voluntary,* as they were sometimes called) child-care agencies. The great majority of these children in placement resided with individual families in foster homes; the remaining children were distributed among facilities such as institutions, group homes, maternity shelters, and so forth.

The private agencies were funded by the city according to a reimbursement formula that was designed to cover approximately 85 to 90 percent of their reimbursable costs. The reimbursement for ongoing programs, such as foster care, was on a per diem basis; that is, the agency received a predetermined amount per day for each child in care. The amount of payment varied according to the type of program (foster home, group home, institution, and so on). A variety of costs either were not reimbursable or—as was the case with adoption—were reimbursed by means of a one-time fee. Payments made to agencies, regardless of whether they were per diem or a one-time fee, came from the Charitable Institutions Budget and totaled some $400 million per year.

Children entered the child-care system for a variety of reasons. In some instances the child's parents made a request to the city because they were unable to provide adequate care in the home; in others the child entered by means of a court mandate for reasons such as neglect, abuse, delinquency, or potential delinquency. Although some children remained in care for only a few months, others remained in the system for several years, often until they reached the age of 21 and were no longer eligible for child welfare services.

A variety of changes had taken place over the past 5 to 10 years which affected not only the relationship between the city and the agencies, but the whole pattern of child care. One such change was in the characteristics of the children in care. Between 1990 and 1996 the mix of children in the child-care system shifted rather dramatically, such that there were now proportionately more older children and more children who were in care because of their own emotional and behavioral problems. As a result of this change, many agencies—and the city as well—had been left with inappropriate programs and service-delivery capabilities; consequently many children were residing in programs that were not appropriate to their needs.

Data

Mr. Brown realized that several complications existed that impinged on his evaluation. First, foster home care cost the city $48 a day, with payments made 365 days a year; this rate had remained unchanged for the full five years. The one-time adoption fee, by contrast, had risen from $1,600 in 1992 to $5,600 in 1996.

Second, over 40 percent of all adoptions in 1996 were "subsidized," that is, the adoptive parents received payments from the city of $5,760 per year. This percentage was up from only 1.1 percent in 1992 (see Exhibit 2).

Third, Mr. Brown had recently obtained some data on the cost to a voluntary agency of an adoptive effort. As he had learned, agencies incurred three types of costs in placing a child in an adoptive home. First, there were the rather standard direct costs for the adoption itself. These expenditures included legal fees, casework time, administrative time, testing, and the like. Second, there was a loss of per diem payments. That is, when a child was adopted, the agency's population level fell; since reimbursement was based on a per-child per-day payment, the agency lost this payment until a replacement child was admitted. The per diem payment was designed to cover both fixed and variable child-care costs, but when a child was adopted only the variable costs stopped—the fixed costs continued. Thus, until the agency could replace the adopted child, it lost reimbursement for the fixed-cost portion of the per diem rate. Third, the child who replaced the one who was adopted was likely to have higher variable costs. Since children who were adopted usually required few special agency services, their variable costs were relatively low. On the other hand, new children entering the child-care system frequently had a need for one or more specialized services, so that when a replacement child was found he/she was likely to have higher variable costs, on the average, than the one who was adopted. As a result, the agency suffered a loss in the surplus of reimbursement over variable costs and consequently had fewer dollars available to cover its fixed costs.

As an example, if the fixed portion of the $48 per-child per-day reimbursement amount was $20, and if a month elapsed before a replacement child was

EXHIBIT 2
Number of Subsidized Adoptions, 1992–1996

	1992	1993	1994	1995	1996
Subsidized adoptions	11	96	218	326	328
Percent of total adoptions.	1.1	9.7	18.7	31.6	40.6

admitted (which frequently was the case), the agency had lost approximately $600 ($20 per day × 30 days) of funds which it had previously planned to use for the payment of rent, salaries, and other expenses to which it had committed itself for the budget year. If the variable costs for the replacement child were $4 more per day than for the one who was adopted, the agency's annual fixed-cost reimbursement was depleted still further. Assuming children were adopted fairly consistently throughout the budget year, the $4 per day loss was in effect for an average of six months for each child adopted; the annual loss in reimbursement for fixed costs was thus about $720 ($4 per day × 180 days) per adopted child. Consequently, using the assumptions of a $20 fixed-cost portion, a one-month lapse before a replacement child was admitted, and $4 per day more in variable costs for the replacement child, an agency's direct adoption costs increased by some $1,320 per placement.

Of further significance was the fact that the direct cost of adoption itself frequently was understated. While the adoption fee might adequately account for the adoption-related costs of any *given* child, there were many children for whom adoption was attempted unsuccessfully. An agency incurred adoption-related costs for these children as well and yet received no reimbursement for them. The schematic diagram in Exhibit 3 illustrates the potential significance of unsuccessful attempts in the computation of adoption costs. In this example 100 children began the adoption process, but only 45 were successfully adopted. Exhibit 4 shows the costs of this process. When only successful attempts are used and when no home finding is necessary, the cost per adoption was $15,240. The inclusion of unsuccessful attempts and home-finding efforts brought the cost to $27,451 per completed adoption; that is, the agency spent a total of $1,235,300 and completed only 45 adoptions.

Dr. Brown noted three points with respect to this example. First, the most significant cost was that of legal fees, which were quite high when there was a charge of permanent neglect because of both the relatively large number of days necessary per case and the fact that in this example the courts decided against the agency in 30 out of 80 cases. Second, not all adoptions followed this pattern. Different legal costs would be incurred, for example, in a case where the child had been surrendered, or where the agency went to court on an abandonment petition. Third, any projected savings would depend on the length of time a child *would have* remained in foster care if he/she were not adopted. He thought 10 years was a reasonable assumption.

In sum, he realized that agencies must consider a variety of costs when deciding whether to proceed toward adoption for a given child. In order to determine more specifically the level of these costs he analyzed 144 children who were adopted through one agency during the three years from 1994 to 1996.

Because this agency had deficit funding for its adoption program, it was able to undertake an adoption whenever it felt that adoption was in the best interests of the child, regardless of the financial consequences. Because it also accepted a relatively high proportion of children classified as "hard to place," it seemed feasible to conclude that the percentage of children adopted would

EXHIBIT 3   Adoption Attempts for Children Considered Permanently Neglected (Each Symbol Represents Five Children)

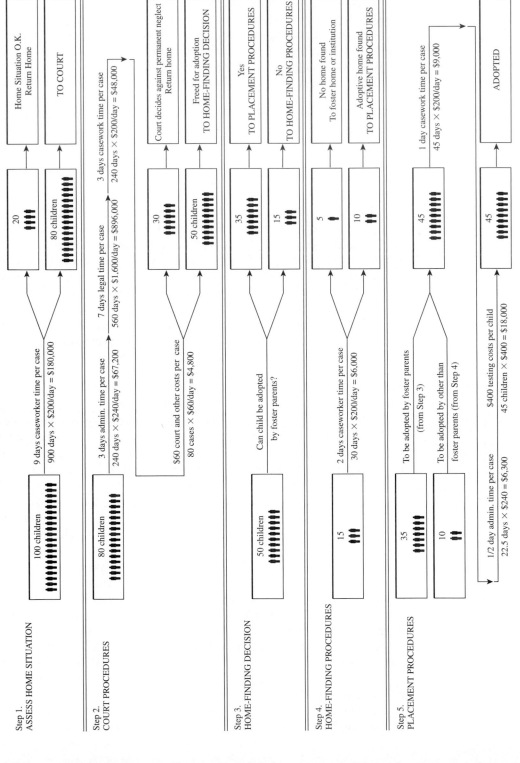

EXHIBIT 4 Adoption Costs for Permanently Neglected Children

		Using 100 Children	
Activity	Cost for One Child	Number of Children Involved	Cost for Children Involved
Caseworker assessment of home situation.............	$ 1,800	100	$ 180,000
Court procedures:			
Administrative time.........................	840	80	67,200
Legal time................................	11,200	80	896,000
Casework time...........................	600	80	48,000
Court and other costs	60	80	4,800
Caseworker time in home-finding procedures*	—	15	6,000
Placement procedures:			
Casework time...........................	200	45	9,000
Administrative time........................	140	45	6,300
Testing costs	400	45	18,000
Total..................................	$15,240	45	$1,235,300
Cost per adopted child..........................			$ 27,451

*Not necessary for the average child. Needed for only 15 children out of the 100. Cost is $400 per child when necessary. Therefore $6,000 is included in the cost for children involved.

EXHIBIT 5 Adoption Analysis

	Actual (1996)				
	Agency		City		Cost per
	Number	Percent*	Number	Percent*	Adoption†
Total children in care	596	—	28,625	—	—
Number of adoptions	43	7.22	807	2.82	—
Adoption breakdown:					
Surrendered	27	4.53	—	—	$12,000
Abandoned	10	1.68			10,800
Permanently neglected	6	1.01	—	—	18,400
Subsidized/unsubsidized breakdown:					
Subsidized	33	5.54	328	1.15	—
Unsubsidized	10	1.68	479	1.67	—

*Percent of total children in care.
†Includes "failures" and other associated costs.

not be biased by the children's characteristics. He classified these children into 36 categories based on legal status, age, and level of handicaps, and found that the average cost per successfully adopted child ranged from $10,800 in the lowest category to $18,400 in the highest.

In order to simplify his analysis, he decided to look only at 43 children whose adoptions were from this agency during 1996, and to collapse his 36 categories into 3, reflecting the most significant factor, legal status: surrendered, abandoned, or permanently neglected. Since this particular agency had had outside funding support for its adoption program, he thought that the results of its efforts might be indicative of what would happen citywide if further financial support for adoptions were made available to the agencies. The results of his analysis are contained in Exhibit 5.

With these data in hand, he began to reflect on the nature of the problem with adoptions, and what changes might be made in the Bureau's reimbursement policy in order to encourage agencies to move toward adoption when it was appropriate for the child.

Questions

1. What is your assessment of Dr. Brown's evaluation methodology? How might it have been improved?

2. Assuming the validity of the data he has gathered, what are the next steps he should take in the evaluation? What changes, if any, would you recommend the Bureau make in its reimbursement policies? In its other policies?

Case 15–2

Timilty Middle School*

Mary Grassa O'Neill, principal of the James P. Timilty Middle School, sat in her unadorned office. The walls were stripped and primed for a much-needed paint job. Ms. O'Neill brought 17 years of middle-school experience to this, her first principalship. Three years had passed since her appointment, and her decision to initiate the Project Promise Pilot Program. Now, after two complete years of the program, and a calm and orderly beginning of the third year, she had the luxury of some time to reflect on two important questions: What had Project Promise promised? and What had it delivered?

Background

The Timilty Middle School, located in historic John Eliot Square of the Fort Hill section of Boston, had a troubled history and had suffered for many years from a poor reputation. Founded in 1937 as a junior high school (Grades 7–9), and transformed to a middle school (Grades 6–8) in 1974, it had seen its racial and ethnic composition change dramatically—from 75 percent white and 25

---

*This case was prepared by Alexander D. Stankowicz under the supervision of Professor David W. Young. Copyright © by David W. Young and Alexander D. Stankowicz.

percent black when founded to 52 percent black, 29 percent Hispanic, 7 percent Asian, and 9 percent white at present.

When Ms. O'Neill took over as principal, the school had a number of problems: low reading and math scores, low student and teacher attendance, high suspension and failure rates, and a general reputation as a low-achieving school. For many, including the press and the surrounding community, it was considered to be the "worst school in town."

In the Boston Public School System (BPS), as in most other cities, students had no choice regarding their school assignment: all middle-school students living in specific neighborhoods were assigned to their geocoded school. As a result, the Timilty's student population consisted of racially mixed, urban poor, living in substandard housing, burdened with the struggles of poverty, drugs and alcohol, teenage pregnancy, family crises, and neighborhood violence. Indeed, according to an AFDC[1] report and free-lunch statistics, the Timilty's students had the second lowest socioeconomic levels in the city.

The Program

Several years ago, Ms. O'Neill had found an application for the Project Promise Pilot Program in her morning mail. She discussed it with her staff, and decided to apply.

Project Promise, as introduced initially in Rochester, New York, was an intensive, academic remediation program designed to improve student performance in reading, mathematics, and writing. It was based on the theory that if underachieving students spent more time on the basics, their skills would improve.

Ms. O'Neill and her staff decided that the program at the Timilty would be for all students, not just those needing remediation. The Timilty's application was approved, and a Pilot Program was initiated. It had seven instructional components:

1. *Extended day.* Students attended school one and a half hours longer Monday through Thursday, from 7:40 A.M. until 3:10 P.M. Friday was a regular 7:40 to 1:40 school day. Teachers worked two hours longer, from 7:25 A.M. until 3:55 P.M., Monday to Friday. Overall, students were in school 37 percent longer; teachers worked 40 percent longer.

2. *Extended week.* Three hours of organized instruction were offered on Saturday mornings. Teachers used a variety of groupings and approaches to involve students in enrichment activities in reading, writing, and math.

3. *Interdisciplinary and team teaching.* Teachers worked together to use thematic teaching across the disciplines. The basic skills of reading and

---

[1]Aid to Families with Dependent Children, a program run by the State Department of Public Welfare.

writing were taught across all subject areas. In order to determine effective ways of teaching across their specializations, teachers worked together in four separate clusters:[2] (*a*) Grade 6, (*b*) Grade 7, (*c*) Grade 8, and (*d*) multilevel, consisting of Grades 6, 7, and 8, with both monolingual and Spanish-speaking bilingual students (designed to assist in "mainstreaming" the Spanish-speaking students). To facilitate interdisciplinary teaching, teachers also created opportunities to teach together.

4. *Smaller class size.* This was achieved by adding academic staff—a teacher and a coordinator—to each cluster.

5. *Flexible schedule.* The traditional day of 45-minute periods was replaced by a flexible schedule, determined by each team, allowing the scheduling of both longer and shorter classes in order to meet instructional needs.

6. *Planning time.* Teachers had common planning time (approximately 4–6 hours per week) to develop interdisciplinary instruction in reading and writing and to discuss any issues relevant to their teaching.

7. *Parent outreach.* To support these school-based innovations, two paid parent outreach workers undertook activities to inform and involve parents in their children's education.

The Program

To implement the program, all academic and resource room position descriptions were rewritten and upgraded, and all former positions were abolished. Ms. O'Neill established a screening committee to fill the new positions, and before implementation of the first full year of Project Promise, 24 Timilty teachers had applied and 21 had been hired. This left 14 vacancies. Ms. O'Neill explained:

> There were three difficulties in attracting staff to the new positions: (1) many teachers simply didn't want to work in Project Promise, (2) the Boston Teachers' Union (BTU) lobbied against Project Promise because they maintained that teachers were being required to apply for their old jobs, and (3) there was a great deal of uncertainty associated with the leap into an educational experiment of this magnitude, involving interdisciplinary teaching.

Although there were some grumblings about the recruitment process, most teachers felt that being chosen for the program bonded them together, and there was a strong belief that the program was going to work. The majority of teachers selected had worked in the school for over 15 years. Of the seven

---

[2]In the Timilty, students at each grade level received all their academic instruction from a small group of teachers; this was called the *cluster.* All nonacademic subjects (physical education, industrial arts, home economics, art) were taught by teachers outside the particular cluster.

new people who were chosen to join the staff, only one was new to teaching. The remainder were experienced teachers, although some were from outside the BPS. According to one veteran, this was very good for the project:

> They had no old habits to break, and they were going to have to plunge in and learn all new habits. Also, they would be mentored by the more experienced teachers in the school. The new people who came in sometimes rose to be stars of the show. One teacher had a really rough time her first year in the school with 30 students in the classroom, unresponsive kids—your typical middle school experience. Now she's in her second year of teaching, this time as a Project Promise teacher. She is teaching what she wants, with a relatively small class size. She has suddenly become a shining star, with all of her talent and ability coming forth.

Administrative staff (consisting of a principal, an assistant principal, and a director of instruction) remained the same, and three additional instructional support teachers were included. According to Clem Pasquale, a veteran of 21 years' teaching at the school:

> What we have here now that we didn't have in the past is the support from the Instructional Coordinators, the Assistant Principal, and the Director of Instruction. There is now a framework of supports where you can go to work through and deal with problems that, in the past, would require you to take time away from your teaching. We now have the organization, a plan and a staff to do whatever has to be done to make the school work.

Jeff Cohen, a 19-year Timilty veteran, added:

> If there is something that happens that you can't handle yourself, you can send the student to someone who can deal with the problem. We are now spending most of the day teaching rather than doing paperwork or disciplining.

Initially, the program was extremely challenging, especially in its attempt to dovetail the normal 6-hour day with a 7½-hour day, and to maintain consistency between Project Promise teachers and other teachers. As a result of this greater intensity, everyone involved had a totally new set of activities for the final 10 weeks of the school year. Teachers had smaller groups to work with—as few as 10 to 15 students for remediation, and approximately 20 to 25 for regular classes, rather than 30 students for both remediation and regular classes.

Although some of the teachers found the coordination demands challenging on occasion, in general, most would do things for the students that they would not have done in situations with larger class sizes. There was a new sense of mood in the building, due largely to the fact that there was now time to work things out. The common planning time that was built into the program allowed the faculty, students, and parents to bond together, and to dedicate themselves to a shared mission of education.

As one observer commented:

> Teachers' Room conversations shifted from weekend activities, complaining about the kids, and counting how many days were left in the school year, to

student-oriented topics like curriculum, sharing successful lessons, and brainstorming new ideas that might be tried in the classroom. There was a new excitement in the school, and both teachers and students seemed to be having fun.

The superintendent of the Boston Public Schools had decided that Project Promise would not be a remedial program, targeted only for students with the lowest scores. Rather, the premise was that if the six academic components were good for students who needed remediation, then they were good for everyone. Jim Fewless, a 21-year veteran of the Timilty, and the 7th grade coordinator, explained the "promise" of Project Promise this way:

> If you are below average, we will work to see that you become an average student; if you are an average student, you can become an above average student; we want the above average student to excel; and if you are already an excellent student, there is always more to learn and more to do, and you will be given the time to do it.

Cost

According to the BPS budget, the Timilty Middle School cost $636,718 more than the average cost of other BPS middle schools. The average per pupil cost for middle schools was $3,746, while the per pupil cost at the Timilty was $5,484, a difference of 46 percent. All of this was attributed to Project Promise. On the average, Project Promise teachers received $6,000–$7,000 more pay per year than other middle-school teachers, most of which was for overtime. The extra money bought several things: common planning time for teachers, smaller class sizes, remedial teachers, extended classroom time (90 minutes) for the students during the week, Saturday classes, and professional development (e.g., training) for the teachers.

Performance Measures

Several indicators of performance were available to Ms. O'Neill. One was student attendance. Prior to Project Promise, attendance at the Timilty ranged from 75 to 85 percent, about average for a middle school. Attendance for the first full year of Project Promise was 90 percent; in the second full year, it rose to about 92 percent. Initially, on Saturdays, attendance was 45 percent, which rose to between 60 to 70 percent in the third year. One explanation given for this was that Timilty students now found school to be a place where they felt a strong sense of belonging, accomplishment, and in the process had some fun.

A second indicator was teacher attendance. Prior to Project Promise, teacher attendance, along with morale, at the Timilty was low. According to one veteran, "The majority of staff members made sure that they took all their personal and sick days, usually right before or after a vacation, when we would have a quarter of the staff absent." Under Project Promise, the Timilty's teacher attendance was the second highest in the city, even though teachers were

EXHIBIT 1   Basic Information

Year	Average Number of Students in School*	Number of Exam School Acceptances	Suspensions	Suspensions per 1000 Students	Potential Nonpromote Percentage
1	462	39	82	n.a.	n.a.
2	510	52	83	n.a.	n.a.
3	492	64	38	8.7	5.0

*Enrollment figures are determined three times each academic year: September, December, and June. This number is an average of the three.

Sources: Average number of students and exam school acceptances from Division of Implementation, Boston Public Schools. Other data were obtained from The Research and Development Department, Boston Public Schools.)

required to put in two extra hours a day and three hours on Saturday. According to Mr. Fewless:

> Project Promise is a great deal of work for the staff. Because of the additional time, our weekends are shortened to a day and a half. Yet, besides the financial remuneration, the professional rewards of working together in a team gives us a sense that we are working together.

A third indicator was exam school[3] acceptances. Before Project Promise, the idea of Timilty's 8th graders applying for exam schools was almost unheard of. With the program, students were encouraged to apply, and the number admitted increased each year. Data on exam school acceptances are contained in Exhibit 1. Moreover, students who had graduated from Project Promise reported that they were not overloaded by the workload of high school, whereas in the past many students had reported being overwhelmed by the demands of regular high school.

A fourth indicator was suspensions, which, as Exhibit 1 indicates, dropped dramatically. By the second full year of Project Promise, the Timilty's suspension rate was 8.7 per 1,000 students, the 10th lowest in the city. Rates at the Cleveland and Thompson Middle Schools, the two other Project Promise Schools, were 7.4 and 15.8, respectively.

A fifth indicator was potential nonpromotes. As Exhibit 1 also indicates, the Timilty's percentage of potential nonpromotes was only 5 percent, the second lowest in the city. Rates at the Cleveland and Thompson Middle Schools were 13.1 and 9.0 percent, respectively.

A sixth indicator was parent involvement. With approximately 426 students in attendance, over 200 parents showed up for the annual open houses. According to Mr. Pasquale, "In the old days there were usually twice as many teachers as parents at open house, and we would be lucky if 13 or 14 parents

[3]BPS had three high schools (Boston Latin, Boston Latin Academy, and Boston Technical High) that were called exam schools, because they required students to take SSAT (Secondary School Aptitude Test) in order to be accepted. These schools, known for their rigorous academic curriculum, prepared students for college.

EXHIBIT 2 Average Percentile Scores for Project Promise versus Non–Project Promise Students

	Project Promise	Non–Project Promise
Reading:[*]		
Grade 6	63	57
Grade 7	50	43
Grade 8	45	41
Math:[†]		
Grade 6	72	64
Grade 7	51	46
Grade 8	54	43

[*]There were statistically significant differences favoring Project Promise in Grades 6 and 7.
[†]There were statistically significant differences favoring Project Promise in Grades 6, 7, and 8.
Note: Figures are based on students who were enrolled for the entire school year. For Project Promise, students had to be in the same Project Promise school for the entire year. Non–Project Promise does not include exam school students.

Source: Office of Research and Development, Boston Public Schools.

showed up." Indeed, following the initiation of Project Promise, over 100 parents frequently came on Saturdays to participate in school activities, such as the science fair, the international festival, and student and teacher appreciation days.

A final indicator was reading and math ability, which was measured by utilizing the MAT (Metropolitan Achievement Test) raw scores to summarize the overall picture for Grades 6, 7, and 8. Students at each grade level were given reading and math tests before they entered Project Promise and again after they had spent one year in the program. The scores of students who participated in Project Promise at the Timilty, as well as the Cleveland and Thompson Middle Schools, were compared to non–Project Promise students in the other BPS middle schools.

The results of these comparisons are shown in Exhibit 2. As this exhibit indicates, Project Promise students scored higher than non–Project Promise students at each grade level on the MAT reading test. In terms of percentile score, the largest difference was at the 7th grade level, where the median percentile was 7 points higher for Project Promise students than non–Project Promise ones. On the MAT math test, the largest difference was at the 8th grade level where Project Promise students had a median percentile 11 points higher than non–Project Promise ones.

Similar results could be seen from an analysis over a two-year period. In the first year, children who were to become Project Promise 6th grade students were 0.3 points behind other 5th grade students. After one year of the program, Project Promise students were 2.6 points ahead of students outside Project Promise. This meant that Project Promise students ended the 5th grade behind other students, went through the program, and at the end of the 6th grade had caught up with and surpassed their counterparts outside Project Promise.

EXHIBIT 3   Median Percentiles for Reading and Math by Grade, Year, and School

	School			
	All Non–Project Promise*	Cleveland	Thompson	Timilty
Grade 6:				
Reading:				
Year 1	50	38	53	48
Year 2	50	44	53	65
Year 3	n.a.	53	62	62
Math:				
Year 1	60	54	49	47
Year 2	57	65	71	71
Year 3	n.a.	63	65	74
Grade 7:				
Reading:				
Year 1	41	37	33	31
Year 2	38	41	45	50
Year 3	n.a.	46	38	50
Math:				
Year 1	47	46	28	30
Year 2	41	50	39	34
Year 3	n.a.	46	46	48
Grade 8:				
Reading:				
Year 1	35	35	29	30
Year 2	37	39	41	37
Year 3	n.a.	41	48	53
Math:				
Year 1	37	43	26	32
Year 2	38	38	34	34
Year 3	n.a.	41	56	54

*"Non–Project Promise" does not include students from the Latin Schools.

Source: Office of Research and Development, Boston Public Schools.

Student performance on a school-by-school basis is shown in Exhibit 3, which shows the median percentile for students outside the program, and that of each Project Promise school. For example, 6th grade students outside the program had a median reading score of 50 in the first year. The Cleveland School started quite behind, with a median score of 38, while Thompson and Timilty students started the 6th grade with scores of 53 and 48, respectively. After the initiation of Project Promise, Cleveland 6th grade students improved somewhat (from 38 to 44), Thompson students stayed about the same, and Timilty students increased to a median score of 65. In the third year, Timilty

EXHIBIT 4 MAT Reading and Math: Progress over Time—Yearly Scaled Score Differences—Project Promise minus Non–Project Promise*

	Year 1	Year 2	Year 3
Reading:			
7th Graders:			
Grade 5	−6		
Grade 6		−3	
Grade 7			+8
8th Graders:			
Grade 6	−8		
Grade 7		+8	
Grade 8			+7
Math:			
7th Graders:			
Grade 5	−11		
Grade 6		+2	
Grade 7			+6
8th Graders:			
Grade 6	−13		
Grade 7		−1	
Grade 8			+12

*Figures are based on students who were enrolled for the entire school years. For Project Promise, students had to be in the same Project Promise school for the entire year. Non–Project Promise does not include exam school students.

Source: Office of Research and Development, Boston Public Schools.

students dropped slightly to 62, while Cleveland and Thompson students continued to improve.

After examining these reading and math scores, the BPS Office of Research and Development concluded:

> Taken together, these data show a pattern of successful outcomes for Project Promise students. The Program seems to work for low-performing students who start out far behind their school counterparts, and also seems to accelerate the achievement of students who do not have a learning lag when they enter the Program.

Long-Term Impact

One important question was whether the impact of Project Promise was cumulative or whether it would begin to wear off over time. Exhibit 4 shows the performance of students who had been in Project Promise for two full years, in comparison with other students for the same period. It suggests that, after participating in Project Promise for two years, current 7th graders had completely overcome the original gap in reading performance and were outperforming their non–Project Promise peers. For current 8th graders, the relative impact of Project Promise had decreased slightly, but this group was still scoring higher than their non–Project Promise peers.

As with reading, future Project Promise students were scoring lower on the MAT math test than other BPS students prior to the start of Project Promise. After one year in the program, Project Promise 6th graders had scored 2 points higher than non–Project Promise 6th graders. Project Promise 7th graders performed similarly. After two years, 7th and 8th graders continued to gain faster in math than other BPS students.

After two complete years of Project Promise, the Office of Research and Development concluded:

> The preliminary results strongly suggest that, as a whole, Project Promise students are improving at a relatively faster rate than their non–Project Promise peers. This is especially true in math. Future analyses will look at changes over time in more detail and information from the CRTs [Criterion Reference Tests]. The final evaluation report will include information from teachers, students and parents regarding the impact of the project.

A Dissenting View

Although there were considerable data available to support the case that the Project Promise Program at the Timilty School was a success, David Whall, the budget director for the BPS, was skeptical. In his view:

> While the Timilty reading and math scores improved, as they did at Cleveland and Thompson, which were also Project Promise schools, there are nonetheless other schools that have shown equivalent improvement without the benefit of Project Promise (Exhibit 5). If you're looking at Year 2 test scores, they are generally up from Year 1 scores, which are down from the prior year. And if you look at the middle school test scores as a whole and compare them from over three years, there isn't any noticeable improvement.
>
> The total expenditure of the BPS went from roughly $256 million prior to Project Promise to $328 million three years later, a 28 percent increase in aggregate expenditures (which is a 15 to 16 percent increase if you correct for inflation) for a student population that has not increased. From my budget perspective, there has been a very large increase in expenditures, but looking at the test scores, there has been no material improvement in academic performance.

Mr. Whall acknowledged that in many ways Project Promise was a desirable and successful program, but, in his view, it did not necessarily represent the optimal use of resources of the BPS.

> Would the system be better off, on a whole, if the money were channeled into other resources? For example, as this analysis that I have prepared [Exhibit 6] shows, there are many ways the $1,265,326 for Project Promise could have been spent last year. Since the students come into middle schools like the Timilty with basic academic deficiencies, it might be a more efficient allocation of resources to target an at-risk elementary population and provide an extended day program with

EXHIBIT 5

MAT Reading and Mathematics: Rankings of Median Percentile Scores for Middle Schools Average Scale Score Change for Last Two Years of Program Project Promise*

School	District	Average Scale Score Change
Reading:		
Lewenberg...............	B	+16.33
M. Curley................	A	+9.33
Dearborn	C	+9.00
McCormack	C	+8.67
Cleveland................	C	+7.00
Mackey	E	+5.67
Timilty	D	+5.33
Barnes	D	+4.00
Thompson	B	+3.67
Tobin	A	+3.00
Edison	A	+2.67
Gavin...................	C	+2.00
Irving..................	B	+2.00
Wheatley	E	+1.33
Rogers	B	+1.00
Holmes.................	C	0.00
R. Shaw	B	0.00
Wilson	C	−0.67
Taft	A	−1.00
Edwards	D	−1.67
Lewis	A	−7.67
King...................	E	−10.67
Mathematics:		
Lewenberg...............	B	+12.67
Timilty	D	+12.00
Tobin	A	+12.00
Thompson	B	+7.33
Edison	A	+7.33
Barnes	D	+5.33
McCormack	C	+5.33
Gavin...................	C	+5.00
Irving..................	B	+2.67
Mackey	E	+2.33
King...................	E	+1.67
Wilson	C	+1.00
Wheatley	E	+0.67
Cleveland................	C	−1.00
Taft	A	−1.67
Holmes.................	C	−2.33
R. Shaw	B	−3.00
Edwards	D	−3.00
M. Curley................	A	−5.00
Dearborn	C	−7.00
Rogers	B	−12.67
Lewis	A	−19.67

*Data for prior years are not available

Source: Department of Educational Testing, Boston Public Schools.

EXHIBIT 6 Budgetary Options*

School	Without Project Promise	School as Percent of Average	With Project Promise	School as Percent of Average	Project Promise Students	School as Percent of Average
Cleveland	$3,665	97.8%	$3,933	105.0%	$4,612	123.1%
Thompson	3,978	106.2	5,165	137.9	5,217	139.3
Timilty	4,165	111.2	5,466	145.9	5,484	146.4

*Middle School average cost per student: $3,746 (does not include overhead, transportation, etc.)

Note: Total city and externally funded budgets for Project Promise came to $1,265,326. By comparison, this sum could have done any of the following:

Purchase an additional 29 guidance counselors, including benefits.

Increase the instructional supply allocation by 26 percent for every student in the BPS.

Raise the BPS's library paraprofessional staff by 162 percent from 59 to 155 FTEs.

Provide another 35 elementary specialist teachers.

Nearly double the targeted reading workforce, raising it from 37 to 69 teachers.

Give the middle schools another 33 instructional support teachers.

Expand outlays for middle school physical education and sports programs by 84 percent.

Double the size of Boston Prep and ACC.

Quadruple the size of our adult ed programs.

Pay for a nearly sixfold expansion of our summer programs.

Create another 35 extended day kdg classes, raising the total number by 71 percent from 49 to 84 FTE.

Push outlays for library and audiovisual materials up by over 1,500 percent.

Establish another 33 AWC classes versus the 55 in place.

Offer sabbaticals to 125 teachers.

Set up another four Barron Assessment Centers.

Double the number of bus monitors.

Or give every teacher a $285 raise.

Source: Budget Office, Boston Public Schools.

academic remediation along with a social-cultural enrichment, including field trips, counseling and other social services.

In short, when evaluating Project Promise, you must look at what it costs the system as a whole, and then you have to ask yourself a couple of questions:

1. It would cost approximately $9 million to replicate Project Promise for the remaining 20 middle schools across the city. Is that the direction that the School Department wants to take?

2. Instead of continuing Project Promise, what else could be done with the money that would yield benefits equal to or greater than what was achieved at the Project Promise schools? Does the 46 percent differential in per pupil cost at the Timilty justify the increase in scores, or are there other alternatives? Does this represent the optimal use of financial resources?

Mr. Whall believed that in terms of cost-benefit analysis, the costs of Project Promise were

perhaps, too high for the benefits derived, and the benefits for the system could have been attained for less money. Or, that equal benefits could have been distributed more widely across the system by doing something for other schools. Of course, that raises the question of scattering your resources across the four winds instead of channeling them into one site. But that gets back to the question: can we afford to replicate Project Promise over the system as a whole, especially during the present period of budgetary constraints?

He also commented about the leadership of Ms. O'Neill.

> Part of Timilty's success has nothing to do with Project Promise, but is due to the leadership of Mary Grassa O'Neill. She is a very dynamic, very good administrator. In my assessment, she is capable of working minor miracles. She has the ability to instill enthusiasm, to communicate to her staff very clear-headed goals and how she wants them accomplished. So I think that leadership was very crucial to the success of the Timilty. Mary could have probably gotten the same results with less of an increase of money.

Ms. O'Neill's Response

Ms. O'Neill believed that Mr. Whall was making some incorrect interpretations of the available information. She also pointed out that Project Promise funds were not completely fungible:

> First of all, you must bear in mind that David Whall is the budget director, not a statistician or researcher. This is important, because the statistics are complex in this field, and an expert is required to interpret them. David says there was no material improvement in academic performance at the Timilty. He definitely is wrong. Moreover, he doesn't mention that all the funding for Project Promise is in grants; that is, everything is outside the "formula" that is used to compute the distribution of the budget among BPS schools. He makes it sound as though we're taking money away from other things that could be funded through grants, which we're not. Also, the $1.2 million he mentions was for 3 schools. The Timilty never got $1.2 million; we got $636,000.

Also involved in the controversy was a statistician from the Office of Research and Development, of the Division of Planning and Resource Allocation, of the Boston Public Schools. The statistician pointed out that Mr. Whall was comparing apples and oranges, and that, if he were to make his case appropriately, he would need to find a school that was comparable to the Timilty. Unfortunately, no such school existed in the Boston school system.

Questions

1. What is your assessment of the data available for Project Promise? What additional information would you like to have? How might it be obtained?

2. What is your assessment of the issues and concerns raised by Mr. Whall?

3. What is your assessment of Ms. O'Neill's and the statistician's responses to Mr. Whall? How might Mr. Whall reply to them?

4. Has Project Promise been a success at the Timilty? Elsewhere? Should it be expanded to other schools in the BPS? In the country?

Case 15–3

Massachusetts Housing Finance Agency[*]

Marvin Siflinger, Director of the Massachusetts Housing Finance Agency (MHFA), was evaluating the results of the State Housing Assistance for Rental Production (SHARP) program, one of several programs under the agency's auspices. SHARP, which had been in existence for only two years, had just completed its second "competitive round," and Mr. Siflinger felt that this was an opportune time to review the program's functioning. He was particularly interested in the system by which projects were selected for assistance, and questioned whether either the selection criteria that had been established and modified once, or the selection process itself, should be modified prior to the third competition.

Background

The Massachusetts Housing Finance Agency (MHFA) was created by a legislative mandate for the purpose of increasing and improving the supply of standard housing for Massachusetts residents. It was intended to focus particular attention on the needs of low income elderly, and other disadvantaged sectors of the population. The agency operated a variety of programs for homeowners and tenants, including mortgage assistance, loan arrangements, and interest subsidy payments for single- and multifamily housing.

Organizationally, the agency was a semi-autonomous arm of the state's Executive Office for Communities and Development (EOCD). The agency's Board of Directors was composed of nine community, housing, and financial representatives selected by the governor, plus two cabinet secretaries. The Board set overall policy and had veto power over virtually all agency activities and decisions. Because the MHFA was a semi-autonomous organization that functioned according to its own internal operating procedures, the state's role normally was limited to the involvement of its representatives on the Board of Directors, although on occasion it had exercised some discretionary authority over agency operations.

The MHFA staff consisted of approximately 200 people, many of whom had a background in banking, management, housing, architecture, and the real estate appraisal industry. An emphasis was placed on recruiting people with "real world experience" and technical expertise in the agency's line of business.

*This case was prepared by Lynn B. Jenkins under the supervision of Professor David W. Young. Copyright © by David W. Young.

History of the SHARP Program

The MHFA traditionally had served as a channel for federal subsidies, including both the "236/Rent Supplement" and "Section 8" programs. These programs were subsidy programs that provided assistance to developers of rental housing, particularly for low-income and elderly residents. They were administered by the federal Department of Housing and Urban Development (HUD). Both programs were exceedingly generous, providing what have been termed "deep" subsidies, and existed in an environment where cost concerns did not significantly interfere with development goals.

As the political and financial support for these programs waned, MHFA was forced not only to develop alternative financing arrangements and to take responsibility for projects remaining in the Section 8 "pipeline," but also to cope with overspending and other programmatic inefficiencies that had developed. SHARP grew out of this need.

The impetus for the SHARP program also came from the realization that without federal (HUD) assistance, no new rental housing would be produced in Massachusetts. Indeed, in one year alone, there was a projected shortage of 200,000 rental units in the state.

The SHARP program was created as part of the state's Comprehensive Housing Act. The SHARP legislation itself was extremely brief and vaguely written. The specific program that emerged was formulated, for the most part, by Joseph Flatley, Assistant Secretary of the EOCD, and Eleanor White, Chief of Operations of the MHFA.

Central to the thinking of SHARP's designers was the desire to dispel the politicized reputation that the MHFA had developed, and to install a fair, consistent system of project appraisal. Drawing on the recommendation of a Housing Task Force, Flatley and White agreed that SHARP should meet some basic criteria. Specifically, it should (*a*) operate on the basis of competitive funding rounds, (*b*) require developers to put up more cash and assume greater financial risk than had been required of them under HUD assistance programs, (*c*) reserve at least 25 percent of the units for low-income tenants, and (*d*) incorporate incentives to use the lowest amount of SHARP funds necessary. The SHARP program was substantially more risky than its predecessors, since it depended largely upon the internal strengths of its chosen developers and their projects. Therefore, as underwriters, the agency needed to be concerned about the extent to which projects were economically successful, which depended in large part on their ability to meet the demands of the market.

Determination of Subsidies

The need for rental housing subsidies existed independently of the 25 percent low-income component that SHARP required of its developers. That is, because of a mismatch between construction costs, financing costs, and market rental rates, even if developers provided only market-rate units—and no low-income units—they generally were unable to build "affordable" rental housing. The result was an absence of rental construction, leading to the previously cited shortage of units. Thus, the SHARP subsidy permitted not only the construction of low-income units but of rental units in general. As a result, since rent for low-income tenants was guaranteed by federal and state assistance programs, a developer's concern lay primarily with marketing the remaining 75 percent of the units.

To determine the maximum annual SHARP subsidy for a given year, the MHFA began with the estimated cost of producing a rental unit (of X number of bedrooms). It then calculated what it would cost the developer to finance construction at market interest rates, and recalculated it at a 5 percent rate. SHARP provided the difference between the two figures. In effect, then, SHARP was designed as a "shallow subsidy," to assist developments that could not be implemented by the private sector alone. For example, for a 2-bedroom unit that cost $60,000 to build, the Section 8 subsidy approached $8,000–$9,000 per year for certain developments; the SHARP subsidy, by contrast, might only provide $2,000–$2,200 per unit. Because it was a shallow subsidy program, SHARP required its developers to find supplemental means of ensuring their projects' viability.

In short, by reducing a developer's interest rate for project financing, SHARP lowered the effective cost of the mortgage loan and, in so doing, lowered the cost-based rent for *all* units to a level that local residents could afford to pay. State subsidies then further lowered the rent for the 25 percent low-income units that the MHFA required its developers to set aside.

Project Financing

In SHARP's first year of operations, the program received a $5 million appropriation from the state. This amount was increased to $13 million in the next year. In both years, the program supplemented its appropriation by raising funds through the sale of tax-exempt bonds to private investors. In addition to relying on the appeal of tax-exempt bonds, the MHFA used mortgage insurance, credit enhancement, and other "creative financing" strategies to make its bonds attractive to investors. The agency then translated the low interest rates it *paid* to its investors into below market interest rates it *charged* developers.

Projects selected for financing were awarded interest reduction subsidies for a maximum 15-year period, during which the subsidy was gradually diminished. Specific terms of both assistance and repayment were negotiated individually between the MHFA and each developer in accordance with the developer's projected cash flows. Importantly, though, the subsidy was not a grant, but a loan that was to be repaid once the project had been in operation for the 15 years (or less).

The Selection Process

SHARP selected its projects according to a set of firmly established guidelines. Once each year there was a "competition" in which developers submitted projects, competing with one another for SHARP assistance. Out of approximately 60 submissions in the first competition, 23 developments were chosen; there were 40 submissions in the second competition, and 13 were chosen.

Projects submitted to the competition were scored and ranked according to a complex set of criteria. In designing these selection criteria, the EOCD and the MHFA asked the question, "What are the critical elements that make a project viable?" The resulting process brought together a variety of professional perspectives on these elements.

In developing the criteria, the MHFA and the EOCD initially disagreed about the balance between financial and social factors in determining the program's operations, although the two agencies agreed from the outset that both sets of criteria were necessary. They eventually agreed to set in place a scoring system prefaced by a group of threshold requirements that established the minimum viability of the project as a real estate venture. Both social and financial criteria were incorporated into the subsequent ranking system, and "gates" and cross-checks ensured that high priority conditions were adequately met. "All other things being equal," said one MHFA executive, "we would like to meet these important social goals, but our primary concerns have to be those of the lender."

In the threshold evaluation, projects were measured in terms of their acceptability as a credit risk and a real estate transaction. These terms included: (1) the quality of the project design, (2) the site, (3) the experience record of the development team, (4) the management company, and (5) the marketability of the project.

Applications that passed the threshold review were distributed within the MHFA for more intensive evaluations by each of the agency's functional subdivisions:

- Design and Technical Department—site specifications and architectural plans.
- Site Evaluation Department—site, market, and community needs.
- Mortgage Department—quality and history of development team, community impact, project's readiness to close, and amount of SHARP subsidy required.
- Equal Opportunity Department—affirmative action conditions.
- Management Department—qualifications of development team and management company.

Detailed evaluation criteria are contained in Exhibit 1.

After the projects were scored and ranked, MHFA selected the highest ranked projects to receive subsidy awards, subject to consideration of two additional program objectives. Some of the selected projects should complement

EXHIBIT 1 SHARP Project Selection Criteria

Projects that passed the set of initial threshold guidelines were competitively scored to determine how well they met certain policy objectives of the SHARP program. This review covered the following objectives:

A. Development Quality Goals: 10 points each, maximum of 50 points. Projects must score a minimum of 30 points and have an acceptable design score in order to remain in the competition.
   1. Design—the quality of the proposed design, including life-cycle costs and the treatment of special environmental conditions.
   2. Development Team—the record and capacity of the development team.
   3. Site—the suitability of the proposed site for housing. The presence of or plans for necessary utilities and amenities. Zoning and site control.
   4. Management—the prospective manageability of the development, the quality of the management plan, and the experience and capacity of the management agent.
   5. Marketability—the likely ability of the units to be marketed at the proposed rents.

B. Overall Impact Goals: 10 points each, maximum of 40 points.
   1. Community impacts—projects with demonstrable impacts upon the community, in support of local policies. Such projects include those which would rehabilitate a critical building in a business district, encourage additional nearby development, or promote investment in a locally targeted revitalization district. Evidence of local support would include contributions to the project from the community. Projects should not encourage displacement. Projects would ideally increase the supply of affordable housing in areas suffering displacement.
   2. Meet housing needs—projects which best meet the overall housing needs of communities in which they will be located (i.e., units of a certain size).
   3. Affirmative action—SHARP encourages developers to provide housing and job opportunities to minorities. Applications which provide vigorous affirmative action efforts, beyond the minimum requirements considered during the threshold review, will be given special preference.
   4. Readiness to move to construction—the readiness of proposals to move quickly to construction. Evidence of readiness would include proper zoning for the proposal, advanced design documents, building permits, etc.

C. Minimal SHARP Subsidy Goal: 10 points. Projects which require less than the maximum permitted amount of SHARP subsidy may earn up to 10 additional points. This criterion is consistent with a desire to generate the greatest level of housing production for the amount of SHARP funds authorized by the Legislature.

Maximum Total Points = 100

efforts to revitalize specific urban neighborhoods, and there should also be a reasonable distribution of selected projects throughout the State.

Following selection of a proposal for SHARP funding, the developer was invited to submit a full mortgage application for MHFA review. At this level of review, the technical feasibility of the accepted loan, and the value and marketability of the completed housing were evaluated.

At this second level of review, both social and financial criteria were given careful consideration. When the MHFA and EOCD designed the scoring system, they established cross-references for priority conditions, such as site, development quality, and zoning. These criteria were evaluated in both the set of initial threshold requirements and in subsequent scoring sections by different departments. This provided an opportunity for various professional viewpoints to be expressed on the merits of a particular aspect of the project. For example, the Design and Technical Department and the Site Evaluation Department might have evaluated different but equally important aspects of a project's site.

According to Ms. White:

> The prime benefit of this strategy is that independent professional views are aired and the process remains open. Everyone on the staff knows what is going on, and the development teams understand the concept of the review process. The more eyes you have on a project, the more objective and defensible the review becomes.

After individual departments completed their reviews, the Mortgage Department studied the resulting ranking order. "It's a bit like grading on a curve," noted Ms. White.

> At this point, we could simply add up the scores, rank them, and fund from the top down . . . but we don't. Rather, the supervisory staff tries to flesh out discrepancies among the project scores, to make standards as uniform as possible. They ask: Did the scoring go properly? Did good projects fall out? Did bad ones rise?
>
> For example, Mr. Jones may have four projects in one competitive round. If he has been given different scores by the Management and Development Departments for certain criteria, the reasons for these differences need to be documented. It may be, for example, that he has experience in inner city rehabilitation but not in new construction, and the differences may therefore make sense. On the other hand, it may be that different individuals have done the scoring and may have judged him differently. Then, top management must be sure that there is consistency among the reviewers.

Following the departmental scoring, Mr. Siflinger, Ms. White, and selected Board members visited each of the proposed development sites to gain yet another angle on the project's desirability. Then, according to Ms. White:

> We return to discuss the scoring with the Mortgage Department and other departmental staff. Evaluations are finely combed for inconsistencies. For example, in a given round, three inner city sites were proposed in one city. Two of them scored a '7' on a particular item, and the third scored a '5.' Yet the latter seemed to be better qualified. Why the discrepancy?
>
> Ninety-nine percent of the time we (senior management, Board members, and the MHFA staff) come to a meeting of the minds on project scores, on problems such as this . . . through a good deal of negotiation, persuasion, discussion. In the 1 percent of the time we can't agree, Marvin and I can overrule the staff's evaluations, though we only do so when we have very compelling reasons to believe that their analysis is incorrect. The Board votes on the results and they, in turn, can overrule us.

Developers were permitted to challenge the scores they received, beginning at the level of the Mortgage Department and rising to the upper administrative levels of the agency, if necessary. As of the second competition, however, not one developer had failed to agree with the staff's score after all challenges had taken place.

According to Ms. White:

> Our atmosphere of open discussion and documentation of results is essential to maintaining the program's credibility and workability. The truth is that a group of individuals—developers, architects, planners, financial analysts—could probably sit around a table and come up with a list of projects that looks quite similar to the results of this elaborate scoring system. We know what kinds of qualities make a development successful . . . but we didn't want to make decisions behind closed doors. If you have a system that is open and fair, and if you show applicants the reasons for the weakness of their proposals and work with them to improve for the next round, they understand that you're not just being arbitrary.

Political Issues

Political issues for SHARP assumed a variety of forms. One was that of community opposition to SHARP-assisted developments. In order to minimize such opposition, the MHFA advised developers to talk with local communities and their leaders before proceeding very far with their plans. As part of the site review process, the MHFA solicited the views of the mayor, chief executive, or selectmen of a project's locality. According to James Power of the MHFA Mortgage Department, in the second competitive round the MHFA had a 95 percent response rate from official community representatives, and letters from citizens and community groups (both favoring and opposing development) had increased manyfold over the first round when there was minimal community participation. "It is not so easy to bulldoze communities any more," said Mr. Power. "If a project doesn't have sufficient political support, it will have trouble all along the way."

With this understanding, the MHFA encouraged developers to balance their interests with those of the businesses and residents in their prospective communities. Difficulties arose when, according to Mr. Power, "the business community wanted to see more multifamily housing, and the residents didn't want more growth in their neighborhoods." However, the MHFA—through its explicit procedures—was seemingly able to keep most political pressure at the level of "small-piece" politics. Said Mr. Power, "we try to help people to respect the system, and encourage cooperation with our goals."

When a project was politically and socially attractive, but financially weak, a second type of political issue arose. An example of this dilemma was a project in an economically depressed area, which had a minority development team and strong political support "from the local politicians all the way up to the EOCD and the legislature," but was deficient in terms of its architectural plans and its proposed rental scale.

According to Ms. White:

> Everybody, including the MHFA, wanted this project to succeed, but it was simply not financially feasible. Marvin met with the EOCD, people from the

governor's office, and the local elected officials—and told them very honestly that the project didn't meet the minimum standards, that it was not a prudent financial risk. They accepted the staff's recommendation, and most of the political pressure was diffused.

The Board could have overruled us, but the last thing that it wants is a foreclosure. That's an embarrassment for everyone. So we worked with the project, and advised them of improvements. The developer reentered the competition this round, and his prospects are vastly improved.

The Future

Given SHARP's popularity in the legislature and the support it enjoyed from developers, there appeared to be no immediate possibility of major changes in the agency's operations. However, central to Mr. Siflinger's thinking as he reflected on the SHARP program's evaluation criteria and process, was the need to address the question of the kinds of changes that might be made to the project selection system to improve its functioning. He had approximately six months prior to the beginning of the third competition.

Questions

1. What are the key elements of SHARP's strategy?

2. What are the incentives for developers? Please be as specific as you can: If you were a developer, how would you make money on a SHARP project as compared to other potential projects?

3. What is your assessment of the project selection system? How does it help SHARP accomplish its goals?

4. What changes, if any, should Mr. Siflinger make to the project selection system?

16

Management Control Systems in Context

In Chapter 1 we positioned management control between strategy formulation and task control, and briefly discussed the structure and process of a management control system. In later chapters we fleshed out the details of both structure and process, devoting Chapter 8 to structure, and chapters 9 to 15 to the phases of the management control process. We preceded those chapters with a discussion of several of the building blocks needed to understand the financial information that lies at the heart of a management control system: the nature of nonprofit organizations (Chapter 2), financial accounting (Chapter 3), financial management (Chapter 4), full and differential cost accounting (Chapters 5 and 6), and pricing (Chapter 7).

The value of these building blocks, and the concepts of structure and process that form the basis of management control systems, is in their application to real-world situations and problems. The ultimate goal is to develop management control systems that facilitate the improved operation of nonprofit organizations. Doing so requires assessing how a management control system fits into its broader organizational context.

We begin this chapter with a very brief summary of the key characteristics of good management control. We then return to the planning and control framework that we discussed in Chapter 1, and place the management control system into it in a more concrete way than we did in that chapter. Finally, we position management control in an organizational context in which it is one of seven organizational processes; this perspective is consistent with much of the shift that is taking place in many organizations toward a focus on cross-functional processes.

Key Characteristics of Good Management Control

In most of our chapters, we had in mind an organization of at least moderate size, say, one with a hundred or more employees and several million dollars of annual operating expenses (smaller organizations can operate successfully with fewer formal management control techniques, although they no doubt will find the basic concepts underlying these techniques helpful). In general, a nonprofit organization of this size that is performing in accordance with the concepts and approaches we have discussed displays several important characteristics:

1. It has a strong governing body. Some members of this body spend considerable time examining program and budget proposals before they are submitted to the full board. Members of the governing body also analyze formal reports on performance and informal communications from clients and others on how well the organization is performing.

2. In performing its functions, the governing body is careful not to infringe on the prerogatives of management. The governing body ensures that the chief executive has full authority to execute policies, and that his or her decisions are supported by the board. The board also ensures that the CEO's compensation is appropriate.

3. Operating managers have the authority to use their judgment in running their responsibility centers and in accomplishing results. However, they are required to operate within somewhat closer budgetary and other constraints than is customary in most for-profit organizations.

4. The control system contains two principal account classifications, one structured in terms of programs and the other in terms of organizational responsibility.

5. Except in unusual circumstances, such as with public goods, the organization charges its clients for the services they receive, sometimes through third-party payers. In this way, the organization generates a monetary measure of the quantity of its outputs, and motivates managers to be concerned about the cost and quantity of services they provide.

6. The unit of pricing is made as specific as feasible because this provides a better measure of the quantity of services rendered and a better basis for decisions on the allocation of resources.

7. Responsibility centers are selected based on senior management's assessment of the resources that a manager controls. Senior management attempts to hold managers responsible only for those resources over which they exert a reasonable amount of control. In general, profit centers are desirable, even when the center "sells" its services internally; in this case,

senior management makes sure that an appropriate set of transfer prices is developed to facilitate the control process.

8. Unless the organization continues with the same activities year after year, it has a strategic planning process that it uses for generating ideas for new programs, analyzing these ideas, reaching decisions on them, and incorporating new or revised programs into an overall plan.

9. Budgeting is viewed as an essential aspect of the management control process because the budget specifies how activities are to be conducted in the coming year. The annual operating budget is derived from the approved programs, and responsibility for the ongoing management of each program is assigned to individual responsibility centers.

10. The organization has a measurement and reporting process that helps to assure that actual spending is kept within the limits specified in the approved budget, unless there are compelling reasons to depart from budgeted amounts. At the same time, the organization has a procedure for revising the budget should circumstances require it.

11. Senior management devotes considerable attention to developing satisfactory output measures. It recognizes that although many output measures are of limited validity, they are better than nothing. As a result, there is a never-ending search for new, more valid measures. At the same time, the limitations of existing output measures are recognized.

12. Despite the fact that many people, especially professionals, dislike the idea of accountability, which is associated with the measurement of outputs, senior management proceeds with such measurements. All levels of management, including senior management, are involved in the monitoring of performance.

13. Managers of each responsibility center receive regular comparisons of actual expenses and revenues with planned expenses and revenues. Reports containing this information are made available in a timely fashion, and are designed so as to highlight significant information. Where appropriate, variances between planned and actual results are isolated by cause: selling price, volume, mix, factor price, and efficiency.

14. In addition to an operations evaluation, senior management undertakes a systematic evaluation of the effectiveness of the organization's programs.

15. Senior management continually satisfies itself that the management control system is consistent with its own management style. It holds meetings with line managers and other subordinates to discuss how information can be used, and expects them to hold similar meetings with their subordinates.

The Management Control Context

Given these criteria for good management control, we now can return to the framework that we laid out in Chapter 1, and use it to put a management control system into a somewhat broader context. Recall from Chapter 1 that we described management control as lying between strategy formulation and task control. Strategy formulation is the process that an organization follows to determine its broad goals and the activities it will undertake to achieve them. From this flows strategic planning, in which the organization selects, modifies, or discontinues its specific programs. Strategic planning is the first phase of the management control process.

Many of the activities that take place in conjunction with the management control effort require the completion of specific tasks: issuing paychecks, ordering inventory, scheduling classes, sending out bills, making appointments for patients, and so forth. These are task control activities. Task control, while generally not considered to be very glamorous, is needed if an organization is to run smoothly on a day-to-day basis.

The relationship among these three activities can perhaps best be seen by using the example of personnel. Strategy formulation is concerned with broad personnel policies, such as whether all faculty are to have Ph.D.s or their equivalent, or whether all physicians are to be board-certified or board-eligible. Management control, by contrast, accepts personnel policies as given, and focuses on the way responsibility centers are designed to encourage behavior that is in the best interest of the organization, including establishing the bases for annual personnel evaluations. Task control is concerned with making sure that annual evaluation forms are distributed and collected in a timely way, that reviews take place on schedule, and that paychecks are issued when due. All of these activities—strategy formulation, management control, and task control—are in some way concerned with personnel. The same can be said of other aspects of the organization, such as clients.

In general, these activities are carried out by different groups of people. Senior management is concerned with strategy formulation and the *design* of the management control system, for example. Senior management also provides the impetus for periodic reviews of operations and programs to make sure that they are consistent with the organization's goals. Middle (or line) managers, by contrast, work within the constraints of the management control system to propose programs and budgets, and to take actions that help the organization move toward its goals. Staff people (and, increasingly, computers) tend to be responsible for task control activities, although usually within the constraints that have been established by the management control system.

Role of Senior Management

This latter point is quite important. No task control activity happens by itself. Rather, a design and implementation effort is needed to make sure that it works in accordance with the organization's needs and is consistent with the management control system. In general, the design of task control activities is the responsibility of either senior or middle management. Indeed, if senior and middle managers do not become involved in the design effort, a set of task control activities is likely to emerge that is not consistent with the organization's best interests. When this happens, senior and middle managers (depending on the size of the organization) may find themselves engaged in actually carrying out task control activities, which is a poor use of their time and takes them away from their more important managerial activities.

More generally, a prime condition for a successful management control or task control system is the active support and involvement of senior management. Ideally, senior management support should come from the chief executive officer. However, if the chief executive is primarily involved in policymaking and relations with the outside world, then the necessary support can come from the principal deputy who in fact exercises most management authority. Without the support of one of these top people, neither activity is likely to work well.

Senior management's support should include more than mere acquiescence. Although its time is precious, it nevertheless must be willing to allocate a significant amount of time and attention to the development of good management control and task control systems. It must understand the objectives and general concepts of the proposed system well enough to see its benefits, and it must explain to operating managers how the system will help them as individuals, and help the organization as a whole. If the system does not function well, or if roadblocks arise during a design (or redesign) effort, senior management must be prepared to listen to the conflicting points of view and then make a decision that moves the system in the right direction.

| **Example** | According to George Turcott, then-associate director of the U.S. Bureau of Land Management, and the person responsible for the introduction of its highly regarded management-by-objectives system, "The 'top dog' has got to get involved. Don't let the assistant director for administration do it. You have to get the line director or the associate to do it. It works. You've also got to have due process. You've got to have management reasonableness the whole way through and be a gentle tyrant."[1] |

One way for senior management to convey its support for the management and task control systems is to assure that operating managers are involved in the systems' design. If such involvement inhibits operating managers' output and hinders their ability to meet performance and evaluation measures, they will have no real incentive to participate. Thus, senior management must "invest" in the system design effort by allowing operating managers such time.

[1]Paraphrased from an interview reported in *GAO Review,* Fall 1981, pp. 23–27.

EXHIBIT 16–1 Information Requirements by Type of Activity

Information Requirements	Type of Activity		
	Strategy Formulation	*Management Control*	*Task Control*
Structured	Client forecasting ROI analysis	Budget analysis (engineered) Short-term forecasting	Accounts receivable General ledger
Semistructured	Merger and acquisition analysis Marketing analysis	Variance analysis Budget preparation (discretionary)	Scheduling and billing Cash management
Unstructured	Product line planning	Client/case mix analysis	Cost analysis

Role of Personal Computers

Widespread availability and use of personal computers has done much to change the nature of management control and task control systems in many nonprofit organizations. The ability either to gather and process data within a single responsibility center, or, via a client server, to access data for analysis at the responsibility center level, has done much to assist managers to obtain management control information in a more timely and action-oriented manner than had been possible previously. Similarly, the availability of accounting and database software has made it easy for even a small organization to have a relatively sophisticated set of accounting reports and other management control reports. Moreover, computing technology offers several advantages, such as lower cost information, quicker introduction of new applications, and more rapid processing turnaround (i.e., from data entry to report preparation).

At the same time that personal computers provide managers with potentially easier and less-expensive access to good management control information, they have also created their own set of managerial issues. These issues arise in the context of a set of information requirements that, for most organizations, can be classified into three categories: structured, semistructured, and unstructured. Each category can be further subdivided in terms of activities corresponding to strategic planning, management control, and task control, The resulting information requirements are shown in Exhibit 16–1.

As Exhibit 16–1 suggests, an organization's information requirements vary depending on the task being undertaken. Specifically, as one goes from the top right corner, where central computers generally are most appropriate, both down and to the left, the value of a personal computer (either alone or in conjunction with a client server) increases. That is, the more strategic the analyses that are undertaken, and the more unstructured the information requirements, the greater the value of a PC.

As a nonprofit organization grows in size and sophistication, its senior management ordinarily finds itself engaging in more management control and strategic planning activities using relatively unstructured information. The flexibility and instant turnaround time if a PC allow managers to play with assumptions, tease them out, and analyze the resulting implications. Generally, in the strategic and unstructured types of analyses, the greater flexibility and rapid turnaround time of a PC outweigh the power advantage of a central computer.

The Broader Organizational Context

As we have discussed in earlier chapters, and as the cases at the end of this chapter illustrate, the management control system cannot be viewed in isolation. Rather, a management control system, by necessity, is part of—and is influenced by—an organization's broader set of managerial activities.[2]

As indicated above, some of these other activities include strategy formulation, since an organization's strategy can be expected to influence its financial and programmatic goals. Other activities relate to conflict resolution, since occasionally organizational (as distinct from interpersonal) conflict can arise concerning matters such as the best programs to adopt, the best approach to client management, or the selection of programmatic objectives. Still other activities relate to the ways that an organization's senior management uses compensation packages and other mechanisms to motivate its employees in an attempt to attain goal congruence.

Beyond these activities, senior management uses recruitment, training, bonuses, praise, promotion, and, at the extreme, severance in an effort to maintain the organization's culture, and it gives considerable thought to how authority and influence flow within the organization, and how that flow affects the way that clients are "managed" within the organization.

Overall, there is a need to attain a *fit* among these various activities. To attain this fit, senior management must address a wide variety of matters. It must, for example, assure itself that the strategy formulation process is addressing the organization's environment, including regulatory and competitive forces. Within strategy formulation, it must be sure that the more specific strategic planning process is leading to programs that support the full range of services needed to achieve the organization's goals.

Other managerial activities tend to flow from these two, but, in many instances, also can influence them. For example, some of the decisions that senior management makes in strategy formulation will depend upon the kind of

---

[2]For a discussion of these activities in the context of integrated delivery systems in health care, see David W. Young and Diana Barrett, "Managing Clinical Integration in Integrated Delivery Systems: A Framework for Action," *Hospital & Health Services Administration* 42, no. 2 (Summer 1997).

information it receives from the management control system. Similarly, depending on its design, the motivation process can encourage professionals to propose new programmatic endeavors, or, more generally, to act in the best interest of the organization overall.

Example

Christine Letts and her colleagues discuss the importance of linking human resource management, benchmarking, quality processes, and product development in nonprofits. They claim that focusing on these processes will assist nonprofits to "carry out their activities in a more businesslike fashion," and will result in the potential to achieve the status of a "high performance organization."[3]

In sum, and as Exhibit 16–2 indicates, beyond assuring that the organization has a good management control system, senior management needs to make sure that there is:

- A *strategy formulation* process that assesses opportunities and risks, and that chooses realistic directions and goals for the organization.

- An *authority and influence* process that fosters collaborative decision making when necessary.

- A *motivation* process that is providing appropriate signals and rewarding people for behavior that is in the best interest of the organization.

- A set of *conflict management* processes that addresses the many kinds of conflict that can arise in the course of achieving the organization's strategy.

- A *cultural maintenance* process that helps to create a set of common values across the organization.

- A *client management* process that helps the organization to attract the kinds of clients that are consistent with its strategy and to provide them with appropriate services at appropriate times.

A list of the kinds of questions that senior management needs to ask itself in conjunction with each of these cross-functional processes is contained in Exhibit 16–3.

As this list indicates, for a nonprofit organization to achieve its strategy, senior management must take action on several related fronts: planning, organizational, and informational. Not only is each of these fronts important in and of itself, but, perhaps most importantly, as the lines in Exhibit 16–2 indicate, the various activities must *fit* with one another. As such, they both reinforce each other and, collectively, help to assure the organization that its clients are receiving appropriate, timely, coordinated, and cost-effective services.[4]

[3]Christine W. Letts, William P. Ryan, and Allen S. Grossman, *High Performance Nonprofit Organizations: Managing Upstream for Greater Impact* (New York: John Wiley & Sons, 1998).
[4]For additional discussion of these ideas, see David W. Young, *Leadership Action: The Seven Levers of Successful CEOs* (Cambridge, MA: The Crimson Press Curriculum Center, 2000).

EXHIBIT 16–2 **Cross-Functional Processes in an Organization**

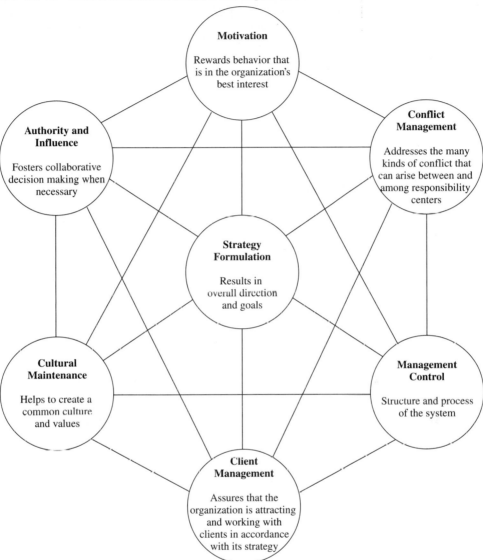

EXHIBIT 16–3 Questions Concerning Cross-Functional Processes

Strategy Formulation
- What sorts of analyses are carried out and by whom?
- Are decisions well formulated, with significant senior management involvement, or a result of individual groups acting independently?
- To what extent does the organization's strategy reflect its values?

Client Processing
- What is the flow of clients through the organization? For instance:
  - > How does a client initially come into contact with the organization?
  - > What decisions are made about how that client will (or will not) be served? Who makes those decisions?
  - > What decisions are made concerning a client leaving the organization? By whom?
- Is care delivered at the best site and by the most appropriate person?

Cultural Maintenance
- What are the principal values of the organization? That is, what does the organization see as its relatively unchanging cultural characteristics?
- How do the organization's programs fit with these values?
- How are the values reinforced and maintained through activities such as recruitment, training, bonuses, promotions, severance, and others?

Authority and Influence
- What does the organizational structure look like?
- What is the flow of authority and influence?
- Does the process reflect the fundamental management and structural changes made as part of the strategy formulation process? Does it foster collaborative decision making?
- What formal mechanisms exist for professionals to influence decision making in the organization? Do these help the organization move toward its strategy?

Motivation
- How are people rewarded for doing good work?
- If there is an incentive compensation system, is it part of the budget formulation process?
- How deeply into the organization does the incentive-compensation system extend? Does it cover paraprofessionals, for example?

Conflict Management
- Where are the potential sources of conflict within the organization? Who typically is involved?

- How is the conflict resolved? That is, what sorts of formal mechanisms are in place (such as permanent or ad hoc committees) to manage the conflict?

Management Control
Strategic Planning
- How and by whom are decisions made to begin new programmatic efforts? To change or drop existing programs?
- Does the process lead to programs that reinforce the organization's strategy? To what extent do programs reflect the strategy?
- How are requests for capital and programs addressed? Do accepted requests move the organization toward its strategy?

Budget Formulation
- Who participates in formulating the organization's annual budget? What is the timetable?
- How does the budget relate to programs?
- What kinds of responsibility centers are in place? What kinds of "drivers" are being used to build the budget? If there is cross-subsidization among programs and responsibility centers, how are the subsidies determined?
- Have transfer prices been established? If so, are responsibility center managers allowed to purchase from outside the system if they think the transfer prices are too high?

Financial Measurement and Reporting
- How are costs and revenues measured and reported to key managers? Are people held responsible for the resources that they control?
- Does the process measure fixed and variable costs for different mixes of clients in different programs, and compute the relevant variances?
- Do the resulting reports help managers to assess their financial performance against the budget in meaningful ways?

Program Measurement and Reporting
- How are programmatic results measured (e.g., quality, client satisfaction)?
- How do program and financial measurement and reporting relate to each other?
- What are the organization's key success factors, and how are these incorporated into the reports? Are these results linked to the motivation process?

Suggested Additional Readings

Andrews, Kenneth R. *The Concept of Corporate Strategy*. Homewood, IL: Dow Jones–Irwin Inc., 1980.

Anthony, Robert N. *The Management Control Function*. Boston: Harvard Business School Press, 1988.

Drucker, Peter. *Management Challenges for the 21st Century*. New York: Harper Collins Publishing, Inc., 1999.

Hamel, Gary, and C.K. Prahalad. *Competing for the Future*. Boston: Harvard Business School Press, 1994.

Hammer, Michael, and James Champy. *Reengineering the Corporation*. New York: Harper Collins, 1993.

Herzberg, Frederick. "One More Time: How Do You Motivate Employees?" *Harvard Business Review OnPoint Enhanced Edition*, January–February 2000.

Kaplan, Robert S., and David P. Norton. *The Balanced Scorecard*. Boston: Harvard Business School Press, 1996.

Kotter, John P. *What Leaders Really Do*. Boston: Harvard Business School Press, 1999.

Labovitz, George, and Victor Rosansky. *The Power of Alignment: How Great Companies Stay Centered and Accomplish Great Things*. New York: John Wiley & Sons, Inc., 1997.

Letts, Christine W., William P. Ryan, and Allen S. Grossman. *High Performance Nonprofit Organizations: Managing Upstream for Greater Impact*. New York: John Wiley & Sons, 1998.

Markides, Constantinos C. *All the Right Moves*. Boston: Harvard Business School Press, 2000.

McKenna, Regis. *Real Time: Preparing for the Age of the Never Satisfied Customer*. Boston: Harvard Business School Press, 1997.

Nelson, Bob. *1001 Ways to Energize Employees*. :Workman Publishing, 1997.

Porter, Michael E. "What Is Strategy?" *Harvard Business Review*, November–December 1996.

Schein, Edgar H. *Organizational Culture and Leadership*, 2nd. ed. San Francisco: Jossey Bass Publishers, 1992.

Smart, Bradford D. *Topgrading*. Englewood Cliffs, NJ: Prentice Hall, Inc., 1999.

Unseem, Michael. *The Leadership Moment: Nine True Stories of Triumph and Disaster and Their Lessons for Us All*. New York: Random House, 1998.

Welch, Jack, with John A. Byrne. *Jack: Straight from the Gut.* New York: Warner Business Books, 2001.

Young, David W., and Sheila M. McCarthy. *Managing Integrated Delivery Systems: A Framework for Action.* Chicago: Health Administration Press, 1999.

Case 16–1

Commonwealth Business School*

IT [Information Technology] is great, and we have a decided comparative advantage. We should have an MBA Program in IT or MIS or whatever, just as we have one in PM [Public Management] and HCM [Health Care Management]. That would be a great move, and would add to our cadre of specialized programs which, in turn, would help to distinguish us as the MBA Program that allows you, the student, to select from several foci where we have expertise and distinction. That could quite easily put us on the map and do so soon.

To make all this work, however, the dean's office needs to focus resources on niche programs and concentrations rather than on the general MBA program. Moreover, students in the General Program must be asked to choose a focus (niche program or concentration). Until this shift in both resources and policy takes place, such that the niche programs can grow and prosper, we'll continue to struggle strategically.

Dexter Yardley, Professor of Management Control

I'm pleased with our progress on concentrations. We have moved aggressively to implement a new MSIM [Master of Science in Investment Management], a new marketing concentration, and perhaps very soon, a new finance concentration. We've hired a new Entrepreneurship person who is going great guns and we're looking for more people in that area. And we're trying to find and hire a top-flight PM person. Judy [Lowell, Director of the Career Center] and the Career Center have been focusing very hard on how to leverage opportunities for concentrators. In terms of resources, the budgets for our specialty programs have risen faster than in any area—and a significant number of our faculty hires were made to support the development of strong concentrations.

I can understand how you might get a different impression from looking only at the small budget that Arnie [Cotler, Director of the Health Care Management

---

*This case was prepared by Professor David W. Young, based on an organization that wishes to remain anonymous. Copyright © by David W. Young.

Program] controls—but these are the realities from the perspective of the overall school budget. I look forward to the day when every one of our MBA students can claim a concentration and receive an equally high level of support. I agree with you that we are not all that we want to be, but we have gone farther faster to develop our concentrated sources of strength in a shorter period of time than I can remember.

I do understand that the workload and management structure issues that you have identified haven't moved as fast as the resources have shifted, and that we need to move there as well. I see the workload issues as being especially critical at this time. The ideas you presented some time ago to the FPC [Faculty Policy Committee] are very relevant to the kinds of changes Joan [Hammond, Associate Dean for Graduate Programs] now talks about. Eventually, we may mature to the point where we can develop the kind of decentralized management structure you also hope for. I think it will be some time before we (and the University) can go there however.

James Malone, Professor of Management and Associate Dean for Operations

The issues being surfaced by Professors Yardley and Malone were on the minds of many faculty in Commonwealth Business School (CBS). Recently, CBS had updated its strategic plan and had shifted the focus from departments to programs. In particular, the school's strategic thinking was now largely about the kinds of programs it should offer to the marketplace, rather than the composition of its departments. Professor Yardley continued:

It's clear from the [program review] process we followed last past year that most students do not buy departments when they come here; they buy programs. However, experience in many other organizations has shown that if we're to be successful in implementing our strategic plans, this shift in strategic thinking needs to be matched with a shift in our management control system (MCS). In our case, the MCS must become program- rather than department-oriented. This is not to diminish the role of departments in the school's infrastructure. They clearly are important as faculty "homes" and as sources of intellectual inspiration. Moreover, when tenure is under consideration, a faculty member's performance generally is assessed by his or her peers in *departments* in other business schools, not by programs. Thus, a program orientation does not imply a reduction in the importance of departments to faculty development, but rather a reorientation of our thinking about how resources are allocated within the school.

At present, however, the school's control system has departments as the main focus, rather than programs. This means that program managers frequently must resort to begging to get a department to hire or make available a faculty member to teach in a particular program. To succeed in a niche program/concentration strategy we must give program/concentration managers resources and let them drive decision making in the departments rather than the other way around.

Professor Yardley had prepared a memorandum for consideration by the school's Faculty Policy Committee (FPC), on which Professor Malone served as a member. Yardley's memo outlined the proposed characteristics of the re-oriented MCS. In particular, it suggested several changes in the way budgets were formulated and faculty workloads were determined within the school. It suggested a MCS with the following characteristics:

1. *Profit Centers.* Programs and departments would be profit centers. All programs would be expected to earn surpluses or break even, whereas departments would be considered successful if they broke even. The system could tolerate deficits occasionally, but not as regular occurrences.

2. *Revenue Computation.* A program's revenue would be computed on the basis of credit units purchased of its course offerings. Since the school was a discretionary expense center in the university, the "revenue" per credit unit would be determined by dividing the school's total budget by the total credit units used by students for the entire academic year. This would assure that all of the school's budget was assigned to programs. A department's revenue would be determined by the sum of (*a*) the "sale" of its faculty members to programs (see below), (*b*) its grant revenues, and (*c*) its alumni and other contributions. Some of the revenue would be taxed to support the school's overhead (see below).

3. *Annual Program Budgets.* Each program's annual revenue budget would be established in May based on anticipated enrollments in its courses for the upcoming academic year. It would be allowed to spend no more than 25 percent of this budgeted amount between July 1 and September 30. Each program's budget would be adjusted in September based on actual enrollments in its fall courses and projections for spring courses. The program would be allowed to spend no more than 35 percent of its budget between October 1 and January 31. A third budget adjustment would take place in January based on actual enrollments in spring courses, and a program would be allowed to spend another 30 percent of its budget between February 1 and May 31. The final budget adjustment would take place in May based on enrollment in summer courses. A program could spend the remaining 10 percent of its budget during the month of June.

4. *Annual Department Budgets.* Department revenue budgets would be computed in a similar way to program budgets, using transfer prices (see below). They would be subject to the same percentage spending limitations as programs.

5. *Tax.* Programs would pay a "tax" that was a combination of a fixed amount each year plus a percent of their tuition and grant revenue. Departments would not pay a fixed annual amount, but they would pay the same percent tax as programs on any grants they received. Alumni and other unrestricted contributions received by either programs or departments would not be taxed.

6. *Financial Aid.* Programs would provide their own financial aid.

7. *Use of Tax Revenue.* The tax revenue would be used to pay for the school's overhead (mainly to provide partial support for the dean's office expenses),

to support the doctoral program, and to support the school's research program. Among other activities, the research program would provide staff to assist faculty with managing existing grants and applying for new ones.

8. *Doctoral Program.* A portion of each year's total tax revenues would be used to support the Doctoral Program (which did not earn tuition revenue in the normal way and had very small classes). Once the annual amount of support had been determined, however, the Doctoral Program would operate in the same way as any other program (i.e., as a profit center, responsible for achieving a surplus or breakeven operation). The same approach would be followed for research and service (see below).

9. *Research Program.* A portion of each year's total tax revenues would be used to support the Research Program (which did not earn tuition revenue). Once the annual amount of support had been determined, the Research Program would operate in the same way as any other program (i.e., as a profit center, responsible for achieving a surplus or breakeven operation).

10. *Tax Formula.* The tax formula (both the fixed amount and the percent rate) would be determined in the first year of the new control system. Tax revenues thus would grow as programs grew in size, and as tuition rates increased. Any change in the fixed proportion of a program's tax, or in the tax *rate* used for programs and departments, would require approval by a majority of the school's voting faculty.

11. *Transfer Prices.* Programs (including the Doctoral, Research, and Service Programs) would "purchase" faculty resources from departments using transfer prices. Within limits, department chairs (DCs) would set each faculty member's transfer price in accordance with his or her salary and the demand for his or her services.[1] A faculty member's transfer price might differ for different programs, depending on the type of course, the expected enrollment, the amount of coordination required, and so forth. DCs would be expected to cover the full cost of their faculty by "selling" them to programs, research projects, or service activities.

12. *Staffing Decisions.* A program director (PD) who was unsatisfied with the value of the services being offered by a department (e.g., the quality of a faculty member's teaching compared to the transfer price for his or her services), would negotiate with the appropriate DCs for the assignment of another faculty member or a lowering of the transfer price. if the results of these negotiations were not acceptable to the PD, he or she would be allowed to hire adjunct faculty to teach the courses in question.

---

[1] In the early years of the new MCS, the transfer price would be established at a different rate for each rank (full professor, associate professor, or assistant professor). Ultimately, however, the rate would be determined as described above.

13. *Service Activities.* Programs would purchase faculty for their PSCs [Program Steering Committees] at rates negotiated with the appropriate DCs. The dean's office would use the Service Program budget to "purchase" faculty time for various school-wide service activities. If the service activity were one to which the faculty member was elected, the dean's office would use the average transfer price that had been negotiated between the DC and the PDs.

14. *Faculty Workloads.* Faculty workload for a 10-month contract consisted of 189 days, computed as follows: One year = 365 days. Weekends = 104 days. Paid holidays = 12 days. Paid vacation = 20 days. Summer = 40 days. Available time = $365 - (104 + 12 + 20 + 40) = 189$ days. Thus, each faculty member on a 10 month contract would be required to "sell" 189 days a year to programs. DCs, in consultation with each of their faculty members, would determine their daily rates.

15. *Course Offerings.* Programs would be allowed to offer courses of any size enrollment they wished, including small seminars. For example, they might use a large enrollment course to subsidize one or more small enrollment courses. They might also negotiate different transfer prices for courses that made different demands on a faculty member. For example, a small enrollment course that a faculty member had taught many times presumably would have a lower transfer price than a large-enrollment course that a faculty member was teaching for the first time.

16. *Financial Management.* Programs and departments would be expected to manage their financial affairs in accordance with the profit center concept. Any surpluses earned would be carried forward into the next year, and accumulate. Programs could use their surpluses in ways that supported their goals and objectives. Departments that accumulated sufficient surpluses could use them to support faculty research (outside of the Research Program) and in other ways that supported their goals and objectives.

17. *Budget Formulation and Approval.* Each PSC would be required to approve its program's budget each year, and to sign off on any changes made during the year as enrollments fluctuated. The budget could be used to provide financial aid, support small course offerings, assist with faculty research, purchase equipment, cover a deficit in a year of low enrollments, or help to support a "sister" program that was in financial difficulty. Programs also could combine their surplus resources with departments to support the research of a particular faculty member.

An Example

An example of how this approach would work is contained in Exhibit 1. As this exhibit indicates, there are six levels of detail. The lowest level of detail

EXHIBIT 1   Management Control System Reports (All Numbers are Hypothetical)

Level 6—Faculty Detail: Department of Accounting

Faculty Member A

Salary (includes fringes) $80,000
Average TP per day $423

Activities	No. Days	Rate	Total Cost	Under Grad	F-T MBA	P-T MBA	Exec MBA	HCM MBA	PM MBA	MIS MBA	Entrepr. MBA	Doctoral	Research	Service	Total
									Purchases by Programs						
Teach 12 classes in UG121	12	$500	$ 6,000	$ 6,000											
Teach 12 classes in UG323	12	$500	$ 6,000	$ 6,000											
GS710 day section	28	$500	$14,000		$14,000										
GS710 evening section	28	$423	$11,852			$11,852									
Teach small elective eve. cours	28	$400	$11,200							$11,200					
Serve on school committee	10	$423	$ 4,233											$4,233	
Serve on Undergrad Committee	9	$423	$ 3,810	$ 3,810											
Coordinate UG221	12	$423	$ 5,079	$ 5,079											
Research	50	$423	$21,164										$21,164		
Totals	189		$83,338	$20,889	$14,000	$11,852	$0	$0	$0	$11,200	$0	$0	$21,164	$4,233	$83,338
Surplus (Deficit)			$ 3,338												

Faculty Member B

Salary (includes fringes) $90,000
Average TP per day $476

Activities	No. Days	Rate	Total Cost	Under Grad	F-T MBA	P-T MBA	Exec MBA	HCM MBA	PM MBA	MIS MBA	Entrepr. MBA	Doctoral	Research	Service	Total
									Purchases by Programs						
Teach UG221	28	$476	$13,333	$13,333											
Teach UG221	28	$476	$13,333	$13,333											
Teach GS710 Day section	28	$476	$13,333		$13,333										
Teach doctoral seminar	28	$476	$13,333									$13,333			
Serve on Graduate Committee	8	$476	$ 3,810		$ 3,810										
Serve on special task force	7	$476	$ 3,333											$3,333	
Research	62	$476	$29,524										$29,524		
Totals	189		$90,000	$26,667	$17,143	$0	$0	$0	$0	$0	$0	$13,333	$29,524	$3,333	$90,000
Surplus (Deficit)			$ 0												

EXHIBIT 1 (Continued)

Faculty Member C

Salary (includes fringes) $120,000
Average TP per day $635

Activities	No. Days	Rate	Total Cost	Under Grad	Purchases by Programs											Total
					F-T MBA	P-T MBA	Exec MBA	HCM MBA	PM MBA	MIS MBA	Entrepr. MBA	Doctoral	Research	Service	
Teach UG221	28	$450	$ 12,600	$12,600											$ 12,600
Teach CS710 Evening section	28	$450	$ 12,600			$12,600									$ 12,600
Teach UG480 (1)	28	$400	$ 11,200	$11,200											$ 11,200
Serve on Committee	10	$635	$ 6,349						$6,349						$ 6,349
Serve on Committee	10	$600	$ 6,000			$ 6,000									$ 6,000
Research	85	$635	$ 53,968										$53,968		$ 53,968
Totals	189		$102,717	$23,800	$0	$18,600	$0	$0	$6,349	$0	$0	$0	$53,968	$0	$102,717
Surplus (Deficit)			($ 17,283)												

Note (1): A small elective day course.

Level 5—Faculty Detail: Undergraduate Program

	Faculty Member							Sub Total	Total
	A	B	C	D	E	F	Etc.		
Department Activity:									
Department of Accounting:									
Teach 12 classes in UG121	$ 6,000							$ 6,000	
Teach 12 classes in UG323	6,000							6,000	
Serve on Undergrad Committee	3,810							3,810	
Coordinate UG221	5,079							5,079	
Teach UG221		13,333						13,333	
Teach UG221		13,333						13,333	
Teach UG221			12,600					12,600	
Teach UG480			11,200					11,200	
Totals for department	$20,889	$26,667	$23,800					$71,356	71,356
Etc. for all departments									512,000
Total expenses									583,356

EXHIBIT 1   (Continued)

Level 4—Department Summary: Department of Accounting

		Total Salary	Purchases by Programs												Surplus (Deficit)
			Under Grad	F-T MBA	P-T MBA	Exec MBA	HCM MBA	PM MBA	MIS MBA	Entrepr. MBA	Doctoral	Research	Service	Total	
Faculty Member	A	$ 80,000	$20,389	$14,000	$11,852	$0	$0	$ 0	$11,200	$0	$ 0	$ 21,164	$4,233	$ 83,338	$ 3,338
Faculty Member	B	$ 90,000	$26,667	$17,143	$ 0	$0	$0	$ 0	$ 0	$0	$13,333	$ 29,524	$3,333	$ 90,000	$ 0
Faculty Member	C	$120,000	$23,800	$ 0	$18,600	$0	$0	$6,349	$ 0	$0	$ 0	$ 53,968	$ 0	$102,717	($17,283)
Department totals		$290,000	$71,356	$31,143	$30,452	$0	$0	$6,349	$11,200	$0	$13,333	$104,656	$7,566	$276,055	($13,945)

Level 3—Course and Activity Detail: Undergraduate Program

Course/Activity	Credit Hours Per Student	Ave. Students per Section	No. Sections	$/Credit Hour	Total Revenue	10% Tax	Net Revenue	Purchases From							Total Cost	Surplus (Deficit)
								AC	FI	OM	OB	MK	IS	BP		
UG221	4	40	3	$1,000	$ 480,000	$ 48,000	$ 432,000	$39,267							$ 39,267	$ 392,733
UG121	4	100	1	$1,000	400,000	40,000	360,000	6,000							6,000	354,000
UG323	4	50	3	$1,000	600,000	60,000	540,000	6,000							6,000	534,000
UG480	2	10	1	$1,000	20,000	2,000	18,000	11,200							11,200	6,800
Etc. for other courses					3,300,000	350,000	3,150,000									
UG221 Coord.								5,079							5,079	(5,079)
Committee								3,810							3,810	(3,810)
Etc.																
Flat tax						500,000	(500,000)									(500,000)
Total					$5,000,000	$1,000,000	$4,000,000	$71,356	$35,000	$120,000	$58,000	$74,000	$45,000	$130,000	$583,356	$3,416,644

EXHIBIT 1 (Concluded)

Level 2—Profit Center Summary: Undergraduate Program

				Department				Sub Total	Total
	AC	FI	IS	OB	OM	MK	BP		
Tuition revenue									$5,000,000
Less tuition-related tax									1,000,000
Net tuition revenue									$4,000,000
Alumni giving									300,000
Other revenue									100,000
Total revenue									$4,400,000
Course/Activity:									
Courses:									
UG121	$ 6,000							$ 6,000	
UG323	6,000							$ 6,000	
UG221	39,267							$ 39,267	
UG480	11,200							$ 11,200	
Etc. for all courses									
Service Activities:									
Undergraduate Committee	3,810							$ 3,810	
Coordination of UG221	5,079							$ 5,079	
Etc. for all service activities									
Total expenses by department	$71,356	$85,000	$120,000	$58,000	$74,000	$45,000	$130,000	$583,356	583,356
Program surplus (deficit)									$3,816,644

Level 1—Profit Center Summary: Schoolwide

	Tuition Generating Programs									Subsidized Programs				
	Under Grads	F-T MBA	P-T MBA	Exec MBA	HCM MBA	PM MBA	MIS MBA	Entrepr. MBA	Subtotal	Doctoral 50% of Tax	Research 30% of Tax	Service 20% of Tax	Subtotal	Total
Tuition revenue	$5,000,000	$3,000,000	$1,500,000	$2,000,000	$1,500,000	$1,000,000	$2,000,000	$1,500,000	$17,500,000	$ 100,000	$ 500,000	$ 700,000	$1,300,000	$18,800,000
Tuition taxes	1,000,000	600,000	350,000	350,000	250,000	200,000	300,000	250,000	3,300,000	1,650,000	990,000	660,000	3,300,000	
Net tuition revenue	$4,000,000	$2,400,000	$1,150,000	$1,650,000	$1,250,000	$ 800,000	$1,700,000	$1,250,000	$14,200,000	$1,750,000	$1,490,000	$1,360,000	$4,600,000	$18,800,000
Alumni giving	300,000													
Other revenue	100,000													
Total revenue	$4,400,000													
Purchases From														
AC	$ 71,356	$ 31,143	$ 30,452	$ 0	$ 0	$ 6,349	$ 11,200	$ 0		$ 13,333	$ 104,656	$ 7,566		$ 276,055
FI	85,000													85,000
OM	120,000													120,000
OB	58,000													58,000
MK	74,000													74,000
IS	45,000													45,000
BP	130,000													130,000
Total	$ 583,356													$ 583,356
Surplus (Deficit)	$3,816,644													$18,216,644

(Level 6) is at the department, where each faculty member's time is "sold" to programs. These totals roll up into program detail (Level 5) and a department summary (Level 4). In this case, the Level 4 summary is for a Department of Accounting with the three faculty members shown in Level 6. As it indicates, this department is in some trouble, not having "sold" all of its faculty resources.

Level 3 shows the tuition revenue a program has generated, its taxes, its "purchases" from the departments, and its surplus or deficit from its teaching-related activities. Level 2 is similar, except it summarizes the tuition revenue and adds any other revenue, such as from alumni contributions. It shows the surplus or deficit for the program when all revenues and all expenses are included.

Finally, Level 1 is the School-wide Profit Center Summary. This level distinguishes between tuition-generating programs and "subsidized" programs, and computes an overall surplus or deficit. As it indicates, the total tax from the tuition-generating programs ($3,300,000 in this hypothetical example) is the same as the total tax revenue for the subsidized programs. Some of the subsidized programs also could earn revenue from tuition (e.g., in the Doctoral Program) or grants (e.g., in the Research Program).

Reactions

The reactions to the proposal were mixed. Neal Kramer, a Professor of Finance, offered the following:

> I believe that if we can create something resembling a market for faculty within CBS, then many of the incentive problems of traditional tenure would go away. As far as faculty time is concerned, I have never liked the idea of points. A point is not a metric that most people can relate to. Percentage of time doesn't work, since we all spend more than 100 percent. I think you are right in thinking along a 189 day scale. It's more transparent.
>
> I agree with the idea of giving programs their "revenue" based on credit units, multiplied by a by a number (price) that is the same as the school's total budget divided by total credit units. That will give program managers an incentive to increase the number of students, and will make each into a true (actually shadow, since the school never sees its revenue) profit center. Importantly, this approach would show the administrative overhead explicitly as a tax.
>
> As far as departments go, why do we need them in the first place? Why can't faculty be free agents? I see some faculty development issues that can happen best in departments but they can be done just as well by a Dean of the faculty. I believe recruiting and course assignment can be done with less formally structured faculty groups. Maybe this is a criticism of the current departmental structure, but I believe departments hinder our ability to apply a fine enough filter at tenure and promotion time—one of my most severe concerns.
>
> Also, we should not mix up workload allocation with performance. Quality of journals is important only in that it increases the attractiveness of a faculty member to a research center. But we should leave things like research quality and teaching

quality out of the workload allocations. Until we have a more comprehensive coverage of research interests in the research centers there will be faculty who do important research but don't find an obvious alignment with a center. My hope is that these situations would be few and could be handled in an ad hoc way.

I also think, however, that our performance evaluation issue is closely linked to workload. The monetary incentives available under our budget are not sufficient to reward faculty for quality work, be it research or teaching. Perhaps this need can be filled if there is a discriminatory pricing of courses (based on teaching quality and demand for the topic). Eventually, these matters will become important when no research center wants to "buy" a non-producing faculty member, and no program wants to "buy" a marginal teacher. In the short run, though, I would exclude them, but I nevertheless think that this is *the* most vital issue facing us today. Please let me know if there any way I can assist you in this quest.

Maureen Sanders, Professor of Operations Management and head of the MBA Program's PDC, offered a different perspective:

My overall concern goes to the heart of the underlying premise. I am not sure I buy the premise that we have shifted from a departmental-driven school to a program-driven one—or that we should. The focus of the strategic planning effort last year was on programs; the focus this year is on departments. I don't think the order is necessarily meant to imply any priorities (although it may). I feel strongly that the influence of programs should be increased relative to departments—and this is happening. But, programs are primarily driven by the teaching mission of the school—they want faculty who contribute directly to the student experience, either through good teaching in the classroom or through curricular development and teaching pedagogy. Departments care more about the scholarly development of faculty. This is not to say departments don't care about teaching, but they balance teaching concerns with individual faculty related research concerns. Too great an emphasis on programs runs the great risk of further denigrating the research mission of the school. I actually feel in terms of marketing ourselves that we do a great disservice by not emphasizing more the research contributions of faculty.

I'm also concerned that the design of the system does not recognize the important role of departments. I agree that students buy programs and that we need to structure incentives in ways that encourage creativity and energy to be devoted to programs. But, to the extent I understand your proposal, it shifts way too much authority to programs—up to almost determining faculty salaries.

In terms of the details, I have the following specific concerns:

1. *Profit Centers.* Why should programs earn surpluses, but not departments? Departments really need surpluses to support junior faculty research efforts.

2. *Annual Program Budgets.* At the undergraduate level, at lot of courses are taken outside of CBS. How would this be handled? Also, do we want to focus on credit hours, or students per credit hour? From your comments here, it seems as though number of students is the driver, not number of courses. This would kill the Health Care Management Program, so it makes me nervous.

3. *Financial Aid.* I don't know what shadow revenue is. Is the point of this that programs have to pay financial aid out of their budgets? I'm a little nervous about this.

4. *Doctoral Program.* There is actually an interesting idea here. We sort of exploit doctoral students through their teaching—think of someone like a Linda Olson. I don't know how much she is paid per course, but she is an outstanding teacher who benefits the school a lot. It would be nice if departments or the doctoral program could capture some of the excess value from having these types of doctoral students.

5. *Research Program.* I am very nervous in general about the extent to which we are beginning to think of school-based research programs. Encouraging research consistent with our vision and providing some "extra" support for this is desirable. But most research is individually generated or generated by small groups of collaborators based on their individual interests. I fear we are going to get into the business of looking at someone's research and not say, "Is this high-quality research that makes a contribution?" but say instead, "Is this research consistent with the vision of the school?" We are unlikely to get good research that way. The notion of a "Research Program" purchasing faculty time for research activities scares me for these reasons. Who is going to manage this? On the other hand, the idea of explicitly recognizing that some percentage of a faculty person's time is devoted to research is important. In our workload planning now, we don't really do this.

6. *Transfer Prices.* This is where I get very nervous. It is easy to set prices in accordance with a faculty member's salary. It is the "demand" for his or her services that makes me nervous. Certain people's prices would be driven very high if programmatic demand was the driver. These would be people who are the best teachers and everybody wanted them. The only way to create any semblance of balance is if chairs had research funds to participate in this market. If I wanted someone to do research, you'd have to meet my price if you wanted them to teach. But, how do I get revenue to fund buying them to do research? There would have to be some division at the school-level of funds available for teaching versus research. These could then be separately allocated to programs versus departments (implicit in this is my disagreement of the notion of a school-wide research program). The appropriate allocation would be a very worthwhile and interesting debate. What would happen with someone who is both an outstanding teacher and researcher? Presumably his or her price would be way out of line with salary For other people, you would not be able to cover their salary through their price. I don't think there are enough individual buyers and sellers in this market for it to work right anyway. Once it is a price-fixed market, we are back where we started. I admit I'm stuck in traditional paradigms, but it is hard for me to even begin to envision how this would work.

7. *Staffing Decisions.* What would you do with tenured faculty whose salary is not covered?

8. *Faculty Workload.* This is tied up with transfer prices. Since I can't imagine how these would really work, it is hard to go very far down this road.

In general, there are some very interesting and intriguing ideas here. I could imagine a whole lot less radical proposal that could operationalize some of these ideas and that could have a major impact on certain types of incentives. I'm amazed that you would devote so much time and thought to something that seems so unlikely to ever occur. But it may engender some interesting discussion.

Professor Yardley responded to these comments:

> Maureen's comments are more about the overall thrust, including the distressing comment near the end: ". . . something that seems so unlikely to ever occur." Nevertheless, most of her comments can be addressed and resolved. For example, her questioning of the underlying premise can be discussed and resolved (I would hope) by pointing out that programs generate tuition revenue, and hence can easily be considered profit centers.
>
> Departments could also be considered profit centers, however. The difference between them and programs is that they would generate most of their "revenue" from internal sales, and would be expected only to break even. To the extent that they generated external revenue, they could earn surpluses; the proposal includes this possibility. Indeed, by encouraging them to generate grant revenue, the proposal does emphasize research. Moreover, by having a Research Program, funded by "taxes," we also manage our unfunded research more directly than we now do.
>
> Maureen's other concerns also could be addressed pretty easily. Certainly, to the extent that we consider "market-based" transfer prices to be disrespectful, we could eliminate them, and create some standard transfer prices. I think, though, that, just like other markets, any time we intervene in our market, we should justify that intervention on the basis of either imperfections or externalities. Otherwise, we will create impediments to the market's smooth functioning.

As spring approached, Professor Malone, in his role as Associate Dean, needed to determine whether to proceed with the redesign of the school's management control system, and, if so, how best to go about it. He commented:

> There are two big issues on my mind. First, should we shift the focus of the school's management control system to programs or remain with departments? Second, if we shift the focus to programs, is Dexter's proposal workable, and, if not, what kinds of changes are needed to make it both workable *and* acceptable to the school's faculty?

Assignment

1. Be sure you understand how the MCS outlined in Exhibit 1 is designed to work. What, in your view, are its strengths and weaknesses? How would you evaluate it against the criteria for a good management control system?

2. What is your response to the two issues expressed by Dean Malone at the end of the case?

3. Assuming that Dean Malone decides to shift the focus of the management control system to programs, how would you change the system designed by Professor Yardley to respond to the concerns expressed by Professor Sanders? What other changes do you think are needed?

4. Assuming that Dean Malone decides to shift the focus of the management control system to programs, how should he go about implementing the changes?

Case 16–2

Apogee Health Care*

> After many long meetings and sometimes heated discussions, we finally succeeded in implementing a new compensation system for our PCPs. Now I'm not so sure that it's appropriate, given that one of our major HMO contracts is switching to capitation next month. We've been working on changing the new system to deal with this, but I worry about changing so soon. I'm also beginning to wonder if its possible to create a fair system when there is both fee-for-service and capitated revenue.

The speaker was Richard Peters, MD, Director of Primary Care for Apogee Health Care (AHC), a physician-hospital organization (PHO) that had been established four years ago by Metropolitan Hospital and several physician groups. Metropolitan Hospital, an academic medical center affiliated with a prestigious medical school, was located in a highly competitive managed care market. The hospital recognized that to be successful it needed to expand its primary care base and solidify its relationships with specialty physicians, and thus formed a PHO. AHC's strategy was to create an integrated delivery system (IDS) that provided cost-effective, quality clinical care and excellent patient service, allowed community physicians and patients easy access, and effectively managed capitated risk.

Historically, in addition to having specialists on staff, the hospital had owned both Metropolitan Physician Group (MPG), a primary care academic medical group that was located on its main campus, as well as several community health centers, all of which had primary care physicians on staff. These groups became part of the newly formed PHO. Moreover, AHC had moved aggressively to acquire primary care medical practices and to establish new practices, which also became part of the PHO. By the end of its first four years, AHC had opened four new primary care practices and expanded eight others. The practices were quite diverse, ranging from some based in community health centers to others with a private practice model, catering to a well-insured population. AHC recognized early on that it needed to develop a competitive primary care compensation system if it was to be successful in recruiting and retaining PCPs.

AHC's Compensation Model

There were several problems with the compensation system that had been in place for MPG and the physician groups at the community health centers. First, some of the more senior physicians were being paid below market rates. Second, there was a belief that some practices had more resources

*This case was prepared by David W. Young and Sheila M. McCarthy. Copyright © by David W. Young.

available to them than others, and hence the ability to earn more money. Third, with the formation of AHC, the hospital had agreed to provide funding for primary care development, and wanted to ensure that its investment was wisely managed.

AHC's first step in redesigning its compensation system was to establish a task force that included the medical directors of each of the group practices, plus Dr. Peters, William Burke, MD, Associate Director of Primary Care, John Paulson, Administrative Director of Primary Care, and Diane Corbin, Associate Vice President of Primary Care. Dr. Peters explained some of the issues:

> We knew from the beginning that establishing a new compensation system would be a complex and difficult undertaking. There was a lot of mistrust among the different primary care practices, particularly between those based in the health centers and the newer groups that were modeled after private practices. There was a lot of tension because no one really knew how the different practices were doing financially but there was a sense that some were not performing as well as others. We looked at this as an opportunity to incorporate some accountability into the system, bring salaries up to market level, and also to build a sense of trust among the different groups.

The task force agreed on two principles at the outset. First, no matter where physicians worked within AHC, they would receive equal pay for equal work, and second, they would have the same resources available to them.

Salary Structure

Using primary care salary ranges in both its own region and nationally, the task force developed an outpatient salary structure. This would be used to recruit new PCPs and also to adjust the salaries of PCPs already on staff to bring their salaries in line with market rates. For internal medicine, the salary ranged from $92,000 for a new physician with no post residency experience to $124,000 for a physician with over seven years experience. The scale was slightly different for pediatricians, starting off at $83,000 and reaching a maximum of $135,000. Additionally, the task force estimated that a physician in internal medicine would generate approximately $25,000 in inpatient income, resulting in maximum total compensation of about $150,000. For a pediatrician, the task force estimated inpatient income at $2,000, resulting in a maximum of $137,000.

The individual physician group exercised discretion regarding the distribution of inpatient revenue. However, the task force recommended that inpatient revenue flow into the practice to facilitate a seamless model of care and the tracking of all revenues and expenses. It also recommended that some portion of this pool of money be used to pay expenses of the outpatient practice. The model assumed that a physician's inpatient revenue would flow into the practice with the practice retaining 20 percent to cover expenses and distributing the remaining 80 percent to the physician. However, this decision rested with the individual practices, as did the amount paid to each physician.

Productivity Standards

Since physicians were being compensated at market rates, the task force wanted to ensure that their productivity was consistent with the market; it therefore developed productivity standards. Additionally, because the hospital was subsidizing the priinary care practices, there was a need to justify its contribution. As Mr. Paulson explained:

> When the issue became one of needed capital and investment, the hospital became more concerned with what they were getting in return. Although the health center practices and the MPG have been around for a long time, from a financial standpoint no one paid much attention to them because they were such a small part of the system. They were subsidized by the hospital and that worked fine when there was a surplus in the system. However, as the hospital started to get squeezed, it began to scrutinize everything.

Through analyses of physicians in their region, the task force arrived at a baseline for outpatient productivity in terms of officc visits: 3,200 for internal medicine and 4,000 for pediatrics. To ensure more accuracy and to allow productivity to be adjusted for time and acuity, they had envisioned translating office visits into units based on RBRVS weights[1], and had determined the average weights for each practice (shown in Exhibit 1). As Dr. Peters explained:

> We had to account for differences among physicians. For example, we know that some patients are more difficult than othcrs; we needed to adjust for this and to find a common unit of work, which is difficult. Do you use visits, bookable hours, or something else? If you ignore visits and use bookable hours, you lose any measure of productivity. We proposed using RBRVS weights to adjust for differences. There were different lcvcls of visits, ranging from Level 1 for a routine visit to Level 5 for the most complicated type of visit. We also adjusted for new patients, realizing that they take longer than an established patient whom the physician knows. Unfortunately, we ended up abandoning this after an analysis of coding showed a high degree of variability across practices. In the end, we ended up using visits as the productivity standard to calculate the level of support the practice was given. However, we allowed the practices to use units, if they wished, to measure productivity internally.

Some of the practices were not happy with the productivity standards set out in the model. A physician who had worked at Meadowbrook Community Health Center for many years commented:

---

[1]The Resource Based Relative Value Scale (RBRVS) was developed by the Health Care Financing Administration as a payment mechanism for physicians. It relies on relative value units to weight different services and visit types.

EXHIBIT 1 RBRVS Average Practice Weights

RBRVS Weights

	Established Patient	New Patient
Level 1..	.21	.40
Level 2..	.40	.77
Level 3..	.70	1.14
Level 4..	.93	1.68
Level 5..	1.46	2.22

Current Practice Weights	Average Weights	Units Needed to Reach Baseline Compensation
Ocean Community Health Center	.74	3,200 × .74 = 2,368
Skyline Community Health Center.............	.78	3,200 × .78 = 2,496
Meadowbrook Community Health Center.......	.71	3,200 × .71 = 2,272
Metropolitan Physician Group	.83	3,200 × .83 = 2,656
Women's Health Group	.98	3,200 × .98 = 3,136
Private Medical Group......................	1.04	3,200 × 1.04 = 3,328
Pediatrics Group Practice...................	.75	4,000 × .75 = 3,000
Ocean Pediatrics	.65	4,000 × .65 = 2,600
Skyline Pediatrics.........................	.62	4,000 × .62 = 2,480
Meadowbrook Pediatrics	.70	4,000 × .70 = 2,800

If I'm an average full-time doctor in our practice, I probably spend about 28 bookable hours seeing patients. But when you factor in running late, it becomes 36 hours seeing patients. Add on completion of charts, and it grows to about 44 hours. Add calls and paperwork associated with each patient (maybe 40 minutes compared to an hour of contact time), and it easily reaches 70 hours a week. At some point I ask myself, what is my time worth? The answer is that they can cut my pay, but I really can't work any harder or do any more than I'm already doing. When I started here 8 years ago, the visits per session were budgeted at 7. They pushed them to 8, and then to 9. Most of the physicians in our practice feel unable to do any more work.

However, other practices, particularly those that were on the lower end of the salary range, had little problem with the new standards. The medical director at Women's Health Group explained:

Prior to the implementation of the compensation model, physicians in our practice were making about half of what some other primary care physicians were making, and our productivity was not that far below the proposed standard. So, with just a small increase in productivity, a physician's salary could almost double.

Support Staff and Space

To provide physicians with the necessary support to meet the new productivity standards, the task force also made recommendations regarding support staff levels per physician FTE (full-time equivalent). For example, for a practice with 8 FTE physicians, the model assumed one business manager at an average annual salary of $40,000, 2 RNs ($48,000 average salary), 4 LPNs ($22,500 average salary), 4 secretaries ($26,500 average salary), 2 file clerks ($21,000 average salary), 2 receptionists ($20,000 average salary), 2 transcriptionists ($24,000 average salary), and 2 managed care secretaries ($25,000 average salary). The productivity standards also assumed that physicians had two rooms available to see patients. If only one room was available, then the task force proposed that a physician be held to a productivity level that was 15 percent below that of a physician with two rooms.

Some of the physicians questioned the assumptions in the model. For example, the model assumed that the support staff at the practices had the same amount of work to do. Many at the health centers were skeptical of this, given the needs and characteristics of their patient population. One of the physicians at Ocean Community Health Center commented:

> We're dealing with a lot of different social issues, including welfare, social security, legal assistance, transportation, cost of medication, and substance abuse. Payer mix may be a rough approximation of poverty in our community. Our practice serves many more folks with Medicaid or free care than the other practices. The folks on Medicaid are in managed care plans, requiring referrals and paperwork related to their social problems. Many of our patients are not well educated or have psychiatric comorbidities, so that they call multiple times for the same request, overloading our phones and personnel. It seems that the amount of work for much of our patient population is enormous.

Role of the Nurse Practitioners

When modeling this plan, using the support staff, productivity and compensation levels described above, the task force found that an all-physician primary care practice lost $23,795 per FTE MD. In an effort to reduce this loss, the model incorporated nurse practitioners (NPs) at a ratio of one nurse practitioner for every three physicians. The NPs, under this model, were not guaranteed a salary but were compensated based on productivity. According to the task force's analysis (see Exhibit 2), this reduced the loss to $10,170 per FTE MD. A full-time nurse practitioner was defined as someone who worked 46 weeks a year with 32 scheduled office hours a week. The NPs estimated that they could see between 2,400 and 2,500 patients a year. They needed the same level of support as physicians, except that no RN support was necessary and only one room was required. However, they would need one hour of physician supervision per week.

EXHIBIT 2
Comparison of
MD/NP and MD
Model*

	MD/NP Model	MD Model
REVENUE		
Inpatient Revenue	$ 337,500	$ 360,000
MD Outpatient Revenue	1,907,892	2,572,800
Lab & Procedure Revenue	923,045	944,656
NP Patient Revenue	502,500	0
Total Net Patient Revenue	$3,670,937	$3,877,456
Other Revenue	$ 85,000	$85,000
Total Revenue	$3,755,937	$3,962,456
EXPENSES		
Physician Salaries	$1,350,000	$1,800,000
Nursing Salaries	460,760	267,542
Admin Salaries	45,000	45,000
Other & Temp. Salaries	333,061	337,761
Total Salaries	$2,188,821	$2,450,303
Fringe Benefits	$ 496,564	$ 548,861
Supplies	137,216	140,429
Outside Services	39,698	40,627
Utilities & Rent	325,500	372,000
Lab Expenses	266,809	273,056
Other	174,037	178,112
Billing Fee	218,821	227,601
Total Expenses	$3,847,466	$4,230,989
Margin	($ 91,529)	($ 268,533)
Surplus/Deficit per MD	($ 10,170)	($ 23,351)
Total Visits	35,958	36,800
ASSUMPTIONS OF MODELS		
Aver. MD Salary	$ 150,000	$ 150,000
Average NP Salary	$ 75,000	N/A
Visits Per MD FTE	3,164	3,200
Visits Per NP FTE	2,500	0
# NP FTEs	3	0
# MD FTEs	9	12

MD to NP Ratio is 3 to 1

NPs work 46 weeks a year, 32 office hours per week, have 1 room, and same support staff as MDs less RN.

MDs will have to spend 1 hour per week supervising NPs.

Number of inpatient days is about 600 days per MD and 450 days per NP. Average net revenue is about $50 per visit assuming a collection rate of 50%.

Average net revenue per outpatient visit is $67, assuming a 67% collection rate.

*Prepared by the task force to analyze the effect of adding nurse practitioners to the model.

Implementation

To implement the new system, the task force asked each practice to budget its yearly volume based on its FTE MDs and the productivity standards outlined in the compensation plan, that is, 3,200 visits for Internists and 4,000 visits for Pediatricians. Revenue was then calculated based upon a practice's payer mix and contractual allowances. On the expense side, support salaries were budgeted based on the standards described above. Physician compensation was budgeted based on anticipated productivity and years of experience. Supplies, rent, and overhead were then added, and the practice signed off on the budget. Once the budgets were developed, the practices had control of their own operations. The task force recommended that a reconciliation process take place at the end of each year for any practice over budget. All overages that were the result of bad decision-making or lack of productivity would be the responsibility of the practice. Overages that were considered to be out of the control of the practice (e.g. lack of patients in the system) would be forgiven.

Risk Sharing

For the most part, the practices were at risk for their own financial viability, and it was up to each practice to decide how to spread the risk among its physicians. The task force outlined several risk sharing suggestions:

1. **Shift the risk to the individual physician.** At the end of each month, individual productivity would determine monthly paychecks. For example, if a physician did 10 percent more units than required under the productivity standard, he or she received a 10 percent higher paycheck. But if at year end there was a shortfall, then physicians would need to take a salary cut in the last pay period.

2. **Spread the risk over all physicians in the practice.** At the end of each month, if the practice was on budget, all physicians would receive their baseline pay. This assumed that productivity would even out over the course of the year, or allowed one physician to take on the responsibility of caring for sicker patients with others in the practice making up the lost productivity.

3. **Voluntarily decrease pay to cover any shortfalls.** Under this option, physicians would forgo some percentage of their monthly paychecks to cover variability. This resulting reserve fund would cover any shortfalls at year-end, and anything left over could be distributed as bonuses to physicians.

In general, the plan was to give the practices as much control over their own operations as possible. Ms. Corbin explained:

All decisions about practice operations lie with the practice. If a practice decides it can forgo a secretary, any resulting savings flow to its bottom line; at the end of the year, any surplus can be distributed as physician compensation or reinvested in the practice.

Physician Compensation

Most of the practices used a straight productivity measure with some kind of weighting system to compensate their physicians. For example, in one practice each visit equivalent was worth $45 to a physician, such that each physician who exceeded budgeted productivity targets earned $45 per visit equivalent in addition to base salary. Conversely, a physician below target was charged $45 per visit equivalent. The practice held inpatient income as a reserve account and any charges were taken from the account. At reconciliation time, the practice distributed 80 percent of a physician's inpatient income, plus or minus any adjustments for outpatient activity.

One or two practices used a straight salary model and relied purely on peer pressure to ensure that the group overall met its budgeted targets. Mark Bower, Medical Director at Skyline Community Health Center, which used a straight salary system, commented on his group's system:

> This type of salary system works for our group. There are seven of us in the practice. We are a pretty close-knit group and are comfortable with each other's practice styles and watch each other's practice. We use pure peer pressure, not financial incentives, to shape behavior. Of course, the risk in this model is that the doctor will slack off, which is unacceptable. However, all of us are pretty closely grouped as far as the number of patients per hour, and we go on the assumption that if you see fewer patients in a day it is because the patients were more difficult. In our view this allows all the doctors to worry about patient care and not the number of widgets produced. It also encourages physicians to take on the more difficult patients. In my view, this type of system has helped our group dynamics. There is less competition. Also, it has not hurt our productivity as a practice. In fact, as a practice we are over our productivity targets set out in our budget.

The First Year

During the first year, there were some problems with implementing the model. One of the main issues was the inability of some practices to get reliable and timely data from fiscal services. Some practices did not receive a quarterly reconciliation and there was a lot of uncertainty about how they were doing financially. For example, one practice knew that it was below productivity and it had worked to reduce expenses to meet its budget. However, at one point, according to the medical director, it looked like the physicians were going to take a 20 percent pay cut. This created a lot of tension within the practice. Others were finding it difficult to meet the productivity targets and balance outside responsibilities. However, without exception, the biggest concern in all the practices was the potential impact of capitation.

Capitation

AHC had expected capitation to grow in the coming years, and believed that if capitation were incorporated into the budget, the deficit shown in Exhibit 2 would be replaced with a surplus. Exhibit 3 shows one scenario envisioned by AHC. As it indicates, a practice with 9 physicians and 3 nurse practitioners would stand to gain $131,979 with an increase in capitation. AHC assumed that capitation would rise to 42 percent of the under-65-year-old population, and 16 percent of the 65-and-older population (line 6), and estimated that the per member per month payment would average $18.00 and $45.00 respectively (line 10). The gain was calculated by subtracting the fee-for-service outpatient revenue that would have been generated if the patients were not capitated from the capitated revenue generated via the per member per month payments (line 11–line 12). The result was a gain of $21,542 for the practice's 65-and-over population, and $110,436 for its under-65-year-old population.

However, as the individual practices and AHC contemplated the current compensation system, they realized that they needed to make some changes to

EXHIBIT 3 **Estimate of the Effect of Capitation on a Group Practice**

			≥ 65 Years Old	< 65 Years Old
	MD Panel Size	1,800 members		
	NP Panel Size	1,200 members		
	Number of Members Covered by Group Practice			
	3 NPs at 1,200 members	3,600		
	9 MDs at 1,800 members	16,200		
Line 1	Total	19,800		
Line 2	Percent of Local Population		17%	83%
Line 3	Number of Members (1 × 2)		3,366	16,434
Line 4	Percent Managed Care		40%	70%
Line 5	Percent Managed Care Which is Capitated		40%	60%
Line 6	Percent of Population Which is Capitated (4 × 5) . . .		16%	42%
Line 7	Number of Capitated Members (3 × 6)		539	6,902
Line 8	Visits per Capitated Member		5	2
Line 9	Total Visits for Capitated Members		2,693	13,805
Line 10	PMPM Payment		$45.00	$18.00
Line 11	Total Revenue per Year (7 × 10 × 12 months)		$290,822	$1,490,892
Line 12	Revenue if Capitated Visits were FFS			
	(estimate $100 per visit)		$269,280	$1,380,456
Line 13	Net Gain from Capitation (11 − 12)		$ 21,542	$ 110,436
			Total	$131,979

Notes
Demographic and managed care penetration data shown in lines 2, 3, 4, and 5 and data regarding visits per member shown in Line 8 are AHC estimates. PMPM payments, shown in line 10 are also estimates from AHC.

deal with capitation. Moreover, because a large HMO contract was due to switch almost immediately, increasing capitated revenue to 30 percent in some practices, these changes had to be made soon. Dr. Peters faced the task of negotiating the level of funds that primary care physicians would receive for a capitated patient under this particular contract and determining how to manage the risk.

The most recent proposal regarding the level of capitated funds for primary care reimbursed a primary care practice $20 per member per month. For this contract, the practice would receive $15 of that amount up front, with the rest going into a risk pool. The practice had the opportunity to earn the risk pool money back by meeting the "medical management goals," shown in Exhibit 4. The document prepared by the AHC established "minimum, target, and stretch goals, which, if the targets are achieved, will provide a financial incentive that puts primary care practices at breakeven for capitation programs with a reasonable incentive to achieve more." Each goal carried a certain weight, which differed by period. For example, in the first 6 months, 50 percent of a practice's risk pool money would be dependent upon reducing inpatient utilization by the target of 1 percent per month.

EXHIBIT 4   Medical Management Goals for Capitation

GOALS

	Minimum	Target	Stretch	
Inpatient Utilization	.5%	1%	2%	Reduce Days/1,000 members (1)
Outpatient Utilization	.5%	1%	2%	Reduce pmpm $s (2)
Open Enrollment	100	300	600	Adjusted members / FTE (3)
Pharmacy	.5%	1.25%	2%	Reduce pmpm $s (4)
Patient Satisfaction	60%	75%	100%	Percent of target achieved (5)
Clinical Goal	60%	75%	100%	Percent of target achieved (6)

WEIGHTING OF EACH GOAL BY PERIOD

	1–6 Months	7–12 Months	13–18 Months	19–24 Months	25–30 Months
Inpatient Utilization	50%	45%	35%	35%	25%
Outpatient Utilization	20%	20%	20%	20%	20%
Open Enrollment	25%	20%	15%	15%	10%
Pharmacy	5%	5%	10%	10%	15%
Patient Satisfaction	0%	5%	10%	10%	15%
Clinical Goal	0%	5%	10%	10%	15%
	100%	100%	100%	100%	100%

Notes
(1) Reduce the inpatient days per 1,000 members by a target goal of 1% per month.
(2) Reduce the per member per month dollars that are allocated to outpatient utilization by a target goal of 1% per month.
    This excludes primary care outpatient visits but includes things like specialty referrals, lab, x-ray and ancillary services.
(3) Increase the number of capitated members per FTE physician.
(4) Reduce the per member per month dollars that are allocated to pharmacy costs by a target goal of 1.25% per month.
(5) Increase the rate of patient satisfaction.
(6) Clinical goals with targets will be established to promote clinical excellence.

This draft proposal had been presented to the physicians at a compensation meeting and reflected the thinking of AHC's senior management. The goal was to use indicators that could be measured by the practices and for which there was available information. This was an important point, raised by one physician who argued:

> If you are going to hold us responsible for meeting these indicators, then we have to have the information available to track our performance. We need information if we are to manage pharmacy use or inpatient utilization.

In addition to the level of funds available to the practices, the other major challenge of capitation was to modify the compensation model so that it was appropriate for both capitation and fee-for-service As Dr. Burke explained:

> Already there are different levels of thinking about capitation among the practices. However, no matter where you think capitation is going or how fast and far it will grow, the reality is that we will never be at 100 percent capitation or 100 percent fee-for-service. There will always be a mixed model. How do you align the incentives under a mixed model?

To deal with this challenge, AHC had drafted a preliminary proposal to address the fact that the practices now would have two significant streams of revenue: fee-for-service and capitated. Therefore, AHC needed to adjust the compensation system to ensure that the right incentives were created. The preliminary proposal is shown in Exhibit 5.

Next Steps

Dr. Peters recognized that designing a compensation system that created the correct incentives for physicians working under a mixed model would be extremely difficult, especially given the diversity of the practices:

> I wonder if the mixed model proposal offers the beginning of a solution that provides the right kind of incentives. While I don't believe that capitation will be the dominant form of payment for some time, the PCPs nevertheless must deal with the fact that from now on, it will be a substantial portion of their revenue.

Questions

1. Consider the different kinds of responsibility centers that can exist in a management control system, and the criteria for their selection. What kind of responsibility centers are the individual practices? What kind of a responsibility center should an individual physician be within a group practice? Why? In answering these questions, think about the relationship among risk, reward, and control and how this relationship works at each level of responsibility center selection.

EXHIBIT 5
Draft Compensation
Proposal Under a
Mixed Model

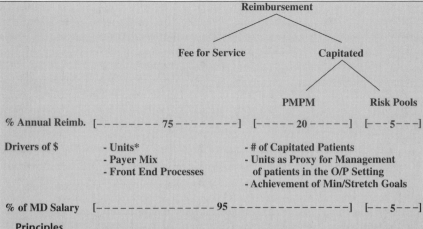

% Annual Reimb. [– – – – – – – – 75 – – – – – – – –] [– – – – 20 – – – – –] [– – 5 – – –]

Drivers of $
- Units*
- Payer Mix
- Front End Processes

- # of Capitated Patients
- Units as Proxy for Management
  of patients in the O/P Setting
- Achievement of Min/Stretch Goals

% of MD Salary [– – – – – – – – – – – – – 95 – – – – – – – – – – – – – –] [– – 5 – – –]

Principles

1. Units are reasonable proxy of effort for both the FFS and capitated component of business.
2. Any physician compensation model must be implemented in the context of overall practice performance. For the practices this is measured in terms of practice income.

Outpatient Salary

Base Salary—Final Settlement: Pay 95% of outpatient salary based on units with incentives for performance above/below standard level of productivity. Standard units based on average weight per visit by practice—so the standard, and consequently $ per unit, will differ by practice. The end result, however, should be that if the practice standard is met, a physician will earn 95% of O/P salary per the Compensation Model. The remaining 5% of salary may be earned through capitated risk pool distribution.

Practice Specific Adjustments to Base Salary: Practices may elect to reduce the unit payment above by a small amount to create a fund to reimburse/incent physician participation in efforts other than direct patient care.

Base Salary/Interim Draw: Set MD Compensation $/Unit at 95% of settlement level above to establish a reserve related to individual MD and overall practice performance. Pay 5% withhold quarterly with incentives if applicable.

Incentives: For each unit above standard, MDs earn same $/unit as in final settlement re: base salary above. For each unit below standard, MDs salary adjusted down by same $/unit as in final settlement re: base salary above plus an additional $15–$38 to cover fixed and possible semivariable overhead costs.

Alternative to Unit Based Compensation for O/P Services: Pay a percent of outpatient collections. This links MD compensation to overall practice performance, but puts MDs at risk for their individual payer mix differences.

Inpatient Salary

Base Salary: Pay I/P salary based on collections for services less 20% for practice overhead related to I/P services.

Payment from Capitated Risk Pools

Allocate/pay dollars from risk pools, in buckets consistent with risk-sharing group for each managed care plan to individual physicians based on member months—regardless of individual MD performance at first. Produce reports that show individual MD performance to be distributed to all member in the risk group and over time determine how to reward individual MD performance within the group.

2. Calculate the contribution of a nurse practitioner and a physician. If a practice has to hire additional providers, which type should it choose? What factors might influence this decision?

3. Consider the four phases of the management control process. How should the six performance criteria that have been introduced be incorporated into the management control process at the individual practice level in a mixed model (i.e., capitation and fee for service)? Should there be additional criteria?

4. How should the performance criteria influence an individual physician's compensation? Should these criteria be applied to both fee-for-service and capitated patients? Consider the impact of a reduction in inpatient utilization on the practice income and individual physician income under the following scenarios: 100 percent fee for service, 100 percent capitation, and 70 percent fee for service/30 percent capitation. Assume that a physician's panel is 2,000 members and that inpatient days are 300 per 1,000 population.

Case 16–3

Northeast Research Laboratory*

On a Friday morning in late December 1973, Sam Lacy, head of the Physical Sciences Division of Northeast Research Laboratory (NRL), thought about two letters which lay on his desk. One, which he had received a few weeks before, was a progress report from Robert Kirk, recently assigned project leader of the Exco project, who reported that earlier frictions between the NRL team and the client had lessened considerably, that high-quality research was under way, and that the prospects for retaining the Exco project on a long-term basis appeared fairly good. The other letter, which had just arrived in the morning's mail, came from Gray Kenney, a vice president of Exco, and stated that the company wished to terminate the Exco contract effective immediately.

Lacy was puzzled. He remembered how pleased Gray Kenney had been only a few months before when the Exco project produced its second patentable process. On the other hand, he also recalled some of the difficulties the project had encountered within NRL which had ultimately led to the replacement of project leader Alan North in order to avoid losing the contract. Lacy decided to call in the participants in an effort to piece together an understanding of what had happened. Some of what he learned is described below. But the problem remained for him to decide what he should report to senior management. What should he recommend to avoid the recurrence of such a situation in the future?

*This case was prepared by Professor Robert N. Anthony. Copyright © by The President and Fellows of Harvard College. Harvard Business School Case 9-175-184.

EXHIBIT 1
Organization Chart
(Simplified)

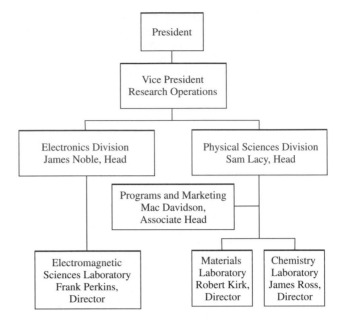

Company Background

Northeast Research Laboratory was a multidisciplinary research and development organization employing approximately 1,000 professionals. It was organized into two main sectors, one for economics and business administration and the other for the physical and natural sciences. Within the physical and natural sciences sector, the organization was essentially by branches of science. The main units were called divisions and the subunits were called laboratories. A partial organization chart is shown in Exhibit 1.

Most of the company's work was done on the basis of contracts with clients. Each contract was a project. Responsibility for the project was vested in a project leader, and through him up the organizational structure in which his laboratory was located. Typically, some members of the project team were drawn from laboratories other than that in which the project leader worked; it was the ability to put together a team with a variety of technical talents that was one of the principal strengths of a multidisciplinary laboratory. Team members worked under the direction of the project leader during the period in which they were assigned to the project. An individual might be working on more than one project concurrently. The project leader could also draw on the resources of central service organizations, such as model shops, computer services, editorial, and drafting. The project was billed for the services of these units at rates which were intended to cover their full costs.

Inception of the Exco Project

In October 1972, Gray Kenney, vice president of Exco, had telephoned Mac Davidson of NRL to outline a research project which would examine the effect of microwaves on various ores and minerals. Davidson was associate head of the Physical Sciences Division and had known Kenney for several years. During the conversation Kenney asserted that NRL ought to be particularly intrigued by the research aspects of the project, and Davidson readily agreed. Davidson was also pleased because the Physical Sciences Division was under pressure to generate more revenue, and this potentially long-term project from Exco would make good use of the available workforce. In addition, senior management of NRL had recently circulated several memos indicating that more emphasis should be put on commercial rather than government work. Davidson was, however, a little concerned that the project did not fall neatly into one laboratory or even one division, but in fact required assistance from the Electronics Division to complement work that would be done in two different Physical Sciences Laboratories (the Chemistry Laboratory and the Materials Laboratory).

A few days later Davidson organized a joint client-NRL conference to determine what Exco wanted and to plan the proposal. Kenney sent his assistant, Tod Denby, who was to serve as the Exco liaison officer for the project. Representing NRL were Davidson; Sam Lacy; Dr. Robert Kirk, director of the Materials Laboratory (one of the two Physical Sciences laboratories involved in the project); Dr. Alan North, manager of Chemical Development and Engineering (and associate director of the Chemistry Laboratory); Dr. James Noble, executive director of the Electronics Division; and a few researchers chosen by Kirk and North. Davidson also would have liked to invite Dr. James Ross, director of the Chemistry Laboratory, but Ross was out of town and couldn't attend the pre-proposal meeting.

Denby described the project as a study of the use of microwaves for the conversion of basic ores and minerals to more valuable commercial products. The study was to consist of two parts:

> Task A—An experimental program to examine the effect of microwaves on 50 ores and minerals, and to select those processes appearing to have the most promise.

> Task B—A basic study to obtain an understanding of how and why microwaves interact with certain minerals.

It was agreed that the project would be a joint effort of three laboratories: (1) Materials, (2) Chemistry, and (3) Electromagnetic. The first two laboratories were in the Physical Sciences Division, and the last was in the Electronics Division.

Denby proposed that the contract be open-ended, with a level of effort of around $10,000–$12,000 per month. Agreement was quickly reached on the content of the proposal. Denby emphasized to the group that an early start was essential if Exco was to remain ahead of its competition.

After the meeting Lacy, who was to have overall responsibility for the project, discussed the choice of project leader with Davidson. Davidson proposed Alan North, a 37-year-old chemist who had had experience as a project leader on several projects. North had impressed Davidson at the pre-proposal meeting and seemed well suited to head the interdisciplinary team. Lacy agreed. Lacy regretted that Dr. Ross (head of the laboratory in which North worked) was unable to participate in the decision of who should head the joint project. In fact, because he was out of town, Ross was neither aware of the Exco project nor of his laboratory's involvement in it.

The following day, Alan North was told of his appointment as project leader. During the next few days, he conferred with Robert Kirk, head of the other Physical Sciences laboratory involved in the project. Toward the end of October Denby began to exert pressure on North to finalize the proposal, stating that the substance had been agreed upon at the pre-proposal conference. North thereupon drafted a five-page letter as a substitute for a formal proposal, describing the nature of the project and outlining the procedures and equipment necessary. At Denby's request, North included a paragraph which authorized members of the client's staff to visit NRL frequently and observe progress of the research program. The proposal's cover sheet contained approval signatures from the laboratories and divisions involved. North signed for his own area and for laboratory director Ross. He telephoned Dr. Noble of the Electronics Division, relayed the client's sense of urgency, and Noble authorized North to sign for him. Davidson signed for the Physical Sciences Division as a whole.

At this stage, North relied principally on the advice of colleagues within his own division. As he did not know personally the individuals in the Electronics Division, they were not called upon at this point. Since North understood informally that the director of the Electromagnetic Sciences Laboratory, Dr. Perkins, was quite busy and often out of town, North did not attempt to discuss the project with Perkins.

After the proposal had been signed and mailed, Dr. Perkins was sent a copy. It listed the engineering equipment which the client wanted purchased for the project and described how it was to be used. Perkins worried that performance characteristics of the power supply (necessary for quantitative measurement) specified in the proposal were inadequate for the task. He asked North about it and North said that the client had made up his mind as to the microwave equipment he wanted and how it was to be used. Denby had said he was paying for that equipment and intended to move it to Exco's laboratories after the completion of the NRL contract.

All these events had transpired rather quickly. By the time Dr. Ross, director of the Chemistry Laboratory, returned, the proposal for the Exco project had been signed and accepted. Ross went to see Lacy and said that he had dealt with Denby on a previous project and had serious misgivings about working with him. Lacy assuaged some of Ross's fears by observing that if anyone could succeed in working with Denby it would be North—a flexible man, professionally competent, who could move with the tide and get along with clients of all types.

Conduct of the Project

Thus the project began. Periodically, when decisions arose, North would seek opinions from division management. However, he was somewhat unclear about whom he should talk to. Davidson had been the person who had actually appointed him project leader. Normally, however, North worked for Ross. Although Kirk's laboratory was heavily involved in the project, Kirk was very busy with other Materials Laboratory work. Adding to his uncertainty, North periodically received telephone calls from Perkins of the Electronics Division, whom he didn't know well. Perkins expected to be heavily involved in the project.

Difficulties and delays began to plague the project. The microwave equipment specified by the client was not delivered by the manufacturer on schedule, and there were problems in filtering the power supply of the radio frequency source. Over the objection of NRL Electromagnetic Sciences engineers, but at the insistence of the client, one of the chemical engineers tried to improve the power supply filter. Eventually the equipment had to be sent back to the manufacturer for modification. This required several months.

In the spring of 1973, Denby, who had made his presence felt from the outset, began to apply strong pressure. "Listen," he said to North, "top management of Exco is starting to get on my back and we need results. Besides, I'm up for review in four months and I can't afford to let this project affect my promotion." Denby was constantly at NRL during the next few months. He was often in the labs conferring individually with members of the NRL teams. Denby also visited North's office frequently.

A number of related problems began to surface. North had agreed to do both experimental and theoretical work for this project, but Denby's constant pushing for experimental results began to tilt the emphasis. Theoretical studies began to lapse, and experimental work became the focus of the Exco project. From time to time North argued that the theoretical work should precede or at least accompany the experimental program, but Denby's insistence on concrete results led North to temporarily deemphasize the theoretical work. Symptoms of this shifting emphasis were evident. One day a senior researcher from Kirk's laboratory came to North to complain that people were being "stolen" from his team. "How can we do a balanced project if the theoretical studies are not given enough workforce?" he asked. North explained the client's position and asked the researcher to bear with this temporary realignment of the project's resources.

As the six-month milestone approached, Denby expressed increasing dissatisfaction with the project's progress. In order to have concrete results to report to Exco management, he directed North a number of times to change the direction of the research. On several occasions various members of the project team had vigorous discussions with Denby about the risks of changing results without laying a careful foundation. North himself spent a good deal of time talking with Denby on this subject, but Denby seemed to discount its importance. Denby began to avoid North and to spend most of his time with the other team members. Eventually the experimental program, initially dedicated to a careful screening of some 50 materials, deteriorated to a somewhat frantic and erratic pursuit of what appeared to be "promising leads." Lacy and Noble played little or no role in this shift of emphasis.

On June 21, 1973, Denby visited North in his office and severely criticized him for proposing a process (hydrochloric acid pickling) that was economically infeasible. In defense, North asked an NRL economist to check his figures. The economist reported back that North's numbers were sound and that, in fact, a source at U.S. Steel indicated that hydrochloric acid pickling was "generally more economic than the traditional process and was increasingly being adopted." Through this and subsequent encounters, the relationship between Denby and North became increasingly strained.

Denby continued to express concern about the Exco project's payoff. In an effort to save time, he discouraged the NRL team from repeating experiments, a practice that was designed to ensure accuracy. Data received from initial experiments were frequently taken as sufficiently accurate, and after hasty analysis were adopted for the purposes of the moment. Not surprisingly, Denby periodically discovered errors in these data. He informed NRL of them.

Denby's visits to NRL became more frequent as the summer progressed. Some days he would visit all three laboratories, talking to the researchers involved and asking them about encouraging leads. North occasionally cautioned Denby against too much optimism. Nonetheless, North continued to oblige the client by restructuring the Exco project to allow for more "production line" scheduling of experiments and for less systematic research.

In August, North discovered that vertile could be obtained from iron ore. This discovery was a significant one, and the client applied for a patent. If the reaction could be proved commercially, its potential would be measured in millions of dollars. Soon thereafter, the NRL team discovered that the operation could, in fact, be handled commercially in a rotary kiln. The client was notified and soon began a pilot plant that would use the rotary kiln process.

Exco's engineering department, after reviewing the plans for the pilot plant, rejected them. It was argued that the rotary process was infeasible and that a fluid bed process would have to be used instead. Denby returned to NRL and insisted on an experiment to test the fluid bed process. North warned Denby that agglomeration (a sticking together of the material) would probably take place. It did. Denby was highly upset, reported to Gray Kenney that he had not received "timely" warning of the probability of agglomeration taking place, and indicated that he had been misled as to the feasibility of the rotary kiln process.[1]

Work continued, and two other "disclosures of invention" were turned over to the client by the end of September.

Personnel Changes

On September 30, Denby came to North's office to request that Charles Fenton be removed from the Exco project. Denby reported he had been watching Fenton in the Electromagnetic Laboratory, which he visited often, and had observed that Fenton spent relatively little time on the Exco project. North, who did not know Fenton well, agreed to look into it. But Denby insisted that Fenton be removed immediately and threatened to terminate the contract if he were allowed to remain.

North was unable to talk to Fenton before taking action because Fenton was on vacation. He did talk to Fenton as soon as he returned, and the researcher admitted that due to the pressure of other work he had not devoted as much time or effort to the Exco work as perhaps he should have.

Three weeks later, Denby called a meeting with Mac Davidson and Sam Lacy. It was their first meeting since the pre-proposal conference for the Exco project. Denby was brief and to the point:

Denby: I'm here because we have to replace North. He's become increasingly difficult to work with and is obstructing the progress of the project.

Lacy: but North is an awfully good man . . .

Davidson: Look, he's come up with some good solid work thus far. What about the process of extracting vertile from iron ore he came up with. And . . .

Denby: I'm sorry, but we have to have a new project leader. I don't mean to be abrupt, but it's either replace North or forget the contract.

Davidson reluctantly appointed Robert Kirk project leader and informed North of the decision. North went to see Davidson a few days later. Davidson told him that although management did not agree with the client, North had been replaced in order to save the contract. Later Dr. Lacy told North the same thing. Neither Lacy nor Davidson made an effort to contact Exco senior management on the matter.

---

[1]Ten months later the client was experimenting with the rotary kiln process for producing vertile from iron ore in his own laboratory.

Following the change of project leadership, the record became more difficult to reconstruct. It appeared that Kirk made many efforts to get the team together, but morale remained low. Denby continued to make periodic visits to NRL but found that the NRL researchers were not talking as freely with him as they had in the past. Denby became skeptical about the project's value. Weeks slipped by. No further breakthroughs emerged.

Lacy's Problem

Dr. Lacy had received weekly status reports on the project, the latest of which is shown in Exhibit 2. He had had a few informal conversations about the project, principally with North and Kirk. He had not read the reports submitted to Exco. If the project had been placed on NRL's "problem list," which comprised about 10 percent of the projects which seemed to be experiencing the most difficulty, Lacy would have received a written report on its status weekly, but the Exco project was not on that list.

With the background given above, Lacy reread Kenney's letter terminating the Exco contract. It seemed likely that Kenney, too, had not had full knowledge of what went on during the project's existence. In his letter, Kenney mentioned the "glowing reports" which reached his ears in the early stages of the work. These reports, which came to him only from Denby, were later significantly modified, and Denby apparently implied that NRL had been "leading him on." Kenney pointed to the complete lack of economic evaluation of alternative processes in the experimentation. He seemed unaware of the fact that at Denby's insistence all economic analysis was supposed to be done by the client. Kenney was most dissatisfied that NRL had not complied with all the provisions of the proposal, particularly those that required full screening of all materials and the completion of the theoretical work.

Lacy wondered why Denby's changes of the proposal had not been documented by the NRL team. Why hadn't he heard more of the problems of the Exco project before? Lacy requested a technical evaluation of the project from the economics process director, and asked Davidson for *his* evaluation of the project. These reports are given in Exhibits 3 and 4. When he reviewed these reports, Lacy wondered what, if any, additional information he should submit to NRL senior management.

Questions

1. Prepare a list of the problems associated with the Exco project, classifying them into categories that you consider meaningful for managerial action.

2. What should Dr. Lacy recommend be done to avoid similar problems in the future?

EXHIBIT 2 Weekly Project Status Report

PROJECT/ACCOUNT STATUS REPORT	ORG 325	PROJ/ACCT 3273	SUB 000	W/O 000	WEEK ENDING DATE 12-22-73	TYPE PROJ	REV TYPE INDUS	PRICE SCA	CLIENT YD		INT/DOM DOMESTIC	NOTICES	PAGE 1

DIVISION PHYSICAL SCI	DEPARTMENT CHEMISTRY LAB	SUPERVISOR ROBERT KIRK	LEADER ROBERT KIRK	PRODUCT TITLE MICROWAVES IN CONVERSION OF BASIC ORES AND MINERALS

INST EXCO	READY DATE 11-06-72	STOP WORK DATE - -	TERM DATE 11-06-74	BURDEN % 28.00	OVERHEAD % 105.00	FEE % 15.00

TRANSACTIONS RECORDED 12-15-73–12-22-73

		LABOR					HOURS	
ORG	ID	W E DATE	T S NO	OBJ	NAME	WEEK	TO DATE
322	02345	12-22-73	363073	13	KIRK	6.0	150
322	02345	12-22-73	363073	22	KIRK	6.0	
322	03212	12-22-73	363082	13	DENSMORE	8.0	25
322	03260	12-22-73	236544	14	COOK	15.0	30
325	12110	12-08-73	C30093	15	HOWARD	15.0	82
325	12110	12-15-73	236548	15	HOWARD	36.0	
325	12110	12-22-73	376147	15	HOWARD	8.0	
325	12357	12-22-73	376149	15	SPELTZ	15.0	68
325	12369	12-22-73	376150	15	GYUIRE	15.0	17
325	12384	12-22-73	R08416	15	DILLON	40.0	44
325	12397	12-22-73	336527	15	NAGY	31.0	31
325	12397	12-22-73	336527	21	NAGY	15.0	
652	12475	12-22-73	236548	15	KAIN	8.0	20
652	12475	12-22-73	236548	21	KAIN	15.0	

Cost Categories (left section):

COST CATEGORIES	(OBJECT CODE)	DOLLARS PTD13WK1	DOLLARS TO DATE	LABOR HOURS ESTIMATE	LABOR HOURS TO DATE	LABOR HOURS BALANCE
SUPERVISOR	(11, 12)		560		36	
SENIOR	(13)	192	17986		1348	
PROFESSIONAL	(14)	150	16787		1678	
TECHNICAL	(15)	529	5299		1037	
CLER/SUPP	(16, 17, 18)		301		84	
OTHER	(10) (19)	72	72		12	
LABOR (S. T.)		943	41005		1644	
BURDEN		248	11481			
OVERHEAD		1227	55110			
OVERTIME PREM	(21)	160	1540			
OVS./OTH. PREM	(22-29)	242	476			
TOTAL PERSONNEL COSTS		2820	109612			
TRAVEL	(56-59)		776			
SUBCONTRACT	(36)					
MATERIAL	(41, 42)		3726			
EQUIPMENT	(43)					
COMPUTER	(37, 45)					
COMMUN	(62, 63, 70, 71)	2	507			
CONSULTANT	(74, 75)					
REPORT COST	(44, 47)					
OTHER M&S		54	99			
TOTAL M&S COST		56	5098			

LAST BILLING DATE 11-30-73
AMOUNT 11350

ACCOUNT STATUS TO DATE
BILLED 154583
PAID 154583

	HOURS	DOLLARS
LABOR (STRAIGHT TIME)	117.0	943
PAYROLL BURDEN		248
OVERHEAD RECOVERY		1227
OVERTIME PREMIUM LABOR	30.0	160
OTHER PREMIUM LABOR	6.0	242
TOTAL PERSONNEL COSTS		2820 S

MATERIALS & SERVICES

PO NO	REF NO	OBJ	DESCRIPTION	REQUESTOR	
61289	54065	48	438	REA EXPRESS	KIRK	42
17234	87413	48	456	GED SUPPLY CO	COOK	10
	04461	71	448	P.T.&T. 326-6200	NAGY	2
			TOTAL M&S COSTS		56 S
		FEE			158
		TRANSACTION TOTAL			3034 T

COMMITMENTS			26847	ESTIMATED	BALANCE
TOTAL LESS FEE		2876	141557	250435	108878
FEE (15.00)		158	24376	37565	13189
TOTAL		3031	165933	288000	122067

TIME BALANCE % 39.4
COST BALANCE % 43.5
TIME BALANCE WKS. 41

COMMITMENT STATUS TO DATE

PO NO		OBJ	VENDOR/DESCRIPTION	TOTAL	CHARGES	BALANCE
A61289	11-21-73	41	MINNESOTA MINING	111	61	50
A61313	11-23-73	41	ALDRICH CHEMICAL	348		348
A95209	11-28-73	43	TENNECO CHEMICAL CO	5		5
A95093	11-15-73	41	UNION CARBIDE CORP	23194		23194
B95104	11-19-73	37	SCIENTIFIC PRODUCTS	600		600
B95232	11-25-73	41	VAN WATERS & ROGERS	2500		2500
018046	12-15-73	57	ROGER MD	300	150	150
					T	26847

EXHIBIT 3
Technical Evaluation

BY RONALD M. BENTON
Director, Process Economics Program

Principal Conclusions

1. The original approach to the investigation as presented in the proposal is technically sound. The accomplishments could have been greater had this been followed throughout the course of the project, but the altered character of the investigation did not prevent accomplishment of fruitful research.

2. The technical conduct of this project on NRL's part was good despite the handicaps under which the work was carried out. Fundamental and theoretical considerations were employed in suggesting the course of research and in interpreting the data. There is no evidence to indicate that the experimental work itself was badly executed.

3. Significant accomplishments of this project were as follows:

   a. *Extraction of vertile from iron ore by several alternative processes.* Conception of these processes was based on fundamental considerations and demonstrated considerable imagination. As far as the work was carried out at NRL, one or more of these processes offers promise of commercial feasibility.

   b. *Nitrogen fixation.* This development resulted from a laboratory observation. The work was not carried far enough to ascertain whether or not the process offers any commercial significance. It was, however, shown that the yield of nitrogen oxides was substantially greater than has previously been achieved by either thermal or plasma processes.

   c. *Reduction of nickel oxide and probably also garnerite to nickel.* These findings were never carried beyond very preliminary stages and the ultimate commercial significance cannot be assessed at this time.

   d. *Discovery that microwave plasmas can be generated at atmospheric pressure.* Again the commercial significance of this finding cannot be appraised at present. However, it opens the possibility that many processes can be conducted economically that would be too costly at the reduced pressures previously thought to be necessary.

4. The proposal specifically stated that the selection of processes for scale-up and economic studies would be the responsibility of the client. I interpret this to mean that NRL was not excluded from making recommendations based on economic considerations. Throughout the course of the investigation, NRL did take economic factors into account in its recommendations.

5. Actual and effective decisions of significance were not documented by NRL and only to a limited extent by the client. There was no attempt on NRL's part to convey the nature or consequences of such decisions to the client's management.

6. The NRL reports were not well prepared, even considering the circumstances under which they were written.

7. It is possible that maximum advantage was not taken of the technical capabilities of personnel in the Electromagnetic Sciences Laboratory. Furthermore, they appeared to have been incompletely informed as to the overall approach to the investigation.

8. There was excessive involvement of the client in the details of experimental work. Moreover, there were frequent changes of direction dictated by the client. Undoubtedly these conditions hampered progress and adequate consideration of major objectives and accomplishments.

9. In the later stages of the project, the client rejected a number of processes and equipment types proposed by NRL for investigation of their commercial feasibility. From the information available to me, I believe that these judgments

EXHIBIT 3
(Continued)

were based on arbitrary opinions as to technical feasibility and superficial extrapolations from other experience as to economic feasibility that are probably not valid.

Evaluation of Client's Complaints

Following are the comments responding to the points raised by the client management during your conversation.

1. *Client anticipated a "full research capability." He had hoped for participation by engineers, chemists, economists, and particularly counted on the provision of an "analytical capability." It was this combination of talents that brought him to NRL rather than [a competitor]. He feels that the project was dominated almost exclusively by chemists.*

    This complaint is completely unfounded. All the disciplines appropriate to the investigation (as called for in the proposal) were engaged on the project to some degree. In addition, men of exceptional capabilities devoted an unusually large amount of time to the project. The client never officially altered the conditions of the proposal stating that no economic studies should be performed by NRL and there was no explicit expression of this desire on the part of the client until near the project termination.

2. *The analytical services were poor. They were sometimes erroneous and there were frequent "deviations." Data was given to the client too hastily, without further experiment and careful analysis, and as a result a significant amount of the data was not reproducible. NRL was inclined to be overly optimistic. "Glowing reports" would be made only to be cancelled or seriously modified later.*

    There is no way of determining whether the analytical services were good or bad, but one can never expect all analytical work to be correct or accurate. Because the client insisted on obtaining raw data, they would certainly receive some analyses that were erroneous. With respect to the allegation that NRL was overly optimistic, there were no recommendations or opinions expressed in the NRL reports or included in the client's notes that can be placed in this category. Whether or not there were verbal statements of this kind cannot of course be ascertained.

3. *There were "errors in the equations and the client was not informed of the changes." This refers to the case of a computer program that had not been "de-bugged." It was the client who discovered the errors and informed NRL of the discrepancies. (The program was eventually straightened out by the Math Sciences Department.)*

    The client's complaint that they were given a computer program which had not been "de-bugged" is valid, but it is not certain that the project leadership gave them the program without exercising normal precautions for its accuracy. The program was developed by a person not presently with NRL and for another project. He transmitted it without any warning that "de-bugging" had not been conducted. It is even possible that the existence and source of error could not have been determined in his usage and would only appear in a different application.

4. *NRL told the client that the "vertile from iron ore" process could be handled commercially in a rotary kiln process and then was informed by his Engineering Division that this was completely infeasible. Plans were then shifted to a fluid bed process and much time and money had been wasted. Client claims that he was not warned that in the fluid bed agglomeration would probably take place. Agglomeration did take place the first time the process was tried ("open boats") and the client was greatly upset.*

EXHIBIT 3
(Continued)

It is unclear whether the original suggestion that a rotary kiln be used in the vertile process came from the client or NRL. In any event, it is a logical choice of equipment and is used for the production of such low-cost items as cement. Without the benefit of at least pilot plant experience that revealed highly abnormal and unfavorable conditions leading to excessive costs, no one would be in a position to state that such equipment would be uneconomic. It is true that a completely standard rotary kiln probably could not be employed, if for no other reason than to prevent the escape of toxic hydrogen sulfide gas from the equipment. At least special design would be needed and probably some mechanical development. However, it is rare that any new process can be installed without special design and development and it is naive to expect otherwise.

I do not know, of course, how much time was actually spent on the "elaborate plans" for the vertile process using a rotary kiln. I can, however, compare it with generally similar types of studies that we carry out in the Process Economics Program. For this kind of process we would expend about 45 engineering man-hours, and the design calculations would be more detailed than the client's engineer made (his cost estimates incidentally reflected inexperience in this field). I doubt, therefore, that this effort represented a serious expenditure of money and would not have been a complete waste even if the process had been based on a partially false premise. The contention that the client was not informed of the agglomeration properties of the vertile while the reaction was taking place seems unlikely. The client's representatives were too intimately concerned with the experimental work that it would be unusual if the subject had not been raised. Moreover, it is doubtful that the client would have been deterred by NRL's warning, in view of their subsequent insistence that considerable effort be devoted to finding means by which a fluid bed could be operated.

5. *The meetings were poorly planned by NRL.*

   There is no way of evaluating this complaint, but certainly the extreme frequency of the meetings would not be conducive to a well-organized meeting.

6. *Experimental procedures were not well planned.*

   Apparently this refers to the client's desire that experiments be planned in detail as much as three months in advance. Such an approach might conceivably be useful merely for purposes of gathering routine data. It is naive to think that research can or should be planned to this degree and certainly if NRL had acceded to the request it would have been a fruitless time-consuming exercise.

7. *Economic support was not given by NRL.*

   As mentioned above, the proposal specifically excluded NRL from economic evaluations, but NRL did make use of economic considerations in its suggestions and recommendations.

8. *NRL promised to obtain some manganese nodules but never produced them.*

   Manganese nodules were obtained by NRL but no experiments were ever run with them. Many other screening experiments originally planned were never carried out because of the changed direction of the project. It seems likely, therefore, that the failure to conduct an experiment with manganese nodules was not NRL's responsibility.

9. *The client claims that he does not criticize NRL for failing "to produce a process." He says that he never expected one, that he wanted a good screening of ores and reactions as called for in the proposal, and that he had hoped for results from the*

EXHIBIT 3
(Concluded)

theoretical studies—Task B. This he feels he did not get. We did not do what the proposal called for.

The statement that a process was not expected seems entirely contrary to the course of the project. There was universal agreement among NRL personnel involved that almost immediately after the project was initiated it was converted into a crash program to find a commercial process. In fact, the whole tenor of the project suggests a degree of urgency incompatible with a systematic research program. It is quite true that the theoretical studies as a part of Task B were never carried out. According to the project leader this part of the proposal was never formally abandoned, it was merely postponed. Unfortunately, this situation was never documented by NRL, as was the case with other significant effective decisions.

Additional Comments

1. It appears that the first indication that the client expected economic studies or evaluations of commercial feasibility occurred during the summer of 1973. At this time the project leader was severely criticized by the client's representatives for having proposed a process (hydrochloric acid pickling) that was economically infeasible. The basis for this criticism was that hydrochloric acid pickling of steel had not proved to be economically feasible. It is totally unreasonable to expect that NRL would have access to information of this kind, and such a reaction would certainly have the effect of discouraging any further contributions of an economic or commercial nature by NRL rather than encouraging them. Actually it is patently ridiculous to directly translate economic experience of the steel industry with steel pickling to leaching a sulfided titanium ore. Nevertheless, I directed an inquiry to a responsible person in U.S. Steel as to the status of hydrochloric acid pickling. His response (based on the consensus of their experts) was diametrically opposite to the client's information. While there are situations that are more favorable to sulfuric acid pickling, hydrochloric acid pickling is generally more economical and is becoming increasingly adopted.

2. The reports written by NRL were requested by the client, but on an urgent and "not fancy" basis. If such were the case, it is understandable that the project leader would be reluctant to expend enough time and money on the report to make it representative of NRL's normal reports. However, the nature of the report seems to indicate that they are directed toward the same individuals with whom NRL was in frequent contact, or persons with a strong interest in the purely scientific aspects. The actual accomplishments of the project were not brought out in a manner that would have been readily understandable to client's management.

Recommendations

It is recommended that consideration be given to the establishment of a simple formal procedure by which high-risk projects could be identified at the proposal stage and brought to the attention of the division vice president. There should also be a formal procedure, operative after project acceptance, in which specific responsibilities are assigned for averting or correcting subsequent developments that would be adverse to NRL's and the client's interests.

Some of the factors that would contribute to a high-risk condition are insufficient funding, insufficient time, low chance of successfully attaining objectives, an unsophisticated client, public or private political conditions, and so forth. The characteristics that made this a high-risk project were certainly apparent at the time the proposal was prepared.

EXHIBIT 4

MEMORANDUM

January 8, 1974

To: Sam Lacy
From: Mac Davidson
Re: The Exco Project—Conclusions

The decision to undertake this project was made without sufficient consideration of the fact that this was a "high-risk" project.

The proposal was technically sound and within the capabilities of the groups assigned to work on the project.

There was virtually no coordination between the working elements of Physical Sciences and Electronics in the preparation of the proposal.

The technical conduct of this project, with few exceptions, was, considering the handicaps under which the work was carried out, good and at times outstanding. The exceptions were primarily due to lack of attention to detail.

The NRL reports were not well prepared, even considering the circumstances under which they were written.

The client, acting under pressure from his own management, involved himself excessively in the details of experimental work and dictated frequent changes of direction and emphasis. The proposal opened the door to this kind of interference.

There was no documentation by NRL of the decisions made by the client which altered the character, direction, and emphasis of the work.

There was no serious attempt on the part of NRL to convey the nature or consequence of the above actions to the client.

Less than half of the major complaints made by the client concerning NRL's performance are valid.

The project team acquiesced too readily in the client's interference and management acquiesced too easily to the client's demands.

Management exercised insufficient supervision and gave inadequate support to the project leader in his relations with the client.

There were no "overruns" either in time or funds.

Case 16–4

Easter Seal Foundation of New Hampshire and Vermont, Inc.*

Larry Gammon, newly elected president of the Easter Seal Foundation of New Hampshire and Vermont, was meeting with a consultant from Easter Seals National to review the Foundation's current situation. He had requested some assistance in addressing several thorny issues he faced in determining the future directions of the organization. On one hand, he was attempting to evaluate the impact of his predecessor's decision to restructure the organization from a single entity into one with four corporate subsidiaries, and the impact that this had had on the quality of decision-making and the level of conflict in the organization. On the other, he was attempting to assess the reasons underlying a growing deficit in the organization's operations, and the changes he might make to give the managers of the subsidiaries greater incentives to operative in a cost-effective manner.

Background

The National Easter Seal Society began in 1919, playing a service and advocacy role for disabled people. Since its inception, many government and other private agencies had entered the rehabilitation movement. National Easter Seals continued to operate, but also to reassess its role, in light of changing demographics, new technology, and the presence of other organizations in the rehabilitation market.

The New Hampshire Easter Seal Society was incorporated as a statewide organization with membership in the National Easter Seal Society. Membership in the National Society brought to affiliated organizations the power of the Easter Seals name, the availability of consulting services, and, perhaps best known, the fund-raising power of a National Telethon.

The Easter Seal Foundation of New Hampshire and Vermont was a $7 million nonprofit organization. Directed by a volunteer board, it provided services to the handicapped, viewing that term in a very broad way. For example, under its sponsorship, elderly citizens were transported and the possibility existed for housing provision, as well. Physical and vocational intervention also was offered to a population of diverse ages in diverse settings. The organization owned a facility in Manchester, New Hampshire, where some of its work was based, and offered contract services in other settings. It also owned a summer camp in New Durham, a building in Plymouth, and recently had taken on a building in Vermont.

*This case was prepared by Dena Rakoff under the supervision of Professor David W. Young. Copyright © by David W. Young.

For over twenty years, the Foundation had operated under the leadership of Robert Cholette, Mr. Gammon's predecessor. Mr. Cholette took the organization from a budget of $89,000 and a staff of 11 to its current size. Mr. Cholette also altered the organization's strategy and structure in significant ways. Faced over fifteen years ago with an erosion in its client base due to the emerging role of hospitals in delivering similar services, the organization—known at the time as the New Hampshire Easter Seal Society—began a process of diversification. Early in his tenure, for example, Mr. Cholette acquired the franchise for the Goodwill Industries, an organization devoted to vocational training, and to recycling salvage clothing and other goods. Ten years later, he divested Easter Seals of the franchise, citing as causes the loss of its building in an eminent domain process, a reduction in client referrals, and a decline in the salvage market.

EXHIBIT 1
Potential Benefits of the Plan

1. The Agency would receive all interest, depreciation, principal or whatever costs which are legitimate in a rental agreement to be reimbursed by third parties.
2. There could be a savings of taxes and profit mark-ups if the Agency owns rather than leases its properties.
3. The corporate reorganization would assist in addressing the question of unrelated revenue.
4. A separate corporation for the Special Transit Service would provide us with an additional shield for liability to the Board of Directors and to the other corporations of the organization.
5. The Board of Directors of the Foundation would approve the grants given to the other subsidiary corporations and would be involved in the decision relating to the limitation of free services.
6. We would at the same time address the New Hampshire/Vermont region in the Agency's corporate structure.
7. It is possible that we would open new doors with SBA, EDA, and other funding sources.
8. We would obtain some flexibility in the negotiations for merger and we would be prepared to handle the ownership of property should additional mergers develop.
9. The corporate structure would offer more opportunity for Board leadership, development and training.
10. There will be little, if any, staff and accounting disruption and very little business office disruption.
11. The cost of the Plan is relatively low in that no large computer or other type of complicated structures will be necessary.
12. The Plan lends itself to the Agency's goal of merger and/or acquisition of other agencies, future housing programs, development of real property gifts program, and many others.
13. Revenues generated by the affiliate corporations, if successful, could ultimately strengthen the Foundation's financial condition.

Throughout his tenure with the organization, Mr. Cholette constantly attempted to balance the dual goals of providing services to needy clients while remaining financially solvent. Toward the end of his twenty-two years with the organization, he became increasingly convinced that financial survival was, in large part, conditioned upon size. As a result, in addition to growth via new services, Mr. Cholette sought growth by merger. Five years prior to his retirement, and with a budget of $3.5 million, the then-named New Hampshire Easter Seal Society and Goodwill Industries merged with three other entities: Special Transit Services, Inc., New Hampshire Youth Advocacy Program, and the Vermont Family Teaching Program.

During the next several years, Mr. Cholette undertook a rather massive corporate reorganization, which formally began when the board of directors voted to cast off the single organizational skin and establish a holding company, which it called the Easter Seal Society/Goodwill Industries Foundation of New Hampshire and Vermont, Inc. The new holding company comprised several subsidiaries: the Easter Seal/Goodwill Industries of New Hampshire and Vermont Society (called "The Society"), the Special Transit Services (STS), and Agency Realty, Inc. (ARI). In his presentation to the Board prior to the vote to establish a holding company, Mr. Cholette outlined several potential benefits of the plan, which are shown in Exhibit 1. The resulting organizational structure is shown in Exhibit 2.

As Exhibit 2 indicates, the Foundation served as a parent company, providing development and other business management services, collecting excess revenues from the subsidiaries, and distributing subsidies in the form of grants or loans where revenue did not cover expenses. The Society was the service arm of the organization, under contract to the national service organization in its name. In the various service facilities there were no longer any full-time administrative personnel; rather, administration was done by vice

EXHIBIT 2
Order of Authority and Reporting

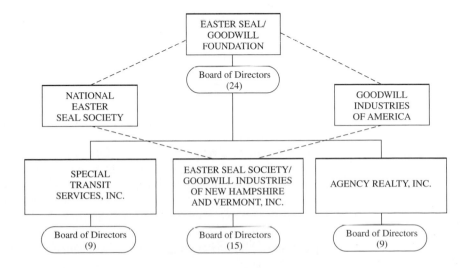

presidents supervising on a functional basis. STS owned or leased, and ran, all the vehicles that Easter Seals and Goodwill needed, and ARI owned or leased all the buildings the organizations used.

Some time later, Easter Seals Management Corporation was added to the organization, resulting in the structure shown in Exhibit 3 (the names in parentheses are those following Mr. Cholette's Departure). Finally, whereas previously there had been a single board of directors, Mr. Cholette devised a series of interlocking boards to oversee the separate and connected workings of all the parts of the organization. The Foundation's board consisted of 24 members with terms varying from one to three years; the Society's board had 15 members with the same terms; the STS and the ARI boards each had nine members, also with terms from one to three years. Six members of both the STS and ARI boards also were on the Foundation board. The Vice Chairman of the Foundation's board was the Chairman of the STS board; the Treasurer of the Foundation's board was the Chairman of the ARI board.

When Mr. Gammon assumed the presidency of the Foundation, the organization consisted of the structure shown in Exhibit 3, with the Foundation as the holding company and four separately incorporated subsidiaries: STS, the Easter Seal Societies of New Hampshire and Vermont, the Easter Seal Management Corporation, and ARI. Essentially, where previously there had been one corporation, there now were four, each with its own set of books, with a great deal of buying and selling of services among the four, and with a need to allocate the overhead of the Foundation among the remaining three if the full cost of services was to be calculated.

Financial Situation

The Foundation and its subsidiaries had been operating at a loss for the past two fiscal years; the losses totaled almost $232,000 and just over $371,000, respectively. Financial statements are contained in Exhibit 4. Year-to-date figures for the first six months of the current fiscal year (Exhibit 5) indicated that the situation was continuing to worsen, showing a $180,000 loss, as compared with a projected surplus of about $38,000.

As Mr. Gammon and his consultant reviewed the growing deficit and the reorganization that had taken place some four years earlier, they focused on several questions. Among them was the matter of the organization's mission of ". . . providing the highest quality of diagnostic, rehabilitative and support services to maximize individual potential through the most comprehensive offering of programs, responsive to needs of the community, to individuals of all ages in the most caring and cost-effective manner." Mr. Gammon wondered if this mission was served most effectively through the current organizational structure. The two also thought they should have a better understanding of why the reorganization had taken place, which they felt would help answer the question of what, if anything, should be changed or salvaged. Finally, if the

EXHIBIT 3   **Organizational Structure**

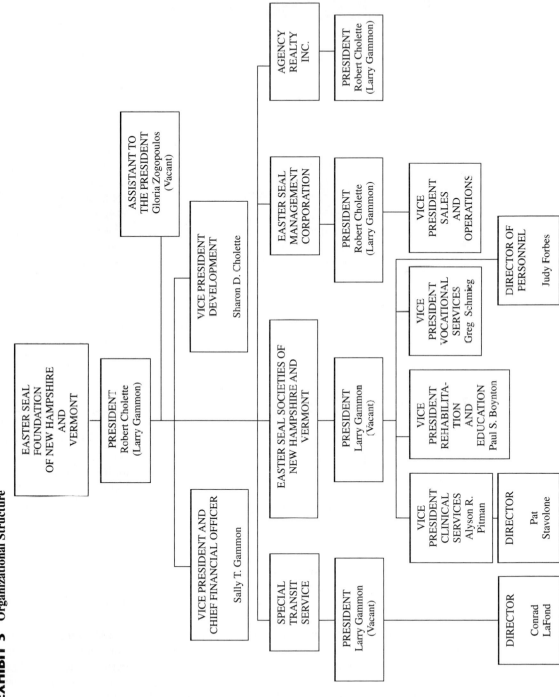

EXHIBIT 4
Financial Statements

EASTER SEAL FOUNDATION AND SUBSIDIARIES		
Consolidated Balance Sheets as of 31 August		
	Last Year	2 Years Ago
ASSETS		
Current assets:		
Cash	$ 127,423	$ 126,533
Accounts receivable, less allowances		
for uncollectible accounts	879,695	1,020,057
Pledges receivable, less allowances		
for uncollectible pledges	165	653
Due from other funds	83,076	124,159
Inventories	15,713	18,547
Prepaid expenses and other current assets.	64,398	75,329
Total current assets	$1,170,470	$1,365,278
Property, plant and equipment (net).	4,369,503	4,394,247
Other assets:		
Unamortized debt issuance costs.	17,814	14,569
Board designated investments:		
Cash and cash equivalents.	4,047	33,532
Investments, at cost.	367,828	318,866
	371,875	352,398
Total assets	$5,929,662	$6,126,492
LIABILITIES AND NET ASSETS		
Current liabilities:		
Notes payable to bank.	480,000	365,000
Accounts payable	394,822	177,922
Accrued expenses	141,194	112,664
Due to other funds	83,076	124,159
Deferred income	60,436	130,044
Current portion of long-term debt.	179,051	144,599
Total current liabilities	$1,338,579	$1,054,388
Long-term debt, less current portion.	1,911,084	2,021,185
Net assets	$2,679,999	$3,050,919
Total liabilities and net assets.	$5,929,662	$6,126,492

current organizational form was to be preserved, Mr. Gammon thought he should be attempting to determine some reasonable goals for the heads of each of the different subsidiaries.

There also were a variety of issues surrounding the management control system. In particular Mr. Gammon wondered about the financial results for which the individual subsidiaries should be held responsible. He also was concerned about the means for allocating the Foundation's overhead to the subsidiaries, and for determining appropriate financial recognition for the

EXHIBIT 4
(Continued)

EASTER SEAL FOUNDATION AND SUBSIDIARIES		
Consolidated Statement of Public Support, Revenue, and Expenses		
	Last Year	**2 Years Ago**
Public support and revenue		
Public support:		
Contributions..........................	$ 220,842	$ 228,266
Bequests	500	92,077
Special events, net of related direct costs, ...	213,571	197,888
Telethon, net of related direct costs	409,304	343,366
Total public support......................	$ 844,217	$ 861,597
Revenue:		
Fees and grants from governmental agencies	$4,200,896	$4,040,347
Program service fees	1,417,251	1,320,111
Sales to public............................	683,512	686,731
Investment income	27,055	32,831
Rental income	14,771	18,310
Management fees	25,986	
Miscellaneous revenue......................	8,337	14,710
Total revenue	$6,377,808	$6,113,040
Total public support and revenue	$7,222,025	$6,974,637
Expenses:		
Program services:		
Public health education	$ 447,516	$ 362,511
Professional education and training	100,359	33,259
Direct services	5,867,689	5,616,693
Total program service......................	$6,415,564	$6,012,463
Support services:		
Management and general.....................	$ 993,496	$ 919,171
Fund-raising	137,739	217,548
Total supporting services	1,131,235	1,136,719
Total program and supporting services	$7,546,799	$7,149,182
Payments to national organizations................	46,522	57,433
Total expenses	$7,593,321	$7,206,615
Surplus (deficit).............................	(371,296)	(231,978)

services that they provided to each other. Finally, he knew he needed a much better understanding than he now had about the causes of the growing deficit so that the trend could be reversed before it was too late.

In an effort to gain a better understanding of some of these issues, Mr. Gammon asked the consultant to meet with some board members as well as several of the key executives in the Foundation and its subsidiaries to get their perspectives on the rationale for reorganization as well as the problems faced by the heads of the subsidiaries.

EXHIBIT 5

EASTER SEAL FOUNDATION OF NEW HAMPSHIRE AND VERMONT, INC.
Profit & Loss Statement Year to Date as of February

By Profit Center	Revenues YTD	Expenses YTD	Profit (Loss)	Projected Profit (Loss)	Variance YTD
Foundation.........	$1,235,279	$1,429,821	($ 194,542)	$ 37,962	($ 232,504)
NH Society.........	3,224,184	3,317,592	(93,408)	10,774	(104,182)
VT Society	178,946	173,465	5,481	144	5,337
STS...............	240,029	247,178	(7,149)	26,365	(33,514)
ARI...............	315,237	243,888	71,349	74,474	(3,125)
	$5,193,675	$5,411,944	($ 218,269)	$ 149,719	($ 367,988)

By Line Item	Monthly Actual	Monthly Proj.	Variance	YTD Actual	YTD Proj.	Variance	Annual Budget
Revenues							
Memorials	$ 95	$ 394	($ 299)	$ 835	$ 1,134	($ 299)	$ 3,500
Mailings	1,150	66,265	(65,115)	112,760	170,416	(57,656)	278,645
Sweeps............	57,462	87,009	(29,547)	147,553	176,235	(28,682)	287,700
Clubs/organizations ..	0	72	(72)	0	72	(72)	500
Special gifts	0	857	(857)	0	857	(857)	6,000
Foundations & trusts .	1,000	227	773	7,408	6,635	773	8,000
Comb. fed campaign .	0	0	0	1,691	1,691	0	3,500
Special events.......	98,647	94,592	4,055	109,320	105,533	3,787	180,260
Telethon events	8,047	18,662	(10,615)	57,427	65,263	(7,836)	235,375
Telethon...........	4,070	46,338	(42,268)	15,242	56,559	(41,317)	363,500
Bequests...........	0	0	0	0	0	0	0
Planned giving	0	4,499	(4,499)	18,507	23,006	(4,499)	50,000
Other contr. income..	0	0	0	1,494	1,494	0	0
Other gifts	0	0	0	0	0	0	20,000
Total contributions ..	170,471	318,915	(148,444)	472,237	608,895	(136,658)	1,436,980
Sale of mail lists	415	4,828	(4,413)	4,932	9,345	(4,413)	19,000
Telemarketing Rev. ...	0	0	0	0	0	0	0
Non Profit Prof Org...	1,919	1,669	250	12,565	12,590	(25)	12,590
Investment income...	3,625	4,226	(601)	22,142	22,743	(601)	48,100
Misc income........	0	0	0	84	0	84	0
Public ed revenue....	0	0	0	400	400	0	400
Reim for subsidiary ...	102,012	111,001	(8,989)	658,719	665,421	(6,702)	1,331,423
Revenue STS........	(5,908)	8,223	(2,315)	(7,149)	26,635	(19,486)	4,586
Revenue ARI	12,129	12,082	47	71,349	74,474	(3,125)	147,297
Total sales..........	126,008	142,029	(16,021)	777,340	811,608	(34,268)	1,563,396
Total revenues......	$ 296,479	$ 460,944	($ 164,465)	$1,249,577	$1,420,503	($170,926)	$3,000,376

EXHIBIT 5 (Continued)

EASTER SEAL FOUNDATION OF NEW HAMPSHIRE AND VERMONT, INC.
Profit & Loss Statement Year to Date as of February

By Line Item	Monthly Actual	Monthly Proj.	Variance	YTD Actual	YTD Proj.	Variance	Annual Budget
Expenses							
Salaries—staff	$ 64,923	$ 86,537	($ 21,614)	$ 450,543	$ 462,625	($ 12,082)	$ 982,587
Taxes & benefits	21,360	15,987	5,373	78,990	71,990	7,000	168,034
Prof. fees.	32,789	54,358	(21,569)	185,348	159,174	26,174	363,457
Supplies	27,172	39,014	(11,842)	75,430	83,452	(8,022)	199,771
Telephone.	1,924	2,142	(218)	9,836	9,946	(110)	36,419
Postage/shipping . . .	53,181	37,073	16,108	104,527	85,046	19,481	144,405
Rents.	2,516	2,516	0	15,091	15,091	0	33,590
Insurance	0	0	0	0	0	0	0
Printing.	7,455	13,853	(6,398)	59,822	47,814	12,008	72,099
Travel—employee . . .	4,572	6,537	(1,965)	10,458	10,737	(279)	27,498
Travel—meetings. . . .	4,552	4,606	(54)	13,253	13,530	(277)	23,601
Travel—agency veh . .	0	581	(581)	3,165	3,671	(506)	5,960
Membership fees. . . .	5,214	4,765	449	30,906	30,305	601	58,916
Equip. tent/serv/minor	(54)	698	(752)	1,472	1,222	250	4,353
Misc. expenses	397	4,231	(3,834)	4,475	7,286	(2,811)	26,155
Interest expense	8,599	5,321	3,278	41,940	35,231	6,709	57,000
Depreciation	4,332	5,132	(800)	25,911	26,710	(799)	57,509
Occup. repairs.	0	57	(57)	0	57	(57)	400
Assist to individ.	0	0	0	0	0	0	
Grants to society	53,109	53,109	0	318,654	318,654	0	637,312
Total expenses	292,041	336,517	(44,476)	1,429,821	1,382,541	47,280	2,899,066
Profit (Loss)	$ 4,438	$ 124,427	($119,989)	($ 180,244)	$ 37,962	($218,206)	$ 101,310

Views of Board Members

Brad Cook

Reorganization was a change that we didn't need, but it's probably worked out all right. Before it, the ESS was everything; at least in appearance, we were a cohesive whole. Bob Cholette was a masterful executive who took advantage of opportunities as he found them. He picked up STS and started ARI. As a Board member in the past, you heard about everything.

We were presented with the restructuring proposal by Bob, whose reasons were three: he was responding to perceived needs, he was hoping for greater flexibility, and, for accounting purposes, he was trying to avoid possible unrelated business income. I had reservations, and I still have them, mainly centering around the time and cost necessarily incurred by this kind of reorganization.

At both meetings where the Board discussed the restructuring proposal, I did express my reservations; in fact, I almost voted against the restructuring when the vote occurred, but all the details had been worked out, so I went along with the 'yes' vote, and it was unanimous.

On the positive side, I look at such improvements as the fact that now the holding company does all the fund-raising, and the agency, busy with program and service delivery, doesn't have to bother about that at all. There are also good results in terms of people. We want to keep people happy, and we have now created some second level presidencies, rather than keeping people as vice presidents under a single president. As president of the holding company, Bob would be free from some day-to-day responsibilities to explore other opportunities, and the people below him would have more power; but they could have had the same power without the corporate reorganization. The flexibility of our new organization allows us to form a new Vermont corporation for our new franchise, the Vermont Easter Seals Society, headed by a Vermont executive. We can have telethons in Vermont, with contributions from Vermont residents, whose money will stay in the state and help Vermont residents. The New Hampshire president can stay within his New Hampshire budget without any losses from Vermont affecting on his results.

But, let's ask a larger question: Is this change good for the organization? There's nothing we couldn't have done before, without the reorganization, that we do now with the restructuring. For instance, one of the changes that we now have in place, an alleged advantage, is that we can identify costs and assign responsibility. We could have done this anyway. Time and money were costs during the restructuring, and they continue to be.

How much have we added to our expenses? There's no complete answer to this, but I can name for you some costs that would not have existed without the change. There are additional accounting fees, filing fees, some computer costs, legal costs, and internal staff costs. There are savings too, but they can't be quantified.

On the positive side, in terms of the Board, we now have more opportunity to watch specific things going on in the organization. More Board members, as they move around to the subsidiary boards, are familiar with the small details and functions of our operations. But the negative side of this is that no group of us looks at the whole any more. That is supposed to be the Foundation Board's job. What we see are book reports when we sit at a full Board meeting. Each member reports what his subsidiary Board is doing. And, of course, we believe everything we hear. I worry that the more diffuse we become, the greater the danger of not knowing. We have to work now to know what's going on with the whole organization. Under the wrong executive this subsidiary system could be manipulated to keep us all dumb.

With bad people, this restructuring will fail; but, with bad people we would have failed with any structure. On the other hand, with good people, and we do have good people, it will work, as it would have worked without the change.

Karl Norwood

I've had over an 11-year affiliation with the organization. We on the Board have had very little direct involvement with actual operations. We play, rather, a policy role. Over the years, ES has become larger and more complex.

I find life after the restructuring much more interesting and productive. Now, we are better able to take advantage of the different expertise that the various

Board members bring; because of their smaller units of responsibility, they can come closer to the day-to-day activities. We can impose more accountability now; we can make sure that budget and goals are met. We are able to develop a more meaningful dialogue with the staff as we get closer to the day-to-day issues.

At the ARI Board meetings, for instance, we are focused solely on real estate. Within the separate Boards, we can meet more frequently. Availability of funds can be quite unpredictable. We can spot reductions of funds more quickly now. Consider one of our major sources of money, the telethons. We don't know ahead of time how much money will be raised from these. And grant cutbacks also have a domino effect. As we identify problems more quickly now, we can react more quickly. We underwent a corporate separation a few years ago in disaffiliating ourselves with Goodwill Industries. If we had had the various separate Boards in place then, we could have acted more quickly, and not waited, as we did, three years longer than we should have.

We're now asking hard questions. I see a change in the fact that we are relying less on government funding, and more looking out for new funding sources. We are reshaping our mission statement, and making sure that we operate within it.

I don't see any disadvantages to this restructuring plan. If you pushed me to suggest an improvement, I might say that continued communication always helps.

Views of Key Executives

Elin Treanor, Comptroller

I've been with ES for seven years. I oversee financial transactions, coordinate the budget, and am responsible for monthly and annual financial statements for both the separate and the consolidated corporations. It's sometimes hard to remember what occurred before and what after the restructuring, but I do have the sense that some of the changes that we've seen recently within the organization might have come about whether or not we restructured.

I've been assessing the costs of running multiple corporations, four of them. We now keep separate records—ledgers, books, financial statements, bank accounts, budgets, and payroll—for each of the four subdivisions. But people like Bob Cholette have said to me, and I guess he may be right, that I was, in effect, doing these separate functions before the restructuring anyway.

We now have four separate accounting specialists, one for each subsidiary, where before we had one accountant. Previously, the one specialist had to know about all the functions of the organization, such as transportation, fund-raising, and rehabilitation. Now each of the four has to know well only the function of the subsidiary he serves; that is an improvement. I know whom to call when there's a question about transportation, for instance, and I can spot the errors more quickly because the packages are smaller. But, you can see that we now have four people on our payroll, where we had only one before.

I can identify another advantage to the present structure for you. I am now able to groom junior accountants on a small subdivision, where before I couldn't have given those same people such useful in-house training; you can't cut your teeth on a large operation, but you can practice on one division. I would have had to hire from the outside, instead.

Sally Gammon and I are finding in our jobs a lot of time taken up by the issues of the restructuring, and a lot of stress. The corporate form is still evolving. For example, before Bob left, I was positioned between two presidents: him and Larry (who was president of both the Society and STS). Now I'll be positioned between Larry and whoever replaces him in the Society and STS. He had gained power over his subordinates, but he found things imposed on him by the parent company, which, I believe, became very frustrating for him. For instance, he wanted control over his overhead costs, rather than having a given percentage imposed on him. He didn't want a standard form lease imposed on him, but rather wanted the flexibility to lease yearly or sublet, actions he might have taken before when real estate was not a separate subsidiary corporation. He did not want costs he couldn't control included in his budget evaluation; he felt he shouldn't be accountable for what he wasn't allowed to control. We are still working out who makes decisions. It will be interesting to see what changes Larry makes now that he is President of the holding company.

When Bob was president, Sally and I found ourselves in the middle. We are still working out jurisdictions.

The budget for the whole corporation used to be worked out before in a single retreat, on a single calendar. Now the Foundation submits its budget in May, and the Society submits a budget in July, having been mandated certain allocations by the previously decided Foundation budget. At budget revision time all four corporations are revising at the same time. Which one does its first is an issue; cuts are done separately, but are dependent on knowledge of what others are cutting, and that information is not freely given.

This business has some external factors that make accurate prediction difficult. For example, we made projections for the past fiscal year based on tuition rates that a state special education funder approved on a preliminary basis last year. Now, in May, a year later, this preliminary approval was denied. That leaves us some $200,000 that will not be reimbursed. We're appealing now. We've put together an external affairs committee that has been lobbying in the state to change things like this.

Bob couldn't oversee everything before. The restructuring freed him to take the entrepreneurial role he wanted, for instance in the ARI project. He was a great salesman who could sell almost anything to the Board. Only once was he voted down by them, and that was on a relatively minor proposal.

We used to have a centralized system, but the different corporations have different needs. This may result in our having to buy new computer systems. Moreover, we now need internal contracts because we have four interacting corporations. And we have the difficult task of assigning transfer costs agreeable to all parties. Accounting finds itself in the middle here.

National ES needs a consolidated set of financial statements. If you zero in on the bottom line, which is always important, you will see that we are still operating at a loss. Because we are now divided into separate corporations, we can show our funders a clearer need for funding than we could when one division's shortfall was made up by another's success.

Funders will often pay for rent where they will not reimburse for interest and carrying charges on a mortgage. They have been trying to tap the corporate veil recently, to understand how the rent figure is derived. Sometimes people think there is double charging of overhead; that's not so: Some items are entered multiple times because of the reporting system. Here's an example of the Society's budget (Exhibit 6).

EXHIBIT 6   Budget for the New Hampshire Society

	Last Year Revised	This Year's Budget	Variance
Fees—Indiv./Ins.	1,587,600	1,710,000	122,400
Govt. Agencies	597,666	630,000	32,334
Tuitions	1,726,809	1,690,000	(36,809)
Housing	657,514	820,000	162,486
Grants	568,057	500,000	(68,057)
Itinerant	363,886	365,000	1,114
Industrial	639,364	675,000	35,636
Salary Reimb. School	14,474	15,000	526
Rent/Sale Property	23,508	10,000	(13,508)
Misc. Income	29,309	25,000	(4,309)
Reimb. from Subsidiary	80,200	83,000	2,800
Free Service Allowance	(150,000)	(150,000)	0
Grants From FD	582,312	697,000	114,688
Total Revenue	6,720,699	7,070,000	349,301
Salaries—Staff	3,044,321	3,144,500	100,179
Salaries—Clients	257,745	270,000	12,255
Taxes and Benefits	572,608	587,000	14,392
Professional Fees	694,595	650,000	(44,595)
Supplies	164,855	174,000	9,145
Telephone	63,678	65,000	1,322
Postage and Shipping	16,344	17,000	656
Rents	581,890	521,000	(60,890)
Building Expense	177,413	165,000	(12,413)
Printing	9,454	10,000	546
Travel—Employee	63,862	70,000	6,138
Travel—Meetings	22,159	45,000	22,841
Agency Vehicles	216,685	220,000	3,315
Assist. to Indiv.	23,505	25,000	1,495
Membership Dues	54,190	56,000	1,810
Minor Equipment	19,117	22,000	2,883
Equipment Rental	12,847	13,000	153
Matching Expenses	12,500	33,000	20,500
Misc. Expense (Ads and Fees)	31,315	10,000	(21,315)
Interest Expense	428	500	72
Depreciation	44,703	37,000	(7,703)
Trans P.Ed from FD	299,306	300,000	694
Trans. Bus. Mgmt. from FD	611,673	625,000	13,327
Bad Debt Expense	40,000	40,000	0
Total Expense	7,035,193	7,100,000	64,807
Net Income (Loss)	(314,494)	(30,000)	284,494

Conrad LaFond, Director of STS

Since I came aboard, the budget of STS has grown from $60,000 to $540,000, and the fleet of vehicles has grown from 9 (Easter Seals had 6 and STS had 3) to 25. We've financed them by grants, fees for service, and donations.

We lease these vehicles to the Easter Seals branch in Laconia, to the Easter Seals people right here in Manchester, and to the camp in New Durham. We also subcontract to outside organizations such as the special education program in the local public school system, an independent living transportation system for senior citizens, and special transportation to the Catholic Medical Center; and, if we have free time in our schedule at the last minute, we provide free service or charge just enough money to cover our expenses.

We rent space from Easter Seals. Those rents are included in our expenses even though they are collected by another Easter Seals agency, ARI. The grant givers are beginning to refuse to pay such overhead. However, I couldn't rent space elsewhere for the low charges they're imposing on me. And no one has said anything about the parking of my vehicles out on the back lot. If I were renting from someone else, they probably would charge for that space.

If Easter Seals in Laconia owned its own vehicles, they could deduct (or charge to funders) the actual out-of-pocket expenses of running them, but not depreciation, which falls in the category of overhead. Since we, STS, own them, and lease to ES, the cost to ES is all expense.

The Foundation runs a public health education program, and charges the costs on to the other corporations. Essentially, we're taxed but have no representation; that is, have no say in the decision to run that program. The president of the Easter Seals is also the president of STS. I'm the director.

Then, there's the revenue side. If the charges for transportation, that is, the fees we are allowed to charge Easter Seals, are not as high as I think they should be, I can't point that out when my revenues don't meet expectations.

I work on the budget with the President of my corporation. He can tell me to allocate, say, $1,000 worth of transportation services to the Adult Day Health Program. If that doesn't provide for all the transportation they need, they would have to contract elsewhere for the services or raise the necessary monies.

How do I know if I have succeeded? The bottom line tells it all. I see how I've done financially from that, and I can tell the services that have been provided from that.

We are forever projecting costs and revenues here; we work on budgets 12 months a year.

Pat Stavolone, Director of Clinical Services

I've been here for seven years. I haven't been affected directly by the reorganization, but I suppose we are more autonomous now. Each department head now makes his or her own projections.

We measure success at budget revision time, which happens in the middle of the year. Also, I have just started to collect weekly reports. I am responsible for measuring how we are doing compared to our projections, for compiling a 1–5 year plan and for drawing up a clinical budget. If I wanted to begin a new program, I would either submit a new budget in the 1–5 year plan or submit a proposal for a new project with accompanying budget at any point during the fiscal year.

Sharon Cholette, Vice President for Development

There were two reasons for the reorganization. First, and the original reason, was to let Easter Seals carry out more entrepreneurial ventures. Bob was considering the Agency Realty project, for instance. He hoped to channel back into the nonprofit agency the proceeds from some profit-making activities. The second reason was to provide protection from any liability claims against the bus fleet that might reach the entire organization. I understand that a finding of negligence would still allow the entire group of corporations to be sued, but without negligence, a plaintiff would likely have to stop with STS's liability.

The Development Department is responsible for raising contributed income and also for agency promotion and publicity. The most visible project, which accomplishes both of these objectives, is the annual telethon, which is broadcast for 21 hours each spring. It is part of the National Easter Seals telethon. We began the telethon in 1976 and raised $60,000. We now raise over $600,000 each year. The telethon involves hundreds of business people and corporations from throughout New Hampshire. The fund-raising projects presented on the telethon go on year round. In addition to supervising all the fund-raising for the telethon, I also write and produce the show.

The telethon is broadcast from our Easter Seals Center. This gives us the opportunity to bring the business people into the center for meetings and for the event itself. Most first-time visitors are surprised at the size and scope of our programs. This dramatically increases our support.

My biggest single fund-raiser is the snowmobile ride-in, which has brought in about $100,000 during each of the last two years. It costs about $10,000 for us to raise that much in that project. It began with a poster girl's father, who was also a snowmobiler, and is now handled totally by the New Hampshire Snowmobile Association, with clubs competing among themselves to raise contributions.

We use about 12 percent of our budget to raise the money we do bring in. If we don't net $5,000 from a project, we wouldn't do it, though it becomes a question as to when to decide to cancel an effort because of inadequate returns. As you might imagine, a project can take a while to build up to speed.

You ask why Easter Seals is still running at a loss. From my point of view, there is increased competition in the rehab market. We're not the only people selling such services. We might project, for instance, that we would have 56 persons in a particular program, and hire people based on that projection. If only 48 people finally enroll, our costs are higher than necessary, and we don't have the revenues we had planned on. Also, sometimes the state funders conditionally approve our fee, and we budget for that. Then, after the year has begun, they let us know that our fee is too high and can't be reimbursed fully.

After the reorganization, there were turf problems. Allocation of costs became an issue. People wanted services, such as brochures, that would advertise these programs, but they didn't want to pay for them. We've had three deficit years in a row now, but this happened once before. We produced better forecasts, and the deficits disappeared. People find it hard to cut back, though.

Sally Gammon, Vice President and Chief Financial Officer

As chief financial officer, I oversee everything related to the budget. I review intercompany methods and work with the accountants. In essence, I oversee all the business functions.

From my point of view, the reorganization was brought about to allow us to have a multibusiness organization, and to create multiple boards that could offer guidance in specific areas. One board could handle program, and another could handle real estate, etc.

Reimbursement was an important issue in the decision to reorganize. Every funder reimbursed differently. The Department of Mental Health covered one set of things, Medicare another; however, they all reimbursed for rent. Reorganization allowed us to create a formula that would build costs consistently.

You ask whether the reorganization was beneficial. You have to look at what was happening fiscally. For three years the balance sheet has been deteriorating, month by month. It's important to pay attention when this becomes a problem. Two years ago, our cohesive team fell apart, which didn't help in solutions. We had hard assets without cash flow. In fact, there was some thought given to increasing the hard assets at the same time we were experiencing declining fund balances. The expansionist mentality was deeply entrenched. We felt invincible.

The last time we faced a deficit, was when I came into the finance position. We looked at everything with an eye toward cutting; we had a different mentality then. At one point, we had $1.2 million in CDs [certificates of deposit]. Now I think we're out on a $900,000 line of credit.

Retrenching is the only answer. The expense of small programs is very high. Overhead has grown tremendously. The subsidiaries are accusing the Foundation of unfair methods of allocation, especially of overhead. But to my mind, that becomes an excuse for not looking at the real problems. We have to look at everything with an eye toward cutting those activities that do not generate a sufficient return.

Mr. Gammon's Recollections

With these views in hand, the consultant then asked Mr. Gammon to reflect on his own experiences during the process of reorganization, and the issues he had faced as president of both the Society and STS. Mr. Gammon's recollections follow.

The agency was in financial trouble, which the restructuring didn't cause, but allowed to keep happening. There were a series of causes for that financial trouble: First, our debt had increased over the preceding 18 months. We had taken on the Vermont franchise, had bought a new building at Plymouth, had merged with two housing programs, and had moved in to the Manchester facility. Second, there was increasing competition for the contributed dollar, especially in New Hampshire where there was an abundance of rehab programs, which meant that the return on fund-raising was lower. Third, we were feeling the effects of government cutbacks. Fourth, the state had developed rate-setting rules that didn't necessarily fit the agency's program/cost structure. Finally, there was increasing inability to recover costs such as public education from grantors. Within the period of one year, we went from a $400,000 surplus to a $400,000 deficit.

At the time of the restructuring many people were outgrowing their jobs. I had been in Easter Seals for 14 years and was second in command. Having started out as a special education teacher, I had risen to executive vice president in charge of all programs. Sharon Cholette was vice president of development and had been in the organization for years since she came as a secretary. Sally Gammon had risen to vice president and chief financial officer since the days when she was a physical therapist, and Bob, who began as a peripatologist, was president.

Bob had created an atmosphere of growth; he was an entrepreneur and creative thinker, but not a good hands-on supervisor. With the reorganization, there was no emphasis on team building. Each subsidiary focused on its own entity. Intercompany solutions were no longer sought. Where, before, we had gone on a budget retreat as a group, now the Foundation's budget was drawn up in May, and the subsidiaries didn't do theirs until the Foundation had spoken. It began to create a system of game playing. There were too many bosses. I had responsibility, but not all the control I needed to create the success I wanted. Bob, the person in ultimate power, could reduce the Foundation's allocation to the Society singlehandedly. I would have to make the adjustment. Since the overhead could not be reduced, we found ourselves having to explain over and over to rate setters the high overhead in our budget. Too many fixed costs end up in an indirect rate that would not be reimbursed by funders.

There was nothing sinister going on. The Foundation's existence created confusion in the organization as a whole. Bob had created an unresponsive bureaucracy, and it was difficult to pinpoint responsibility for nonachievement.

We misused the structure; we kidded ourselves. The cost to run the Foundation and raise $1.3 million became exorbitant; the system took over. The Foundation allocated its costs to the agencies in a fixed manner. Of our $7 million budget, $2 million was fixed, as the holding company began feeding off its subsidiaries. With a focus on these fixed transfer costs, we in the Society backed into our budget, knowing we had to either raise more money or cut other costs. Neither of these could be done without eliminating services. If that was done, overhead was not cut and simply had to be borne by the remaining programs.

The system of allocations confused everyone. No one knew how much the fund-raising was costing, and some didn't want to know. And, we were giving the board too much information for them to make sense of it. I finally convinced them a few months ago using a stepdown analysis. Look, if costs of $240,000 include an imposed allocation of $30,000, if my revenues and fees bring in $210,000, and then if I shut down completely, this $30,000 imposed charge won't go away. The allocated fee was charged on the basis of the size of the agency, and included rents on the Plymouth facility that ARI owned even when I no longer wanted to run the program there.

Seven-eighths of our budget comes from grants and fees; National Easter Seals has called that a very high proportion, and recommend nothing more extreme than 40–60 percent split or vice versa. Since we raise the other one-eighth of our revenues by fund-raising, with a $1 per capita yield, which is very high for a grass roots organization, we aren't going to increase that side of the budget. A stable organization seems to be promised by cutting some of the expenses and the programs, concentrating only on the bigger projects.

You might ask about increasing productivity. Let me tell you about that. When I hold exit interviews with employees, some say they want more education benefits; others want more vacation time. But everyone says that we expect too much from them. This tells me that productivity is as high as it will go; we cannot push these people any more.

I'm thinking about concentrating our fund-raising effort on major events, and telling people what their money is paying for. I'd rather raise fewer gross dollars if that will increase our net.

What incentives move us? We have had MBO programs in the past, whose goals were based on meeting our approved budget. Salaries were dependent upon that. It didn't work as well as we wanted because it caused people to focus just on their own part of the organization; the rest of the organization could be going down the tubes, but the person who met his or her budget would get a bonus.

Then later there were incentive plans based on the agency's doing all right; those were harder. Under this kind of plan, Sharon and Sally were given incentive plans with goals that were unachievable. I had a plan where if I made my budget, I got one-half of a stated bonus; the rest was dependent upon the success of others.

Now, I'd like to see goals based not only on budget. Perhaps we could identify, together, goals such as a development of new programs, or increase in number of clients served. When these are reached, bonuses would be due.

Next Steps

With this information in mind, Mr. Gammon and the consultant felt they were ready to think creatively about some solutions to the Foundation's problems.

Questions

1. What are the principal problems that Mr. Gammon faces? Please classify these problems into categories that are useful for analysis.

2. How should Mr. Gammon resolve these problems?

Case 16–5
Fletcher Allen Health Care*

In a fee-for-service environment, surgeons can go out and generate more revenue to support their research, and so cross-subsidizing another department would not be that big a problem. But in a capitated system, we're working more and getting paid less, so we have to think about how we protect our revenue sources. We are not simply a department that is going to go out and do clinical work. We have a research mission and an educational mission.

Dr. Steven Shackford, Clinical Leader of the Surgery Healthcare Service at the newly formed Fletcher Allen Health Care (FAHC), continued:

*This case was prepared by Sheila M. McCarthy under the supervision of Professor David W. Young. Copyright © by The President and Fellows of Harvard College and by David W. Young.

As chair of surgery, I worry about both protecting my department's revenue stream and, at the same time, maintaining the viability of the institution. That's a complex issue because you have to balance teaching, research, and clinical practice, but you have to have clinical productivity to support the teaching and research. For example, the Dean has put together something called FTARS [Faculty Teaching And Reward System] to provide departments with appropriate resources to do their teaching. After collecting data for a year, our analysis showed that surgery was being underpaid by about $900,000 a year, while another department was being overpaid by about $2 million. A few years ago, this wouldn't have been a big deal but in this environment, we now need those funds. We can't attract tertiary care providers to this place unless we can find innovative ways to support them.

Dr. Shackford's concerns were based, in large part, on FAHC's first two years of operations. The integrated clinical enterprise had been financially sound in its first year, but had run into financial difficulties in its second year. Although Surgery had done well, it had not been spared the resulting budget cutting. FAHC's financial difficulties, and the resulting actions to correct them, had led to a lot of stress within the organization and dissatisfaction among some of the surgeons. Now, in November 1996, as FAHC entered its third year of existence, some of them felt that the commitments and assurances given by the administration at the time of the merger agreement had been abandoned, leading them to question whether they should remain a part of the enterprise.

Background

Fletcher Allen Health Care was formed in January 1995 by the merger of University Health Center (UHC), Medical Center Hospital of Vermont (MCHV), and Fanny Allen Hospital. The resulting entity included 250 physicians and 600 beds. It was responsible for operating a regional system of care and coordinating the clinical medical education programs for the University of Vermont College of Medicine. It provided approximately 60 percent of Vermont's patient care services.

The Market

Fletcher Allen was located in Burlington, Vermont, one of the country's most rural states, with a 1995 population of slightly over half a million. It relied on the local market for about one-half of its business and was working to build market share. The market was predominantly fee for service, but managed care and capitation were growing steadily. FAHC's senior management predicted that by 2000 managed care penetration would reach about 70 percent, leading to downward pressure on the premium dollar, and hence on providers to control costs.

The major insurance products in the market were Community Health Plan (CHP) and Blue Cross and Blue Shield of Vermont. CHP was a New York–based

HMO that dominated the managed care market, covering some 85,000 people. Blue Cross and Blue Shield insured about 200,000 Vermonters, mainly under indemnity programs. However, it had begun to move members into managed care, and in 1996 had launched a new managed care product in conjunction with FAHC.

In several counties, FAHC competed with Dartmouth-Hitchcock Medical Center, which was located in Lebanon, New Hampshire, about 125 miles southeast of Burlington via an interstate highway. Dartmouth-Hitchcock was a tertiary care academic medical center that was part of the Lahey Hitchcock Clinic, an integrated delivery system that spanned parts of Massachusetts, New Hampshire, and Vermont. As tertiary care providers, FAHC and Dartmouth-Hitchcock compared favorably on quality and service. Although FAHC historically had had lower costs, Dartmouth-Hitchcock was working to eliminate this advantage, and had announced plans to reduce its costs by $10 million during 1996–97. It also had expanded its referral base by forming a number of affiliations with community providers.

The Merging Organizations

UHC, MCHV, and the College of Medicine had a long history of working together in the area of education and, more recently, in service delivery. UHC was the practice plan of the College of Medicine and comprised 10 departmental practice groups and a parent organization that acted as a management service organization (MSO). The MSO was responsible for common functions among the 10 practice groups, including contracting, developing fee schedules, negotiating capitation arrangements, budgeting, and designing systems for quality assurance, medical information, and accounting.

Prior to the merger, each practice group had been an independent corporation that was responsible for its own profitability. Each was assessed a Dean's tax to help finance teaching and research at the College of Medicine, and each paid a flat tax of 8.75 percent of gross billings to the MSO for its services, as well as to subsidize research and education within UHC. The remaining funds stayed within the group, usually for distribution to the physician members.

The 250 physicians in the departmental practice groups provided about 550,000 ambulatory care visits annually, and accounted for two-thirds of all admissions to the MCHV. In some specialties, the practice group physicians represented the majority of providers in the area. Indeed, in some surgery subspecialties, all surgeons in the local county were members of the UHC group.

The MCHV was a 500-bed tertiary care hospital that was the primary teaching hospital for the University of Vermont College of Medicine. It employed 3,600 people at the time of the merger and had an annual budget of $174 million. The departmental chairs at the College of Medicine served as the clinical chiefs at MCHV and the clinical leaders of their respective practice groups.

Fanny Allen Hospital, named after a descendent of Ethan Allen (of the Green Mountain Boys), was a 100-bed Catholic community hospital with strong local community support. At the time of the merger, it employed 500 people and had an annual budget of $23 million.

The Merger

In 1990 UHC and MCHV had adopted a common planning process across the academic medical center. In 1993 Fanny Allen was invited to join them in a short-term planning process to explore opportunities for a closer affiliation. Within two months, the leadership of the three organizations recognized that a single organization made sense, and began to move forward with the merger process. This process was unusual in that it involved not only these three organizations but the College of Medicine as well. According to the leadership, the major goals of the merger were to create an organization that would be positioned to (*a*) maximize patient value by understanding and improving quality of services, outcomes, and lowering per capita healthcare costs, (*b*) integrate physicians into leadership positions at all levels, including governance, strategic planning, and operations, as well as in managing the delivery of care, and (*c*) fully coordinate care and the educational mission but allow the academic process to be retained by the university.

One of the critical pieces of the merger process was gaining the acceptance of the UHC physicians, particularly because of their hold on the local market. However, before they would vote to move forward with a merger, the physicians outlined several conditions. These included a strategic plan, an operating structure, and a physician compensation plan. As Churchill Hindes, Ph.D., FAHC's Vice President of Financial Services, explained:

> The physicians wanted to see a strategic plan to know where the new organization would take them. They wanted to see an operating structure to see how decisions would be made. And finally, they wanted to know who was going to be in charge of their compensation. The physicians wanted to ensure that FAHC would uphold the academic mission and preserve the entrepreneurial spirit of the practice plans.

A strategic plan was accepted by all parties at the time of the merger. Although the plan had evolved during the first two years of operations, it remained true to the one originally developed. A summary of the 1996–1997 version is shown in Exhibit 1.

FAHC's organizational model and operating structure are shown in Exhibit 2. The model organized clinical areas into Healthcare Services (HCS) teams that ultimately would have fully integrated budgets across all the professional and institutional activities. To prevent problems between clinical units and the academic process, the chair of each department was appointed the clinical leader of the relevant HCS. The clinical leader then chose the administrative leader and the nursing leader who completed the leadership triad of each HCS. HCSs were supported by Key Support Processes (KSPs) that included such activities as registration, scheduling, billing, quality assurance, and education.

EXHIBIT 1   Strategic Blueprint for 1996–97

THE CRITICAL ISSUES THAT CONFRONT US

Managed Care	Competition	Networks	Communities	Teaching and Research	Culture	Health Improvement
• Stiff penalties for costs, utilization and price above market • Service quality and clinical outcomes no longer taken for granted by consumers	• Competition for referral care • Overall value counts heavily • Consumers want the best providers and the best system	• Strength through connections • Rural communities want access to continuum of services and strong local care systems	• Deliver care where people live • Keep medical leadership and decision making at a local level	• Financial support for teaching and research decreasing • Opportunity for the region's 3 referral centers and 2 medical schools to collaborate.	• In the face of rapid change, maintain and enhance: - quality of relationships - quality of work life - individual and team performance	• Shift focus to improving health status of population served. • Partnerships must be forged with other community health and human service organizations

WHY WE EXIST

The mission of FAHC is to improve the health of people of the communities that it serves. FAHC will continuously improve the quality, the cost, and accessibility of health care for those communities. FAHC will work with other providers, both local and regional, to integrate services. FAHC will not restrict the availability or compromise the quality of essential care on any basis. FAHC will integrate its health care services and programs with teaching and research to ensure that learning occurs in an environment that stresses prevention and health improvement, patient focused care systems and processes, and the delivery of services that maximize value in a caring environment.

OUR VISION FOR THE FUTURE

We envision Fletcher Allen Health Care as an organization committed to improving the health status of the people and contributing to the achievement of health communities in the region. We see a future where FAHC is:
• directly providing health care services, training future clinicians, and developing new knowledge through research.
• working collaboratively with other care givers and organizations in our region designing new care processes which add value to those served
• accountable that services and programs are accessible, cost-effective, and of high quality.

WHAT WE VALUE

1. We respect the dignity of all individuals and are responsive to their physical, emotional, spiritual, and social needs and cultural diversity.
2. We are just and prudent stewards of limited natural and financial resources.
3. We foster a climate which encourages both those receiving and providing care to make responsible choices.
4. We strive for excellence in quality of care and seek to continually learn and improve.
5. We acknowledge a partnership with the community to ensure the best possible care at the right time in the right place, by the right provider.
6. We are caring and compassionate to each other and to those we serve.
7. We communicate openly and honestly with the community we serve.

HOW WE WILL ACHIEVE OUR VISION

1. Redesign our care management system and infrastructure	2. Build an internal corporate culture that fosters caring, innovations, and results	3. Improve the health status of the communities that we serve	4. Create a new health plan to serve the people of our region	5. Respond to the needs of local care management systems	6. Make strategic investments in primary care
Provide the right care, at the right time, in the right place, by the right provider. Make info. systems, facilities, staffing, and patient research support this goal.	Help everyone who works at FAHC achieve their potential. Strengthen communication. Retain appropriate workforce through aggressive retraining opportunities. Recognize individual and team effort.	Work within community partnerships to improve health status, reduce morbidity and mortality and enhance quality of life.	Integrate care delivery and financing to promote health; provide affordable, high quality care; and achieve healthier communities.	Develop relationships with hospitals, physicians, and other health care providers in the region.	Improve FAHC's capacity to provide primary care for area residents.

HOW MY WORK TEAM AND I CAN HELP

• Select a patient care or a support process and improve it. • Ask others for ideas about improving value overall • Contribute your ideas	• Keep an ongoing list of innovations your team is working on • Contribute to a caring environment for patients, their families, and friends • Contribute your ideas	• Extend the focus of care to include prevention • Help patients manage disease independently • Contribute your ideas	• Provide/support excellent care at lowest possible cost • Develop products and services plan members want • Contribute your ideas	• Ensure a rapid response to referring provider requests • Reach out to other communities • Contribute your ideas	• Support high quality patient care within the primary care practices • Make it easy to access specialty care when required • Contribute your ideas

EXHIBIT 2 **Organizational Chart**

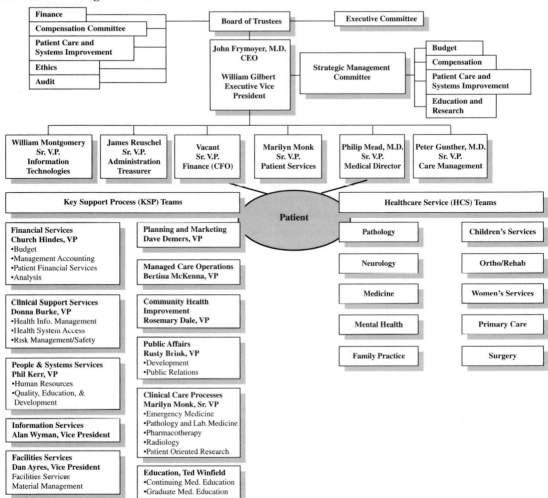

During the merger negotiations, the leadership from the four organizations (UHC, MCHV, College of Medicine, and Fanny Allen) selected John Frymoyer, MD, Dean of the College of Medicine, as FAHC's first CEO. Dr. Frymoyer had been instrumental in the creation of FAHC and was considered by many to be the "visionary" behind the merger. Moreover, with this choice, everyone was assured that the academic mission would be upheld. Additionally, the leadership established the Strategic Management Committee (SMC), which included the CEO, the Executive Vice President, all senior vice presidents, and all physician clinical leaders of the health care service teams. The SMC was designated as the main policy-making body of the new enterprise.

Another issue that was addressed by the leadership was the flow of research dollars. An agreement was negotiated at the time of the merger that created a clear division between funds from nonprofit organizations, including the federal government funds, and funds from private for-profit organizations, such as pharmaceutical companies. The nonprofit funds would go to the College of Medicine, because it relied heavily on them for financial support and it had the administrative capacity to manage them. The for-profit funds would go to Fletcher Allen. One senior manager estimated that nonprofit funds were at least 10 times the amount of the private funds.

Physician Compensation

Prior to the merger, individual physicians had received university base salaries and practice plan supplements. There was no uniformity among the departments, no productivity requirements, and many salaries were below the national median of other academic and nonacademic physicians. Nevertheless, the individual practice plans had significant autonomy, and some were concerned about losing it under a merged system. This was particularly troublesome for the department of surgery. According to Frank Ittleman, MD, Division Head of Cardiovascular Surgery:

> Many of us were concerned about losing our autonomy. The department had evolved under Dr. Davis [Dr. Shackford's predecessor] into a close-knit group. Many things were done on a handshake or a verbal agreement, and we felt that we would always be taken care of over the long term. Dr. Davis acted in many ways as a surrogate father to the younger surgeons. We didn't feel threatened and felt we were reasonably well compensated. While we knew we could make more at other institutions at a certain point in our career, we also were led to believe that, as our careers progressed, our compensation would not be dramatically reduced. We never really envisioned that this would change, and we didn't understand that the whole medical scene and reimbursement policy could alter our careers.
>
> When Steve arrived about five or six years ago, he had a somewhat different attitude toward compensation. He felt that if you worked harder you should get paid more for your work. This was well received and worked quite well. While we still made less than we would have elsewhere, the lifestyle and camaraderie here were worth a great deal. The culture of the surgery group, although somewhat modified by age and retirement, was preserved under Steve's leadership.
>
> With Fletcher Allen, we saw ourselves potentially losing the one-on-one relationship with the chief and the way we were treated financially. We were concerned that as the groups and the hospital amalgamated, this relationship would be lost in the shuffle.
>
> Another concern we had about Fletcher Allen was losing control of revenues. Under the old system we had a moderate amount of control. We knew that our revenues were taxed and some of it went to the medical school and to residency training and research. We had no problem with that and gladly supported it. However, many of us were concerned that, with the merger, money would be used to support other groups that did not work as hard. This had happened to a certain extent before, but we felt it would be magnified with the new system. As we

considered whether to become part of Fletcher Allen, the compensation plan was the linchpin.

Additionally, the compensation plan needed to address some of the concerns that many of the physicians had about the impact of the merger on the entrepreneurial culture of the physician groups. As Dr. Hindes saw the situation:

> The physicians wanted to make sure that with a merger, the entrepreneurial spirit of the practice plans was preserved. Under the UHC system, the different practice plans were independent corporations with a bottom line. Each was a tub on its own bottom, so to speak. At the end of the year, significant portions of profit or surplus were distributed to physicians as bonuses. Also, through a flat tax of 8.75 percent of gross billings and a number of other mechanisms, we had developed a very unique system of cross subsidization. This system allowed UHC to uphold the principle that with equal effort everyone would have an equal opportunity to profit. In a good year, every group was able to pay bonuses and reward effort. Also, the clinical leaders were accustomed to being fully accountable for their bottom lines. We felt we had cracked the riddle of how to motivate physicians in academic medicine. We maintained a very high entrepreneurial spirit in fully academic practices. They were scholars but every year they drove the bottom line. It was this spirit and the academic mission that the physicians did not want to lose.

As part of the merger negotiations, a compensation committee was selected to deal with these issues. Its goal was to design a new system that would move salaries to the market level and link compensation to market-based productivity standards with incentives for improved efficiency. The committee worked over a six-month period to develop a physician compensation plan that would meet the demands of an evolving system and satisfy the practice plan physicians.

One of the key pieces of this plan was the funds flow among the physicians, the medical center, and the College of Medicine. A diagram of this funds flow is shown in Exhibit 3. As it indicates, a physician's compensation would still consist of a base salary funded in part by the College of Medicine and in part by FAHC. Additionally, clinical activities would continue to provide support for the College of Medicine.

In addition, a key aspect of the plan, according to Dr. Hindes, was the remaining funds professional (RFP):

> The RFP was the core of the whole plan. It was designed to approximate much of what before had been the bottom line, and to maintain the entrepreneurial spirit. The RFP was the "price of admission" for physicians. We guaranteed that we would design the system in such a way that there would be a defined bottom line for the professional side. We were willing to do this because we wanted the deal to work and we wanted to maintain the culture. To make it binding each physician signed an employment contract with FAHC that lasted until October 1997. The contract guaranteed them the continuation of their existing salaries assuming the same productivity, and that their compensation would be in accordance with the compensation plan. We also guaranteed them that we would not modify the

EXHIBIT 3 Funds Flow

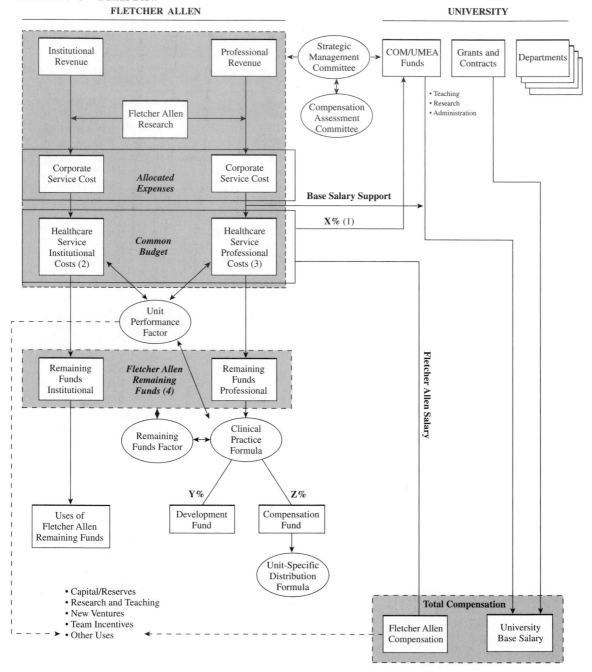

See case text for explanation of notes.

compensation plan during that time. With these provisions, the physicians voted to become part of Fletcher Allen.

According to the RFP's designers, the following were important elements of the computation:

- The distinction between Hospital and Professional Fee Revenues was an accounting provision to facilitate management and to demonstrate how Fletcher Allen would manage its various categories of revenues and expenses.

- X% [shown as (1) on Exhibit 3] was comparable to current arrangements regarding hospital and practice plan support of COM/UMEA. Practice plan support in FY 1994 was calculated as 0.5 percent of gross charges.

- Institutional cost (2) and Professional costs (3) were terms of convenience. The former included items generally referred to as hospital, facility, and/or technical costs. The latter included items generally referred to as physician costs and traditionally incurred by UHC and/or practice plans.

- Fletcher Allen Remaining Funds (4) comprised the aggregate nonprofessional and professional Healthcare Service Remaining Funds and Losses.

- The Unit Performance Factor(s) would adjust the Compensation Fund upward or downward, depending upon the performance of the HCS. The criteria used to measure the performance of the HCS were to be based upon qualitative, financial, volume, and/or other measures of success prospectively determined by the HCS and approved by the SMC. No measures had yet been developed.

- Financial performance in excess of prospective budget targets provided funds to adjust the RFP upward through the Remaining Funds Factor. If there was a significant shortfall, the Remaining Funds Factor could also be used to adjust the RFP downward. The Board of Trustees had specified that the RFP was to be adjusted based upon a methodology prospectively agreed upon during the budget process.

The plan was designed to be implemented in three phases. In the first phase, the physicians were protected from institutional risk, and performance rewards were based solely on the professional side. Thus, the RFP would not be affected by the performance against budget on the hospital or institutional side. In the second phase, as shown in Exhibit 3, there was a linkage between the professional and institutional side. Using a unit performance factor, the RFP could be increased or decreased depending on the HCS's performance. In the third phase, the scope of accountability was to be expanded to incorporate overall organizational performance.

The Transition

In fiscal year (FY) 1995 (1 October 1994 to 30 September 1995), which included nine months of the merger, Fletcher Allen did well financially and worked toward merging the multiple systems within the various organizations. However, during FY 1996, it suffered a financial crisis. This crisis was created in part because, with the merging of the systems, the organization had no financial data until five months into the fiscal year. At that point, senior management realized it was running a $5 to $6 million deficit.

To deal with the crisis, FAHC's senior management hired as, Executive Vice President of Operations, William Gilbert, an attorney with broad-based experience in the federal and state regulatory arenas. Mr. Gilbert had served as a cabinet-level official with the former Governor of Vermont, and most recently had managed a law firm. In the early 1980s, he had chaired the board of the University Health Center.

Mr. Gilbert used several "budget tools," which included a hiring freeze and an across the board cut of 5 percent. He described the process:

> The use of the budget tools was ugly and painful, but at the time it worked. What was unfortunate was that some of the managers who had stepped up to the plate early paid the price. Some of the best managers got hurt. It was an extremely difficult time all around. The meetings of the Strategic Management Committee often involved budget fights that were destructive to morale. There was no certainty that anything we were doing would work. The Board was up in arms and the physicians were uncomfortable.

The mandate to achieve a 5 percent reduction led to layoffs in the spring of about 123 people, which had a detrimental effect on employee morale. Members of senior management, physicians, and administrators commented that there was poor communication and a lot of misinformation exchanged among administration, employees, and physicians, which eroded trust within the organization. By the end of the second year, three of the highest members of senior management had left.

FAHC ended FY1996 in the black. (FAHC's balance sheets and income statements for FY1995 and 1996 are shown in Exhibits 4 and 5.) However, by all accounts the expense reduction process was extremely difficult. To prevent a crisis of this sort from happening again, and in recognition that Fletcher Allen had to continue to reduce its costs, the Strategic Management Committee launched a redesign effort. The effort was to take place during FY1997, and was to be guided by FAHC's key physician leaders. Jim Reuschel, Senior Vice President and Chief Operating Officer, explained its goals:

> I see two main goals of the redesign effort. The first involves a bottom-up approach, working with the line managers and staff to improve their units. The second is the formation of core teams that will look at core processes across the system. The first I see as a 9–12 month effort. The second will be a two-to-three-year effort.

Dr. Shackford was selected to lead the redesign, part of which included a gainsharing model to be used in FY1997. Gainsharing would be open to all employees except physicians and senior administration. The goal for FY1997 was to take $6 million out of the system. If the $6 million in savings were

EXHIBIT 4 Balance Sheets

| | As of 30 September | |
	1996	1995
GENERAL FUNDS		
Assets		
CURRENT ASSETS:		
Cash and Cash Equivalents	0	1,916,289
Assets Whose Use Is Limited and That Are Required for		
Current Liabilities	7,430,177	3,484,410
Patient Accounts Receivable, Net	55,251,733	58,864,819
Short-Term Investments	287,900	869,585
Inventory at Lower of Cost or Market	4,670,529	4,600,277
Due from Related Parties	3,686,562	379,301
Other Current Assets	5,182,415	2,759,802
TOTAL CURRENT ASSETS.	76,509,316	72,874,483
ASSETS WHOSE USE IS LIMITED:		
By Board Designation	86,387,665	73,506,497
Under Bond Agreements, Held by Trustee	139,158	15,645,711
Self Insurance Trust.	581,247	0
TOTAL ASSETS WHOSE USE IS LIMITED.	87,108,070	89,152,208
Less Assets Whose Use Is Limited and That Are Required for		
Current Liabilities	7,430,177	3,484,410
NONCURRENT ASSETS WHOSE USE IS LIMITED	79,677,893	85,667,798
PROPERTY AND EQUIPMENT, NET.	102,545,656	93,768,289
OTHER ASSETS:		
Deferred Financing Costs	3,068,150	1,686,046
Notes Receivable	511,373	699,668
Investment in Affiliated Companies.	1,028,068	328,747
TOTAL OTHER ASSETS.	4,607,591	2,714,461
TOTAL GENERAL FUND ASSETS	263,340,456	255,025,031

achieved, $3 million would go to employees through gainsharing and the other $3 million would go to the system.

Integration of Financial Information

As FAHC moved ahead with the redesign effort, the Strategic Management Committee was simultaneously moving forward on a number of other matters related to increased integration and accountability. One area of attention was financial systems, which many people felt were impeding FAHC's ability to achieve integration across the institutional and professional budgets.

One problem with the financial systems was institutional revenue. The existing reports showed *professional* revenue and expenses for each HCS (see Exhibit 6). Thus, for example, when surgery ordered a test from pathology, pathology billed for and received the professional revenue and was responsible for the professional expenses. However, there was no counterpart on the

EXHIBIT 4 (Continued)

	As of 30 September	
	1996	*1995*
Liabilities and Fund Balances		
CURRENT LIABILITIES:		
Current Installments of Long-Term Debt..................	3,162,110	3,342,490
Current Installments of Capital Lease Obligations............	168,067	141,920
Line of Credit..	4,100,000	0
Accounts Payable.....................................	8,713,165	5,862,364
Accrued Expenses.....................................	6,954,179	6,531,310
Accrued Payroll and Related Benefits......................	14,028,378	15,731,597
Estimated Third-Party Settlements	3,481,306	3,639,600
Due to Other Funds	394,418	2,617,743
TOTAL CURRENT LIABILITIES............................	41,001,623	37,867,024
POST RETIREMENT BENEFITS OBLIGATION	3,245,322	3,477,131
LONG-TERM DEBT, Excluding Current Installments	79,768,727	82,887,438
CAPITAL LEASE, Excluding Current Installments	238,295	406,363
FUND BALANCE.......................................	139,086,488	130,387,075
TOTAL GENERAL FUND LIABILITIES & FUND BALANCE.......	263,340,455	255,025,031
DONOR RESTRICTED FUNDS		
Assets		
ENDOWMENT FUNDS:		
Cash and Equivalents..................................	14,502,777	0
TOTAL ENDOWMENT FUNDS..........................	14,502,777	0
SPECIFIC PURPOSE FUNDS:		
Due from Other Funds.................................	3,760,626	2,617,743
Due from Related Companies............................	0	750
TOTAL SPECIFIC PURPOSE FUNDS	3,760,626	2,618,493
Liabilities and Fund Balances		
ENDOWMENT FUNDS:		
Due to Other Funds...................................	3,366,208	0
Accounts Payable and Accrued Liabilities	54,009	0
Fund Balance..	11,082,560	0
TOTAL ENDOWMENT FUNDS..........................	14,502,777	0
SPECIFIC PURPOSE FUNDS:		
Accounts Payable.....................................	4,447	4,037
Fund Balance..	3,756,180	2,614,456
TOTAL SPECIFIC PURPOSE FUNDS	3,760,627	2,618,493

institutional side, such that HCSs saw only institutional expenses, and their expense budgets were developed based on *estimated* volume. Moreover, if surgery ordered more tests than budgeted, pathology incurred the additional expenses, not surgery. According to Dr. Hindes, efforts were underway to improve the systems so that the HCSs would see revenue and expenses on the institutional as well as on professional side.

EXHIBIT 5 Income Statements

	Audited 1995 Actual	1995 Budget	30 September 1996 YTD Actual	30 September 1996 YTD Budget	30 September 1996 Variance
Patient Service Revenue:					
Hospital Inpatient Revenue	210,649,675	214,043,301	207,375,876	214,043,301	(6,667,425)
Outpatient Ancillary Services	56,506,242	65,390,449	65,165,336	65,390,449	(225,113)
Physician Service Revenue	70,753,968	93,015,100	100,346,414	93,015,100	7,331,314
GROSS CHARGES	337,909,885	372,448,850	372,887,626	372,448,850	438,776
Managed Care FFS EQ.	(8,321,853)	(10,599,283)	(12,831,618)	(10,599,283)	(2,232,335)
Charity Care	(9,030,067)	(7,924,101)	(8,262,169)	(7,924,101)	(338,068)
GROSS PATIENT SERVICE REVENUE	320,557,965	353,925,466	351,793,839	353,925,466	(2,131,627)
MANAGED CARE INCOME	7,706,462	8,961,033	11,361,653	8,961,033	2,400,620
ADJUSTED GROSS PATIENT SERVICE REVENUE	328,264,427	362,886,499	363,155,492	362,886,499	268,993
DEDUCTIONS FROM PATIENT REVENUE	68,667,328	80,910,113	82,282,467	80,910,113	1,372,354
NET PATIENT SERVICE REVENUE	259,597,099	281,976,386	280,873,025	281,976,386	(1,103,361)
RESEARCH GRANTS & CONTRACTS	3,546,926	4,260,477	3,962,076	4,260,477	(298,401)
OTHER REVENUE	7,708,018	9,313,518	9,090,051	9,313,518	(223,467)
TOTAL REVENUE	270,852,043	295,550,381	293,925,152	295,550,381	(1,625,229)
Expenses:					
Salaries, Payroll Taxes and Fringe Benefits	159,943,675	178,181,822	181,304,849	178,181,822	(3,123,027)
Professional Fees	869,690	447,033	91,221	447,033	355,812
Medical and Surgical Supplies	20,363,886	20,420,184	24,920,287	20,420,184	(4,500,103)
Pharmaceuticals	9,718,082	11,027,810	10,309,390	11,027,810	718,420
Dietary Supplies	1,956,673	1,900,206	2,083,228	1,900,206	(183,022)
Utilities	5,864,811	6,477,195	6,970,834	6,477,195	(493,639)
Insurance	4,585,452	4,800,236	4,852,773	4,800,236	(52,537)
Other Expenses	28,125,802	22,974,865	25,754,849	22,974,865	(2,779,984)
Purchased Services	10,644,040	12,320,449	12,301,014	12,320,449	19,435
Depreciation	11,453,189	13,879,091	13,393,803	13,879,091	485,288
Interest Expense	5,540,133	5,723,129	4,947,163	5,723,129	775,966
Provision for Bad Debt	7,314,905	8,250,503	6,870,971	8,250,503	1,379,532
TOTAL EXPENSES	266,380,338	286,402,523	293,800,382	286,402,523	(7,397,859)
Income from Operations	4,471,705	9,147,858	124,770	9,147,858	(9,023,088)
NONOPERATING GAINS					
Unrestricted Gifts and Bequests	214,814	384,763	539,463	384,763	154,700
Income on Investments/Limited by Board	4,165,937	5,157,200	6,984,154	5,157,200	1,826,954
Income on Investments/Endowment Funds	153,505	202,412	238,693	202,412	36,281
Income on Investments/Affiliates	(596,277)	0	741,385	0	741,385
Other Investment Income	204,924	218,937	(390,942)	218,937	(609,879)
NONOPERATING GAINS	4,142,903	5,963,312	8,112,753	5,963,312	2,149,441
Revenues and Gains in Excess of Expenses	$ 8,614,608	$ 15,111,170	$ 8,237,523	$ 15,111,170	($6,873,647)

EXHIBIT 6 FY96 (actual) Professional Revenue and Expenses for each Healthcare Service
(The names of the HCSs have been disguised to preserve confidentiality*)

	Medicine 1	Medicine 2	Medicine 3	Primary Care 1
Revenue:				
Physician Rev. (FFS)	21,962,159	2,029,557	1,524,487	1,739,856
Physician Rev. (Man. Care FFS).	1,624,943	199,502	570,763	979,880
Gross Patient Revenue.	23,587,102	2,229,059	2,095,250	2,719,736
Deductions from Revenue:				
Managed Care FFS Equivalent	1,625,843	199,890	570,369	981,168
Other Deductions from Revenue	9,610,574	671,304	450,501	474,159
Total Deductions from Revenue	11,236,417	871,194	1,020,870	1,455,327
Net Patient Revenue	12,350,685	1,357,865	1,074,380	1,264,409
Managed Care.	1,248,775	156,322	541,201	877,469
Research Grants and Contracts.	164,514	34,640	1,295,202	16,947
Other Operating Revenue	160,410	295,061	661,660	323,837
Total	1,573,699	486,023	2,498,063	1,218,253
Total Net Revenues	13,924,384	1,843,888	3,572,443	2,482,662
Operating Expenses:				
Salaries	6,795,732	1,078,909	2,727,478	1,507,211
Payroll Tax and Fringe	788,128	121,242	177,712	84,255
Medical/Surgical Supply.	105,616	4,391	41	63,484
Pharmaceuticals.	311,322	28	0	8,331
Utilities	159,387	33,384	54,403	47,947
Insurance and Bonding	203,577	37,087	54,615	35,581
Purchased Services.	75,426	68,185	239,639	26,284
Supplies Other.	578,758	88,789	130,128	114,965
Research/Grant Expenses	91,730	1,756	21,359	0
Bad Debt	804,434	76,583	59,301	60,959
Depreciation	88,106	19,365	26,384	13,643
Interest Expense.	0	206	0	0
	10,002,216	1,529,925	3,491,060	1,962,660
Income from Operations	3,922,168	313,963	81,383	520,002
Nonoperating Revenue	0	(123)	0	(6,422)
Excess Revenue Over Expenses	3,922,168	313,840	81,383	513,580
Allocated Overhead.	5,338,830	651,296	1,407,060	1,560,990
Net Gain (Loss) After Allocation	(1,416,662)	(337,456)	(1,325,677)	(1,047,410)

*The medical HCS are classified at Medical 1, 2, or 3. The primary care HCS are shown as Primary Care 1, 2, 3, and 4. Surgery 1 is the Department of Surgery.

A second problem was overhead allocation. There was a total of about $120 million in budgeted overhead for FY1997, including costs for the executive offices and the KSPs. FAHC was refining the existing model for allocating this overhead to the HCSs. To do so, several physicians' leaders were working with the financial services department.

Although $120 million was the *budgeted* overhead figure, it was not necessarily the amount that actually would be allocated to the HCSs. Rather, *actual* overhead would be allocated. While FAHC did not have a formal process in place to address an increase in overhead spending over the budgeted amount, several senior administrators explained that all the KSPs

Primary Care 2	Primary Care 3	Primary Care 4	Surgery 1	Surgery 2	Surgery 3	Total
4,096,352	3,599,108	6,215,162	25,500,349	11,336,109	3,410,399	81,413,538
836,353	1,816,011	1,706,476	2,725,178	1,252,769	507,174	12,219,049
4,932,705	5,415,119	7,921,638	28,225,527	12,588,878	3,917,573	93,632,587
835,130	1,816,234	1,706,052	2,744,737	1,253,594	506,542	12,239,559
1,289,517	1,148,279	1,577,622	9,835,977	3,548,857	959,823	29,566,613
2,124,647	2,964,513	3,283,674	12,580,714	4,802,451	1,466,365	41,806,172
2,808,058	2,450,606	4,637,964	15,644,813	7,786,427	2,451,208	51,826,415
772,260	2,074,705	1,481,270	2,337,205	1,001,899	398,250	10,889,356
126,355	79,590	55,794	146,336	47,109	(4,028)	1,962,459
172,845	147,366	467,161	209,034	224,102	201,528	2,863,004
1,071,460	2,301,661	2,004,225	2,692,575	1,273,110	595,750	15,714,819
3,879,518	4,752,267	6,642,189	18,337,388	9,059,537	3,046,958	67,541,234
2,760,110	3,238,275	3,908,651	8,524,963	5,394,427	2,333,190	38,268,946
253,985	277,554	380,794	1,152,311	554,383	415,175	4,205,539
36,839	86,786	127,585	232,112	148,580	0	805,434
57,413	40,825	(349)	64,656	6,428	0	488,654
59,031	78,609	99,649	207,180	9,936	4,088	753,614
56,190	52,215	397,760	521,862	99,078	51,726	1,509,691
96,896	50,361	23,753	258,422	257,880	147,240	1,244,086
152,891	282,441	279,937	841,490	128,764	321,550	2,919,713
0	0	22,444	31,834	323,619	219	492,961
156,150	142,563	236,026	895,632	427,221	120,015	2,978,884
30,963	69,436	83,247	272,466	232,897	110,085	946,592
0	0	0	0	60,309	0	60,515
3,660,468	4,319,065	5,559,497	13,002,928	7,643,522	3,503,288	54,674,629
219,050	433,202	1,082,692	5,334,460	1,416,015	(456,330)	12,866,605
0	(2,644)	1,293	0	0	0	(7,896)
219,050	430,558	1,083,985	5,334,460	1,416,015	(456,330)	12,858,709
1,432,648	2,117,453	3,375,827	4,832,841	2,956,020	1,599,448	25,272,413
(1,213,598)	(1,686,895)	(2,291,842)	501,619	(1,540,005)	(2,055,778)	(12,413,704)

and the executive offices were accountable for their budgets. Therefore, in Dr. Hindes' view, the issue was not the amount to be allocated, but *how* it was to be allocated. He explained:

> The $120 million in budgeted overhead has already been agreed to. Everyone on the Strategic Management Committee agreed to this amount when they approved the budgets for the different KSPs. There are 11 core KSPs that have several smaller KSPs within them. For example, I head up the Financial Core that includes 4 KSPs—accounting, billing, budgeting and analysis. All together, there are about 30 KSPs. All the managers understand that they are accountable for their budgets and that there will be consequences if they significantly go over budget.

The major concern of the HCS clinical leaders was fairness of the allocation model. The allocation model, shown in Exhibit 7, had been distributed to the Strategic Management Committee in late November at one of its Thursday evening meetings for discussion and a vote. The administration was anxious to have the model approved because the fiscal year had begun in October and they wanted to begin preparing financial reports that incorporated the allocated overhead.

For the most part, the clinical leaders accepted the model but were a bit hesitant to fully support it without more time to consider the implications. There was discussion around some of the statistics chosen, such as how to allocate the cost of residents. Some clinical leaders wanted to base the allocation on where residents spent their time, rather than on the HCSs to which they were assigned. For example, if an Ob/Gyn resident spent time in surgery, some felt that a portion of the resident's salary should be allocated to surgery. However, Dr. Shackford disagreed, arguing that surgery already absorbed the cost of teaching residents from other HCSs, and should not be allocated any additional costs. Ultimately, the group decided to allocate residents to their assigned services, rather than where they spent time. Additionally, the SMC agreed to test the model using last year's numbers to determine how each HCS would be affected by the new methodology.

Department of Surgery

Like the other clinical leaders, Dr. Shackford was struggling to balance the clinical, educational, and research missions of his service in light of the limited resources available to him. He faced the ongoing challenge of cost reduction, which was complicated by the systems in place and the budget cuts that took place the prior year. He also needed to address physician compensation and the issues surrounding the RFP for the upcoming years.

Cost Reduction

Prior to the merger, the department of surgery had begun a reengineering effort to become more efficient. This effort had continued after the merger and involved moving to a clinic mode and closing some solo offices to create greater efficiency. Overall, Dr. Shackford believed that the department had been quite successful at reducing costs. During the budget crisis, when surgery was required to cut an additional 5 percent, the department felt it had been hit particularly hard. As Lisa Goodrich, Administrative Service Leader for the Surgery Healthcare Service, explained:

> Different services started at different places. We felt that we were a little leaner than some because we'd already made some cuts. But that didn't matter when the crisis hit. It's frustrating—you play by what you thought were the rules and that doesn't always work to your advantage.

EXHIBIT 7   Cost Allocation Model

Overhead Group	Total Allocated	Allocation Statistic	Statistic Explanation
Registration	$4,149,629	Total Costs—HCS only	Allocates to cost centers in HCS—no allocation to the cost centers in the KSPs.
Executive Office	20,832,693	Total Direct Cost	Based on total cost in all FAHC cost centers.
Bad Debt and Insurance	3,636,312	Hospital Cost Center Revenue	Allocates to institutional cost centers only—based on revenues.
Budget Modifications	2,821,208	Salaries for Nursing Units	Allocates to institutional nursing units only—based on total salaries and wages.
Extraordinary Items	577,761	Professional Revenues	Allocates only to cost centers that have professional revenues.
Nursing Administration	1,624,068	Nursing FTEs	Allocates to cost centers that have nursing FTEs—SN, LPNs, etc.
Employee Benefits	23,748,781	Nonphysician salaries	Allocates to cost centers that have nonphysician salary dollars.
Human Resources	2,474,688	Total Employees by Cost Center	Allocates by employee head count—not FTEs—to all cost centers.
Graduate Medical Education	8,735,791	Medicare Intern and Resident Count	Allocates to cost centers on the time spent by residents according to rotation schedules.
Patient Relations	4,675,152	Patient Days	Allocates to institutional cost centers by number of patient days.
Patient Fin. Services—Physicians	2,287,606	Physician Billing Volumes	Allocates to professional cost centers—based on percentage of total bills produced.
Patient Fin. Services—Institution	8,864,889	Institutional Revenues	Allocates to institutional cost centers—based on total revenues.
Environmental Services	16,597,129	Total Square Feet	Allocates to all cost centers based on their total square feet.
Nutrition Services	6,422,707	Total Cost Institutional only	Allocates to institutional cost centers—based on their total expenses.
Clinical Nutrition Services	1,737,175	Patient Meals Served	Allocates only to cost centers that serve patient meals.
Materials Management	3,553,467	Total Supply Expense	Allocates to cost centers based on their total supply expense.
Laundry and Linen	2,080,764	Total Laundry Pounds	Allocates to cost centers based on their pounds of laundry processed.
Quality Systems Improvement	1,176,823	Total FTEs	Allocates to all cost centers based on total FTEs.
MHCIC—Poison Center	238,760	100% to ED	100% to the Emergency Department.
Grand Total	$116,235,403		

Nevertheless, given the need to continue to take costs out of the system, the service was moving forward to improve performance. Dr. Shackford used what he called a "Performance Spider" to monitor surgery's performance. Surgery's Performance Spider for the first month of the fiscal year is shown in Exhibit 8. This diagram illustrates the department's performance on 26 specific indicators within four categories: system performance, outcomes, customer satisfaction, and resource utilization. Dr. Shackford explained its value:

> These go to the board to show them how the HCSs are doing. I use it for my own department so that, in a minute, I can look at the dashboard and see where we're going. The middle circle serves as the benchmark and the outside circle is the ideal. I can look at this and know where we are.

Data and Systems

One issue that made many of the reengineering and improvement efforts difficult was the lack of systems and data. For example, in an effort to improve efficiency, each HCS was looking at its top five or six procedures and then focusing on two, with the goal of reducing utilization and eventually developing clinical pathways. The approach compared different surgeons on different indicators such as length of stay and number of laboratory tests. An example is shown in Exhibit 9. However, as Larry Goetschius, Administrative Leader for the Surgery Healthcare Service, explained, it was extremely difficult to get timely information:

> Right now the data are pulled from three different databases and compiled into this report [Exhibit 9]. This isn't so bad for the first one, but when you ask the systems people for the data every month, they almost fall off their chairs because it takes so long to do. They just don't have time to do it on a regular basis. We are just not integrated with our information systems. Nevertheless, the information is extremely useful and has resulted in improvement.

The lack of systems was also particularly problematic when it came to managing the budget. One example was the issue of medical and surgical supplies. The operating room revenue and expenses, which included the line item medical and surgical supplies, fell under the Surgery Healthcare Service budget. This line item had increased dramatically, but the Surgery Healthcare Service had no way of knowing why. As one administrator explained:

> In many areas we lack the data we need. We don't have the systems right now to drill down to the level that we need to understand what drivers are related to medical and surgery supplies. We've been working for six or seven months to get a handle on what the drivers are so we can begin to control them.

There was also some question about the accuracy of the data, which made it even more difficult to use and also hurt the credibility of the administrators. Mr. Goetschius explained:

EXHIBIT 8 Performance Spider

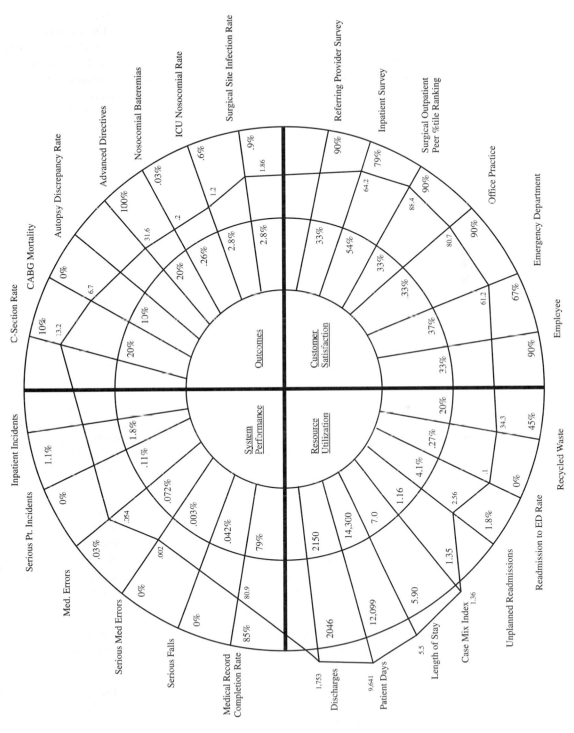

EXHIBIT 9 Cost Comparisons by Procedure

DRG 3812 HEAD NECK ENDARTER NEC							
	Volume	Average LOS	Average Total Cost	Average Lab Cost	Average X-Ray Cost	Average OR Cost	Average Drug Cost
Physician A	30	4.13	$5,841	$406	$448	$1,747	$288
Physician B	31	3.10	4,056	229	205	1,729	180
Physician C	44	2.86	4,191	187	259	1,615	127
Fletcher Group	357	3.73	None	None	None	None	None
National Teaching	1,669	4.12	None	None	None	None	None

Notes:
1. Data from Discharge History, HCM Cost Accounting System and CFIS
2. Discharge Service = 007104,015529,013581,013714—"Vascular"
3. During January 1, 1995–December 31, 1995
4. Top six volume procedures for service chosen for national comparison.
5. Costs for national groups not provided due to costing methodology differences between CFIS and HCM

> People in my position lose credibility when we use data that a surgeon can look at and say, "I know that's not right." Our data systems are lacking so much that they hurt our ability to make good decisions and to get buy-in from surgeons. So we end up trying to raise everyone's general awareness because we cannot go to individual surgeons or to services that use the operating room and say, "Medical surgical supplies have gone up because you're using this more expensive product."

The process was complicated by the fact that other HCSs, such as orthopedics, used the operating room but were not held accountable for operating room costs. According to Mr. Goetschius:

> Right now the OR falls under surgery's budget. So surgery gets the institutional revenue through the room charges and other institutional charges, and is responsible for all expenses. This is difficult to manage because when an orthopedist performs surgery, he or she receives the professional revenue but not the institutional revenue, nor is he or she accountable for the costs associated with the operating room. So if the orthopedist decides to use the most expensive prosthesis, it does not affect his or her bottom line but it does affect Surgery's. There is no alignment of responsibility for making the decision and accountability for that decision. The problem is worse because the margins are shrinking and we need to be able to hold people accountable for costs.

On the outpatient side, the service was in somewhat better shape as far as systems because a shadow system had been created prior to the merger. Ms. Goodrich explained:

> I came into UHC prior to the merger and I had created the financial systems internally, where information was lacking in the UHC system. When information came in from accounting, I manipulated it to make it meet our needs. Presenting the division heads or physicians with a report straight from Accounting was not meaningful. We were trying to make the physicians accountable for their bottom lines. We had to create financial statements for each surgeon, including all expenses and revenues from the professional side of the business. I used to do

these on a monthly basis. Now, the responsibility has been shifted to someone else who creates them on an annual basis. Other things have taken priority.

Performance Evaluation

To help ensure accountability of surgeons for performance in the clinical, teaching, and research spheres, Dr. Shackford had designed a compensation system that was linked to specific criteria in each area. This system was quite different from the one that had been used before the merger. He explained:

> Until 1995, gross billings drove salary increases and bonuses. There was cross-subsidization among surgeons to support research and teaching and that was okay. The surgeons bought into it and they trusted that I would do it appropriately. They also trusted me to ensure that everyone in the department was working hard enough. This trust was built upon open books and clear goals.

With the merger, Dr. Shackford had begun to evaluate each surgeon's performance using much broader criteria, shown in Exhibit 10. He also had developed his own database on the surgeons in his department to evaluate their performance:

> I created the database. I wrote the computer program and entered the data myself because I wanted to make sure it was done right. This is really important when you are moving to a new system. I then evaluated each of the 44 surgeons in my service, weighting the criteria differently for each physician depending on his or her activities.
>
> This year, I'm shifting this responsibility to the division heads, which is where I think it should rest. I can do it for my own division, but I have no credibility to go into the ENT division and tell them how long a radical neck should stay in the hospital. But the division head can. Additionally, they will also have their own development funds.

Most division heads were looking forward to having Dr. Shackford decentralize some of the decision making around compensation, but they had some concerns as well. In the view of Robert Sofferman, MD, Division Head of Otolaryngology:

> It's an interesting and complicated process. For the people who just do the clinical work and generate a lot of revenue, the information is objective and easy to get. But it's more difficult to measure someone who teaches and does of lot of other things to help the organization or department. Steve has tried to capture this in his database, but it's very complicated. I would probably need some help getting my arms around it to make it work for me. However, I do think comprehensive performance evaluation is very valuable and important.
>
> More generally, I think it's appropriate for us to manage our own lives, so to speak. It's extremely difficult to do things when you don't have control and have to go to the chair and ask permission. The recent budget crisis was extremely difficult for us. I don't know if our selected changes would be any different, but getting here was painful and tough.

EXHIBIT 10 Criteria for Productivity Awards

Clinical Competency and Productivity as determined by (not in order of priority):
- Dollars Billed
- RVUs
- Patient Satisfaction (letters, comments)
- Nights on Call/Call Units
- Utilization Data (when available)
- Complication Rate (wound infections)

Teaching Competency and Productivity as determined by (not in order of priority):
- Support of Clinical Core Lectures
- Support of Senior Major Lectures
- Support of Resident Didactic Lectures/Conferences/Teaching Rounds
- Student Advisees
- Teaching Scores/Evaluations
- Teaching Awards

Research Competency and Productivity as determined by (not in order of priority):
- Number of Published Pages as First Faculty Author
  - Peer Review, Chapters, Case Reports, Letters to Editor, Book Review, etc.
- Grant Dollars Awarded
- Grant Dollars Requested (with pink sheet requests)
- Research Awards/Recognition
  - Editorial Boards
  - Editor
- Evaluations or Research Mentorship—if applicable

Service Competency and Productivity as determined by (not in order of priority):
- Willingness to Serve
- Committee Work (chair, member)
  - Fletcher Allen Health Care
  - College of Medicine
  - Professional Society (officer)

Administrative Competency and Productivity as determined by (not in order of priority):
- Administrative Responsibility
  - Division Chair
  - Clinical Director
  - Program Director
- Willingness to Serve
- Timely Completion of Assigned Tasks
- Emotional Intelligence
- People Skills

Dr. Dennis Vane, Division Head of Pediatric Surgery, agreed that decentralizing responsibility to the division heads was appropriate. He felt that this shift would make the divisions more aware of their own profitability:

> There are some divisions that are more than self-supporting and others that are not self-supporting. I think that putting more responsibility on the division heads makes us more aware of those issues. We understand that some divisions will make money and some will not. We don't have an ability to draw from infinite

patient population, and we've had to decide as a department what we will and won't have here. But, I think that there are some divisions that are not financially solvent that need to be. Hopefully, by putting the responsibility at the division head level, people will take that to heart.

Decentralization did not mean that each division necessarily had to have a positive bottom line financially, but each needed to demonstrate how its physicians were spending their time. Dr. Vane continued:

The whole issue is to determine what everything costs us. It may make money, it may lose money, but we need to know what it costs so we can make an intelligent decision. For example, a pediatric surgeon may have a negative bottom line, but perhaps he is doing all the difficult newborn cases, or has terrible payer mix. It's not an intelligent decision to get rid of that person. For one thing the work would just accrue to other physicians. The issue is that we need information. We need to understand how hard everyone is working, on the academic side, in research, and clinically. It's now the division head's job to balance all these, which is appropriate, because the division head is better able to judge the activities of the surgeons in his division.

However, Dr. Vane also commented that the decentralization would require some transition and a change of mind set, due to the traditional relationship that surgeons had with their chair:

When you are hired, you are hired by the chair and you work for the chair, and that is where the ultimate authority rests. Now, with decentralization, it's the division head who will regulate your salary and your academic mission and that's a change of mind set that will take some transition. The chair, in this case Steve, will need to be there as a mediator, and the surgeons have to feel like they have access to him, but he has to be careful not to undermine the authority of the division heads or the decentralization won't work.

Remaining Funds Professional

Dr. Shackford's ability to pay bonuses or distribute funds to the division heads to pay bonuses was largely dependent on the existence of the RFP that had been built into FAHC's physician compensation plan at the time of the merger. However, given the financial difficulties of FY1996, the Strategic Management Committee had agreed that there would be no RFP for FY1997. This decision had the greatest financial impact on surgery, medicine, and pathology, as they were the only HCSs that had positive RFPs for FY1996—surgery with over $1 million, medicine with $500,000, and pathology with $40,000.

The RFP calculation involved more than the bottom line on the professional side that is shown in Exhibit 6. Dr. Hindes described some of the differences:

To calculate an HCS's RFP in 1996, we made several adjustments to the bottom line on the professional side. For example, we needed to adjust for salary sharing across the professional and institutional budgets for the HCS leadership team.

These salaries were split 50–50 between the professional and institutional side. Another example was the deduction of FY96 budget recovery savings that occurred in the professional cost centers. If these savings were not backed out, then the RFP would have increased. These were just two of the special RFP calculations.

The computation methodology was particularly important for surgery, not only because of its historical surplus, but because of a discrepancy that had arisen around the amount of its RFP for FY1996. As Dr. Shackford explained:

> The issue with the 1996 RFP is difficult. The 5 percent reduction should have dropped to our bottom line, but interestingly enough they [administration] said, "No, that goes to the institution." Finally, we ended up getting a legal opinion and believe that under the contract they cannot take it away from us.

Dr. Ittleman commented on the effect this issue had had on the surgeons:

> When you have to start getting lawyers and legal opinions involved, it really takes us out of our element. We all want to work and be free of these financial issues, but the issues keep cropping up. It doesn't seem as if the surgeons and administration are working on the same page, but rather we are more adversarial. If there was a higher sense of trust between the administration and surgeons, then I think we would be more sanguine about the proposed changes. We all want this merger to work and are proud of this institution, but at the same time we have to protect ourselves.

Dr. Shackford hoped that in FY1997 the surgeons would benefit from some of the savings from redesign, an effort that the surgeons believed essential to the system's success. In his view:

> Most of us understood the fee-for-service environment. We understood how to run that type of business on the professional side. However, in the integrated system we now have to understand the institutional side because we now have institutional risk. We understand why there is no RFP for FY97 and we buy into that. We have to get $6 million out of the system to be on the target to achieve the strategic plan. Everyone that I know of has bought into the good of the strategic plan. They see it in their best interests that we achieve that plan. Pretty much we all went through the strategic plan when it came out and agreed to it. Yes, we have to build primary care, and yes, money will have to leave surgery and go to primary care. However, the surgeons want to make sure that they understand the allocation of funds that leave surgery and that it is done fairly and in concert with the strategic plan. The biggest issue for the surgeons is trust—they have to trust their chairman and trust who their chairman is taking leadership from.

In this regard, Dr. Shackford was suggesting that in the redesign effort, if the system achieved savings above and beyond the $6 million, the doctors should share in them. He explained:

> The departments that are making a difference should share in the savings. For example, if surgery squeezes out another million, then the doctors should get a percentage, say 20 percent, of that savings. This is the only way you're going to

get the doctors on board here. If all goes as planned, the RFP will be reinstituted for FY98. However, physician contracts come up for renewal in October 1997 [the first month of FY98] and we need their buy-in.

Many at FAHC understood that the renewal of the contracts in October 1997 was not guaranteed. Some physicians were clearly frustrated with FAHC, and several surgeons had suggested the possibility of forming their own group outside of the FAHC system. Although they quickly pointed out that this was not their goal, nor the ideal outcome, the idea was not considered impossible.

Questions

1. Considering the strategic blueprint in Exhibit 1 and other information in the case, how would you characterize FAHC's strategy? In particular, what are its unique features? Its strengths and weaknesses?

2. How does the RFP work? Is it achieving the goals that were established for it at the time of the merger? What, if any, are its flaws? As FAHC moves towards further integration of the professional and institutional budgets, what should the heads of the HCSs worry about in terms of the RFP?

. What types of responsibility centers are the HCSs, the divisions, and the physicians? Are they well designed?

4. What impact will the decentralization of responsibility to the division heads have on the department of surgery? What should Dr. Shackford be concerned about as he moves toward decentralization within the department?

5. Are the performance spider and Dr. Shackford's compensation criteria aligned? Do they fit with the strategic plan?

6. What is your assessment of the change process at FAHC? In particular, could the budget crisis have been avoided? If so, how?

Appendix

Solutions to Practice Cases

Overview

This is a tricky case that may cause a bit of difficulty. The problem is that some errors have been made by Oceanside Nursing Rome in constructing its financial statements, and you need to correct them. You will need to do some reasoning to make the corrections.

Question 1

T accounts with beginning balances are shown in Exhibit A. Exhibit A also contains transactions for items 1 through 6 in the case. Journal entries have been made in Exhibit B; each is accompanied by an explanation.

Note that there are a couple of problems with the retained earnings account. First, it is $10,000 too high. To figure out why, we need to recognize that its $24,500 balance in Exhibit 1 was *after* the $10,000 income (shown in Exhibit 1) was added. Effectively, the statement of retained earnings for 1998 must have looked as follows:

Retained earnings at beginning of year	$14,500
Add surplus	10,000
Retained earnings at end of year	$24,500

[1]This solution was prepared by David W. Young. Copyright © by David W. Young.

EXHIBIT A   T-Accounts

Cash	
(BB) 1,500	
1,500	

Accounts Receivable	
(BB) 13,000	800 (6)
12,200	

Supplies Inventory	
(BB) 4,000	1,000 (1)
3,000	

Prepaid Expenses	
(2) 2,000	
2,000	

Property & Equipment	
(BB) 48,000	
48,000	

Accumulated Dep. B&E	
	2,000 (3)
	2,000 (3a)
	4,000

Other Assets	
(BB) 12,000	
12,000	

Accounts Payable	
	9,000 (BB)
	9,000

Salaries & Wages Payable	
	4,000 (4)
	4,000

Unearned Revenue	
	4,000 (5)
	4,000

Income Summary	
(B) 44,000	106,000 (A)
(C) 25,000	
(D) 33,800	
(E) 1,000	
(F) 2,000	
(G) 200	

Contributions	
	45,000 (BB)
	45,000

Retained Earnings	
(3a) 2,000	14,500 (BB)
	200 (G)
	12,700

Revenue	
(5) 4,000	110,000 (BB)
(A) 106,000	

Salary Expense	
(BB) 40,000	44,000 (B)
(4) 4,000	

Maintenance Expense	
(BB) 25,000	25,000 (C)

Other Expense	
(BB) 35,000	2,000 (2)
(6) 800	33,800 (D)

Supply Expense	
(1) 1,000	1,000 (E)

Depreciation Expense	
(3) 2,000	2,000 (F)

EXHIBIT B   Journal Entries

1. Supply expense   1,000
         Supply inventory   1,000

   This entry adjusts the ending balance of the inventory to $3,000. Thus, supply expenses must be higher than originally thought.

2. Prepaid expenses   2,000
         Other expenses   2,000

   Too much had been debited to other expenses. This entry reduces other expenses and puts the $2,000 into prepaid expenses (insurance).

3. Depreciation expense   2,000
         Accumulated depreciation   2,000

   Property and equipment depreciation should be $2,000 per year, computed as follows:
   $48,000 − $8,000 = $40,000. $40,000 ÷ 20 years = $2,000 per year.

3a. Retained earnings   2,000
         Accumulated depreciation   2,000

   This transaction records the 1997 depreciation amount that was not recorded in 1997 (otherwise, the property and equipment would have had a balance of $46,000 on the balance sheet).

4. Salary expense   4,000
         Salaries and wages payable   4,000

   Since there is no salaries and wages payable account on the balance sheet, we assume that this item was not recorded.

5. Revenue   4,000
         Unearned revenue   4,000

   Too much revenue had been credited to the account. This entry corrects for that. Since the $4,000 is unearned, the liability account is created.

6. Other Expense   800
         Accounts receivable   800

   This puts the bad debt expense (an estimate) into other expenses and reduces accounts receivable by a corresponding amount.

A to F   These are closing entries based on the new balances in the operating statement accounts. They are made to the income summary.

G   This closes the income summary, resulting in a $200 credit to retained earnings.

We are redoing these calculations by changing the operating statement accounts. To be accurate, we must "reset the clock" to where is was at the beginning of the year. To do so, we must put in a beginning balance of $14,500.

The second problem is that we must correct prior-period earnings (1997) to account for the depreciation in that year (see entry 3a). You may not have not been exposed to this concept before, and so may struggle with it a bit. What's important is that you cannot make the correction to this year's operating statement; rather, the correction must be made directly to the retained earnings account. Alternatively, you could correct the retained earnings account in the same way that you corrected other accounts. The results are contained in Exhibit C.

Either approach can be used: adjusting retained earnings for the incorrect entries or adjusting the expense accounts and redoing the closing. if we choose the

EXHIBIT C Reconciliation of Retained Earnings

	Assets	=	Liabilities	+	Equity
Beginning balance, retained earnings..................					$24,500
Inventory adjustment................................	−1,000				−1,000
Prepaid expense adjustment........................	+2,000				+2,000
Depreciation adjustment for 1998	−2,000				−2,000
Depreciation adjustment for 1997	−2,000				−2,000
Salary adjustment.................................			+4,000		−4,000
Unearned revenue adjustment......................			+4,000		−4,000
Bad debt adjustment	−800				−800
Ending balance, retained earnings					$12,700

EXHIBIT D Financial Statements

Operating Statement for 1998

Operating revenues		$106,000
Operating expenses:		
Salaries and wages	$44,000	
Maintenance....................	25,000	
Supplies........................	1,000	
Depreciation	2,000	
Other	33,800	
Total operating expenses............		105,800
Operating income (loss)		$ 200

Balance Sheet as of December 31, 1998

Assets			Liabilities + Equity	
Cash.....................		$ 1,500	Accounts payable	$ 9,000
Accounts receivable (net)....		12,200	Salaries and wages payable....	4,000
Inventory		3,000	Unearned revenue	4,000
Prepaid expenses		2,000		
Total current assets.........		$18,700	Total current liabilities........	$17,000
Property & equipment	$48,000		Contributions..............	45,000
Less: Accumulated dep......	4,000		Retained earnings...........	12,700
Net		44,000		
Other assets..............		12,000		
Total assets..............		$74,700	Total liabilities + equity	$74,700

Statement of Retained Earnings

Retained earnings at beginning of year	$14,500
Less: Correction to prior period....................	(2,000)
Plus: Operating income..........................	200
Retained earnings at end of year	$12,700

latter approach, we must reset retained earnings to the January 1, 1997, level of $14,500, and we must include the adjustment for 1998 depreciation.

Corrected financial statements are contained in Exhibit D.

Question 2

Oceanside still operated in the black, but barely so. Whether its Surplus is about right, too small, or too large is a subject that will be discussed in Chapter 4.

Chapter 4 Practice Case: Energy Associates (A) Solution[2]

Overview

This is a pretty basic case designed to assist you to refresh your memory about preparing statements of cash flows and performing ratio analyses.

Question 1

The SCF is contained in Exhibit A.

Question 2

A set of ratios and the formulas used to calculate them are contained in Exhibit B. This exhibit has been set up on a spreadsheet, which can be replicated quite easily. Once a spreadsheet of this sort exists, it can be used for ratio analyses of other organizations simply by copying it and entering a new set of key financial statement figures. The ratios then will be calculated automatically.

Question 3

The SCF There are several things we can learn from the SCF that are not readily apparent on the other financial statements. First, although our revenues were $200,000, we actually collected $209,000 in cash; this is because our accounts receivable balance fell by $9,000 (from $24,000 to $15,000). We, of course, know nothing about the behavior of individual accounts in the accounts receivable account. That is, we could have collected the entire $24,000 that was owed at the beginning of the period, such that the $15,000 that is owed at the end of the period is from the sales during the period. Or we could have collected the entire amount of the $200,000 sales during the period plus $9,000 of the $24,000 that was owed at the beginning of the period. If this were the case, we would have $15,000 in accounts receivable that are over one year old, giving rise to some concern about the collectability of the amount that is owed.

Only by "aging" the accounts receivable can we make this determination. That is, we would need to calculate how much of the $15,000 has been owed for various time periods. The time periods frequently used in an aging analysis are fewer than 30 days, 30 to 59 days, 60 to 89 days, 90 to 120 days, and over 120 days. Of course, the older the account receivable, the less likely it is to be collected.

[2]This solution was prepared by Professor David W. Young. Copyright © by David W. Young.

EXHIBIT A   A Statement of Cash Flows

1. Calculate Cash Flows from Operations:

a. Direct Method:

Beginning balance Accounts Receivable	$ 24,000	
Plus: Revenues	200,000	
Less: Ending balance Accounts Receivable	15,000	
Equals: Cash collected from customers		$ 209,000
Beginning balance Inventory	$ 31,000	
Plus: Purchases	??	
Less: Cost of Goods Sold	130,000	
Equals: Ending balance Inventory	59,000	
Therefore $31 + x - 130 = 59$; $x = 158$		
Therefore purchases = ...	158,000	
Beginning balance Accounts Payable	16,000	
Plus: Purchases	158,000	
Less: Payments	??	
Equals: Ending balance Accounts Payable	20,000	
Therefore cash payments to suppliers = ...		(154,000)
Other cash payments		(33,000)
Net cash provided by operating activities		$ 22,000

b. Indirect Method:

Change in net assets		$ 25,000
Adjustments to reconcile to cash		
provided by operating activities:		
Depreciation	$ 12,000	
Decrease in Accounts Receivable	9,000	
Increase in Inventory	(28,000)	
Increase in Accounts Payable	4,000	(3,000)
Net cash provided by operating activities		$ 22,000

2. Calculate Cash Flows from Financing and Investing Activities:

Investing activities		
Increase in plant and equipment		$(24,000)
Financing activities		
Decrease in notes payable	(7,000)	
Increase in bonds payable	20,000	13,000

3. Determine Change in Cash . . . . $ 11,000

4. Reconcile to Cash Balances:

Plus: Beginning balance cash		19,000
Equals: Ending balance cash		$ 30,000

EXHIBIT B   Financial Ratios

Reference No.	Key Financial Statement Figures	1997	1998
1	Cash	19,000	30,000
2	Accounts receivable.	24,000	15,000
3	Inventory	31,000	59,000
4	Total current assets	74,000	104,000
5	Net fixed assets.	56,000	68,000
6	Total assets	130,000	172,000
7	Total current liabilities	23,000	20,000
8	Long-term liabilities.	0	20,000
9	Total liabilities	23,000	40,000
10	Total net assets	107,000	132,000
11	Revenues.		200,000
12	COGS		130,000
13	Depreciation		12,000
14	Interest payments		1,900
15	Total expenses.		175,000
16	Change in net assets		25,000
17	Principal payments		N.A.

Formulas (1)	Ratios	1997	1998
	Profitability		
16 ÷ 11	Profit margin.		0.125
16 ÷ 6	Return on assets		0.145
16 : 10	Return on equity.		0.189
	Liquidity		
4 ÷ 7	Current ratio.	3.22	5.20
(1 + 2) ÷ 7	Quick ratio	1.87	2.25
2 ÷ (11 ÷ 365)	Ave. days receivable		27.4
	Asset management		
11 ÷ 6	Asset turnover.		1.16
11 ÷ 5	Fixed-asset turnover		2.94
3 ÷ (12 ÷ 365)	Ave. days inventory.		165.7
	Long-term solvency		
9 ÷ 10	Debt/equity		0.30
6 ÷ 10	Leverage		1.30
8 ÷ 10	Long-term debt/equity		0.15
(16 + 13 + 14) ÷ (17 + 14)	Debt-service coverage.		N.A
(16 + 13 + 14) ÷ (13 + 14)	Modified debt service coverage (assumes depreciation is equal to principal payments)		2.80
(16 + 14)/14	Times interest earned		14.16

Note 1: Formulas use reference numbers above.

Second, we can see that operations provided us with $22,000 in cash; this is very difficult to determine from the other financial statements, and, indeed, to do so would require an analysis of the sort we have done with the SCF. Note that both the direct and the indirect method arrive at this number.

Third, not all of the $22,000 from operations made its way into the cash account, since we spent $24,000 for additional plant and equipment. To avoid a decrease in cash as a result of the plant and equipment acquisition, we increased our borrowing by $13,000. The net result of these three items—operations, investing, and financing—was that cash increased by $11,000. The cash increase is readily apparent from the two balance sheets, but the causes of the change are less clear without the SCF.

Finally, we did some refinancing, which also is fairly obvious on the balance sheet but is clarified somewhat on the SCF. In particular, we shifted our debt structure from a short-term note payable to long-term bonds payable. While we know nothing about the bonds other than their long-term nature, it is encouraging to see the shift, since acquisitions of fixed assets generally should be financed with some combination of long-term debt and equity, and not with short-term debt.

The Ratios   The ratios tell us a great deal about EA that we didn't already know. First, in 1998, it had a return on assets of 14.5 percent. This is quite likely well above inflation, suggesting that the organization is financially healthy.

In the area of liquidity, we see a marked improvement between the two years, including an impressive increase in the current ratio from 3.2 to 5.2.

Finally, we see that the organization has taken on additional long-term debt, increasing its leverage slightly. This is how it has financed a large portion of its new fixed assets, and how it raised its 14.5 percent ROA to an 18.9 percent ROE. Despite this increase in debt, its times-interest-earned ratio indicates that it is earning more than 14 times its interest payments; thus it seems to be facing relatively little risk that it will not be able to meet its debt-service obligations. Its modified debt service coverage ratio seems to confirm this.

Question 4

It would be helpful to have more years of data so that we could see whether the changes taking place in the ratios in 1998 are part of a trend or an aberration. It also would be helpful to have some figures from the industry so we could get an idea of what a reasonable current ratio would be, how long other firms keep their products in inventory, and how long clients typically take to pay their bills. Finally, it would be helpful to have some sense of management's objectives for liquidity, and its desired balance between debt and equity, so we could assess the debt/equity ratio.

Chapter 5 Practice Case 1: Mossy Bog Transportation Agency Solution[3]

Overview

This is a relatively simple case in calculating full costs. It requires you to assign costs to cost centers and to determine appropriate bases of allocation for service center costs. Most of the information is provided in the case itself.

Question 1

| | | | | Service Centers | | |
Department	Initial Costs	Allocated Costs	Total to Allocate	Main- tenance	Adminis- tration	Total
Maintenance (1)	$ 1,160	0	$1,160			
Administration (2)	2,400	400	2,800	$ 400		
Rapid Transit	8,000			600	$ 560	$ 9,160
Slow Transit	4,000			160	2,240	6,400
Total	$15,560			$1,160	$2,800	$15,560

Notes:

1. $1,160,000 maintenance costs ÷ $5,800,000 depreciation dollars (excludes depreciation dollars in the maintenance department) = $.20 per depreciation dollar.

2. $2,800,000 (2,400,000 + 400,000) administration costs ÷ 50,000 labor hours (only uses labor hours in Rapid Transit and Slow Transit departments) = $56.00 per labor hour.

Question 2

The next step is to use this information to set prices (or to compare existing revenue with full costs). Specifically, we would need to estimate total number of rides on each form of transit, and divide total costs by that figure to get a cost per ride. This would then need to be marked up by a percentage to give us the surplus we required.

Chapter 5 Practice Case 2: Museum of Frozen History Solution[4]

Overview

This is a case in working through the basics of activity-based costing. ABC was discussed in the chapter, but can be difficult to apply in practice. This case provides an opportunity to experience the nitty gritty of ABC.

Question 1

Overhead rate = total manufacturing overhead cost ÷ budgeted direct labor dollars
= $3,000,000 ÷ $600,000 = $5 per DL$

[3]This solution was prepared by Professor David W. Young. Copyright © by David W. Young.
[4]This solution was prepared by Professor David W. Young. Copyright © by David W. Young.

	Colombian Cocoa	Miami Mango
Direct materials	$4.20	$3.20
Direct labor	.30	.30
Overhead (.30 × $5.00)	1.50	1.50
Full production cost.	$6.00	$5.00
Markup (30%).	1.80	1.50
Selling price.	$7.80	$6.50

Question 2

Activity	Cost Driver	Budgeted Activity	Budgeted Cost	Unit Cost
Purchasing	Purchase orders	1,158	$579,000	$500
Material handing	Setups	1,800	720,000	400
Quality contol	Batches	720	144,000	200
Cream freezing	Machine hours	96,100	961,000	10
Flavor blending	Blending hours	33,600	336,000	10
Packaging	Packaging hours	26,000	260,000	10

Formulas

Purchasing	# purchase orders × $500 ÷ number of pints of output
Material handling	# setups × $400 ÷ number of pints of output
Quality control	# batches × $200 ÷ number of pints of output
Cream freezing	# hours × $10 ÷ number of pints of output
Flavor blending	# hours × $10 ÷ number of pints of output
Packaging	# hours × $10 ÷ number of pints of output

Cost of Colombian Cocoa

1. Direct material 4.20
2. Direct labor. 30
3. Purchasing (4 orders × $500 ÷ 100,000 pints). 02
4. Material handling (30 setups × $400 ÷ 100,000 pints) 12
5. Quality control (10 batches × $200 ÷ 100,000 pints) 02
6. Cream freezing (1,000 hours × $10 ÷ 100,000 pints) 10
7. Blending (500 hours × $10 ÷ 100,000 pints). 05
8. Packaging (100 hours × $10 ÷ 100,000 pints). 01
Total $4.82

Cost of Miami Mango

1. Direct material 3.20
2. Direct labor. 30
3. Purchasing (4 orders × $500 ÷ 2,000 pints). 1.00
4. Material handling (12 setups × $400 ÷ 2,000 pints) 2.40
5. Quality control (4 batches × $200 ÷ 2,000 pints) 40
6. Cream freezing (20 hours × $10 ÷ 2,000 pints). 10
7. Blending (10 hours × $10 ÷ 2,000 pints). 05
8. Packaging (2 hours × $10 ÷ 2,000 pints). 01
Total $7.46

Question 3

The museum's strategy appears to be to sell both popular (high-volume, produced in large batches) and esoteric (low-volume, produced in small batches) blends of ice cream. If this is the case, direct labor hours may not be the best cost driver for it to use for absorbing manufacturing overhead into a pint of ice cream. Rather, the ABC analysis seems more appropriate, given that small batches of ice cream require more manufacturing overhead.

The differences are not trivial, as the following comparison shows:

	Colombian Cocoa	Miami Mango
Current System:		
Price per pint.	$ 7.80	$ 6.50
"Perceived cost" per pint.	6.00	5.00
Contribution per pint to profits	$ 1.80	$ 1.50
Number of pints	100,000	2,000
Total contribution to profits.	$180,000	$ 3,000
Proposed System:		
Price per pint.	$ 7.80	$ 6.50
"True cost" per pint.	4.82	7.46
Contribution per pint to profits	$ 2.98	$ (0.96)
Number of pints	100,000	2,000
Total contribution to profits.	$298,000	$(1,920)

While the museum may wish to continue to sell Miami Mango as a small loss leader, it can at least evaluate it as such, rather than as a small winner. Moreover, the museum may be able to price the flavor more appropriately, reflecting its premium nature.

Chapter 6 Practice Case: Energy Associates (B) Solution[5]

Overview

This a case on cost-volume-profit analysis with multiple products. Although relatively basic, it bridges into some alternative-choice decision making, requiring you to assess how you would manage costs, how you would make a choice under constraints, and whether you would eliminate a losing product line.

Question 1

The weighted average contribution margin is calculated as follows:

$$(\$74,000 - \$67,900) \div 1,500 = \$4.07$$

Therefore, breakeven is

$$\$50,700 \div \$4.07 = 12,457 \text{ items}$$

[5]This solution was prepared by Professor David W. Young. Copyright © by David W. Young.

Some of the concerns about this breakeven figure are the following:

- A change in the mix of products will change breakeven.

- The number is so much higher than the projected volume that breaking even seems out of the question.

- With the exception of storm windows, we don't know if there are any unique fixed costs per product (since all fixed costs are allocated). If we did, we would have a better chance of seeing which products are in the most trouble. This is particularly true since allocated fixed costs include labor. It is likely that some products are not even covering their unique fixed costs, and it would be helpful to know which ones.

- Storm windows actually is budget to exceed breakdown on its unique fixed costs: $2,000 ÷ $5 = 400 units, versus 500 units budgeted.

You may be concerned with the fixed-cost allocation, but this is unnecessary. The breakeven figure calculated above is totally independent of the way fixed costs have been allocated. Thus, changing the allocation of fixed costs does not have any effect on breakeven.

Question 2

There are essentially five options for eliminating the budgeted loss:

- Increase price.

- Decrease unit variable costs.

- Change mix.

- Decrease fixed costs.

- Increase volume.

Question 3

The key issue here is not *unit* contribution margin (UCM) but *total* contribution, which depends on how many additional units will be sold of each product *as a result of spending $1,000 to advertise it.* Thus, you do not want to consider existing total contribution, but only the differential effects on total contribution of the advertising. Thus, the question is not which product to emphasize, but rather how EA should *decide* which product to emphasize. The answer to that question depends on the following kind of analysis:

	Shower Nozzles	Thermo-stats	Storm Windows
UCM	$2	$10	$5
Breakeven (# of units to cover $1,000).	500	100	200

For example, if EA assumes that the following results can be achieved exclusively from spending $1,000 on advertising, it should advertise the shower nozzles, even though they have the lowest UCM:

	Shower Nozzles	Thermo- stats	Storm Windows
Additional sales (in units)	1,500	250	100
Additional contribution	$3,000	$2,500	$ 500
Less: Advertising.	(1,000)	(1,000)	(1,000)
Net contribution	$2,000	$1,500	$ (500)

The key here is to see the distinction between UCM and total contribution

Question 4

Contribution from storm windows is $2,500 ($5 per item × 500 items). Therefore, don't discontinue unless doing so will allow you to do one or some combination of the following:

- Reduce fixed costs by $2,500 or more.

- Increase thermostat sales by 250 or more (250 × $10 = $2,500).

- Increase shower nozzle sales by 1250 or more (1250 × $2 = $2,500).

Of course, these changes must come about directly as a result of discontinuing storm windows; that is, they must be the *opportunity costs* of continuing to sell storm windows. If the changes can be made without reducing sales of storm windows, then do so, but don't discontinue them.

Chapter 7 Practice Case: Job Enrichment Center Solution[5]

Overview

This is a case on pricing, although it could also be used for expense budgeting or breakeven analysis. It use depends on what you select as the unknown element in the equation.

Question 1

The budget might look something like that shown in Exhibit A. As it indicates, the price per trainee is $551.25 for Basic Literacy and $1,564.50 for English as a Second Language. As the budget also indicates, JEC is anticipating a surplus of $14,970 for the year.

In calculating this budget, you needed to pay attention to the following issues:

- Distinguishing between programs. Each program should be budgeted for separately.

---

[6]This solution was prepared by Professor David W. Young. Copyright © by David W. Young.

EXHIBIT A   Costs, Prices, and Operating Margin

Line	Item	Formula	Program Basic Literacy	Program English as a Second Language	Total
1	Faculty:	5 faculty @ $20,000 each	$100,000		$100,000
2		3 faculty @ $25,000 each		$75,000	75,000
3	Books/Workbooks	5 × 400 × $15	30,000		30,000
4		2 × 60 × $20		2,400	2,400
5	Total direct costs	Sum of lines 1 through 4	$130,000	$77,400	$207,400
6	Administration and general	($92,000 ÷ 460) * Line 8	80,000	12,000	92,000
7	Total costs	Sum of lines 5 and 6	$210,000	$89,400	$299,400
8	Anticipated number of trainees		400	60	
9	Full cost per trainee	Line 7 ÷ Line 8	$ 525	$ 1,490	
10	Margin		0.05	0.05	
11	Price	(1 + Line 10) * Line 9	$ 551.25	$ 1,564.50	
12	Total budgeted surplus	(Line 11 − Line 9) * Line 8	$ 10,500	$ 4,470	$ 14,970

- Allocating administrative and general to programs.

- Calculating total costs and an average cost per trainee. Increasing this cost by 5 percent to arrive at the price.

- Computing the total budget margin at the anticipated costs and prices.

Question 2

Since JEC has been operating for two years, it presumably has some good knowledge about the acceptability of its prices and its various costs. It's main source of uncertainty would appear to be the number of trainees. Since local companies pay the prices, the number of trainees are not the number of people who desire JEC's programs, but rather the number of people the local companies intend to hire after they have completed one or both of JEC's training programs.

Chapter 8 Practice Case: Valley Hospital Solution[7]

Overview

This is a fairly basic case on transfer pricing, but one that illustrates the problem of goal congruence rather neatly. You should have little or no trouble making the computations, so that you can focus on the bigger question of how to resolve the issues that arise as a result of the computations.

Question 1

The computations on a per-test basis are as follows:

[7]This solution was prepared by Professor David W. Young. Copyright © by David W. Young.

	Amb Care Division	Laboratory Division	Hospital Overall
Option 1—Buy from Hospital Lab Division			
Revenue	$11.00	$6.00	$11.00
Variable cost	6.00	2.00	2.00
Contribution.	$ 5.00	$4.00	$ 9.00
Option 2—Buy from Biolab			
Revenue	$11.00	$0.00	$11.00
Variable cost	4.50	0.00	4.50
Contribution.	$ 6.50	$0.00	$ 6.50

Question 2

The problem depicted by the figures in this table is an absence of goal congruence. Specifically, although Dr. Martin could improve the surplus in her division by having urinalyses prepared by Biolab, the overall surplus of Valley Hospital would decline if she were to do so. That is, the hospital pays $2.00 "out of pocket" for every urinalysis done by the Laboratory Division for Dr. Martin's division. All other costs are fixed. Therefore each urinalysis done by the Laboratory Division reduces the hospital's surplus by $2.00.

If Dr. Martin buys urinalyses from the Biolab, the hospital incurs an incremental cost of $4.50 instead of $2.00, and its surplus therefore is reduced by $4.50. This is because, when urinalyses are purchased from Biolab, the hospital pays a price that includes not just variable costs, but a portion of Biolab's fixed costs, plus a profit margin. Clearly, the hospital would prefer to have Dr. Martin purchase urinalyses from the Laboratory Division rather than from the freestanding laboratory.

The problem is that when Dr. Martin purchases urinalyses from the hospital's Laboratory Division, she is charged $6.00, not $2.00. As a result, for each urinalyses she purchases from the Laboratory Division, her division's surplus falls by $6.00, as compared to only $4.50 if she purchases urinalyses from the freestanding laboratory.

In summary, to allow Dr. Martin to purchase from outside the hospital increases her division's surplus but reduces the hospital's overall surplus. To force her to buy from the Laboratory Division maximizes the hospital's overall surplus but reduces the surplus of her division. Since she is paid a bonus, it also reduces her bonus. Clearly, Dr. Martin's goals are not congruent with those of the hospital as a whole.

Question 3

The resolution of transfer pricing problems such as these is one of the most complicated aspects of designing a management control structure. In arriving at a transfer price, senior management typically chooses among three options: (1) market price, (2) full cost, and (3) marginal cost. Different organizations use different options depending on a variety of circumstances, including matters such as the availability of information concerning market price, and the effect of the choice on managers' motivation. As such, there is no correct option.

Although there is no right answer to the resolution of this problem, there are four basic issues that Mr. Black might consider in making a transfer pricing decision.

1. Rules of the Game. The rules of the game must be clear. In the above example, Dr. Martin must know her options at the beginning of her budget year. If she must buy from inside the hospital, this needs to be well understood and agreed to.

2. Incentives. The price (or pricing formula) needs to be established in advance, and held constant throughout the budget year. Dr. Martin should not be forced to pay for inefficiencies in the laboratory if its actual costs diverge from its budgeted ones. To allow this would be to remove any incentive for the laboratory manager to control costs.

3. Setting a Fair Transfer Price. If Dr. Martin is to be required to buy from inside the hospital, the transfer price probably should be a negotiated one. In many organization's the rule is that the transfer price must be at the "market rate," or $4.50 in the above situation, but this is not always possible due to the unavailability of market price information. In the above example, the market price for a urinalysis probably is readily available from a free-standing lab, but free-standing labs most likely to not do lymph node dissections; hence, a market price for this test would be difficult to determine.

4. Autonomy versus Central Control. Perhaps most importantly, Mr. Black must decide how much autonomy he wishes to give to the hospital's divisions. Will he allow them to set their own prices without intervention, or will he intervene to set negotiated prices? Will he allow purchasing divisions to go outside if they can get a better deal than selling divisions offer them?

If Mr. Black chooses to give selling divisions the autonomy to set prices at the level they choose, and purchasing divisions the autonomy to buy from the outside, he must be prepared to lose some intraorganizational transactions, and to have the organization's overall profits fall as a result. He must believe, therefore, that the increased autonomy will give individual division managers the motivation to increase their profits, and that the resulting increases will more than offset the declines in overall profits caused by the use of outside purchases.

If, on the other hand, Mr. Black intervenes in the divisions, price-setting and outside-purchase decisions, he must be prepared to engage in many detailed price-setting activities, and to assist in the resolution of the frequent conflicts that will arise between divisional managers.

Both courses of action have advantages and disadvantages, and successful organizations can be found that have chosen each course. The key question that must be asked is the following: *Do the transfer pricing rules motivate managers to take actions that are simultaneously in the best interest of both their individual responsibility centers and the organization as a whole?* If not, then there would appear to be good reason to change the transfer pricing rules.

Chapter 9 Practice Case: Erie Museum Solution[8]

Overview

This is a case that will allow you to work through some of the basic elements of capital budgeting. It also introduces some tricky issues that go beyond the basic computations.

Question 1

The internal rate of return of the proposal can be calculated as follows:

$$\text{Investment} \div \text{Annual cash flows} = \text{Present value factor}$$

$$\$150,000 \div \$30,000 = 5.000$$

$$\text{Economic life} = 10 \text{ years}$$

Internal rate of return = 15% (The present value factor that lies at the intersection of the 10-year row and the 15% column is 5.019.)

Question 2

Part A   As a discount rate of 20 percent, the net present value can be calculated as follows:

Cash flows:	$30,000
Economic life:	10 years
Investment amount:	$150,000
Interest rate:	20%
Net present value:	= ($30,000 × 4.192) − $150,000
	= $125,760 − $150,000
	= ($24,240)

At 20 percent, the investment is not financially feasible. This makes sense, of course, since its internal rate of return was only 15 percent.

Part B   At a discount rate of 5 percent, the net present value can be calculated as follows:

Cash flows	$30,000
Economic life:	10 years
Investment amount:	$150,000
Interest rate:	5%
Net present value	= ($30,000 × 7.7355) − $150,000
	= $232,065 − $150,000
	= $82,065

[8]This solution was prepared by Professor David W. Young. Copyright © by David W. Young.

At 5 percent, we need to estimate the present value factor using the midpoint between 4 percent and 6 percent. When we do so, the investment is financially feasible. This also makes sense given an internal rate of return of 15 percent.

Part C   The appropriate rate to use is the weighted cost of capital, or, more specifically, the weighted cost of capital after the additional borrowing takes place (which is not, incidentally, the same as the interest rate on the incremental borrowing). This raises the question of how to calculate the weighted cost of capital.

The key point here is that donated funds generally are not free. In the first place, there usually is some fund-raising cost associated with donations. Second, donors may expect that the earnings on their funds are to be used rather than the principal; under these circumstances, the rate of return must be equivalent to the interest that could be earned on the funds. Finally, in an inflationary economy, unless donated funds earn a rate of return equivalent to inflation, their purchasing power will be eroded. Thus, the interest rate used should be at least equal to inflation, and possibly should reflect the opportunity cost of the funds. Let's use a rate of 10 percent, which is a fairly reasonable amount for a conservatively invested portfolio of funds. The result is the following weighted cost of capital:

	Percent of Total	Average Interest Rate	Weighted Interest Rate
Debt.	40.0%	12.0%	4.8%
Equity.	60.0	10.0	6.0
Total.	100.0%		10.8%

Given the arbitrary nature of these computations, 11 percent would serve the purpose. We might even use 12 percent if we were expecting to take on some additional debt during the coming year at a higher interest rate. Alternatively, if the cost of debt were declining, we might lower the rate to 10 percent. The result will be a figure that is somewhat higher than 4.8 percent but certainly not as high as 20 percent.

Question 3

The mistake came about because the economic life was estimated at 10 years when it in fact was only 2 years. If Ms. Michaels' proposed equipment has an economic life of only two years, it would have an internal rate of return of less than 1 percent, as the following calculations show:

$$\text{Investment} \div \text{Annual cash flows} = \text{Present value factor}$$

$$\$150,\!000 \div \$30,\!000 = 5.000$$

$$\text{Economic life} = 2 \text{ years}$$

The present value factor that lies at the intersection of the 2-year row and the 1% column is 1.970. Therefore, the internal rate of return is less than 1 percent. If a two-year economic life had been used for the previous request, it would not have been financially feasible either.

The fact that a mistake was made in the past does not change the conclusion that the new investment is financially feasible at 15 percent, *assuming* that the economic life and cash flows have been estimated accurately this time. Thus, the past decision is a sunk cost and must not be incorporated into the calculations for the present decision.

What is relevant here, however, is Ms. Michaels' ability to estimate economic lives. Mr. Larson should question Ms. Michaels' 10-year estimate carefully, in order to satisfy himself that it is as accurate as possible. No matter how much he questions Ms. Michaels, though, it is impossible to predict the future with certainty, and thus a similar mistake may be made again.

Question 4

There are a variety of nonquantitative factors to consider in this decision—product quality, competition, curator satisfaction, the kind of technology needed to preserve the art, and others. Indeed, it is nonquantitative factors that would usually tip the balance, especially if preserving the integrity of the art is at stake. The three issues that seem the most important here are the following:

- Erie's strategy. What is it, and how does this project help to achieve it?

- The credibility of Ms. Michaels. She did not do a good job of estimating the economic life of her last project. What confidence do we have in her estimate for this one?

- The pace of technological change. What will happen a few years from now with the technology in her area.

Chapter 10 Practice Case: Bandon Medical Associates (A) Solution[9]

Overview

This case lends itself to the use of a rather simple spreadsheet, which can be used to both build the budget and to examine opportunities for increasing the budgeted surplus.

Question 1

Exhibit A contains a spreadsheet with the budget, and shows the three factors that will be useful for budget revision: number and mix of visits, resources per visit, and cost per resource unit. Exhibit B contains the formulas used in the computations.

[9]This solution was prepared by Professor David W. Young. Copyright © David W. Young.

EXHIBIT A   Original Budget

Overall Budget	Initial Consult	Routine Physical	Intensive Visit	Routine Visit	Total
Number of visits	3,000	4,000	6,000	6,000	19,000
Price per visit	$ 150.00	$ 110.00	$ 80.00	$ 60.00	
Total revenue	$450,000	$440,000	$480,000	$360,000	$1,730,000
Variable expenses per visit.	$ 106.50	$ 77.75	$ 44.00	$ 31.00	
Total variable expenses	$319,500	$311,000	$264,000	$186,000	1,080,500
Contribution.	$130,500	$129,000	$216,000	$174,000	$ 649,500
Total fixed expenses					300,000
Allocated overhead.					250,000
Surplus					$ 99,500
Variable expense detail:					
Physician care:					
Average # minutes per visit . . .	60	45	20	10	
Average wage per minute	$ 1.35	$ 1.35	$ 1.35	$ 1.35	
Total expense per visit	$ 81.00	$ 60.75	$ 27.00	$ 13.50	
Extender care:					
Average # minutes per visit . . .	15	10	10	15	
Average wage per minute	$ 0.90	$ 0.90	$ 0.90	$ 0.90	
Total expense per visit	$ 13.50	$ 9.00	$ 9.00	$ 13.50	
Medical supplies:					
Average # units per visit.	3	2	2	1	
Average expense per unit.	$ 4.00	$ 4.00	$ 4.00	$ 4.00	
Total expense per visit	$ 12.00	$ 8.00	$ 8.00	$ 4.00	
Total average per variable					
expense per visit	$ 106.50	$ 77.75	$ 44.00	$ 31.00	

Exhibit A demonstrates that initial consults and routine physicals each make up only about 20 percent of the contribution. An intensive follow-up visit makes up about a third, and a routine visit about 25 percent.

Question 2

Dr. Desautels has several options, as follows:

- *Increase revenues.* In general, this option is the easiest to put into a budget but the hardest to actually make happen. It would be unwise for Dr. Desautels to increase his budgeted surplus by taking this route. If he does, there are three ways to go about it:

    1. Raise prices. We are told little about the market, however, so it is hard to say whether a price increase could be instituted without a loss in volume. Frequently, HMOs and other third-party payers dictate prices, so the group practice quite likely is a price taker.

EXHIBIT B Formulas for Original Budget

	A	B Initial Consult	C Routine Physical	D Intensive Visit	E Routine Visit	F Total
	Overall Budget					
7	Number of visits	3,000	4,000	6,000	6,000	= SUM(B7:E7)
8	Price per visit	150	110	80	60	
9	Total revenue	= B7 * B8	= C7 * C8	= D7 * D8	= E7 * E8	= SUM(B9:E9)
10						
11	Variable expenses per visit	= B35	= C35	= D35	= E35	
12	Total variable expenses	= B7 * B11	= C7 * C11	= D7 * D11	= E7 * E11	= SUM(B12:E12)
13	Contribution	= B9 – B12	= C9 – C12	= D9 – D12	= E9 – E12	= SUM(B13:E13)
14	Total fixed expenses					300000
15	Allocated overhead					250000
16	Surplus					= F13 – F14 – F15
17						
18	**Variable expense detail:**					
19	Physician care:					
20	Average # minutes per visit	60	45	20	10	
21	Average wage per minute	1.35	= B21	= B21	= B21	
22	Total expense per visit	= B20 * B21	= C20 * C21	= D20 * D21	= E20 * E21	
23						
24	Extender care:					
25	Average # minutes per visit	15	10	10	15	
26	Average wage per minute	0.9	= B26	= B26	= B26	
27	Total expense per visit	= B25 * B26	= C25 * C26	= D25 * D26	= E25 * E26	
28						
29	Medical supplies:					
30	Average # units per visit	3	2	2	1	
31	Average expense per unit	4	= B31	= C31	= D31	
32	Total expense per visit	= B30 * B31	= C30 * C31	= D30 * D31	= E30 * E31	
33						
34	**Total average per variable**					
35	**expense per visit**	= B22 + B32 + B27	= C22 + C32 + C27	= D22 + D32 + D27	= E22 + E32 + E27	

2. Increase volume. Presumably, Dr. Desautels is trying to do this already, however, and this set of figures quite likely represents his best guess. It may even be optimistic.

3. Change the mix of business toward more higher contribution cases. The analysis of this option is a little tricky. Assuming capacity constraints, the question is not which visit type has the highest contribution margin, but how much total contribution can be attained. If, for example, Dr. Desautels's physicians could see only one more patient (and were interested primarily in the impact on surplus), they would see a patient for an initial consult. If, however, they have one hour of capacity available, they presumably would prefer to see six routine follow-up patients. Since each visit is only 10 minutes, this approach would provide total contribution of $174 ($29 × 6), compared to only $43.50 for a single initial consult (which lasts 60 minutes). These computations are shown in the first box in Exhibit C, which shows the impact of a shift of 333 hours from intensive follow-up visits to routine follow-up visits. As this exhibit indicates, the financial impact is $22,000. However, when the extender time is included (shown in the second box at the bottom of Exhibit C), the number of visits that are possible in an hour changes (assuming extender time cannot overlap with physician time). The result is the availability of 500 hours (rather than 333 hours). However, given that total time is only 5 minutes less for the routine follow-up visits, the number of additional visits is only 1,200. Overall, the result is a decline in contribution.

- *Reduce costs.* This is probably the most viable option. There are two ways to go about it:

  1. Reduce fixed costs. We are told little about these, so it is hard to say whether this is a viable option. In most organizations, it usually is feasible since costs of this sort tend to grow as the business grows but not to decline as growth declines. From all we can tell, the allocated overhead is something that is outside Dr. Desautels's control.

  2. Reduce variable expense per case. There are two ways to do this:

     a. Reduce the number of resource units per case. For example, fewer physician minutes, extender minutes, or medical supplies per case.

     b. Reduce the expense per resource unit. This can be done by lowering factor prices (e.g., lower physician wages, extender wages, supply expense per unit).

If we examine these options, we can see that it probably will be difficult to reduce factor prices. We could ask physicians and extenders to work for less, but, depending on opportunities in the area, that would probably result in some of them leaving. Replacing them with lower-wage people could be difficult. Similarly, we presumably have the best prices that we can get from suppliers, although this certainly is a possibility.

EXHIBIT C   Original Budget with Variations in Visit Mix

Overall Budget	Initial Consult	Routine Physical	Intensive Visit	Routine Visit	Total
Number of visits	3,000	4,000	6,000	6,000	19,000
Price per visit	$ 150.00	$ 110.00	$ 80.00	$ 60.00	
Total revenue	$450,000	$440,000	$480,000	$360,000	$1,730,000
Variable expenses per visit	$ 106.50	$ 77.75	$ 44.00	$ 31.00	
Total variable expenses	$319,500	$311,000	$264,000	$186,000	1,080,500
Contribution	$130,500	$129,000	$216,000	$174,000	$ 649,500
Total fixed expenses					300,000
Allocated overhead					250,000
Surplus					$ 99,500
Variable expense detail:					
Physician care:					
Average # minutes per visit	60	45	20	10	
Average wage per minute	$ 1.35	$ 1.35	$ 1.35	$ 1.35	
Total expense per visit	$ 81.00	$ 60.75	$ 27.00	$ 13.50	
Extender care:					
Average # minutes per visit	15	10	10	15	
Average wage per minute	$ 0.90	$ 0.90	$ 0.90	$ 0.90	
Total expense per visit	$ 13.50	$ 9.00	$ 9.00	$ 13.50	
Medical supplies:					
Average # units per visit	3	2	2	1	
Average expense per unit	$ 4.00	$ 4.00	$ 4.00	$ 4.00	
Total expense per visit	$ 12.00	$ 8.00	$ 8.00	$ 4.00	
Total average per variable expense per visit	$ 106.50	$ 77.75	$ 44.00	$ 31.00	

Financial Implications of a Change in Visit Mix—Physicians Only					
Unit Contribution margin	$ 43.50	$ 32.25	$ 36.00	$ 29.00	
# visits possible in an hour	1.0	1.3	3.0	6.0	
Potential total contribution in 1 hour	$ 43.50	$ 43.00	$ 108.00	$ 174.00	
# visits planned	3,000	4,000	6,000	6,000	
Planned contribution	130,500	129,000	216,000	174,000	$ 649,500
Change in visits			−1,000	2,000	
Hours used (saved) with visit change			−333	333	
New contribution	130,500	129,000	180,000	232,000	$ 671,500
Change in contribution	0	0	−36,000	58,000	$ 22,000
New surplus					$ 121,500

Financial Implications of a Change in Visit Mix—Physicians and Extenders					
Unit contribution margin	$ 43.50	$ 32.25	$ 36.00	$ 29.00	
# visits possible in an hour	0.8	1.1	2.0	2.4	
Potential total contribution in 1 hour	$ 34.80	$ 35.18	$ 72.00	$ 69.60	
# visits planned	3,000	4,000	6,000	6,000	
Planned contribution	130,500	129,000	216,000	174,000	$ 649,500
Change in visits			−1,000	1,200	
Hours used (saved) with visit change			−500	500	
New contribution	130,500	129,000	180,000	208,800	$ 648,300
Change in contribution	0	0	−36,000	34,800	($ 1,200)
New surplus					$ 98,300

EXHIBIT D   Original Budget with Increases in Provider Productivity

Overall Budget	Initial Consult	Routine Physical	Intensive Visit	Routine Visit	Total
Number of visits	3,000	4,000	6,000	6,000	19,000
Price per visit	$ 150.00	$ 110.00	$ 80.00	$ 60.00	
Total revenue	$450,000	$440,000	$480,000	$360,000	$1,730,000
Variable expenses per visit.	$ 106.50	$ 77.75	$ 44.00	$ 31.00	
Total variable expenses	$319,500	$311,000	$264,000	$186,000	1,080,500
Contribution.	$130,500	$129,000	$216,000	$174,000	$ 649,500
Total fixed expenses					300,000
Allocated overhead.					250,000
Surplus					$ 99,500
Variable expense detail:					
Physician care:					
Average # minutes per visit . . .	60	45	20	10	
Average wage per minute	$ 1.35	$ 1.35	$ 1.35	$ 1.35	
Total expense per visit	$ 81.00	$ 60.75	$ 27.00	$ 13.50	
Extender care:					
Average # minutes per visit . . .	15	10	10	15	
Average wage per minute	$ 0.90	$ 0.90	$ 0.90	$ 0.90	
Total expense per visit	$ 13.50	$ 9.00	$ 9.00	$ 13.50	
Medical supplies:					
Average # units per visit.	3	2	2	1	
Average expense per unit.	$ 4.00	$ 4.00	$ 4.00	$ 4.00	
Total expense per visit	$ 12.00	$ 8.00	$ 8.00	$ 4.00	
Total average per variable					
expense per visit	$ 106.50	$ 77.75	$ 44.00	$ 31.00	

Financial Implications of Productivity Changes					
Original Budget					
Number physicians needed.	6.0				
Number extenders needed	2.8				
With 10% Physician Productivity Increase					
Minutes per visit	54	40.5	18	9	
Number physicians needed.	5.4				
New surplus					$ 172,400
Increase over original surplus					$ 72,900
With 10% Extender Productivity Increase					
Minutes per visit	13.5	9	9	13.5	
Number extenders needed	2.5				
New surplus					$ 120,650
Increase over original surplus					$ 21,150

This leaves us with option 2a. It appears that this area is where the greatest opportunities exist. By working with the physicians and extenders in the group, Dr. Desautels may be able to reduce the time spent per visit. As Exhibit D shows, the big payoff is with physicians, not with extenders. That is, a 10 percent increase in productivity for physicians across all visit types improves the surplus by $72,900, whereas a similar increase for extenders improves it by only $21,150. All of this comes with no change in budgeted fixed costs, except that the implication is the use of fewer physicians: 5.4 FTEs rather than 6 FTEs.

Note, incidentally, that with the projected visit volume and productivity figures, the group will need another .8 FTE extender.

Question 3

There are several problems that might arise. First, and perhaps most importantly, with the bonus based on revenue generation, there is a considerable incentive for physicians to obtain productivity increases by shifting some of the responsibility for a visit to an extender. Doing so will free up the physicians to either see more patients or spend time in other activities. This problem surfaces in the (B) case.

Second, Dr. Desautels probably will want to see greater detail on fixed expenses to see how they might be reduced. For example, some breakdown among the usual categories of rent, utilities, cleaning, administration, and the like might shed some light on the feasibility of reducing these expenses.

Third, Dr. Desautels probably should work with the CFO to see if the allocation can be restructured either as a fixed commitment or, if there is a measurable unit of activity, based on a transfer price. Otherwise, excessive spending by Coos Bay will quite likely affect BMA's bottom line in a way that Dr. Desautels cannot control. If transfer prices can be established, he will need to work with the CFO (and others in the hospital) to determine where they are appropriate and where they are not. It should be easy to have a transfer price for laundry services, for example, but would be quite difficulty to have one for the "administration and general" cost center.

Finally, as Dr. Desautels already has seen at the retreat, there no doubt will be considerable resistance from physicians to spending their time on financial matters. Developing per-visit standards and linking them to financial matters can be time-consuming and frustrating. Developing transfer prices for service departments can be similarly difficult.

Chapter 13 Practice Case: El Conjo Family Planning Clinic Solution[10]

Overview

This case lends itself to the use of a rather simple spreadsheet, which can be used to compute the variances. Once one variance has been computed accurately, the

[10]This solution was prepared by Professor David W. Young. Copyright © David W. Young.

formula used in that cell then can be copied and pasted into the remaining cells of a like kind.

Question 1

Exhibit 3 is simply the same format as Exhibit 1 but using the actual results from Exhibit 2. Exhibit 4, as described in the text, keeps everything at the budgeted levels, but uses the actual number of visits of each type to make the computations. As it indicates, although the number of visits increased by 50 from the budget, the mix changed in such a way that the surplus should have been $750 lower than budgeted.

Exhibit 4 also computes the revenue price variances using the formulas described in the Appendix to the chapter.

Question 2

Some of the other reasons for the large total variance might be the following:

- More or fewer physician minutes, nursing minutes, medical supply units, or laboratory tests per visit, on average, than budgeted.

EXHIBIT A　Productivity/Usage Variances

Type of Service	IUD 1st Visit	Oral Conc 1st Visit	Special Follow-Up	Routine Follow-Up	Total
Physician Care:					
Budgeted—actual minutes per visit . . .	5	5	−5	−5	
Budgeted wage per minute	$ 1.00	$ 1.00	$ 1.00	$ 1.00	
Productivity variance per visit.	$ 5.00	$ 5.00	($ 5.00)	($ 5.00)	
Total productivity variances	$ 13,750	$11,000	($ 5,000)	($3,000)	$ 16,750
Nursing Care:					
Budgeted—actual minutes per visit . . .	−10	−10	5	5	
Budgeted wage per minute	$ 0.50	$ 0.50	$ 0.50	$ 0.50	
Productivity variance per visit.	($ 5.00)	($ 5.00)	$ 2.50	$ 2.50	
Total productivity variances	($ 13,750)	($11,000)	$ 2,500	$1,500	($ 20,750)
Medical Supplies:					
Budgeted—actual # units per visit	−1	−1	0	0	
Budgeted expense per unit	$ 25.00	$ 25.00	$ 25.00	$25.00	
Usage variance per visit	($ 25.00)	($ 25.00)	$ 0.00	$ 0.00	
Total usage variances	($ 68,750)	($55,000)	$ 0	$ 0	($123,750)
Laboratory:					
Budgeted—actual tests per visit	−2	−1	−3	0	
Budgeted expense per test.	$ 15.00	$ 15.00	$ 15.00	$15.00	
Usage variance per visit	($ 30.00)	($ 15.00)	($ 45.00)	$ 0.00	
Total usage variances	($ 82,500)	($33,000)	($45,000)	$ 0	($160,500)
Total productivity/usage variances per visit.	($ 55.00)	($ 40.00)	($ 47.50)	($ 2.50)	
Actual # visits	2,750	2,200	1,000	600	
Total productivity/usage variances	($151,250)	($88,000)	($47,500)	($1,500)	($288,250)

- Higher or lower average physician wage per minute, nursing wage per minute, expense per medical supply unit, or expense per laboratory test than budgeted.

- Higher or lower fixed expenses.

Question 3

The computations are shown in Exhibit A, B, and C. These exhibits indicate the following:

- *Exhibit A.* Productivity and usage variances (the first set of reasons above) accounted for a negative $288,250 variance. Looking along the type-of-service dimension, we can see that over half of the total ($160,500) was for laboratory tests. Looking along the visit-type dimension, we can see that over half

EXHIBIT B   Wage, Price, and Efficiency Variances

	IUD 1st Visit	Oral Conc 1st Visit	Special Follow-Up	Routine Follow-Up	Total
Actual # visits	2,750	2,200	1,000	600	
Type of Service:					
Physician care:					
Budgeted—actual wage per minute	($ 0.20)	($ 0.20)	($ 0.20)	($ 0.20)	
Actual # minutes per visit	25	5	20	10	
Wage rate variance per visit	($ 5.00)	($ 1.00)	($ 4.00)	($ 2.00)	
Total wage rate variance	($13,750)	($ 2,200)	($4,000)	($1,200)	($21,150)
Nursing care:					
Budgeted—actual wage per minute	($ 0.10)	($ 0.10)	($ 0.10)	($ 0.10)	
Actual # minutes per visit	40	30	25	5	
Wage rate variance per visit	($ 4.00)	($ 3.00)	($ 2.50)	($ 0.50)	
Total wage rate variance	($11,000)	($ 6,600)	($2,500)	($ 300)	($20,400)
Medical supplies:					
Budgeted—actual expense per unit	$ 4.00	$ 4.00	$ 4.00	$ 4.00	
Actual # units per visit	4	2	2	0	
Price/efficiency variance per visit	$ 16.00	$ 8.00	$ 8.00	$ 0.00	
Total price/efficiency variance	$44,000	$17,600	$8,000	$ 0	$69,600
Laboratory:					
Budgeted—actual expense per test	($ 1.00)	($ 1.00)	($ 1.00)	($ 1.00)	
Actual # tests per visit	5	3	5	0	
Price/efficiency variance per visit	($ 5.00)	($ 3.00)	($ 5.00)	$ 0.00	
Total price/efficiency variance	($13,750)	($ 6,600)	($5,000)	$ 0	($25,350)
Total wage, price, and efficiency variances	$ 5,500	$ 2,200	($3,500)	($1,500)	$ 2,700

($151,250) was for an IUD first visit. The highest single item was laboratory tests for an IUD first visit.

- *Exhibit B.* Wage, price, and efficiency variances (the second set of reasons above) accounted for only a small portion of the total and actually summed to a positive variance of $2,700. The $2,700 masked some more significant variances, however, but none was as substantial as the productivity and usage variances.

- Actual fixed expenses did not differ from the budget.

- *Exhibit C.* Summary of variances indicates that the total variance was $303,300 (budget of a positive $85,000 to actual of negative $218,300 is a total variance of $303,300). In terms of responsible groups, the area that had the largest problem was the laboratory, but everyone had a negative variance.

In terms of managing the clinic, Ms. Ruiz might start by examining why more lab tests were ordered for every visit type except a routine follow-up. She might also ask the nurses why they are spending 10 minutes more per first visits than budgeted. Is it possible, for example, that physicians are saving 5 minutes per visit

EXHIBIT C   Summary of Variances

	IUD 1st Visit	Oral Conc 1st Visit	Special Follow-Up	Routine Follow-Up	Total
Contribution margin variances	($ 8,750)	$ 5,000	$ 0	$3,000	($ 750)
Revenue price variances	0	(22,000)	5,000	0	(17,000)
Subtotal.	($ 8,750)	($ 17,000)	$ 5,000	$3,000	($ 17,750)
Productivity/usage variances:					
Physician care	$ 13,750	$ 11,000	($ 5,000)	($3,000)	$ 16,750
Nursing care	(13,750)	(11,000)	2,500	1,500	(20,750)
Medical supplies	(68,750)	(55,000)	0	0	(123,750)
Laboratory.	(82,500)	(33,000)	(45,000)	0	(160,500)
Subtotal.	($151,250)	($ 88,000)	($47,500)	($1,500)	($288,250)
Wage, price, and efficiency variances:					
Physician care	($ 13,750)	($ 2,200)	($ 4,000)	($1,200)	($ 21,150)
Nursing care	(11,000)	(6,600)	(2,500)	(300)	(20,400)
Medical supplies	44,000	17,600	8,000	0	69,600
Laboratory.	(13,750)	(6,600)	(5,000)	0	(25,350)
Subtotal.	$ 5,500	$ 2,200	($ 3,500)	($1,500)	$ 2,700
Total variances.	($154,500)	($102,800)	($46,000)	$ 0	($303,300)
Variances by responsible group					
Physicians	$ 0	$ 8,800	($ 9,000)	($4,200)	($ 4,400)
Nurses.	(24,750)	(17,600)	0	1,200	(41,150)
Medical supply department.	(24,750)	(37,400)	8,000	0	(54,150)
Laboratory.	(96,250)	(39,600)	(50,000)	0	(185,850)
Senior management	(8,750)	(17,000)	5,000	3,000	(17,750)
Total	($154,500)	($102,800)	($46,000)	$ 0	($303,300)

by giving the nurses more work? If so, perhaps that is appropriate, but there may be quality-of-care issues that need to be examined. Moreover, there is no savings if it takes a nurse (at half the per-minute wage of a physician) 10 minutes to do what a physician could do in 5 minutes.

In general, however, the big problem appears to be in the laboratory, and, to a lesser extent, with medical supplies. Ms. Ruiz needs to focus on these two areas, and especially on resource usage within them to see if the actual usage patterns are appropriate or a result of excessive ordering.

Name index

Case index

Subject index